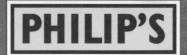

G000299433

STREET ATLAS
East Kent

First published in 1989 by

Philip's, a division of
Octopus Publishing Group Ltd
2-4 Heron Quays, London E14 4JP

Third colour edition 2005
First impression 2005

ISBN-10   0-540-08664-9 (spiral)
ISBN-13   978-0-540-08664-1 (spiral)

© Philip's 2005

Ordnance Survey®

This product includes mapping data licensed
from Ordnance Survey® with the permission of
the Controller of Her Majesty's Stationery Office.
© Crown copyright 2005. All rights reserved.
Licence number 100011710.

Printed and bound in Spain
by Cayfosa-Quebecor

Contents

III   **Key to map symbols**

IV   **Key to map pages**

VI   **Route planning**

VIII   **Administrative and Postcode boundaries**

1   **Street maps** at 3½ inches to 1 mile

210   **Index** of towns and villages

212   **Index** of streets, hospitals, industrial estates, railway
stations, schools, shopping centres, universities
and places of interest

Digital Data

The exceptionally high-quality mapping found in this atlas is available as digital data in TIFF
format, which is easily convertible to other bitmapped (raster) image formats.

The index is also available in digital form as a standard database table. It contains all the details
found in the printed index together with the National Grid reference for the map square in which
each entry is named.

For further information and to discuss your requirements, please contact Philip's on
020 7644 6932 or james.mann@philips-maps.co.uk

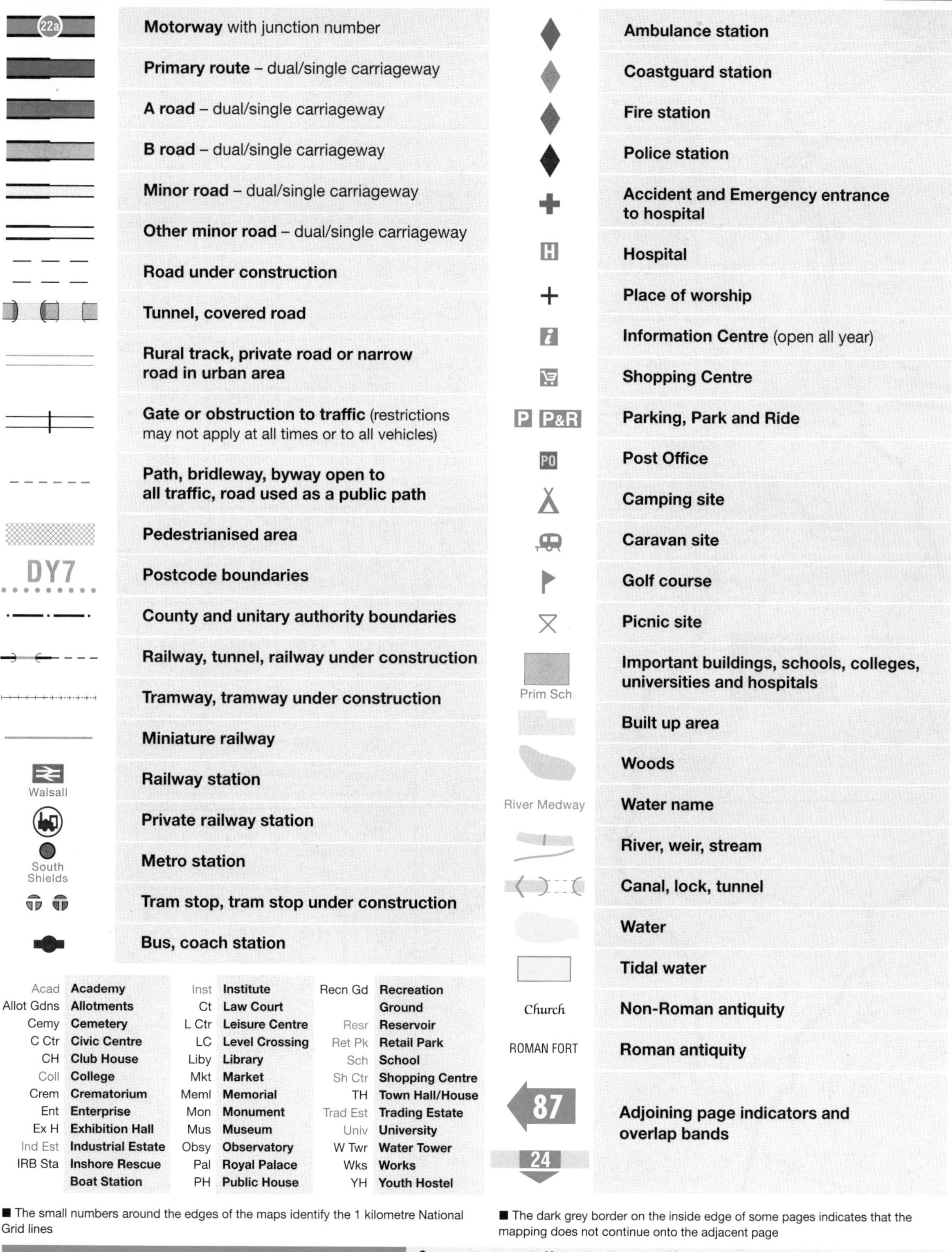

Symbol	Description
	Motorway with junction number
	Primary route – dual/single carriageway
	A road – dual/single carriageway
	B road – dual/single carriageway
	Minor road – dual/single carriageway
	Other minor road – dual/single carriageway
	Road under construction
	Tunnel, covered road
	Rural track, private road or narrow road in urban area
	Gate or obstruction to traffic (restrictions may not apply at all times or to all vehicles)
	Path, bridleway, byway open to all traffic, road used as a public path
	Pedestrianised area
DY7	**Postcode boundaries**
	County and unitary authority boundaries
	Railway, tunnel, railway under construction
	Tramway, tramway under construction
	Miniature railway
Walsall	**Railway station**
	Private railway station
South Shields	**Metro station**
	Tram stop, tram stop under construction
	Bus, coach station

Symbol	Description
◆	**Ambulance station**
◆	**Coastguard station**
◆	**Fire station**
◆	**Police station**
✚	**Accident and Emergency entrance to hospital**
H	**Hospital**
+	**Place of worship**
i	**Information Centre** (open all year)
🛒	**Shopping Centre**
P P&R	**Parking, Park and Ride**
PO	**Post Office**
Å	**Camping site**
	Caravan site
▶	**Golf course**
✕	**Picnic site**
Prim Sch	**Important buildings, schools, colleges, universities and hospitals**
	Built up area
	Woods
River Medway	**Water name**
	River, weir, stream
	Canal, lock, tunnel
	Water
	Tidal water
Church	**Non-Roman antiquity**
ROMAN FORT	**Roman antiquity**
87 / 24	**Adjoining page indicators and overlap bands**

Acad	**Academy**	Inst	**Institute**	Recn Gd	**Recreation Ground**
Allot Gdns	**Allotments**	Ct	**Law Court**		
Cemy	**Cemetery**	L Ctr	**Leisure Centre**	Resr	**Reservoir**
C Ctr	**Civic Centre**	LC	**Level Crossing**	Ret Pk	**Retail Park**
CH	**Club House**	Liby	**Library**	Sch	**School**
Coll	**College**	Mkt	**Market**	Sh Ctr	**Shopping Centre**
Crem	**Crematorium**	Meml	**Memorial**	TH	**Town Hall/House**
Ent	**Enterprise**	Mon	**Monument**	Trad Est	**Trading Estate**
Ex H	**Exhibition Hall**	Mus	**Museum**	Univ	**University**
Ind Est	**Industrial Estate**	Obsy	**Observatory**	W Twr	**Water Tower**
IRB Sta	**Inshore Rescue Boat Station**	Pal	**Royal Palace**	Wks	**Works**
		PH	**Public House**	YH	**Youth Hostel**

■ The small numbers around the edges of the maps identify the 1 kilometre National Grid lines

■ The dark grey border on the inside edge of some pages indicates that the mapping does not continue onto the adjacent page

The scale of the maps on the pages numbered in blue is 5.52 cm to 1 km • 3½ inches to 1 mile • 1: 18103

0	¼	½	¾	1 mile
0	250m 500m 750m	1 kilometre		

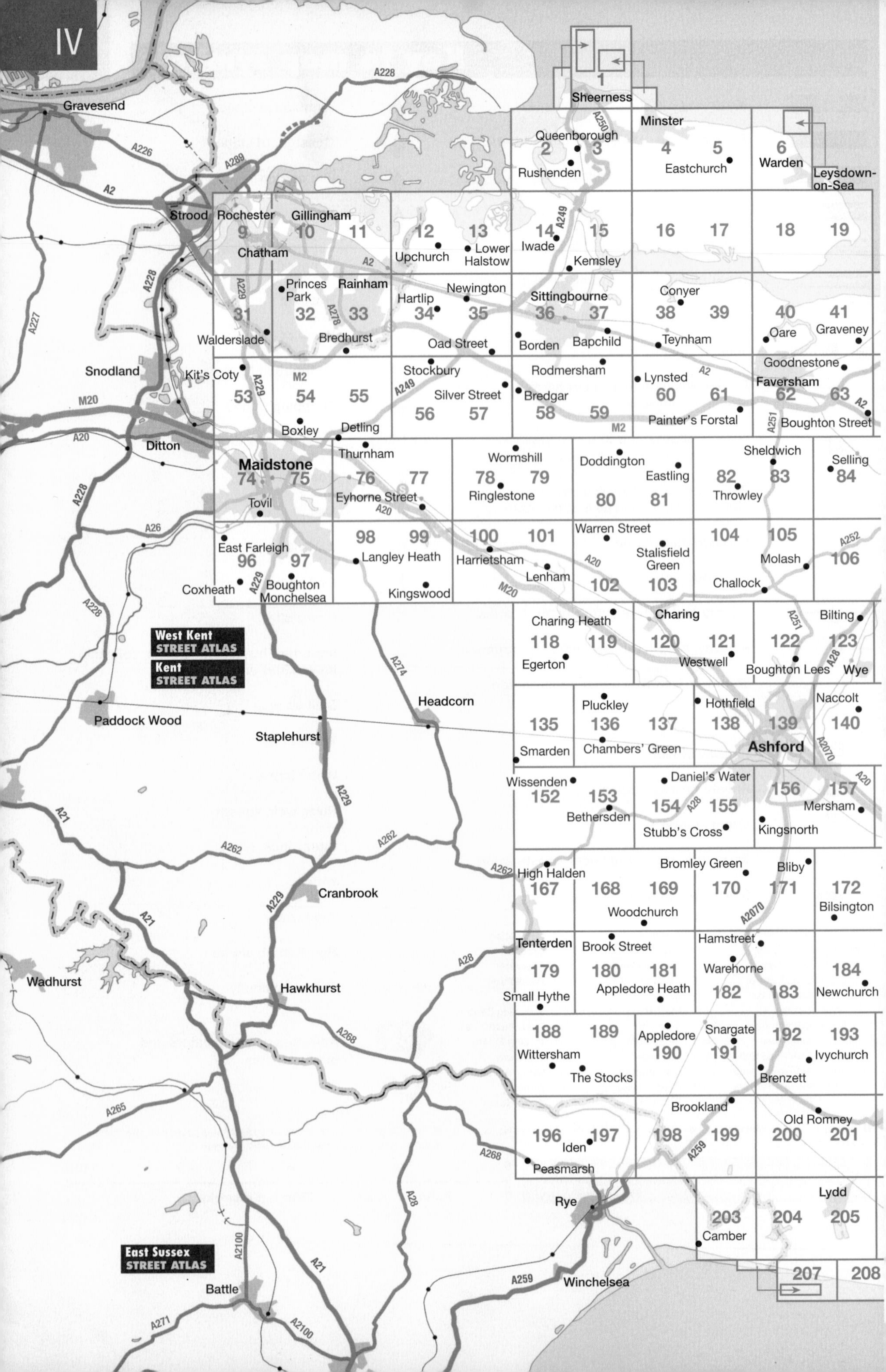

Gravesend

Sheerness

Minster

Queenborough
2 **3**
Rushenden

4 **5**
Eastchurch

6
Warden

Leysdown-
on-Sea

Strood Rochester Gillingham
9 **10** **11**
Chatham

12 **13** **14** **15**
Upchurch Lower Iwade
Halstow Kemsley

16 **17**

18 **19**

Princes Rainham
Park
31 **32** **33**
Walderslade
Bredhurst

Hartlip Newington
34 **35**
Oad Street

Sittingbourne
36 **37**
Borden Bapchild

Conyer
38 **39**
Teynham

40 **41**
Oare Graveney

Snodland

Kit's Coty

Ditton

M2
53 **54** **55**
Boxley Detling

Stockbury
Silver Street
56 **57**

Rodmersham
Bredgar
58 **59**

Lynsted
60 **61**
Painter's Forstal

Goodnestone
Faversham
62 **63**
Boughton Street

Maidstone
74 **75**
Tovil

Thurnham
76 **77**
Eyhorne Street

Wormshill
78 **79**
Ringlestone

Doddington
Eastling
80 **81**

Sheldwich
82 **83**
Throwley

Selling
84

East Farleigh
96 **97**
Coxheath Boughton
Monchelsea

98 **99**
Langley Heath

Kingswood

100 **101**
Harrietsham
Lenham

Warren Street
102 **103**
Stalisfield
Green

104 **105**
Molash
Challock

106

West Kent
STREET ATLAS
Kent
STREET ATLAS

Charing Heath
118 **119**
Egerton

Charing
120 **121**
Westwell

122 **123**
Boughton Lees Wye

Bilting

Headcorn

Pluckley
135 **136** **137**
Smarden Chambers' Green

Hothfield
138 **139**

Naccolt
140

Ashford

Paddock Wood

Staplehurst

Wissenden
152 **153**
Bethersden

Daniel's Water
154 **155**
Stubb's Cross

156 **157**
Mersham
Kingsnorth

Cranbrook

High Halden
167 **168** **169**
Woodchurch

Bromley Green
170 **171**

Bliby

172
Bilsington

Wadhurst

Hawkhurst

Tenterden
179 **180** **181**
Small Hythe Appledore Heath

Brook Street

Hamstreet
182 **183**
Warehorne

184
Newchurch

188 **189**
Wittersham
The Stocks

Appledore
190 **191**
Snargate

192 **193**
Ivychurch
Brenzett

196 **197**
Iden
Peasmarsh

Brookland
198 **199**

Old Romney
200 **201**

Rye

Winchelsea

Battle

Lydd
203 **204** **205**
Camber

207 **208**

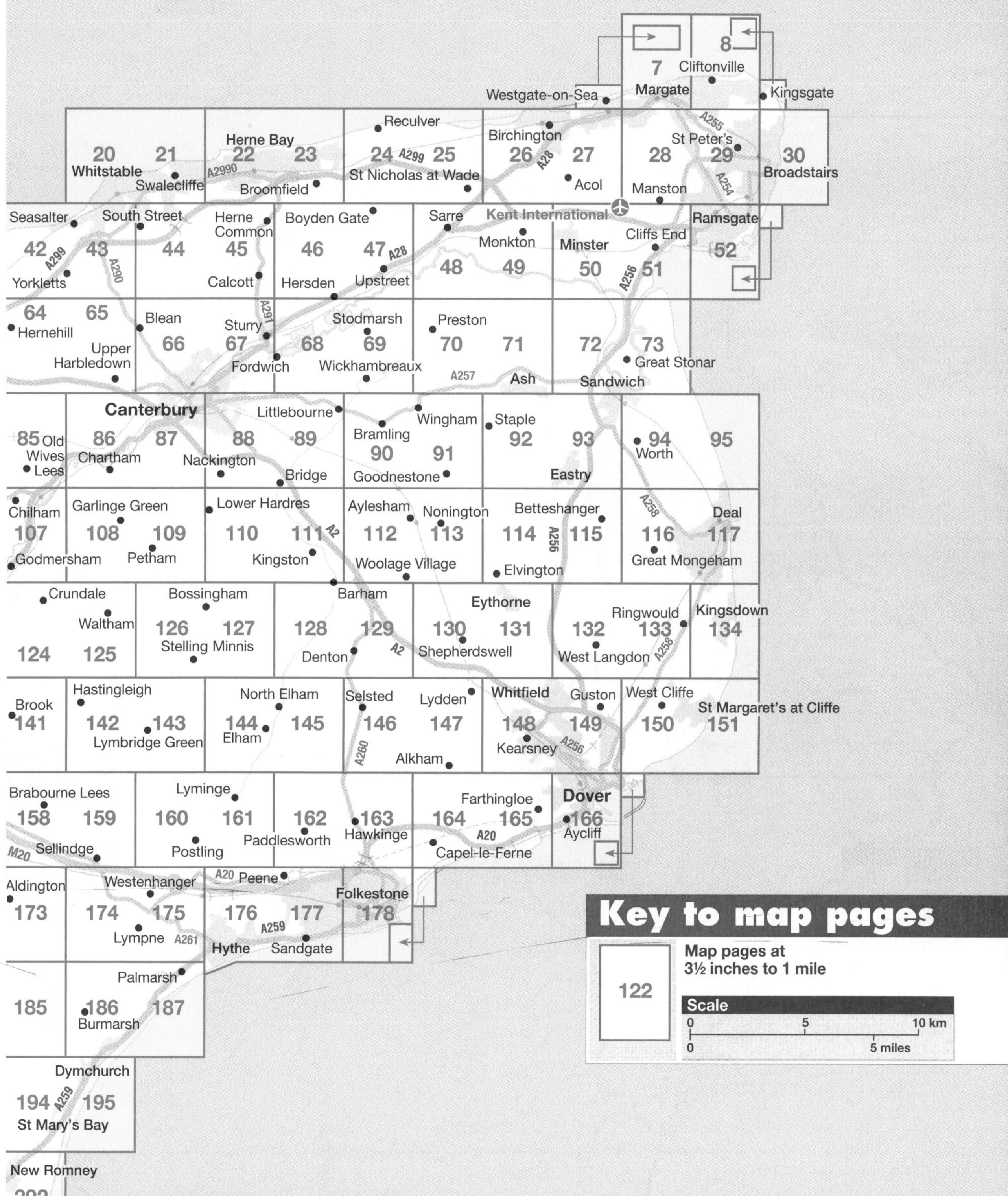

7

8

Cliftonville

Westgate-on-Sea   Margate   Kingsgate

20 Whitstable   **21**   Herne Bay   **22**   **23**   Reculver   **24** A299 **25**   Birchington   **26** A28 **27**   St Peter's   **28**   **29**   **30** Broadstairs

Swalecliffe   Broomfield   St Nicholas at Wade   Acol   Manston

Seasalter   South Street   Herne Common   Boyden Gate   Sarre   Kent International ✈   Cliffs End   Ramsgate

42 A299 **43** A290 **44**   **45**   **46**   **47** A28   Monkton   Minster   **52**

Yorkletts   Calcott   Hersden   Upstreet   **48**   **49**   **50** A256 **51**

64   **65**   Blean   Sturry   Stodmarsh   Preston

Hernehill   **66**   **67**   **68**   **69**   **70**   **71**   **72**   **73**

Upper Harbledown   Fordwich   Wickhambreaux   A257   Great Stonar

Ash   Sandwich

Canterbury   Littlebourne   Wingham   Staple

85 Old Wives Lees   **86** Chartham   **87**   **88**   **89**   Bramling   **90**   **91**   **92**   **93**   **94** Worth   **95**

Nackington   Bridge   Goodnestone   Eastry

Chilham   Garlinge Green   Lower Hardres   Aylesham   Nonington   Betteshanger   Deal

107   **108**   **109**   **110**   **111** A2 **112**   **113**   **114** A256 **115**   **116**   **117**

Godmersham   Petham   Kingston   Woolage Village   Elvington   Great Mongeham

Crundale   Bossingham   Barham   Eythorne   Ringwould   Kingsdown

Waltham   **126**   **127**   **128**   **129**   **130**   **131**   **132**   **133**   **134**

124   **125**   Stelling Minnis   Denton   A2 Shepherdswell   West Langdon A258

Brook   Hastingleigh   North Elham   Selsted   Lydden   Whitfield   Guston   West Cliffe

141   **142**   **143**   **144**   **145**   **146**   **147**   **148**   **149**   **150**   **151**   St Margaret's at Cliffe

Lymbridge Green   Elham   A260   Alkham   Kearsney A256

Brabourne Lees   Lyminge   Farthingloe   Dover

158   **159**   **160**   **161**   **162**   **163**   **164**   **165**   **166**   Aycliff

M20 Sellindge   Postling   Paddlesworth   Hawkinge   Capel-le-Ferne   A20

Aldington   Westenhanger   A20 Peene   Folkestone

173   **174**   **175**   **176**   A259 **177**   **178**

Lympne   A261   Hythe   Sandgate

Palmarsh

185   **186**   **187**

Burmarsh

Dymchurch

194 A259 **195**

St Mary's Bay

New Romney

202

Greatstone-on-Sea

Lade

206

Lydd-on-Sea

209

Dungeness

Key to map pages

| 122 | Map pages at 3½ inches to 1 mile |

Scale

0 — 5 — 10 km

0 — 5 miles

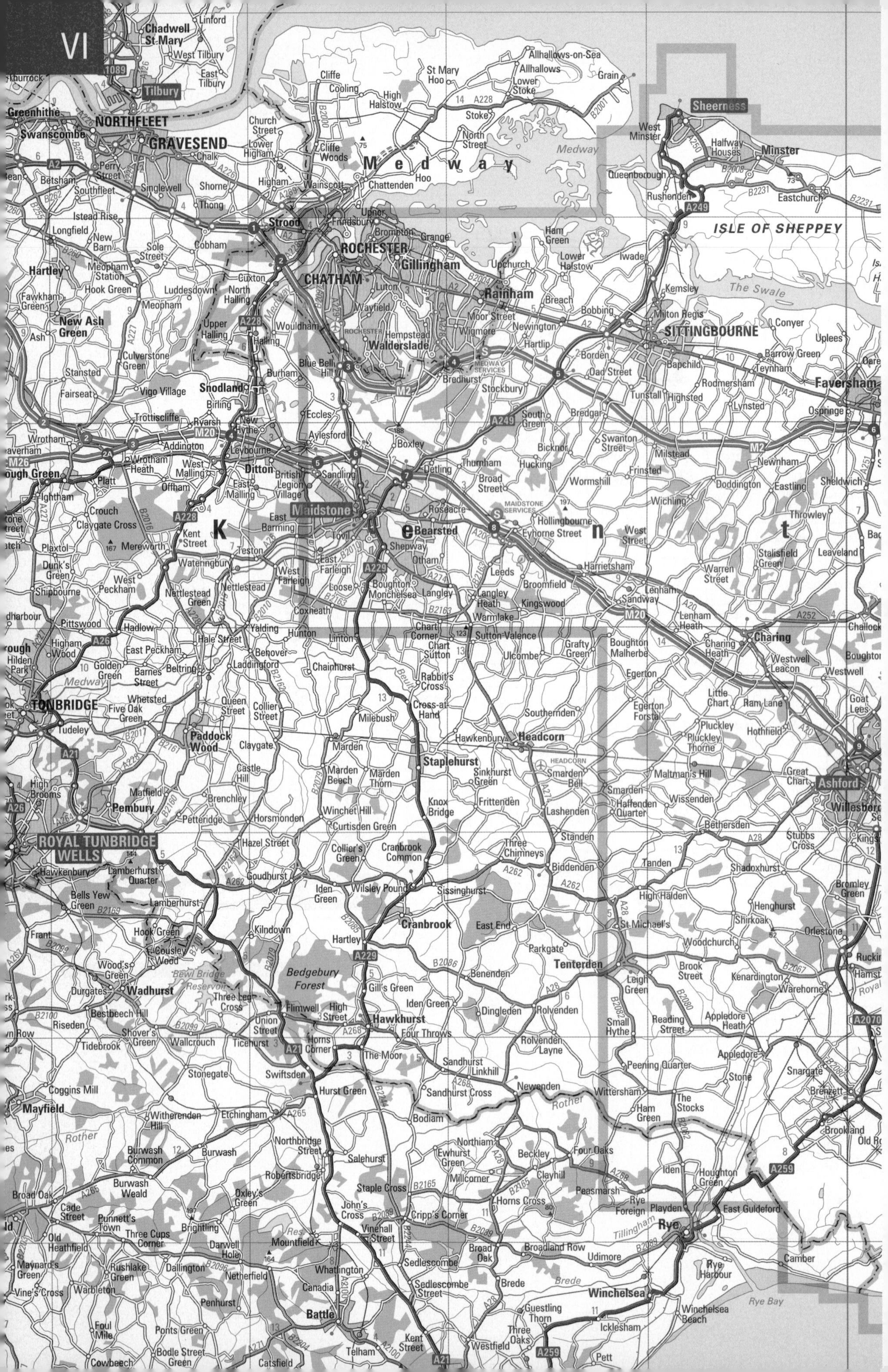
Chadwell St Mary
Linford
West Tilbury
East Tilbury
Tilbury
Thurrock
Greenhithe
NORTHFLEET
Swanscombe
GRAVESEND
Chalk
Perry Street
Betsham
Southfleet
Singlewell
Shorne
Thong
Istead Rise
Longfield
New Barn
Hartley
Sole Street
Cobham
Meopham Station
Hook Green
Meopham
Luddesdown
Fawkham Green
New Ash Green
Ash
Culverstone Green
Stansted
Fairseat
Vigo Village
Trottiscliffe
Wrotham
Wrotham Heath
Platt
Ightham
Borough Green
Crouch
Claygate Cross
Mereworth
Plaxtol
Dunk's Green
Shipbourne
West Peckham
Hadlow
Pittswood
Higham Wood
Hilden Park
Golden Green
East Peckham
Barnes Street
Beltring
Medway
TONBRIDGE
Five Oak Green
Whetsted
Tudeley
Paddock Wood
Claygate
High Brooms
Pembury
Matfield
Brenchley
Petteridge
ROYAL TUNBRIDGE WELLS
Hawkenbury
Lamberhurst Quarter
Lamberhurst
Bells Yew Green
Frant
Hook Green
Cousley Wood
Wood's Green
Wadhurst
Durgates
Bewl Bridge Reservoir
Three Leg Cross
Bestbeech Hill
Riseden
Shover's Green
Wallcrouch
Tidebrook
Ticehurst
Stonegate
Coggins Mill
Mayfield
Witherenden Hill
Etchingham
Rother
Burwash Common
Burwash
Burwash Weald
Broad Oak
Cade Street
Punnett's Town
Three Cups Corner
Old Heathfield
Brightling
Darwell Hole
Dallington
Maynard's Green
Rushlake Green
Vine's Cross
Warbleton
Netherfield
Penhurst
Foul Mile
Ponts Green
Bodle Street Green
Cowbeech
Catsfield
Cliffe
Cooling
High Halstow
Church Street
Lower Higham
Cliffe Woods
Higham
Wainscott
Chattenden
Medway
Hoo
St Mary Hoo
Allhallows-on-Sea
Allhallows
Lower Stoke
Stoke
North Street
Grain
Strood
Frindsbury
Upnor
Brompton
Grange
ROCHESTER
Gillingham
CHATHAM
Luton
Wayfield
Cuxton
North Halling
Upper Halling
Halling
Wouldham
Burham
Snodland
Birling
Ryarsh
New Hythe
Leybourne
Addington
West Malling
East Malling
Offham
Ditton
Kent Street
Teston
Wateringbury
Nettlestead
Nettlestead Green
Hempstead
Walderslade
Blue Bell Hill
Eccles
Aylesford
Sandling
British Legion Village
Maidstone
East Barming
Tovil
East Farleigh
West Farleigh
Loose
Coxheath
Yalding
Hunton
Hale Street
Laddingford
Benover
Collier Street
Queen Street
Chainhurst
Linton
Boughton Monchelsea
Shepway
Otham
Langley
Bearsted
Roseacre
Detling
Boxley
Thurnham
Upchurch
Rainham
Moor Street
Wigmore
Bredhurst
Stockbury
Hartlip
Newington
Breach
Lower Halstow
Ham Green
Iwade
Bobbing
Kemsley
Milton Regis
SITTINGBOURNE
Borden
Oad Street
Bapchild
Tunstall
Highsted
Rodmersham
South Green
Bredgar
Swanton Street
Bicknor
Hucking
Broad Street
Hollingbourne
Eyhorne Street
Leeds
Broomfield
Langley Heath
Kingswood
Warmlake
Chart Corner
Chart Sutton
Sutton Valence
Ulcombe
Grafty Green
Boughton Malherbe
Harrietsham
Lenham
Sandway
Lenham Heath
Charing
Charing Heath
Westwell Leacon
Westwell
Challock
Egerton
Egerton Forstal
Little Chart
Ram Lane
Hothfield
Pluckley
Pluckley Thorne
Maltman's Hill
Great Chart
Ashford
Willesborough
Smarden
Smarden Bell
Haffenden Quarter
Wissenden
Bethersden
Headcorn
Hawkenbury
Southernden
Staplehurst
Sinkhurst Green
Frittenden
Lashenden
Standen
Biddenden
Three Chimneys
Sissinghurst
Rabbit's Cross
Cross-at-Hand
Milebush
Marden
Marden Beech
Marden Thorn
Knox Bridge
Winchet Hill
Curtisden Green
Horsmonden
Hazel Street
Collier's Green
Cranbrook Common
Goudhurst
Iden Green
Wilsley Pound
Kilndown
Hartley
Cranbrook
East End
Parkgate
Bedgebury Forest
Gill's Green
Flimwell
High Street
Hawkhurst
Iden Green
Benenden
Dingleden
Rolvenden
Four Throws
Rolvenden Layne
Union Street
Horns Corner
The Moor
Swiftsden
Sandhurst
Linkhill
Sandhurst Cross
Hurst Green
Bodiam
Newenden
Tenterden
Leigh Green
St Michael's
High Halden
Tanden
Small Hythe
Reading Street
Peening Quarter
Wittersham
Ham Green
The Stocks
Northiam
Ewhurst Green
Beckley
Four Oaks
Clayhill
Millcorner
Peasmarsh
Northbridge Street
Salehurst
Robertsbridge
Staple Cross
John's Cross
Cripp's Corner
Horns Cross
Vinehall Street
Mountfield
Sedlescombe
Sedlescombe Street
Whatlington
Canadia
Battle
Brede
Broad Oak
Broadland Row
Udimore
Telham
Kent Street
Westfield
Three Oaks
Guestling Thorn
Icklesham
Pett
Winchelsea
Winchelsea Beach
Rye
Rye Harbour
Rye Foreign
Playden
Iden
Houghton Green
East Guldeford
Camber
Rye Bay
Tillingham
Brede
Sheerness
West Minster
Halfway Houses
Minster
Queenborough
Rushenden
Eastchurch
ISLE OF SHEPPEY
The Swale
Conyer
Uplees
Barrow Green
Teynham
Faversham
Ospringe
Lynsted
Milstead
Frinsted
Wormshill
Newnham
Doddington
Eastling
Sheldwich
Throwley
Wichling
West Street
Stalisfield Green
Warren Street
Leaveland
Goat Lees
Stubbs Cross
Shadoxhurst
Bromley Green
Henghurst
Shirkoak
Orlestone
Woodchurch
Brook Street
Kenardington
Warehorne
Appledore Heath
Appledore
Stone
Snargate
Brenzett
Brookland
Ruckinge
Hamstreet
K e n t
M e d w a y
M2
M20
M26
M25
A2
A20
A21
A26
A28
A228
A229
A249
A259
A262
A268
A2070
A1089
MAIDSTONE SERVICES
MEDWAY SERVICES
HEADCORN
ROCHESTER

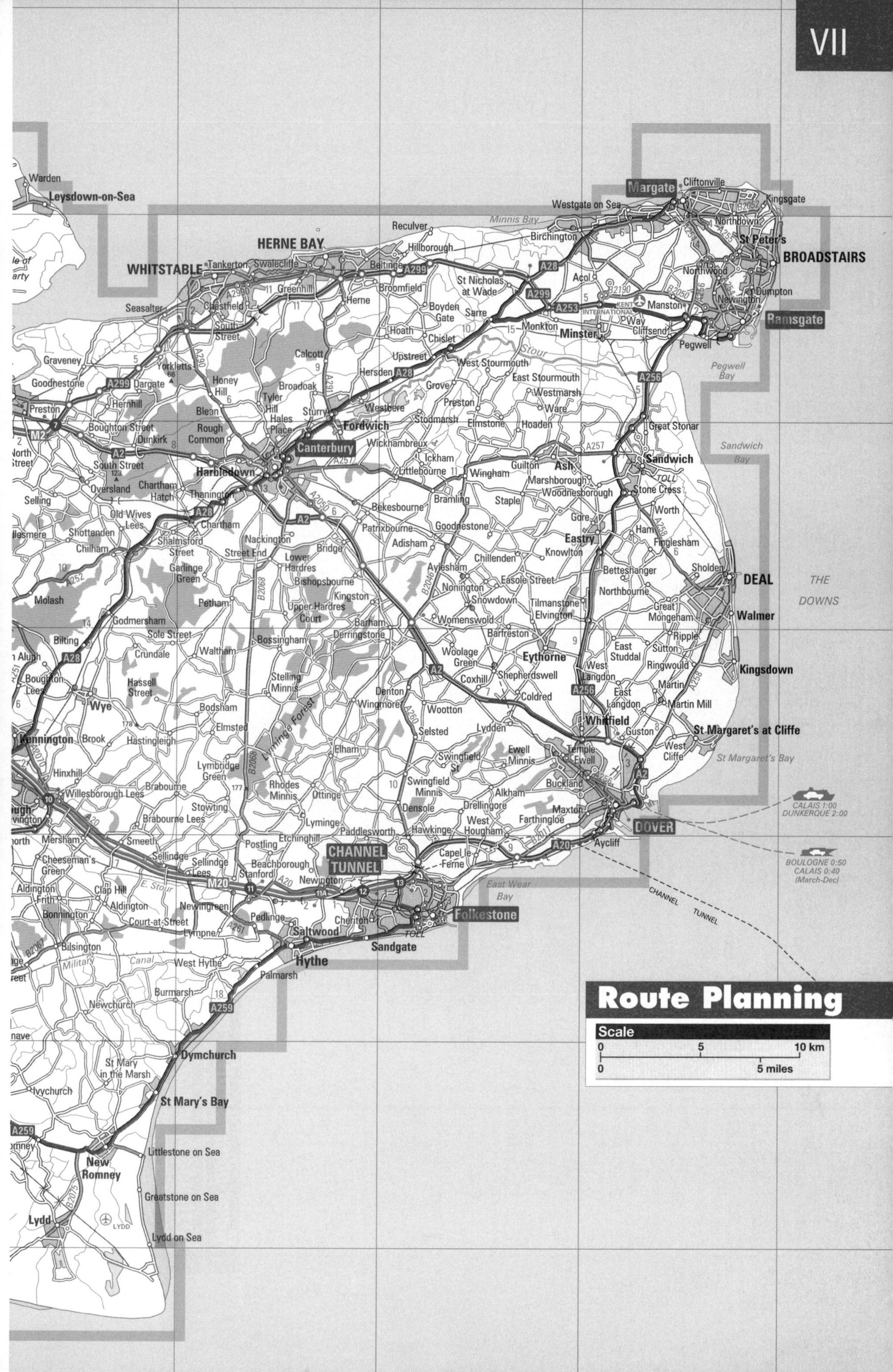
Route Planning
Scale
0
5
10 km
0
5 miles
Warden
Leysdown-on-Sea
Margate
Cliftonville
Kingsgate
Westgate on Sea
Minnis Bay
Birchington
Northdown
St Peter's
BROADSTAIRS
Reculver
Hillborough
HERNE BAY
WHITSTABLE
Tankerton
Swalecliffe
Beltinge
Greenhill
Herne
Broomfield
St Nicholas at Wade
Acol
Northwood
Dumpton
Newington
Seasalter
Chestfield
South Street
Boyden Gate
Sarre
Monkton
Minster
Manston
KENT INTERNATIONAL
Way
Cliffsend
Ramsgate
Pegwell
Pegwell Bay
Hoath
Chislet
Graveney
Yorkletts
Calcott
Upstreet
West Stourmouth
Stour
Goodnestone
Dargate
Honey Hill
Broadoak
Hersden
Grove
East Stourmouth
Westmarsh
Preston
Hernhill
Tyler Hill
Hales Place
Sturry
Westbere
Fordwich
Stodmarsh
Elmstone
Ware
Hoaden
Blean
Rough Common
Boughton Street
Dunkirk
Canterbury
Wickhambreux
Great Stonar
Sandwich
Sandwich Bay
North Street
South Street
Harbledown
Ickham
Littlebourne
Wingham
Guilton
Ash
Marshborough
Woodnesborough
TOLL
Stone Cross
Worth
Selling
Oversland
Chartham Hatch
Thanington
Bekesbourne
Bramling
Staple
Old Wives Lees
Chartham
Patrixbourne
Goodnestone
Gore
Ham
Finglesham
Shottenden
Chilham
Shalmsford Street
Nackington
Street End
Bridge
Adisham
Eastry
Knowlton
Sholden
DEAL
THE DOWNS
Garlinge Green
Lower Hardres
Aylesham
Chillenden
Betteshanger
Northbourne
Molash
Petham
Bishopsbourne
Kingston
Nonington
Easole Street
Snowdown
Tilmanstone
Elvington
Upper Hardres Court
Womenswold
Great Mongeham
Walmer
Godmersham
Barham
Derringstone
Barfreston
Ripple
Bilting
Sole Street
Crundale
Waltham
Bossingham
Woolage Green
Eythorne
East Studdal
Sutton
Ringwould
Kingsdown
Hassell Street
Stelling Minnis
Coxhill
Shepherdswell
West Langdon
Martin
Boughton Lees
Wye
Denton
Wingmore
Coldred
East Langdon
Martin Mill
Bodsham
Lyminge Forest
Wootton
Whitfield
Guston
St Margaret's at Cliffe
Kennington
Brook
Hastingleigh
Elmsted
Selsted
Lydden
Temple Ewell
West Cliffe
St Margaret's Bay
Elham
Swingfield St
Ewell Minnis
Hinxhill
Lymbridge Green
Swingfield Minnis
Alkham
Buckland
Willesborough Lees
Brabourne
Rhodes Minnis
Ottinge
Densole
Drellingore
Maxton
CALAIS 1:00
DUNKERQUE 2:00
Stowting
West Hougham
Farthingloe
Brabourne Lees
Lyminge
Mersham
Smeeth
Etchinghill
Paddlesworth
Hawkinge
DOVER
Postling
CHANNEL TUNNEL
Capel le Ferne
Aycliff
Cheeseman's Green
Sellindge
Sellindge Lees
Beachborough
BOULOGNE 0:50
CALAIS 0:40
(March-Dec)
Aldington Frith
Clap Hill
Aldington
E. Stour
Stanford
Newington
CHANNEL TUNNEL
East Wear Bay
Bonnington
Newingreen
Pedlinge
Cheriton
Folkestone
Court-at-Street
Lympne
Saltwood
Sandgate
Bilsington
Military Canal
West Hythe
Hythe
Palmarsh
Burmarsh
Newchurch
Dymchurch
St Mary in the Marsh
Ivychurch
St Mary's Bay
Littlestone on Sea
New Romney
Greatstone on Sea
Lydd
LYDD
Lydd on Sea
M2
M20
A2
A20
A28
A299
A253
A256
A257
A258
A259
A260
A261
A290
A291
A2050
A252
A251
A2070
A255
A254
B2052
B2050
B2190
B2068
B2046
B2011
B2067
B2075

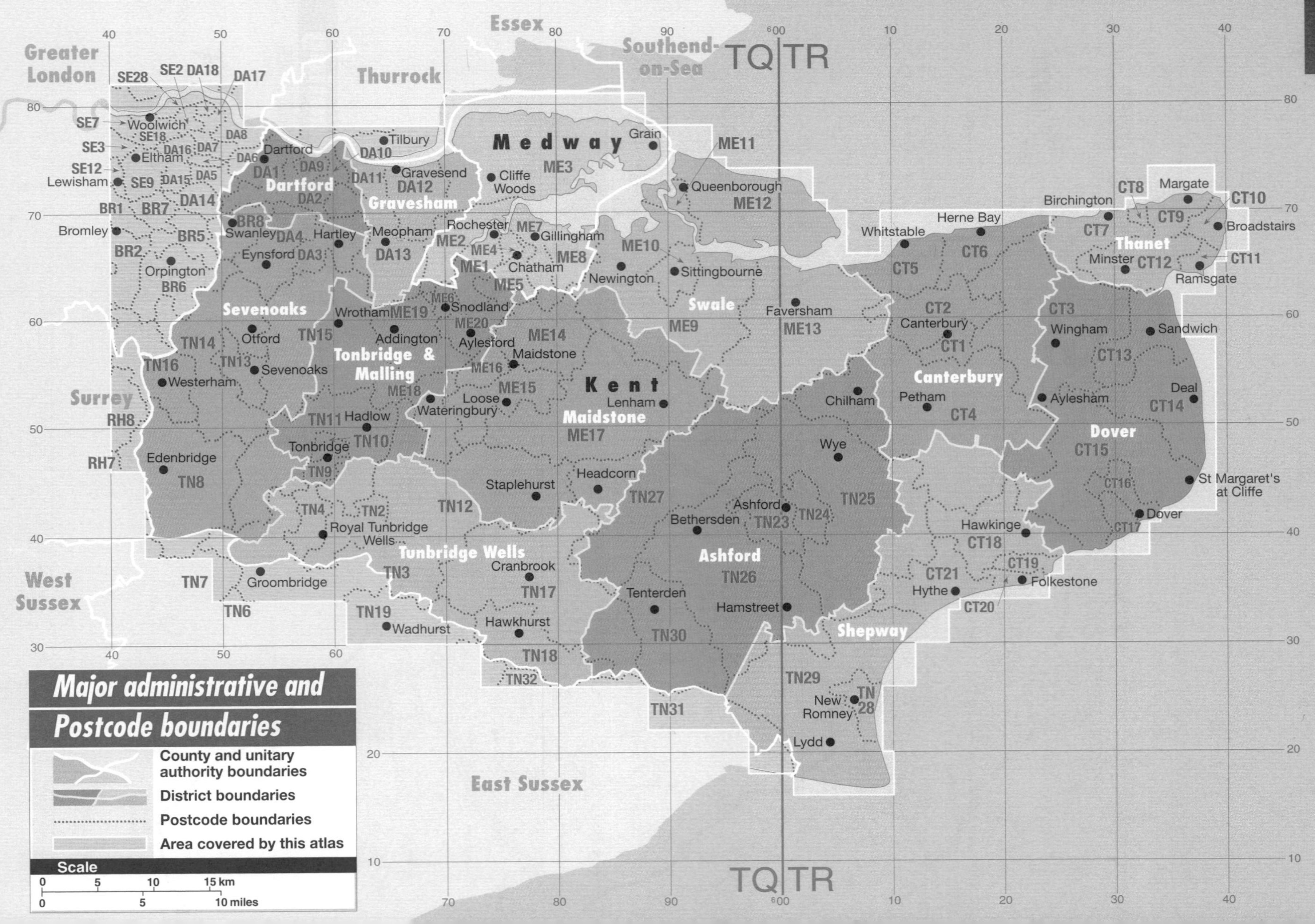

Major administrative and
Postcode boundaries

County and unitary
authority boundaries

District boundaries

Postcode boundaries

Area covered by this atlas

Scale

| | 5 | 10 | 15 km |
| 0 | 5 | 10 miles |

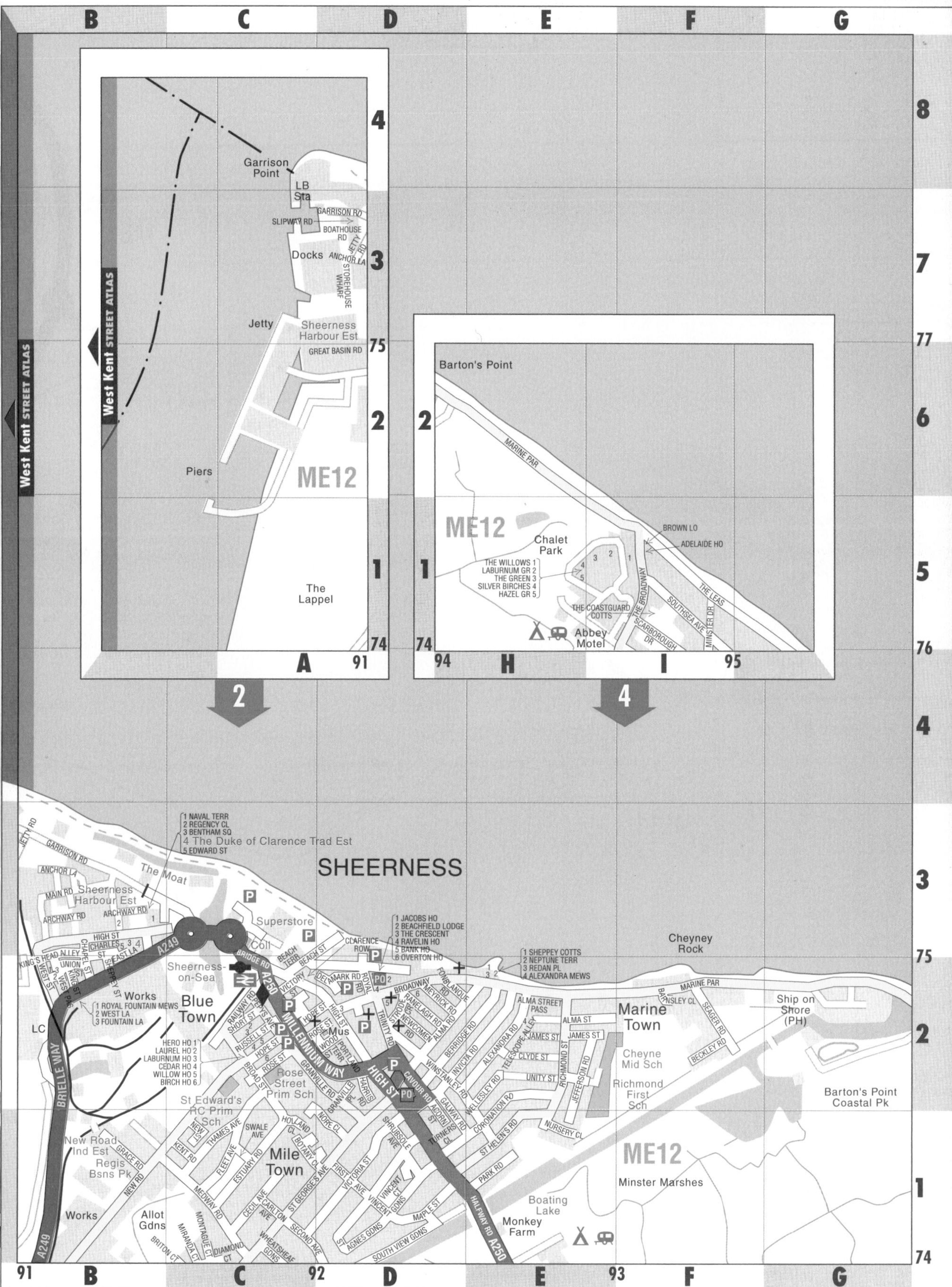

West Kent STREET ATLAS

B   **C**   **D**   **E**   **F**   **G**

8

Garrison
Point

LB
Sta

GARRISON RD

SLIPWAY RD

BOATHOUSE
RD

Docks

7

STOREHOUSE
WHARF

ANCHOR LA

Jetty

Sheerness
Harbour Est

GREAT BASIN RD

75

77

2

ME12

6

Piers

The Lappel

1

The Moat

ME12

Barton's Point

MARINE PAR

ME12

Chalet
Park

BROWN LO

Adelaide Ho

THE WILLOWS 1
LABURNUM GR 2
THE GREEN 3
SILVER BIRCHES 4
HAZEL GR 5

THE COASTGUARD
COTTS

Abbey
Motel

THE LEAS

MINSTER DR

SOUTHSEA AVE

THE BROADWAY

SCARBOROUGH DR

76

A   91

94   **H**   **I**   95

2

4

4

3

SHEERNESS

1 NAVAL TERR
2 REGENCY CL
3 BENTHAM SQ
4 The Duke of Clarence Trad Est
5 EDWARD ST

JETTY RD

GARRISON RD

ANCHOR LA

MAIN RD

Sheerness
Harbour Est

ARCHWAY RD

CHAPEL ST

HIGH ST

CHARLES ST

KING'S HEAD

ALLEY

UNION ST

Works
1 ROYAL FOUNTAIN MEWS
2 WEST LA
3 FOUNTAIN LA

Blue
Town

HERO HO 1
LAUREL HO 2
LABURNUM HO 3
CEDAR HO 4
WILLOW HO 5
BIRCH HO 6

St Edward's
RC Prim
Sch

A249

BRIELLE WAY

LC

New Road
Ind Est
Regis
Bsns Pk

Works

Allot
Gdns

A249

Superstore

Coll

BRIDGE RD

BEACH ST

CLARENCE
ROW

1 JACOBS HO
2 BEACHFIELD LODGE
3 THE CRESCENT
4 RAVELIN HO
5 BANK HO
6 OVERTON HO

DEL-MARK RD

BROADWAY

Sheerness-
on-Sea

VICTORY

RAILWAY RD

SHORT ST

RUSSELL ST

HOPE ST

Mus

HIGH ST

MILLENNIUM WAY

TRINITY RD

WOOD ST

PORTLAND

Rose
Street
Prim Sch

GRANVILLE RD

GRANVILLE

CAVOUR RD

MARDEN RD

HIGH ST

HOLLAND

HOPE ST

Mile
Town

SWALE
AVE

FLEET LANE

Thames Ave

GRAPE RD

KENT RD

NEW RD

MEDWAY RD

MONTAGUE CT

MIRANDA CT

DIAMOND
CT

BRITON CT

WHEATSHEAF
GDNS

CECIL AVE

CARLTON
AVE

ST GEORGE'S AVE

FIRST AVE

VICTORIA ST

AGNES GDNS

SOUTH VIEW GDNS

SHRUBSOLE

TURNER ST

CANNON ST

JACOB ST

ST HELEN'S RD

CORONATION RD

VINCENT
GDNS

VINCENT ST

MAPLE ST

SECOND AVE

A250

HALFWAY RD

PARK RD

1 SHEPPEY COTTS
2 NEPTUNE TERR
3 REDAN PL
4 ALEXANDRA MEWS

PANELAGH RD

METRICK RD

ALMA STREET
PASS

ALMA ST

BERRIDGE RD

INVICTA RD

ALEXANDRA RD

JAMES ST

JAMES ST

CLYDE ST

UNITY ST

WELLESLEY RD

RICHMOND RD

JEFFERSON RD

NURSERY CL

Cheyney
Rock

Marine
Town

Cheyne
Mid Sch

Richmond
First
Sch

MARINE PAR

BARNSLEY CL

SEAGER RD

BECKLEY RD

Ship on
Shore
(PH)

Barton's Point
Coastal Pk

ME12

Minster Marshes

Boating
Lake

Monkey
Farm

74

B   **C**   **D**   **E**   **F**   **G**

91   92   93

3

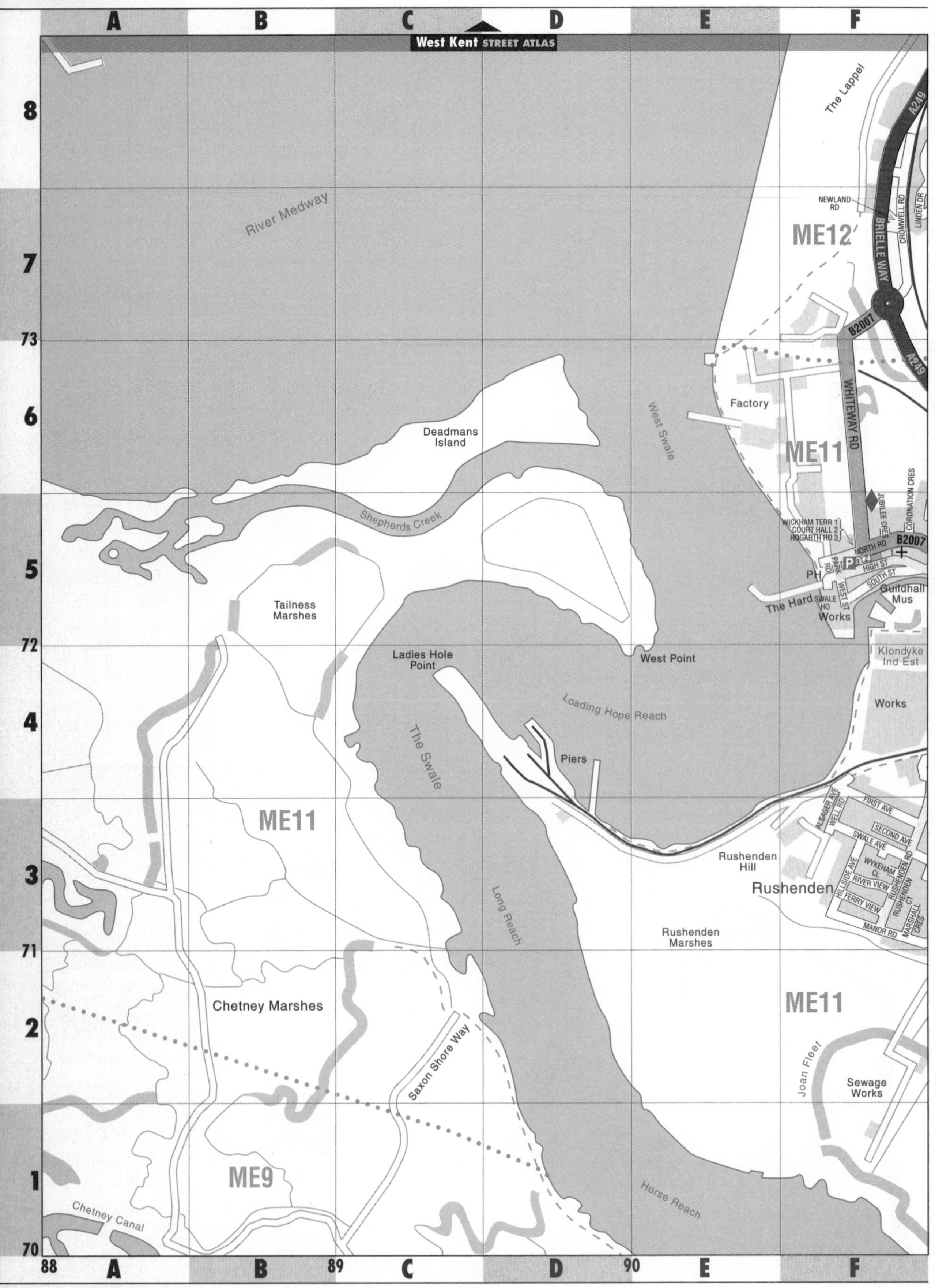

West Kent STREET ATLAS

A   B   C   D   E   F

8

7

73

6

5

72

4

3

71

2

1

70

88   A   B   89   C   D   90   E   F

The Lappel

A249

ME12

NEWLAND RD

CROMWELL RD

LINDEN DR

BRIELLE WAY

B2007

WHITEWAY RD

A249

River Medway

West Swale

Factory

ME11

CORONATION CRES

JUBILEE CRES

WICKHAM TERR 1
COURT HALL 2
HOGARTH HO 3

B2007

Deadmans
Island

NORTH RD

HIGH ST

SWALE RD

WEST ST

PARK RD

Shepherds Creek

Tailness
Marshes

PH

The Hard

P

SOUTH ST

SWALE
HO

Works

Guildhall
Mus

Klondyke
Ind Est

Ladies Hole
Point

West Point

Works

Loading Hope Reach

The Swale

Piers

ALSAGER AVE

WELL RD

FIRST AVE

SECOND AVE

ME11

SWALE AVE

HILLSIDE AVE

WYKEHAM
CL

RIVER VIEW

RUSHENDEN RD

Rushenden
Hill

Rushenden

Long Reach

71

FERRY VIEW

MANOR RD

MARSHALL
CRES

Rushenden
Marshes

ME11

Chetney Marshes

Saxon Shore Way

Joan Fleet

Sewage
Works

ME9

Horse Reach

Chetney Canal

1
4

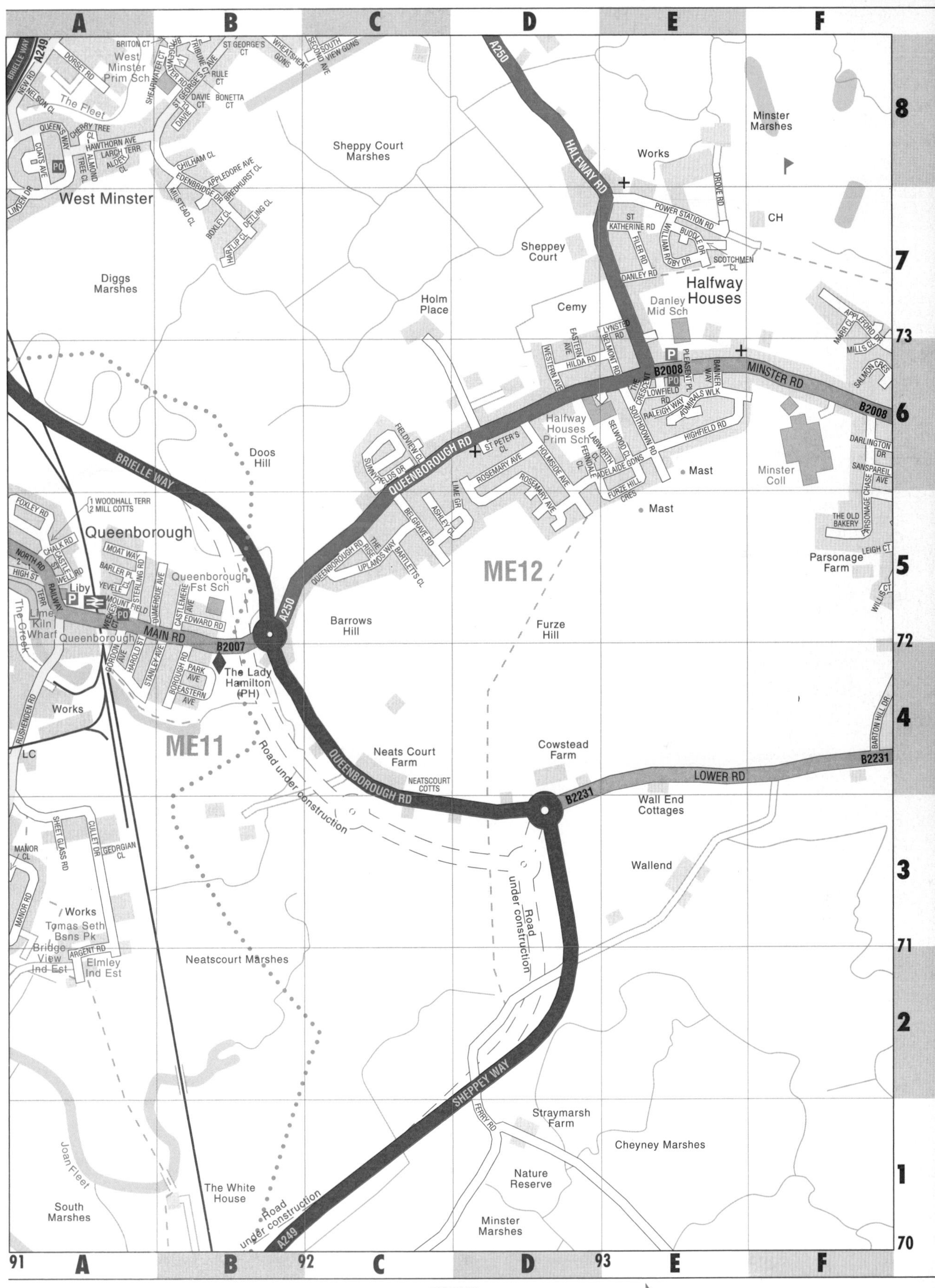
West Minster
West Minster Prim Sch
The Fleet
Diggs Marshes
Sheppy Court Marshes
Sheppey Court
Holm Place
Cemy
Works
Minster Marshes
CH
Halfway Houses
Danley Mid Sch
HALFWAY RD
POWER STATION RD
MINSTER RD
QUEENBOROUGH RD
BRIELLE WAY
Doos Hill
Halfway Houses Prim Sch
Mast
Minster Coll
Parsonage Farm
Queenborough
Queenborough Fst Sch
ME12
ME11
Barrows Hill
Furze Hill
MAIN RD
The Lady Hamilton (PH)
Works
Road under construction
Neats Court Farm
Cowstead Farm
LOWER RD
Wall End Cottages
Wallend
Tomas Seth Bsns Pk
Bridge View Ind Est
Elmley Ind Est
Neatscourt Marshes
SHEPPEY WAY
Straymarsh Farm
Cheyney Marshes
Nature Reserve
Minster Marshes
The White House
South Marshes
Joan Fleet
A249
A250
B2007
B2008
B2231
A B C D E F
8 7 6 5 4 3 2 1
73 72 71 70
91 92 93

15
4

1 3

A B C D E F

8 Ripney Hill Farm

The Leas
Merryman's Hill
Southsea Ave
Sexburga Dr
Minster Dr
Augustine Rd
Seaside Ave
Scarborough Dr

Royal Oak Point

7 Elliott Park Sch

Clovelly Dr
The Glen
Glendale Rd
Wards Hill Rd
Rodmer
The Glen
Broadway
Woodland Dr
Waverley Ave
Hillside Rd
Marina Dr
Scrapsgate Rd
Johnson Way
Kent Ave

Minster

Noreen Ave
The Rowans
Queenborough Dr
Abbeyview Dr
Shurland Ave
Glanwood Dr
Orchard Gro
Bellevue Rd

Haybornes Chase
Northwood Rise
Highview Rd
Alston Cl
Howard Rd
Santorre Ave
Lymouth Dr
Love La

Sheppey
H

Kings Rd
Princes Ave
Imperial Ave
Westcliff Rd

Church Terr
Cardinal Cl
Carriage Cl
Queens Rd
Stanley Rd
Baldwin Rd
Churchill Rd

Round Hill

Seacliff

East End Farm

73

Stiles Cl
Appleford Dr
St Mary's Row
Silverdale Ave
Croidene Ct
The Maples
Trafalgar Par
Saxon Ave
Shurland Ave

Brecon Chase
Minster-in-Sheppey Prim Sch
Waterloo Hill
Mus
Minster Abbey
HIGH ST
BACK LA
PO
Chapel St

Cliff Gdns
Mill Hill
Windmill Rise

Oak La
Caravan Pk

6 B2008
Porter Rd
PO
MINSTER RD
Fleetwood
Darlington Dr
Dreadnought Ave
Matilda Ct
Parish Rd

Worcester
Liby
Blatcher Cl
Copland Ave
George Parris Ct
Harps Ave
New Rd
Bramston Rd
Prince Charles Ave
Petfield
Abbey La

Chiddingford Cl
Tams Gdns
Echo Wlk
Broadway
Sports Gd
St George's CE Mid Sch

Chequers Rd
Pigtail Cnr
Oak Ave
Danedale Ave

B2008
Plough Rd
Eastchurch Rd
Bell La
Sheppey Terr

Sanspareil Ave
Summerville Ave
Tyson Cl
Saunders Ct
Hilltop Rd
Lapwing Cl
Heron Dr
Blatcher Cl
Harps Ave
Hopkins Pl

Nelson Ave
Drake Ave
Elm La

Tadwell Farm

5 Lovell Cl
Allen Cl
Wain Cl
Miller Cl
Barton Hill Dr
Plover Rd
Sheppey Community
H
Rape Hill

1 Alaseun Terr
2 Murthwaite Ct
3 Menzies Ct
4 Turmine St

Thistle Hill Way
Scocles Cotts
Scocles Rd

Boarers Farm
Woottons Farm

Brambledown

Shrubsoles Hill

The Mount

72

Buckthorne Ho
Lower Ave
Thistle Hill
Buckthorne Rd
Orchid
Harebell Cl
Penny Cft
Thistle Hill Way

Scocles Farm

ME12

Shardens Farm
Brambledown Spring

4 Marshlands Farm
B2231
LOWER RD
Piggery
FORTY ACRES HILL

LOWER RD

Elm Tree Inn (PH)
Primrose Cottage
Greyhound Rd

Brambledown

B2231

3 Flatcreek Head

71

South Lees

Elmley Rd

Poors

Windmill
Jay Rd
New Hook Farm

Old Hook Rd

2

Southlees Marshes

1

Newhook Marshes

Old Hook Farm

70

94 A B 95 C D 96 E F

3 16

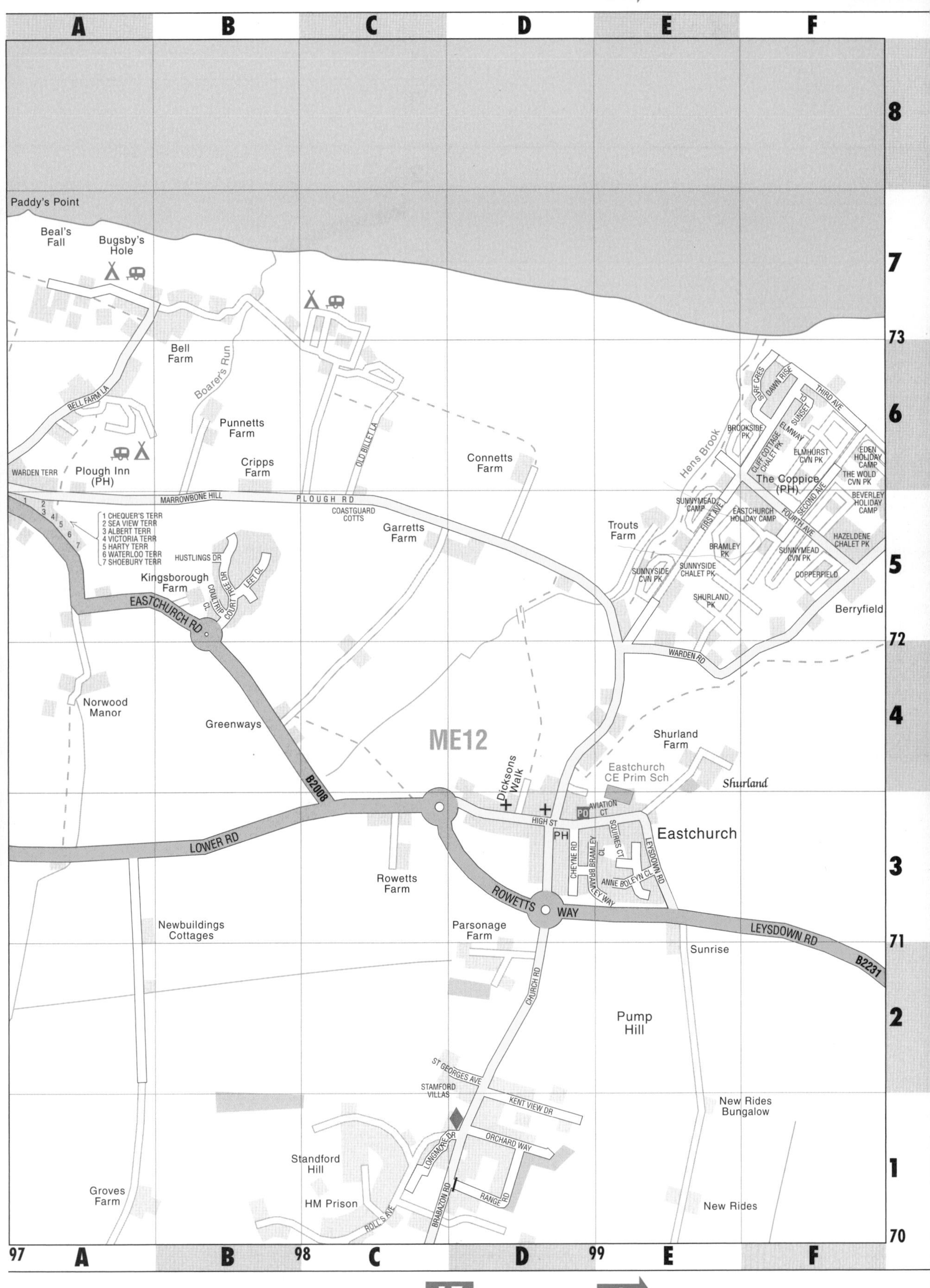

Paddy's Point

Beal's Fall

Bugsby's Hole

Bell Farm

Boarer's Run

Punnetts Farm

Cripps Farm

Warden Terr

Plough Inn (PH)

Bell Farm La

Marrowbone Hill

PLOUGH RD

Old Billet La

Coastguard Cotts

Connetts Farm

Garretts Farm

1 Chequer's Terr
2 Sea View Terr
3 Albert Terr
4 Victoria Terr
5 Harty Terr
6 Waterloo Terr
7 Shoebury Terr

Hustlings Dr

Kingsborough Farm

EASTCHURCH RD

COULTER CL

CASLET

LEE CL

FIRST AVE

Norwood Manor

Greenways

B2008

LOWER RD

ME12

Dicksons Walk

Rowetts Farm

Newbuildings Cottages

Parsonage Farm

ROWETTS WAY

Trouts Farm

SURF CRES

DAWN RISE

THIRD AVE

SUNSET

Brookside PK

ELMWAY

CLIFF COTTAGE CHALET PK

ELMHURST CVN PK

THE WOLD CVN PK

EDEN HOLIDAY CAMP

The Coppice (PH)

Sunnymead Camp

Eastchurch Holiday Camp

Second Ave

Fourth Ave

Beverley Holiday Camp

Hazeldene Chalet PK

Bramley PK

Sunnyside CVN PK

Sunnyside Chalet PK

Sunnymead CVN PK

Copperfield

Shurland PK

Berryfield

WARDEN RD

Shurland Farm

Eastchurch CE Prim Sch

Shurland

HIGH ST

PO

AVIATION CT

PH

CHEYNE RD

SQUIRES CT

BRAMLEY

BRAMLEY CL

ANNE BOLEYN CL

BRAMLEY WAY

LEYSDOWN RD

Eastchurch

LEYSDOWN RD

B2231

Sunrise

CHURCH RD

Pump Hill

New Rides Bungalow

ST GEORGES AVE

Stamford Villas

KENT VIEW DR

Standford Hill

HM Prison

LONGMORE DR

BRABAZON RD

ORCHARD WAY

RANGE RD

ROLL'S AVE

Groves Farm

New Rides

5

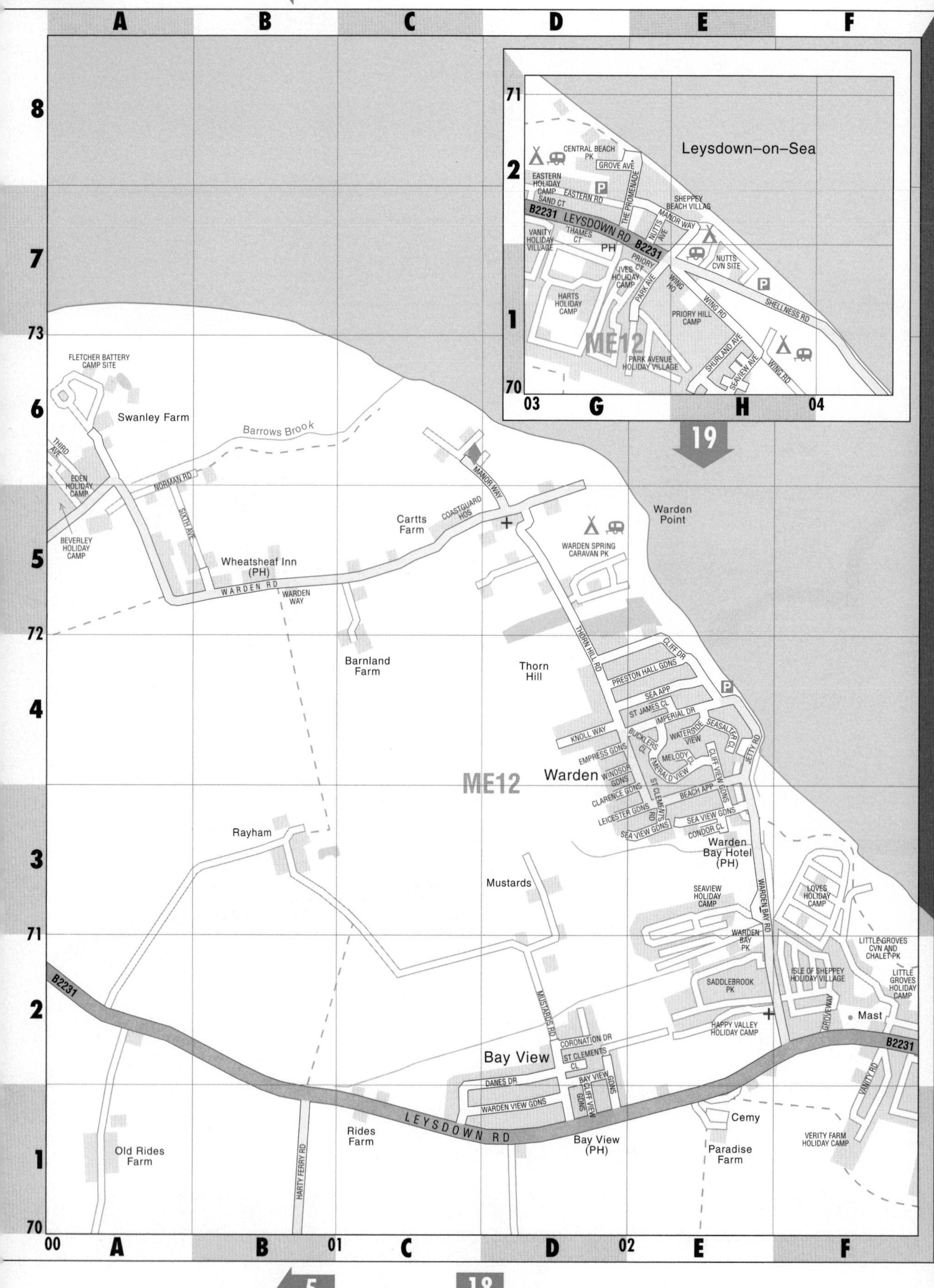

A   B   C   D   E   F

8

7

73

6

5

72

4

3

71

2

1

70

71

Leysdown-on-Sea

2

CENTRAL BEACH PK
GROVE AVE
EASTERN HOLIDAY CAMP
EASTERN RD
SAND CT
SHEPPEY BEACH VILLAS
MANOR WAY
B2231   LEYSDOWN RD   B2231
THAMES CT
NUTTS AVE
VANITY HOLIDAY VILLAGE
PH
PRIORY
IVES CT HOLIDAY CAMP
NUTTS CVN SITE
SHELLNESS RD

1

HARTS HOLIDAY CAMP
PARK AVE
PRIORY HILL CAMP
WING HO
WING RD
ME12
PARK AVENUE HOLIDAY VILLAGE
SHURLAND AVE
SEAVIEW AVE
WING RD

70

03   G   H   04

19

FLETCHER BATTERY CAMP SITE
Swanley Farm
Barrows Brook
THIRD AVE
EDEN HOLIDAY CAMP
NORMAN RD
BEVERLEY HOLIDAY CAMP
SIXTH AVE
Wheatsheaf Inn (PH)
WARDEN RD
WARDEN WAY
Cartts Farm
COASTGUARD HOS
MANOR WAY
Warden Point
WARDEN SPRING CARAVAN PK
Barnland Farm
Thorn Hill
THORN HILL RD
CLIFF DR
PRESTON HALL GDNS
SEA APP
ST JAMES CL
IMPERIAL DR
KNOLL WAY
BUCKLERS
WATERSIDE VIEW
SEASALT CL
MELODY
EMPRESS GDNS
WINDSOR GDNS
EMERALD VIEW
CLIFF VIEW GDNS
JETTY RD
ME12
Warden
CLARENCE GDNS
ST CLEMENTS RD
BEACH APP
LEICESTER GDNS
SEA VIEW GDNS
CONDOR CL
SEA VIEW GDNS
Rayham
Mustards
Warden Bay Hotel (PH)
SEAVIEW HOLIDAY CAMP
LOVES HOLIDAY CAMP
WARDEN BAY PK
WARDEN BAY RD
LITTLE GROVES CVN AND CHALET PK
LITTLE GROVES HOLIDAY CAMP
SADDLEBROOK PK
ISLE OF SHEPPEY HOLIDAY VILLAGE
B2231
MUSTARDS RD
CORONATION DR
ST CLEMENTS CL
HAPPY VALLEY HOLIDAY CAMP
GROVEWAY
Mast
B2231
Bay View
DANES DR
BAY VIEW GDNS
CLIFF VIEW GDNS
WARDEN VIEW GDNS
LEYSDOWN RD
Cemy
VERITY RD
Old Rides Farm
HARTY FERRY RD
Rides Farm
Bay View (PH)
Paradise Farm
VERITY FARM HOLIDAY CAMP

00   A   B   01   C   D   02   E   F

8

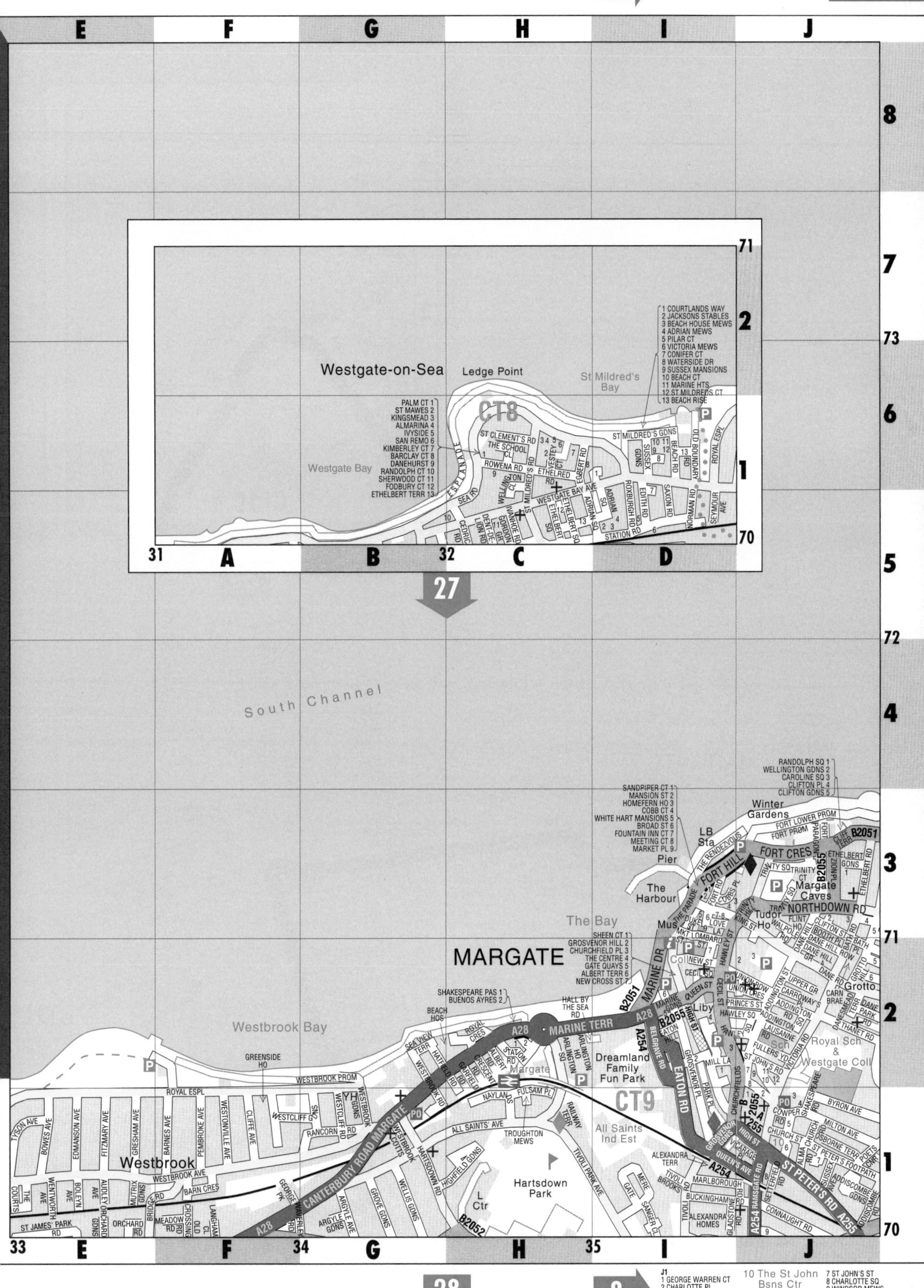

J1
1 GEORGE WARREN CT
2 CHARLOTTE PL
3 SPARROW CASTLE
4 MILTON SQ
5 ARNOLD RD
6 OXFORD ST
7 HOMESTEAD CL
8 VICARAGE CRES
9 CONNAUGHT GDNS
10 The St John Bsns Ctr

J2
1 PUMP LA
2 COLLEGE SQ
3 COLLEGE WLK
4 ANCHOR HILL
5 GROTTO RD
6 GROTTO GDNS
7 ST JOHN'S ST
8 CHARLOTTE SQ
9 WINDSOR MEWS
10 PRINCES CRES
11 LAUSANNE TERR
12 VENTNOR LA

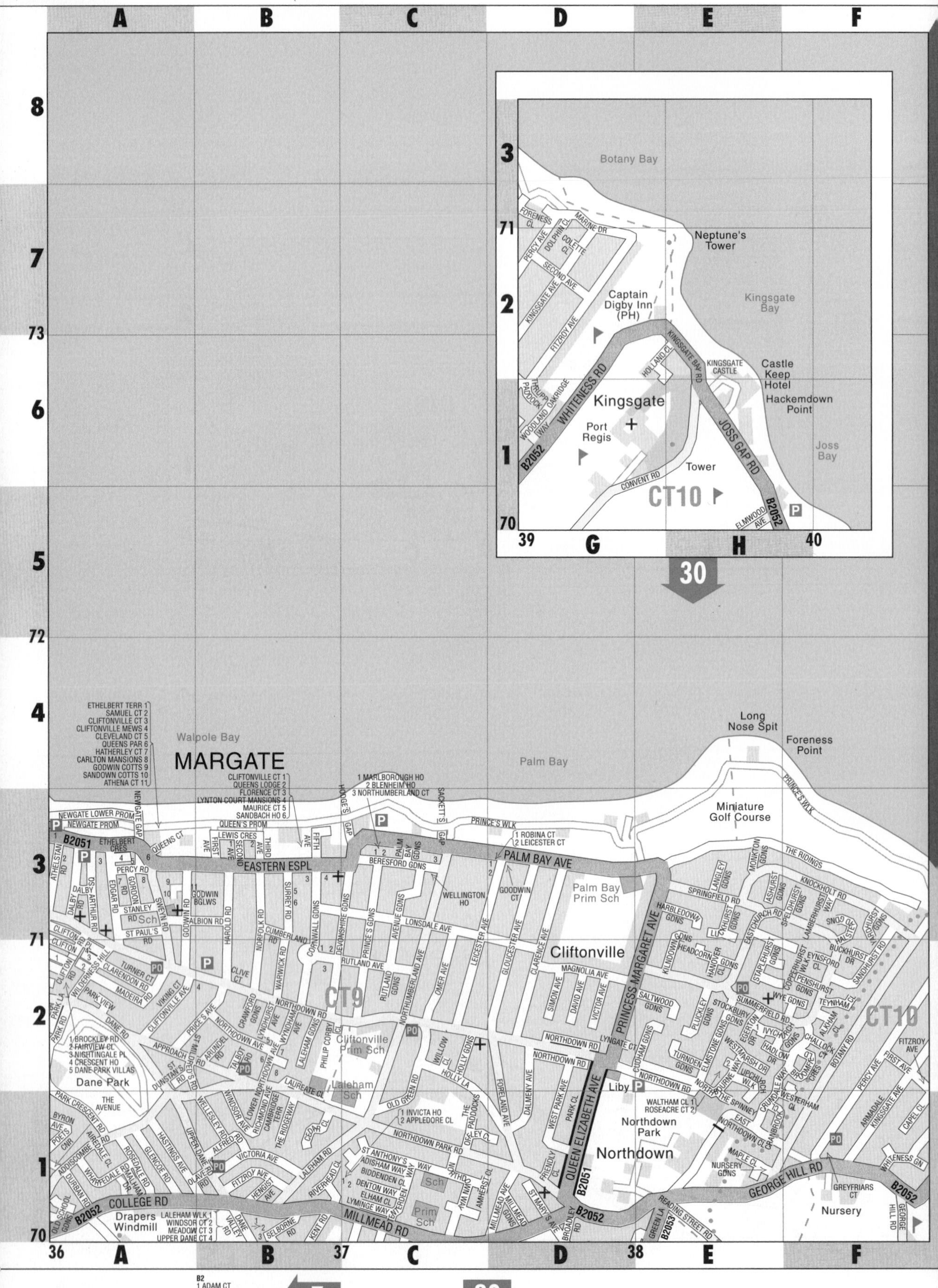

A B C D E F

8

7

73

6

5

72

4

3

71

2

1

70

Inset map (CT10)

3

71

2

1

70

Botany Bay

FORENESS CL
PERCY AVE
DOL PRIN CL
COLETTE
MARINE DR

Neptune's Tower

KINGSGATE AVE
SECOND AVE

Kingsgate Bay

Captain Digby Inn (PH)

FITZROY AVE

HOLLAND CL

KINGSGATE BAY RD

Castle Keep Hotel

Hackemdown Point

Kingsgate

KINGSGATE CASTLE

Port Regis

WOODLAND DRAKERIDGE WAY
THRUSH CL
PADDOCK CL
B2052
WHITENESS RD

CONVENT RD

JOSS GAP RD

Joss Bay

Tower

CT10

ELMWOOD AVE
B2052

P

39   G   40   H

↓ 30

ETHELBERT TERR 1
SAMUEL CT 2
CLIFTONVILLE CT 3
CLIFTONVILLE MEWS 4
CLEVELAND CT 5
QUEENS PAR 6
HATHERLEY CT 7
CARLTON MANSIONS 8
GODWIN COTTS 9
SANDOWN COTTS 10
ATHENA CT 11

Long Nose Spit
Foreness Point

Walpole Bay

MARGATE

Palm Bay

CLIFTONVILLE CT 1
QUEENS LODGE 2
FLORENCE CT 3
LYNTON COURT MANSIONS 4
MAURICE CT 5
SANDBACH HO 6

1 MARLBOROUGH HO
2 BLENHEIM HO
3 NORTHUMBERLAND CT

Miniature Golf Course

PRINCE'S WLK

NEWGATE LOWER PROM
P NEWGATE PROM

Queen's Prom

QUEENS CT

LEWIS CRES

PRINCE'S WLK

B2051
ATHEL STAN RD
ETHELBERT CRES
PERCY RD
EDGAR RD
GORDON
QUEENS ST
FIRST
SECOND
THIRD
FIFTH
AVE
KING'S GAP
P
PALM BAY AVE

Eastern Espl

1 ROBINA CT
2 LEICESTER CT

Palm Bay Prim Sch

Cliftonville

CLIFTON RD
CLIFTON
TURNER RD
CLARENDON RD
MADEIRA RD
DALBY
ARTHUR RD
STANLEY RD
ST PAUL'S RD
GODWIN BGLWS
ALBION RD
HAROLD RD
WARWICK RD
NORFOLK RD
CUMBERLAND RD
CORNWALL GDNS
DEVONSHIRE GDNS
PRINCE'S GDNS
AVENUE RD
LONSDALE AVE
WELLINGTON HO
GOODWIN CT

BERESFORD GDNS

PALM
BAY

SURREY RD

CT9

RUTLAND AVE

OMER AVE
LEICESTER AVE
GLOUCESTER AVE
CLARENCE AVE

Magnolia Ave
SIMON AVE
DAVID AVE
VICTOR AVE

PRINCESS MARGARET AVE

SPRINGFIELD RD
HARBLEDOWN GDNS
KILNDOWN GDNS
HEADCORN RD
HARNET CT
SALTWOOD GDNS
LYNGATE CT

KNOCKHOLT RD
THE RIDINGS
MONKTON
LANGLEY GDNS
ASHURST GDNS
CASTROPH GDNS
LAMBERHURST WAY
SNOD GDNS
BUCKHURST RD
SANDHURST RD
STAPLEHURST GDNS
PENSHURST GDNS
COPPERHURST DR
EYNSFORD RD
IVYCHURCH GDNS
STOCKBURY GDNS
SUMMERFIELD GDNS
WYE GDNS
TEYNHAM
CHALLOCK
MALL
TELL

CT10

PARK LA
PARK VIEW
WILTON RD
VIKING AVE
SWEYN RD
CLIVE CT
CrescentHO
Dane Park

1 BROCKLEY RD
2 FAIRVIEW CT
3 NIGHTINGALE PL
4 CRESCENT HO
5 DANE PARK VILLAS

CLIFTONVILLE AVE
PRICE'S AVE
CRAWFORD RD
NORTHDOWN AVE
WYNDHAM AVE
ARUNDEL GDNS
NORTHDOWN RD
WILLOW

Cliftonville Prim Sch
Philip Corby

HOLLY AVE
HOLLY LA
DALMENY AVE
FORELAND AVE
WEST PARK AVE
PARK CL

NORTHDOWN RD

Liby P
NORTHDOWN RD

TURNDEN GDNS
WESTMARSH DR
UPCHURCH WLK
HADLOW
EAST
CRUNDALE GDNS
WESTERHAM

PERCY AVE

ARMADALE
KINGSGATE GN

BYRON AVE
POE'S LA
CNR
ADDISCOMBE RD
WHARFEDALE RD
ARDALE CT
ROSEGATE RD
GLENCOE RD
DURBAN RD
DUNSTAN RD
WESTFIELD RD
Laureate CL
Laleham Sch
OLD GREEN RD
REDLEY CL
THE PADDOCKS
WALTHAM CL 1
ROSEACRE CT 2
Northdown Park

Northdown

NURSERY GDNS
MAPLE CL
THE SPINNEY
EAST
WESTERHAM

FITZROY AVE

P0

B2052
COLLEGE RD

Drapers Windmill

LALEHAM WLK 1
WINDSOR CT 2
MEADOW CT 3
UPPER DANE CT 4

THE AVENUE
PARK CRESCENT RD
HASTINGS AVE
UPPER DANE
GEORGE
VICTORIA AVE
RIVERHEAD RD
KENT RD
FITZROY AVE
HENGIST AVE
SELBORNE RD
DANE VALLEY

ST ANTHONY'S WAY
ADISHAM WAY
BIDDENDEN WAY
DENTON WAY
ELHAM CL
LYMINGE WAY
Sch
Prim Sch

WM MAR
AMHERST
ST MARY'S AVE

QUEEN ELIZABETH AVE

1 INVICTA HO
2 APPLEDORE CL

B2051

FRIENDLY
BROADLEY
B2052

READING STREET RD
GREEN LA
B2053

Nursery

GEORGE HILL RD

Greyfriars

WHITENESS GN

B2052

GEORGE HILL RD

MILLMEAD RD

36 A 37 B C 38 D E F

B2
1 ADAM CT
2 JAMES CT
3 RUTLAND HO
4 WESTMOUNT HO
5 HIGHFIELD CT
6 REBECCA CT
7 RICHARD CT
8 LEONA CT

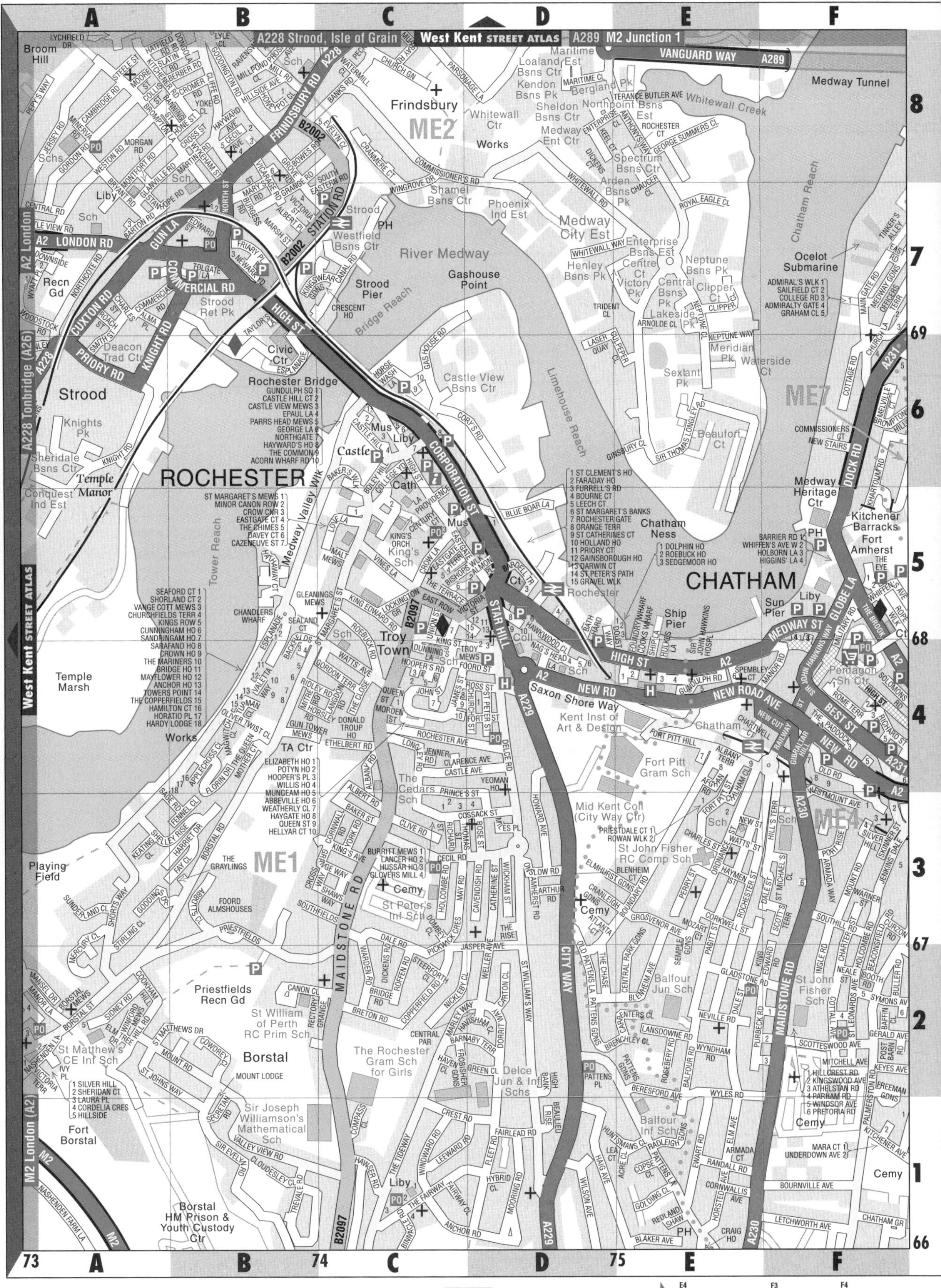

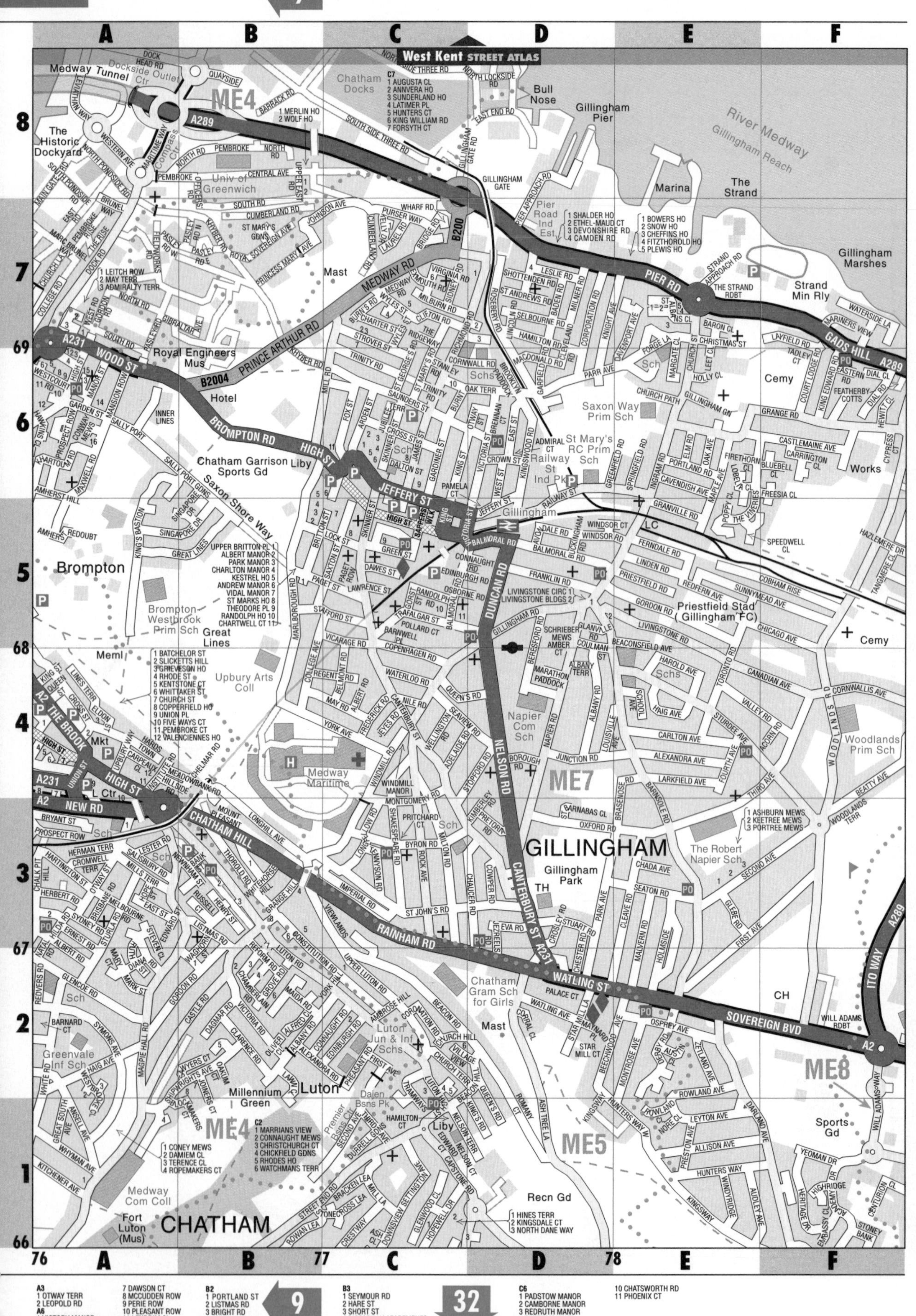

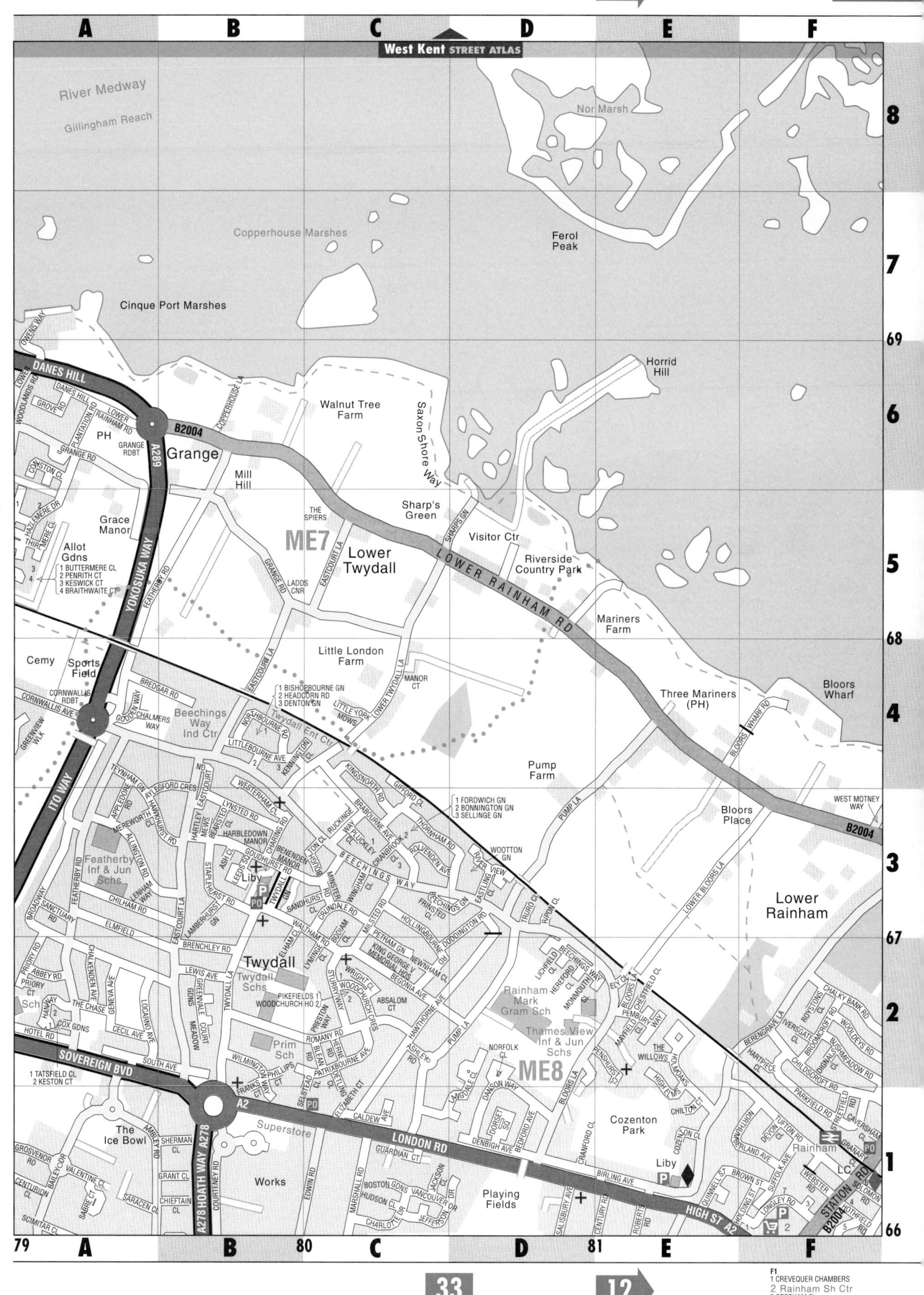

West Kent STREET ATLAS

A B C D E F

River Medway
Gillingham Reach

Nor Marsh

Copperhouse Marshes

Ferol Peak

8

Cinque Port Marshes

Horrid Hill

7

69

DANES HILL
B2004
Grange
Walnut Tree Farm
Saxon Shore Way

6

ME7
Lower Twydall
Sharp's Green
Visitor Ctr
Riverside Country Park
LOWER RAINHAM RD

5

68

Cemy
Sports Field
Little London Farm
Mariners Farm
Three Mariners (PH)
Bloors Wharf

4

1 FORDWICH GN
2 BONNINGTON GN
3 SELLINGE GN
Pump Farm
Bloors Place
WEST MOTNEY WAY
B2004

3

67

Twydall
Rainham Mark Gram Sch
Lower Rainham

2

ME8
Cozenton Park
Rainham

1

Sovereign Blvd
Superstore
LONDON RD
The Ice Bowl
Playing Fields
HIGH ST A2
B2004
STATION RD

66

79 A 80 B 81 C D E F

F1
1 CREVEQUER CHAMBERS
2 Rainham Sh Ctr
3 GRESHAM CL
4 HARRISON CT
5 MAPLINS CL
6 SIGNAL CT
7 SUFFOLK CT

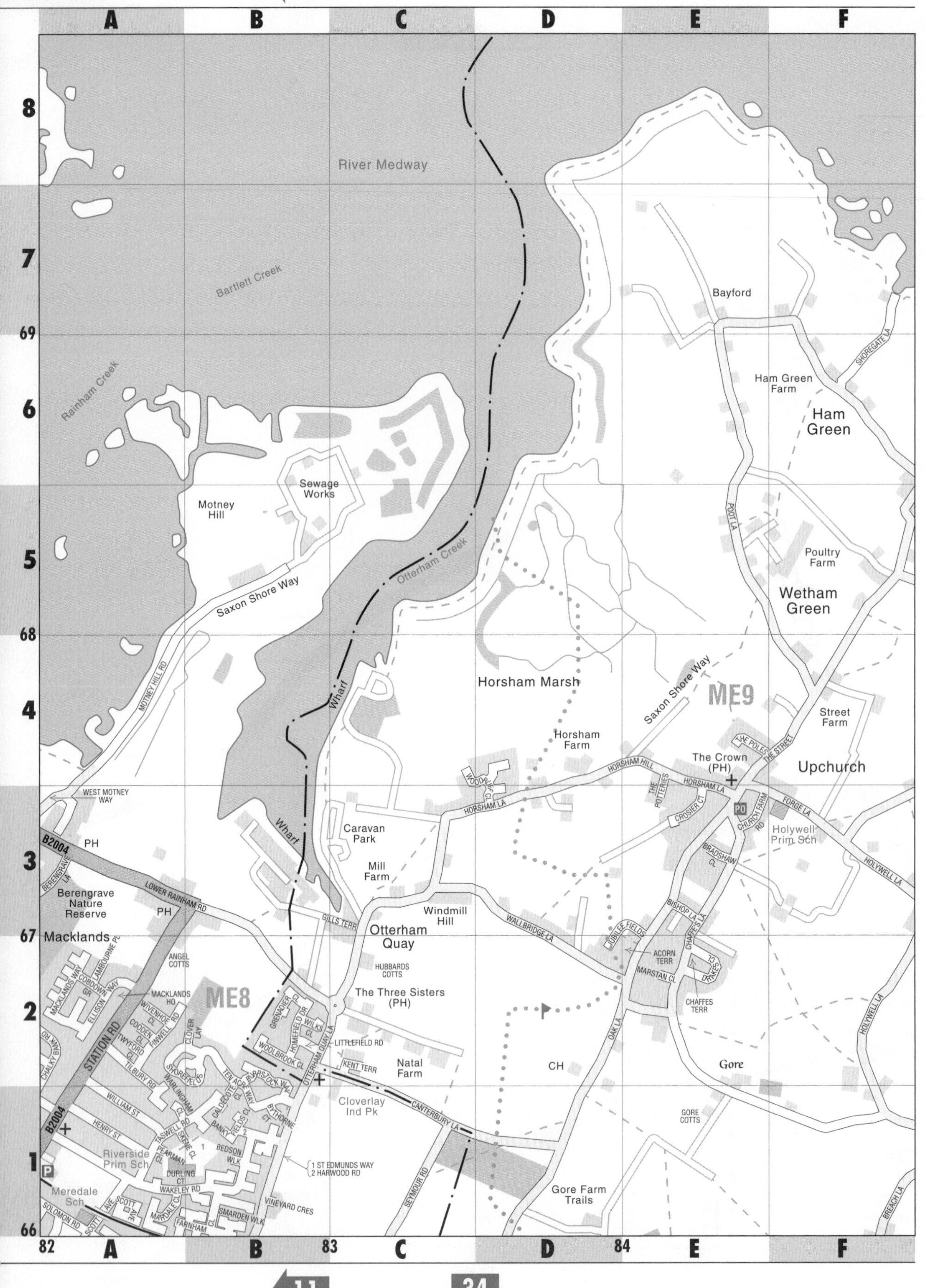

A B C D E F

8

River Medway

7

Bartlett Creek

69

6

Rainham Creek

Ham Green Farm

Bayford

Ham Green

SHOREGATE LA

POOT LA

Sewage Works

Motney Hill

Poultry Farm

Wetham Green

5

Saxon Shore Way

Otterham Creek

68

Wharf

Horsham Marsh

Saxon Shore Way

ME9

Street Farm

4

Horsham Farm

THE POLES

THE STREET

Upchurch

WEST MOTNEY WAY

Horsham Hill

Horsham LA

The Crown (PH)

THE POTTERIES

CROSIER CT

Horsham LA

PO

FORGE LA

B2004

PH

Caravan Park

WOOD LA

Horsham LA

Holywell Prim Sch

HOLYWELL LA

Berengrave Nature Reserve

LOWER RAINHAM RD

Mill Farm

BRADSHAW CL

3

PH

BISHOP LA

CHAFFES LA

67

Macklands

GILLS TERR

Windmill Hill

WALLBRIDGE LA

JUBILEE FIELDS

ACORN TERR

Otterham Quay

TO CRES

MARSTAN CL

ANGEL COTTS

MACKLANDS HO

HUBBARDS COTTS

CHAFFES TERR

2

MACKLANDS WAY

CAMBOURNE PL

ME8

GRENADIER

WILKS

The Three Sisters (PH)

OAK LA

Gore

ELLISON WAY

WIVENHOE CL

CL

HOMEFIELD DR

OTTERHAM QUAY LA

GORE COTTS

STATION RD

COLPS CL

FINWELL RD

CLOVER LA

WOOLBROOK CL

LITTLEFIELD RD

CH

WILLIAM ST

TILBURY RD

KENT TERR

Natal Farm

CALDECOTT CL

BANKS

BETHORNE

1

B2004

HENRY ST

Riverside Prim Sch

P

Cloverlay Ind Pk

CANTERBURY LA

Gore Farm Trails

Meredale Sch

DURLING CT

WAKELEY RD

SELMOUR RD

1 ST EDMUNDS WAY
2 HARWOOD RD

SOLOMON RD

SMARDEN WLK

VINEYARD CRES

BREACH LA

66

82 A B 83 C D 84 E F

14

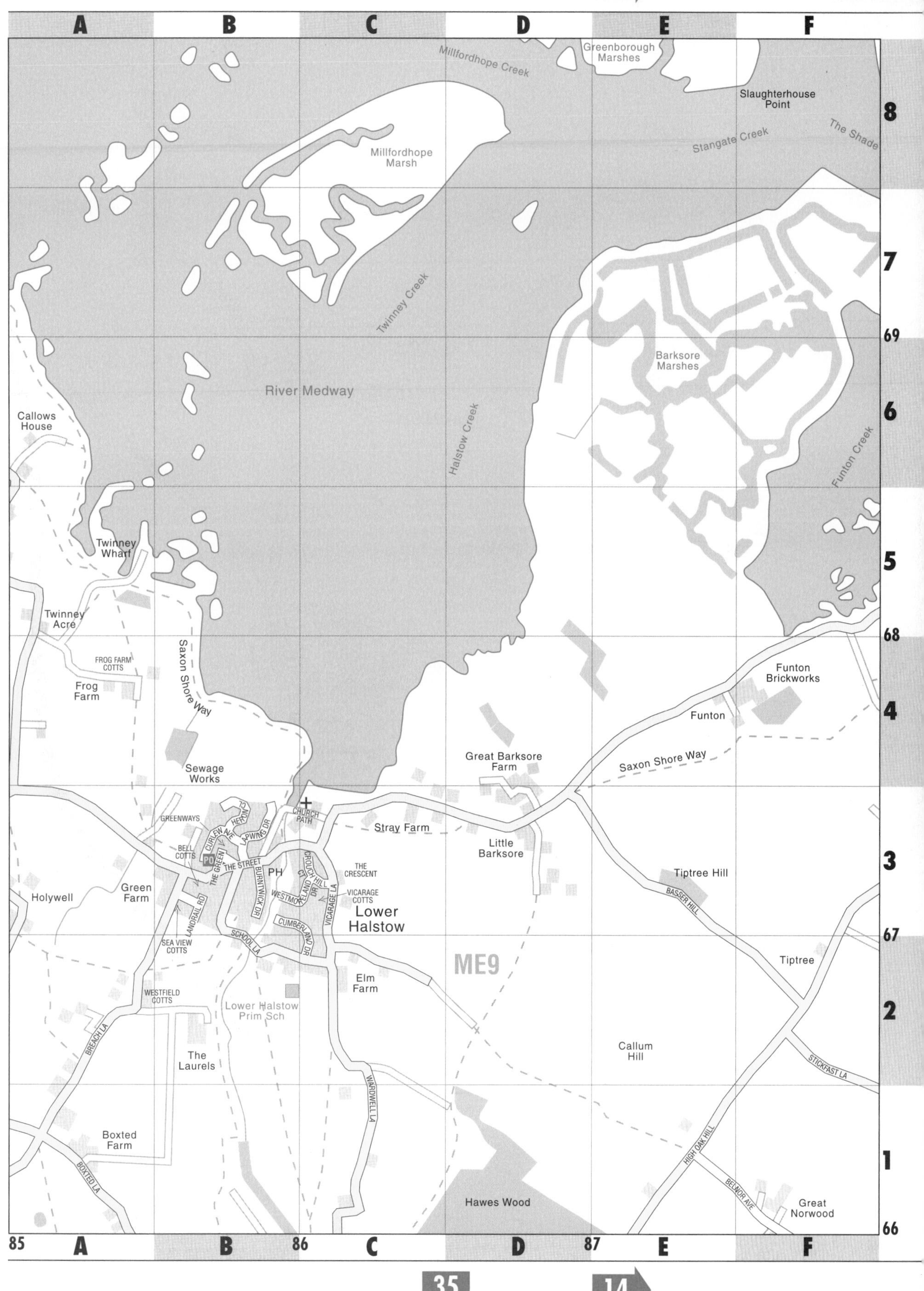

A
B
C
D
E
F
Greenborough Marshes
Millfordhope Creek
Slaughterhouse Point
Stangate Creek
The Shade
Millfordhope Marsh
Twinney Creek
Barksore Marshes
River Medway
Halstow Creek
Funton Creek
Callows House
Twinney Wharf
Twinney Acre
FROG FARM COTTS
Frog Farm
Saxon Shore Way
Sewage Works
Funton Brickworks
Funton
Great Barksore Farm
Saxon Shore Way
GREENWAYS
CHURCH PATH
Stray Farm
Little Barksore
BELL COTTS
PO
CURLEW AVE
HERON CL
LAPWING DR
THE GREEN
THE STREET
BURNTWICK DR
CROUCH HILL CT
ELAND DR
WESTMORLAND
VICARAGE LA
THE CRESCENT
VICARAGE COTTS
PH
Lower Halstow
Tiptree Hill
BASSER HILL
Holywell
Green Farm
LANDRAIL RD
SEA VIEW COTTS
SCHOOL LA
CUMBERLAND DR
ME9
Tiptree
Elm Farm
WESTFIELD COTTS
Lower Halstow Prim Sch
BREACH LA
The Laurels
Callum Hill
STICKFAST LA
WARDWELL LA
Boxted Farm
BOXTED LA
HIGH OAK HILL
BELMOR AVE
Hawes Wood
Great Norwood
8
7
69
6
5
68
4
3
67
2
1
66
85
86
87

35

14

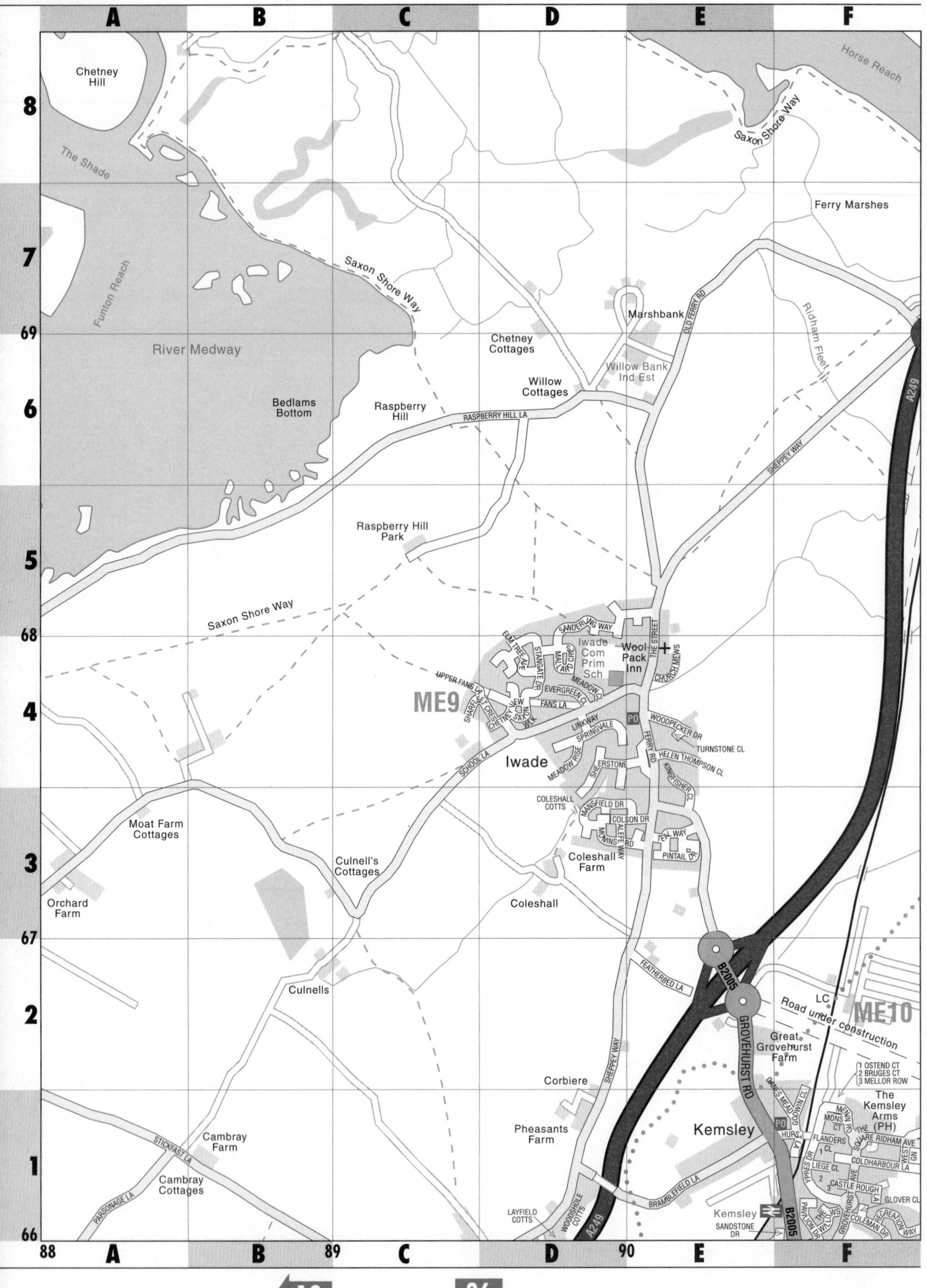

A   B   C   D   E   F

Chetney Hill

The Shade

Horse Reach

Saxon Shore Way

Ferry Marshes

Funton Reach

River Medway

Saxon Shore Way

Marshbank

Chetney Cottages

Old Ferry Rd

Ridham Fleet

Bedlams Bottom

Raspberry Hill

Willow Bank Ind Est

Willow Cottages

Raspberry Hill La

Sheppey Way

A249

Raspberry Hill Park

Saxon Shore Way

Sander Jag Way

The Street

Iwade Com Prim Sch

Wool Pack Inn

Church Mews

ME9

Upper Fans La

Flint Tree Ave

Stangate Dr

New Rd

Meadow Cl

Evergreen Cl

Fans La

Woodpecker Dr

PO

Turnstone Cl

School La

Linkway

Springvale

Meadow Rise

Erstone

Ferry Rd

Kingsfisher Cl

Helen Thompson Cl

Iwade

Moat Farm Cottages

Coleshall Cotts

Mansfield Dr

Colson Dr

Alef Rd

McInnes Way

Teal Way

Pintail Cl

Culnell's Cottages

Coleshall Farm

Orchard Farm

Coleshall

Featherbed La

B2005

LC

ME10

Road under construction

Culnells

Sheppey Way

Grovehurst Rd

Great Grovehurst Farm

1 OSTEND CT
2 BRUGES CT
3 MELLOR ROW

Corbiere

Dames Meadow

The Kemsley Arms (PH)

Ridham Ave

Stickfast La

Cambray Farm

Pheasants Farm

Kemsley

PO

Flanders Cl

Coldharbour Ave

Castle Rough

Glover Cl

Parsonage La

Cambray Cottages

Woodsholt Cotts

Bramblefield La

A249

Layfield Cotts

Kemsley

Sandstone Dr

B2005

Coleman Dr

Creaton Way

88   A   B   89   C   D   90   E   F

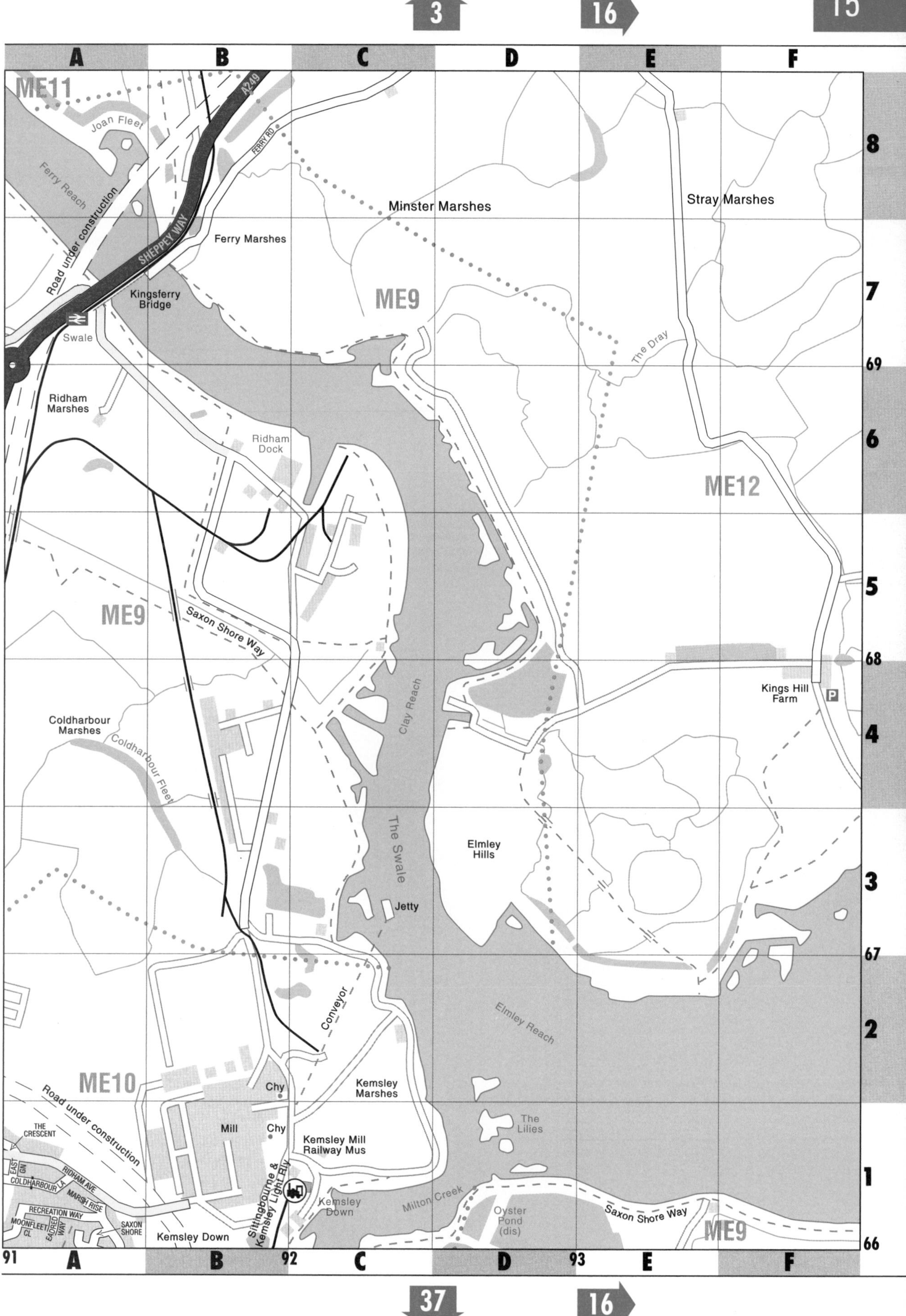

ME11

Joan Fleet

Ferry Reach

SHEPPEY WAY

FERRY RD

A249

Road under construction

Ferry Marshes

Minster Marshes

Stray Marshes

ME9

Kingsferry Bridge

Swale

Ridham Marshes

The Dray

ME12

Ridham Dock

Saxon Shore Way

ME9

Clay Reach

Kings Hill Farm

P

Coldharbour Marshes

Coldharbour Fleet

The Swale

Elmley Hills

Jetty

Conveyor

Elmley Reach

ME10

Road under construction

Kemsley Marshes

THE CRESCENT

EAST GN

RIDHAM AVE

MARSH RISE

COLDHARBOUR LA

RECREATION WAY

MOONFLEET CL

EADRED WAY

SAXON SHORE

Chy

Mill

Chy

Kemsley Mill Railway Mus

Sittingbourne & Kemsley Light Rly

Kemsley Down

The Lilies

Milton Creek

Oyster Pond (dis)

Saxon Shore Way

ME9

Kemsley Down

8
7
69
6
5
68
4
3
67
2
1
66

91 A B 92 C D 93 E F

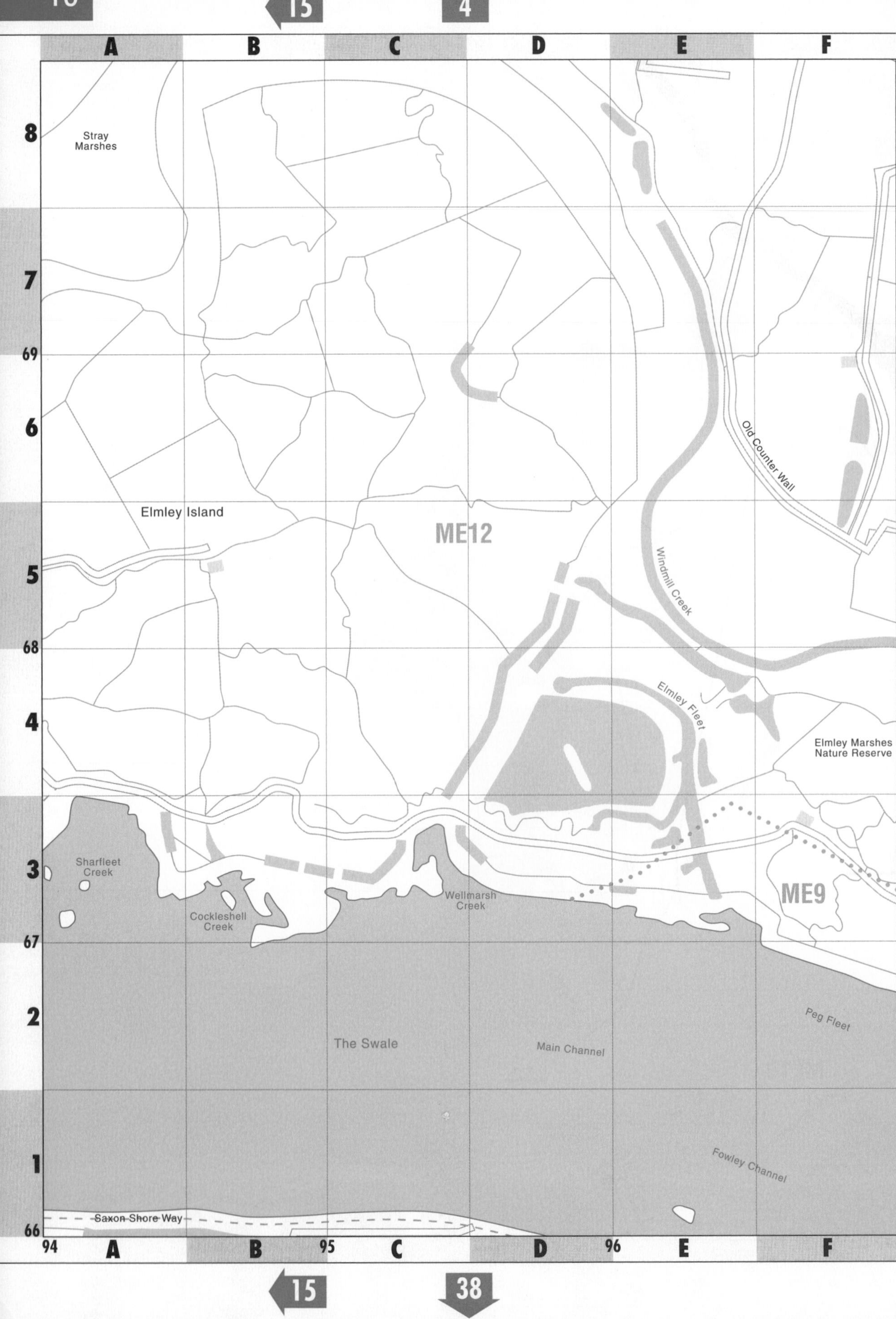

A B C D E F

8

Stray
Marshes

7

69

6

Elmley Island

ME12

Old Counter Wall

Windmill Creek

5

68

Elmley Fleet

4

Elmley Marshes
Nature Reserve

3

Sharfleet
Creek

Cockleshell
Creek

Wellmarsh
Creek

ME9

67

2

The Swale

Main Channel

Peg Fleet

1

Fowley Channel

66

Saxon Shore Way

94 A B 95 C D 96 E F

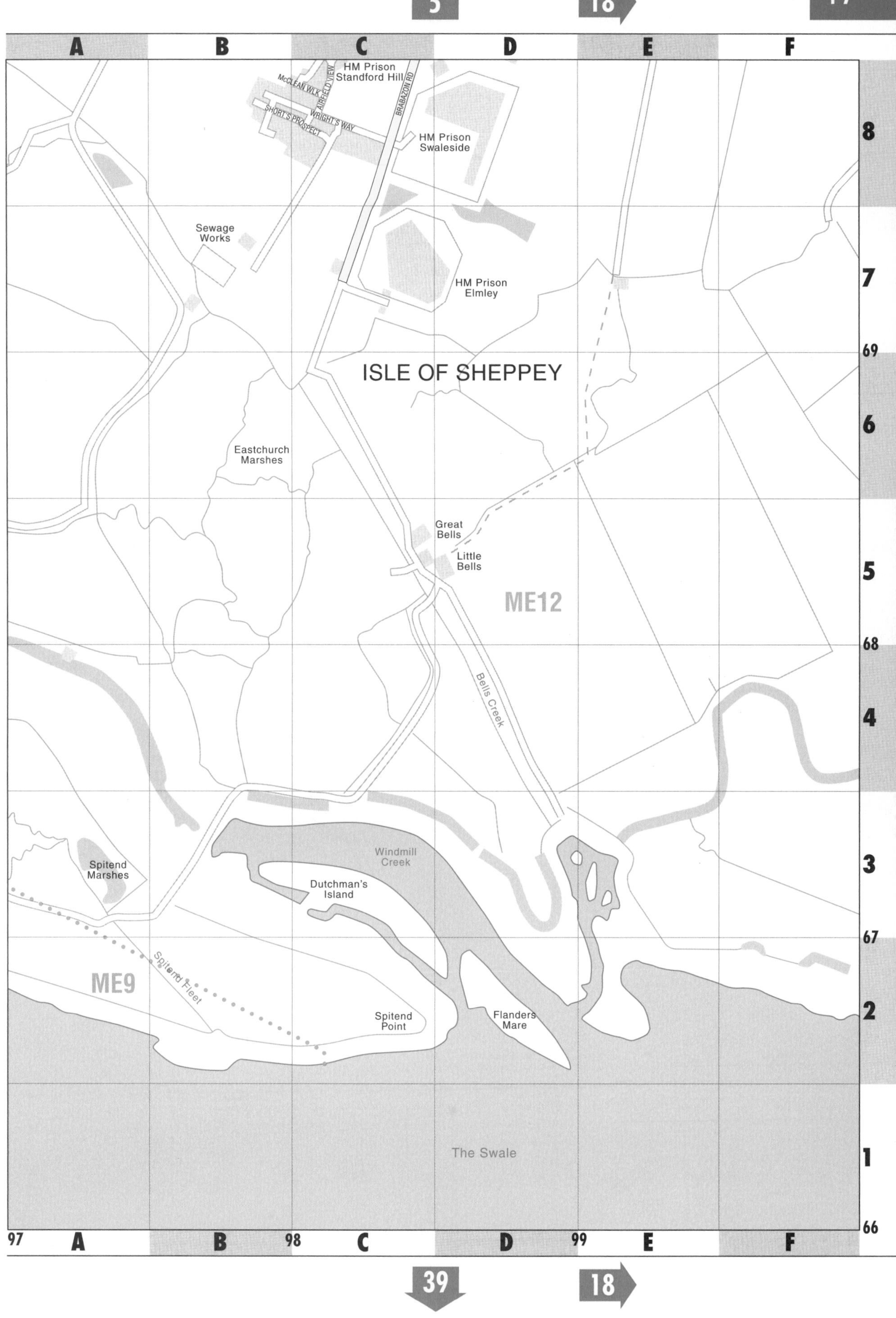

A   B   C   D   E   F

HM Prison
Standford Hill

McCLEAN WLK
AIRFIELD VIEW
WRIGHT'S WAY
SHORT'S PROSPECT
BRABAZON RD

HM Prison
Swaleside

8

Sewage
Works

HM Prison
Elmley

7

69

ISLE OF SHEPPEY

6

Eastchurch
Marshes

Great
Bells

Little
Bells

ME12

5

68

Bells Creek

4

Spitend
Marshes

Windmill
Creek

Dutchman's
Island

3

67

ME9

Spitend Fleet

Spitend
Point

Flanders
Mare

2

The Swale

1

66

97   A   B   98   C   D   99   E   F

A　　B　　C　　D　　E　　F

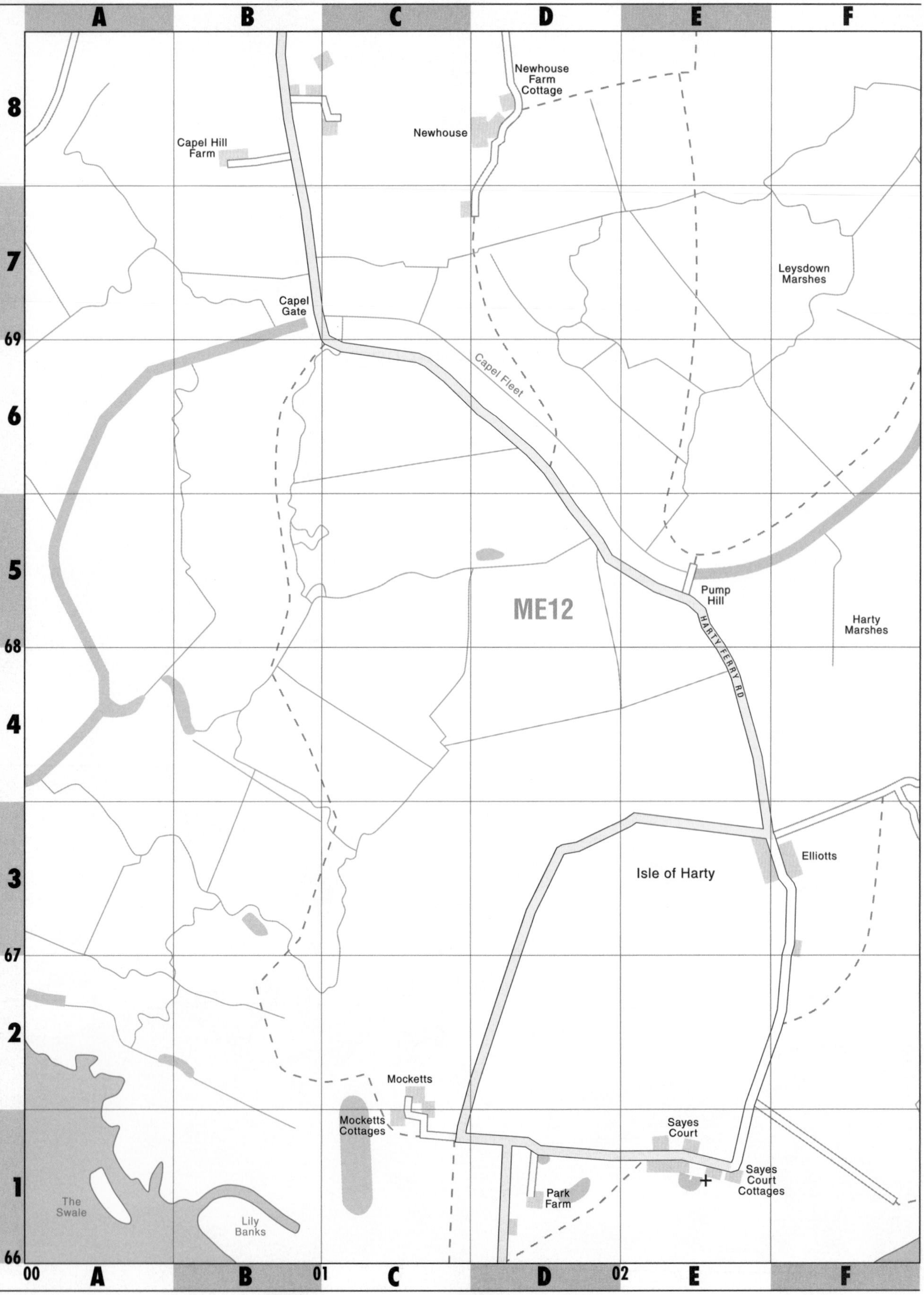

8

Newhouse
Farm
Cottage

Newhouse

Capel Hill
Farm

7

Leysdown
Marshes

Capel
Gate

69

Capel Fleet

6

5

ME12

Pump
Hill

HARTY FERRY RD

Harty
Marshes

68

4

3

Isle of Harty

Elliotts

67

2

Mocketts

Mocketts
Cottages

Sayes
Court

Sayes
Court
Cottages

+

1

The
Swale

Lily
Banks

Park
Farm

66

00　　A　　B　　01　　C　　D　　02　　E　　F

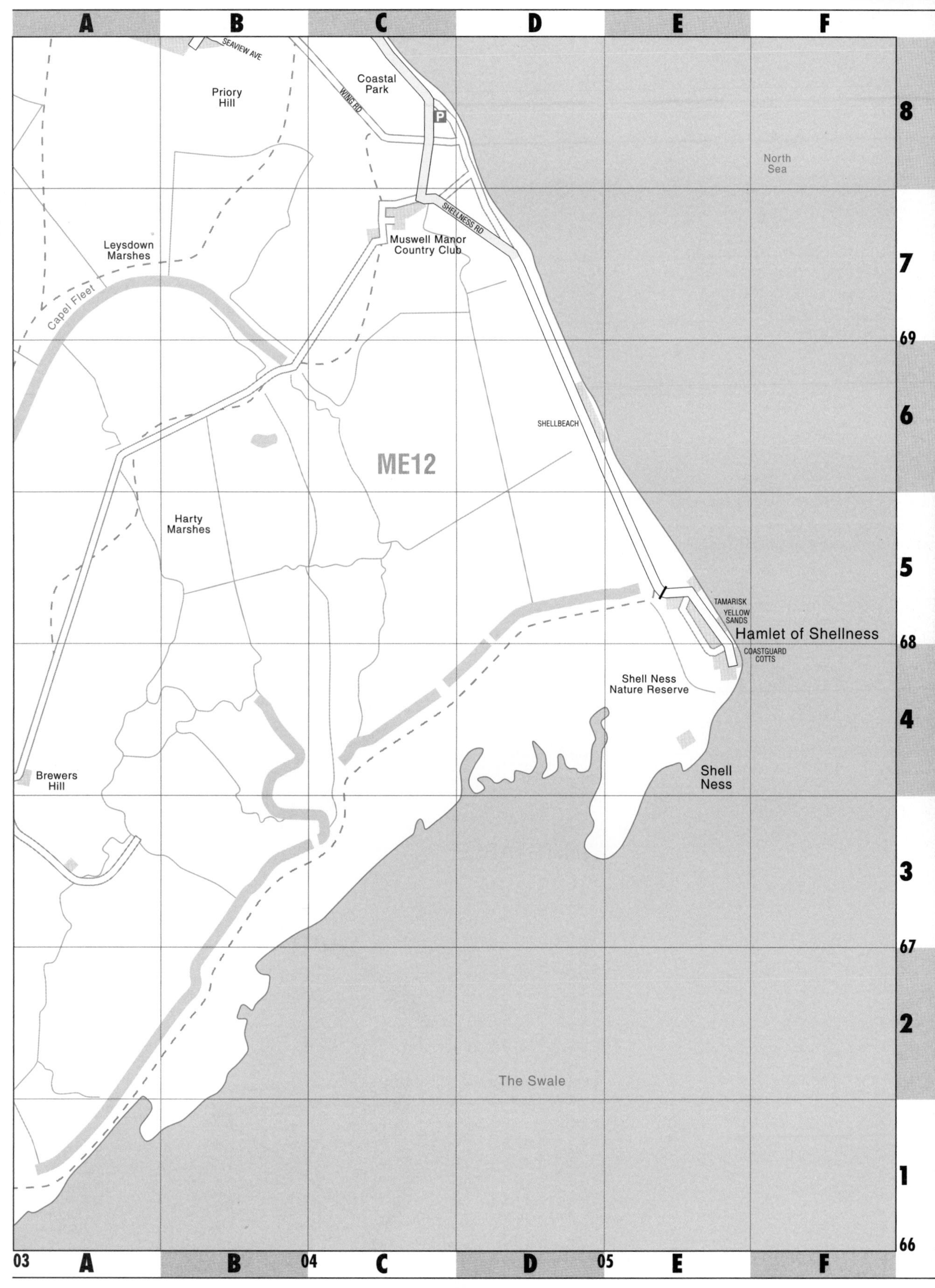

A B C D E F

8

North
Sea

SEAVIEW AVE

Coastal
Park

Priory
Hill

WING RD

P

SHELLNESS RD

7

Leysdown
Marshes

Muswell Manor
Country Club

69

Capel Fleet

6

SHELLBEACH

ME12

5

Harty
Marshes

TAMARISK
YELLOW
SANDS

Hamlet of Shellness

68

COASTGUARD
COTTS

Shell Ness
Nature Reserve

4

Shell
Ness

Brewers
Hill

3

67

2

The Swale

1

66

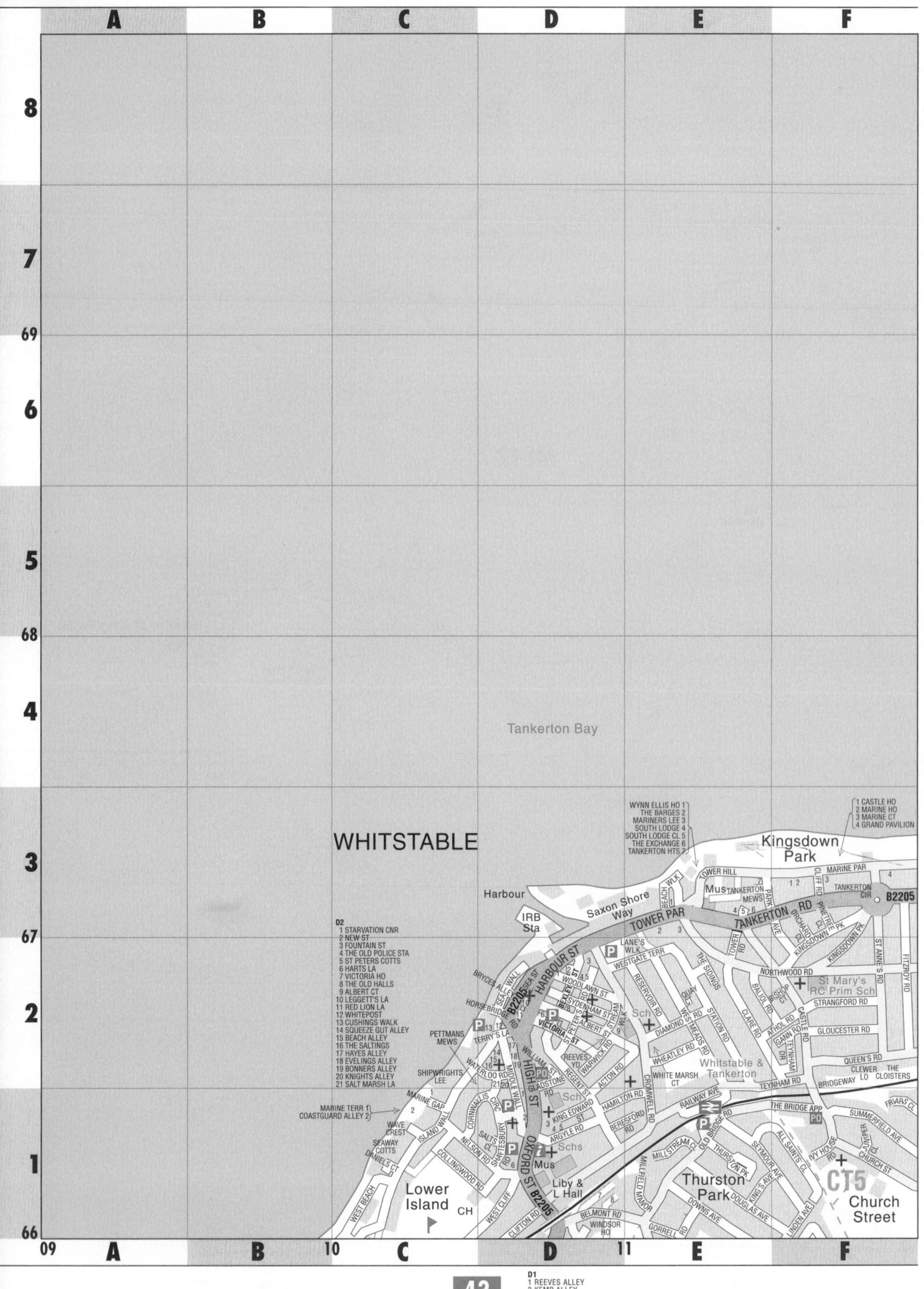

WHITSTABLE

Tankerton Bay

Kingsdown Park

Harbour

Saxon Shore Way

D2
1 STARVATION CNR
2 NEW ST
3 FOUNTAIN ST
4 THE OLD POLICE STA
5 ST PETERS COTTS
6 HARTS LA
7 VICTORIA HO
8 THE OLD HALLS
9 ALBERT CT
10 LEGGETT'S LA
11 RED LION LA
12 WHITEPOST
13 CUSHINGS WALK
14 SQUEEZE GUT ALLEY
15 BEACH ALLEY
16 THE SALTINGS
17 HAYES ALLEY
18 EVELINGS ALLEY
19 BONNERS ALLEY
20 KNIGHTS ALLEY
21 SALT MARSH LA

1 WYNN ELLIS HO
2 THE BARGES
3 MARINERS LEE
4 SOUTH LODGE
5 SOUTH LODGE CL
6 THE EXCHANGE
TANKERTON HTS

1 CASTLE HO
2 MARINE HO
3 MARINE CT
4 GRAND PAVILION

MARINE TERR 1
COASTGUARD ALLEY 2

Lower Island

Thurston Park

CT5
Church Street

D1
1 REEVES ALLEY
2 KEMP ALLEY
3 SKINNER'S ALLEY
4 OYSTER MEWS
5 OXFORD CL
6 OXFORD MANS
7 THE OLD COAL YD
8 BELMONT YD

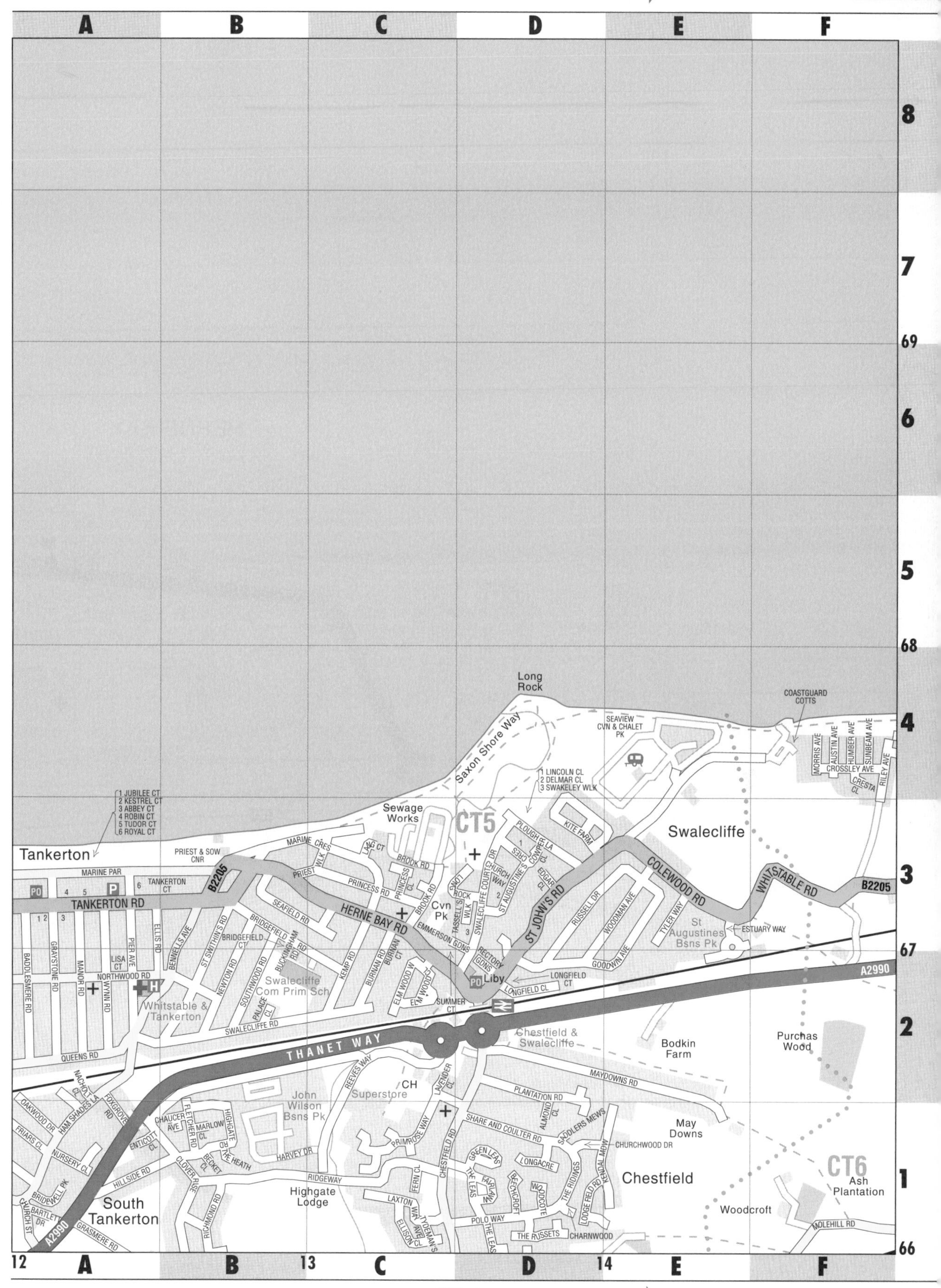

Long Rock

COASTGUARD COTTS

SEAVIEW CVN & CHALET PK

4

1 LINCOLN CL
2 DELMAR CL
3 SWAKELEY WLK

MORRIS AVE
AUSTIN AVE
HUMBER AVE
SUNBEAM AVE
CROSSLEY AVE
CRESTA CL
RILEY AVE

Saxon Shore Way

1 JUBILEE CT
2 KESTREL CT
3 ABBEY CT
4 ROBIN CT
5 TUDOR CT
6 ROYAL CT

Sewage Works

CT5

KITE FARM

Swalecliffe

B2205

Tankerton

PRIEST & SOW CNR

MARINE CRES

PRIEST WLK

LAG CT

BROOK RD

PLOUGH LA

ST AUGUSTINE'S CL

ST AUGUSTINE'S CONIFF

EDGER

COLEWOOD RD

WHITSTABLE RD

B2205

3

MARINE PAR

TANKERTON CT

6

PO

P

TANKERTON RD

B2205

PALACE

SEAFIELD RD

PRINCESS RD

PRINCESS

BROOK RD

CHURCH WAY

TASSELL'S WLK

SWALECLIFFE COURT DR

ST JOHN'S RD

RUSSELL DR

WOODMAN AVE

TYLER WAY

St Augustines Bsns Pk

ESTUARY WAY

1 2 3

GRAYSTONE RD

BADDLESMERE RD

MANOR RD

WYNN RD

PIER AVE

ELLIS RD

BENNELLS AVE

ST SWITHIN'S RD

NEWTON RD

SOUTHWOOD RD

BRIDGEFIELD RD

BRIDGEFIELD CT

BUCKINGHAM RD

KEMP RD

BURNAN RD

BURNAN RD

ELM WOOD W

ELM WOODS

HERNE BAY RD

EMMERSON GDNS

Cvn Pk

RECTORY GDNS

GOODWIN AVE

67

LISA CT

NORTHWOOD RD

H

Whitstable & Tankerton

Swalecliffe Com Prim Sch

SWALECLIFFE RD

SUMMER CT

PO

Liby

LONGFIELD RD

LONGFIELD CT

LONGFIELD CL

A2990

2

QUEENS RD

THANET WAY

Chestfield & Swalecliffe

Bodkin Farm

Purchas Wood

MAYDOWNS RD

NICHOLLS RD

FOXGROVE RD

OAKWOOD DR

HAM SHADES LA

CHAUCER AVE

FLETCHER RD

MARLOW CL

HIGHGATE

BECKET AVE

THE HEATH

HARVEY DR

REEVES WAY

John Wilson Bsns Pk

Superstore

CH

LAVENDER

PRIMROSE WAY

CHESTFIELD RD

SHARE AND COULTER RD

PLANTATION RD

ALMOND

SADDLERS MEWS

CHURCHWOOD DR

May Downs

CT6

Ash Plantation

FRIARS CL

BRIDEWELL PK

CHURCH ST

BARTLETT DR

A2990

GRASMERE RD

HILLSIDE RD

RICHMOND RD

CLOVER RISE

ENDICOTT CL

NURSERY CL

Highgate Lodge

RIDGEWAY

FERN CL

LAXTON

ELLISON CL

TYDEMAN'S AVE

POLO WAY

THE LEAS

GREEN LEAS

FAIRWAY

GREENACRE

WOODCOTE

LODGE FIELD RD

KENDAL MDW

LONGACRE

THE RIDINGS

THE RUSSETS

CHARNWOOD

Chestfield

Woodcroft

MOLEHILL RD

South Tankerton

1

66

12 A B 13 C D 14 E F

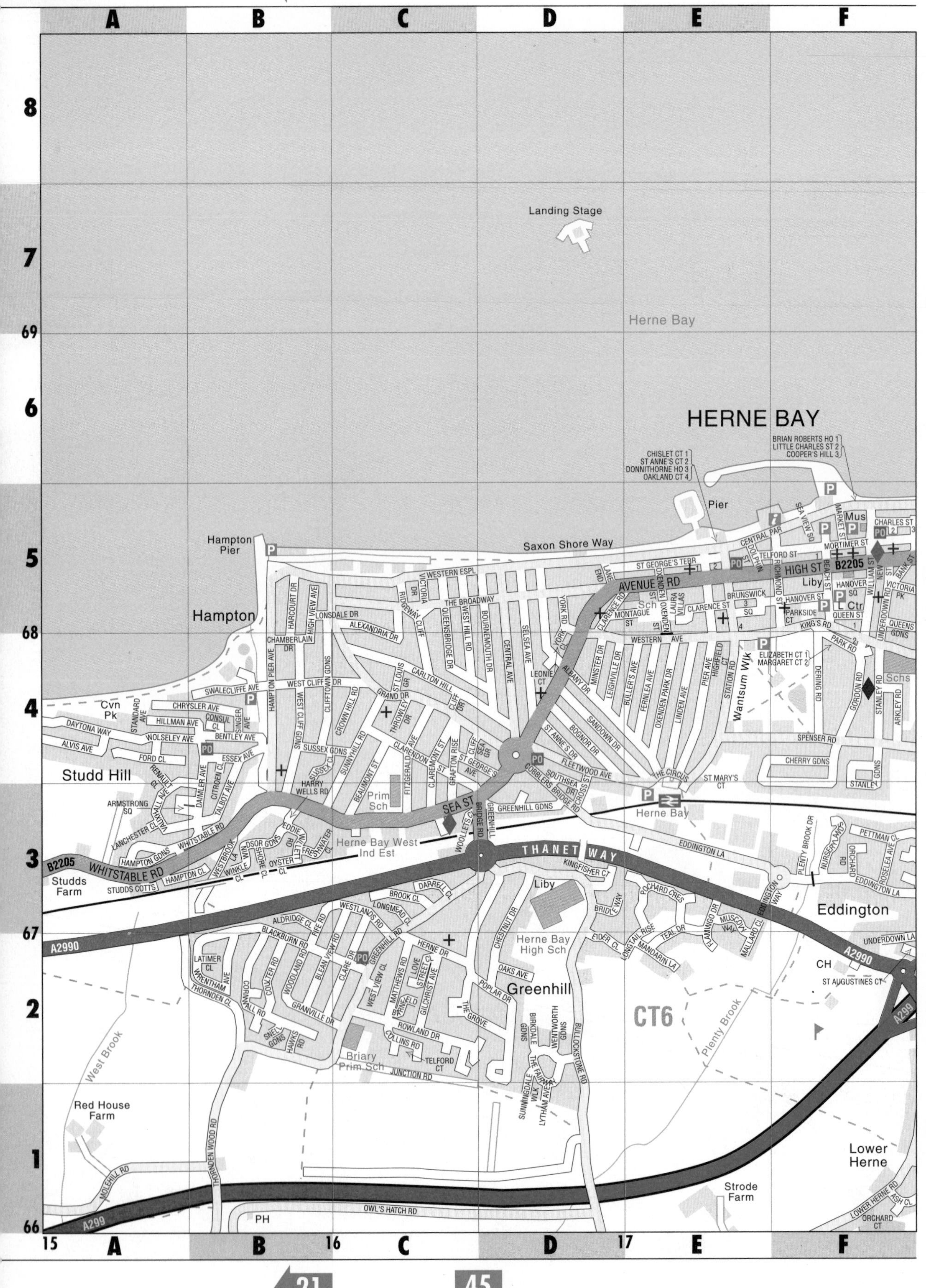

Map grid references (top)

A   B   C   D   E   F

8

7

69

6

5

68

4

3

67

2

1

66

15   A   B   16   C   D   17   E   F

Map labels

Landing Stage

Herne Bay

HERNE BAY

CHISLET CT 1
ST ANNE'S CT 2
DONNITHORNE HO 3
OAKLAND CT 4

BRIAN ROBERTS HO 1
LITTLE CHARLES ST 2
COOPER'S HILL 3)

Pier

Hampton Pier

Saxon Shore Way

CENTRAL PAR

CHARLES ST

Mus

SEA VIEW SQ

Hampton

ST GEORGE'S TERR

AVENUE RD

HIGH ST

B2205

Liby

Western Espl

VICTORIA

Brunswick

Parkside

HANOVER ST

QUEEN ST

The Broadway

QUEENSBRIDGE DR

WEST HILL RD

BOURNEMOUTH DR

CENTRAL AVE

YORK RD

CLARENCE ST

KING'S RD

Sch

Montague

WESTERN   AVE

Wantsum Wlk

Elizabeth CT 1
Margaret CT 2

Schs

Hampton
Pier

West Cliff Gdns

CLIFTON GDNS

CROWN HILL RD

GRAND AVE

CARLTON HILL

CLIFF AVE

ST ANNE'S DR

SANDOWN DR

OXENDEN PARK DR

LINDEN AVE

PARK RD

DENNIS RD

GORDON RD

STANLEY RD

ARKLEY RD

Cvn
Pk

CHRYSLER AVE

HILLMAN AVE

CONSUL
CT

BENTLEY AVE

SUSSEX GDNS

SUNNYHILL RD

CLARENDON RD

FLEETWOOD RD

THE CIRCUS

ST MARY'S
CT

CHERRY GDNS

SPENSER RD

STANLE

DAYTONA WAY

ALVIS AVE

FORD CL

NOLSELEY AVE

ESSEX AVE

BEAUMONT ST

FITZGERALD AVE

GRAFTON RD

ST GEORGE'S
AVE

SOUTHSEA DR

COBBLERS BRIDGE RD

GREENHILL GDNS

Herne Bay

Studd Hill

ARMSTRONG
SQ

LANCHESTER CL

HAMPTON GDNS

WHITSTABLE RD

DAIMLER AVE

TALBOT AVE

Harry
Wells Rd

Prim
Sch

SEA ST

WOOLLET

Herne Bay West
Ind Est

B2205

WHITSTABLE RD

HAMPTON CL

WESTBROOK

WINDSOR GDNS

EDDIE LN

OYSTER
CL

THANET   WAY

Kingfisher CT

POCHARD CRES

EDDINGTON LA

PLENTY BROOK DR

NURSERY RD

ORCHARD

PETTMAN CL

CHELSEA AVE

EDDINGTON LA

Eddington

Studds
Farm

STUDDS COTTS

Herne Bay West
Ind Est

A2990

ALDRIDGE CL

BLACKBURN RD

WESTLANDS RD

LONGMEAD

DARRELL CL

BROOK CL

Liby

BRIDLE WAY

EIDER CL

LONGTAIL RISE

MANDARIN LA

TEAL DR

FLAMINGO DR

MUSCOVY
DR

MALLARD CL

EDDINGTON WAY

A2990

UNDERDOWN LA

A299

West Brook

LATIMER
CL

WRENTHAM

THORNDEN CL

COXTER RD

COLWER RD

CORNWALL RD

WOODLAND RD

BEAN VIEW RD

GREENHILL RD

CLARE DR

MATTHEWS RD

WEST VIEW CL

LOVE
STREET

GILCHRIST AVE

HERNE RD

POPLAR DR

OAKS AVE

CHESTNUT DR

Herne Bay
High Sch

Greenhill

CT6

Plenty Brook

CH

ST AUGUSTINES CT

Red House
Farm

MOLEHILL RD

THORNDEN WOOD RD

GRANVILLE DR

SNELL
GDNS

HAWKS

COLLINS AVE

ROWLAND DR

TELFORD
CT

Briary
Prim Sch

JUNCTION RD

THE GROVE

BIRDALE
GDNS

SISKIN GDNS

WELLMANS DR

HURON DR

BULLOCKSTONE RD

THE FAIRWAY

HEATHMY WAY

A299

OWL'S HATCH RD

PH

Strode
Farm

**Lower
Herne**

LOWER HERNE RD

ASH CL

ORCHARD
CT

A299

24

A B C D E F

8
7
69
6
5
68
4
3
67
2
1
66

1 PROSPECT HILL
2 CHAPEL ST
3 CAVENDISH CT
4 HERTFORD HO

EAST CLIFF PAR
The Downs
Saxon Shore Way
Beltinge Cliff
Wantsum Wlk
Bishopstone
Beltinge
Works
Hillborough Bsns Pk
Elm Court Farm
Maystreet Bridge
Sweech Bridge
Sewage Works
Mast
MAYSTREET CROSS
Queen Victoria Meml
Sch
Blacksole Farm
CT6
Herne Bay Court
THANET WAY
A299
B2205 CANTERBURY RD
Cemy
Windmill
Hunters Forstal
Broomfield
Hawe Farm
Claver House
Heart in Hand
HEART IN HAND CNR
Oxenden House Farm
OXENDEN CNR
CT3
Strode Park
A291 CANTERBURY RD
POND COTTS

CHARLES ST, NORTH ST, EAST ST, CANTERBURY RD, HIGH ST, BEACON WLK, BELLE VUE RD, HILL TOP RD, BEACON HILL, HILLBOROUGH RD, BELTINGE RD, ALMA RD, SALISBURY RD, THE LEES, THURLOW AVE, ASHBEE GDNS, KNOWLER WAY, SYCAMORE CL, CLIFF AVE, QUEENS AVE, REGENTS WLK, BURLINGTON DR, HAZLEMERE DR, LISMORE RD, CONYNGHAM RD, BELTINGE DR, RECULVER RD, RECULVER DR, FRESHLANDS, GLENBERVIE DR, OCEAN VIEW, GAINSBOROUGH DR, HOGARTH CL, SEAVILLE DR, PINE WLK, THE PADDOCKS, WANTSUM CL, PRIEST FIELDS, FAIRFAX DR, MANOR RD, MANOR CL, HAVEN DR, HILLBOROUGH DR, BISHOPSTONE DR, RECULVER CL, BISHOPSTONE LA, SANDERLING RD, KINGSTON CL, LOVE CL, CORMORANT WAY, KEAT FARM CL, KITTIWAKE CL, FULMAR WAY, PETREL CL, PUFFIN RD, ROSEBERY AVE, ROWLAND CRES, RICHMOND DR, COVENTRY GDNS, LANCASTER GDNS, TERMINUS DR, GLENBROOK CL, THE HORSHAMS, HOLMSCROFT RD, OSBORNE GDNS, CHURCHILL AVE, CLEMENTINE CL, WINSTON GDNS, THORNHURST, WILLOW TREE CL, ORCHARD PK, MAXTED CT, MALVERN PK, HIGHFIELDS VIEW, HIGHFIELDS AVE, CHARTWELL AVE, HILARY CL, SEA VIEW RD, GLEN AVE, ROSE GDNS, ASHBURN GDNS, LANDON RD, REEDS CL, GRANGE RD, MEADOW CL, LAWRENCE GDNS, CHURCH VIEW, MARITIME AVE, BHUTAN RD, THE ACRES CL, AROLLA RD, ELLIOT CT, SELSEY CL, AMOS CL, CORNWALLIS AVE, CAMPBELL CL, SHAPLAND CL, CORSICAN WLK, VICTORIA PK, FENOULHET WAY, SOUTH RD, CAVENDISH RD, CECIL PK, CECIL CT, BEACON RD, DOWNS PK, TYNDALE PK, HADLEIGH GDNS, REYNOLDS CL, DENCE CL, DENCE PK, BEACON AVE, KING EDWARD AVE, KING EDWARD CT, MICKLEBURGH HILL, MICKLEBURGH AVE, HERNEVILLE GDNS, BURTON FIELDS, THUNDERSLAND RD, ASH TREES, FAIROAKS, COURTLANDS, ELIZABETH WAY, COLLARD CL, MAYFIELD RD, HERNE AVE, IVANHOE RD, OAKDALE RD, DOUGLAS RD, SPENSER RD, GOSFIELD RD, QUEEN'S CT, ST ANDREWS CL, ST CLEMENT'S CT, PARSONAGE RD, BEAUMANOR, PRIORY LA, BOWES LA, MILL LA, MARGATE RD, WALCOT PL, BOSSHOLE LA, MAY ST, SWEECHBRIDGE RD, HEART IN HAND RD, FORD HILL

SWALE CL, HILLCROFT RD, EASTGATE CL, GREEN ACRES CL, RAVENSBOURNE AVE, DARENTH CL, HILLBROW AVE, PIGEON LA, LIMES CL, THE DOWNINGS, UPPER FREE DOWN, SONDES CL, WINDMILL CL, WINDMILL RD, MILL COURT CL, MOUNT VIEW RD, PEARTREE RD, HELDING CL, ELLIS WAY, PARTRIDGE CL, GOLDFINCH CL, CURLEW CL, PINTAIL WAY, KINGSFIELD RD, WILLOW FARM WAY, HOOPERS LA, BRAMLEY GDNS, SPICERS FIELD, MARGATE RD, HUNTERS FORSTAL RD, BRAMBLEFIELDS CL, ROCKINGHAM PL, LAKE DR, EPPING CL, HAWE FARM WAY, DEAN CROFT CL, HALFORD CL, BOWLAND CL, ARDEN RD, SHERWOOD CL, GORSE LA, HUNTERS CHASE, THE MEADOWS, PLOUGH CT, RYE WLK, BARLEY CL, CHALFONT DR, LADYFIELDS, SILVERDALE DR, MERRYWOOD GR, MAGNOLIA RISE, WICK WAY, STRANGFORD PL, ASHDOWN CL, CHARNWOOD RD, RADNOR CL, BROOMFIELD RD, STRODE PARK RD, MILL VIEW RD, WOODROW CHASE, SEYMOUR CL, SCHOOL LA, STREETFIELD, BLENHEIM CL, LOWER HERNE RD, ORCHARD ROW, RUSKINS VIEW, BENSTEDE CL

18 A B 19 C D 20 E F

46

24

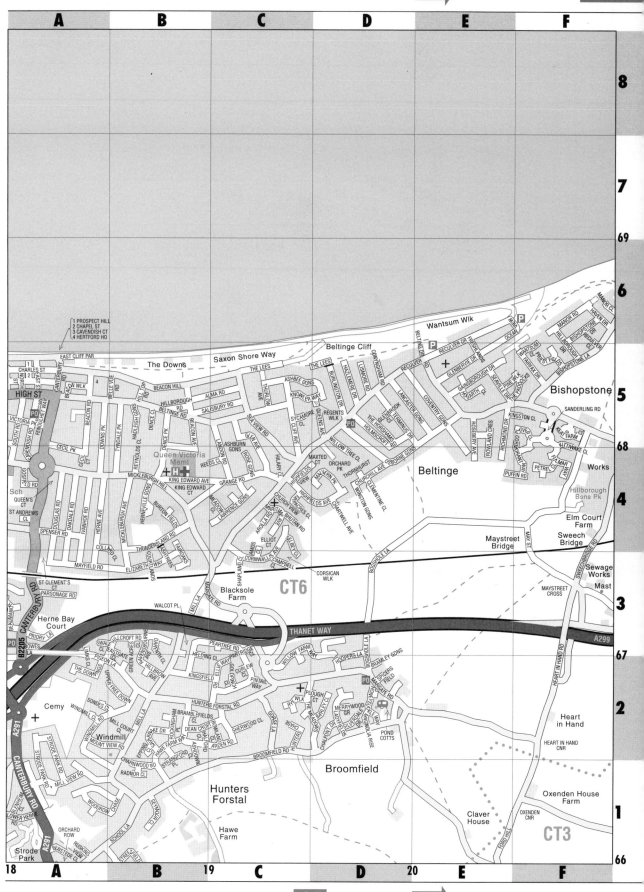

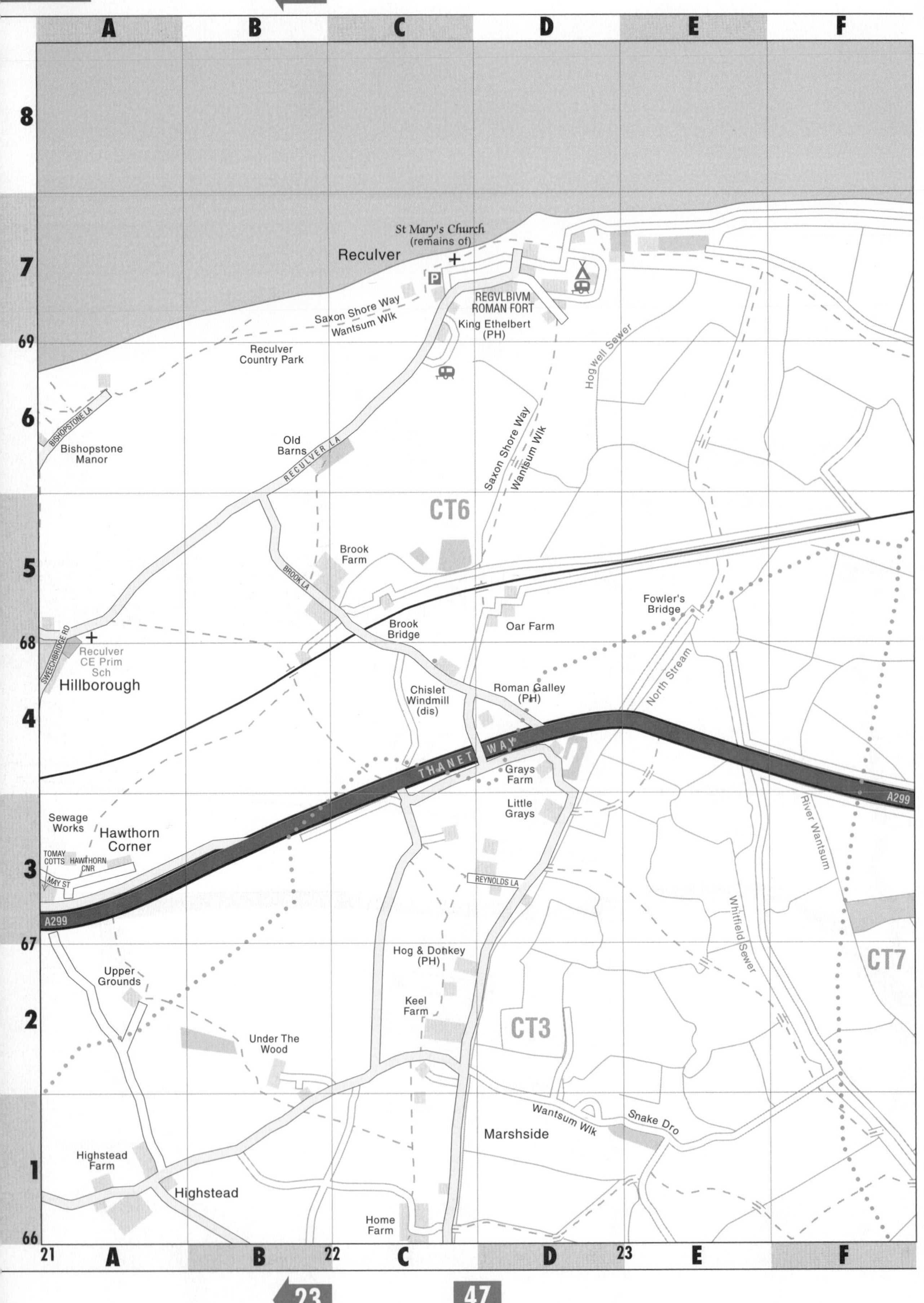

A B C D E F

8

7 Reculver

St Mary's Church
(remains of)

REGVLBIVM
ROMAN FORT
King Ethelbert
(PH)

69

Saxon Shore Way
Wantsum Wlk

Reculver
Country Park

Hog well Sewer

6

BISHOPSTONE LA

Bishopstone
Manor

Old
Barns

RECULVER LA

Saxon Shore Way
Wantsum Wlk

CT6

5

BROOK LA

Brook
Farm

Fowler's
Bridge

68

SKEECHBRIDGE RD

Reculver
CE Prim
Sch

Hillborough

Brook
Bridge

Oar Farm

North Stream

4

Chislet
Windmill
(dis)

Roman Galley
(PH)

THANET WAY

Grays
Farm

A299

River Wantsum

3

Sewage
Works

Hawthorn
Corner

TOMAY
COTTS HAWTHORN
CNR

MAY ST

Little
Grays

REYNOLDS LA

Whitfield Sewer

CT7

A299

67

Upper
Grounds

Hog & Donkey
(PH)

2

Keel
Farm

CT3

Under The
Wood

Wantsum Wlk

Snake Dro

1

Highstead
Farm

Highstead

Marshside

66

21 A B 22 C D 23 E F

26

A
B
C
D
E
F
8
7
69
6
5
68
4
3
67
2
1
66
24
25
26
Knock Point
CT6
Thanet Coastal Path
Twelve Foot Dike
River Wantsum
LC
LC
LC
LC
LC
Wade Marsh
Wade Farm
Wantsum Wlk
Wantsum Wlk
Shuart
Bartletts
Chambers Wall
Warehorn
CT7
Potten Street
Wade House
Hedgend Ind Est
SHUART LA
THANET WAY
POTTEN STREET RD
A299
Wagtail
Wade Marsh Stream
Cemy
Frost Farm
WANTSUM WAY
COURT RD
COURT COTTS
SHUART LA
St Nicholas Court
Belle Isle
St Nicholas at Wade CE Prim Sch
Snake Dro
THE STREET
SUN LA
PO
BRIDGES CL
THE OAKS
THE FINCHES
MANSUM CT
Bell Inn (PH)
THE LENGTH
THANET VIEW
MANOR LEA RD
BEDFORD WAY
St Nicholas at Wade
SANDALWOOD
MANOR RD
SOLOCOTS
DOWN BARTON RD
SUMMER RD
PROSPECT PL
Down Barton
River Wantsum
DOWN BARTON FARM COTTS
ST NICHOLAS CNR
CANTERBURY RD
A28
A28
ORCHARD LA

48
26

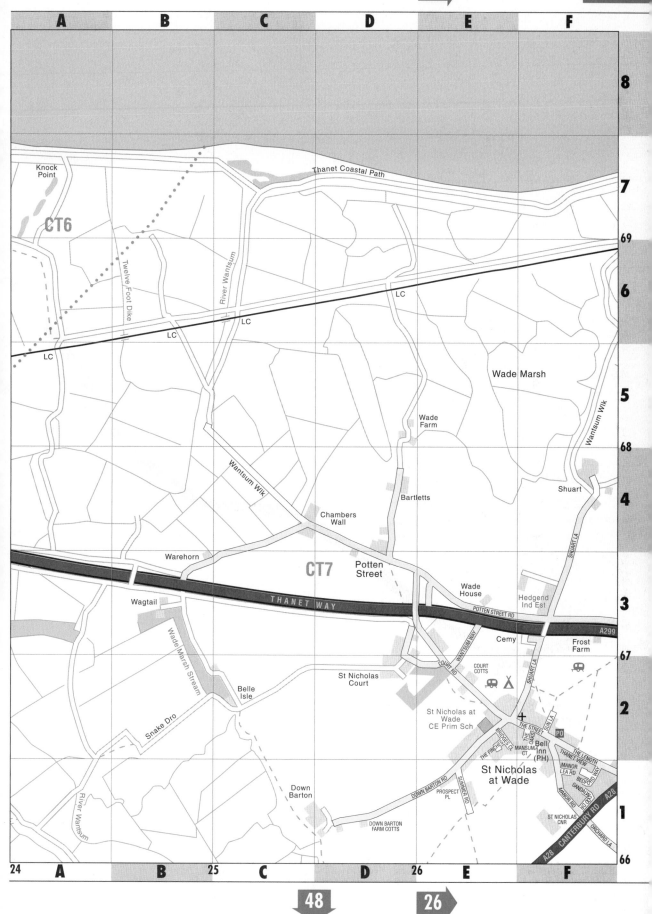

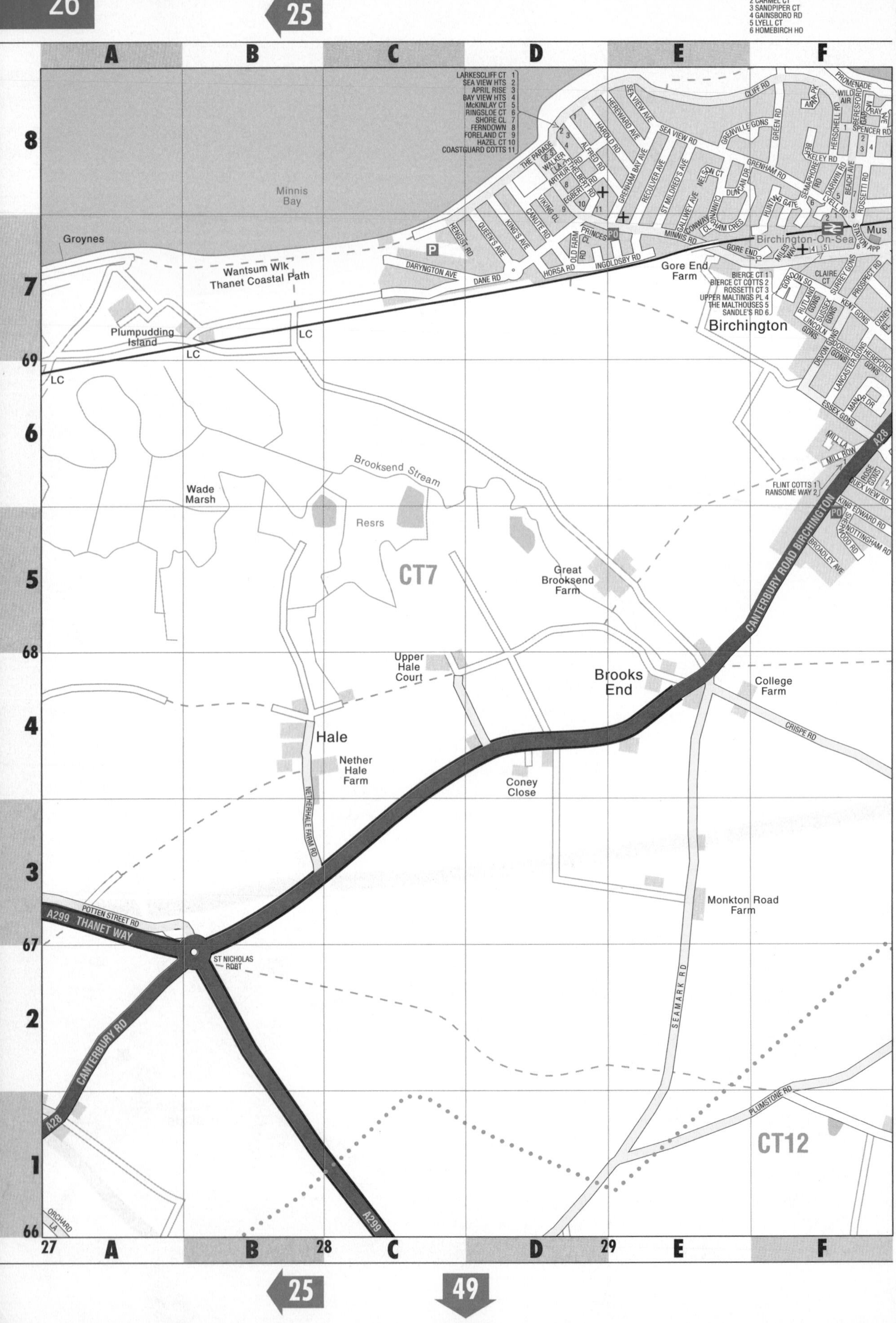

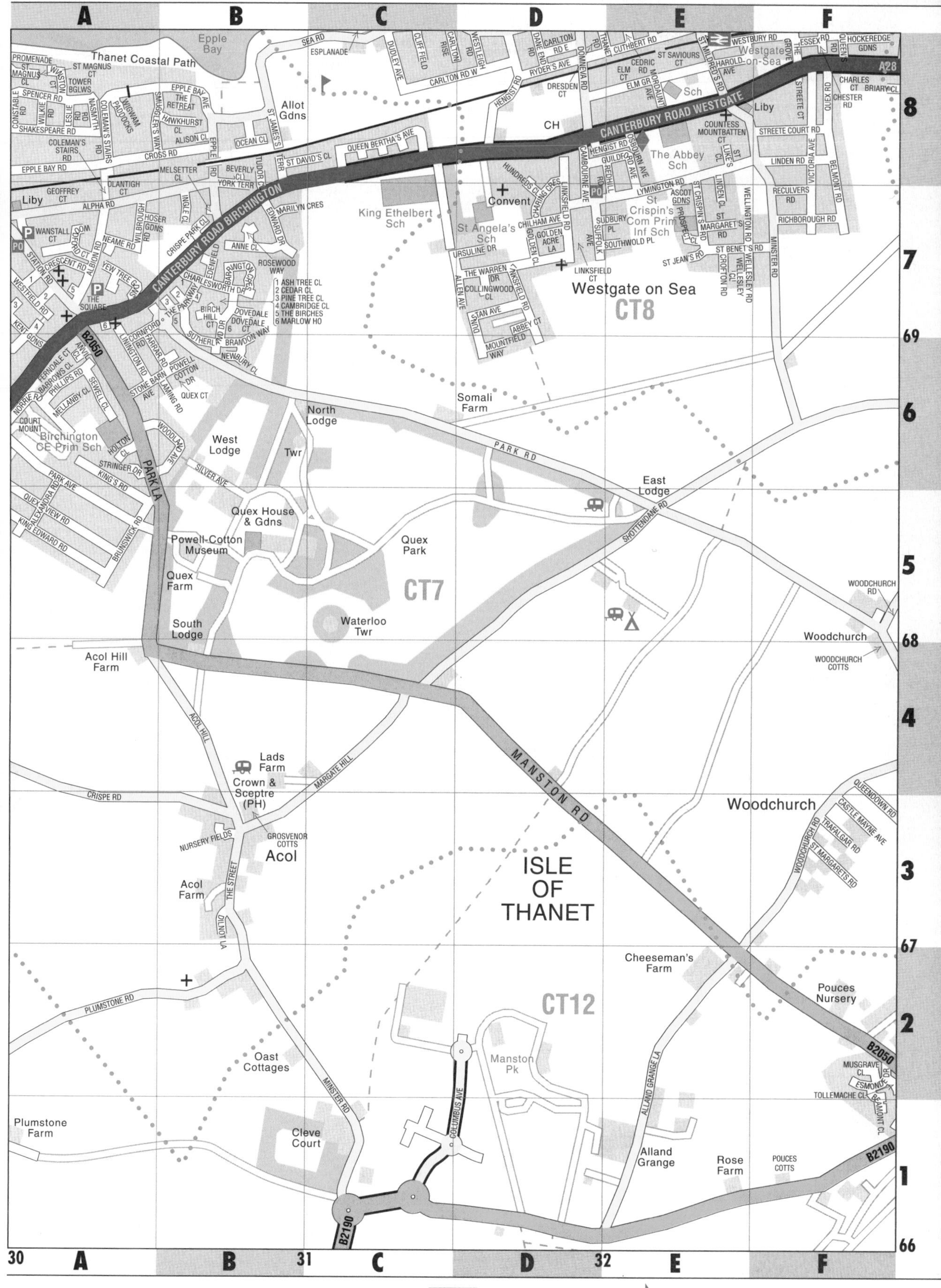

A7
1 EASTFIELD RD
2 PADDOCK RD
3 SHEPPEY CL
4 ROMNEY CL
5 TAPLIN CT
6 WALNUT TREE CL

Epple
Bay

Thanet Coastal Path

CANTERBURY ROAD WESTGATE

Westgate-on-Sea

Allot
Gdns

King Ethelbert
Sch

Convent

St Angela's
Sch

St Crispin's
Com Prim
Inf Sch

The Abbey
Sch

Westgate on Sea
CT8

CANTERBURY ROAD BIRCHINGTON

1 ASH TREE CL
2 CEDAR CL
3 PINE TREE CL
4 CAMBRIDGE CL
5 THE BIRCHES
6 MARLOW HO

Rosewood
Way

The Warren
Dr
Collingwood
CL

Somali
Farm

North
Lodge

PARK RD

East
Lodge

Birchington
CE Prim Sch

West
Lodge

Twr

Quex House
& Gdns

Quex
Park

Woodchurch
RD

Powell-Cotton
Museum

Quex
Farm

CT7

Woodchurch

WOODCHURCH
COTTS

South
Lodge

Waterloo
Twr

Acol Hill
Farm

MANSTON RD

Woodchurch

Lads
Farm

Crown &
Sceptre
(PH)

Crispe Rd

Nursery Fields

Grosvenor
Cotts

Acol

Cheeseman's
Farm

Pouces
Nursery

Acol
Farm

ISLE
OF
THANET

Plumstone Rd

CT12

B2050

Oast
Cottages

Manston
Pk

Plumstone
Farm

Cleve
Court

COLUMBUS AVE

Alland
Grange

Rose
Farm

Pouces
Cotts

B2190

B2190

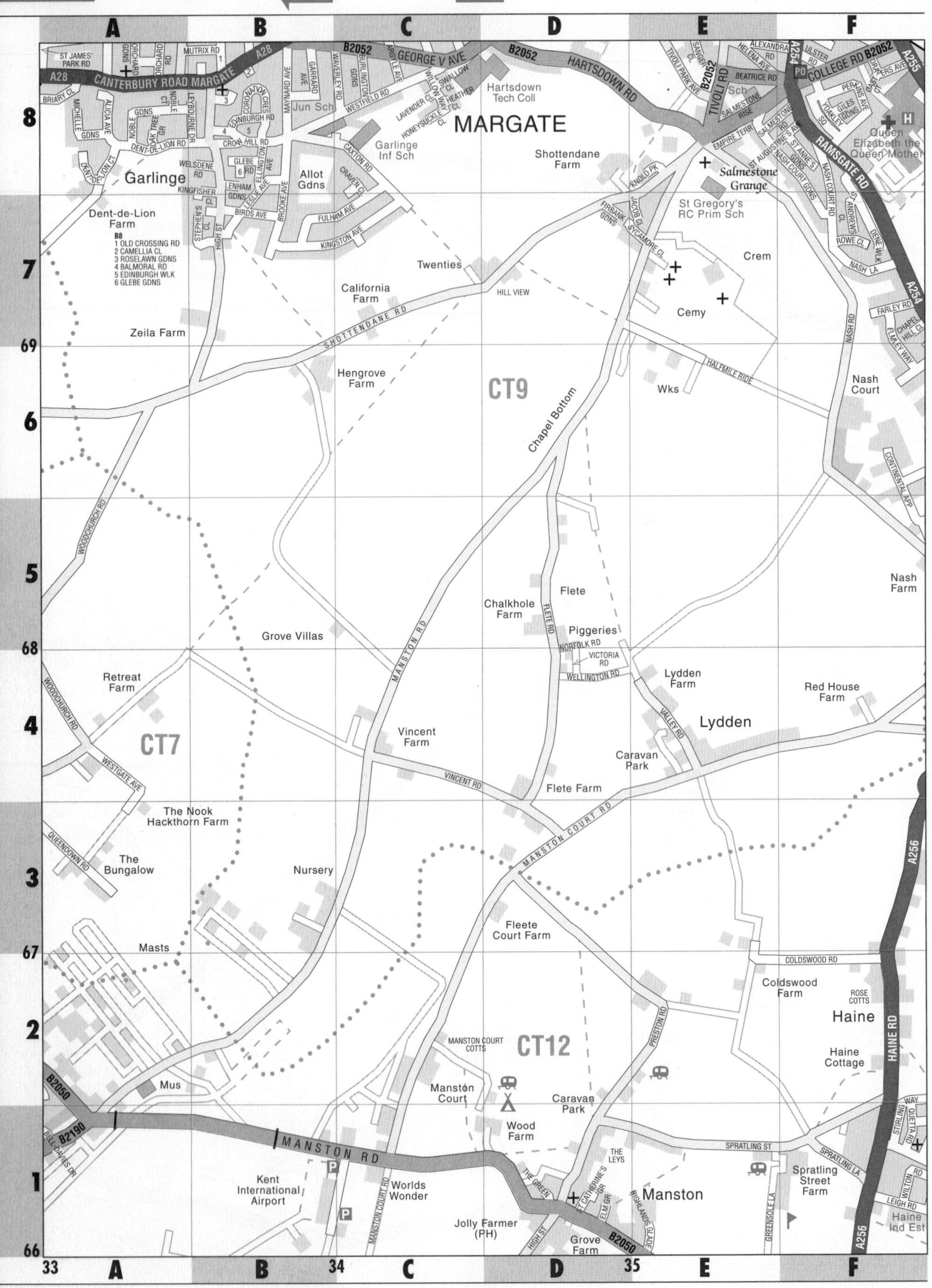

MARGATE

St James'
Park Rd

CANTERBURY ROAD MARGATE
A28

Garlinge

Dent-de-Lion
Farm

88
1 OLD CROSSING RD
2 CAMELLIA CL
3 ROSELAWN GDNS
4 BALMORAL RD
5 EDINBURGH WLK
6 GLEBE GDNS

Jun Sch

Garlinge
Inf Sch

Allot
Gdns

MUTRIX RD

GEORGE V AVE

HARTSDOWN RD

B2052

B2052

Hartsdown
Tech Coll

Shottendane
Farm

Salmestone
Grange

St Gregory's
RC Prim Sch

Crem

COLLEGE RD

Queen
Elizabeth the
Queen Mother

Tivoli
Sch

Zeila Farm

California
Farm

Twenties

HILL VIEW

SHOTTENDANE RD

Hengrove
Farm

CT9

Chapel Bottom

Cemy

Wks

Nash
Court

HALFMILE RIDE

Nash
Farm

Grove Villas

MANSTON RD

Retreat
Farm

CT7

WOODCHURCH RD

WESTGATE AVE

The Nook
Hackthorn Farm

QUEENDOWN RD

The
Bungalow

Nursery

Masts

Mus

Vincent
Farm

VINCENT RD

Chalkhole
Farm

Flete

FLETE RD

Piggeries

NORFOLK RD
VICTORIA
RD
WELLINGTON RD

Flete Farm

Lydden
Farm

VALLEY RD

Lydden

Caravan
Park

Red House
Farm

MANSTON COURT RD

Fleete
Court Farm

PRESTON RD

COLDSWOOD RD

Coldswood
Farm

ROSE
COTTS

Haine

Haine
Cottage

HAINE RD

B2050

B2190

MANSTON RD

Kent
International
Airport

Worlds
Wonder

Manston Court
Cotts

CT12

Manston
Court

Wood
Farm

Caravan
Park

THE
LEYS

SPRATLING ST

Spratling
Street
Farm

Jolly Farmer
(PH)

THE GREEN

HIGH ST

St Catherine's

ELM GR

Manston

B2050

Grove
Farm

Haine
Ind Est

A256

8
30

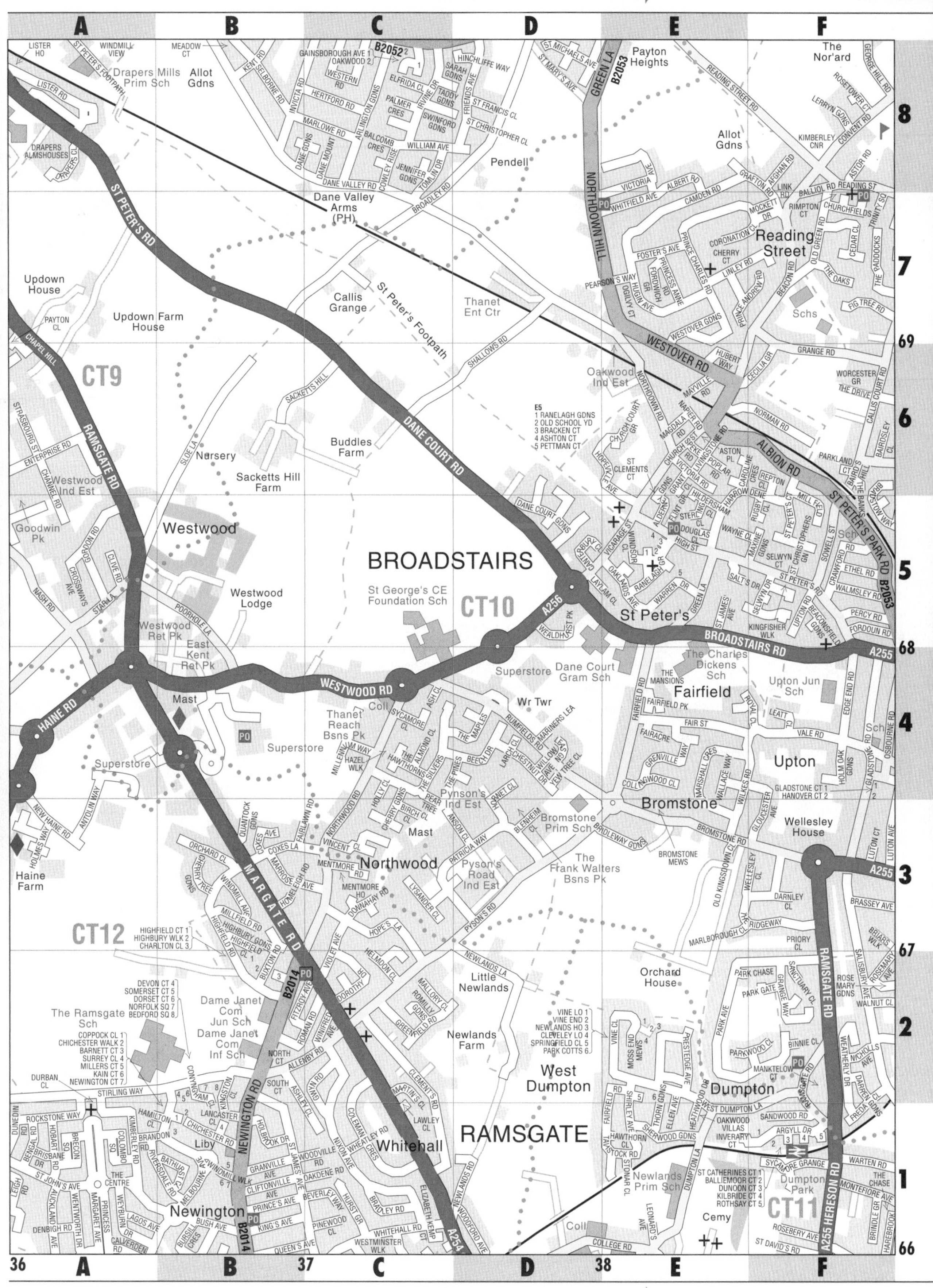
A
B
C
D
E
F
8
7
69
6
5
68
4
3
67
2
1
66
36
37
38
Drapers Mills Prim Sch
Allot Gdns
Payton Heights
The Nor'ard
Allot Gdns
Pendell
Dane Valley Arms (PH)
Reading Street
Updown House
Updown Farm House
Callis Grange
St Peter's Footpath
Thanet Ent Ctr
Schs
Oakwood Ind Est
CT9
Nursery
Sacketts Hill Farm
Buddles Farm
Westwood Ind Est
Goodwin Pk
Westwood
BROADSTAIRS
Westwood Lodge
St George's CE Foundation Sch
CT10
St Peter's
Westwood Ret Pk
East Kent Ret Pk
Superstore
Dane Court Gram Sch
The Charles Dickens Sch
Fairfield
Upton Jun Sch
Mast
Thanet Reach Bsns Pk
Coll
Wr Twr
Superstore
Upton
Superstore
Pyson's Ind Est
Bromstone
Bromstone Prim Sch
Wellesley House
Haine Farm
Mast
Northwood
Pyson's Road Ind Est
The Frank Walters Bsns Pk
CT12
Little Newlands
Orchard House
The Ramsgate Sch
Dame Janet Com Jun Sch
Dame Janet Com Inf Sch
Newlands Farm
West Dumpton
Dumpton
Liby
Whitehall
RAMSGATE
Newington
Newlands Prim Sch
Dumpton Park
CT11
Cemy
Coll
ST PETER'S RD
DANE COURT RD
RAMSGATE RD
WESTWOOD RD
HAINE RD
MARGATE RD
NEWINGTON RD
NORTHDOWN HILL
GREEN LA
WESTOVER RD
ALBION RD
ST PETER'S PARK RD
BROADSTAIRS RD
A255 HERESON RD
B2052
B2053
B2014
A254
A255
A256
E5
1 RANELAGH GDNS
2 OLD SCHOOL YD
3 BRACKEN CT
4 ASHTON CT
5 PETTMAN CT
HIGHFIELD CT 1
HIGHBURY WLK 2
CHARLTON CL 3
DEVON CT 4
SOMERSET CT 5
DORSET CT 6
NORFOLK SQ 7
BEDFORD SQ 8
COPPOCK CL 1
CHICHESTER WALK 2
BARNETT CT 3
SURREY CL 4
MILLERS CT 5
KAIN CT 6
NEWINGTON CT 7
VINE LO 1
VINE END 2
NEWLANDS HO 3
CLEVELEY LO 4
SPRINGFIELD CL 5
PARK COTTS 6
GLADSTONE CT 1
HANOVER CT 2
ST CATHERINES CT 1
BALLIEMOOR CT 2
DUNOON CT 3
KILBRIDE CT 4
ROTHSAY CT 5
GAINSBOROUGH AVE 1
OAKWOOD 2

52
30

8
29

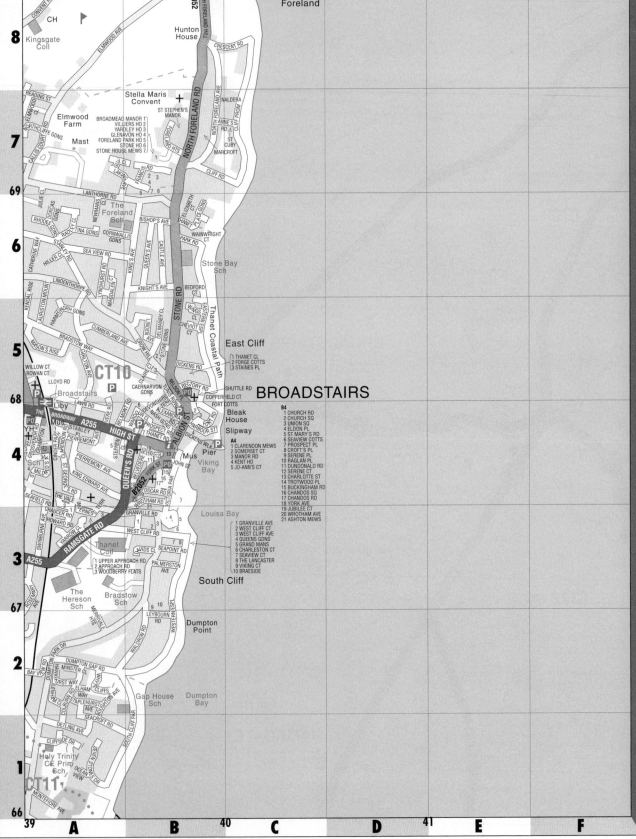
A
B
C
D
E
F
8
7
69
6
5
68
4
3
67
2
1
66
39
40
41
North Foreland
Kingsgate Coll
CH
CONVENT RD
ELMWOOD AVE
B2052
NORTH FORELAND HILL
Hunton House
CRESCENT RD
Stella Maris Convent
READING ST
ELMWOOD CL
Elmwood Farm
NORTHCLIFFE GDNS
CALLIS COURT RD
Mast
BROADMEAD MANOR 1
VILLIERS HO 2
YARDLEY HO 3
GLENAVON HO 4
FORELAND PARK HO 5
STONE HO 6
STONE HOUSE MEWS 7
ST STEPHEN'S MANOR
FORELAND HTS
NORTH FORELAND RD
NORTH FORELAND AVE
NALDERA
ANNE'S RD
CLIFF PROM
ST CUBY
MARCROFT
CLIFF RD
GUY CL
LAKING AVE
FRANCIS RD
LANTHORNE RD
JULIE CL
DORCAS GDNS
NEWMANS CL
The Foreland Sch
RHODES GDNS
RADLEY CL
TINA GDNS
CORNWALLIS GDNS
BISHOP'S AVE
ELIZABETH CT
THANET PLACE GDNS
WAINWRIGHT CT
PARK RD
CATHERINE WAY
STANLEY RD
HILLER CL
SEA VIEW RD
LYNDHURST RD
MAGDALEN CT
KING'S AVE
QUEEN'S AVE
CASTLE AVE
Stone Bay Sch
KNIGHT'S AVE
BEDFORD CT
LINDENTHORPE RD
KENDAL RISE
LAURISTON MOUNT
HARMSWORTH GDNS
STONE RD
WINGS CL
EASTERN ESPL
CHEVIOT CT
Thanet Coastal Path
LINDEN AVE
DELMANEY CL
CUMBERLAND AVE
CROW HILL
STONE GDNS
East Cliff
BRADSTOW WAY
MASON'S RISE
CARLTON AVE
1 THANET CL
2 FORGE COTTS
3 STAINES PL
DICKENS RD
WILLOW CT
ROWAN CT
CT10
CLARE CT
LLOYD RD
Broadstairs
CAERNARVON GDNS
RECTORY RD
SHUTTLE RD
NELSON PL
TUNIS ROW
COPPERFIELD CT
BROADSTAIRS
FORT COTTS
LAWN RD
Liby
DEVONSHIRE TERR
ALEXANDRA RD
NASH GDNS
Bleak House
THE BROADWAY
A255
HIGH ST
ALBION ST
HARBOUR ST
FORT RD
Mus
BELMONT RD
VERE RD
PROSPECT RD
THANET RD
Slipway
YH
STANLEY PL
PIERREMONT
DICKENS WLK
Pier
CRAMPTON
GROSVENOR RD
CINDER PATH
CLARENDON RD
STEPHEN CL
QUEEN'S RD
BELVEDERE RD
JOHN ST
Viking Bay
Sch
PIERREMONT AVE
YORK ST
ST GEORGE'S RD
KING EDWARD AVE
B2052
VICTORIA PAR
OSCAR RD
WROTHAM RD
SEAFIELD RD
THE VALE
INVERNESS TERR
CHAUCER RD
HOWARD RD
GRANVILLE RD
Louisa Bay
SWINBURNE AVE
YARROW CL
WEST CLIFF RD
RAMSGATE RD
Thanet Coll
DAVIDS CL
SEAPOINT RD
A255
1 UPPER APPROACH RD
2 APPROACH RD
3 WOODBERRY FLATS
PALMERSTON AVE
South Cliff
The Hereson Sch
Bradstow Sch
ROSEMARY AVE
MERRIVALE HTS
LEYBOURN RD
WESTERN ESPL
Dumpton Point
WALDRON RD
DUMPTON PARK DR
DUMPTON GAP RD
MINSTER CL
BAY VIEW RD
HAWTHORN CL
ELHAM WAY
CLIFFS
STAPLEHURST AVE
BOUGHTON AVE
Gap House Sch
Dumpton Bay
SEACROFT RD
DETLING AVE
SOUTH CLIFF PAR
CLIFFSIDE DR
Holy Trinity CE Prim Sch
SEVEN STONES DR
OCEAN VIEW
CT11
MONTEFIORE AVE
B4
1 CHURCH RD
2 CHURCH SQ
3 UNION SQ
4 ELDON PL
5 ST MARY'S RD
6 SEAVIEW COTTS
7 PROSPECT PL
8 CROFT'S PL
9 SERENE PL
10 RAGLAN PL
11 DUNDONALD RD
12 SERENE CT
13 CHARLOTTE ST
14 TROTWOOD PL
15 BUCKINGHAM RD
16 CHANDOS SQ
17 CHANDOS RD
18 YORK AVE
19 JUBILEE CT
20 WROTHAM AVE
21 ASHTON MEWS
A4
1 CLARENDON MEWS
2 SOMERSET CT
3 MANOR RD
4 KENT HO
5 JO-ANN'S CT
1 GRANVILLE AVE
2 WEST CLIFF CT
3 WEST CLIFF AVE
4 QUEENS GDNS
5 GRAND MANS
6 CHARLESTON CT
7 SEAVIEW CT
8 THE LANCASTER
9 VIKING CT
10 BRAESIDE

52
29

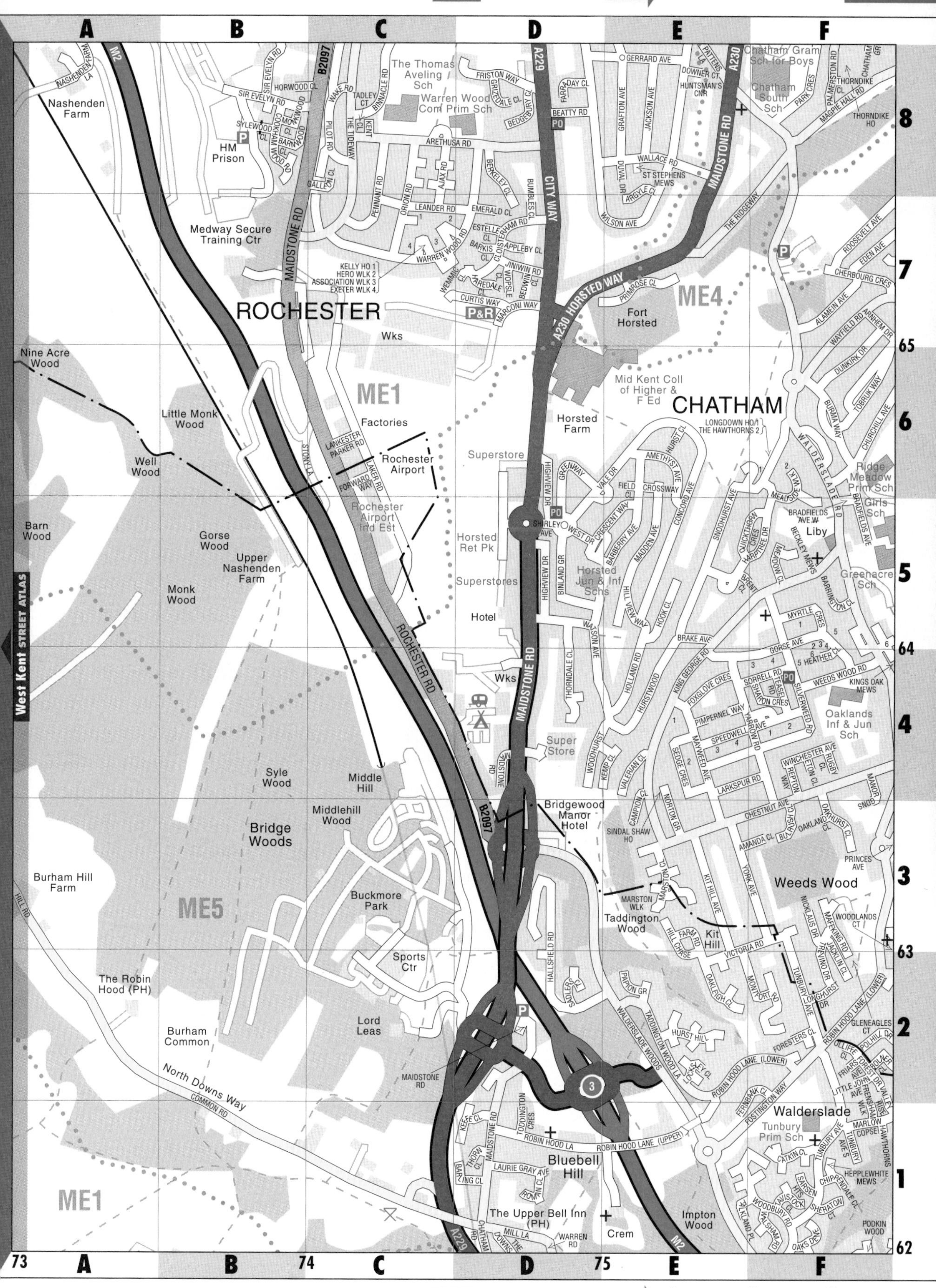

E4
1 LAVENDER CL
2 ASPEN WAY
3 HONEYSUCKLE CL
4 GENTIAN CL

F4
1 MALLOW WAY
2 JASMINE CL
3 HAREBELL CL
4 ROSEMARY CL
5 LINDEN HO
6 OAK HO

F5
1 SAFFRON WAY
2 WILLOW HO
3 PINE HO
4 ROWAN HO
5 HAWTHORN HO
6 BLEAKWOOD RD

31
10

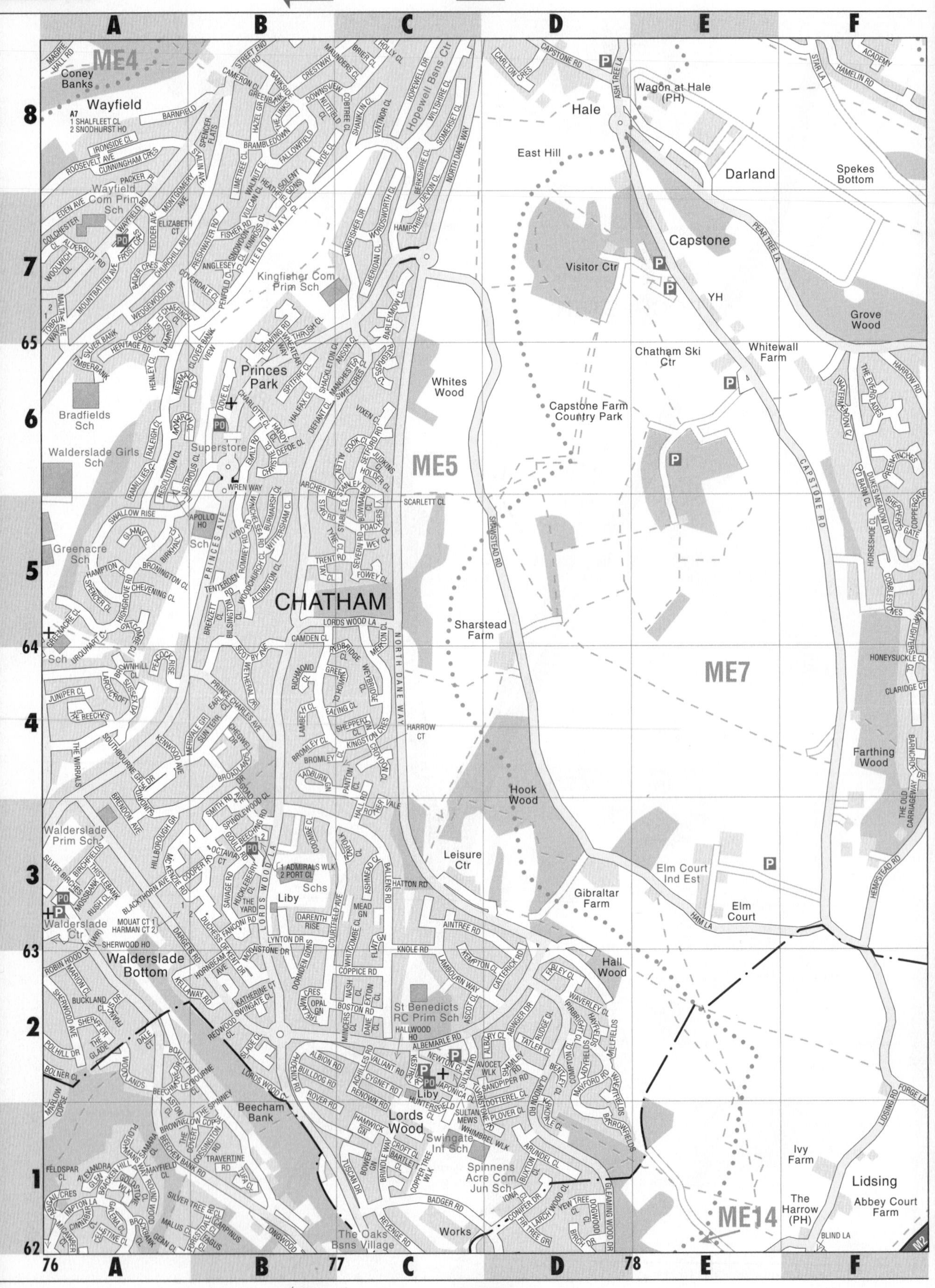
A B C D E F
8 7 65 6 5 64 4 3 63 2 1 62
76 77 78
ME4
Coney Banks
Wayfield
A7
1 SHALFLEET CL
2 SNODHURST HO
Wayfield Com Prim Sch
Hale
Wagon at Hale (PH)
East Hill
Darland
Spekes Bottom
Capstone
Visitor Ctr
YH
Grove Wood
Kingfisher Com Prim Sch
Chatham Ski Ctr
Whitewall Farm
Princes Park
Whites Wood
Bradfields Sch
Capstone Farm Country Park
Walderslade Girls Sch
Superstore
ME5
Greenacre Sch
CHATHAM
Sharstead Farm
ME7
Farthing Wood
Hook Wood
Walderslade Prim Sch
Leisure Ctr
Schs
Liby
Elm Court Ind Est
Gibraltar Farm
Elm Court
Walderslade Ctr
Walderslade Bottom
Hall Wood
St Benedicts RC Prim Sch
Beecham Bank
Lords Wood
Swingate Inf Sch
Spinnens Acre Com Jun Sch
Ivy Farm
Lidsing
The Harrow (PH)
Abbey Court Farm
ME14
Works
The Oaks Bsns Village
Hopewell Bsns Ctr
NORTH DANE WAY
CAPSTONE RD
SHARSTEAD RD
PRINCES AVE
LORDS WOOD LA
HAM LA
PEAR TREE LA
ASH TREE LA
BLIND LA
M2

11
34

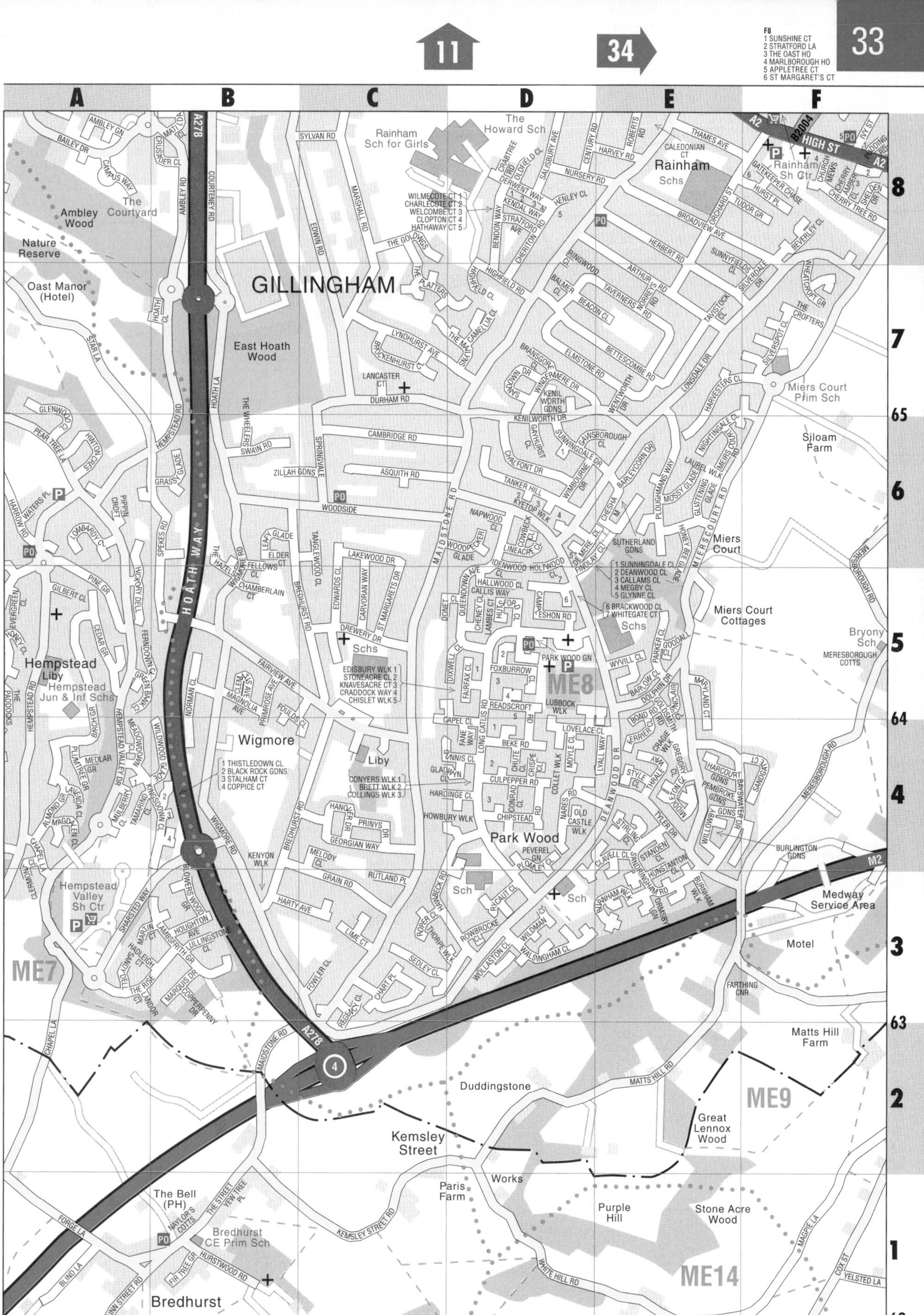
F8
1 SUNSHINE CT
2 STRATFORD LA
3 THE OAST HO
4 MARLBOROUGH HO
5 APPLETREE CT
6 ST MARGARET'S CT
A
B
C
D
E
F
GILLINGHAM
Rainham Sch for Girls
The Howard Sch
Rainham
Schs
Rainham Sh Ctr
HIGH ST
A2
B2004
A278
HOATH WAY
Ambley Wood
The Courtyard
Nature Reserve
Oast Manor (Hotel)
East Hoath Wood
WILMECOTE CT 1
CHARLECOTE CT 2
WELCOMBE CT 3
CLOPTON CT 4
HATHAWAY CT 5
Miers Court Prim Sch
Siloam Farm
Miers Court
Miers Court Cottages
Bryony Sch
MERESBOROUGH COTTS
1 SUNNINGDALE CL
2 DEANWOOD CL
3 CALLAMS CL
4 MEGBY CL
5 GLYNNE CL
6 BRACKWOOD CL
7 WHITEGATE CT
Schs
Hempstead
Liby
Hempstead Jun & Inf Schs
EDISBURY WLK 1
STONEACRE CL 2
KNAVESACRE CT 3
CRADDOCK WAY 4
CHISLET WLK 5
ME8
Wigmore
Liby
CONYERS WLK 1
BRETT WLK 2
COLLINGS WLK 3
1 THISTLEDOWN CL
2 BLACK ROCK GDNS
3 STALHAM CT
4 COPPICE CT
Park Wood
Sch
Hempstead Valley Sh Ctr
ME7
Medway Service Area
Motel
M2
FARTHING CNR
Matts Hill Farm
Duddingstone
ME9
Kemsley Street
Great Lennox Wood
Paris Farm
Works
Purple Hill
Stone Acre Wood
The Bell (PH)
Bredhurst CE Prim Sch
Bredhurst
ME14
8
7
65
6
5
64
4
3
63
2
1
62
79
80
81

55
34

33
12

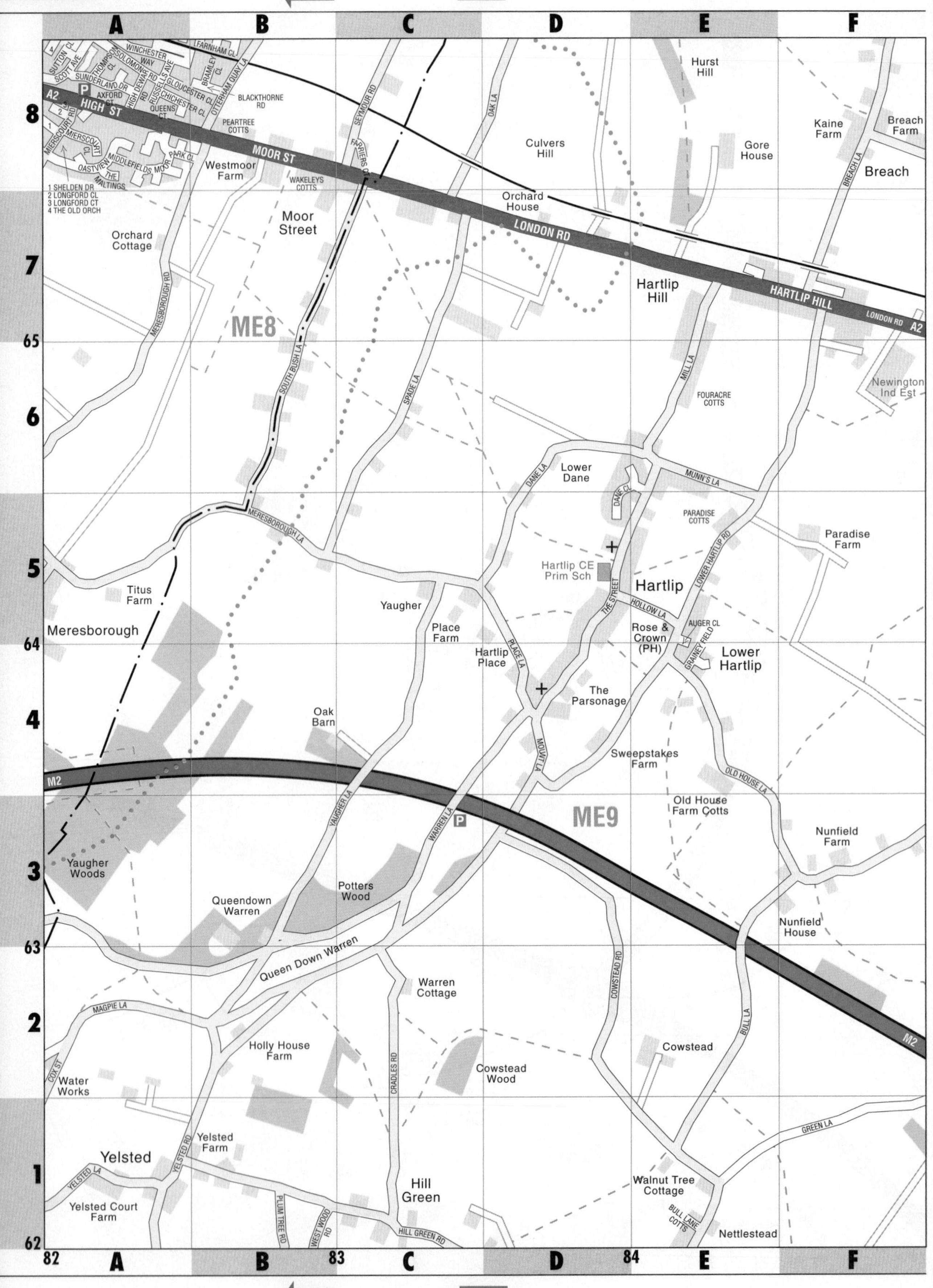
A
B
C
D
E
F
Hurst Hill
Breach Farm
Kaine Farm
Gore House
Breach
Culvers Hill
Orchard House
Westmoor Farm
Moor Street
Orchard Cottage
Hartlip Hill
ME8
Newington Ind Est
Lower Dane
Paradise Farm
Hartlip CE Prim Sch
Hartlip
Titus Farm
Meresborough
Yaugher
Place Farm
Hartlip Place
Rose & Crown (PH)
Lower Hartlip
The Parsonage
Oak Barn
Sweepstakes Farm
ME9
Old House Farm Cotts
Nunfield Farm
Yaugher Woods
Potters Wood
Queendown Warren
Nunfield House
Queen Down Warren
Warren Cottage
Holly House Farm
Cowstead
Cowstead Wood
Water Works
Yelsted
Yelsted Farm
Hill Green
Walnut Tree Cottage
Yelsted Court Farm
Nettlestead
A2 HIGH ST
MOOR ST
LONDON RD
HARTLIP HILL
M2
1 SHELDEN DR
2 LONGFORD CL
3 LONGFORD CT
4 THE OLD ORCH
8
7
6
5
4
3
2
1
65
64
63
62
82
83
84

33
56

A   B   C   D   E   F

8

BELNOR AVE

Wardwell Farm
Wardwell Wood

Oak Hill Farm

HIGH OAK HILL

Rook Wood

Cemy

Newington Ent Ctr

SCHOOL LA

Mill Hill

Newington CE Prim Sch

7

Rook Lodge

VICARAGE CT

DENHAM RD

WESTWOOD WLK

Newington

1 ST MARY'S PL
2 EDWINS PL
3 ST MARK'S CL
4 ST STEPHEN'S CL
5 ST MATTHEW'S CL
6 ST MARTINS CL

Cold Harbour

65

LONDON RD

STATION RD

CHURCH RD

COLD HARBOUR LA

P

Pond Farm

Keycol Hill

Demelza House Hospice

6

Newington

LONDON RD

ALLSWORTH CL

THE WILLOWS

PO

HIGH ST

BROOKES PL

THE TRACIES

ELLEN'S PL

BOYCES HILL

Keycol

ROOK LA

PLAYSTOL

PEAR TREE WLK

FRANKAPPS CL

WILCOOKS CL

DENNIS

CALLAWAYS LA

1 RED ROBIN COTTS
2 CHERRY HILL CT
3 ALBION PL

LADYFIELDS CL

KEYCOL HILL

ORCHARD DR

BRAMLEY CL

Newington Manor

A2

OLD MAIDSTONE RD

5

ME9

A249

Gwelo Farm

BULL LA

Standard Hill

Cranbrook Wood

PH

64

4

Chesley Farm

WORMDALE RD

Wormdale

Cold Store

CHESTNUT ST

Chestnut Street

CHESTNUT ST

SCHOOL LA

Chesley

Borden CE Prim Sch

LIMEPITS CROSS

Thrognall Farm

WORMDALE HILL

CH

Rock Meadows

Sunnyhill

3

DANAWAY COTTS

WESTFIELD GDNS

Danaway

Munsgore Farm

MUNSGORE LA

63

Eyehorn Farm

Pond Farm

2

WOODGATE LA

GREEN LA

5

Stockbury Valley

Woodgate Farm

Vinson Farm

Oad Street

POND FARM RD

DUVARD'S PL

1

Church Wood

A249

Bowl Reed

M2

Plough and Harrow (PH)

62

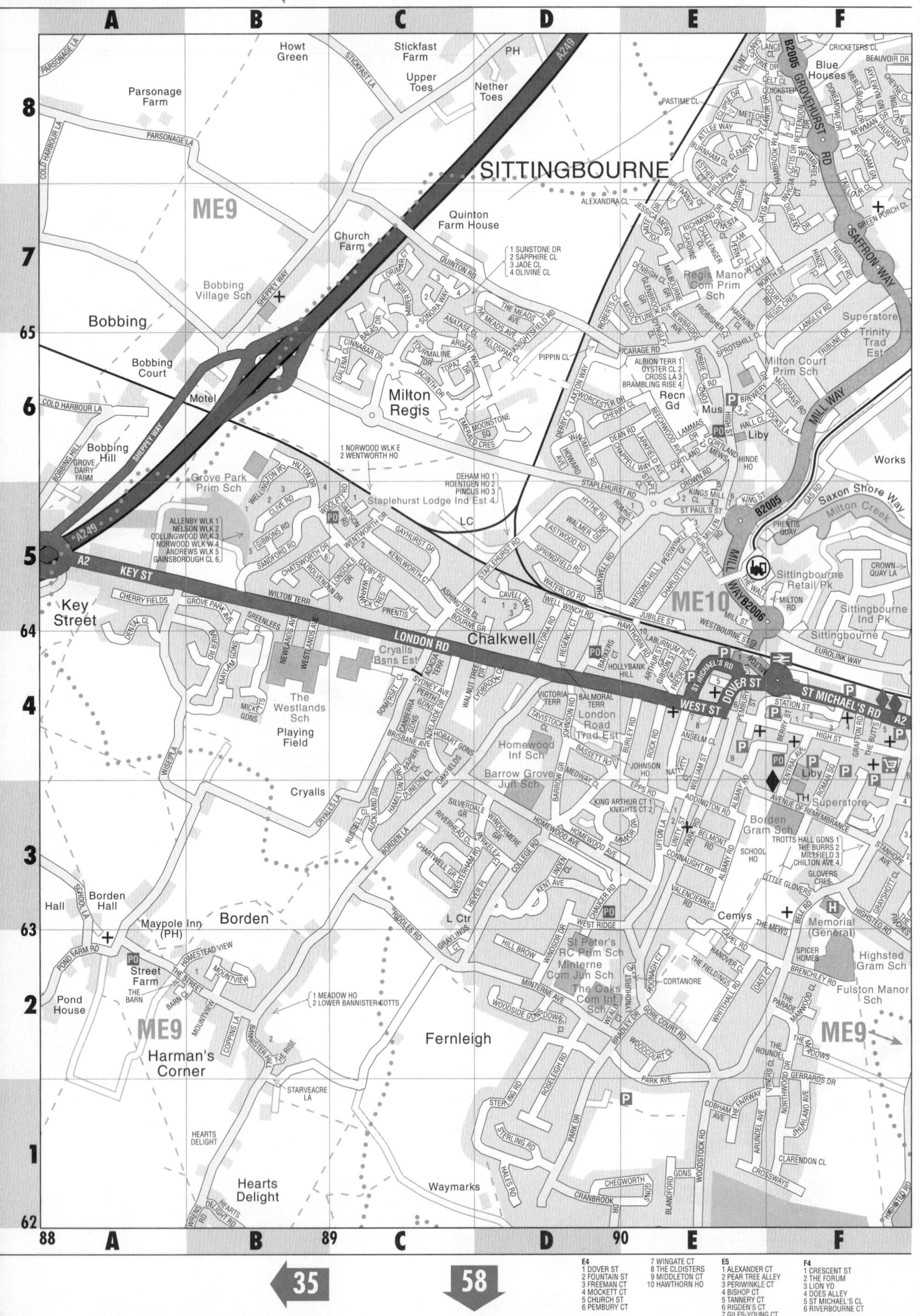

ME9

SITTINGBOURNE

Bobbing

Milton Regis

Key Street

Chalkwell

ME10

Borden

Harman's Corner

Fernleigh

Hearts Delight

Waymarks

ME9

E4
1 DOVER ST
2 FOUNTAIN ST
3 FREEMAN CT
4 MOCKETT CT
5 CHURCH ST
6 PEMBURY CT
7 WINGATE CT
8 THE CLOISTERS
9 MIDDLETON CT
10 HAWTHORN HO

E5
1 ALEXANDER CT
2 PEAR TREE ALLEY
3 PERIWINKLE CT
4 BISHOP CT
5 TANNERY CT
6 RIGDEN'S CT
7 GILES-YOUNG CT

F4
1 CRESCENT ST
2 THE FORUM
3 LION YD
4 DOES ALLEY
5 ST MICHAEL'S CL
6 RIVERBOURNE CT

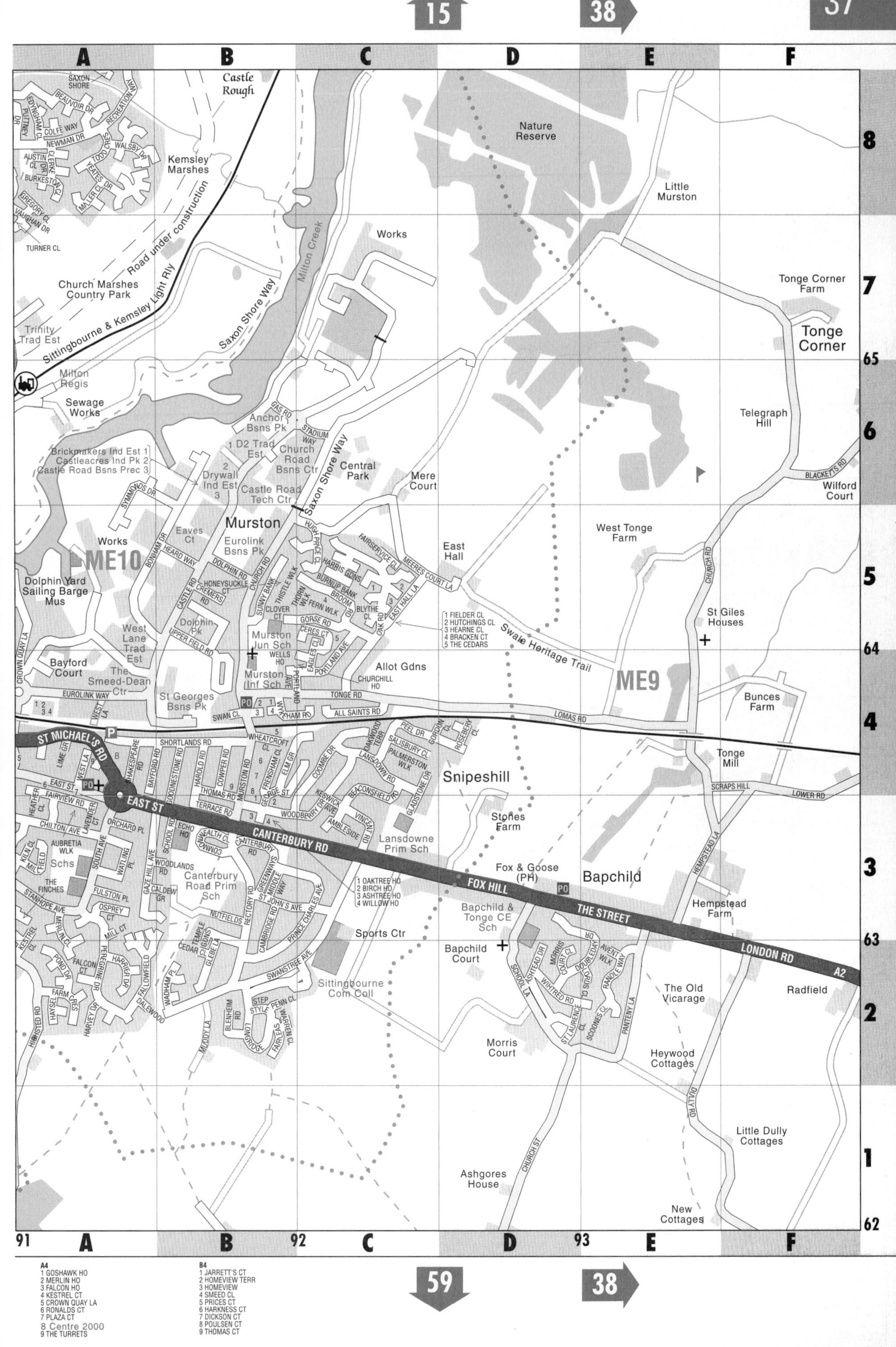

A
B
C
D
E
F

8
7
65
6
5
64
4
3
63
2
1
62

Castle
Rough

Nature
Reserve

Little
Murston

Saxon Shore

Kemsley
Marshes

Tonge Corner
Farm

Works

Tonge
Corner

Church Marshes
Country Park

Sittingbourne & Kemsley Light Rly

Saxon Shore Way

Milton Creek

Telegraph
Hill

Trinity
Trad Est

Milton
Regis

Blacketts Rd

Wilford
Court

Sewage
Works

Anchor
Bsns Pk

Gas Rd

Stadium Way

Church
Road
Bsns Ctr

Central
Park

Mere
Court

West Tonge
Farm

Church Rd

Brickmakers Ind Est 1
Castleacres Ind Pk 2
Castle Road Bsns Prec 3

1 D2 Trad
Est

Drywall
Ind Est

Saxon Shore Way

Castle Road
Tech Ctr

Murston

Eaves
Ct

Eurolink
Bsns Pk

East
Hall

St Giles
Houses

Works

ME10

Heard Way

Dolphin Yard
Sailing Barge
Mus

Dolphin
Pk

Upper Field Rd

Murston
Jun Sch

Swale Heritage Trail

ME9

West
Lane
Trad
Est

Murston
Inf Sch

Allot Gdns

Bunces
Farm

Bayford
Court

The
Smeed-Dean
Ctr

St Georges
Bsns Pk

Churchill
Ho

1 FIELDER CL
2 HUTCHINGS CL
3 HEARNE CL
4 BRACKEN CT
5 THE CEDARS

Tonge Rd

Eurolink Way

Swan Cl

All Saints Rd

Lomas Rd

Tonge
Mill

St Michael's Rd

Wheatcroft
Cl

Scraps Hill

Lower Rd

East St

Canterbury Rd

Snipeshill

Stones
Farm

Bapchild

Lansdowne
Prim Sch

Fox & Goose
(PH)

Fox Hill

Hempstead
Farm

Canterbury
Road Prim
Sch

1 OAKTREE HO
2 BIRCH HO
3 ASHTREE HO
4 WILLOW HO

The Street

London Rd

A2

Bapchild &
Tonge CE
Sch

Bapchild
Court

The Old
Vicarage

Radfield

Sports Ctr

Sittingbourne
Com Coll

Morris
Court

Heywood
Cottages

Little Dully
Cottages

Ashgores
House

Church St

New
Cottages

A   B   C   D   E   F

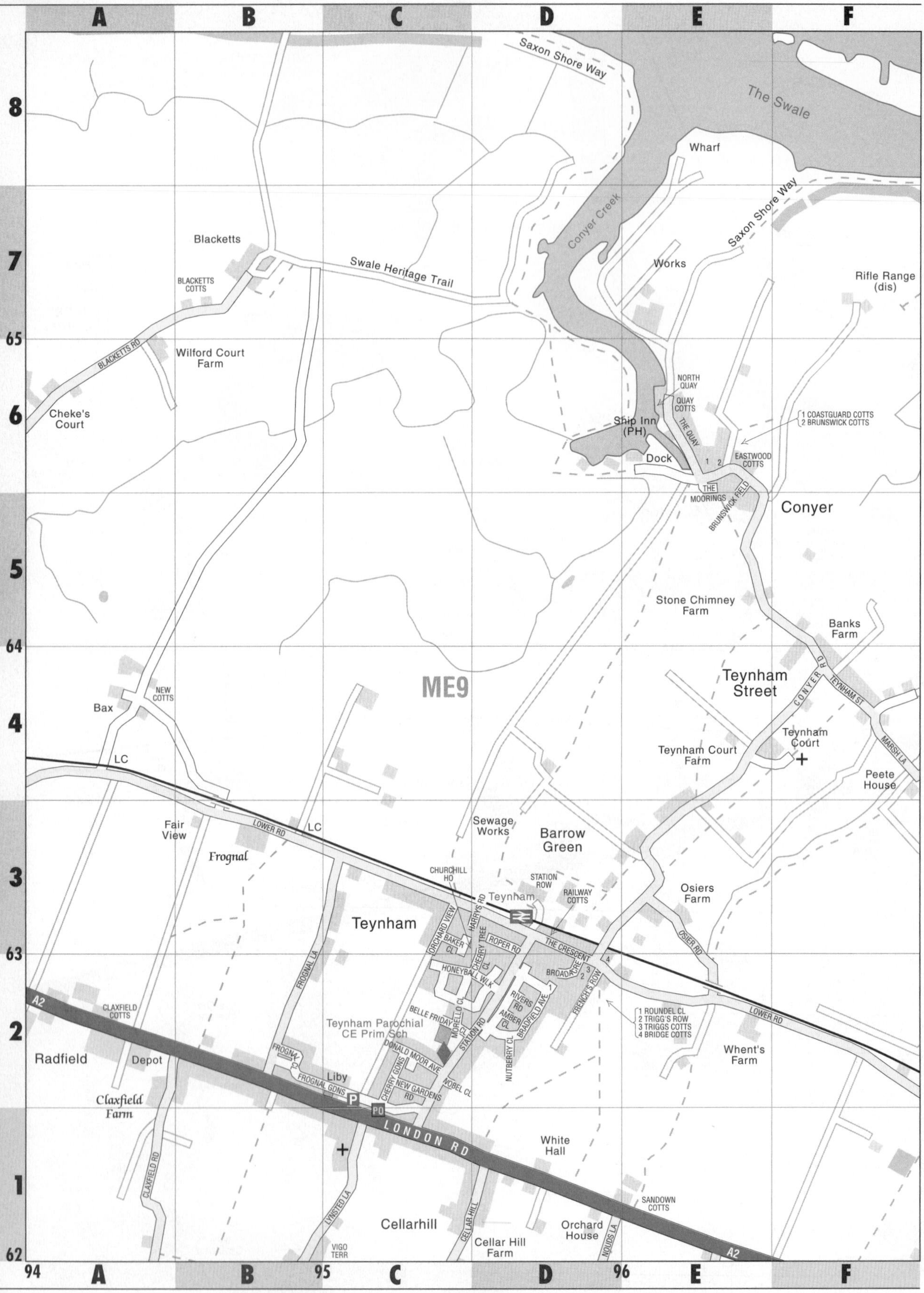

8

Saxon Shore Way

The Swale

Wharf

7 Blacketts

Swale Heritage Trail

Conyer Creek

Works

Rifle Range (dis)

BLACKETTS COTTS

65

Wilford Court Farm

BLACKETTS RD

NORTH QUAY

6 Cheke's Court

QUAY COTTS

Ship Inn (PH)

THE QUAY

1 COASTGUARD COTTS
2 BRUNSWICK COTTS

Dock

1 2

EASTWOOD COTTS

THE MOORINGS

BRUNSWICK FIELD

Conyer

5

Stone Chimney Farm

Banks Farm

64

ME9

Teynham Street

CONYER RD

TEYNHAM ST

Bax

NEW COTTS

Teynham Court Farm

Teynham Court

MARSH LA

4

LC

Peete House

LOWER RD LC

Fair View

Frognal

Sewage Works

Barrow Green

Osiers Farm

3

CHURCHILL HO

STATION ROW

RAILWAY COTTS

Teynham

ORCHARD VIEW

BAKER CL

HARRYS RD

CHERRY TREE CL

ROPER RD

THE CRESCENT

OSIER RD

63

FROGNAL LA

HONEYBALL WLK

BELLE FRIDAY CL

MORPELLO CL

STATION RD

RITERS RD

AMBER CL

BROADACRE

3
2

BRENCHLEY ROW

4

1 ROUNDEL CL
2 TRIGG'S ROW
3 TRIGGS COTTS
4 BRIDGE COTTS

2 Radfield

A2

CLAXFIELD COTTS

Depot

FROGNAL

FROGNAL GDNS

Teynham Parochial CE Prim Sch

DONALD MOOR AVE

CHERRY GDNS

NEW GARDENS RD

NOBEL CL

NUTBERRY CL

BRADFIELD AVE

Whent's Farm

Liby

P

PO

1

Claxfield Farm

CLAXFIELD RD

LONDON RD

White Hall

SANDOWN COTTS

LYNSTED LA

Cellarhill

Cellar Hill Farm

Orchard House

NOURDS LA

A2

62

VIGO TERR

CELLAR HILL

94 A   B   95   C   D   96   E   F

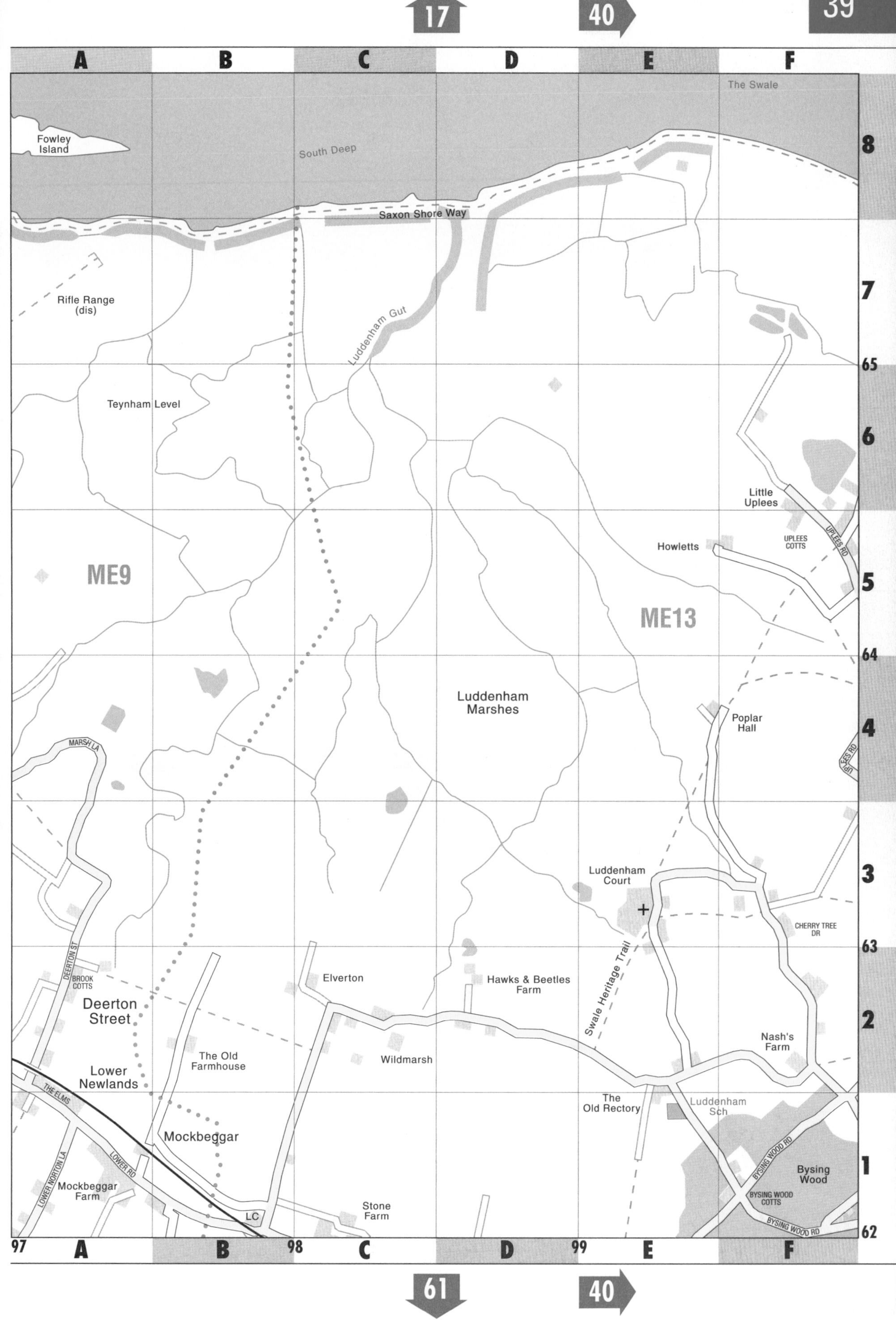

A **B** **C** **D** **E** **F**

The Swale

8

Fowley
Island

South Deep

Saxon Shore Way

7

Rifle Range
(dis)

Luddenham Gut

65

Teynham Level

6

Little
Uplees

UPLEES
COTTS

Howletts

UPLEES RD

ME9

5

ME13

64

Luddenham
Marshes

Poplar
Hall

4

MARSH LA

UPLEES RD

Luddenham
Court

3

+

CHERRY TREE
DR

63

DEERTON ST

BROOK
COTTS

Elverton

Hawks & Beetles
Farm

Swale Heritage Trail

Deerton
Street

Nash's
Farm

2

Lower
Newlands

The Old
Farmhouse

Wildmarsh

The
Old Rectory

Luddenham
Sch

THE ELMS

Mockbeggar

BYSING WOOD RD

Bysing
Wood

LOWER NORTON LA

LOWER RD

Mockbeggar
Farm

Stone
Farm

LC

BYSING WOOD
COTTS

1

BYSING WOOD RD

62

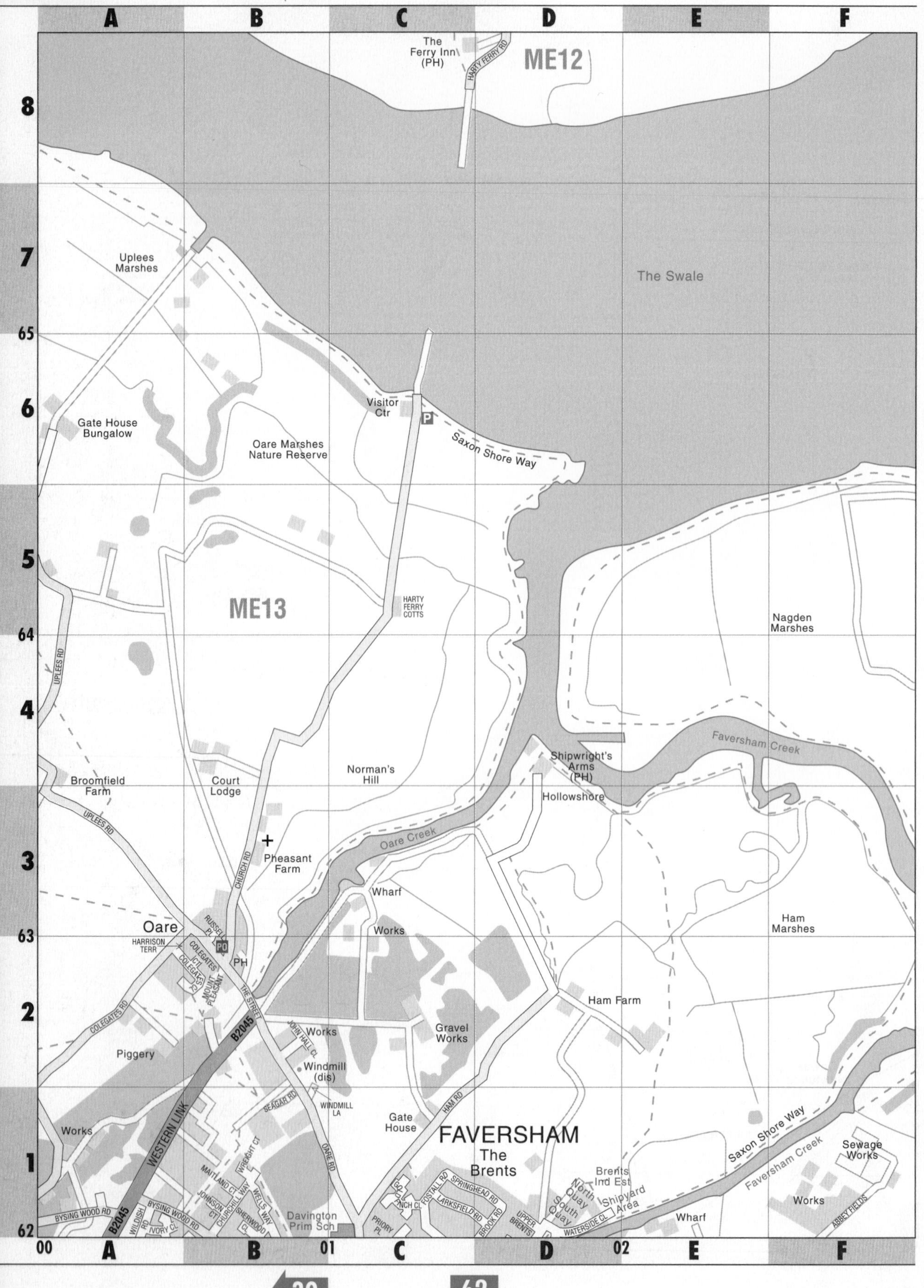

	A	B	C	D	E	F

The Ferry Inn (PH)

HARTY FERRY RD

ME12

8

Uplees Marshes

The Swale

7

65

Visitor Ctr

P

6

Gate House Bungalow

Oare Marshes Nature Reserve

Saxon Shore Way

5

ME13

HARTY FERRY COTTS

Nagden Marshes

64

UPLEES RD

Faversham Creek

4

Broomfield Farm

Court Lodge

Norman's Hill

Shipwright's Arms (PH)

Hollowshore

Ham Marshes

UPLEES RD

CHURCH RD

Pheasant Farm

Oare Creek

3

Wharf

Works

Ham Farm

Oare

RUSSELL RD

HARRISON TERR

PD

PH

COLEGATES CL

63

MOUNT PLEASANT

COLEGATES

THE STREET

Ham Farm

2

COLEGATES RD

B2045

JOHNHALL CL

Works

Gravel Works

Piggery

Windmill (dis)

WIRRENT CL

SEAGAR RD

WINDMILL LA

HAM RD

WESTERN LINK

OARE RD

Gate House

FAVERSHAM

The Brents

Saxon Shore Way

Sewage Works

1

Works

MAITLAND CT

WELLS WAY

SHERWOOD CL

Brents Ind Est

North Quay

South Quay

Shipyard Area

Faversham Creek

Works

BYSING WOOD RD

B2045

WILLUSH

BYSING WOOD RD

IVORY CL

JOHNSON CL

CHURCHILL WAY

C2

FESTIVAL RD

SPRINGHEAD RD

LARKSFIELD RD

BROOK RD

UPPER BRENTS

WATERSIDE CL

Wharf

ABBEY FIELDS

62

Davington Prim Sch

PRIORY PL

FINCH CL

00
01
02

	A	B	C	D	E	F

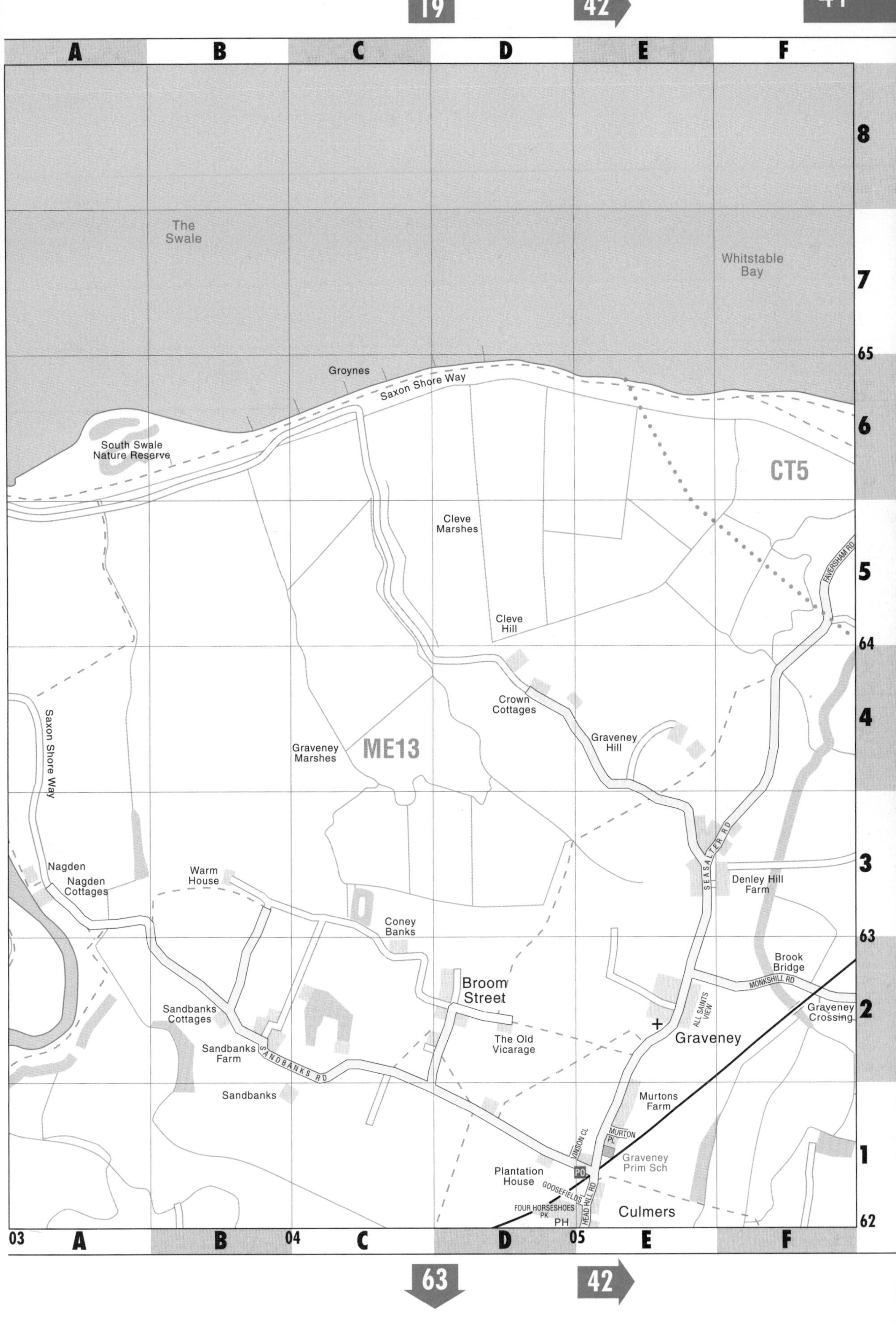

The Swale

Whitstable Bay

Groynes

Saxon Shore Way

South Swale
Nature Reserve

CT5

FAVERSHAM RD

Cleve
Marshes

Cleve
Hill

Crown
Cottages

Graveney
Hill

Graveney
Marshes

ME13

SEASALTER RD

Nagden

Nagden
Cottages

Saxon Shore Way

Warm
House

Denley Hill
Farm

Coney
Banks

Brook
Bridge

MONKSHILL RD

Broom
Street

Sandbanks
Cottages

ALL SAINTS VIEW

Graveney
Crossing

Sandbanks
Farm

SANDBANKS RD

The Old
Vicarage

Graveney

Sandbanks

Murtons
Farm

MURTON
PL

VINSON CL

Graveney
Prim Sch

Plantation
House

PO

GOOSEFIELDS

HEAD HILL RD

Graveney
Prim Sch

Culmers

FOUR HORSESHOES
PK

PH

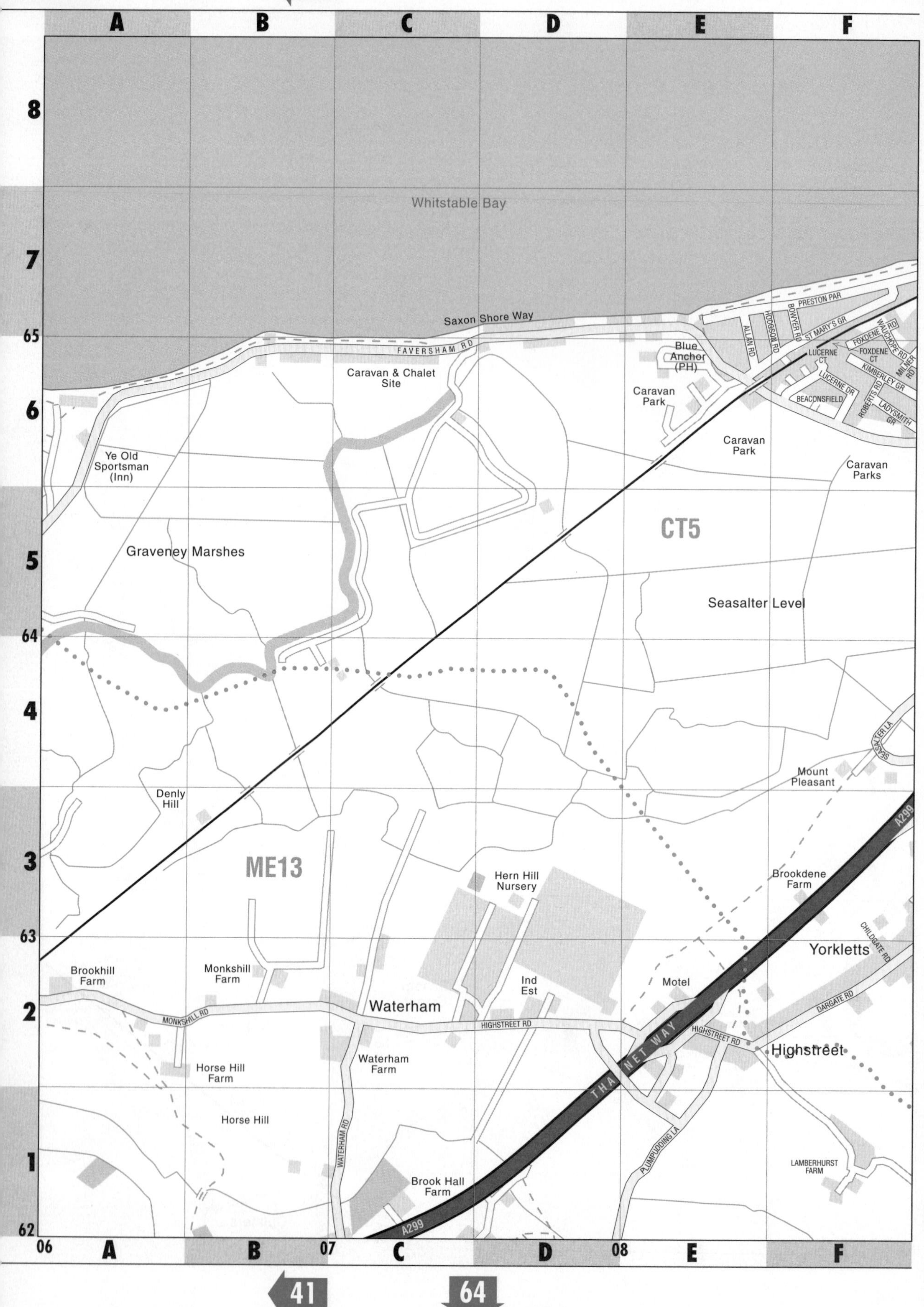

Whitstable Bay

Saxon Shore Way

FAVERSHAM RD

Caravan & Chalet Site

Blue Anchor (PH)

PRESTON PAR

ST MARY'S GR

FOXDENE RD

FOXDENE CT

HUDSON RD

BOWYER RD

WALDERS RD

ALLAN RD

LUCERNE CT

LUCERNE DR

KIMBERLEY GR

BEACONSFIELD

ROBERTS RD

LADYSMITH GR

MILL RD

Caravan Park

Caravan Park

Caravan Parks

Ye Old Sportsman (Inn)

CT5

Graveney Marshes

Seasalter Level

SEASALTER LA

Mount Pleasant

A299

Denly Hill

ME13

Hern Hill Nursery

Brookdene Farm

CHILDGATE RD

Yorkletts

Brookhill Farm

Monkshill Farm

Ind Est

Motel

DARGATE RD

Waterham

THANET WAY

HIGHSTREET RD

Highstreet

MONKSHILL RD

HIGHSTREET RD

Horse Hill Farm

Waterham Farm

WATERHAM RD

PLUMPUDDING LA

LAMBERHURST FARM

Horse Hill

Brook Hall Farm

A299

06   07   08

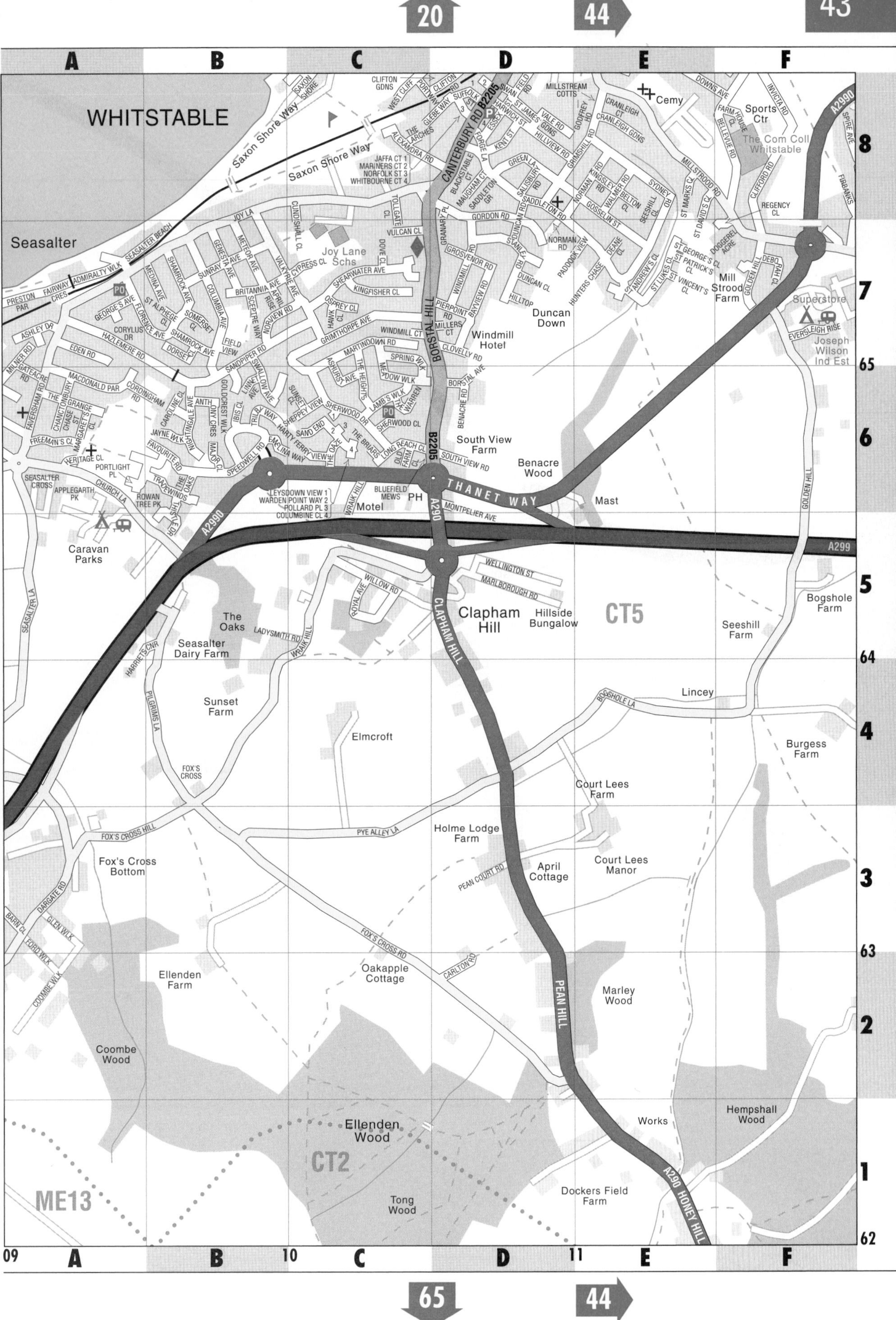
20
44
WHITSTABLE
Seasalter
Saxon Shore Way
Joy Lane Schs
Duncan Down
Windmill Hotel
South View Farm
Benacre Wood
Mast
Motel
PH
THANET WAY
Caravan Parks
The Oaks
Seasalter Dairy Farm
Clapham Hill
Hillside Bungalow
CT5
Seeshill Farm
Bogshole Farm
Mill Strood Farm
Sports Ctr
The Com Coll Whitstable
Superstore
Joseph Wilson Ind Est
Cemy
Sunset Farm
Elmcroft
Lincey
Burgess Farm
Court Lees Farm
Holme Lodge Farm
April Cottage
Court Lees Manor
Fox's Cross Bottom
Oakapple Cottage
Ellenden Farm
Marley Wood
Coombe Wood
Ellenden Wood
CT2
Tong Wood
Works
Hempshall Wood
Dockers Field Farm
ME13
BORSTAL HILL
CANTERBURY RD
CLAPHAM HILL
PEAN HILL
A290 HONEY HILL
A2990
A299
B2205
A290
65
44

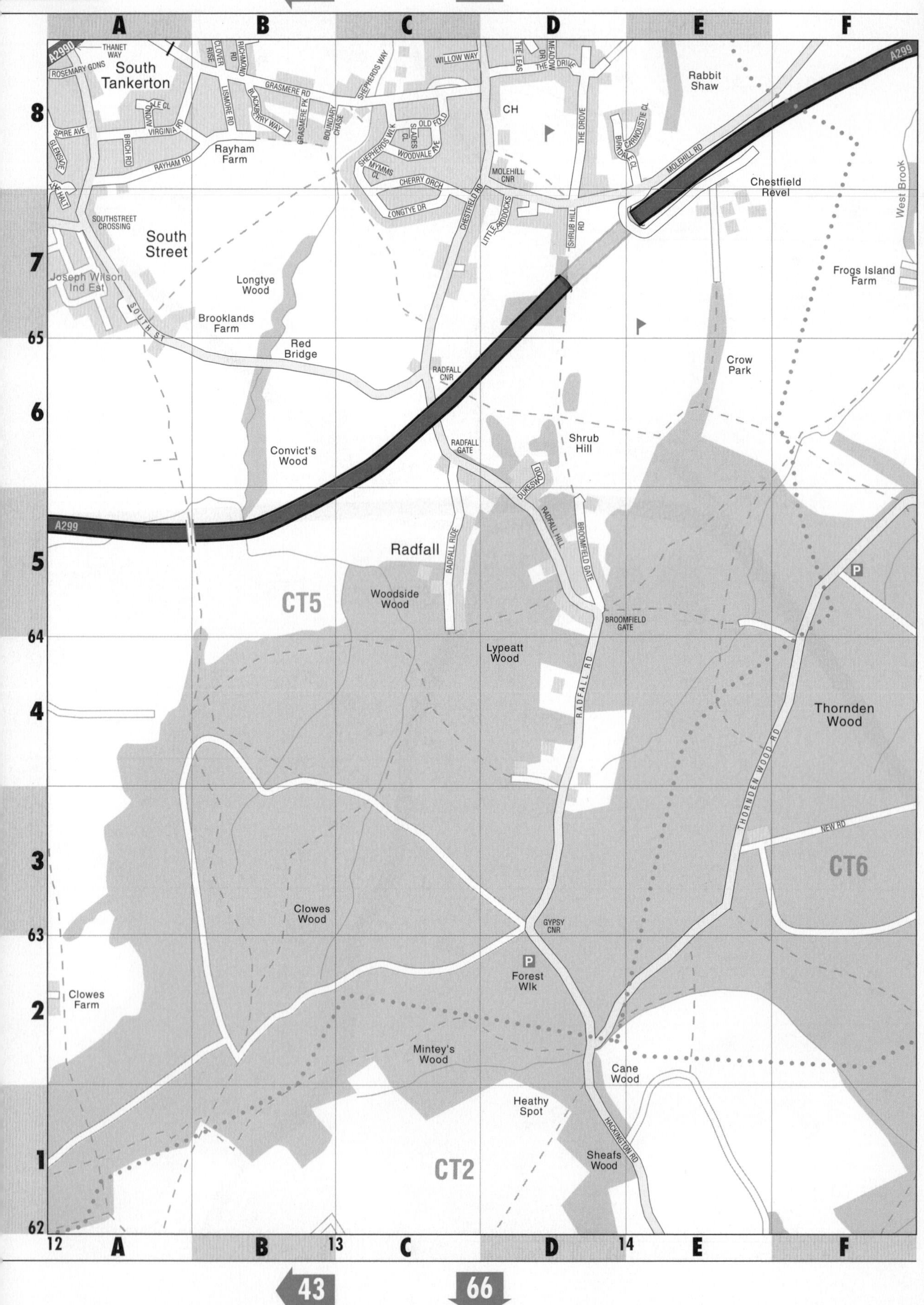

43
21

A299
THANET WAY
ROSEMARY GDNS
South
Tankerton
CLOVER RISE
RICHMOND RD
BLACKBERRY WAY
GRASMERE RD
GRASMERE PK
SHEPHERDS WAY
WILLOW WAY
THE LEAS
MEADOW DR
THE DRIVE
CH
Rabbit
Shaw
A299
West Brook
SPIRE AVE
GLENSIDE
SEASALTER
VALE CL
SOMMY
VIRGINIA RD
BIRCH RD
Rayham
Farm
BOUNDARY CHASE
SHEPHERDS WK
MYMMS CL
OLD FOLD
WOODVALE AVE
SLADES CL
CHERRY ORCH
MOLEHILL
CNR
SHRUB HILL RD
BIRKDALE CL
CARNOUSTIE CL
MOLEHILL RD
Chestfield
Revel
RAYHAM RD
LISMORE RD

SOUTHSTREET
CROSSING
South
Street
LONGTYE DR
CHESTFIELD RD
LITTLE PADDOCKS
Frogs Island
Farm

7

Joseph Wilson
Ind Est
SOUTH ST
Longtye
Wood
Brooklands
Farm
Red
Bridge
RADFALL
CNR
Crow
Park

65

6
Convict's
Wood
RADFALL
GATE
Shrub
Hill

DUKES WK
RADFALL HILL
BROOMFIELD GATE
A299
Radfall
RADFALL RIDE

5
CT5
Woodside
Wood
BROOMFIELD
GATE
P

64
Lypeatt
Wood
RADFALL RD
Thornden
Wood

4

THORNDEN WOOD RD
NEW RD

3
Clowes
Wood
CT6

63
GYPSY
CNR

Clowes
Farm
P
Forest
Wlk

2
Mintey's
Wood
Cane
Wood

HACKINGTON RD

1
Heathy
Spot
Sheafs
Wood
CT2

62
12
A
B
13
C
D
14
E
F

43
66

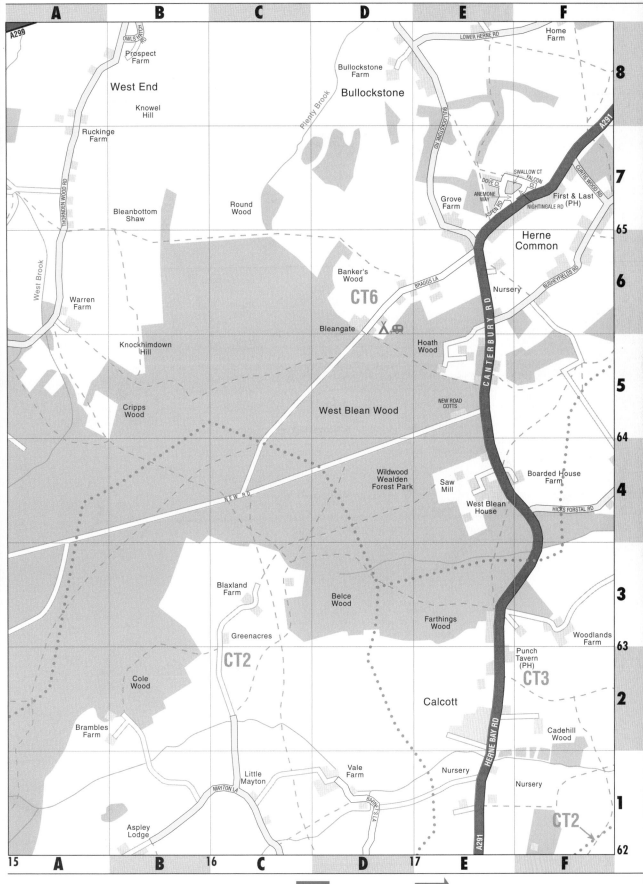

22
46

A B C D E F
A299
OWLS HATCH RD
Prospect Farm
West End
Knowel Hill
Ruckinge Farm
THORNDEN WOOD RD
Bleanbottom Shaw
West Brook
Warren Farm
Knockhimdown Hill
Cripps Wood
Bullockstone Farm
Bullockstone
Plenty Brook
Round Wood
Banker's Wood
CT6
Bleangate
West Blean Wood
NEW RD
LOWER HERNE RD
Home Farm
BULLOCKSTONE RD
SWALLOW CT
FALCON CL
DOVE CL
ANEMONE WAY
ASPEN RD
NIGHTINGALE RD
CURTIS WOOD RD
First & Last (PH)
A291
Grove Farm
Herne Common
BRAGGS LA
Nursery
BUSHEYFIELDS RD
CANTERBURY RD
Hoath Wood
NEW ROAD COTTS
Wildwood Wealden Forest Park
Saw Mill
West Blean House
Boarded House Farm
HICKS FORSTAL RD
Blaxland Farm
Belce Wood
Farthings Wood
Greenacres
CT2
Woodlands Farm
Punch Tavern (PH)
CT3
Cole Wood
Calcott
Cadehill Wood
Brambles Farm
HERNE BAY RD
Little Mayton
MAYTON LA
Vale Farm
BARNETS LA
Nursery
Nursery
CT2
Aspley Lodge
A291
8
7
65
6
5
64
4
3
63
2
1
62
15
16
17
A B C D E F
67
46

45
23

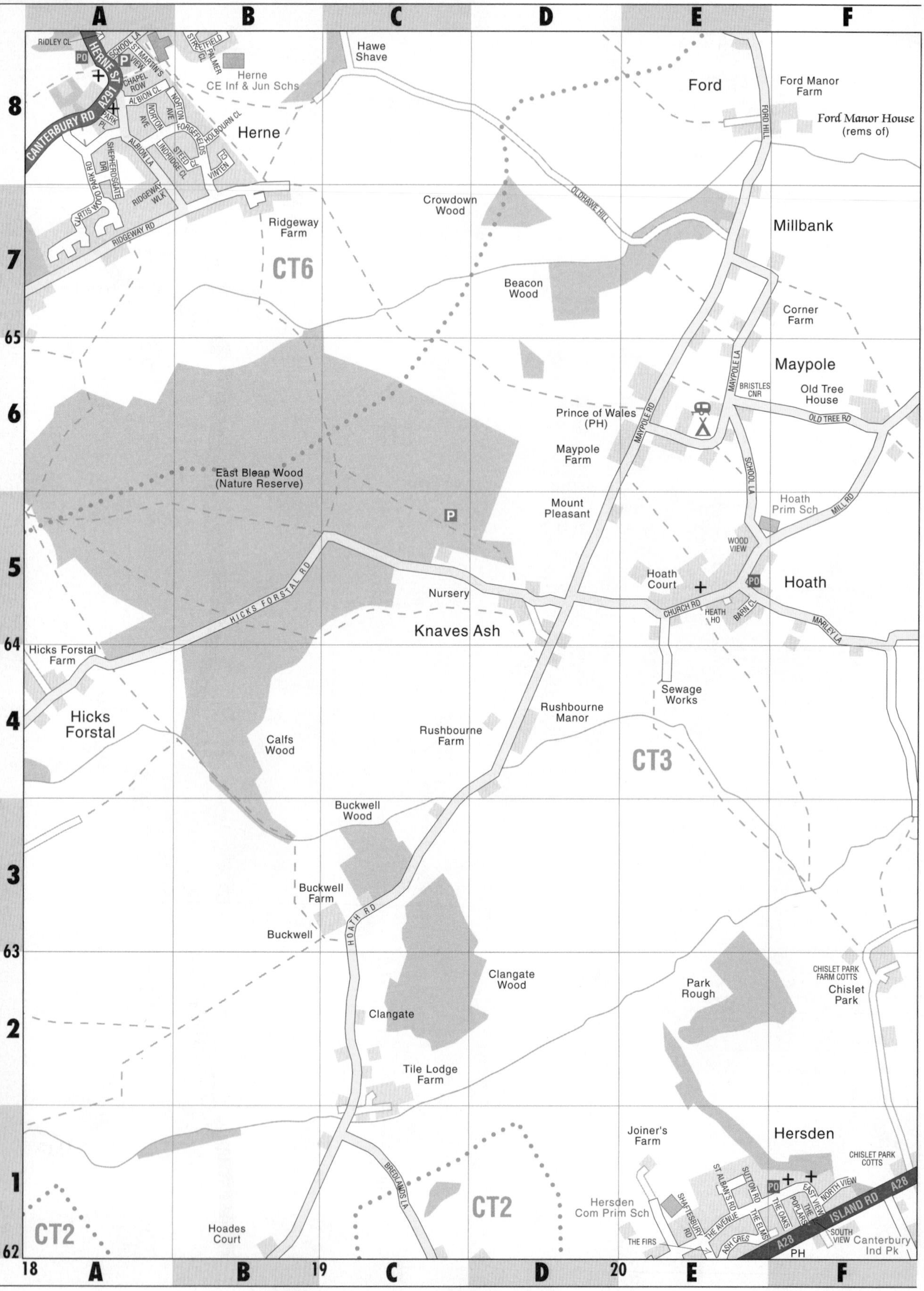

A **B** **C** **D** **E** **F**

RIDLEY CL
PO
HERNE ST
SCHOOL LA
ST MARTIN'S VIEW
CHAPEL ROW
STREETFIELD
PALMER
Hawe Shave
Ford
Ford Manor Farm
Ford Manor House (rems of)

CANTERBURY RD
A291
ALBION CL
NORTON
FORGEFIELDS
HOLBORN CL
Herne CE Inf & Jun Schs

8

SHEPHERDSGATE DR
CURTIS WAY
RIDGEWAY WLK
ALMAN LA
STEED CL
LINGROVE CL
VINTEN CL
Herne

Millbank

7

RIDGEWAY RD
Ridgeway Farm
CT6
Crowdown Wood
OLDHAWE HILL
FORD HILL

Corner Farm

Maypole

65

Beacon Wood

MAYPOLE LA
BRISTLES CNR
Old Tree House

6

East Blean Wood (Nature Reserve)
Prince of Wales (PH)
Maypole Farm
MAYPOLE RD
SCHOOL LA
OLD TREE RD

Hoath Prim Sch
MILL RD

Mount Pleasant
WOOD VIEW

5

P
HICKS FORSTAL RD
Nursery
Hoath Court
Heath Ho
BARN CL
PO
Hoath
MARLEY LA

64

Hicks Forstal Farm
Knaves Ash
CHURCH RD

4

Hicks Forstal
Calfs Wood
Rushbourne Farm
Rushbourne Manor
Sewage Works
CT3

3

Buckwell Wood
Buckwell Farm
HOATH RD

63

Buckwell
Clangate Wood
Park Rough
CHISLET PARK FARM COTTS
Chislet Park

2

Clangate
Tile Lodge Farm

1

Joiner's Farm
Hersden
CHISLET PARK COTTS

BREDLANDS LA
CT2
Hersden Com Prim Sch
ST ALBAN'S RD
SHAFTESBURY RD
SUTTON RD
PO
THE AVENUE
THE OAKS
THE ELMS
THE POPLARS
EAST VIEW
NORTH VIEW
ISLAND RD
A28
CHISLET PARK IND PK

CT2
Hoades Court
The Firs
ASH CRES
SOUTH VIEW
PH
Canterbury Ind Pk

62

45
68

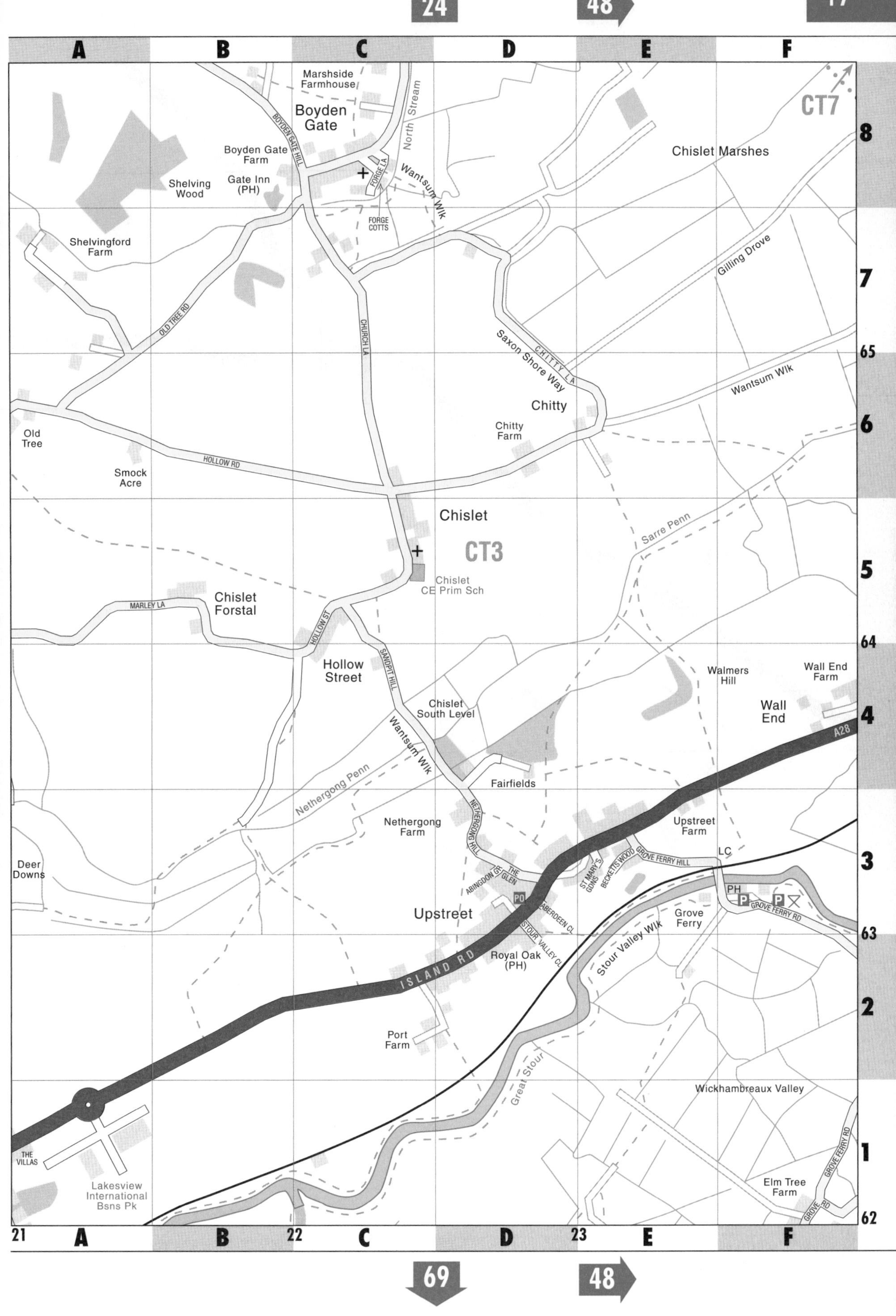

CT7

Chislet Marshes

Marshside Farmhouse

Boyden Gate

Boyden Gate Farm

Gate Inn (PH)

FORGE LA

FORGE COTTS

North Stream

Wantsum Wlk

Shelving Wood

Shelvingford Farm

OLD TREE RD

BOYDEN GATE HILL

CHURCH LA

Gilling Drove

Saxon Shore Way

CHITTY LA

Wantsum Wlk

Chitty

Chitty Farm

Old Tree

HOLLOW RD

Smock Acre

Chislet

CT3

Chislet CE Prim Sch

Sarre Penn

MARLEY LA

Chislet Forstal

HOLLOW ST

SANDPIT HILL

Hollow Street

Walmers Hill

Wall End Farm

Wall End

A28

Chislet South Level

Wantsum Wlk

Nethergong Penn

Fairfields

Upstreet Farm

LC

Deer Downs

Nethergong Farm

NETHERGONG HILL

THE GLEN

ABINGDON CL

ST MARY'S GDNS

BECKETS WOOD

GROVE FERRY HILL

PH

P

P

Upstreet

PO

ABERDEEN CL

STOUR VALLEY CL

Grove Ferry

GROVE FERRY RD

LC

Royal Oak (PH)

ISLAND RD

Stour Valley Wlk

Port Farm

Great Stour

Wickhambreaux Valley

THE VILLAS

Lakesview International Bsns Pk

Elm Tree Farm

GROVE FERRY RD

GROVE RD

47
25

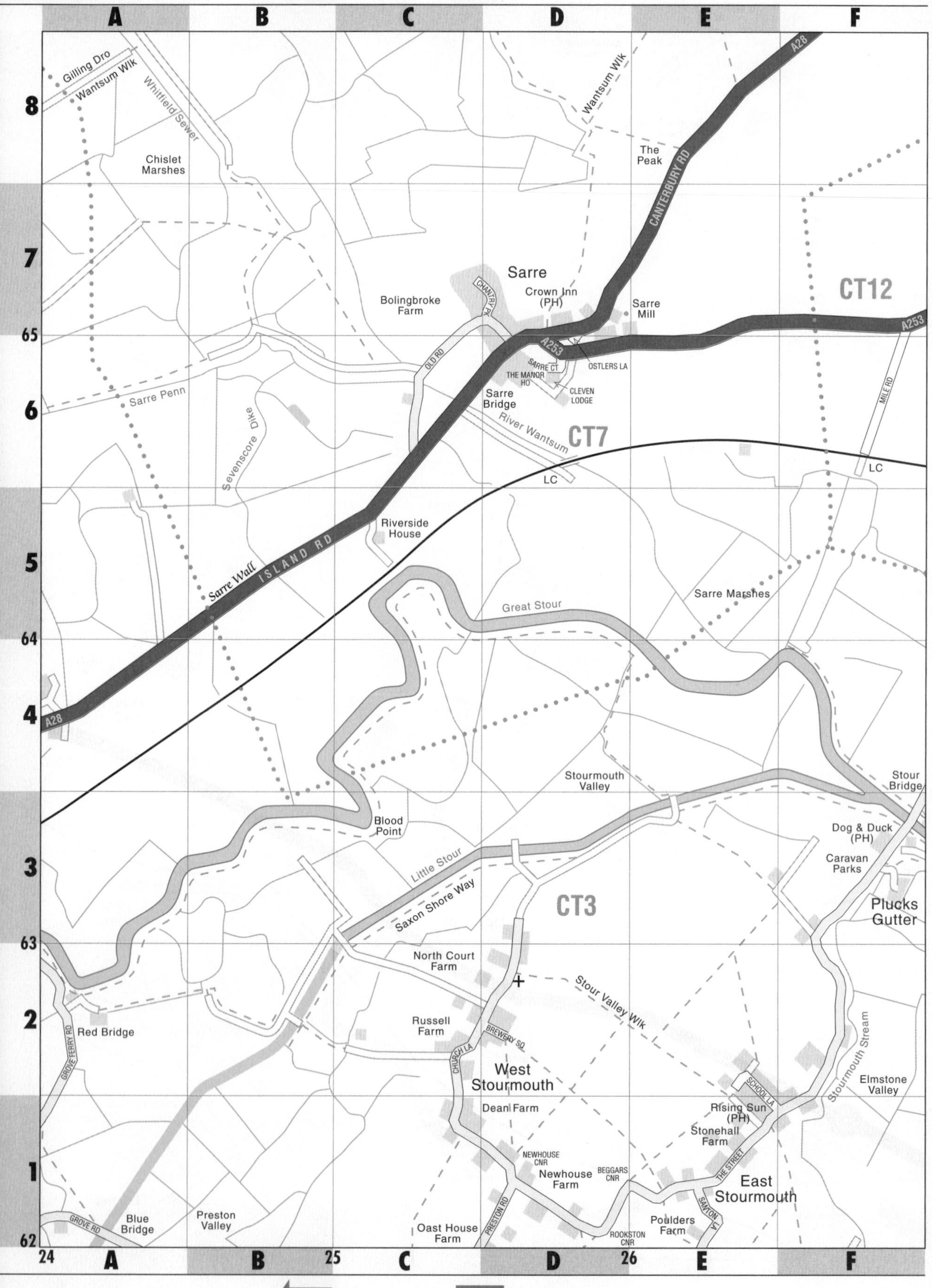
A
B
C
D
E
F
8
7
65
6
5
64
4
3
63
2
1
62
24
25
26
Gilling Dro
Wantsum Wlk
Whitfield Sewer
Chislet Marshes
Wantsum Wlk
The Peak
CANTERBURY RD
A28
Sarre
Crown Inn (PH)
Sarre Mill
CHANTRY PL
Bolingbroke Farm
CT12
A253
OLD RD
SARRE CT
THE MANOR HO
OSTLERS LA
CLEVEN LODGE
Sarre Bridge
Sarre Penn
Sevenscore Dike
River Wantsum
CT7
MILE RD
LC
Riverside House
Sarre Wall
ISLAND RD
Sarre Marshes
Great Stour
Stourmouth Valley
Stour Bridge
Blood Point
Dog & Duck (PH)
Caravan Parks
Little Stour
Saxon Shore Way
CT3
Plucks Gutter
North Court Farm
Stour Valley Wlk
Russell Farm
Red Bridge
GROVE FERRY RD
BREWERY SQ
CHURCH LA
West Stourmouth
Dean Farm
SCHOOL LA
Rising Sun (PH)
Stonehall Farm
Stourmouth Stream
Elmstone Valley
NEWHOUSE CNR
Newhouse Farm
BEGGARS CNR
THE STREET
East Stourmouth
GROVE RD
Blue Bridge
Preston Valley
Oast House Farm
PRESTON RD
ROOKSTON CNR
Poulders Farm
SANTON LA

47
70

26
50

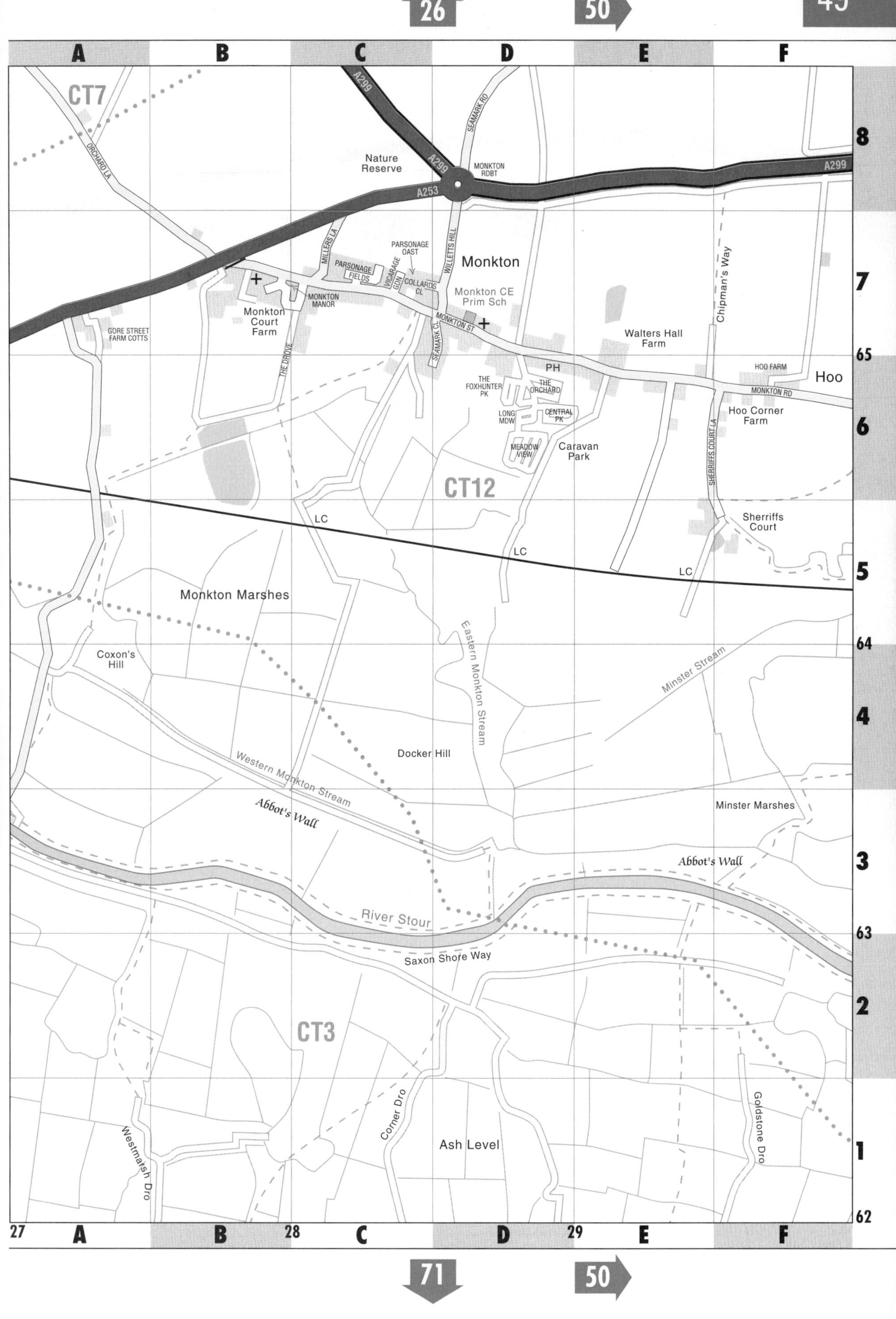
A
B
C
D
E
F
CT7
ORCHARD LA
A299
SEAMARK RD
Nature
Reserve
MONKTON
RDBT
A253
MILLERS LA
PARSONAGE
OAST
WILLETTS HILL
Monkton
PARSONAGE
FIELDS
VICARAGE
GDN
COLLARDS
CL
MONKTON
MANOR
Monkton CE
Prim Sch
Monkton
Court
Farm
GORE STREET
FARM COTTS
MONKTON ST
SEAMARK CL
THE DROVE
Chipman's Way
Walters Hall
Farm
PH
HOO FARM
Hoo
MONKTON RD
THE
FOXHUNTER
PK
THE
ORCHARD
LONG
MDW
CENTRAL
PK
Hoo Corner
Farm
MEADOW
VIEW
Caravan
Park
SHERRIFFS COURT LA
CT12
LC
Sherriffs
Court
LC
LC
Monkton Marshes
Eastern Monkton Stream
Coxon's
Hill
Minster Stream
Docker Hill
Western Monkton Stream
Abbot's Wall
Minster Marshes
Abbot's Wall
River Stour
Saxon Shore Way
CT3
Corner Dro
Ash Level
Westmarsh Dro
Goldstone Dro
8
7
65
6
5
64
4
3
63
2
1
62
27
28
29

71
50

49
27

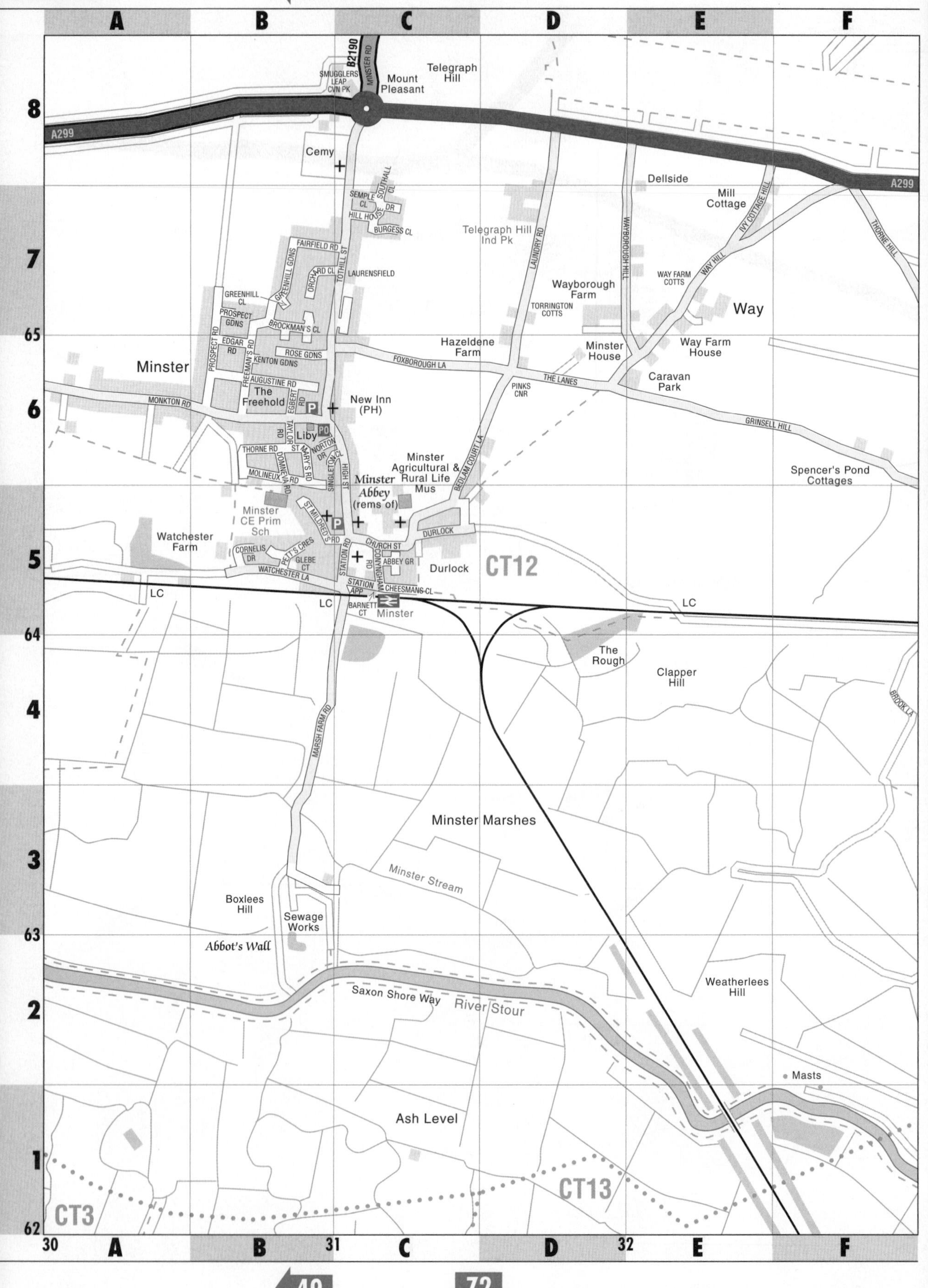
A
B
C
D
E
F
B2190
MINSTER RD
SMUGGLERS LEAP CVN PK
Mount Pleasant
Telegraph Hill
A299
Cemy
SOUTHALL CL
SEMPLE CL
HILL HOUSE DR
BURGESS CL
FAIRFIELD RD
TOTHILL ST
ORCHARD CL
LAURENSFIELD
GREENHILL GDNS
GREENHILL CL
PROSPECT GDNS
BROCKMAN'S CL
PROSPECT RD
EDGAR RD
FREEMAN'S RD
KENTON GDNS
ROSE GDNS
AUGUSTINE RD
Minster
The Freehold
EGBERT RD
MONKTON RD
New Inn (PH)
Liby
PO
TAYLOR RD
THORNE RD
ST MARY'S RD
NORTON DR
SINGLETON CL
HIGH ST
DOMNEVA RD
MOLINEUX RD
Minster Abbey (rems of)
ST MILDRED'S RD
Minster CE Prim Sch
Watchester Farm
CORNELIS DR
PETT'S CRES
GLEBE CT
STATION RD
CHURCH ST
CONYNGHAM RD
ABBEY GR
WATCHESTER LA
STATION APP
CHEESMANS CL
BARNETT CT
Minster
LC
Minster Agricultural & Rural Life Mus
DURLOCK
Durlock
CT12
Telegraph Hill Ind Pk
LAUNDRY RD
Hazeldene Farm
FOXBOROUGH LA
PINKS CNR
THE LANES
BEDLAM COURT LA
Wayborough Farm
TORRINGTON COTTS
WAYBOROUGH HILL
Minster House
Dellside
Mill Cottage
IVY COTTAGE HILL
WAY HILL
WAY FARM COTTS
Way
Way Farm House
Caravan Park
GRINSELL HILL
THORNE HILL
Spencer's Pond Cottages
The Rough
Clapper Hill
BROOK LA
MARSH FARM RD
Minster Marshes
Minster Stream
Boxlees Hill
Sewage Works
Abbot's Wall
Saxon Shore Way
River Stour
Weatherlees Hill
Masts
Ash Level
CT13
CT3
8
7
65
6
5
64
4
3
63
2
1
62
30
31
32

49
72

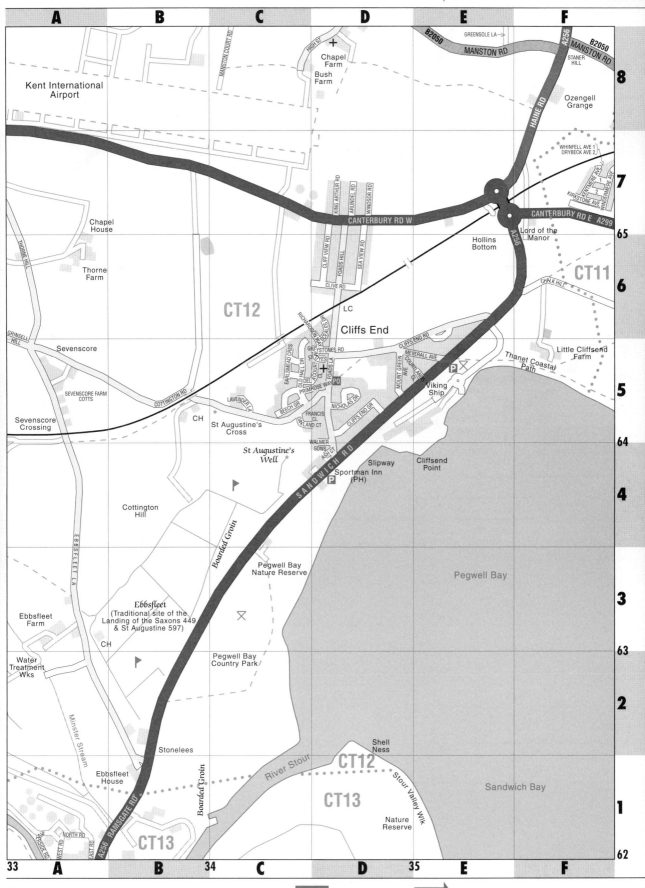

B2050

GREENSOLE LA →

MANSTON RD

B2050
MANSTON RD

STANER HILL

8

Kent International Airport

Chapel Farm

Bush Farm

HAINE RD

Ozengell Grange

WHINFELL AVE 1
DRYBECK AVE 2

Chapel House

KING ARTHUR RD
ARUNDEL RD
WINDSOR RD

CONEYMERE AVE
KIRKSTONE AVE
WINDERMERE AVE

7

Thorne Farm

CLIFF VIEW RD
FOADS HILL
SEA VIEW RD

CANTERBURY RD W

CANTERBURY RD E   A299

Lord of the Manor

65

Sevenscore

A256

Hollins Bottom

CHALK HILL

CT11

6

GRINSELL HILL

CT12

CLIVE RD

LC

Cliffs End

Little Cliffsend Farm

RICHARDSON RD
HOLLICONDANE RD
FOADS LA

GREYSTONES RD

CLIFFS END RD

MEVERALL AVE

Thanet Coastal Path

Sevenscore Farm Cotts

COTTINGTON RD

LAVENDER LA

BARLSMEAD CRES
OLD HALL DR
DELACOURT
YEW CL
PRIMROSE WAY

MOUNT GREEN
COURTLANDS AVE

P

Viking Ship

5

Sevenscore Crossing

CH

BEECH GR
OAKLAND CT
NICHOLAS DR

FRANCIS CL

CLIFFS END GR

PO

St Augustine's Cross

WALMER GDNS
ASH CT

64

St Augustine's Well

SANDWICH RD

Slipway

Cliffsend Point

4

EBBSFLEET LA

Cottington Hill

P

Sportman Inn (PH)

Ebbsfleet Farm

Bourded Groin

Pegwell Bay Nature Reserve

Pegwell Bay

3

Ebbsfleet
(Traditional site of the Landing of the Saxons 449 & St Augustine 597)

CH

Water Treatment Wks

Pegwell Bay Country Park

63

2

Minster Stream

Stonelees

Shell Ness

RAMSGATE RD

Bourded Groin

River Stour

CT12

Stour Valley Wlk

Sandwich Bay

Ebbsfleet House

CT13

1

A256

PARKSIDE RD
WEST RD
NORTH RD
EAST RD

CT13

Nature Reserve

62

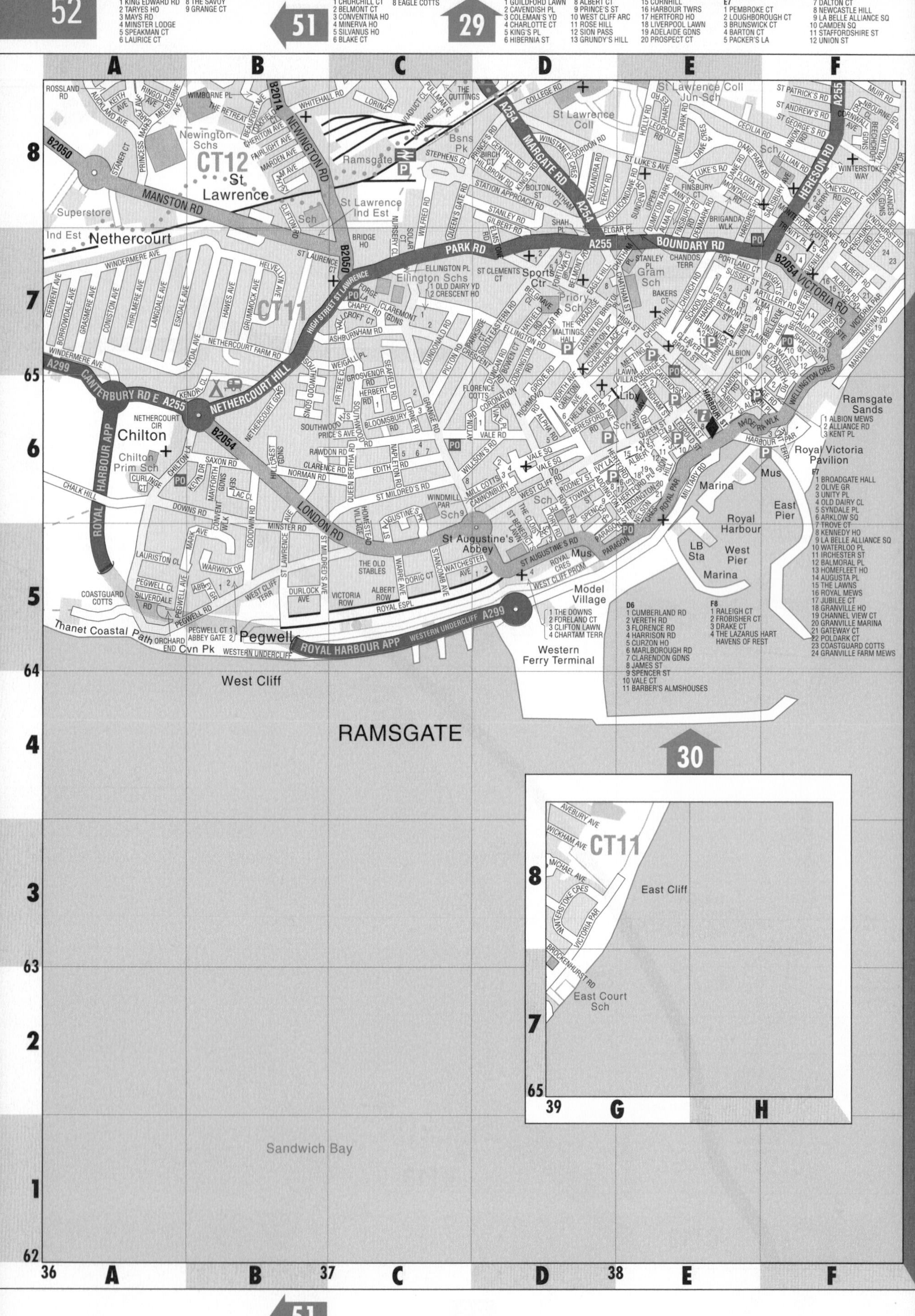
52
C6
1 KING EDWARD RD
2 TARYES HO
3 MAYS RD
4 MINSTER LODGE
5 SPEAKMAN CT
6 LAURICE CT
7 NAPLETON CT
8 THE SAVOY
9 GRANGE CT
51
D7
1 CHURCHILL CT
2 BELMONT CT
3 CONVENTINA HO
4 MINERVA HO
5 SILVANUS HO
6 BLAKE CT
7 COLLINGWOOD CT
8 EAGLE COTTS
29
E6
1 GUILDFORD LAWN
2 CAVENDISH PL
3 COLEMAN'S YD
4 CHARLOTTE CT
5 KING'S PL
6 HIBERNIA ST
7 ALBION HILL
8 ALBERT CT
9 PRINCE'S ST
10 WEST CLIFF ARC
11 ROSE HILL
12 SION PASS
13 GRUNDY'S HILL
14 ST MICHAEL'S ALLEY
15 CORNHILL
16 HARBOUR TWRS
17 HERTFORD HO
18 LIVERPOOL LAWN
19 ADELAIDE GDNS
20 PROSPECT CT
21 PROSPECT TERR
E7
1 PEMBROKE CT
2 LOUGHBOROUGH CT
3 BRUNSWICK CT
4 BARTON CT
5 PACKER'S LA
6 DOVE CT
7 DALTON CT
8 NEWCASTLE HILL
9 LA BELLE ALLIANCE SQ
10 CAMDEN SQ
11 STAFFORDSHIRE ST
12 UNION ST
A B C D E F
8 7 65 6 5 64 4 3 63 2 1 62
36 37 38
CT12
CT11
St Lawrence
Newington Schs
Nethercourt
Superstore
Ind Est
Ramsgate
St Lawrence Ind Est
St Lawrence Coll
Ellington Schs
Sports Ctr
Gram Sch
Priory Sch
The Maltings Hall
Liby
Chilton
Chilton Prim Sch
St Augustine's Abbey
Model Village
Mus
Marina
Royal Harbour
West Pier
East Pier
LB Sta
Ramsgate Sands
Royal Victoria Pavilion
Pegwell
Thanet Coastal Path
Orchard End Cvn Pk
West Cliff
Western Ferry Terminal
RAMSGATE
Sandwich Bay
MANSTON RD
NEWINGTON RD
PARK RD
BOUNDARY RD
MARGATE RD
HERESON RD
VICTORIA RD
HIGH STREET ST LAWRENCE
NETHERCOURT HILL
CANTERBURY RD E
ROYAL HARBOUR APP
LONDON RD
WESTERN UNDERCLIFF
ROYAL ESPL
1 ALBION MEWS
2 ALLIANCE RD
3 KENT PL
F7
1 BROADGATE HALL
2 OLIVE GR
3 UNITY PL
4 OLD DAIRY CL
5 SYNDALE PL
6 ARKLOW SQ
7 TROVE CT
8 KENNEDY HO
9 LA BELLE ALLIANCE SQ
10 WATERLOO PL
11 IRCHESTER ST
12 BALMORAL PL
13 HOMEFLEET HO
14 AUGUSTA PL
15 THE LAWNS
16 ROYAL MEWS
17 JUBILEE CT
18 GRANVILLE HO
19 CHANNEL VIEW CT
20 GRANVILLE MARINA
21 GATEWAY CT
22 POLDARK CT
23 COASTGUARD COTTS
24 GRANVILLE FARM MEWS
D6
1 CUMBERLAND RD
2 VERETH RD
3 FLORENCE RD
4 HARRISON RD
5 CURZON HO
6 MARLBOROUGH RD
7 CLARENDON GDNS
8 JAMES ST
9 SPENCER ST
10 VALE CT
11 BARBER'S ALMSHOUSES
F8
1 RALEIGH CT
2 FROBISHER CT
3 DRAKE CT
4 THE LAZARUS HART HAVENS OF REST
1 THE DOWNS
2 FORELAND CT
3 CLIFTON LAWN
4 CHARTAM TERR
30
East Cliff
East Court Sch
39 G H
51

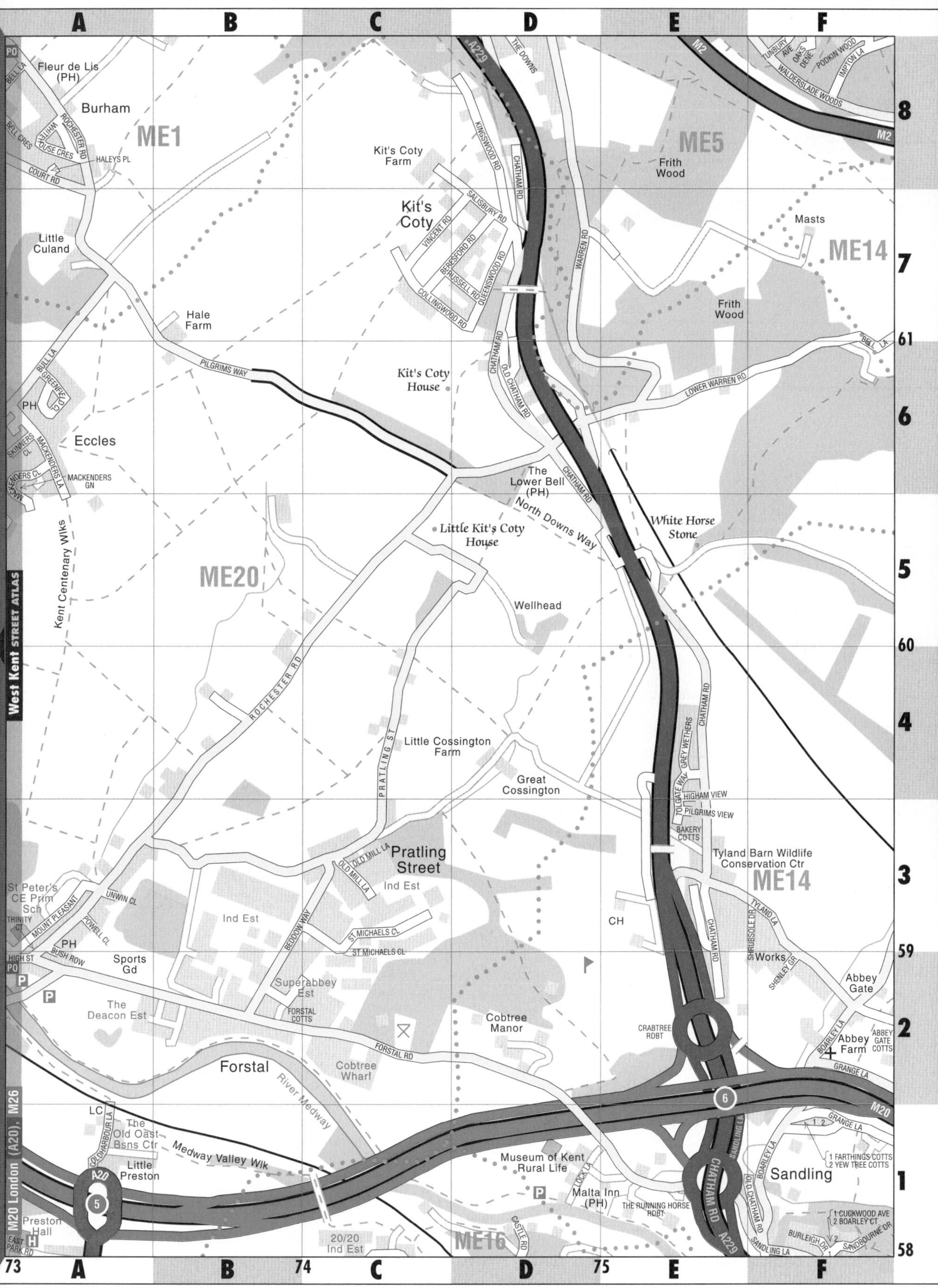

A   B   C   D   E   F

8

7

61

6

5

60

4

3

59

2

1

58

PO
BELL LA
Fleur de Lis (PH)
Burham
ME1
HALEYS PL
ROCHESTER RD
WHITE HOUSE CRES
BELL CRES
COURT RD
Little Culand
BU'LLA
GREENE RD
PH
Eccles
SKINNERS CL
MACKENDERS CL
MACKENDERS GN
MACKENDERS LA
Hale Farm
PILGRIMS WAY
Kit's Coty Farm
Kit's Coty
SALISBURY RD
VINCENT RD
BERESFORD RD
BRUSSELL RD
QUEENSWOOD RD
COLLINGWOOD RD
Kit's Coty House
Little Kit's Coty House
ME20
Wellhead
ROCHESTER RD
PRATLING ST
Little Cossington Farm
Great Cossington
OLD MILL LA
OLD MILL LA
Pratling Street
Ind Est
St Peter's CE Prim Sch
TRINITY CT
MOUNT PLEASANT
UNWIN CL
POWELL CL
PH
BUSH ROW
HIGH ST
PO
P
P
Sports Gd
The Deacon Est
Superabbey Est
FORSTAL COTTS
BEDDOW WAY
ST MICHAELS CL
ST MICHAELS CL
Forstal
FORSTAL RD
Cobtree Wharf
Cobtree Manor
Cobtree Manor
River Medway
LC
COLDHARBOUR LA
The Old Oast Bsns Ctr
Medway Valley Wlk
Little Preston
A20
5
Preston Hall
EAST PARK RD
H
20/20 Ind Est
ME16
Museum of Kent Rural Life
COCK LA
P
Malta Inn (PH)
CASTLE RD
THE RUNNING HORSE RDBT
Kent Centenary Wlks
West Kent STREET ATLAS
M20 London (A20), M26

A29
THE DOWNS
M2
KINGSWOOD RD
CHATHAM RD
M2
ME5
Frith Wood
TUNBURY AVE
OAKS DENE
PODKIN WOOD
WALDERSLADE WOODS
TIMPTON LA
Masts
ME14
Frith Wood
BELL LA
WARREN RD
LOWER WARREN RD
OLD CHATHAM RD
CHATHAM RD
The Lower Bell (PH)
North Downs Way
White Horse Stone
CHATHAM RD
GREY WETHERS
TO GATE WAY
HIGHAM VIEW
PILGRIMS VIEW
BAKERY COTTS
Tyland Barn Wildlife Conservation Ctr
ME14
CH
CHATHAM RD
SHRUBSOLE DR
TYLAND LA
SHENLEY GR
Works
CRABTREE RDBT
6
Abbey Gate
BOURLEY LA
Abbey Farm
ABBEY GATE COTTS
GRANGE LA
M20
CHATHAM RD
A29
SANDLING LA
GRANGE LA
Sandling
BOARLEY LA
1 2
1 FARTHINGS COTTS
2 YEW TREE COTTS
1 CUCKWOOD AVE
2 BOARLEY CT
BURLEIGH DR
SANDLING LA
SANDBOURNE DR

53
32

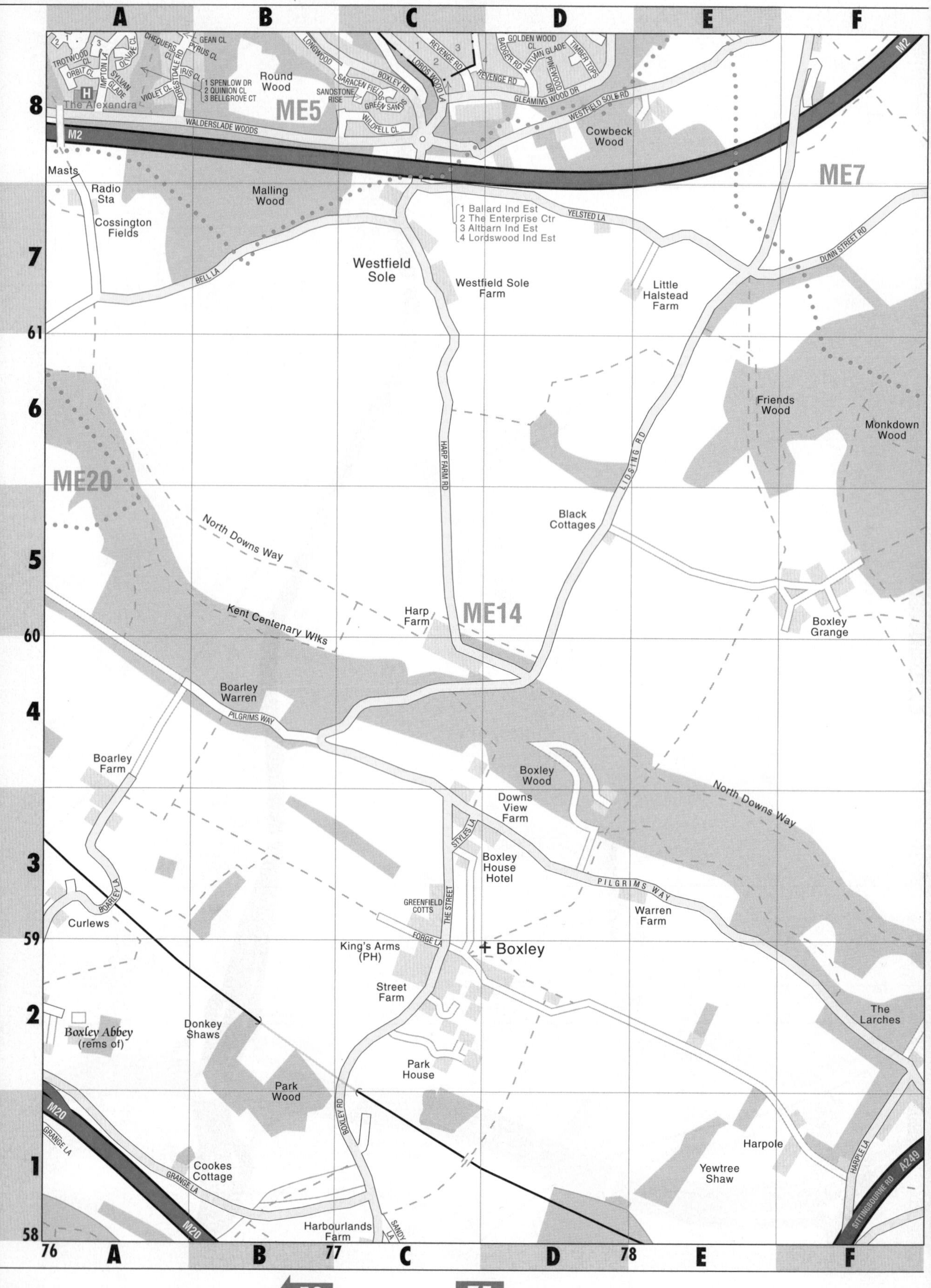
A
B
C
D
E
F
8
7
61
6
5
60
4
3
59
2
1
58
76
77
78
ME5
ME7
ME20
ME14
M2
M20
A249
The Alexandra
Round Wood
Malling Wood
Masts
Radio Sta
Cossington Fields
Westfield Sole
Westfield Sole Farm
Cowbeck Wood
Little Halstead Farm
1 Ballard Ind Est
2 The Enterprise Ctr
3 Altbarn Ind Est
4 Lordswood Ind Est
1 SPENLOW DR
2 QUINION CL
3 BELLGROVE CT
WALDERSLADE WOODS
YELSTED LA
DUNN STREET RD
BELL LA
HARP FARM RD
LIDSING RD
Friends Wood
Monkdown Wood
Black Cottages
North Downs Way
Kent Centenary Wlks
Harp Farm
Boxley Grange
Boarley Warren
PILGRIMS WAY
Boarley Farm
Boxley Wood
Downs View Farm
Boxley House Hotel
STYLES LA
THE STREET
GREENFIELD COTTS
FORGE LA
King's Arms (PH)
Boxley
Warren Farm
Curlews
BOARLEY LA
Street Farm
Boxley Abbey (rems of)
Donkey Shaws
Park House
Park Wood
The Larches
BOXLEY RD
Harpole
Yewtree Shaw
Cookes Cottage
GRANGE LA
Harbourlands Farm
SANDY LA
HARPLE LA
SITTINGBOURNE RD

53
75

33
56

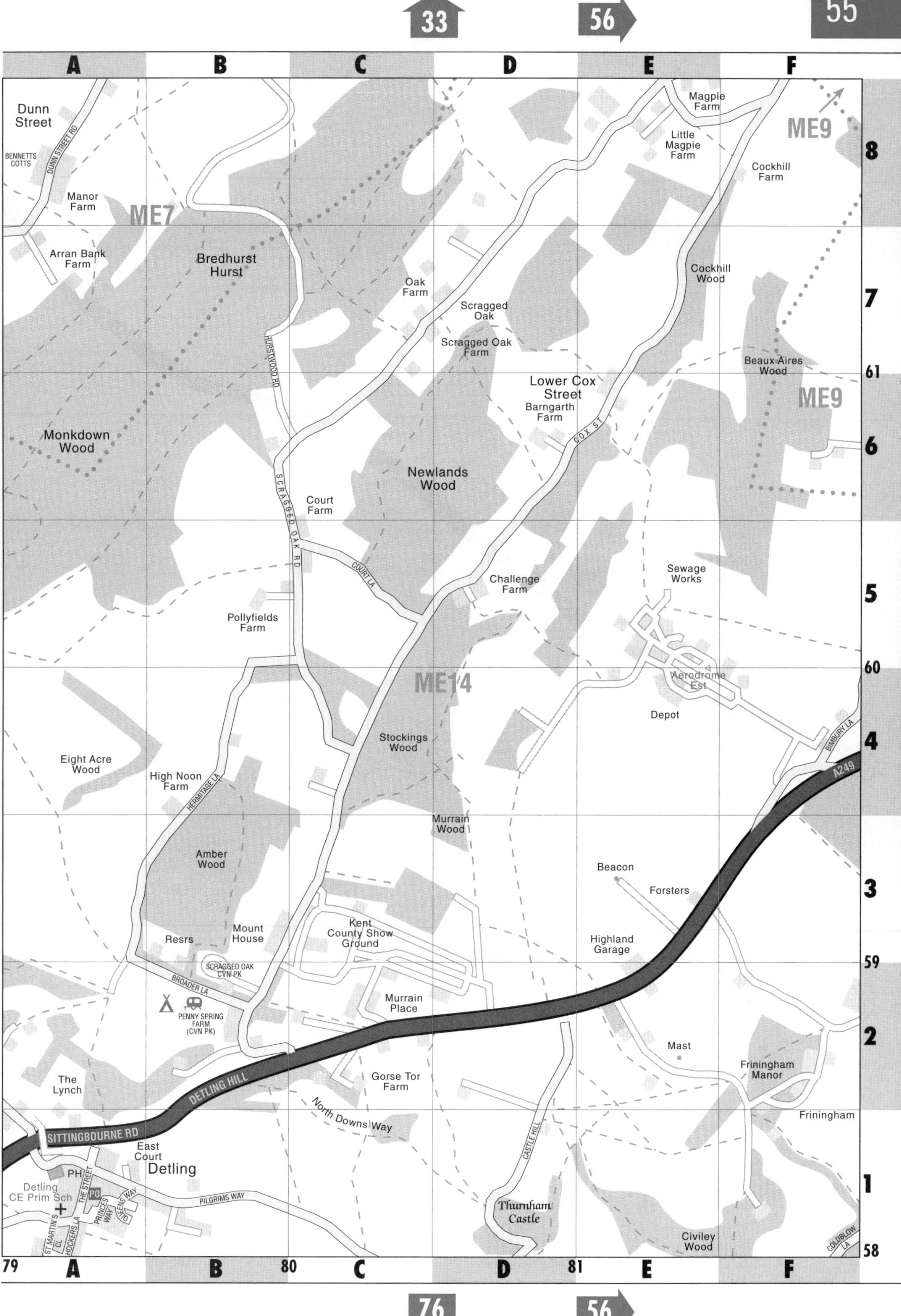
A
B
C
D
E
F
Dunn Street
BENNETTS COTTS
DUNN STREET RD
Manor Farm
ME7
Arran Bank Farm
Bredhurst Hurst
Magpie Farm
Little Magpie Farm
ME9
Cockhill Farm
8
Oak Farm
Scragged Oak
Scragged Oak Farm
Cockhill Wood
7
HURSTWOOD RD
Beaux Aires Wood
61
Lower Cox Street
Barngarth Farm
ME9
COX ST
Monkdown Wood
Newlands Wood
6
SCRAGGED OAK RD
Court Farm
COURT LA
Sewage Works
Challenge Farm
5
Pollyfields Farm
ME14
Aerodrome Est
60
Depot
Stockings Wood
BIMBURY LA
4
Eight Acre Wood
High Noon Farm
HERMITAGE LA
A249
Murrain Wood
Amber Wood
Beacon
Forsters
3
Kent County Show Ground
Resrs
Mount House
Highland Garage
SCRAGGED OAK CVN PK
59
BROADER LA
PENNY SPRING FARM (CVN PK)
Murrain Place
Mast
2
The Lynch
DETLING HILL
Gorse Tor Farm
Friningham Manor
North Downs Way
Friningham
SITTINGBOURNE RD
East Court
Detling
PH
THE STREET
CASTLE HILL
Detling CE Prim Sch
PO
QUEENS WAY
PILGRIMS WAY
1
PRINCES WAY
ST MARTIN'S CL
HOCKERS LA
Thurnham Castle
Civiley Wood
COLDBLOW LA
58
79
80
81

76
56

55
34

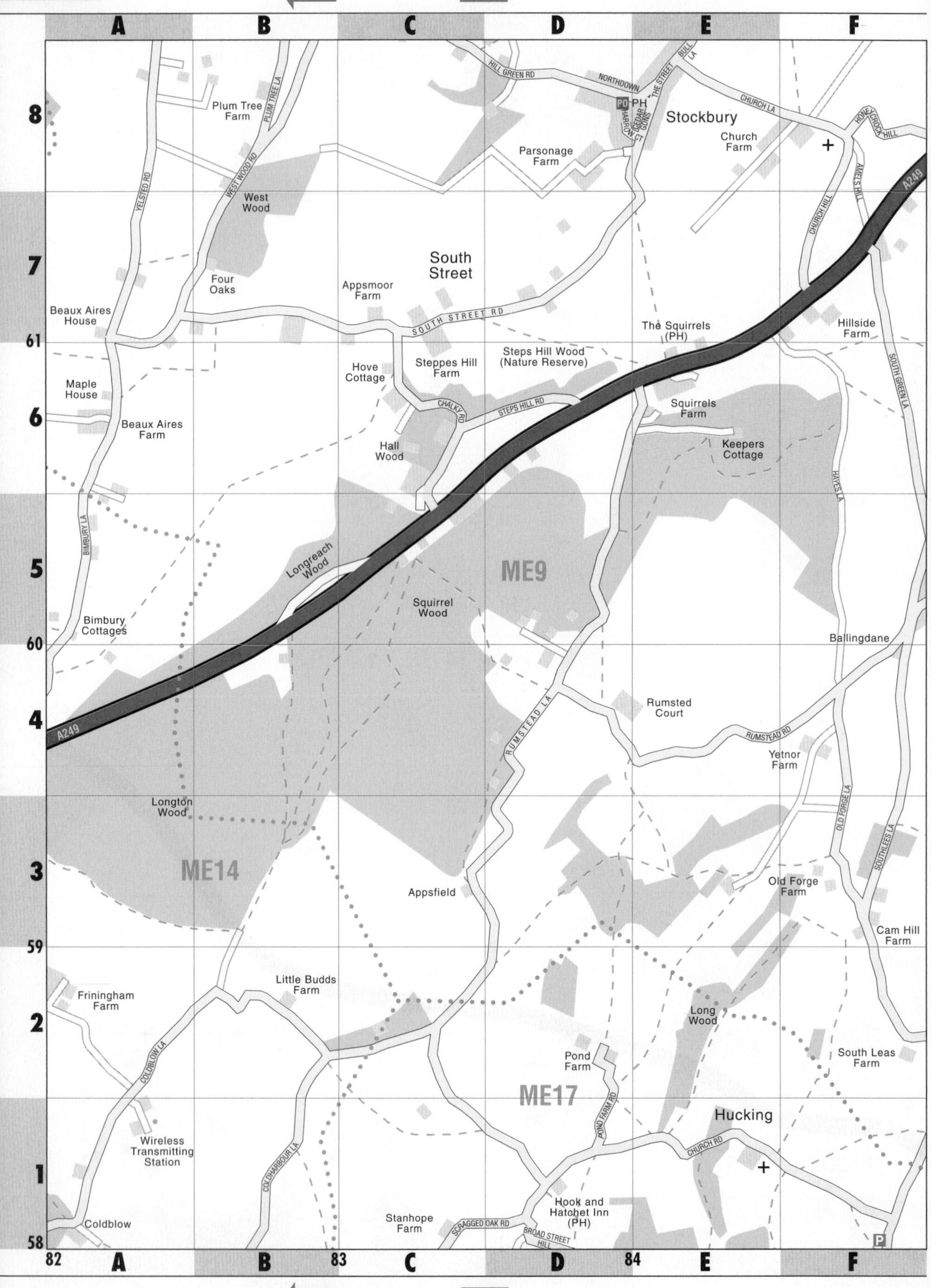
A
B
C
D
E
F
8
7
61
6
5
60
4
3
59
2
1
58
82
83
84
Plum Tree Farm
PLUM TREE LA
HILL GREEN RD
NORTHDOWN
THE STREET
BULL LA
PO
PH
Stockbury
CHURCH LA
Church Farm
HONEYCROCK HILL
Parsonage Farm
YELSTED RD
WEST WOOD RD
West Wood
AMELS HILL
CHURCH HILL
A249
South Street
Four Oaks
Appsmoor Farm
Beaux Aires House
SOUTH STREET RD
The Squirrels (PH)
Hillside Farm
Hove Cottage
Steppes Hill Farm
Steps Hill Wood (Nature Reserve)
Maple House
CHALKY RD
STEPS HILL RD
Squirrels Farm
SOUTH GREEN LA
Beaux Aires Farm
Hall Wood
Keepers Cottage
HAYES LA
BIMBURY LA
Longreach Wood
ME9
Squirrel Wood
Bimbury Cottages
Ballingdane
RUMSTEAD LA
Rumsted Court
RUMSTEAD RD
Yetnor Farm
Longton Wood
OLD FORGE LA
SOUTHLEES LA
ME14
Appsfield
Old Forge Farm
Cam Hill Farm
Little Budds Farm
Friningham Farm
Long Wood
South Leas Farm
COLDBLOW LA
Pond Farm
ME17
POND FARM RD
Hucking
CHURCH RD
Wireless Transmitting Station
COLDHARBOUR LA
Hook and Hatchet Inn (PH)
Stanhope Farm
SCRAGGED OAK RD
BROAD STREET HILL
Coldblow
P

55
77

35
58

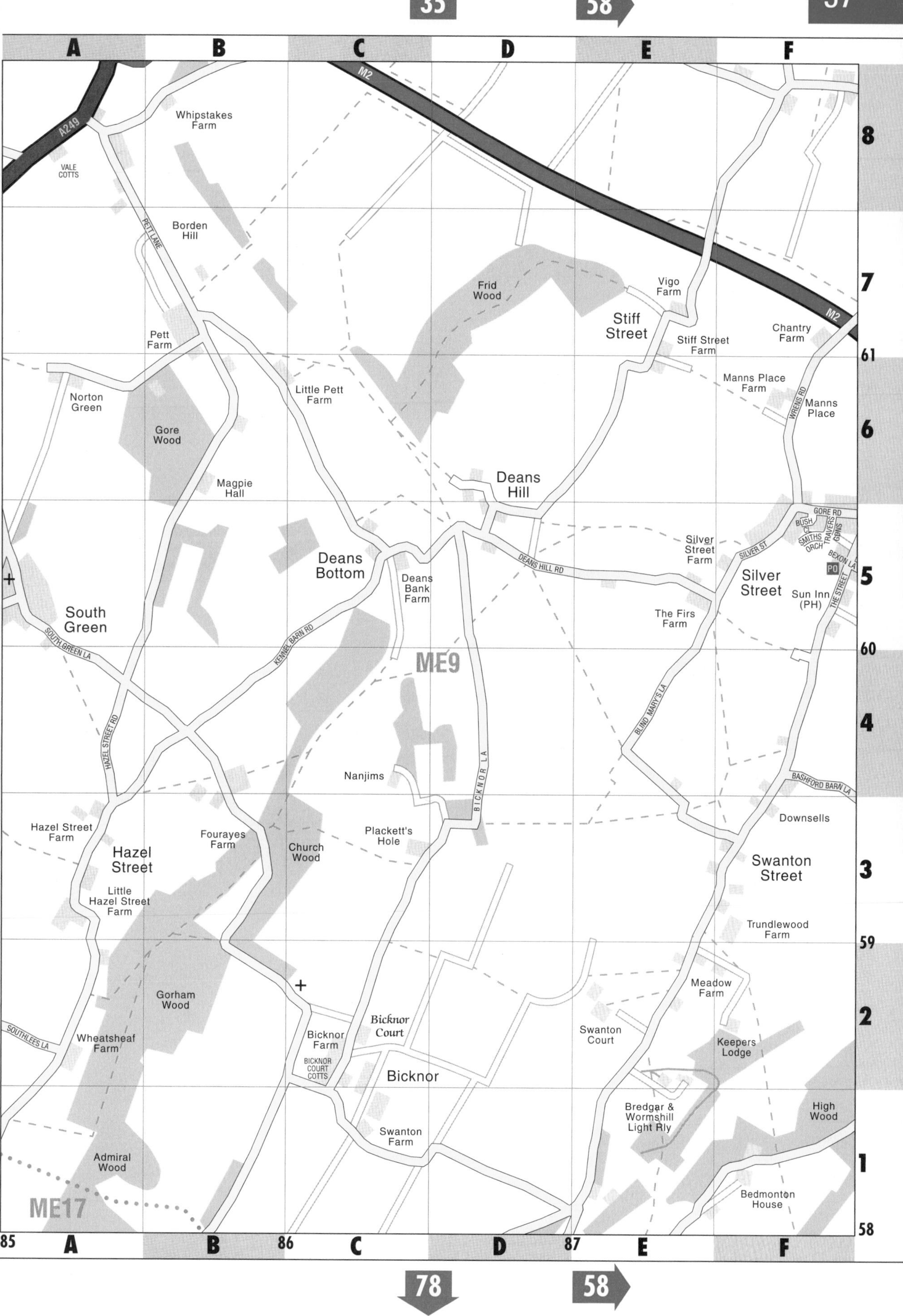
A
B
C
D
E
F
8
7
61
6
5
60
4
3
59
2
1
58
85
86
87
M2
A249
VALE COTTS
Whipstakes Farm
Borden Hill
PETT LANE
Pett Farm
Norton Green
Gore Wood
Magpie Hall
Little Pett Farm
Frid Wood
Vigo Farm
Stiff Street
Stiff Street Farm
Chantry Farm
Manns Place Farm
WRENS RD
Manns Place
Deans Hill
Deans Bottom
Deans Bank Farm
DEANS HILL RD
Silver Street Farm
SILVER ST
GORE RD
BUSH CL
SMITHS ORCH
TRAVERS GDNS
BEXON LA
PO
THE STREET
Silver Street
Sun Inn (PH)
The Firs Farm
South Green
SOUTH GREEN LA
KENNEL BARN RD
ME9
BLIND MARY'S LA
HAZEL STREET RD
Nanjims
BICKNOR LA
BASHFORD BARN LA
Downsells
Hazel Street Farm
Hazel Street
Fourayes Farm
Church Wood
Plackett's Hole
Swanton Street
Little Hazel Street Farm
Trundlewood Farm
Meadow Farm
Gorham Wood
Bicknor Court
Swanton Court
Keepers Lodge
SOUTHLEES LA
Wheatsheaf Farm
Bicknor Farm
BICKNOR COURT COTTS
Bicknor
Bredgar & Wormshill Light Rly
High Wood
Swanton Farm
Admiral Wood
Bedmonton House
ME17

78
58

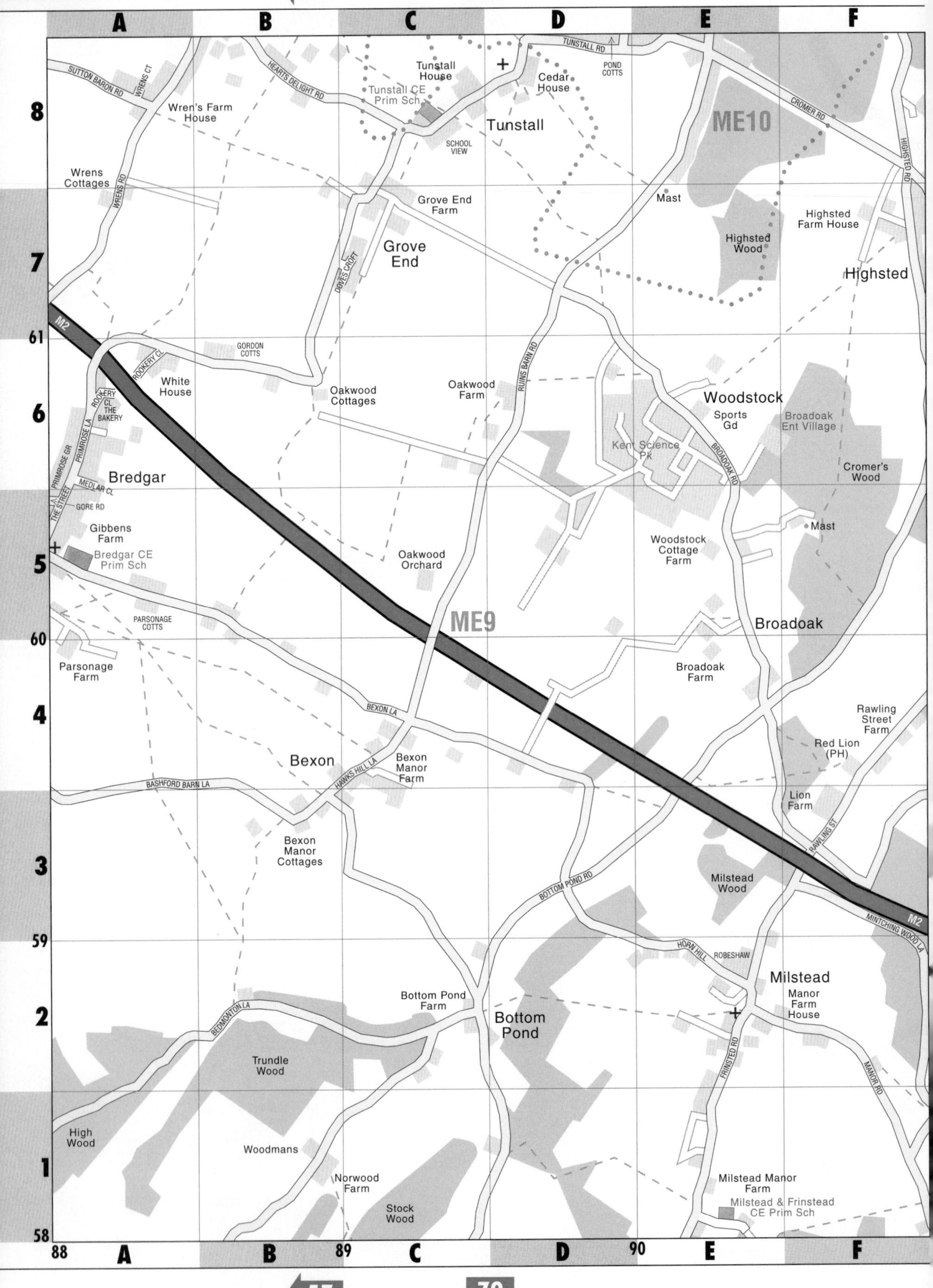
A
B
C
D
E
F
8
7
61
6
5
60
4
3
59
2
1
58
88
89
90
SUTTON BARON RD
WRENS CT
HEARTS DELIGHT RD
Tunstall House
Tunstall CE Prim Sch
Cedar House
TUNSTALL RD
POND COTTS
Wren's Farm House
Tunstall
SCHOOL VIEW
CROMER RD
ME10
HIGHSTED RD
Wrens Cottages
WRENS RD
Grove End Farm
Mast
Highsted Farm House
Highsted Wood
Grove End
DOVES CROFT
Highsted
M2
GORDON COTTS
ROOKERY CL
White House
ROOKERY CL
THE BAKERY
Oakwood Cottages
Oakwood Farm
RUINS BARN RD
Woodstock
Sports Gd
Broadoak Ent Village
PRIMROSE GR
PRIMROSE LA
Kent Science Pk
BROADOAK RD
Cromer's Wood
Bredgar
MEDLAR CL
THE STREET
GORE RD
Gibbens Farm
Mast
Bredgar CE Prim Sch
Woodstock Cottage Farm
Oakwood Orchard
ME9
PARSONAGE COTTS
Broadoak
Parsonage Farm
Broadoak Farm
BEXON LA
Rawling Street Farm
Red Lion (PH)
Bexon
Bexon Manor Farm
HAWKS HILL LA
BASHFORD BARN LA
Lion Farm
Bexon Manor Cottages
RAWLING ST
Milstead Wood
BOTTOM POND RD
MINTCHING WOOD LA
HORN HILL
ROBESHAW
Milstead
BEDMONTON LA
Bottom Pond Farm
Manor Farm House
Bottom Pond
FRINSTED RD
Trundle Wood
MANOR RD
High Wood
Woodmans
Norwood Farm
Stock Wood
Milstead Manor Farm
Milstead & Frinstead CE Prim Sch

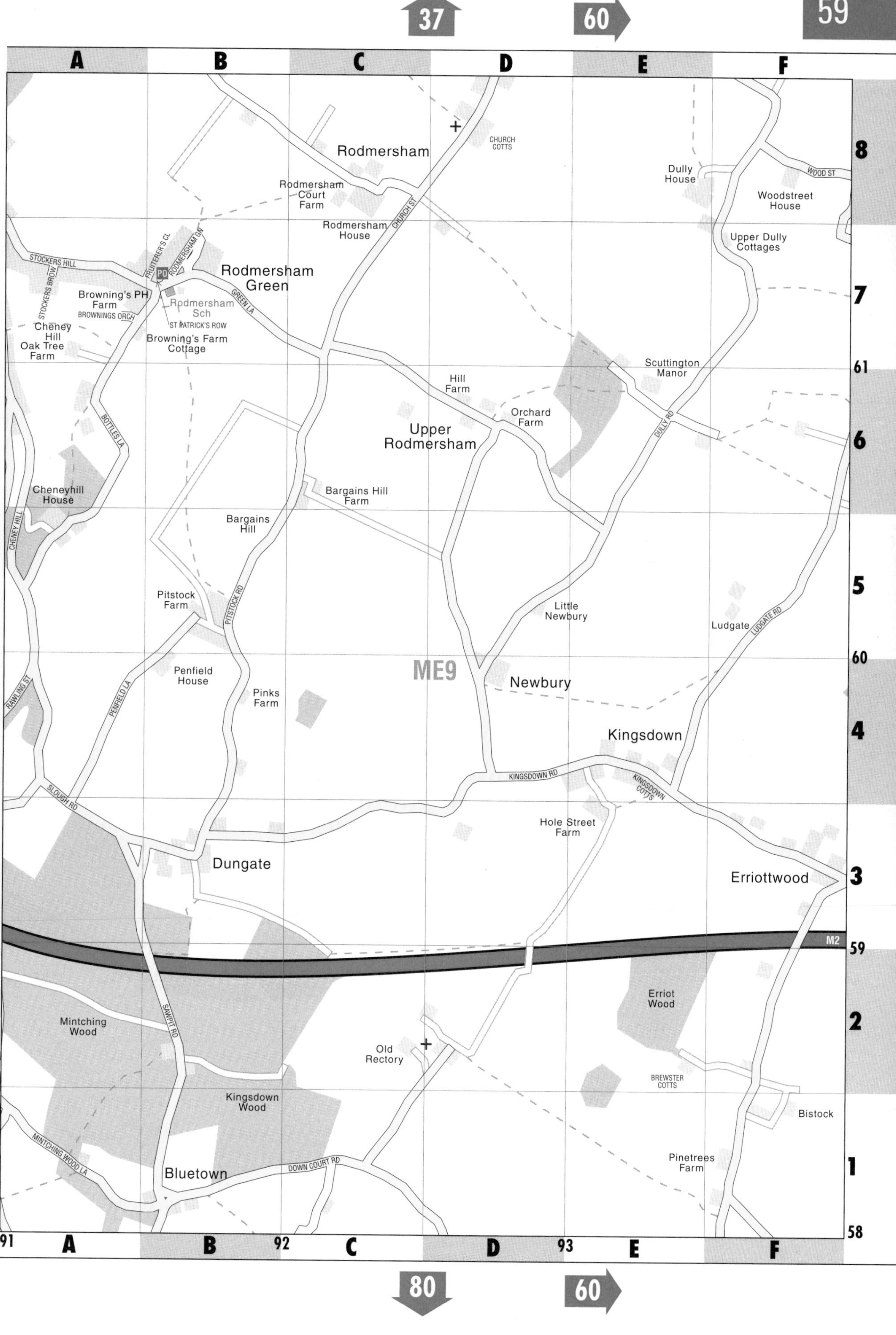
37
60
A
B
C
D
E
F
Rodmersham
CHURCH COTTS
Rodmersham Court Farm
Rodmersham House
CHURCH ST
Dully House
WOOD ST
Woodstreet House
Upper Dully Cottages
STOCKERS HILL
STOCKERS BROW
FRUITERER'S CL
RODMERSHAM GN
PO
Rodmersham Green
Browning's PH
Farm
BROWNINGS ORCH
Rodmersham Sch
GREEN LA
ST PATRICK'S ROW
Cheney Hill
Oak Tree Farm
Browning's Farm Cottage
Hill Farm
Scuttington Manor
Orchard Farm
Upper Rodmersham
DULLY RD
BOTTLES LA
Cheneyhill House
CHENEY HILL
Bargains Hill Farm
Bargains Hill
Pitstock Farm
PITSTOCK RD
Little Newbury
Ludgate
LUDGATE RD
ME9
Penfield House
PENFIELD LA
RAWLING ST
Pinks Farm
Newbury
Kingsdown
KINGSDOWN RD
KINGSDOWN COTTS
SLOUGH RD
Hole Street Farm
Dungate
Erriottwood
M2
Erriot Wood
Mintching Wood
SAWPIT RD
Old Rectory
BREWSTER COTTS
Bistock
Kingsdown Wood
MINTCHING WOOD LA
Pinetrees Farm
Bluetown
DOWN COURT RD
8
7
61
6
5
60
4
3
59
2
1
58
91
92
93
80
60

A | B | C | D | E | F

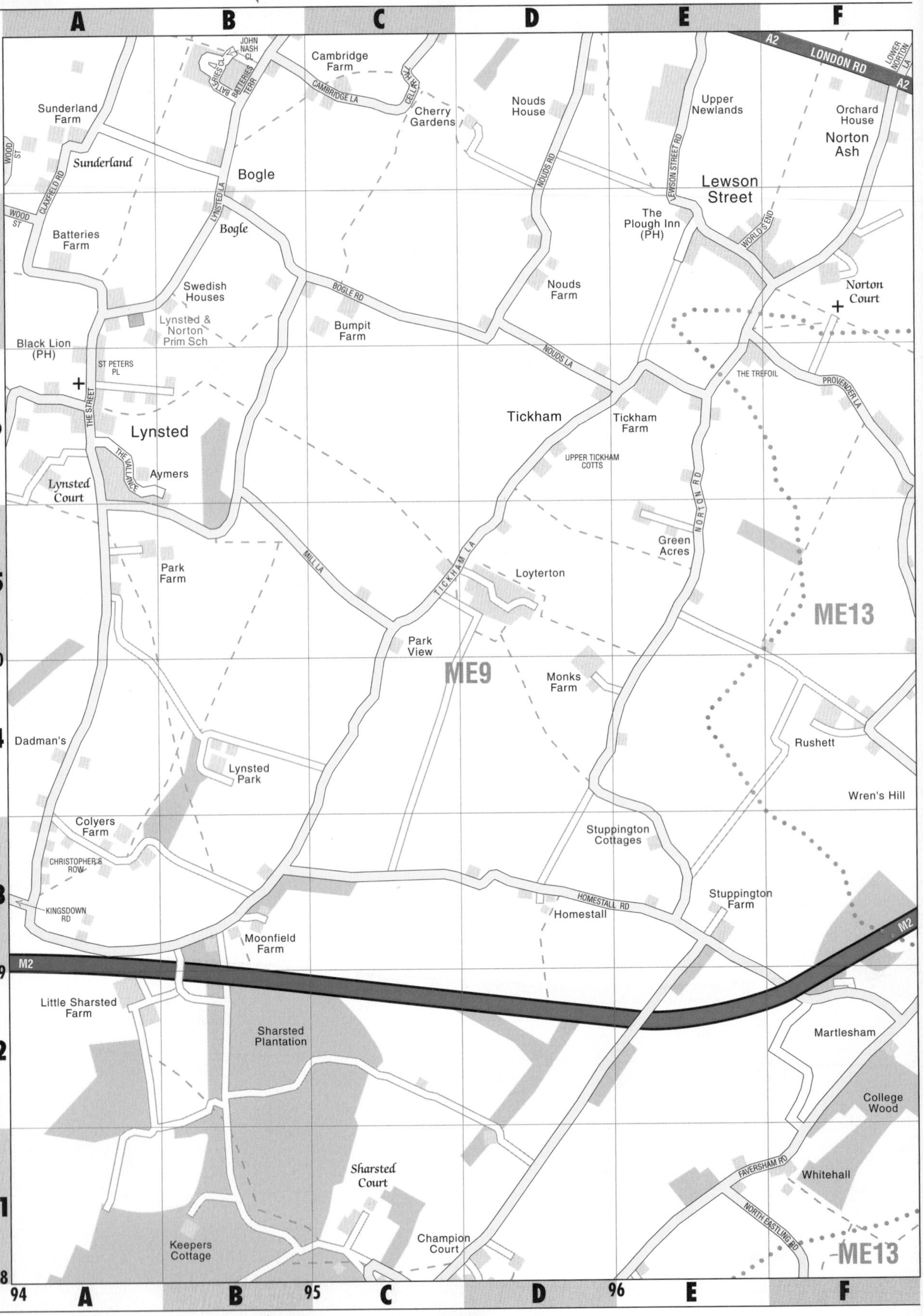

A2 LONDON RD
LOWER NORTON LA
A2

8

Sunderland Farm

Sunderland

JOHN NASH CL

GILES CL

BATTERIES TERR

Cambridge Farm

CAMBRIDGE LA

CELLAR HILL

Cherry Gardens

Nouds House

Upper Newlands

Orchard House

Norton Ash

Bogle

Bogle

LYNSTED LA

NOUDS RD

Lewson Street

LEWSON STREET RD

7

Batteries Farm

WOOD ST

CLAXFIELD RD

Swedish Houses

Lynsted & Norton Prim Sch

BOGLE RD

Bumpit Farm

Nouds Farm

The Plough Inn (PH)

WORLD'S END

Norton Court

THE TREFOIL

PROVENDER LA

61

Black Lion (PH)

ST PETERS PL

NOUDS LA

6

THE STREET

Lynsted

THE VALLANCE

Aymers

Tickham

Tickham Farm

UPPER TICKHAM COTTS

NORTON RD

Lynsted Court

MILL LA

Park Farm

TICKHAM LA

Loyterton

Green Acres

ME13

5

Park View

ME9

60

Monks Farm

4

Dadman's

Lynsted Park

Rushett

Wren's Hill

Colyers Farm

CHRISTOPHER'S ROW

Stuppington Cottages

3

KINGSDOWN RD

HOMESTALL RD

Homestall

Stuppington Farm

M2

Moonfield Farm

59

M2

Little Sharsted Farm

2

Sharsted Plantation

Martlesham

College Wood

FAVERSHAM RD

Whitehall

1

NORTH EASTLING RD

Sharsted Court

Keepers Cottage

Champion Court

ME13

58

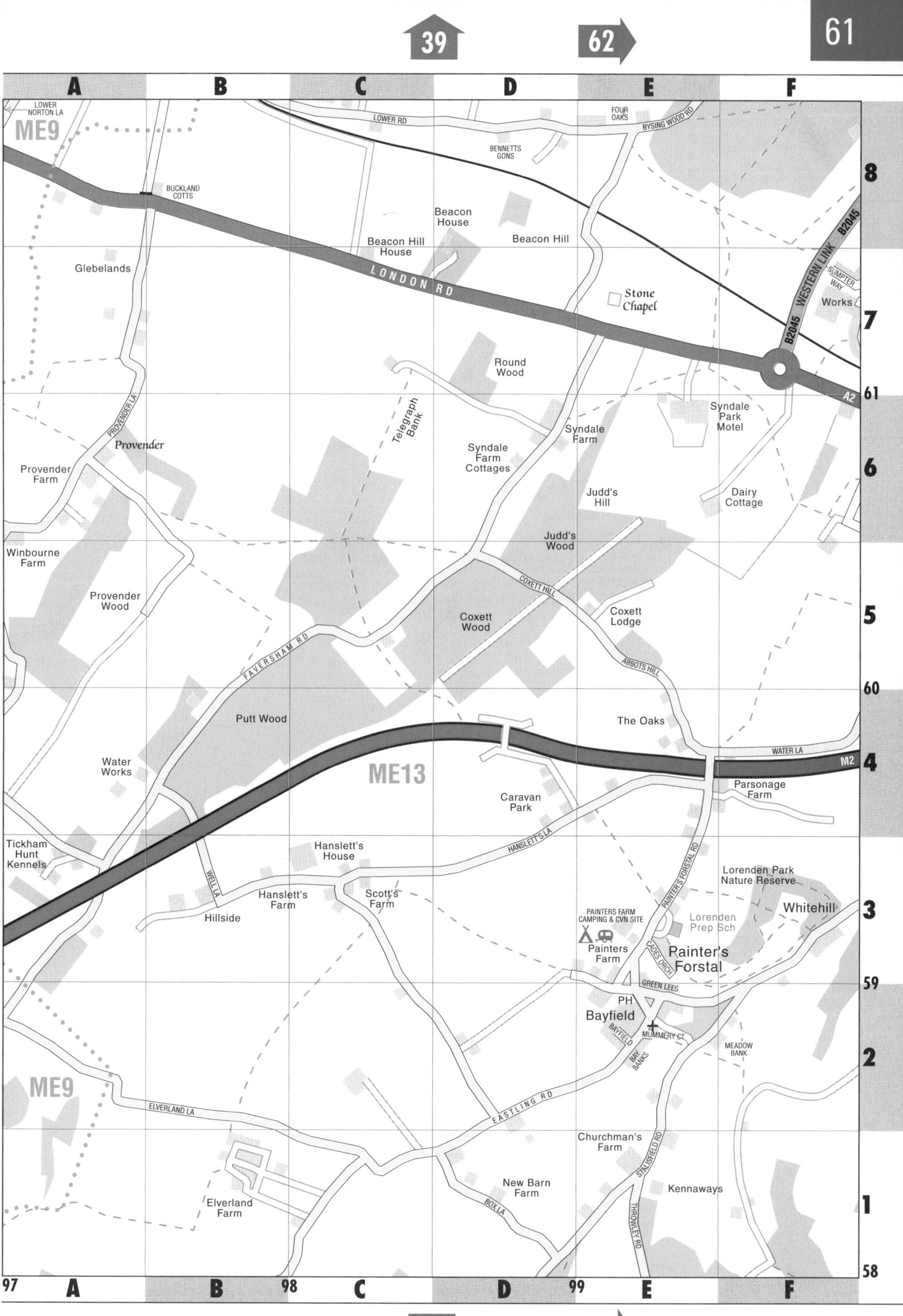

A B C D E F

8
7
61
6
5
60
4
3
59
2
1
58

LOWER NORTON LA
ME9
Glebelands
BUCKLAND COTTS
LOWER RD
BENNETTS GDNS
FOUR OAKS
BYSING WOOD RD
Beacon House
Beacon Hill House
Beacon Hill
LONDON RD
Stone Chapel
WESTERN LINK
B2045
SUMPTER WAY
Works
B2045
A2
PROVENDER LA
Provender
Provender Farm
Telegraph Bank
Round Wood
Syndale Farm Cottages
Syndale Farm
Syndale Park Motel
Winbourne Farm
Provender Wood
Judd's Hill
Judd's Wood
Dairy Cottage
FAVERSHAM RD
Coxett Wood
COXETT HILL
Coxett Lodge
ABBOTS HILL
Putt Wood
The Oaks
WATER LA
M2
Water Works
ME13
Caravan Park
Parsonage Farm
Tickham Hunt Kennels
WELL LA
Hanslett's House
HANSLETT'S LA
PAINTER'S FORSTAL RD
Lorenden Park Nature Reserve
Whitehill
Hanslett's Farm
Hillside
Scott's Farm
PAINTERS FARM CAMPING & CVN SITE
Painters Farm
CAGES ORCH
Lorenden Prep Sch
Painter's Forstal
GREEN LEES
ME9
PH
Bayfield
BAYFIELD
MUMMERY CT
59
MEADOW BANK
ELVERLAND LA
BAY BANKS
EASTLING RD
Churchman's Farm
STALISFIELD RD
Elverland Farm
BOX LA
New Barn Farm
THROWLEY RD
Kennaways

97 A 98 B C 98 D 99 E F

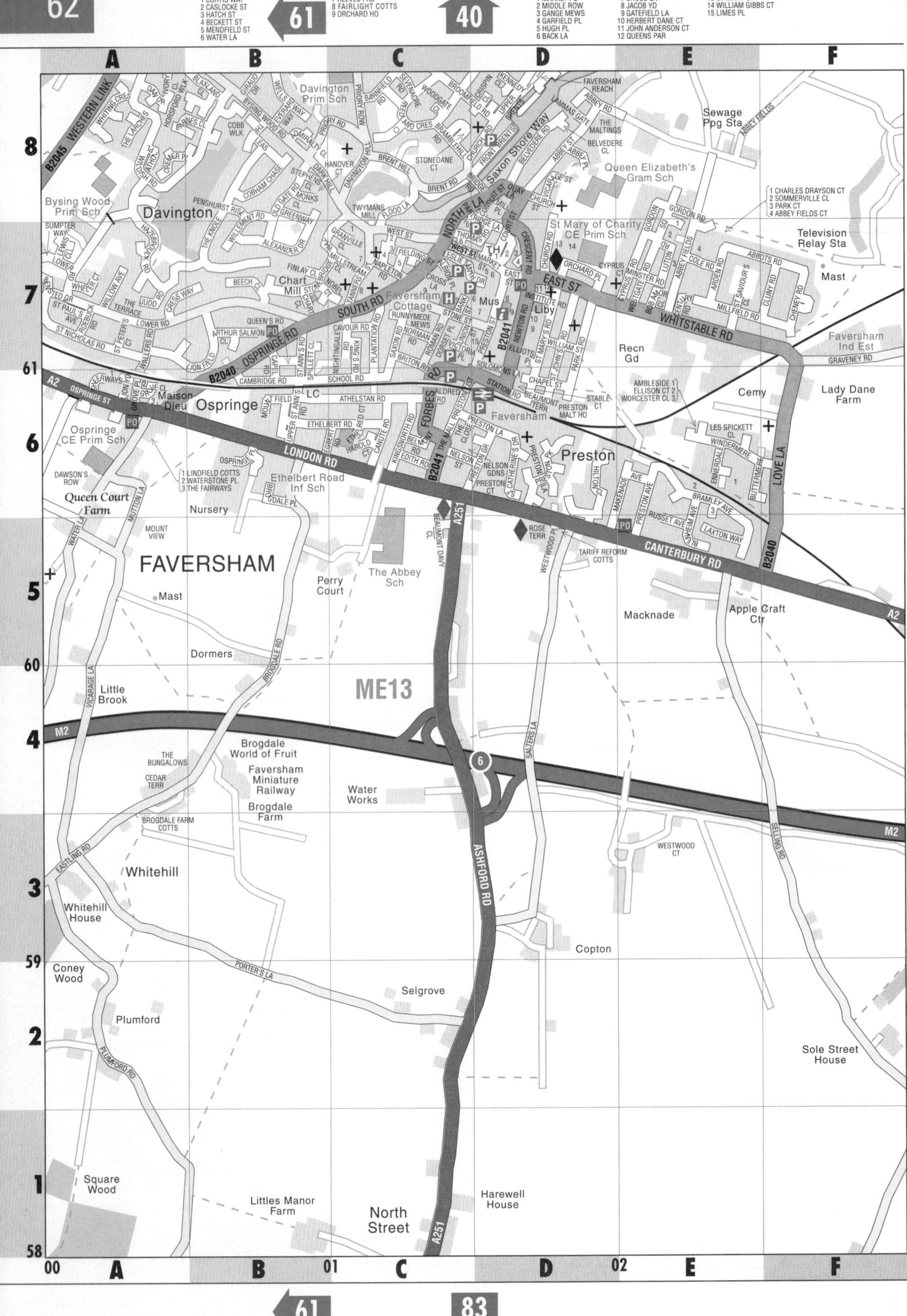

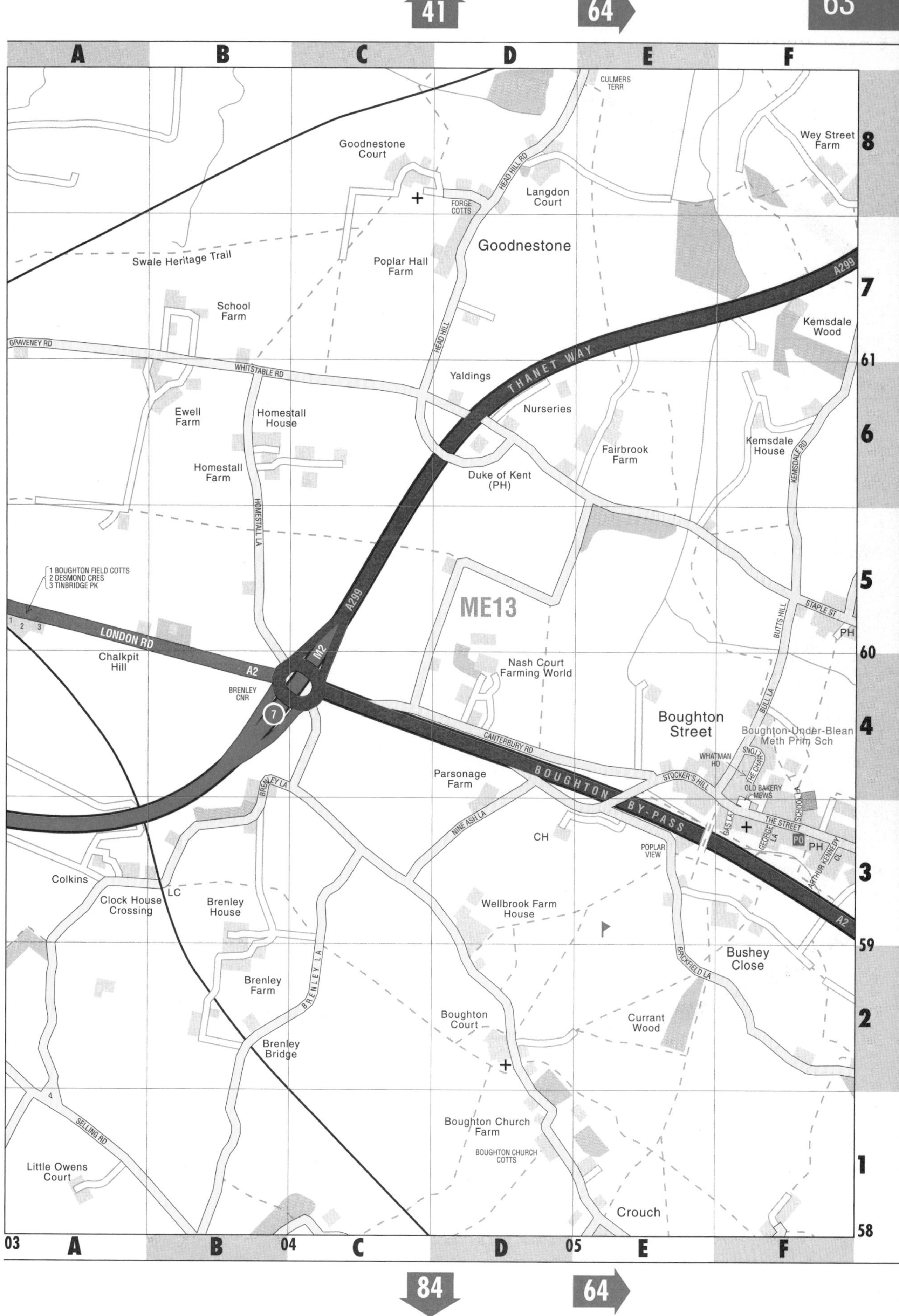

41
64
A
B
C
D
E
F
CULMERS TERR
Wey Street Farm
8
Goodnestone Court
HEAD HILL RD
Langdon Court
FORGE COTTS
Goodnestone
Swale Heritage Trail
Poplar Hall Farm
A299
7
School Farm
Kemsdale Wood
GRAVENEY RD
HEAD HILL
WHITSTABLE RD
Yaldings
THANET WAY
61
Ewell Farm
Homestall House
Nurseries
6
Fairbrook Farm
Kemsdale House
KEMSDALE RD
Homestall Farm
Duke of Kent (PH)
HOMESTALL LA
1 BOUGHTON FIELD COTTS
2 DESMOND CRES
3 TINBRIDGE PK
5
ME13
A299
STAPLE ST
BUTTS HILL
LONDON RD
PH
Chalkpit Hill
M2
Nash Court Farming World
60
A2
BRENLEY CNR
7
Boughton Street
BULL LA
4
Boughton-Under-Blean Meth Prim Sch
CANTERBURY RD
WHATMAN HO
Parsonage Farm
BOUGHTON BY-PASS
STOCKER'S HILL
THE CHAR
OLD BAKERY MEWS
BRENLEY LA
NINE ASH LA
SCHOOL LA
CH
GAS LA
THE STREET
GEORGE LA
POPLAR VIEW
PO
PH
ARTHUR KENNEDY CL
Colkins
LC
3
Clock House Crossing
Brenley House
Wellbrook Farm House
A2
59
BRICKFIELD LA
Bushey Close
Brenley Farm
BRENLEY LA
Boughton Court
Currant Wood
2
Brenley Bridge
SELLING RD
Boughton Church Farm
BOUGHTON CHURCH COTTS
Little Owens Court
1
Crouch
58
03
04
05
84
64

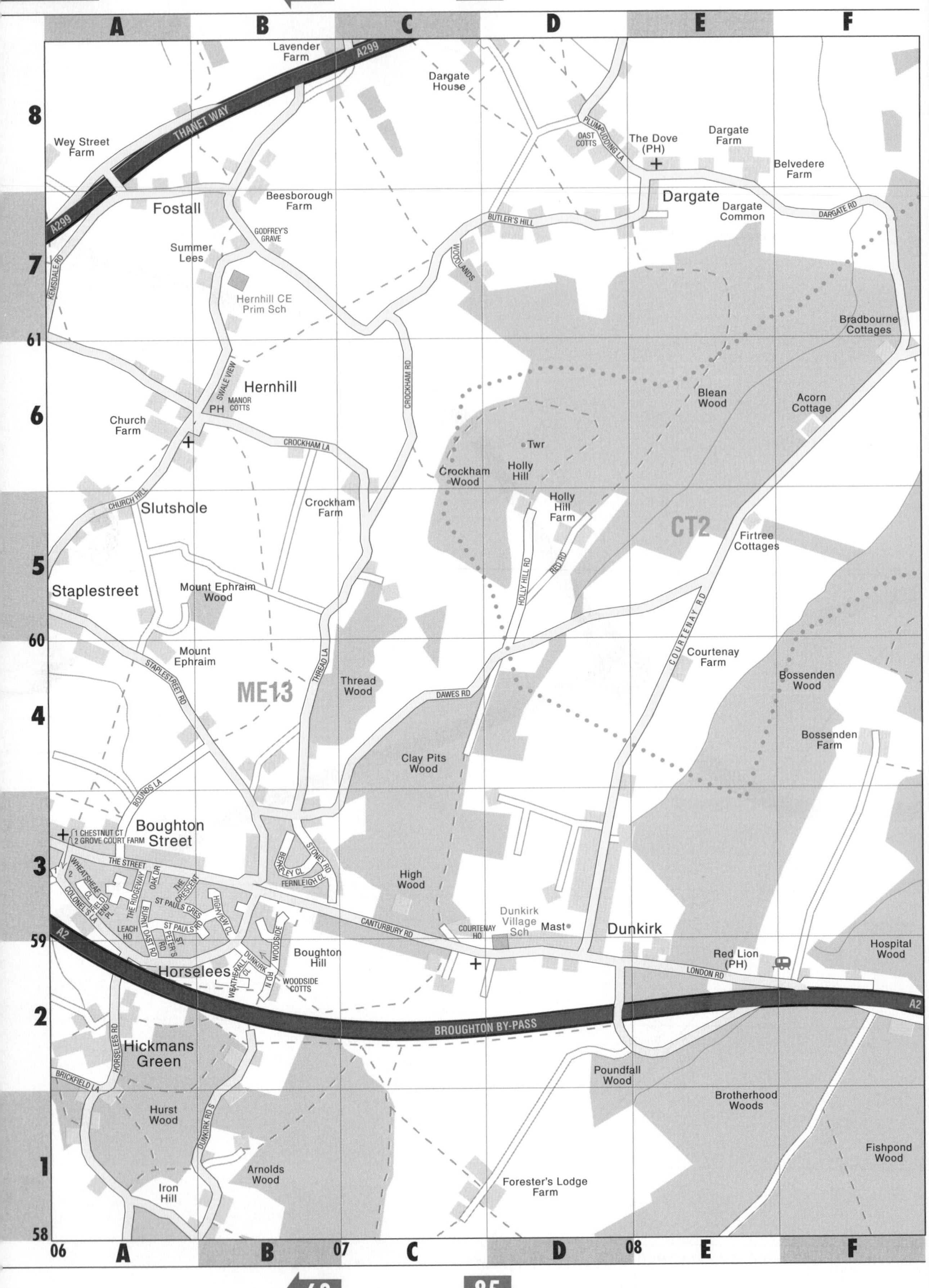

A B C D E F

8

Lavender Farm
A299
THANET WAY

Dargate House

Wey Street Farm

PLUM PUDDING LA

OAST COTTS

The Dove (PH)

Dargate Farm

Dargate

Belvedere Farm

Fostall

Beesborough Farm

7

A299
KEMSDALE RD

Summer Lees

GODFREY'S GRAVE

BUTLER'S HILL

WOODLANDS

Dargate Common

DARGATE RD

61

Hernhill CE Prim Sch

Bradbourne Cottages

6

SWALE VIEW

Hernhill
PH

MANOR COTTS

CROCKHAM RD

Blean Wood

Acorn Cottage

Church Farm

CROCKHAM LA

Twr

Crockham Wood

Holly Hill

CT2

Firtree Cottages

Slutshole

CHURCH HILL

Crockham Farm

Holly Hill Farm

HOLLY HILL RD

RD RD

5

Staplestreet

Mount Ephraim Wood

THREAD LA

COURTENAY RD

60

STAPLESTREET RD

Mount Ephraim

Thread Wood

DAWES RD

Courtenay Farm

Bossenden Wood

4

ME13

Clay Pits Wood

Bossenden Farm

BOUNS LA

Boughton Street

STONEY RD

BERKLEY CL

High Wood

1 CHESTNUT CT
2 GROVE COURT FARM

3

THE STREET

WHEATSHEAM CL
CLOSE END

OAK DR

THE CRESCENT

ST PAULS CRESS

FERNLEIGH CT

HIGHVIEW RD

CANTURBURY RD

Dunkirk Village Sch

Mast

Dunkirk

Hospital Wood

THE RIDGEWAY
COLONEL'S LA

LEACH HO

ST PAULS

ST PETER'S

WOODSIDE

COURTENAY HO

59

A2

DUNKIRK RD N

Boughton Hill

Red Lion (PH)

LONDON RD

Horselees

WEATHERS CL

WOODSIDE COTTS

2

HORSELEES RD

Hickmans Green

BROUGHTON BY-PASS

A2

BRICKFIELD LA

Poundfall Wood

Brotherhood Woods

Hurst Wood

DUNKIRK RD S

1

Arnolds Wood

Forester's Lodge Farm

Fishpond Wood

Iron Hill

58

06 A B 07 C D 08 E F

43
66

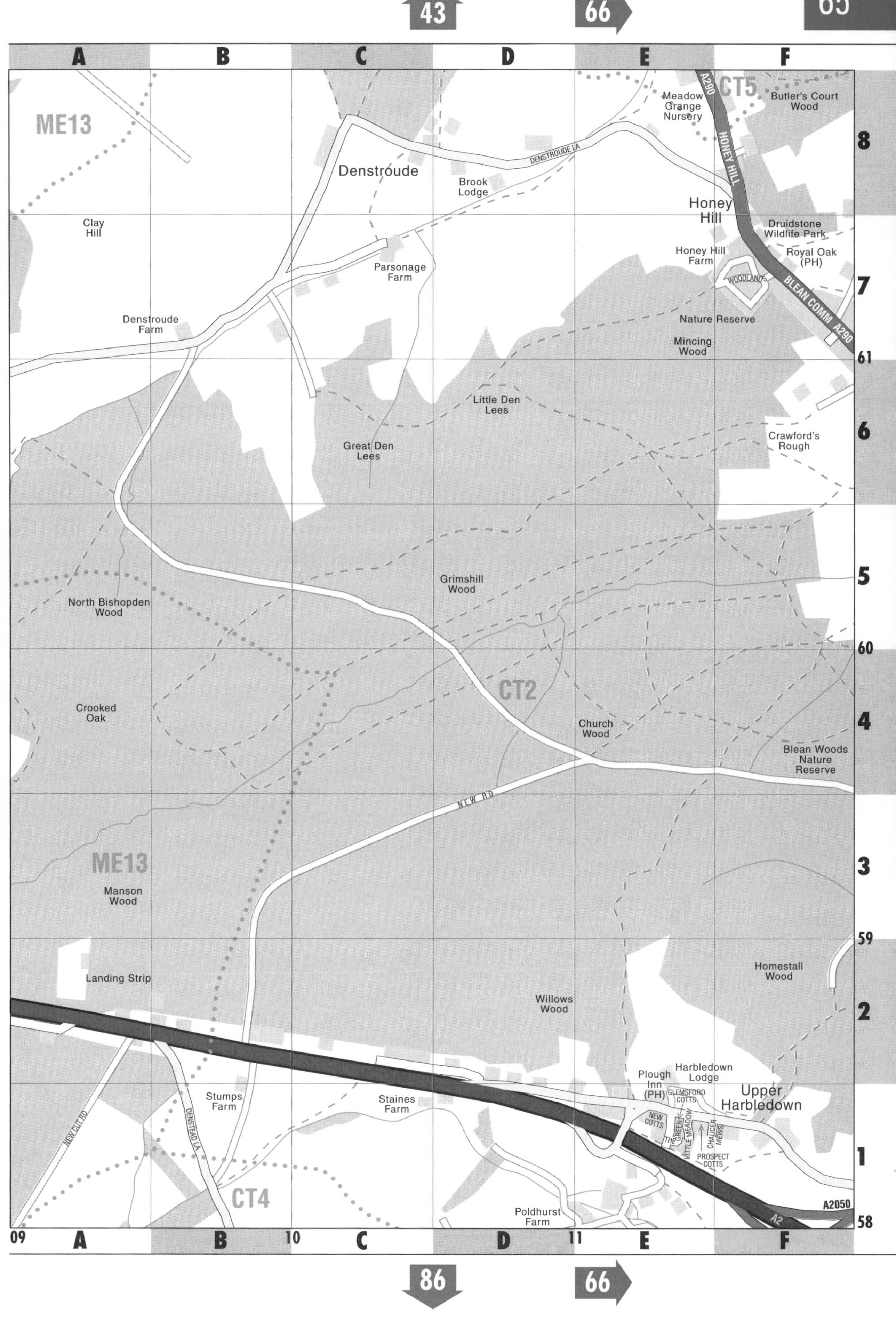
A
B
C
D
E
F
ME13
Denstroude
Brook Lodge
DENSTROUDE LA
Meadow Grange Nursery
A290
CT5
Butler's Court Wood
HONEY HILL
Honey Hill
Clay Hill
Druidstone Wildlife Park
Honey Hill Farm
Royal Oak (PH)
Parsonage Farm
WOODLANDS
BLEAN COMM
A290
Denstroude Farm
Nature Reserve
Mincing Wood
Little Den Lees
Great Den Lees
Crawford's Rough
Grimshill Wood
North Bishopden Wood
CT2
Crooked Oak
Church Wood
Blean Woods Nature Reserve
NEW RD
ME13
Manson Wood
Homestall Wood
Landing Strip
Willows Wood
Plough Inn (PH)
Harbledown Lodge
Stumps Farm
Staines Farm
GLEMSFORD COTTS
Upper Harbledown
NEW COTTS
THE GREEN
LITTLE MEADOW
CHAUCER MEWS
PROSPECT COTTS
NEW CUT RD
DENSTEAD LA
CT4
Poldhurst Farm
A2050
A2
8
7
61
6
5
60
4
3
59
2
1
58
09
10
11

86
66

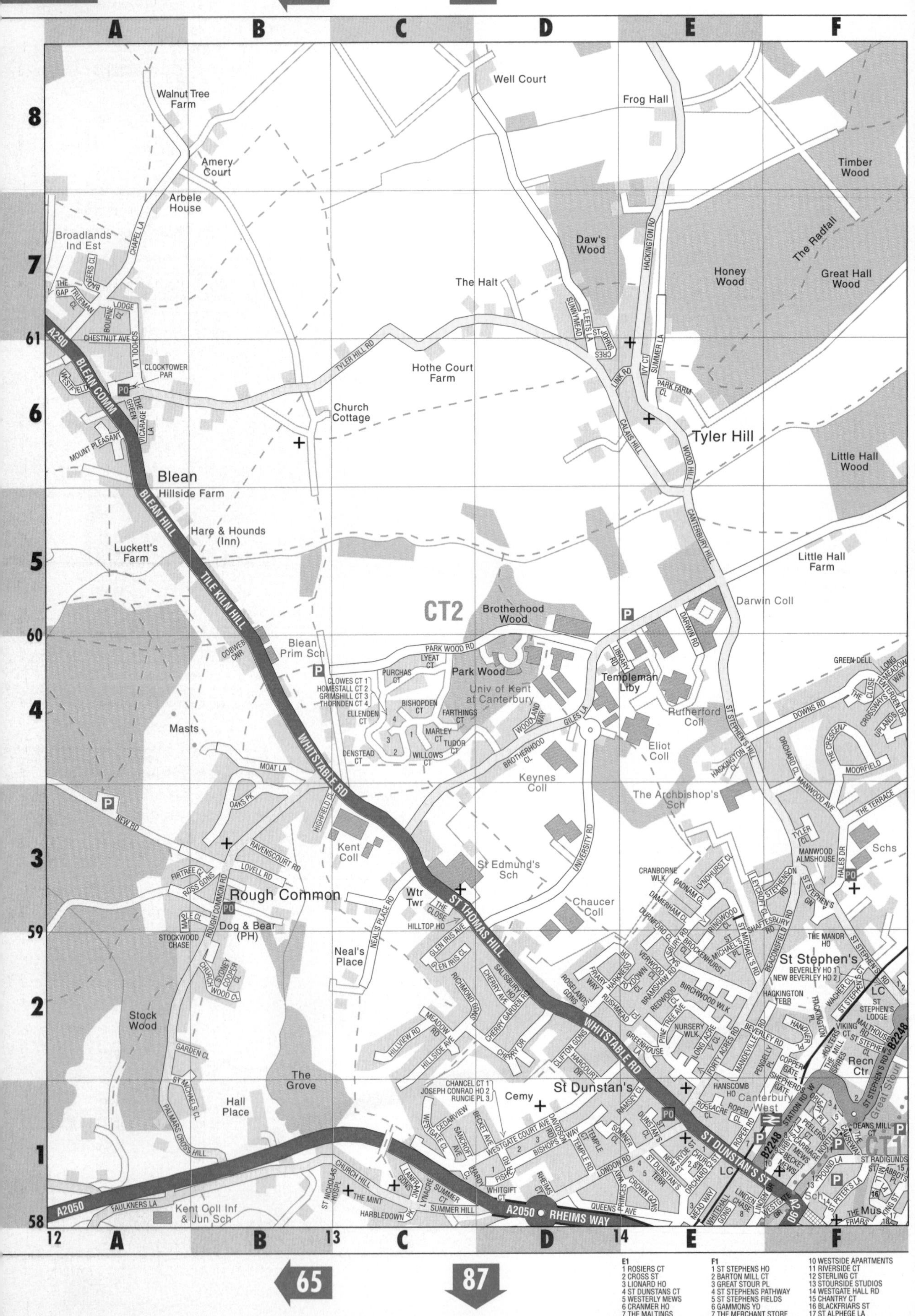

E1
1 ROSIERS CT
2 CROSS ST
3 LIONARD HO
4 ST DUNSTANS CT
5 WESTERLY MEWS
6 CRANMER HO
7 THE MALTINGS
8 WESTGATE CT

F1
1 ST STEPHENS HO
2 BARTON MILL CT
3 GREAT STOUR PL
4 ST STEPHENS PATHWAY
5 ST STEPHENS FIELDS
6 GAMMONS YD
7 THE MERCHANT STORE
8 KIRBY'S HEIGHTS
9 TEMPLAR CT

10 WESTSIDE APARTMENTS
11 RIVERSIDE CT
12 STERLING CT
13 STOURSIDE STUDIOS
14 WESTGATE HALL RD
15 CHANTRY CT
16 BLACKFRIARS ST
17 ST ALPHEGE LA
18 THE CLOISTERS

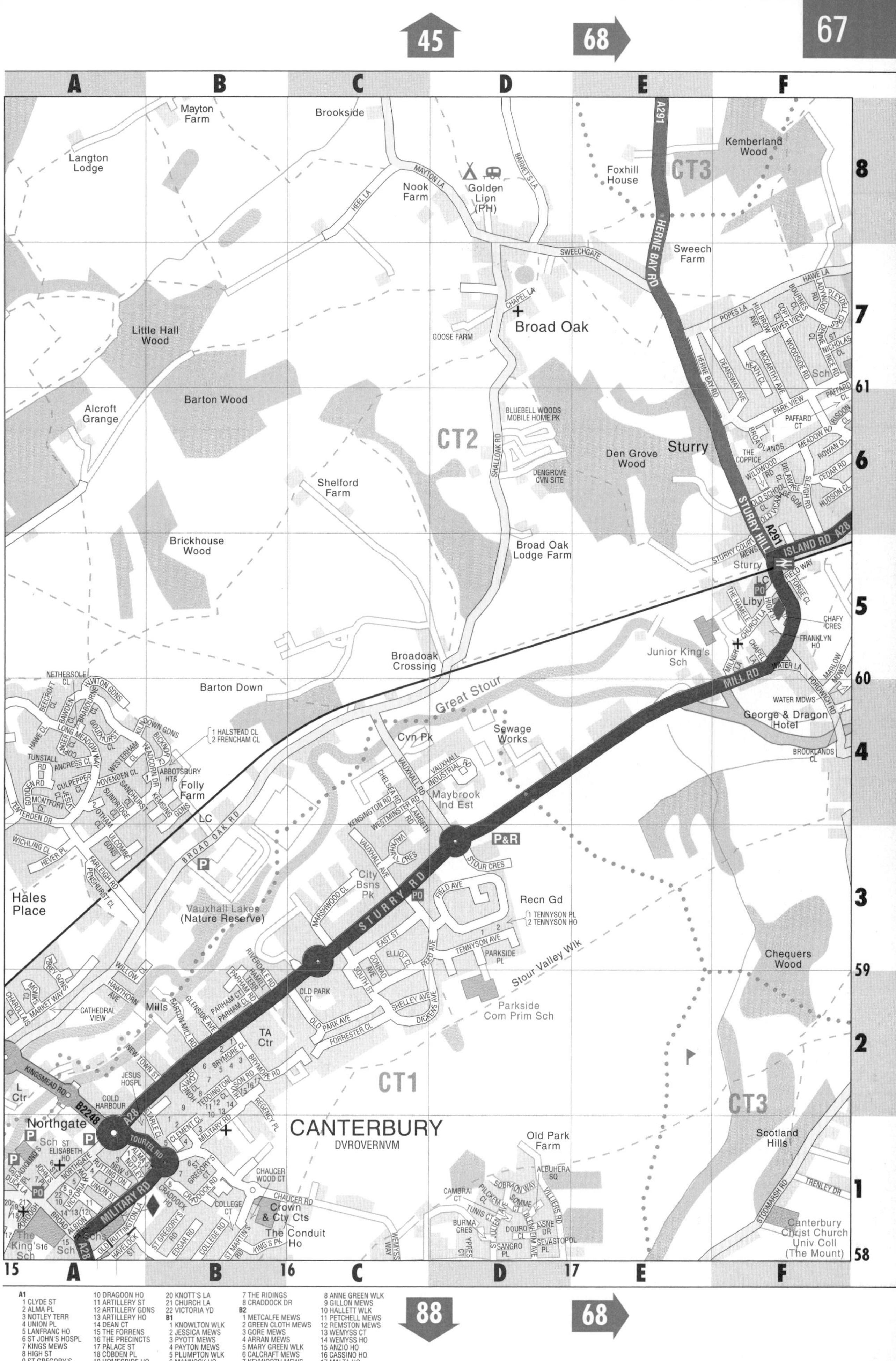

67
46

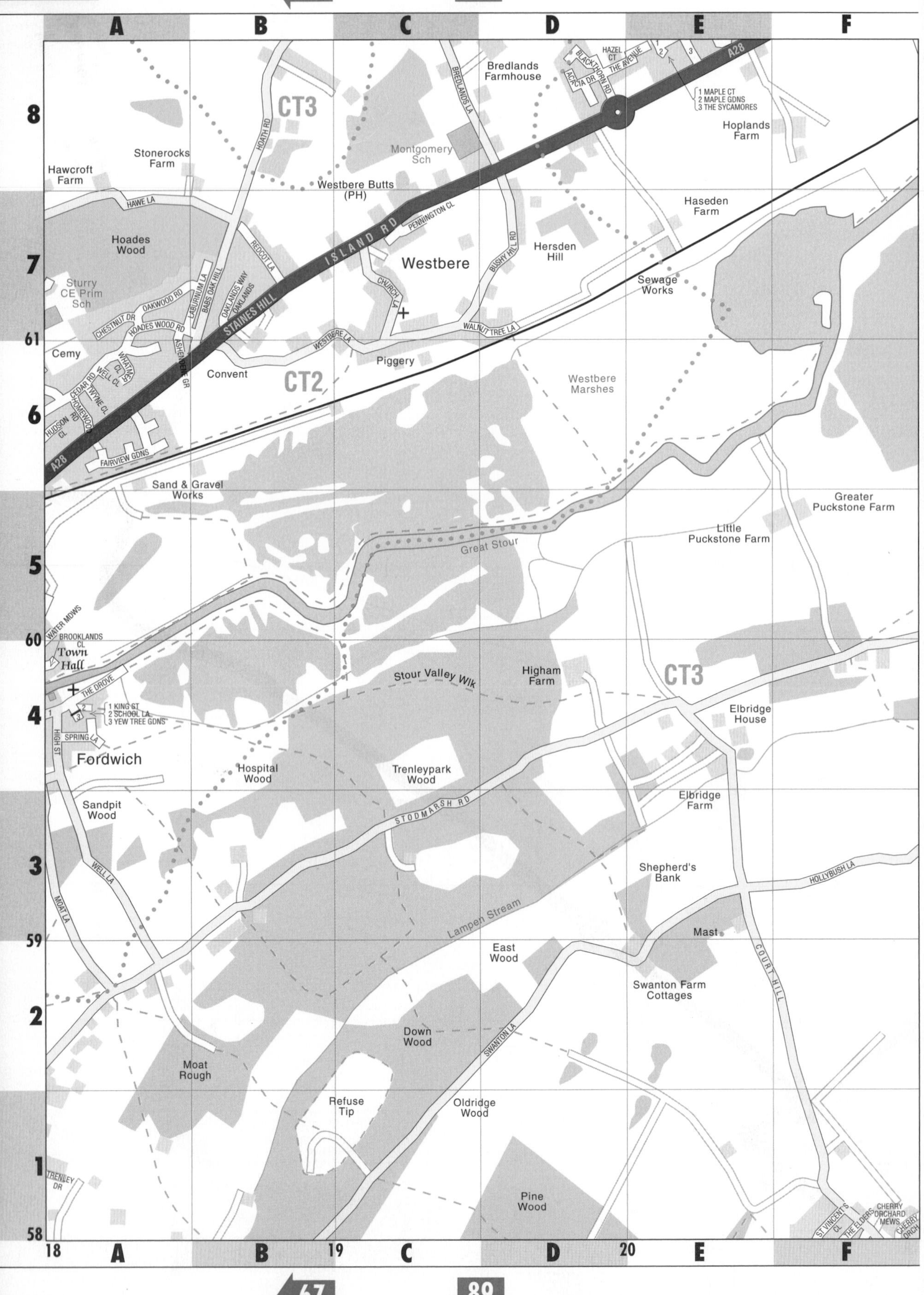
A
B
C
D
E
F
8
7
61
6
5
60
4
3
59
2
1
58
18
19
20
CT3
CT2
CT3
A28
Bredlands Farmhouse
HAZEL CT
THE AVENUE
BLACKTHORN RD
ACACIA DR
1 MAPLE CT
2 MAPLE GDNS
3 THE SYCAMORES
Hoplands Farm
Stonerocks Farm
Hawcroft Farm
HOATH RD
BREDLANDS LA
Montgomery Sch
Westbere Butts (PH)
HAWE LA
PENNINGTON CL
Haseden Farm
Hoades Wood
REDCOT LA
ISLAND RD
BUSHY HILL RD
Hersden Hill
Westbere
Sturry CE Prim Sch
LABURNUM LA
BABS OAK HILL
OAKLANDS WAY
OAKLANDS
OAKWOOD RD
CHESTNUT DR
HOADES WOOD RD
STAINES HILL
CHURCH LA
Sewage Works
WALNUT TREE LA
WESTBERE LA
Cemy
Convent
Piggery
Westbere Marshes
ASHENDEN GR
WHATMER CL
WELL CL
CEDAR RD
TWYNE CL
HOMEWOOD RD
HUDSON CL
FAIRVIEW GDNS
Sand & Gravel Works
Greater Puckstone Farm
Little Puckstone Farm
Great Stour
WATER MDWS
BROOKLANDS CL
Town Hall
THE DROVE
Stour Valley Wlk
Higham Farm
1 KING ST
2 SCHOOL LA
3 YEW TREE GDNS
Elbridge House
HIGH ST
SPRING LA
Fordwich
Hospital Wood
Trenleypark Wood
Elbridge Farm
Sandpit Wood
STODMARSH RD
WELL LA
Shepherd's Bank
HOLLYBUSH LA
MOAT LA
Lampen Stream
Mast
East Wood
COURT HILL
Swanton Farm Cottages
Down Wood
SWANTON LA
Moat Rough
Refuse Tip
Oldridge Wood
TRENLEY DR
Pine Wood
ST VINCENT'S CL
THE ELDERS
CHERRY ORCHARD MEWS
CHERRY ORCH

67
89

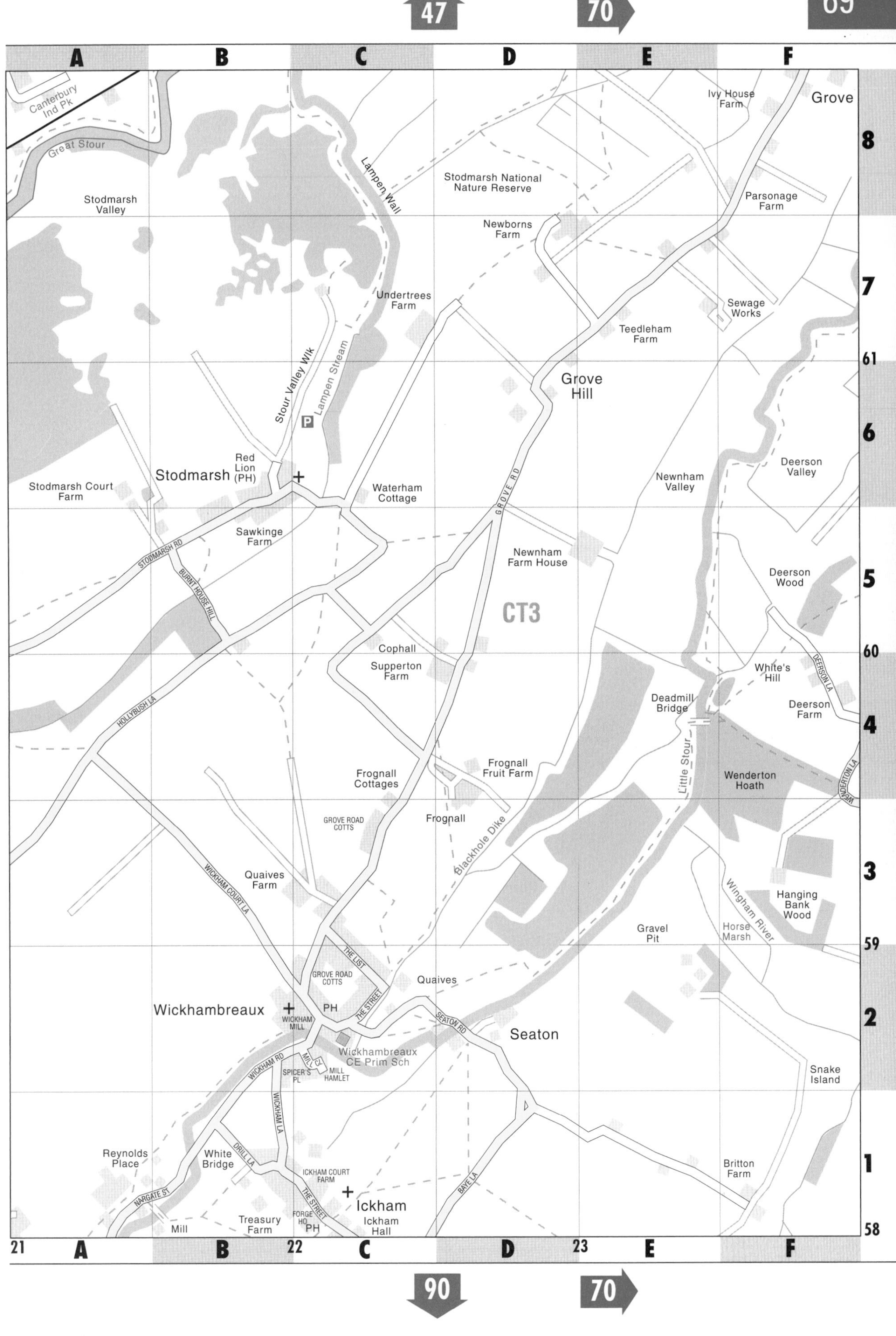
47
70
A
B
C
D
E
F
Canterbury Ind Pk
Great Stour
Stodmarsh Valley
Lampen Wall
Stodmarsh National Nature Reserve
Ivy House Farm
Grove
Parsonage Farm
Newborns Farm
Undertrees Farm
Sewage Works
Teedleham Farm
Grove Hill
Stour Valley Wlk
Lampen Stream
Red Lion (PH)
Stodmarsh
Stodmarsh Court Farm
Waterham Cottage
Newnham Valley
Deerson Valley
Sawkinge Farm
STODMARSH RD
BURNT HOUSE HILL
GROVE RD
Newnham Farm House
Deerson Wood
CT3
Cophall
Supperton Farm
White's Hill
DEERSON LA
Deadmill Bridge
Deerson Farm
HOLLYBUSH LA
Frognall Cottages
Frognall Fruit Farm
Little Stour
Wenderton Hoath
WENDERTON LA
GROVE ROAD COTTS
Frognall
Blackhole Dike
Quaives Farm
WICKHAM COURT LA
Wingham River
Hanging Bank Wood
Horse Marsh
Gravel Pit
THE LIST
GROVE ROAD COTTS
Quaives
Wickhambreaux
WICKHAM MILL
PH
THE STREET
SEATON RD
Seaton
Wickhambreaux CE Prim Sch
WICKHAM RD
MILL CL
SPICER'S PL
MILL HAMLET
WICKHAM LA
Snake Island
Reynolds Place
White Bridge
DRILL LA
ICKHAM COURT FARM
BAYE LA
Britton Farm
NARGATE ST
THE STREET
Ickham
FORGE HO
Treasury Farm
Ickham Hall
Mill
PH
8
7
61
6
5
60
4
3
59
2
1
58
21
22
23
90
70

69
48

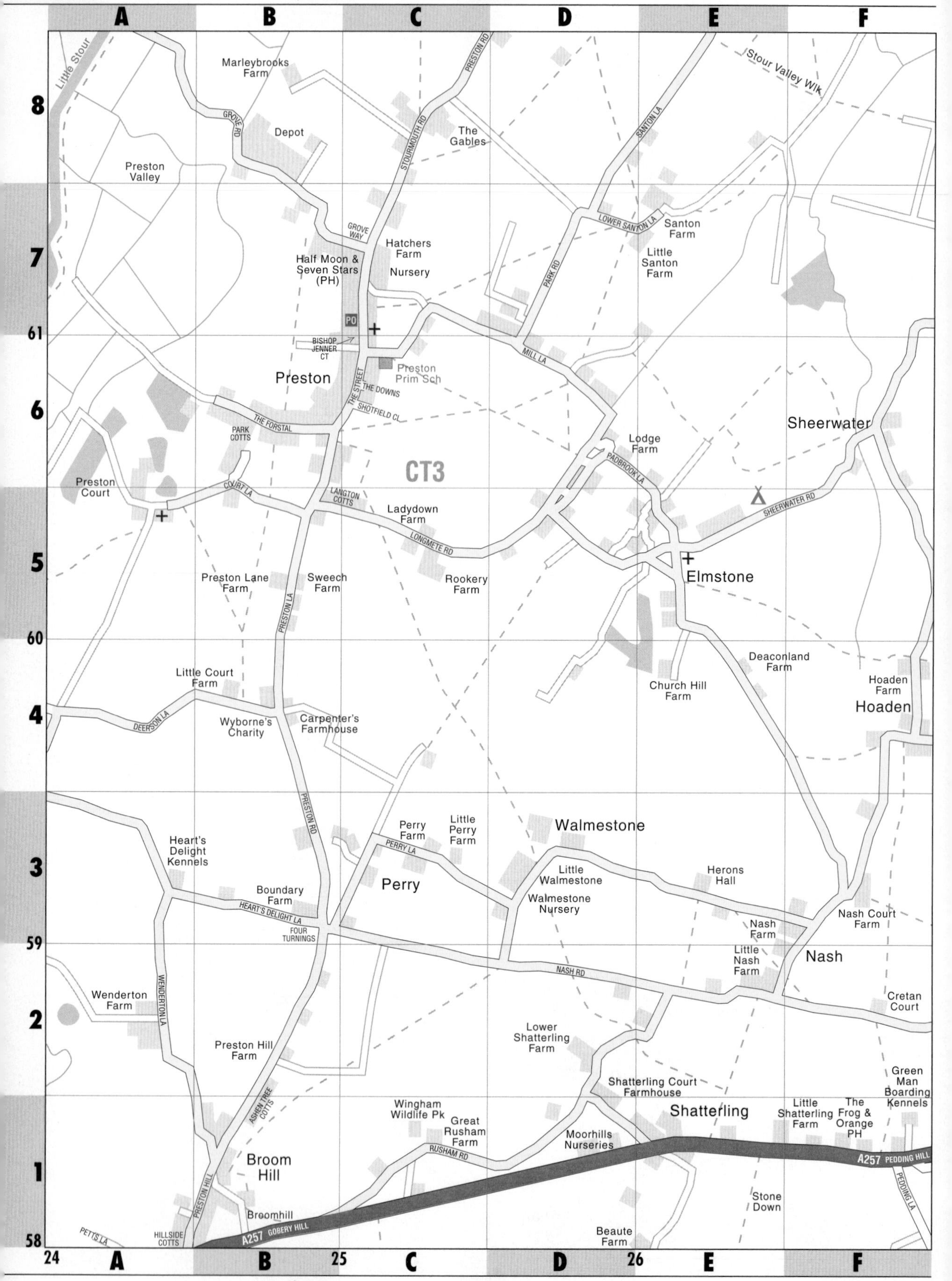

A B C D E F

8

7

61

6

5

60

4

3

59

2

1

58

Little Stour

Marleybrooks Farm

GROVE RD

Depot

Preston Valley

PRESTON RD

STOURMOUTH RD

The Gables

SANTON LA

Stour Valley Wlk

GROVE WAY

Hatchers Farm Nursery

LOWER SANTON LA

Santon Farm

Little Santon Farm

Half Moon & Seven Stars (PH)

PO

PARK RD

MILL LA

BISHOP JENNER CT

Preston Prim Sch

Preston

THE STREET

THE DOWNS

SHOTFIELD CL

THE FORSTAL

PARK COTTS

Lodge Farm

Sheerwater

PADBROOK LA

CT3

Preston Court

COURT LA

LANGTON COTTS

Ladydown Farm

LONGMETE RD

Sheerwater Rd

SHEERWATER RD

Elmstone

Preston Lane Farm

PRESTON LA

Sweech Farm

Rookery Farm

Deaconland Farm

Hoaden Farm

Hoaden

Little Court Farm

DEERSON LA

Wyborne's Charity

Carpenter's Farmhouse

Church Hill Farm

Heart's Delight Kennels

PRESTON RD

Perry Farm

PERRY LA

Little Perry Farm

Walmestone

Herons Hall

Nash Court Farm

Boundary Farm

HEART'S DELIGHT LA

Perry

Little Walmestone

Walmestone Nursery

Nash Farm

Nash

FOUR TURNINGS

NASH RD

Little Nash Farm

Wenderton Farm

WENDERTON LA

Cretan Court

Preston Hill Farm

ASH IN TREE COTTS

Lower Shatterling Farm

Shatterling Court Farmhouse

Shatterling

Little Shatterling Farm

The Frog & Orange PH

Green Man Boarding Kennels

Broom Hill

Wingham Wildlife Pk

Great Rusham Farm

RUSHAM RD

Moorhills Nurseries

A257 PEDDING HILL

PEDDING LA

PRESTON HILL

Broomhill

Stone Down

Beaute Farm

PETTS LA

HILLSIDE COTTS

A257 GOBERY HILL

24 25 26

A B C D E F

A B C D E F

8
Richborough Stream
Corner Dro
WESTMARSH DRO
The Way Out Inn (PH)
Lower Paramour Farm
Ash Level
Westmarsh
GOLDSTONE DRO
WASS DRO
Barton Farm
7
Wingham Barton Manor
Stour Valley Wlk
Paramour Street
Fruit Packing Sta
Lower Goldstone
61
Little Ware Farm
Uphousden Farm
Hawthorn Farm
Lower Ware Farm
6
Warehorne
MOLLAND LA
Ware
Downfield Farm
Great Ware Farm
Upper Goldstone
Sandhills Farm
5
THE ROW
Great Knell Farm
CT3
Hoaden Court
Piggery
60
Bruges Nursery
Overland Farm
Belle-Vue Farm
4
Cop Street
Southlands Farm
Greenlands Farm
Little Knell Farm
Finchley Farm
OVERLAND LA
COP STREET RD
Knell Farm
Weddington
3
KNELL LANE
Great Weddington Farm
Little Weddington Farm
Europa Nurseries
Chequer Court
59
WEDDINGTON LA
COP STREET RD
Kingsland Farm
2
MOLLAND LA
MOLLAND LEA
HOLNESS RD
JAMES CL
MOLLAND CL
WOODS LEY
QUEEN'S RD
CHEQUER LA
CHILTON GDNS
Recn Gd
ST NICHOLAS HO
Hills Court
Molland Farm
SCHOOL RD
CARTWRIGHT CL
FIELD CL
BECKET CL
Ash
LAY LA
White Post Farm
GLEBELANDS
Sch
CHILTON SQ
GOODBAN SQ
CHILTON PL
Liby
BURFORD'S ALLEY
HAVELOCK PL
WHITE POST GDNS
A257
SANDWICH RD
CHERRY GARDEN LA
THE STREET
Guilton
PUDDING LA
PO
PEDDING HILL
GUILTON
St Faith's at Ash Sch
STREET END
1
Moat Farm
Guilton Farm
MOAT LA
MILL FIELD
NEW ST
POULTON LA
DURLOCK RD
ORCHARD VIEW
SAUNDERS LA
COOMBE LA
LANGDON AVE
58

27 A B 28 C D 29 E F

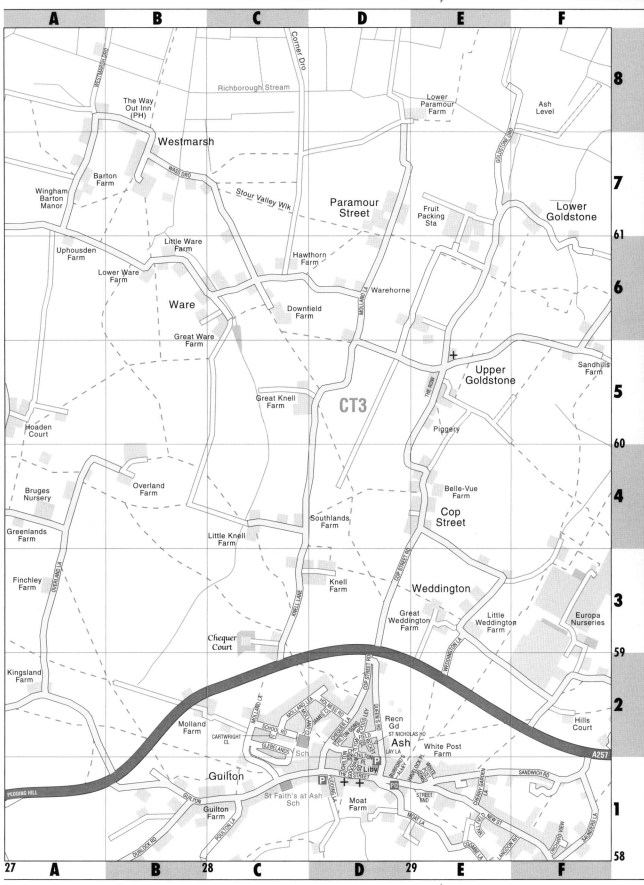

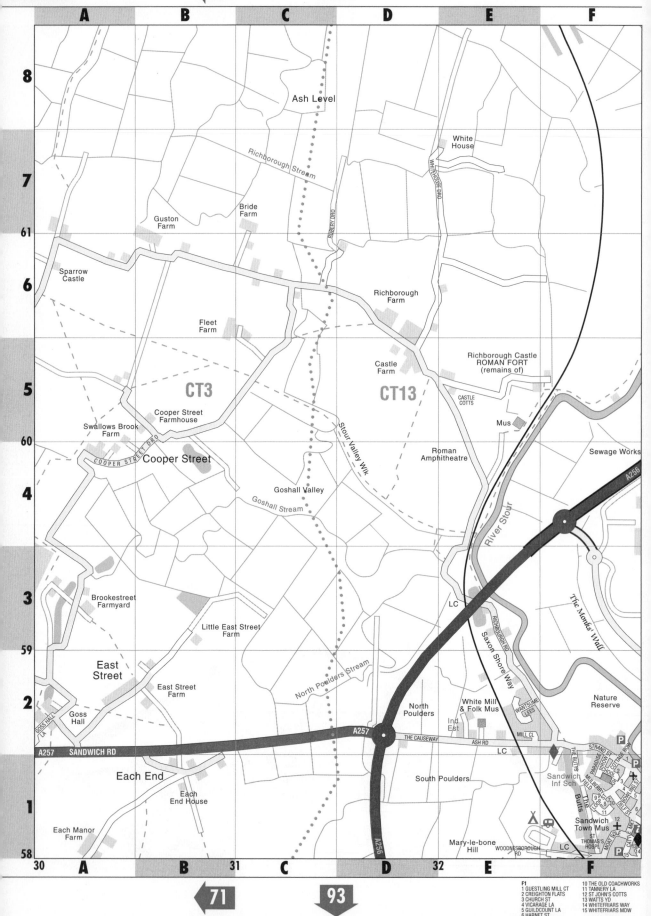

F1
1 GUESTLING MILL CT
2 CREIGHTON FLATS
3 CHURCH ST
4 VICARAGE LA
5 GUILDCOUNT LA
6 HARNET ST
7 WANTSUM MEWS
8 STOUR CT
9 LOOP COURT MEWS
10 THE OLD COACHWORKS
11 TANNERY LA
12 ST JOHN'S COTTS
13 WATTS YD
14 WHITEFRIARS WAY
15 WHITEFRIARS MDW

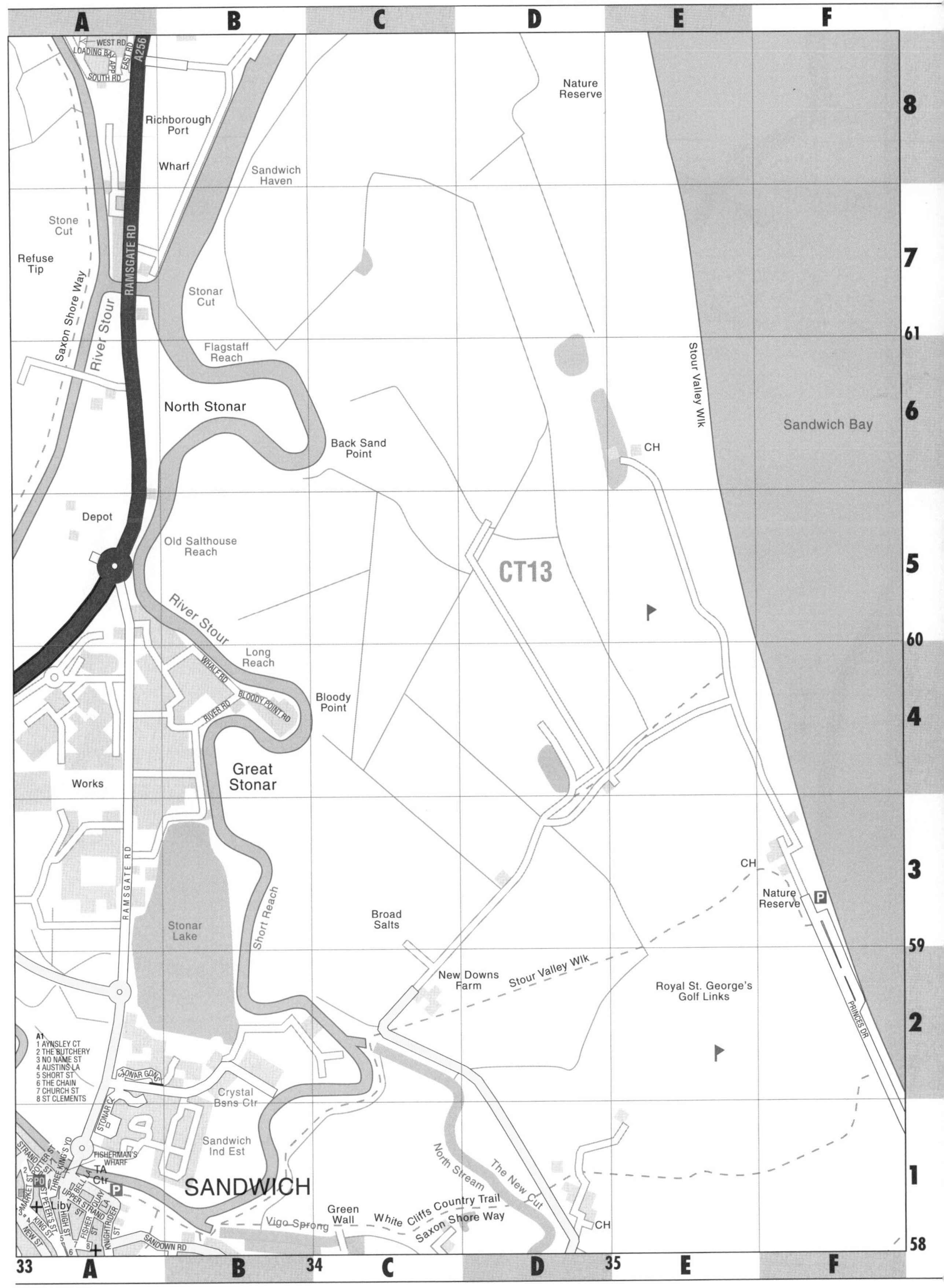

A B C D E F

8

7

61

6 Sandwich Bay

5

60

4

3

59

2

1

58

West Rd
Loading Bay
South Rd
A256
EAST RD
RAMSGATE RD

Richborough
Port

Wharf

Sandwich
Haven

Nature
Reserve

Stone
Cut

Refuse
Tip

Saxon Shore Way

River Stour

Stonar
Cut

Flagstaff
Reach

North Stonar

Back Sand
Point

Stour Valley Wlk

CH

Depot

Old Salthouse
Reach

CT13

River Stour

WHALE RD
RIVER RD
BLOODY POINT RD

Long
Reach

Bloody
Point

Works

Great
Stonar

RAMSGATE RD

Stonar
Lake

Short Reach

CH

Nature
Reserve

P

Broad
Salts

New Downs
Farm

Stour Valley Wlk

Royal St. George's
Golf Links

PRINCES DR

A1
1 AYNSLEY CT
2 THE BUTCHERY
3 NO NAME ST
4 AUSTINS LA
5 SHORT ST
6 THE CHAIN
7 CHURCH ST
8 ST CLEMENTS

STONAR CL
STONAR PL

Crystal
Bsns Ctr

Sandwich
Ind Est

Fisherman's
Wharf

TA
Ctr

STRAND ST
QUAY ST
THREE KING'S YD
FISHER ST
UPPER ST
PETER ST
HIGH ST
NEW ST
MARKET ST
KING ST
KNIGHTRIDER
STRAND ST

PO
P

SANDWICH

Lby

SANDOWN RD

Vigo Sprong

Green
Wall

White Cliffs Country Trail

Saxon Shore Way

North Stream

The New Cut

CH

33 A B 34 C D 35 E F

F7
1 GAGETOWN TERR
2 GILBERT TERR

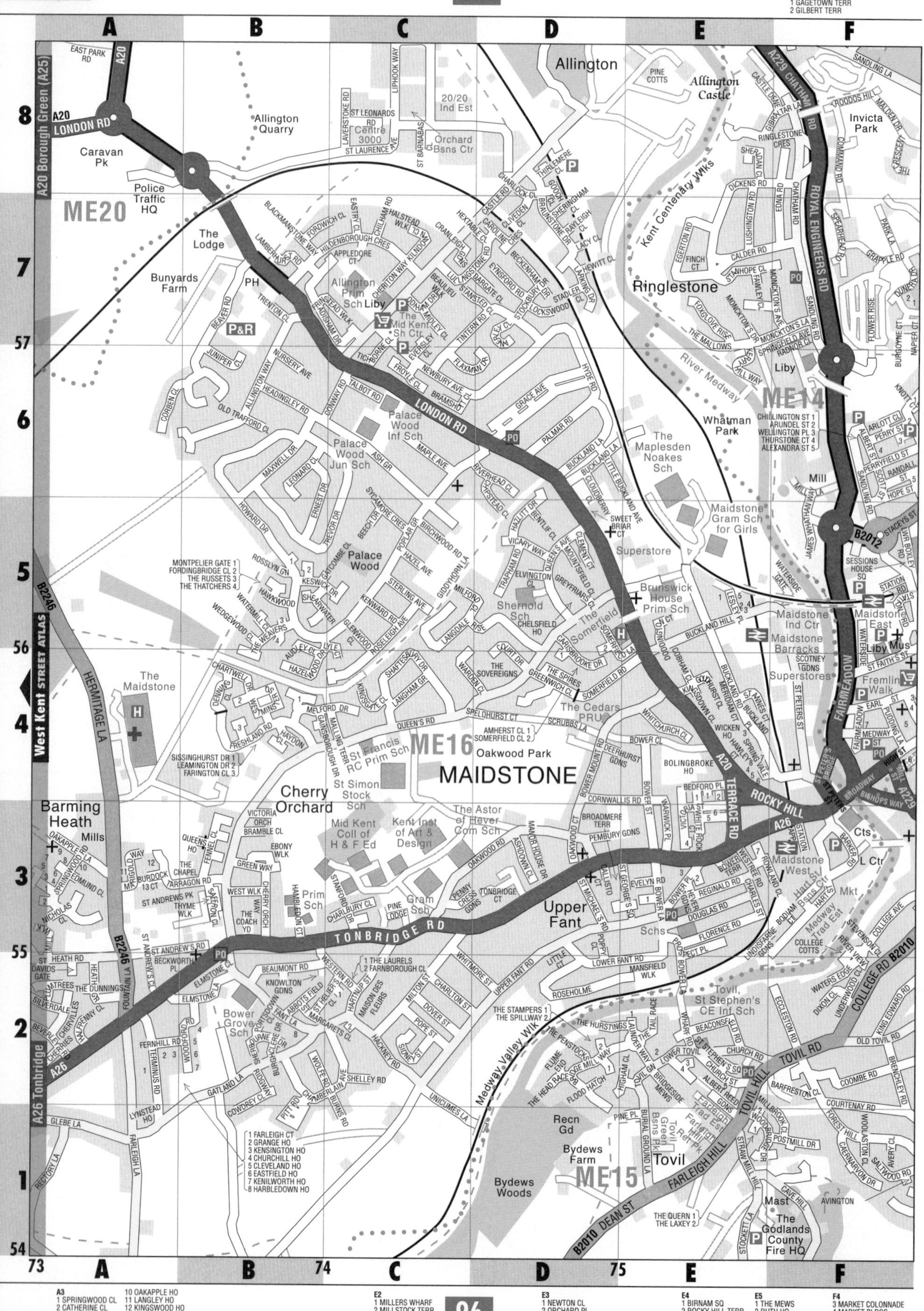

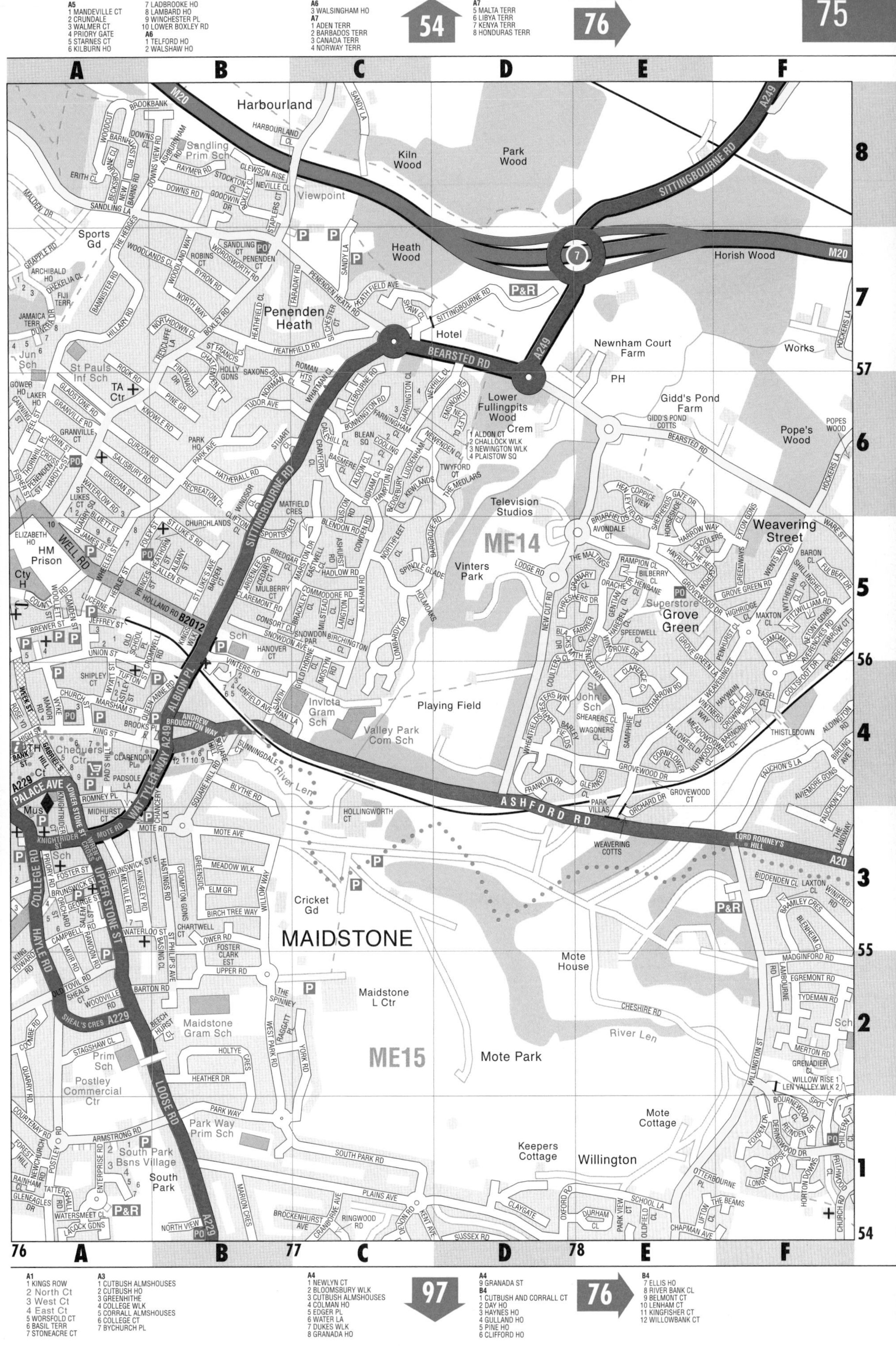

75
A5
1 MANDEVILLE CT
2 CRUNDALE
3 WALMER CT
4 PRIORY GATE
5 STARNES CT
6 KILBURN HO
7 LADBROOKE HO
8 LAMBARD HO
9 WINCHESTER PL
10 LOWER BOXLEY RD
A6
1 TELFORD HO
2 WALSHAW HO
A6
3 WALSINGHAM HO
A7
1 ADEN TERR
2 BARBADOS TERR
3 CANADA TERR
4 NORWAY TERR
54
A7
5 MALTA TERR
6 LIBYA TERR
7 KENYA TERR
8 HONDURAS TERR
76
Harbourland
Kiln Wood
Park Wood
Sandling Prim Sch
Viewpoint
Sports Gd
Heath Wood
Horish Wood
M20
SITTINGBOURNE RD
A249
Penenden Heath
Hotel
BEARSTED RD
Newnham Court Farm
Works
Jun Sch
St Pauls Inf Sch
TA Ctr
Lower Fullingpits Wood
Crem
PH
Gidd's Pond Farm
Pope's Wood
Television Studios
ME14
Vinters Park
Weavering Street
HM Prison
Cty H
WELL RD
HOLLAND RD
B2012
Superstore
Grove Green
St John's Sch
Invicta Gram Sch
Valley Park Com Sch
Playing Field
Chequers Ctr
River Len
ASHFORD RD
A20
PALACE AVE
A229
Mus
COLLEGE RD
HAYLE RD
UPPER STONE ST
Cricket Gd
MAIDSTONE
Mote House
Maidstone L Ctr
Maidstone Gram Sch
ME15
Mote Park
Prim Sch
Postley Commercial Ctr
Park Way Prim Sch
South Park Bsns Village
South Park
LOOSE RD
Keepers Cottage
Willington
Mote Cottage
76
77
78
A1
1 KINGS ROW
2 North Ct
3 West Ct
4 East Ct
5 WORSFOLD CT
6 BASIL TERR
7 STONEACRE CT
A3
1 CUTBUSH ALMSHOUSES
2 CUTBUSH HO
3 GREENHITHE
4 COLLEGE WLK
5 CORRALL ALMSHOUSES
6 COLLEGE CT
7 BYCHURCH PL
A4
1 NEWLYN CT
2 BLOOMSBURY WLK
3 CUTBUSH ALMSHOUSES
4 COLMAN HO
5 EDGER PL
6 WATER LA
7 DUKES WLK
8 GRANADA HO
97
A4
9 GRANADA ST
B4
1 CUTBUSH AND CORRALL CT
2 DAY HO
3 HAYNES HO
4 GULLAND HO
5 PINE HO
6 CLIFFORD HO
76
B4
7 ELLIS HO
8 RIVER BANK CL
9 BELMONT CT
10 LENHAM CT
11 KINGFISHER CT
12 WILLOWBANK CT

A B C D E F
8 7 57 6 5 56 4 3 55 2 1 54
Works
ORCHARD VIEW
HOCKERS CL
Detling
HOCKERS LA
Black Horse (PH)
CASTLE HILL
North Downs Way
Fox Farm Cotts
COLDBLOW LA
PILGRIMS WAY
Thurnham Court
Thurnham
ALDINGTON LA
M20
Thurnham Keep Farm
Court Farm
Cobham Manor Riding Centre
Gorewood Farm
THURNHAM LA
Honeyhills Wood
Gore Wood
The Lilk
WATER LA
Clayswood
Birling House
Chapel Lane Farm
ME14
Longham Wood
1 PORT CL
2 AVERENCHES RD
3 CREVE COEUR CL
4 MAMIGNOT CL
CHAPEL LA
Ware Street
FANCY ROW
CH
Bearsted
1 INVICTA VILLAS
2 FORGE LA
3 SMARTS COTTS
4 MOTE HALL VILLAS
5 THE OASTS
6 THE OLD CORN STORES
7 OLIVERS ROW
Howe Court
Liby
Bearsted Green Bsns Ctr
PO
PH
Bridge Farm
CRISMILL LA
The Green
Barty Farm
Roseacre Jun Sch
Bearsted
Thurnham CE Inf Sch
Roseacre
PLANTATION LA
THE GROVE
PO
A20
P
ASHFORD RD
LILK HILL
CH
Woodcut Farm
Tudor Park Hotel & Country Club
Milgate Park
River Len
Milgate House
PINE LODGE TOURING PK
Mantle's
Silver Hill
ME17
Liby
Jun & Inf Schs
1 SMALL HYTHE CL
2 GASCOYNE CL
3 RYAN DR
Nursery
CARING LA
OTHAM LA
OTHAM ST
CARING RD
Orchard Spot (PH)
ME15
GREEN HILL
Caring Farm
Caring
Fulling Mill Farm
OLD MILL RD
1 ELLENSWOOD CL
2 REDSELLS CL
3 RAVENS DANE CL
79 80 81

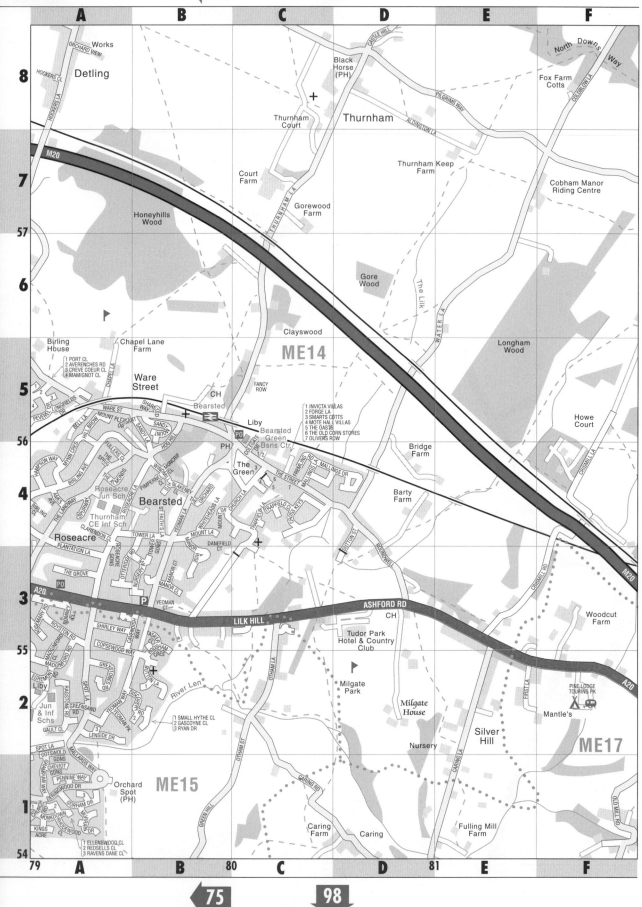

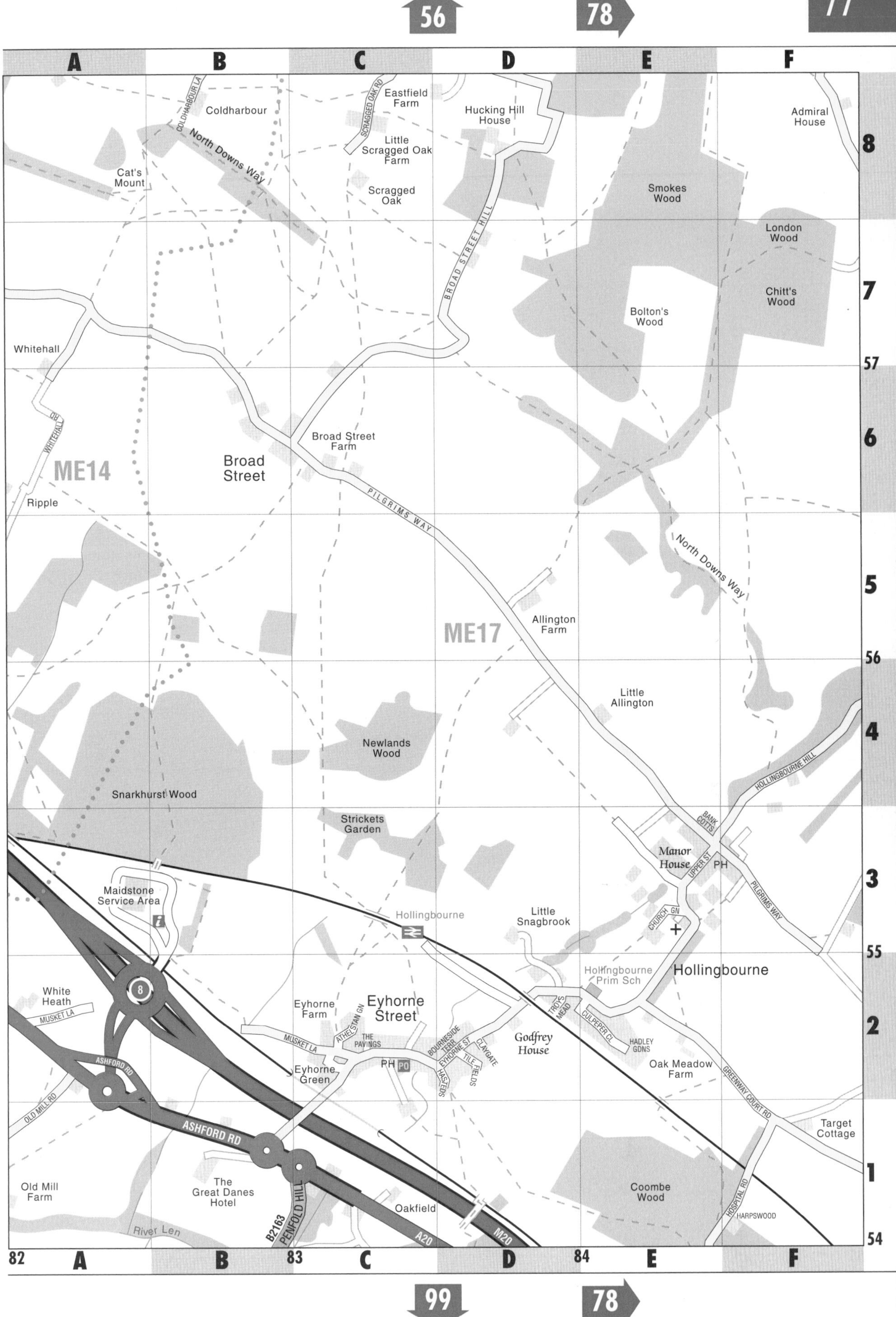

56
78
A
B
C
D
E
F
Eastfield Farm
Hucking Hill House
Admiral House
Coldharbour
COLDHARBOUR LA
SCRAGGED OAK RD
Little Scragged Oak Farm
North Downs Way
Cat's Mount
Scragged Oak
Smokes Wood
London Wood
BROAD STREET HILL
Bolton's Wood
Chitt's Wood
Whitehall
WHITEHALL RD
Broad Street Farm
ME14
Broad Street
Ripple
PILGRIMS WAY
North Downs Way
Allington Farm
ME17
Little Allington
Newlands Wood
HOLLINGBOURNE HILL
Snarkhurst Wood
Strickets Garden
BANK COTTS
Manor House
UPPER ST
PH
PILGRIMS WAY
Maidstone Service Area
Hollingbourne
Little Snagbrook
CHURCH GN
Hollingbourne Prim Sch
Hollingbourne
White Heath
MUSKET LA
8
Eyhorne Farm
Eyhorne Street
ATHELSTAN GN
THE PAVINGS
MUSKET LA
BOURNESIDE TERR
EYHORNE ST
CLAYGATE
TILE FIELDS
HASTEDS
PH
PO
Godfrey House
TROYS MEAD
CULPEPER CL
HADLEY GDNS
Oak Meadow Farm
GREENWAY COURT RD
ASHFORD RD
Eyhorne Green
OLD MILL RD
ASHFORD RD
Target Cottage
Old Mill Farm
The Great Danes Hotel
B2163
PENFOLD HILL
Oakfield
Coombe Wood
HOSPITAL RD
HARPSWOOD
River Len
A20
M20
8
7
57
6
5
56
4
3
55
2
1
54
82
83
84
99
78

8 Bicknor Park

Bedmonton Manor Farm

Bedmonton

Hill House

Colyers Wents

Stockbury Wood

Saywell Farm

Wormshill

7 Cooper's Farm

ME9

Blacksmith's Arms (PH)

MATTINSON PL

THE STREET

57 Park Wood

Gotteridge

6 Mordenden Wood

Yewtree Farm

Drake Lane Plantation

Water Tower

WHITE POST

5 Smith's Farm

Marshall's Farm

Drake La

Hollingbourne Farm

Morning Dawn

56 HOLLINGBOURNE HILL

Hollingbourne House

Tile Barn

Stock Wood

West Leas

Ringlestone

4 ME17

RINGLESTONE RD

BLACK POST

Ringlestone Inn (PH)

3 Frogshole

High Wood

Salisbury Wood

Merlewood Farm

STEDE HILL

Horsalls

55

2

Lower Deans Farm

Dean's Hill

HOGBARN LA

North Downs Way

Mile Hill

1 Greenway Court Farm

GREENWAY COURT RD

Greenway Court

Harrietsham Manor

54

GREENWAY COURT FARM COTTS

| 85 | A | | B | 86 | C | | D | 87 | E | | F |

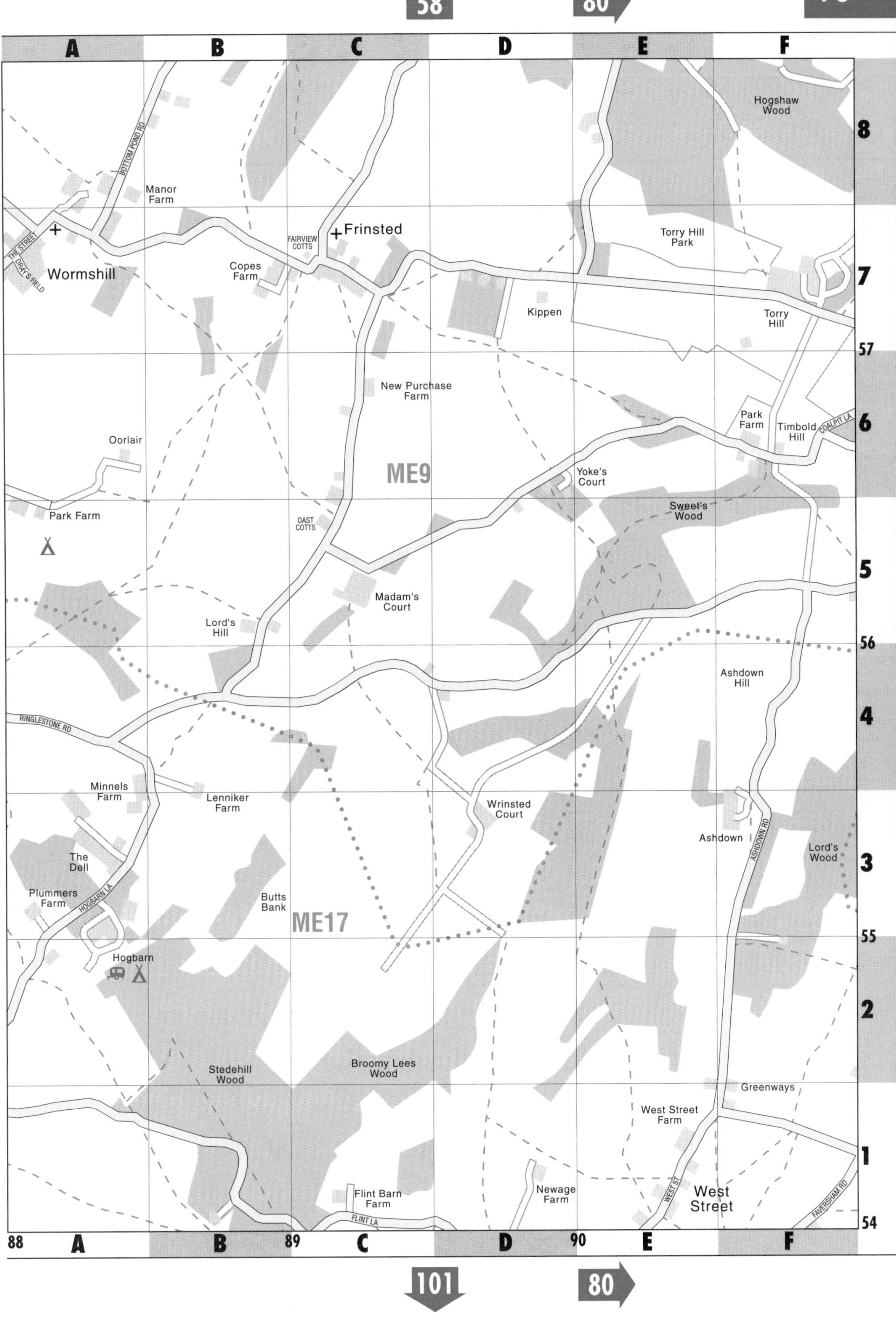

A B C D E F

8

Hogshaw
Wood

Manor
Farm

+ Frinsted

FAIRVIEW
COTTS

Torry Hill
Park

7

THE STREET

DRAY'S FIELD

Wormshill

Copes
Farm

BOTTOM POND RD

Kippen

Torry
Hill

57

New Purchase
Farm

Park
Farm

Timbold
Hill

COALPIT LA

6

Oorlair

ME9

Yoke's
Court

Sweet's
Wood

Park Farm

OAST
COTTS

Madam's
Court

5

Lord's
Hill

Ashdown
Hill

56

RINGLESTONE RD

4

Minnels
Farm

Lenniker
Farm

Wrinsted
Court

Ashdown

ASHDOWN RD

Lord's
Wood

3

The
Dell

HOGBARN LA

Butts
Bank

ME17

Plummers
Farm

55

Hogbarn

2

Stedehill
Wood

Broomy Lees
Wood

Greenways

West Street
Farm

West
Street

WEST ST

1

Flint Barn
Farm

FLINT LA

Newage
Farm

FAVERSHAM RD

54

88 A B 89 C D 90 E F

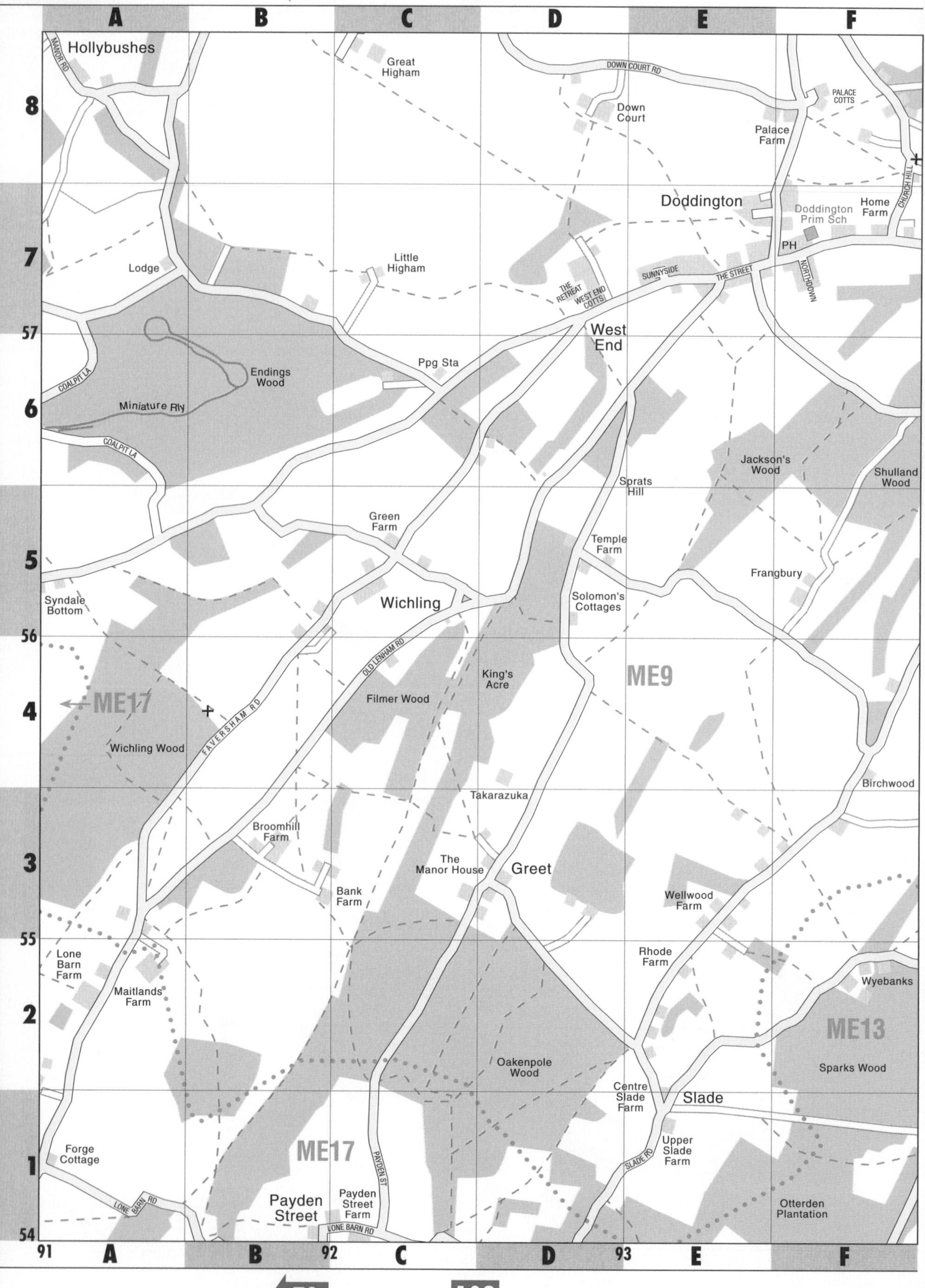

Hollybushes

Great Higham

DOWN COURT RD

Down Court

PALACE COTTS

Palace Cotts

8

Palace Farm

Doddington

Doddington Prim Sch

Home Farm

Lodge

7

Little Higham

THE RETREAT

WEST END COTTS

SUNNYSIDE

THE STREET

PH

NORTH DOWN

CHURCH HILL

57

Ppg Sta

West End

Endings Wood

COALPIT LA

Miniature Rly

COALPIT LA

6

Sprats Hill

Jackson's Wood

Shulland Wood

Green Farm

Temple Farm

Frangbury

5

Wichling

Solomon's Cottages

Syndale Bottom

56

ME9

ME17 ←

King's Acre

4

FAVERSHAM RD

OLD LENHAM RD

Filmer Wood

Wichling Wood

Birchwood

Takarazuka

Broomhill Farm

3

The Manor House

Greet

Wellwood Farm

Bank Farm

55

Rhode Farm

Lone Barn Farm

Wyebanks

Maitlands Farm

2

ME13

Oakenpole Wood

Sparks Wood

Centre Slade Farm

Slade

Forge Cottage

1

ME17

SLADE RD

PAYDEN ST

Upper Slade Farm

Otterden Plantation

LONE BARN RD

Payden Street

Payden Street Farm

LONE BARN RD

54

91

A

B

92

C

D

93

E

F

60
82

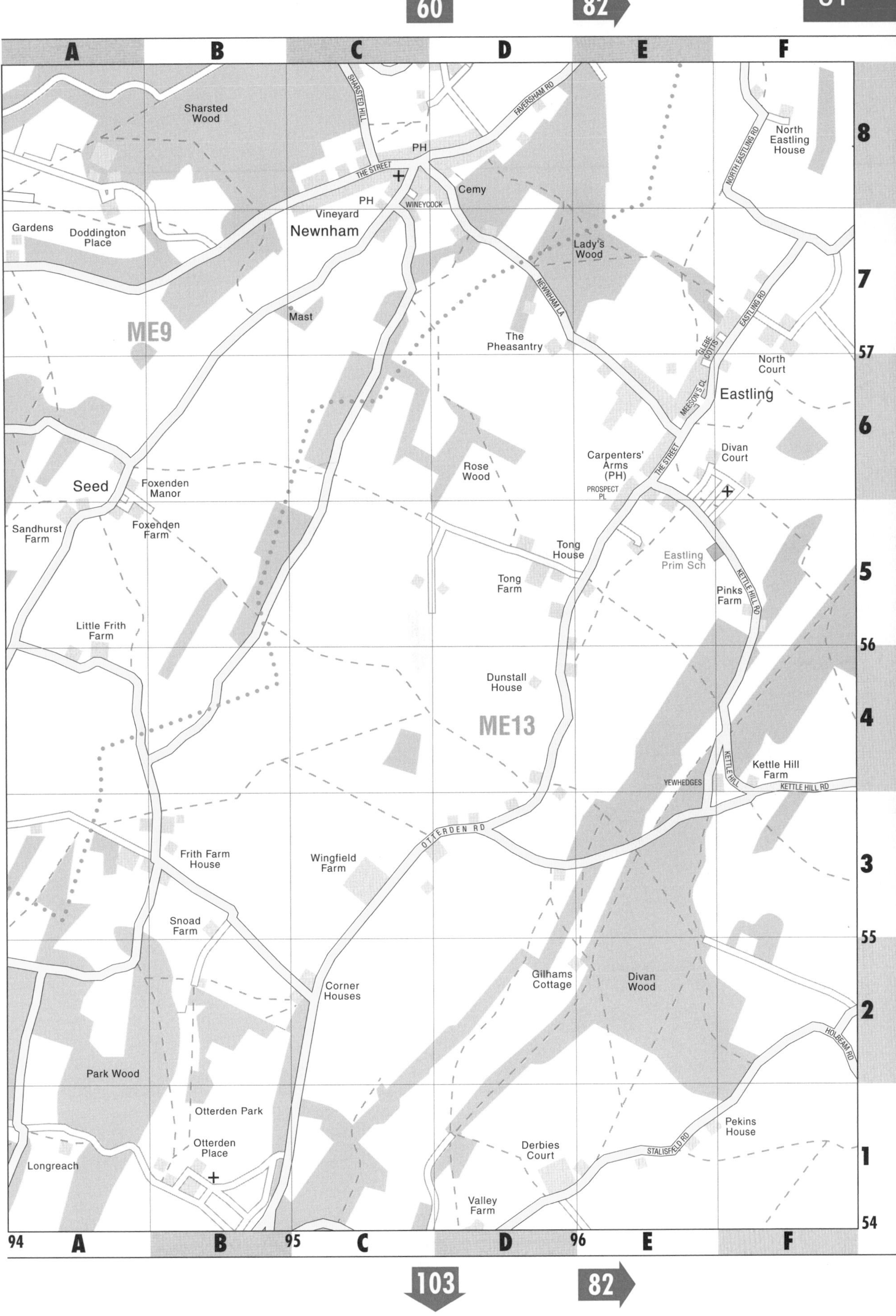
A
B
C
D
E
F
Sharsted Wood
SHARSTED HILL
FAVERSHAM RD
PH
THE STREET
PH
Cemy
WINEYCOCK
Vineyard
Newnham
Gardens
Doddington Place
North Eastling House
NORTH EASTLING RD
Lady's Wood
NEWNHAM LA
EASTLING RD
ME9
Mast
The Pheasantry
GLEBE COTTS
North Court
MEESON'S CL
Eastling
Rose Wood
Carpenters' Arms (PH)
Divan Court
PROSPECT PL
THE STREET
Seed
Foxenden Manor
Foxenden Farm
Sandhurst Farm
Tong House
Eastling Prim Sch
Tong Farm
KETTLE HILL RD
Pinks Farm
Little Frith Farm
Dunstall House
ME13
Kettle Hill Farm
YEWHEDGES
KETTLE HILL
KETTLE HILL RD
OTTERDEN RD
Frith Farm House
Wingfield Farm
Snoad Farm
Gilhams Cottage
Divan Wood
Corner Houses
HOLBEAM RD
Park Wood
Otterden Park
Pekins House
Otterden Place
Derbies Court
STALISFIELD RD
Longreach
Valley Farm
8
7
57
6
5
56
4
3
55
2
1
54
94
95
96

103
82

81
61

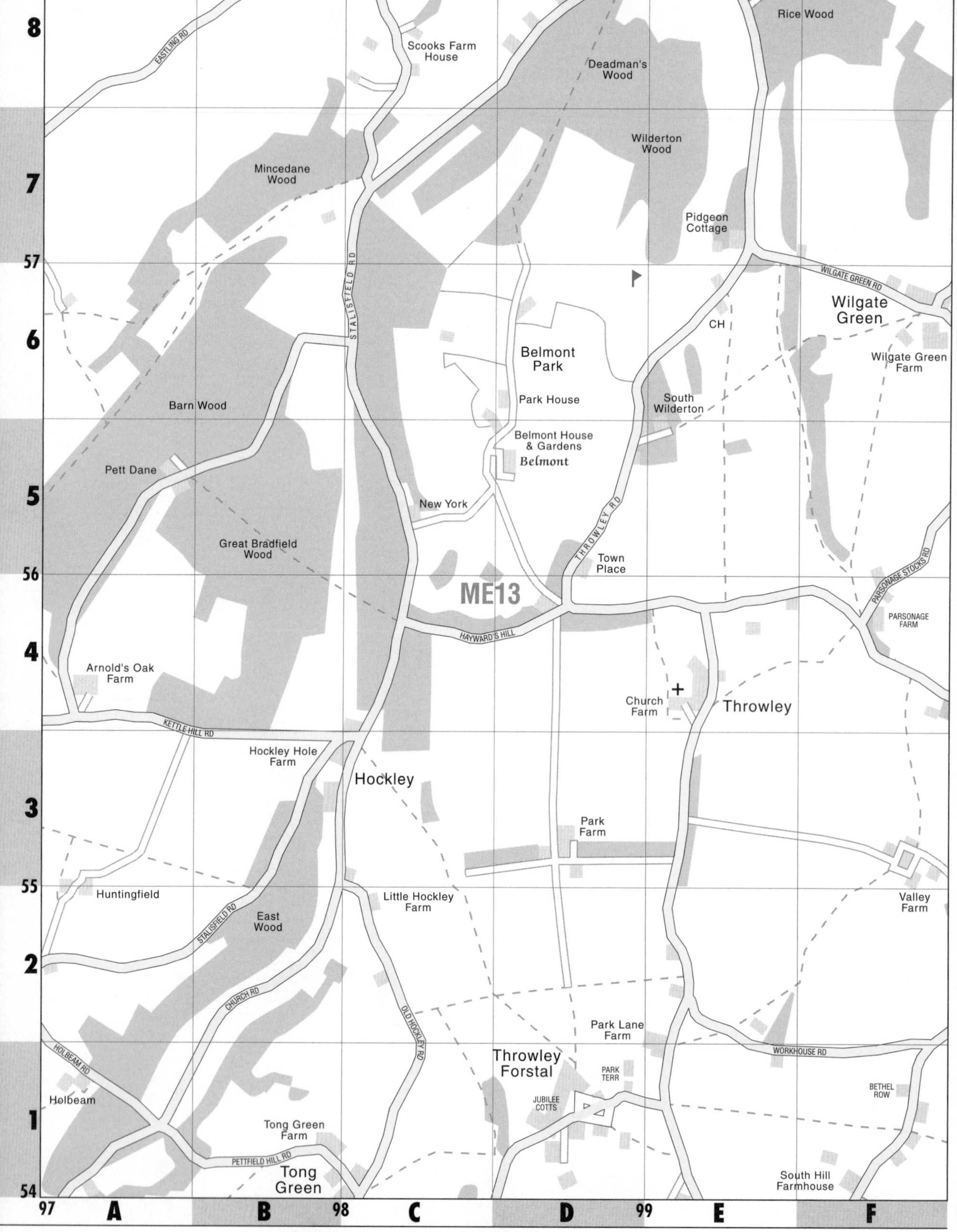

A B C D E F
8
7
57
6
5
56
4
3
55
2
1
54
97 A B 98 C D 99 E F
EASTLING RD
Scooks Farm House
Deadman's Wood
Rice Wood
Wilderton Wood
Mincedane Wood
Pidgeon Cottage
STALISFIELD RD
WILGATE GREEN RD
Wilgate Green
CH
Belmont Park
Wilgate Green Farm
Park House
South Wilderton
Barn Wood
Belmont House & Gardens
Belmont
Pett Dane
New York
THROWLEY RD
Great Bradfield Wood
Town Place
PARSONAGE STOCKS RD
ME13
PARSONAGE FARM
HAYWARD'S HILL
Arnold's Oak Farm
Church Farm
Throwley
KETTLE HILL RD
Hockley Hole Farm
Hockley
Park Farm
Huntingfield
Little Hockley Farm
Valley Farm
STALISFIELD RD
East Wood
CHURCH RD
Park Lane Farm
OLD HOCKLEY RD
HOLBEAM RD
WORKHOUSE RD
Throwley Forstal
PARK TERR
BETHEL ROW
JUBILEE COTTS
Holbeam
Tong Green Farm
PETTFIELD HILL RD
Tong Green
South Hill Farmhouse

81
104

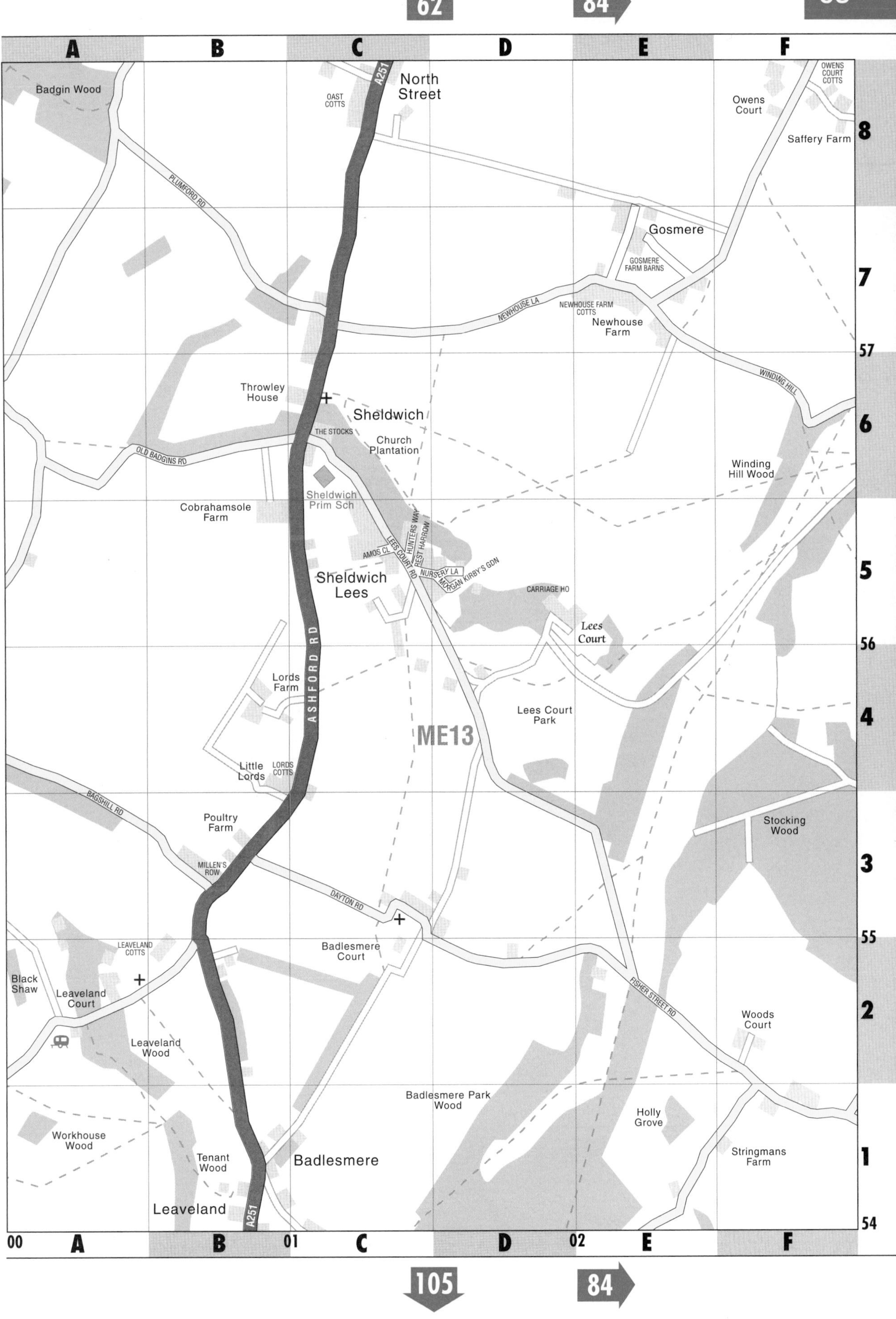

62

84

A   B   C   D   E   F

North
Street

Badgin Wood

OAST
COTTS

A251

OWENS
COURT
COTTS

Owens
Court

Saffery Farm

8

PLUMFORD RD

Gosmere

GOSMERE
FARM BARNS

7

NEWHOUSE LA

NEWHOUSE FARM
COTTS

Newhouse
Farm

57

WINDING HILL

Throwley
House

Sheldwich

OLD BADGINS RD

THE STOCKS

Church
Plantation

Winding
Hill Wood

6

Cobrahamsole
Farm

Sheldwich
Prim Sch

HUNTERS WAY

REST HARROW

Sheldwich
Lees

LEES COURT RD

AMOS CL

NURSERY LA

MEG AN KIRBY'S GDN

CARRIAGE HO

Lees
Court

5

56

Lords
Farm

ME13

Lees Court
Park

4

ASHFORD RD

BAGSHILL RD

Little
Lords

LORDS
COTTS

Stocking
Wood

Poultry
Farm

3

MILLEN'S
ROW

DAYTON RD

55

Badlesmere
Court

FISHER STREET RD

Black
Shaw

LEAVELAND
COTTS

Leaveland
Court

Woods
Court

2

Leaveland
Wood

Badlesmere Park
Wood

Holly
Grove

Workhouse
Wood

Stringmans
Farm

1

Tenant
Wood

Badlesmere

A251

Leaveland

54

A B C D E F

8

Poppington
Bungalow

Gushmere

Danecourt
Bridge

KIT HILL

CROUCH
COTTS

WALNUT TREE
COTTS

NORTH LA

SOUTH ST

CROUCH LA

South
Street

FEATHERBED LA

Pumping
Sta

Brookes
Croft

7

Selling

STATION
COTTS

Overland

BLACKLEYS

57

WINDING HILL

Hogben's
Hill

WORTAGE LA

Sondes
Arms
(PH)

NEAMES
FORSTAL

WOODGATE
CT

THE WARREN

BRIDGE
COTTS

Neames
Forstal

6

2
1

1 THE SQUARE
2 PEACOCK PL

SELLING ST

CHURCH LA

White Lion
(PH)

Selling

SELLING RD

MONICA PL

Harefield
Farm

Selling
CE Prim
Sch

THE STREET

SELLING RD

Selling Court
Farm

Rhode
Court

Rhode
Farm

5

Grove
Wood

ME13

56

Shepherds
Hill

GROVE RD

OAK
COTTS

Perry Wood
Local
Nature Reserve

Little Stone Stile
Farm

Greenlane
Wood

4

Step
Wood

Works

Perrywood

P

Perry
Wood

LITTLE
STONE STILE
COTTS

Albox
Wood

Priviss
Wood

Stone Stile
Farm

3

Fridhill
Wood

SUTTON
COTTS

Rose &
Crown
(PH)

Conduit
Wood

Cheese
Wood

55

Round
Wood

The
Mount

Wales
Wood

2

Franklins
Wood

CT4

Pole
Wood

GOLDUPS LANE
COTTS

GOLDUPS LA

STONE STILE LA

Shottenden

Playing
Field

1

FISHER STREET RD

BEANEY'S LA

BEANEY'S LA
COTTS

DENNE MANOR LA

POST OFFICE
ROW

Howletts
Farm

SOLESHILL RD

Old House
Wood

Cheyneys
Farm

SHOTTENDEN RD

54

03 A B 04 C D 05 E F

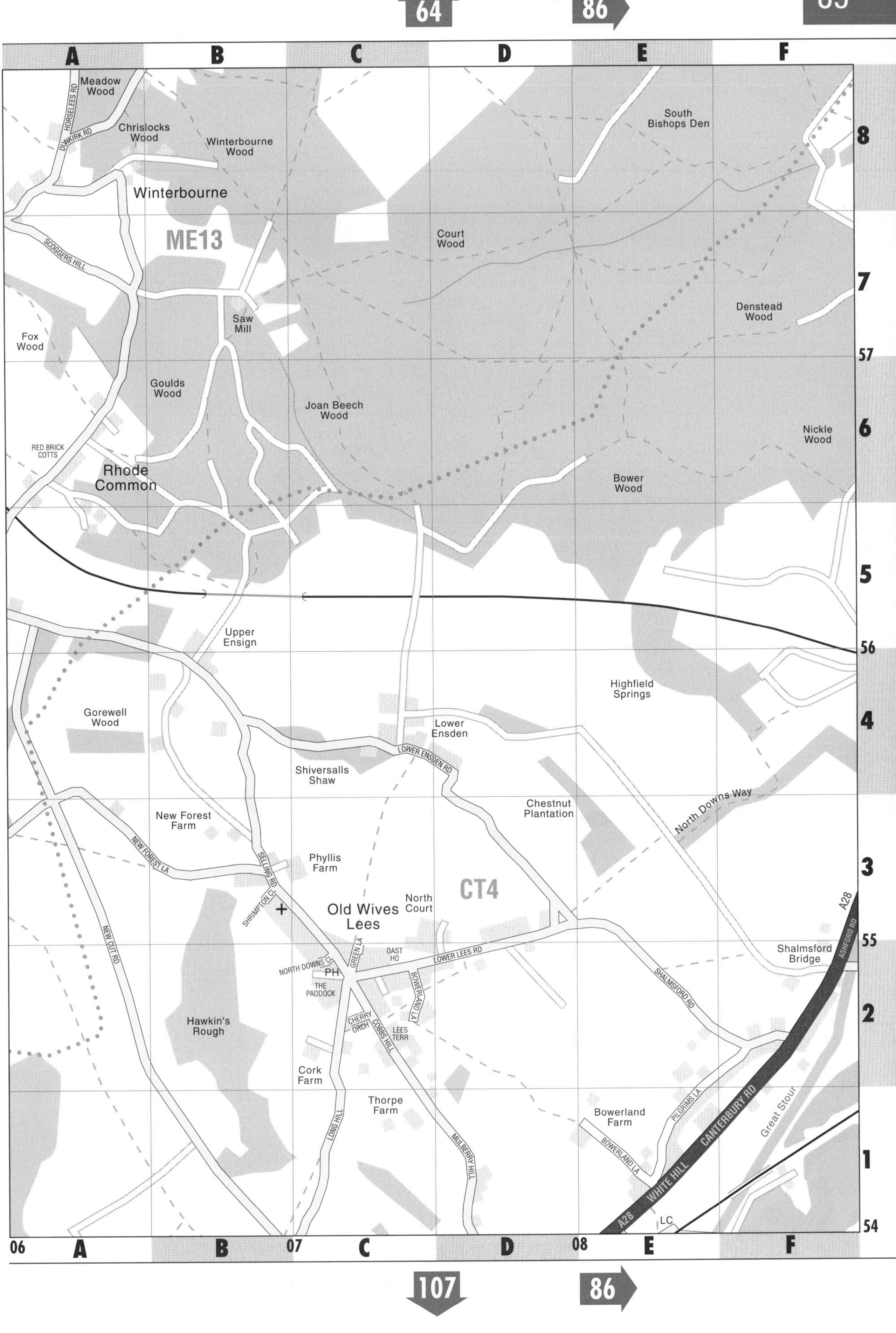
64
86
A
B
C
D
E
F
8
7
57
6
5
56
4
3
55
2
1
54
06
07
08
107
86
Meadow Wood
HORSELEES RD
DUNKIRK RD
Chrislocks Wood
Winterbourne Wood
Winterbourne
South Bishops Den
ME13
SCOGGERS HILL
Court Wood
Saw Mill
Denstead Wood
Fox Wood
Goulds Wood
Joan Beech Wood
Nickle Wood
RED BRICK COTTS
Rhode Common
Bower Wood
Upper Ensign
Highfield Springs
Gorewell Wood
Lower Ensden
LOWER ENSDEN RD
Shiversalls Shaw
Chestnut Plantation
North Downs Way
New Forest Farm
NEW FOREST LA
Phyllis Farm
SELLING RD
SHRIMPTON CL
CT4
Old Wives Lees
North Court
A28
ASHFORD RD
Shalmsford Bridge
NEW CUT RD
NORTH DOWNS CL
PH
GREEN LA
OAST HO
LOWER LEES RD
THE PADDOCK
BOWERLAND LA
SHALMSFORD RD
CHERRY ORCH
COBBS HILL
LEES TERR
Hawkin's Rough
Cork Farm
Thorpe Farm
Bowerland Farm
PILGRIMS LA
CANTERBURY RD
Great Stour
LONG HILL
MULBERRY HILL
BOWERLAND LA
WHITE HILL
A28
LC

A · B · C · D · E · F

ME13

8

Denstead
Cotts

Denstead
Oast

Poldhurst
Farm

CT2

Denstead
Farm

Bigbury
Camp

Howfield Wood

Bigbury
House

7

Petty
France

Bigbury
Wood

PRIMROSE HILL

North Downs Way

BIGBURY RD

57

Hunstead
Wood

Bigberry
Farm

Howfield Wood
Farm

6

TOWN LA

NIGHTINGALE CL

Chartham
Hatch

The Royal Oak
(PH)

HOWFIELD LA

Fright Wood

The
Rough

Howfield
Farm

5

NEW TOWN ST

Nickle
Farm

Mast

A28

56

HATCH LA

Langdane
Wood

Works

CT4

LC

Dunning
Shaw

Stour Valley
Ind Est

4

NICKLE
COTTS

HORTON
GDNS

HORTON
COTTS

Cemy

LC

Stour Valley Wlk

Sewage
Works

Horton

ASHFORD RD

Great Stour

RIVERSIDE

STATION RD

3

A28

The Deanery

LC

Chartham

1 APSLEY COTTS
2 DE L'ANGLE ROW
3 MILL TERR
4 DE L'ANGLE HO

THE GREEN

CHURCH LA

55

LC

PARISH RD

RIVER

STOUR RD

STOUR CL

Chartham

Mill

CARMEL CL

OLD SCHOOL
MEWS

THE HYDE

BOLTS HILL

RENTAIN RD

BALTINGTON ST

2

Ye Olde
England
(PH)

PO

ASHDOWN
FIELD

SHALMSFORD ST

ARNOLD RD

HIGHLAND RD

BAKER'S LA

COCKERING RD

BRUNDELL
TERR

BOBBIN LODGE HILL

SHALMSFORD CT

CREMER

WOODSIDE
AVE

LAWSON
CL

LARKEY VIEW

1 REDWOOD CL
2 LIME CL
3 CHAPLAINS WLK
4 AINSLEY WAY
5 TOWER VIEW
6 THE CHAPEL

THRUXLED LA

Shalmsford
Street

Chartham
Prim Sch

BRICE AVE

POMFRET
HO

POMFRET RD

Stour Valley Wlk

THE CRESCENT

PH

JASMINE CT

BEECH AVE

LINDEN RD

ASPEN RD

LAUREL WAY

ALMOND

OLD GARDEN
CT

LITTLE COPSE

OLD CHURCH RD

GODFREY GDNS

UPDOWN WAY

CHESTNUT CL

GARDENERS
PL

1

MYSTOLE LA

THE DOWNS

MAGNOLIA DR

SYCAMORE CL

Chartham
Downs

54

09
A · B · 10 · C · D · 11 · E · F

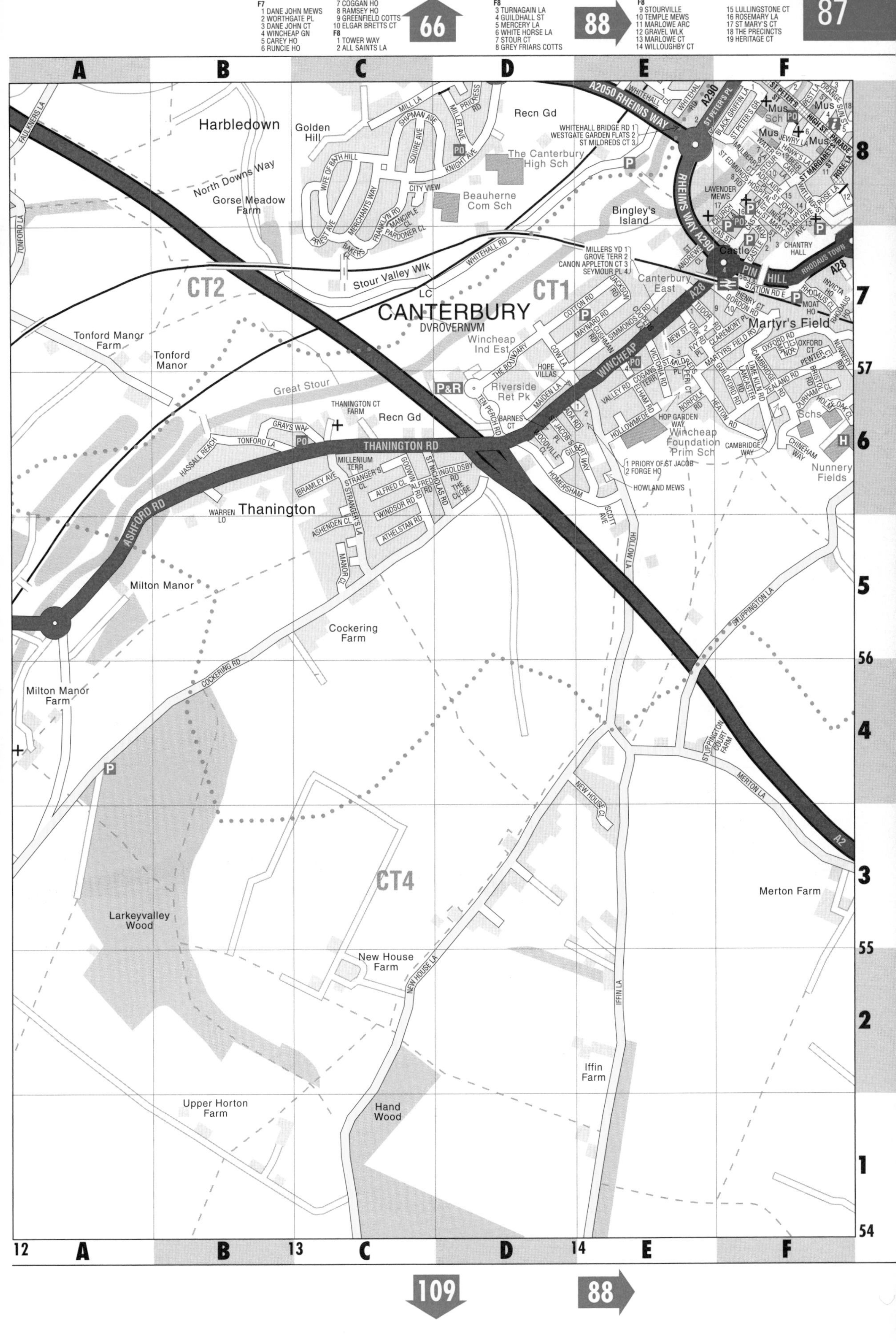

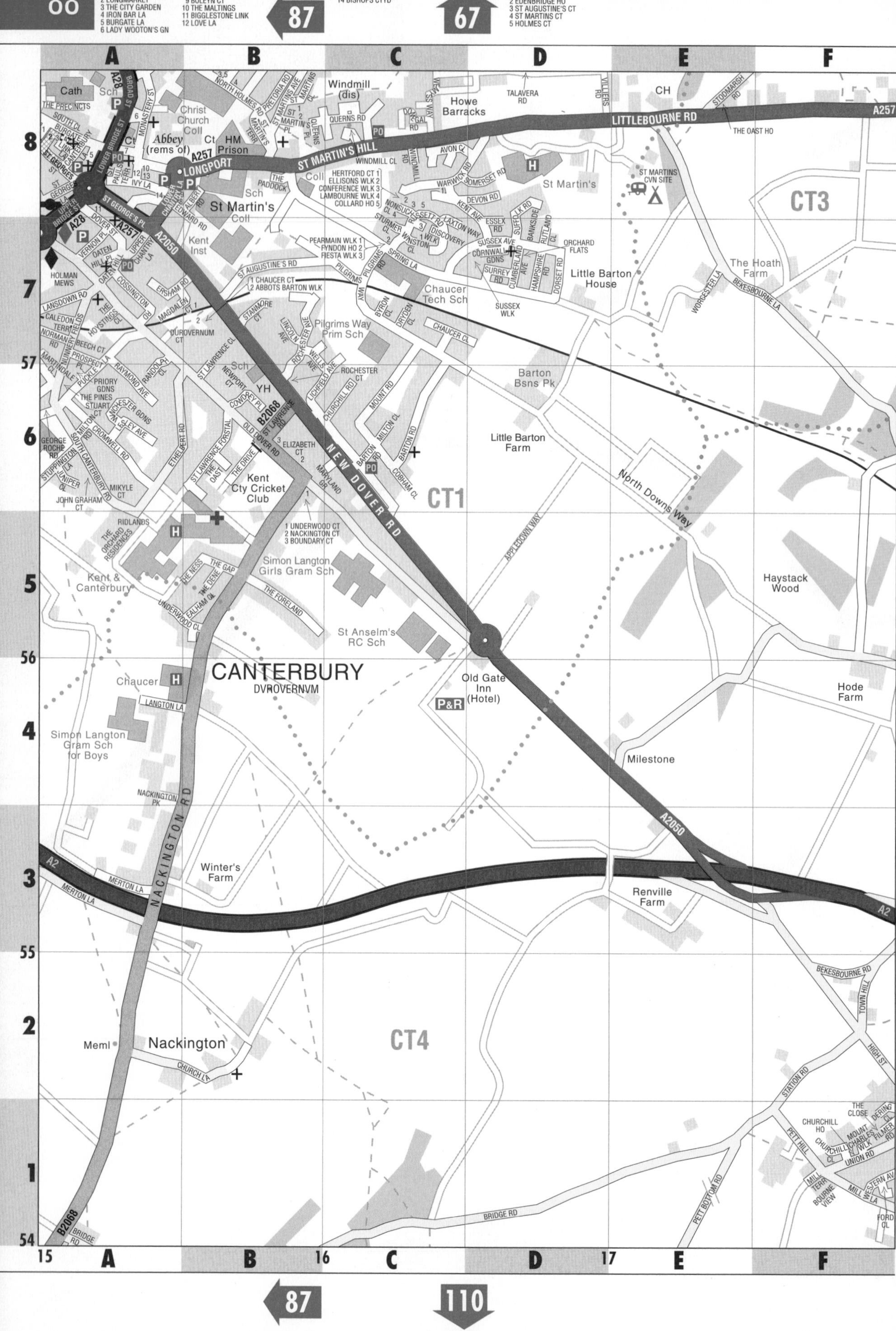

68
90

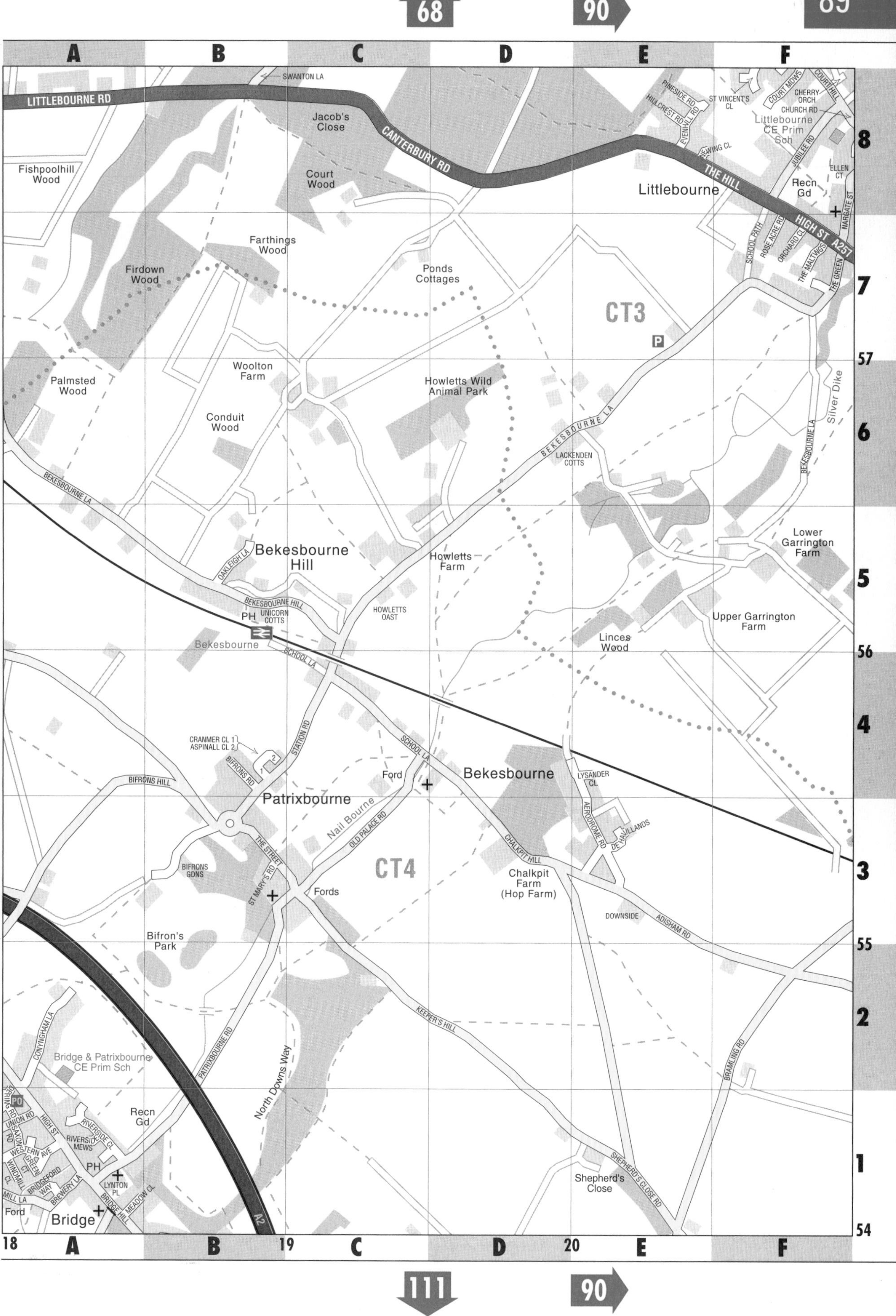
A
B
C
D
E
F
LITTLEBOURNE RD
SWANTON LA
Jacob's Close
CANTERBURY RD
Court Wood
Fishpoolhill Wood
Farthings Wood
Firdown Wood
Ponds Cottages
Palmsted Wood
Woolton Farm
Conduit Wood
Howletts Wild Animal Park
CT3
Littlebourne
THE HILL
HIGH ST A257
Littlebourne CE Prim Sch
Recn Gd
PINESIDE RD
HILLCREST RD
EVENHILL RD
ST VINCENT'S CL
COURT MDWS
CHERRY ORCH
CHURCH RD
COURT HILL
JUBILEE RD
ELLEN CT
NARGATE ST
SCHOOL PATH
ROSE ACRE RD
ORCHARD CL
THE MALTINGS
THE GREEN
BEKESBOURNE LA
LACKENDEN COTTS
Silver Dike
Lower Garrington Farm
Upper Garrington Farm
Linces Wood
Bekesbourne Hill
OAKLEIGH LA
BEKESBOURNE HILL
PH
UNICORN COTTS
Bekesbourne
HOWLETTS OAST
Howletts Farm
SCHOOL LA
STATION RD
CRANMER CL 1
ASPINALL CL 2
BIFRONS RD
BIFRONS HILL
Patrixbourne
Ford
Bekesbourne
LYSANDER CL
AERODROME RD
DE HAVILLANDS
Nail Bourne
OLD PALACE RD
THE STREET
BIFRONS GDNS
ST MARY'S RD
Fords
CT4
CHALKPIT HILL
Chalkpit Farm (Hop Farm)
DOWNSIDE
ADISHAM RD
Bifron's Park
KEEPER'S HILL
CONYNGHAM LA
Bridge & Patrixbourne CE Prim Sch
PATRIXBOURNE RD
North Downs Way
BRAMLING RD
Recn Gd
PO
SPRING RD
UNION RD
SAXON RD
HIGH ST
WESTERN AVE
GREEN CT
WINDMILL CL
RIVERSIDE CL
RIVERSIDE MEWS
BRIDGEFORD WAY
BREWERY LA
LYNTON PL
PH
MEADOW CL
BRIDGE HILL
MILL LA
Ford
Bridge
A2
Shepherd's Close
SHEPHERD'S CLOSE RD
8
7
57
6
5
56
4
3
55
2
1
54
18
19
20

111
90

89
69

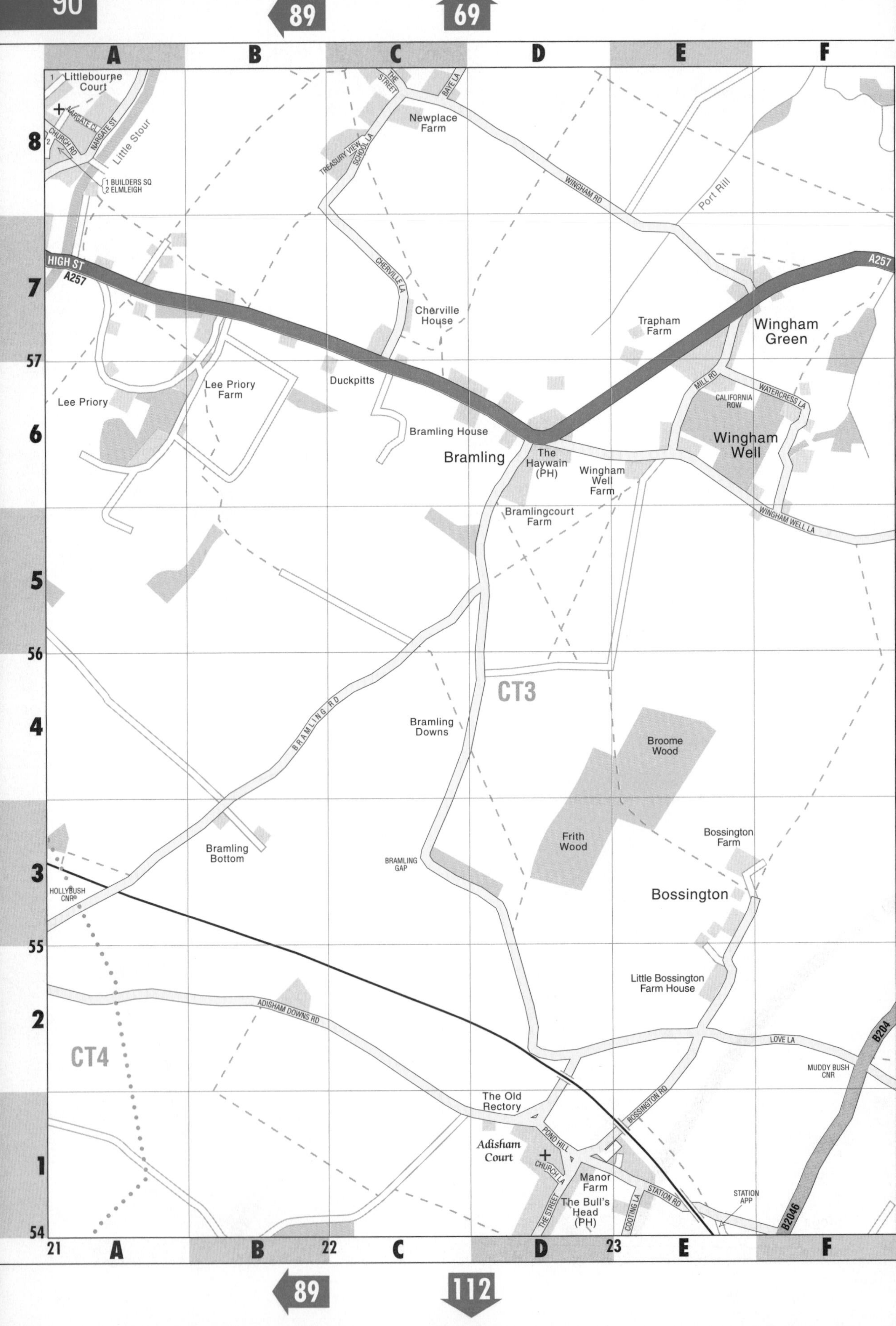
Littlebourne Court
MARGATE CL
NARGATE ST
CHURCH RD
Little Stour
1 BUILDERS SQ
2 ELMLEIGH
THE STREET
BAYE LA
Newplace Farm
TREASURY VIEW
SCHOOL LA
WINGHAM RD
Port Rill
HIGH ST
A257
CHERVILLE LA
Cherville House
Trapham Farm
Wingham Green
Lee Priory Farm
Duckpitts
Lee Priory
MILL RD
WATERCRESS LA
CALIFORNIA ROW
Bramling House
Wingham Well
Bramling
The Haywain (PH)
Wingham Well Farm
Bramlingcourt Farm
WINGHAM WELL LA
CT3
BRAMLING RD
Bramling Downs
Broome Wood
Frith Wood
Bossington Farm
Bramling Bottom
BRAMLING GAP
HOLLYBUSH CNR
Bossington
Little Bossington Farm House
ADISHAM DOWNS RD
LOVE LA
B2046
CT4
MUDDY BUSH CNR
The Old Rectory
BOSSINGTON RD
POND HILL
Adisham Court
CHURCH LA
Manor Farm
The Bull's Head (PH)
THE STREET
COOTING LA
STATION RD
STATION APP
A B C D E F
8 7 57 6 5 56 4 3 55 2 1 54
21 22 23

89
112

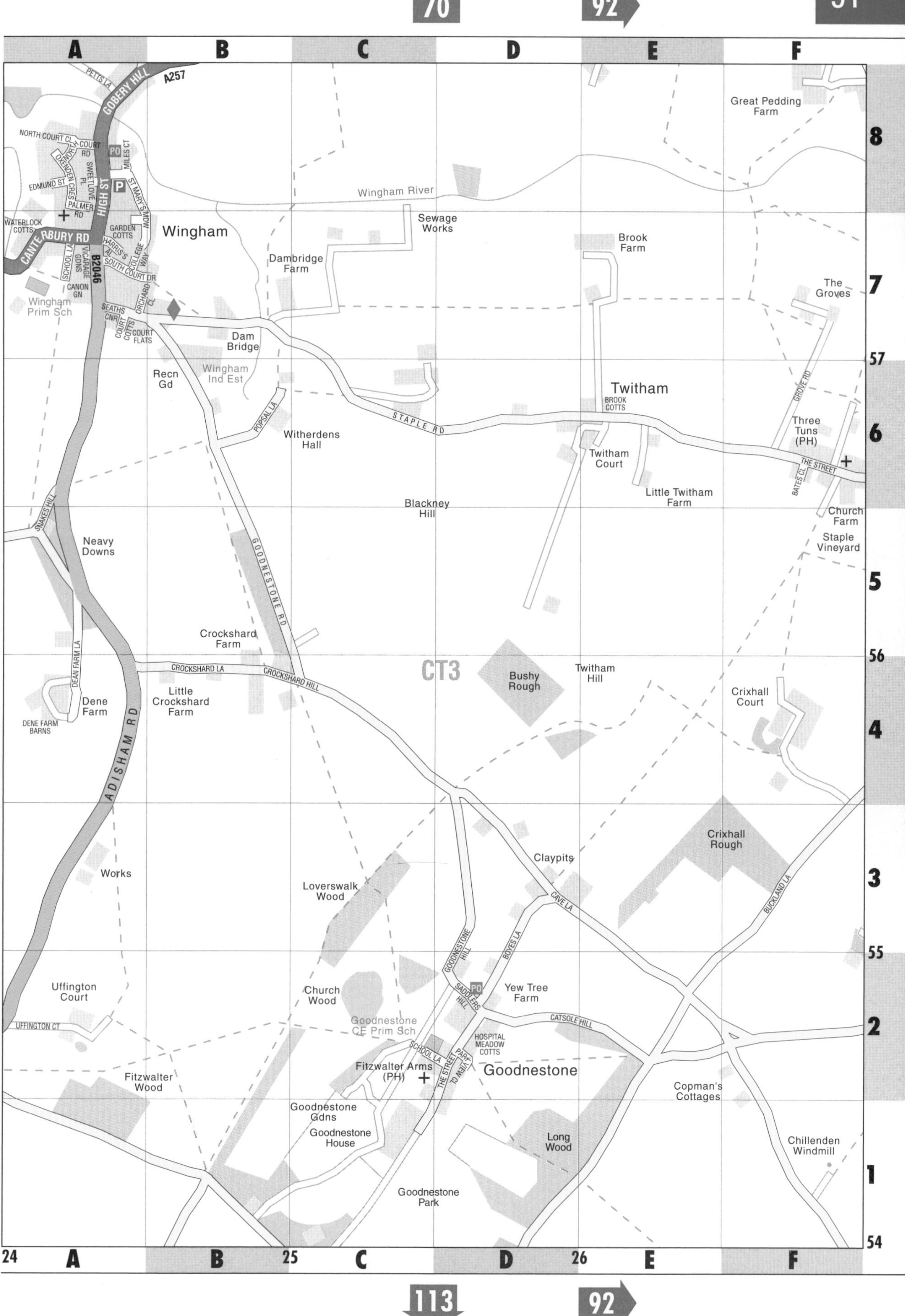

A B C D E F

PETTS LA
GOBERY HILL
A257
NORTH COURT CL
COURT RD
PO
MILES CT
COVENTRY CRES
SWEETLOVE PL
EDMUND ST
PALMER RD
HIGH ST
ST MARY'S WK
GARDEN COTTS
WATERLOCK COTTS
CANTERBURY RD
VICARAGE GDNS
COLLEGE WAY
CANON GN
Wingham
B2046
Wingham Prim Sch
SEATHS CNR
COURT COTTS
SOUTH COURT DR
ORCHARD CL
COURT FLATS
Dam Bridge

Great Pedding Farm

Wingham River

Sewage Works

Brook Farm

The Groves

Dambridge Farm

Recn Gd

Wingham Ind Est

Witherdens Hall

POPSALL LA

STAPLE RD

Twitham

BROOK COTTS

Three Tuns (PH)

GROVE RD

Twitham Court

THE STREET

BATS CL

Little Twitham Farm

Church Farm

Staple Vineyard

SNAKES HILL

Neavy Downs

Blackney Hill

GOODNESTONE RD

DEAN FARM LA

Crockshard Farm

CROCKSHARD LA

CROCKSHARD HILL

CT3

Bushy Rough

Twitham Hill

Crixhall Court

Dene Farm

DENE FARM BARNS

ADISHAM RD

Little Crockshard Farm

Works

Loverswalk Wood

Claypits

CAVE LA

Crixhall Rough

BUCKLAND LA

GOODNESTONE HILL

BOYES LA

Church Wood

SADDLERS HILL

PO

Yew Tree Farm

CATSOLE HILL

Uffington Court

UFFINGTON CT

Goodnestone CE Prim Sch

SCHOOL LA

HOSPITAL MEADOW COTTS

Fitzwalter Arms (PH)

THE STREET (PART)
TD AND I

Goodnestone

Copman's Cottages

Fitzwalter Wood

Goodnestone Gdns

Goodnestone House

Long Wood

Chillenden Windmill

Goodnestone Park

91
71

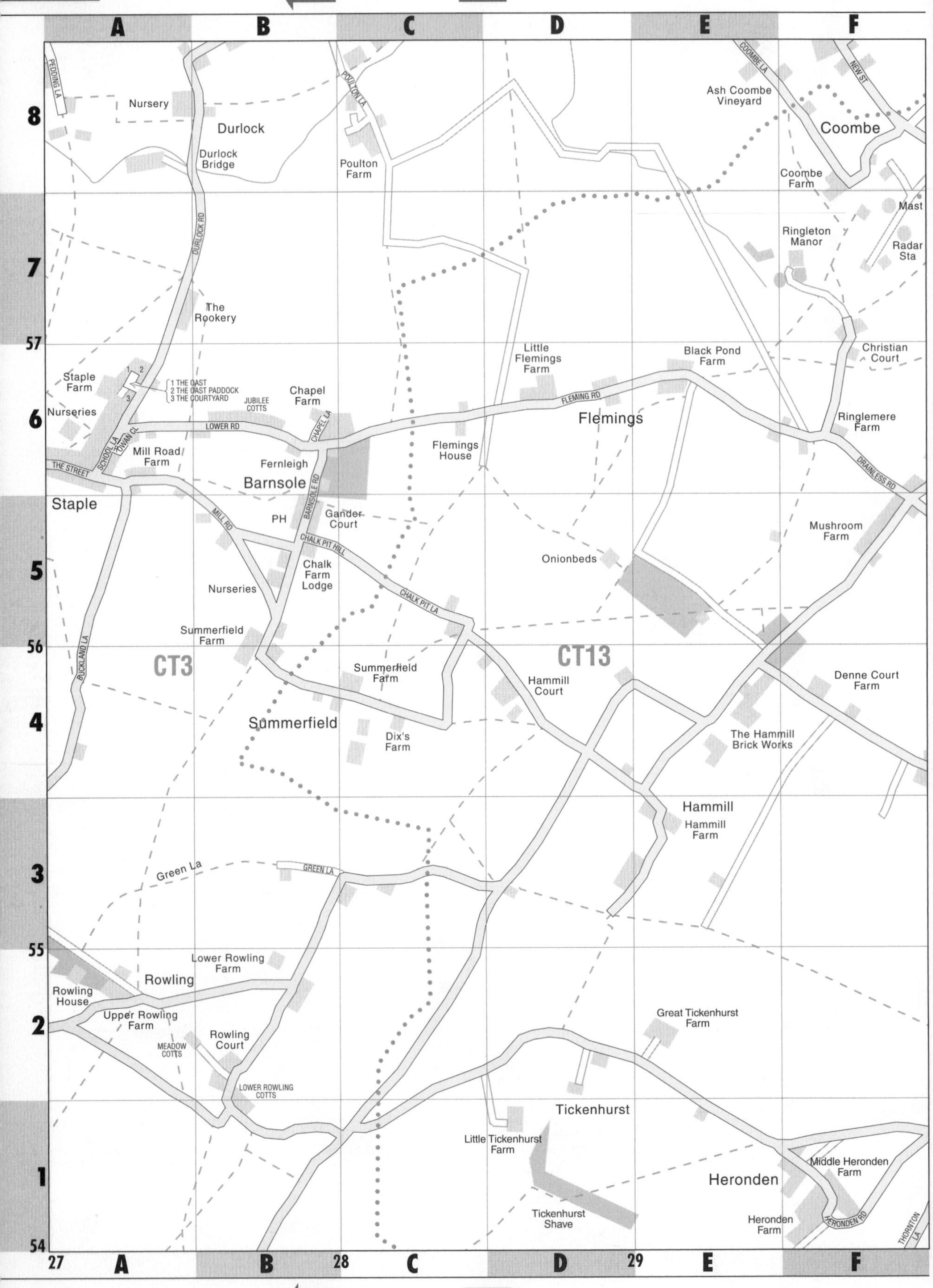
A
B
C
D
E
F
8
7
57
6
5
56
4
3
55
2
1
54
27
28
29
PEDDING LA
Nursery
Durlock
Durlock Bridge
POULTON LA
Poulton Farm
COOMBE LA
NEW ST
Ash Coombe Vineyard
Coombe
Coombe Farm
Mast
Ringleton Manor
Radar Sta
DURLOCK RD
The Rookery
Little Flemings Farm
Black Pond Farm
Christian Court
Staple Farm
1 THE OAST
2 THE OAST PADDOCK
3 THE COURTYARD
JUBILEE COTTS
Chapel Farm
FLEMING RD
Flemings
Ringlemere Farm
Nurseries
LOWER RD
CHAPEL LA
SCHOOL LA
LOWAN CL
Mill Road Farm
Flemings House
THE STREET
Fernleigh
Barnsole
DRAINLESS RD
Staple
MILL RD
BARNSOLE RD
PH
Gander Court
Mushroom Farm
CHALK PIT HILL
Chalk Farm Lodge
Onionbeds
Nurseries
CHALK PIT LA
Summerfield Farm
CT3
CT13
BUCKLAND LA
Summerfield Farm
Hammill Court
Denne Court Farm
Summerfield
Dix's Farm
The Hammill Brick Works
Hammill
Hammill Farm
Green La
GREEN LA
Lower Rowling Farm
Rowling
Rowling House
Upper Rowling Farm
Rowling Court
MEADOW COTTS
Great Tickenhurst Farm
LOWER ROWLING COTTS
Tickenhurst
Little Tickenhurst Farm
Middle Heronden Farm
Heronden
Tickenhurst Shave
Heronden Farm
HERONDEN RD
THORNTON LA

91
114

72
94

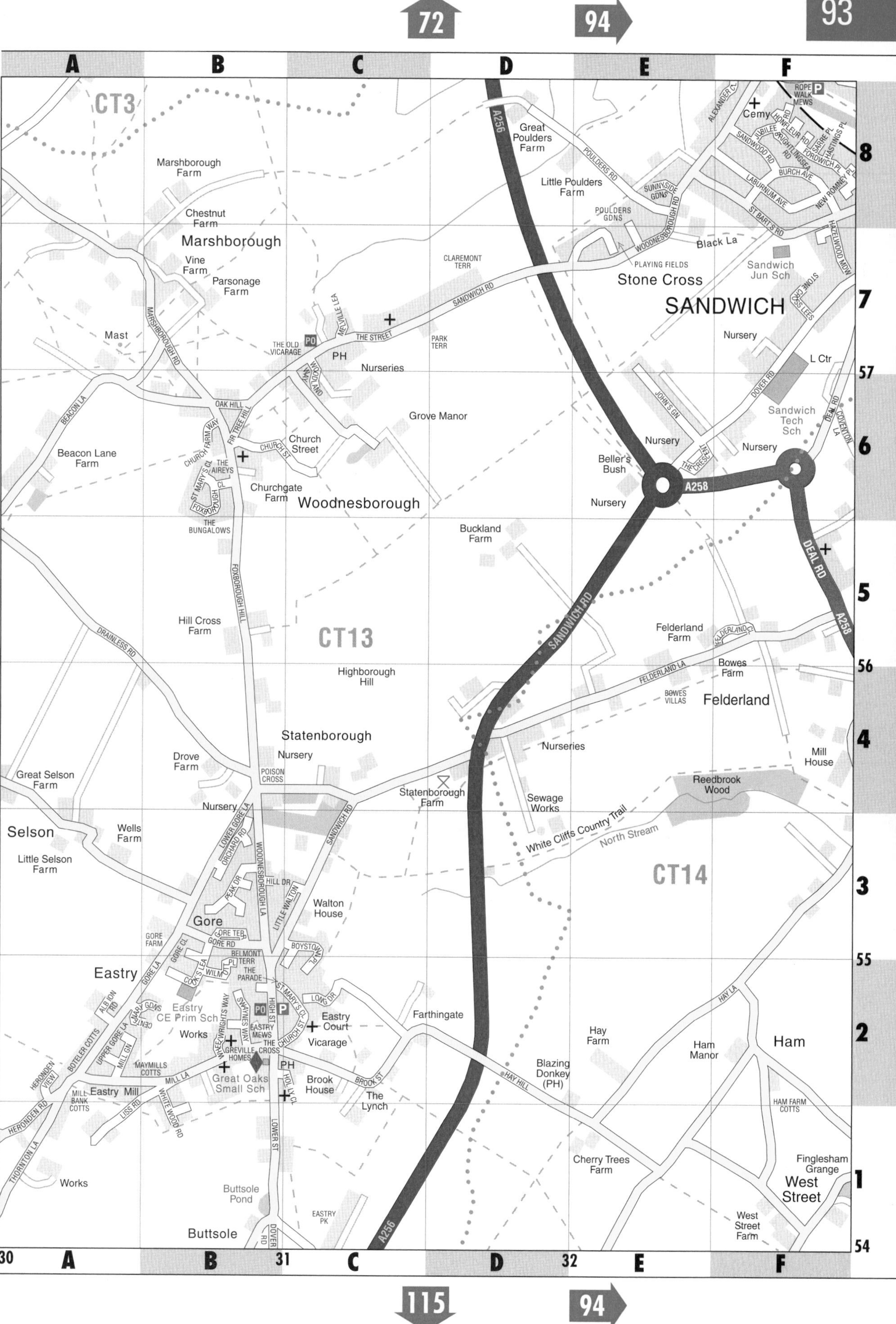
CT3
CT13
CT14
SANDWICH
Stone Cross
Marshborough
Marshborough Farm
Chestnut Farm
Vine Farm
Parsonage Farm
Mast
Beacon Lane Farm
Woodnesborough
Church Street
Churchgate Farm
Great Poulders Farm
Little Poulders Farm
Grove Manor
Nurseries
Buckland Farm
Beller's Bush
Nursery
Sandwich Jun Sch
Sandwich Tech Sch
L Ctr
Black La
Hill Cross Farm
Highborough Hill
Statenborough
Statenborough Farm
Drove Farm
Great Selson Farm
Selson
Little Selson Farm
Wells Farm
Felderland
Felderland Farm
Bowes Farm
Mill House
Reedbrook Wood
Sewage Works
White Cliffs Country Trail
North Stream
Gore
Eastry
Eastry CE Prim Sch
Works
Great Oaks Small Sch
Eastry Mill
Walton House
Eastry Court
Vicarage
Brook House
The Lynch
Farthingate
Hay Farm
Blazing Donkey (PH)
Ham Manor
Ham
Cherry Trees Farm
Finglesham Grange
West Street
West Street Farm
Buttsole Pond
Buttsole
A256
A258
SANDWICH RD
DEAL RD
DOVER RD
FELDERLAND LA
HAY HILL
HAY LA
DRAINLESS RD
FOXBOROUGH HILL
MARSHBOROUGH RD
BEACON LA
WOODNESBOROUGH LA
LOWER ST

115
94

93
73

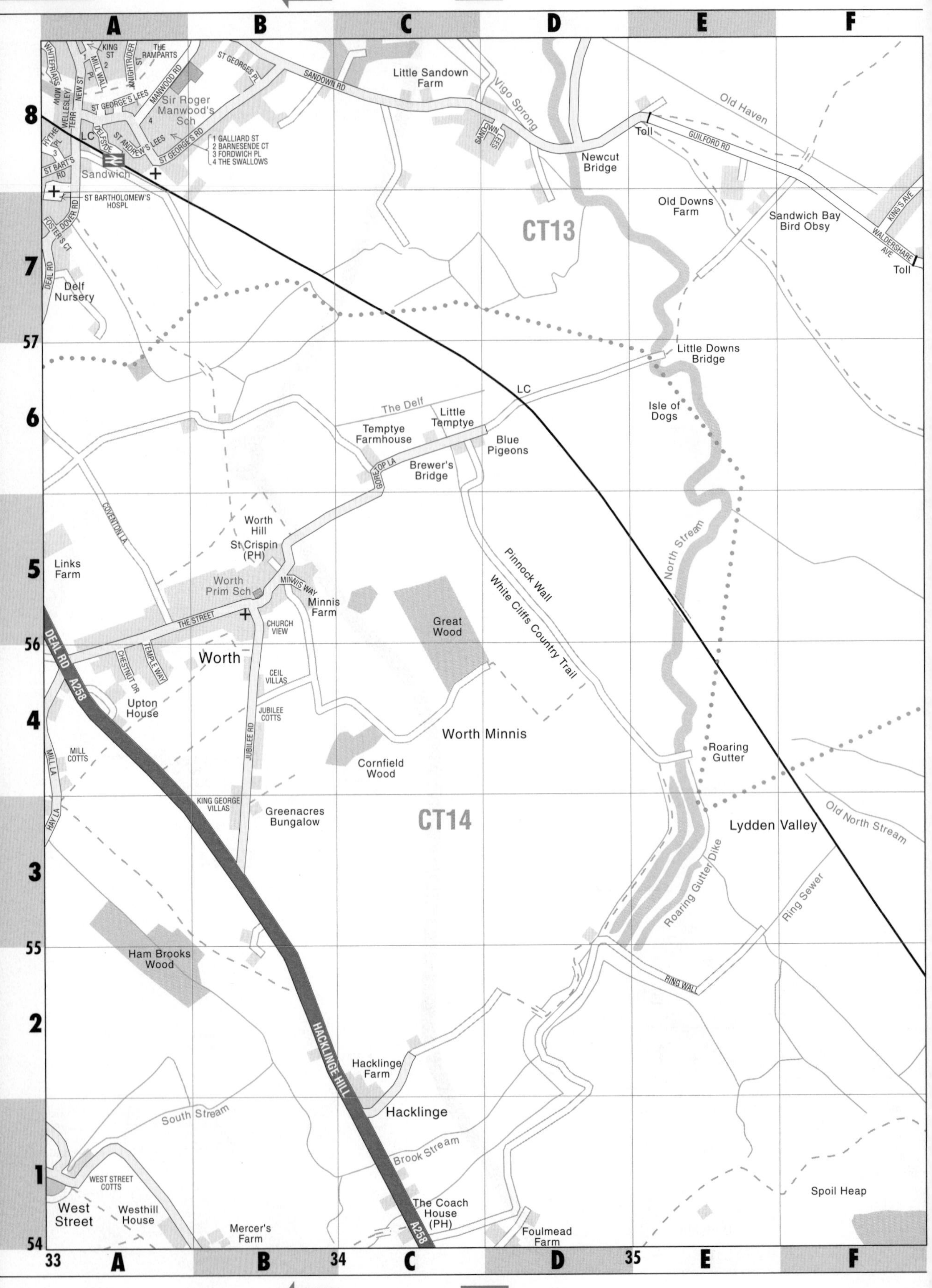
A
B
C
D
E
F
8
7
57
6
5
56
4
3
55
2
1
54
33
34
35
Little Sandown Farm
Sir Roger Manwood's Sch
Sandwich
ST BARTHOLOMEW'S HOSPL
1 GALLIARD ST
2 BARNESENDE CT
3 FORDWICH PL
4 THE SWALLOWS
SANDOWN RD
Vigo Sprong
Newcut Bridge
Old Haven
Toll
GUILFORD RD
Old Downs Farm
Sandwich Bay Bird Obsy
CT13
Delf Nursery
Little Downs Bridge
Isle of Dogs
The Delf
Little Temptye
Temptye Farmhouse
Blue Pigeons
Brewer's Bridge
Worth Hill
St Crispin (PH)
Links Farm
Worth Prim Sch
Minnis Farm
Great Wood
Pinnock Wall
White Cliffs Country Trail
North Stream
Worth
Upton House
Worth Minnis
Cornfield Wood
Roaring Gutter
Greenacres Bungalow
CT14
Lydden Valley
Old North Stream
Roaring Gutter Dike
Ring Sewer
Ham Brooks Wood
RING WALL
HACKLINGE HILL
A258
DEAL RD
Hacklinge Farm
Hacklinge
South Stream
Brook Stream
West Street
Westhill House
Mercer's Farm
The Coach House (PH)
Foulmead Farm
Spoil Heap

93
116

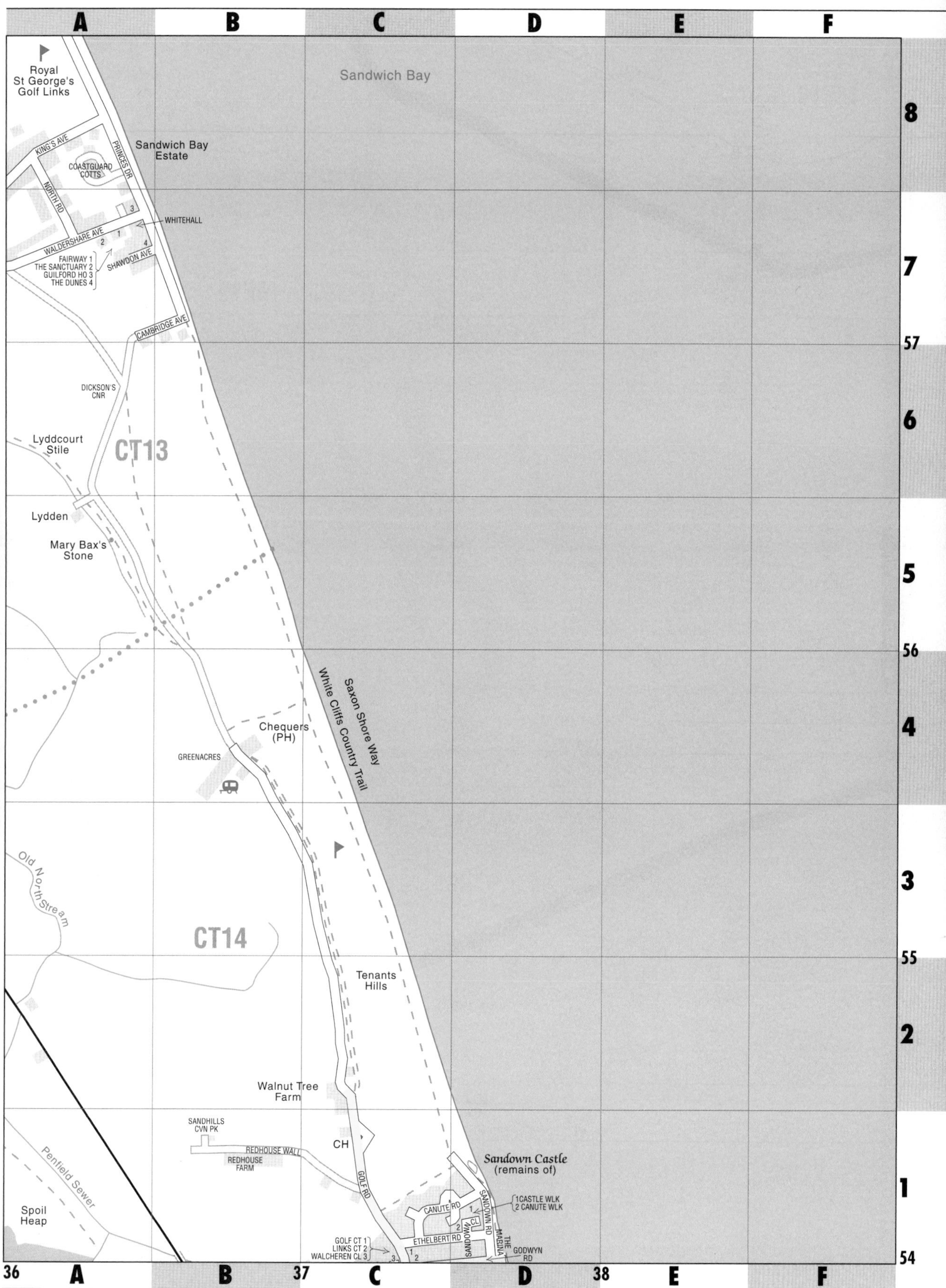

Royal
St George's
Golf Links

Sandwich Bay

KING'S AVE

Sandwich Bay
Estate

COASTGUARD
COTTS

PRINCES DR

NORTH RD

3

WHITEHALL

WALDERSHARE AVE

2   1   4

FAIRWAY 1
THE SANCTUARY 2
GUILFORD HO 3
THE DUNES 4

SHAWDON AVE

CAMBRIDGE AVE

57

DICKSON'S
CNR

6

Lyddcourt
Stile

CT13

Lydden

Mary Bax's
Stone

5

56

White Cliffs Country Trail

Saxon Shore Way

Chequers
(PH)

4

GREENACRES

Old North Stream

CT14

Tenants
Hills

55

2

Walnut Tree
Farm

SANDHILLS
CVN PK

REDHOUSE WALL

REDHOUSE
FARM

CH

GOLF RD

Sandown Castle
(remains of)

CASTLE WLK
CANUTE WLK

1

Penfield Sewer

CANUTE RD

SANDOWN RD

THE MARINA

1

CL

2

Spoil
Heap

GOLF CT 1
LINKS CT 2
WALCHEREN CL 3

ETHELBERT RD

3   1   2

SANDOWN
RD

GODWYN
RD

54

36   A   B   37   C   D   38   E   F

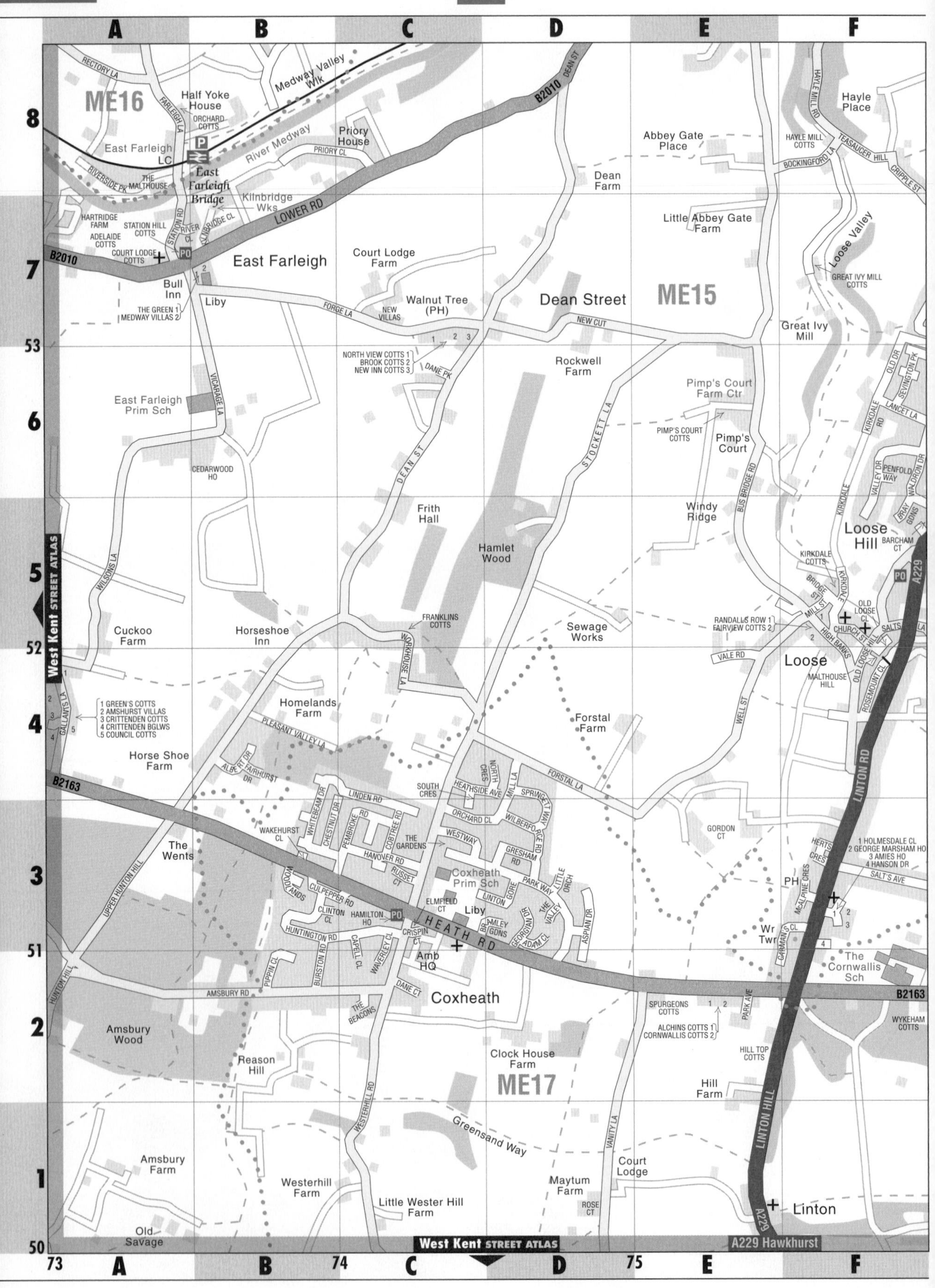
74
A
B
C
D
E
F
8
7
53
6
5
52
4
3
51
2
1
50
73
74
75
ME16
Half Yoke House
Medway Valley Wlk
Orchard Cotts
Priory House
East Farleigh
LC
River Medway
Priory Cl
East Farleigh Bridge
Kilnbridge Wks
Riverside Pk
The Malthouse
Hartridge Farm
Station Hill Cotts
Adelaide Cotts
Court Lodge Cotts
Lower Rd
B2010
East Farleigh
Court Lodge Farm
Bull Inn
Liby
The Green 1
Medway Villas 2
Forge La
New Villas
Walnut Tree (PH)
Dean Street
ME15
New Cut
Abbey Gate Place
Dean Farm
Little Abbey Gate Farm
Hayle Place
Hayle Mill Cotts
Bockingford La
Teasaucer Hill
Cripple St
Loose Valley
Great Ivy Mill Cotts
Great Ivy Mill
North View Cotts 1
Brook Cotts 2
New Inn Cotts 3
Dane Pk
Rockwell Farm
Pimp's Court Farm Ctr
Pimp's Court Cotts
Pimp's Court
East Farleigh Prim Sch
Vicarage La
Cedarwood Ho
Dean St
Stockett La
Bus Bridge Rd
Frith Hall
Windy Ridge
Hamlet Wood
Wilsons La
Loose Hill
Kirkdale Cotts
Barcham Ct
Cuckoo Farm
Horseshoe Inn
Franklins Cotts
Workhouse La
Sewage Works
Randalls Row 1
Fairview Cotts 2
Vale Rd
Loose
Malthouse Hill
Old Loose Cl
Church St
High Banks
Rosemount Cl
1 Green's Cotts
2 Amshurst Villas
3 Crittenden Cotts
4 Crittenden Bglws
5 Council Cotts
Gallants La
Homelands Farm
Pleasant Valley La
Forstal Farm
Well St
Horse Shoe Farm
Albert Dr
Fairhurst Dr
B2163
Linden Rd
South Cres
Heathside Ave
North Cres
Mill La
Springett Way
Forstal La
Linton Rd
A229
Wakehurst Cl
Whitebeam Dr
Chestnut Dr
Pembroke Rd
Cobtree Rd
The Gardens
Orchard Cl
Westway
Wilberforce Rd
Gresham Rd
Gordon Ct
1 Holmesdale Cl
2 George Marsham Ho
3 Amies Ho
4 Hanson Dr
Herts Cres
The Wents
Hanover Rd
Russet Ct
Coxheath Prim Sch
Park Way
Little Orch
Salt's Ave
PH
McAlpine Cres
Woodlands
Culpepper Rd
Elmfield Ct
Liby
Linton Gore
The Valley
Aspian Dr
Upper Hunton Hill
Clinton Cl
Hamilton Ho
PO
Heath Rd
Bramley Gdns
Georgian Dr
Adam Cl
Huntington Rd
Capell Cl
Waverley Cl
Crispin Ct
Wr Twr
Carmans Cl
The Cornwallis Sch
Hunton Hill
Pippin Cl
Burston Rd
Amb HQ
Dane Ct
Amsbury Rd
The Beacons
Coxheath
Spurgeons Cotts
Alchins Cotts 1
Cornwallis Cotts 2
Park Ave
Wykeham Cotts
Amsbury Wood
Reason Hill
Clock House Farm
ME17
Hill Top Cotts
Hill Farm
Westerhill Rd
Greensand Way
Vanity La
Linton Hill
Amsbury Farm
Westerhill Farm
Maytum Farm
Court Lodge
Little Wester Hill Farm
Rose Ct
Linton
Old Savage
West Kent STREET ATLAS
A229 Hawkhurst

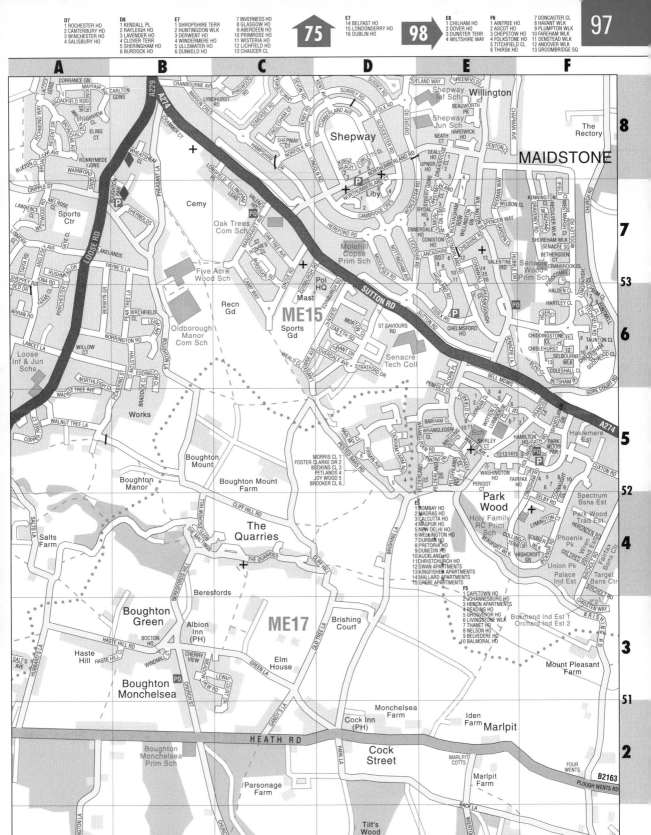

97
76

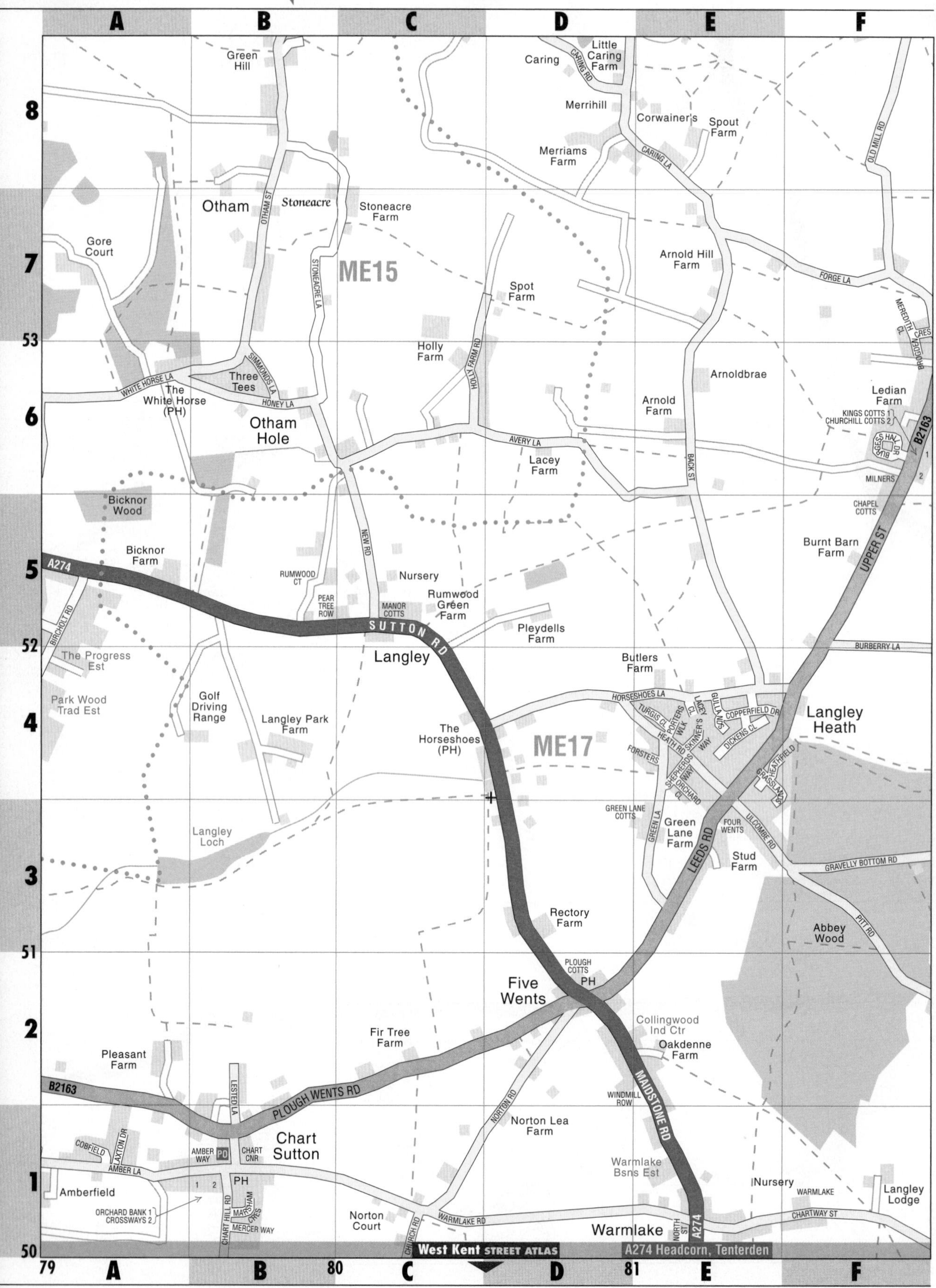
Green Hill
Caring
Little Caring Farm
Merrihill
Corwainer's
Spout Farm
Merriams Farm
Otham
Stoneacre
Stoneacre Farm
Gore Court
ME15
Arnold Hill Farm
Spot Farm
Holly Farm
Arnoldbrae
Three Tees
The White Horse (PH)
Otham Hole
Arnold Farm
Ledian Farm
Lacey Farm
Bicknor Wood
Bicknor Farm
Burnt Barn Farm
Nursery
Rumwood Green Farm
Pleydells Farm
Langley
Butlers Farm
The Progress Est
Park Wood Trad Est
Golf Driving Range
Langley Park Farm
The Horseshoes (PH)
ME17
Langley Heath
Langley Loch
Green Lane Farm
Stud Farm
Rectory Farm
Abbey Wood
Five Wents
Collingwood Ind Ctr
Oakdenne Farm
Fir Tree Farm
Pleasant Farm
Norton Lea Farm
Chart Sutton
Warmlake Bsns Est
Amberfield
Nursery
Langley Lodge
Norton Court
Warmlake
A274
B2163
SUTTON RD
PLOUGH WENTS RD
MAIDSTONE RD
LEEDS RD
UPPER ST
West Kent STREET ATLAS
A274 Headcorn, Tenterden

97

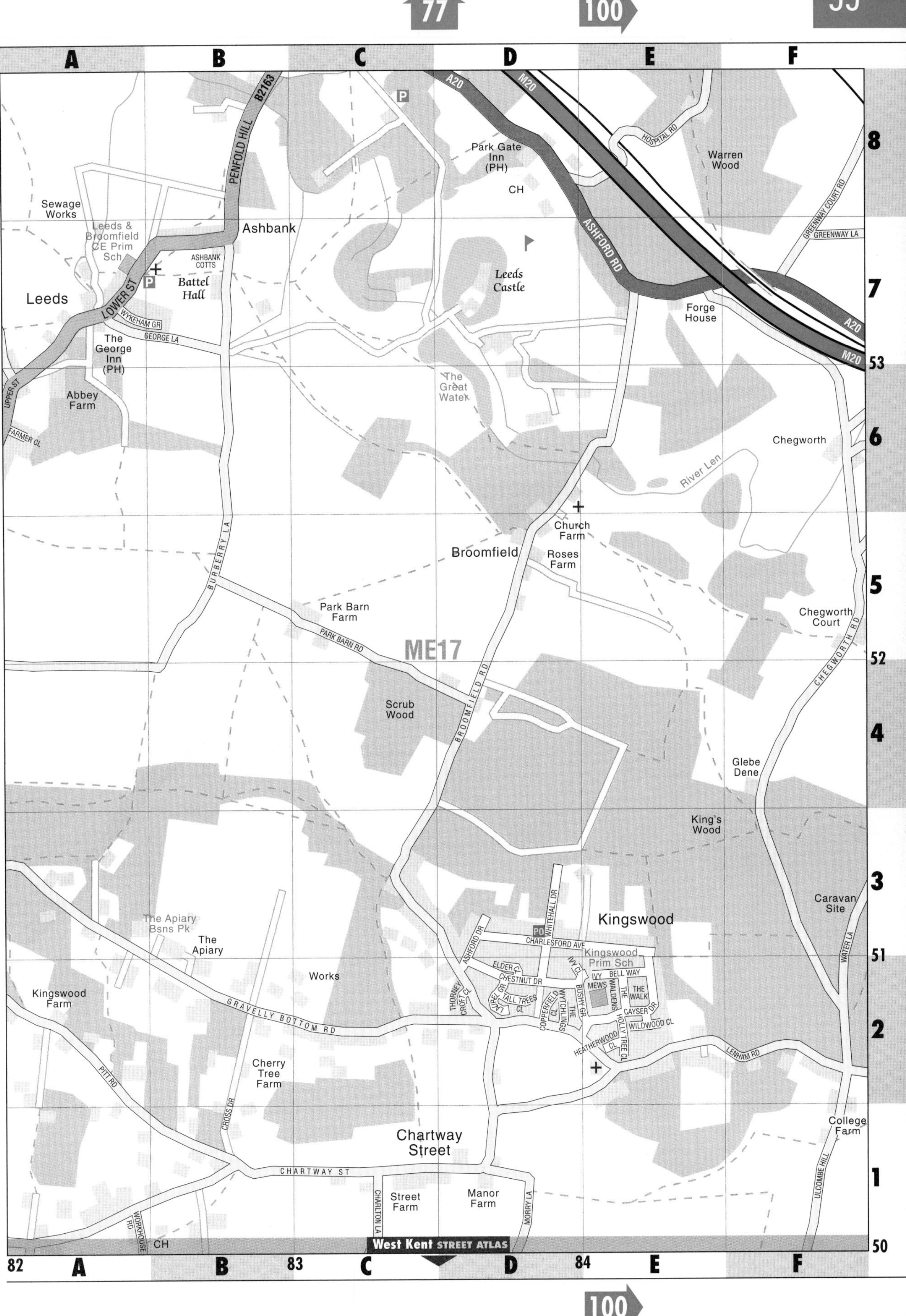

A B C D E F

8
7
53
6
5
52
4
3
51
2
1
50

Leeds

Sewage Works

Leeds & Broomfield CE Prim Sch

Ashbank

ASHBANK COTTS

Battel Hall

The George Inn (PH)

Abbey Farm

PENFOLD HILL

B2163

LOWER ST

WYKEHAM GR

GEORGE LA

UPPER ST

FARMER CL

BURBERRY LA

Park Gate Inn (PH)

CH

Leeds Castle

ASHFORD RD

A20

M20

HOSPITAL RD

Warren Wood

GREENWAY LA

GREENWAY COURT RD

Forge House

A20

M20

The Great Water

Chegworth

River Len

Church Farm

Broomfield

Roses Farm

Park Barn Farm

PARK BARN RD

Chegworth Court

CHEGWORTH RD

ME17

Scrub Wood

BROOMFIELD RD

Glebe Dene

King's Wood

Caravan Site

The Apiary Bsns Pk

The Apiary

Works

Kingswood Farm

GRAVELLY BOTTOM RD

WHITEHALL DR

PO

CHARLESFORD AVE

ASHFORD DR

THORNEY

CROFT CL

ELDER CL

CHESTNUT DR

LACEY CL

TALL TREES CL

COPPERFIELD CL

THE WYCHLINGS

BUSHY GR

IVY CL

IVY

Kingswood

Kingswood Prim Sch

BELL WAY

MEWS

THE WALDENS

THE WALK

CAYSER DR

WILDWOOD CL

HEATHERWOOD

HOLT TREE CL

LENHAM RD

WATER LA

College Farm

ULCOMBE HILL

PITT RD

CROSS DR

Cherry Tree Farm

Chartway Street

CHARTWAY ST

CHARLTON LA

Street Farm

Manor Farm

MORRY LA

WORKHOUSE RD

CH

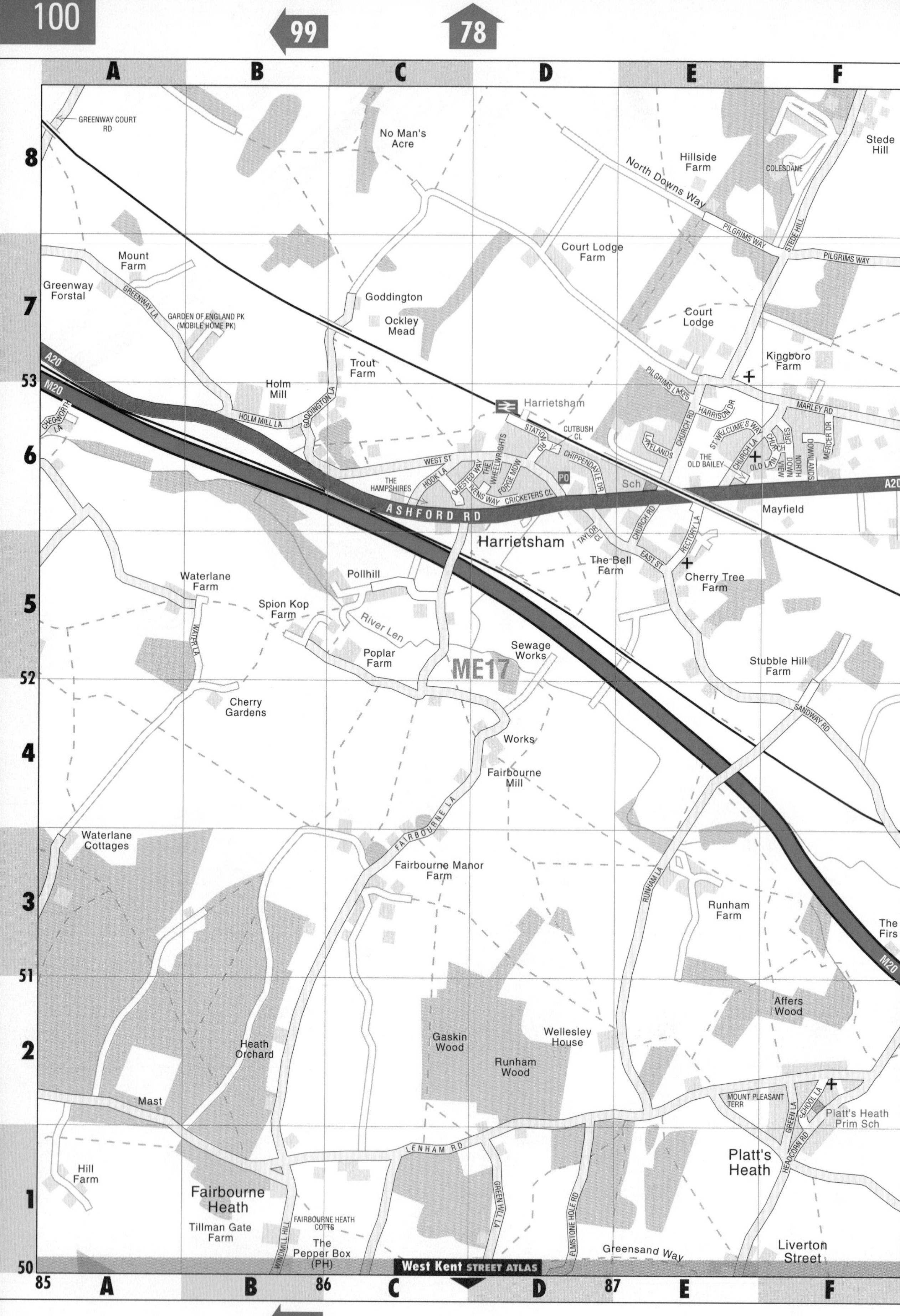

A **B** **C** **D** **E** **F**

8

Greenway Court RD

Stede Hill

No Man's Acre

North Downs Way

Hillside Farm

COLESDANE

Court Lodge Farm

PILGRIMS WAY

STEDE HILL

7

Mount Farm

Greenway Forstal

GREENWAY LA

Garden of England PK (MOBILE HOME PK)

Goddington

Ockley Mead

Court Lodge

PILGRIMS WAY

Kingboro Farm

MARLEY RD

A20

Trout Farm

Holm Mill

HOLM MILL LA

GODDINGTON LA

PILGRIMS (MCE'S

CHURCH RD

HARRISON DR

ST WLCOME'S WAY

OLD LA

MERCER DR

DOWNSLAND

53

M20

CHEGWORTH LA

Harrietsham

STATION RD

CUTBUSH CL

CHIPPENDAYLE DR

KELANDS

The Old Bailey

OLD LA

HUBON

6

WEST ST

HOOK LA

QUESTED WAY

THE WHEELWRIGHTS

FORGE MDW

PO

Sch

A20

THE HAMPSHIRES

KENS WAY

CRICKETERS CL

Mayfield

ASHFORD RD

Harrietsham

TAYLOR CL

CHURCH RD

EAST ST

RECTORY LA

Waterlane Farm

Pollhill

The Bell Farm

Cherry Tree Farm

5

Spion Kop Farm

River Len

Sewage Works

Stubble Hill Farm

WATER LA

Poplar Farm

ME17

SANDWAY RD

52

Cherry Gardens

Works

Fairbourne Mill

4

FAIRBOURNE LA

RUNHAM LA

Runham Farm

The Firs

3

Waterlane Cottages

Fairbourne Manor Farm

Runham Farm

M20

51

Affers Wood

Heath Orchard

Gaskin Wood

Wellesley House

MOUNT PLEASANT TERR

SCHOOL LA

Platt's Heath Prim Sch

2

Mast

Runham Wood

GREEN LA

HEADCORN RD

Platt's Heath

Hill Farm

LENHAM RD

GREEN HILL LA

ELMSTONE HOLE RD

Liverton Street

1

Fairbourne Heath

Tillman Gate Farm

WINDMILL HILL

FAIRBOURNE HEATH COTTS

The Pepper Box (PH)

Greensand Way

50

85 **A** **86** **B** **C** **86** **D** **87** **E** **F**

79
102

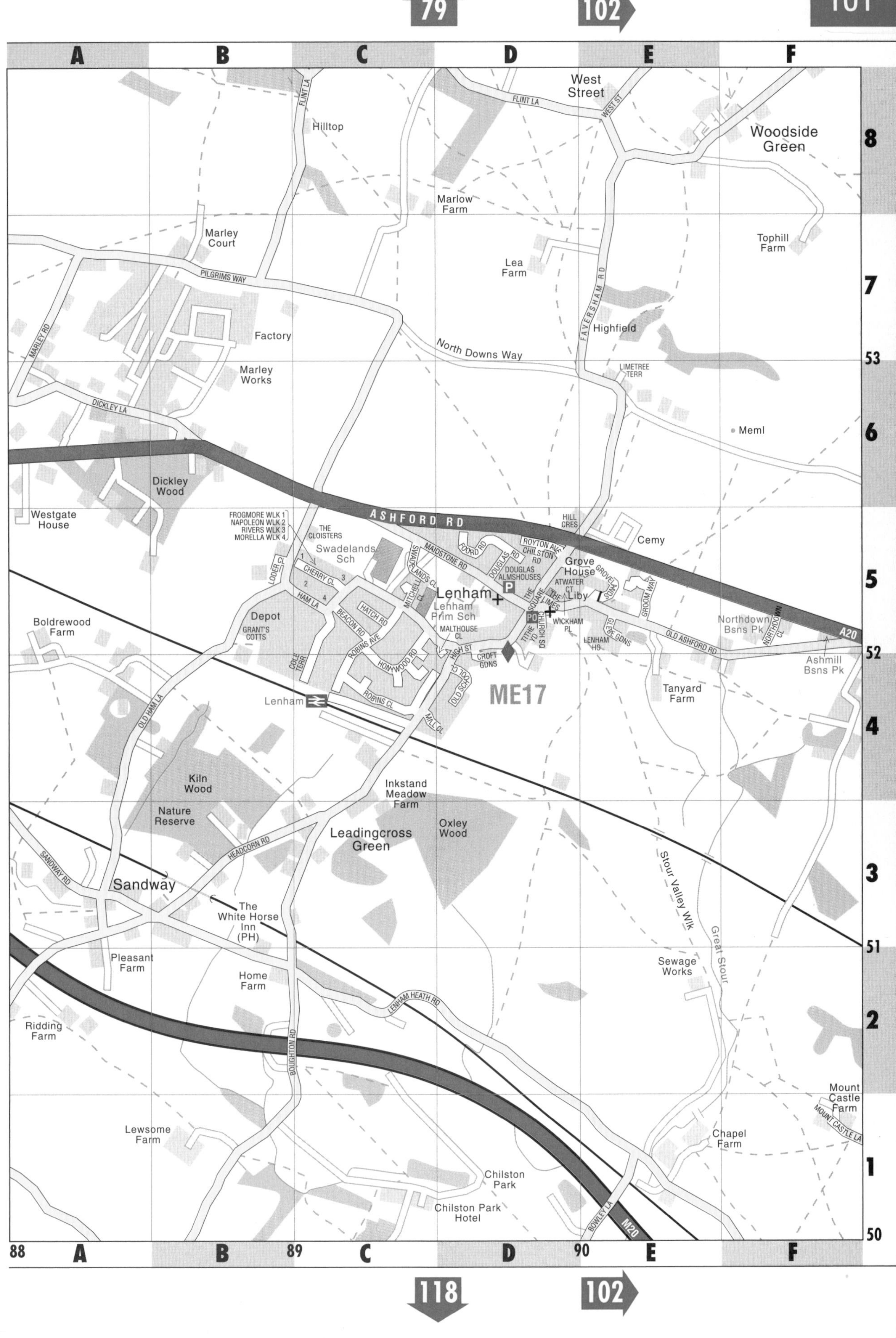
A
B
C
D
E
F
West Street
FLINT LA
WEST ST
Hilltop
Woodside Green
8
Marlow Farm
Marley Court
Tophill Farm
Lea Farm
PILGRIMS WAY
7
FAVERSHAM RD
Highfield
Factory
MARLEY RD
North Downs Way
53
LIMETREE TERR
Marley Works
DICKLEY LA
Meml
6
Dickley Wood
Westgate House
ASHFORD RD
HILL CRES
FROGMORE WLK 1
NAPOLEON WLK 2
RIVERS WLK 3
MORELLA WLK 4
THE CLOISTERS
Swadelands Sch
Cemy
ROYTON AVE
CHILSTON RD
Grove House
FOORD RD
MAIDSTONE RD
DOUGLAS RD
DOUGLAS ALMSHOUSES
LODER CL
CHERRY CL
GROVELANDS
GROOM WAY
5
MITCHELL CL
Lenham
ATWATER CT
Liby
HAM LA
Lenham Prim Sch
THE SQUARE
THE LIMES
Depot
HATCH RD
PO
CHURCH SQ
WICKHAM PL
Northdown Bsns Pk
NORTHDOWN CL
Boldrewood Farm
GRANT'S COTTS
BEACON RD
MALTHOUSE CL
TITHE YD
GLEBE GDNS
LENHAM HO
OLD ASHFORD RD
A20
ROBINS AVE
HONYWOOD RD
HIGH ST
CROFT GDNS
52
COLE TERR
Ashmill Bsns Pk
Tanyard Farm
OLD SCH CL
ME17
Lenham
ROBINS CL
OLD HAM LA
MILL CL
4
Kiln Wood
Inkstand Meadow Farm
Nature Reserve
Oxley Wood
Leadingcross Green
HEADCORN RD
SANDWAY RD
Stour Valley Wlk
Sandway
3
The White Horse Inn (PH)
Great Stour
51
Pleasant Farm
Sewage Works
Home Farm
LENHAM HEATH RD
Ridding Farm
2
BOUGHTON RD
Mount Castle Farm
MOUNT CASTLE LA
Lewsome Farm
Chapel Farm
1
Chilston Park
Chilston Park Hotel
BOWLEY LA
M20
50
88
89
90

118
102

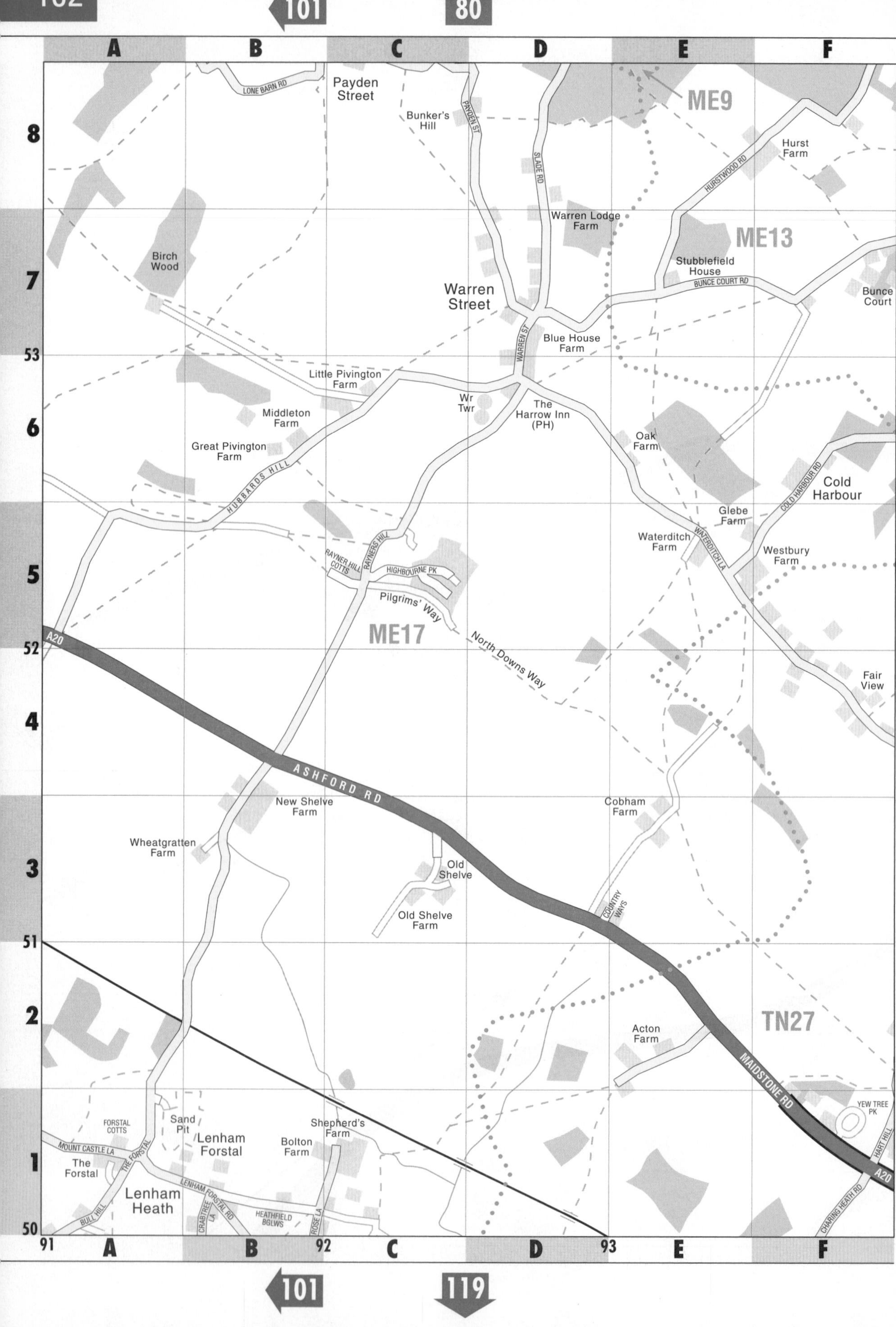

A B C D E F

8

7

53

6

5

52

4

3

51

2

50

A B C D E F

91 92 93

Lone Barn Rd
Payden Street
Bunker's Hill
Payden St
Slade Rd
Hurstwood Rd
ME9
Hurst Farm
ME13
Warren Lodge Farm
Stubblefield House
Bunce Court Rd
Bunce Court
Birch Wood
Warren Street
Blue House Farm
Warren St
Little Pivington Farm
Middleton Farm
Wr Twr
The Harrow Inn (PH)
Oak Farm
Great Pivington Farm
Hubbards Hill
Cold Harbour Rd
Cold Harbour
Glebe Farm
Rayner Hill Cotts
Raynes Hill
Highbourne Pk
Waterditch Farm
Waterditch La
Westbury Farm
Pilgrims' Way
ME17
North Downs Way
Fair View
A20
Ashford Rd
New Shelve Farm
Cobham Farm
Wheatgratten Farm
Old Shelve
Country Ways
Old Shelve Farm
Maidstone Rd
TN27
Acton Farm
Yew Tree Pk
Hart Hill
Forstal Cotts
Sand Pit
Shepherd's Farm
Mount Castle La
The Forstal
Lenham Forstal
Bolton Farm
A20
The Forstal
Lenham Forstal Rd
Crabtree La
Heathfield Bglws
Rise La
Charing Heath Rd
Bull Hill
Lenham Heath

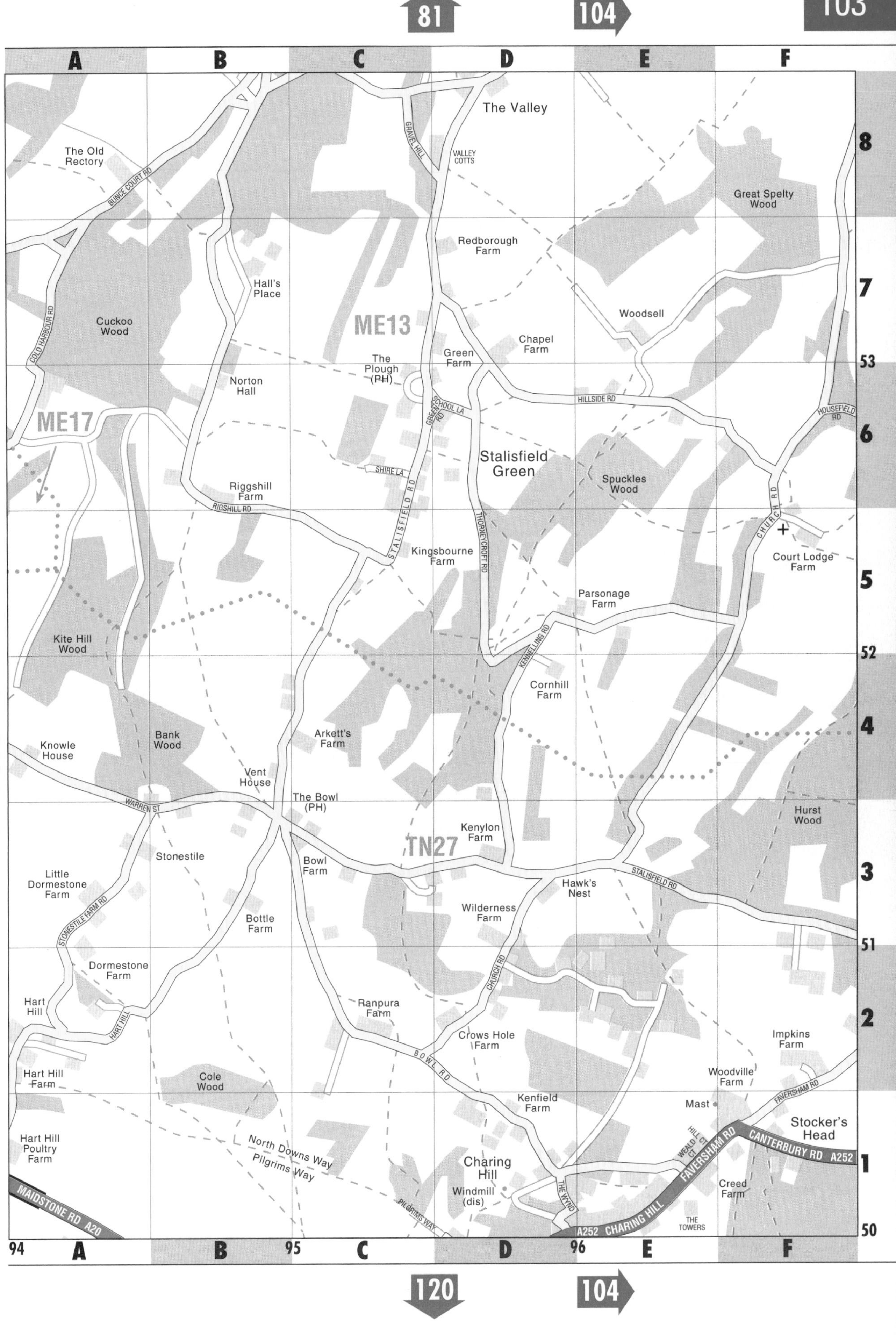
A
B
C
D
E
F
The Valley
The Old Rectory
BUNCE COURT RD
GRAVEL HILL
VALLEY COTTS
Great Spelty Wood
Redborough Farm
Hall's Place
Cuckoo Wood
COLD HARBOUR RD
ME13
Woodsell
Chapel Farm
Green Farm
The Plough (PH)
Norton Hall
ME17
SCHOOL LA
GREEN RD
HILLSIDE RD
HOUSEFIELD RD
Stalisfield Green
SHIRE LA
Spuckles Wood
Riggshill Farm
RIGGSHILL RD
STALISFIELD RD
THORNEYCROFT RD
CHURCH RD
Kingsbourne Farm
Court Lodge Farm
Parsonage Farm
Kite Hill Wood
KENNELLING RD
Cornhill Farm
Knowle House
Bank Wood
Arkett's Farm
Vent House
The Bowl (PH)
WARREN ST
Hurst Wood
Kenylon Farm
Stonestile
TN27
Little Dormestone Farm
Bowl Farm
Hawk's Nest
STALISFIELD RD
STONESTILE FARM RD
Bottle Farm
Wilderness Farm
Dormestone Farm
CHURCH RD
Hart Hill
HART HILL
Ranpura Farm
Crows Hole Farm
Impkins Farm
BOWL RD
Hart Hill Farm
Cole Wood
Woodville Farm
Kenfield Farm
FAVERSHAM RD
Mast
Stocker's Head
Hart Hill Poultry Farm
North Downs Way
Pilgrims Way
HILL CT
WEALD CT
FAVERSHAM RD
CANTERBURY RD A252
Charing Hill
Creed Farm
Windmill (dis)
MAIDSTONE RD A20
PILGRIMS WAY
THE WYND
A252 CHARING HILL
THE TOWERS
8
7
53
6
5
52
4
3
51
2
1
50
94
95
96

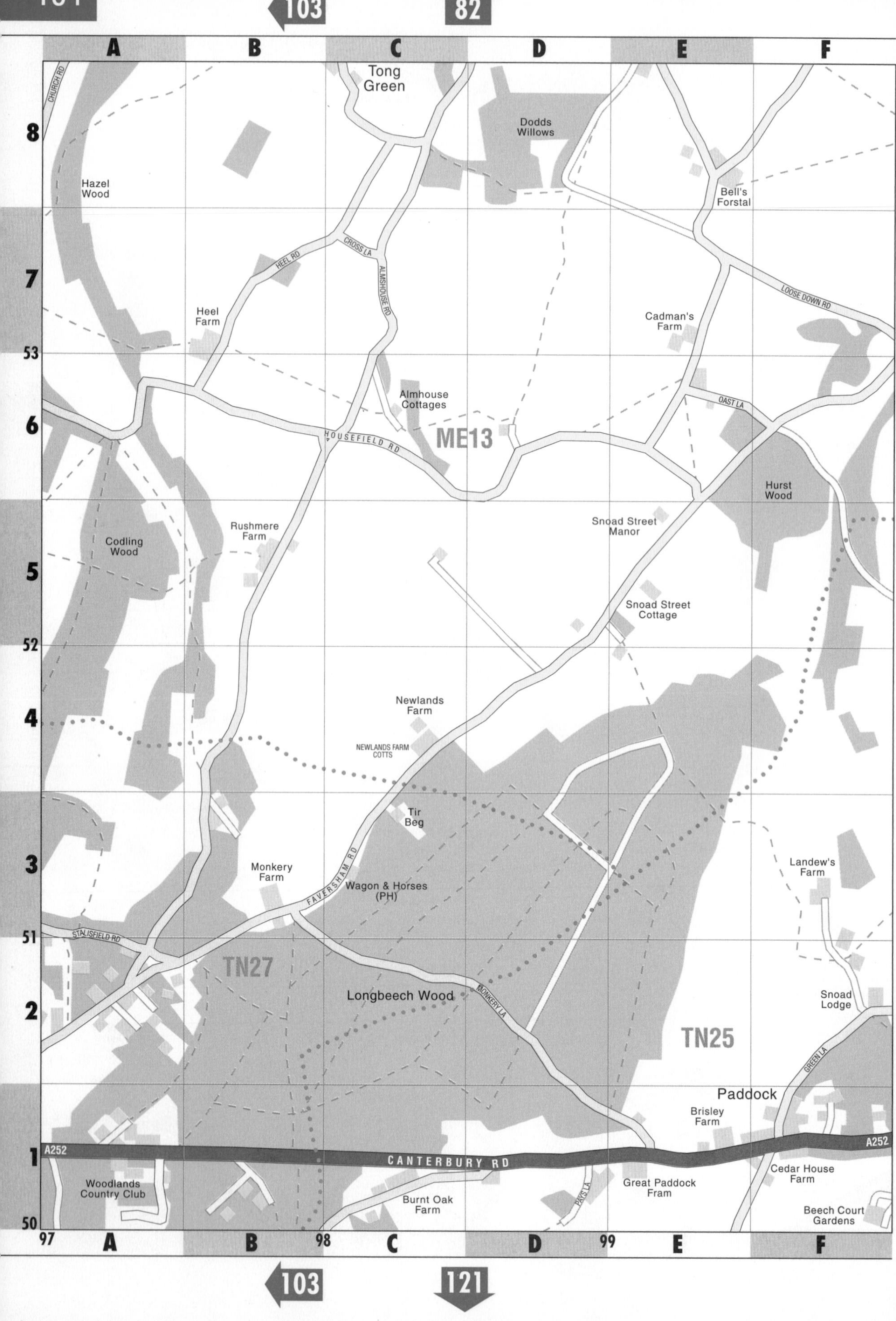

A   B   C   D   E   F

Tong
Green

Dodds
Willows

8

Hazel
Wood

Bell's
Forstal

7

CROSS LA

HEEL RD

ALMSHOUSE RD

LOOSE DOWN RD

Heel
Farm

Cadman's
Farm

53

OAST LA

Almhouse
Cottages

6

HOUSEFIELD RD

ME13

Hurst
Wood

Rushmere
Farm

Snoad Street
Manor

Codling
Wood

5

Snoad Street
Cottage

52

Newlands
Farm

4

NEWLANDS FARM
COTTS

Tir
Beg

Landew's
Farm

3

Monkery
Farm

FAVERSHAM RD

Wagon & Horses
(PH)

STALISFIELD RD

51

TN27

Snoad
Lodge

Longbeech Wood

MONKERY LA

2

TN25

Paddock

GREEN LA

Brisley
Farm

A252

1

A252

CANTERBURY RD

Cedar House
Farm

Woodlands
Country Club

Burnt Oak
Farm

PARK LA

Great Paddock
Fram

Beech Court
Gardens

50

97   A   B   98   C   D   99   E   F

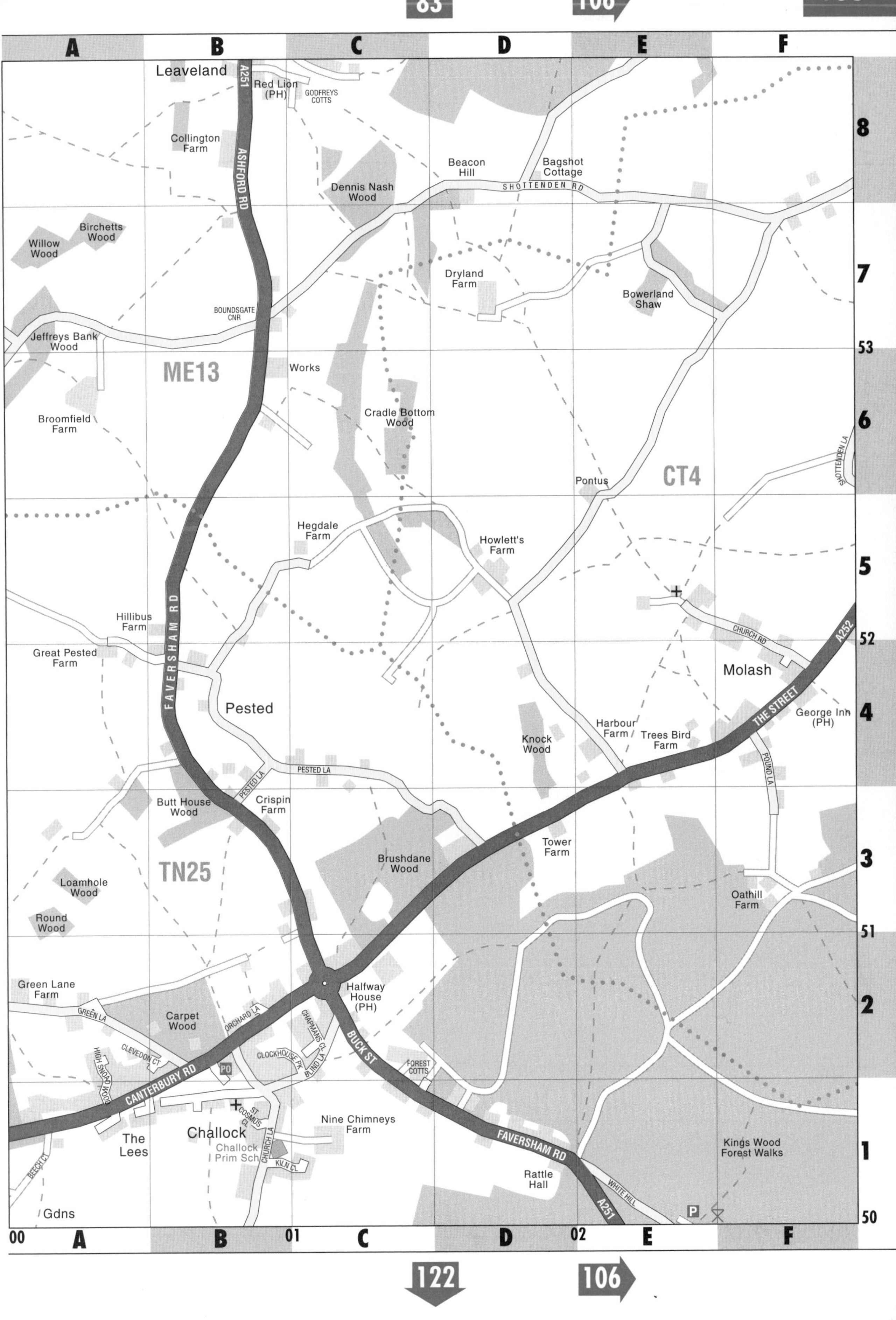
A
B
C
D
E
F
Leaveland
A251
Red Lion (PH)
GODFREYS COTTS
Collington Farm
ASHFORD RD
Beacon Hill
Bagshot Cottage
SHOTTENDEN RD
Dennis Nash Wood
Birchetts Wood
Willow Wood
Dryland Farm
Bowerland Shaw
BOUNDSGATE CNR
Jeffreys Bank Wood
ME13
Works
Broomfield Farm
Cradle Bottom Wood
Pontus
CT4
SHOTTENDEN LA
Hegdale Farm
Howlett's Farm
Hillibus Farm
Great Pested Farm
FAVERSHAM RD
CHURCH RD
A252
Molash
Pested
Harbour Farm
Trees Bird Farm
Knock Wood
THE STREET
George Inn (PH)
POUND LA
PESTED LA
Butt House Wood
Crispin Farm
Tower Farm
Brushdane Wood
TN25
Loamhole Wood
Oathill Farm
Round Wood
Green Lane Farm
Halfway House (PH)
GREEN LA
Carpet Wood
ORCHARD LA
CHAPMANS CL
BUCK ST
CLEVEDON CT
HIGH SNOAD WOOD
CLOCKHOUSE PK
BLIND LA
FOREST COTTS
CANTERBURY RD
PO
ST COSMUS CL
Nine Chimneys Farm
FAVERSHAM RD
The Lees
Challock
Challock Prim Sch
CHURCH LA
KILN CL
Kings Wood Forest Walks
Rattle Hall
BEECH CL
WHITE HILL
A251
P
Gdns
8
7
53
6
5
52
4
3
51
2
1
50
00
01
02

A **B** **C** **D** **E** **F**

8

Chequers Farm

SHOTTENDEN RD

Little Hurst Wood

Harts Farm

DENNE MANOR LA

Dolfinch Wood

Great Hurst Wood

Maggrllyden

7

Little Bower

SHOTTENDEN LA

Wytherling Court

Denne Manor Farm

Danecourt Shaw

Pigeonhouse Wood

Dane Court

A252

53

Great Bower

CT4

Old Park Shaw

Dane Street

6

Flemings

Park Wood

Young Manor Farm

SHOTTENDEN LA

Ridge Wood

5

A252

Stanners Wood

Cutlers

Cutlers Wood

52

Coppins Farm

4

Godmersham Park

3

North Downs Way

51

King's Wood

2

Godmersham Downs

1

TN25

50

03 **A** **B** 04 **C** **D** 05 **E** **F**

85
108

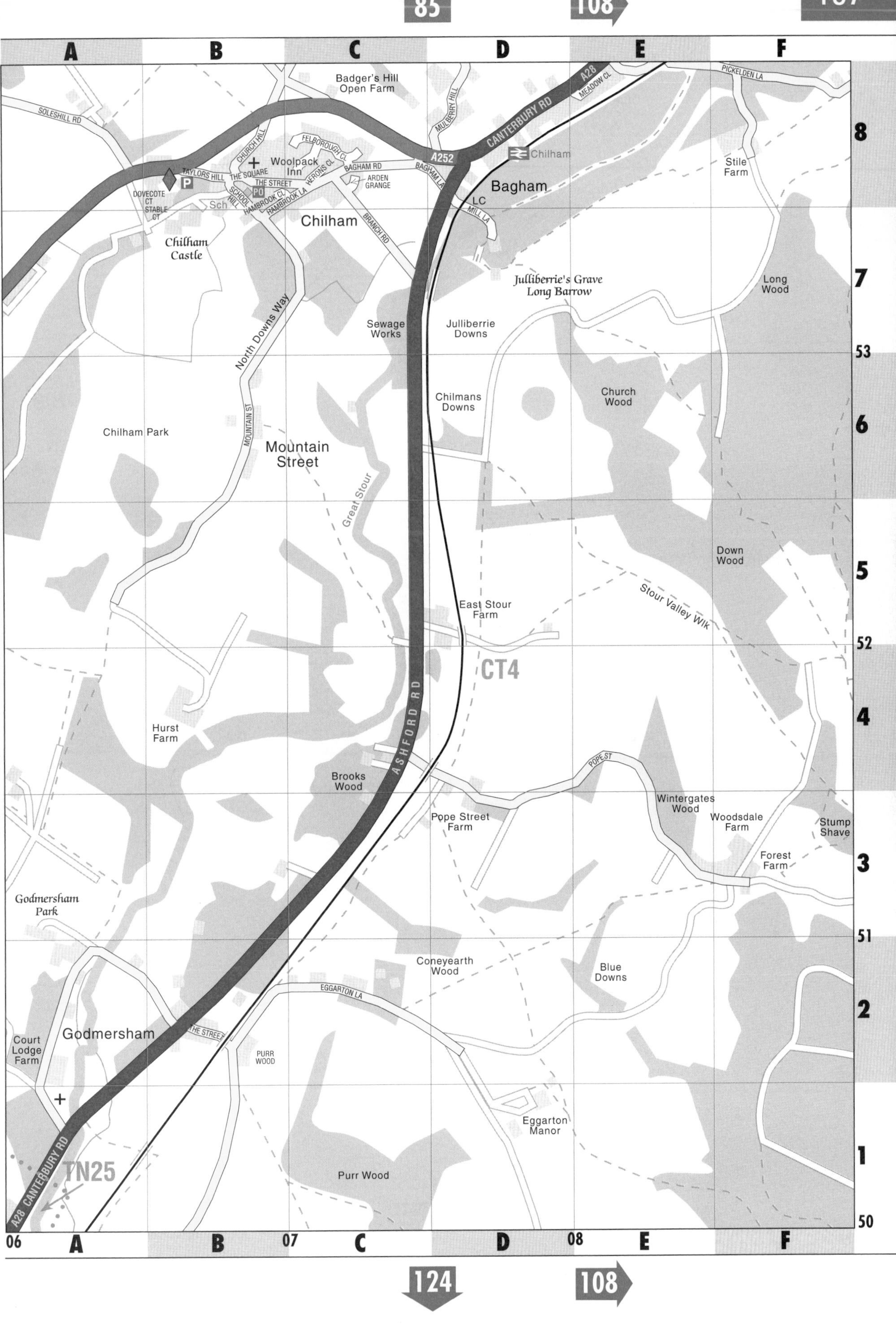
A
B
C
D
E
F
8
7
53
6
5
52
4
3
51
2
1
50
06
07
08
Badger's Hill
Open Farm
SOLESHILL RD
MULBERRY HILL
CANTERBURY RD
A28
MEADOW CL
PICKELDEN LA
A252
Chilham
Bagham
Stile
Farm
FELBOROUGH CL
CHURCH HILL
Woolpack
Inn
HERONS CL
BAGHAM RD
BAGHAM LA
TAYLORS HILL
THE SQUARE
THE STREET
PO
ARDEN
GRANGE
DOVECOTE
CT
STABLE
CT
SCHOOL
HILL
Sch
HAMBROOK CL
HAMBROOK LA
LC
MILL LA
Chilham
BRANCH RD
Chilham
Castle
Julliberrie's Grave
Long Barrow
Long
Wood
Sewage
Works
Julliberrie
Downs
North Downs Way
Chilmans
Downs
Church
Wood
MOUNTAIN ST
Chilham Park
Mountain
Street
Great Stour
Down
Wood
East Stour
Farm
Stour Valley Wlk
CT4
ASHFORD RD
Hurst
Farm
POPE ST
Brooks
Wood
Wintergates
Wood
Woodsdale
Farm
Stump
Shave
Pope Street
Farm
Forest
Farm
Godmersham
Park
Coneyearth
Wood
Blue
Downs
EGGARTON LA
THE STREET
Godmersham
Court
Lodge
Farm
PURR
WOOD
Eggarton
Manor
CANTERBURY RD
A28
TN25
Purr Wood

124
108

107
86

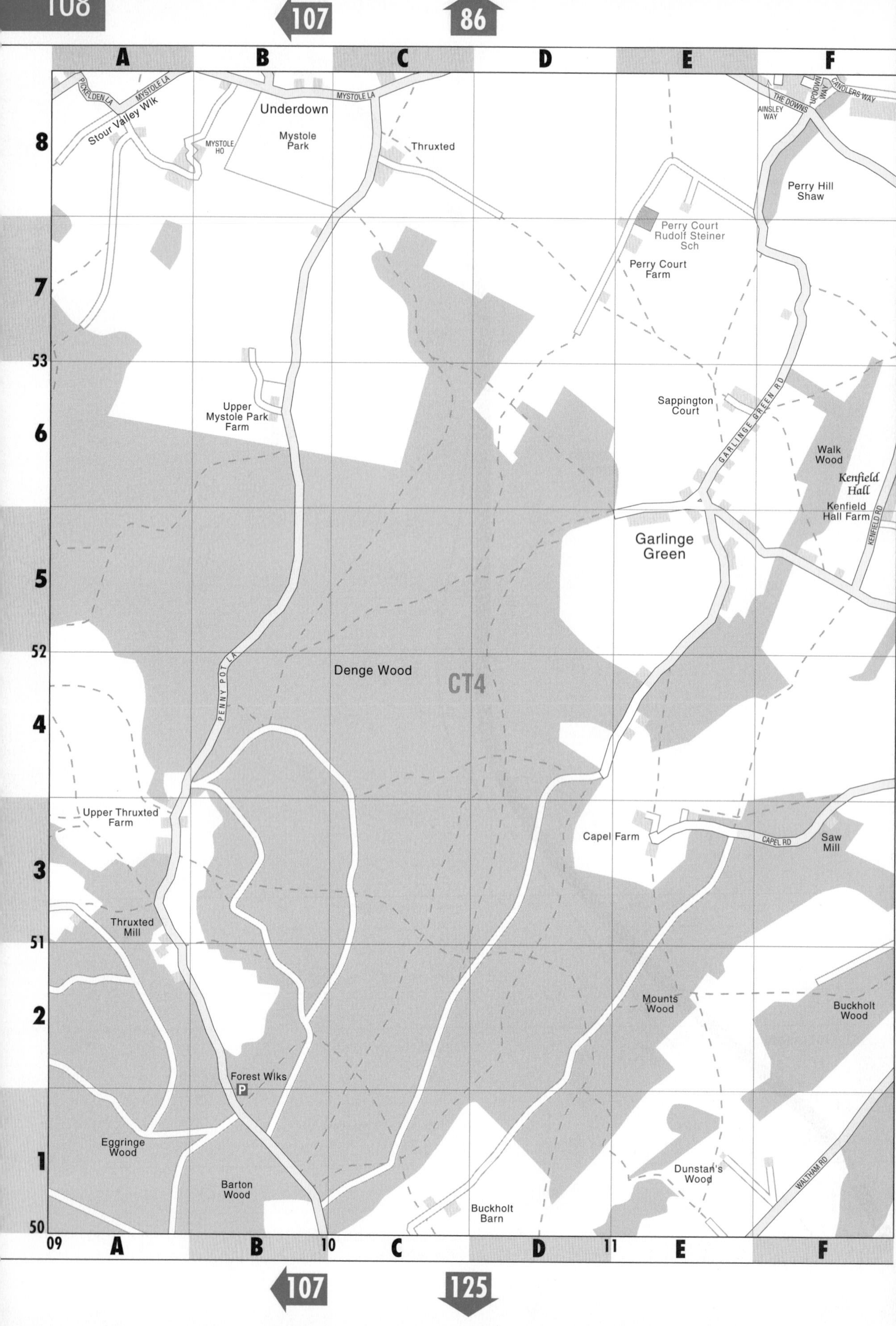
A
B
C
D
E
F
PICKELDEN LA
MYSTOLE LA
Stour Valley Wlk
Underdown
MYSTOLE HO
Mystole Park
Thruxted
THE DOWNS
AINSLEY WAY
UPDOWN WAY
CANDLERS WAY
Perry Hill Shaw
Perry Court Rudolf Steiner Sch
Perry Court Farm
8
7
53
6
Upper Mystole Park Farm
Sappington Court
GARLINGE GREEN RD
Walk Wood
Kenfield Hall
Kenfield Hall Farm
KENFIELD RD
Garlinge Green
5
52
Denge Wood
CT4
PENNY POT LA
4
Upper Thruxted Farm
Capel Farm
CAPEL RD
Saw Mill
3
Thruxted Mill
51
2
Mounts Wood
Buckholt Wood
Forest Wlks
P
Eggringe Wood
1
Barton Wood
Dunstan's Wood
WALTHAM RD
Buckholt Barn
50
09
10
11

107
125

87
110

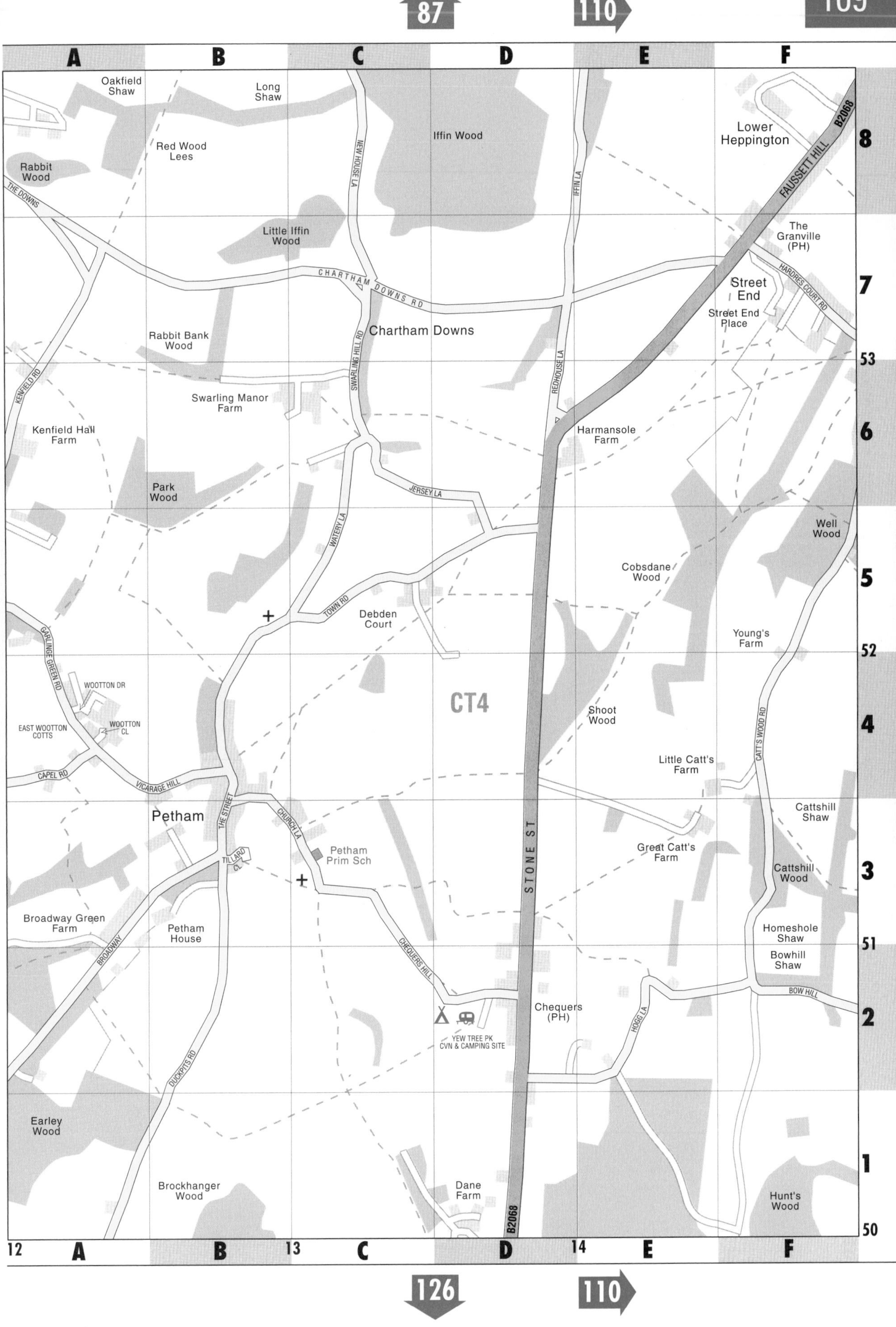
A
B
C
D
E
F
Oakfield Shaw
Long Shaw
Iffin Wood
Lower Heppington
B2068
Rabbit Wood
Red Wood Lees
NEW HOUSE LA
IFFIN LA
FAUSSETT HILL
THE DOWNS
Little Iffin Wood
The Granville (PH)
CHARTHAM DOWNS RD
Street End
HARDRES COURT RD
Street End Place
Rabbit Bank Wood
Chartham Downs
SWARLING HILL RD
REDHOUSE LA
KENFIELD RD
Swarling Manor Farm
Kenfield Hall Farm
Harmansole Farm
Park Wood
JERSEY LA
WATERY LA
Well Wood
Cobsdane Wood
TOWN RD
Debden Court
Young's Farm
GARLINGE GREEN RD
WOOTTON DR
CT4
EAST WOOTTON COTTS
WOOTTON CL
Shoot Wood
CATT'S WOOD RD
Little Catt's Farm
CAPEL RD
VICARAGE HILL
THE STREET
Petham
CHURCH LA
Cattshill Shaw
TILLARD CL
Petham Prim Sch
STONE ST
Great Catt's Farm
Cattshill Wood
Broadway Green Farm
Petham House
Homeshole Shaw
BROADWAY
CHEQUERS HILL
Bowhill Shaw
BOW HILL
HOGG LA
Chequers (PH)
YEW TREE PK CVN & CAMPING SITE
DUCKPITS RD
Earley Wood
Brockhanger Wood
Dane Farm
Hunt's Wood
8
7
53
6
5
52
4
3
51
2
1
50
12
13
14

126
110

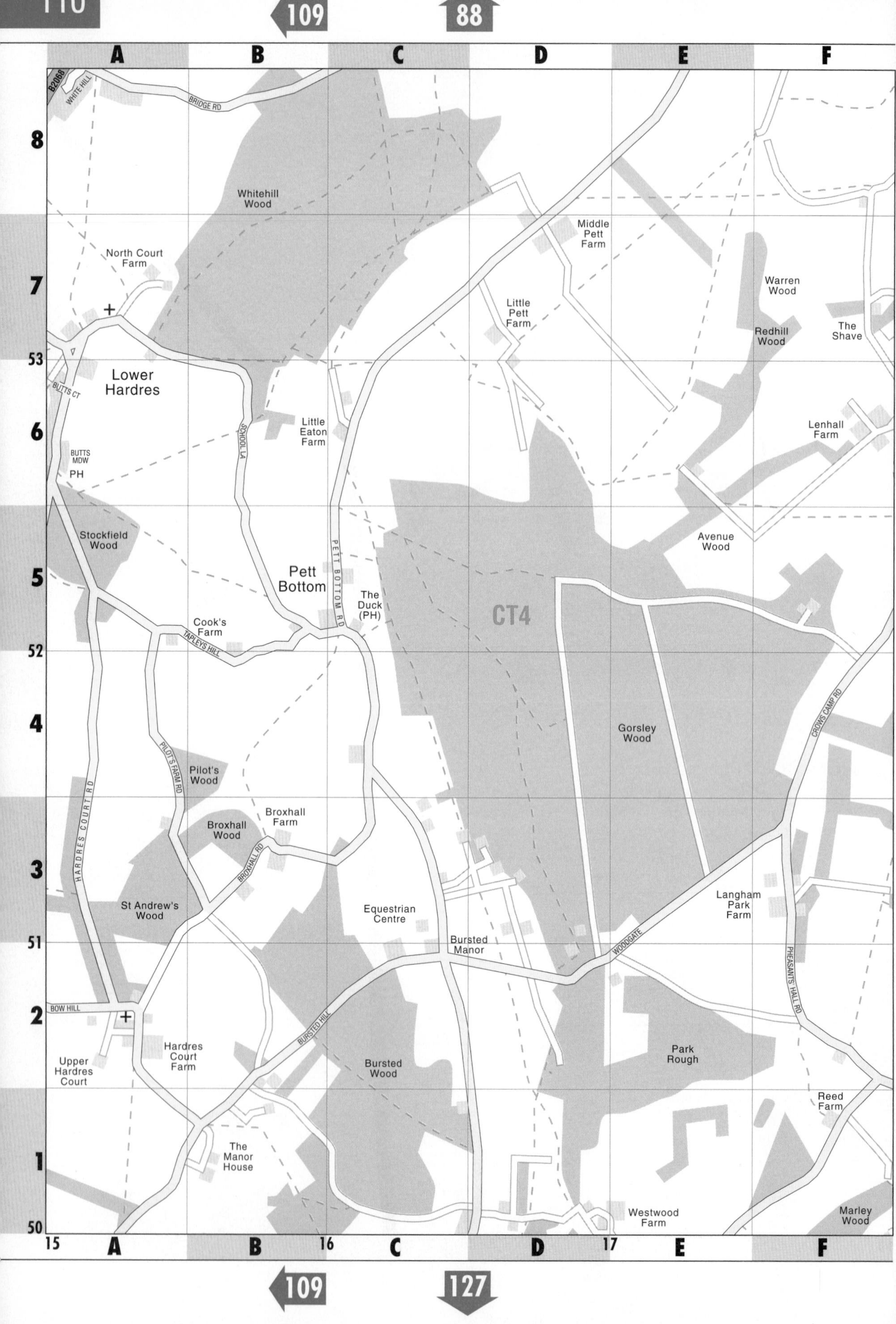

109
88

B2068
WHITE HILL
BRIDGE RD
Whitehill
Wood
Middle
Pett
Farm
North Court
Farm
Warren
Wood
Little
Pett
Farm
Redhill
Wood
The
Shave
Lower
Hardres
BUTTS CT
Little
Eaton
Farm
Lenhall
Farm
SCHOOL LA
BUTTS
MDW
PH
Stockfield
Wood
Avenue
Wood
Pett
Bottom
PETT BOTTOM RD
The
Duck
(PH)
CT4
Cook's
Farm
TAPLEYS HILL
Gorsley
Wood
Pilot's
Wood
PILOT'S FARM RD
HARDRES COURT RD
Broxhall
Farm
Broxhall
Wood
BROXHALL RD
St Andrew's
Wood
Equestrian
Centre
Langham
Park
Farm
WOODGATE
Bursted
Manor
PHEASANT'S HALL RD
CROWS CAMP RD
BOW HILL
BURSTED HILL
Upper
Hardres
Court
Hardres
Court
Farm
Bursted
Wood
Park
Rough
Reed
Farm
The
Manor
House
Westwood
Farm
Marley
Wood

109
127

89
112

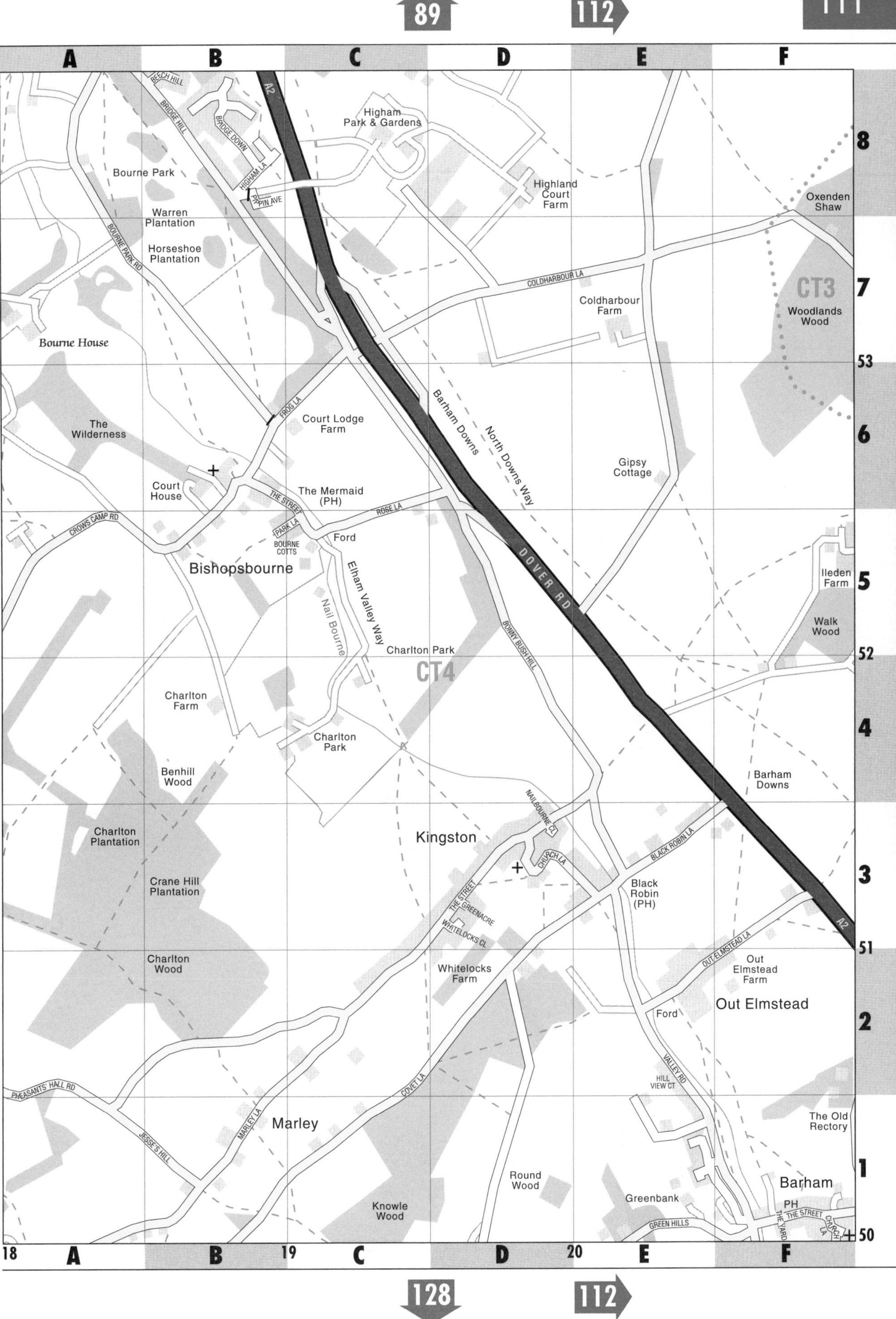
A
B
C
D
E
F
A2
BEECH HILL
BRIDGE HILL
BRIDGE DOWN
HIGHAM LA
PIPPIN AVE
Higham
Park & Gardens
Highland
Court
Farm
Oxenden
Shaw
8
Bourne Park
Warren
Plantation
Horseshoe
Plantation
BOURNE PARK RD
COLDHARBOUR LA
Coldharbour
Farm
CT3
Woodlands
Wood
7
Bourne House
53
FROG LA
Court Lodge
Farm
Barham Downs
North Downs Way
The
Wilderness
6
Gipsy
Cottage
Court
House
The Mermaid
(PH)
THE STREET
ROSE LA
CROWS CAMP RD
PARK LA
Ford
BOURNE
COTTS
DOVER RD
Bishopsbourne
Ileden
Farm
5
Elham Valley Way
Nail Bourne
Walk
Wood
BONNY BUSH HILL
Charlton Park
CT4
52
Charlton
Farm
Charlton
Park
4
Benhill
Wood
Barham
Downs
NAILBOURNE CL
Charlton
Plantation
Kingston
CHURCH LA
BLACK ROBIN LA
Crane Hill
Plantation
Black
Robin
(PH)
3
THE STREET
GREENACRE
WHITELOCKS CL
A2
51
OUT ELMSTEAD LA
Charlton
Wood
Whitelocks
Farm
Out
Elmstead
Farm
Out Elmstead
Ford
2
PHEASANTS' HALL RD
VALLEY RD
HILL
VIEW CT
COVET LA
MARLEY LA
Marley
The Old
Rectory
JESSE'S HILL
1
Round
Wood
Barham
Knowle
Wood
Greenbank
PH
THE STREET
GREEN HILLS
THE YARD
CHURCH
LA
50
18
A
B
19
C
D
20
E
F

128
112

111
90

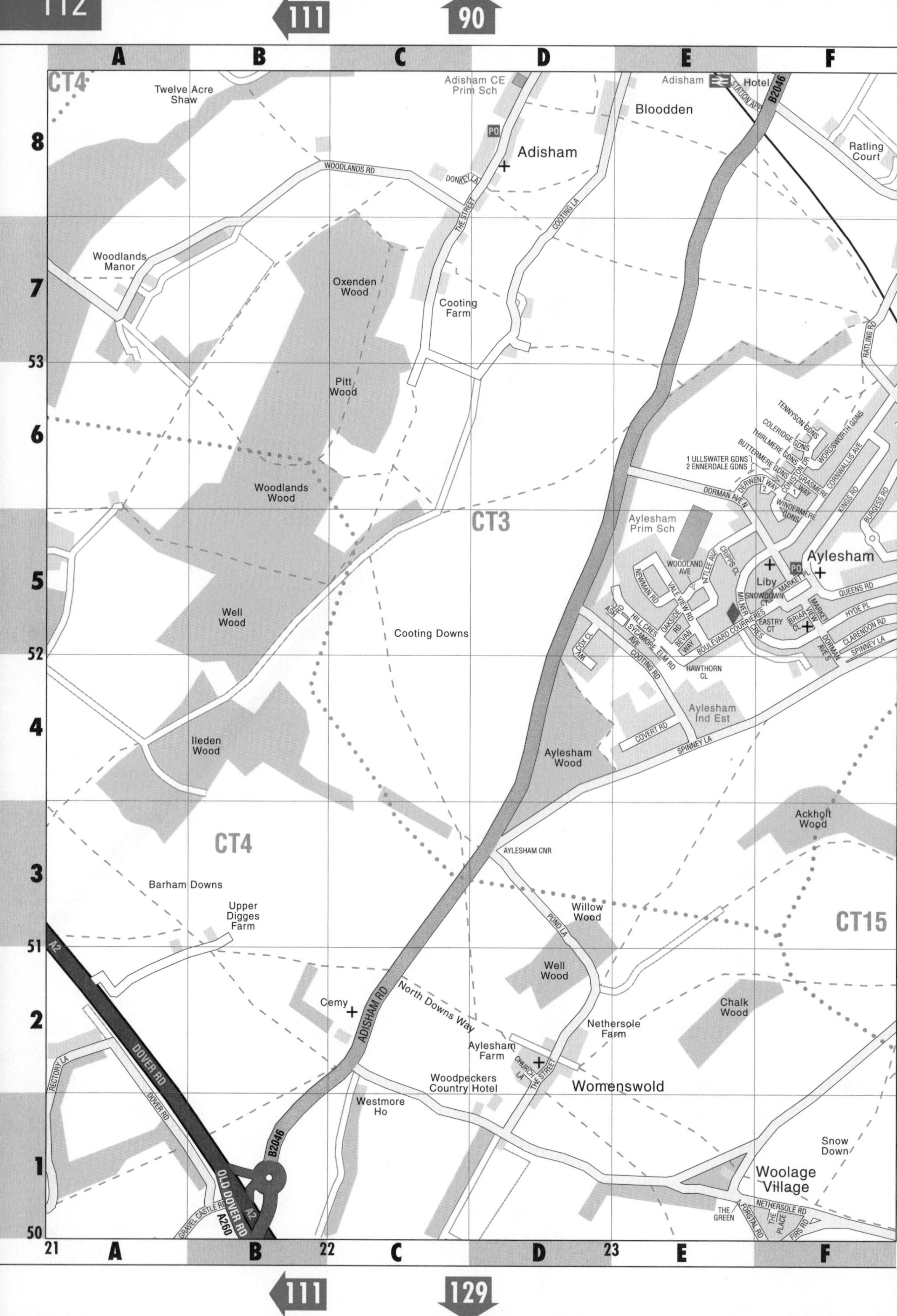
A
B
C
D
E
F
CT4
Twelve Acre Shaw
Adisham CE Prim Sch
Adisham
Hotel
STATION APP
B2046
Bloodden
PO
Adisham
Ratling Court
WOODLANDS RD
DONKEY LA
THE STREET
COOTING LA
Woodlands Manor
Oxenden Wood
Cooting Farm
RATLING RD
Pitt Wood
TENNYSON GDNS
COLERIDGE GDNS
WORDSWORTH GDNS
THIRLMERE GDNS
BUTTERMERE GDNS
CONISTON DR
CORNWALLIS AVE
1 ULLSWATER GDNS
2 ENNERDALE GDNS
GRASMERE WAY
DERWENT WAY
DORMAN AVE N
WINDERMERE GDNS
KINGS RD
BURGESS RD
Woodlands Wood
CT3
Aylesham Prim Sch
Aylesham
WOODLAND AVE
ATTLEE AVE
CRIPPS CL
Liby
PO
MARKET PL
QUEENS RD
NEWMAN RD
VALE VIEW RD
SNOWDOWN CT
MILNER CRES
MARKET
HYDE PL
Well Wood
Cooting Downs
ASH CL
HILL CRES
OAKSIDE RD
BEVAN WAY
BOULEVARD COURRIERES
EASTRY CT
BRIAR CL
VIEW
CLARENDON RD
COX CL
SYCAMORE AVE
ELM RD
DORMAN AVE S
SPINNEY LA
COOTING RD
HAWTHORN CL
Aylesham Ind Est
COVERT RD
SPINNEY LA
Ileden Wood
Aylesham Wood
Ackholt Wood
CT4
AYLESHAM CNR
Barham Downs
Upper Digges Farm
Willow Wood
POND LA
CT15
A2
Well Wood
ADISHAM RD
North Downs Way
Cemy
Chalk Wood
Nethersole Farm
RECTORY LA
DOVER RD
Aylesham Farm
CHURCH LA
THE STREET
Womenswold
Woodpeckers Country Hotel
DOVER RD
Westmore Ho
B2046
Snow Down
OLD DOVER RD
Woolage Village
A2
GRAVEL CASTLE RD
A260
THE GREEN
FORSTAL RD
NETHERSOLE RD
THE PLACE
FIRS RD
8
7
53
6
5
52
4
3
51
2
1
50
21
22
23

111
129

91
114

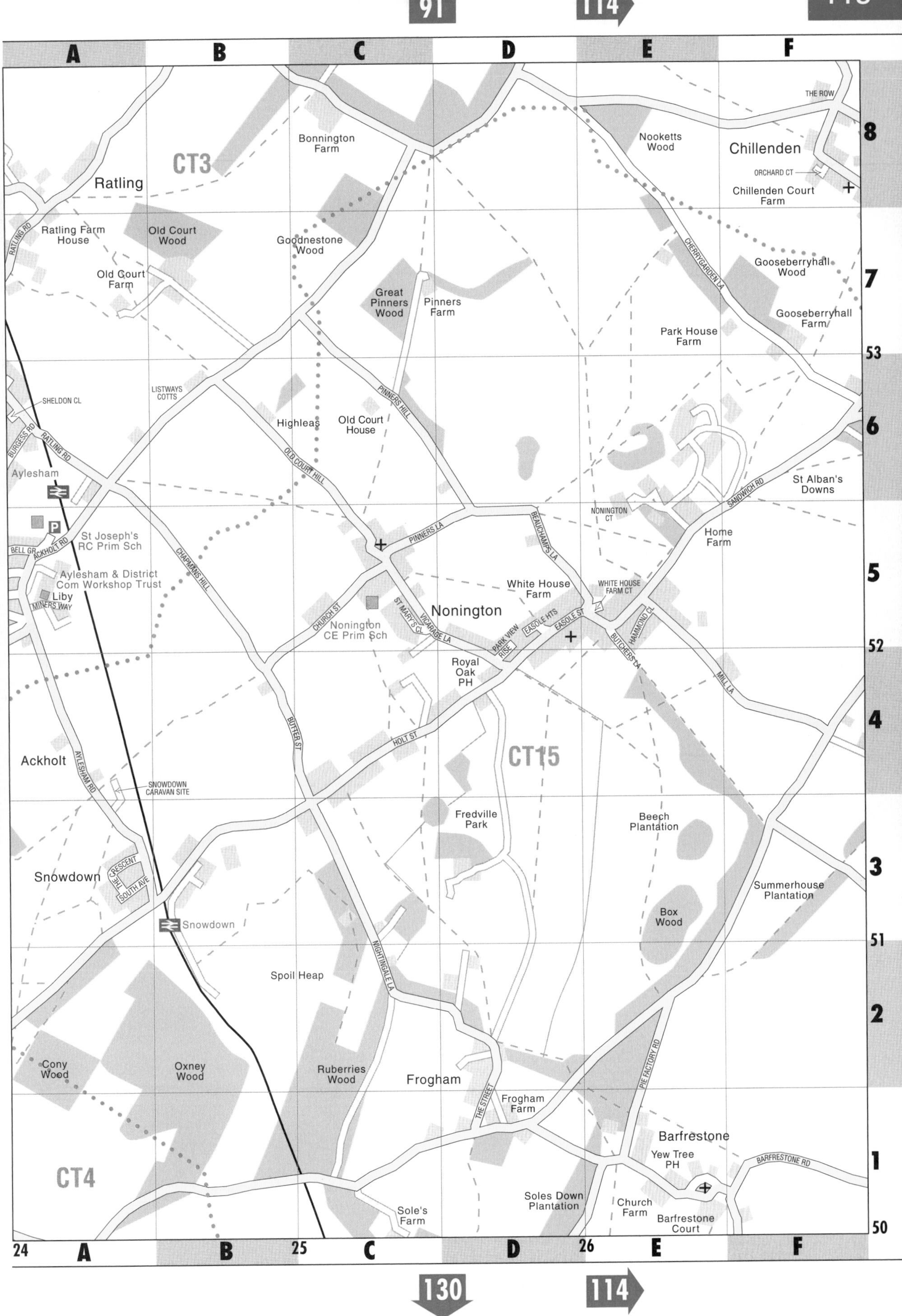
A
B
C
D
E
F
THE ROW
8
Bonnington Farm
Nooketts Wood
Chillenden
CT3
Ratling
ORCHARD CT
Chillenden Court Farm
RATLING RD
Ratling Farm House
Old Court Wood
Goodnestone Wood
CHERRYGARDEN LA
Gooseberryhall Wood
Old Court Farm
7
Great Pinners Wood
Pinners Farm
Gooseberryhall Farm
Park House Farm
53
LISTWAYS COTTS
SHELDON CL
PINNERS HILL
6
Highleas
Old Court House
BURGESS RD
RATLING RD
OLD COURT HILL
Aylesham
SANDWICH RD
St Alban's Downs
NONINGTON CT
BEAUCHAMPS LA
PINNERS LA
Home Farm
St Joseph's RC Prim Sch
BELL GR
ACKHOLT RD
5
Aylesham & District Com Workshop Trust
CHAPMANS HILL
White House Farm
WHITE HOUSE FARM CT
Liby
MINERS WAY
Nonington
HAMMOND CL
ST MARY'S CL
CHURCH ST
EASOLE HTS
EASOLE ST
Nonington CE Prim Sch
VICARAGE LA
PARK VIEW RISE
BUTCHERS LA
52
Royal Oak PH
MILL LA
4
BUTTER ST
HOLT ST
CT15
Ackholt
AYLESHAM RD
SNOWDOWN CARAVAN SITE
Fredville Park
Beech Plantation
3
Snowdown
THE CRESCENT
SOUTH AVE
Summerhouse Plantation
Box Wood
Snowdown
51
NIGHTINGALE LA
Spoil Heap
2
Cony Wood
Oxney Wood
Ruberries Wood
Frogham
PIE FACTORY RD
THE STREET
Frogham Farm
Barfrestone
1
Yew Tree PH
BARFRESTONE RD
CT4
Soles Down Plantation
Church Farm
Sole's Farm
Barfrestone Court
50
24
A
B
25
C
D
26
E
F

130
114

113
92

	A	B	C	D	E	F

8

YEW TREE FARM

SHORT ST

Griffin's Head (PH)

War Meml

Home Wood

CT13

7

The Warren

CT3

Home Farm

Home Farm

Knowlton

Knowlton Court

Black La

Knowlton Park

CUCKOLDS CNR

SANDWICH RD

53

The Grove

THORNTON LW

6

Manorial Earthworks

Shingleton Wood

Dover Lodge Cottages

Shingleton Farm

Venson Farm

St Alban's Downs

Round Wood

Shingleton Cottages

CT14

5

Kelk Hill

Thorntonhill Cottages

Thornton Farm

Kittington Cottages

52

Brown Pudding Plantation

Thornton Wood

Garden Wood

4

Kittington Farm

The Downs

DANE CT

PIKE RD

SCHOOL RD

3

Beeches Farm

51

CT15

Spoil Heap

Craythorne Firs

2

POPLAR DR

CYPRESS GR

SWEETBRIAR LA

ASH GR

BEECH DR

CHERRY GR

ROMAN WAY

CHAUCER RD

ST JOHNS RD

FAIRVIEW RD

OAK GR

Burgess Hill

Works

BARVILLE RD

PO

LARCH RD

ADELAIDE RD

MILNER CT

MILNER RD

TERRACE RD

Elvington

MILNER

ELMATON LA

MILYARD WAY

WIGMORE LA

SANDWICH RD

1

BARFRESTONE RD

Sports Gd

50

27	A		B	28	C		D	29	E		F

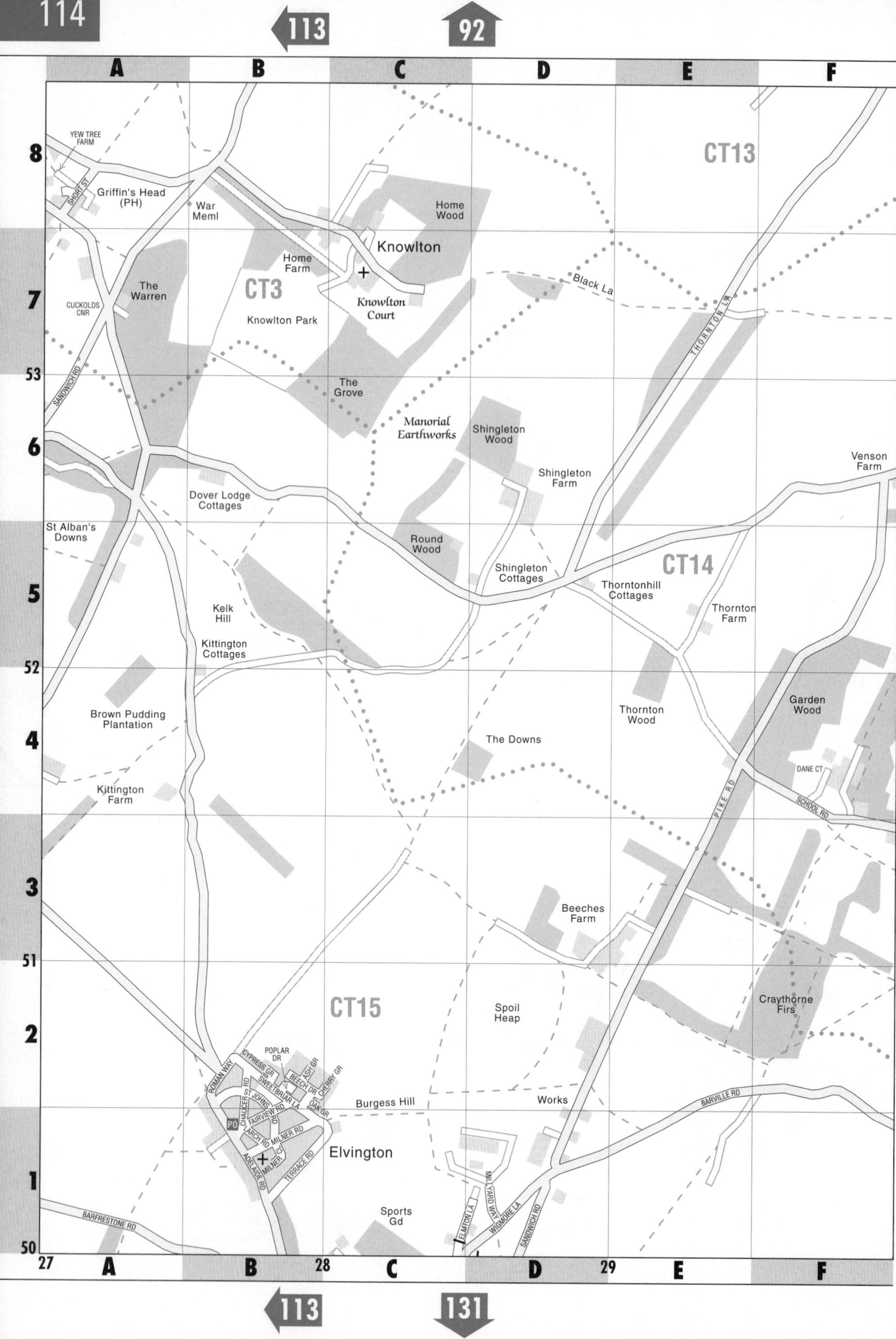

113
131

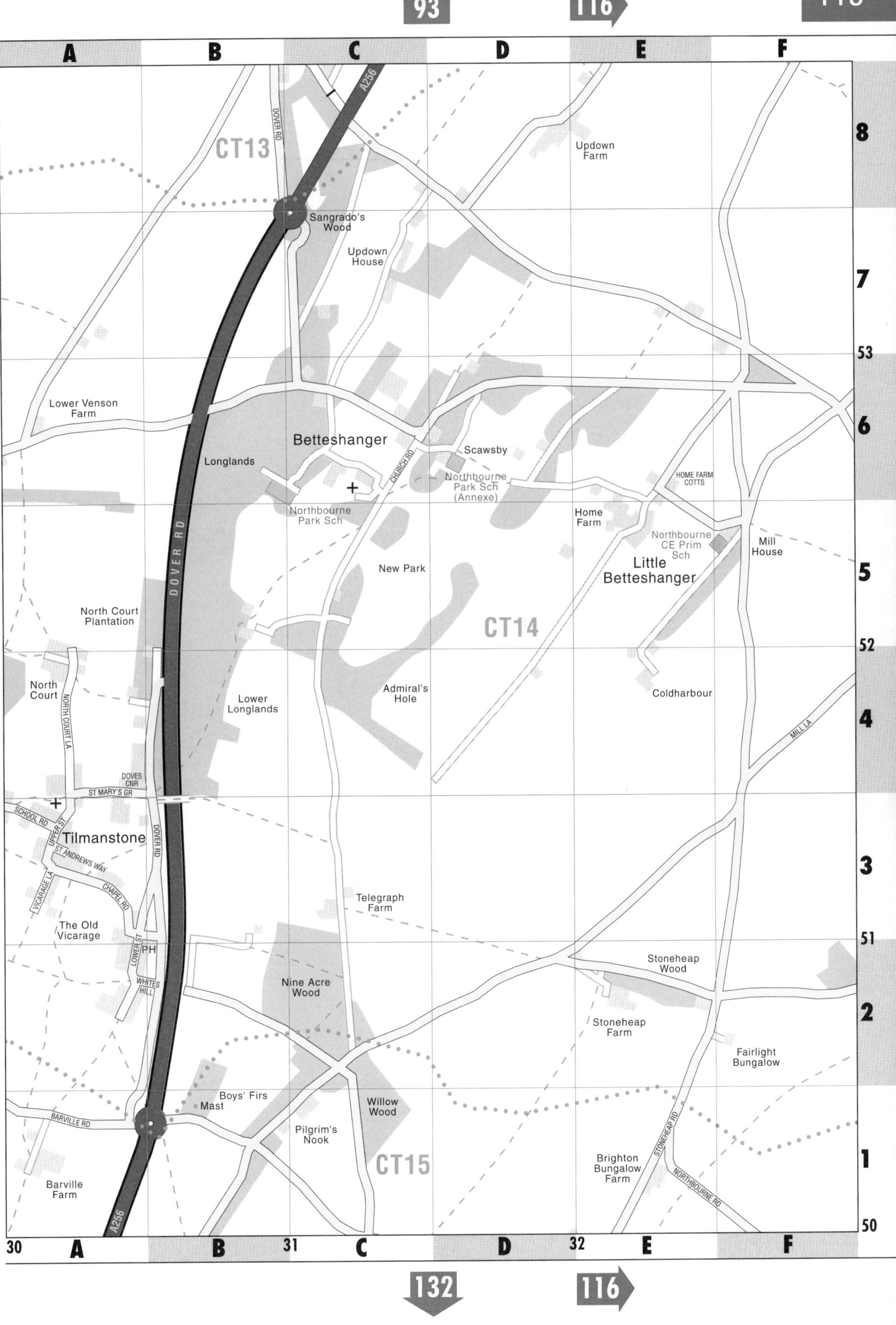
93
116
A
B
C
D
E
F
8
7
53
6
5
52
4
3
51
2
1
50
30
31
32
A256
DOVER RD
CT13
Updown Farm
Sangrado's Wood
Updown House
Lower Venson Farm
Betteshanger
Longlands
Scawsby
CHURCH RD
Northbourne Park Sch (Annexe)
Northbourne Park Sch
HOME FARM COTTS
Home Farm
Northbourne CE Prim Sch
Mill House
Little Betteshanger
New Park
North Court Plantation
CT14
DOVER RD
North Court
NORTH COURT LA
Lower Longlands
Admiral's Hole
Coldharbour
MILL LA
DOVES CNR
ST MARY'S GR
SCHOOL RD
UPPER ST
Tilmanstone
ST ANDREWS WAY
DOVER RD
VICARAGE LA
CHAPEL RD
Telegraph Farm
The Old Vicarage
LOWER ST
PH
WHITES HILL
Nine Acre Wood
Stoneheap Wood
Stoneheap Farm
Fairlight Bungalow
Boys' Firs
Mast
Willow Wood
BARVILLE RD
Pilgrim's Nook
STONEHEAP RD
Brighton Bungalow Farm
NORTHBOURNE RD
CT15
Barville Farm
A256
132
116

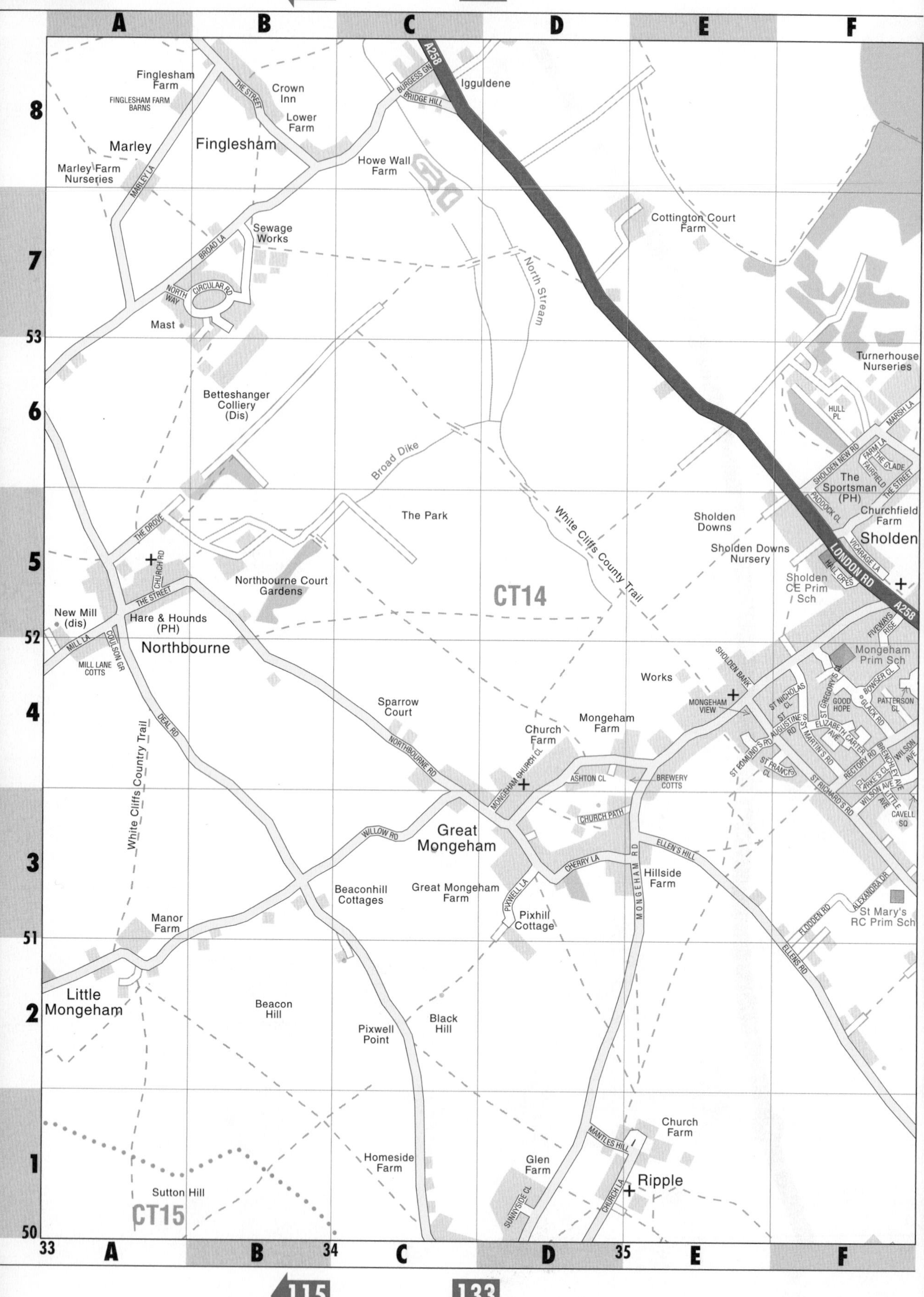

115
94

A B C D E F

8

Finglesham
Farm
Crown
Inn
FINGLESHAM FARM
BARNS
Lower
Farm
Iggulidene

Marley
Finglesham
Howe Wall
Farm
Marley Farm
Nurseries

7
Sewage
Works
Cottington Court
Farm

MARLEY LA
BROAD LA

NORTH
WAY
CIRCULAR RD
North Stream

53
Mast

Turnerhouse
Nurseries

6
Betteshanger
Colliery
(Dis)
Broad Dike
HULL
PL
MARSH LA

SHOLDEN NEW RD
FARM LA
THE GLADE
FAIRFIELD
THE STREET

The
Sportsman
(PH)
Churchfield
Farm
Sholden

The Park
White Cliffs County Trail
Sholden
Downs

PADDOCK CL
VICARAGE LA

5

THE DROVE
CHURCH RD

Northbourne Court
Gardens
CT14
Sholden Downs
Nursery
Sholden
CE Prim
/ Sch

THE STREET

LONDON RD
A258

52
New Mill
(dis)
Hare & Hounds
(PH)
FIVEWAYS
RISE

MILL LA
COULSON GR
Northbourne
Works
SHOLDEN BANK
Mongeham
Prim Sch

4
MILL LANE
COTTS
Sparrow
Court
Mongeham
View
St Nicholas
CL
BONSOR RD

NORTHBOURNE RD

Church
Farm
Mongeham
Farm
GOOD
HOPE
BLACK RD
PATTERSON
GL

DEAL RD
MONGEHAM CHURCH CL

St GREGORY'S

ST NICHOLAS CL
ST AUGUSTINE'S
ST ELIZABETH CARTER
RECTORY RD
WILSON AVE
CAVELL
SQ

ASHTON CL
Brewery
Cotts
ST EDMUND'S RD
ST FRANCIS
CL
ST MARTIN'S
ST RICHARD'S RD
WILKE'S CL
WILSON AVE E

3

WILLOW RD
Great
Mongeham
CHURCH PATH
CHERRY LA
Hillside
Farm
ALEXANDRA DR

White Cliffs Country Trail
Beaconhill
Cottages
Great Mongeham
Farm
PIXWELL LA
Pixhill
Cottage
ELLEN'S HILL
St Mary's
RC Prim Sch

51
Manor
Farm
MONGEHAM RD
FLODDEN RD
ELLENS RD

2
Little
Mongeham
Beacon
Hill
Black
Hill

Pixwell
Point

1

Church
Farm

Homeside
Farm
Glen
Farm
MANTLES HILL
Ripple

Sutton Hill
CT15
SUNNYSIDE CL
CHURCH LA

50

33 A B 34 C D E 35 F

95

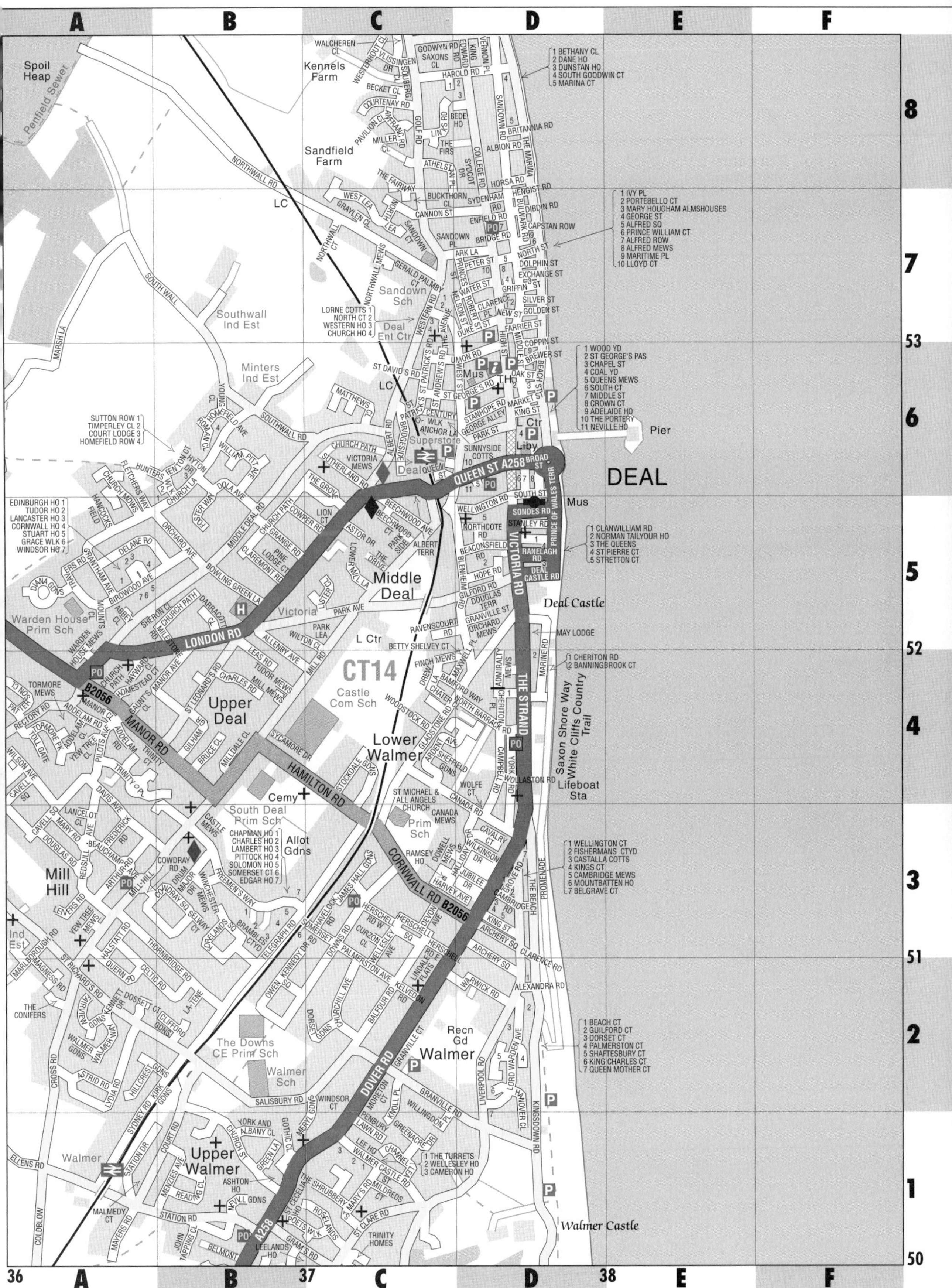
A
B
C
D
E
F
8
7
53
6
5
52
4
3
51
2
1
50
36
37
38
Spoil Heap
Kennels Farm
Sandfield Farm
Southwall Ind Est
Minters Ind Est
Sandown Sch
Deal Ent Ctr
Superstore
Deal
DEAL
Pier
Mus
L Ctr
Liby
Middle Deal
Victoria
Deal Castle
CT14
Castle Com Sch
Upper Deal
Lower Walmer
Warden House Prim Sch
Mill Hill
South Deal Prim Sch
Allot Gdns
Cemy
Prim Sch
Saxon Shore Way White Cliffs Country Trail
Lifeboat Sta
Recn Gd
Walmer
The Downs CE Prim Sch
Walmer Sch
Upper Walmer
Walmer Castle
QUEEN ST A258
LONDON RD
B2056
MANOR RD
HAMILTON RD
CORNWALL RD B2056
VICTORIA RD
THE STRAND
DOVER RD
A258
1 BETHANY CL
2 DANE HO
3 DUNSTAN HO
4 SOUTH GOODWIN CT
5 MARINA CT
1 IVY PL
2 PORTEBELLO CT
3 MARY HOUGHAM ALMSHOUSES
4 GEORGE ST
5 ALFRED SQ
6 PRINCE WILLIAM CT
7 ALFRED ROW
8 ALFRED MEWS
9 MARITIME PL
10 LLOYD CT
LORNE COTTS 1
NORTH CT 2
WESTERN HO 3
CHURCH HO 4
1 WOOD YD
2 ST GEORGE'S PAS
3 CHAPEL ST
4 COAL YD
5 QUEENS MEWS
6 SOUTH CT
7 MIDDLE ST
8 CROWN CT
9 ADELAIDE HO
10 THE PORTERY
11 NEVILLE HO
SUTTON ROW 1
TIMPERLEY CL 2
COURT LODGE 3
HOMEFIELD ROW 4
EDINBURGH HO 1
TUDOR HO 2
LANCASTER HO 3
CORNWALL HO 4
STUART HO 5
GRACE WLK 6
WINDSOR HO 7
1 CLANWILLIAM RD
2 NORMAN TAILYOUR HO
3 THE QUEENS
4 ST PIERRE CT
5 STRETTON CT
MAY LODGE
1 CHERITON RD
2 BANNINGBROOK CT
CHAPMAN HO 1
CHARLES HO 2
LAMBERT HO 3
PITTOCK HO 4
SOLOMON HO 5
SOMERSET CT 6
EDGAR HO 7
1 WELLINGTON CT
2 FISHERMANS CTYD
3 CASTALLA COTTS
4 KINGS CT
5 CAMBRIDGE MEWS
6 MOUNTBATTEN HO
7 BELGRAVE CT
1 BEACH CT
2 GUILFORD CT
3 DORSET CT
4 PALMERSTON CT
5 SHAFTESBURY CT
6 KING CHARLES CT
7 QUEEN MOTHER CT
1 THE TURRETS
2 WELLESLEY HO
3 CAMERON HO

134

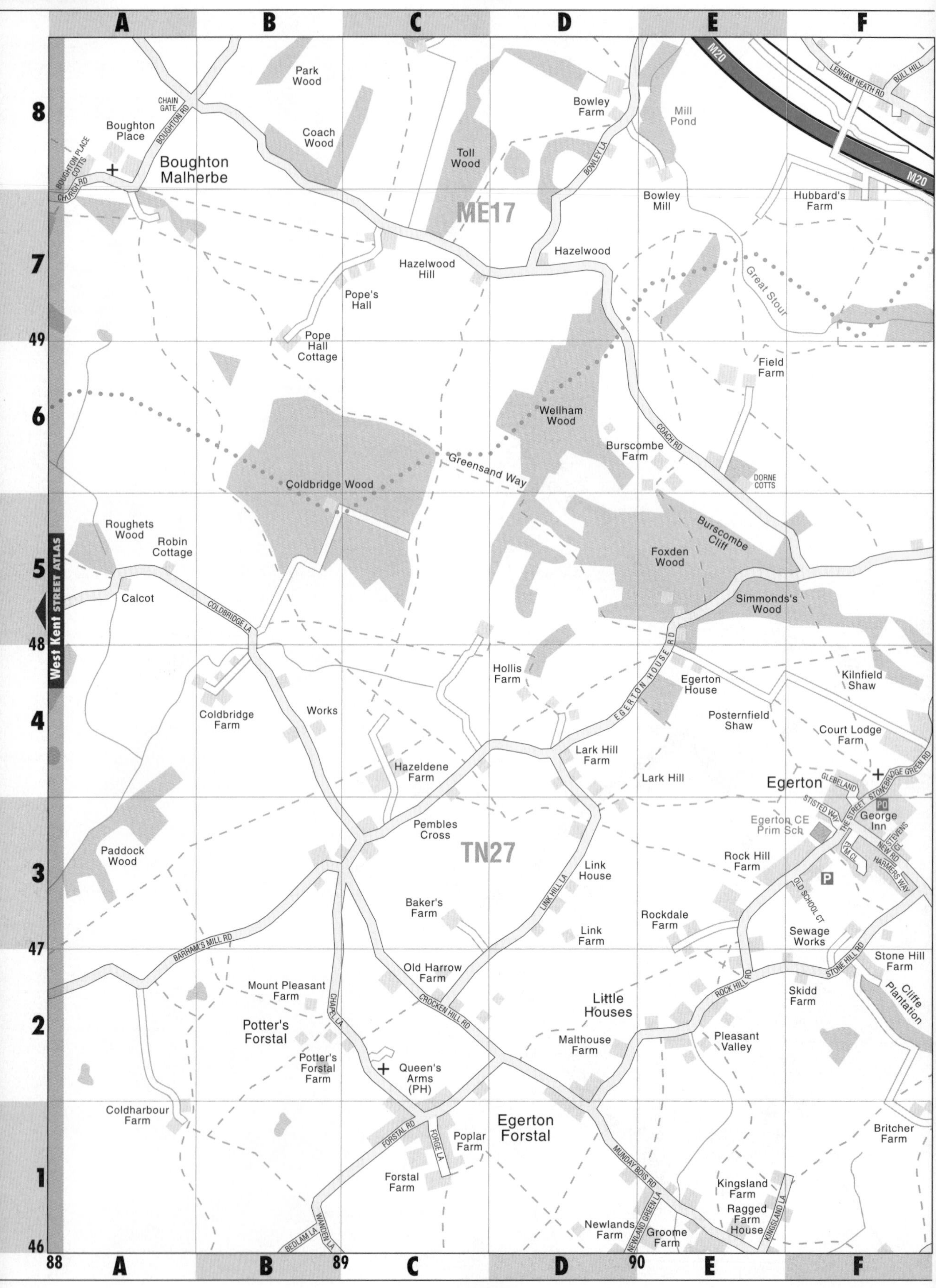

West Kent STREET ATLAS

Park
Wood

CHAIN
GATE
Boughton
Place

Boughton
Malherbe

Coach
Wood

Toll
Wood

Bowley
Farm

Mill
Pond

LENHAM HEATH RD

BULL HILL

M20

M20

ME17

Bowley
Mill

Hubbard's
Farm

Hazelwood Hill

Hazelwood

BOWLEY LA

Pope's
Hall

Great Stour

Pope
Hall
Cottage

Field
Farm

Wellham
Wood

COACH RD

Burscombe
Farm

Greensand Way

DORNE
COTTS

Coldbridge Wood

Burscombe
Cliff

Roughets
Wood

Robin
Cottage

Foxden
Wood

Calcot

COLDBRIDGE LA

Simmonds's
Wood

Hollis
Farm

Egerton
House

Kilnfield
Shaw

Coldbridge
Farm

Works

Posternfield
Shaw

Court Lodge
Farm

EGERTON HOUSE RD

Hazeldene
Farm

Lark Hill
Farm

Lark Hill

Egerton

GLEBELAND

STOKEBRIDGE GYEM RD

Paddock
Wood

Pembles
Cross

TN27

Link
House

Rock Hill
Farm

Egerton CE
Prim Sch

STISTED WAY

George
Inn

P.O

STEVENS

NEW RD

HARMERS WAY

Baker's
Farm

LINK HILL LA

Link
Farm

Rockdale
Farm

OLD SCHOOL CT

P

Sewage
Works

Stone Hill
Farm

Cliffe
Plantation

BARHAM'S MILL RD

Mount Pleasant
Farm

Old Harrow
Farm

CROCKEN HILL RD

Little
Houses

ROCK HILL

STONE HILL RD

Skidd
Farm

CHART LA

Potter's
Forstal

Malthouse
Farm

Pleasant
Valley

Potter's
Forstal
Farm

Queen's
Arms
(PH)

Egerton
Forstal

Coldharbour
Farm

FORSTAL RD

FORGE LA

Poplar
Farm

MUNDAY BOIS RD

Britcher
Farm

Forstal
Farm

BEDLAM LA

VANDEN LA

NEWLAND GREEN LA

Newlands
Farm

Groome
Farm

Kingsland
Farm

KINGSLAND LA

Ragged
Farm
House

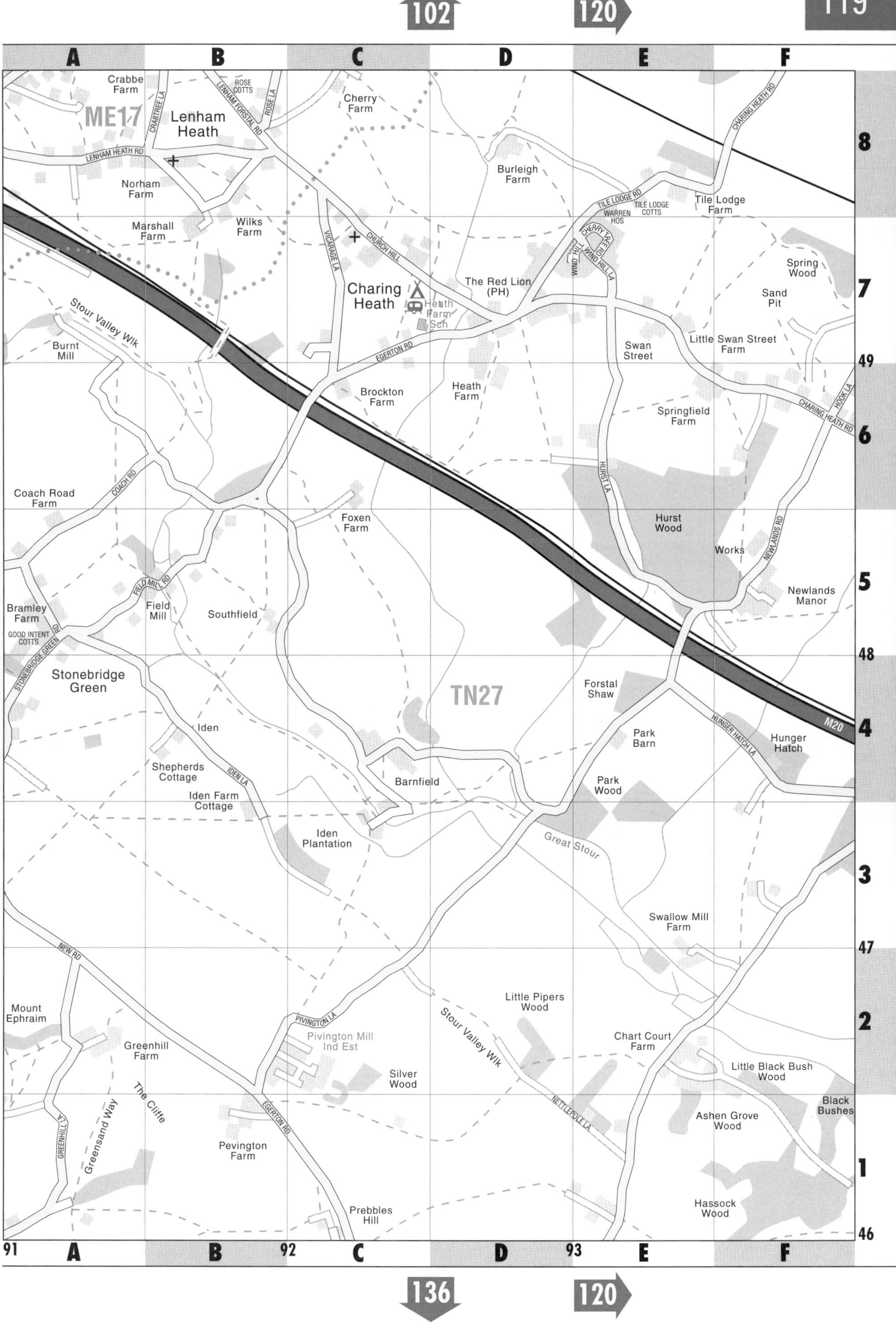
A
B
C
D
E
F
Crabbe Farm
ROSE COTTS
LENHAM FORSTAL RD
ROSE LA
CRABTREE LA
ME17
Lenham Heath
Cherry Farm
CHARING HEATH RD
8
LENHAM HEATH RD
Norham Farm
Burleigh Farm
TILE LODGE RD
WARREN HOS
TILE LODGE COTTS
Tile Lodge Farm
Marshall Farm
Wilks Farm
VICARAGE LA
CHURCH HILL
CHERRY TREE RD
WIND HILL
WIND HILL LA
Spring Wood
The Red Lion (PH)
Charing Heath
Heath Farm Sch
Sand Pit
7
Stour Valley Wlk
Burnt Mill
EGERTON RD
Swan Street
Little Swan Street Farm
49
Brockton Farm
Heath Farm
HOOK LA
CHARING HEATH RD
Springfield Farm
6
Coach Road Farm
COACH RD
HURST LA
Foxen Farm
Hurst Wood
Works
NEWLANDS RD
FIELD MILL RD
5
Bramley Farm
Field Mill
Southfield
Newlands Manor
GOOD INTENT COTTS
STONEBRIDGE GREEN RD
48
Stonebridge Green
TN27
Forstal Shaw
Iden
Park Barn
HUNGER HATCH LA
Hunger Hatch
M20
4
Shepherds Cottage
IDEN LA
Barnfield
Park Wood
Iden Farm Cottage
Iden Plantation
Great Stour
3
Swallow Mill Farm
NEW RD
47
Mount Ephraim
Little Pipers Wood
PIVINGTON LA
Stour Valley Wlk
Chart Court Farm
2
Pivington Mill Ind Est
Greenhill Farm
Silver Wood
Little Black Bush Wood
The Cliffe
Black Bushes
Greensand Way
GREENHILL LA
EGERTON RD
NETTLEPOLE LA
Ashen Grove Wood
Pevington Farm
1
Prebbles Hill
Hassock Wood
46
91
92
93

119
103

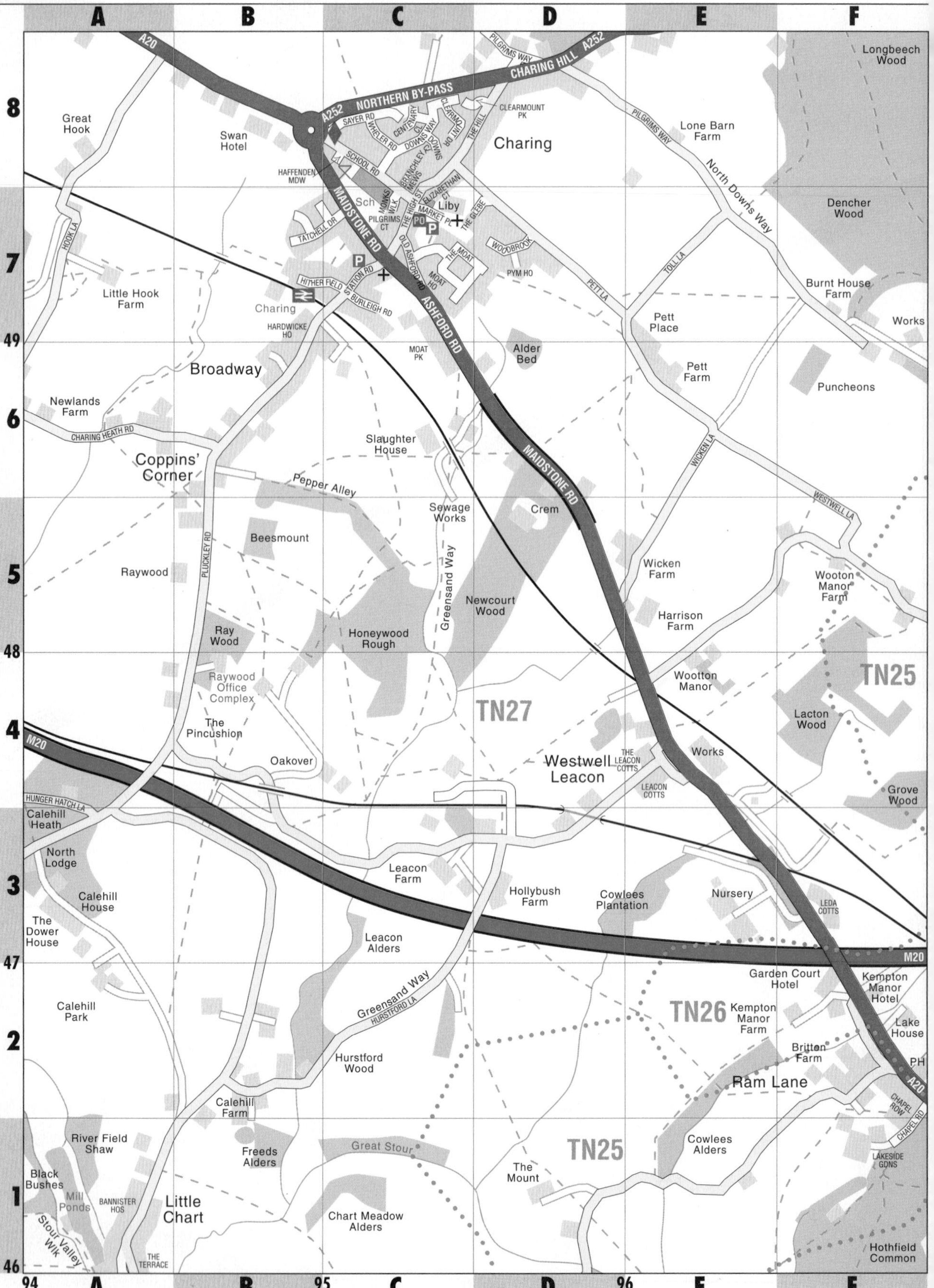

A B C D E F

8

A20

Great Hook

NORTHERN BY-PASS

Swan Hotel

A252

CHARING HILL A252

PILGRIMS WAY

Longbeech Wood

SAYER RD

WHEELER RD

SCHOOL RD

DOWNS WAY

CENTENARY

CLEARMOUNT PK

PILGRIMS WAY

Lone Barn Farm

Charing

HAFFENDEN MDW

MAIDSTONE RD

TATCHELL DR

PILGRIMS CT

MORRIS WLK

BRANCHLEY MEWS

THE HIGH ST

ELIZABETH CT

MARKET PL

Sch

Liby

PO

P

P

THE GLEBE

North Downs Way

Dencher Wood

7

HITHER FIELD

STATION RD

BURLEIGH RD

ASHFORD RD

OLD ASHFORD

WOODBROOK

PYM HO

MOAT HO

THE MOAT

PETT LA

TOLL LA

Burnt House Farm

Works

Charing

HARDWICKE HO

49

MOAT PK

Alder Bed

Pett Place

Puncheons

Broadway

Newlands Farm

6

CHARING HEATH RD

Slaughter House

MAIDSTONE RD

Pett Farm

WICKEN LA

WESTWELL LA

Coppins' Corner

PLUCKLEY RD

Pepper Alley

Sewage Works

Crem

Wicken Farm

Wooton Manor Farm

Beesmount

Greensand Way

5

Raywood

Ray Wood

Honeywood Rough

Newcourt Wood

Harrison Farm

Lacton Wood

48

Raywood Office Complex

Wootton Manor

TN27

TN25

4

M20

The Pincushion

Oakover

THE LEACON COTTS

Westwell Leacon

LEACON COTTS

Works

Grove Wood

HUNGER HATCH LA

Calehill Heath

North Lodge

Leacon Farm

Hollybush Farm

Cowlees Plantation

Nursery

LEDA COTTS

3

Calehill House

Leacon Alders

M20

The Dower House

Greensand Way

HURSTFORD LA

Garden Court Hotel

Kempton Manor Hotel

47

Calehill Park

TN26

Kempton Manor Farm

Lake House

Britten Farm

A20

PH

2

Hurstford Wood

Ram Lane

CHAPEL ROW

River Field Shaw

Calehill Farm

Great Stour

The Mount

TN25

Cowlees Alders

LAKESIDE GDNS

Black Bushes

Mill Ponds

BANNISTER HOS

Freeds Alders

Chart Meadow Alders

Hothfield Common

1

Stour Valley Wlk

Little Chart

THE TERRACE

46

94 A B 95 C D 96 E F

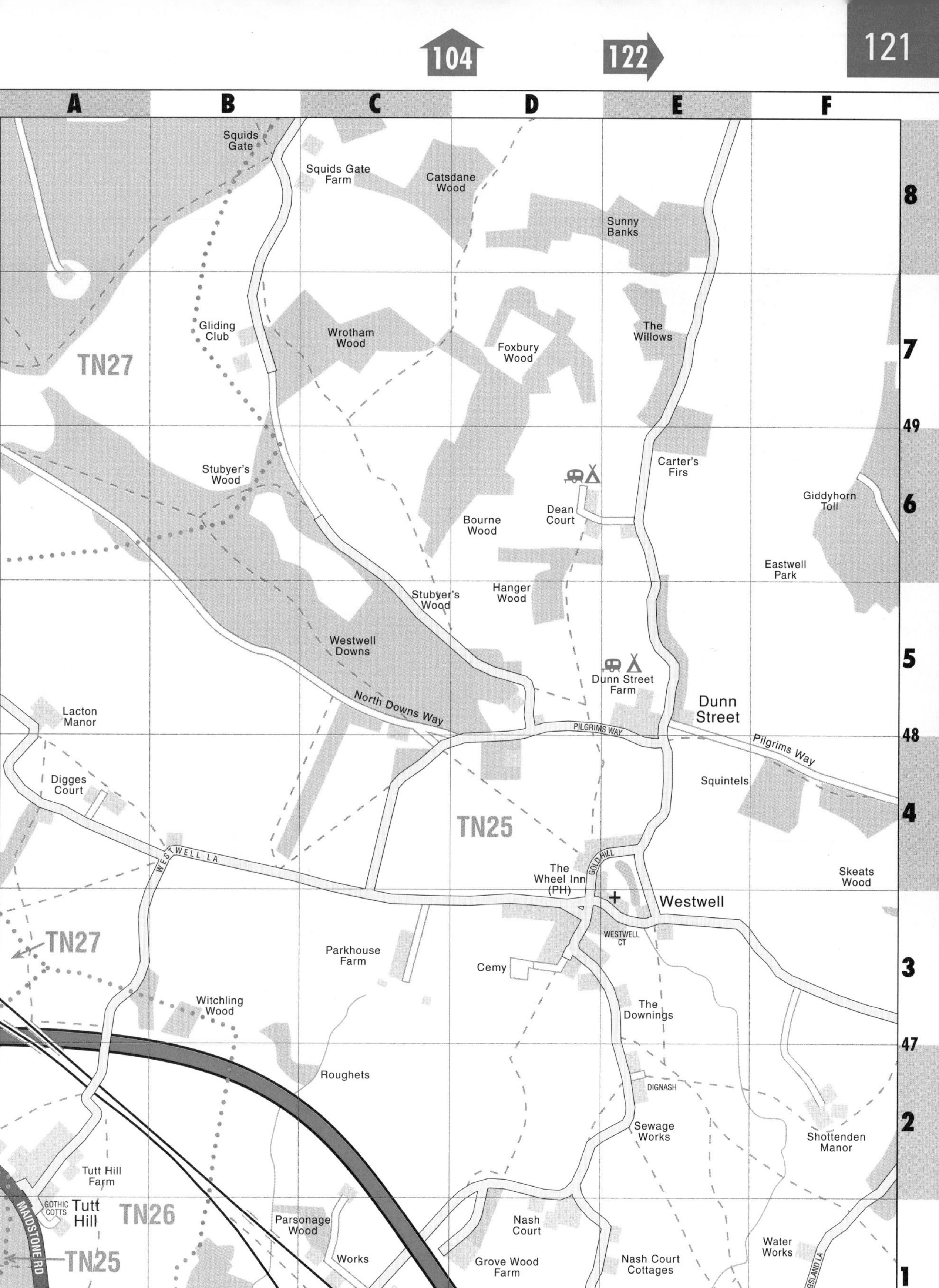

A B C D E F

8
7
49
6

5
48
4

3
47
2
1
46

97 A B 98 C D 99 E F

Squids Gate
Squids Gate Farm
Catsdane Wood
Sunny Banks
Gliding Club
Wrotham Wood
Foxbury Wood
The Willows
TN27
Stubyer's Wood
Carter's Firs
Giddyhorn Toll
Dean Court
Bourne Wood
Eastwell Park
Stubyer's Wood
Hanger Wood
Westwell Downs
Dunn Street Farm
Dunn Street
North Downs Way
PILGRIMS WAY
Pilgrims Way
Lacton Manor
Squintels
Digges Court
TN25
WESTWELL LA
The Wheel Inn (PH)
GOLD HILL
Skeats Wood
Westwell
TN27
WESTWELL CT
Parkhouse Farm
Cemy
Witchling Wood
The Downings
Roughets
DIGNASH
Sewage Works
Shottenden Manor
MAIDSTONE RD
Tutt Hill Farm
GOTHIC COTTS
Tutt Hill
TN26
Parsonage Wood
Nash Court
Water Works
Works
Grove Wood Farm
Nash Court Cottages
KINGSLAND LA
TN25
A20
Ripple Wood
Sunnybridge Farm
M20

121
105

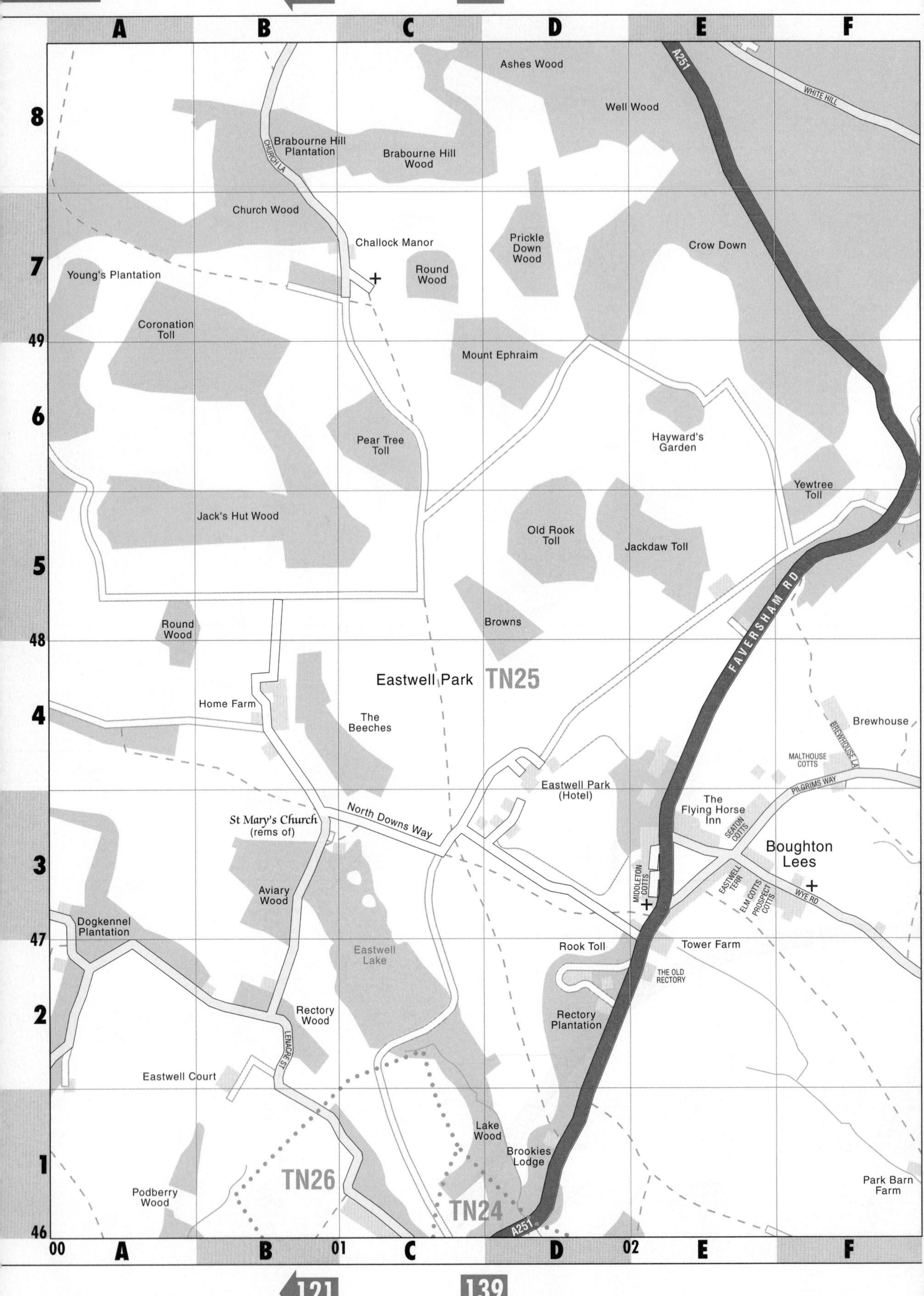
A
B
C
D
E
F
8
7
49
6
5
48
4
3
47
2
1
46
00
01
02
Ashes Wood
Well Wood
A251
WHITE HILL
Brabourne Hill Plantation
CHURCH LA
Brabourne Hill Wood
Church Wood
Challock Manor
Prickle Down Wood
Crow Down
Young's Plantation
Round Wood
Coronation Toll
Mount Ephraim
Pear Tree Toll
Hayward's Garden
Yewtree Toll
Jack's Hut Wood
Old Rook Toll
Jackdaw Toll
Round Wood
Browns
FAVERSHAM RD
Eastwell Park
TN25
Home Farm
The Beeches
Brewhouse
BREWHOUSE LA
MALTHOUSE COTTS
PILGRIMS WAY
Eastwell Park (Hotel)
The Flying Horse Inn
SEATON COTTS
North Downs Way
St Mary's Church (rems of)
Boughton Lees
MIDDLETON COTTS
EASTWELL TERR
ELM COTTS
PROSPECT COTTS
WYE RD
Aviary Wood
Dogkennel Plantation
Eastwell Lake
Rook Toll
Tower Farm
THE OLD RECTORY
Rectory Wood
Rectory Plantation
LENACRE ST
Eastwell Court
Lake Wood
Brookies Lodge
TN26
Podberry Wood
Park Barn Farm
TN24
A251

121
139

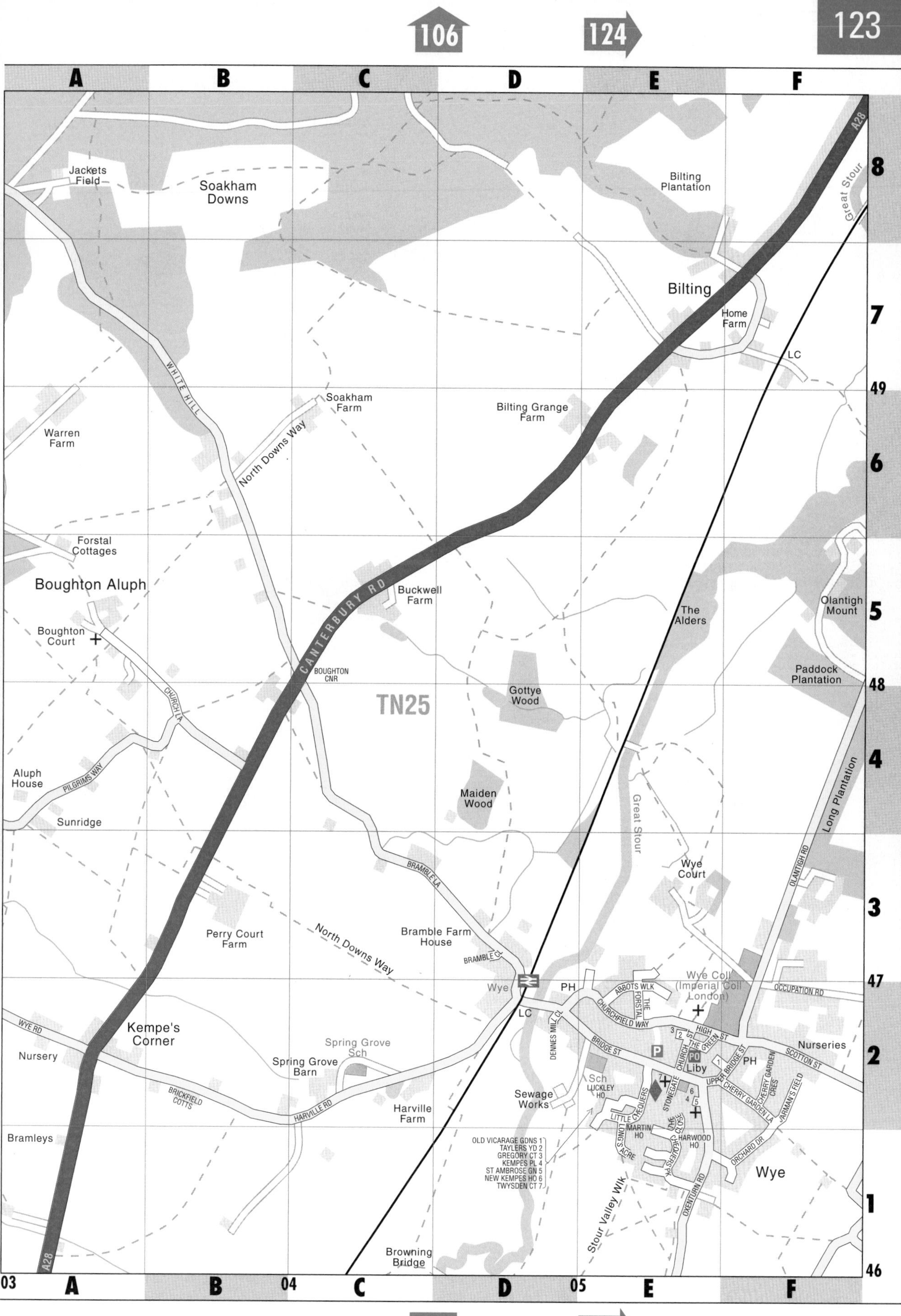

A   B   C   D   E   F

8

Jackets Field

Soakham Downs

Bilting Plantation

Bilting

7

Home Farm

LC

49

WHITE HILL

Warren Farm

North Downs Way

Soakham Farm

Bilting Grange Farm

6

Forstal Cottages

Boughton Aluph

CANTERBURY RD

Buckwell Farm

The Alders

Olantigh Mount

5

Boughton Court

BOUGHTON CNR

TN25

Paddock Plantation

48

CHURCH LA

Aluph House

PILGRIMS WAY

Gottye Wood

Long Plantation

4

Sunridge

Maiden Wood

Great Stour

OLANTIGH RD

BRAMBLE LA

Wye Court

3

Perry Court Farm

North Downs Way

Bramble Farm House

BRAMBLE CT

OCCUPATION RD

Wye

PH

Wye Coll (Imperial Coll London)

47

LC

ABBOTS WLK

CHURCHFIELD WAY

THE FORSTAL

HIGH ST

Nurseries

SCOTTON ST

2

WYE RD

Nursery

Kempe's Corner

Spring Grove Sch

Spring Grove Barn

DENNES MILL

BRIDGE ST

P

PO Liby

CHURCH ST

THE GREEN

STONEGATE

UPPER BRIDGE ST

PH

CHERRY GARDEN LA

CHERRY GARDEN CRES

JARMAN'S FIELD

BRICKFIELD COTTS

HARVILLE RD

Harville Farm

Sewage Works

Sch LUCKLEY HO

3

6

4 5

Bramleys

OLD VICARAGE GDNS 1
TAYLERS YD 2
GREGORY CT 3
KEMPES PL 4
ST AMBROSE GN 5
NEW KEMPES HO 6
TWYSDEN CT 7

STOUR VALLEY WLK

LITTLE CROUCHERS

LONG'S ACRE

MARTIN HO

LIME CLOSE

OXENTURN RD

HARWOOD HO

ORCHARD DR

Wye

1

A28

Browning Bridge

46

123
107

A B C D E F

8

Great Stour

A28

Ripple
Farm

Trimworth
Manor

Works

Thornham
Lodge

Little
Winchcombe

7

Tye
Wood

Great Stour

Crundale

CT4

Glenwood
Farm

Fairisle
Farm

Winchcombe
Farm

Viney's
Wood

Church
Wood

49

Oxen Lees
Wood

Black Edge
Wood

Crundale
House

6

Little Olantigh
Farm

Warren
Wood

Crundale
Downs

OLANTIGH RD

Nursery

Marriage
Wood

5

Roughets

48

Kidney
Clump

Round
Wood

Marriage
Hill

4

Beech
Wood

Stour Valley Wlk

Marriage
Farm

Sheepfold

TN25

3

Mast

Pett Street
Farm

North Downs Way

47

HASSELL ST

Down
Farm

Prout's
Spinney

2

Meml
(Crown)

Collyerhill
Wood

Hurst
Wood

Woodmans
Arms
(PH)

SCOTTON ST

COLDHARBOUR LA

1
2
3

Withersdane
Hall

1 WITHERSDANE COTTS
2 BERNARD SUNLEY HALL
3 THE GARDEN HALL

Coldharbour
Farm

AMAGE ROAD
COTTS

AMAGE RD

Coombe
Manor

Centre for
European
Agri-Enviromental
Studies

Wye
Downs

Little
Combe

1

46

06 A 07 B C 08 D E F

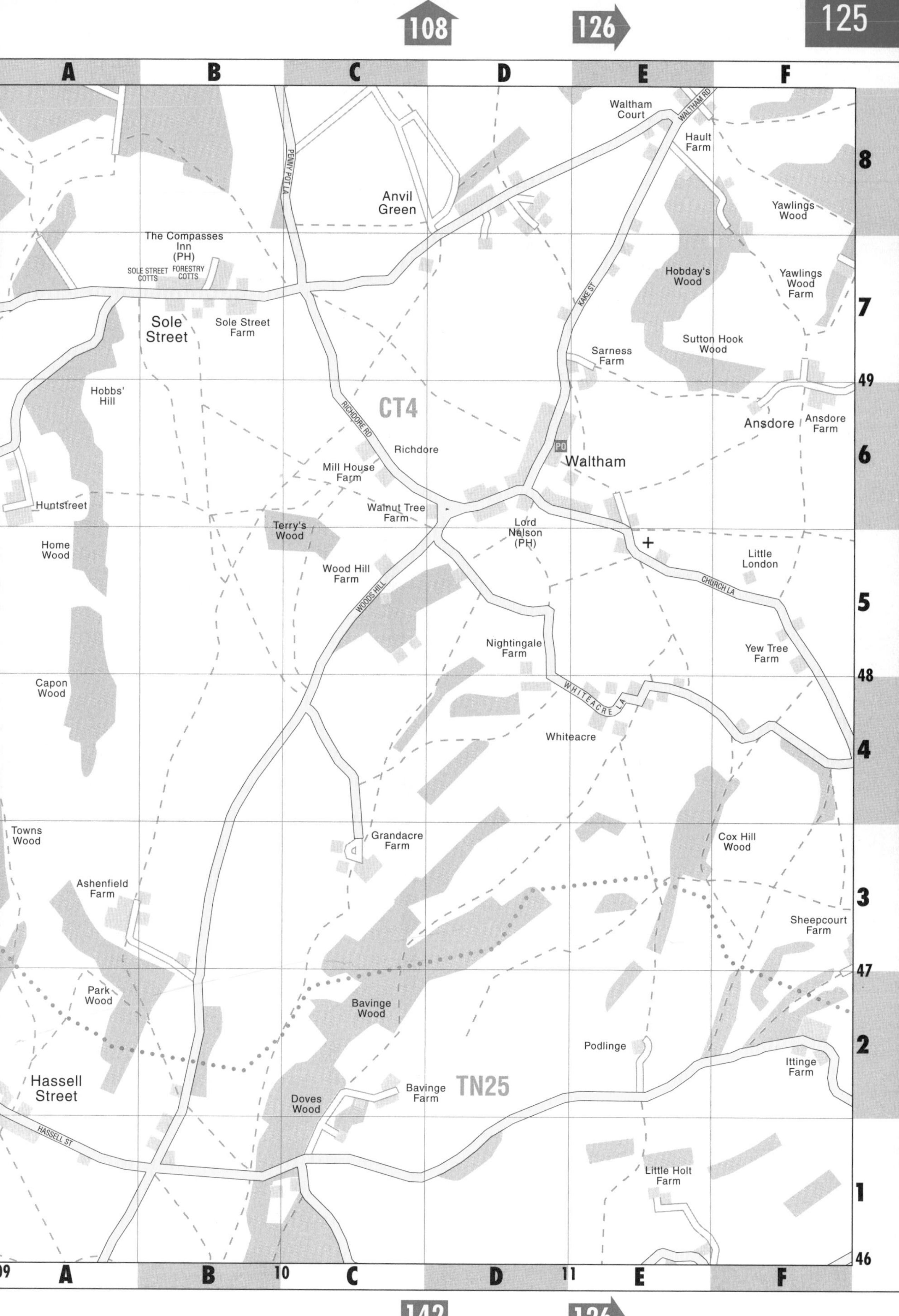

A B C D E F

8

Waltham
Court
WALTHAM RD
Hault
Farm

Yawlings
Wood

Anvil
Green

The Compasses
Inn
(PH)
SOLE STREET   FORESTRY
COTTS   COTTS

Hobday's
Wood

Yawlings
Wood
Farm

7

Sole
Street

Sole Street
Farm

KAKE ST

Sutton Hook
Wood

49

Hobbs'
Hill

CT4

Sarness
Farm

Ansdore   Ansdore
Farm

6

Richdore

PO

Waltham

Huntstreet

Mill House
Farm

Walnut Tree
Farm

Lord
Nelson
(PH)

+

Little
London

Terry's
Wood

RICHDORE RD

Home
Wood

Wood Hill
Farm

CHURCH LA

5

Nightingale
Farm

Yew Tree
Farm

WOODS HILL

48

Capon
Wood

WHITEACRE LA

Whiteacre

4

Towns
Wood

Grandacre
Farm

Cox Hill
Wood

Ashenfield
Farm

3

Sheepcourt
Farm

47

Park
Wood

Bavinge
Wood

Podlinge

Ittinge
Farm

2

Hassell
Street

Bavinge
Farm

TN25

Doves
Wood

Little Holt
Farm

1

HASSELL ST

46

A B C D E F

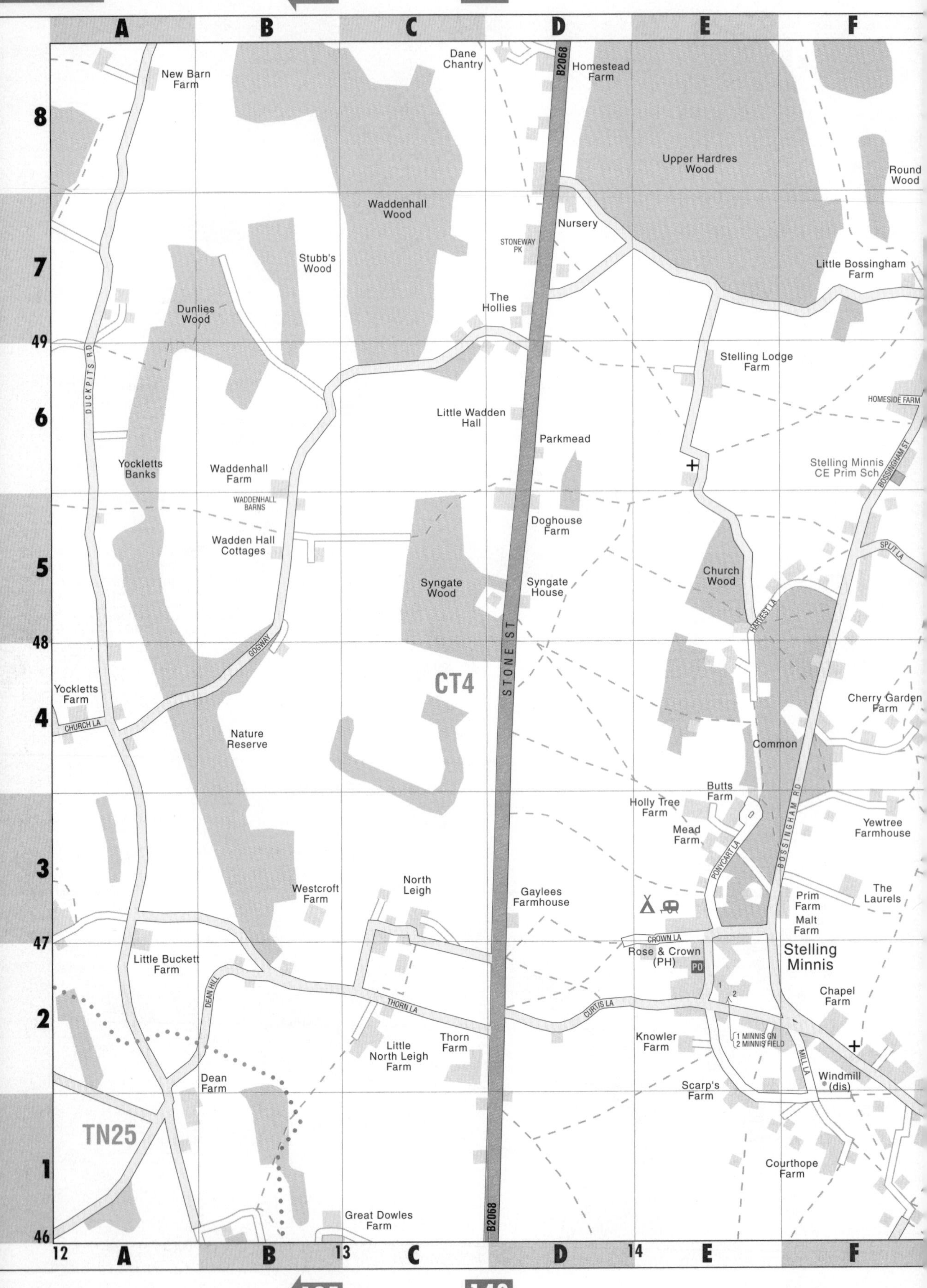

A   B   C   D   E   F

8

New Barn
Farm

Dane
Chantry

Homestead
Farm

Upper Hardres
Wood

Round
Wood

Waddenhall
Wood

Nursery

7

Stubb's
Wood

STONEWAY
PK

Little Bossingham
Farm

The
Hollies

49

Dunlies
Wood

Stelling Lodge
Farm

HOMESIDE FARM

6

Little Wadden
Hall

Parkmead

Yockletts
Banks

Waddenhall
Farm

Stelling Minnis
CE Prim Sch

WADDENHALL
BARNS

Doghouse
Farm

SPLIT LA

5

Wadden Hall
Cottages

Church
Wood

48

Syngate
Wood

Syngate
House

HARVEST LA

Yockletts
Farm

CHURCH LA

CT4

STONE ST

Cherry Garden
Farm

4

Nature
Reserve

Common

3

Westcroft
Farm

North
Leigh

Gaylees
Farmhouse

Holly Tree
Farm

Butts
Farm

Yewtree
Farmhouse

Mead
Farm

Prim
Farm

The
Laurels

47

Little Buckett
Farm

DEAN HILL

THORN LA

CURTIS LA

CROWN LA

Rose & Crown
(PH)

PO

Malt
Farm

Stelling
Minnis

2

Little
North Leigh
Farm

Thorn
Farm

Knowler
Farm

1 MINNIS GN
2 MINNIS FIELD

Chapel
Farm

Dean
Farm

Scarp's
Farm

MILL LA

Windmill
(dis)

TN25

1

Courthope
Farm

46

Great Dowles
Farm

B2068

12   A   B   13   C   D   14   E   F

DUCKPITS RD

GOGWAY

POTCART LA

BOSSINGHAM RD

BOSSINGHAM ST

B2068

A B C D E F

Little Westwood Farm
Reed's Mill (dis)
Westwood
8
MARLEY LA
HARDRES COURT RD
Lynsore Bottom
Quilters Wood
Covet Wood Cottages
Hop Packet (PH)
Great Bossingham Farm
Manns Wood
7
COVET LA
THE STREET
PETT BOTTOM RD
49
Bossingham
Lynsore Court
Kingswood Farm
TERRACE COTTS
MANNS HILL
6
Covet Wood
Clambercrown
Atchester Wood
CT4
Great Palmstead Farm
5
Palmstead
SPLIT LA
Split Lane Farm
48
Little Palmstead Farm
Dane Farm
4
PEAFIELD WOOD RD
Peafield Wood
Abbotswood
High Chimney Farm
Fryarne Park Wood
South Lodge Farm
Charcoal Farm
Beech Villa
3
Fryarne Park
Little Wildage Farm
47
Bladbean
Lodge Wood
Bladbean Stud Farm
2
Farthingsole Farm
Madams Wood
Boormanhatch Farm
Jacques Court
1
PARK GATE
46

15 A B 16 C D 17 E F

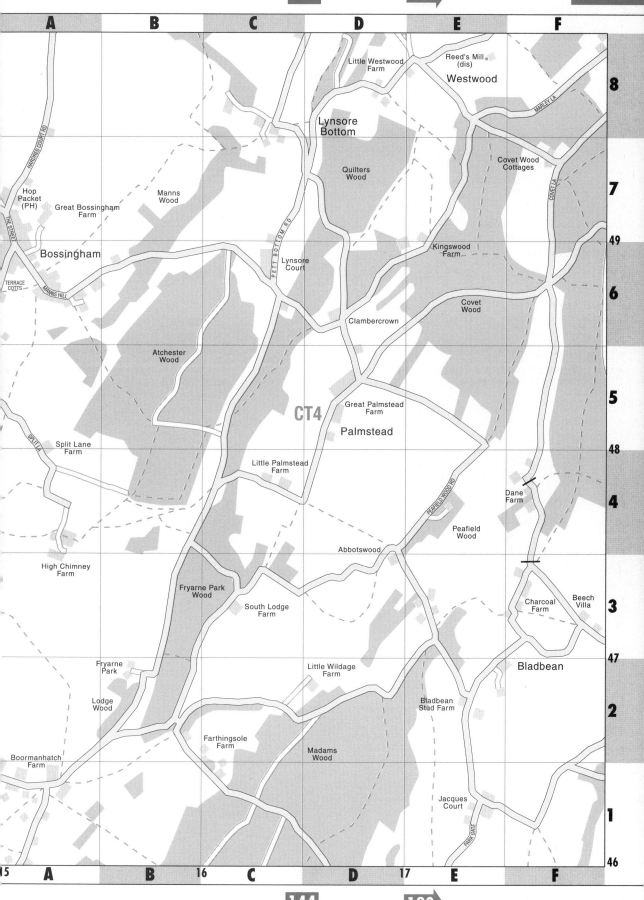

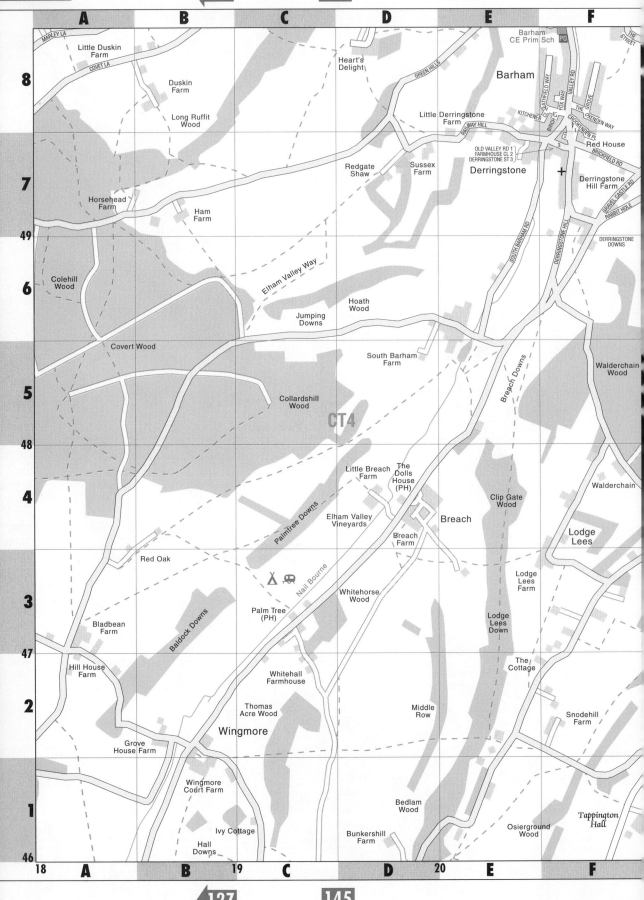

8

Marley La
Little Duskin Farm
Covet La
Duskin Farm
Long Ruffit Wood
Heart's Delight
Green Hills
Barham CE Prim Sch
PO
THE STREET
Barham
Kitchener
Birch Ct
Heathfield Way
Fox Way
Valley Rd
The Grove
Oxenden Way
Crockenden Pl
Red House
Brickfield Rd

7

Horsehead Farm
Ham Farm
Redgate Shaw
Sussex Farm
Little Derringstone Farm
Way Hill
Railway Hill
Old Valley Rd 1
Farmhouse Cl 2
Derringstone St 3
Derringstone
Derringstone Hill Farm
Gravel Castle Rd
Rabbit Hole

49

Colehill Wood
Elham Valley Way
Hoath Wood
South Barham Rd
Derringstone Hill
Derringstone Downs

6

Jumping Downs

Covert Wood
South Barham Farm
Breach Downs
Walderchain Wood

5

Collardshill Wood
CT4

48

Little Breach Farm
The Dolls House (PH)
Clip Gate Wood
Walderchain

4

Palmtree Downs
Elham Valley Vineyards
Breach
Lodge Lees

Red Oak
Nail Bourne
Breach Farm
Lodge Lees Farm

3

Bladbean Farm
Baldock Downs
Palm Tree (PH)
Whitehorse Wood
Lodge Lees Down
The Cottage

47

Hill House Farm
Whitehall Farmhouse
Thomas Acre Wood
Middle Row
Snodehill Farm

2

Wingmore
Grove House Farm
Bedlam Wood

1

Wingmore Court Farm
Osierground Wood
Tappington Hall

Ivy Cottage
Bunkershill Farm
Hall Downs

46

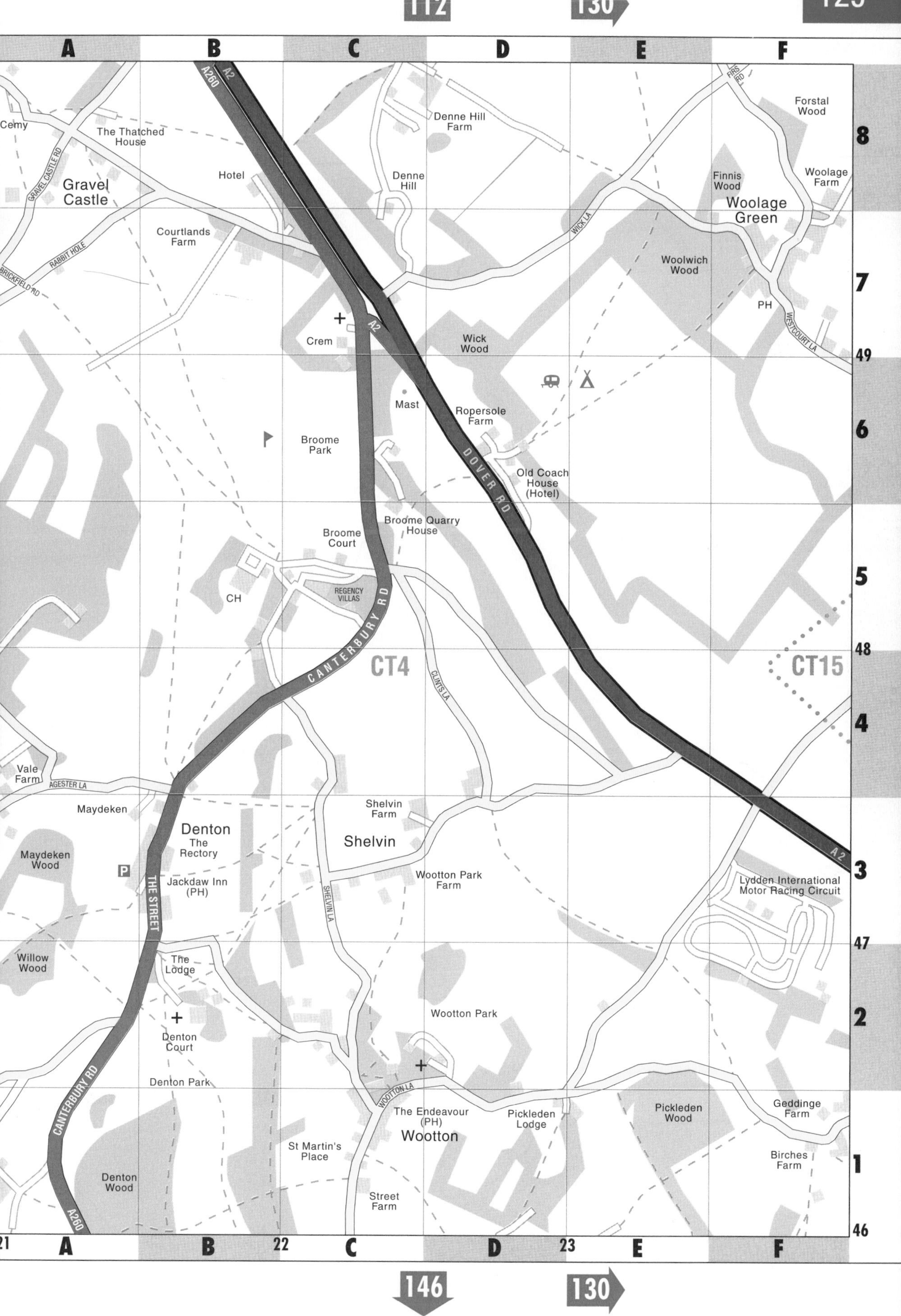
112
130
A
B
C
D
E
F
8
7
49
6
5
48
4
3
47
2
1
46
21
22
23
146
Cemy
The Thatched House
Gravel Castle
GRAVEL CASTLE RD
Hotel
Courtlands Farm
RABBIT HOLE
BRICKFIELD RD
A260
A2
Denne Hill Farm
Denne Hill
Crem
Wick Wood
WICK LA
Forstal Wood
Finnis Wood
Woolage Farm
Woolage Green
Woolwich Wood
PH
WESTCOURT LA
FIRS RD
Mast
Ropersole Farm
Broome Park
DOVER RD
Old Coach House (Hotel)
Broome Court
Broome Quarry House
REGENCY VILLAS
CH
CANTERBURY RD
CT4
CLINTS LA
CT15
Vale Farm
AGESTER LA
Maydeken
Denton
The Rectory
Maydeken Wood
Shelvin Farm
Shelvin
Jackdaw Inn (PH)
Wootton Park Farm
Lydden International Motor Racing Circuit
THE STREET
SHELVIN LA
Willow Wood
The Lodge
Wootton Park
Denton Court
Denton Park
WOOTTON LA
The Endeavour (PH)
Wootton
Pickleden Lodge
Pickleden Wood
Geddinge Farm
St Martin's Place
Birches Farm
Denton Wood
Street Farm

129
113

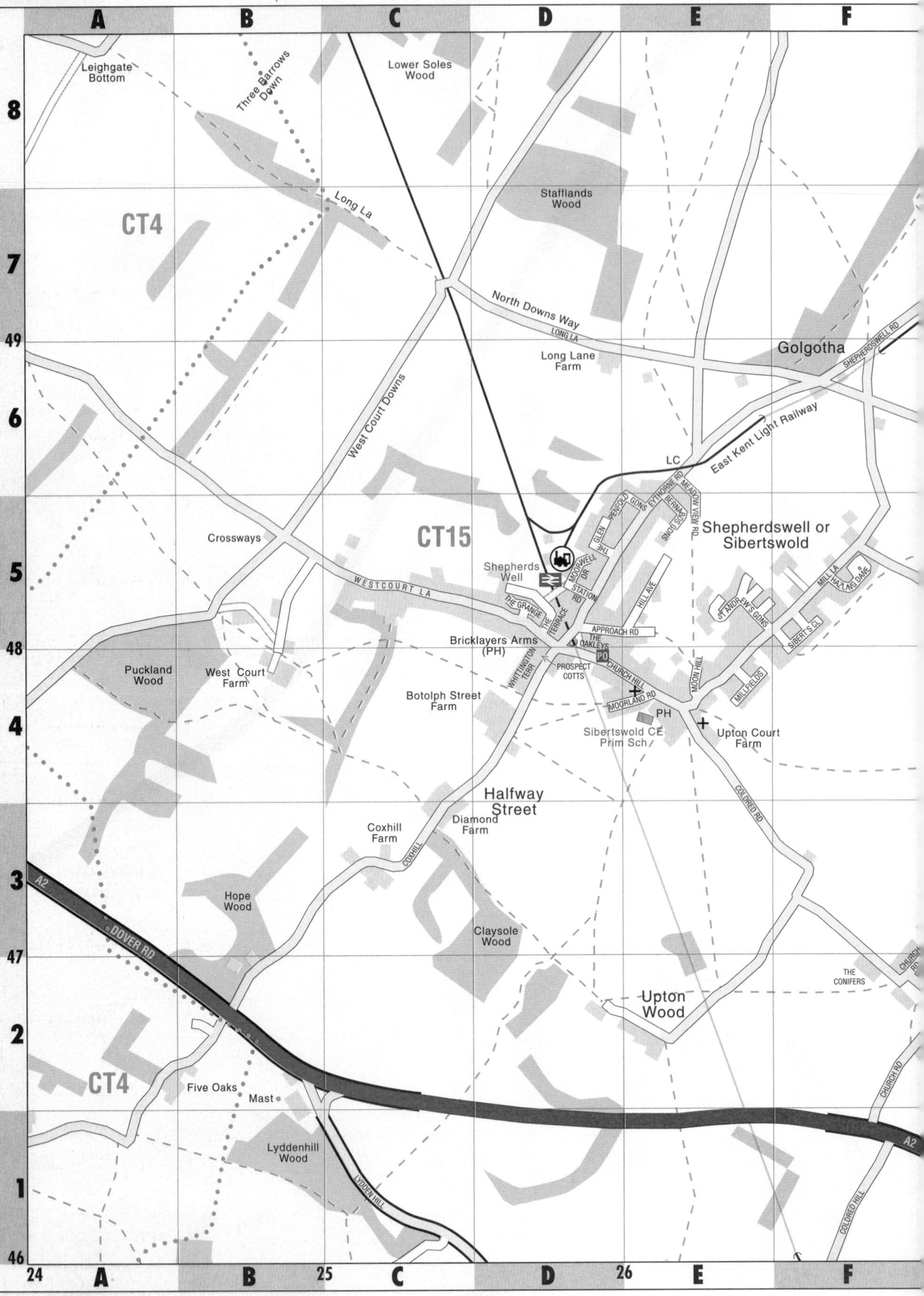

	A	B	C	D	E	F

Leighgate Bottom

Three Barrows Down

Lower Soles Wood

8

CT4

Long La

Stafflands Wood

7

North Downs Way

LONG LA

49

Golgotha

West Court Downs

Long Lane Farm

6

East Kent Light Railway

LC

Crossways

CT15

Shepherdswell or Sibertswold

PEVFOLD GDNS
THE GLEN
MOORWELL DR
EYTHORNE RD
BERNAL
MEADOW VIEW RD
SPRING GDNS

5

Shepherds Well

WESTCOURT LA

THE GRANGE

MOORWELL STATION RD

HILL AVE

ST ANDREWS GDNS

MILL LA
MAXINE DRIVE

Puckland Wood

West Court Farm

THE TERRACE

APPROACH RD

SIBERT S CL

48

Bricklayers Arms (PH)

WHITTINGTON TERR

THE OAKLEYS

PROSPECT COTTS

PO

CHURCH HILL

UNION HILL

MILLFIELDS

Botolph Street Farm

MOORLAND RD

PH

Upton Court Farm

4

Sibertswold CE Prim Sch

COLDRED RD

Halfway Street

Coxhill Farm

COXHILL

Diamond Farm

3

A2

DOVER RD

Hope Wood

Claysole Wood

THE CONIFERS

CHURCH RD

47

Upton Wood

2

CT4

Five Oaks

Mast

A2

Lyddenhill Wood

LYDDEN HILL

COLDRED HILL

CHURCH HILL

1

46

24	A	B	25	C	D	26	E	F

129
147

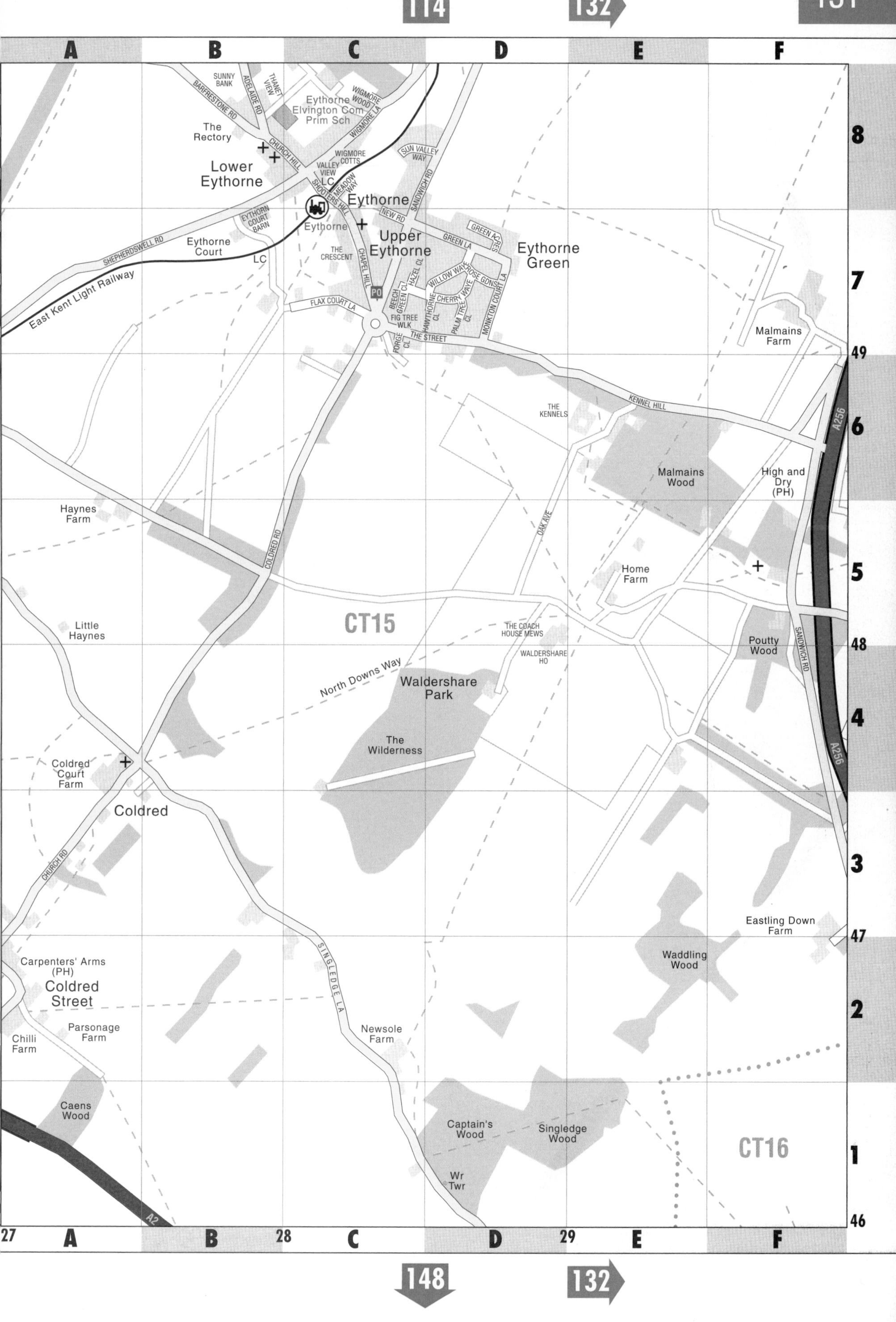

SUNNY BANK
BARFRESTONE RD
ADELAIDE RD
THANET VIEW
CHURCH HILL
The Rectory
Eythorne
Elvington Com
Prim Sch
WIGMORE WOOD
WIGMORE LA
Lower Eythorne
VALLEY VIEW
WIGMORE COTTS
SUN VALLEY WAY
SANDWICH RD
LC
Eythorne
SCHOTTS HILL
MEADOW WAY
Eythorne
Eythorne
Upper Eythorne
EYTHORN COURT BARN
THE CRESCENT
CHAPEL HILL
Eythorne
Eythorne
LC
SHEPHERDSWELL RD
Eythorne Court
NEW RD
GREEN LA
GREEN ACRES
Eythorne Green
FLAX COURT LA
East Kent Light Railway
PO
BEECH CL
FORGE CL
HAZEL CL
HAWTHORNE CL
FIG TREE WLK
CHERRY CL
PALM TREE CL
WILLOW WAY
ROSE GDNS
WATTLE
MONKTON COURT LA
THE STREET
Malmains Farm
A256
THE KENNELS
KENNEL HILL
Malmains Wood
High and Dry (PH)
Haynes Farm
COLDRED RD
OAK AVE
Home Farm
+
SANDWICH RD
CT15
Little Haynes
THE COACH HOUSE MEWS
WALDERSHARE HO
Poutty Wood
North Downs Way
Waldershare Park
+
Coldred Court Farm
The Wilderness
Coldred
CHURCH RD
Eastling Down Farm
Carpenters' Arms (PH)
SINGLEDGE LA
Waddling Wood
Coldred Street
Chilli Farm
Parsonage Farm
Newsole Farm
Caens Wood
Captain's Wood
Singledge Wood
CT16
A2
Wr Twr

131
115

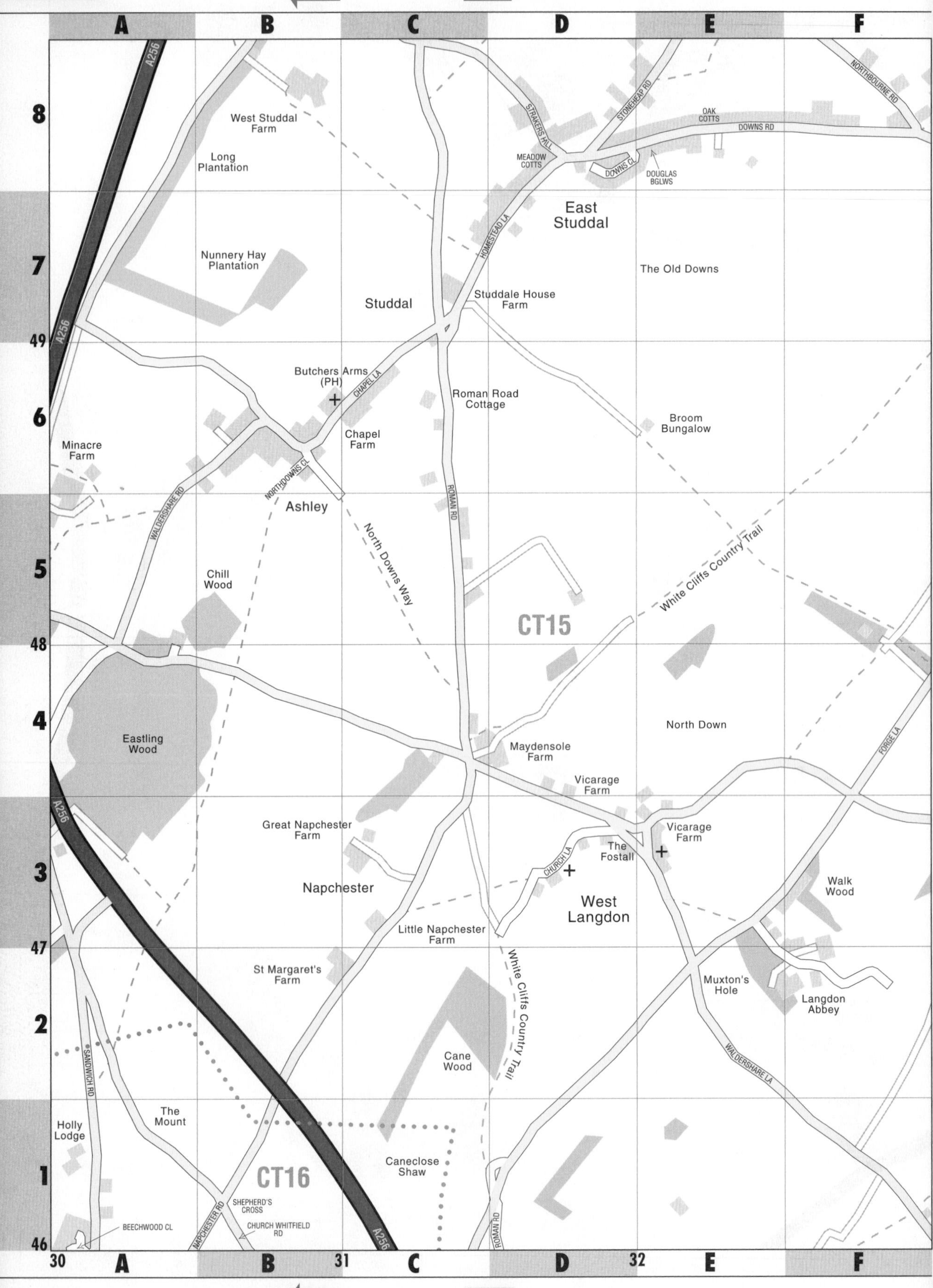
A
B
C
D
E
F
8
7
49
6
5
48
4
3
47
2
1
46
30
31
32
A256
West Studdal Farm
Long Plantation
Nunnery Hay Plantation
STRAKERS HILL
STONEHEAP RD
OAK COTTS
DOWNS RD
NORTHBOURNE RD
MEADOW COTTS
DOWNS CL
DOUGLAS BGLWS
East Studdal
HOMESTEAD LA
The Old Downs
Studdal
Studdale House Farm
Butchers Arms (PH)
CHAPEL LA
Roman Road Cottage
Broom Bungalow
Minacre Farm
Chapel Farm
NORTHDOWNS CL
Ashley
WALDERSHARE RD
ROMAN RD
North Downs Way
White Cliffs Country Trail
Chill Wood
CT15
North Down
Eastling Wood
Maydensole Farm
FORGE LA
Vicarage Farm
Great Napchester Farm
Vicarage Farm
The Fostall
CHURCH LA
Napchester
West Langdon
Walk Wood
Little Napchester Farm
St Margaret's Farm
Muxton's Hole
Langdon Abbey
White Cliffs Country Trail
WALDERSHARE LA
SANDWICH RD
Cane Wood
Holly Lodge
The Mount
Caneclose Shaw
CT16
NAPCHESTER RD
SHEPHERD'S CROSS
BEECHWOOD CL
CHURCH WHITFIELD RD
ROMAN RD

131
149

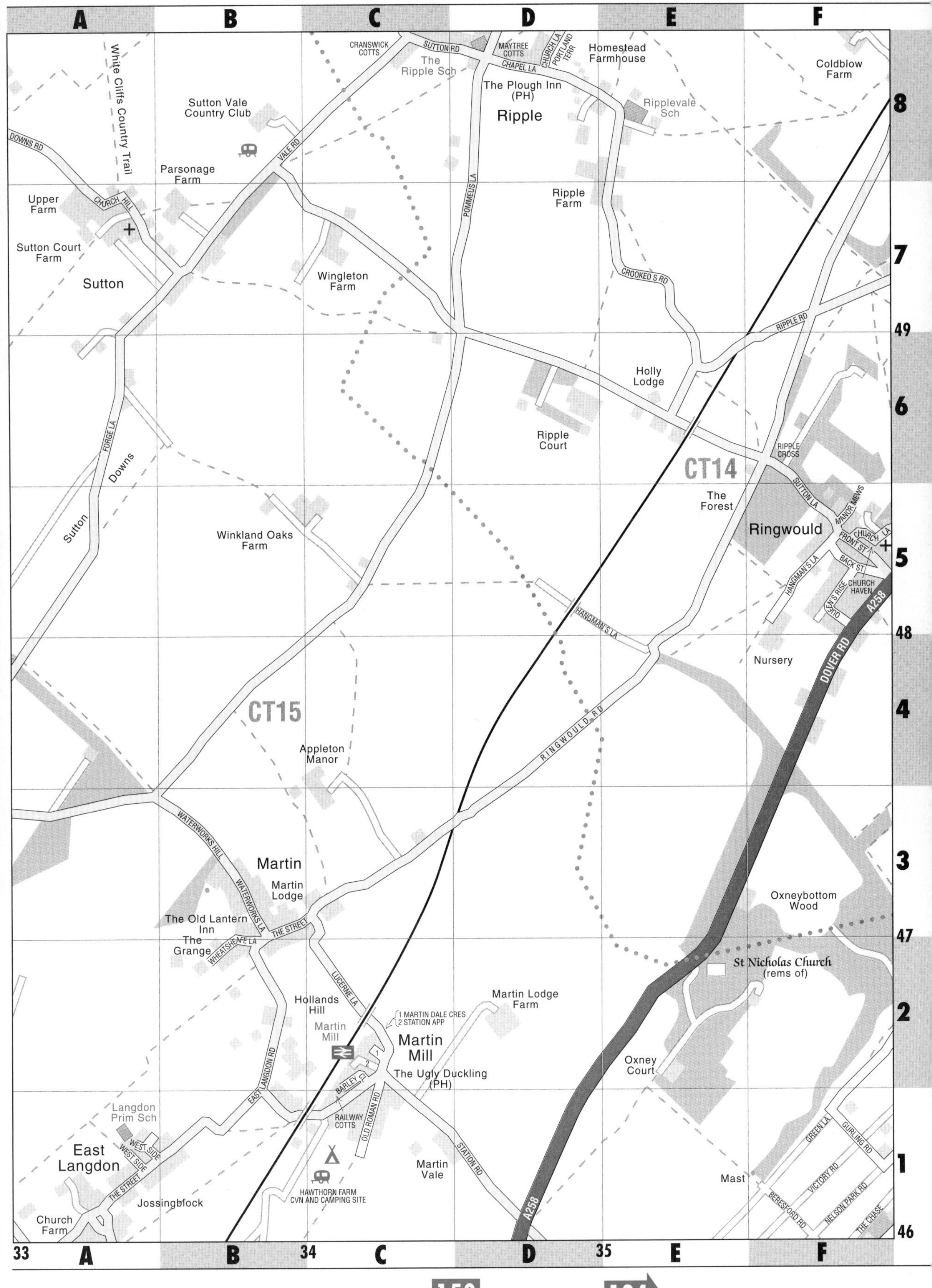
A
B
C
D
E
F
8
7
49
6
5
48
4
3
47
2
1
46
33
34
35
White Cliffs Country Trail
Sutton Vale Country Club
Parsonage Farm
Upper Farm
Sutton Court Farm
Sutton
DOWNS RD
CHURCH HILL
VALE RD
CRANSWICK COTTS
SUTTON RD
The Ripple Sch
MAYTREE COTTS
CHAPEL LA
CHURCH LA
PORTLAND TERR
The Plough Inn (PH)
Ripple
Homestead Farmhouse
Ripplevale Sch
Coldblow Farm
POMMEUS LA
Ripple Farm
Wingleton Farm
CROOKED S RD
RIPPLE RD
Holly Lodge
Ripple Court
RIPPLE CROSS
CT14
The Forest
Ringwould
SUTTON LA
MANOR MEWS
CHURCH LA
FRONT ST
BACK ST
HANGMAN'S LA
CHURCH HAVEN
QUEEN'S RISE
A258
DOVER RD
Nursery
FORGE LA
Sutton Downs
Winkland Oaks Farm
HANGMAN'S LA
RINGWOULD RD
CT15
Appleton Manor
WATERWORKS HILL
Martin
Martin Lodge
WATERWORKS LA
The Old Lantern Inn
THE STREET
The Grange
WHEATSHEAFE LA
Oxneybottom Wood
St Nicholas Church (rems of)
Hollands Hill
LUCERNE LA
1 MARTIN DALE CRES
2 STATION APP
Martin Mill
Martin Mill
Martin Lodge Farm
The Ugly Duckling (PH)
Oxney Court
EAST LANGDON RD
BARLEY CL
RAILWAY COTTS
OLD ROMAN RD
Langdon Prim Sch
WEST SIDE
WEST SIDE
East Langdon
THE STREET
Jossingblock
Church Farm
HAWTHORN FARM CVN AND CAMPING SITE
Martin Vale
STATION RD
A258
Mast
GREEN LA
GURLING RD
VICTORY RD
BERESFORD RD
NELSON PARK RD
THE CHASE

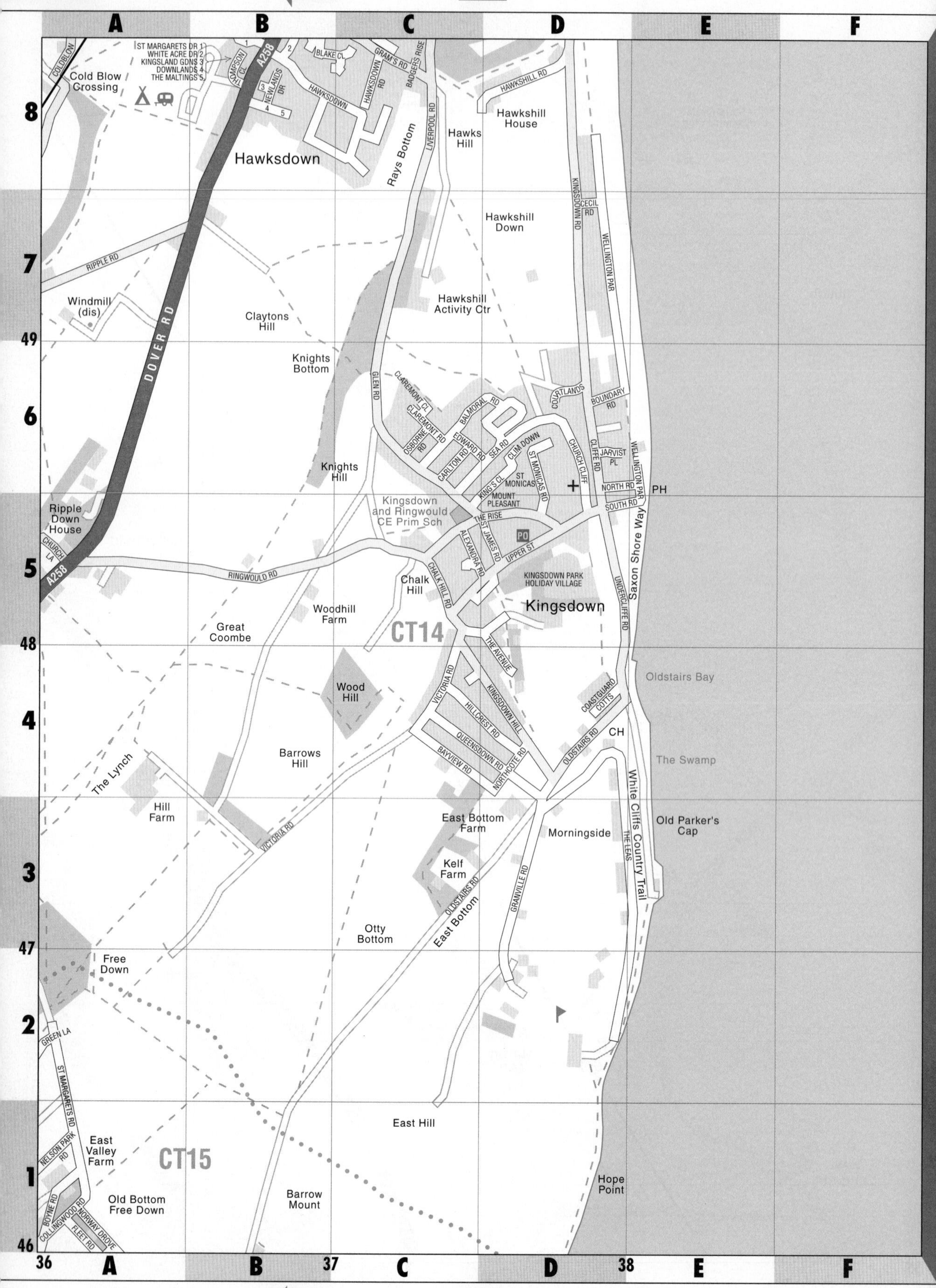
Cold Blow Crossing
ST MARGARETS DR 1
WHITE ACRE DR 2
KINGSLAND GDNS 3
DOWNLANDS 4
THE MALTINGS 5
Hawksdown
Hawks Hill
Hawkshill House
Rays Bottom
Hawkshill Down
Hawkshill Activity Ctr
RIPPLE RD
Windmill (dis)
Claytons Hill
DOVER RD
A258
Knights Bottom
Knights Hill
Kingsdown and Ringwould CE Prim Sch
Ripple Down House
RINGWOULD RD
Chalk Hill
Woodhill Farm
Great Coombe
CT14
Kingsdown
KINGSDOWN PARK HOLIDAY VILLAGE
Saxon Shore Way
PH
Oldstairs Bay
Wood Hill
Barrows Hill
The Swamp
The Lynch
Hill Farm
VICTORIA RD
East Bottom Farm
Morningside
Old Parker's Cap
Kelf Farm
Otty Bottom
East Bottom
White Cliffs Country Trail
Free Down
East Hill
East Valley Farm
CT15
Old Bottom Free Down
Barrow Mount
Hope Point

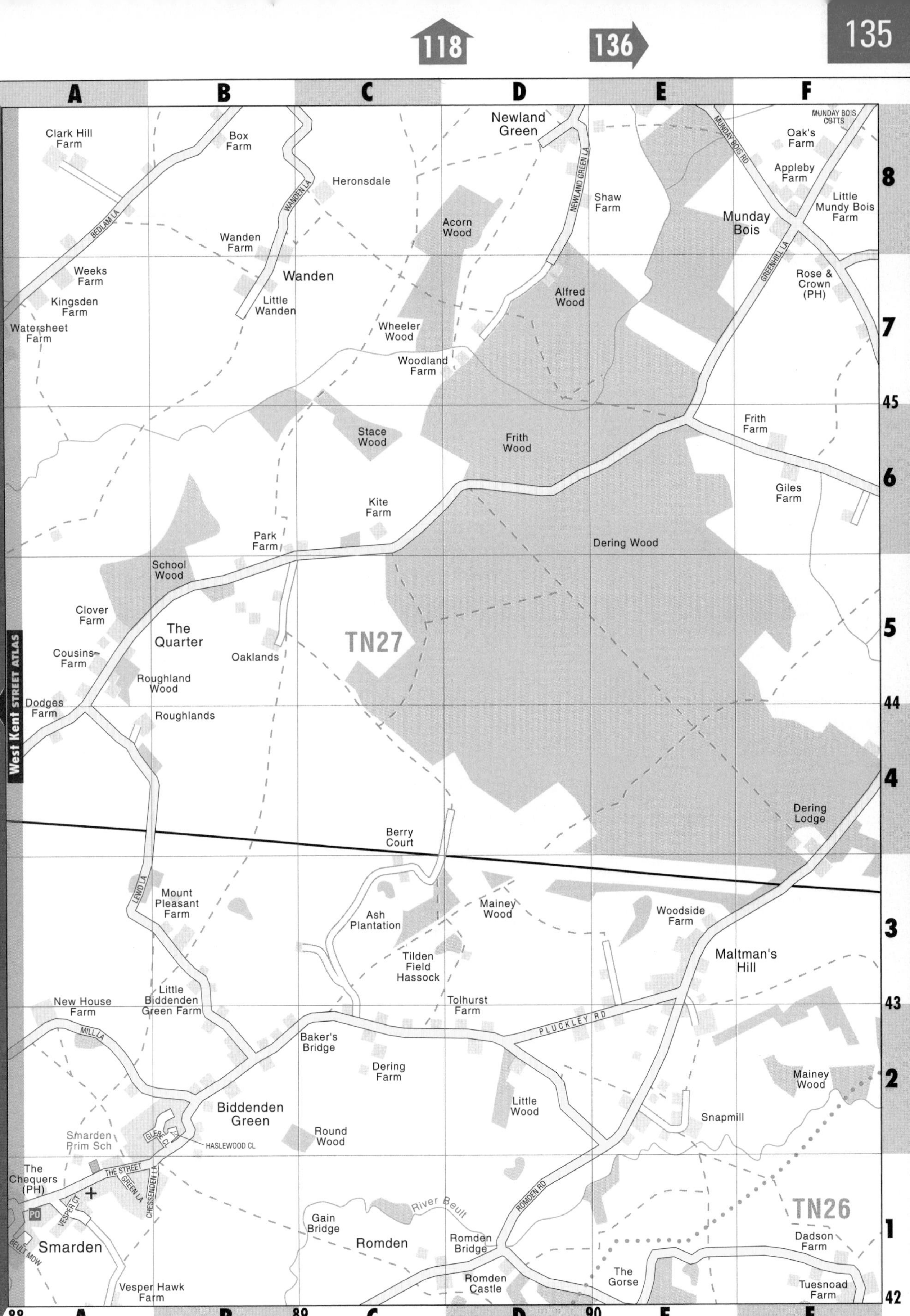
A
B
C
D
E
F
Clark Hill Farm
Box Farm
Newland Green
MUNDAY BOIS COTTS
Oak's Farm
Appleby Farm
Heronsdale
WANDEN LA
NEWLAND GREEN LA
MUNDAY BOIS RD
Shaw Farm
Little Mundy Bois Farm
Munday Bois
Acorn Wood
BEDLAM LA
Wanden Farm
GREENHILL LA
Weeks Farm
Wanden
Rose & Crown (PH)
Alfred Wood
Kingsden Farm
Little Wanden
Wheeler Wood
Watersheet Farm
Woodland Farm
Frith Farm
Stace Wood
Frith Wood
Giles Farm
Kite Farm
Park Farm
Dering Wood
School Wood
Clover Farm
The Quarter
TN27
Cousins Farm
Oaklands
Roughland Wood
Dodges Farm
Roughlands
Dering Lodge
Berry Court
LEWD LA
Mount Pleasant Farm
Ash Plantation
Mainey Wood
Woodside Farm
Maltman's Hill
Tilden Field Hassock
Little Biddenden Green Farm
New House Farm
Tolhurst Farm
MILL LA
PLUCKLEY RD
Baker's Bridge
Dering Farm
Mainey Wood
Little Wood
Biddenden Green
Snapmill
Smarden Prim Sch
GLEBE CL
HASLEWOOD CL
Round Wood
The Chequers (PH)
THE STREET
GREEN LA
CHESSENDEN LA
River Beult
ROMDEN RD
TN26
PO
VESPER CT
Gain Bridge
Romden
Romden Bridge
Dadson Farm
BEULT MDW
Smarden
The Gorse
Romden Castle
Tuesnoad Farm
Vesper Hawk Farm
8
7
45
6
5
44
4
3
43
2
1
42
88
89
90
West Kent STREET ATLAS

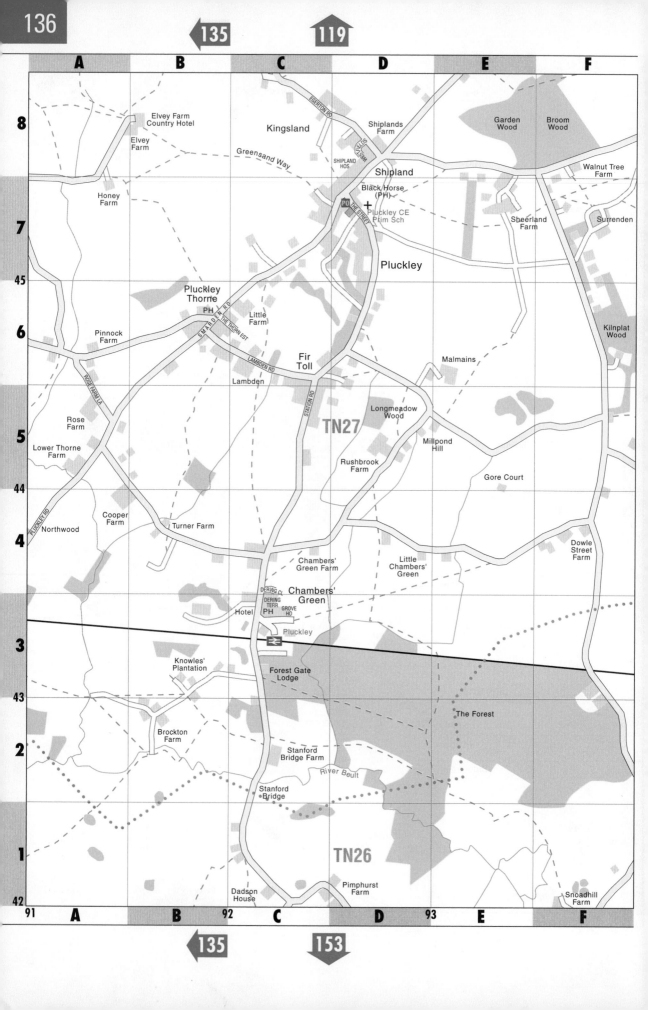

A B C D E F

8

Elvey Farm
Country Hotel
Elvey
Farm

Kingsland

Greensand Way

Shiplands
Farm

EGERTON RD

WESTGATE ST

SHIPLAND
HOS

Shipland

Garden
Wood

Broom
Wood

Walnut Tree
Farm

Honey
Farm

Black Horse
(PH)

PO THE STREET

Pluckley CE
Prim Sch

Pluckley

Sheerland
Farm

Surrenden

7

45

Pluckley
Thorne

PH

Pinnock
Farm

SMARDEN RD

THE THORN EST

Little
Farm

LAMBDEN RD

Fir
Toll

Malmains

Kilnplat
Wood

6

Lambden

STATION RD

TN27

Longmeadow
Wood

Millpond
Hill

Rose
Farm

Rushbrook
Farm

Gore Court

5

44

Lower Thorne
Farm

PLUCKLEY RD

ROSE FARM LA

Cooper
Farm

Turner Farm

Chambers'
Green Farm

Little
Chambers'
Green

Dowle
Street
Farm

4

Northwood

DERING CL

DERING
TERR

GROVE RD

Chambers'
Green

Hotel

PH

Pluckley

Knowles'
Plantation

Forest Gate
Lodge

The Forest

3

43

Brockton
Farm

Stanford
Bridge Farm

River Beult

2

Stanford
Bridge

TN26

Dadson
House

Pimphurst
Farm

Snoadhill
Farm

1

42

91 A B 92 C D 93 E F

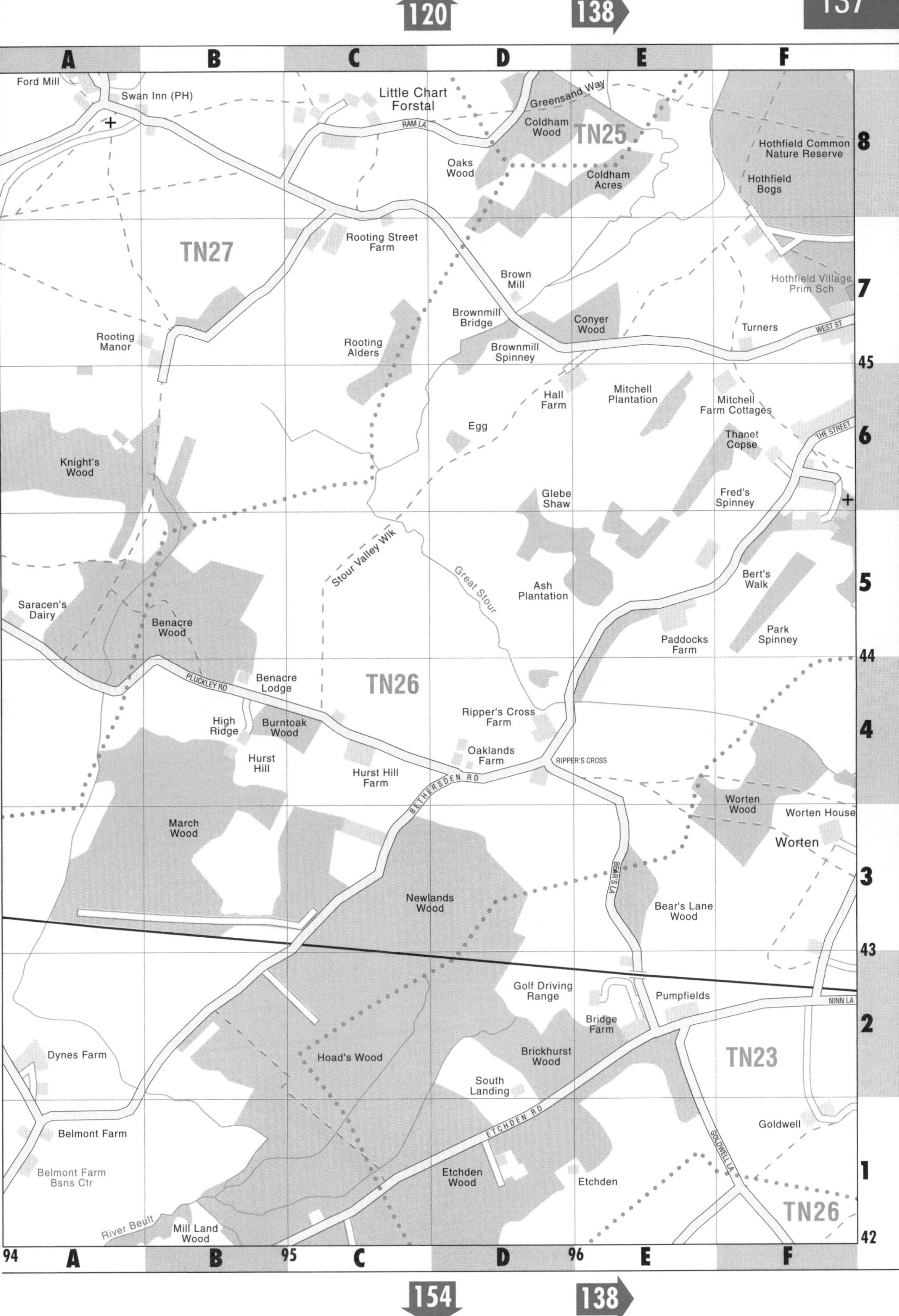

120
138
154
138

137 121

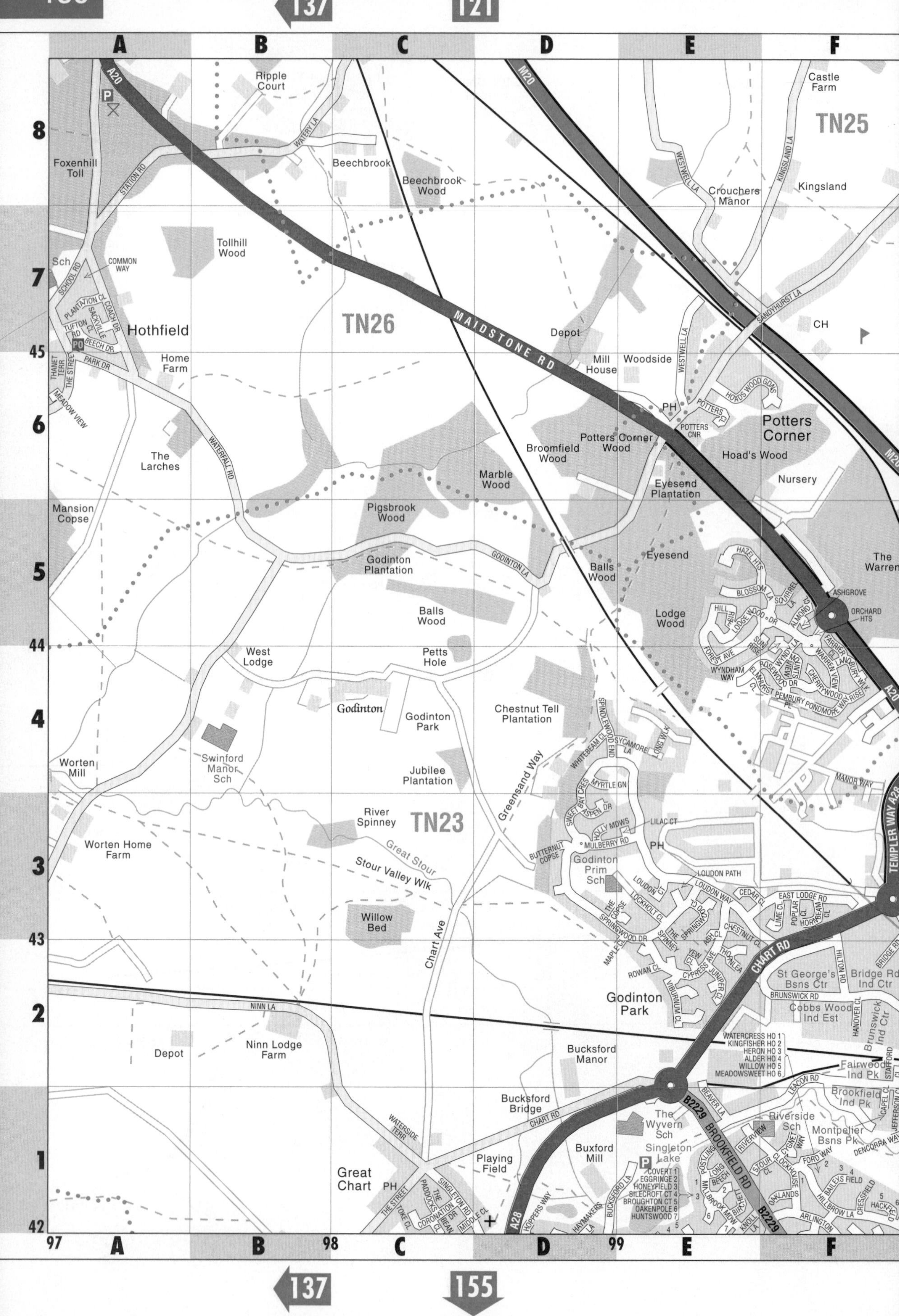
A B C D E F
8 7 6 5 4 3 2 1
45 44 43 42
97 98 99
Ripple Court
Foxenhill Toll
Beechbrook
Beechbrook Wood
Castle Farm
TN25
Crouchers Manor
Kingsland
Tollhill Wood
Sch
Hothfield
TN26
MAIDSTONE RD
Depot
CH
Home Farm
Mill House
Woodside
Potters Corner
The Larches
Potters Corner Wood
Broomfield Wood
Hoad's Wood
Marble Wood
Eyesend Plantation
Nursery
Mansion Copse
Pigsbrook Wood
Godinton Plantation
Balls Wood
Eyesend
The Warren
Lodge Wood
West Lodge
Petts Hole
Godinton
Godinton Park
Chestnut Tell Plantation
Swinford Manor Sch
Worten Mill
Jubilee Plantation
Greensand Way
River Spinney
TN23
Worten Home Farm
Great Stour
Stour Valley Wlk
Godinton Prim Sch
Willow Bed
Chart Ave
CHART RD
St George's Bsns Ctr
Bridge Rd Ind Ctr
Godinton Park
Cobbs Wood Ind Est
Brunswick Ind Ctr
Depot
Ninn Lodge Farm
Bucksford Manor
Fairwood Ind Pk
Brookfield Ind Pk
Bucksford Bridge
The Wyvern Sch
Riverside Sch
Montpelier Bsns Pk
Buxford Mill
Singleton Lake
Playing Field
Great Chart
PH
BROOKFIELD RD
TEMPLER WAY A28
A20
M20
B2229
A28

137 155

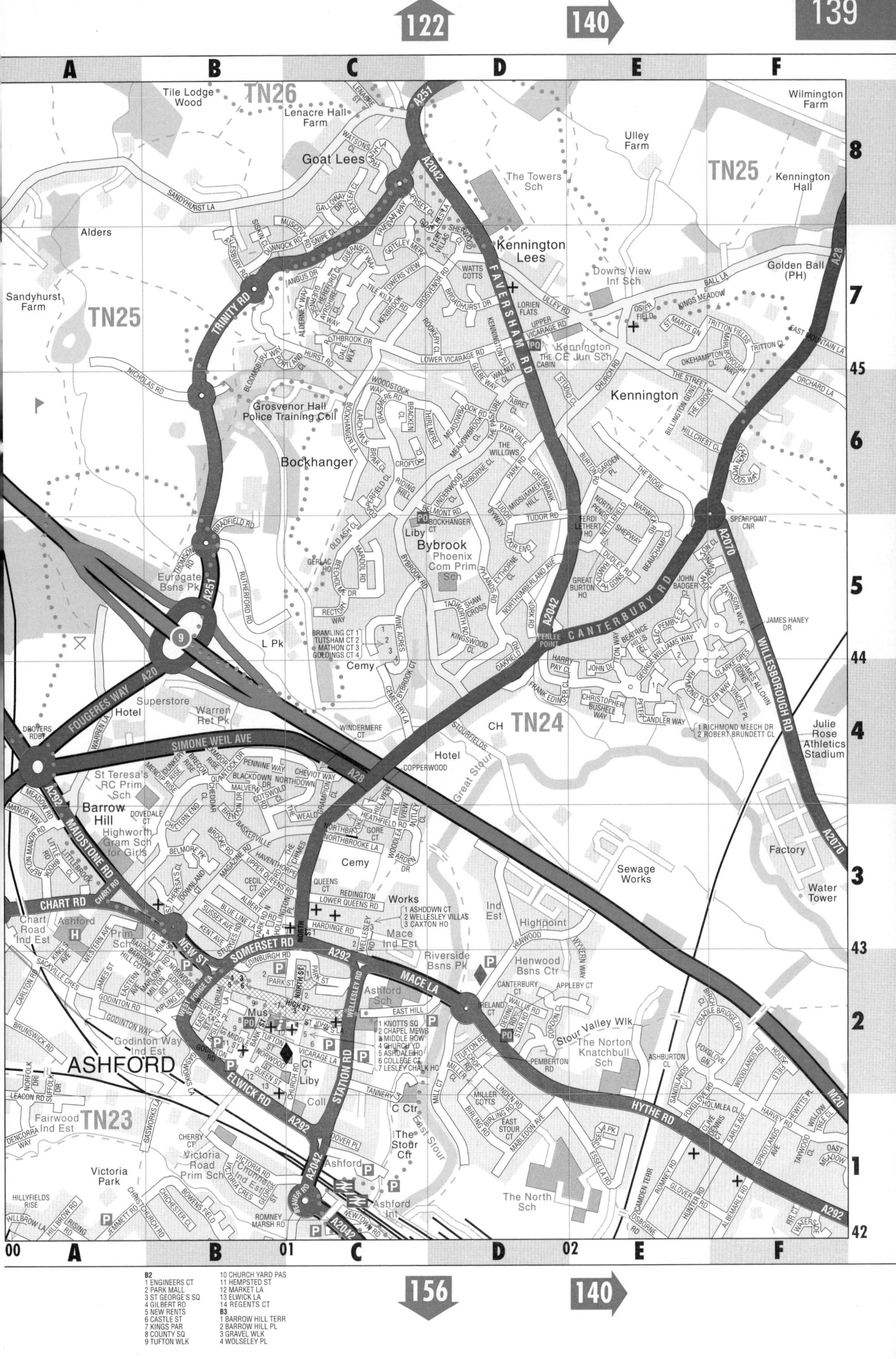

139
123

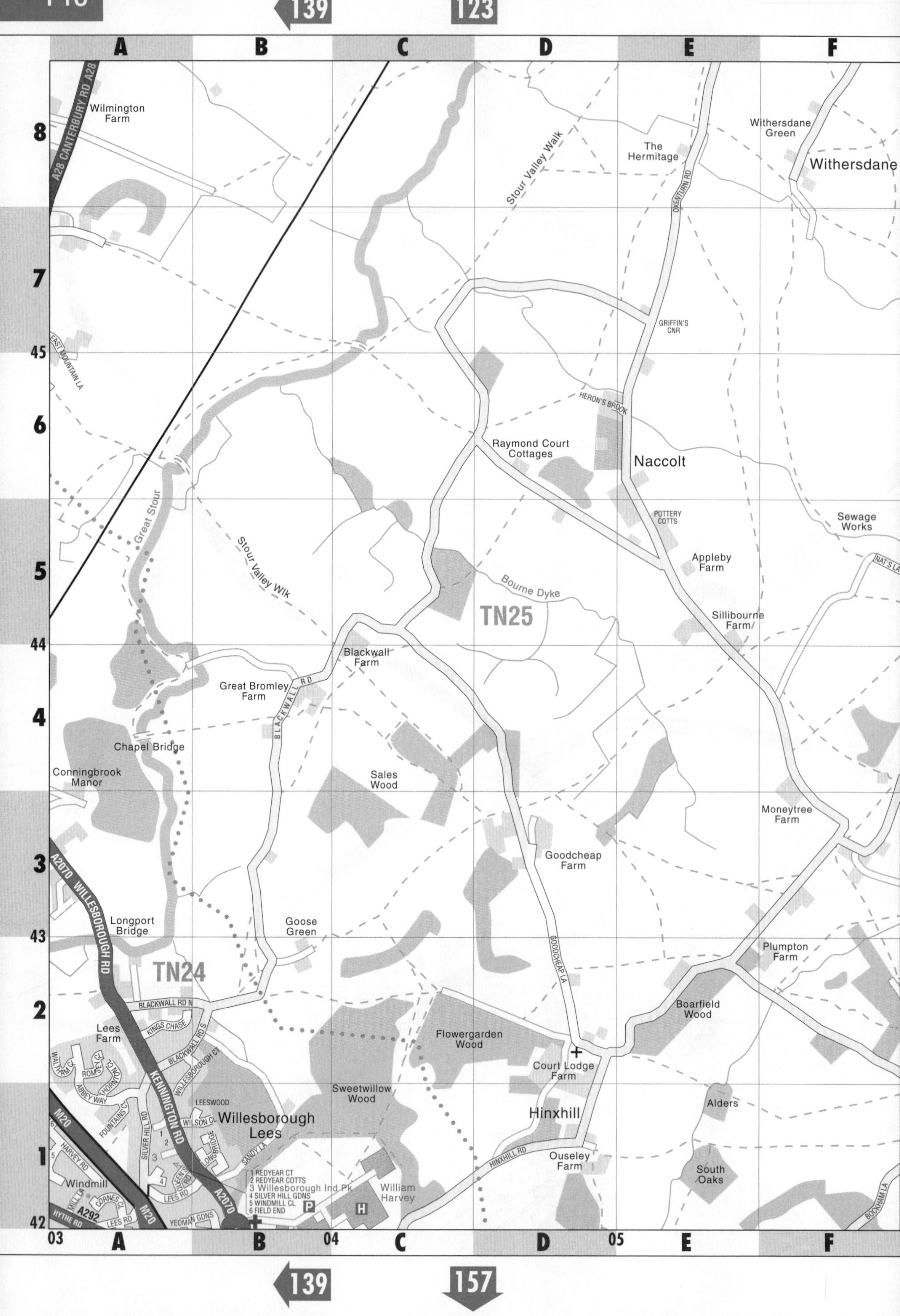
A
B
C
D
E
F
8
7
45
6
5
44
4
3
43
2
1
42
03
04
05
A28 CANTERBURY RD A28
Wilmington
Farm
Withersdane
Green
Withersdane
The
Hermitage
Stour Valley Walk
OXENTURN RD
GRIFFIN'S
CNR
EAST MOUNTAIN LA
HERON'S BROOK
Raymond Court
Cottages
Naccolt
POTTERY
COTTS
Sewage
Works
Appleby
Farm
NAT'S LA
Great Stour
Stour Valley Wlk
Bourne Dyke
TN25
Sillibourne
Farm
Blackwall
Farm
Great Bromley
Farm
BLACKWALL RD
Chapel Bridge
Conningbrook
Manor
Sales
Wood
Moneytree
Farm
A2070 WILLESBOROUGH RD
Goodcheap
Farm
Longport
Bridge
Goose
Green
GOODCHEAP LA
Plumpton
Farm
TN24
BLACKWALL RD N
Boarfield
Wood
Lees
Farm
KINGS CHASE
BLACKWALL RD S
Flowergarden
Wood
Court Lodge
Farm
WILLESBOROUGH CT
KENNINGTON RD
Sweetwillow
Wood
Alders
ABBEY WAY
LEESWOOD
Willesborough
Lees
Hinxhill
M20
FOUNTAINS CL
SILVER HILL RD
WILSON CL
SANDY LA
HINXHILL RD
Ouseley
Farm
South
Oaks
HARVEY RD
1 REDYEAR CT
2 REDYEAR COTTS
3 Willesborough Ind Pk
4 SILVER HILL GDNS
5 WINDMILL CL
6 FIELD END
Windmill
William
Harvey
A2070
A292
HYTHE RD
LEES RD
YEOMAN GDNS
BOCKHAM LA

139
157

124
142

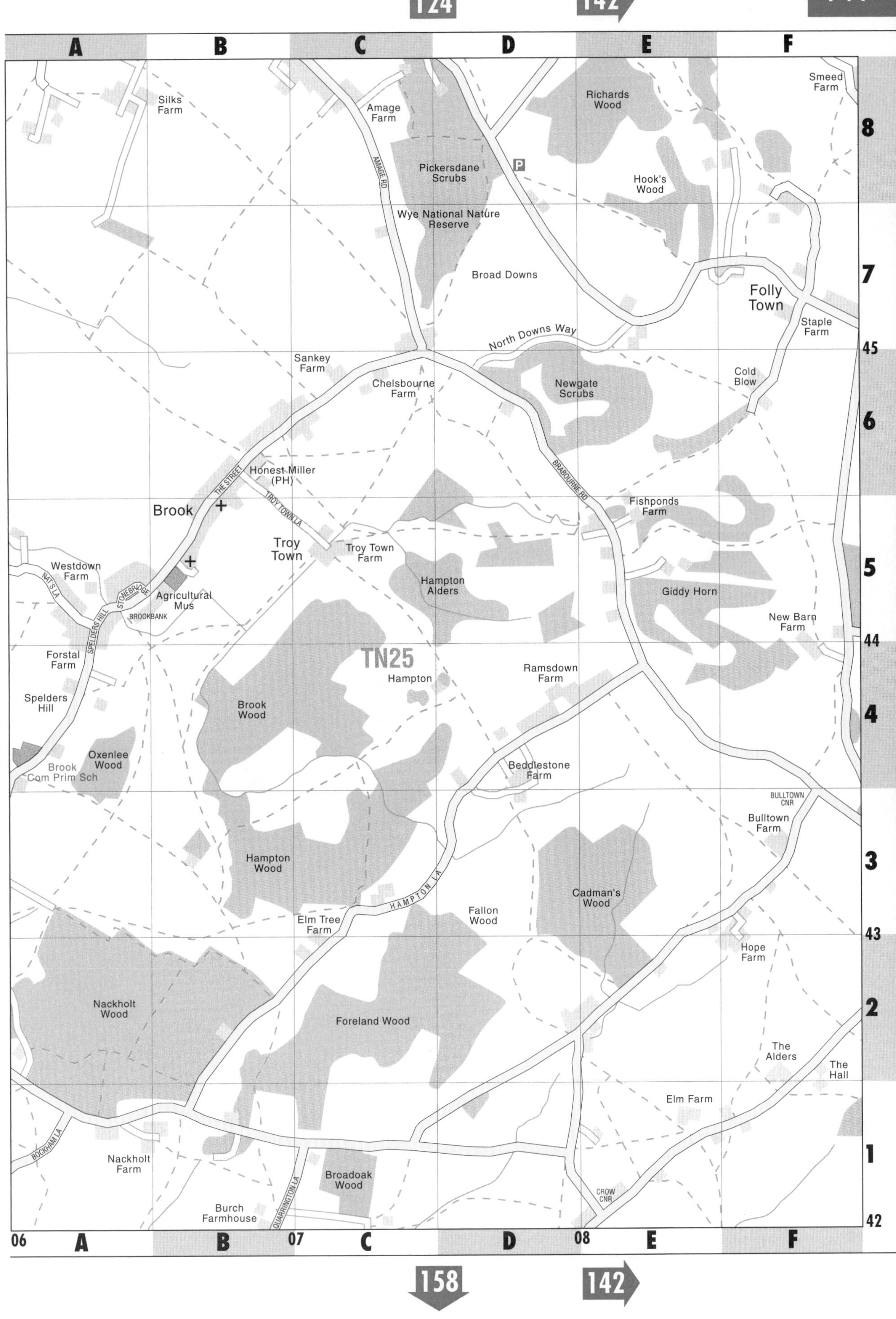

158
142

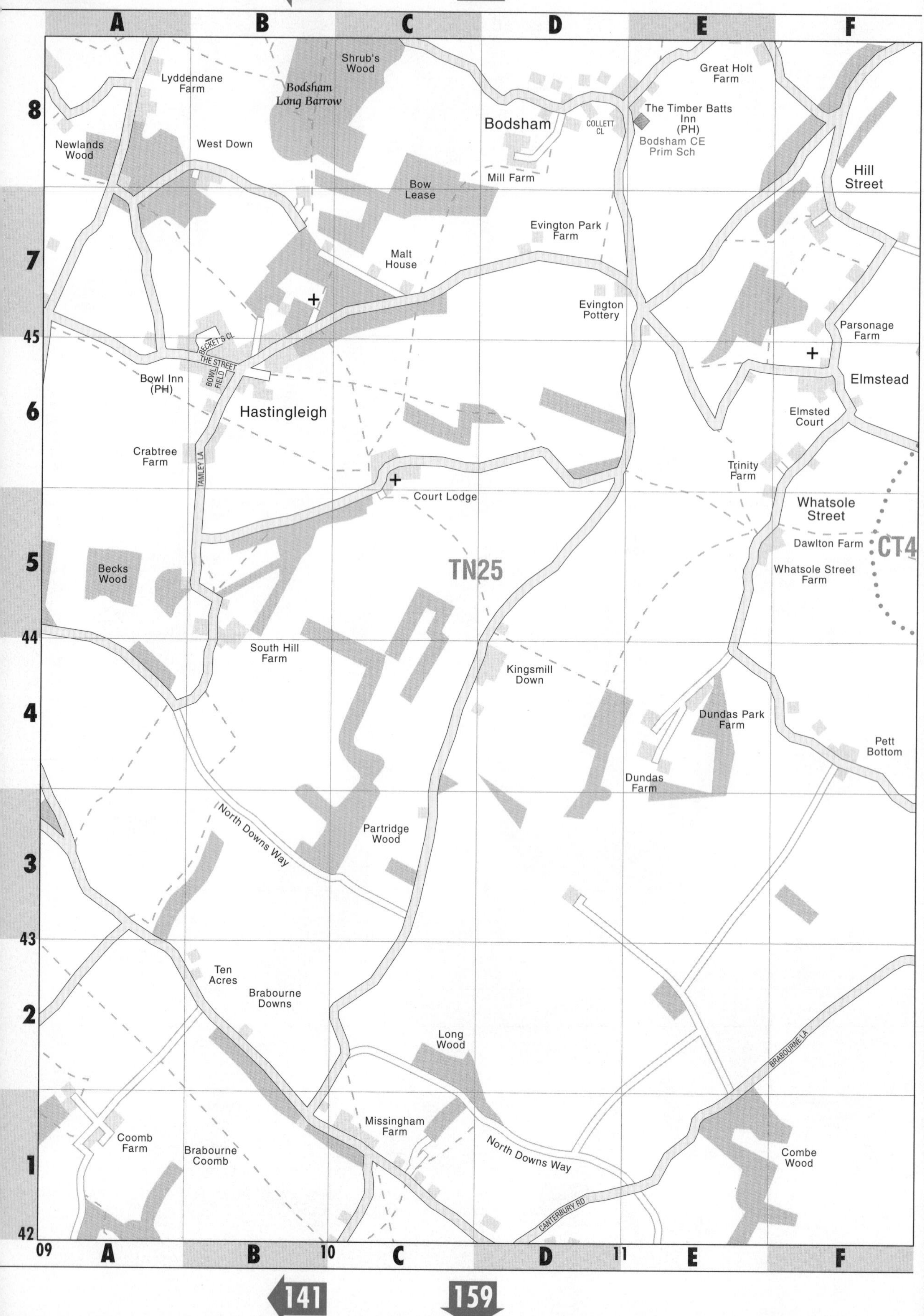

A B C D E F

8

Lyddendane
Farm

Shrub's
Wood

Bodsham
Long Barrow

Great Holt
Farm

Bodsham

COLLETT
CL

The Timber Batts
Inn
(PH)

Bodsham CE
Prim Sch

Newlands
Wood

West Down

Hill
Street

Bow
Lease

Mill Farm

7

Malt
House

Evington Park
Farm

45

BECKET'S CL

THE STREET

BOWL FIELD

Evington
Pottery

Parsonage
Farm

Bowl Inn
(PH)

Hastingleigh

Elmstead

6

Elmsted
Court

Crabtree
Farm

TAMLEY LA

Trinity
Farm

Court Lodge

Whatsole
Street

CT4

5

Becks
Wood

TN25

Dawlton Farm

Whatsole Street
Farm

44

South Hill
Farm

Kingsmill
Down

Dundas Park
Farm

4

Pett
Bottom

Dundas
Farm

North Downs Way

Partridge
Wood

3

43

Ten
Acres

Brabourne
Downs

2

Long
Wood

BRABOURNE LA

Coomb
Farm

Missingham
Farm

Combe
Wood

1

Brabourne
Coomb

North Downs Way

42

CANTERBURY RD

09 A B 10 C D 11 E F

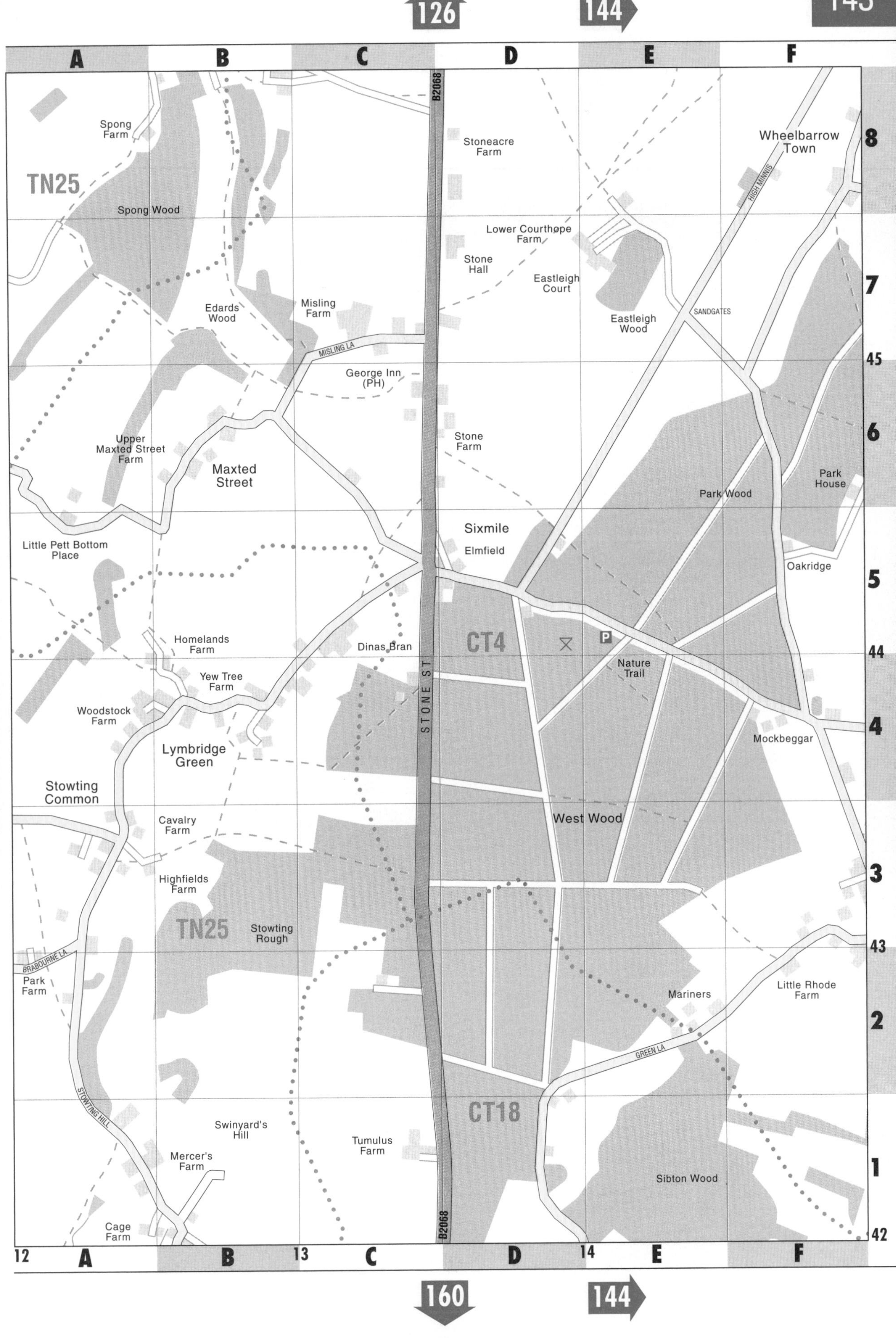
126
144
A
B
C
D
E
F
8
7
45
6
5
44
4
3
43
2
1
42
12
13
14
160
144
B2068
Spong Farm
TN25
Spong Wood
Stoneacre Farm
Wheelbarrow Town
HIGH MINNIS
Lower Courthope Farm
Stone Hall
Eastleigh Court
Eastleigh Wood
SANDGATES
Edards Wood
Misling Farm
MISLING LA
George Inn (PH)
Upper Maxted Street Farm
Maxted Street
Stone Farm
Park House
Park Wood
Sixmile
Elmfield
Little Pett Bottom Place
Oakridge
CT4
Nature Trail
Homelands Farm
Dinas Bran
Yew Tree Farm
Woodstock Farm
STONE ST
Mockbeggar
Lymbridge Green
Stowting Common
West Wood
Cavalry Farm
Highfields Farm
TN25
Stowting Rough
BRABOURNE LA
Park Farm
Mariners
Little Rhode Farm
GREEN LA
STOWTING HILL
CT18
Swinyard's Hill
Tumulus Farm
Mercer's Farm
Sibton Wood
Cage Farm

143 127

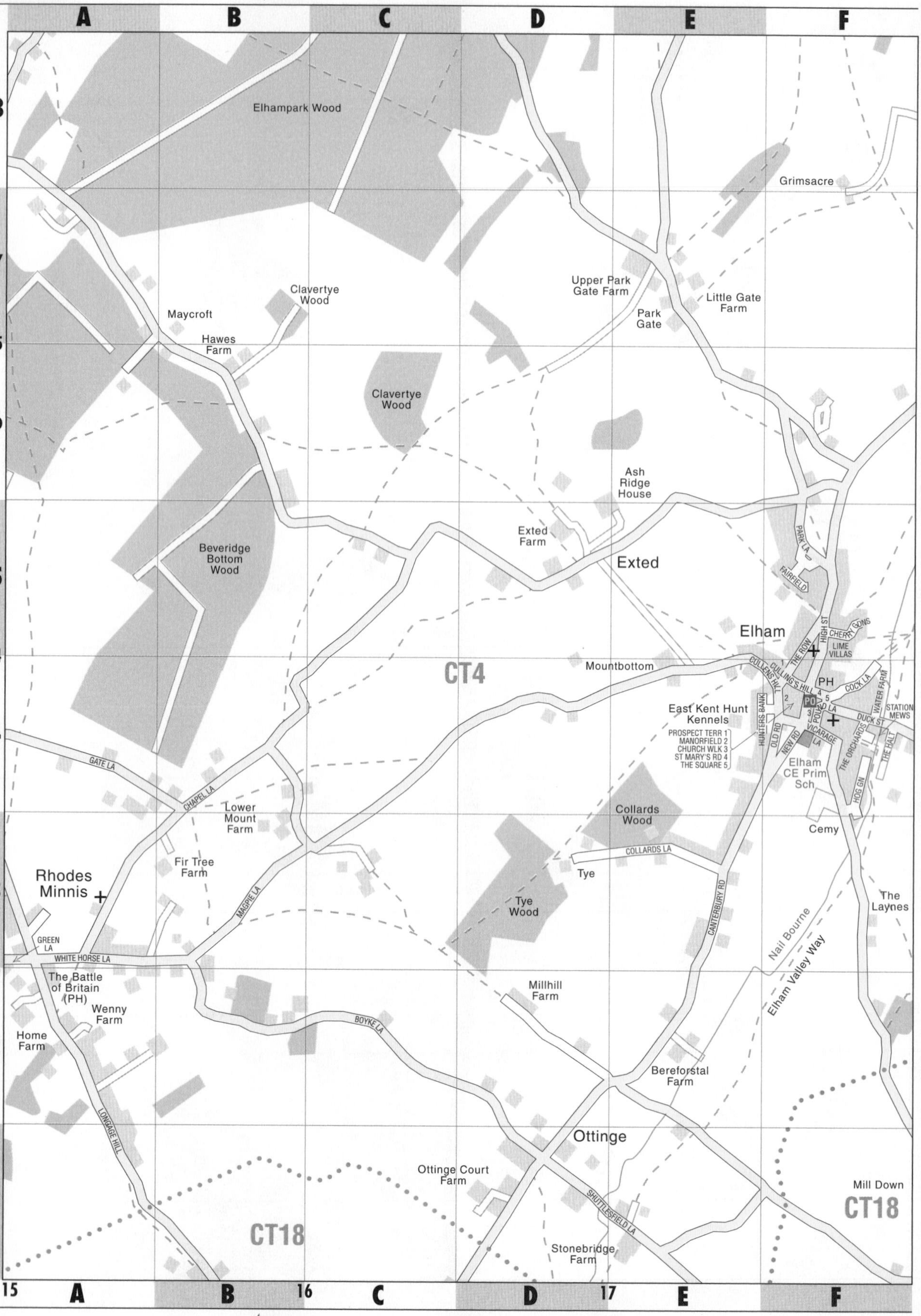

A B C D E F

8

Elhampark Wood

Grimsacre

7

Clavertye Wood

Maycroft

Upper Park Gate Farm

Little Gate Farm

45

Hawes Farm

Park Gate

Clavertye Wood

6

Ash Ridge House

Beveridge Bottom Wood

Exted Farm

Exted

5

Elham

PARK LA

FAIRFIELD

44

Mountbottom

CT4

HIGH CHERRY SONS

LIME VILLAS

CULLING'S HILL

PH

COCK LA

WATER FARM

East Kent Hunt Kennels

PO

POUND LA

STATION MEWS

HUNTERS BANK

OLD RD

NEW RD

VICARAGE LA

DUCK ST

THE ORCHARDS

THE HALL

4

GATE LA

PROSPECT TERR 1
MANORFIELD 2
CHURCH WLK 3
ST MARY'S RD 4
THE SQUARE 5

Elham CE Prim Sch

HOG GN

CHAPEL LA

Lower Mount Farm

Collards Wood

Cemy

Fir Tree Farm

MAGPIE LA

Collards La

The Laynes

3

Rhodes Minnis

Tye

COLLARDS LA

CANTERBURY RD

GREEN LA

Tye Wood

Nail Bourne

WHITE HORSE LA

Elham Valley Way

43

The Battle of Britain (PH)

Wenny Farm

Millhill Farm

2

Home Farm

BOYKE LA

Bereforstal Farm

LONGAGE HILL

Ottinge

1

Ottinge Court Farm

Mill Down

CT18

SHUTTLESFIELD LA

CT18

Stonebridge Farm

42

15 A B 16 C D 17 E F

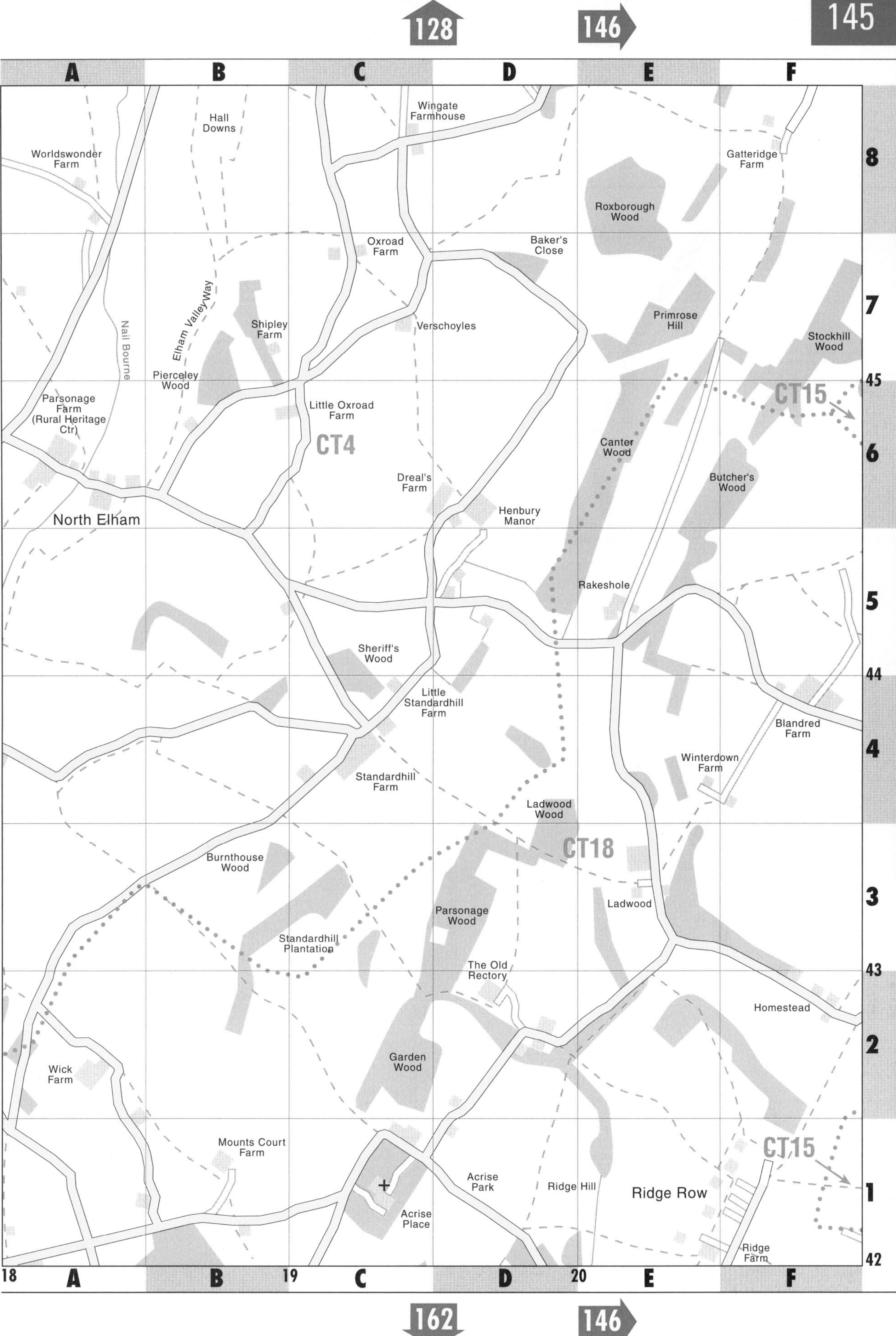

A B C D E F

8

Worldswonder Farm

Hall Downs

Wingate Farmhouse

Gatteridge Farm

Roxborough Wood

Oxroad Farm

Baker's Close

7

Elham Valley Way

Shipley Farm

Verschoyles

Primrose Hill

Stockhill Wood

45

Nail Bourne

Pierceley Wood

Parsonage Farm (Rural Heritage Ctr)

Little Oxroad Farm

CT4

CT15

6

Canter Wood

Butcher's Wood

North Elham

Dreal's Farm

Henbury Manor

Rakeshole

5

Sheriff's Wood

44

Little Standardhill Farm

Blandred Farm

4

Standardhill Farm

Ladwood Wood

Winterdown Farm

CT18

Burnthouse Wood

Ladwood

3

Standardhill Plantation

Parsonage Wood

43

The Old Rectory

Homestead

2

Wick Farm

Garden Wood

Mounts Court Farm

Acrise Park

Ridge Hill

CT15

1

Acrise Place

Ridge Row

Ridge Farm

42

18 A B 19 C D 20 E F

145
129

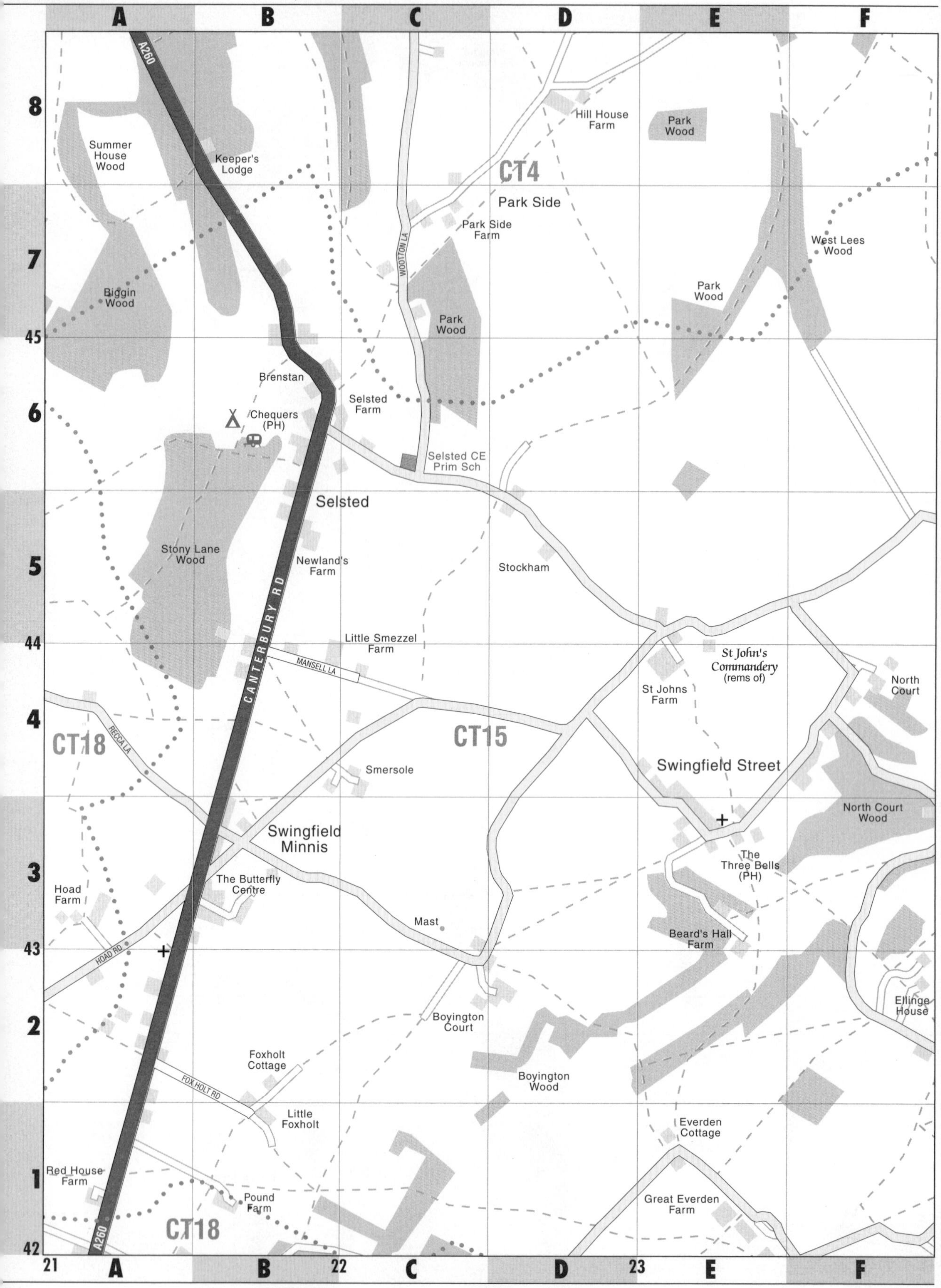

A B C D E F

8

7

45

6

5

44

4

3

43

2

1

42

21 A B 22 C D 23 E F

Summer House Wood

Keeper's Lodge

Biggin Wood

A260

Hill House Farm

Park Wood

CT4

Park Side

Park Side Farm

WOOTTON LA

West Lees Wood

Park Wood

Brenstan

Chequers (PH)

Selsted Farm

Selsted CE Prim Sch

Selsted

CANTERBURY RD

Stony Lane Wood

Newland's Farm

Stockham

Little Smezzel Farm

MANSELL LA

St John's Commandery (rems of)

St Johns Farm

North Court

CT18

BECCA LA

CT15

Smersole

Swingfield Street

North Court Wood

Swingfield Minnis

The Butterfly Centre

Mast

The Three Bells (PH)

Beard's Hall Farm

Ellinge House

Hoad Farm

HOAD RD

Boyington Court

Foxholt Cottage

FOX HOLT RD

Little Foxholt

Boyington Wood

Everden Cottage

Red House Farm

Pound Farm

Great Everden Farm

CT18

130
148

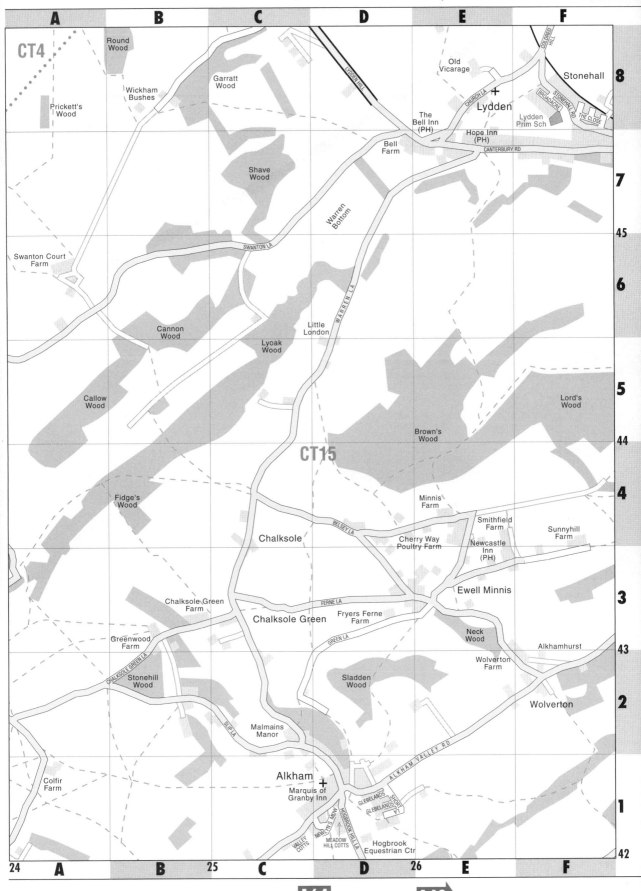
A
B
C
D
E
F
CT4
Round Wood
Garratt Wood
Old Vicarage
Stonehall
Prickett's Wood
Wickham Bushes
LYDDEN HILL
COLDRED HILL
CHURCH LA
Lydden
BROADACRE
STONEHALL RD
THE CLOSE
Lydden Prim Sch
The Bell Inn (PH)
Hope Inn (PH)
Bell Farm
CANTERBURY RD
Shave Wood
Warren Bottom
Swanton Court Farm
SWANTON LA
Cannon Wood
Little London
WARREN LA
Lyoak Wood
Callow Wood
Lord's Wood
Brown's Wood
CT15
Fidge's Wood
Minnis Farm
Smithfield Farm
Sunnyhill Farm
BELSEY LA
Chalksole
Cherry Way Poultry Farm
Newcastle Inn (PH)
Ewell Minnis
Chalksole Green Farm
FERNE LA
Chalksole Green
Fryers Ferne Farm
Neck Wood
Greenwood Farm
GREEN LA
Alkhamhurst
Wolverton Farm
CHALKSOLE GREEN LA
Stonehill Wood
Sladden Wood
Wolverton
SLIP LA
Malmains Manor
ALKHAM VALLEY RD
Colfir Farm
Alkham
Marquis of Granby Inn
GLEBELANDS
SHORT LA
NEWLYN'S MDW
HOGBROOK HILL LA
VALLEY COTTS
MEADOW HILL COTTS
Hogbrook Equestrian Ctr
8
7
45
6
5
44
4
3
43
2
1
42
24
25
26

164
148

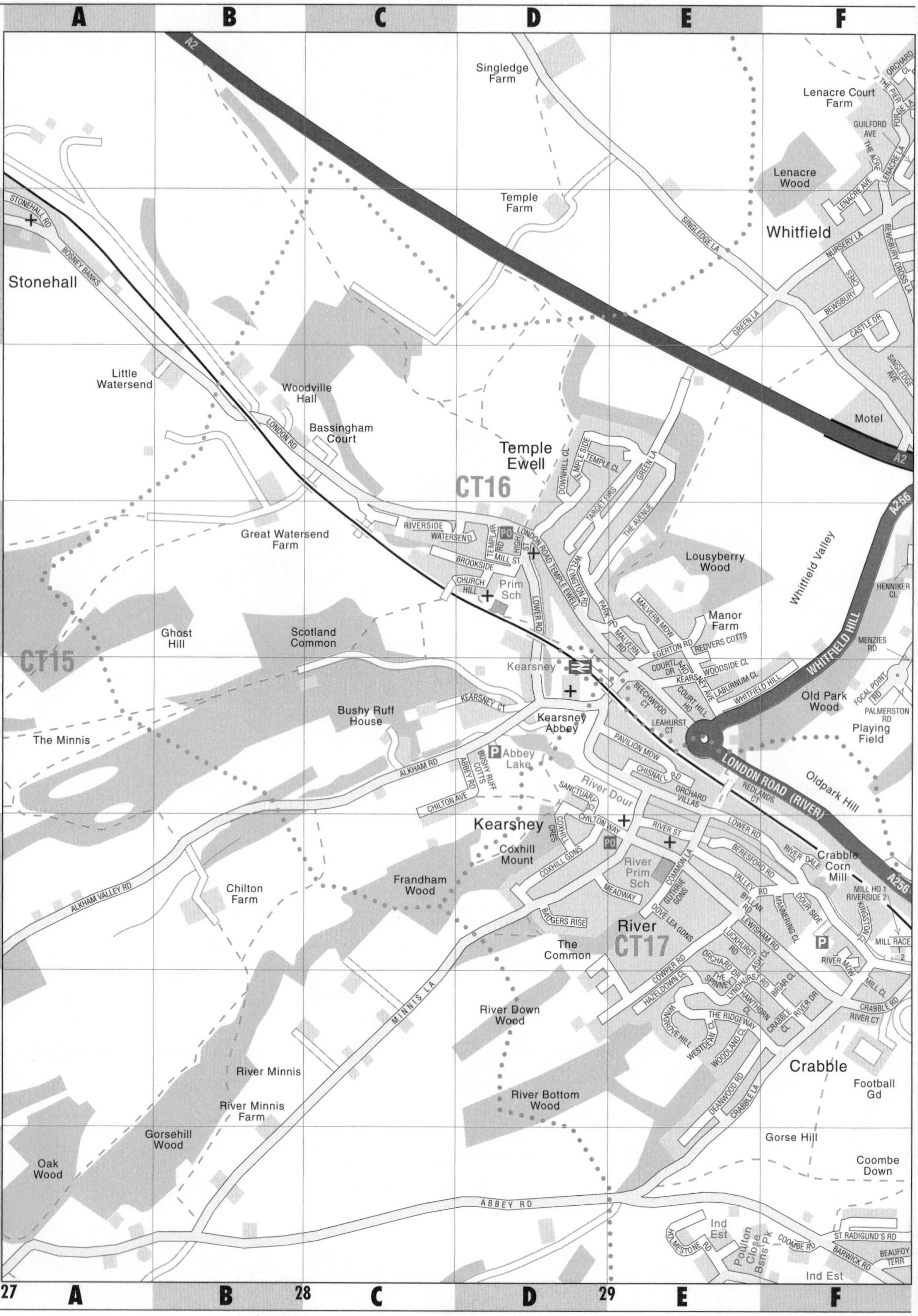

A B C D E F

8

7

45

6

5

44

4

3

43

2

1

42

A2

Stonehall

STONEHALL RD

BUSHEY BANKS

Little Watersend

Woodville Hall

LONDON RD

Bassingham Court

Great Watersend Farm

RIVERSIDE
WATERSEND
BROOKSIDE
CHURCH HILL

CT16

Temple Ewell

DOWNHILL CL
TEMPLE SIDE
TEMPLE CL

TARGET FIRS

PO
LONDON ROAD TEMPLE EWELL
TEMPLAR RD
WELLINGTON RD
MILL ST
Prim Sch
LOWER RD

GREEN LA

THE AVENUE

Lousyberry Wood

Manor Farm

MALVERN MDW
PARK RD
MALVERN RD
EGERTON RD
COURT HILL
REDVERS COTTS
WOODSIDE CL

Whitfield Valley

WHITFIELD HILL

A256

Motel

A2

HENNIKER CL
MENZIES RD

Old Park Wood

FOCAL POINT RD
PALMERSTON RD

Playing Field

Singledge Farm

Temple Farm

SINGLEDGE LA

Whitfield

Lenacre Court Farm
THE PIER
ORCHARD CL
FORGE LA
GUILFORD AVE
LENACRE LA

Lenacre Wood

NURSERY LA
SEED
BEWSBURY LA
BEWSBURY CROSS LA
CASTLE DR
GREEN LA

SINGLEDGE AVE

CT15

Ghost Hill

Scotland Common

The Minnis

Bushy Ruff House

KEARSNEY CT

Kearsney

Kearsney Abbey

Abbey Lake

ALKHAM RD
BUSHY RUFF COTTS
ABBEY RD
CHILTON AVE

SANCTUARY
River Dour
CHISNALL RD
ORCHARD VILLAS

PAVILION MDW

BEECHWOOD CT
LEAHURST CT
COURT HO
COURT LAND
KEARSNEY AVE
LABURNUM CL
WHITFIELD HILL

LONDON ROAD (RIVER)
REDLANDS CT

Oldpark Hill

Crabble Corn Mill

RIVER DALE

Chilton Farm

ALKHAM VALLEY RD

Frandham Wood

Coxhill Mount

COXHILL CRES
COXHILL GDNS
BADGERS RISE

CHILTON WAY

Kearsney

PO

River Prim Sch
MEADWAY

The Common

RIVER ST
LOWER RD
BERESFORD RD
COMMON LA
ROTHERA
DOVE LEA GDNS

River

CT17

RIVER MDW

VALLEY RD
BYLLAN
LEWISHAM RD
DOUR SIDE

MANNERING CL

MILL HO 1
RIVERSIDE 2
KINGSTON ST
P
MILL RACE

MINNIS LA

River Down Wood

River Bottom Wood

River Minnis

River Minnis Farm

Gorsehill Wood

Oak Wood

ABBEY RD

LUCKHURST CL
YNGHURST RD
COWPER RD
ORCHARD DR
HAZELDOWN CL
THE SPINNEY
BRIAR CL
RIVER DR
HAWTHORN

HARGROVE HILL
WESTYDON CL
THE RIDGEWAY
WOODLAND CL
DEANWOOD RD
CRABBLE LA

CRABBLE CL
RIVER CT
MILL CL
CRABBLE RD

Crabble

Football Gd

Gorse Hill

Coombe Down

Ind Est

HOLMESTONE RD
Podium Close Bsns Pk

St RADIGUND'S RD
BARWICK RD
COOMBE PK
BEAUFOY TERR

Ind Est

A256

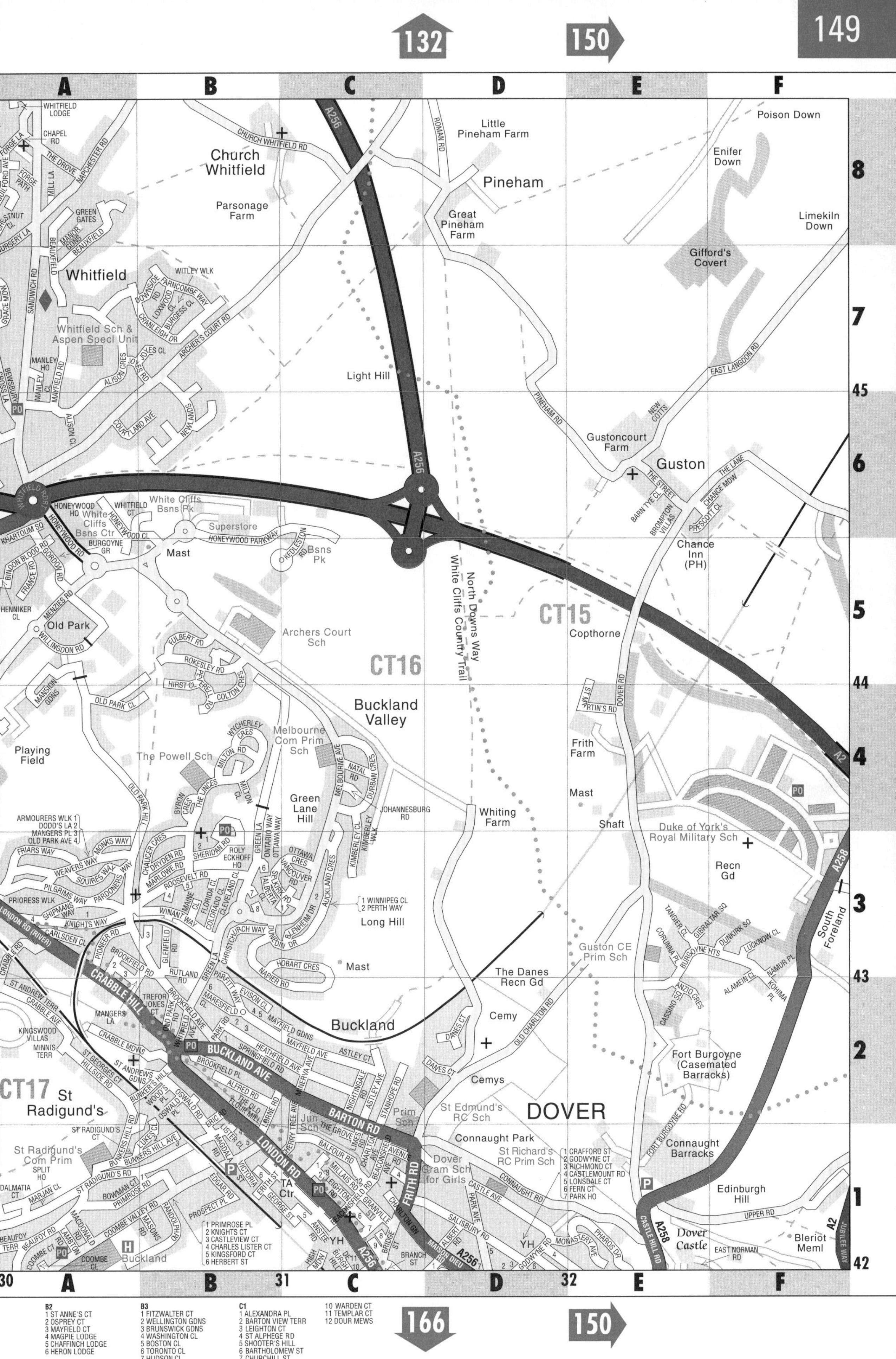
132
150
166
150
Church Whitfield
Parsonage Farm
Little Pineham Farm
Pineham
Great Pineham Farm
Poison Down
Enifer Down
Limekiln Down
Gifford's Covert
Whitfield
Whitfield Sch & Aspen Specl Unit
Light Hill
Gustoncourt Farm
Guston
Chance Inn (PH)
White Cliffs Bsns Pk
White Cliffs Bsns Ctr
Superstore
Bsns Pk
Mast
Old Park
Archers Court Sch
CT16
CT15
Copthorne
North Downs Way
White Cliffs Country Trail
Buckland Valley
Playing Field
The Powell Sch
Melbourne Com Prim Sch
Green Lane Hill
Frith Farm
Whiting Farm
Shaft
Duke of York's Royal Military Sch
Recn Gd
Long Hill
Guston CE Prim Sch
The Danes Recn Gd
Buckland
Cemy
Cemys
Fort Burgoyne (Casemated Barracks)
South Foreland
CT17
St Radigund's
St Radigund's Com Prim
St Edmund's RC Sch
DOVER
Connaught Park
St Richard's RC Prim Sch
Connaught Barracks
Dover Gram Sch for Girls
Edinburgh Hill
Dover Castle
Bleriot Meml
Buckland
1 WINNIPEG CL
2 PERTH WAY
ARMOURERS WLK 1
DODD'S LA 2
MANGERS PL 3
OLD PARK AVE 4
1 CRAFFORD ST
2 GODWYNE CT
3 RICHMOND CT
4 CASTLEMOUNT RD
5 LONSDALE CT
6 FERN CT
7 PARK HO
1 PRIMROSE PL
2 KNIGHTS CT
3 CASTLEVIEW CT
4 CHARLES LISTER CT
5 KINGSFORD CT
6 HERBERT ST
B2
1 ST ANNE'S CT
2 OSPREY CT
3 MAYFIELD CT
4 MAGPIE LODGE
5 CHAFFINCH LODGE
6 HERON LODGE
B3
1 FITZWALTER CT
2 WELLINGTON GDNS
3 BRUNSWICK GDNS
4 WASHINGTON CL
5 BOSTON CL
6 TORONTO CL
7 HUDSON CL
8 MONTREAL CL
C1
1 ALEXANDRA PL
2 BARTON VIEW TERR
3 LEIGHTON CT
4 ST ALPHEGE RD
5 SHOOTER'S HILL
6 BARTHOLOMEW ST
7 CHURCHILL ST
8 PAUL'S PL
9 MATTHEW'S PL
10 WARDEN CT
11 TEMPLAR CT
12 DOUR MEWS

A **B** **C** **D** **E** **F**

WALDERSHARE LA

EAST LANGDON RD

GUSTON RD

8

White Hill

Solton Close

Famine Down

Solton Manor Farm

LANGDON CROSS

A258

Mill Hill

GREEN LA

VICTORY RD

NELSON PARK RD

SEYMOUR RD

HARDY RD

COLLINGWOOD RD

BOWIE PL

STATION RD

ST VINCENT RD

Nelson Park

7

45

MILLFIELD

Liby

KINGSDOWN RD

Townsend Farm

THE CHASE

AVENUE

HIGH ST

TOWNSEND FARM RD

ST KNOTTS LA

CRIPPS LA

6

West Cliffe Farm

DOVER RD

POND LA

Wallet's Court

West Cliffe

CLIFFE HO 1
HEATH CT 2

WELLA

VICARAGE LA

ROYSTON GDNS

REACH CL

GEORGES PL

LANGDON CL

REACH RD

ROMAN WAY

CHURCHILL

REACH CL

Cherry Tree Cottage

East Hill

Guston Mill (dis)

THE LANE

St Margarets Holiday Park

5

Brickfield Cottages

South Foreland

CT15

Reach Court Farm

44

The Swingate Inn (PH)

Bere Wood

4

A2

A258

Bere Farm

LIGHTHOUSE RD

SEA VIEW RD

GOODWIN RD

3

JUBILEE WAY

Wanstone Farm

South Foreland Lighthouse

43

Masts

WT Sta

Memls

UPPER RD

Bantam Hole

Fan Point

Fan Bay

2

CT16

Saxon Shore Way

White Cliffs Country Trail

Langdon Hole

Crab Bay

Mast

CLIFF RD

Langdon Bay

1

A2

Broadlees Bottom

South Foreland

Fox Hill Down

Gateway to the White Cliffs Visitor Ctr

Langdon Cliffs

NORTH CAMBER WAY

SOUTH CAMBER WAY

CIRCULAR RD

Eastern Docks

42

33 **A** **B** **34** **C** **D** **35** **E** **F**

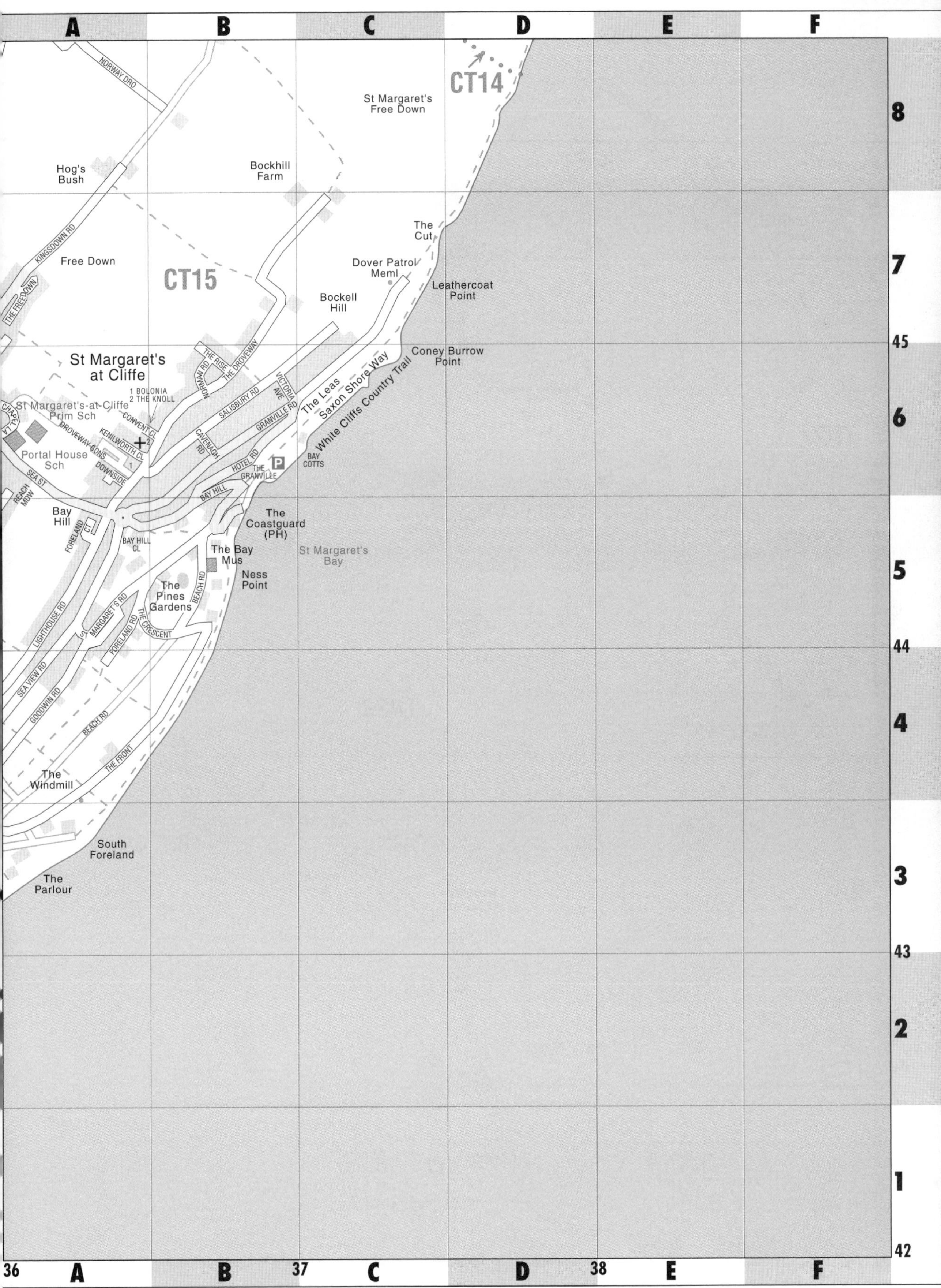

134

A B C D E F

CT14

St Margaret's
Free Down

8

NORWAY DRO

Hog's
Bush

Bockhill
Farm

The
Cut

7

KINGSDOWN RD

Free Down

CT15

Dover Patrol
Meml

Leathercoat
Point

THE FREEDOWN

Bockell
Hill

45

Coney Burrow
Point

St Margaret's
at Cliffe

THE RISE

THE DROVEWAY

IVY DRO

SALISBURY RD

VICTORIA AVE

GRANVILLE RD

The Leas

Saxon Shore Way

White Cliffs Country Trail

6

1 BOLONIA
2 THE KNOLL

St Margaret's-at-Cliffe
Prim Sch

CONVENT CL

CAVENDISH RD

BAY
COTTS

QUARRY CT

DROVEWAY GDNS

KENILWORTH CL

DOWNSIDE

HOTEL RD

THE
GRANVILLE

P

Portal House
Sch

SEA ST

REACH MDW

BAY HILL

The
Coastguard
(PH)

5

Bay
Hill

FORELAND CT

BAY HILL
CL

BEACH RD

The Bay
Mus

St Margaret's
Bay

Ness
Point

LIGHTHOUSE RD

MARGARET'S RD

FORELAND RD

THE CRESCENT

The Pines
Gardens

44

SEA VIEW RD

GOODWIN RD

BEACH RD

4

THE FRONT

The
Windmill

South
Foreland

3

The
Parlour

43

2

1

42

36 A B 37 C D 38 E F

135

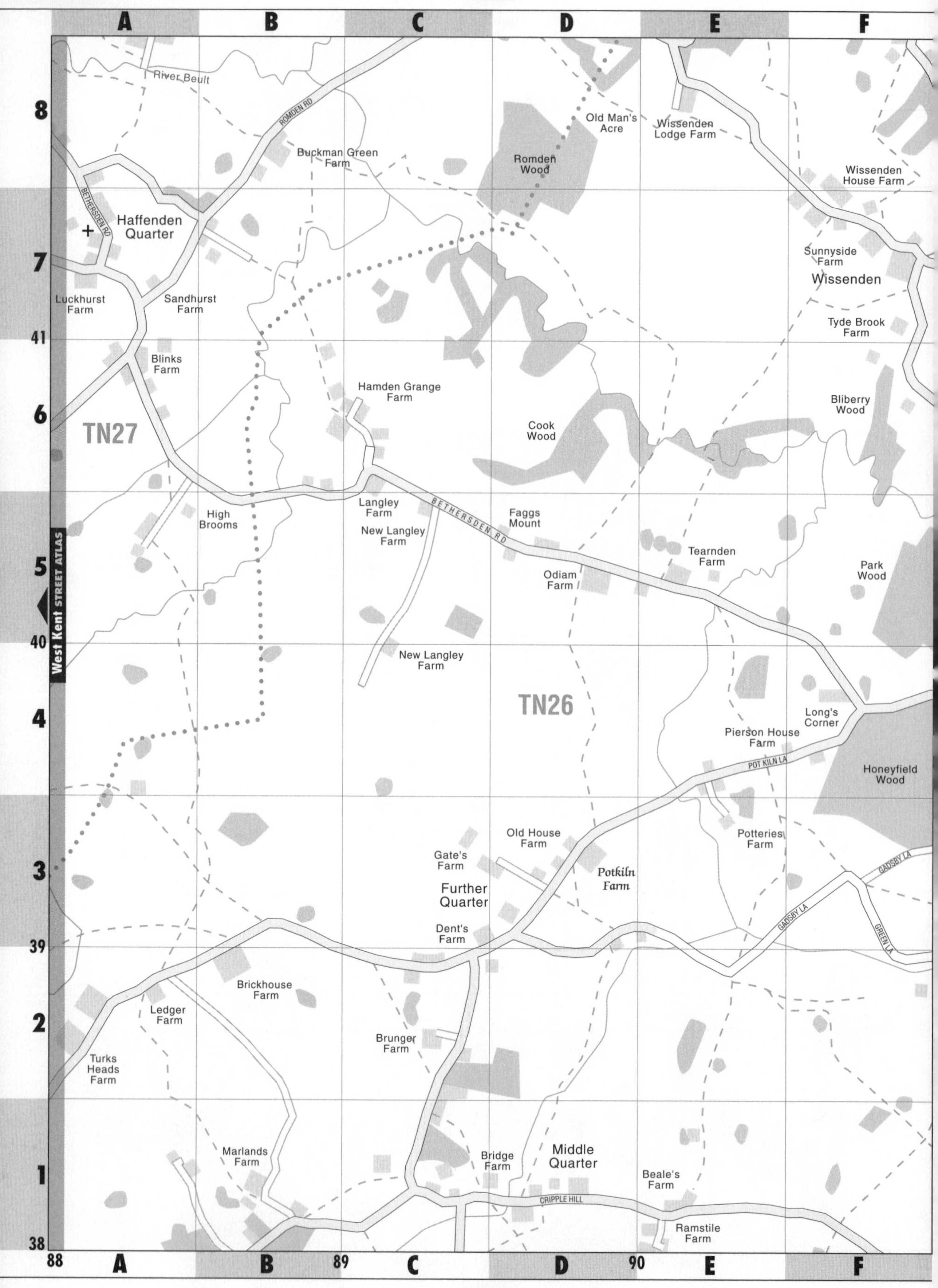
A
B
C
D
E
F
8
7
41
6
5
40
4
3
39
2
1
38
88
89
90
River Beult
ROMDEN RD
Old Man's Acre
Wissenden Lodge Farm
Buckman Green Farm
Romden Wood
Wissenden House Farm
BETHERSDEN RD
Haffenden Quarter
Sunnyside Farm
Wissenden
Luckhurst Farm
Sandhurst Farm
Tyde Brook Farm
Blinks Farm
Hamden Grange Farm
Bliberry Wood
TN27
Cook Wood
Langley Farm
BETHERSDEN RD
Faggs Mount
High Brooms
New Langley Farm
Tearnden Farm
Park Wood
Odiam Farm
West Kent STREET ATLAS
New Langley Farm
TN26
Long's Corner
Pierson House Farm
POT KILN LA
Honeyfield Wood
Old House Farm
Potteries Farm
Gate's Farm
Potkiln Farm
GADSBY LA
Further Quarter
Dent's Farm
GADSBY LA
GREEN LA
Brickhouse Farm
Ledger Farm
Brunger Farm
Turks Heads Farm
Marlands Farm
Bridge Farm
Middle Quarter
Beale's Farm
CRIPPLE HILL
Ramstile Farm

167

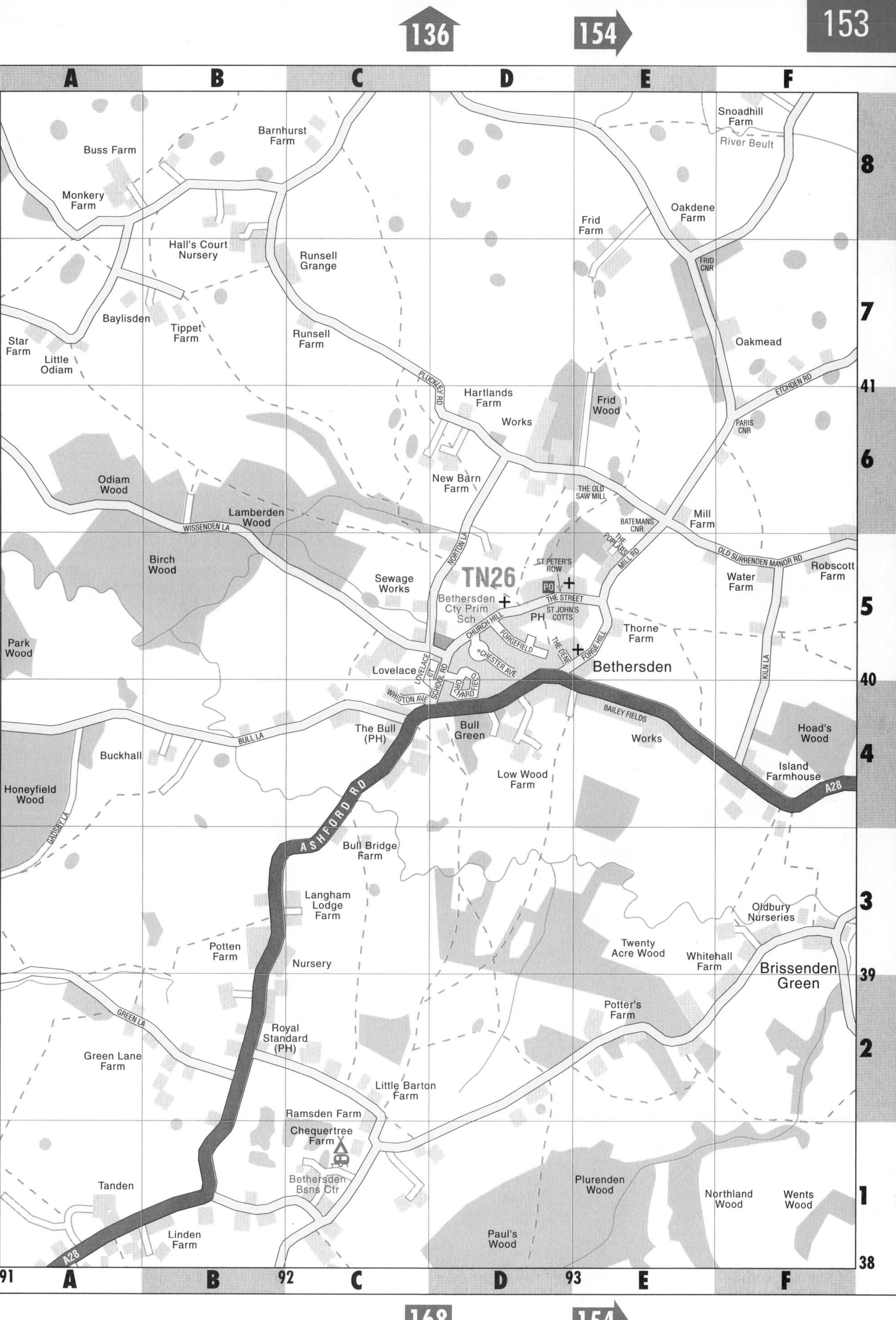
136
154
Buss Farm
Barnhurst Farm
Monkery Farm
Hall's Court Nursery
Runsell Grange
Snoadhill Farm
River Beult
Oakdene Farm
Frid Farm
FRID CNR
Baylisden
Tippet Farm
Star Farm
Little Odiam
Runsell Farm
Oakmead
PLUCKLEY RD
Hartlands Farm
Works
Frid Wood
ETCHDEN RD
PARIS CNR
Odiam Wood
New Barn Farm
THE OLD SAW MILL
Lamberden Wood
WISSENDEN LA
BATEMANS CNR
THE POPLARS
Mill Farm
Birch Wood
NORTON LA
MILL RD
OLD SURRENDEN MANOR RD
Robscott Farm
Sewage Works
TN26
ST PETER'S ROW
PO
Water Farm
Bethersden Cty Prim Sch
THE STREET
ST JOHN'S COTTS
PH
CHURCH HILL
Thorne Farm
Park Wood
FORGEFIELD
THE DENE
FORGE HILL
KILN LA
CHESTER AVE
LOVELACE CT
SCHOOL RD
ORCHARD FIELD
Lovelace
Bethersden
WHISTON AVE
BAILEY FIELDS
The Bull (PH)
Bull Green
Works
Hoad's Wood
BULL LA
Buckhall
Low Wood Farm
Island Farmhouse
Honeyfield Wood
ASHFORD RD
A28
GADSBY LA
Bull Bridge Farm
Langham Lodge Farm
Oldbury Nurseries
Potten Farm
Twenty Acre Wood
Whitehall Farm
Nursery
Brissenden Green
GREEN LA
Potter's Farm
Royal Standard (PH)
Green Lane Farm
Little Barton Farm
Ramsden Farm
Chequertree Farm
Tanden
Bethersden Bsns Ctr
Plurenden Wood
Northland Wood
Wents Wood
Linden Farm
Paul's Wood
A28
A B C D E F
8 7 41 6 5 40 4 3 39 2 1 38
91 92 93
168
154

A **B** **C** **D** **E** **F**

8

River Beult

Etchden Farm

ETCHDEN RD

TN23

Coldharbour Farm

Little Goldwell

GOLDWELL LA

PURCHASE LA

7

Longberry Farm

PARK LA

Daniel's Water

Malt House Farm

Yardhurst

Daniel's Water Farm

Fleeden

Purchase Wood

TN23

41

Surrenden Lakes

Forstal Farm

River Beult

SANDY LA

6

Mannering Wood

Vitters Oak

Court Reed Farm

A28

Winters Farm

Wetlands Wood

OLD SURRENDEN MANOR RD

Barton Farm

SANDY CNR

5

Butcher Wood

St Margarets Farm

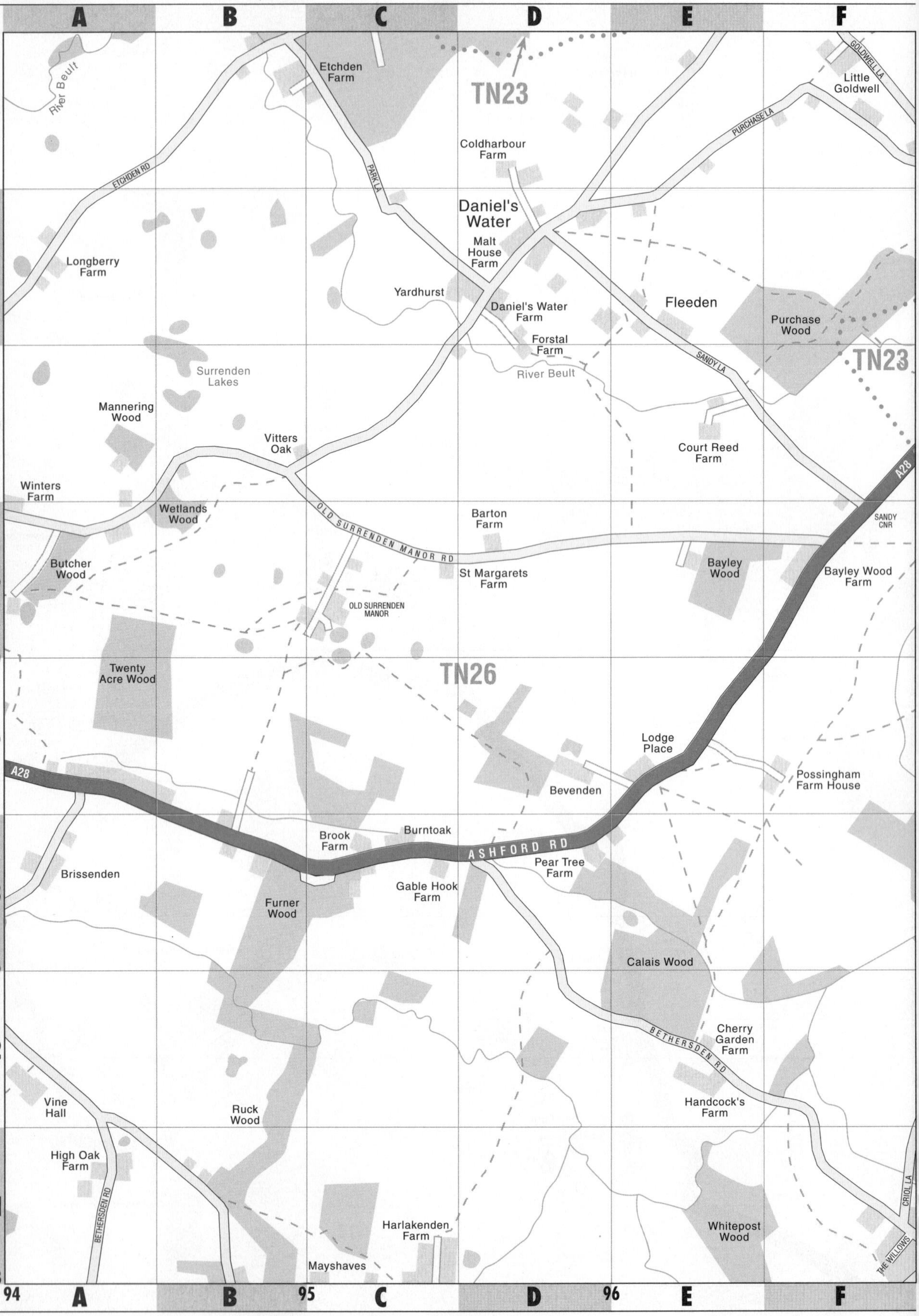

Bayley Wood

Bayley Wood Farm

OLD SURRENDEN MANOR

40

Twenty Acre Wood

TN26

4

A28

Lodge Place

Possingham Farm House

Brissenden

Brook Farm

Burntoak

Bevenden

Pear Tree Farm

ASHFORD RD

3

Furner Wood

Gable Hook Farm

Calais Wood

39

Cherry Garden Farm

BETHERSDEN RD

2

Vine Hall

Ruck Wood

Handcock's Farm

BETHERSDEN RD

High Oak Farm

Harlakenden Farm

Whitepost Wood

CRIOL LA

1

Mayshaves

THE WILLOWS

38

94 **A** **B** 95 **C** **D** 96 **E** **F**

138
156

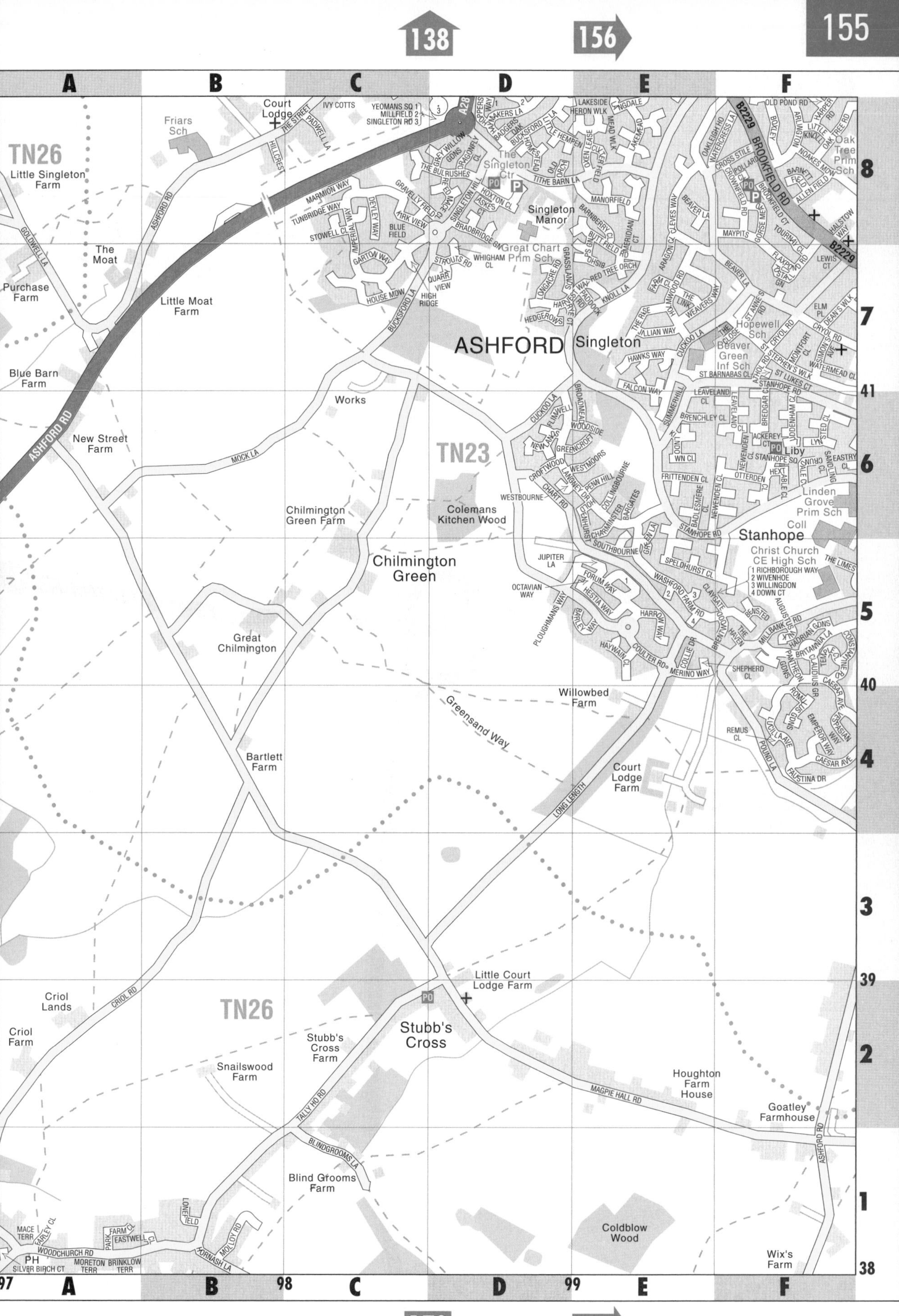
A
B
C
D
E
F
TN26
Little Singleton Farm
Friars Sch
Court Lodge
The Moat
Purchase Farm
Little Moat Farm
Blue Barn Farm
ASHFORD RD
New Street Farm
Works
MOCK LA
ASHFORD
Singleton
Singleton Manor
The Singleton Ctr
Great Chart Prim Sch
TN23
Colemans Kitchen Wood
Chilmington Green Farm
Chilmington Green
Great Chilmington
Bartlett Farm
Greensand Way
Willowbed Farm
Court Lodge Farm
LONG LENGTH
Hopewell Sch
Beaver Green Inf Sch
Oak Tree Prim Sch
Linden Grove Prim Sch
Coll
Stanhope
Christ Church CE High Sch
1 RICHBOROUGH WAY
2 WIVENHOE
3 WILLINGDON
4 DOWN CT
B2229
BROOKFIELD RD
Little Court Lodge Farm
Stubb's Cross
Stubb's Cross Farm
Snailswood Farm
Criol Lands
Criol Farm
CRIOL RD
TN26
TALLY HO RD
BLINDGROOMS LA
Blind Grooms Farm
MAGPIE HALL RD
Houghton Farm House
Goatley Farmhouse
ASHFORD RD
Coldblow Wood
Wix's Farm
WOODCHURCH RD
HORNASH LA
MOLLOY RD
PH
8
7
41
6
5
40
4
3
39
2
1
38
97
98
99

170
156

155
139

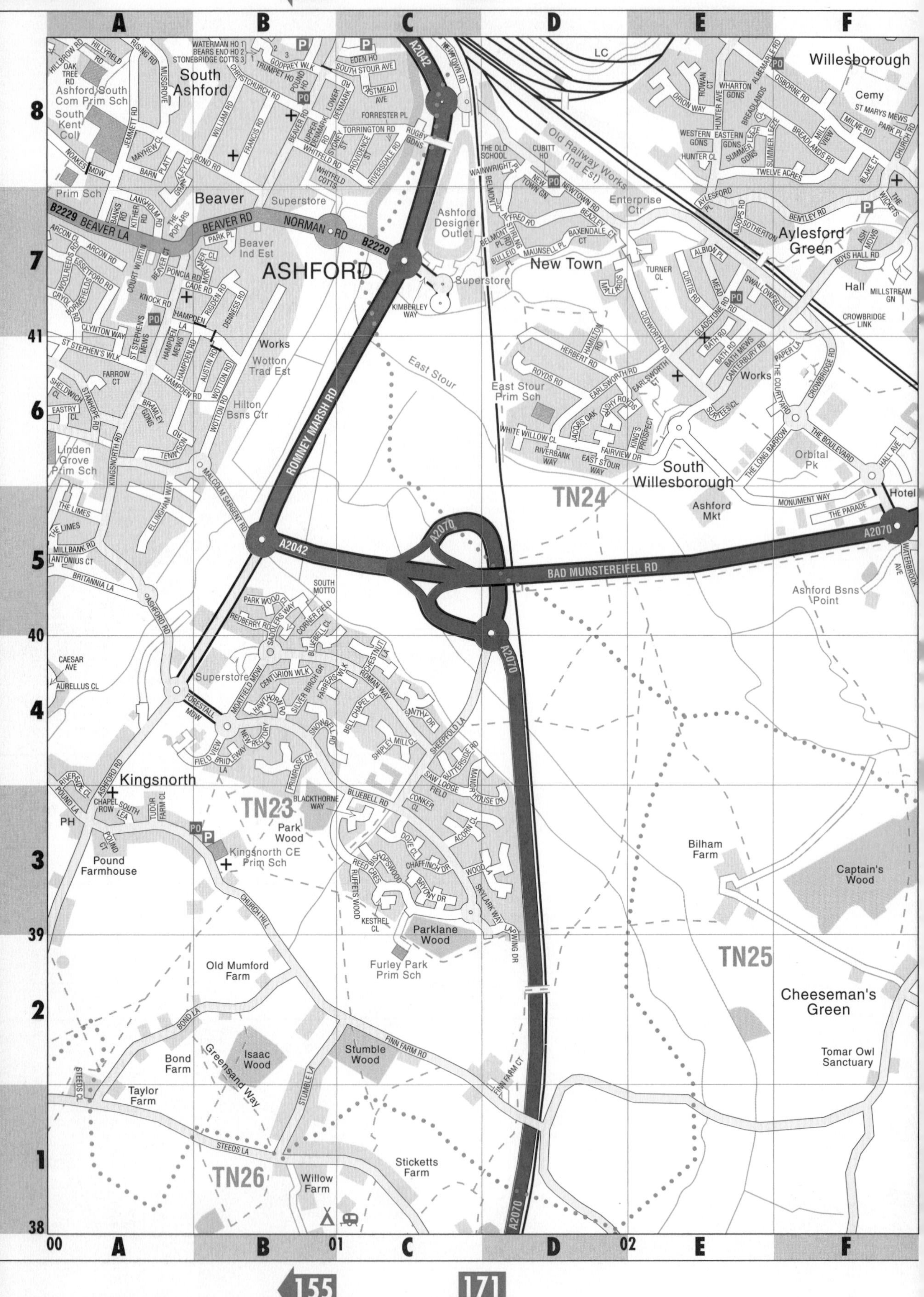
South Ashford
Willesborough
ASHFORD
Beaver
New Town
Aylesford Green
South Willesborough
Kingsnorth
TN23
TN24
TN25
TN26
Ashford Designer Outlet
East Stour
ROMNEY MARSH RD
BAD MUNSTEREIFEL RD
A2042
A2070
B2229
Park Wood
Pound Farmhouse
Kingsnorth CE Prim Sch
Old Mumford Farm
Parklane Wood
Furley Park Prim Sch
Bond Farm
Isaac Wood
Stumble Wood
Taylor Farm
Sticketts Farm
Willow Farm
Bilham Farm
Captain's Wood
Cheeseman's Green
Tomar Owl Sanctuary
Orbital Pk
Ashford Mkt
Ashford Bsns Point
East Stour Prim Sch
Linden Grove Prim Sch
Hilton Bsns Ctr
Wotton Trad Est
Beaver Ind Est
Enterprise Ctr
Greensand Way

155
171

140
158

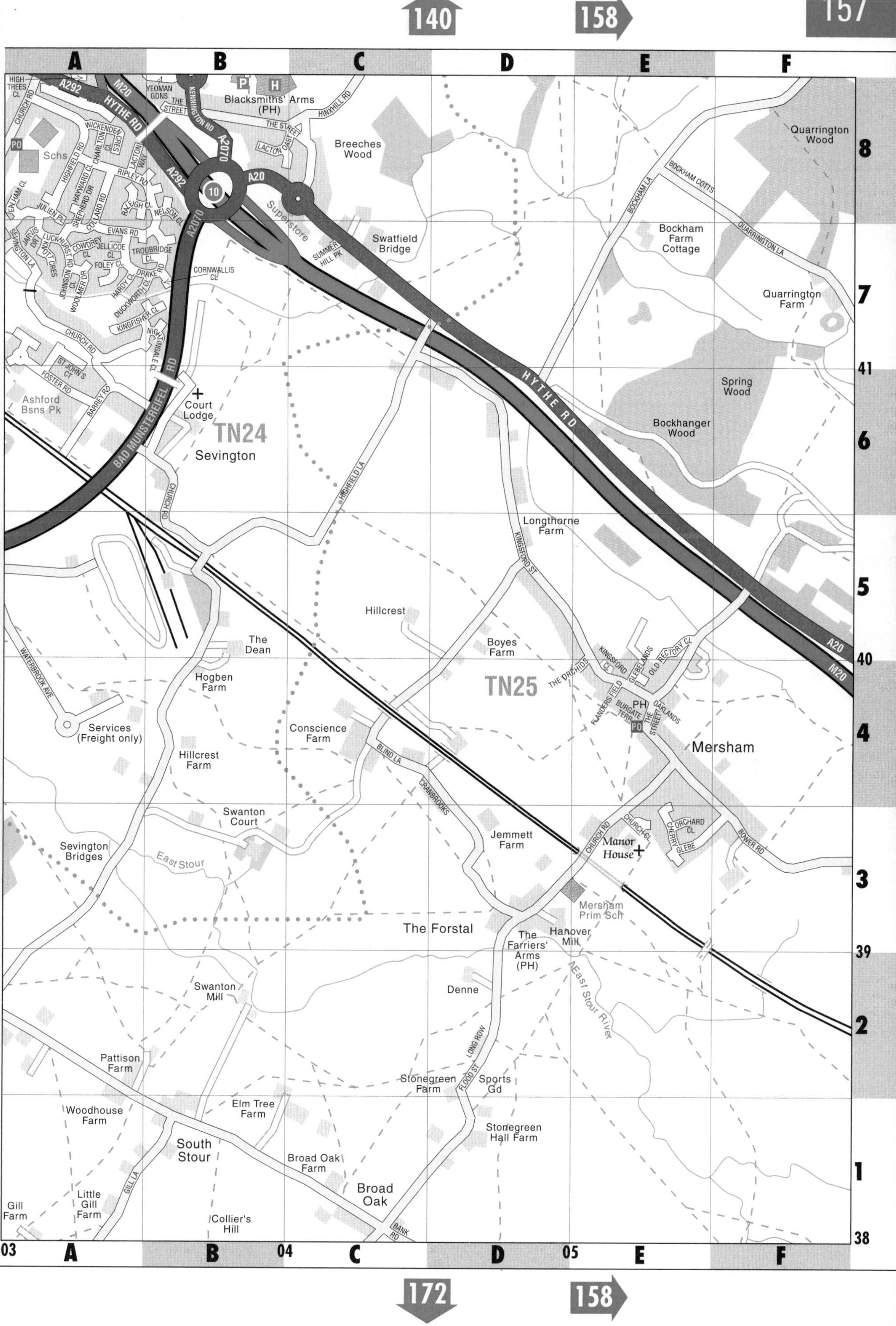
A
B
C
D
E
F
8
7
41
6
5
40
4
3
39
2
1
38
03
04
05
Blacksmiths' Arms (PH)
Breeches Wood
Quarrington Wood
Schs
Swatfield Bridge
Superstore
Bockham Farm Cottage
Quarrington Farm
Spring Wood
Bockhanger Wood
Ashford Bsns Pk
Court Lodge
TN24
Sevington
Longthorne Farm
Hillcrest
The Dean
Boyes Farm
Hogben Farm
TN25
Services (Freight only)
Conscience Farm
Mersham
Hillcrest Farm
Swanton Court
Jemmett Farm
Sevington Bridges
East Stour
Manor House
Mersham Prim Sch
The Forstal
The Farriers' Arms (PH)
Hanover Mill
Swanton Mill
Denne
East Stour River
Pattison Farm
Stonegreen Farm
Sports Gd
Woodhouse Farm
Elm Tree Farm
Stonegreen Hall Farm
South Stour
Broad Oak Farm
Broad Oak
Little Gill Farm
Gill Farm
Collier's Hill
A292
M20
A2070
A20
HYTHE RD
BAD MUNSTEREIFEL RD
KINGSFORD ST
HIGHFIELD LA
CHURCH RD
BLIND LA
CRANBROOKS
BOCKHAM LA
QUARRINGTON LA
BOCKHAM COTTS
WATERBROOK AVE
LONG ROW
FLOOD ST
BANK RD
GILL LA
BOWER RD
THE STREET
OAKLANDS
OLD RECTORY CL
GLEBELANDS
THE ORCHIDS
FLANDERS FIELD
BURGATE TERR
CHURCH CL
CHERRY GLEBE
ORCHARD CL
PH
PO
HINXHILL RD
KENNINGTON RD
YEOMAN GDNS
LACTON OAST
LACTON WAY
SUMMER HILL PK
CORNWALLIS CL
NIGHTINGALE CL
KINGFISHER CL
DUCKWORTH CL
HARDY CL
DRAKE RD
TROUBRIDGE CL
FOLEY CL
JELLICOE CL
EVANS RD
NELSON CL
RALEIGH CL
RIPLEY RD
COLLARD RD
SHEPHERD DR
HAYWARD CL
HIGHFIELD RD
CHARLTON CL
WICKENDEN CRES
HIGH TREES CL
COWDREY CL
LUCKHURST RD
JOHNSON CL
WOOLMER DR
KNOTT CRES
JARVIS DR
JULIEN PL
PELHAM CL
SEVINGTON LA
ST JOHN'S CT
FOSTER RD
BARREY RD

172
158

157
141

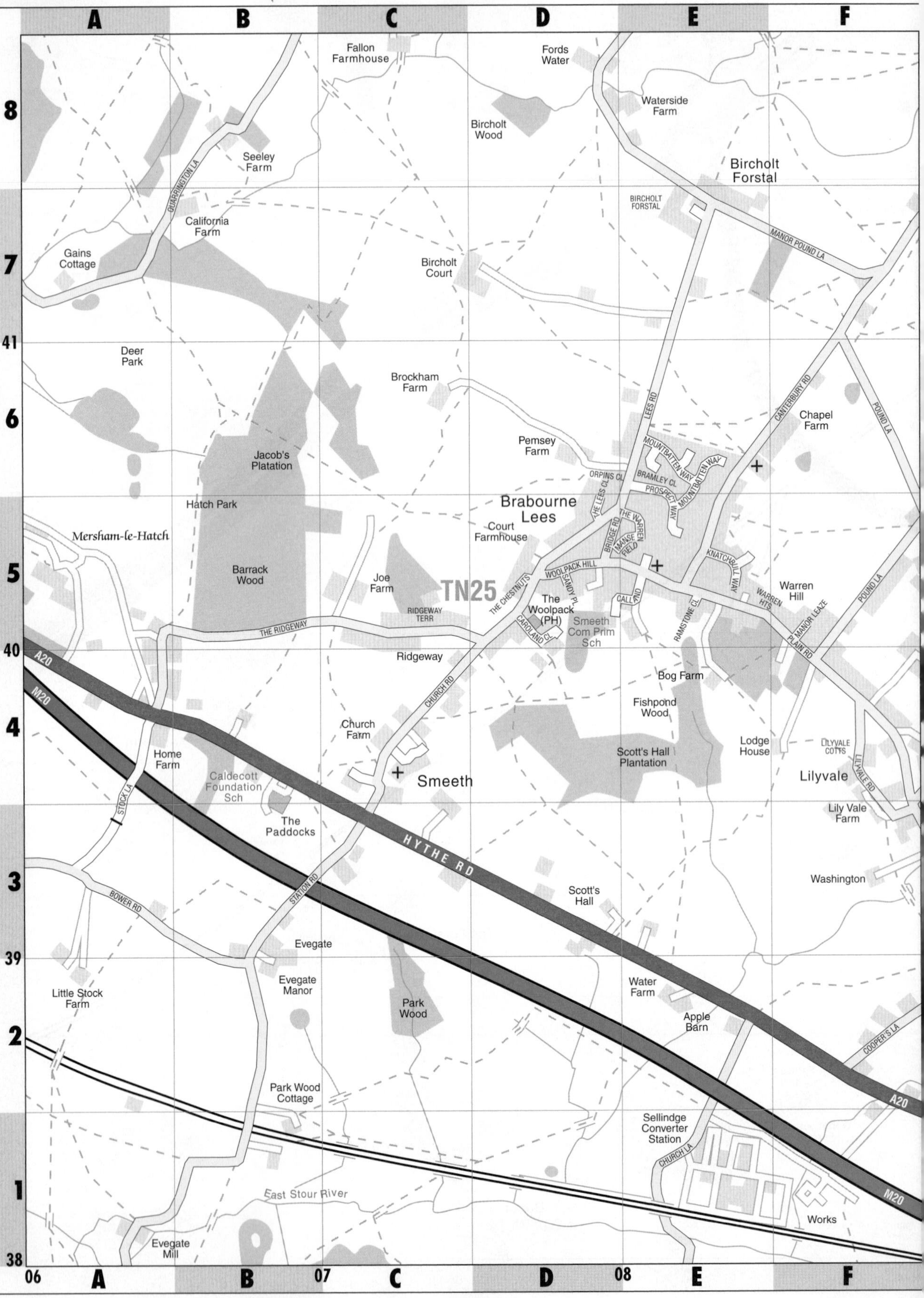

A B C D E F

8

7

41

6

5

40

4

39

3

2

1

38

Fallon Farmhouse

Fords Water

Waterside Farm

Bircholt Wood

Bircholt Forstal

BIRCHOLT FORSTAL

Seeley Farm

California Farm

Gains Cottage

Bircholt Court

MANOR POUND LA

Deer Park

Brockham Farm

Chapel Farm

Jacob's Platation

Pemsey Farm

CANTERBURY RD

POUND LA

Hatch Park

Brabourne Lees

Mersham-le-Hatch

Court Farmhouse

MOUNTBATTEN WAY

BRAMLEY CL

THE LEES CL

PROSPECT WAY

MOUNTBATTEN WAY

Barrack Wood

Joe Farm

TN25

THE WOOLPACK (PH)

Smeeth Com Prim Sch

Warren Hill

WARREN HTS

THE RIDGEWAY

RIDGEWAY TERR

THE CHESTNUTS

WOOLPACK HILL

THE WARREN

BRIDGE RD

IMAGE FIELD

KNATCHBULL WAY

MANOR LEAZE

A20

Ridgeway

CHURCH RD

CAROLAND CL

RAMSTONE CL

Bog Farm

PLAIN RD

LILYVALE COTTS

M20

Church Farm

Fishpond Wood

Lodge House

Lilyvale

Home Farm

Caldecott Foundation Sch

Smeeth

Scott's Hall Plantation

Lily Vale Farm

The Paddocks

HYTHE RD

Washington

STOCK LA

BOWER RD

STATION RD

Scott's Hall

Little Stock Farm

Evegate

Water Farm

Apple Barn

COOPER'S LA

Evegate Manor

Park Wood

A20

Park Wood Cottage

Sellindge Converter Station

M20

East Stour River

CHURCH LA

Evegate Mill

Works

157
173

142
160

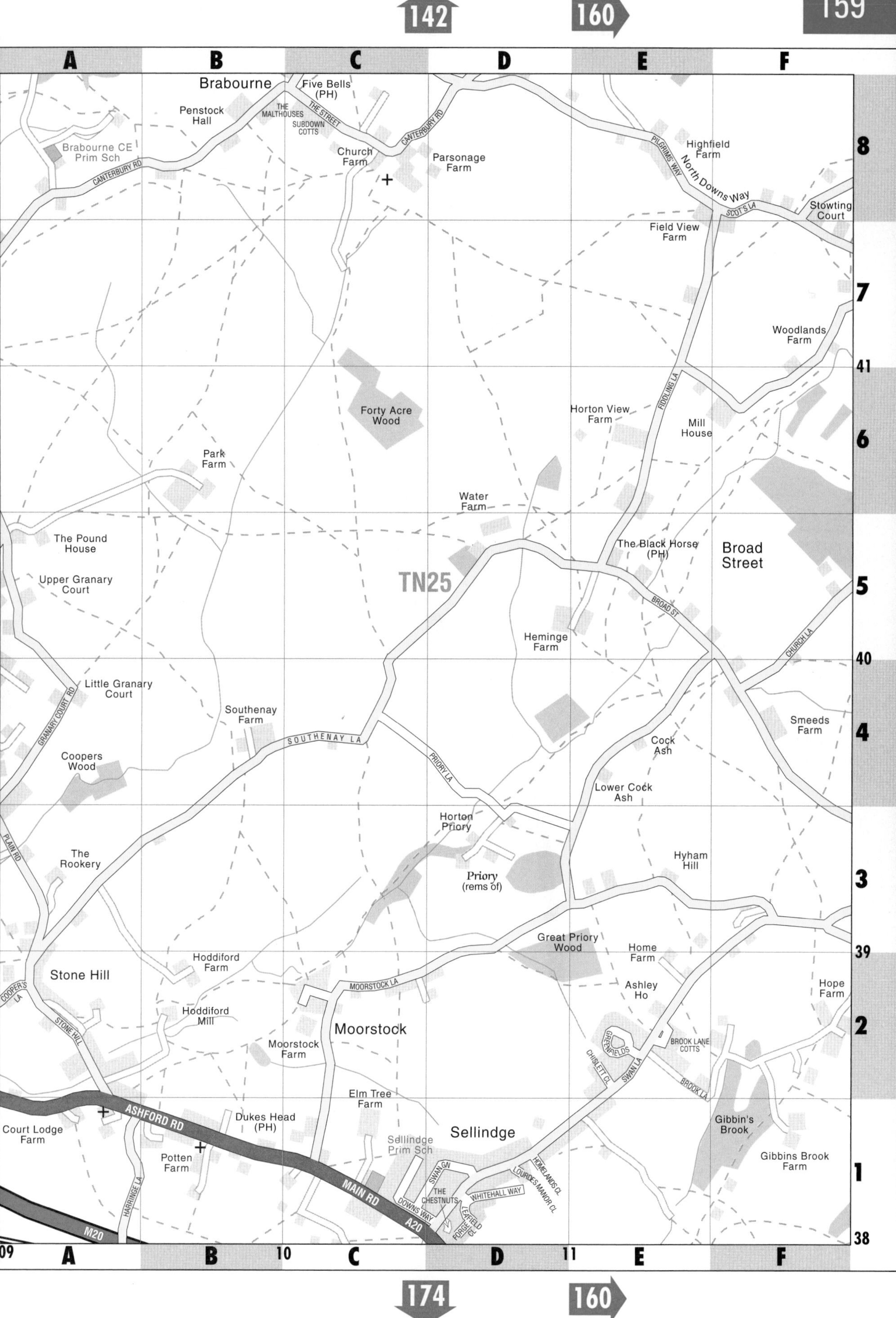
A
B
C
D
E
F
Brabourne
Five Bells (PH)
Penstock Hall
THE MALTHOUSES
THE STREET
SUBDOWN COTTS
CANTERBURY RD
Brabourne CE Prim Sch
Church Farm
Parsonage Farm
Highfield Farm
PILGRIMS' WAY
North Downs Way
SCOT'S LA
Stowting Court
Field View Farm
8
7
Woodlands Farm
41
FIDDLING LA
Forty Acre Wood
Horton View Farm
Mill House
6
Park Farm
Water Farm
The Pound House
The Black Horse (PH)
Broad Street
Upper Granary Court
TN25
5
BROAD ST
Heminge Farm
CHURCH LA
40
Little Granary Court
GRANARY COURT RD
Southenay Farm
SOUTHENAY LA
Smeeds Farm
4
Cock Ash
Coopers Wood
PRIORY LA
Lower Cock Ash
Horton Priory
PLAIN RD
The Rookery
Hyham Hill
Priory (rems of)
3
Great Priory Wood
Home Farm
39
Hoddiford Farm
Stone Hill
MOORSTOCK LA
Ashley Ho
Hope Farm
COOPER'S LA
STONE HILL
Hoddiford Mill
2
Moorstock
Moorstock Farm
GREENFIELDS
BROOK LANE COTTS
CHISLETT CL
SWAN LA
BROOK LA
Elm Tree Farm
ASHFORD RD
Dukes Head (PH)
Court Lodge Farm
Sellindge
Gibbin's Brook
Sellindge Prim Sch
Potten Farm
Gibbins Brook Farm
1
SWAN GN
HOMELANDS CL
LOURDES MANOR CL
THE CHESTNUTS
WHITEHALL WAY
MAIN RD
HARRINGE LA
DOWNS WAY
LEEFIELD CL
FORGE CL
A20
M20
38
09
10
11

174
160

159
143

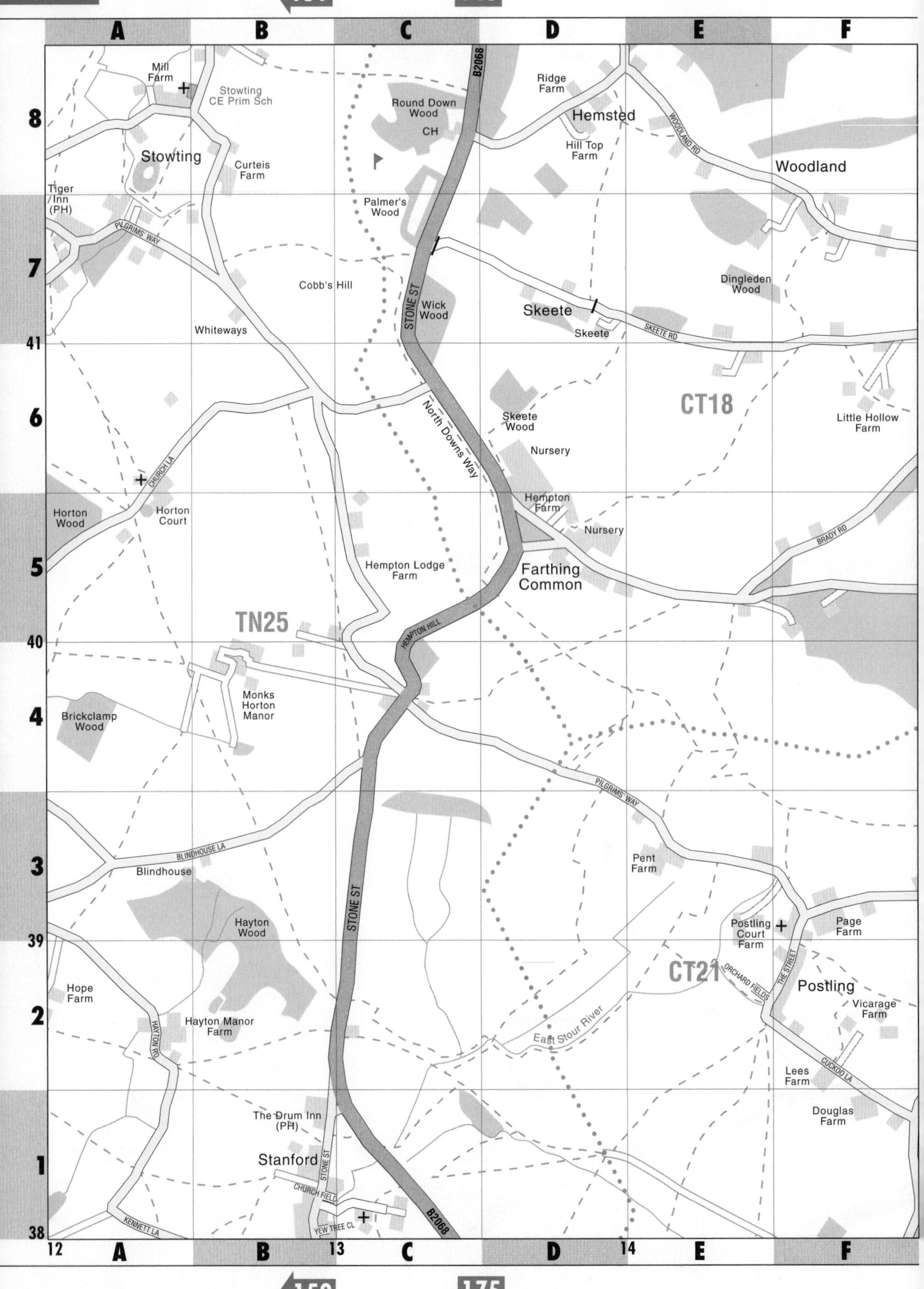
A
B
C
D
E
F
8
7
41
6
5
40
4
3
39
2
1
38
12
13
14
Mill Farm
Stowting CE Prim Sch
Round Down Wood
CH
Ridge Farm
Hemsted
Hill Top Farm
WOODLAND RD
Woodland
B2068
Stowting
Curteis Farm
Tiger Inn (PH)
Palmer's Wood
PILGRIMS' WAY
Cobb's Hill
STONE ST
Wick Wood
Skeete
Skeete
SKEETE RD
Dingleden Wood
Whiteways
CT18
Little Hollow Farm
Skeete Wood
Nursery
North Downs Way
CHURCH LA
Horton Wood
Horton Court
Hempton Farm
Nursery
BRADY RD
Hempton Lodge Farm
Farthing Common
TN25
HEMPTON HILL
Monks Horton Manor
Brickclamp Wood
PILGRIMS' WAY
BLINDHOUSE LA
Blindhouse
Pent Farm
Hayton Wood
STONE ST
Postling Court Farm
Page Farm
CT21
ORCHARD FIELDS
THE STREET
Postling
Hope Farm
Vicarage Farm
HAYTON RD
Hayton Manor Farm
East Stour River
CUCKOO LA
Lees Farm
Douglas Farm
The Drum Inn (PH)
Stanford
STONE ST
CHURCH FIELD
YEW TREE CL
KENNETT LA
B2068

159
175

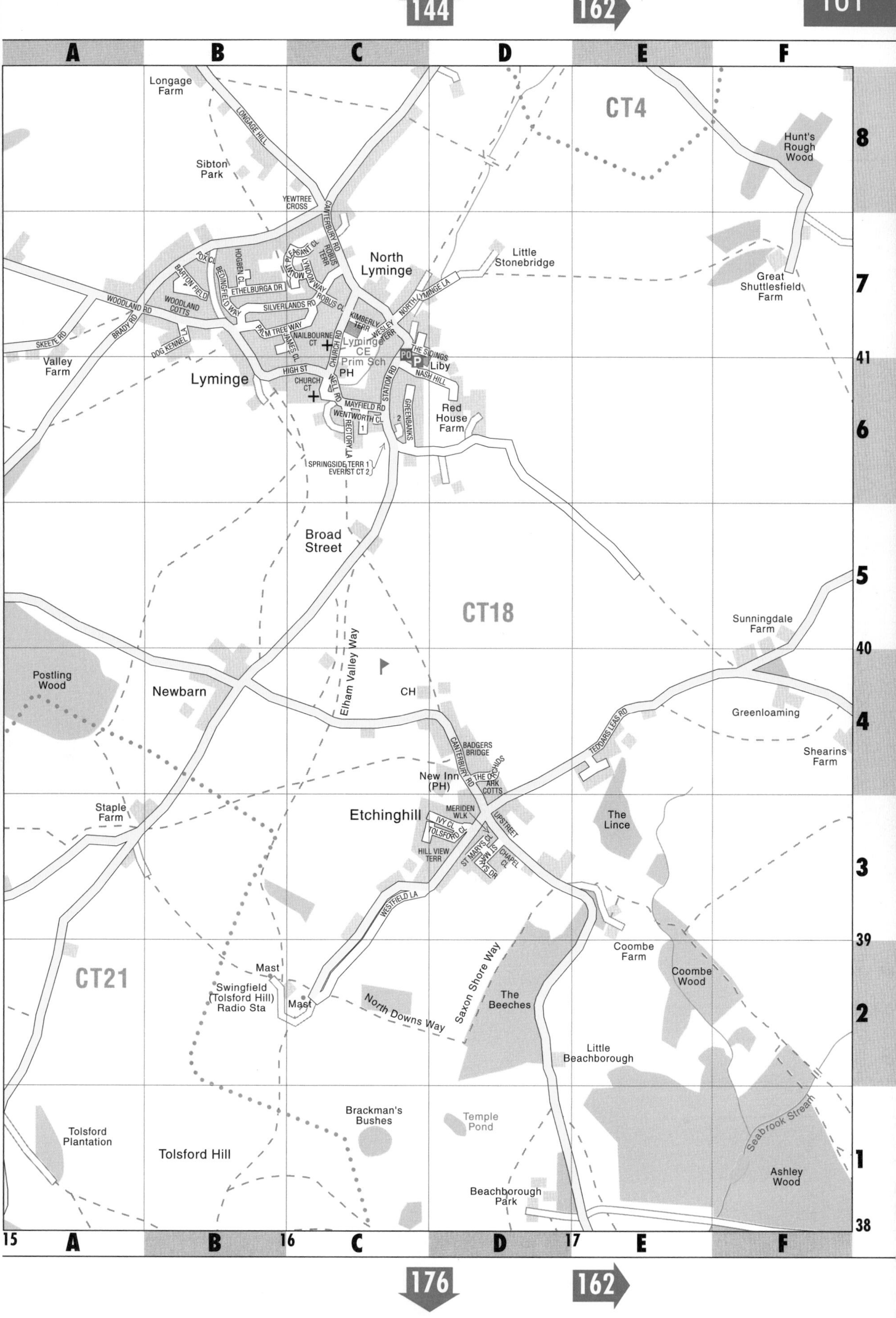
144
162
A
B
C
D
E
F
Longage
Farm
LONGAGE HILL
CT4
8
Hunt's
Rough
Wood
Sibton
Park
YEWTREE
CROSS
CANTERBURY RD
ROBUS
TERR
North
Lyminge
Little
Stonebridge
7
Great
Shuttlesfield
Farm
FOX CL
HOGBEN CL
MT PLEASANT CL
LYNDON WAY
BARTON FIELD
BEDINGFIELD WAY
ETHELBURGA DR
WOODLAND RD
WOODLAND
COTTS
SILVERLANDS RD
ROBUS CL
NORTH LYMINGE LA
BRADY RD
SKEETE RD
PALM TREE WAY
JAMES CL
NAILBOURNE
CT
KIMBERLY
TERR
WESLEY
TERR
CHURCH RD
Lyminge
CE
Prim Sch
THE SIDINGS
PO
P
Liby
41
DOG KENNEL LA
Valley
Farm
Lyminge
HIGH ST
CHURCH
CT
WELL RD
PH
STATION RD
NASH HILL
MAYFIELD RD
WENTWORTH CL
RECTORY LA
GREENBANKS
Red
House
Farm
6
SPRINGSIDE TERR 1
EVERIST CT 2
Broad
Street
5
CT18
Sunningdale
Farm
40
Elham Valley Way
Postling
Wood
Newbarn
CH
Greenloaming
TEDDARS LEAS RD
4
Shearins
Farm
BADGERS
BRIDGE
CANTERBURY RD
THE ORCHIDS
New Inn
(PH)
ARK
COTTS
Staple
Farm
Etchinghill
MERIDEN
WALK
IVY CL
TOLSFORD CL
UPSTREET
The
Lince
HILL VIEW
TERR
ST MARYS CL
CHAPEL
CL
3
WESTFIELD LA
Coombe
Farm
39
Mast
Coombe
Wood
CT21
Swingfield
(Tolsford Hill)
Radio Sta
Mast
Saxon Shore Way
The
Beeches
North Downs Way
2
Little
Beachborough
Brackman's
Bushes
Temple
Pond
Seabrook Stream
Tolsford
Plantation
Tolsford Hill
1
Ashley
Wood
Beachborough
Park
38
15
16
17
176
162

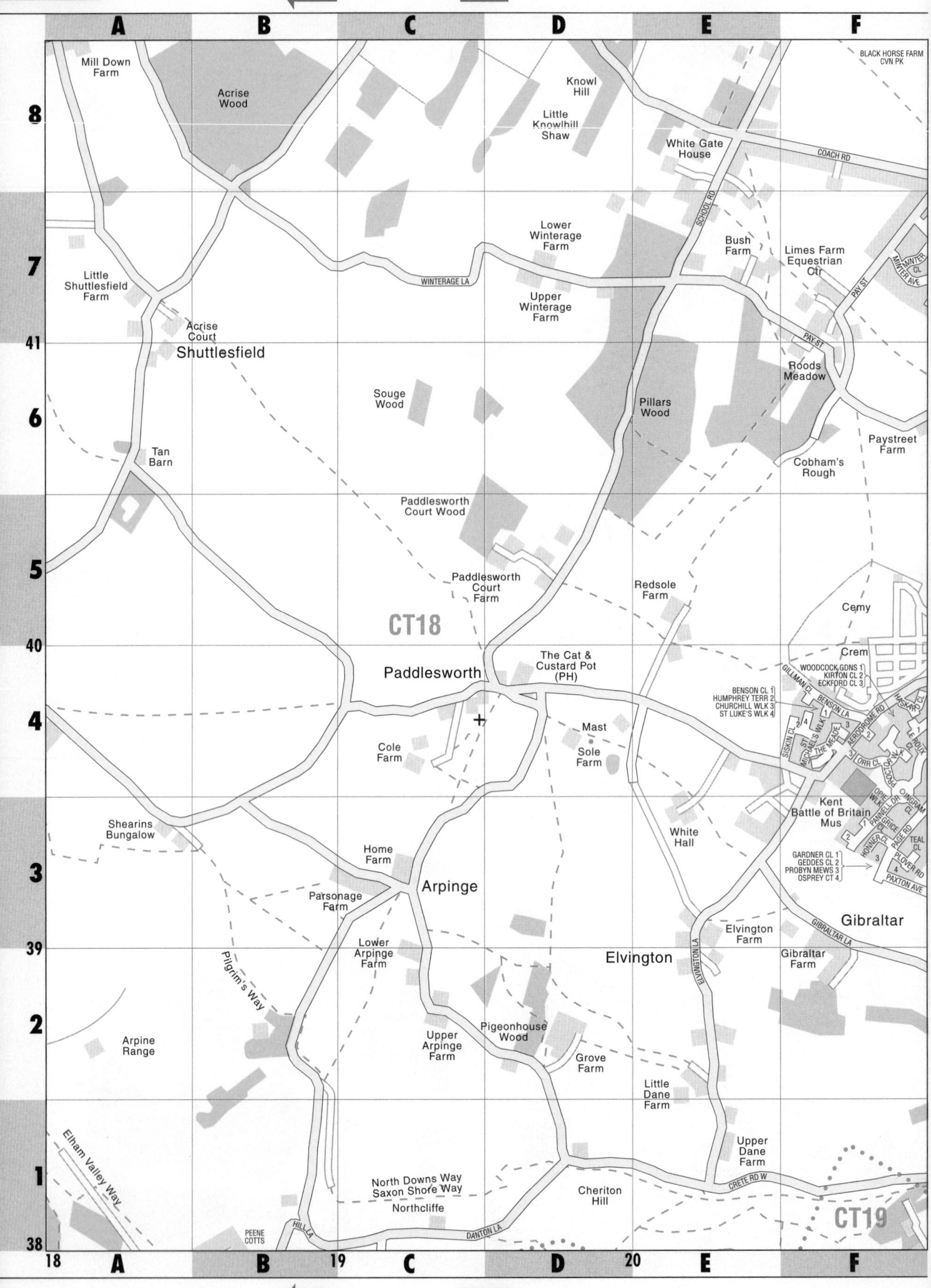

A B C D E F

8

Mill Down Farm

Acrise Wood

Knowl Hill

Little Knowlhill Shaw

White Gate House

COACH RD

BLACK HORSE FARM CVN PK

7

Little Shuttlesfield Farm

WINTERAGE LA

Lower Winterage Farm

Upper Winterage Farm

Bush Farm

SCHOOL RD

Limes Farm Equestrian Ctr

PAY ST

MINTER CL

MINTER AVE

41

Acrise Court

Shuttlesfield

PAY ST

Roods Meadow

6

Souge Wood

Pillars Wood

Paystreet Farm

Tan Barn

Cobham's Rough

5

Paddlesworth Court Wood

Paddlesworth Court Farm

Redsole Farm

Cemy

CT18

40

Paddlesworth

The Cat & Custard Pot (PH)

Crem

WOODCOCK GDNS 1
KIRTON CL 2
ECKFORD CL 3

4

Cole Farm

Mast

Sole Farm

BENSON CL 1
HUMPHREY TERR 2
CHURCHILL WLK 3
ST LUKE'S WLK 4

BENSON LA

GILLMAN CL

KERSBROOKE RD

SISKIN CL

MITCHELL'S WLK

ST MICHAEL'S WLK

THE MEADE

ORR CL

LE ROUX

3

Shearins Bungalow

Home Farm

White Hall

Kent Battle of Britain Mus

PANNELL DR

CREE CT

PRICE RD

PIERCE CL

HORNET CL

TEAL CL

PLOVER RD

GARDNER CL 1
GEDDES CL 2
PROBYN MEWS 3
OSPREY CT 4

PAXTON AVE

Gibraltar

GIBRALTAR LA

39

Parsonage Farm

Pilgrim's Way

Arpinge

Lower Arpinge Farm

Elvington

Elvington Farm

ELVINGTON LA

Gibraltar Farm

2

Arpine Range

Upper Arpinge Farm

Pigeonhouse Wood

Grove Farm

Little Dane Farm

1

Eltham Valley Way

North Downs Way
Saxon Shore Way

Northcliffe

Cheriton Hill

Upper Dane Farm

CRETE RD W

CT19

38

PEENE COTTS

HILL LA

DANTON LA

18   A   B   19   C   D   20   E   F

146
164

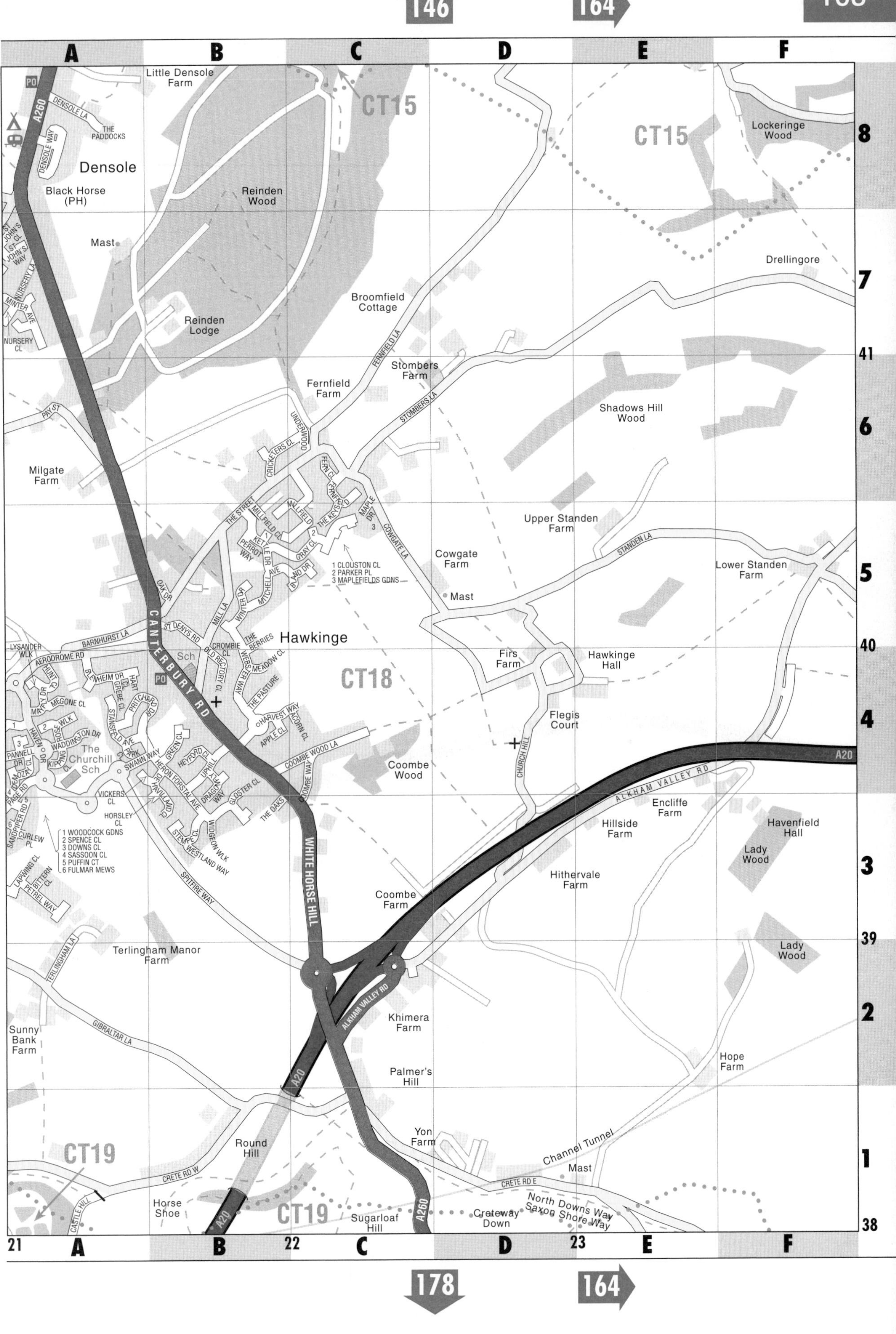
Little Densole Farm
CT15
Lockeringe Wood
Densole
Black Horse (PH)
Reinden Wood
Mast
Drellingore
Broomfield Cottage
Reinden Lodge
Stombers Farm
Fernfield Farm
Shadows Hill Wood
Milgate Farm
Upper Standen Farm
Cowgate Farm
Lower Standen Farm
1 CLOUSTON CL
2 PARKER PL
3 MAPLEFIELDS GDNS
Mast
Hawkinge
Firs Farm
Hawkinge Hall
CT18
Flegis Court
The Churchill Sch
Coombe Wood
A20
Encliffe Farm
Hillside Farm
Havenfield Hall
1 WOODCOCK GDNS
2 SPENCE CL
3 DOWNS CL
4 SASSOON CL
5 PUFFIN CT
6 FULMAR MEWS
Lady Wood
Hithervale Farm
Coombe Farm
Terlingham Manor Farm
Lady Wood
Khimera Farm
Sunny Bank Farm
Hope Farm
Palmer's Hill
Yon Farm
Round Hill
CT19
Channel Tunnel
Mast
Horse Shoe
CT19
Sugarloaf Hill
Creteway Down
North Downs Way
Saxon Shore Way
A260
CANTERBURY RD
WHITE HORSE HILL
ALKHAM VALLEY RD
A
B
C
D
E
F
8
7
41
6
5
40
4
3
39
2
1
38
21
22
23

178
164

163
147

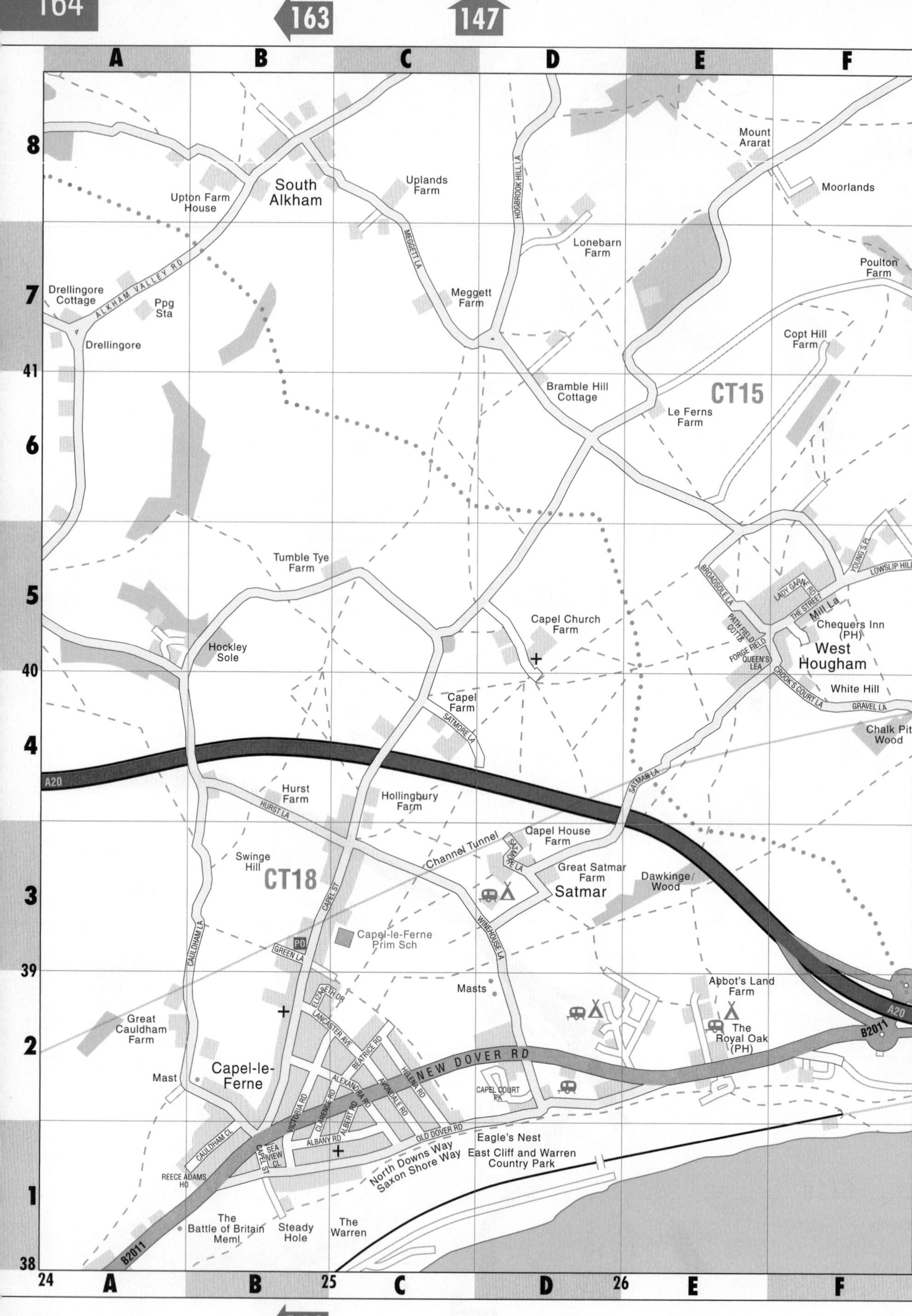
A
B
C
D
E
F
8
7
41
6
5
40
4
3
39
2
1
38
24
25
26
South Alkham
Upton Farm House
Uplands Farm
Mount Ararat
Moorlands
HOGBROOK HILL LA
MEGGETT LA
Lonebarn Farm
Poulton Farm
Drellingore Cottage
ALKHAM VALLEY RD
Ppg Sta
Meggett Farm
Drellingore
Copt Hill Farm
Bramble Hill Cottage
CT15
Le Ferns Farm
Tumble Tye Farm
BROADSOLE LA
LADY GARNE RD
YOUNG'S PL
LOWSLIP HILL
THE STREET
Mill La
Capel Church Farm
Chequers Inn (PH)
PATH FIELD COTTS
FORGE FIELD
QUEEN'S LEA
West Hougham
Hockley Sole
CROOK'S COURT LA
White Hill
GRAVEL LA
Capel Farm
SATMORE LA
Chalk Pit Wood
A20
SATMAR LA
Hurst Farm
Hollingbury Farm
HURST LA
Capel House Farm
Channel Tunnel
SATMAR LA
Swinge Hill
Great Satmar Farm
Dawkinge Wood
CT18
Satmar
CAPEL ST
CAULDHAM LA
WINEHOUSE LA
PO
Capel-le-Ferne Prim Sch
GREEN LA
ELIZABETH DR
Masts
Abbot's Land Farm
Great Cauldham Farm
LANCASTER AVE
BEATRICE RD
A20
The Royal Oak (PH)
B2011
NEW DOVER RD
HELENA RD
Mast
Capel-le-Ferne
ALEXANDRA RD
AVONDALE RD
CAPEL COURT PK
VICTORIA RD
CLARENCE RD
ALBERT RD
OLD DOVER RD
Eagle's Nest
CAULDHAM CL
ALBANY RD
SEA VIEW CL
East Cliff and Warren Country Park
North Downs Way
Saxon Shore Way
CAPEL ST
REECE ADAMS HO
The Battle of Britain Meml
Steady Hole
The Warren
B2011

163

148
166

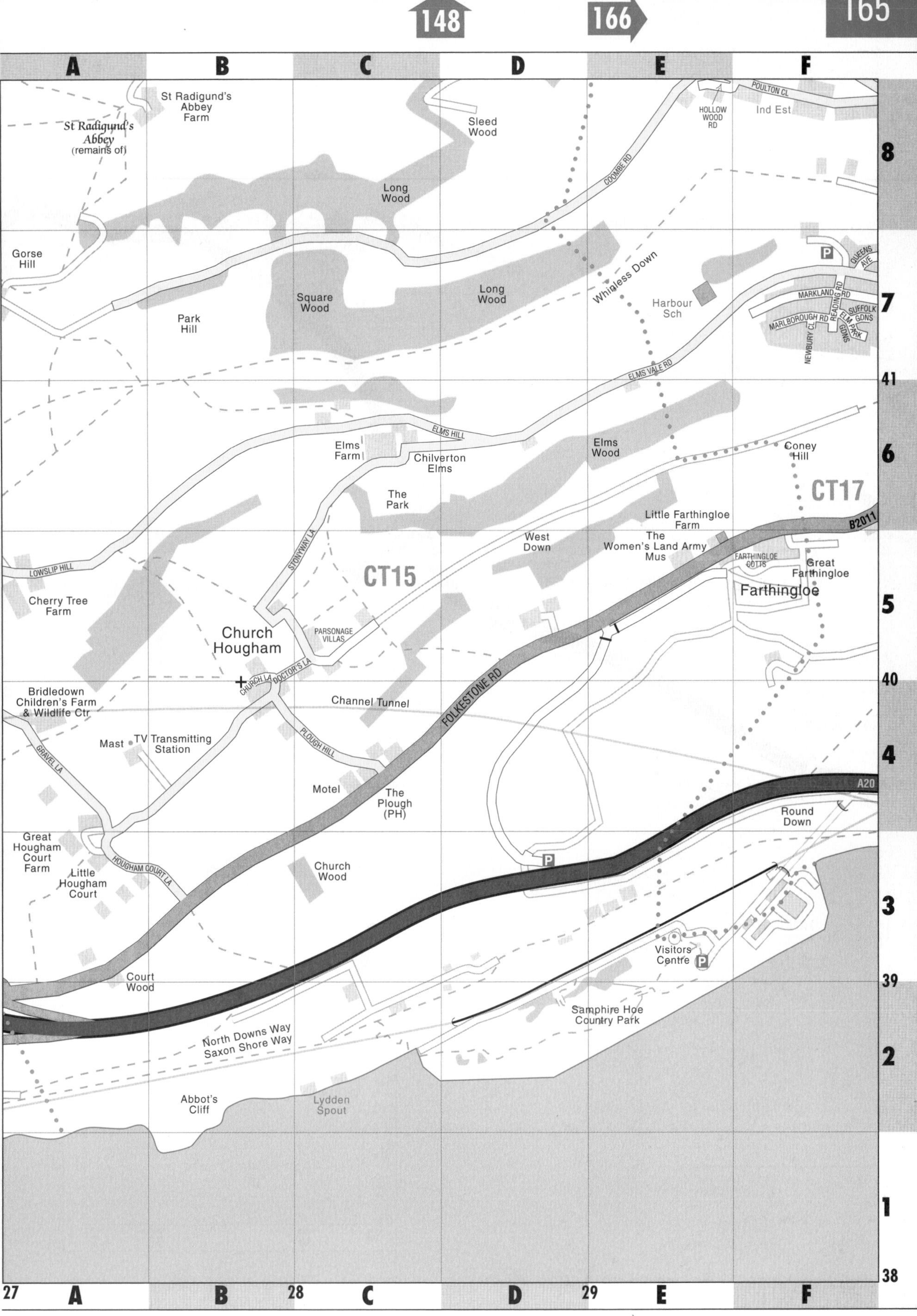
St Radigund's Abbey Farm
St Radigund's Abbey (remains of)
Sleed Wood
Long Wood
Gorse Hill
Park Hill
Square Wood
Long Wood
Whinless Down
Harbour Sch
Ind Est
POULTON CL
HOLLOW WOOD RD
COOMBE RD
QUEENS AVE
MARKLAND RD
READING RD
SUFFOLK GDNS
ELM PARK GDNS
MARLBOROUGH RD
NEWBURY CL
ELMS VALE RD
ELMS HILL
Elms Farm
Chilverton Elms
Elms Wood
Coney Hill
The Park
CT17
Little Farthingloe Farm
B2011
West Down
The Women's Land Army Mus
FARTHINGLOE COTTS
Great Farthingloe
Farthingloe
LOWSLIP HILL
STONYWAY LA
CT15
Cherry Tree Farm
Church Hougham
PARSONAGE VILLAS
CHURCH LA
DOCTOR'S LA
FOLKESTONE RD
Bridledown Children's Farm & Wildlife Ctr
Channel Tunnel
Mast
TV Transmitting Station
GRAVEL LA
PLOUGH HILL
Motel
The Plough (PH)
A20
Round Down
Great Hougham Court Farm
Little Hougham Court
HOUGHAM COURT LA
Church Wood
Visitors Centre
Court Wood
Samphire Hoe Country Park
North Downs Way
Saxon Shore Way
Abbot's Cliff
Lydden Spout
A B C D E F
8 7 41 6 5 40 4 3 39 2 1 38
27 28 29

166

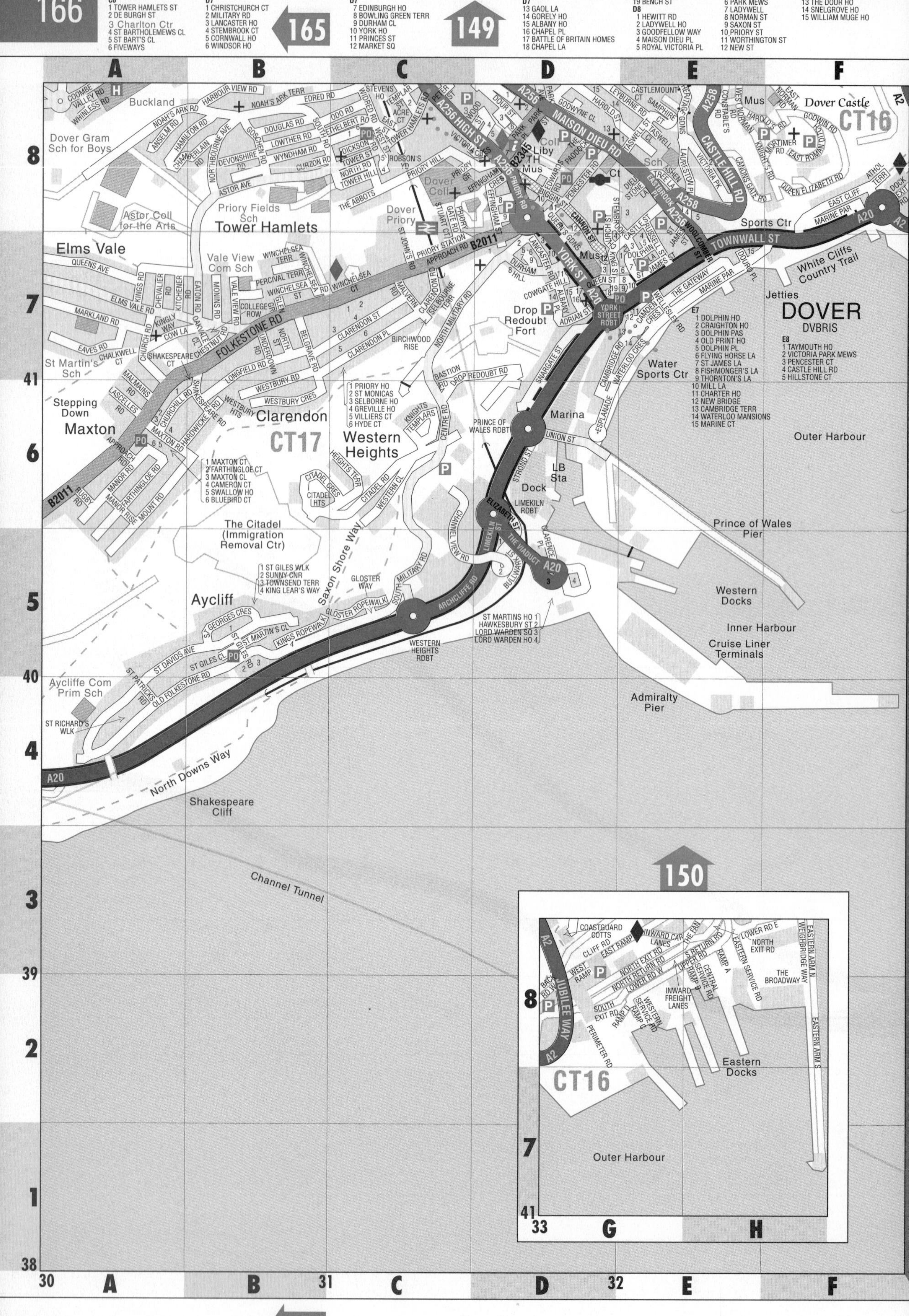

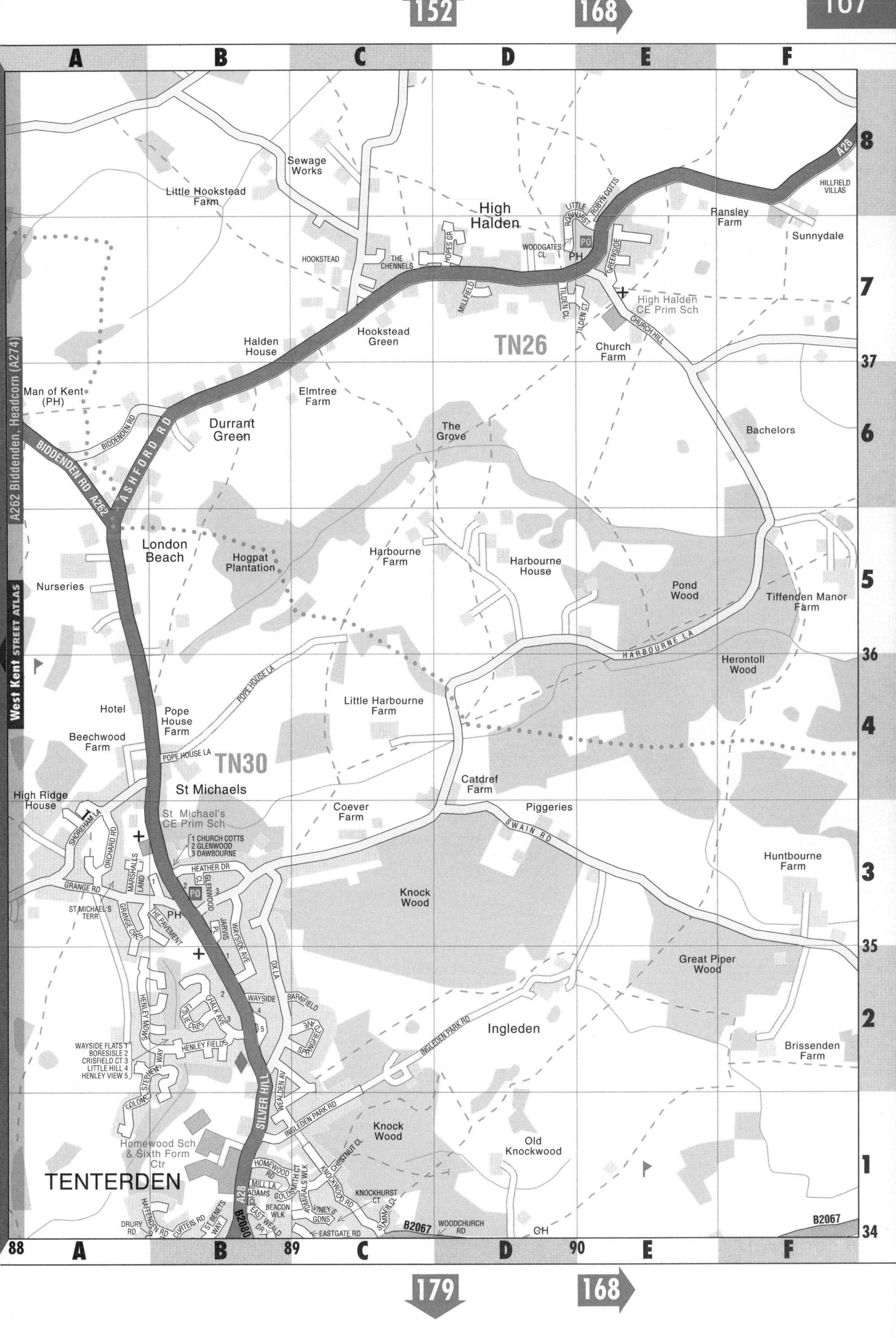
152
168
A
B
C
D
E
F
8
7
37
6
5
36
4
3
35
2
1
34
88
89
90
Sewage Works
Little Hookstead Farm
High Halden
HOOKSTEAD
THE CHENNELS
HOPES GR
MILLFIELD
WOODGATES CL
PH
PO
ROBYN COTTS
GREENSIDE
TILDEN CL
TILDEN CT
CHURCH HILL
High Halden CE Prim Sch
Ransley Farm
HILLFIELD VILLAS
Sunnydale
A28
Hookstead Green
Halden House
TN26
Church Farm
Man of Kent (PH)
BIDDENDEN RD
Elmtree Farm
Durrant Green
ASHFORD RD
The Grove
Bachelors
A262
London Beach
Hogpat Plantation
Harbourne Farm
Harbourne House
Pond Wood
Tiffenden Manor Farm
Nurseries
HARBOURNE LA
Herontoll Wood
POPE HOUSE LA
Little Harbourne Farm
Hotel
Pope House Farm
Beechwood Farm
TN30
St Michaels
Catdref Farm
High Ridge House
Coever Farm
Piggeries
St Michael's CE Prim Sch
SHOREHAM LA
ORCHARD RD
1 CHURCH COTTS
2 GLENWOOD
3 DAWBOURNE
SWAIN RD
HEATHER DR
MARSHALLS LAND
GLENWOOD
Knock Wood
Huntbourne Farm
GRANGE RD
ST MICHAEL'S TERR
GRANGE CRES
THE PAVEMENT
JARVIS PL
WAYSIDE AVE
OX LA
Great Piper Wood
WAYSIDE
BARNFIELD
CHALK AVE
LESLIE CRES
HENLEY MDWS
INGLEDEN PARK RD
Ingleden
SPRINGFIELD AVE
HENLEY FIELDS
Brissenden Farm
WAYSIDE FLATS 1
BORESISLE 2
CRISFIELD CT 3
LITTLE HILL 4
HENLEY VIEW 5
STEPHENS WAY
COLONEL'S WAY
SILVER HILL
WEALDEN AV
Knock Wood
Old Knockwood
Homewood Sch & Sixth Form Ctr
TENTERDEN
HOMEWOOD RD
MILL LA
ADAMS CL
GOLDSMITH CT
ADMIRALS WLK
CHESTNUT CL
KNOCKWOOD RD
KNOCKHURST CT
BEACON WLK
EAST WEALD DR
VINEY'S GDNS
SUMMER CL
EASTGATE RD
B2067
WOODCHURCH RD
CH
B2067
A28
B2080
DRURY RD
HAFFENDEN RD
CURTEIS RD
ST BENETS WAY
A262 Biddenden, Headcorn (A274)
West Kent STREET ATLAS
179
168

167
153

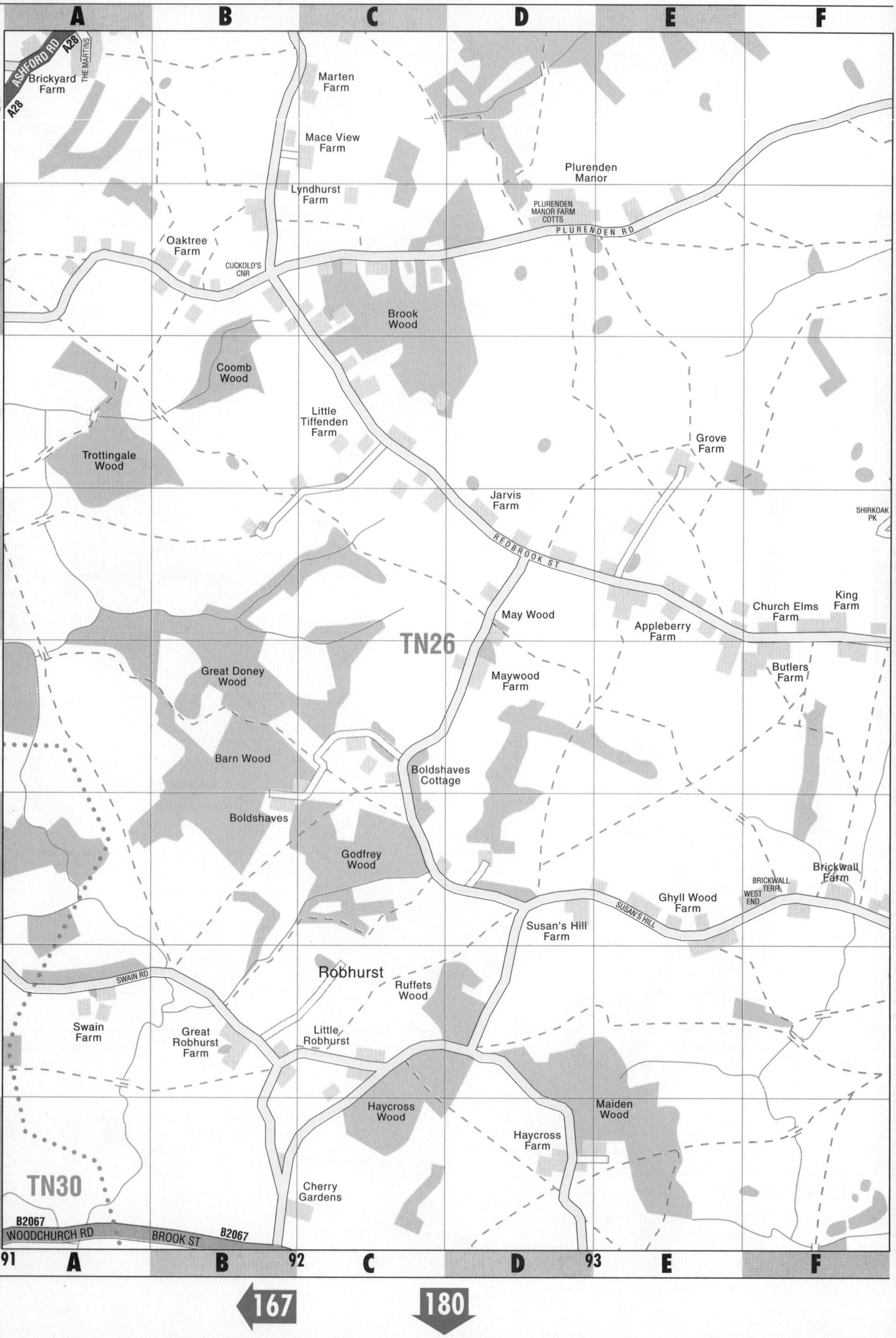

A B C D E F

8

ASHFORD RD
A28
THE MARTINS
Brickyard
Farm
A28

Marten
Farm

Mace View
Farm

Plurenden
Manor

7

Oaktree
Farm

Lyndhurst
Farm

CUCKOLD'S
CNR

PLURENDEN MANOR
FARM COTTS

PLURENDEN RD

Brook
Wood

37

Coomb
Wood

Grove
Farm

6

Trottingale
Wood

Little
Tiffenden
Farm

SHIRKOAK
PK

Jarvis
Farm

REDBROOK ST

5

May Wood

Appleberry
Farm

Church Elms
Farm

King
Farm

36

TN26

Great Doney
Wood

Maywood
Farm

Butlers
Farm

4

Barn Wood

Boldshaves
Cottage

Boldshaves

Godfrey
Wood

Ghyll Wood
Farm

BRICKWALL
TERR
WEST
END

Brickwall
Farm

3

SUSAN'S HILL

Susan's Hill
Farm

35

SWAIN RD

Robhurst

Ruffets
Wood

2

Swain
Farm

Great
Robhurst
Farm

Little
Robhurst

Haycross
Wood

Maiden
Wood

Haycross
Farm

1

TN30

Cherry
Gardens

B2067
WOODCHURCH RD
BROOK ST
B2067

34

91 A B 92 C D 93 E F

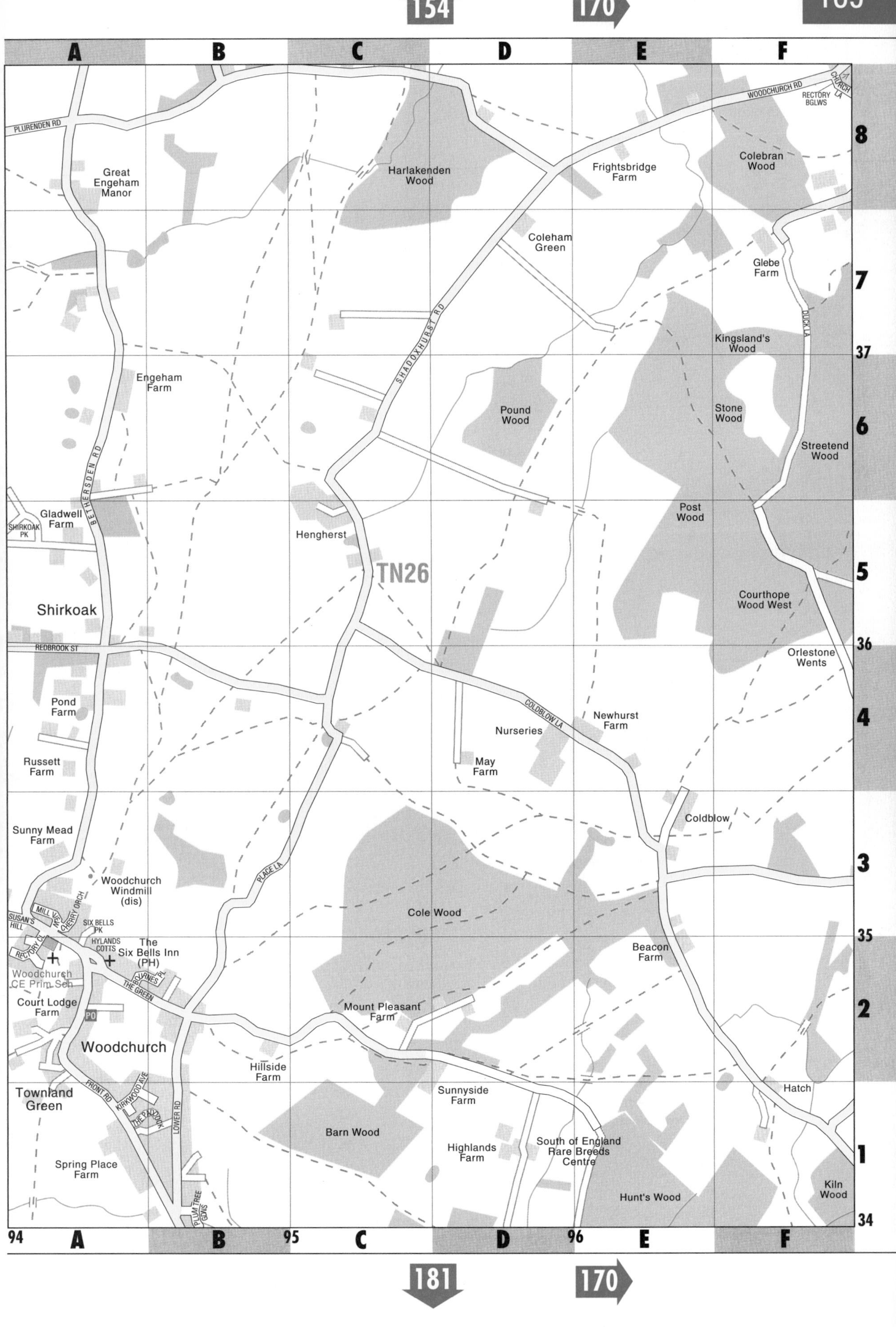

PLURENDEN RD

WOODCHURCH RD

CHURCH LA

RECTORY BGLWS

Great Engeham Manor

Harlakenden Wood

Frightsbridge Farm

Colebran Wood

Coleham Green

Glebe Farm

SHADOXHURST RD

Kingsland's Wood

DUCK LA

Engeham Farm

Pound Wood

Stone Wood

Streetend Wood

BETHERSDEN RD

SHIRKOAK PK

Gladwell Farm

Hengherst

Post Wood

TN26

Shirkoak

Courthope Wood West

REDBROOK ST

Orlestone Wents

Pond Farm

Nurseries

COLDBLOW LA

Newhurst Farm

Russett Farm

May Farm

Coldblow

Sunny Mead Farm

PLACE LA

Woodchurch Windmill (dis)

SUSAN'S HILL

CHERRY ORCH

MILL VW

SIX BELLS PK

HYLANDS COTTS

The Six Bells Inn (PH)

Cole Wood

Beacon Farm

RECTORY CL

Woodchurch CE Prim Sch

VINES CL

THE GREEN

Court Lodge Farm

PO

Mount Pleasant Farm

Woodchurch

FRONT RD

KIRKWOOD AVE

THE PADDOCK

LOWER RD

Hillside Farm

Townland Green

Sunnyside Farm

Hatch

Spring Place Farm

PLUM TREE GDNS

Barn Wood

Highlands Farm

South of England Rare Breeds Centre

Hunt's Wood

Kiln Wood

169
155

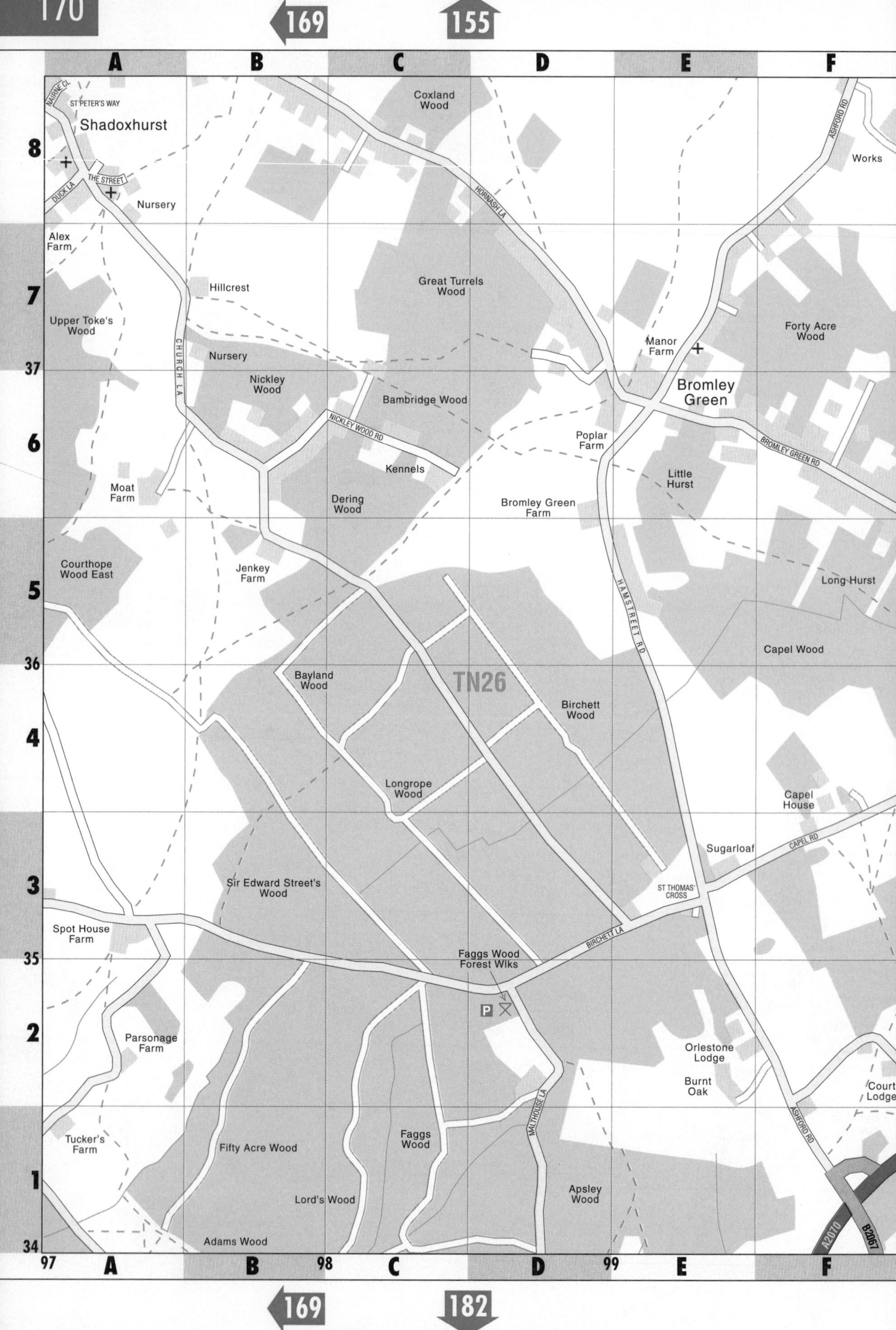
A
B
C
D
E
F
8
7
37
6
5
36
4
3
35
2
1
34
97
98
99
NAIRNE CL
ST PETER'S WAY
Shadoxhurst
DUCK LA
THE STREET
Nursery
Alex Farm
Upper Toke's Wood
Hillcrest
CHURCH LA
Nursery
Nickley Wood
Moat Farm
Courthope Wood East
Jenkey Farm
Coxland Wood
HORNASH LA
Great Turrels Wood
Bambridge Wood
NICKLEY WOOD RD
Kennels
Dering Wood
Bromley Green Farm
Poplar Farm
Manor Farm
Bromley Green
BROMLEY GREEN RD
Little Hurst
ASHFORD RD
Works
Forty Acre Wood
Long Hurst
Capel Wood
HAMSTREET RD
Bayland Wood
TN26
Birchett Wood
Longrope Wood
Capel House
Sugarloaf
CAPEL RD
ST THOMAS' CROSS
Sir Edward Street's Wood
Spot House Farm
BIRCHETT LA
Faggs Wood Forest Wlks
P
Parsonage Farm
MALTHOUSE LA
Orlestone Lodge
Burnt Oak
Court Lodge
ASHFORD RD
Tucker's Farm
Fifty Acre Wood
Faggs Wood
Lord's Wood
Apsley Wood
Adams Wood
A2070
B2067

169
182

156
172

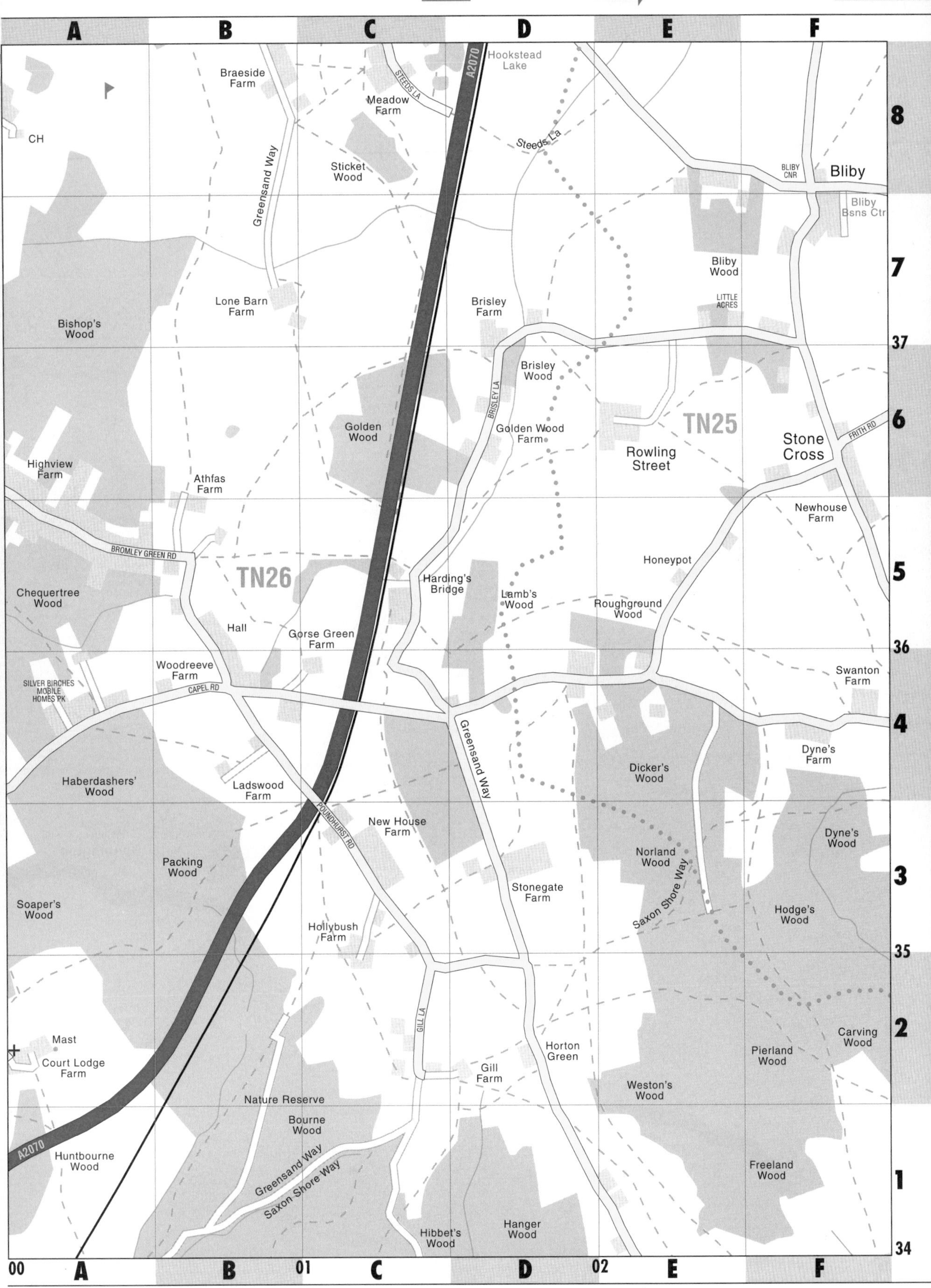
A
B
C
D
E
F
Hookstead Lake
A2070
Braeside Farm
Meadow Farm
STEEDS LA
Steeds La
CH
Greensand Way
Sticket Wood
BLIBY CNR
Bliby
Bliby Bsns Ctr
Bliby Wood
LITTLE ACRES
Lone Barn Farm
Brisley Farm
Bishop's Wood
Brisley Wood
BRISLEY LA
Golden Wood
Golden Wood Farm
TN25
Rowling Street
Stone Cross
FRITH RD
Highview Farm
Athfas Farm
Newhouse Farm
BROMLEY GREEN RD
Honeypot
TN26
Harding's Bridge
Chequertree Wood
Lamb's Wood
Roughground Wood
Hall
Gorse Green Farm
Woodreeve Farm
Swanton Farm
SILVER BIRCHES MOBILE HOMES PK
CAPEL RD
Greensand Way
Dyne's Farm
Dicker's Wood
Haberdashers' Wood
Ladswood Farm
POUNDHURST RD
New House Farm
Dyne's Wood
Norland Wood
Packing Wood
Stonegate Farm
Saxon Shore Way
Soaper's Wood
Hodge's Wood
Hollybush Farm
GILL LA
Mast
Horton Green
Carving Wood
Pierland Wood
Court Lodge Farm
Gill Farm
Weston's Wood
Nature Reserve
Bourne Wood
A2070
Huntbourne Wood
Greensand Way
Saxon Shore Way
Freeland Wood
Hibbet's Wood
Hanger Wood
8
7
37
6
5
36
4
3
35
2
1
34
00
01
02

183
172

171
157

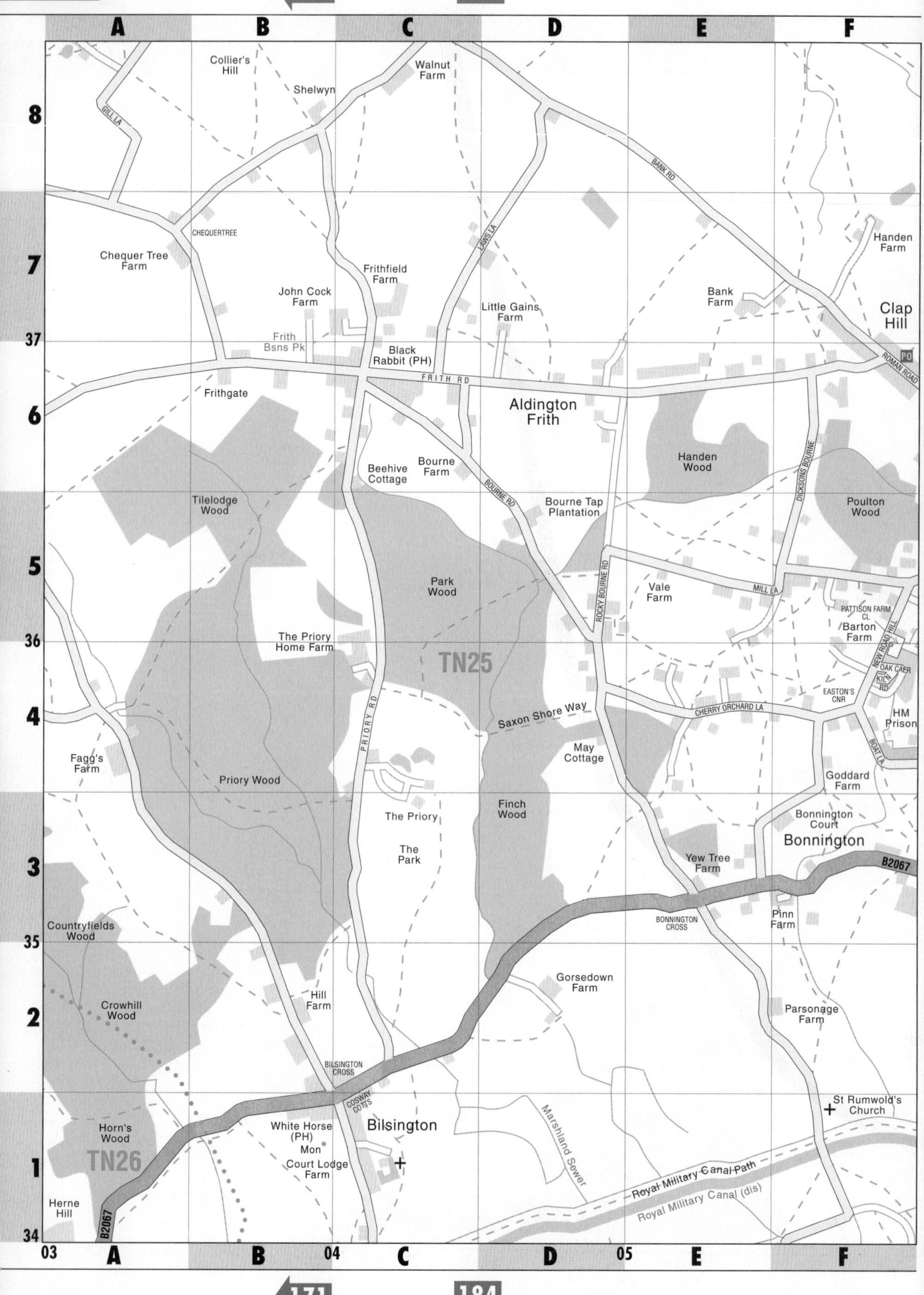
A
B
C
D
E
F
Collier's Hill
Walnut Farm
Shelwyn
GILL LA
BANK RD
CHEQUERTREE
Chequer Tree Farm
LAWS LA
Handen Farm
Frithfield Farm
John Cock Farm
Little Gains Farm
Bank Farm
Clap Hill
Frith Bsns Pk
Black Rabbit (PH)
FRITH RD
ROMAN ROAD
PO
Frithgate
Aldington Frith
Beehive Cottage
Bourne Farm
Handen Wood
DICKSONS BOURNE
BOURNE RD
Tilelodge Wood
Bourne Tap Plantation
Poulton Wood
Park Wood
ROCKY BOURNE RD
Vale Farm
MILL LA
PATTISON FARM CL
Barton Farm
NEW ROAD HILL
The Priory Home Farm
TN25
OAK CAER
KILN RD
EASTON'S CNR
CHERRY ORCHARD LA
HM Prison
Saxon Shore Way
PRIORY RD
BOAT LA
Fagg's Farm
May Cottage
Goddard Farm
Priory Wood
Finch Wood
The Priory
Bonnington Court
Bonnington
The Park
Yew Tree Farm
B2067
BONNINGTON CROSS
Pinn Farm
Countryfields Wood
Gorsedown Farm
Crowhill Wood
Hill Farm
Parsonage Farm
BILSINGTON CROSS
COSWAY COTTS
St Rumwold's Church
Marshland Sewer
Horn's Wood
White Horse (PH)
Bilsington
Mon
Court Lodge Farm
TN26
Royal Military Canal Path
Royal Military Canal (dis)
Herne Hill
B2067
8
7
37
6
5
36
4
3
35
2
1
34
03
04
05

171
184

158
174

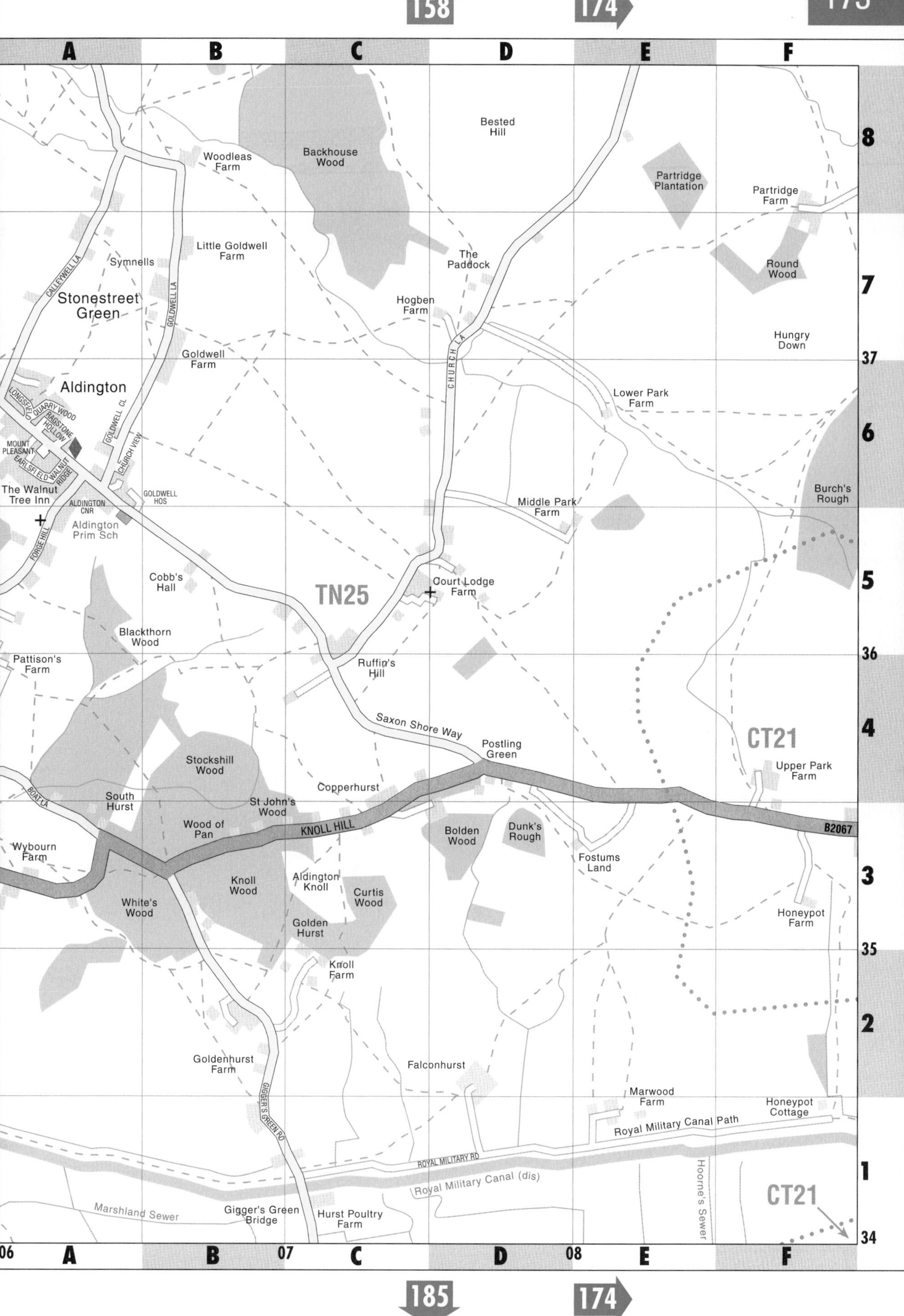
A
B
C
D
E
F
8
7
37
6
5
36
4
3
35
2
1
34
06
07
08
Bested Hill
Backhouse Wood
Woodleas Farm
Partridge Plantation
Partridge Farm
Little Goldwell Farm
Symnells
The Paddock
Round Wood
Stonestreet Green
CALLEYWELL LA
GOLDWELL LA
Hogben Farm
Hungry Down
Goldwell Farm
CHURCH LA
Aldington
Lower Park Farm
LONGSFIELD
QUARRY WOOD
RAGSTONE HOLLOW
GOLDWELL CL
MOUNT PLEASANT
EARLSFIELD
WALNUT RIDGE
CHURCH VIEW
The Walnut Tree Inn
ALDINGTON CNR
GOLDWELL HOS
Middle Park Farm
Burch's Rough
Aldington Prim Sch
FORGE HILL
Cobb's Hall
TN25
Court Lodge Farm
Blackthorn Wood
Pattison's Farm
Ruffin's Hill
Saxon Shore Way
CT21
Postling Green
Stockshill Wood
Upper Park Farm
Copperhurst
BOAT LA
South Hurst
St John's Wood
Wood of Pan
KNOLL HILL
Bolden Wood
Dunk's Rough
B2067
Wybourn Farm
Fostums Land
Knoll Wood
Aldington Knoll
Curtis Wood
White's Wood
Honeypot Farm
Golden Hurst
Knoll Farm
Goldenhurst Farm
Falconhurst
GIGGER'S GREEN RD
Marwood Farm
Honeypot Cottage
Royal Military Canal Path
ROYAL MILITARY RD
Royal Military Canal (dis)
Hoorne's Sewer
CT21
Marshland Sewer
Gigger's Green Bridge
Hurst Poultry Farm

185
174

173
159

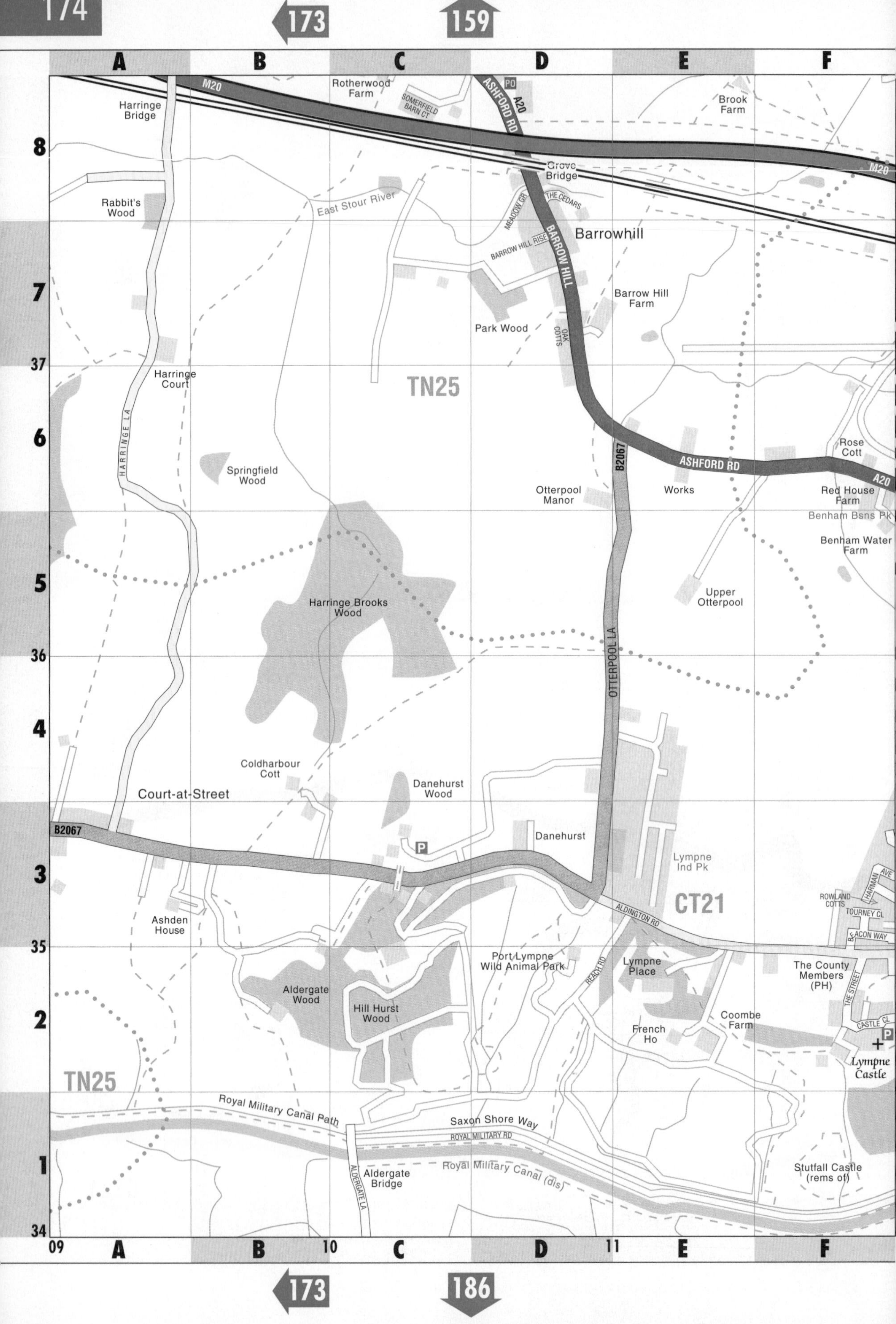
A
B
C
D
E
F
M20
Harringe Bridge
Rotherwood Farm
SOMERFIELD BARN CT
ASHFORD RD
PO
A20
Brook Farm
8
Grove Bridge
Rabbit's Wood
East Stour River
MEADOW GR
THE CEDARS
Barrowhill
BARROW HILL RISE
BARROW HILL
7
Barrow Hill Farm
Park Wood
OAK COTTS
37
Harringe Court
TN25
HARRINGE LA
6
Rose Cott
B2067
ASHFORD RD
A20
Springfield Wood
Otterpool Manor
Works
Red House Farm
Benham Bsns Pk
Benham Water Farm
5
Harringe Brooks Wood
Upper Otterpool
36
OTTERPOOL LA
4
Coldharbour Cott
Danehurst Wood
Court-at-Street
B2067
P
Danehurst
3
Lympne Ind Pk
CT21
ROWLAND COTTS
HARMAN AVE
TOURNEY CL
BEACON WAY
Ashden House
ALDINGTON RD
35
Port Lympne Wild Animal Park
REACH RD
Lympne Place
The County Members (PH)
THE STREET
Aldergate Wood
Hill Hurst Wood
2
French Ho
Coombe Farm
CASTLE CL
P
Lympne Castle
TN25
Royal Military Canal Path
Saxon Shore Way
ROYAL MILITARY RD
1
ALDERGATE LA
Aldergate Bridge
Royal Military Canal (dis)
Stutfall Castle (rems of)
34
09
10
11

173
186

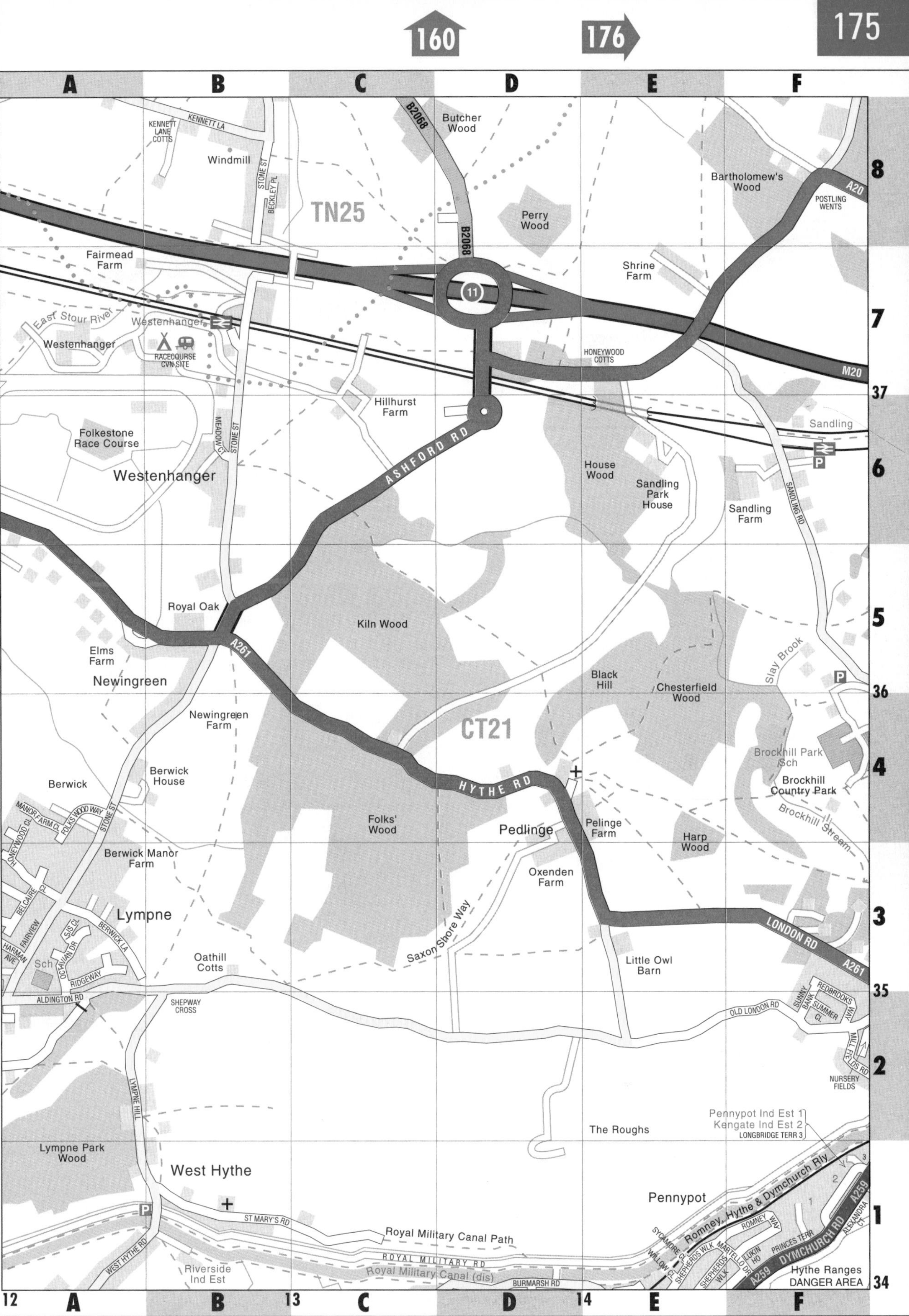
160
176
A
B
C
D
E
F
8
7
37
6
5
36
4
3
35
2
1
34
12
13
14
TN25
CT21
Butcher Wood
Windmill
Perry Wood
Bartholomew's Wood
Fairmead Farm
Shrine Farm
Westenhanger
Racecourse Cvn Site
Hillhurst Farm
Folkestone Race Course
Westenhanger
House Wood
Sandling Park House
Sandling Farm
Sandling
Royal Oak
Kiln Wood
Elms Farm
Newingreen
Black Hill
Chesterfield Wood
Newingreen Farm
Berwick
Berwick House
Folks' Wood
Pedlinge
Pelinge Farm
Harp Wood
Brockhill Park Sch
Brockhill Country Park
Berwick Manor Farm
Oxenden Farm
Lympne
Oathill Cotts
Saxon Shore Way
Little Owl Barn
Shepway Cross
The Roughs
Pennypot Ind Est 1
Kengate Ind Est 2
Longbridge Terr 3
Lympne Park Wood
West Hythe
Pennypot
Royal Military Canal Path
Riverside Ind Est
Royal Military Canal (dis)
Hythe Ranges
DANGER AREA
Ashford Rd
Hythe Rd
London Rd
A261
A20
M20
B2068
A259
Stone St
Kennett La
Sandling Rd
Old London Rd
Aldington Rd
Lympne Hill
St Mary's Rd
Royal Military Rd
Burmarsh Rd
Dymchurch Rd
Romney, Hythe & Dymchurch Rly
East Stour River
Slay Brook
Brockhill Stream
Honeywood Cotts
Postling Wents
Nursery Fields
187
176

175
161

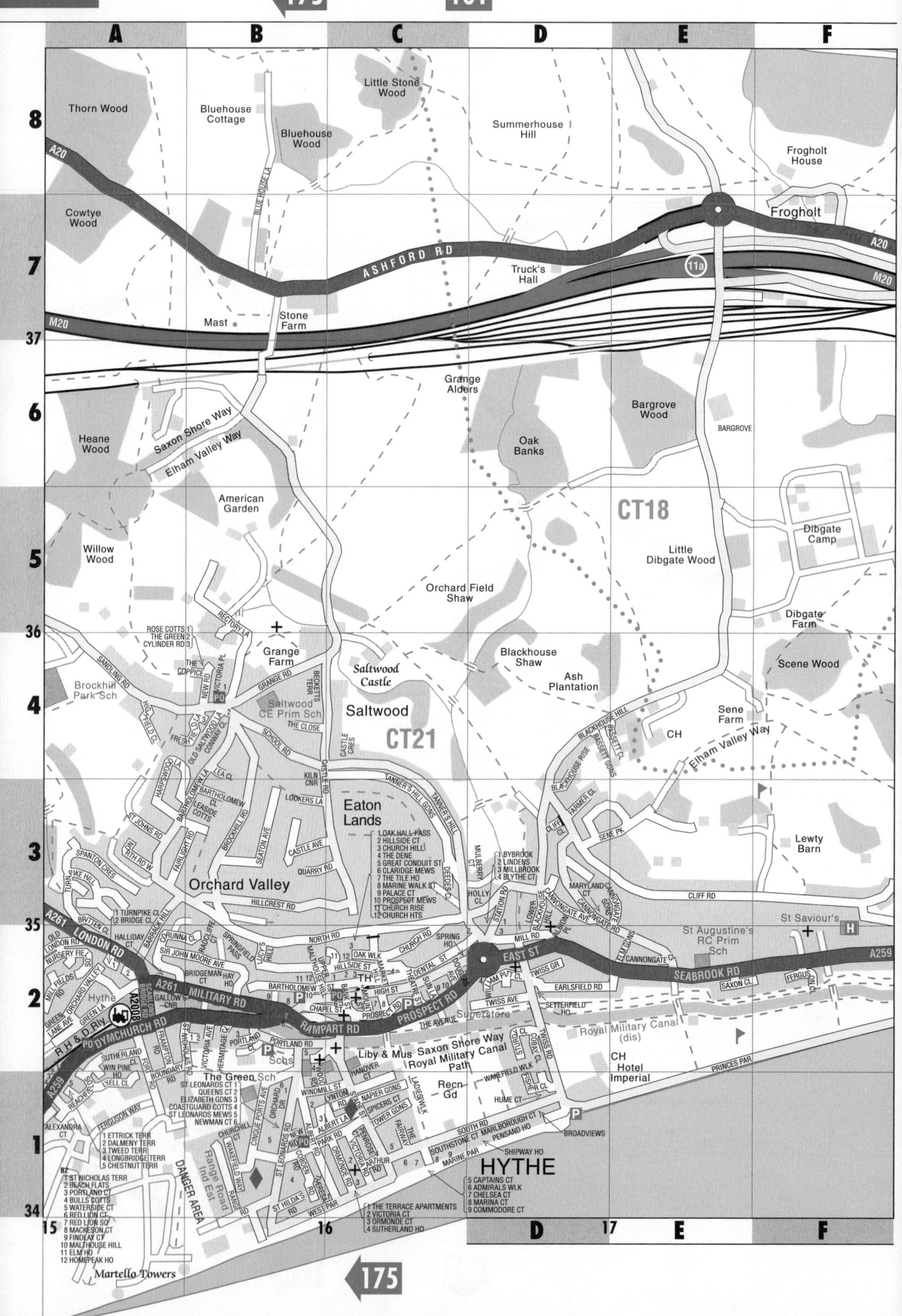
A
B
C
D
E
F
8
7
37
6
5
36
4
3
35
2
1
34
15
16
17
Thorn Wood
Bluehouse Cottage
Bluehouse Wood
Little Stone Wood
Summerhouse Hill
Frogholt House
Frogholt
A20
Cowtye Wood
BLUE HOUSE LA
ASHFORD RD
Truck's Hall
11a
M20
Mast
Stone Farm
Grange Alders
Bargrove Wood
BARGROVE
Heane Wood
Saxon Shore Way
Elham Valley Way
Oak Banks
American Garden
CT18
Dibgate Camp
Willow Wood
Little Dibgate Wood
Orchard Field Shaw
Dibgate Farm
RECTORY LA
ROSE COTTS 1
THE GREEN 2
CYLINDER RD 3
Grange Farm
Saltwood Castle
Blackhouse Shaw
Ash Plantation
Scene Wood
SANDLING RD
THE COPPICE
VICTORIA PL
NEW RD
GRANGE RD
BECKETTS TERR
Brockhill Park Sch
Saltwood CE Prim Sch
Saltwood
THE CLOSE
CT21
Sene Farm
CH
BLACKHOUSE HILL
BASSETT CL
BASSETT GDNS
SCHOOL RD
CASTLE CRES
KILN CNR
CASTLE RD
TANNER'S HILL GDNS
TANNER'S HILL
Eaton Lands
LOOKERS LA
BLACKHOUSE RISE
FARMER CL
CLIFF CL
SENE PK
Lewty Barn
HARPSWOOD LA
OLD SALTWOOD LA
CONWAY CL
BARTHOLOMEW LA
BARTHOLOMEW CL
LEASIDE COTTS
FAIRLIGHT RD
BROCKHILL RD
SEATON AVE
CASTLE AVE
QUARRY RD
1 OAK HALL PASS
2 HILLSIDE CT
3 CHURCH HILL
4 THE DENE
5 GREAT CONDUIT ST
6 CLARIDGE MEWS
7 THE TILE HO
8 MARINE WALK ST
9 PALACE CT
10 PROSPECT MEWS
11 CHURCH RISE
12 CHURCH HTS
MULBERRY CT
1 BYBROOK
2 LINDENS
3 MILLBROOK
4 BLYTHE CT
DEEDES CL
HOLLY CL
ST JOHNS RD
SPANTON CRES
TURNPIKE HILL
Orchard Valley
HILLCREST RD
MARYLAND CT
CANNONGATE GDNS
CANNONGATE AVE
CANNONGATE RD
CLIFF RD
St Saviour's
H
1 TURNPIKE CL
2 BRIDGE CL
A261
LONDON RD
HALLIDAY CT
BARRACK HILL
CORUNNA CL
RADCLIFFE CT
SPRINGFIELD PASS
LUCY'S HILL
NORTH RD
CHURCH RD
SPRING HO
STATION RD
LOWER BLACKHOUSE HILL
ALBION PL
MILL RD
ELM GDNS
St Augustine's RC Prim Sch
CANNONGATE CL
A259
SIR JOHN MOORE AVE
BRIDGEMAN CT
HAY HO
OAK WLK
HILLSIDE ST
DENTAL ST
EAST ST
WILLIAM PITT CL
TWISS GR
SEABROOK RD
SAXON CL
FERGUS
Hythe
A2008
A261 MILITARY RD
GALLOWS CNR
BARTHOLOMEW ST
HIGH ST
THEATRE ST
SUN LA
EARLSFIELD RD
CHAPEL ST
RAMPART RD
PROSPECT RD
TWISS AVE
SETTERFIELD HO
Superstore
THE AVENUE
Royal Military Canal (dis)
DYMCHURCH RD
R H & D Rly
FRAMPTON RD
ST NICHOLAS RD
VICTORIA AVE
HERMITAGE CL
PORTLAND CL
PORTLAND RD
Schs
Liby & Mus
Saxon Shore Way
Royal Military Canal Path
STURDEE CL
COBAY CL
TWISS RD
CH
Hotel Imperial
PRINCES PAR
SUTHERLAND RD
WIN PINE HO
FORT RD
BOUNDARY RD
The Green Sch
HANOVER CT
WINDMILL ST
LADIES WLK
Recn Gd
WAKEFIELD WLK
FISHER CL
HUME CT
ST LEONARDS CT 1
QUEENS CT 2
ELIZABETH GDNS 3
COASTGUARD COTTS 4
ST LEONARDS MEWS 5
NEWMAN CT 6
CINQUE PORTS AVE
ORCHARD DR
LYNTON RD
NAPIER GDNS
SPICERS CT
TOWER GDNS
THE FAIRWAY
SOUTH RD
MARLBOROUGH CT
PENSAND HO
SOUTHSTONE CT
BROADVIEWS
ALEXANDRA CT
FERGUSON WAY
REACHFIELDS
1 ETTRICK TERR
2 DALMENY TERR
3 TWEED TERR
4 LONGBRIDGE TERR
5 CHESTNUT TERR
CHURCHILL CT
WAKEFIELD WAY
ST LEONARDS RD
ALBERT RD
COBDEN RD
ALBERT LA
PARK RD
ORMONDE RD
VICTORIA RD
PENROSE CT
ARTHUR RD
SHIPWAY HO
MARINE PAR
HYTHE
B2
1 ST NICHOLAS TERR
2 BEACH FLATS
3 PORTLAND CT
4 BULLS COTTS
5 WATERSIDE CT
6 RED LION CT
7 RED LION SQ
8 MACKESON CT
9 FINDLAY CT
10 MALTHOUSE HILL
11 ELM HO
12 HOMEPEAK HO
DANGER AREA
Range Road Ind Est
ST HILDA'S RD
THERESA RD
WEST PAR
1 THE TERRACE APARTMENTS
2 VICTORIA CT
3 ORMONDE CT
4 SUTHERLAND HO
5 CAPTAINS CT
6 ADMIRALS WLK
7 CHELSEA CT
8 MARINA CT
9 COMMODORE CT
Martello Towers

175

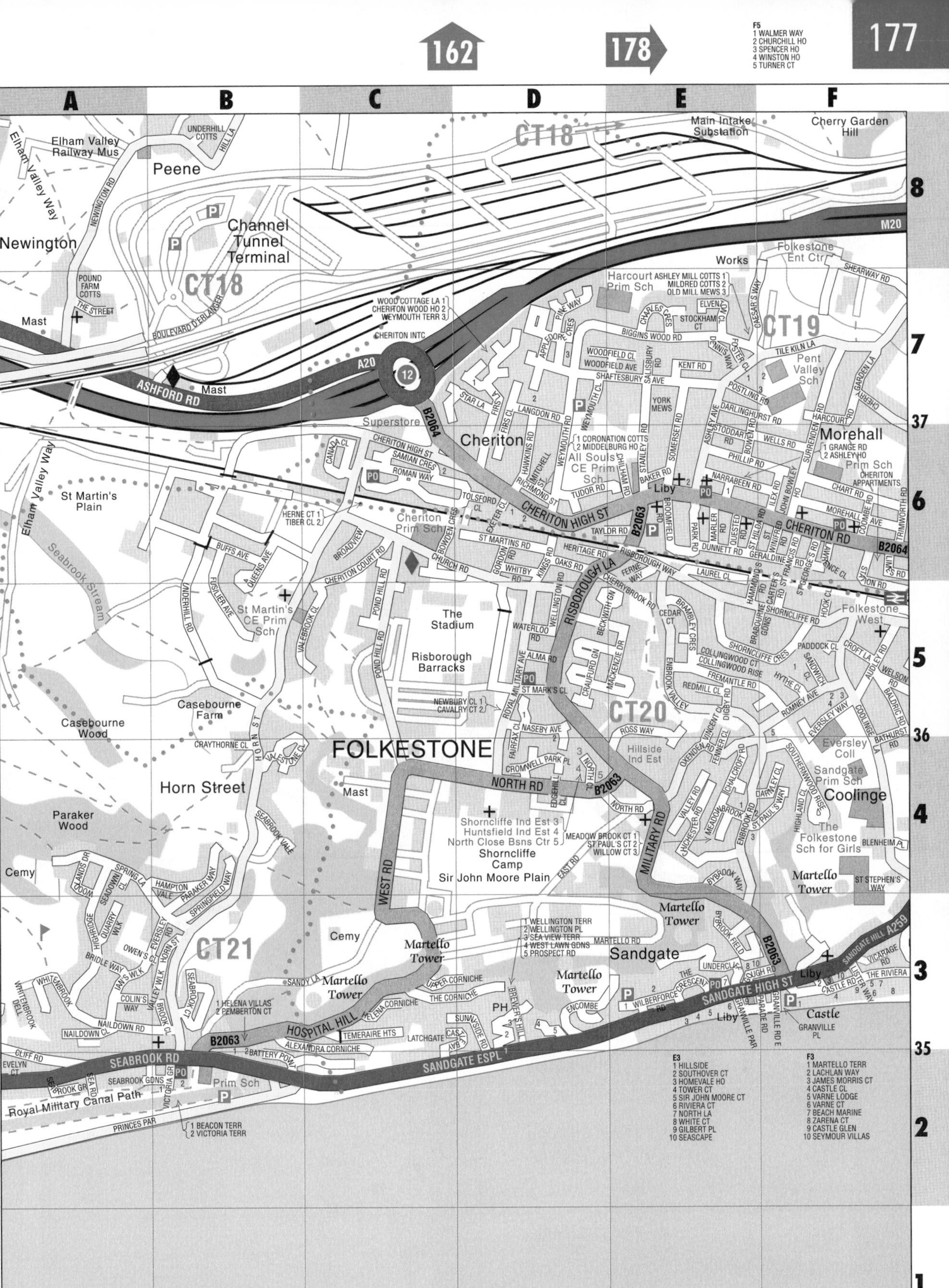

162
178
F5
1 WALMER WAY
2 CHURCHILL HO
3 SPENCER HO
4 WINSTON HO
5 TURNER CT

177

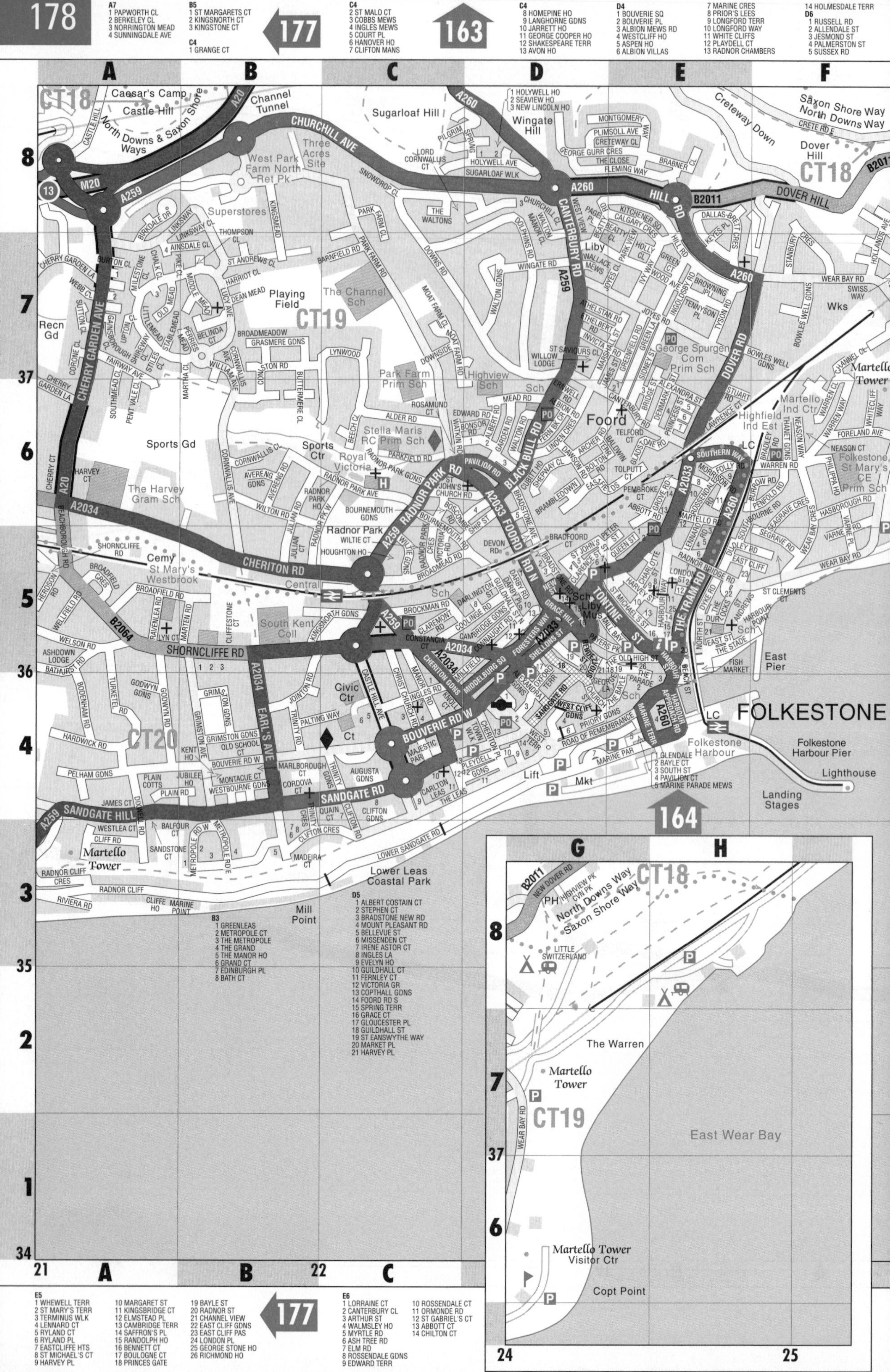
A7
1 PAPWORTH CL
2 BERKELEY CL
3 NORRINGTON MEAD
4 SUNNINGDALE AVE
B5
1 ST MARGARETS CT
2 KINGSNORTH CT
3 KINGSTONE CT
C4
1 GRANGE CT
177
C4
2 ST MALO CT
3 COBBS MEWS
4 INGLES MEWS
5 COURT PL
6 HANOVER HO
7 CLIFTON MANS
163
C4
8 HOMEPINE HO
9 LANGHORNE GDNS
10 JARRETT HO
11 GEORGE COOPER HO
12 SHAKESPEARE TERR
13 AVON HO
D4
1 BOUVERIE SQ
2 BOUVERIE PL
3 ALBION MEWS RD
4 WESTCLIFF HO
5 ASPEN HO
6 ALBION VILLAS
7 MARINE CRES
8 PRIOR'S LEES
9 LONGFORD TERR
10 LONGFORD WAY
11 WHITE CLIFFS
12 PLAYDELL CT
13 RADNOR CHAMBERS
14 HOLMESDALE TERR
D6
1 RUSSELL RD
2 ALLENDALE ST
3 JESMOND ST
4 PALMERSTON ST
5 SUSSEX RD
A
B
C
D
E
F
CT18
Caesar's Camp
Castle Hill
North Downs & Saxon Shore Ways
Channel Tunnel
CHURCHILL AVE
Sugarloaf Hill
Wingate Hill
Creteway Down
Saxon Shore Way
North Downs Way
Dover Hill
DOVER HILL
West Park Farm North Ret Pk
Three Acres Site
Superstores
Playing Field
The Channel Sch
CT19
Recn Gd
Park Farm Prim Sch
Highview Sch
Stella Maris RC Prim Sch
Sports Gd
Sports Ctr
Royal Victoria
The Harvey Gram Sch
Radnor Park
CHERITON RD
Cemy
St Mary's Westbrook
Central
South Kent Coll
SHORNCLIFFE RD
Civic Ctr
CT20
SANDGATE RD
SANDGATE HILL
Martello Tower
Lower Leas Coastal Park
Mill Point
Foord
George Spurgen Com Prim Sch
Martello Ind Ctr
Highfield Ind Est
Folkestone, St Mary's CE Prim Sch
Wks
East Pier
FOLKESTONE
Folkestone Harbour
Folkestone Harbour Pier
Lighthouse
Landing Stages
1 GLENDALE
2 BAYLE CT
3 SOUTH ST
4 PAVILION CT
5 MARINE PARADE MEWS
164
B3
1 GREENLEAS
2 METROPOLE CT
3 THE METROPOLE
4 THE GRAND
5 THE MANOR HO
6 GRAND CT
7 EDINBURGH PL
8 BATH CT
D5
1 ALBERT COSTAIN CT
2 STEPHEN CT
3 BRADSTONE NEW RD
4 MOUNT PLEASANT RD
5 BELLEVUE ST
6 MISSENDEN CT
7 IRENE ASTOR CT
8 INGLES LA
9 EVELYN HO
10 GUILDHALL CT
11 FERNLEY CT
12 VICTORIA GR
13 COPTHALL GDNS
14 FOORD RD S
15 SPRING TERR
16 GRACE CT
17 GLOUCESTER PL
18 GUILDHALL ST
19 ST EANSWYTHE WAY
20 MARKET PL
21 HARVEY PL
G
H
CT18
North Downs Way
Saxon Shore Way
LITTLE SWITZERLAND
The Warren
Martello Tower
CT19
East Wear Bay
Martello Tower Visitor Ctr
Copt Point
24
25
21
22
E5
1 WHEWELL TERR
2 ST MARY'S TERR
3 TERMINUS WLK
4 LENNARD CT
5 RYLAND CT
6 RYLAND PL
7 EASTCLIFFE HTS
8 ST MICHAEL'S CT
9 HARVEY PL
10 MARGARET ST
11 KINGSBRIDGE CT
12 ELMSTEAD PL
13 CAMBRIDGE TERR
14 SAFFRON'S PL
15 RANDOLPH HO
16 BENNETT CT
17 BOULOGNE CT
18 PRINCES GATE
19 BAYLE ST
20 RADNOR ST
21 CHANNEL VIEW
22 EAST CLIFF GDNS
23 EAST CLIFF PAS
24 LONDON PL
25 GEORGE STONE HO
26 RICHMOND HO
177
E6
1 LORRAINE CT
2 CANTERBURY CL
3 ARTHUR ST
4 WALMSLEY HO
5 MYRTLE RD
6 ASH TREE RD
7 ELM RD
8 ROSSENDALE GDNS
9 EDWARD TERR
10 ROSSENDALE CT
11 ORMONDE RD
12 ST GABRIEL'S CT
13 ABBOTT CT
14 CHILTON CT

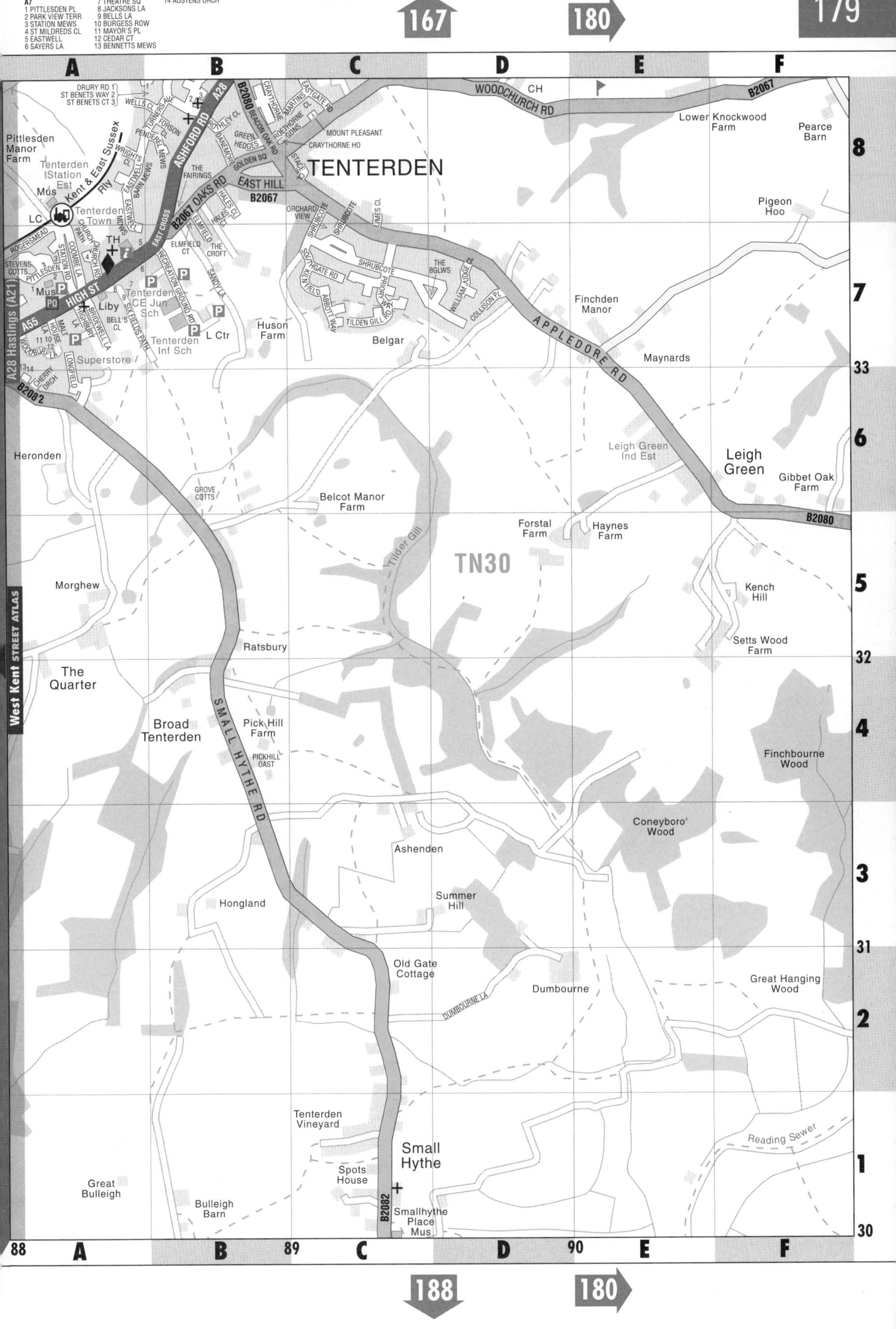

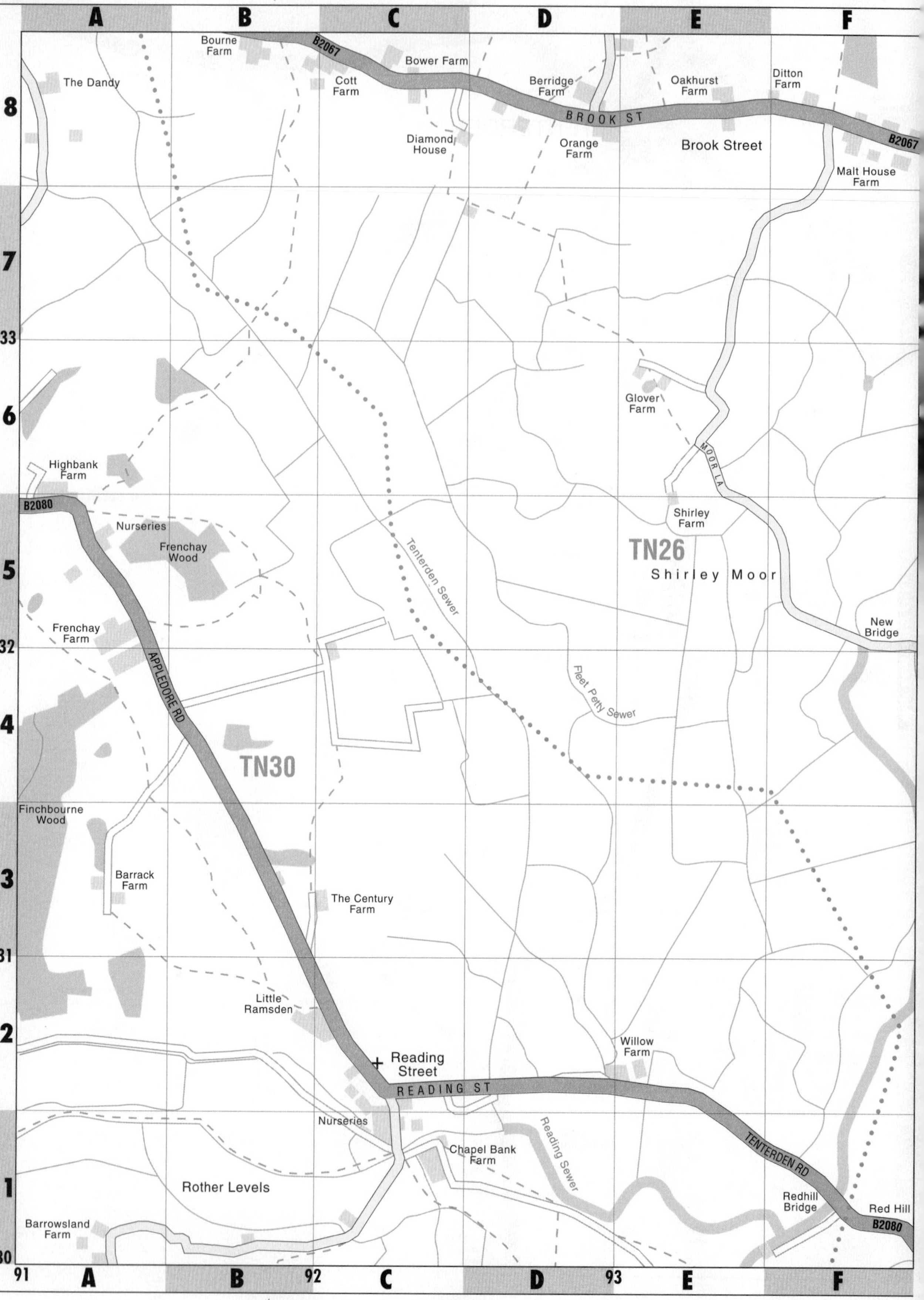

A **B** **C** **D** **E** **F**

The Dandy

Bourne Farm

B2067

Bower Farm

Cott Farm

Berridge Farm

Oakhurst Farm

Ditton Farm

8

Diamond House

Orange Farm

BROOK ST

Brook Street

B2067

Malt House Farm

7

33

Glover Farm

MOOR LA

6

Highbank Farm

B2080

Shirley Farm

Nurseries

Frenchay Wood

TN26

SHIRLEY MOOR

5

Frenchay Farm

Tenterden Sewer

New Bridge

32

APPLEDORE RD

TN30

4

Fleet Petty Sewer

Finchbourne Wood

Barrack Farm

3

The Century Farm

31

Little Ramsden

2

Willow Farm

Reading Street

READING ST

Nurseries

Reading Sewer

TENTERDEN RD

Chapel Bank Farm

Rother Levels

1

Redhill Bridge

Red Hill

Barrowsland Farm

B2080

30

91 **A** **B** 92 **C** **D** 93 **E** **F**

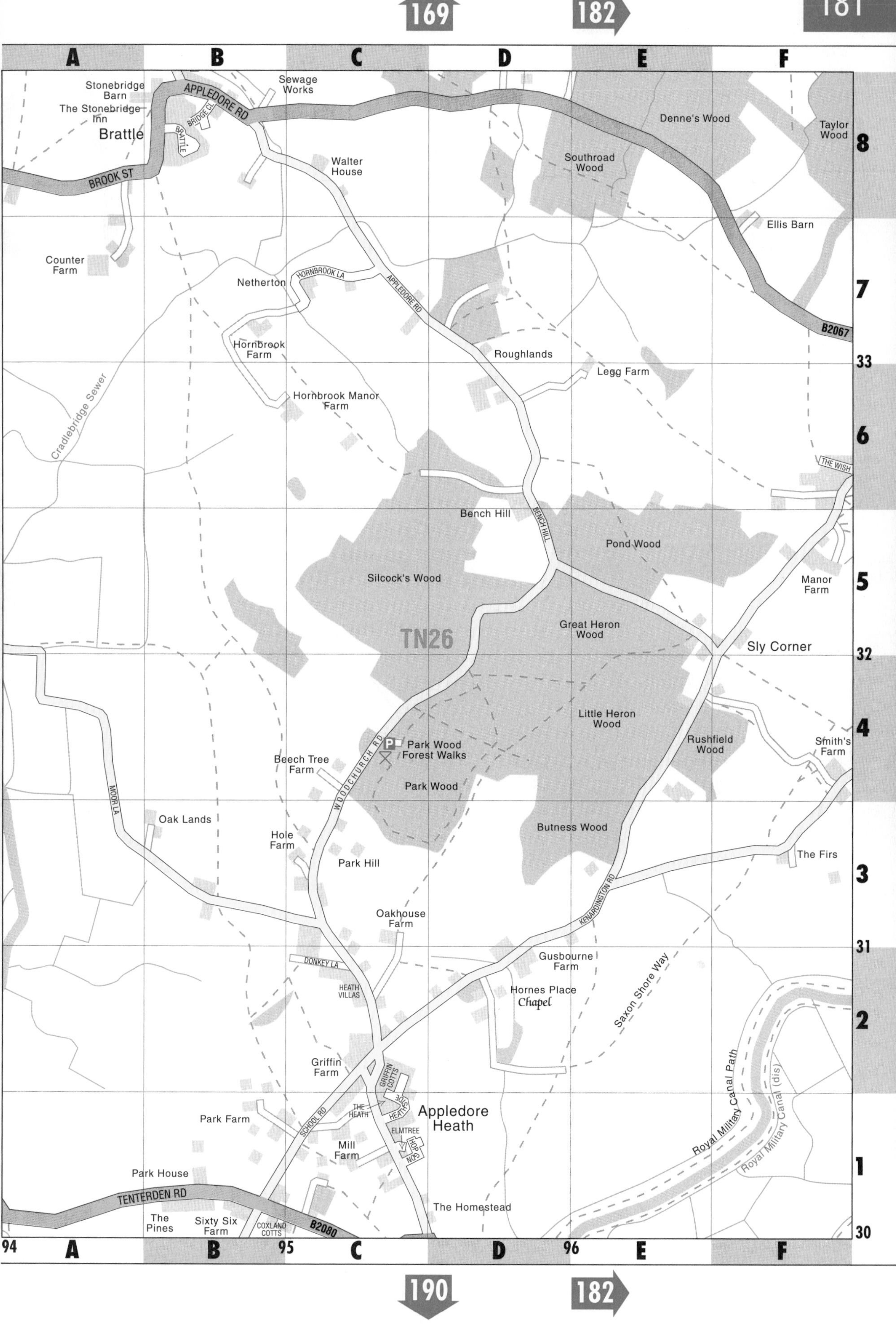
A
B
C
D
E
F
Stonebridge Barn
The Stonebridge Inn
Brattle
Sewage Works
APPLEDORE RD
BRIDGE CL
BRATTLE
BROOK ST
Walter House
Denne's Wood
Southroad Wood
Taylor Wood
Ellis Barn
Counter Farm
Netherton
HORNBROOK LA
APPLEDORE RD
B2067
Hornbrook Farm
Roughlands
Legg Farm
Hornbrook Manor Farm
Cradlebridge Sewer
THE WISH
Bench Hill
BENCH HILL
Pond Wood
Silcock's Wood
Manor Farm
Great Heron Wood
TN26
Sly Corner
Little Heron Wood
Park Wood Forest Walks
Rushfield Wood
Smith's Farm
Beech Tree Farm
WOODCHURCH RD
Park Wood
MOOR LA
Oak Lands
Hole Farm
Butness Wood
The Firs
Park Hill
KENARDINGTON RD
Oakhouse Farm
Gusbourne Farm
DONKEY LA
Hornes Place
Chapel
Saxon Shore Way
HEATH VILLAS
Griffin Farm
GRIFFIN COTTS
THE HEATH
HEATH SIDE
Appledore Heath
Royal Military Canal Path
Royal Military Canal (dis)
Park Farm
SCHOOL RD
ELMTREE
HOP
Mill Farm
Park House
TENTERDEN RD
The Homestead
The Pines
Sixty Six Farm
COXLAND COTTS
B2080
8
7
33
6
5
32
4
3
31
2
1
30
94
95
96

181 170

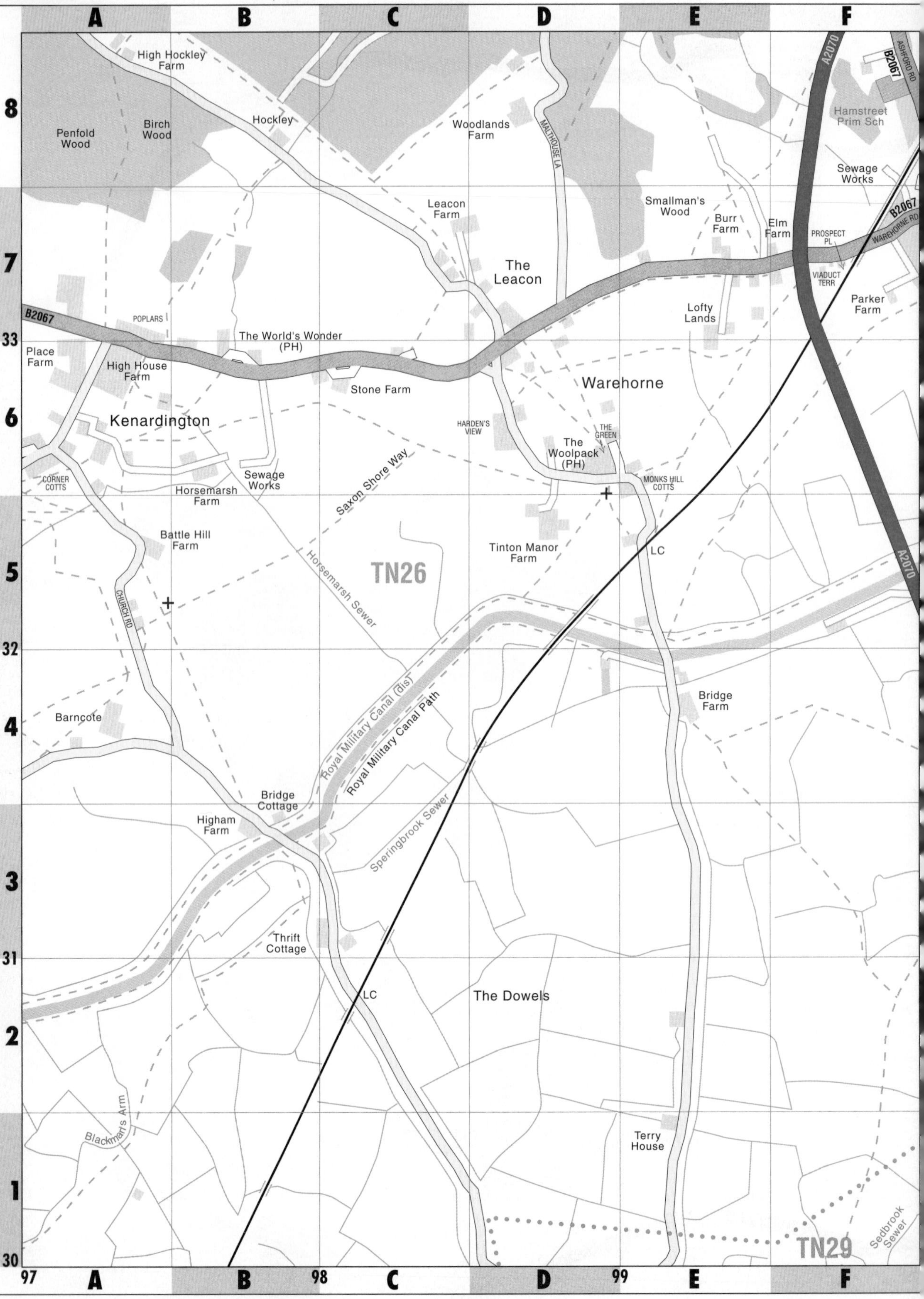

A B C D E F

8

High Hockley Farm

Penfold Wood

Birch Wood

Hockley

Woodlands Farm

MALTHOUSE LA

Smallman's Wood

Burr Farm

Elm Farm

A2070

B2067

ASHFORD RD

Hamstreet Prim Sch

Sewage Works

7

Leacon Farm

The Leacon

PROSPECT PL

VIADUCT TERR

WAREHORNE RD

B2067

Parker Farm

33

B2067

Place Farm

POPLARS

The World's Wonder (PH)

High House Farm

Stone Farm

Warehorne

Lofty Lands

6

Kenardington

HARDEN'S VIEW

The Woolpack (PH)

THE GREEN

MONKS HILL COTTS

CORNER COTTS

Sewage Works

Horsemarsh Farm

Saxon Shore Way

5

Battle Hill Farm

CHURCH RD

Horsemarsh Sewer

TN26

Tinton Manor Farm

LC

32

Bridge Farm

4

Barncote

Royal Military Canal (dis)

Royal Military Canal Path

Bridge Cottage

Higham Farm

Speringbrook Sewer

3

Thrift Cottage

31

LC

The Dowels

2

Blackmans Arm

Terry House

1

Sedbrook Sewer

30

TN29

97 A B 98 C D 99 E F

181 191

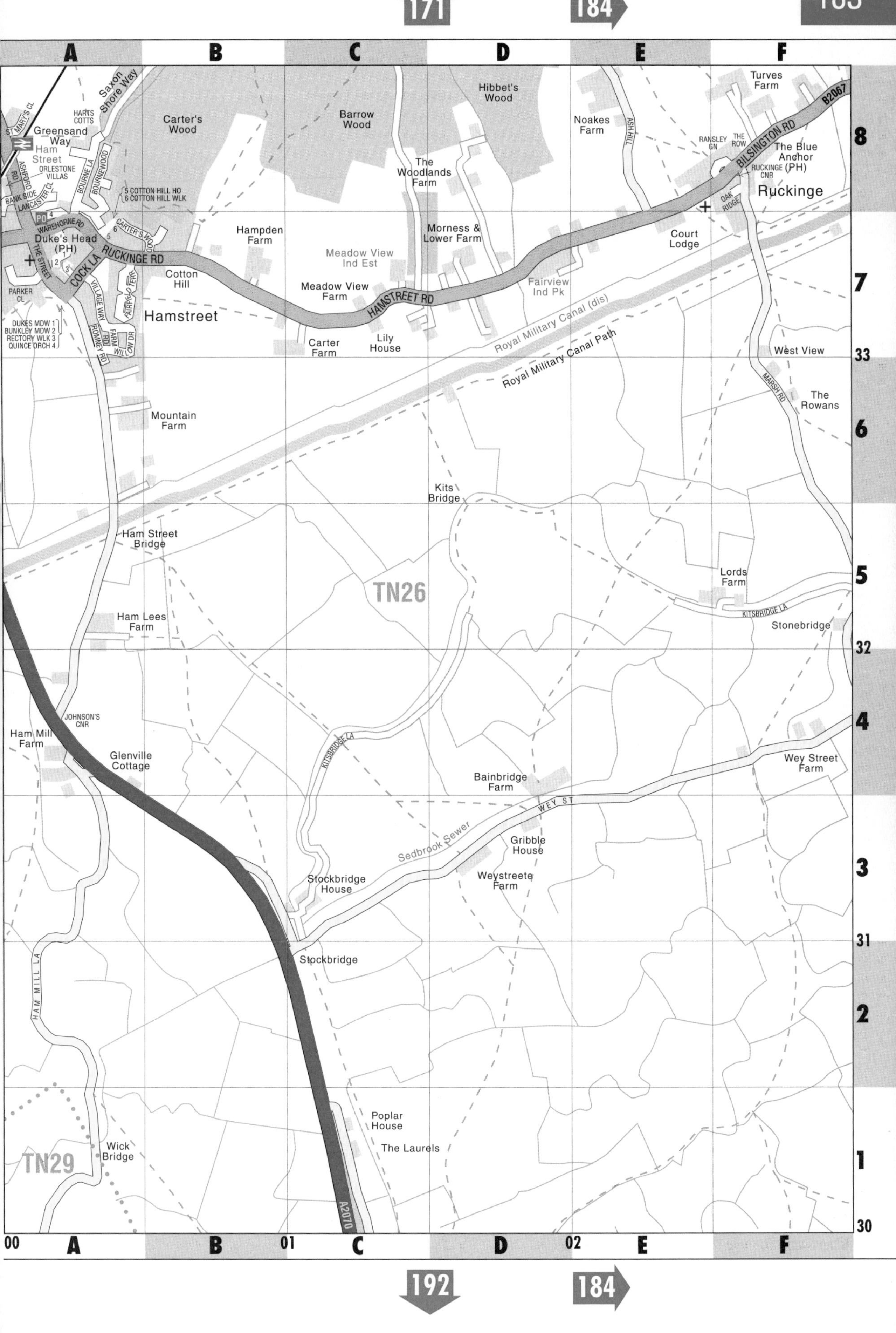

ST MARY'S CL

Greensand
Way

Saxon Shore Way

HARTS COTTS

Ham
Street

ORLESTONE
VILLAS

BOURNE LA

BOURNEWOOD

CARTER'S WOOD

Carter's
Wood

Barrow
Wood

Hibbet's
Wood

The
Woodlands
Farm

Noakes
Farm

ASH HILL

Turves
Farm

B2067

8

RANSLEY
GN

THE
ROW

BILSINGTON RD

The Blue
Anchor
(PH)

Ruckinge

OAK
RIDGE

RUCKINGE
CNR

BANK SIDE
LANCASTER CL

ASHFORD RD

PO

WAREHORNE RD

Duke's Head
(PH)

COCK LA

THE STREET

5 COTTON HILL HO
6 COTTON HILL WLK

RUCKINGE RD

Hampden
Farm

Cotton
Hill

Meadow View
Ind Est

Morness &
Lower Farm

Court
Lodge

PARKER
CL

VILLAGE WAY

FAIRVIEW TERR

ROMNEY RD

Hamstreet

Meadow View
Farm

HAMSTREET RD

Fairview
Ind Pk

7

DUKES MDW 1
BUNKLEY MDW 2
RECTORY WLK 3
QUINCE ORCH 4

FARM WLK
LOW DR

Carter
Farm

Lily
House

Royal Military Canal (dis)

West View

33

Royal Military Canal Path

MARSH RD

The
Rowans

Mountain
Farm

6

Kits
Bridge

Ham Street
Bridge

Lords
Farm

5

TN26

KITSBRIDGE LA

Stonebridge

Ham Lees
Farm

32

JOHNSON'S
CNR

4

Ham Mill
Farm

Glenville
Cottage

KITSBRIDGE LA

Bainbridge
Farm

Wey Street
Farm

WEY ST

Gribble
House

Sedbrook Sewer

Weystreete
Farm

3

HAM MILL LA

Stockbridge
House

31

Stockbridge

2

Poplar
House

The Laurels

Wick
Bridge

1

TN29

A2070

30

183
172

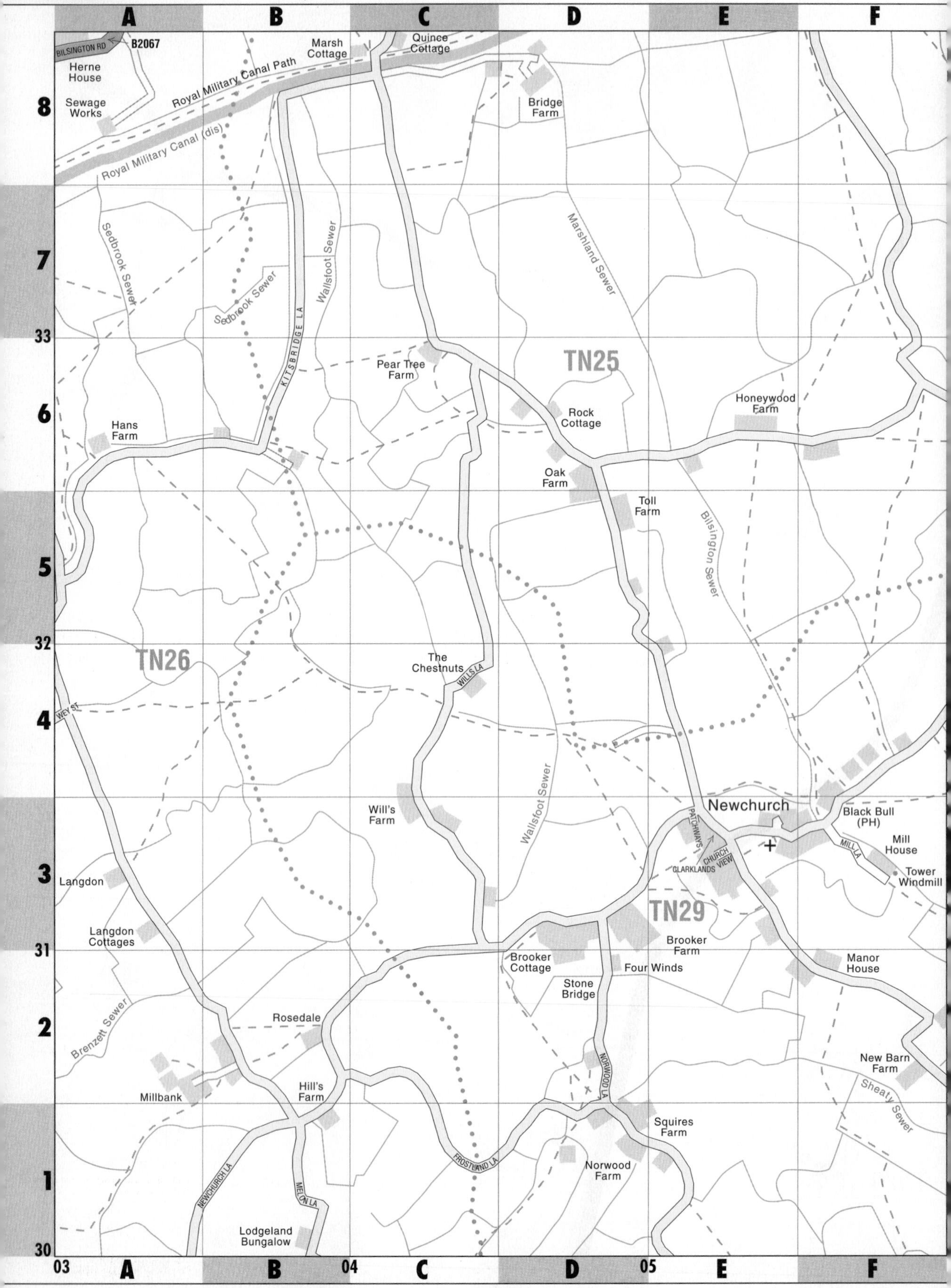

A **B** **C** **D** **E** **F**

8

BILSINGTON RD
Herne House
B2067
Sewage Works
Marsh Cottage
Quince Cottage
Bridge Farm
Royal Military Canal Path
Royal Military Canal (dis)

7

Sedbrook Sewer
Sedbrook Sewer
Wallsfoot Sewer
KITSBRIDGE LA
Marshland Sewer

33

Pear Tree Farm
Rock Cottage
TN25
Honeywood Farm

6

Hans Farm
Oak Farm
Toll Farm
Bilsington Sewer

5

32

TN26
The Chestnuts
WILLS LA

4

WEY ST
Will's Farm
Wallsfoot Sewer
Newchurch
Black Bull (PH)
Mill House

3

Langdon
Langdon Cottages
PATCHWAYS
CHURCH VIEW
CLARKLANDS
MILL LA
Tower Windmill
TN29
Brooker Farm
Manor House

31

Brenzett Sewer
Rosedale
Brooker Cottage
Stone Bridge
Four Winds

2

Millbank
Hill's Farm
NORWOOD LA
New Barn Farm
Sheaty Sewer

1

NEWCHURCH LA
MELTON LA
FROSTLAND LA
Norwood Farm
Squires Farm

30

Lodgeland Bungalow

03 **A** **B** 04 **C** **D** 05 **E** **F**

183
193

173
186

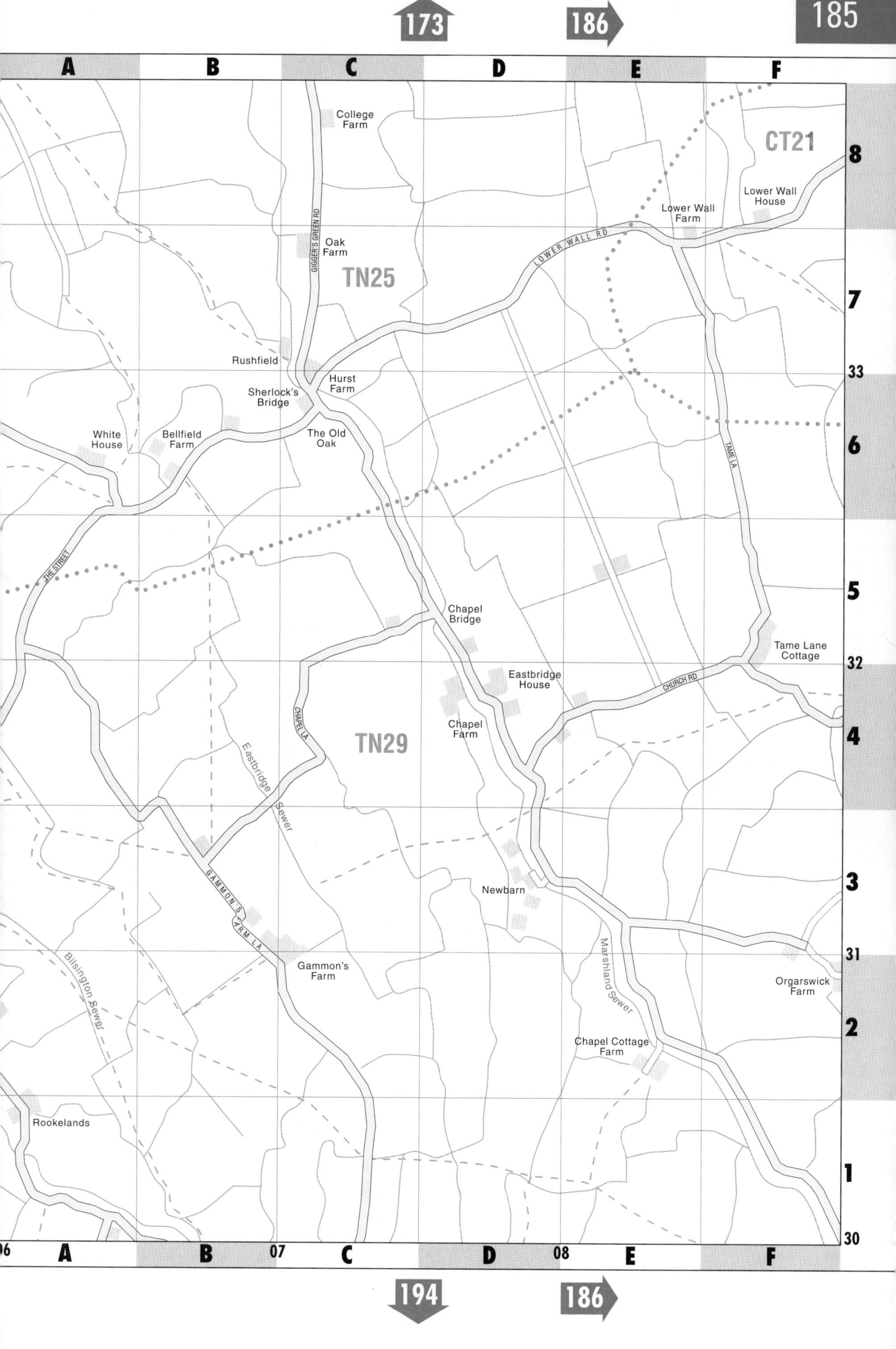
A
B
C
D
E
F
8
7
33
6
5
32
4
3
31
2
1
30
06
07
08
College Farm
CT21
Lower Wall House
Lower Wall Farm
LOWER WALL RD
GIGGER'S GREEN RD
Oak Farm
TN25
Rushfield
Hurst Farm
Sherlock's Bridge
White House
Bellfield Farm
The Old Oak
TAME LA
THE STREET
Chapel Bridge
Tame Lane Cottage
Eastbridge House
CHURCH RD
CHAPEL LA
TN29
Chapel Farm
Eastbridge Sewer
GAMMON'S FARM LA
Newbarn
Marshland Sewer
Gammon's Farm
Orgarswick Farm
Bilsington Sewer
Chapel Cottage Farm
Rookelands

194
186

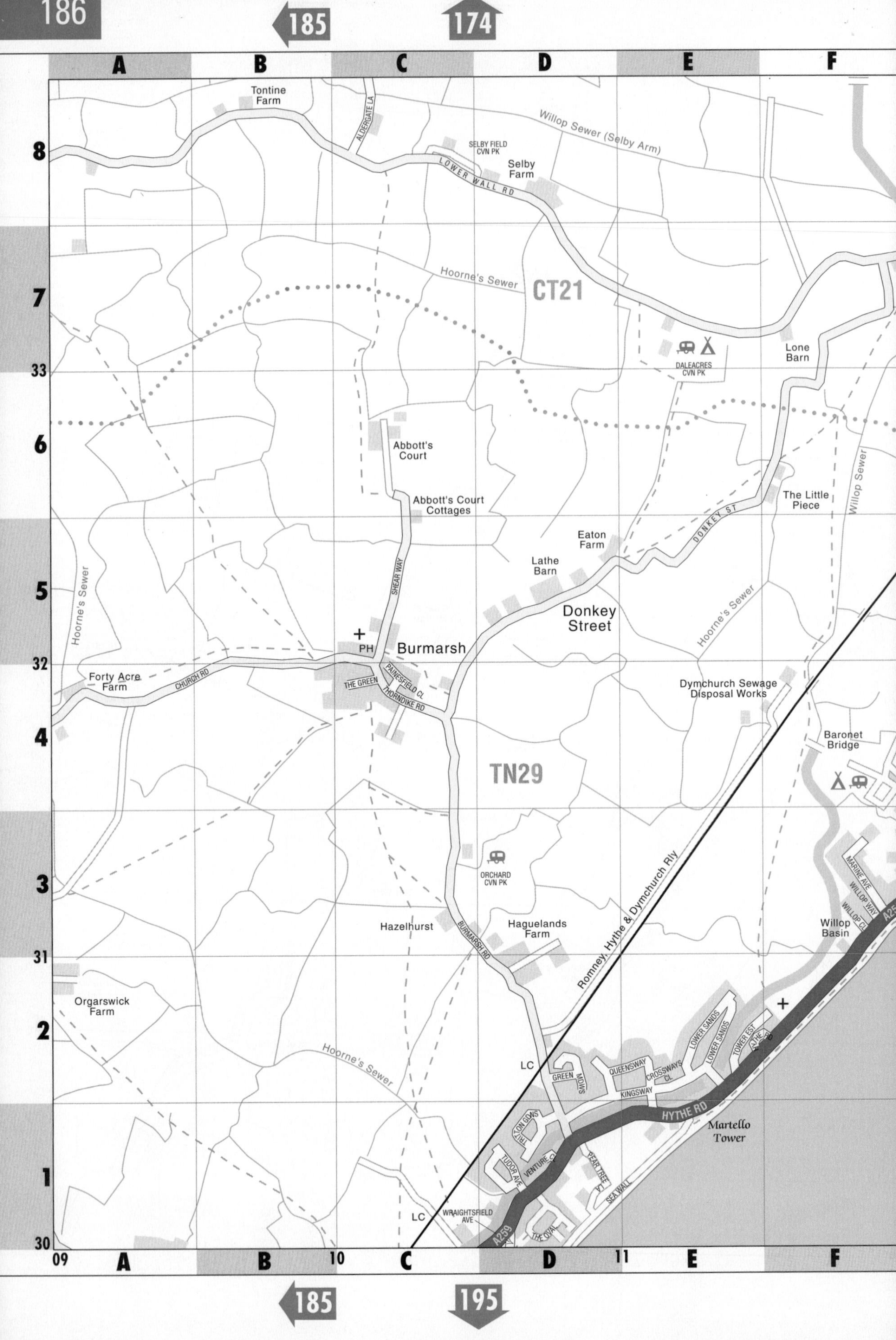
A
B
C
D
E
F
8
7
33
6
5
32
4
3
31
2
1
30
09
10
11
Tontine Farm
ALDERGATE LA
Willop Sewer (Selby Arm)
SELBY FIELD CVN PK
Selby Farm
LOWER WALL RD
Hoorne's Sewer
CT21
DALEACRES CVN PK
Lone Barn
Abbott's Court
Abbott's Court Cottages
The Little Piece
Willop Sewer
DONKEY ST
Eaton Farm
Lathe Barn
SHEAR WAY
Hoorne's Sewer
Donkey Street
Hoorne's Sewer
PH
Burmarsh
Forty Acre Farm
CHURCH RD
PAINESFIELD CL
THE GREEN
THORNDIKE RD
Dymchurch Sewage Disposal Works
Baronet Bridge
TN29
ORCHARD CVN PK
Romney, Hythe & Dymchurch Rly
MARINE AVE
WILLOP WAY
WILLOP CL
Willop Basin
A259
Hazelhurst
BURMARSH RD
Haguelands Farm
Orgarswick Farm
LOWER SANDS
LOWER SANDS
TOWER EST
LATHE RD
Hoorne's Sewer
LC
GREEN MDWS
QUEENSWAY
CROSSWAYS CL
KINGSWAY
HYTHE RD
Martello Tower
TRITON GDNS
TUDOR AVE
VENTURE CL
PEAR TREE LA
SEA WALL
LC
WRAIGHTSFIELD AVE
A259
THE OVAL

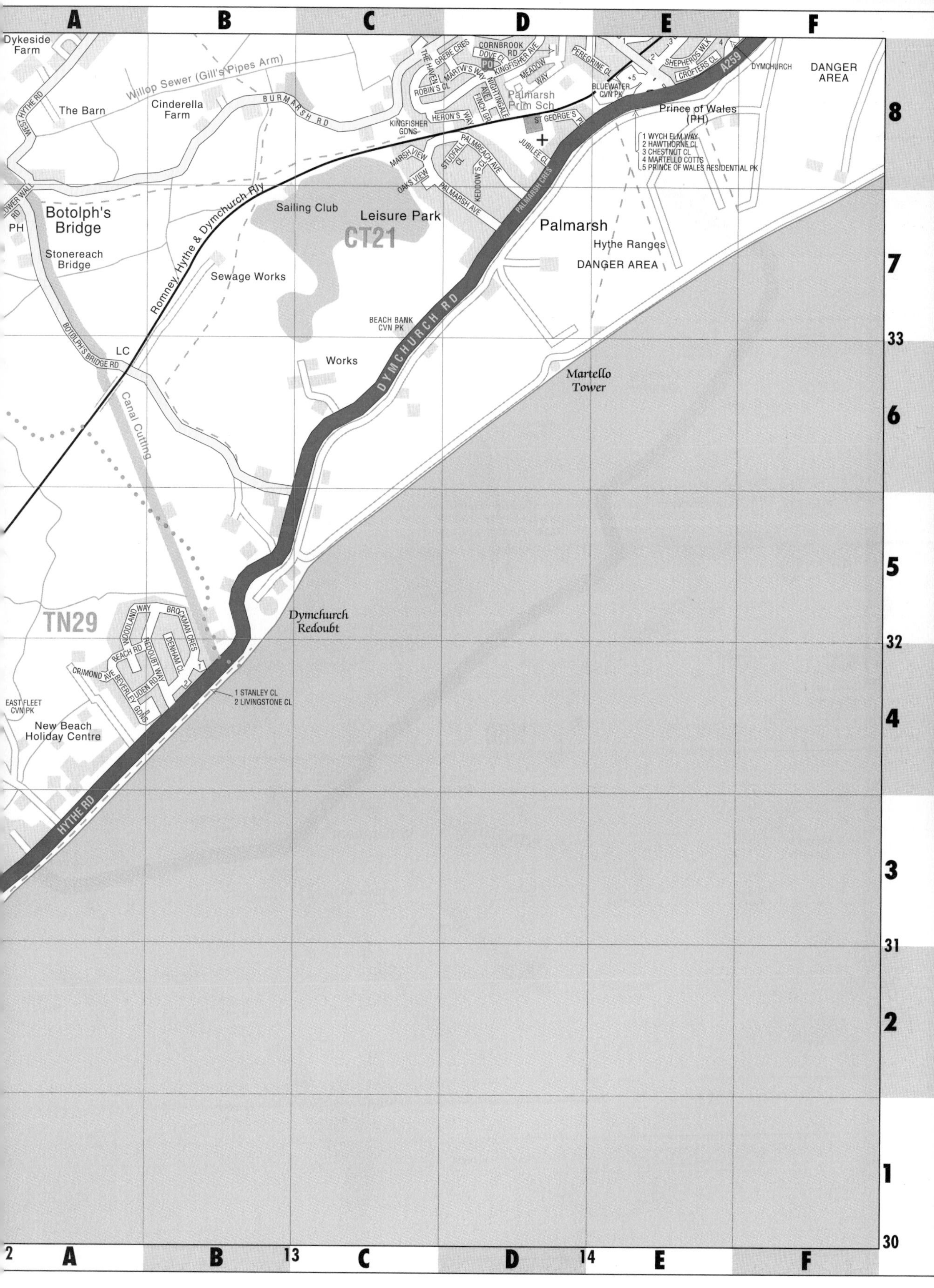

A   B   C   D   E   F

Dykeside
Farm

The Barn

Cinderella
Farm

BURMARSH RD

Willop Sewer (Gill's Pipes Arm)

CORNBROOK
RD

DOVE CL

GREBE CRES

ROBIN'S CL

THE HAVEN

MARTIN'S WAY

NIGHTINGALE

PANEL

FINCH GRO

MEADOW
WAY

KINGFISHER AVE

HERON'S WY

KINGFISHER
GDNS

MARSH VIEW

ST GEORGE'S PL

STUDFALL
CL

PALMBEACH AVE

OAK'S VIEW

KEEDOW'S CL

PALM MARSH AVE

JUBILEE CL

Palmarsh
Prim Sch

PEREGRINE CL

BLUEWATER
CVN PK

SHEPHERD'S WLK

CROFTERS CL

A259

Dymchurch

DANGER
AREA

Prince of Wales
(PH)

8

1 WYCH ELM WAY
2 HAWTHORNE CL
3 CHESTNUT CL
4 MARTELLO COTTS
5 PRINCE OF WALES RESIDENTIAL PK

WEST HYTHE RD

LOWER RD

PH

Botolph's
Bridge

Stonereach
Bridge

BOTOLPH'S BRIDGE RD

LC

Canal Cutting

Romney, Hythe & Dymchurch Rly

Sailing Club

CT21

Leisure Park

Sewage Works

Works

BEACH BANK
CVN PK

DYMCHURCH RD

PALMARSH CRES

Palmarsh

Hythe Ranges

DANGER AREA

Martello
Tower

7

33

6

TN29

WOODLAND WAY

BEACH RD

REDOUBT WAY

BROOKMAN CRES

DENHAM CL

CRIMOND AVE

BEVERLEY GDNS

LYDDEN WAY

Dymchurch
Redoubt

5

32

4

EAST FLEET
CVN PK

New Beach
Holiday Centre

1 STANLEY CL
2 LIVINGSTONE CL

HYTHE RD

3

31

2

1

30

2   A   B   13   C   D   14   E   F

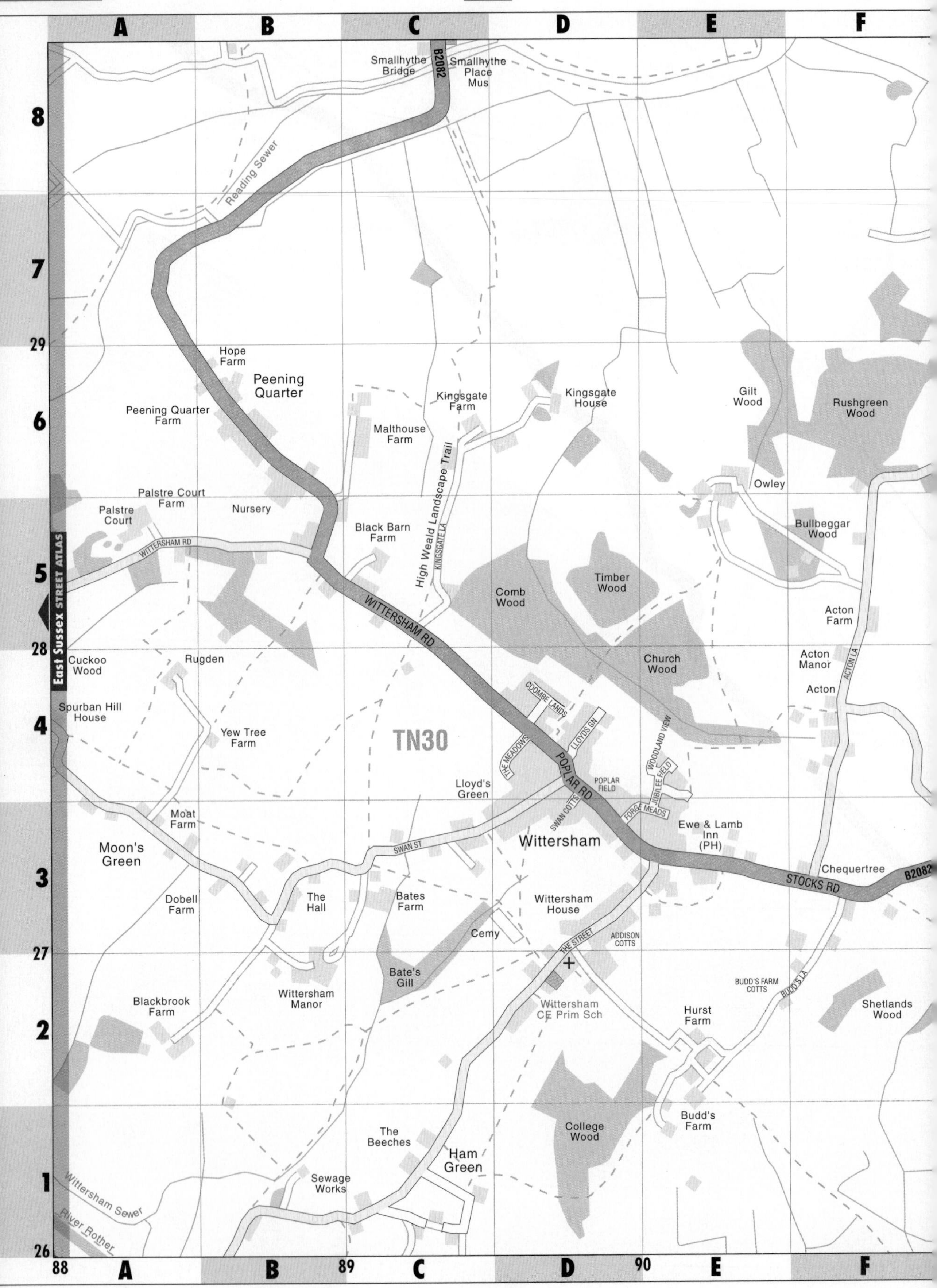

East Sussex STREET ATLAS

A **B** **C** **D** **E** **F**

8

7

29

Reading Sewer

Smallhythe Bridge
B2082
Smallhythe Place Mus

6

Hope Farm

Peening Quarter

Kingsgate Farm

Kingsgate House

Gilt Wood

Rushgreen Wood

Peening Quarter Farm

Malthouse Farm

High Weald Landscape Trail

Owley

Bullbeggar Wood

Palstre Court Farm

Nursery

Black Barn Farm

KINGSGATE LA

5

Palstre Court

WITTERSHAM RD

WITTERSHAM RD

Comb Wood

Timber Wood

Acton Farm

28

Cuckoo Wood

Rugden

Church Wood

Acton Manor

ACTON LA

Acton

4

Spurban Hill House

Yew Tree Farm

TN30

THE MEADOWS

COOMBE LANDS

LLOYDS GN

POPLAR RD

WOODLAND VIEW

JUBILEE FIELD

Moat Farm

Lloyd's Green

POPLAR RD

SWAN COTTS

Poplar Field

FORCE MEADS

Ewe & Lamb Inn (PH)

Moon's Green

SWAN ST

Wittersham

Chequertree

B2082

3

Dobell Farm

The Hall

Bates Farm

STOCKS RD

Wittersham House

27

Cemy

Bate's Gill

THE STREET

ADDISON COTTS

BUDD'S FARM COTTS

BUDD'S LA

Blackbrook Farm

Wittersham Manor

Wittersham CE Prim Sch

Hurst Farm

Shetlands Wood

2

The Beeches

Ham Green

College Wood

Budd's Farm

1

Wittersham Sewer

Sewage Works

River Rother

26

88 **A** **B** 89 **C** **D** 90 **E** **F**

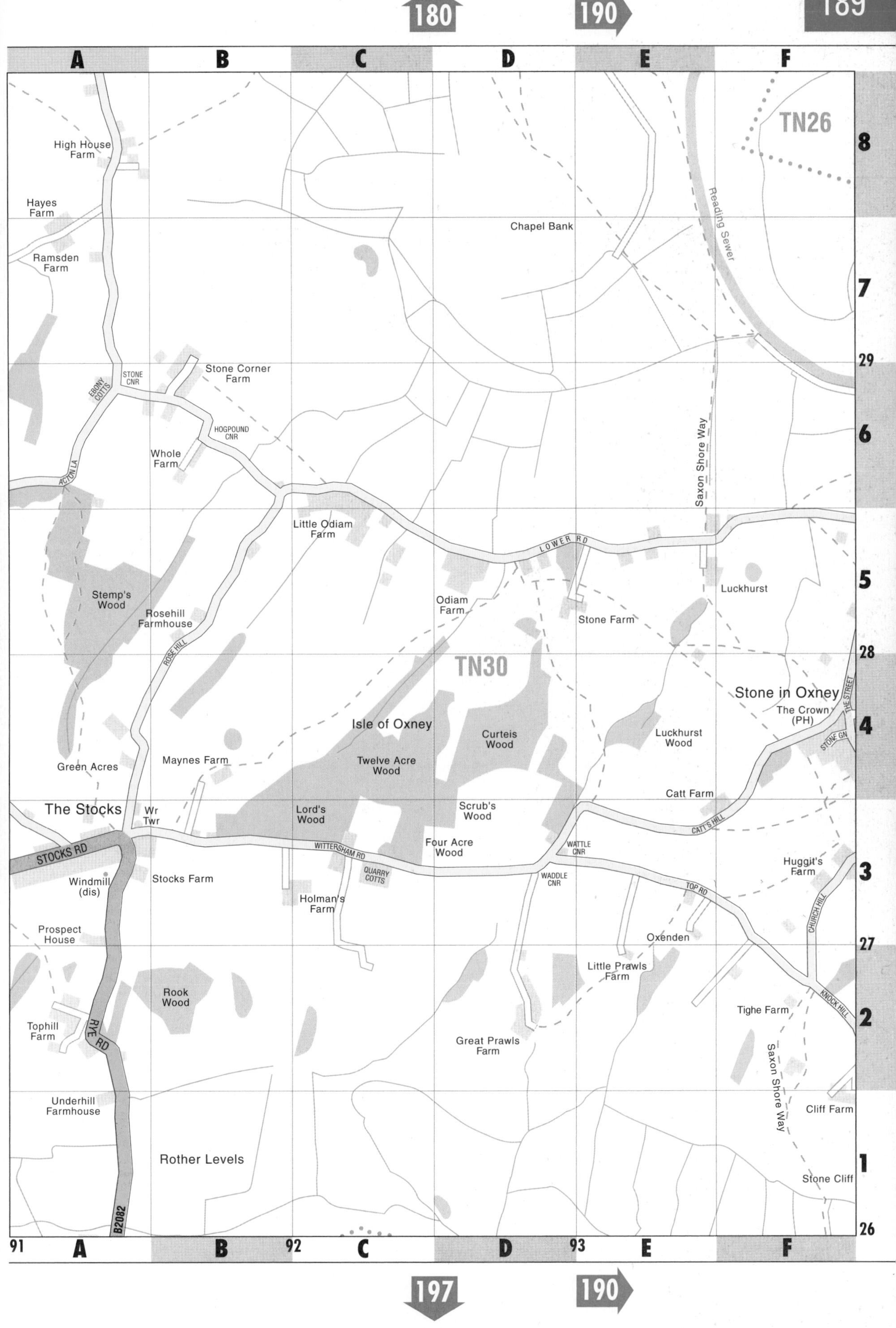

A B C D E F

8

High House Farm

Hayes Farm

Chapel Bank

7

Ramsden Farm

29

Stone Corner Farm

STONE CNR

EBONY COTTS

HOGPOUND CNR

6

Whole Farm

ACTON LA

Reading Sewer

Little Odiam Farm

LOWER RD

Saxon Shore Way

Luckhurst

5

Stemp's Wood

Rosehill Farmhouse

Odiam Farm

Stone Farm

ROSE HILL

28

TN30

Stone in Oxney

The Crown (PH)

THE STREET

4

Isle of Oxney

Curteis Wood

Luckhurst Wood

STONE GN

Green Acres

Maynes Farm

Twelve Acre Wood

Catt Farm

CATT'S HILL

The Stocks

Wr Twr

Lord's Wood

Scrub's Wood

Four Acre Wood

WATTLE CNR

Huggit's Farm

3

STOCKS RD

Stocks Farm

WITTERSHAM RD

QUARRY COTTS

WADDLE CNR

TOP RD

CHURCH HILL

Windmill (dis)

Holman's Farm

Oxenden

27

Prospect House

Little Prawls Farm

RYE RD

Tighe Farm

KNOCK HILL

2

Tophill Farm

Rook Wood

Great Prawls Farm

Saxon Shore Way

Cliff Farm

Underhill Farmhouse

1

Rother Levels

Stone Cliff

B2082

26

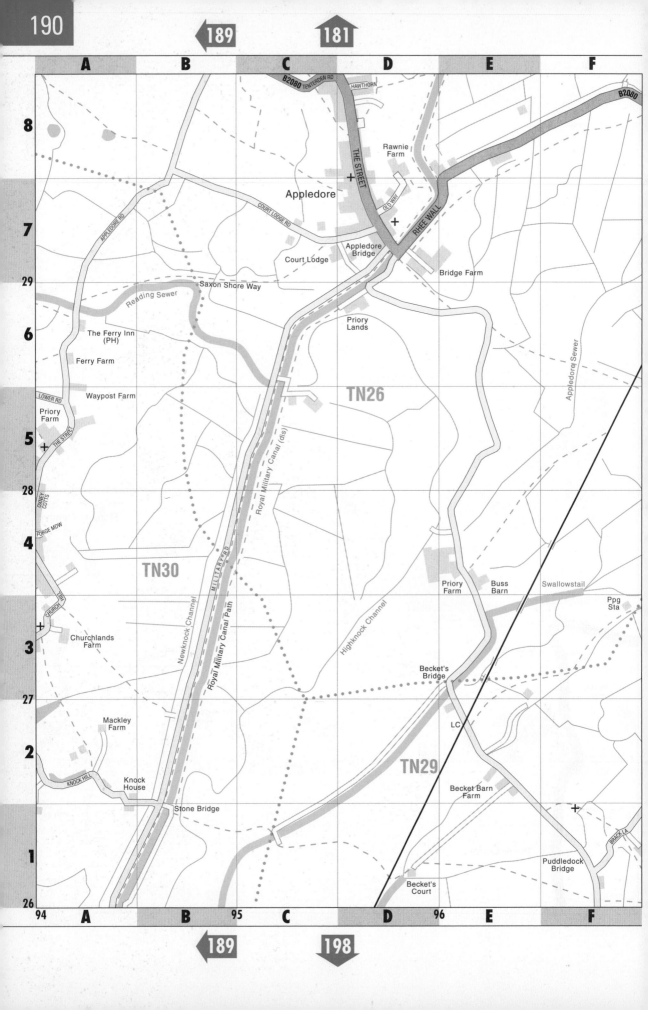

B2080 TENTERDEN RD

HAWTHORN

THE STREET

Rawnie
Farm

Appledore

COURT LODGE RD

OLD WAY

RHEE WALL

B2080

Court Lodge

Appledore
Bridge

Bridge Farm

APPLEDORE RD

Saxon Shore Way

29

Reading Sewer

Priory
Lands

6

The Ferry Inn
(PH)

Ferry Farm

TN26

Appledore Sewer

Waypost Farm

LOWER RD

Priory
Farm

THE STREET

5

DIXNEY
COTTS

28

FORGE MDW

Royal Military Canal (dis)

4

TN30

MILITARY RD

Priory
Farm

Buss
Barn

Swallowstail

CHURCH LN

Newknock Channel

Royal Military Canal Path

Highknock Channel

Ppg
Sta

Churchlands
Farm

Becket's
Bridge

3

27

LC

Mackley
Farm

TN29

2

KNOCK HILL

Knock
House

Becket Barn
Farm

Stone Bridge

Puddledock
Bridge

BRACK LA

1

26

Becket's
Court

94

A

B

95

C

D

96

E

F

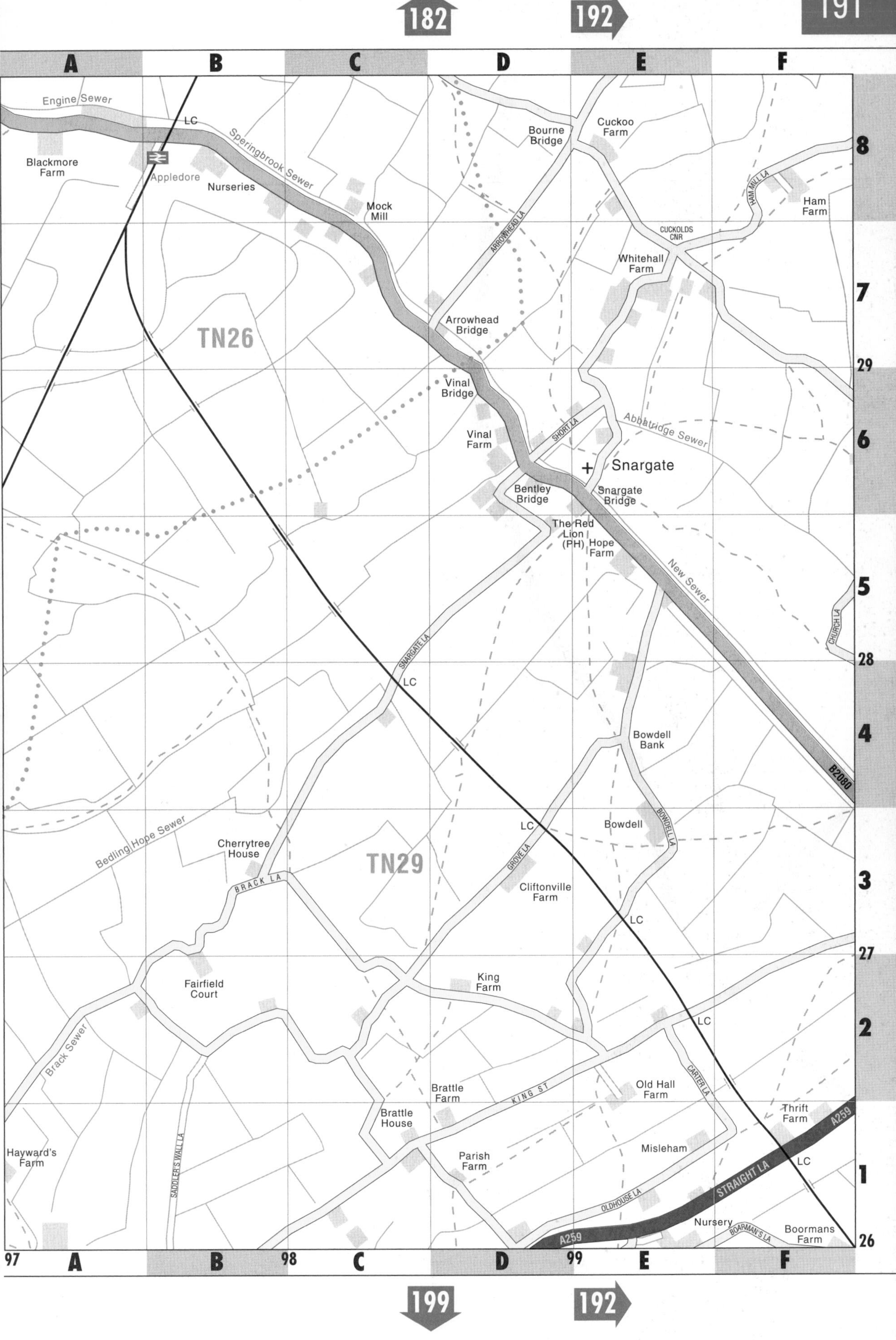
A
B
C
D
E
F
Engine Sewer
LC
Springbrook Sewer
Blackmore Farm
Appledore
Nurseries
Bourne Bridge
Cuckoo Farm
Mock Mill
Ham Farm
HAM MILL LA
CUCKOLDS CNR
ARROWHEAD LA
Whitehall Farm
TN26
Arrowhead Bridge
Vinal Bridge
Vinal Farm
SHORT LA
Abbatridge Sewer
Snargate
Bentley Bridge
Snargate Bridge
The Red Lion (PH)
Hope Farm
New Sewer
CHURCH LA
SNARGATE LA
LC
Bowdell Bank
B2080
LC
Bowdell
BOWDELL LA
Bedling Hope Sewer
Cherrytree House
TN29
GROVE LA
BRACK LA
Cliftonville Farm
LC
Fairfield Court
King Farm
LC
Brack Sewer
Brattle Farm
KING ST
Old Hall Farm
CARTER LA
Brattle House
Thrift Farm
A259
Hayward's Farm
SADDLER'S WALL LA
Parish Farm
Misleham
LC
STRAIGHT LA
OLDHOUSE LA
Nursery
BOARMAN'S LA
Boormans Farm
A259
8
7
29
6
5
28
4
3
27
2
1
26
97
98
99

A   B   C   D   E   F

8

Snave
Manor Farm
TN26

Court-at-Wick

Abbatridge Sewer

Walnut Tree Farm

7

Brenzett Sewer

Hangman's Toll Bridge

29

Chapel Farm

Poplar Farm

6

Codhall

Brenzett Green

Moat House

NEWCHURCH LA

CHURCH LA

Springfarm Rd

Poplar Farm

5

Hook House

New House Farm

28

SPRING FARM

MELON LA

4

TN29

MOOR LA

The Bell Inn (PH)

THE GARDENS

Marsh's Farm

Abbatridge Sewer

CHURCH LA

Cemy

Brenzett Corner Bridge

Brenzett Aeronautical Mus

Ivychurch

OASTHOUSE FIELD

Knowlden Farm

B2080

PH

MOORE CL

KING ST

THE HAVEN

Brenzett

BRENZETT CNR

3

Brenzett Place

Sumnerhouse Bridge

IVYCHURCH RD

A2070

B2080

27

Brenzett CE Prim Sch

A2070

A259

WENHAM LA

Mast

New Sewer

2

STRAIGHT LA

Blue House Farm

Owen's Bridge

A259

Finn Farm

Rhee Wall

Callington Court Farm

Beacon

TICKNER'S LA

TILLERY LA

1

New Sewer

YOKES LA

Rheewall Farm

Yoakes Bridge

A259

26

00   A   B   01   C   D   02   E   F

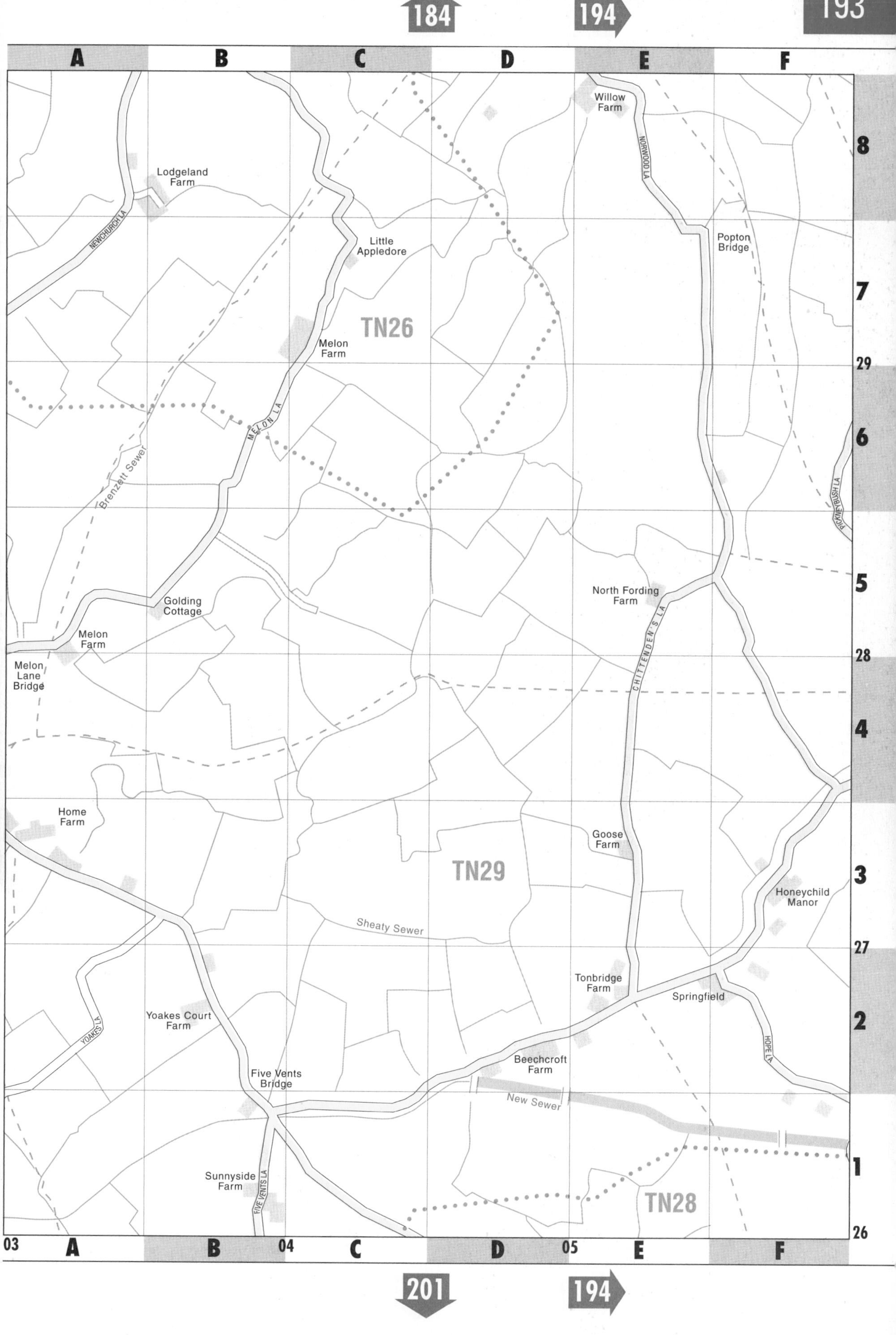

184
194
194

Willow Farm

Lodgeland Farm

Little Appledore

TN26

Melon Farm

MELON LA

NEWCHURCH LA

Brenzett Sewer

Popton Bridge

FLOODGATE LA

PLURENDEN LA

Golding Cottage

Melon Farm

Melon Lane Bridge

North Fording Farm

CHITTENDEN'S LA

Home Farm

TN29

Goose Farm

Honeychild Manor

Sheaty Sewer

Tonbridge Farm

Springfield

YOAKES LA

Yoakes Court Farm

HOPE LA

Five Vents Bridge

Beechcroft Farm

New Sewer

FIVE VENTS LA

Sunnyside Farm

TN28

A B C D E F

8

Oldhouse
Bridge

Blue House
Farm

Blackmanstone
Bridge

GANNON'S FARM LA

Eastbridge Sewer

Pickneybush
Bridge

Mast

Tatnam
Farm

JEFFERSTONE SEWER

7

Pickney Bush
Farm

Sheaty Sewer

Clobsden Sewer

Tatnam
Bridge

Sellinge
Farm

29

Pickney Bush
Farm Cotts

Marten
Farm

Swallowtail
Bridge

6

PICKNEYBUSH LA

Turngates
Bridge

TN29

Wild
Refuge

5

PICKNEYBUSH LA

Haffenden
Farm

ST MARY'S RD

Shingle Hall
Farm

Sports
Gd

Golden Sands
Holiday Centre

28

RECTORY RD
WADES CL

+

St Mary's
Bay

JEFFERSTONE GDNS

JEFFERSTONE LA

Jesson Court
CVN PK

NSRD RD

SEAWAY GDNS
SEAWAY RD
SEAWAY CRES

LC

Star
Inn

St Mary in the Marsh

Jefferstone Sewer

OLD BAKERY
CL

PO

4

School
Farm

Brodnyx

LAUREL AVE
PINE TREE RD
ASPEN
WILLOW DR
ELM RD
HAWTHORN CL
HOLLY RD

MAPLE DR
BEECHWOOD
OAK DR

ASH TREE CL 1
TURNSTONE CT 2
FULMAR CT 3

CEDAR CRES

Romney, Hythe & Dymchurch Rly

3

New Sewer

Slinches

MEADS
WAY
GRASSMERE

TAYLORS CL

TAYLORS

NEW BRIDGE WAY
JENNER'S WAY
NEWLANDS

BRIARS
FAIRWAY
CL

GAZEDOWN

A259

COAST DR

27

New Sewer

TN28

Winford
Bridge

DYMCHURCH RD

P

The
Warren

2

Paternosterford
Bridge

1

HOPE LA

Brodynex
Farm

Romney Warren
Country Park

Marlie
Farm

A259

COAST RD

26

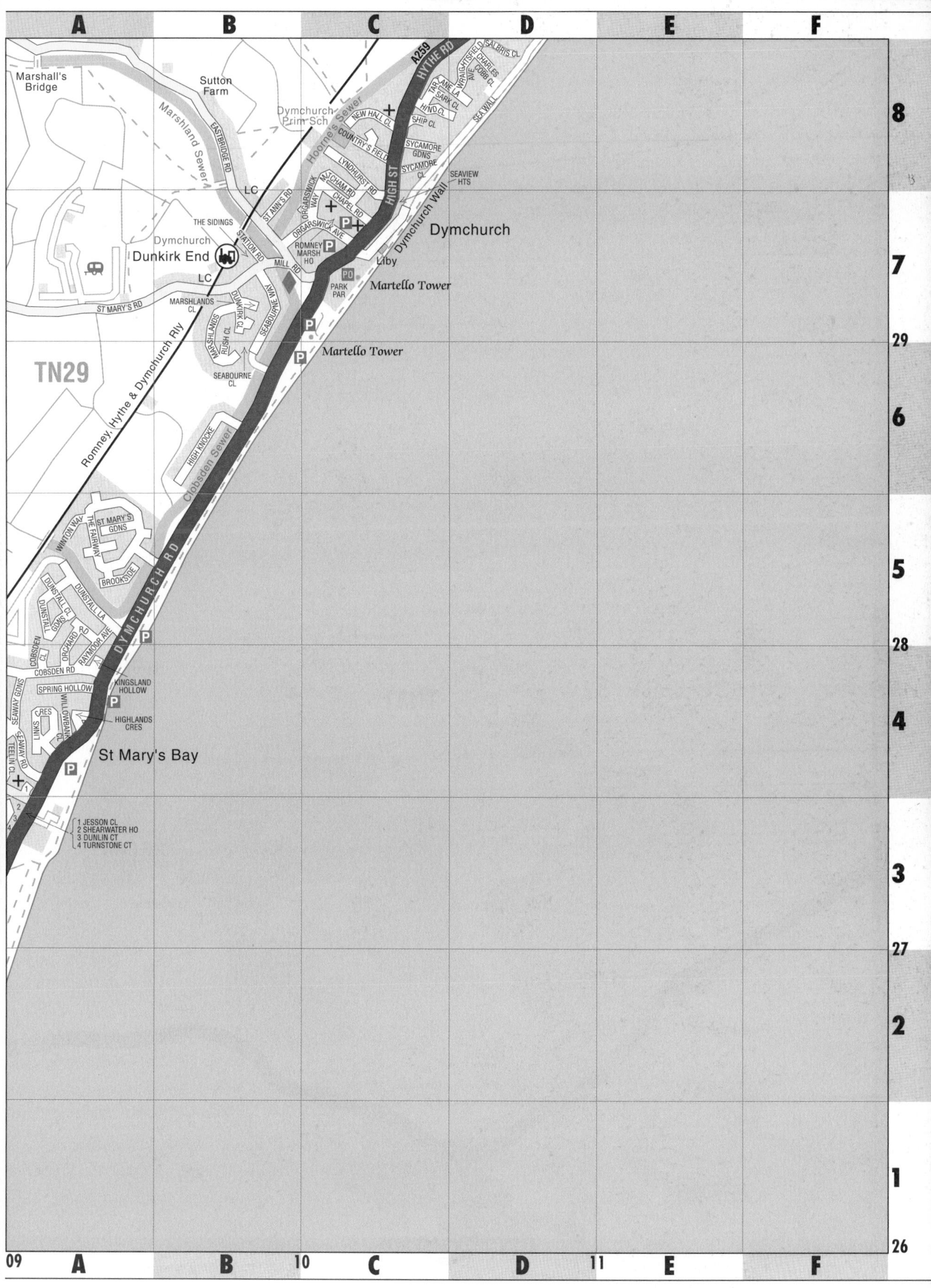

Marshall's Bridge

Sutton Farm

Dymchurch Prim Sch

Marshland Sewer

EASTBRIDGE RD

LC

THE SIDINGS

Dymchurch
Dunkirk End

STATION RD

LC

MILL RD

ST MARY'S RD

MARSHLANDS CL

MARSHLANDS

RUSH CL

DUNKIRK CL

SEABOURNE WAY

SEABOURNE CL

HIGH KNOCKE

Oldesden Sewer

Romney, Hythe & Dymchurch Rly

DYMCHURCH RD

TN29

Hoorne Sewer

COUNTRY'S FIELD

NEW HALL CL

ST ANN'S RD

ORGARSWICK WAY

LYNDHURST RD

CHAPEL RD

EACHAM RD

ORGARSWICK AVE

ROMNEY MARSH HO

HIGH ST

A259
HYTHE RD

SARK CL

LANE LA

HIND CL

SHIP CL

SYCAMORE GDNS

SYCAMORE CL

Dymchurch Wall

WRIGHTSFIELD

SALBRIS CL

CHARLES COBB CL

SEA WALL

SEAVIEW HTS

Dymchurch

Liby

PARK PAR

Martello Tower

Martello Tower

WINTON WAY

THE FAIRWAY

ST MARY'S GDNS

BROOKSIDE

DUNSTALL CL

DUNSTALL LA

DUNSTALL GDNS

ORCHARD RD

RAYMOOR AVE

COBSDEN CL

COBSDEN RD

SEAWAY GDNS

SPRING HOLLOW

WILLOWBANK

SEAWAY RD

TEELIN CL

CRES

KINGSLAND HOLLOW

HIGHLANDS CRES

St Mary's Bay

1 JESSON CL
2 SHEARWATER HO
3 DUNLIN CT
4 TURNSTONE CT

09   A   B   10   C   D   11   E   F   26

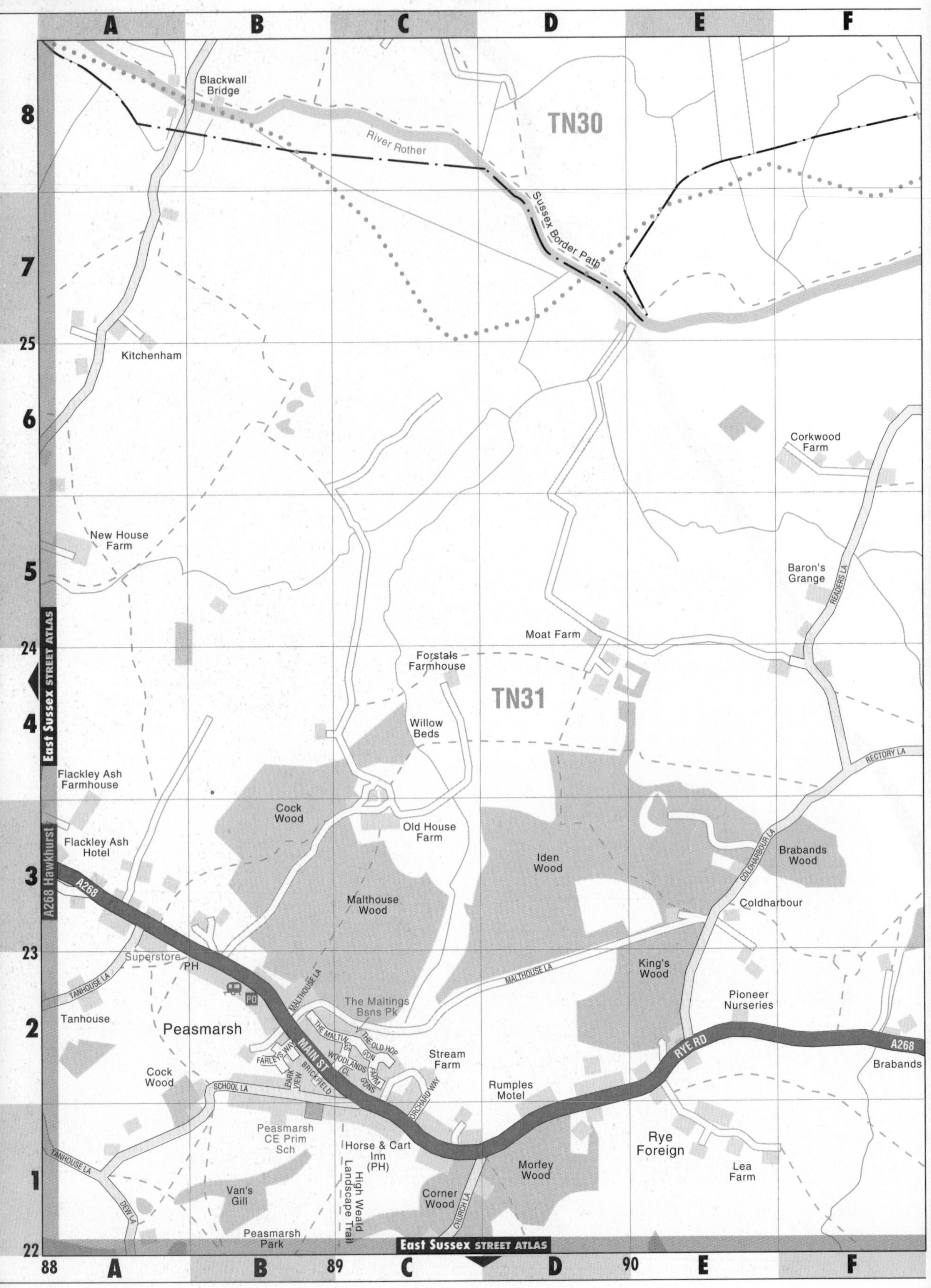

A · B · C · D · E · F

8
7
25
6
5
24
4
23
3
2
1
22

88 · A · B · 89 · C · D · 90 · E · F

Blackwall Bridge

River Rother

TN30

Sussex Border Path

Kitchenham

Corkwood Farm

New House Farm

Baron's Grange

Moat Farm

Forstals Farmhouse

TN31

Willow Beds

Flackley Ash Farmhouse

Cock Wood

Old House Farm

Iden Wood

Brabands Wood

Flackley Ash Hotel

A268

Malthouse Wood

Coldharbour

East Sussex STREET ATLAS

A268 Hawkhurst

Superstore

PH

MALTHOUSE LA

King's Wood

MALTHOUSE LA

Pioneer Nurseries

TANHOUSE LA

PO

The Maltings Bsns Pk

Tanhouse

The Maltings

Peasmarsh

MAIN ST

The Old Hop

Woodlands Cl

Stream Farm

Rumples Motel

RYE RD

A268

Brabands

Cock Wood

FARLEY'S WAY

BARN VIEW

BRICKFIELD

SCHOOL LA

ORCHARD WAY

Rye Foreign

Lea Farm

Peasmarsh CE Prim Sch

Horse & Cart Inn (PH)

Morfey Wood

Van's Gill

High Weald Landscape Trail

Corner Wood

CHURCH LA

TANHOUSE LA

DEW LA

Peasmarsh Park

East Sussex STREET ATLAS

READERS LA

RECTORY LA

COLDHARBOUR LA

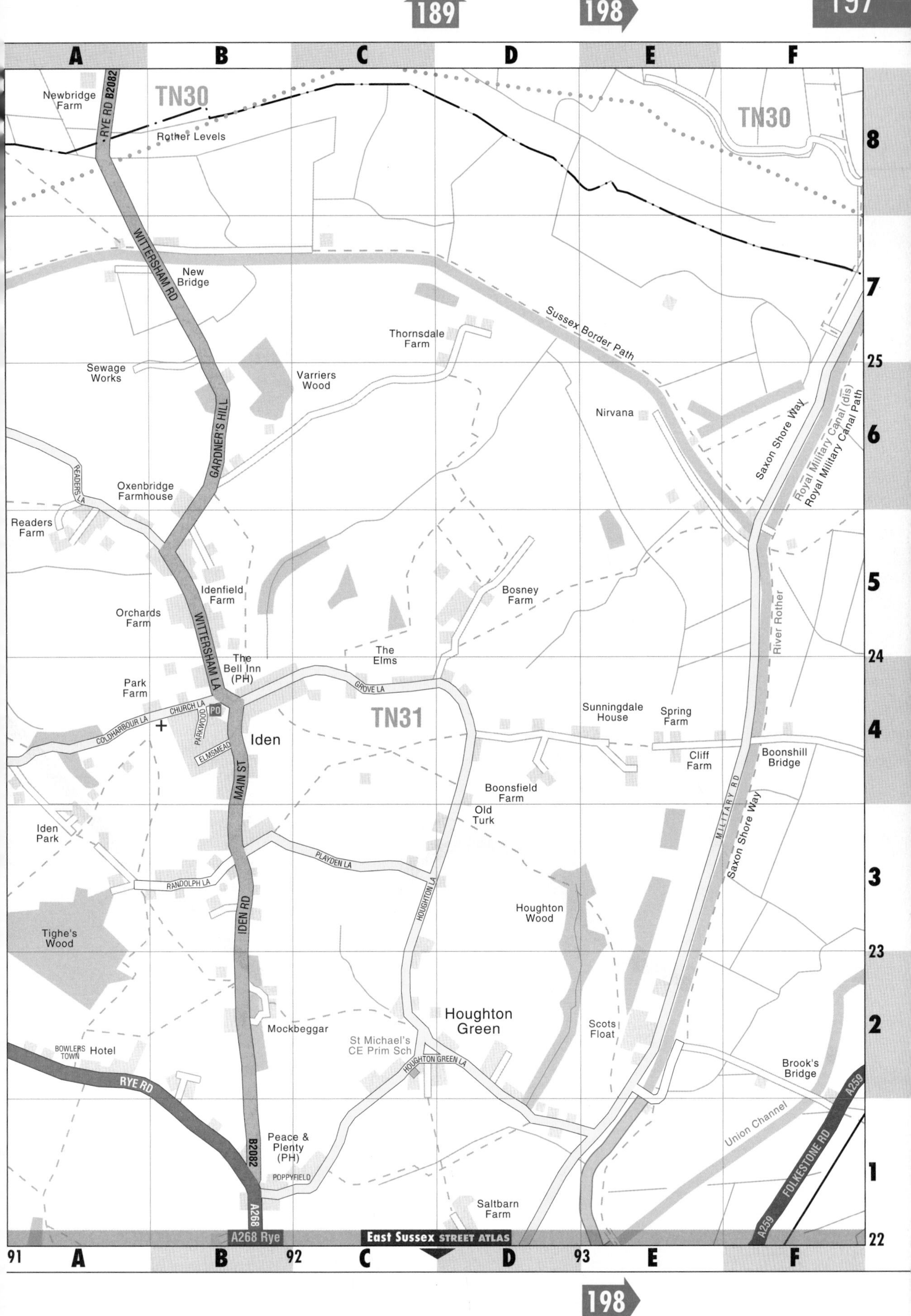
A
B
C
D
E
F
8
7
25
6
5
24
4
3
23
2
1
22
91
92
93
TN30
TN30
TN31
Newbridge Farm
RYE RD B2082
Rother Levels
WITTERSHAM RD
New Bridge
Sussex Border Path
Thornsdale Farm
Sewage Works
Varriers Wood
Nirvana
GARDNER'S HILL
READERS LA
Oxenbridge Farmhouse
Saxon Shore Way
Royal Military Canal (dis)
Royal Military Canal Path
Readers Farm
Idenfield Farm
Bosney Farm
Orchards Farm
WITTERSHAM LA
River Rother
The Bell Inn (PH)
The Elms
Park Farm
GROVE LA
CHURCH LA
PO
COLDHARBOUR LA
PARKWOOD
ELMSMEAD
Iden
MAIN ST
Sunningdale House
Spring Farm
Cliff Farm
Boonshill Bridge
Boonsfield Farm
Old Turk
MILITARY RD
Saxon Shore Way
Iden Park
PLAYDEN LA
RANDOLPH LA
HOUGHTON LA
IDEN RD
Houghton Wood
Tighe's Wood
Houghton Green
Scots Float
Mockbeggar
St Michael's CE Prim Sch
BOWLERS TOWN
Hotel
HOUGHTON GREEN LA
RYE RD
Brook's Bridge
A259
Union Channel
Peace & Plenty (PH)
B2082
POPPYFIELD
FOLKESTONE RD
Saltbarn Farm
A268
A259
A268 Rye

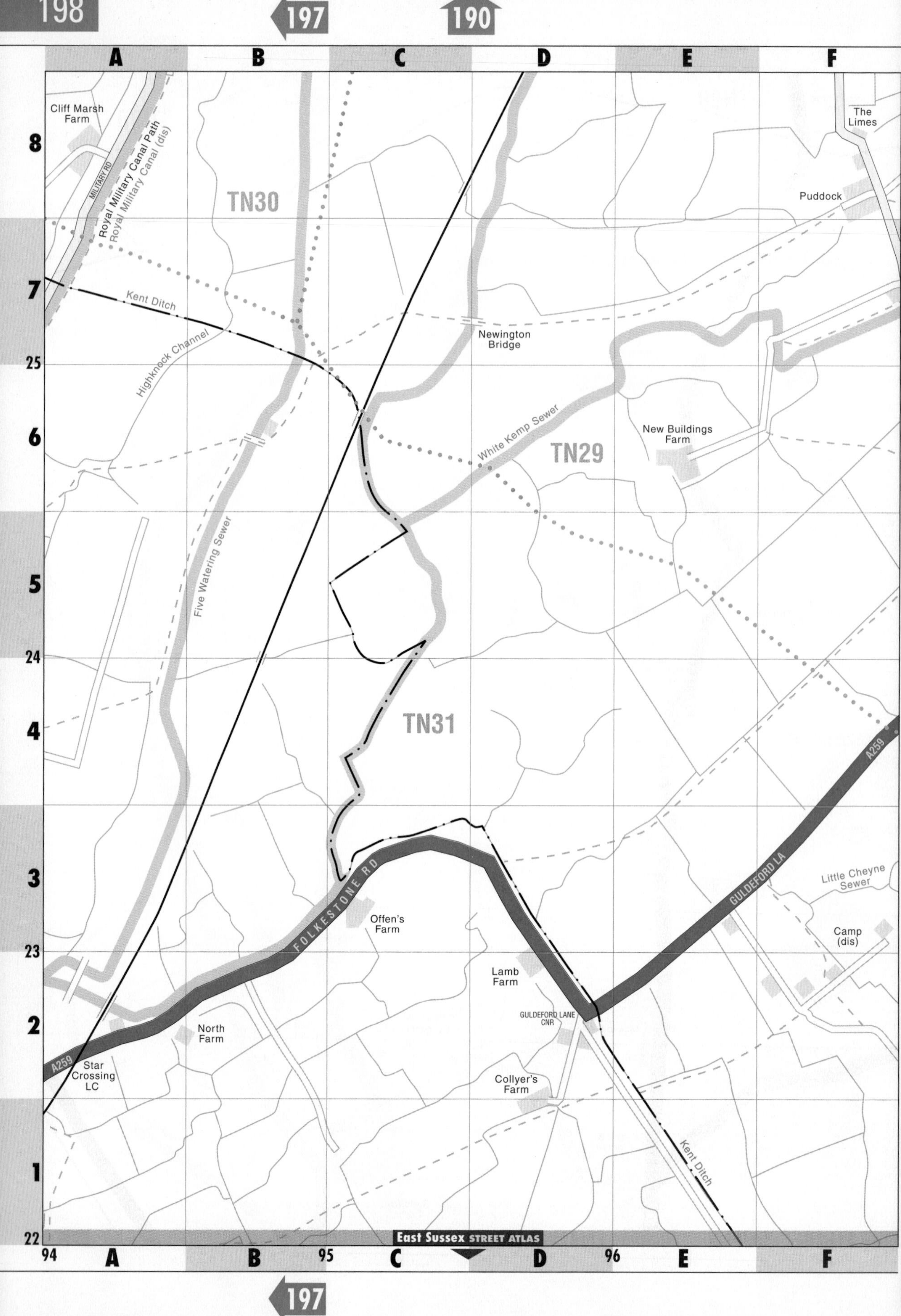

A B C D E F

8

Cliff Marsh
Farm

The
Limes

TN30

Puddock

7

Kent Ditch

25

Newington
Bridge

6

White Kemp Sewer

TN29

New Buildings
Farm

Royal Military Canal Path
Royal Military Canal (dis)

MILITARY RD

Highknock Channel

Five Watering Sewer

5

24

4

TN31

A259

GULDEFORD LA

Little Cheyne
Sewer

3

FOLKESTONE RD

Offen's
Farm

Camp
(dis)

23

Lamb
Farm

2

North
Farm

GULDEFORD LANE
CNR

A259

Star
Crossing
LC

Collyer's
Farm

Kent Ditch

1

22

94 A B 95 C D 96 E F

191
200

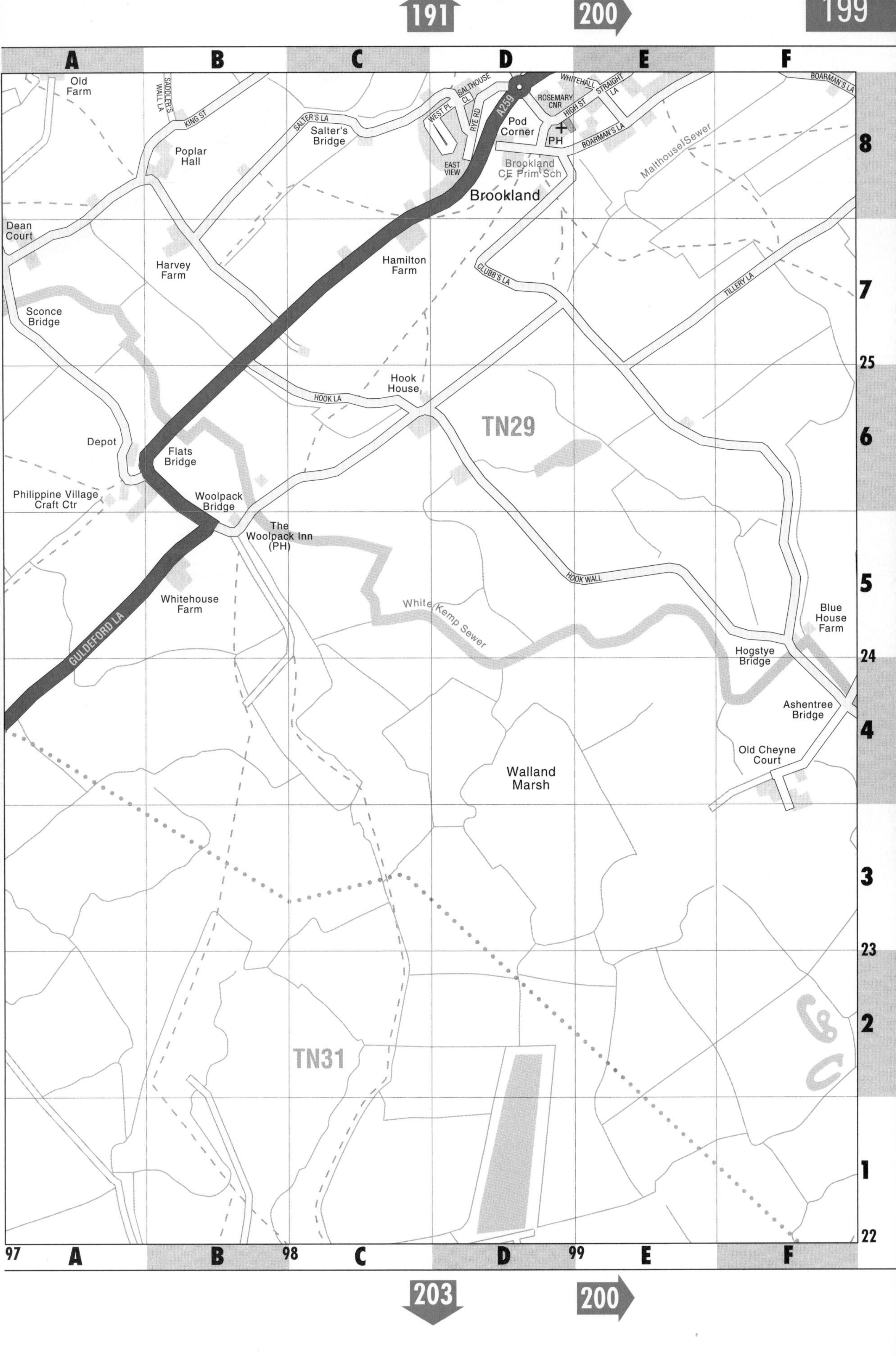
A
B
C
D
E
F
Old Farm
SADDLER'S WALL LA
KING ST
SALTER'S LA
Salter's Bridge
WEST PL
SALTHOUSE CL
RYE RD
A259
Pod Corner
ROSEMARY CNR
WHITEHALL
HIGH ST
STRAIGHT LA
BOARMAN'S LA
PH
Poplar Hall
EAST VIEW
Brookland CE Prim Sch
Brookland
Malthouse Sewer
Dean Court
Harvey Farm
Hamilton Farm
CLUBB'S LA
TILLERY LA
Sconce Bridge
Hook House
HOOK LA
TN29
Depot
Flats Bridge
Philippine Village Craft Ctr
Woolpack Bridge
The Woolpack Inn (PH)
HOOK WALL
Whitehouse Farm
White Kemp Sewer
Blue House Farm
GULDEFORD LA
Hogstye Bridge
Ashentree Bridge
Old Cheyne Court
Walland Marsh
TN31
8
7
25
6
5
24
4
3
23
2
1
22
97
98
99

203
200

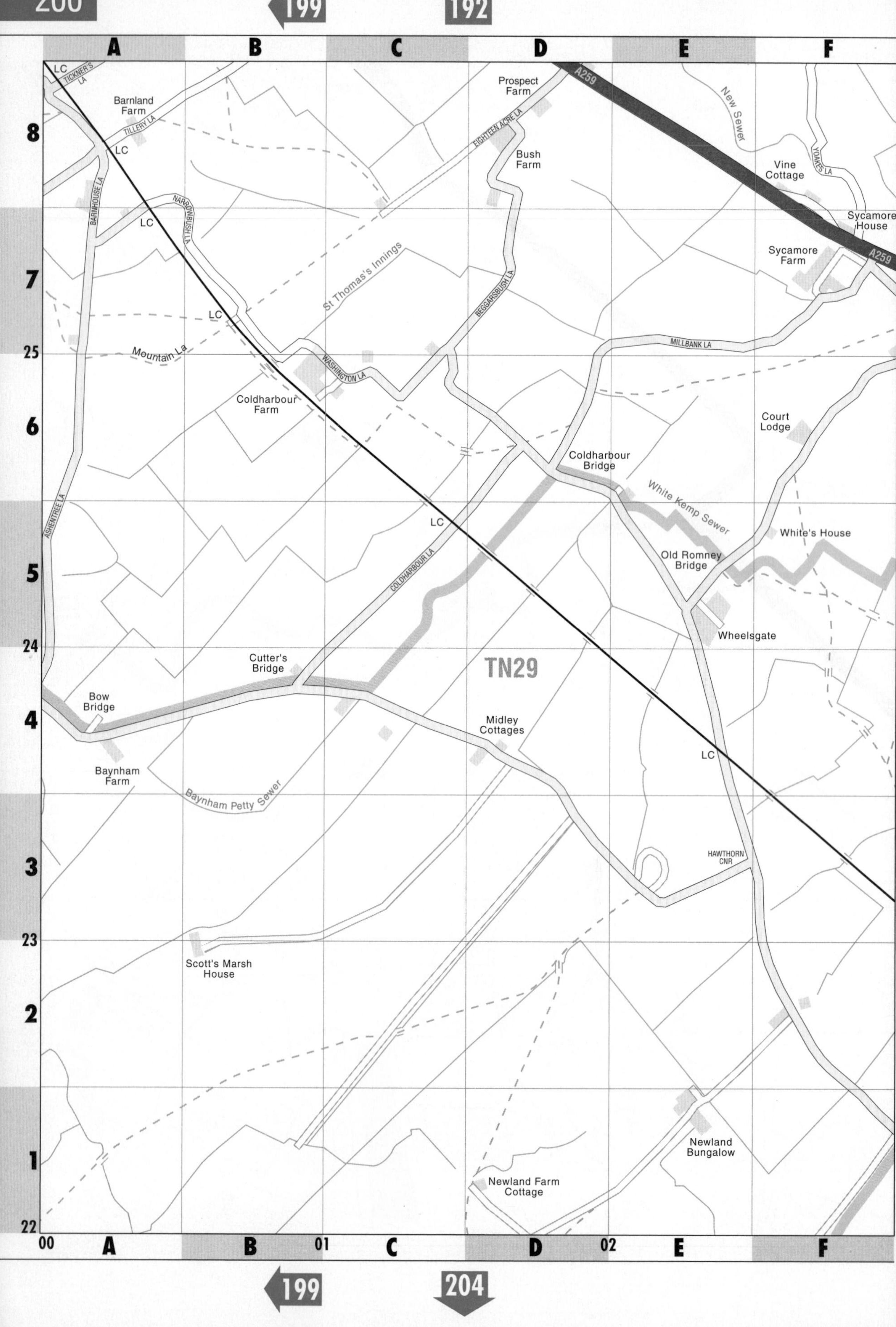
A
B
C
D
E
F
8
7
25
6
5
24
4
3
23
2
1
22
00
01
02
LC
TICKNER'S LA
Barnland Farm
TILLERY LA
BARNHOUSE LA
NARROWBUSH LA
Prospect Farm
A259
New Sewer
EIGHTEEN ACRE LA
Bush Farm
Vine Cottage
YOAKES LA
Sycamore House
Sycamore Farm
St Thomas's Innings
BEGGARSBUSH LA
Mountain La
MILLBANK LA
WASHINGTON LA
Coldharbour Farm
Court Lodge
Coldharbour Bridge
White Kemp Sewer
White's House
ASHENTREE LA
Old Romney Bridge
COLDHARBOUR LA
Wheelsgate
TN29
Cutter's Bridge
Bow Bridge
Midley Cottages
Baynham Farm
Baynham Petty Sewer
HAWTHORN CNR
Scott's Marsh House
Newland Bungalow
Newland Farm Cottage

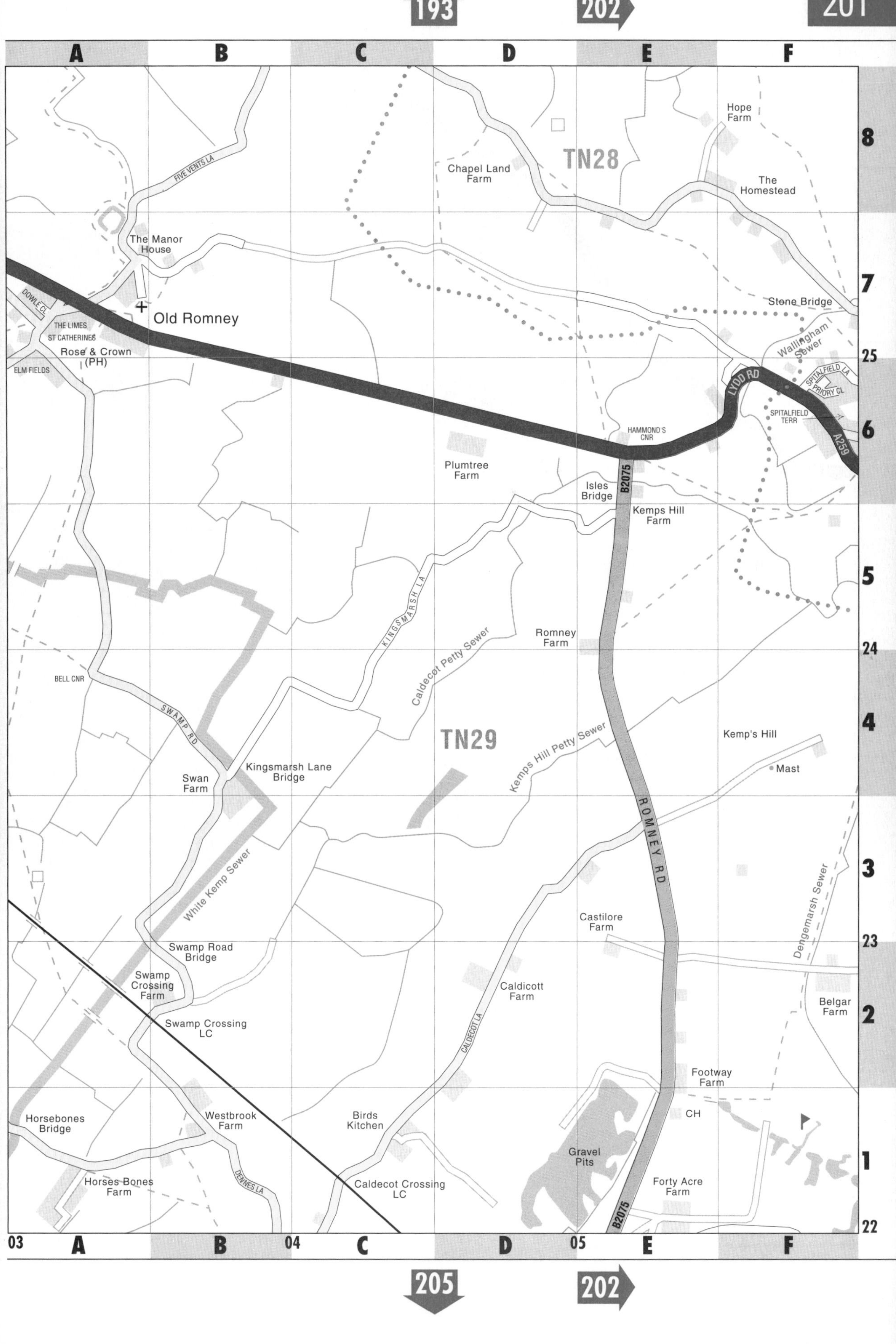
A
B
C
D
E
F
Hope Farm
TN28
Chapel Land Farm
The Homestead
FIVE VENTS LA
The Manor House
Old Romney
DOWLE CL
THE LIMES
ST CATHERINES
Rose & Crown (PH)
ELM FIELDS
Stone Bridge
Wallingham Sewer
LYDD RD
SPITALFIELD LA
PRIORY CL
SPITALFIELD TERR
A259
HAMMOND'S CNR
Plumtree Farm
Isles Bridge
B2075
Kemps Hill Farm
KINGSMARSH LA
Romney Farm
Caldecot Petty Sewer
BELL CNR
SWAMP RD
TN29
Kemps Hill Petty Sewer
Kemp's Hill
Mast
Kingsmarsh Lane Bridge
Swan Farm
ROMNEY RD
White Kemp Sewer
Castilore Farm
Dengemarsh Sewer
Swamp Road Bridge
Swamp Crossing Farm
Caldicott Farm
Belgar Farm
Swamp Crossing LC
CALDECOT LA
Footway Farm
CH
Horsebones Bridge
Westbrook Farm
Birds Kitchen
Gravel Pits
Horses Bones Farm
DENNES LA
Caldecot Crossing LC
Forty Acre Farm
B2075
8
7
25
6
5
24
4
3
23
2
1
22
03
04
05

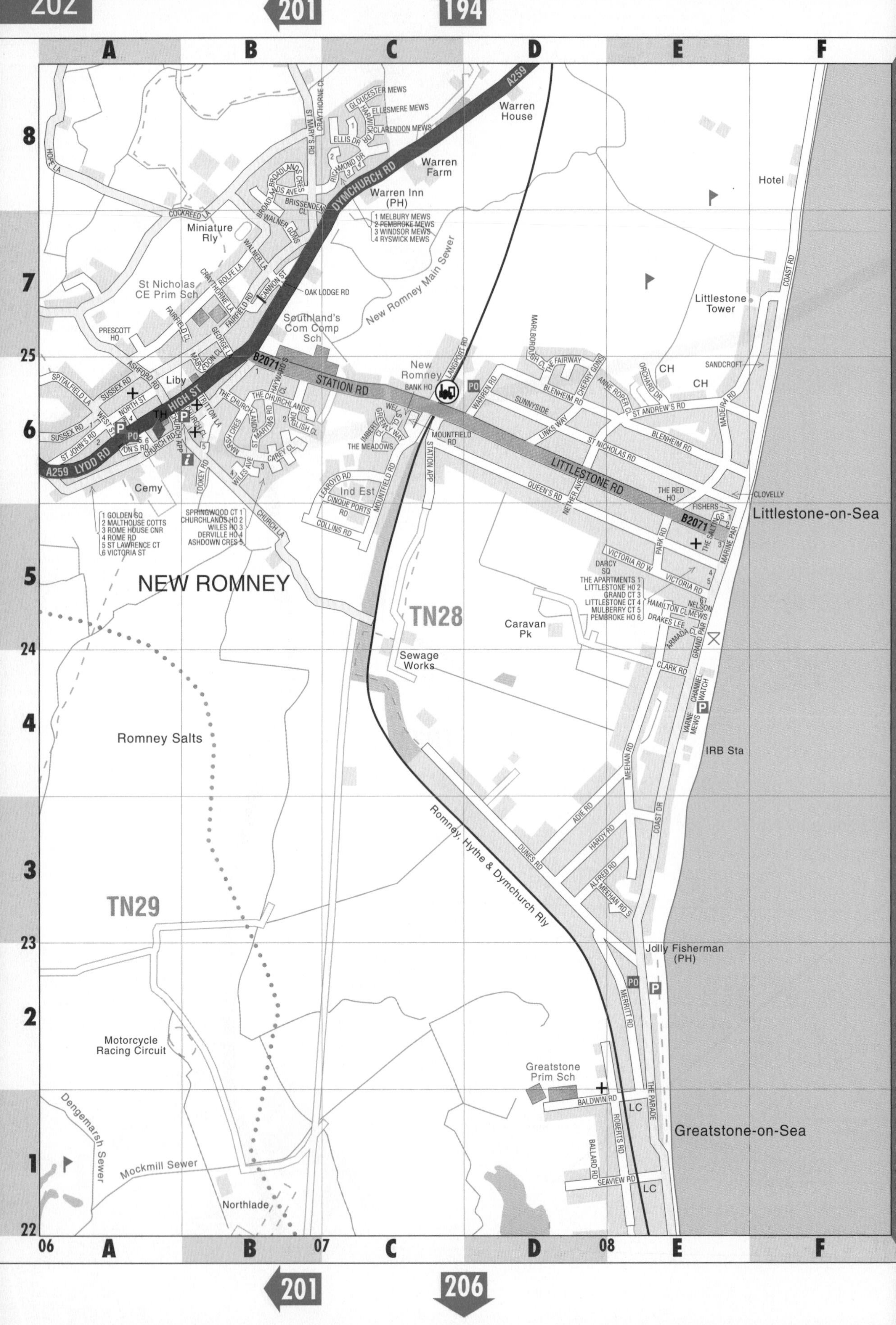

A   B   C   D   E   F

8

Warren
House

Hotel

7

St Nicholas
CE Prim Sch

Littlestone
Tower

25

SANDCROFT

New
Romney
Bank Ho

Clovelly

Littlestone-on-Sea

6

NEW ROMNEY

LITTLESTONE RD

THE RED
HO

FISHERS

Cemy

1 GOLDEN SQ
2 MALTHOUSE COTTS
3 ROME HOUSE CNR
4 ROME RD
5 ST LAWRENCE CT
6 VICTORIA ST

SPRINGWOOD CT 1
CHURCHLANDS HO 2
WILES HO 3
DERVILLE HO 4
ASHDOWN CRES 5

Ind Est

5

TN28

THE APARTMENTS 1
LITTLESTONE HO 2
GRAND CT 3
LITTLESTONE CT 4
MULBERRY CT 5
PEMBROKE HO 6

Caravan
Pk

24

Sewage
Works

IRB Sta

4

Romney Salts

3

TN29

23

Jolly Fisherman
(PH)

2

Motorcycle
Racing Circuit

Greatstone
Prim Sch

1

Dengemarsh Sewer

Mockmill Sewer

Northlade

LC

Greatstone-on-Sea

LC

22

06   A   B   07   C   D   08   E   F

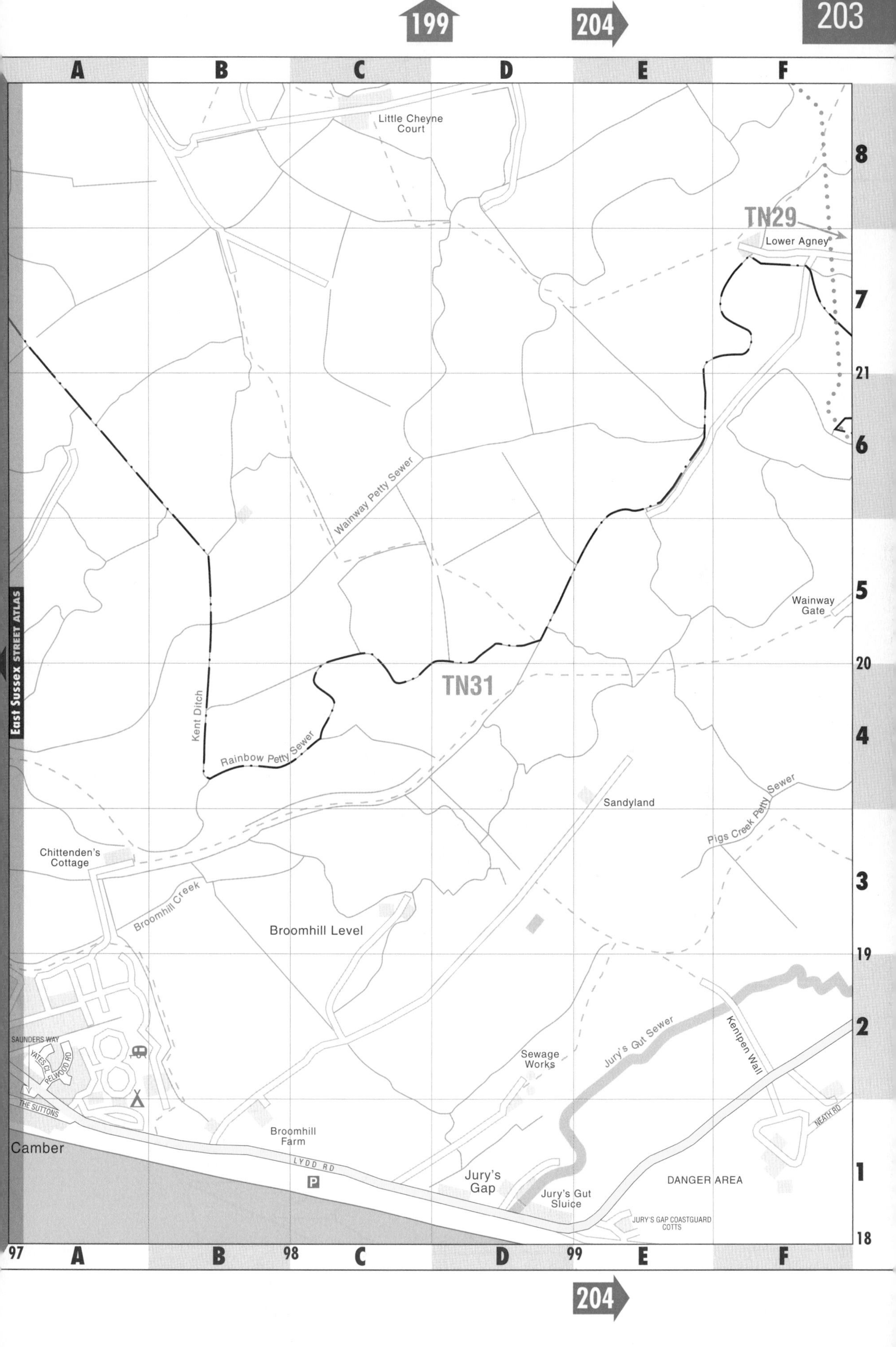

8

TN29

Lower Agney

7

21

6

Little Cheyne
Court

Wainway Petty Sewer

Wainway
Gate

5

TN31

20

Kent Ditch

4

Rainbow Petty Sewer

Sandyland

Pigs Creek Petty Sewer

Chittenden's
Cottage

3

Broomhill Creek

Broomhill Level

19

SAUNDERS WAY

2

YALES ST

BELWOOD RD

THE SUTTONS

Jury's Gut Sewer

Kempen Wall

NEATH RD

Camber

Broomhill
Farm

LYDD RD

P

Sewage
Works

Jury's
Gap

Jury's Gut
Sluice

JURY'S GAP COASTGUARD
COTTS

DANGER AREA

1

18

East Sussex STREET ATLAS

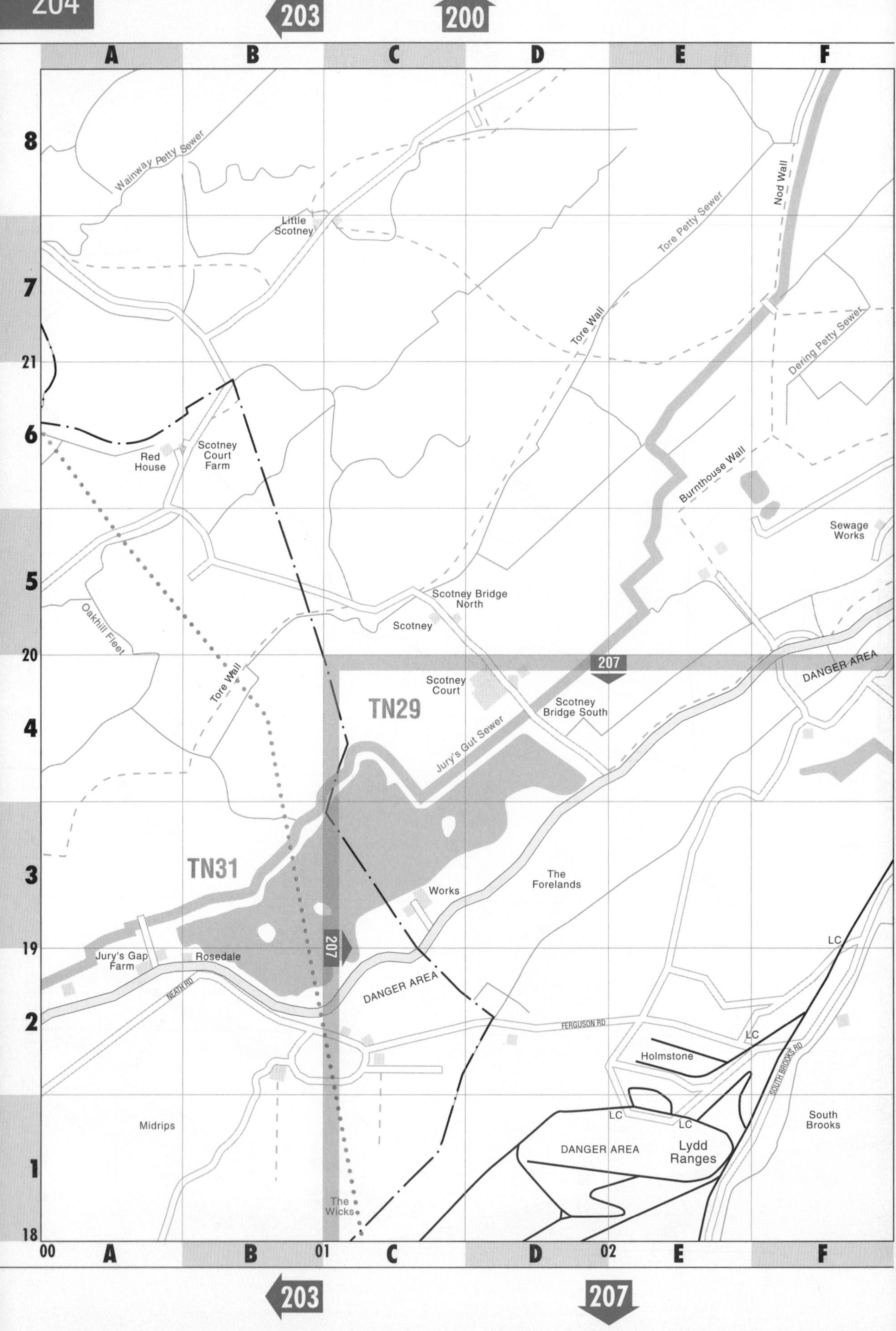

203
200

A B C D E F

8

7

21

6

5

20

4

3

19

2

1

18

Wainway Petty Sewer

Little
Scotney

Tore Petty Sewer

Nod Wall

Dering Petty Sewer

Red
House

Scotney
Court
Farm

Burnthouse Wall

Sewage
Works

Oakhill Fleet

Tore Wall

Scotney Bridge
North

Scotney

Tore Wall

207

DANGER AREA

TN29

Scotney
Court

Scotney
Bridge South

Jury's Gut Sewer

TN31

207

The
Forelands

Works

LC

Jury's Gap
Farm

Rosedale

19

NEATH RD

207

DANGER AREA

FERGUSON RD

LC

Holmstone

SOUTH BROOKS RD

Midrips

LC   LC

DANGER AREA

Lydd
Ranges

South
Brooks

The
Wicks

00 A B 01 C D 02 E F

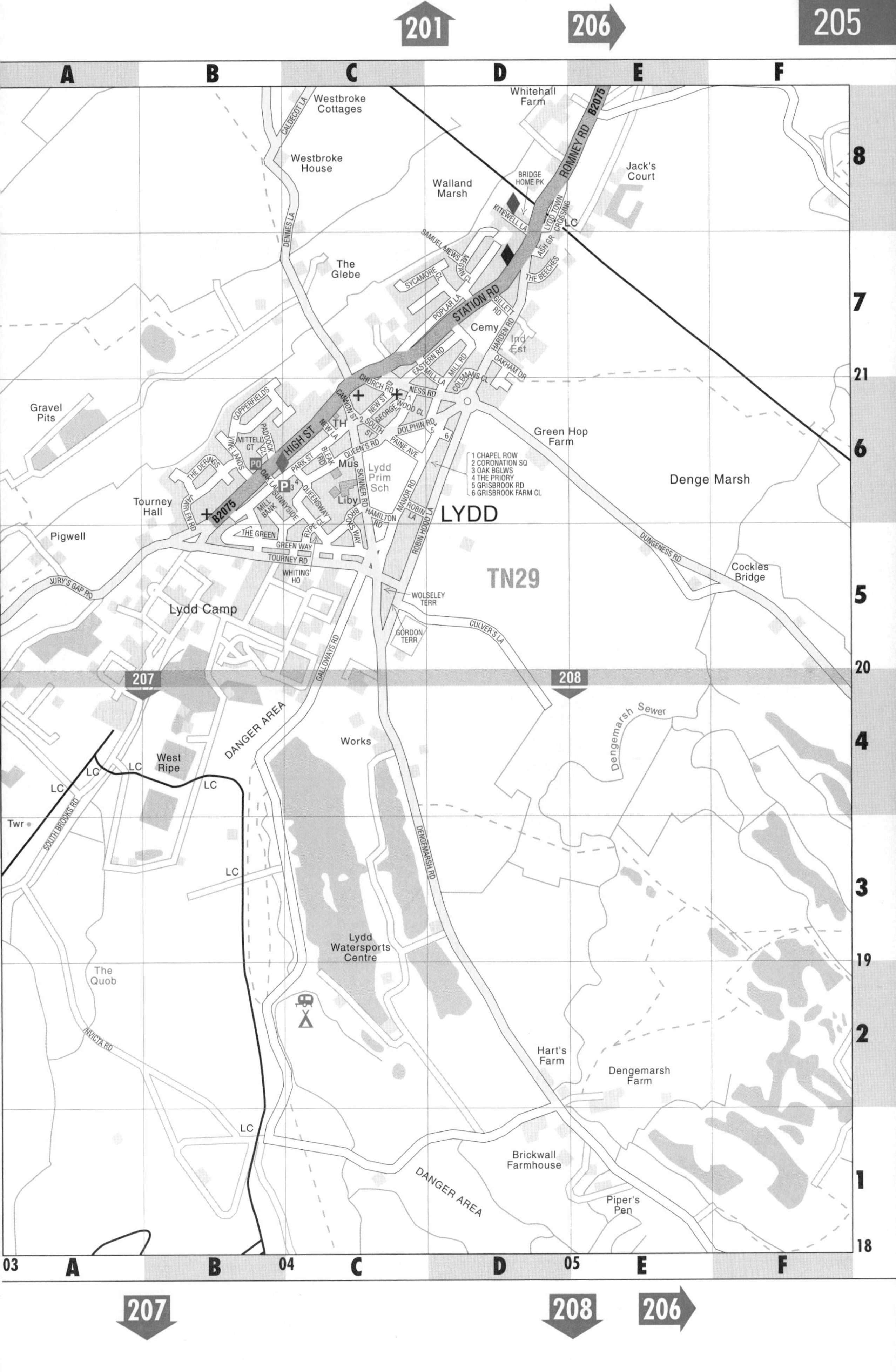
201
206
A
B
C
D
E
F
8
7
21
6
5
20
4
3
19
2
1
18
03
04
05
Westbroke Cottages
Westbroke House
Whitehall Farm
Walland Marsh
Jack's Court
BRIDGE HOME PK
ROMNEY RD
B2075
LYDD TOWN CROSSING
KITEWELL LA
SAMUEL MEWS
MEGAN CL
ASH GR
THE BEECHES
The Glebe
SYCAMORE CL
POPLAR LA
STATION RD
GILLETT RD
Cemy
Ind Est
HARDEN RD
OAKHAM DR
CALDECOT LA
DENNES LA
EASTERN RD
MILL LA
MILL RD
COLEMANS CL
CHURCH RD
NESS RD
WOOD CL
DOLPHIN RD
PAINE AVE
Gravel Pits
COPPERFIELDS
HIGH ST
CANNON ST
NEW ST
GEORGE ST
SOUTH ST
NEW LA
TH
MITTELL CT
PADDOCK CL
VINE LANDS
THE DERINGS
PO
PARK ST
BLEAK RD
QUEEN'S RD
Mus
Lydd Prim Sch
Liby
Green Hop Farm
1 CHAPEL ROW
2 CORONATION SQ
3 OAK BGLWS
4 THE PRIORY
5 GRISBROOK RD
6 GRISBROOK FARM CL
Denge Marsh
Tourney Hall
JARLEN RD
OAK LA
SUNNYSIDE
MILL BANK
QUEENSWAY
SKINNER RD
BROOKS WAY
HAMILTON RD
MANOR RD
ROBIN LA
ROBIN HOOD LA
LYDD
Pigwell
THE GREEN
RYPE CL
GREEN WAY
TOURNEY RD
WHITING HO
DUNGENESS RD
Cockles Bridge
TN29
JURY'S GAP RD
Lydd Camp
WOLSELEY TERR
GORDON TERR
CULVER'S LA
GALLOWAYS RD
207
208
DANGER AREA
Works
Dengemarsh Sewer
LC
West Ripe
Twr
SOUTH BROOKS RD
DENGEMARSH RD
Lydd Watersports Centre
The Quob
INVICTA RD
Hart's Farm
Dengemarsh Farm
Brickwall Farmhouse
Piper's Pen
207
208
206

205
202

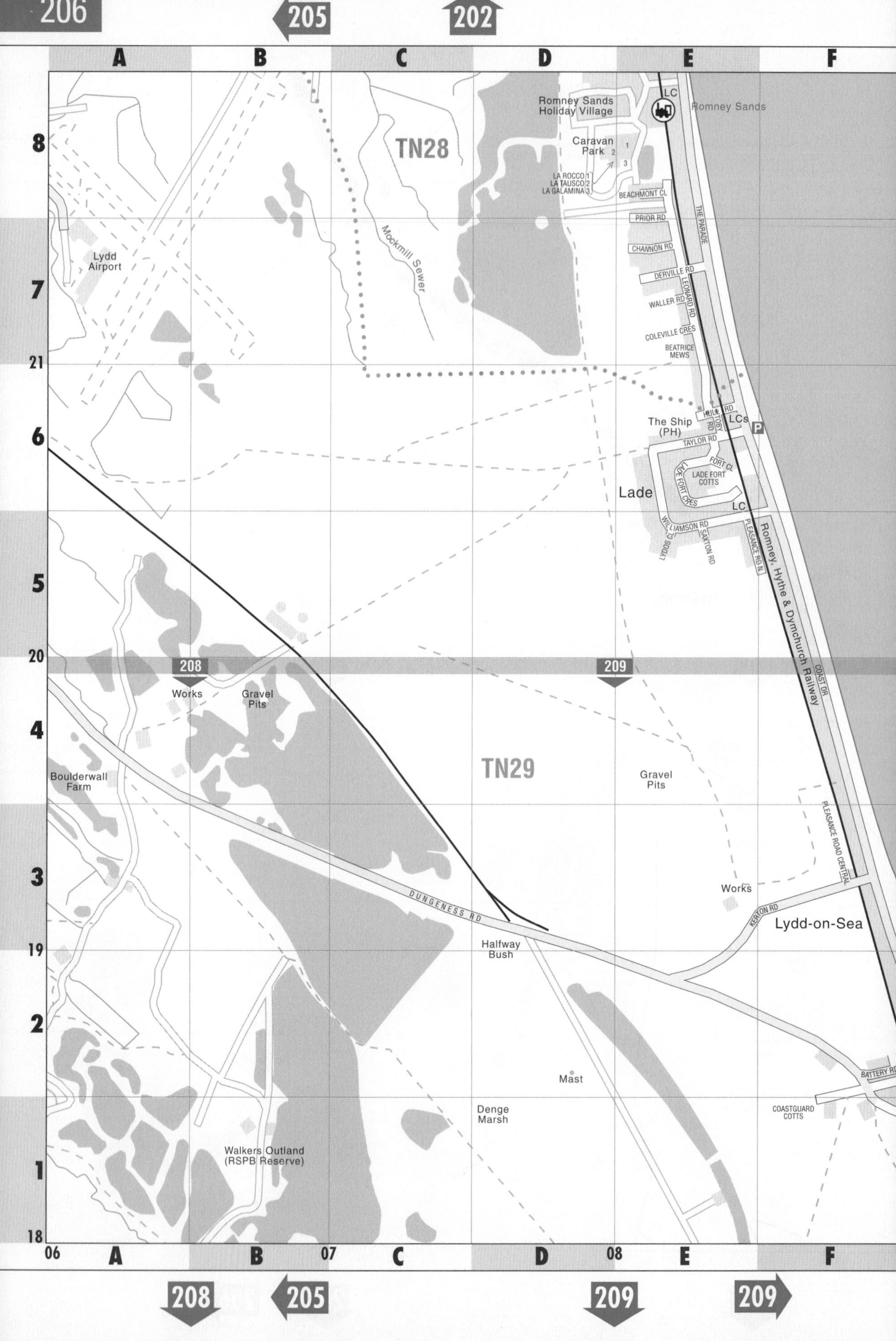

TN28

Lydd
Airport

Mockmill Sewer

Romney Sands
Holiday Village

LC
Romney Sands

Caravan
Park

LA ROCCO 1
LA TAUSCO 2
LA GALAMINA 3

BEACHMONT CL
PRIOR RD
CHANNON RD

DERVILLE RD
WALLER RD
LEONARD RD

COLEVILLE CRES
BEATRICE
MEWS

THE PARADE

The Ship
(PH)

LCs

HULL RD
VICTORY RD
TAYLOR RD
FORT CL
LADE FORT
COTTS
LADE FORT CRES

Lade

WILLIAMSON RD
LYDDS CLOSE
SAXTON RD
PLEASANCE RD N

LC

P

Romney, Hythe & Dymchurch Railway

COAST DR.

208
Works
Gravel
Pits

209

TN29

Gravel
Pits

Boulderwall
Farm

DUNGENESS RD

Works

PLEASANCE ROAD CENTRAL

KERTON RD

Lydd-on-Sea

Halfway
Bush

Mast

BATTERY RD

Denge
Marsh

COASTGUARD
COTTS

Walkers Outland
(RSPB Reserve)

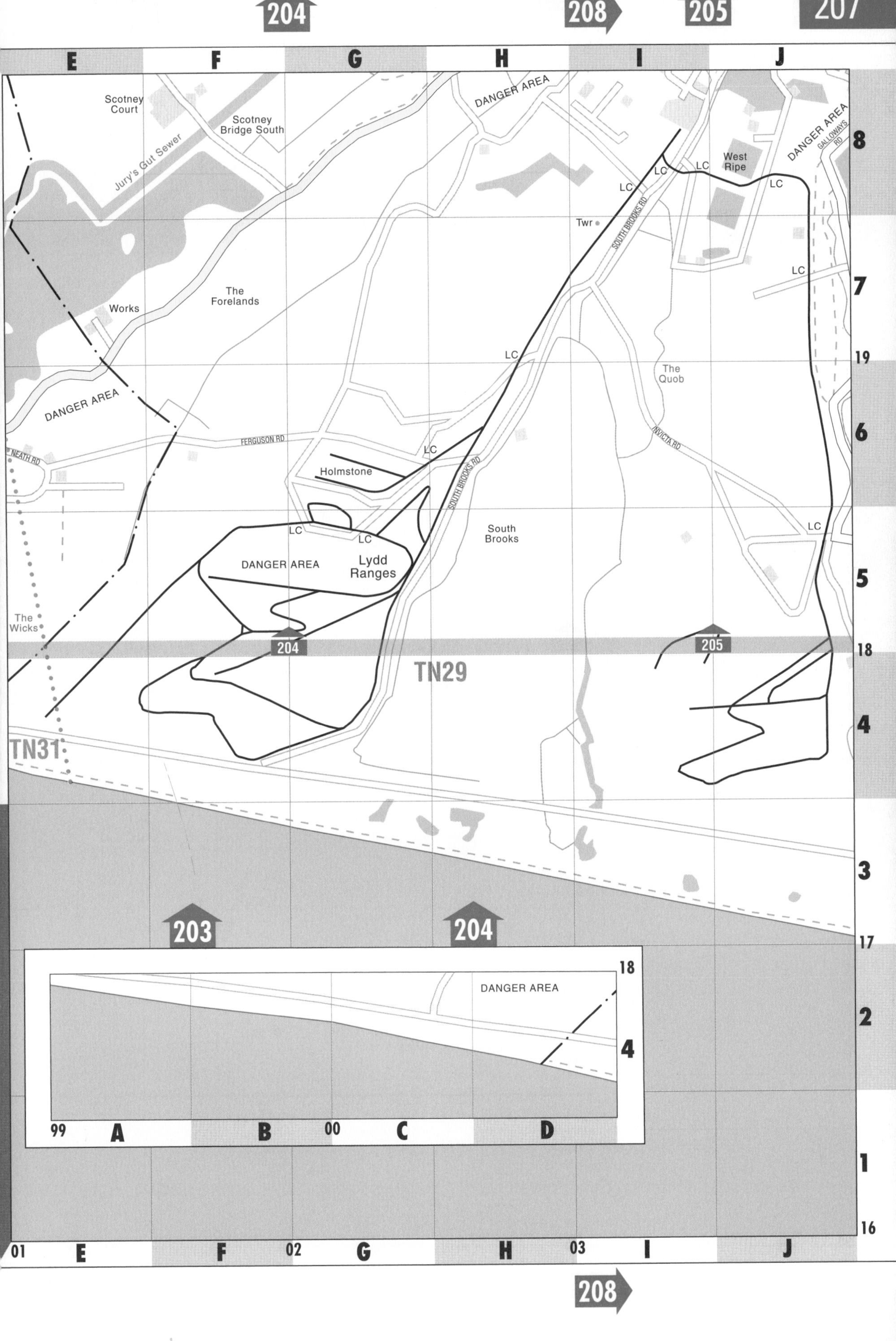

E   F   G   H   I   J

Scotney Court

Scotney Bridge South

DANGER AREA

West Ripe

DANGER AREA

GALLOWAYS RD

8

Jury's Gut Sewer

Twr

SOUTH BROOKS RD

LC
LC
LC
LC

LC

The Forelands

Works

7

LC

19

The Quob

DANGER AREA

NEATH RD

FERGUSON RD

LC

INVICTA RD

6

Holmstone

South Brooks

LC

The Wicks

LC   LC

DANGER AREA   Lydd Ranges

LC

5

204

205

18

TN29

TN31

4

203   204

17

DANGER AREA

18

2

4

99   A   B   00   C   D

16

01   E   F   02   G   H   03   I   J

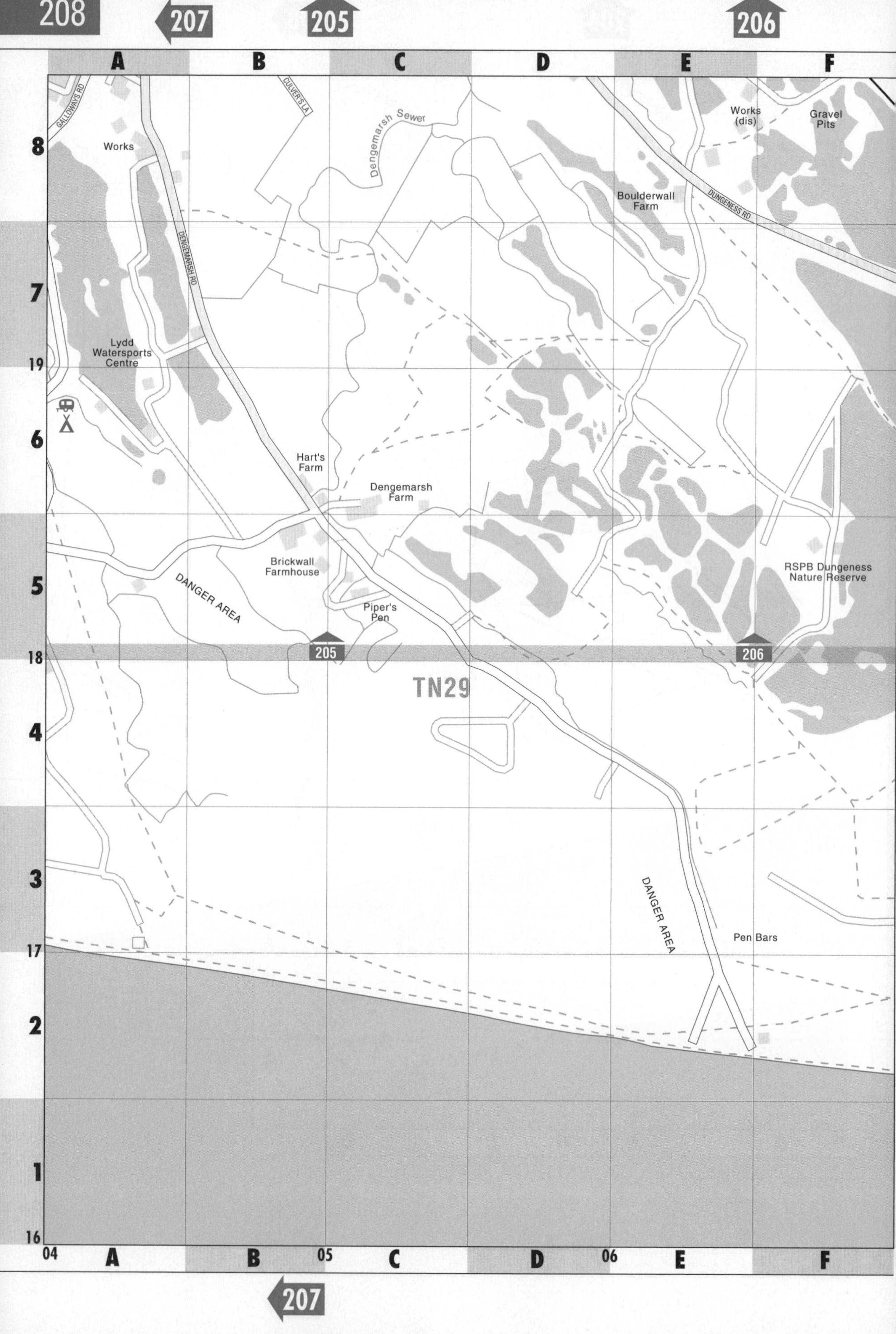
A   B   C   D   E   F

8   Works
Works (dis)   Gravel Pits
Dengemarsh Sewer
CULVER'S LA
GALLOWAYS RD
Boulderwall Farm
DUNGENESS RD

7

19   Lydd Watersports Centre
DENGEMARSH RD

6   Hart's Farm
Dengemarsh Farm

Brickwall Farmhouse
RSPB Dungeness Nature Reserve

5   DANGER AREA
Piper's Pen

18   ▲ 205   ▲ 206

TN29

4

DANGER AREA

3
Pen Bars

17

2

1

16   04   A   B   05   C   D   06   E   F

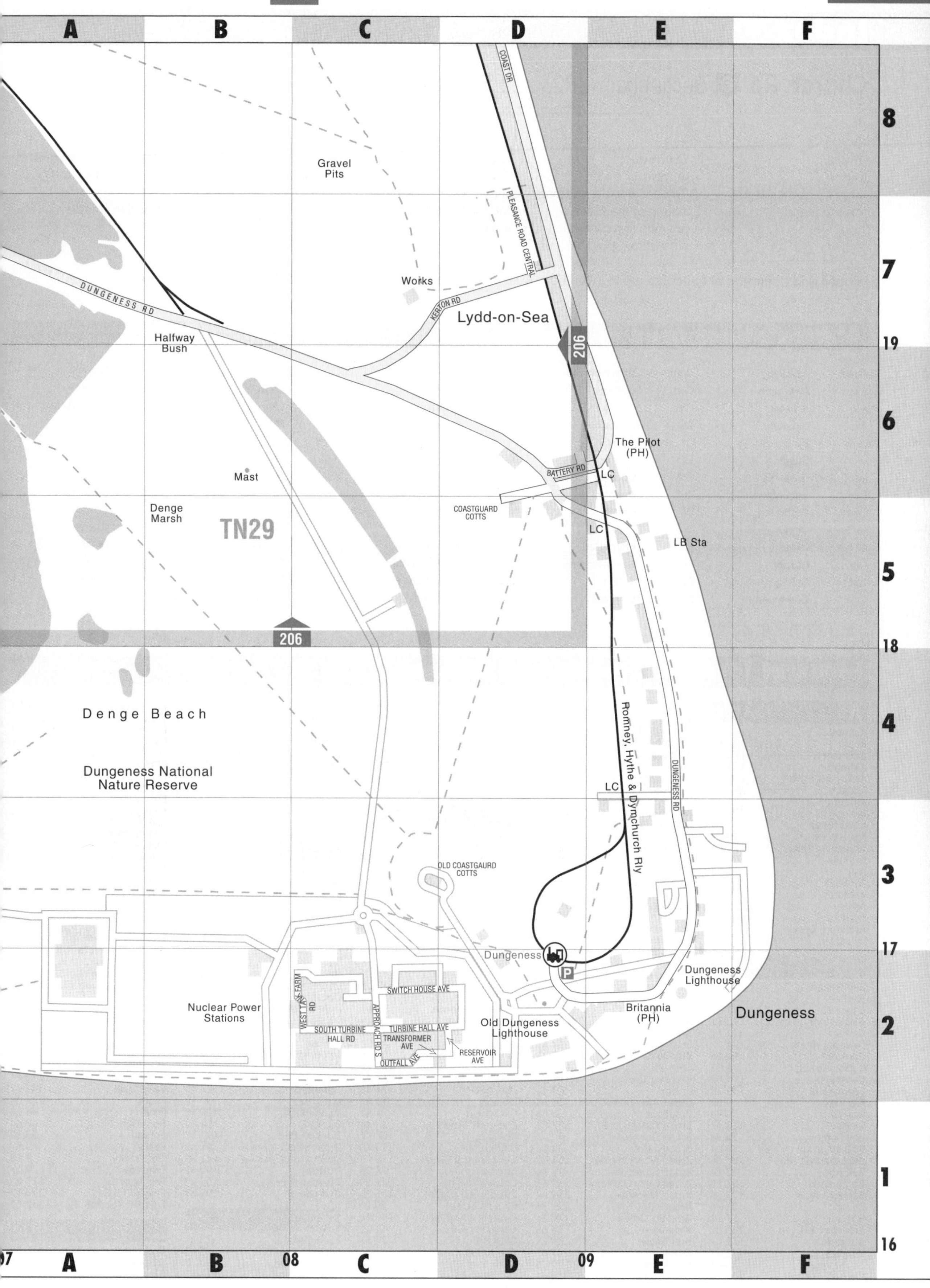

A B C D E F

8

Gravel
Pits

7

Works

COAST DR

PLEASANCE ROAD CENTRAL

KERTON RD

Lydd-on-Sea

19

206

Halfway
Bush

DUNGENESS RD

The Pilot
(PH)

6

Mast

BATTERY RD

LC

Denge
Marsh

COASTGUARD
COTTS

LC

TN29

LB Sta

5

206

18

Romney, Hythe & Dymchurch Rly

4

Denge Beach

Dungeness National
Nature Reserve

DUNGENESS RD

LC

OLD COASTGAURD
COTTS

3

17

Dungeness

Dungeness
Lighthouse

Nuclear Power
Stations

WEST LADE FARM RD

SWITCH HOUSE AVE

APPROACH RD S

SOUTH TURBINE
HALL RD

TURBINE HALL AVE

TRANSFORMER
AVE

OUTFALL AVE

RESERVOIR
AVE

Old Dungeness
Lighthouse

P

Britannia
(PH)

Dungeness

2

1

07 A B 08 C D 09 E F

16

Index

Church Rd **6** Beckenham BR2..........**53** C6

Place name	**Location number**	**Locality, town or village**	**Postcode district**	**Page and grid square**
May be abbreviated on the map	Present when a number indicates the place's position in a crowded area of mapping	Shown when more than one place has the same name	District for the indexed place	Page number and grid reference for the standard mapping

Public and commercial buildings are highlighted in magenta **Places of interest** are highlighted in blue with a star★

Abbreviations used in the index

Acad	**Academy**	Comm	**Common**	Gd	**Ground**	L	**Leisure**	Prom	**Prom**
App	**Approach**	Cott	**Cottage**	Gdn	**Garden**	La	**Lane**	Rd	**Road**
Arc	**Arcade**	Cres	**Crescent**	Gn	**Green**	Liby	**Library**	Recn	**Recreation**
Ave	**Avenue**	Cswy	**Causeway**	Gr	**Grove**	Mdw	**Meadow**	Ret	**Retail**
Bglw	**Bungalow**	Ct	**Court**	H	**Hall**	Meml	**Memorial**	Sh	**Shopping**
Bldg	**Building**	Ctr	**Centre**	Ho	**House**	Mkt	**Market**	Sq	**Square**
Bsns, Bus	**Business**	Ctry	**Country**	Hospl	**Hospital**	Mus	**Museum**	St	**Street**
Bvd	**Boulevard**	Cty	**County**	HQ	**Headquarters**	Orch	**Orchard**	Sta	**Station**
Cath	**Cathedral**	Dr	**Drive**	Hts	**Heights**	Pal	**Palace**	Terr	**Terrace**
Cir	**Circus**	Dro	**Drove**	Ind	**Industrial**	Par	**Parade**	TH	**Town Hall**
Cl	**Close**	Ed	**Education**	Inst	**Institute**	Pas	**Passage**	Univ	**University**
Cnr	**Corner**	Emb	**Embankment**	Int	**International**	Pk	**Park**	Wk, Wlk	**Walk**
Coll	**College**	Est	**Estate**	Intc	**Interchange**	Pl	**Place**	Wr	**Water**
Com	**Community**	Ex	**Exhibition**	Junc	**Junction**	Prec	**Precinct**	Yd	**Yard**

Index of localities, towns and villages

Golgotha 130 F6
Goodnestone Faversham 63 D7
Goodnestone Wingham 91 D2
Gore 93 B3
Grange 11 B6
Gravel Castle 129 A8
Graveney 41 E2
Great Chart 138 C1
Great Mongeham 116 C3
Great Stonar 73 B4
Greatstone-on-Sea 202 E1
Greenhill 22 D2
Greet 80 D3
Grove 69 F8
Grove End 58 C7
Grove Green 75 E5
Grove Hill 69 D6
Guilton 71 C1
Gushmere 84 C8
Guston 149 E6

H

Hacklinge 94 C1
Haffenden Quarter 152 A7
Haine 28 F2
Hale Birchington 26 B4
Hale Chatham 32 D8
Hales Place 67 A3
Halfway Houses 3 E7
Halfway Street 130 D4
Ham 93 F2
Ham Green Upchurch 12 F6
Ham Green Wittersham 188 C1
Hamlet of Shellness 19 E5
Hammill 92 E3
Hampton 22 B5
Hamstreet 183 B7
Harbledown 87 B8
Harbourland 75 B8
Harman's Corner 36 A2
Harrietsham 100 D5
Hartlip 34 E5
Hassell Street 125 A2
Hastingleigh 142 B6
Hawkinge 163 C5
Hawksdown 134 B8
Hawthorn Corner 24 A3
Hazel Street 57 A3
Hearts Delight 36 B1
Hempstead 33 A5
Hemsted 160 D8
Herne 46 B8
Herne Bay 22 E6
Herne Common 45 F6
Hernhill 64 B6
Heronden 92 F1
Hersden 46 F1
Hickmans Green 64 A2
Hicks Forstal 46 A4
High Halden 167 D7
Highstead 24 A1
Highsted 58 F7
Highstreet 42 F2
Hillborough 24 A4
Hill Green 34 C1
Hill Street 142 F8
Hinxhill 140 D1
Hoaden 70 F4
Hoath 46 F5
Hockley 82 C3
Hogben's Hill 84 A6
Hollingbourne 77 E2
Hollow Street 47 C4
Hollybushes 80 A8
Honey Hill 65 E8
Hoo 49 F6
Horn Street 177 B4
Horselees 64 A2
Horton 86 F3
Hothfield 138 A7
Houghton Green 197 D2
Hucking 56 E1
Hunters Forstal 23 C1
Hythe 176 D1

I

Ickham 69 C1
Iden 197 B4
Ivychurch 192 E3
Iwade 14 D4

J

Jury's Gap 203 D1

K

Kearsney 148 D3
Kemsley 14 E1
Kemsley Street 33 C2
Kenardington 182 A6
Kennington 139 E6
Kennington Lees 139 D7
Keycol 35 E6
Key Street 36 A5
Kingsdown Deal 134 D5
Kingsdown Lynsted 59 E4
Kingsdown Park 20 F3
Kingsgate 8 G1
Kingsland 136 C8
Kingsnorth 156 A4
Kingston 111 D3
Kingswood 99 E3
Kit's Coty 53 C7
Knaves Ash 46 C5
Knowlton 114 C7

L

Lade 206 E6
Langley 98 C4
Langley Heath 98 F4
Leadingcross Green 101 C3
Leaveland 105 B8
Leeds 99 A7
Leigh Green 179 F6
Lenham 101 D5
Lenham Forstal 102 B1
Lenham Heath 119 B8
Lewson Street 60 E7
Leysdown-on-Sea 6 H2
Lidsing 32 F1
Lilyvale 158 F4
Linton 96 F1
Little Betteshanger 115 E5
Littlebourne 89 E8
Little Chart 120 A1
Little Chart Forstal 137 C8
Little Houses 118 D2
Little Mongeham 116 A2
Littlestone-on-Sea 202 F5
Liverton Street 100 F1
Lodge Lees 128 F4
London Beach 167 B5
Loose 96 F4
Loose Hill 96 F5
Lords Wood 32 C1
Lower Cox Street 55 D6
Lower Eythorne 131 B8
Lower Goldstone 71 F7
Lower Halstow 13 C3
Lower Hardres 110 A6
Lower Hartlip 34 E4
Lower Heppington 109 F8
Lower Herne 22 F1
Lower Island 20 C1
Lower Newlands 39 A2
Lower Rainham 11 F3
Lower Twydall 11 C5
Lower Walmer 117 C4
Luton 10 B2
Lydd 205 D6
Lydd Camp 205 B5
Lydden 147 E8
Lydd-on-Sea 209 D7
Lymbridge Green 143 B4
Lyminge 161 B6
Lympne 175 A3
Lynsore Bottom 127 D8
Lynsted 60 A6

M

Macklands 12 A2
Maidstone 75 C3
Maltman's Hill 135 E3
Manston 28 E1
Margate 7 H2
Marine Town 1 F2
Marley Barham 111 B1
Marley Deal 116 A8
Marlpit 97 E2
Marshborough 93 B7
Marshside 24 D1
Martin 133 B3
Martin Mill 133 C2
Martyr's Field 87 F7
Maxted Street 143 B6
Maxton 166 A6
Maypole 46 F6
Meresborough 34 A5
Merryman's Hill 4 C8
Mersham 157 E4
Middle Deal 117 C5
Middle Quarter 152 D1
Mile Town 1 C1
Millbank 46 F7
Mill Hill 117 A3
Milstead 58 E2
Milton Regis 36 C6
Minster Sheppey 4 B7
Minster Thanet 50 A6
Mockbeggar 39 B1
Molash 105 F4
Monkton 49 D7
Moon's Green 188 A3
Moorstock 159 C2
Moor Street 34 B7
Morehall 177 F6
Mountain Street 107 B6
Munday Bois 135 F8
Murston 37 B5

N

Naccolt 140 E6
Nackington 88 A2
Napchester 132 C3
Nash 70 F2
Neames Forstal 84 E6
Nethercourt 52 A7
Newbarn 161 B4
Newbury 59 D4
Newchurch 184 E3
Newingreen 175 A5
Newington Folkestone 177 A8
Newington Ramsgate 29 B1
Newington Sittingbourne 35 A6
Newland Green 135 D8
Newnham 81 C7
New Romney 202 A5
New Town 156 D7
Nonington 113 D5
Northbourne 116 A4
Northdown 8 D1
North Elham 145 A6
Northgate 67 A1
North Lyminge 161 C7
North Stonar 73 B6
North Street 62 C1
Northwood 29 C3

O

Oad Street 35 E1
Oare 40 A3
Old Romney 201 B7
Old Wives Lees 85 C3
Orchard Valley 176 B3
Ospringe 62 B6
Otham 98 B7
Otham Hole 98 B6
Otterham Quay 12 C3
Ottinge 144 D1
Out Elmstead 111 F2
Oversland 84 F7

P

Paddlesworth 162 C4
Paddock 104 E1
Painter's Forstal 61 E3
Palmarsh 187 D7
Palmstead 127 D5
Paramour Street 71 D7
Park Wood Gillingham 33 D4
Park Wood Maidstone 97 E4
Patrixbourne 89 B3
Payden Street 80 B1
Peasmarsh 196 A2
Pedlinge 175 D4
Peene 177 B8
Peening Quarter 188 B6
Pegwell 52 B5
Penenden Heath 75 B7
Pennypot 175 E1
Perry 70 C3
Perrywood 84 C4
Pested 105 B4
Petham 109 B3
Pett Bottom 110 B5
Pineham 149 D8
Platt's Heath 100 E1
Pluckley 136 D7
Pluckley Thorne 136 B6
Plucks Gutter 48 F3
Postling 160 F2
Potten Street 25 D3
Potters Corner 138 F6
Potter's Forstal 118 B2
Pratling Street 53 C3
Preston Ash 70 B6
Preston Faversham 62 D6
Princes Park 32 B6

Q

Queenborough 3 A5

R

Radfall 44 C5
Radfield 38 A2
Rainham 33 E8
Ram Lane 120 E2
Ramsgate 52 C4
Ratling 113 A8
Reading Street Broadstairs 29 F7
Reading Street Tenterden 180 C2
Reculver 24 C7
Rhode Common 85 A6
Rhodes Minnis 144 A3
Ridge Row 145 E1
Ringlestone Harrietsham 78 F4
Ringlestone Maidstone 74 E7
Ringwould 133 F5
Ripple 133 D8
River 148 E3
Robhurst 168 C2
Rochester 9 B6
Rodmersham 59 C8
Rodmersham Green 59 B7
Romden 135 C1
Roseacre 76 A4
Rough Common 66 B3
Rowling 92 A2
Rowling Street 171 E6
Ruckinge 183 F8
Rushenden 2 F3
Rye Foreign 196 E1

S

St Dunstan's 66 D1
St Lawrence 52 B8
St Margaret's at Cliffe 151 A6
St Martin's 88 B8
St Mary in the Marsh 194 B4
St Mary's Bay 195 A4
St Michaels 167 B4
St Nicholas at Wade 25 E1
St Peter's 29 E5
St Radigund's 149 A2
St Stephen's 66 F2
Saltwood 176 C4
Sandgate 177 E3
Sandling 53 F1
Sandway 101 A3
Sandwich 73 B1
Sarre 48 D7
Satmar 164 D3
Seasalter 43 A7
Seaton 69 D2
Seed 81 A6
Sellindge 159 D1
Selling 84 C6
Selson 93 A3
Selsted 146 B5
Sevington 157 B6
Shadoxhurst 170 A8
Shalmsford Street 86 B1
Shatterling 70 E1
Sheerness 1 D3
Sheerwater 70 F6
Sheldwich 83 C6
Sheldwich Lees 83 C5
Shelvin 129 C3
Shepherds Hill 84 A4
Shepherdswell
or Sibertswold 130 E5
Shepway 97 D8
Shipland 136 D8
Shirkoak 169 A5
Sholden 116 F5
Shottenden 84 D1
Shuttlesfield 162 A6
Sibertswold
or Shepherdswell 130 E5
Silver Street 57 F5
Singleton 155 E7
Sittingbourne 36 D8
Sixmile 143 D5
Skeete 160 D7
Slade 80 E1
Slutshole 64 A5
Sly Corner 181 F5
Small Hythe 179 C1
Smarden 135 A1
Smeeth 158 C4
Snargate 191 E6
Snipeshill 37 D4
Snowdown 113 A3
Sole Street 125 B7
South Alkham 164 B8
South Ashford 156 A8
South Green 57 A5
South Stour 157 B1
South Street Selling 84 F8
South Street Stockbury 56 C7
South Street Whitstable 44 A7
South Tankerton 21 A1
South Willesborough 156 E6
Stalisfield Green 103 D6
Stanford 160 B1
Stanhope 155 F6
Staple 92 A5
Staplestreet 64 A5
Statenborough 93 C4
Stelling Minnis 126 F2
Stiff Street 57 E7
Stockbury 56 E8
Stocker's Head 103 F1
Stodmarsh 69 B6
Stonebridge Green 119 A4
Stone Cross
Aldington Frith 171 F6
Stone Cross Sandwich 93 E7
Stonehall 147 F8
Stone Hill 159 A2
Stone in Oxney 189 F4
Stonestreet Green 173 A7
Stowting 160 A8
Stowting Common 143 A4
Street End 109 F7
Strood 9 A6
Stubb's Cross 155 C2
Studdal 132 C7
Studd Hill 22 A4
Sturry 67 E6
Summerfield 92 B4
Sutton 133 A7
Swalecliffe 21 E3
Swanton Street 57 F3
Swingfield Minnis 146 B3
Swingfield Street 146 E4

T

Tankerton 21 A3
Temple Ewell 148 D6
Tenterden 179 C8
Teynham 38 C3
Teynham Street 38 E4
Thanington 87 B6
The Brents 40 D1
The Forstal 157 D3
The Leacon 182 D7
The Lees 105 A1
The Quarries 97 C4
The Quarter Headcorn 135 B5
The Quarter Tenterden 179 A4
The Stocks 189 A3
The Valley 103 D8
Throwley 82 E4
Throwley Forstal 82 D1
Thurnham 76 D8
Thurston Park 20 E1
Tickenhurst 92 D1
Tickham 60 D6
Tilmanstone 115 A3
Tonge Corner 37 F7
Tong Green 82 B1
Tovil 74 E1
Tower Hamlets 166 B8
Townland Green 169 A1
Troy Town Brook 141 B5
Troy Town Rochester 9 C5
Tunstall 58 D8
Tutt Hill 121 A1
Twitham 91 E6
Twydall 11 B2
Tyler Hill 66 E6

U

Underdown 108 B8
Upchurch 12 F4
Upper Deal 117 B4
Upper Eythorne 131 C7
Upper Fant 74 D3
Upper Goldstone 71 E5
Upper Harbledown 65 F1
Upper Rodmersham 59 C6
Upper Walmer 117 B1
Upstreet 47 D3
Upton 29 F4
Upton Wood 130 E2

W

Walderslade 31 F1
Walderslade Bottom 32 A2
Walmer 117 C2
Walmestone 70 D3
Waltham 125 E6
Wanden 135 B7
Warden 6 D4
Warehorne 182 D6
Ware Street 76 B5
Warmlake 98 D1
Warren Street 102 D7
Waterham 42 C2
Way 50 E7
Wayfield 32 A8
Weavering Street 75 F5
Weddington 71 E3
Weeds Wood 31 F3
Westbere 68 C7
Westbrook 7 E1
West Cliffe 150 D6
West Dumpton 29 D2
West End Doddington 80 D7
West End Herne Bay 45 B8
Westenhanger 175 B6
Western Heights 166 C6
Westfield Sole 54 C7
Westgate-on-Sea 7 B2
West Hougham 164 F5
West Hythe 175 B1
West Langdon 132 D3
Westmarsh 71 B7
West Minster 3 A7
West Stourmouth 48 D2
West Street Eastry 93 F1
West Street Lenham 79 E1
Westwell 121 E3
Westwell Leacon 120 D4
Westwood Barham 127 E8
Westwood Broadstairs 29 B5
Wetham Green 12 F5
Whatsole Street 142 F5
Wheelbarrow Town 143 F8
Whitehall 29 C1
Whitfield 149 A7
Whitstable 20 C3
Wichling 80 C5
Wickhambreaux 69 B2
Wigmore 33 B4
Wilgate Green 82 F6
Willesborough 156 F8
Willesborough Lees 140 B1
Willington 75 E1
Wingham 91 B7
Wingham Green 90 F7
Wingham Well 90 E6
Wingmore 128 B2
Winterbourne 85 A8
Wissenden 152 F7
Withersdane 140 F8
Wittersham 188 D3
Wolverton 147 F2
Womenswold 112 D2
Woodchurch Margate 27 F3
Woodchurch Tenterden 169 A2
Woodland 160 F8
Woodnesborough 93 C6
Woodside Green 101 F8
Woodstock 58 E6
Woolage Green 129 F8
Woolage Village 112 F1
Wooton 129 C1
Wormshill 79 A7
Worten 137 F3
Worth 94 B4
Wye 123 F1

Y

Yelsted 34 A1
Yorkletts 42 F2

20/20 Ind Est ME16 ...74 C8

A

Abbeville Ho ME1 ...9 C4
Abbey Cl Deal CT14 ...117 A5
Minster (Sheppey) ME12 ...4 D6
Abbey Ct
Westgate-on-S CT8 ...27 D7
Whitstable CT5 ...21 A3
Abbey Fields ME13 ...62 E7
Abbey Fields Ct ME13 ...62 E7
Abbey Gate CT11 ...52 B5
Abbey Gate Cotts ME14 ...53 F2
Abbey Gdns CT2 ...67 A2
Abbey Gr
Minster (Thanet) CT12 ...50 C5
Ramsgate CT11 ...52 B5
Abbey Pl ME13 ...62 D8
Abbey Rd Faversham ME13 .62 D8
Gillingham ME8 ...11 A2
Kearsney CT16 ...148 D4
River CT15,CT17 ...148 D1
Abbey Sch The
Faversham ME13 ...62 C5
Westgate-on-S CT8 ...27 E8
Abbey St ME13 ...62 D8
Abbey Way TN24 ...140 A1
Abbeyview Dr ME12 ...4 B6
Abbot's Hill CT11 ...52 E6
Abbots Barton Wlk CT1 ...88 B7
Abbots Field ME16 ...74 B2
Abbots Hill ME13 ...61 E5
Abbots Pl CT1 ...66 F1
Abbots Rd ME13 ...62 F7
Abbots The CT17 ...166 C8
Abbots Wlk TN25 ...123 E2
Abbotsbury Hts CT2 ...67 B4
Abbott Ct 13 CT20 ...178 E6
Abbott Rd CT20 ...178 E6
Abbott Way TN30 ...179 C7
Abbotts Cl ME1 ...9 B3
Aberdeen Cl CT3 ...47 D3
Aberdeen Ho 9 ME15 ...97 E7
Abigail Cres ME5 ...32 A1
Abingdon Gr CT3 ...47 D3
Abinger Dr ME5 ...32 D2
Absalom Ct ME8 ...11 C2
Acacia Dr CT3 ...68 D8
Acacia Terr ME10 ...36 C4
Academy Dr ME7 ...10 F1
Achilles Rd ME5 ...32 C2
Ackerey Ct TN23 ...155 F6
Ackholt Rd CT3 ...113 A5
Acol Hill CT7 ...27 B4
Acorn Cl Hawkinge CT18 ..163 C4
Kingsnorth TN23 ...156 C3
Acorn Pl ME15 ...97 E6
Acorn Rd ME7 ...10 F4
Acorn St ME12 ...1 D1
Acorn Terr ME9 ...12 E2
Acorn Wharf Rd ME1 ...9 C6
Acre Cl ME1 ...9 E1
Acre Ct CT17 ...166 C8
Acre The CT16 ...148 F8
Acton La TN30 ...188 F4
Acton Rd CT5 ...20 D2
Ada Rd CT1 ...87 D6
Adam Cl ME17 ...96 D3
Adam Ct 1 CT9 ...8 B2
Adams Cl TN30 ...167 B1
Adbert Dr ME15 ...96 B4
Addelam Cl CT14 ...117 A4
Addelam Rd CT14 ...117 A4
Addington Pl CT11 ...52 E6
Addington Rd Margate CT9 ..7 J2
Sittingbourne ME10 ...36 E3
Addington Sq CT9 ...7 J2
Addington St Margate CT9 ..7 J2
Ramsgate CT11 ...52 D6
Addiscombe Gdns CT9 ...7 J1
Addiscombe Rd CT9 ...8 A1
Addison Cotts TN30 ...188 D3
Adelaide Dr ME10 ...36 C4
Adelaide Gdns
Halfway Houses ME12 ...3 E6
10 Ramsgate CT11 ...52 E6
Adelaide Ho Deal CT14 ...117 D6
Sheerness ME12 ...1 I1
Adelaide Pl CT1 ...87 F8
Adelaide Rd
Elvington CT15 ...114 B1
Gillingham ME7 ...10 C4
Aden Terr 1 ME14 ...75 A7
Adie Rd TN28 ...202 D3
Adisham CE Prim Sch
CT3 ...112 D8
Adisham Downs Rd CT3,
CT4 ...90 B2
Adisham Dr ME16 ...74 B7
Adisham Gn ME10 ...36 F8
Adisham Rd
Bekesbourne CT4 ...89 E3
Wingham CT3 ...91 A4
Womenswold CT4,CT3 ...112 C2
Adisham Sta CT3 ...112 E8
Adisham Way CT9 ...8 C1
Admiral Ct ME7 ...10 D6
Admiral's Wlk ME4 ...9 F7
Admirals Wlk
Chatham ME5 ...32 B3
Halfway Houses ME12 ...3 E6
Hythe CT21 ...176 C1
Admirals Wlk *continued*
Tenterden TN30 ...167 C1
Admiralty Cl ME13 ...62 B8
Admiralty Mews CT14 ...117 D4
Admiralty Terr 1 ME7 ...10 A7
Admiralty Wlk CT5 ...43 A7
Adrian Mews CT8 ...7 D1
Adrian Sq CT8 ...7 D1
Adrian St CT17 ...166 D7
Aerodrome Est ME14 ...55 E4
Aerodrome Rd
Bekesbourne CT4 ...89 E3
Hawkinge CT18 ...163 A4
Afghan Rd
Broadstairs CT10 ...29 F8
Chatham ME4 ...9 E4
Agester La CT4 ...129 A4
Agricultural Mus Brook The*
TN25 ...141 B5
Ainsdale Cl CT19 ...178 B7
Ainsley Way CT4 ...108 F8
Aintree Ho 1 ME15 ...97 F6
Aintree Rd ME5 ...32 C3
Airedale Cl CT9 ...8 A1
Aireys The CT13 ...93 B6
Airfield View ME12 ...17 C8
Aisne Dr CT1 ...67 D1
Ajax Rd ME1 ...31 C8
Alamein Ave ME5 ...31 F7
Alamein Cl CT15 ...149 F3
Alaseun Terr ME12 ...4 A5
Albany Dr CT6 ...22 D4
Albany Ho 15 CT17 ...166 D7
Albany Pl CT17 ...166 D7
Albany Rd
Capel-le-F CT18 ...164 C1
Chatham ME4 ...10 B2
Gillingham ME7 ...10 D4
Rochester ME1 ...9 C4
Sittingbourne ME10 ...36 E3
Albany St ME14 ...75 B5
Albany Terr Chatham ME4 ...9 E4
Gillingham ME7 ...10 D4
Albemarle Rd
Ashford TN24 ...139 F1
Chatham ME5 ...32 C2
Albert Costain Ct 1
CT20 ...178 D5
Albert Ct
8 Ramsgate CT12 ...52 E6
9 Whitstable CT5 ...20 D2
Albert La CT21 ...176 C1
Albert Manor ME7 ...10 B5
Albert Pl ME2 ...9 B7
Albert Rd Ashford TN24 ...139 B3
Broadstairs CT10 ...29 E8
Canterbury CT1 ...88 B8
Capel-le-F CT18 ...164 C2
Chatham ME4 ...10 A3
Deal CT14 ...117 C6
Dover CT16 ...149 D1
Folkestone CT19 ...178 D6
Gillingham ME7 ...10 C4
Hythe CT21 ...176 B1
Margate CT9 ...7 H2
Ramsgate CT11 ...52 F7
Rochester ME1 ...9 C3
Albert Reed Gdns ME15 ...74 E2
Albert Row CT11 ...52 C5
Albert St Maidstone ME14 ..74 F6
Ramsgate CT11 ...52 E6
Whitstable CT5 ...20 D2
Albert Terr Deal CT14 ...117 C5
Margate CT9 ...7 I2
Minster (Sheppey) ME12 ...5 A5
Alberta Cl CT16 ...149 B3
Albion Cl CT6 ...46 A8
Albion Ct CT11 ...52 E6
Albion Hill 7 CT11 ...52 E6
Albion La CT6 ...46 A8
Albion Mews CT11 ...52 F6
Albion Mews Rd 3
CT20 ...178 D4
Albion Pl Ashford TN24 ...156 E7
Canterbury CT1 ...67 A1
Faversham ME13 ...62 C7
Hythe CT21 ...176 D2
Maidstone ME14 ...75 B4
Newington ME9 ...35 B6
Ramsgate CT11 ...52 E6
Albion Rd Birchington CT7 ..27 A7
Broadstairs CT10 ...29 F6
Chatham ME5 ...32 B2
Deal CT14 ...117 D8
Eastry CT13 ...93 A2
Folkestone CT19 ...178 D6
Margate CT9 ...8 B3
Ramsgate CT11 ...52 F7
Albion St CT10 ...30 B4
Albion Terr ME10 ...36 E6
Albion Villas 6 CT20 ...178 D4
Albuhera Sq CT1 ...67 D1
Albury Cl ME5 ...32 D2
Alchins Cotts ME17 ...96 E2
Alder Cl ME12 ...3 A8
Alder Ho TN23 ...138 F1
Alder Rd CT19 ...178 C6
Aldergate La CT21 ...174 C1
Alderney Gdns CT10 ...29 E5
Alderney Way TN24 ...139 C7
Aldershot Rd ME5 ...32 A7
Aldington Cl ME5 ...32 B5
Aldington Cnr TN25 ...173 A6
Aldington La ME14 ...76 D8
Aldington Prim Sch
TN25 ...173 A5
Aldington Rd
Lympne CT21 ...174 E3
Aldington Rd *continued*
Maidstone ME14 ...75 F4
Aldon Cl ME14 ...75 C6
Aldon Ct ME14 ...75 C6
Aldred Rd ME13 ...62 C6
Aldridge Cl CT6 ...22 B3
Alec Pemble Cl TN24 ...139 E5
Alefe Way ME9 ...14 D3
Alexander Cl CT13 ...93 F8
Alexander Ct
1 Rochester ME2 ...9 B8
1 Sittingbourne ME10 ...36 E5
Alexander Dr ME13 ...62 B7
Alexandra Ave ME7 ...10 E4
Alexandra Cl ME10 ...36 E7
Alexandra Corniche
CT20,CT21 ...177 C3
Alexandra Ct CT21 ...176 A1
Alexandra Dr CT14 ...116 F3
Alexandra Gdns CT20 ...178 D4
Alexandra Glen ME5 ...32 A1
Alexandra Homes CT9 ...7 I1
Alexandra Hospl The
ME5 ...54 A8
Alexandra Mews ME12 ...1 E2
Alexandra Pl 1 CT17 ...149 C1
Alexandra Rd
Birchington CT7 ...27 A5
Broadstairs CT10 ...30 B4
Capel-le-F CT18 ...164 C2
Chatham ME4 ...10 B2
Deal CT14 ...117 D2
Kingsdown CT14 ...134 C5
Margate CT9 ...28 E8
Ramsgate CT11 ...52 D8
Sheerness ME12 ...1 E2
Whitstable CT5 ...43 C8
Alexandra St
Folkestone CT19 ...178 E6
Maidstone ME14 ...74 F6
Alexandra Terr CT9 ...7 I1
Alexandria Dr CT6 ...22 C5
Alfred Cl Canterbury CT1 ...87 C6
Chatham ME4 ...10 B2
Alfred Mews CT14 ...117 D7
Alfred Rd Ashford TN24 ...156 D7
Birchington CT7 ...26 D8
Canterbury CT1 ...87 C6
Dover CT16 ...149 B2
Greatstone-on-Sea TN28 ..202 D3
Margate CT9 ...8 B1
Alfred Row CT14 ...117 D7
Alfred Sq CT14 ...117 D7
Alicia Ave CT9 ...28 A8
Alison Cl Birchington CT7 ...27 B8
Whitfield CT16 ...149 A6
Alison Cres CT16 ...149 A7
Alkham Cl CT9 ...8 F2
Alkham Rd
Maidstone ME14 ...75 C5
Temple Ewell CT15,CT16 ...148 C4
Alkham Valley Rd
Alkham CT15 ...147 E1
Hawkinge CT18,CT15 ...163 E4
All Saints CE Prim Sch
ME15 ...75 A3
All Saints Ind Est CT9 ...7 I1
All Saints La 2 CT1 ...87 F8
All Saints Rd ME10 ...37 C4
All Saints View ME13 ...41 E2
All Saints' Ave CT9 ...7 H1
All Saints' CE Prim Sch
ME4 ...10 A3
All Saints' Cl CT5 ...20 F1
All Souls' CE Prim Sch
CT19 ...177 E6
Allan Rd CT5 ...42 E6
Alland Grange La CT12 ...27 E2
Allen Ave CT8 ...27 D7
Allen Cl ME5 ...32 C6
Allen Ct ME12 ...4 A5
Allen Field TN23 ...155 F8
Allen St ME14 ...75 B5
Allenby Ave CT14 ...117 B5
Allenby Rd CT12 ...29 C2
Allenby Wlk ME10 ...36 B5
Allendale St 2 CT19 ...178 D6
Alliance Rd CT11 ...52 F6
Allington Prim Sch ME16 .74 C7
Allington Rd ME8 ...11 A3
Allington Way ME16 ...74 B6
Allison Ave ME7 ...10 E1
Allnutt Mill Cl 4 ME15 ...74 E2
Allsworth Cl ME9 ...35 B6
Alma Pl 2 Canterbury CT1 .67 A1
Ramsgate CT11 ...52 E7
Rochester ME2 ...9 A7
Alma Rd Folkestone CT20 .177 D5
Herne Bay CT6 ...23 C5
Margate CT9 ...7 J1
Ramsgate CT11 ...52 E8
Sheerness ME12 ...1 D2
Alma St Canterbury CT1 ...67 A1
Sheerness ME12 ...1 E2
Alma Street Pas ME12 ...1 E2
Almarina CT8 ...7 C1
Almon Pl ME1 ...9 D5
Almond Cl Ashford TN23 ..138 F5
Broadstairs CT10 ...29 C4
Whitstable CT5 ...21 D1
Almond Ct CT4 ...86 E1
Almond Gr ME7 ...33 A4
Almond Ho 9 ME16 ...74 A3
Almond Tree Cl ME12 ...3 A8
Almonds The ME14 ...76 A4
Almshouse Rd ME13 ...104 C7
Almshouses 8 CT1 ...88 A8
Alpha Rd Birchington CT7 ...27 A7
Alpha Rd *continued*
Ramsgate CT11 ...52 D6
Alsager Ave ME11 ...2 F3
Alsops Rd TN24 ...156 E7
Alston Cl ME12 ...4 C7
Altbarn Ind Est ME5 ...54 C8
Alvis Ave CT6 ...22 A4
Amage Rd TN25 ...141 C8
Amage Road Cotts
TN25 ...124 B1
Amanda Cl ME5 ...31 F3
Amber Cl ME9 ...38 D2
Amber Ct ME7 ...10 D5
Amber La ME17 ...98 A1
Amber Rise ME10 ...36 C7
Amber Way ME17 ...98 B1
Ambleside
Faversham ME13 ...62 E6
Sittingbourne ME10 ...37 C3
Ambley Gn ME8 ...33 A8
Ambley Rd ME8 ...33 B8
Ambley Wood Nature
Reserve* ME7,ME8 ...33 A8
Ambrose Hill ME5 ...10 C2
Amels Hill ME9 ...56 F8
Ames Ave ME14 ...76 A4
Amethyst Ave ME5 ...31 E6
Amherst Cl
Maidstone ME16 ...74 D4
Margate CT9 ...8 C1
Amherst Hill ME7 ...10 A6
Amherst Rd ME1 ...9 D3
Amherst Redoubt ME4 ...10 A5
Amies Ho ME15 ...96 F3
Amos Cl Herne Bay CT6 ...23 C3
Sheldwich ME13 ...83 C5
Amsbury Rd ME15,ME17 ...96 B2
Amshurst Villas ME15 ...96 A4
Anatase Cl ME10 ...36 C7
Anchor Bsns Pk ME10 ...37 B6
Anchor Hill 4 CT9 ...7 J2
Anchor Ho ME1 ...9 B4
Anchor La Deal CT14 ...117 C6
Sheerness ME12 ...1 B3
Anchor Rd ME1 ...9 C1
Ancress Cl CT2 ...67 A4
Andover Wlk 12 ME15 ...97 F6
Andrew Broughton Way
ME14 ...75 B4
Andrew Manor ME7 ...10 C6
Andrews Wlk ME10 ...36 B5
Anemone Way CT6 ...45 E7
Anerley Cl ME16 ...74 D7
Angel Cotts ME8 ...12 A2
Anglesey Ave ME15 ...97 A7
Anglesey Cl ME5 ...32 B7
Angus Dr TN24 ...139 C7
Ann's Rd CT11 ...52 E8
Anna Pk CT7 ...26 F8
Anne Boleyn Cl ME12 ...5 E3
Anne Cl CT7 ...27 B7
Anne Green Wlk 8 CT1 ...67 B2
Anne Roper Cl TN28 ...202 E6
Anne's Rd CT10 ...30 C7
Annvera Ho 2 ME7 ...10 C7
Ansell Ave ME4 ...10 A1
Anselm Cl ME10 ...36 E4
Anselm Rd CT17 ...166 A8
Anson Cl Broadstairs CT10 .29 D3
Chatham ME5 ...32 C6
Anstee Rd CT17 ...149 C1
Anthony Cres CT5 ...43 B6
Anthonys Way ME2 ...9 E8
Antolin Way CT10,CT12 ...29 A3
Antonius Ct TN23 ...156 A5
Anvil Cl CT7 ...27 A6
Anzio Cres CT15 ...149 E2
Anzio Ho 15 CT1 ...67 B2
Apartments The TN28 ...202 E5
Apiary Bsns Pk The
ME17 ...99 B3
Apollo Ho ME5 ...32 A6
Apple Cl CT18 ...163 B4
Apple Craft Ctr* ME13 ...62 E5
Appleby Cl ME1 ...31 D7
Appleby Ct TN24 ...139 D2
Applecross Cl ME1 ...9 B4
Appledore Ave ME12 ...3 B8
Appledore Cl CT9 ...8 C1
Appledore Cres CT19 ...177 D7
Appledore Ct ME16 ...74 C7
Appledore Rd
Appledore TN26,TN30 ...190 A7
Brattle TN26 ...181 C7
Gillingham ME8 ...11 A3
Tenterden TN30 ...179 E7
Appledore Sta TN26 ...191 B8
Appledown Way CT1 ...88 D5
Appleford Dr ME12 ...3 F7
Applegarth Pk CT5 ...43 A6
Appletree Ct 5 ME8 ...33 F8
Approach Rd
Broadstairs CT10 ...30 A4
Dover CT17 ...166 A6
Margate CT9 ...8 A2
Shepherdswell CT15 ...130 D5
Approach Rd S TN29 ...209 C2
April Rise Birchington CT7 ..26 D8
Whitstable CT5 ...43 B7
Apsley Cotts CT4 ...86 D3
Apsley St TN23 ...139 B2
Aragon Cl TN23 ...155 E7
Archbishop's Sch The
CT2 ...66 E3
Archcliffe Rd CT17 ...166 C5
Archer Rd Chatham ME5 ...32 B6
Folkestone CT19 ...178 D6
Archer's Court Rd CT15,
CT16 ...149 B7
Archers Court Sch CT16 .149 B5
Archery Sq CT14 ...117 D3
Archibald Ho ME14 ...75 A7
Archway Ct 4 ME2 ...9 B8
Archway Rd
Ramsgate CT11 ...52 E6
Sheerness ME12 ...1 B3
Arcon Cl TN23 ...156 A7
Arcon Rd TN23 ...156 A7
Arden Bsns Pk ME2 ...9 E7
Arden Dr TN24 ...139 C3
Arden Grange CT4 ...107 C8
Arden Jun Sch ME7 ...10 D6
Arden Rd Faversham ME13 .62 E7
Herne Bay CT6 ...23 C2
Arden St ME7 ...10 C6
Ardenlee Dr ME14 ...75 B5
Ardent Ave CT14 ...117 C4
Arethusa Rd ME1 ...31 C8
Argent Rd ME11 ...3 A2
Argent Way ME10 ...36 C6
Argyle Ave CT9 ...7 G1
Argyle Cl ME1 ...31 E8
Argyle Gdns CT9 ...7 G1
Argyle Rd CT5 ...20 D1
Argyll Dr CT11 ...29 F1
Ark Cotts CT18 ...161 D4
Ark La CT14 ...117 D7
Arkley Rd CT6 ...22 F4
Arklow Sq 6 CT11 ...52 F7
Arlington TN23 ...155 F8
Arlington Gdns CT9 ...29 C8
Arlington Ho CT9 ...7 H2
Arlington Sq CT9 ...7 H2
Arlott Cl ME14 ...74 F6
Armada Cl TN28 ...202 E5
Armada Ct ME4 ...9 E1
Armada Way ME4 ...9 F3
Armadale CT10 ...8 F1
Armourers Wlk CT16 ...149 A3
Armstrong Rd ME15 ...75 A1
Armstrong Sq CT6 ...22 A3
Arnhem Dr ME5 ...31 F7
Arnold Rd Chartham CT4 ...86 C2
5 Margate CT9 ...7 J1
Arnolde Cl ME2 ...9 E7
Arolla Rd CT6 ...23 C4
Arran Mews 4 CT1 ...67 B2
Arran Rd ME15 ...97 A6
Arrowhead La TN26,
TN29 ...191 D7
Arthur Kennedy Cl ME13 ..63 F3
Arthur Rd Birchington CT7 ..26 D8
Deal CT14 ...117 A3
Gillingham ME8 ...33 E7
Hythe CT21 ...176 C1
Margate CT9 ...8 A3
Rochester ME1 ...9 D3
Arthur Salmon Cl ME13 ...62 B7
Arthur St
3 Folkestone CT19 ...178 E6
Sittingbourne ME10 ...36 E4
Artillery Gdns 12 CT1 ...67 A1
Artillery Ho 13 CT1 ...67 A1
Artillery Rd CT11 ...52 F7
Artillery St 11 CT1 ...67 A1
Arundel Ave ME10 ...36 E1
Arundel Cl ME5 ...32 D1
Arundel Rd Cliffs End CT12 .51 D7
Margate CT9 ...8 B2
Arundel St ME14 ...74 F6
Ascot Cl ME5 ...32 C2
Ascot Gdns CT8 ...27 E7
Ascot Ho 2 ME15 ...97 F6
Ash Cl Ashford TN23 ...138 E3
Broadstairs CT10 ...29 C4
Chatham ME5 ...10 C1
Crabble CT17 ...148 E3
Gillingham ME8 ...11 B3
Herne Bay CT6 ...22 F1
Ash Cres CT3 ...46 E1
Ash Ct CT12 ...51 D4
Ash Gr Elvington CT15 ...114 B2
Lydd TN29 ...205 D7
Maidstone ME16 ...74 C6
Ash Mdws TN24 ...156 F7
Ash Rd Aylesham CT3 ...112 E5
Sandwich CT13 ...72 E2
Ash Tree Cl
Birchington CT7 ...27 B7
St Mary's Bay TN29 ...194 F3
Ash Tree La ME5 ...10 D1
Ash Tree Rd 6 CT19 ...178 E6
Ashbank Cotts ME17 ...99 B7
Ashbee Gdns CT6 ...23 C5
Ashborne Cl TN24 ...139 D6
Ashburn Gdns CT6 ...23 C5
Ashburn Mews ME7 ...10 E3
Ashburnham Rd
Maidstone ME14 ...75 B8
Ramsgate CT11 ...52 C7
Ashburton Cl TN24 ...139 E2
Ashdale Ho TN23 ...139 C2
Ashdown Cl
Herne Bay CT6 ...23 B2
Maidstone ME16 ...74 D3
Ashdown Cres TN28 ...202 B6
Ashdown Ct TN24 ...139 C3
Ashdown Field CT4 ...86 B2
Ashdown Lodge CT20 ...178 A5
Ashdown Rd ME17,ME9 ...79 F3
Ashen Tree Cotts CT3 ...70 B1
Ashen Tree La CT16 ...166 E8
Ashenden Cl CT1 ...87 C5
Ashendene Gr CT2 ...68 A6
Ashentree La TN29 ...200 A5

Ash – Bee 213

Ashford Borough Mus★ TN23 139 B2
Ashford Bsns Pk TN24 157 A6
Ashford Bsns Point TN24 156 F5
Ashford Designer Outlet TN24 156 C7
Ashford Dr ME17 99 D3
Ashford Hospl TN23 139 A3
Ashford Int Sta TN24 139 C1
Ashford Rd Ashford TN23 155 B8
Bethersden TN26,TN23 153 C4
Charing TN27 120 C7
Chartham CT4,CT1 86 C3
Folkestone CT18,CT19 177 B7
Godmersham CT4 107 C4
Hamstreet TN26 170 F1
Harrietsham ME17 100 C6
Kingsnorth TN23,TN26 156 A4
Maidstone ME14 76 D3
Maidstone,Grove Green ME14 75 D4
New Romney TN28 202 A6
Sellindge TN25 159 B1
Sheldwich ME13 83 C4
Tenterden TN30 179 B8
Tenterden,High Halden TN26,TN30 167 A6
Westenhanger CT21,TN25, CT18 175 C6
Ashford Sch TN23 139 C2
Ashford South Com Prim Sch TN23 156 A8
Ashford Sta TN24 139 C1
Ashgrove TN23 138 F5
Ashington Cl ME10 36 C5
Ashley Ave CT19 177 E6
Ashley Cl
Halfway Houses ME12 3 C5
Ramsgate CT12 29 B2
Ashley Dr CT5 43 A7
Ashley Ho CT19 177 E6
Ashley Mill Cotts CT19 177 E7
Ashley Rd ME8 11 C2
Ashmead Cl ME5 32 C3
Ashmill Bsns Pk ME17 101 F6
Ashtead Dr ME9 37 D2
Ashton Cl CT14 116 D4
Ashton Ct 4 CT10 29 E5
Ashton Ho CT14 117 B1
Ashton Mews 21 CT10 30 B4
Ashtree Ho ME10 37 B3
Ashtrees CT6 23 B3
Ashurst Ave CT5 43 C6
Ashurst Gdns CT9 8 E3
Ashurst Rd ME14 75 C5
Askes Ct TN23 155 D8
Aspen Cl TN29 194 F3
Aspen Dr TN23 138 D3
Aspen Ho 5 CT20 178 D4
Aspen Rd Chartham CT4 86 E1
Herne CT6 45 E7
Aspen Way 2 ME5 31 E4
Aspian Dr ME17 96 D3
Aspinall Cl CT4 89 B4
Asquith Rd ME8 33 C6
Association Wlk ME1 31 C7
Astley Ave CT16 149 C2
Astley Ct CT16 149 C2
Astley St ME14 75 A4
Aston Cl ME5 32 A2
Aston Pl CT10 29 E6
Astor Ave CT17 166 B8
Astor Coll for the Arts CT17 166 A8
Astor Dr CT14 117 C5
Astor of Hever Com Sch The ME16 74 C3
Astor Rd CT10 29 F8
Astrid Rd CT14 117 A2
Athelstan Gn ME17 77 C2
Athelstan Pl CT14 117 C8
Athelstan Rd
Canterbury CT1 87 C5
Chatham ME4 9 F2
Faversham ME13 62 C6
Folkestone CT19 178 D7
Margate CT9 8 A3
Athena Ct CT9 8 A3
Athol Pl ME13 62 A8
Athol Rd Ashford TN23 155 F7
Whitstable CT5 20 F2
Athol Terr CT16 166 F8
Atkinson Wlk TN24 139 F5
Atlanta Ct ME4 9 D3
Attlee Ave CT3 112 E5
Attlee Way ME10 36 E8
Atwater Ct ME17 101 D5
Aubretia Wlk ME10 37 A3
Auckland Ave CT12 52 A8
Auckland Cres CT16 149 C3
Auckland Dr ME10 36 C3
Auckland Ho 10 ME15 97 E5
Audley Ave
Gillingham ME7 10 E1
Margate CT9 7 E1
Audley Cl ME16 74 B5
Audley Rd CT20 177 F5
Auger Cl ME9 34 E5
Augusta Cl 1 ME7 10 C7
Augusta Gdns CT20 178 C4
Augusta Pl 14 CT11 52 F7
Augusta Rd CT11 52 F7
Augustine Rd
Minster (Sheppey) ME12 4 B8
Minster (Thanet) CT12 50 B6
Augustus Wlk TN23 155 F5
Aurellus Cl TN23 156 A4
Austell Manor 5 ME7 10 C6
Austens Orch 14 TN30 179 A7
Austin Ave CT6 21 F4
Austin Cl Gillingham ME5 10 E2
Sittingbourne ME10 37 A8
Austin Rd TN23 156 B6
Austins La 4 CT13 73 A1
Autumn Glade ME5 54 D8
Avebury Ave CT11 52 G8
Aveling Ct 2 ME2 9 B7
Avent Wlk ME9 37 E2
Avenue Gdns CT9 8 C3
Avenue of Remembrance ME10 36 F3
Avenue Rd Dover CT16 149 C1
Herne Bay CT6 22 E5
Ramsgate CT11 52 F7
Avenue The Deal CT14 117 C7
Hersden CT3 46 E1
Hythe CT21 176 C2
Kingsdown CT14 134 D4
Margate CT9 8 A1
St Margaret's at Cliffe CT15 150 F6
Temple Ewell CT16 148 E5
Averenches Rd ME14 75 F5
Avereng Gdns CT19 178 B6
Avereng Rd CT19 178 B6
Avery Cl ME15 74 F1
Avery La ME15, ME17 98 D6
Aviation Ct ME12 5 E3
Aviemore Gdns ME14 75 F4
Avington Cl ME15 74 F1
Avocet Wlk ME5 32 D2
Avon Cl CT1 88 C8
Avon Ho 13 CT20 178 C4
Avondale Cl CT5 44 A8
Avondale Ct ME14 75 E5
Avondale Rd
Capel-le-F CT18 164 C2
Gillingham ME7 10 D5
Axford Ct ME8 34 A8
Aycliffe Com Prim Sch CT17 166 A4
Aylesbury Rd TN25 139 B7
Aylesford Cres ME8 11 B4
Aylesford Pl TN24 156 E7
Aylesham & District Com Workshop Trust CT3 113 A5
Aylesham Cnr CT3 112 D3
Aylesham Ind Est CT3 112 E4
Aylesham Prim Sch CT3 112 E5
Aylesham Rd CT15,CT3 113 A4
Aylesham Sta CT3 113 A6
Aylewyn Gn ME10 36 F8
Aynsley Ct 1 CT13 73 A1
Ayrshire Cl TN24 139 C7
Ayton Rd CT11 52 C6

B

Babs Oak Hill CT2 68 B7
Back La
6 Faversham ME13 62 D7
Maidstone ME17 97 E1
Minster (Sheppey) ME12 4 D6
Back Rd W CT16 166 G8
Back St Leeds ME17 98 E6
Ringwould CT14 133 F5
Backfields ME1 9 B4
Bad Munstereifel Rd TN23,TN24 156 D5
Baddlesmere Rd CT5 21 A2
Baden Rd ME7 10 D7
Bader Cres ME5 32 A7
Badger Rd ME5 32 C1
Badger's Hill Open Farm★ CT4 107 C8
Badgers Bridge CT18 161 D4
Badgers Cl CT2 66 A7
Badgers Oak TN23 155 D8
Badgers Rise Deal CT14 134 C8
Kearsney CT17 148 D3
Badlesmere Cl TN23 155 E6
Baffin Cl ME4 9 F2
Bagham La CT4 107 D8
Bagham Rd CT4 107 C8
Bagshill Rd ME13 83 A3
Bailey Dr ME7 11 A1
Bailey Fields TN26 153 E4
Baileys Field TN23 138 F1
Baird's Hill CT10 29 F6
Bairdsley Cl CT10 29 F6
Bakenham Ho 1 ME1 9 C1
Baker Cl ME9 38 C2
Baker Rd CT19 177 E6
Baker St ME1 9 C3
Baker's La CT4 86 D2
Baker's Wlk ME1 9 C6
Bakers Cl CT2 87 C7
Bakers Ct CT11 52 E7
Bakery Cotts ME14 53 E3
Bakery The ME9 58 A6
Balas Dr ME10 36 C7
Balcomb Cres CT9 29 C8
Baldric Rd CT20 177 F5
Baldwin Rd
Greatstone-on-Sea TN28 202 D1
Minster (Sheppey) ME12 4 D7
Baldwin Terr CT19 178 D6
Balfour Ct CT20 178 B3
Balfour Inf Sch ME1 9 E1
Balfour Jun Sch ME4 9 E2
Balfour Rd Chatham ME4 9 E2
Deal CT14 117 C2
Dover CT16 149 C1
Baliol Rd CT5 20 E2
Ball La TN24 139 F7
Ballard Ind Est ME5 54 C8
Ballard Rd TN28 202 D1
Ballens Rd ME5 32 C3
Balliemoor Ct CT11 29 F1
Balliol Rd CT10 29 F8
Balmer Cl ME8 33 D7
Balmoral Ho 10 ME15 97 F5
Balmoral Pl 12 CT11 52 F7
Balmoral Rd
Gillingham ME7 10 D5
Kingsdown CT14 134 C6
4 Margate CT9 28 B8
Balmoral Terr ME10 36 D4
Bamford Way CT14 117 C4
Bank Cotts ME17 77 E3
Bank Ho
New Romney TN28 202 C6
Sheerness ME12 1 D2
Bank Rd TN25 172 E8
Bank Side TN26 183 A8
Bank St Ashford TN23 139 B2
Chatham ME4 10 B3
Faversham ME13 62 C7
Herne Bay CT6 22 F5
Hythe CT21 176 C2
Maidstone ME14 75 A4
Bank View 5 ME15 74 E2
Banks Rd Ashford TN23 156 A7
Rochester ME2 9 C8
Banks The CT10 29 F6
Bankside Canterbury CT1 88 D7
Chatham ME5 32 B8
Banky Fields Cl ME8 12 B1
Banner Way ME12 3 E6
Banning St ME2 9 B8
Banningbrook Ct CT14 117 D4
Bannister Hill ME9 36 B2
Bannister Hos TN26 120 A1
Bannister Rd ME14 75 A7
Bapchild & Tonge CE Prim Sch ME9 37 D3
Barbados Terr 2 ME14 75 A7
Barber's Almshouses 11 CT11 52 D6
Barberry Ave ME5 31 E5
Barcham Ct ME15 96 F5
Barclay Ct CT8 7 C1
Bardell Terr ME1 9 D5
Barden Ct ME14 75 B5
Barfleur Manor 3 ME7 10 A6
Barfreston Cl ME15 74 F2
Barfrestone Rd CT15 114 A1
Bargates TN23 155 E6
Barges The CT5 20 E3
Bargrove CT18 176 E6
Bargrove Rd ME14 75 C5
Barham CE Prim Sch CT4 128 F8
Barham Cl ME15 97 E5
Barham's Mill Rd TN27 118 B3
Barker Rd ME16 74 F3
Barkers Ct ME10 36 D4
Barkis Cl ME1 31 D7
Barler Pl ME11 3 A5
Barley Cl Herne Bay CT6 23 D2
Martin Mill CT15 133 C2
Barley Fields ME14 75 D4
Barley Way TN23 155 E5
Barleycorn Dr ME8 33 E6
Barleymow Cl ME5 32 C7
Barling Cl ME5 31 D1
Barlow Cl ME8 33 E5
Barn Cl Borden ME9 36 A2
Hoath CT3 46 E5
Yorkletts CT5 43 A3
Barn Cres CT9 7 F1
Barn Platt TN23 156 A8
Barn The ME9 36 A2
Barn Tye Cl CT15 149 E6
Barnaby Terr ME1 9 D2
Barnard Ct ME4 10 A2
Barnberry Cl TN23 155 E8
Barncroft Cl ME14 75 F4
Barncroft Dr ME7 32 F4
Barnes Ave CT9 7 F1
Barnes Cl ME13 62 B8
Barnes Ct CT1 87 D6
Barnesende Ct CT13 94 A8
Barnet's La CT2 67 D8
Barnett Ct
Minster (Thanet) CT12 50 C5
Ramsgate CT12 29 B1
Barnett Field TN23 155 F8
Barnfield Chatham ME5 32 A8
Herne Bay CT6 22 C2
Tenterden TN30 167 C2
Barnfield Rd
Faversham ME13 62 C8
Folkestone CT19 178 C7
Barnhouse La TN29 200 A8
Barnhurst La CT18 163 A5
Barnhurst Rd ME14 75 A8
Barnsley Cl ME12 1 F2
Barnsole Inf Sch ME7 10 E4
Barnsole Jun Sch ME7 10 E4
Barnsole Rd
Gillingham ME7 10 E3
Staple CT3 92 B5
Barnwell Pl ME7 10 C5
Barnwood Cl ME1 31 B8
Baron Cl Gillingham ME7 10 E7
Maidstone ME14 75 F5
Barrack Hill CT21 176 A2
Barrack Rd ME4 10 B8
Barrey Rd TN24 157 A6
Barrier Rd ME4 9 F5
Barrington Cl ME5 31 F5
Barrington Cres CT7 27 B7
Barrow Gr ME10 36 D3
Barrow Grove Jun Sch ME10 36 D3
Barrow Hill
Ashford TN23 139 B2
Barrowhill TN25 174 D7
Barrow Hill Cotts TN23 139 A2
Barrow Hill Pl 2 TN23 139 B3
Barrow Hill Rise TN25 174 D7
Barrow Hill Terr 1 TN23 139 B3
Barrowfields ME5 32 D1
Barrows Cl CT7 27 A6
Bartholomew Cl CT21 176 B3
Bartholomew La CT21 176 B3
Bartholomew St
6 Dover CT16 149 C1
Hythe CT21 176 B2
Bartlett Cl ME5 32 C1
Bartlett Dr CT5 21 A1
Bartletts Cl ME12 3 C5
Barton Bsns Pk CT1 88 D6
Barton Court Gram Sch CT1 88 B8
Barton Ct 4 CT11 52 E7
Barton Field CT18 161 B7
Barton Hill Dr ME12 4 A5
Barton Jun Sch CT16 149 C2
Barton Mill Ct 2 CT2 66 F1
Barton Mill Rd CT1 67 B2
Barton Rd Canterbury CT1 88 C6
Dover CT16 149 C2
Maidstone ME15 75 A2
Rochester ME2 9 A7
Barton View Terr 2 CT17 149 C1
Barton's Point Coastal Pk★ ME12 1 G2
Barville Rd CT15 114 E2
Barwick Rd CT17 148 F1
Bashford Barn La ME9 58 A4
Basil Terr 6 ME15 75 A1
Basing Cl ME15 75 B3
Baskerville TN24 139 B3
Basmere Cl ME14 75 C6
Basser Hill ME9 13 E3
Bassett Cl CT21 176 E4
Bassett Gdns CT21 176 D4
Bassett Rd ME10 36 D4
Bastion Rd CT17 166 C6
Batchelor St ME4 10 A4
Bateman Cnr TN26 153 E6
Bates Cl CT3 91 F6
Bath Ct 8 CT20 178 B3
Bath Hard ME1 9 D5
Bath Mews TN24 156 E6
Bath Pl CT9 7 J2
Bath Rd Ashford TN24 156 E6
Margate CT9 7 J2
Bathurst Cl CT12 29 B1
Bathurst Rd CT20 178 A5
Batteries Cl ME9 60 B8
Batteries Terr ME9 60 B8
Battery Point CT21 177 B2
Battery Rd TN29 209 D6
Battle of Britain Homes 17 CT17 166 D7
Battle of Britain Meml The★ CT18 164 A1
Bawden Cl CT2 67 A4
Baxendale Ct TN24 156 D7
Bay Banks ME13 61 E2
Bay Cotts CT15 151 C6
Bay Hill CT15 151 B6
Bay Hill Cl CT15 151 A5
Bay Mus The★ CT15 151 B5
Bay View Gdns ME12 6 D2
Bay View Hts CT7 26 D8
Bay View Rd CT10 30 A2
Baye La CT3 69 D1
Bayfield ME13 61 E2
Bayford Rd ME10 37 A4
Bayle Ct CT20 178 E4
Bayle St 19 CT20 178 E5
Bayle The CT20 178 E4
Bayswater Dr ME8 33 E4
Bayview Rd
Kingsdown CT14 134 C4
Whitstable CT5 43 D7
Beach Alley 15 CT5 20 D2
Beach App ME12 6 E3
Beach Ave CT7 26 F8
Beach Bank Cvn Pk CT21 187 C7
Beach Ct Deal CT14 117 D2
Westgate-on-S CT8 7 D1
Beach Flats 2 CT21 176 B2
Beach Hos CT9 7 G2
Beach House Mews CT8 7 D1
Beach Marine 7 CT20 177 F3
Beach Rd
Dymchurch TN29 187 A4
St Margaret's at Cliffe CT15 151 B5
Westgate-on-S CT8 7 D1
Beach Rise CT8 7 D1
Beach St Deal CT14 117 D6
Folkestone CT20 178 E4
Herne Bay CT6 22 F5
Sheerness ME12 1 C2
Beach Terr ME12 1 C2
Beach The CT14 117 D3
Beach Wlk CT5 20 E3
Beachborough Rd CT19, CT20 178 A5
Beachfield Lodge ME12 1 D2
Beachmont Cl TN28 206 E8
Beacon Ave CT6 23 B5
Beacon Cl ME8 33 D7
Beacon Hill
Gillingham ME5 10 D2
Herne Bay CT6 23 B5
Beacon La CT13 93 A6
Beacon Oak Rd TN30 179 B8
Beacon Rd
Broadstairs CT10 29 F7
Chatham ME5 10 C2
Herne Bay CT6 23 A5
Lenham ME17 101 C5
Beacon Terr CT21 177 B2
Beacon Way CT21 174 F3
Beacon Wlk
Herne Bay CT6 23 A5
Tenterden TN30 167 B1
Beacons The ME17 96 C2
Beaconsfield CT5 42 F6
Beaconsfield Ave
Dover CT16 149 C1
Gillingham ME7 10 E5
Beaconsfield Gdns CT10 29 F5
Beaconsfield Rd
Canterbury CT2 66 F2
Chatham ME4 9 F3
Deal CT14 117 D5
Dover CT16 149 C1
Maidstone ME15 74 E2
Sittingbourne ME10 37 C4
Beamont Cl CT12 27 F2
Beams The ME15 75 F1
Bean Cl TN23 138 C1
Beaney's La CT4 84 C1
Beaney's La Cotts CT4 84 C1
Bear's La TN23,TN26 137 E3
Bears End Ho TN23 156 B8
Bearsted Cl ME8 11 B3
Bearsted Green Bsns Ctr ME14 76 C4
Bearsted Rd ME14 75 E6
Bearsted Sta ME14 76 B5
Beatrice Hills Cl TN24 139 E5
Beatrice Mews TN28 206 E7
Beatrice Rd
Capel-le-F CT18 164 C2
Margate CT9 28 E8
Beatty Ave ME7 10 F4
Beatty Cl CT19 178 E8
Beatty Rd
Folkestone CT19 178 D8
Rochester ME1 31 D8
Beauchamp Ave CT14 117 A3
Beauchamp Cl TN24 139 E5
Beauchamps La CT15 113 D5
Beaufort Ave CT12 52 B8
Beaufort Ct ME2 9 E6
Beaufort Wlk ME15 97 E4
Beaufoy Rd CT17 149 A1
Beaufoy Terr CT17 148 F1
Beauherne Com Sch CT2 87 D8
Beaulieu Rise ME1 9 D1
Beaulieu Wlk ME16 74 C7
Beaumanor CT6 23 A3
Beaumont Davy Cl ME13 62 C5
Beaumont Rd ME16 74 B2
Beaumont St CT6 22 C4
Beaumont Terr ME13 62 D6
Beauvoir Dr ME10 37 A8
Beauworth Pk ME15 97 E8
Beauxfield CT16 149 A7
Beaver Ct TN23 156 A7
Beaver Green Inf Sch TN23 155 E7
Beaver Ind Est TN23 156 B7
Beaver La Ashford TN23 138 E1
Ashford,Beaver TN23 156 A7
Ashford,Singleton TN23 155 F7
Beaver Rd Ashford TN23 156 B8
Maidstone ME16 74 B7
Beazley Ct TN24 156 D7
Beckenham Dr ME16 74 D7
Becket Ave CT2 66 D1
Becket Cl Ash CT3 71 D2
Deal CT14 117 C8
Whitstable CT5 21 B1
Becket Mews CT2 66 F1
Becket's Cl TN25 142 B6
Beckett St 4 ME13 62 C7
Becketts Terr CT21 176 B4
Becketts Wood CT3 47 E3
Beckley Mews ME5 31 F5
Beckley Pl TN25 175 B8
Beckley Rd ME12 1 F2
Becksbourne Cl ME14 75 A8
Beckwith Gn CT20 177 E5
Beckworth Pl ME16 74 B2
Beddow Way ME20 53 B3
Bede Ho CT14 117 D8
Bedford Ave ME8 11 D1
Bedford Ct CT10 30 B6
Bedford Pl ME16 74 E4
Bedford Sq CT12 29 B2
Bedford Way CT7 25 F1
Bedgebury Cl
Maidstone ME14 75 C6
Rochester ME1 31 D8
Bedingfield Way CT18 161 B7
Bedlam Court La CT12 50 C6
Bedlam La TN27 135 A8
Bedmonton La ME9 58 B2
Bedson Wlk ME8 12 B1
Bedwin Cl ME1 31 D7
Beech Ave CT4 86 E1
Beech Cl Faversham ME13 62 B7

Beech Cl continued
Folkestone CT19 178 C6
Beech Court Gdns★
TN25 104 F1
Beech Ct CT1 88 A7
Beech Dr Broadstairs CT10 29 D4
Elvington CT15 114 B2
Hothfield TN26 138 A7
Maidstone ME16 74 C5
Beech Gr CT12 51 C5
Beech Green Cl CT15 131 C7
Beech Hill CT4 111 B8
Beech Hurst Cl ME15 75 B2
Beechcroft CT5 21 D1
Beechcroft Gdns CT11 52 F8
Beechen Bank Rd ME5 32 A1
Beeches The
Chatham ME5 32 A4
Lydd TN29 205 D7
Beeching Rd ME5 32 B3
Beechings Gn ME8 11 C3
Beechings Way ME8 11 C3
Beechings Way Ind Ctr
ME8 11 B4
Beechmore Dr ME5 32 A2
Beecholme Dr TN24 139 C5
Beechwood Ave
Deal CT14 117 C5
Gillingham ME5 10 D2
Sittingbourne ME10 36 E6
Beechwood Cl
St Mary's Bay TN29 194 F3
Whitfield CT16 132 A1
Beechwood Ct
Deal CT14 117 C5
Temple Ewell CT16 148 E4
Beecroft Cl CT2 67 A4
Beer Cart La CT1 87 F8
Beggars Cnr CT3 48 D1
Beggarsbush La TN29 200 D7
Begonia Ave ME8 11 C2
Beke Rd ME8 33 D4
Bekesbourne Hill CT4 89 B5
Bekesbourne La
Bekesbourne CT3,CT4 89 E6
Canterbury CT3 88 F7
Littlebourne CT3 89 F6
Bekesbourne Rd CT4 88 F2
Bekesbourne Sta CT4 89 B5
Belcaire Cl CT21 175 A3
Belfast Ho 14 ME15 97 E7
Belgrave Cl CT11 52 D7
Belgrave Ct CT14 117 D3
Belgrave Rd Dover CT17 166 B7
Halfway Houses ME12 3 C5
Margate CT9 7 I2
Belinda Ct CT19 178 B7
Bell Chapel Cl TN23 156 C4
Bell Cnr TN29 201 A4
Bell Cotts ME9 13 B3
Bell Cres ME1 53 A8
Bell Farm La ME12 5 A6
Bell Gr CT3 113 A5
Bell La Burham ME1 53 A8
Chatham ME14 54 B7
Maidstone ME14 76 A5
Sandwich CT13 73 A1
Bell Mdw ME15 97 E6
Bell Rd Maidstone ME15 97 E5
Sittingbourne ME10 36 F3
Bell Sh Ctr ME10 36 F4
Bell Way ME17 99 E2
Bell Wood Prim Sch
ME15 97 E5
Bell's Cl TN30 179 A7
Bell-Davies Dr CT12 28 A1
Belle Friday Cl ME9 38 C2
Belle Vue Rd CT6 23 B5
Bellevue Ave CT11 52 F7
Bellevue Rd
Minster (Sheppey) ME12 4 C6
Ramsgate CT11 52 F7
Whitstable CT5 43 F8
Bellevue St 5 CT20 178 D5
Bellflower Ave ME12 4 A4
Bellgrove Ct ME5 54 A8
Bells La 9 TN30 179 A7
Belmont CT14 117 B1
Belmont Ct
9 Maidstone ME15 75 B4
2 Ramsgate CT11 52 D7
Belmont Farm Bsns Ctr
TN26 137 A1
Belmont House & Gdns★
ME13 82 D5
Belmont Pl TN24 156 D7
Belmont Rd
Ashford TN24 139 D6
Broadstairs CT10 30 A4
Faversham ME13 62 C6
Gillingham ME7 10 C4
Halfway Houses ME12 3 E6
Margate CT9 8 C1
Ramsgate CT11 52 D7
Sittingbourne ME10 36 E3
Westgate-on-S CT8 27 F8
Whitstable CT5 20 D1
Belmont St CT11 52 E7
Belmont Terr CT13 93 B3
Belmont Yd 8 CT5 20 D1
Belmore Pk TN24 139 B3
Belnor Ave ME9 13 F1
Belsey La CT15 147 D4
Belting Dr CT6 23 E5
Beltinge Rd CT6 23 B5
Belton Cl CT5 43 E8
Belvedere Cl ME13 62 D8
Belvedere Ho 9 ME15 97 F5
Belvedere Rd
Broadstairs CT10 30 B4
Faversham ME13 62 D8
Benacre Rd CT5 43 D6
Bench Hill TN26 181 D5
Bench St 19 CT16 166 D7
Bendon Way ME8 33 D8
Benenden Manor ME8 11 B3
Bengal Rd CT12 29 A1
Benham Bsns Pk CT21 174 F5
Bennells Ave CT5 21 B3
Bennett Ct 16 CT20 178 E5
Bennetts Cotts ME7 55 A8
Bennetts Gdns ME13 61 D8
Bennetts Mews 13 TN30 179 A7
Benson Cl CT18 162 F4
Benson La CT18 162 F4
Bensted TN23 155 F5
Bensted Gr ME13 62 A7
Benstede Cl CT6 23 A1
Bentham Sq ME12 1 B3
Bentley Ave CT6 22 B4
Bentley Cl ME5 32 D2
Bentley Rd TN24 156 F7
Bentlif Cl ME16 74 D5
Berber Rd ME2 9 B8
Berengrave La ME8 11 F2
Berengrave Nature Reserve★
ME8 12 A3
Beresford Ave ME1 9 E2
Beresford Ct 7 CT7 26 F8
Beresford Gap CT7 26 F8
Beresford Gdns CT9 8 C3
Beresford Rd
Gillingham ME7 10 D4
Kit's Coty ME20 53 D7
Ramsgate CT11 52 D6
River CT17 148 E3
St Margaret's at Cliffe
CT15 133 F1
Whitstable CT5 20 D1
Beresfords Hill ME17 97 B4
Bergland Pk ME2 9 D8
Berkeley Cl
Boughton Street ME13 64 B3
2 Folkestone CT19 178 A7
Rochester ME1 31 D8
Berkeley Ct ME10 36 D3
Berkeley Mount 8 ME4 9 F4
Berkeley Rd CT7 26 F8
Berkshire Cl ME5 32 C8
Bernard Sunley Hall
TN25 124 A2
Bernards Gdns CT15 130 E5
Berridge Rd ME12 1 D2
Berries The CT18 163 B5
Berry St ME10 36 F4
Berwick La CT21 175 A3
Berwyn Gr ME15 97 A6
Best La CT1 87 F8
Best St ME4 9 F4
Bethany Cl CT14 117 C8
Bethel Row ME13 82 F1
Bethersden Bsns Ctr
TN26 153 C1
Bethersden Ct ME15 97 F7
Bethersden Cty Prim Sch
TN26 153 D5
Bethersden Rd
Hothfield TN26 137 D4
Shadoxhurst TN26 154 E2
Smarden TN27,TN26 152 C5
Woodchurch TN26 169 A6
Betony Gdns ME14 75 F5
Betsham Rd ME15 97 F6
Bettescombe Rd ME8 33 E7
Betty Shelvey Ct CT14 117 D4
Beult Mdw TN27 135 A1
Bevan Way CT3 112 E5
Beverley Cl ME8 33 F8
Beverley Gdns TN29 187 A4
Beverley Ho CT2 66 F2
Beverley Holiday Camp
ME12 6 A5
Beverley Rd
Canterbury CT2 66 E2
Maidstone ME16 74 A2
Beverley Way CT12 29 C1
Beverly Cl CT7 27 B8
Bewsbury Cres CT16 148 F7
Bewsbury Cross La
CT16 148 F7
Bexley St CT5 20 D2
Bexon La ME9 58 C4
Bglws The TN30 179 D7
Bhutan Rd CT6 23 C4
Bicknor Cl CT2 67 B4
Bicknor Court Cotts ME9 57 C2
Bicknor La ME9 57 D3
Bicknor Rd ME15 97 F4
Biddenden Cl
Maidstone ME15 75 F3
Margate CT9 8 C1
Biddenden Rd TN26,
TN26 167 A6
Bierce Ct CT7 26 F7
Bierce Ct Cotts CT7 26 F7
Bifrons Gdns CT4 89 B3
Bifrons Hill CT4 89 B4
Bifrons Rd CT4 89 B4
Bigbury Rd CT2,CT4 86 E7
Biggin St CT16 166 D8
Biggins Wood Rd CT19 177 E7
Bigglestone Link 11 CT1 88 A8
Bilberry Cl ME14 75 E5
Bill Street Rd 1 ME2 9 C8
Billington Gdns TN24 139 E6
Bilsington Cl ME5 32 B5
Bilsington Cross TN25 172 C2
Bimbury La ME14,ME9 56 A5
Bindon Blood Rd CT16 149 A5
Bingley Rd 1 ME1 9 E4
Binland Gr ME5 31 D5
Binnacle Rd ME1 31 C8
Binnie Cl CT10 29 F2
Birch Cl Ashford TN24 139 F2
Broadstairs CT10 29 C3
Birch Ct Barham CT4 128 F8
Ramsgate CT11 52 D8
Birch Dr ME5 32 D1
Birch Gr ME7 33 A4
Birch Hill Ct CT7 27 B7
Birch Ho
6 Maidstone ME16 74 A3
Sheerness ME12 1 C2
Sittingbourne ME10 37 B3
Birch Rd CT5 44 A8
Birch Tree Way ME15 75 B3
Birches The CT7 27 B7
Birchett TN23 138 E1
Birchett La TN26 170 D3
Birchfield Cl ME15 97 B6
Birchfields ME5 32 A3
Birchington CE Prim Sch
CT7 27 A6
Birchington Cl ME14 75 C5
Birchington-On-Sea Sta
CT7 26 F7
Bircholt Forstal TN25 158 E7
Bircholt Rd ME15 97 F4
Birchwood Rd ME16 74 C5
Birchwood Rise CT17 166 C7
Birchwood Wlk CT2 66 E2
Birds Ave CT9 28 B7
Birdwood Ave CT14 117 A5
Birkdale Cl CT5 44 D8
Birkdale Ct 3 ME16 74 E4
Birkdale Dr CT19 178 A8
Birkdale Gdns CT6 22 D2
Birkhall Cl ME5 32 A5
Birling Ave Gillingham ME8 11 E1
Maidstone ME14 76 A4
Birling Cl ME14 76 A4
Birling Rd TN24 139 D1
Birnam Sq 1 ME16 74 E4
Bishop Ct
4 Sittingbourne ME10 36 E5
Whitstable CT5 20 F2
Bishop Jenner Ct CT3 70 C6
Bishop La ME9 12 E3
Bishop's Ave CT10 30 B6
Bishopbourne Gn ME8 11 B4
Bishopden Ct CT2 66 C4
Bishops Ctyd 14 CT1 88 A8
Bishops Gn TN23 155 E7
Bishops Way
Canterbury CT2 66 D1
Maidstone ME15 74 F4
Bishops Wlk ME1 9 C5
Bishopstone Dr CT6 23 F6
Bishopstone La CT6 23 F5
Bishopswood TN23 156 C3
Bittern Cl CT18 163 A3
Black Bull Rd CT19 178 D6
Black Griffin La CT1 87 F8
Black Horse Farm Cvn Pk
CT18 162 F8
Black Post ME17 78 E4
Black Robin La CT4 111 E3
Black Rock Gdns ME7 33 B4
Blackberry Way CT5 44 B8
Blackburn Rd CT6 22 B2
Blackdown Dr TN24 139 B4
Blacketts Cotts ME9 38 B7
Blacketts Rd ME9 38 A6
Blackfriars St 16 CT1 66 F1
Blackhouse Hill CT18,
CT21 176 D4
Blackhouse Rise CT21 176 D3
Blackleys ME13 84 F7
Blackmanstone Way
ME16 74 B7
Blacksmith Dr ME14 75 D5
Blackstable Ct CT5 43 D8
Blackthorn Ave ME5 32 A3
Blackthorn Rd CT3 68 D8
Blackthorne Rd ME8 34 B8
Blackthorne Way TN23 156 C3
Blackwall Rd TN24,TN25 140 B4
Blackwall Rd N TN24 140 A2
Blackwall Rd S TN24 140 A2
Blake Cl CT14 134 C8
Blake Ct Ashford TN24 156 F8
6 Ramsgate CT11 52 D7
Blakeney Cl ME14 76 B4
Blaker Ave ME1 9 E1
Bland Dr CT18 163 C5
Blandford Gdns ME10 36 E1
Blatcher Cl ME12 4 B6
Blaxland Cl ME13 62 B8
Bleak Ho★ CT10 30 B4
Bleak Rd TN29 205 C6
Bleakwood Rd 6 ME5 31 F5
Blean Comm CT2 66 A6
Blean Hill CT2 66 A5
Blean Prim Sch CT2 66 B4
Blean Rd ME8 11 C2
Blean Sq ME14 75 C6
Blean View Rd CT6 22 B2
Blean Woods Nature
Reserve★ CT2 65 F4
Blendon Rd ME14 75 C5
Blenheim Ave
Canterbury CT1 67 D1
Blenheim Ave continued
Chatham ME4 9 E2
Faversham ME13 62 E5
Blenheim Cl
Broadstairs CT10 29 D3
Herne Bay CT6 23 A1
Maidstone ME15 75 F3
Blenheim Ct ME4 9 E3
Blenheim Dr Dover CT16 149 C3
Hawkinge CT18 163 A4
Blenheim Ho CT9 8 C3
Blenheim Pl CT20 177 F4
Blenheim Rd Deal CT14 117 D5
Littlestone-on-Sea TN28 202 D6
Sittingbourne ME10 37 B2
Bleriot Meml★ CT16 149 F1
Bliby Bsns Ctr TN25 171 F7
Bliby Cnr TN25 171 F8
Blind La Bredhurst ME7 33 A1
Challock TN25 105 C2
Gillingham ME7 32 F1
Mersham TN25 157 C4
Blind Mary's La ME9 57 E4
Blindgrooms La TN26 155 C1
Blindhouse La TN25 160 B3
Blockmakers Ct ME4 10 B1
Bloody Point Rd CT13 73 B4
Bloomsbury Rd CT11 52 C6
Bloomsbury Way TN24 139 B7
Bloomsbury Wlk 2
ME15 75 A4
Bloors La ME8 11 D1
Bloors Wharf Rd ME7 11 F4
Blossom La TN25 138 E5
Blowers Wood Gr ME7 33 B3
Blue Boar La ME1 9 D5
Blue Field TN23 155 C8
Blue House La CT21 176 B8
Blue Line La TN24 139 B3
Bluebell Cl Gillingham ME7 10 F6
Kingsnorth TN23 156 B4
Bluebell Rd TN23 156 C3
Bluebell Woods Mobile Home
Pk CT2 67 D6
Bluebird Ct CT17 166 A6
Bluefield Mews CT5 43 C6
Bluett St ME14 75 A5
Bluewater Cvn Pk CT21 187 E8
Blythe Cl ME10 37 C5
Blythe Ct CT21 176 D2
Blythe Rd ME15 75 B4
Boarley Ct ME14 53 F1
Boarley La ME14 53 F2
Boarman's La TN29 199 E8
Boat La TN25 173 A4
Boathouse Rd ME12 1 A3
Bob Amor Cl ME13 62 E7
Bobbin Lodge Hill CT4 86 B2
Bobbing Hill ME9 36 A6
Bobbing Village Sch ME9 36 B7
Bockham Cotts TN25 157 E8
Bockham La
Ashford TN25 141 A1
Mersham TN25 157 E8
Bockhanger Ct TN24 139 D5
Bockhanger La TN24 139 C6
Bockingford La ME15 96 F8
Bocton Ho ME17 97 B3
Bodenham Rd CT20 178 A4
Bodiam Cl ME8 11 C3
Bodiam Ct ME16 74 F3
Bodkins Cl ME17 97 D5
Bodsham CE Prim Sch
TN25 142 E8
Bodsham Cres ME15 76 B3
Bogle Rd ME9 60 C7
Bognor Dr CT6 22 D4
Bogshole La
Herne Bay CT6 23 D3
Whitstable CT5 43 E4
Boley Hill ME1 9 C6
Boleyn Ave CT9 7 E1
Boleyn Ct 9 CT1 88 A8
Bolingbroke Ho ME16 74 E3
Bolner Cl ME5 31 F2
Bolonia CT15 151 A6
Bolton Rd CT19 178 D6
Bolton St CT11 52 D8
Bolts Hill CT4 86 C2
Bombay Ho 1 ME15 97 E5
Bond La TN23 156 A2
Bond Rd Ashford TN23 156 B8
Gillingham ME8 33 E5
Bonetta Ct ME12 3 B8
Bonham Dr ME10 37 B5
Bonners Alley 19 CT5 20 D2
Bonnington Cross TN25 172 E3
Bonnington Gn ME8 11 C3
Bonnington Rd ME14 75 C6
Bonny Bush Hill CT4 111 D5
Bonsor Rd CT19 178 D6
Booth Pl CT9 7 J3
Booth Rd ME4 9 F2
Borden CE Prim Sch ME9 35 F3
Borden Gram Sch ME10 36 F3
Borden La ME10,ME9 36 C3
Boresisle TN30 167 B2
Bornefields TN23 156 A7
Borough CT1 67 A1
Borough Rd
Gillingham ME7 10 D4
Queenborough ME11 3 B4
Borrowdale Ave CT11 52 A7
Borstal Ave CT5 43 D6
Borstal Hill CT5 43 D7
Borstal HM Prison & Youth
Custody Ctr ME1 9 B1
Borstal Mews ME1 9 A2
Borstal Rd ME1 9 B3
Borstal St ME1 9 A2
Boscombe Rd CT19 178 C6
Bosney Banks CT15 148 A7
Bossingham Rd CT4 126 F3
Bossingham St CT4 126 F6
Bossington Rd CT3 90 E1
Boston Cl 5 CT16 149 B3
Boston Gdns ME8 11 C1
Boston Rd ME5 32 C2
Botany Cl ME12 1 C1
Botany Rd CT10 8 F2
Boteler Cotts CT13 93 A2
Botolph's Bridge Rd
CT21 187 A6
Bottles La ME9 59 A6
Bottlescrew Hill ME17 97 B4
Bottom Pond Rd ME9 58 D3
Boughton Ave CT10 30 A2
Boughton Church Cotts
ME13 63 D1
Boughton Cl ME8 11 B3
Boughton Cnr TN25 123 C5
Boughton Field Cotts
ME13 63 A5
Boughton Hill ME13 64 C3
Boughton La ME15 97 B6
Boughton Monchelsea Prim
Sch ME17 97 B2
Boughton Par ME15 97 A7
Boughton Place Cotts
ME17 118 A8
Boughton Rd ME17 101 B2
Boughton-Under-Blean Meth
Prim Sch ME13 63 F3
Boulevard Courrieres
CT3 112 E5
Boulevard D'erlanger
CT18 177 B7
Boulevard The TN24 156 F6
Boulogne Ct 17 CT20 178 E5
Boundary Chase CT5 44 B8
Boundary Cl ME12 4 E6
Boundary Ct CT1 88 B6
Boundary Rd Chatham ME4 9 E3
Deal CT14 134 D6
Hythe CT21 176 A2
Ramsgate CT11 52 E7
Boundary The CT1 87 D7
Bounds La ME13 64 A3
Boundsgate Cnr ME13 105 B7
Bourne Cotts CT4 111 C5
Bourne Ct ME1 9 D5
Bourne Gr ME10 36 C5
Bourne La TN26 183 A8
Bourne Lodge Cl CT2 66 A7
Bourne Park Rd CT4 111 A7
Bourne Rd TN25 172 D5
Bourne View CT4 88 F1
Bournemouth Dr CT6 22 D4
Bournemouth Gdns
CT19 178 C6
Bournemouth Rd CT19 178 C5
Bournes Cl CT2 67 F7
Bournes Pl TN26 169 A2
Bourneside Terr ME17 77 D2
Bournewood TN26 183 A8
Bournewood Cl ME15 75 F1
Bournville Ave ME4 9 F1
Bouverie Pl 2 CT20 178 D4
Bouverie Rd W CT20 178 C4
Bouverie Sq 1 CT20 178 D4
Bow Hill CT4 109 F2
Bowdell La TN29 191 E3
Bowden Cres CT20 177 C6
Bowen Ct CT11 52 D7
Bowen Rd CT19 177 E6
Bowens Field TN23 139 B1
Bower Cl ME16 74 E4
Bower Gn ME5 32 C1
Bower Grove Sch ME16 74 B2
Bower La ME16 74 E3
Bower Mount Rd ME16 74 D4
Bower Pl ME16 74 E3
Bower Rd TN25 158 A3
Bower St ME16 74 E4
Bower Terr ME16 74 E3
Bowerland La
Chilham CT4 85 E1
Old Wives Lees CT4 85 C2
Bowers Ho ME7 10 E7
Bowes Ave CT9 7 E1
Bowes La CT6 23 A3
Bowes Rd ME2 9 B8
Bowes Villas CT14 93 E4
Bowl Field TN25 142 B6
Bowl Rd TN27 103 D2
Bowland Cl CT6 23 C2
Bowlers Town TN31 197 A2
Bowles Well Gdns CT19 178 F7
Bowley La ME17 118 D8
Bowling Green La CT14 117 B5
Bowling Green Terr 8
CT17 166 D7
Bowling St CT13 72 F1
Bowman Cl ME5 32 C5
Bowman Ct CT17 149 A1
Bowser Cl CT14 116 F4
Bowyer Rd CT5 42 F7
Box La ME13 61 D1
Boxley TN23 155 F8
Boxley Cl Maidstone ME14 75 B8
West Minst ME12 3 B7
Boxley Rd Chatham ME5 32 B2
Maidstone ME14 75 B7
Boxmend Ind Est ME15 97 F3
Boxted La ME9 13 A1
Boyces Hill ME9 35 D6

Boyden Gate Hill CT3 . . . . .47 B8
Boyes La CT3 . . . . .91 D3
Boyke La CT4 . . . . .144 C2
Boyne Rd CT15 . . . . .134 A1
Boys Hall Rd TN24 . . . . . .156 F7
Boystown Pl CT13 . . . . .93 C3
Brabazon Rd ME12 . . . . .5 C1
Brabner Cl CT19 . . . . .178 E8
Brabourne Ave ME8 . . . . . .11 C3
Brabourne CE Prim Sch TN25 . . . . .159 A8
Brabourne Cl CT2 . . . . .67 A4
Brabourne Gdns CT20 . . .177 E5
Brabourne La TN25 . . . . . .142 F2
Brabourne Rd TN25 . . . . .141 D6
Brack La TN29 . . . . .191 B3
Bracken Cl TN24 . . . . .139 C6
Bracken Ct
3 Broadstairs CT10 . . . . . . .29 E5
Sittingbourne ME10 . . . . . . .37 C5
Bracken Hill ME5 . . . . .32 A1
Bracken Lea ME5 . . . . .10 C1
Brackley Cl ME14 . . . . .75 C5
Brackwood Cl ME8 . . . . . . .33 D5
Bradbridge Gn TN23 . . . .155 D8
Braddick Cl ME15 . . . . .97 B6
Bradfield Ave ME9 . . . . . . .38 D2
Bradfield Rd TN24 . . . . . .139 B5
Bradfields Ave ME5 . . . . . . .31 F5
Bradfields Ave W ME5 . . . .31 F5
Bradfields Sch ME5 . . . . . .32 A6
Bradfoord Ct CT20 . . . . . .178 D5
Bradley Dr ME10 . . . . .36 E2
Bradley Rd
Folkestone CT19 . . . . .178 F6
Ramsgate CT12 . . . . .29 C1
Bradshaw Cl ME9 . . . . .12 E3
Bradstone Ave CT19 . . . . .178 D6
Bradstone New Rd 3 CT20 . . . . .178 D5
Bradstone Rd CT20 . . . . .178 D5
Bradstow Sch CT10 . . . . . .30 A3
Bradstow Way CT10 . . . . . .30 A5
Brady Rd CT18 . . . . .161 A7
Braeside CT10 . . . . .30 B3
Braggs La CT6 . . . . .45 E6
Braithwaite Ct ME7 . . . . . .11 A5
Brake Ave ME5 . . . . .31 E5
Bramble Cl
Maidstone ME16 . . . . .74 B3
Wye TN25 . . . . .123 D3
Bramble La TN25 . . . . . . .123 C3
Brambledown
Chatham ME5 . . . . .32 B8
Folkestone CT19 . . . . .178 D6
Bramblefield La ME10, ME9 . . . . .14 E1
Bramblefields Cl CT6 . . . . .23 B2
Bramblehill Rd ME13 . . . . .62 C8
Brambles Ctyd CT14 . . . . .117 B3
Brambley Cres CT20 . . . . .177 E5
Brambling Rise ME10 . . . . .36 E6
Bramley Ave
Canterbury CT1 . . . . .87 C6
Faversham ME13 . . . . .62 E6
Bramley Cl
Brabourne Lees TN25 . . . . .158 E6
Eastchurch ME12 . . . . .5 D3
Gillingham ME8 . . . . .34 B8
Newington ME9 . . . . .35 A5
Bramley Cres ME15 . . . . . .75 F3
Bramley Gdns
Ashford TN23 . . . . .156 A6
Coxheath ME17 . . . . .96 C3
Herne Bay CT6 . . . . .23 D2
Bramley Pk ME12 . . . . .5 E5
Bramley Way ME12 . . . . .5 D3
Bramling Gap CT3 . . . . .90 C3
Bramling Rd CT3,CT4 . . . . .90 B4
Bramshaw Rd CT2 . . . . .66 E2
Bramshott Cl ME16 . . . . . .74 C6
Bramston Rd ME12 . . . . .4 C6
Branch Rd CT4 . . . . .107 C7
Branch St CT16 . . . . .149 C1
Branchley Mews TN27 . . .120 C8
Brandon Rd CT12 . . . . .29 A1
Brandon Way CT7 . . . . .27 B6
Bransgore Cl ME8 . . . . .33 D7
Brasenose Rd ME7 . . . . . . .10 E4
Brasier Ct ME12 . . . . .4 A5
Brassey Ave CT10 . . . . .29 F3
Brattle TN26 . . . . .181 B8
Braunstone Dr ME16 . . . . .74 D7
Bray Gdns ME15 . . . . .96 F5
Breach La ME9 . . . . .13 A2
Breadlands Cl TN24 . . . . .156 E8
Breadlands Rd TN24 . . . . .156 F8
Brecon Chase ME12 . . . . . . .4 C7
Brecon Rise TN24 . . . . . . .139 B4
Brecon Sq CT12 . . . . .29 A1
Bredgar & Wormshill Light Rly★ ME9 . . . . .57 E1
Bredgar CE Prim Sch ME9 .58 A5
Bredgar Cl Ashford TN23 . . .155 F6
Maidstone ME14 . . . . .75 C5
Bredgar Rd ME8 . . . . .11 B4
Bredhurst CE Prim Sch ME7 .33 B1
Bredhurst Cl ME12 . . . . .3 B7
Bredhurst Rd ME8 . . . . .33 B4
Bredlands La CT3,CT2 . . . .46 C1
Brenchley Ave CT14 . . . . .116 F4
Brenchley Cl
Ashford TN23 . . . . .155 E6
Rochester ME1 . . . . .9 D2
Brenchley Rd
Gillingham ME8 . . . . .11 B2
Brenchley Rd continued
Maidstone ME15 . . . . .74 F2
Sittingbourne ME10 . . . . .36 F2
Brendon Ave ME5 . . . . .32 A3
Brendon Dr TN24 . . . . . . .139 B3
Brenley Cnr ME13 . . . . . . .63 B4
Brenley La ME13 . . . . .63 C2
Brennan Ct ME7 . . . . .10 D6
Brent Cl ME5 . . . . .31 E5
Brent Hill ME13 . . . . .62 C8
Brent Rd ME13 . . . . .62 C8
Brents Ind Est ME13 . . . . . .40 D1
Brentwood TN23 . . . . .155 F5
Brenzett Aeronautical Mus★ TN29 . . . . .192 B3
Brenzett CE Prim Sch TN29 . . . . .192 A2
Brenzett Cl ME5 . . . . .32 B5
Brenzett Cnr TN29 . . . . . .192 A3
Breton Rd ME1 . . . . .9 C2
Brett Wlk ME8 . . . . .33 D4
Brewer St Deal CT14 . . . . .117 D6
Maidstone ME14 . . . . .75 A5
Brewer's Hill CT20 . . . . . .177 D3
Brewery Cotts CT14 . . . . .116 E4
Brewery La CT4 . . . . .89 A1
Brewery Rd ME10 . . . . .36 E6
Brewery Sq CT3 . . . . .48 D2
Brewhouse La TN25 . . . . .122 F4
Brewster Cotts ME9 . . . . . .59 E2
Brian Roberts Ho CT6 . . . .22 F5
Briar Cl Ashford TN24 . . . . .139 C6
Aylesham CT3 . . . . .112 F5
Crabble CT17 . . . . .148 F2
Briar Fields ME14 . . . . .75 E5
Briars Rd TN29 . . . . .194 F3
Briars The CT5 . . . . .43 C6
Briars Wlk CT10 . . . . .29 F3
Briary Cl CT9 . . . . .28 A8
Briary Prim Sch CT6 . . . . . .22 C2
Brice Ave CT4 . . . . .86 C1
Brickfield TN31 . . . . .196 B2
Brickfield Cotts TN25 . . . .123 B2
Brickfield La ME13 . . . . . . .63 E2
Brickfield Rd CT4 . . . . . . .128 F7
Brickmakers Ind Est ME10 . . . . .37 B6
Brickwall Terr TN26 . . . . .168 F3
Bridewell La TN30 . . . . . .179 A7
Bridewell Pk CT5 . . . . .21 A1
Bridge & Patrixbourne CE Prim Sch CT4 . . . . .89 A2
Bridge App The CT5 . . . . . .20 F1
Bridge Cl Hythe CT21 . . . . .176 A2
Woodchurch TN26 . . . . . . .181 B8
Bridge Cotts Selling ME13 . . .84 E7
Teynham ME9 . . . . .38 D2
Bridge Down CT4 . . . . . . .111 B8
Bridge Hill Bridge CT4 . . . .111 B8
Finglesham CT14 . . . . .116 C8
Bridge Ho Ramsgate CT11 . .52 F7
Rochester ME1 . . . . .9 B4
Bridge Home Pk TN29 . . .205 D8
Bridge Mill Way ME15 . . . .74 D2
Bridge Rd Ashford TN23 . . .138 F2
Brabourne Lees TN25 . . . . .158 D5
Bridge CT4 . . . . .88 D1
Deal CT14 . . . . .117 D7
Faversham ME13 . . . . .62 D8
Gillingham ME7 . . . . .10 C7
Margate CT9 . . . . .7 E1
Rochester ME1 . . . . .9 C2
Sheerness ME12 . . . . .1 C2
Bridge Rd Ind Ctr TN23 . . .138 F2
Bridge St Dover CT16 . . . .149 C1
Folkestone CT19 . . . . .178 E6
Maidstone ME15 . . . . .96 F5
Wye TN25 . . . . .123 E2
Bridge View Ind Est ME11 . . .3 A2
Bridgefield Ct CT5 . . . . . . .21 B3
Bridgefield Rd CT5 . . . . . . .21 B3
Bridgeford Way CT4 . . . . . .89 A1
Bridgeman Ct CT21 . . . . .176 B2
Bridges Cl CT7 . . . . .25 E2
Bridgeside CT14 . . . . .117 C6
Bridgeside Mews ME15 . . .74 E2
Bridgewater Rd ME12 . . . . . .3 B8
Bridgeway CT5 . . . . .20 F2
Bridle Way Herne Bay CT6 . .22 D3
Hythe CT21 . . . . .177 A3
Bridledown Children's Farm & Wildlife Ctr★ CT15 . . .165 A4
Bridleway Gdns CT10 . . . .29 E3
Bridleway La TN23 . . . . . .156 B4
Brielle Way
Queenborough ME11,ME12 . . .3 A6
Sheerness ME12 . . . . .1 B2
Brier Cl ME5 . . . . .32 C8
Brier Rd ME10 . . . . .36 B4
Briganda Wlk CT11 . . . . . . .52 E8
Bright Rd 3 ME4 . . . . .10 B2
Bright's Pl CT11 . . . . .52 F7
Brightlingsea Rd CT13 . . . .93 F8
Brindle Gr CT11 . . . . .29 F1
Brindle Way ME5 . . . . .32 C1
Brinklow Terr TN26 . . . . .155 A1
Brisbane Ave ME10 . . . . . .36 C4
Brisbane Dr CT12 . . . . .29 A1
Brisbane Rd ME4 . . . . .10 A3
Brishing Cl ME15 . . . . .97 E5
Brishing La ME17 . . . . .97 D4
Brishing Rd ME15,ME17 . . .97 F3
Brisley La TN26 . . . . .171 D6
Brissenden Cl TN28 . . . . .202 B8
Bristles Cnr CT3 . . . . .46 E6
Bristol Pl CT11 . . . . .52 D7
Bristol Rd CT1 . . . . .87 F6
Britannia Ave CT5 . . . . .43 B7
Britannia Cl ME10 . . . . .36 E7
Britannia La TN23 . . . . . . .155 F5
Britannia Rd CT14 . . . . . .117 D8
Briton Ct ME12 . . . . .3 B8
Briton Rd ME13 . . . . .62 C7
Britten Cl CT21 . . . . .176 A3
Britton St ME7 . . . . .10 B5
Broad La CT14 . . . . .116 B7
Broad Oak Rd CT2 . . . . . . .67 B3
Broad St Canterbury CT1 . . .67 A1
Deal CT14 . . . . .117 D6
Margate CT9 . . . . .7 I3
Ramsgate CT11 . . . . .52 E7
Sellindge TN25 . . . . .159 E5
Sheerness ME12 . . . . .1 C2
Broad Street Hill ME17 . . .77 D7
Broadacre Lydden CT15 . . .147 F8
Teynham ME9 . . . . .38 D2
Broader La ME14 . . . . .55 B2
Broadfield Cres CT20 . . . .178 A5
Broadfield Rd
Folkestone CT20 . . . . .178 A5
Loose ME15 . . . . .97 A8
Broadgate Hall 1 CT11 . . . .52 F7
Broadhurst Dr TN24 . . . . .139 D7
Broadlands CT2 . . . . .67 F6
Broadlands Ave TN28 . . .202 B8
Broadlands Cres TN28 . . .202 B8
Broadlands Dr ME5 . . . . . .32 B4
Broadlands Ind Est CT2 . . .66 A7
Broadley Ave CT7 . . . . .26 F5
Broadley Rd CT10,CT9 . . . .29 C7
Broadmead TN23 . . . . . . .155 E6
Broadmead Manor CT10 . . .30 B7
Broadmead Rd CT19 . . . .178 C5
Broadmeadow CT19 . . . . .178 B7
Broadmere Terr ME16 . . . .74 D3
Broadoak Ave ME15 . . . . . .97 A8
Broadoak Ent Village ME9 .58 F6
Broadoak Rd ME9 . . . . .58 E6
Broadsole La CT15 . . . . . .164 E5
Broadstairs Rd CT10 . . . . .29 E5
Broadstairs Sta CT10 . . . . .30 A4
Broadview CT20 . . . . .177 C6
Broadview Ave ME8 . . . . . .33 E8
Broadviews CT21 . . . . . . .176 D1
Broadway Gillingham ME8 . . .11 A3
Maidstone ME14 . . . . .74 F4
Petham CT4 . . . . .109 A2
Sheerness ME12 . . . . .1 D2
Broadway The
Broadstairs CT10 . . . . .30 A4
Dover CT16 . . . . .166 H8
Herne Bay CT6 . . . . .22 C5
Minster (Sheppey) ME12 . . . . .4 B7
Brockbank Cl ME5 . . . . . . .32 A1
Brockenhurst Ave ME15 . . .75 C1
Brockenhurst Cl
Canterbury CT2 . . . . .66 E2
Gillingham ME8 . . . . .33 C7
Brockenhurst Rd CT11 . . . .52 G8
Brockhill Ctry Pk★ CT21 . . . . .175 F4
Brockhill Park Sch CT21 . . . . .175 F4
Brockhill Rd CT21 . . . . . . .176 B3
Brockley Rd CT9 . . . . .8 A2
Brockman Cres TN29 . . . .187 B4
Brockman Rd CT20 . . . . . .178 C5
Brockman's Cl CT12 . . . . . .50 B7
Brogdale Farm★ ME13 . . . .62 B4
Brogdale Farm Cotts ME13 . . . . .62 A3
Brogdale Pl ME13 . . . . .62 B6
Brogdale Rd ME13 . . . . . . .62 B5
Brogdale World of Fruit★ ME13 . . . . .62 B4
Brogden Cres ME17 . . . . . .98 F7
Bromley Cl ME5 . . . . .32 B4
Bromley Green Rd TN26 . . . . .171 A5
Brompton Hill ME4 . . . . .9 F6
Brompton La ME2 . . . . .9 A8
Brompton Rd ME7 . . . . .10 B6
Brompton Villas CT15 . . . .149 E6
Brompton-Westbrook Prim Sch ME7 . . . . .10 A5
Bromstone Mews CT10 . . . .29 E3
Bromstone Prim Sch CT10 . . . . .29 D3
Bromstone Rd CT10 . . . . . .29 E3
Bronington Cl ME5 . . . . . . .32 A5
Brook Cl Herne Bay CT6 . . . .22 C3
Hythe CT21 . . . . .177 B3
Brook Com Prim Sch TN25 . . . . .141 A4
Brook Cotts
East Farleigh ME15 . . . . . . .96 C7
Staple CT3 . . . . .91 E6
Teynham ME9 . . . . .39 A2
Brook La Cliffs End CT12 . . . .50 F4
Reculver CT6 . . . . .24 B5
Sellindge TN25 . . . . .159 E2
Brook La Cotts TN25 . . . . .159 E2
Brook Rd Faversham ME13 . .40 D1
Whitstable CT5 . . . . .21 C3
Brook St Eastry CT13 . . . . . .93 C2
Woodchurch TN26 . . . . . . .180 D8
Brook The ME4 . . . . .10 A4
Brookbank Brook TN25 . . . .141 A5
Maidstone ME14 . . . . .75 A8
Brooke Ave CT9 . . . . .28 B7
Brooke Rd TN24 . . . . .139 B3
Brooker Cl ME17 . . . . .97 D5
Brookes Pl ME9 . . . . .35 B6
Brookfield Ave CT16 . . . . .149 B2
Brookfield Ct TN23 . . . . . .155 F8
Brookfield Ind Pk TN23 . .138 F1
Brookfield Pl CT16 . . . . . .149 B2
Brookfield Rd
Ashford TN23 . . . . .155 F8
Dover CT16 . . . . .149 A3
Brookland CE Prim Sch TN29 . . . . .199 D8
Brooklands Cl CT2 . . . . . . .67 F4
Brooklyn Paddock ME7 . . .10 D6
Brooks Pl ME14 . . . . .75 A4
Brooks Way TN29 . . . . . . .205 C5
Brookside
St Mary's Bay TN29 . . . . . . .195 A5
Temple Ewell CT16 . . . . . . .148 D5
Brookside Pk ME12 . . . . .5 F6
Broom Rd ME10 . . . . .37 C5
Broomcroft Rd ME8 . . . . . .11 F2
Broomfield Cres CT9 . . . . . .8 F2
Broomfield Gate CT5 . . . . .44 D5
Broomfield Rd
Faversham ME13 . . . . .62 C8
Folkestone CT19 . . . . .177 E6
Herne Bay CT6 . . . . .23 C2
Kingswood ME17 . . . . .99 D4
Brotherhood Cl CT2 . . . . . .66 D4
Broughton By-Pass ME13 . . . . .64 C2
Broughton Ct TN23 . . . . . .138 E1
Brown Lo ME12 . . . . .1 I1
Brown St ME8 . . . . .11 F1
Brownelow Copse ME5 . . . .32 B1
Brownhill Cl ME5 . . . . .32 A4
Browning Pl CT19 . . . . . . .178 E7
Brownings Orch ME9 . . . . . .59 A7
Broxhall Rd CT4 . . . . .110 B3
Bruce Cl CT14 . . . . .117 B4
Bruges Ct ME10 . . . . .14 F1
Brundell Terr CT4 . . . . .86 B2
Brunel Way ME4 . . . . .10 A7
Brunswick Cotts ME9 . . . . .38 E6
Brunswick Ct 3 CT11 . . . . .52 E7
Brunswick Field ME9 . . . . .38 E6
Brunswick Gdns 3 CT16 . . . . .149 B3
Brunswick House Prim Sch ME16 . . . . .74 E5
Brunswick Ind Ctr TN23 . .138 F2
Brunswick Rd
Ashford TN23 . . . . .138 F2
Birchington CT7 . . . . .27 A5
Brunswick Sq CT6 . . . . .22 E5
Brunswick St
Maidstone ME15 . . . . .75 A3
Ramsgate CT11 . . . . .52 E7
Brunswick St E ME15 . . . . .75 A3
Bryant Rd ME2 . . . . .9 A7
Bryant St ME4 . . . . .10 A3
Bryces Alley CT5 . . . . .20 D2
Brymore Cl CT1 . . . . .67 B2
Brymore Rd CT1 . . . . .67 B2
Bryony Dr TN23 . . . . .156 C3
Bryony Sch ME8 . . . . .33 F5
Buck St TN25 . . . . .105 C2
Buckhurst Dr CT9 . . . . .8 F2
Buckingham Rd
15 Broadstairs CT10 . . . . . . .30 B4
Gillingham ME7 . . . . .10 D5
Margate CT9 . . . . .7 I1
Whitstable CT5 . . . . .21 B2
Buckingham Row ME15 . . . .97 E7
Buckland Ave CT16 . . . . . .149 B2
Buckland Cl ME5 . . . . .32 A2
Buckland Cotts ME13 . . . . .61 B8
Buckland Hill ME16 . . . . . .74 E5
Buckland Hospl CT17 . . . .149 A1
Buckland La
Maidstone ME16 . . . . .74 D6
Staple CT3 . . . . .92 A4
Buckland Pl ME16 . . . . .74 E4
Buckland Rd ME16 . . . . . . .74 E4
Bucklers Cl ME12 . . . . .6 E4
Bucksford La TN23 . . . . . .155 C7
Buckthorn Cl CT14 . . . . . .117 C7
Buckthorne Ho ME12 . . . . . .4 A4
Buckthorne Rd ME12 . . . . . .4 A4
Budd's Farm Cotts TN30 . .188 E2
Budd's La TN30 . . . . .188 F2
Buddle Dr ME12 . . . . .3 E7
Buenos Ayres CT9 . . . . .7 H2
Buffs Ave CT20 . . . . .177 B6
Builders Sq CT3 . . . . .90 A8
Bull Hill ME17 . . . . .102 A1
Bull La Bethersden TN26 . . .153 B4
Boughton Street ME13 . . . . . .63 F4
Eccles ME20 . . . . .53 A6
Yelsted ME9 . . . . .34 E2
Bull Lane Cotts ME9 . . . . . .34 E1
Bulldog Rd ME5 . . . . .32 B2
Bulleid Pl TN24 . . . . .156 D7
Buller Rd ME4 . . . . .9 F2
Buller's Ave CT6 . . . . .22 E4
Bullockstone Rd CT6 . . . . .45 E7
Bulls Cotts 4 CT21 . . . . . .176 B2
Bulltown Cnr TN25 . . . . . .141 F3
Bullwark St CT17 . . . . . . .166 D5
Bulrush Cl ME5 . . . . .31 F3
Bulrushes The TN23 . . . . .155 D8
Bulwark Rd CT14 . . . . . . .117 D7
Bumbles Cl ME1 . . . . .31 D7
Bunce Court Rd ME13, ME17 . . . . .102 E7
Bungalows The
Faversham ME13 . . . . .62 A4
Woodnesborough CT13 . . . . .93 B5
Bunker's Hill CT17 . . . . . .149 B2
Bunkers Hill Ave CT17 . . .149 B1
Bunkers Hill Rd CT17 . . . .149 A1
Bunkley Mdw TN26 . . . . . .183 A7
Burberry La ME17 . . . . .99 B5
Burch Ave CT13 . . . . .93 F8
Burdock Ct ME16 . . . . .74 A3
Burdock Ho 6 ME15 . . . . . .97 D8
Burford's Alley CT3 . . . . . .71 D1
Burgate CT1 . . . . .88 A8
Burgate La 5 CT1 . . . . .88 A8
Burgate Terr TN25 . . . . . . .157 E4
Burgess Cl
Minster (Thanet) CT12 . . . . .50 C7
Whitfield CT16 . . . . .149 B7
Burgess Gn CT14 . . . . .116 C8
Burgess Hall Dr ME17 . . . . .98 F6
Burgess Rd
Aylesham CT3 . . . . .112 F6
Rochester ME2 . . . . .9 B7
Burgess Row 10 TN30 . . . .179 A7
Burghclere Dr ME16 . . . . . .74 B2
Burgoyne Ct ME14 . . . . .74 F7
Burgoyne Gr CT16 . . . . . . .149 A5
Burgoyne Hts CT15 . . . . . .149 E3
Burial Ground La ME15 . . .74 E1
Burkeston Cl ME10 . . . . . . .37 A8
Burleigh Dr ME14 . . . . .53 F1
Burleigh Rd TN27 . . . . . . .120 C7
Burley Rd ME10 . . . . .36 E4
Burlington Dr CT6 . . . . . . .23 D5
Burlington Gdns
Gillingham ME8 . . . . .33 E4
Margate CT9 . . . . .28 C8
Burma Cres CT1 . . . . .67 D1
Burma Way ME5 . . . . .31 F6
Burmarsh Cl ME5 . . . . .32 B5
Burmarsh Rd
Burmarsh TN29 . . . . .186 C3
Hythe CT21 . . . . .187 C8
Burn's Rd ME7 . . . . .10 C7
Burnan Ct CT5 . . . . .21 C2
Burnan Rd CT5 . . . . .21 C2
Burnham Cl ME10 . . . . .36 E8
Burnham Wlk ME8 . . . . .33 E3
Burns Rd ME16 . . . . .74 C2
Burnt House Hill CT3 . . . . .69 B5
Burnt Oak Terr ME7 . . . . . .10 D6
Burnt Oast Rd ME13 . . . . . .64 A3
Burntwick Dr ME9 . . . . .13 B3
Burnup Bank ME10 . . . . . . .37 C5
Burritt Mews ME1 . . . . .9 C3
Burrow Rd CT19 . . . . .178 F6
Burrs The ME10 . . . . .36 F3
Burrstock Way ME8 . . . . . .12 B2
Bursill Cres CT12 . . . . .29 B1
Bursted Hill CT4 . . . . .110 B2
Burston Rd ME17 . . . . .96 B2
Burton Cl CT19 . . . . .178 A7
Burton Fields CT6 . . . . .23 B4
Burton Rd TN24 . . . . .139 E6
Bus Bridge Rd ME15 . . . . . .96 E6
Bush Ave CT12 . . . . .29 B1
Bush Cl ME9 . . . . .57 F5
Bush Row ME20 . . . . .53 A3
Bushey Cl ME13 . . . . .63 F3
Busheyfields Rd CT6 . . . . .45 F6
Bushmeadow Rd ME8 . . . . .11 F2
Bushy Gr ME17 . . . . .99 D2
Bushy Hill Rd CT2 . . . . . . .68 D7
Bushy Royds TN24 . . . . . .156 D6
Bushy Ruff Cotts CT16 . . .148 D4
Butchers La CT15 . . . . . . .113 E5
Butchery La 1 CT1 . . . . . . .88 A8
Butchery The 2 CT13 . . . . .73 A1
Butler's Hill ME13 . . . . .64 D7
Butt Field Rd TN23 . . . . . .155 E7
Butter St CT15 . . . . .113 C4
Butterfly Centre The★ CT15 . . . . .146 B3
Buttermere ME13 . . . . .62 E6
Buttermere Cl
Folkestone CT19 . . . . .178 B6
Gillingham ME7 . . . . .11 A5
Buttermere Gdns CT3 . . .112 F6
Butternut Copse TN23 . . .138 D3
Butterside Rd TN23 . . . . .156 C4
Button La ME15 . . . . .76 B2
Butts Ct CT4 . . . . .110 A6
Butts Hill ME13 . . . . .63 F5
Butts Mdw CT4 . . . . .110 A6
Butts The Sandwich CT13 . . .72 F1
Sittingbourne ME10 . . . . .36 F4
Buxton Cl Chatham ME5 . . . .32 D1
Loose ME15 . . . . .97 A8
Buxton Rd CT12 . . . . .29 B2
Bybrook CT21 . . . . .176 D3
Bybrook Ct TN24 . . . . .139 C4
Bybrook Field CT20 . . . . .177 E3
Bybrook Rd TN24 . . . . . . .139 C5
Bybrook Way CT20 . . . . . .177 E4
Bychurch Pl 7 ME15 . . . . .75 A3
Byllan Rd CT17 . . . . .148 E3
Byron Ave CT9 . . . . .7 J1
Byron Cl CT1 . . . . .88 C7
Byron Cres CT16 . . . . .149 B4
Byron Prim Sch ME7 . . . . .10 C3
Byron Rd Gillingham ME7 . . .10 C3
Maidstone ME14 . . . . .75 B7
Bysing Wood Cotts ME13 . . .39 F1
Bysing Wood Prim Sch ME13 . . . . .62 A8
Bysing Wood Rd ME13 . . . .62 B8
Bythorne Ct ME8 . . . . .12 B1

C

Cabin The TN24 . . . . .139 D7

Cade Rd TN23 156 B7
Cades Orch ME13 61 E3
Cadnam Cl CT2 66 E3
Caernarvon Dr ME15 74 F1
Caernarvon Gdns CT10 30 B5
Caesar Ave TN23 155 F4
Caesar's Way CT19 177 E7
Calais Hill CT2 66 E6
Calcraft Mews 6 CT1 67 B2
Calcutta Ho 3 ME15 97 E5
Caldecot La TN29 201 D2
Caldecote Cl ME8 12 B1
Caldecott Foundation Sch TN25 158 B4
Calder Rd ME14 74 E7
Caldew Ave ME8 11 C1
Caldew Gr ME10 37 A3
Caledon Terr CT1 88 A7
Caledonian Ct ME8 33 E8
Calehill Cl ME14 75 C6
Calgary Cres CT19 178 E8
California Row CT3 90 E6
Callams Cl ME8 33 D6
Calland TN25 158 E5
Callaways La ME9 35 B6
Calleywell La TN25 173 A7
Callis Court Rd CT10 29 F6
Callis Grange Inf Sch CT10 29 F7
Callis Way ME8 33 D5
Callisto Ct ME16 74 D3
Calverden Rd CT12 29 A1
Camborne Manor 2 ME7 10 C6
Cambourne Ave CT8 27 D8
Cambrai Ct CT1 67 D1
Cambridge Ave CT13 95 B7
Cambridge Cl CT7 27 B7
Cambridge Cres ME15 97 D7
Cambridge Gdns CT20 178 D5
Cambridge La ME9 60 C8
Cambridge Mews CT14 117 D3
Cambridge Rd
Canterbury CT1 87 F6
Deal CT14 117 D3
Dover CT17 166 D7
Faversham ME13 62 B6
Gillingham ME8 33 C6
Rochester ME2 9 A8
Sittingbourne ME10 37 B3
Cambridge Terr
1 Chatham ME4 9 F4
13 Dover CT16,CT17 166 E7
13 Folkestone CT20 178 E5
Margate CT9 8 B1
Cambridge Way CT1 87 F6
Camden Cl ME5 32 B5
Camden Cres CT16 166 E7
Camden Rd
Broadstairs CT10 29 E7
Gillingham ME7 10 D7
Ramsgate CT11 52 E6
Camden Sq 10 CT11 52 E7
Camden St ME14 75 A5
Camden Terr TN24 139 E1
Camellia Cl
Gillingham ME8 33 D7
2 Margate CT9 28 B8
Cameron Cl ME5 32 B8
Cameron Ct CT17 166 A6
Cameron Ho CT14 117 C1
Camomile Dr ME14 75 F5
Camp Way ME15 97 C6
Campbell Cl CT6 23 C3
Campbell Rd Deal CT14 117 D4
Maidstone ME15 75 A3
Camperdown Manor 5 ME7 10 A6
Campion Cl ME5 31 E3
Campleshon Rd ME8 33 D5
Campus Way ME8 33 A8
Canada Cl CT19 177 C6
Canada Mews CT14 117 C3
Canada Rd CT14 117 D3
Canada Terr 3 ME14 75 A7
Canadian Ave ME7 10 F4
Canal Rd ME2 9 C7
Canberra Gdns ME10 36 C4
Candlers Way CT4 108 F8
Canning St ME14 75 A6
Cannon Rd CT11 52 D7
Cannon St Deal CT14 117 C7
Dover CT16 166 D8
Lydd TN29 205 C6
New Romney TN28 202 B7
Cannonbury Rd CT11 52 D6
Cannongate Ave CT21 176 D3
Cannongate Cl CT21 176 E2
Cannongate Gdns CT21 176 E3
Cannongate Rd CT21 176 D3
Canon Appleton Ct CT1 87 E7
Canon Cl ME1 9 B2
Canon Gn CT3 91 A7
Canon Woods Way TN24 139 F6
Canons Gate Rd CT16 166 E8
Canterbury Cathedral★ CT1 88 A8
Canterbury Centre The (Mus)★ CT1 66 F1
Canterbury Christ Church Univ Coll CT10 29 C4
Canterbury Christ Church Univ Coll (The Mount) CT3 67 F1
Canterbury Cl
Broadstairs CT10 29 D5
2 Folkestone CT19 178 E6
Canterbury Coll CT1 88 B8
Canterbury Ct TN24 139 D2
Canterbury East Sta CT1 87 F7
Canterbury High Sch The CT2 87 D8
Canterbury Hill CT2 66 E5
Canterbury Ho 2 ME15 97 D7
Canterbury Ind Pk CT3 69 A8
Canterbury La
Canterbury CT1 88 A8
Gillingham ME8,ME9 12 C1
Canterbury Rd
Ashford TN24 156 E6
Ashford,Kennington TN24 139 E5
Barham CT4 129 C5
Boughton Aluph TN25 123 C5
Boughton Street ME13 63 D4
Brabourne TN25 159 C8
Brabourne Lees TN25 158 F6
Challock TN25,TN27 104 C1
Chilham CT4 85 F1
Denton CT4 129 A1
Dunkirk ME13 64 C3
Elham CT4 144 E3
Etchinghill CT18 161 D4
Faversham ME13 62 E5
Folkestone CT19 178 D7
Folkestone,Foord CT19 178 E6
Hawkinge CT18,CT19,CT15, CT4 163 B4
Herne CT3,CT6 45 E5
Herne Bay CT6 23 A3
Littlebourne CT3 89 C8
Lydden CT15 147 E7
Lyminge CT18 161 C7
Sarre CT7 48 E7
Sittingbourne ME10 37 B3
Whitstable CT5 43 D8
Wingham CT3 91 A7
Canterbury Rd E CT11, CT12 52 A6
Canterbury Rd W CT12 51 D7
Canterbury Road Birchington CT7 27 B7
Canterbury Road Margate CT9 7 G1
Canterbury Road Prim Sch ME10 37 B3
Canterbury Road Westgate CT8,CT9 27 E8
Canterbury St ME7 10 C4
Canterbury Tale The★ CT1 87 F8
Canterbury West Sta CT2 66 F1
Canute Rd Birchington CT7 26 D7
Deal CT14 95 C1
Faversham ME13 62 C6
Canute Wlk CT14 95 D1
Capel Cl Ashford TN23 138 F1
Broadstairs CT10 8 F1
Gillingham ME8 33 D4
Capel Court Pk CT18 164 D2
Capel Rd
Bromley Green TN26 171 B4
Faversham ME13 62 B7
Petham CT4 108 F3
Sittingbourne ME10 36 E2
Capel St CT18 164 B3
Capel-le-Ferne Prim Sch CT18 164 C3
Capell Cl ME17 96 C3
Capetown Ho 1 ME15 97 F5
Capstan Row CT14 117 D7
Capstone Farm Country Pk★ ME7 32 D5
Capstone Rd
Chatham ME5 10 D1
Gillingham ME7 32 F6
Captains Ct CT21 176 C1
Cardinal Cl ME12 4 D7
Cardine Cl ME10 36 E7
Carey Cl TN28 202 B6
Carey Ho 5 CT1 87 F7
Caring La ME14,ME17 76 E1
Caring Rd ME15,ME17 76 C1
Carisbrooke Dr ME16 74 D4
Carlsden Cl CT17 149 A3
Carlton Ave
Broadstairs CT10 30 A5
Gillingham ME7 10 E4
Ramsgate CT11 52 D6
Sheerness ME12 1 C1
Carlton Cres ME5 32 D8
Carlton Gdns ME15 97 B8
Carlton Hill CT6 22 C4
Carlton Leas CT20 178 C4
Carlton Mans CT9 8 A3
Carlton Rd Ashford TN23 139 A2
Kingsdown CT14 134 C6
Whitstable CT5 43 D2
Carlton Rd E CT8 27 D8
Carlton Rd W CT8 27 D8
Carlton Rise CT8 27 C8
Carman's Cl ME15,ME17 96 F3
Carmel Cl CT4 86 B2
Carmel Ct 2 CT7 26 F8
Carn Brae CT9 7 J2
Carnoustie Cl CT5 44 E8
Caroland Cl TN25 158 D5
Caroline Cl CT5 43 B6
Caroline Cres
Broadstairs CT10 29 E6
Maidstone ME16 74 D7
Caroline Sq CT9 7 J3
Carpeaux Cl ME4 10 A4
Carpenters Cl ME1 9 E2
Carpinus Cl ME5 32 B1
Carriage Ho ME13 83 D5
Carriage Mews CT2 66 F1
Carrie Ho 3 ME16 74 E5
Carrington Cl ME7 10 F6
Carroway's Pl CT9 7 J2
Carter La TN29 191 E2
Carter's Rd CT20 177 F5
Carter's Wood TN26 183 B7
Carton Cl ME1 9 D2
Cartwright & Kelsey CE Prim Sch CT3 71 C2
Cartwright Cl CT3 71 C2
Carvoran Way ME8 33 C5
Caslocke St 2 ME13 62 C7
Cassino Ho 16 CT1 67 B2
Cassino Sq CT15 149 E2
Castalla Cotts CT14 117 D3
Castle Ave
Broadstairs CT10 30 B6
Dover CT16 149 D1
Hythe CT21 176 B3
Rochester ME1 9 C4
Castle Bay CT20 177 D3
Castle Cl
4 Folkestone CT20 177 F3
Lympne CT21 174 F2
Castle Com Sch CT14 117 C4
Castle Cotts CT13 72 E5
Castle Cres CT21 176 C4
Castle Dene ME14 74 F8
Castle Dr CT16 148 F7
Castle Glen 9 CT20 177 F3
Castle Hill
Folkestone CT19,CT18 178 A8
Rochester ME1 9 C6
Thurnham ME14 55 D1
Castle Hill Ave CT20 178 C4
Castle Hill Ct ME1 9 C6
Castle Hill Rd 4 CT16 166 E8
Castle Ho CT5 20 D2
Castle Mayne Ave CT7 27 F3
Castle Mews CT14 117 A4
Castle Rd Chatham ME4 10 B2
Folkestone CT20 177 F3
Hythe CT21 176 B4
Maidstone ME16 74 D7
Sittingbourne ME10 37 B5
Whitstable CT5 20 F2
Castle Road Bsns Prec ME10 37 B6
Castle Road Tech Ctr ME10 37 B6
Castle Rough La ME10 14 F1
Castle Row CT1 87 F7
Castle St
6 Ashford TN23 139 B2
Canterbury CT1 87 F8
Dover CT16 166 E8
Queenborough ME11 3 A5
Castle View Bsns Ctr ME1 9 C6
Castle View Mews ME1 9 C6
Castle View Rd ME2 9 A7
Castle Wlk CT14 95 D1
Castleacres Ind Pk ME10 37 B6
Castlemaine Ave ME7 10 F6
Castlemere Ave ME11 3 B5
Castlemount Ct CT16 166 E8
Castlemount Rd CT16 149 D1
Castleview Ct CT17 149 B1
Cathedral View CT2 67 A2
Catherine Cl 2 ME16 74 A3
Catherine St ME1 9 D3
Catherine Way CT10 30 A6
Catkin Cl ME5 31 F1
Catsole Hill CT3 91 D2
Catt's Hill TN30 189 E3
Catt's Wood Rd CT4 109 F4
Catterick Rd ME5 32 D2
Cattle Market CT13 72 F1
Cauldham Cl CT18 164 B1
Cauldham La CT18 164 B3
Caulkers Ho 7 ME4 10 B2
Causeway The
Canterbury CT1 66 F1
Sandwich CT13 72 D2
Cavalry Ct Deal CT14 117 D3
Folkestone CT20 177 D5
Cave Hill ME15 74 F1
Cave La CT3 91 D3
Cavell Sq CT14 117 A3
Cavell Way ME10 36 D5
Cavenagh Rd CT15 151 B6
Cavendish Ave ME7 10 E6
Cavendish Ct CT6 23 A5
Cavendish Pl 2 CT11 52 E6
Cavendish Rd
Herne Bay CT6 23 A5
Rochester ME1 9 D3
Cavendish St CT11 52 E6
Cavendish Way ME15 76 B3
Caversham Cl ME8 11 F1
Cavour Rd
Faversham ME13 62 C7
Sheerness ME12 1 D2
Caxton Ho TN24 139 C3
Caxton Rd CT9 28 C8
Cayser Dr ME17 99 E2
Cazeneuve St ME1 9 C5
Cecil Ave Gillingham ME8 11 A2
Rochester ME2 9 B8
Sheerness ME12 1 C1
Cecil Ct Ashford TN24 139 B3
Herne Bay CT6 23 A4
Cecil Pk CT6 23 A4
Cecil Rd Kingsdown CT14 134 D7
Rochester ME1 9 C3
Cecil Sq CT9 7 I2
Cecil St CT9 7 I2
Cecilia Gr CT10 29 F6
Cecilia Rd CT11 52 E8
Cedar Cl Ashford TN23 138 E3
Birchington CT8 27 B7
Broadstairs CT10 29 F7
Margate CT9 8 B1
Sittingbourne ME10 37 B2
Cedar Cres TN29 194 F3
Cedar Ct Folkestone CT20 177 E5
Maidstone ME14 75 B5
12 Tenterden TN30 179 A7
Cedar Gdns ME9 56 E8
Cedar Gr ME7 33 A5
Cedar Ho ME12 1 C2
Cedar Rd CT2 68 A6
Cedar Terr ME13 62 A4
Cedars PRU The ME16 74 D4
Cedars Sch The ME1 9 C4
Cedars The
Barrowhill TN25 174 D8
Sittingbourne ME10 37 C5
Cedarview CT2 66 C1
Cedarwood Ho ME15 96 B6
Cedric Rd CT8 7 C1
Ceil Villas CT14 94 B4
Celestine Cl ME5 32 A1
Cellar Hill ME9 60 C8
Celt Cl ME10 36 F8
Celtic Rd CT14 117 A2
Cemetery La TN24 139 C4
Centenary Cl TN27 120 C8
Centenary Gdns CT13 93 A2
Central Ave Chatham ME4 10 B8
Herne Bay CT6 22 D4
Sittingbourne ME10 36 F4
Central Beach Pk ME12 6 G2
Central Bsns Pk ME2 9 E7
Central Par Herne Bay CT6 22 E5
Rochester ME1 9 D2
Central Park Gdns ME4 9 E2
Central Pk CT12 49 D6
Central Rd Ramsgate CT11 52 D8
Rochester ME2 9 A7
Central Service Rd CT16 166 H8
Central Sta CT19 178 C5
Centre 2000
Maidstone ME16 74 C8
8 Sittingbourne ME10 37 A4
Centre Ct ME2 9 E7
Centre Rd CT17 166 C6
Centre The Margate CT9 7 I2
Ramsgate CT12 29 A1
Centurion Cl ME8 10 F1
Centurion Wlk TN23 156 B4
Century Ct ME1 9 C5
Century Rd
Faversham ME13 62 E7
Gillingham ME8 33 D8
Century Wlk CT14 117 C6
Ceres Ct ME10 37 C5
Chada Ave ME7 10 E3
Chaffe's La ME9 12 E3
Chaffes Terr ME9 12 E2
Chaffinch Cl ME5 32 A7
Chaffinch Dr TN23 156 C3
Chaffinch Lodge 5 CT16 149 B2
Chafy Cres CT2 67 F5
Chain Gate ME17 118 A8
Chain The 6 CT13 73 A1
Chalcroft Rd CT20 177 E4
Chalfont Dr
Gillingham ME8 33 D6
Herne Bay CT6 23 D2
Chalk Ave TN30 167 B2
Chalk Cl CT19 178 A7
Chalk Hill CT11,CT12 51 F6
Chalk Hill Rd CT14 134 C5
Chalk Pit Hill
Chatham ME4 10 A3
Staple CT3 92 B5
Chalk Pit La CT13,CT3 92 C5
Chalk Rd ME11 3 A5
Chalkenden Ave ME8 11 A2
Chalkers Way ME8 11 B4
Chalkpit Hill CT4 89 D3
Chalksole Green La CT15 147 B2
Chalkwell Ct CT17 166 A7
Chalkwell Rd ME10 36 D5
Chalky Bank Rd ME8 11 F2
Chalky Rd ME9 56 C6
Challenger Cl ME10 36 E7
Challock Ct CT9 8 F2
Challock Prim Sch TN25 105 B1
Challock Wlk ME14 75 C6
Chalmers Way ME8 11 A4
Chamberlain Ave ME16 74 C2
Chamberlain Ct ME8 33 B5
Chamberlain Dr CT6 22 B4
Chamberlain Rd
Chatham ME4 10 B2
Dover CT17 166 B8
Chance Mdw CT15 149 E6
Chancel Ct CT2 66 D1
Chancery La ME15 75 B3
Chanctonbury Chase CT5 43 A6
Chandlers Wharf ME1 9 B5
Chandos Rd 17 CT10 30 B4
Chandos Sq 16 CT10 30 B4
Chandos Terr CT12 52 E7
Channel Cl CT19 178 F7
Channel Lea CT14 117 C1
Channel Rd CT9 29 A6
Channel Sch The CT19 178 C7
Channel Tunnel Terminal CT18 177 B8
Channel View 21 CT19 178 E5
Channel View Ct 19 CT11 52 F7
Channel View Rd CT17 166 C5
Channel Watch TN28 202 E4
Channon Rd TN28 206 E7
Chantry Ct 15 CT1 67 F1
Chantry Hall CT1 87 F7
Chantry Pk CT7 48 D7
Chapel Cl CT18 161 D3
Chapel Cotts ME17 98 F5
Chapel Hill
Eythorne CT15 131 C7
Margate CT9 29 A6
Chapel Hill Cl CT9 28 F7
Chapel La Blean CT2 66 A7
Bredhurst ME7 33 A2
Broad Oak CT2 67 D7
18 Dover CT16 166 D7
East Studdal CT15 132 C6
Egerton Forstal TN27 118 B2
Gillingham ME7 33 A4
Maidstone ME14 76 A5
Newchurch TN29 185 C4
Rhodes Minnis CT4 144 B4
Ripple CT14 133 D8
St Margaret's at Cliffe CT15 150 F6
Staple CT3 92 B6
Sturry CT2 67 F5
Chapel Mews TN23 139 C2
Chapel Pl 16 Dover CT17 166 D7
Ramsgate CT11 52 D7
Chapel Place La CT11 52 D7
Chapel Rd
Dymchurch TN29 195 C7
Ram Lane TN26 120 F1
Ramsgate CT11 52 C7
Tilmanstone CT14 115 A3
Whitfield CT16 149 A8
Chapel Row Herne CT6 46 A8
Kingsnorth TN23 156 A3
Lydd TN29 205 C6
Ram Lane TN26 120 F2
Chapel St Deal CT14 117 D6
Faversham ME13 62 D6
Herne Bay CT6 23 A5
Hythe CT21 176 B2
Minster (Sheppey) ME12 4 D6
Sheerness ME12 1 B2
Chapel The Chartham CT4 86 F1
Maidstone ME16 74 B3
Chaplains Wlk CT4 86 E1
Chapman Ave ME15 97 E8
Chapman Ho CT14 117 B3
Chapmans Cl TN25 105 C2
Chapmans Hill CT15,CT3 113 B5
Chappell Way ME10 36 E6
Charing CE Prim Sch TN27 120 C8
Charing Cl CT12 52 C8
Charing Cres CT8 27 D7
Charing Heath Rd
Charing TN27 120 A6
Charing Heath TN27 119 F8
Charing Hill TN27 103 E1
Charing Rd ME8 11 B3
Charing Sta TN27 120 B7
Charlbury Cl ME16 74 C3
Charlecote Ct ME8 33 D8
Charles Cobb Cl TN29 195 D8
Charles Cres CT19 177 E7
Charles Ct CT8 27 F8
Charles Dickens Ctr (Mus)★ ME1 9 C5
Charles Dickens Sch The CT10 29 E4
Charles Drayson Ct ME13 62 E7
Charles Ho CT14 117 B3
Charles Lister Ct CT17 149 B1
Charles Rd Deal CT14 117 B4
Ramsgate CT11 52 E8
Charles St Chatham ME4 9 E3
Herne Bay CT6 23 A5
Maidstone ME16 74 E3
Rochester ME2 9 A7
Sheerness ME12 1 B3
Charlesford Ave ME17 99 D3
Charleston Ct CT10 30 B3
Charlesworth Dr CT7 27 B7
Charlock Cl ME16 74 D8
Charlotte Cl ME5 32 B6
Charlotte Ct 4 CT11 52 E6
Charlotte Dr ME8 11 C1
Charlotte Pl 2 CT9 7 J1
Charlotte Sq 8 CT9 7 J2
Charlotte St
13 Broadstairs CT10 30 B4
Folkestone CT20 178 E5
Sittingbourne ME10 36 E5
Charlton Ave CT16 149 C1
Charlton CE Prim Sch CT16 149 C1
Charlton Cl
Ashford TN24 157 A8
Ramsgate CT12 29 B2
Charlton Ctr 3 CT17 166 C8
Charlton Gn CT16 149 C1
Charlton La ME17 99 C1
Charlton Manor ME7 10 B5
Charlton St ME16 74 C2
Charltons The ME13 63 F4
Charminster TN23 155 E6
Charnwood CT5 21 D1
Charnwood Rd CT6 23 B1

Charollais Cl CT2 67 A2
Chart Cl ME13 62 B7
Chart Cnr ME17 98 B1
Chart Hill Rd ME17 98 B1
Chart Mill Gun Powder Mills★ ME13 62 B7
Chart Pl ME8 33 C3
Chart Rd
Ashford,Godinton Park TN23 138 F2
Ashford,Great Chart TN23 138 D1
Ashford,Stanhope TN23 155 D6
Folkestone CT19 177 F6
Chart Road Ind Est TN23 139 A3
Chartam Terr CT11 52 D5
Charter Ho 11 CT16 166 E7
Charter St Chatham ME4 9 F2
Gillingham ME7 10 C7
Chartham Downs Rd CT4 109 C7
Chartham Prim Sch CT4 86 C2
Chartham Sta CT4 86 D3
Chartway St ME17 99 C1
Chartwell Ave CT6 23 D4
Chartwell Ct Chatham ME4 9 E4
Maidstone ME15 75 B3
Chartwell Dr ME16 74 B4
Chartwell Gr ME10 36 C3
Chase The Chatham ME4 9 D2
Gillingham ME8 11 A2
Ramsgate CT11 29 F1
St Margaret's at Cliffe CT15 133 F1
Chater Cl CT14 117 C4
Chatham Ct CT11 52 D8
Chatham Gr ME4 9 F1
Chatham Gram Sch for Boys ME4 31 F8
Chatham Gram Sch for Girls ME5 10 C2
Chatham Hill ME4 10 B3
Chatham House Gram Sch for Boys CT11 52 E7
Chatham Pl CT11 52 E7
Chatham Rd
Kit's Coty ME20 53 D6
Maidstone ME14 53 E1
Sandling ME14 53 E4
Chatham Ski Ctr ME7 32 E6
Chatham South Sch ME4 31 F8
Chatham St CT11 52 E7
Chatham Sta ME4 9 E4
Chatsworth Dr ME10 36 B5
Chatsworth Rd 10 ME7 10 C6
Chattenden Ct ME14 75 B6
Chatwell Ct ME7 10 C5
Chaucer Ave CT5 21 B1
Chaucer Cl
Canterbury CT1 88 C7
13 Maidstone ME15 97 E7
Rochester ME2 9 E8
Chaucer Coll CT2 66 D3
Chaucer Cres CT16 149 B3
Chaucer Ct CT1 88 B7
Chaucer Hospl CT4 88 A4
Chaucer Mews CT2 65 E1
Chaucer Rd
Broadstairs CT10 30 A3
Canterbury CT1 67 C1
Elvington CT15 114 B2
Gillingham ME7 10 D3
Sittingbourne ME10 36 D3
Chaucer Tech Sch CT1 88 C7
Chaucer Wood Ct CT1 67 B1
Cheddar Cl TN24 139 B4
Cheesmans Cl CT12 50 C5
Cheffins Ho ME7 10 E7
Chegwell Dr ME5 32 B4
Chegworth Gdns ME10 36 E1
Chegworth La ME17 100 A6
Chegworth Rd ME17 99 F5
Chelmar Rd ME7 10 B4
Chelmsford Ho ME15 97 E6
Chelsea Ct CT21 176 C1
Chelsea Rd CT1 67 C4
Chelsfield Ho ME16 74 D5
Cheltenham Cl ME15 97 F6
Cheney Cl ME8 33 D5
Cheney Hill ME9 59 A5
Cheney Rd ME13 62 F7
Chennels The TN26 167 C7
Chepstow Ho 3 ME15 97 F6
Chequer La CT3 71 D2
Chequer's Terr ME12 5 A5
Chequers Cl ME5 54 A8
Chequers Ctr ME15 75 A4
Chequers Hill CT4 109 C2
Chequers Pk TN25 123 E1
Chequers Rd ME12 4 E6
Chequertree TN25 172 B7
Cherbourg Cres ME5 31 F7
Cheriton Appartments CT19 177 F6
Cheriton Ave CT12 52 B8
Cheriton Court Rd CT20 177 C6
Cheriton Gdns CT20 178 C4
Cheriton High St CT19 177 D6
Cheriton Intc CT19 177 C7
Cheriton Pl Deal CT14 117 D4
Folkestone CT20 178 D4
Cheriton Prim Sch CT20 177 C6
Cheriton Rd Deal CT14 117 D4
Folkestone CT19,CT20 178 B5
Folkestone, Morehall CT19 177 F6
Gillingham ME8 33 D8
Cheriton Way ME16 74 C7
Cheriton Wood Ho CT19 177 D7
Cherries The ME16 74 A2
Cherry Amber Cl ME8 33 F8
Cherry Ave CT2 66 D2
Cherry Cl Lenham ME17 101 C5
Sittingbourne ME10 36 D6
Cherry Ct Ashford TN23 139 B1
Broadstairs CT10 29 E7
Folkestone CT19 178 A6
Cherry Dr CT2 66 D2
Cherry Fields ME10 36 A5
Cherry Garden Ave CT19 178 A7
Cherry Garden Cres TN25 123 F2
Cherry Garden La
Ash CT3 71 E1
Folkestone CT19 177 F7
Wye TN25 123 F2
Cherry Garden Rd CT2 66 D2
Cherry Gdns
Broadstairs CT10 29 C3
Elham CT4 144 F5
Herne Bay CT6 22 F4
Littlestone-on-Sea TN28 202 D6
Teynham ME9 38 C2
Cherry Glebe TN25 157 E3
Cherry Gr CT15 114 B2
Cherry Hill Ct ME9 35 B6
Cherry La CT14 116 D3
Cherry Orch
Littlebourne CT3 68 F1
Old Wives Lees CT4 85 C2
Tenterden TN30 179 A6
Whitstable CT5 44 C8
Woodchurch TN26 169 A3
Cherry Orchard La TN25 172 E4
Cherry Orchard Mews CT3 68 F1
Cherry Orchard Way ME16 74 B3
Cherry Tree Ave CT16 149 C1
Cherry Tree Cl
Teynham ME9 38 D2
West Minst ME12 3 A8
Cherry Tree Dr ME13 39 F3
Cherry Tree Gdns CT12 29 B3
Cherry Tree Rd
Charing Heath TN27 119 E7
Gillingham ME8 33 F8
Cherry View ME17 97 B3
Cherry Waye CT15 131 D7
Cherrybrook Rd CT20 177 D6
Cherrygarden La CT15, CT3 113 E7
Cherrywood Rise TN25 138 F4
Cherville La CT3 90 C7
Chervilles ME16 74 A2
Chesham Dr ME8 33 E6
Cheshire Rd
Maidstone ME15 97 E7
Maidstone,Willington ME15 75 E2
Chessenden La TN27 135 A1
Chester Ave TN26 153 D5
Chester Rd
Gillingham ME7 10 D2
Westgate-on-S CT8 27 F8
Chestfield & Swalecliffe Sta CT5 21 D2
Chestfield Cl ME8 11 E2
Chestfield Rd CT5 44 C7
Chestnut Ave Blean CT2 66 A7
Chatham ME5 31 F3
Chestnut Cl
Ashford TN23 138 E3
Hythe CT21 187 E8
Tenterden TN30 167 C1
Whitfield CT16 149 A8
Chartham CT4 86 F1
Chestnut Ct ME13 64 A3
Chestnut Dr
Broadstairs CT10 29 D4
Coxheath ME17 96 B3
Herne Bay CT6 22 D3
Kingswood ME17 99 D2
Sturry CT2 68 A7
Worth CT14 94 A4
Chestnut Ho 5 ME16 74 A3
Chestnut La TN23 156 C4
Chestnut Rd CT17 166 B7
Chestnut St ME9 35 E4
Chestnut Terr CT21 176 A1
Chestnut Wood La ME9 35 E3
Chestnuts The
Brabourne Lees TN25 158 D5
Sellindge TN25 159 D1
Chetney View ME9 14 D4
Chevalier Rd CT17 166 A7
Chevening Cl ME5 32 A5
Cheviot Ct CT10 30 B5
Cheviot Gdns ME15 76 A1
Cheviot Way TN24 139 C4
Cheyne Cl ME10 36 F8
Cheyne Mid Sch The ME12 1 E2
Cheyne Rd ME12 5 D3
Chicago Ave ME7 10 F5
Chichester Cl
Ashford TN23 139 B1
Gillingham ME8 34 A8
Chichester Rd
Folkestone CT20 177 E4
Ramsgate CT12 29 B1
Chichester Wlk CT12 29 B1
Chickfield Gdns 4 ME5 10 C2
Chiddingfold Cl ME12 4 D6
Chiddingstone Cl ME15 97 F6
Chieftain Cl ME7 11 B1
Childgate Rd CT5 42 F2
Childscroft Rd ME8 11 F2
Chilham Ave CT8 27 D7
Chilham Cl Chatham ME4 9 E3
West Minst ME12 3 B8
Chilham Ho 1 ME15 97 E8
Chilham Rd
Folkestone CT19 177 E6
Gillingham ME8 11 A3
Maidstone ME16 74 C7
Chilham Sta CT4 107 D8
Chillenden Windmill★ CT3 91 F1
Chillington St ME14 74 F6
Chilston Rd ME17 101 D5
Chiltern Cl ME15 75 F1
Chiltern End TN24 139 B3
Chilton Ave
Sittingbourne ME10 37 A3
Temple Ewell CT16 148 C4
Chilton Ct
14 Folkestone CT20 178 E6
Gillingham ME8 11 E1
Chilton Field CT3 71 D2
Chilton Gdns CT3 71 D2
Chilton La CT11 52 A6
Chilton Pl CT3 71 D2
Chilton Prim Sch CT11 52 A6
Chilton Sq CT3 71 D2
Chilton Way CT17 148 D3
Chimes The
Ashford TN24 139 C3
Rochester ME1 9 C5
Chineham Way CT1 87 F6
Chippendale Cl ME5 31 F1
Chippendayle Dr ME17 100 D6
Chipstead Cl ME16 74 D6
Chipstead Rd ME8 33 D4
Chislehurst Cl ME15 97 F6
Chislet CE Prim Sch CT3 47 C5
Chislet Ct CT6 22 E5
Chislet Park Cotts CT3 46 F1
Chislet Park Farm Cotts CT3 46 F2
Chislet Wlk ME8 33 D5
Chislett Cl TN25 159 E2
Chisnall Rd CT17 148 E4
Chittenden's La TN29 193 E5
Chitty La CT3 47 D6
Christ Church CE High Sch TN23 155 F5
Christ Church CE Jun Sch CT11 52 C6
Christ Church Coll CT1 88 B8
Christ Church Rd CT20 178 C4
Christchurch Ct
3 Chatham ME5 10 C2
1 Dover CT17 166 D7
Christchurch Ho 11 ME15 97 E5
Christchurch Rd TN23 156 B8
Christchurch Way CT16 149 B3
Christen Way ME15,ME17 97 F3
Christian Ct 3 ME2 9 C8
Christie Cl ME5 32 B6
Christmas St ME7 10 E7
Christopher Bushell Way TN24 139 E4
Christopher's Row ME9 60 A3
Chrysler Ave CT6 22 B4
Chunnel Ind Est TN23 139 B1
Church App TN28 202 A6
Church Cl Mersham TN25 157 E3
New Romney TN28 202 B6
Church Cliff CT14 134 D6
Church Cotts
Rodmersham ME9 59 D8
Tenterden TN30 167 B3
Church Court Gr CT10 29 E6
Church Cres ME17 100 F6
Church Ct CT18 161 C6
Church Farm Rd ME9 12 E3
Church Farm Way CT13 93 B6
Church Field TN25 160 B1
Church Gn
Hollingbourne ME17 77 E3
Rochester ME2 9 C8
Church Haven CT14 133 F5
Church Hill
Bethersden TN26 153 D5
Boughton Street ME13 64 A5
Canterbury CT2 66 C1
Charing Heath ME17,TN27 119 C7
Chatham ME5 10 C2
Chilham CT4 107 B8
Doddington ME9 80 F8
Eythorne CT15 131 C8
Hawkinge CT18 163 D4
High Halden TN26 167 E7
Hythe CT21 176 C2
Kingsnorth TN23 156 B3
Loose ME17 97 C1
Ramsgate CT11 52 E7
Shepherdswell CT15 130 D4
Stockbury ME9 56 F7
Stone in Oxney TN30 189 F3
Sutton CT15 133 A7
Temple Ewell CT16 148 D5
Church Ho CT14 117 C7
Church Hts CT21 176 C2
Church La Adisham CT3 90 D1
Aldington TN25 173 D7
Barham CT4 111 F1
Boughton Aluph TN25 123 B4
Boyden Gate CT3 47 C7
Brenzett TN29 191 F5
Canterbury CT1 87 F8
Church La *continued*
21 Canterbury,Northgate CT1 67 A1
Challock TN25 122 B8
Chartham CT4 86 D3
Chatham ME4 9 F6
Church Hougham CT15 165 B5
Deal CT14 117 B6
Harrietsham ME17 100 E6
Iden TN31 197 B4
Kingston CT4 111 D3
Lower Hardres CT4 88 B2
Lydden CT15 147 E8
Maidstone,Bearsted ME14 76 C4
New Romney TN28 202 B5
Newington ME9 35 B6
Peasmarsh TN31 196 C1
Petham CT4 109 C3
Ringwould CT14 133 F5
Ripple CT14 116 D1
Selling ME13 84 B6
Shadoxhurst TN26 170 A7
Stockbury ME9 56 E8
Stourmouth CT3 48 C2
Stowting TN25 160 A6
Sturry CT2 67 F5
Waltham CT4 125 F5
West Langdon CT15 132 D3
Westbere CT2 68 C7
Whitstable CT5 43 A6
Womenswold CT4 112 D2
Church Marshes Ctry Pk★ ME10 37 A7
Church Mdws CT14 117 A6
Church Mews
Gillingham ME8 33 F8
Iwade ME9 14 E4
Church Path Deal CT14 117 B5
Gillingham ME7 10 E6
Great Mongeham CT14 116 D3
Lower Halstow ME9 13 C3
Church Rd Ashford TN23 139 C2
Ashford,Aylesford Green TN24 157 A7
Ashford,Kennington TN24 139 E6
Ashford,Willesborough TN24 157 A8
Boughton Malherbe ME17 118 A8
1 Broadstairs CT10 30 B4
Burmarsh TN29 185 E4
Charing TN27 103 D2
Chart Sutton ME17 98 C1
Coldred CT15 131 A3
Dover CT17 166 A7
Eastchurch ME12 5 D2
Eastling ME13 82 B2
Faversham ME13 62 D7
Faversham,Oare ME13 40 B3
Faversham,The Brents ME13 62 D8
Folkestone CT20 177 C6
Harrietsham ME17 100 E6
Hoath CT3 46 E5
Hucking ME17 56 E1
Hythe CT21 176 C2
Kenardington TN26 182 A5
Littlebourne CT3 90 A8
Lydd TN29 205 C6
Lyminge CT18 161 C7
Maidstone ME15 97 F7
Maidstone,Tovil ME15 74 E2
Margate CT9 7 J1
Mersham TN25 157 E3
Molash CT4 105 F5
New Romney TN28 202 A6
Northbourne CT14 116 A5
Northbourne,Betteshanger CT14 115 C6
Ramsgate CT11 52 E7
Sevington TN24 157 B6
Sittingbourne ME9 37 E5
Sittingbourne,Murston ME10 37 B5
Smeeth TN25 158 C4
Stalisfield Green ME13 103 F5
Tenterden TN30 179 A7
Church Rise CT21 176 C2
Church Road Bsns Ctr ME10 37 B6
Church Sq
2 Broadstairs CT10 30 B4
Lenham ME17 101 D5
Church St
Broadstairs CT10 29 E6
Canterbury CT2 66 E1
Chatham ME4 10 A4
Deal CT14 117 B1
Dover CT16 166 D7
Eastry CT13 93 C2
Faversham ME13 62 D8
Folkestone CT20 178 D4
Gillingham ME7 10 E6
Maidstone ME14 75 A4
Maidstone, Boughton Monchelsea ME17 97 B2
Maidstone,Loose ME15 96 F5
Maidstone,Tovil ME15 74 E2
Margate CT9 7 J1
Minster (Thanet) CT12 50 C5
Nonington CT15 113 C5
Rochester ME1 9 D4
Rodmersham ME9 59 C8
7 Sandwich CT13 73 A1
3 Sandwich,The Butts CT13 72 F1
5 Sittingbourne ME10 36 E4
Sittingbourne ME10 36 E5
Whitstable CT5 20 F1
Church St *continued*
Woodnesborough CT13 93 B6
Wye TN25 123 E2
Church Street (St Pauls) 7 CT1 88 A8
Church Terr Chatham ME5 10 C2
Minster (Sheppey) ME12 4 C7
Church View
Aldington TN25 173 A6
Herne Bay CT6 23 C4
Newchurch TN29 184 E3
Worth CT14 94 B5
Church Way CT5 21 D3
Church Whitfield Rd CT16 149 B8
Church Wlk CT4 144 F4
Church Wood Cl CT2 66 B2
Church Yard Pas 10 TN23 139 B2
Church Yd TN23 139 C2
Churchfield Pl CT9 7 I2
Churchfield Way TN25 123 E2
Churchfields
Broadstairs CT10 29 F7
Margate CT9 7 J1
Churchfields Terr ME1 9 B4
Churchill Ave
Chatham ME5 32 A7
Deal CT14 117 C2
Folkestone CT19 178 C8
Herne Bay CT6 23 D4
Churchill Cl Bridge CT4 88 F1
Folkestone CT19 178 D8
St Margaret's at Cliffe CT15 150 F5
Churchill Cotts ME17 98 F6
Churchill Ct Hythe CT21 176 B1
1 Ramsgate CT11 52 D7
Churchill Ho Bridge CT4 88 F1
2 Folkestone CT20 177 F5
Maidstone ME16 74 B2
Sittingbourne ME10 37 C4
Teynham ME9 38 C3
Churchill Rd
Canterbury CT1 88 C6
Dover CT17 166 A6
Minster (Sheppey) ME12 4 D6
Churchill Sch The CT18 163 A4
Churchill St 7 CT16 149 C1
Churchill Way ME13 40 B1
Churchill Wlk CT18 162 F4
Churchlands ME14 75 B5
Churchlands Ho TN28 202 B6
Churchlands The TN28 202 B6
Churchwood Dr CT5 21 D1
Chute Cl ME8 33 D4
Cinder Path CT10 30 A4
Cinnabar Cl ME5 32 A1
Cinnabar Dr ME10 36 C6
Cinque Ports Ave CT21 176 B1
Cinque Ports Rd TN28 202 C5
Circular Rd Dover CT16 150 B1
Finglesham CT14 116 B7
Circus The CT6 22 E4
Citadel Cres CT17 166 B6
Citadel Hts CT17 166 B6
Citadel Rd CT17 166 C6
Citadel The (Immigration Removal Ctr) CT17 166 B5
Citroen Cl CT6 22 B4
City Bsns Pk CT1 67 C3
City Garden The 3 CT1 88 A8
City View CT2 87 C8
City Way ME1 9 D2
Claire Ct Birchington CT7 26 F7
Broadstairs CT10 30 B5
Claire Ho 4 ME16 74 E5
Clandon Rd ME5 32 D2
Clanwilliam Rd CT14 117 D5
Clapham Hill CT5 43 D5
Clare Dr CT6 22 C2
Clare Rd CT5 20 E2
Claremont Cl CT14 134 C6
Claremont Gdns CT11 52 C7
Claremont Pl CT1 87 F7
Claremont Rd Deal CT14 117 B5
Folkestone CT20 178 C5
Kingsdown CT14 134 C6
Maidstone ME14 75 B5
Claremont St CT6 22 C4
Claremont Terr CT13 93 D7
Claremont Way 2 ME4 9 F3
Clarence Ave Margate CT9 8 D2
Rochester ME1 9 C4
Clarence Ct ME14 75 E4
Clarence Gdns ME12 6 E3
Clarence Pl Deal CT14 117 D7
Dover CT17 166 D5
Clarence Rd
Capel-le-F CT18 164 B2
Chatham ME4 10 B2
Deal CT14 117 D3
Herne Bay CT6 22 D5
Ramsgate CT11 52 C6
Clarence Row ME12 1 C2
Clarence St
Folkestone CT20 178 D5
Herne Bay CT6 22 E5
Clarendon Cl
Maidstone ME14 76 A4
Sittingbourne ME10 36 F1
Clarendon Gdns 7 CT11 52 D6
Clarendon House Gram Sch CT11 52 E6

Clarendon Mews
1 Broadstairs CT10 . . . . . . .30 A4
New Romney TN28 . . . . . . .202 C8
Clarendon Pl
Dover CT17 . . . . .166 C7
Maidstone ME14 . . . . . . .75 A4
Clarendon Rd
Aylesham CT3 . . . . .112 F5
Broadstairs CT10 . . . . .30 A4
Dover CT17 . . . . .166 C7
Margate CT9 . . . . .8 A2
Clarendon St
Dover CT17 . . . . .166 C7
Herne Bay CT6 . . . . .22 C4
Claridge Ct ME7 . . . . .32 F4
Claridge Mews CT21 . . . . .176 C2
Clark Rd TN28 . . . . .202 E4
Clarke Cres TN24 . . . . . . .139 F4
Clarke's Cl CT14 . . . . .116 F4
Clarklands TN29 . . . . . . .184 E3
Claudius Gr TN23 . . . . . . .155 F5
Clavell Cl ME8 . . . . .33 E4
Claxfield Cotts ME9 . . . . . .38 A2
Claxfield Rd ME9 . . . . .60 A8
Claygate Ashford TN23 . . . .155 F5
Eyhorne Street ME17 . . . . . .77 D2
Maidstone ME15 . . . . .75 D1
Clearmount Dr TN22 . . . . .120 C8
Clearmount Pk TN27 . . . . .120 D8
Cleave Rd ME7 . . . . .10 E3
Cleaver La CT11 . . . . .52 E7
Clematis Ave ME8 . . . . . . .33 B5
Clement Cl
Canterbury CT1 . . . . .67 B1
Sittingbourne ME10 . . . . . .36 E8
Clement Ct ME8 . . . . .74 D5
Clement's Rd CT12 . . . . . . .29 C2
Clementine Cl CT6 . . . . . . .23 D4
Clerke Dr ME10 . . . . .37 A8
Clermont Cl ME7 . . . . .33 A4
Clevedon Ct TN25 . . . . . . .105 B2
Cleveland Cl CT16 . . . . . . .149 B3
Cleveland Ct CT9 . . . . .8 A3
Cleveland Ho ME16 . . . . . .74 B2
Cleveland Rd ME7 . . . . . . .10 D6
Cleveley Lo CT11 . . . . .29 E2
Cleven Lodge CT7 . . . . . . .48 D6
Cleves Way TN23 . . . . . . .155 E8
Clewer Lo CT5 . . . . .20 F2
Clewson Rise ME14 . . . . . .75 B8
Cliff Ave CT6 . . . . .23 C5
Cliff Cl CT21 . . . . .176 D3
Cliff Cottage Chalet Pk
ME12 . . . . .5 F6
Cliff Dr Herne Bay CT6 . . . . .22 C4
Warden ME12 . . . . .6 E4
Cliff Field CT8 . . . . .27 C8
Cliff Gdns ME12 . . . . .4 E7
Cliff Hill ME17 . . . . .97 D4
Cliff Hill Rd ME17 . . . . .97 C4
Cliff Prom CT10 . . . . .30 C7
Cliff Rd Birchington CT7 . . . .26 F8
Broadstairs CT10 . . . . .30 B7
Dover CT15,CT16 . . . . . . .150 C1
Folkestone CT20 . . . . . . .178 A3
Hythe CT21 . . . . .176 E3
Whitstable CT5 . . . . .20 F3
Cliff Sea Gr CT6 . . . . .22 C4
Cliff St CT11 . . . . .52 E6
Cliff Terr CT9 . . . . .7 J3
Cliff View Gdns
Leysdown-on-S ME12 . . . . . .6 D1
Warden ME12 . . . . .6 E4
Cliff View Rd CT12 . . . . . . .51 D6
Cliffe Ave CT9 . . . . .7 F1
Cliffe Ho
Folkestone CT20 . . . . . . .178 A3
St Margaret's at Cliffe
CT15 . . . . .150 F6
Cliffe Rd Deal CT14 . . . . . .134 D4
Rochester ME2 . . . . .9 B8
Cliffestone Ct CT20 . . . . . .178 B5
Clifford Gdns CT14 . . . . . .117 B2
Clifford Ho 6 ME14 . . . . . .75 B4
Clifford Rd CT5 . . . . .43 F8
Cliffs End Gr CT12 . . . . . . .51 D5
Cliffs End Rd CT12 . . . . . . .51 E5
Cliffside Dr CT10 . . . . .30 A1
Clifftown Gdns CT6 . . . . . .22 B4
Clifton Cl ME14 . . . . .75 B5
Clifton Cres CT20 . . . . . . .178 B3
Clifton Gdns
Canterbury CT2 . . . . .66 D2
Folkestone CT20 . . . . . . .178 C4
Margate CT9 . . . . .7 J3
Whitstable CT5 . . . . .43 D8
Clifton Lawn CT11 . . . . . . .52 D5
Clifton Mans 7 CT20 . . . . .178 C4
Clifton Pl CT9 . . . . .8 A3
Clifton Rd
Folkestone CT20 . . . . . . .178 C4
Gillingham ME7 . . . . .10 C7
Margate CT9 . . . . .8 A2
Ramsgate CT11 . . . . .52 B8
Whitstable CT5 . . . . .20 D1
Clifton St CT9 . . . . .7 J3
Cliftonville Ave
Margate CT9 . . . . .8 A2
Ramsgate CT12 . . . . .29 B1
Cliftonville Ct Margate CT9 . .8 A3
Margate,Cliftonville CT9 . . . . .8 B3
Cliftonville Mews CT9 . . . . .8 A3
Cliftonville Prim Sch CT9 . . .8 C2
Clim Down CT14 . . . . .134 D6
Clinton Cl ME17 . . . . .96 B3

Clints La CT4 . . . . .129 D4
Clipper Cl ME2 . . . . .9 E7
Clipper Ct ME2 . . . . .9 E7
Clive Ct CT9 . . . . .8 B2
Clive Dennis Ct TN24 . . . . .139 E1
Clive Rd Cliffs End CT12 . . . .51 D6
Margate CT9 . . . . .29 A5
Rochester ME1 . . . . .9 C3
Sittingbourne ME10 . . . . . .36 B5
Cliveden Cl ME16 . . . . .74 D7
Clockhouse TN23 . . . . . . .138 F1
Clockhouse Pk TN25 . . . . .105 C2
Clocktower Par CT2 . . . . . .66 A6
Cloisterham Rd ME1 . . . . . .31 D7
Cloisters The
18 Canterbury CT1 . . . . . .66 F1
Lenham ME17 . . . . .101 C5
Ramsgate CT11 . . . . .52 D5
8 Sittingbourne ME10 . . . .36 E4
Whitstable CT5 . . . . .20 F2
Clopton Ct ME8 . . . . .33 D8
Close The Ashford TN23 . . . .155 F7
Bridge CT4 . . . . .88 F1
Canterbury CT1 . . . . .87 D6
Canterbury,Hales Place CT2 . .66 F4
Canterbury,St Dunstan's
CT2 . . . . .66 C3
Faversham ME13 . . . . .62 C6
Folkestone CT19 . . . . . . .178 E8
Hythe CT21 . . . . .176 B4
Lydden CT15 . . . . .147 F8
Rochester ME1 . . . . .9 C4
Wye TN25 . . . . .123 E2
Cloudberry Cl ME16 . . . . . .74 D6
Cloudesley Cl ME1 . . . . . . .9 B1
Clouston Cl CT18 . . . . .163 B5
Clovelly TN28 . . . . .202 E6
Clovelly Dr ME12 . . . . .4 B8
Clovelly Rd CT5 . . . . .43 D7
Clover Bank View ME5 . . . .32 B6
Clover Ct ME10 . . . . .37 B5
Clover Lay ME8 . . . . .12 B2
Clover Rise CT5 . . . . .21 B1
Clover St 3 ME4 . . . . .9 F4
Clover Terr 4 ME15 . . . . . .97 D8
Cloverlay Ind Pk ME8 . . . . .12 C1
Clowes Ct CT2 . . . . .66 C4
Clubb's La TN29 . . . . .199 D7
Cluny Rd ME13 . . . . .62 F7
Clyde St
1 Canterbury CT1 . . . . . .67 A1
Sheerness ME12 . . . . .1 E2
Clynton Way TN23 . . . . . .156 A7
Coach Dr TN26 . . . . .138 A7
Coach House Mews The
CT15 . . . . .131 D5
Coach Rd
Charing Heath TN27 . . . . .119 A6
Densole CT18 . . . . .162 F8
Egerton ME17,TN27 . . . . .118 E6
Coach Yd The ME16 . . . . . .74 B3
Coalpit La ME9 . . . . .80 A6
Coast Dr
Greatstone-on-Sea TN28 . . .202 E3
Lydd-on-Sea TN29 . . . . . .209 D8
St Mary's Bay TN29 . . . . . .194 F2
Coast Rd TN28 . . . . .202 F7
Coastguard Alley CT5 . . . . .20 C1
Coastguard Cotts
Conyer ME9 . . . . .38 E6
Dover CT16 . . . . .166 G8
Herne Bay CT6 . . . . .21 F4
Hythe CT21 . . . . .176 B1
Kingsdown CT14 . . . . . . .134 D4
Leysdown-on-S ME12 . . . . .19 E4
Lydd-on-S TN29 . . . . .209 D5
Minster (Sheppey) ME12 . . . .5 C5
23 Ramsgate,East Cliff
CT11 . . . . .52 F7
Ramsgate,Pegwell CT11 . . . .52 A5
Sandwich CT13 . . . . .95 A8
Birchington CT7 . . . . .26 D8
Coastguard Cotts The
ME12 . . . . .1 I1
Coastguard Hos ME12 . . . . .6 C5
Coats Ave ME12 . . . . .3 A8
Cobay Ct CT21 . . . . .176 D2
Cobb Ct CT9 . . . . .7 I3
Cobb Wlk ME13 . . . . .62 B8
Cobblers Bridge Rd CT6 . . .22 D3
Cobblestones ME7 . . . . . . .32 F5
Cobbs Hill CT4 . . . . .85 C2
Cobbs Mews 3 CT20 . . . . .178 C4
Cobbs Pl CT9 . . . . .7 I3
Cobbs Wood Ind Est
TN23 . . . . .138 F2
Cobden Pl 18 CT1 . . . . . . .67 A1
Cobden Rd
4 Chatham ME4 . . . . . . .10 B2
Hythe CT21 . . . . .176 B1
Cobdown Gr ME8 . . . . .12 A2
Cobfield ME17 . . . . .98 A1
Cobham Ave ME10 . . . . . . .36 E1
Cobham Chase ME13 . . . . .62 B8
Cobham Cl
Canterbury CT1 . . . . .88 C6
Maidstone ME16 . . . . .74 E4
Cobham Rise ME7 . . . . . . .10 F5
Cobsden Cl TN29 . . . . .195 A4
Cobsden Rd TN29 . . . . . . .195 A4
Cobtree Cl ME5 . . . . .32 C8
Cobtree Rd ME17 . . . . .96 C3
Cobweb Cnr CT2 . . . . .66 B4
Cock La Elham CT4 . . . . . . .144 F4
Hamstreet TN26 . . . . .183 A7
Cockering Rd
Canterbury CT1,CT4 . . . . . .87 B4

Cockering Rd continued
Chartham CT4 . . . . .86 E2
Cockreed La TN28 . . . . . . .202 B7
Codrington Rd CT11 . . . . . .52 D7
Cogans Terr CT1 . . . . .87 E6
Coggan Ho 7 CT1 . . . . . . .87 F7
Colburn Rd CT10 . . . . .30 A2
Colchester Cl ME5 . . . . .32 A7
Cold Harbour CT1 . . . . .67 A2
Cold Harbour La ME9 . . . . .35 F6
Cold Harbour Rd ME13 . . . .103 A7
Coldblow CT14 . . . . .117 A1
Coldblow La
Hucking ME14 . . . . .56 A2
Woodchurch TN26 . . . . . .169 D4
Coldbridge La TN27 . . . . . .118 B5
Coldharbour La
Bridge CT4,CT3 . . . . .111 D7
Forstal ME20 . . . . .53 A1
Hucking ME14,ME9 . . . . . .56 B1
Old Romney TN29 . . . . . . .200 C5
Peasmarsh TN31 . . . . . . .196 E3
Sittingbourne ME10 . . . . . .124 A1
Wye TN25 . . . . .124 A2
Coldred Hill CT15 . . . . .130 F1
Coldred Rd Coldred CT15 . . .131 B5
Maidstone ME15 . . . . .97 F4
Shepherdswell CT15 . . . . .130 E3
Coldswood Rd CT12 . . . . . .28 F2
Cole Rd ME13 . . . . .62 E7
Cole Terr ME17 . . . . .101 C4
Colegate Dr ME14 . . . . .76 C4
Colegates Cl ME13 . . . . . . .40 B2
Colegates Ct ME13 . . . . . . .40 B2
Colegates Rd ME13 . . . . . . .40 A2
Coleman Cres CT12 . . . . . . .29 C1
Coleman Dr ME10 . . . . .14 F1
Coleman's Stairs Rd CT7 . . .27 A8
Coleman's Yd 9 CT11 . . . . .52 E6
Colemans La TN29 . . . . . . .205 D7
Coleridge Gdns CT3 . . . . . .112 F6
Colesdane ME17 . . . . .100 E8
Coleshall Cl ME15 . . . . .97 F6
Coleshall Cotts ME9 . . . . . .14 D3
Colette Cl CT10 . . . . .8 G2
Coleville Cres TN28 . . . . . .206 E7
Colewood Rd CT5 . . . . .21 E3
Colfe Way ME10 . . . . .37 A8
Colin's Way CT21 . . . . .177 A3
Collard Ct CT6 . . . . .23 A4
Collard Ho CT1 . . . . .88 C8
Collard Rd TN24 . . . . .157 A8
Collards Cl CT17 . . . . .49 D7
Collards La CT4 . . . . .144 E3
College Ave
Gillingham ME7 . . . . .10 B4
Maidstone ME15 . . . . .74 F3
College Cotts ME16 . . . . . . .74 F3
College Ct Ashford TN23 . . .139 C2
Canterbury CT1 . . . . .67 B1
6 Maidstone ME15 . . . . . .75 A3
College Row CT17 . . . . . . .166 B7
College Sq 2 CT9 . . . . .7 J2
College Way CT3 . . . . .91 A7
College Wlk
4 Maidstone ME15 . . . . . .75 A3
3 Margate CT9 . . . . .7 J2
College Yd ME1 . . . . .9 C6
Collet Wlk ME8 . . . . .33 D4
Collett Cl TN25 . . . . .142 D8
Collie Dr TN23 . . . . .155 E5
Collingbourne TN23 . . . . . .155 E6
Collings Wlk ME8 . . . . .33 D4
Collington Terr ME15 . . . . . .97 E4
Collingwood Cl
Broadstairs CT10 . . . . .29 E4
Westgate-on-S CT8 . . . . . .27 D7
Collingwood Ct
Folkestone CT20 . . . . . . .177 E5
7 Ramsgate CT11 . . . . . .52 D7
Collingwood Ind Ctr
ME17 . . . . .98 E2
Collingwood Rd
Kit's Coty ME20 . . . . .53 C7
St Margaret's at Cliffe
CT15 . . . . .150 F8
Whitstable CT5 . . . . .20 C1
Collingwood Rise CT20 . . . .177 E5
Collingwood Wlk ME10 . . . .36 B5
Collins Rd Herne Bay CT6 . . .22 C2
New Romney TN28 . . . . . .202 C5
Collis St ME2 . . . . .9 A8
Collison Pl TN30 . . . . .179 D7
Colman Ho 4 ME14 . . . . . .75 A4
Colombo Sq CT12 . . . . .29 A1
Colonel Stephens Way
TN30 . . . . .167 B2
Colonel's La ME13 . . . . .64 A3
Colorado Cl CT16 . . . . .149 B3
Colson Dr ME9 . . . . .14 E3
Colton Cres CT16 . . . . .149 B4
Coltsfoot Dr ME14 . . . . .75 F4
Columbia Ave CT5 . . . . .43 B7
Columbine Cl CT5 . . . . .43 C6
Columbus Ave CT12 . . . . . .27 D1
Com Coll Whitstable The
CT5 . . . . .43 F8
Command Rd ME14 . . . . . . .74 F8
Commercial Rd ME2 . . . . . . .9 C8
Commissioner's Rd ME2 . . . .9 C8
Commissioners Ct ME4 . . . . .9 F4

Commodore Ct CT21 . . . . .176 C1
Commodore Rd ME14 . . . . .75 C5
Common La CT17 . . . . .148 E3
Common Rd ME5 . . . . .31 B1
Common The ME1 . . . . .9 C6
Common Way TN26 . . . . . .138 A7
Commonwealth Cl ME10 . . . .37 B3
Compass Cl ME1 . . . . .9 C1
Compass Ctr ME4 . . . . .10 A8
Compton Cl ME5 . . . . .32 D2
Concord Ave ME5 . . . . .31 E5
Condor Cl ME12 . . . . .6 E3
Conduit Ho The ✱ CT1 . . . . .67 B1
Conduit St ME13 . . . . .62 D8
Coney Mews ME4 . . . . .10 A1
Conference Wlk CT1 . . . . . .88 C8
Conifer Ct CT8 . . . . .7 D1
Conifer Dr ME5 . . . . .32 D1
Conifers The Deal CT14 . . . .117 A2
Shepherdswell CT15 . . . . .130 F2
Coniston Ave CT11 . . . . . . .52 A7
Coniston Dr CT3 . . . . .112 F6
Coniston Ho ME15 . . . . .97 E7
Coniston Rd CT19 . . . . . . .178 B7
Conker Cl TN23 . . . . .156 C3
Connaught Barracks
CT16 . . . . .149 E1
Connaught Cl ME15 . . . . . . .97 F4
Connaught Gdns 9 CT9 . . . .7 J1
Connaught Mews 2 ME4 . .10 C2
Connaught Rd
Chatham ME4 . . . . .10 C2
Dover CT16 . . . . .149 D1
Folkestone CT20 . . . . . . .178 D5
Gillingham ME7 . . . . .10 D5
Margate CT9 . . . . .7 J1
Sittingbourne ME10 . . . . . .36 E3
Conquest Ind Est ME2 . . . . .9 A5
Conrad Ave CT1 . . . . .67 C3
Conrad Cl ME8 . . . . .33 D4
Consort Cl ME14 . . . . .75 B5
Constable Rd CT7 . . . . .27 A8
Constable's Rd CT16 . . . . . .166 E8
Constancia Ct CT20 . . . . . .178 C5
Constantine Rd TN23 . . . . . .155 F5
Constitution Hill 8 ME5 . . .10 B3
Constitution Rd ME5 . . . . . .10 B2
Consul Cl CT6 . . . . .22 B4
Continental App CT9 . . . . . .28 F6
Convent Cl CT15 . . . . .151 B6
Convent Rd CT10 . . . . .8 G1
Convent Wlk CT11 . . . . .52 D7
Conventina Ho 3 CT11 . . . .52 D7
Conway Cl Birchington CT7 . . .26 C7
Hythe CT21 . . . . .176 B4
Conway Hall 18 ME7 . . . . . .10 A6
Conway Mews ME7 . . . . . . .10 A6
Conway Rd ME16 . . . . .74 C6
Conyer Rd ME9 . . . . .38 F4
Conyers Wlk ME8 . . . . .33 D4
Conyngham Ct CT12 . . . . . .29 B2
Conyngham La CT4 . . . . . . .89 A2
Conyngham Rd
Herne Bay CT6 . . . . .23 D5
Minster (Thanet) CT12 . . . .50 C5
Cooden Cl ME8 . . . . .12 A2
Cook Cl ME5 . . . . .32 C6
Cook's Lea CT13 . . . . .93 B2
Cookham Hill ME1 . . . . .9 A2
Cookham Wood Rd ME1 . . . .31 B8
Cooks La ME10 . . . . .36 F6
Cooks Wharf ME1 . . . . .9 E4
Cooling Cl ME14 . . . . .75 C6
Coolinge La CT20 . . . . .177 F4
Coolinge Rd CT20 . . . . .178 A4
Coombe Cl Chatham ME5 . . . .32 B3
Dover CT17 . . . . .149 A1
Coombe Ct CT17 . . . . .149 A1
Coombe Dr ME10 . . . . .37 C4
Coombe La Ash CT13,CT3 . . .92 A8
Tenterden TN30 . . . . .179 A7
Coombe Lands TN30 . . . . . .188 D4
Coombe Rd Crabble CT17 . . .148 F1
Dover CT15,CT17 . . . . . . .165 E8
Folkestone CT19 . . . . . . .177 F6
Maidstone ME15 . . . . .74 F2
Coombe Valley Rd CT17 . . .149 A1
Coombe Way CT18 . . . . . . .163 C4
Coombe Wlk CT5 . . . . .43 A2
Coombe Wood La CT18 . . . .163 C4
Cooper Rd ME5 . . . . .32 B3
Cooper Street Dro CT3 . . . . .72 B4
Cooper's Hill CT3 . . . . .72 F5
Cooper's La TN25 . . . . .158 F2
Coopers La CT1 . . . . .87 E7
Cooting La CT3 . . . . .112 D8
Cooting Rd CT3 . . . . .112 E4
Cop Street Rd CT3 . . . . .71 D3
Copenhagen Rd ME7 . . . . . .10 C4
Copinger Cl CT2 . . . . .67 A4
Copland Ave ME12 . . . . . . .4 C6
Copper Tree Ct ME15 . . . . . .97 A5
Copper Tree Wlk ME5 . . . . .32 C1
Copperfield ME12 . . . . .5 F5
Copperfield Cl
Ashford TN24 . . . . .139 C6
Kingswood ME17 . . . . .99 D2
Copperfield Ct CT10 . . . . . . .30 B5
Copperfield Dr ME17 . . . . . .98 E4
Copperfield Ho 6 ME4 . . . . .9 F4
Copperfield Rd ME1 . . . . . . .9 C2
Copperfields TN29 . . . . . . .205 B6
Copperfields The ME1 . . . . . .9 B4
Coppergate
Canterbury CT2 . . . . .66 F4
Gillingham ME7 . . . . .32 F5
Copperhouse La ME7 . . . . . .11 B6

Copperhurst Wlk CT9 . . . . . .8 F2
Copperpenny Dr ME7 . . . . . .33 B3
Copperwood TN24 . . . . . . .139 C4
Coppice Ct ME7 . . . . .33 B4
Coppice Rd ME5 . . . . .32 C2
Coppice The Hythe CT21 . . .176 B4
Sturry CT2 . . . . .67 F6
Coppice View ME14 . . . . . . .75 E6
Coppin St CT14 . . . . .117 D6
Coppins La ME9 . . . . .36 F6
Coppock Cl CT12 . . . . .29 B1
Copse Cl ME1 . . . . .9 E1
Copse The TN23 . . . . .138 D3
Copsewood Way ME15 . . . . .76 A3
Copt Cl CT2 . . . . .67 F7
Copthall Gdns 13 CT20 . . . .178 D5
Corben Cl ME16 . . . . .74 B6
Cordelia Cres ME1 . . . . .9 A2
Cordingham Rd CT5 . . . . . . .43 A6
Cordova Ct CT20 . . . . .178 B4
Corkwell St ME4 . . . . .9 E3
Cormorant Way CT6 . . . . . .23 F4
Cornbrook Rd CT21 . . . . . .187 D8
Cornelis Dr CT12 . . . . .50 B5
Corner Cotts TN26 . . . . . . .182 A6
Corner Field TN23 . . . . . . .156 B5
Cornes Cl TN24 . . . . .140 A1
Cornflower Cl ME14 . . . . . . .75 E4
Cornford Rd CT7 . . . . .27 A7
Cornhill 15 CT11 . . . . .52 E6
Corniche The CT20 . . . . . . .177 C3
Cornwall Ave CT11 . . . . . . .52 F8
Cornwall Cl ME15 . . . . .97 E7
Cornwall Gdns
Canterbury CT1 . . . . .88 D7
Margate CT9 . . . . .8 B3
Cornwall Ho Deal CT14 . . . .117 A5
5 Dover CT17 . . . . .166 C7
Cornwall Rd Deal CT14 . . . .117 C3
Gillingham ME7 . . . . .10 D6
Herne Bay CT6 . . . . .22 B2
Rochester ME1 . . . . .9 C3
Cornwallis Ave
Aylesham CT3 . . . . .112 F6
Chatham ME4 . . . . .9 E1
Folkestone CT19 . . . . . . .178 B6
Gillingham ME8 . . . . .11 A4
Herne Bay CT6 . . . . .23 C3
Cornwallis Circ CT5 . . . . . . .20 C1
Cornwallis Cl
Ashford TN24 . . . . .157 A7
Folkestone CT19 . . . . . . .178 B6
Cornwallis Cotts ME17 . . . . .96 E2
Cornwallis Gdns CT10 . . . . .30 A6
Cornwallis Rd ME16 . . . . . .74 D4
Cornwallis Rdbt ME8 . . . . . .11 A4
Cornwallis Sch The ME15 . . .96 F2
Coronation Cl CT10 . . . . . . .29 E7
Coronation Cotts CT19 . . . .177 D6
Coronation Cres
Margate CT9 . . . . .28 B8
Queenborough ME11 . . . . . .2 F5
Coronation Dr
Ashford TN23 . . . . .138 C1
Leysdown-on-S ME12 . . . . . .6 D2
Coronation Flats 5 ME4 . . . .9 F3
Coronation Rd
Chatham ME5 . . . . .10 C2
Ramsgate CT11 . . . . .52 D6
Sheerness ME12 . . . . .1 E1
Coronation Sq TN29 . . . . . .205 C6
Corone Cl CT19 . . . . .178 A7
Corporation Rd ME7 . . . . . . .10 D7
Corporation St ME1 . . . . . . .9 C6
Corral Cl ME5 . . . . .10 D2
Corrall Almshouses 5
ME15 . . . . .75 A3
Corrance Gn ME15 . . . . .97 A3
Corsican Wlk CT6 . . . . .23 C3
Cortanore ME10 . . . . .36 E2
Cortland Cl ME10 . . . . .36 E6
Cortland Mews ME10 . . . . . .36 E6
Corunna Cl CT21 . . . . .176 A2
Corunna Pl CT15 . . . . .149 E3
Cory's Rd ME1 . . . . .9 D6
Corylus Dr CT5 . . . . .43 A7
Cossack St ME1 . . . . .9 D3
Cossington Rd
Canterbury CT1 . . . . .88 A7
Chatham ME5 . . . . .32 B1
Cosway Cotts TN25 . . . . . . .172 C1
Cotswold Cl TN24 . . . . . . .139 B4
Cotswold Gdns ME4 . . . . . . .76 A2
Cottage Rd Chatham ME4 . . . .9 F6
Ramsgate CT11 . . . . .52 E6
Cottage Row CT13 . . . . .72 F1
Cottall Ave ME4 . . . . .9 F2
Cottington Rd CT12 . . . . . . .51 B5
Cotton Hill Ho TN26 . . . . . .183 A7
Cotton Hill Wlk TN26 . . . . .183 A7
Cotton Rd CT1 . . . . .87 E7
Coulman St ME7 . . . . .10 D5
Coulson Gr CT14 . . . . .116 A5
Coulter Rd Ashford TN23 . . .155 E5
Herne Bay CT6 . . . . .22 B2
Coulters Cl ME14 . . . . .75 D5
Coultrip Cl ME12 . . . . .5 B5
Council Cotts ME15 . . . . . . .96 A4
Countess Mountbatten Ct
CT8 . . . . .27 E8
Country Ways ME17 . . . . . .102 D3
Country's Field TN29 . . . . . .195 C8
County Rd ME14 . . . . .75 A5
County Sq 8 TN23 . . . . . . .139 B2
Court Cotts
St Nicholas at Wade CT7 . . . .25 E2
Wingham CT3 . . . . .91 A7
Court Dr ME16 . . . . .74 D4

Court Flats CT3 ....91 A7
Court Hall ME11 ....2 F5
Court Hall Mus★ ME10 ..36 E6
Court Hill CT3 ....68 E2
Court Hill Ho CT16 ......148 E4
Court La Detling ME14 .....55 C5
Preston CT3 ....70 B6
Court Lodge CT14 ....117 B6
Court Lodge Cotts ME15 ..96 A7
Court Lodge Rd
Appledore TN26 ....190 C7
Gillingham ME7 ....10 F6
Court Mdw ME8 ....11 B2
Court Mdws CT3 ....89 F8
Court Mount CT7 ....27 A6
Court Pl 5 CT20 ....178 C4
Court Rd Burham ME1 .....53 A8
Deal CT14 ....117 B1
Sittingbourne ME10 ....36 F7
St Nicholas at Wade CT7 ....25 E2
Court St ME13 ....62 D7
Court Tree Dr ME12 ....5 B5
Court Wurtin TN23 ......156 A7
Courtenay Ho ME13 ......64 C3
Courtenay Rd
Boughton Street CT2,ME13 ..64 E5
Deal CT14 ....117 C8
Maidstone ME15 ....74 F2
Courteney Rd ME8 ....33 B8
Courtfield Ave ME5 ....32 B3
Courtland Ave CT16 .....149 A6
Courtland Dr CT16 ......148 E4
Courtlands Deal CT14 ....134 D6
Herne Bay CT6 ....23 B3
Courtlands Cl CT12 ....51 E5
Courtlands Way CT8 ....7 D1
Courts The CT9 ....7 E1
Courtyard The
Ashford TN24 ....156 F6
Gillingham ME8 ....33 A8
Staple CT3 ....92 A6
Coventon La CT14 ....94 A5
Coventry Gdns CT6 ....23 E5
Coverdale Ave ME15 ......97 D6
Coverdale Cl ME5 ....32 B7
Covert TN23 ....138 E1
Covert Rd CT3 ....112 E4
Covert The ME5 ....32 B1
Covet La CT4 ....111 C2
Cow La Canterbury CT1 ....87 D7
Dover CT17 ....166 A7
Cowbeck Cl ME8 ....33 D6
Cowden Rd ME14 ....75 C5
Cowdray Rd CT14 ....117 A3
Cowdray Sq CT14 ....117 A3
Cowdrey Cl
Ashford TN24 ....157 A7
Maidstone ME16 ....74 B2
Rochester ME1 ....9 B2
Cowdrey Pl CT1 ....88 B6
Cowgate Hill CT17 ......166 D7
Cowgate La CT18 ....163 C5
Cowley Rise CT9 ....29 C8
Cowper Cl CT5 ....21 D3
Cowper Rd Crabble CT17 ..148 E3
Deal CT14 ....117 C5
Gillingham ME7 ....10 D3
Margate CT9 ....7 J1
Sittingbourne ME10 ....37 B4
Cowstead Rd ME9 ....34 D2
Cox Gdns ME8 ....11 A2
Cox St ME14 ....55 E6
Coxes Ave CT12 ....29 B3
Coxes La CT12 ....29 B3
Coxett Hill ME13 ....61 D5
Coxheath Prim Sch ME17 .96 C3
Coxhill CT15 ....130 C3
Coxhill Cres CT17 ....148 D3
Coxhill Gdns CT17 ......148 D3
Coxland Cotts TN26 .....181 B1
Cozenton Cl ME8 ....11 E1
Crabble Ave CT17 ....149 A2
Crabble Cl CT17 ....148 F2
Crabble Corn Mill★
CT17 ....148 F3
Crabble Hill CT16,CT17 ..149 A2
Crabble La CT17 ....148 E2
Crabble Mdws CT17 .....149 A2
Crabble Rd CT17 ....149 A3
Crabtree La ME17 ....119 B8
Crabtree Rd ME8 ....33 D8
Crabtree Rdbt ME14 ......53 E2
Craddock Dr 8 CT1 ......67 B1
Craddock Ho CT1 ....67 B1
Craddock Rd CT1 ....67 B1
Craddock Way ME8 ....33 D5
Cradle Bridge Dr TN24 ..139 F2
Cradles Rd ME9 ....34 C2
Crafford St CT16 ....149 D1
Cragie Wlk ME8 ....33 E4
Craig Ho ME1 ....9 E1
Craighton Ho 2 CT16 ...166 E7
Crampton Ct CT10 ....30 A4
Cranborne Ave ME15 ......75 C1
Cranborne Wlk CT2 ......66 E3
Cranbourne Ave ME15 ....97 B8
Cranbourne Cl CT11 ......52 F8
Cranbrook Cl
Gillingham ME8 ....11 C3
Maidstone ME15 ....97 F7
Margate CT9 ....8 E1
Cranbrook Dr ME10 ......36 D1
Cranbrooks TN25 ....157 D4
Cranford Cl ME8 ....11 D1
Cranleigh Ct CT5 ....43 E8
Cranleigh Dr CT16 ......149 B7
Cranleigh Gdns
Chatham ME4 ....9 D3
Cranleigh Gdns *continued*
Maidstone ME16 ....74 C7
Whitstable CT5 ....43 E8
Cranmer Cl CT4 ....89 B4
Cranmer Ct ME15 ....97 B8
Cranmer Ho 6 CT2 ....66 E1
Cranmere Ct ME2 ....9 C8
Cranswick Cotts CT14 ...133 C8
Craufurd Gn CT20 ....177 D5
Craven Cl CT9 ....28 C8
Crawford Gdns CT9 ....8 B2
Crawford Rd CT10 ....29 F5
Crayford Cl ME14 ....75 C6
Craythorne TN30 ....179 B8
Craythorne Cl
Hythe CT21 ....177 B4
New Romney TN28 ....202 B8
Craythorne Ho TN30 ....179 B8
Craythorne La TN28 .....202 B7
Creighton Flats 2 CT13 ...72 F1
Cremer Cl CT4 ....86 C2
Cremer Pl ME13 ....62 A8
Cremers Rd ME10 ....37 B5
Crescent Ho Margate CT9 ...8 A2
Ramsgate CT12 ....52 C7
Rochester ME2 ....9 C7
Crescent Rd
Birchington CT7 ....27 A7
Broadstairs CT10 ....30 C8
Faversham ME13 ....62 D7
Margate CT9 ....7 H2
Ramsgate CT11 ....52 D7
Crescent St 1 ME10 ......36 F4
Crescent The
Aylesham CT15 ....113 A3
Boughton Street ME13 .....64 A3
Canterbury CT2 ....66 F4
Chartham CT4 ....86 D1
Eythorne CT15 ....131 C7
Folkestone CT20 ....177 E3
Halfway Houses ME12 ......3 E6
Lower Halstow ME9 ....13 C3
Maidstone ME14 ....74 F8
Sandwich CT13 ....93 E6
Sheerness ME12 ....1 D2
Sittingbourne ME10 ....15 A1
St Margaret's at Cliffe
CT15 ....151 A5
Teynham ME9 ....38 D3
Crescent Way ME5 ....31 D5
Cress Way ME13 ....62 A7
Cressey Ct 7 ME4 ....9 E4
Cressfield TN23 ....138 F1
Crest Rd ME1 ....9 C1
Cresta Cl CT6 ....21 F4
Crestway ME5 ....32 B8
Crete Rd E CT18,CT19 ...163 D1
Crete Rd W CT18 ....163 B1
Creteway Cl CT19 ......178 E8
Creve Coeur Cl ME14 .....76 A5
Crevequer Chambers 1
ME8 ....11 F1
Cricketers Cl
Harrietsham ME17 ....100 D6
Hawkinge CT18 ....163 B6
Sittingbourne ME10 ....36 F8
Crimond Ave TN29 ....187 A4
Criol Rd TN26 ....155 A2
Cripple Hill TN26 ....152 D1
Cripple St ME15 ....97 A7
Cripps Cl CT3 ....112 E5
Cripps' La CT15 ....150 F6
Crisfield Ct TN30 ....167 B2
Crismill La ME14 ....76 F4
Crismill Rd ME14,ME17 ....76 F3
Crispe Cl ME8 ....33 D4
Crispe Park Cl CT7 ......27 B7
Crispe Rd CT7 ....27 A3
Crispin Cl ME13 ....62 D8
Crispin Ct ME17 ....96 C3
Crittenden Bglws ME15 ...96 A4
Crittenden Cotts ME15 ...96 A4
Crocken Hill Rd TN27 ...118 C2
Crockham La ME13 ....64 B6
Crockham Rd ME13 ....64 C6
Crockshard Hill CT3 ......91 B4
Crockshard La CT3 ....91 B4
Croft Cl ME5 ....32 C1
Croft Gdns ME17 ....101 D4
Croft La CT20 ....177 F5
Croft Rd TN24 ....139 D2
Croft The TN30 ....179 B7
Croft's Pl 8 CT10 ....30 B4
Crofters Cl CT21 ....187 E8
Crofters The ME8 ....33 F7
Crofton Cl TN24 ....139 C6
Crofton Rd CT8 ....27 E7
Croftwood TN23 ....155 D6
Croidene Ct ME12 ....4 A6
Crombie Cl CT18 ....163 B5
Cromer Rd Rochester ME2 ...9 B8
Sittingbourne ME9,ME10 ...58 F8
Crompton Gdns ME15 .....75 B3
Crompton Tower Rly Mus★
CT10 ....30 A4
Cromwell Park Pl CT20 ..177 D4
Cromwell Rd
Canterbury CT1 ....88 A6
Maidstone ME14 ....75 B5
West Minst ME11 ....2 F7
Whitstable CT5 ....20 E1
Cromwell Terr ME4 ....10 A3
Crook's Court La CT15 ..164 F4
Crooked S Rd CT14 ......133 E7
Crookenden Pl CT4 .....128 F8
Crosier Ct ME9 ....12 E3
Crosley Rd ME7 ....10 D3
Cross Dr ME17 ....99 B1
Cross Keys ME14 ....76 C4
Cross La
7 Faversham ME13 ....62 D7
Sittingbourne ME10 ....36 E6
Throwley Forstal ME13 ...104 C7
Cross Rd Birchington CT7 ...27 B8
Deal CT14 ....117 A2
Cross St
2 Canterbury CT2 ....66 E1
Chatham ME4 ....10 A4
Gillingham ME7 ....10 C6
Herne Bay CT6 ....22 D3
Maidstone ME14 ....75 A6
Rochester ME2 ....9 B8
Cross Stile TN23 ....155 F8
Cross The CT13 ....93 B2
Cross Way ME1 ....9 C3
Crossley Ave CT6 ....21 F4
Crossway ME5 ....31 E6
Crossways Canterbury CT2 ...66 F4
Chart Sutton ME17 ....98 B1
Sittingbourne ME10 ....36 F1
Crossways Ave CT9 ....29 A5
Crossways Cl TN29 ......186 E2
Crouch Cotts ME13 ....84 E8
Crouch Hill Ct ME9 ....13 C3
Crouch La ME13 ....84 E8
Crow Cnr
Brabourne TN25 ....141 E1
Rochester ME1 ....9 C5
Crow Hill CT10 ....30 B5
Crow Hill Rd CT9 ....28 B8
Crow La ME1 ....9 C5
Crowbridge Link TN24 ...156 F7
Crowbridge Rd TN24 ....156 F6
Crown Ct CT14 ....117 D6
Crown Gdns CT2 ....66 E1
Crown Hill Rd CT6 ....22 C4
Crown Ho ME1 ....9 B4
Crown La CT4 ....126 E3
Crown Quay La 5 ME10 ...37 A4
Crown Rd ME10 ....36 E6
Crown St ME7 ....10 D6
Crownfield Rd TN23 .....155 F8
Crownfields ME14 ....75 F4
Crows Camp Rd CT4 .....111 A5
Croydon Cl ME5 ....32 C4
Cruise Liner Terminal
CT17 ....166 E4
Crundale 2 ME14 ....75 A5
Crundale Cl TN23 ....155 F6
Crundale Rd ME8 ....11 C3
Crundale Way CT9 ....8 E1
Crusader Cl ME8 ....33 B8
Cryalls Bsns Est ME10 ....36 C4
Cryalls La ME10,ME9 .....36 C3
Cryol Rd TN23 ....156 A7
Crystal Bsns Ctr CT13 ....73 B2
Ctr for European
Agri-Enviromental Studies
TN25 ....124 A1
Cubitt Ho CT19 ....178 D6
Cuckold's Cnr TN26 .....168 B7
Cuckolds Cnr
Chillenden CT3 ....114 A7
Snargate TN29 ....191 E7
Cuckoo La Ashford TN23 ..155 D6
Ashford,Singleton TN23 ..155 E7
Postling CT21 ....160 F2
Cuckoowood Ave ME14 ....53 F1
Cudham Cl ME14 ....75 C6
Cudham Gdns CT9 ....8 E2
Cudworth Rd TN24 ......156 E7
Cullens Hill CT4 ....144 F4
Cullet Dr ME11 ....3 A3
Culling's Hill CT4 ....144 F4
Culmers Terr ME13 ....63 E8
Culpeper Cl
Hollingbourne ME17 ....77 E2
Rochester ME2 ....9 E6
Culpepper Cl CT2 ....67 A4
Culpepper Rd
Coxheath ME17 ....96 B3
Gillingham ME8 ....33 D4
Culter Field TN23 ....155 E8
Culver's La TN29 ....205 D5
Cumberland Ave
Broadstairs CT10 ....30 A5
Canterbury CT1 ....88 D7
Maidstone ME15 ....97 D8
Cumberland Dr ME9 ......13 C3
Cumberland Rd
Chatham ME4,ME7 ....10 B7
Gillingham ME7 ....10 C7
Margate CT9 ....8 B3
1 Ramsgate CT11 ....52 D6
Cundishall Cl CT5 ....43 C8
Cunningham Cres
Birchington CT7 ....26 E7
Chatham ME5 ....32 A8
Cunningham Ho ME1 ....9 B4
Curlew Ave ME9 ....13 B3
Curlew Cl CT6 ....23 C2
Curlew Pl CT18 ....163 A3
Curling Ct CT11 ....52 A6
Curteis Rd TN30 ....167 B1
Curtis La CT4 ....126 D2
Curtis Rd TN24 ....156 E7
Curtis Way
1 Faversham ME13 ....62 C7
Rochester ME1 ....31 D7
Curtis Wood Park Rd
CT6 ....46 A7
Curtis Wood Rd CT6 ......45 F7
Curzon Cl CT14 ....117 C3
Curzon Ho 5 CT11 ....52 D6
Curzon Rd Chatham ME4 ....9 F3
Dover CT17 ....166 B8
Curzon Rd *continued*
Maidstone ME14 ....75 A6
Cushings Wlk 18 CT5 .....20 D2
Cushman Rd CT1 ....87 E7
Cutbush & Corrall Ct 1
ME14 ....75 B4
Cutbush Almshouses
3 Maidstone ME14 ....75 A4
1 Maidstone ME15 ....75 A3
Cutbush Cl ME17 ....100 D6
Cutbush Ho 2 ME15 ......75 A3
Cuthbert Rd CT8 ....27 E8
Cuttings The CT12 ....52 C8
Cuxton Rd
Maidstone ME15 ....97 F5
Rochester ME2 ....9 A7
Cygnet Rd ME5 ....32 C2
Cygnet Way TN23 ....138 F1
Cylinder Rd CT21 ....176 B4
Cypress Ave TN23 ......138 E2
Cypress Cl CT5 ....43 C7
Cypress Ct ME7 ....10 F6
Cypress Gr CT15 ....114 B2
Cyprus Ct ME13 ....62 E7
Cyprus Rd ME13 ....62 E7

D

D'este Rd CT11 ....52 F7
D2 Trad Est ME10 ....37 B6
Daglish Cl TN28 ....202 B6
Dagmar Rd ME4 ....10 B2
Daimler Ave CT6 ....22 B3
Dajen Bsns Pk ME4 ....10 C1
Dalby Rd CT9 ....8 A3
Dalby Sq CT9 ....8 A3
Dale Ct ME5 ....32 A2
Dale Rd ME1 ....9 C3
Dale St ME4 ....9 E2
Dale Wlk TN24 ....139 C7
Daleacres Cvn Pk CT21 ..186 E7
Dalewood ME10 ....37 A2
Dallas-Brett Cres CT19 ..178 E8
Dallinger Rd 1 CT7 ....26 F8
Dalmatia Ct CT17 ....149 A1
Dalmeny Ave CT9 ....8 D1
Dalmeny Terr CT21 ......176 A1
Dalton Ct 7 CT11 ....52 E7
Dalton St ME7 ....10 C6
Dame Janet Com Inf Sch
CT12 ....29 B2
Dame Janet Com Jun Sch
CT12 ....29 B2
Damerham Cl CT2 ....66 E3
Damiem Cl ME4 ....10 A2
Dan Dr ME13 ....62 A8
Danaway Cotts ME9 ....35 C3
Dane Cl Chatham ME5 .....32 C2
Hartlip ME9 ....34 D6
Dane Court Gdns CT10 ....29 D5
Dane Court Gram Sch
CT10 ....29 E4
Dane Court Rd CT10 ......29 C6
Dane Cres CT11 ....52 E8
Dane Ct Coxheath ME17 ...96 C2
Tilmanstone CT14 ....114 F4
Dane End Rd CT8 ....27 D8
Dane Gdns CT9 ....29 B8
Dane Hill CT9 ....7 J3
Dane Hill Gr CT9 ....7 J2
Dane Hill Row CT9 ....7 J2
Dane Ho CT14 ....117 D8
Dane John Ct 3 CT1 ......87 F7
Dane John Mews 1 CT1 ...87 F7
Dane La ME9 ....34 D6
Dane Mount CT9 ....29 C8
Dane Park Rd Margate CT9 ..7 J2
Ramsgate CT11 ....52 E8
Dane Park Villas CT9 ......8 A2
Dane Pk ME15 ....96 C6
Dane Rd Birchington CT7 ...26 D7
Margate CT9 ....8 A2
Ramsgate CT11 ....52 E8
Dane Valley Rd CT10,CT9 ..29 C8
Danecourt Com Sch ME8 .11 A2
Danedale Ave ME12 ....4 F6
Danefield Ct ME14 ....76 B4
Danehurst CT8 ....7 C1
Danemore TN30 ....179 B8
Danes Ct CT16 ....149 D2
Danes Dr ME12 ....6 D2
Danes Hill ME7 ....11 A6
Danes Mead ME10 ....14 F1
Danesmead Terr CT9 ....7 J2
Daniel Ho 5 ME16 ....74 E5
Daniels Ct CT5 ....20 C1
Danley Mid Sch ME12 ......3 E7
Danley Rd ME12 ....3 E7
Danson Way ME8 ....11 D2
Danton La CT18 ....162 C1
Darby Pl CT20 ....178 D5
Darby Rd CT20 ....178 D5
Darcy Sq TN28 ....202 E5
Darenth Cl CT6 ....23 B3
Darenth Rise ME5 ....32 B3
Dargate Cl ME16 ....74 D7
Dargate Rd
Dargate CT2,ME13 ....64 F7
Yorkletts CT5 ....43 A3
Dargets Rd ME5 ....32 A3
Dark Hill ME13 ....62 C8
Darland Ave ME7 ....10 E1
Darlinghurst Rd CT19 ...177 E7
Darlington Dr ME12 ....4 A6
Darlington St CT20 ......178 D5
Darnley Cl
Broadstairs CT10 ....29 F3
Darnley Cl *continued*
Folkestone CT20 ....177 F4
Darnley Rd ME2 ....9 A6
Darracott Cl CT14 ....117 B5
Darrell Cl CT6 ....22 C3
Darren Gdns CT10 ....29 F2
Darwin Coll CT2 ....66 E5
Darwin Ct ME1 ....9 D5
Darwin Rd Birchington CT7 .26 F8
Canterbury CT2 ....66 E5
Darynngton Ave CT7 ......26 C7
Davenport Ave ME7 ......10 E7
Davey Ct ME1 ....9 C5
David Ave CT9 ....8 D2
Davids Cl CT10 ....30 B3
Davidson Rd CT2 ....66 D1
Davie Cl ME12 ....3 B8
Davie Ct ME12 ....3 B8
Davington Hill ME13 .....62 C8
Davington Prim Sch
ME13 ....62 C8
Davis Ave CT14 ....117 A4
Dawbourne TN30 ....167 B3
Dawes Rd CT2,ME13 ......64 C4
Dawes St ME7 ....10 C5
Dawn Rise ME12 ....5 F6
Dawson Ct 7 ME7 ....10 A6
Dawson Rd CT19 ....178 D6
Dawson's Row ME13 .....62 A6
Day Ho 2 ME14 ....75 B4
Dayton Rd ME13 ....83 C3
Daytona Way CT6 ....22 A4
De Burgh Hill CT17 .....149 C1
De Burgh St 2 CT17 ....166 C8
De Havilland Cl CT18 ...163 B4
De Havillands CT4 ....89 E3
De L'angle Ho CT4 ....86 D3
De L'angle Row CT4 ......86 D3
De Mere Cl ME8 ....33 D6
Deacon Est The ME20 .....53 A2
Deacon Trad Ctr ME2 ......9 A6
Deal Castle★ CT14 .....117 D5
Deal Castle Rd CT14 ....117 D5
Deal Ent Ctr CT14 ......117 C7
Deal Ho ME15 ....97 E8
Deal Maritime & Local
History Mus★ CT14 ....117 D6
Deal Parochial CE Prim Sch
CT14 ....117 C3
Deal Rd
Northbourne CT14 ....116 A4
Sandwich CT13,CT14 ......93 F5
Deal Sta CT14 ....117 C6
Dean Croft CT6 ....23 B2
Dean Ct 14 CT1 ....67 A1
Dean Hill CT4,TN25 .....126 B2
Dean Mead CT19 ....178 B7
Dean Rd ME10 ....36 E6
Dean St ME15 ....96 C6
Dean's Wlk TN23 ....155 F7
Deane Cl CT5 ....43 E7
Deane Ct 8 ME7 ....10 C6
Deans Hill Rd ME9 ....57 D5
Deans Mill Ct CT1 ....66 F1
Deansway Ave CT2 ....67 F7
Deanwood Cl ME8 ....33 D6
Deanwood Dr ME8 ....33 E4
Deanwood Prim Education
Tech Sch ME8 ....33 D3
Deanwood Rd CT17 .....148 E2
Deborah Cl CT5 ....43 F7
Deedes Cl CT21 ....176 C3
Deerhurst Gdns ME16 .....74 D4
Deerson La CT3 ....70 A4
Deerton St ME9 ....39 A2
Defiant Cl ME5 ....32 B6
Defoe Cl ME5 ....32 B6
Deham Ho ME10 ....36 D5
Delacourt Cl CT12 ....51 D5
Delamark Rd ME12 ....1 D2
Delane Rd CT14 ....117 A5
Delaware Cl CT2 ....67 F6
Delce Jun & Inf Schs ME1 ..9 D2
Delce Rd ME1 ....9 D4
Delf St CT13 ....72 F1
Delfside CT13 ....94 A8
Delmaney Cl CT10 ....30 B5
Delmar Cl CT5 ....21 D3
Demelza House Hospice
ME9 ....35 F6
Demozay Cl CT18 ....163 A4
Denbigh Ave ME8 ....11 D1
Denbigh Cl ME10 ....36 E7
Denbigh Rd CT12 ....29 A1
Dence Cl CT6 ....23 B5
Dence Pk CT6 ....23 B4
Dencorra Way TN23 .....139 A1
Dene Farm Barns CT3 ....91 A4
Dene Farm La CT3 ....91 A4
Dene The
Bethersden TN26 ....153 D5
Canterbury CT1 ....88 B5
Hythe CT21 ....176 C2
Dene Wlk CT9 ....28 F7
Dengemarsh Rd TN29 ...208 A7
Dengrove Cvn Site CT2 ...67 D6
Denham Cl TN29 ....187 B4
Denham Rd ME9 ....35 B7
Denmark Rd CT11 ....52 E8
Denmark St CT19 ....178 E6
Denne Cl CT2 ....67 F7
Denne Manor La CT4 ....106 C8
Dennes La TN29 ....205 C8
Dennes Mill Cl TN25 ....123 D2
Denness Rd TN23 ....156 B7

Denning Cl ME16 . . . . .74 B4
Dennis Way CT19 . . . . .177 E7
Dennis Wilcocks Cl ME9 . . . .35 B6
Densole La CT18 . . . . .163 A8
Densole Way CT18 . . . . . . .163 A8
Denstead Cotts CT4 . . . . . . .86 B8
Denstead Ct CT2 . . . . .66 C4
Denstead La CT4,ME13 . . . . .86 C7
Denstead Oast CT4 . . . . .86 B8
Denstead Wlk **11** ME15 . . . . .97 F6
Denstroude La CT2 . . . . .65 D8
Dent-De-Lion Ct CT9 . . . . . . .28 A8
Dent-De-Lion Rd
  Margate CT9 . . . . .28 A8
  Westgate-on-S CT8 . . . . .7 C1
Dental Cl ME10 . . . . .36 A5
Dental St CT21 . . . . .176 C2
Denton Cl ME15 . . . . .97 E8
Denton Gn ME8 . . . . .11 B4
Denton Way CT9 . . . . .8 C1
Derby Cl ME10 . . . . .36 D6
Derby Rd Gillingham ME5 . . . .10 E2
  Maidstone ME15 . . . . .97 C8
Dering Cl Bridge CT4 . . . . . .88 F1
  Pluckley TN27 . . . . .136 C4
Dering Rd Ashford TN24 . . . .139 D2
  Bridge CT4 . . . . .89 A1
  Herne Bay CT6 . . . . .22 F4
Dering Terr TN27 . . . . .136 C3
Derings The TN29 . . . . .205 B6
Deringwood Dr ME15 . . . . . .75 F1
Derringstone Downs
  CT4 . . . . .128 F6
Derringstone Hill CT4 . . . . .128 F7
Derringstone St CT4 . . . . . .128 F7
Derville Ho TN28 . . . . .202 B6
Derville Rd TN29 . . . . .206 E7
Derwent Ave CT11 . . . . .52 A7
Derwent Ho **3** ME15 . . . . . .97 E7
Derwent Way
  Aylesham CT3 . . . . .112 F6
  Gillingham ME8 . . . . .33 D8
Desmond Cres ME13 . . . . . . .63 A5
Detling Ave CT10 . . . . .30 A1
Detling CE Prim Sch
  ME14 . . . . .55 A1
Detling Cl Gillingham ME8 . . .11 C2
  West Minst ME12 . . . . .3 B7
Detling Hill ME14 . . . . .55 B2
Devon Ave CT14 . . . . .117 C3
Devon Cl Chatham ME5 . . . . .32 C7
  Gillingham ME8 . . . . .11 F1
Devon Ct CT12 . . . . .29 B2
Devon Gdns CT7 . . . . .26 F7
Devon Rd Canterbury CT1 . . .88 D8
  Folkestone CT19 . . . . .178 D5
  Maidstone ME15 . . . . .97 C8
Devonshire Gdns CT9 . . . . . . .8 C3
Devonshire Rd
  Dover CT17 . . . . .166 B8
  Gillingham ME7 . . . . .10 D7
Devonshire Terr CT10 . . . . . .30 B5
Dew La TN31 . . . . .196 A1
Dexter Cl TN25 . . . . .139 C8
Deyley Way TN23 . . . . .155 C8
Dhekelia Cl ME14 . . . . .75 A7
Dial Cl ME7 . . . . .10 F6
Dial Rd ME7 . . . . .10 F6
Diamond Ct ME12 . . . . .1 C1
Diamond Rd CT5 . . . . .20 E2
Diana Gdns CT14 . . . . .117 A5
Diana Rd ME4 . . . . .10 A2
Dibdin Rd CT14 . . . . .117 D7
Dickens Ave CT1 . . . . .67 D2
Dickens Cl ME17 . . . . .98 E4
Dickens Ct ME2 . . . . .9 D8
Dickens House Mus★
  CT10 . . . . .30 B4
Dickens Rd
  Broadstairs CT10 . . . . .30 B5
  Maidstone ME14 . . . . .74 E8
  Rochester ME1 . . . . .9 C2
Dickens Wlk CT10 . . . . .30 B4
Dickley La ME17 . . . . .101 A6
Dickson Ct **7** ME10 . . . . . .37 B4
Dickson Rd CT17 . . . . .166 C8
Dickson's Cnr CT13 . . . . .95 A6
Dicksons Bourne TN25 . . . .172 F4
Dieu Stone La CT16 . . . . . .166 E8
Digby Rd CT20 . . . . .177 E5
Dignals Cl ME8 . . . . .11 F2
Dignash TN25 . . . . .121 E2
Diligent Dr ME10 . . . . .36 F7
Dilnot La CT7 . . . . .27 B3
Diocesan & Payne Smith CE
  Prim Sch CT1 . . . . .67 A1
Discovery Rd ME15 . . . . .76 B2
Discovery Wlk CT7 . . . . .88 C7
Disraeli Cl ME15 . . . . .97 E5
Dixon Cl ME15 . . . . .74 F2
Dixwell Cl ME8 . . . . .33 D5
Dixwell Rd CT20 . . . . .178 A4
Dobbie Cl ME10 . . . . .36 E6
Dock Exit Rd CT16 . . . . . . .166 F8
Dock Head Rd ME4 . . . . . . .10 A8
Dock Rd ME4 . . . . .9 F6
Dockside Outlet Ctr ME4 . . . .10 A8
Doctor's La CT15 . . . . .165 B5
Dodd's La CT16 . . . . .149 A3
Doddington Ct ME16 . . . . . . .74 E5
Doddington Place Gdns★
  ME9 . . . . .81 A7
Doddington Prim Sch
  ME9 . . . . .80 F7
Doddington Rd ME8 . . . . . . .11 D3

Does Alley **4** ME10 . . . . . . .36 F4
Dog Kennel La CT18 . . . . . .161 B7
Doggerel Acre CT5 . . . . .43 F7
Dogwood Cl ME5 . . . . .32 D1
Dola Ave CT14 . . . . .117 A6
Dolphin Cl CT10 . . . . .8 G3
Dolphin Dr ME8 . . . . .33 E5
Dolphin Ho
  1 Dover CT16 . . . . .166 E7
  Rochester ME1 . . . . .9 E5
Dolphin La CT16 . . . . .166 E7
Dolphin Pas **3** CT16 . . . . .166 E7
Dolphin Pk ME10 . . . . .37 B5
Dolphin Pl **5** CT16 . . . . . .166 E7
Dolphin Rd Lydd TN29 . . . . .205 C6
  Sittingbourne ME10 . . . . .37 B5
Dolphin St Deal CT14 . . . . . .117 D7
  Herne Bay CT6 . . . . .22 E5
Dolphin Yard Sailing Barge
  Mus★ ME10 . . . . .37 A5
Dolphins ME13 . . . . .62 D7
Dolphins Rd CT19 . . . . .178 D7
Dombey Cl ME1 . . . . .9 C3
Domneva Rd
  Minster (Thanet) CT12 . . . . .50 B6
  Westgate-on-S CT8 . . . . .27 D8
Donald Moor Ave ME4 . . . . . .38 C2
Donald Troup Ho ME1 . . . . . . .9 C4
Doncaster Cl **7** ME15 . . . . .97 F6
Donegal Rd CT1 . . . . .88 C8
Donemowe Dr ME10 . . . . . . .36 F8
Donet Cl ME8 . . . . .33 C5
Dongola Rd ME2 . . . . .9 B8
Donkey La Adisham CT3 . . . .112 C8
  Appledore Heath TN26 . . . . .181 C2
Donkey St CT21,TN29 . . . . . .186 E5
Donnahay Rd CT12 . . . . .29 C3
Donnithorne Ho CT10 . . . . . .22 E5
Dorcas Gdns CT10 . . . . .30 A6
Dorman Ave N CT3 . . . . . . .112 E6
Dorman Ave S CT3 . . . . . . .112 F5
Dornden Gdns ME5 . . . . .32 B2
Dorne Cotts TN27 . . . . .118 E6
Dorothy Dr CT12 . . . . .29 C2
Dorrit Way ME1 . . . . .9 D2
Dorset Cl CT5 . . . . .43 B7
Dorset Ct Deal CT14 . . . . .117 D2
  Ramsgate CT12 . . . . .29 B2
Dorset Gdns
  Birchington CT7 . . . . .26 F7
  Deal CT14 . . . . .117 C2
Dorset Pl ME13 . . . . .62 C7
Dorset Rd Canterbury CT1 . . .88 D7
  West Minst ME12 . . . . .3 A8
Dorset Sq ME8 . . . . .11 D1
Dorset Way ME15 . . . . .97 C8
Dossett Ct CT14 . . . . .117 A2
Dotterel Cl ME5 . . . . .32 D2
Doubleday Dr ME9 . . . . .37 E2
Douglas Almshouses
  ME17 . . . . .101 D5
Douglas Ave Hythe CT21 . . . .176 C2
  Whitstable CT5 . . . . .20 E1
Douglas Bglws CT15 . . . . . .132 E8
Douglas Cl CT10 . . . . .29 E5
Douglas Rd Deal CT14 . . . . .117 A3
  Dover CT17 . . . . .166 B8
  Herne Bay CT6 . . . . .23 A4
  Lenham ME17 . . . . .101 D5
  Maidstone ME16 . . . . .74 E3
Douglas Terr CT14 . . . . .117 D5
Dour Ho The **13** CT16 . . . .166 D8
Dour Mews **12** CT16 . . . . .149 C1
Dour Side CT17 . . . . .148 F3
Dour St CT16 . . . . .166 D8
Douro Cl CT1 . . . . .67 D1
Douro Pl CT16 . . . . .166 E7
Doust Way ME1 . . . . .9 D5
Dove Cl Chatham ME5 . . . . . .32 B6
  Herne CT6 . . . . .45 E7
  Hythe CT21 . . . . .187 D8
  Kingsnorth TN23 . . . . .156 C3
  Whitstable CT5 . . . . .43 C7
Dove Ct **6** CT16 . . . . .52 E7
Dove Lea Gdns CT17 . . . . . .148 E3
Dovecote Ct CT4 . . . . .107 B8
Dovedale CT7 . . . . .27 B7
Dovedale Ct
  Ashford TN24 . . . . .139 B4
  Birchington CT7 . . . . .27 B7
Dover Castle & Princess of
  Wales Regiment Mus★
  CT16 . . . . .166 F8
Dover Coll CT17 . . . . .166 C8
Dover Gram Sch for Boys
  CT17 . . . . .166 A8
Dover Gram Sch for Girls
  CT16 . . . . .149 C1
Dover Hill CT19 . . . . .178 F8
Dover Ho **2** ME16 . . . . . . .97 E8
Dover Mus★ CT16 . . . . .166 D7
Dover Patrol Meml★
  CT15 . . . . .151 C7
Dover Pl TN23 . . . . .139 C1
Dover Priory Sta CT17 . . . .166 C8
Dover Rd Barham CT4 . . . . . .112 A1
  Bishopsbourne CT4 . . . . . . .111 D5
  Dover CT15 . . . . .149 E4
  Folkestone CT19,CT20 . . . . .178 E7
  Ringwould CT14 . . . . .134 A4
  Sandwich CT13 . . . . .93 F6
  St Margaret's at Cliffe
    CT15 . . . . .150 D6
  Tilmanstone CT13,CT14 . . . .115 B5
  Woolage Green CT4 . . . . . .129 D6
Dover St Canterbury CT1 . . . .88 A7
  Maidstone ME16 . . . . .74 C2
  1 Sittingbourne ME10 . . . .36 E4

Doves Cnr CT14 . . . . .115 A4
Dowell Mews CT14 . . . . . . .117 C3
Dowle Cl TN29 . . . . .201 A4
Down Barton Farm Cotts
  CT7 . . . . .25 D1
Down Barton Rd CT7 . . . . . . .25 E1
Down Court Rd ME9 . . . . . . .59 C1
Down Ct TN23 . . . . .155 E5
Downer Ct ME1 . . . . .31 E8
Downhill Cl CT16 . . . . .148 D6
Downings The CT6 . . . . .23 A2
Downland Ct TN24 . . . . . . .139 B3
Downlands Deal CT14 . . . . .134 B8
  Harrietsham ME17 . . . . . . .100 F6
Downs Ave CT5 . . . . .20 E1
Downs CE Prim Sch The
  CT14 . . . . .117 B2
Downs Cl Charing TN27 . . . .120 C8
  East Studdal CT15 . . . . . . .132 D8
  Hawkinge CT18 . . . . .163 A4
  Maidstone ME14 . . . . .75 B8
  Sittingbourne ME10 . . . . . . .36 D2
Downs Pk CT6 . . . . .23 A5
Downs Rd Canterbury CT2 . . .66 F4
  Deal CT14 . . . . .117 C3
  East Studdal CT15 . . . . . . .132 E8
  Folkestone CT19 . . . . .178 C7
  Maidstone ME14 . . . . .75 B8
  Ramsgate CT11 . . . . .52 B6
Downs The Chartham CT4 . . . .86 E1
  Chatham ME5 . . . . .31 D1
  Preston CT3 . . . . .70 C6
  Ramsgate CT11 . . . . .52 D5
Downs View Inf Sch
  TN24 . . . . .139 E7
Downs View Rd ME14 . . . . . .75 B8
Downs Way
  Charing TN27 . . . . .120 C8
  Sellindge TN25 . . . . .159 C1
Downside
  Bekesbourne CT4 . . . . .89 E3
  Folkestone CT19 . . . . .178 C7
  Rochester ME2 . . . . .9 A7
  St Margaret's at Cliffe
    CT15 . . . . .151 A6
Downside Rd CT16 . . . . . . .149 B7
Downsview ME5 . . . . .32 C8
Dragonfly Cl TN23 . . . . . . .155 D8
Dragonfly Way CT18 . . . . . .163 B4
Dragoon Ho **10** CT1 . . . . . .67 A1
Drainless Rd CT13 . . . . .93 A5
Drake Ave ME12 . . . . .4 C5
Drake Ct **3** CT11 . . . . .52 F8
Drake Rd TN24 . . . . .157 B7
Drakes Cl ME9 . . . . .12 E2
Drakes Lee TN28 . . . . .202 E5
Drapers Almshouses CT9 . . .29 A8
Drapers Ave CT9 . . . . .28 F8
Drapers Cl CT9 . . . . .29 A8
Drapers Mills Prim Sch
  CT9 . . . . .29 A8
Drapers Windmill★ CT9 . . . . .8 A1
Drawbridge Cl ME15 . . . . . . .97 E8
Dray's Field ME9 . . . . .79 A7
Dreadnought Ave ME12 . . . . . .4 C5
Dreamland Family Fun Pk★
  CT9 . . . . .7 I2
Dresden Ct CT8 . . . . .27 D8
Drew La CT14 . . . . .117 C4
Drewery Dr ME8 . . . . .33 C5
Drill La CT3 . . . . .69 B1
Drive The
  Broadstairs CT10 . . . . .29 F6
  Canterbury CT1 . . . . .88 B4
  Deal CT14 . . . . .117 C5
  Whitstable CT5 . . . . .44 D8
Drop Redoubt Fort★
  CT17 . . . . .166 D7
Drop Redoubt Rd CT17 . . . .166 D7
Drove Rd ME12 . . . . .3 E7
Drove The Fordwich CT2 . . . .68 A4
  Monkton CT12 . . . . .49 B6
  Northbourne CT14 . . . . . . .116 A5
  Whitfield CT16 . . . . .149 A8
  Whitstable CT5 . . . . .44 D8
Drovers Rdbt TN24 . . . . . . .139 A4
Droveway Gdns CT15 . . . . . .151 A6
Droveway The CT15 . . . . . . .151 B6
Druidstone Wildlife Pk★
  CT2 . . . . .65 F7
Drum La TN23 . . . . .139 B2
Drum Major Dr CT14 . . . . . .117 B3
Drury Rd TN30 . . . . .167 B1
Drybeck Ave CT11 . . . . .51 F7
Dryden Cl CT1 . . . . .88 C7
Dryden Rd CT16 . . . . .149 B3
Drywall Ind Est ME10 . . . . . .37 B6
Dublin Ho **16** ME15 . . . . . .97 E7
Duchess Of Kent Dr ME5 . . . .32 B3
Duck La Canterbury CT1 . . . . .67 A1
  Shadoxhurst TN26 . . . . . . .169 F7
Duck St CT14 . . . . .144 F4
Duckpits Rd CT4 . . . . .126 A6
Duckworth Cl TN24 . . . . . . .157 B7
Dudley Ave CT11 . . . . .52 C8
Dudley Rd Ashford TN24 . . . .139 C5
  Folkestone CT19 . . . . .178 E5
Duke of Clarence Trad Est
  The ME12 . . . . .1 B3
Duke of York's Royal Military
  Sch CT15 . . . . .149 F4
Duke St Deal CT14 . . . . . . .117 D7
  Margate CT9 . . . . .7 I3
Dukes Mdw TN26 . . . . .183 A7
Dukes Meadow Dr ME7 . . . . .32 F6
Dukes Wlk **7** ME15 . . . . . .75 A4
Dukeswood CT5 . . . . .44 D8
Dully Rd Lynsted ME9 . . . . . .59 E6

Dully Rd continued
  Sittingbourne ME9 . . . . .37 E1
Dumbourne La TN30 . . . . . .179 D2
Dumergue Ave ME11 . . . . .3 B5
Dumpton Gap Rd CT10 . . . . . .30 A2
Dumpton La CT11 . . . . .29 E1
Dumpton Park Dr CT10,
  CT11 . . . . .30 A2
Dumpton Park Rd CT11 . . . . .52 E8
Dumpton Park Sta CT11 . . . .29 F1
Duncan Cl CT5 . . . . .43 D7
Duncan Dr CT7 . . . . .26 E8
Duncan Rd
  Gillingham ME7 . . . . .10 C5
  Ramsgate CT11 . . . . .52 C7
  Whitstable CT5 . . . . .43 D7
Dundonald Rd
  11 Broadstairs CT10 . . . . .30 B4
  Ramsgate CT11 . . . . .52 C7
Dunedin Cl ME10 . . . . .36 C3
Dunedin Dr CT16 . . . . .149 B3
Dunedin Ho **9** ME15 . . . . . .97 E5
Dunedin Rd CT12 . . . . .29 A1
Dunera Dr ME14 . . . . .75 A7
Dunes Rd TN28 . . . . .202 D3
Dunes The CT13 . . . . .95 A7
Dungeness Nature National
  Reserve★ TN29 . . . . .209 B4
Dungeness Rd TN29 . . . . . .209 A4
Dungeness Sta★ TN29 . . . .209 D2
Dunkeld Ho **6** ME15 . . . . . .97 E7
Dunkery Rise TN24 . . . . . . .139 B4
Dunkirk Cl TN29 . . . . .195 B7
Dunkirk Dr ME5 . . . . .31 F6
Dunkirk Rd N ME13 . . . . .64 B2
Dunkirk Rd S ME13 . . . . .64 B1
Dunkirk Sq CT15 . . . . .149 F3
Dunkirk Village Sch
  ME13 . . . . .64 C2
Dunlin Cl TN29 . . . . .195 A3
Dunn Street Rd ME7 . . . . . . .55 A8
Dunnett Rd CT19 . . . . .177 E6
Dunning's La ME1 . . . . .9 C4
Dunnings The ME16 . . . . .74 A2
Dunnock Rd TN25 . . . . .139 B7
Dunoon Ct CT11 . . . . .29 F1
Dunstall Cl TN29 . . . . .195 A5
Dunstall Gdns TN29 . . . . . .195 A5
Dunstall La TN29 . . . . .195 A5
Dunstan Ave CT8 . . . . .27 D7
Dunstan Ho CT14 . . . . .117 D8
Dunster Terr **3** ME15 . . . . .97 E8
Durban Cl CT12 . . . . .29 A2
Durban Cres CT13 . . . . .149 C4
Durban Ho **7** ME15 . . . . . .97 E5
Durban Rd CT13 . . . . .93 A1
Durham Cl Canterbury CT1 . . .87 F6
  9 Dover CT17 . . . . .166 D7
  Maidstone ME15 . . . . .75 E1
Durham Hill CT17 . . . . .166 D7
Durham Rd ME8 . . . . .33 C7
Durling Ct ME8 . . . . .12 A1
Durlock Cl CT12 . . . . .50 C5
Durlock Ave CT11 . . . . .52 B5
Durlock Rd CT3 . . . . .92 B7
Durlocks The CT19 . . . . .178 E5
Durnford Cl CT2 . . . . .66 E2
Durovernum CT1 . . . . .88 A7
Durrell Gdns ME5 . . . . .10 C1
Duval Dr ME1 . . . . .31 E8
Duvard's Pl ME9 . . . . .35 F1
Dyke Rd CT19 . . . . .178 E5
Dymchurch Ho **1** CT1 . . . . .88 B8
Dymchurch Prim Sch
  TN29 . . . . .195 C8
Dymchurch Rd
  Hythe CT21,TN29 . . . . . . .187 C6
  St Mary's Bay TN29,TN28 . . .195 A5
Dymchurch Sta★ TN29 . . . .195 B7
Dyngley Cl ME10 . . . . .36 E6

E

Eadred Way ME10 . . . . .15 A1
Eagle Cotts **8** CT11 . . . . . .52 D7
Eagle Hill CT11 . . . . .52 D7
Eagles Cl ME10 . . . . .37 C4
Ealham Cl Ashford TN24 . . . .157 A8
  Canterbury CT4 . . . . .88 B5
Ealing Cl ME5 . . . . .32 C4
Earl Cl ME5 . . . . .32 B4
Earl St ME14 . . . . .74 F4
Earl's Ave CT20 . . . . .178 B4
Earls Ave TN24 . . . . .139 F1
Earlsfield TN25 . . . . .173 A6
Earlsfield Rd CT21 . . . . .176 D2
Earlsmead Cres CT12 . . . . . .51 C5
Earlsworth Ct TN24 . . . . . . .156 D6
Earlsworth Rd TN24 . . . . . . .156 D6
Easole Hts CT15 . . . . .113 D5
Easole St CT15 . . . . .113 D5
East Blean Wood (Nature
  Reserve)★ CT3,CT6 . . . . . .46 B6
East Borough Prim Sch
  ME14 . . . . .75 B5
East Cliff Dover CT16 . . . . . .166 F8
  Folkestone CT19 . . . . .178 E5
East Cliff & Warren Ctry Pk★
  CT18 . . . . .164 D1
East Cliff Gdns **22** CT19 . . .178 E5
East Cliff Pas **23** CT19 . . . .178 E5
East Court Sch CT11 . . . . . . .52 C7
East Cross TN30 . . . . .179 B7
East Ct **4** ME15 . . . . .75 A1
East End ME4,ME7 . . . . .10 D8

East Farleigh Prim Sch
  ME15 . . . . .96 B6
East Farleigh Sta ME16 . . . . .96 B8
East Fleet Cvn Pk TN29 . . . .187 A4
East Gn ME10 . . . . .15 A1
East Hall La ME10 . . . . .37 C5
East Hill Ashford TN24 . . . . .139 C2
East Hill Ashford TN24,
  Tenterden TN30 . . . . .179 B8
East Kent Light Rly★
  CT15 . . . . .131 A7
East Kent Light Rly★
  CT15 . . . . .130 E6
East Kent Ret Pk CT10 . . . . . .29 B4
East La CT1 . . . . .1 B2
East Langdon Rd
  Guston CT15 . . . . .149 F7
  Martin Mill CT15 . . . . .133 B2
East Lodge Rd TN23 . . . . . .138 F3
East Mountain La TN24 . . . . .139 F7
East Norman Rd CT16 . . . . .149 E1
East Northdown CT9 . . . . .8 E1
East Park Rd ME20 . . . . . . .74 A8
East Ramp CT16 . . . . .166 G8
East Rd Chatham ME4 . . . . . .10 A7
  Folkestone CT20 . . . . .177 D4
  Sandwich CT13 . . . . .73 A8
East Roman Ditch CT16 . . . .166 F8
East Row ME1 . . . . .9 C5
East St Ashford TN23 . . . . . .139 B2
  Canterbury CT1 . . . . .67 C3
  Chatham ME4 . . . . .10 A3
  Dover CT17 . . . . .166 C8
  Faversham ME13 . . . . .62 D7
  Folkestone CT19 . . . . .178 E5
  Gillingham ME7 . . . . .10 D6
  Harrietsham ME17 . . . . . . .100 C5
  Herne Bay CT6 . . . . .23 A5
  Hythe CT21 . . . . .176 D2
  Sittingbourne ME10 . . . . . . .37 A4
East Stour Ct TN24 . . . . . . .139 D1
East Stour Prim Sch
  TN24 . . . . .156 D6
East Stour Way TN24 . . . . . .156 D6
East View
  Brookland TN29 . . . . .199 D8
  Hersden CT3 . . . . .46 F1
East Weald Dr TN30 . . . . . .167 B1
East Wootton Cotts CT4 . . . .109 A4
Eastbridge Rd TN29 . . . . . .195 B8
Eastbrook Pl CT16 . . . . .166 E8
Eastchurch CE Prim Sch
  ME12 . . . . .5 E4
Eastchurch Holiday Camp
  ME12 . . . . .5 F5
Eastchurch Rd Margate CT9 . . .8 E3
  Minster (Sheppey) ME12 . . . . .5 B5
Eastcliffe Hts **7** CT20 . . . . .178 E5
Eastcourt Gn ME8 . . . . .11 B4
Eastcourt La
  Gillingham ME8 . . . . .11 B3
  Gillingham,Lwr Twydal ME7,
    ME8 . . . . .11 C5
Eastern Arm N CT16 . . . . . .166 H8
Eastern Arm S CT16 . . . . . .166 H8
Eastern Ave
  Ashford TN23 . . . . .139 A2
  Halfway Houses ME12 . . . . . .3 D6
  Queenborough ME11 . . . . . . .3 B4
Eastern Espl
  Broadstairs CT10 . . . . .30 B5
  Margate CT9 . . . . .8 B3
Eastern Gdns TN24 . . . . . . .156 E4
Eastern Holiday Camp
  ME12 . . . . .5 F5
Eastern Rd Gillingham ME7 . . .10 F6
  Leysdown-on-S ME12 . . . . . . .6 G2
  Lydd TN29 . . . . .205 D2
Eastern Service Rd
  CT16 . . . . .166 H8
Eastfield Ho ME16 . . . . .74 E2
Eastfield **1** CT7 . . . . .27 A7
Eastfields CT19 . . . . .178 D6
Eastgate ME1 . . . . .9 C5
Eastgate Cl CT6 . . . . .23 B3
Eastgate Ct ME1 . . . . .9 C5
Eastgate Rd TN30 . . . . .179 C8
Eastgate Terr ME1 . . . . .9 C5
Eastling Cl ME8 . . . . .11 D3
Eastling Prim Sch ME13 . . . .81 F5
Eastling Rd Eastling ME13 . . . .81 F7
  Painters Forstal ME13 . . . . . .61 D2
Eastmead Ave TN23 . . . . . . .156 C1
Easton's Cnr TN25 . . . . . . .172 F4
Eastry CE Prim Sch CT13 . . .93 B2
Eastry Cl Ashford TN23 . . . . .156 A6
  Maidstone ME16 . . . . .74 C7
Eastry Ct CT3 . . . . .112 F5
Eastry Mews CT13 . . . . .93 B2
Eastry Pk CT13 . . . . .93 C1
Eastwell **5** TN30 . . . . .179 A7
Eastwell Barn Mews
  TN30 . . . . .179 A8
Eastwell Cl
  Maidstone ME14 . . . . .75 C5
  Shadoxhurst TN26 . . . . . . .155 B1
Eastwell Mdws TN30 . . . . . .179 A8
Eastwell Terr TN25 . . . . . . .122 C3
Eastwood Cotts ME9 . . . . . . .38 E6
Eastwood Rd ME10 . . . . .36 D5
Eaton Hill CT9 . . . . .7 I2
Eaton Rd Dover CT17 . . . . . .166 C8
  Margate CT9 . . . . .7 I1
Eaves Ct ME10 . . . . .37 B5
Eaves Rd CT17 . . . . .166 A7
Ebbsfleet La CT12 . . . . .51 A3
Ebony Cotts TN30 . . . . .189 A6
Ebony Wlk ME16 . . . . .74 B3
Eccleston Rd ME15 . . . . .74 F2

Echo Cl ME15 97 F6
Echo Ho ME10 37 B3
Echo Wlk ME12 4 D6
Eckford Cl CT18 162 F4
Eclipse Dr ME10 36 E8
Eddie Willet Rd CT6 22 B3
Eddington Cl ME15 97 B6
Eddington La CT6 22 F3
Eddington Way CT6 22 E3
Eden Ave ME5 32 A7
Eden Ho TN23 156 C8
Eden Holiday Camp ME12 6 A5
Eden Rd CT5 43 A7
Edenbridge Dr ME12 3 B8
Edenbridge Ho 2 CT1 88 B8
Edenfield CT7 27 B7
Edgar Cl CT5 21 D3
Edgar Ho CT14 117 B3
Edgar Rd Canterbury CT1 67 B1
Dover CT17 149 B1
Margate CT9 8 A3
Minster (Thanet) CT12 50 B6
Edge End Rd CT10 29 F4
Edgehill Cl CT20 177 D4
Edger Pl 5 ME15 75 A4
Edinburgh Ho Deal CT14 117 A5
7 Dover CT17 166 D7
Edinburgh Pl 7 CT20 178 B3
Edinburgh Rd
Ashford TN24 139 B2
Chatham ME4 10 C2
Gillingham ME7 10 D5
Margate CT9 28 B8
Edinburgh Sq ME15 97 C7
Edinburgh Wlk 5 CT9 28 B8
Edisbury Wlk ME8 33 D5
Edith Rd Faversham ME13 62 C6
Ramsgate CT11 52 C6
Westgate-on-S CT8 7 D1
Edmanson Ave CT9 7 E1
Edmund Cl ME16 74 A3
Edmund St CT3 91 A8
Edna Rd ME14 74 F8
Edred Rd CT17 166 B8
Edward Ct ME5 10 C1
Edward Dr CT7 27 B7
Edward Rd Canterbury CT1 88 A8
Folkestone CT19 178 D6
Kingsdown CT14 134 C6
Queenborough ME11 3 B5
Edward St Chatham ME4 10 A3
Rochester ME2 9 B7
Sheerness ME12 1 B3
Edward Terr 9 CT20 178 E6
Edwards Cl ME8 33 C5
Edwards Rd CT16 166 D8
Edwin Rd ME8 33 C8
Edwina Ave ME12 4 A7
Edwins Pl ME9 35 C7
Edyngham Cl ME10 37 A8
Effingham Cres CT17 166 D8
Effingham St
Dover CT17 166 D8
Ramsgate CT11 52 E6
Egbert Rd Birchington CT7 26 D8
Faversham ME13 62 C6
Minster (Thanet) CT12 50 B6
Westgate-on-S CT8 7 C1
Egerton CE Prim Sch
TN27 118 F3
Egerton Dr CT9 8 E2
Egerton House Rd TN27 118 E4
Egerton Rd
Charing Heath TN27 119 C7
Maidstone ME14 74 E7
Pluckley TN27 119 B1
Temple Ewell CT16 148 E5
Eggarton La CT4 107 C2
Eggringe TN23 138 E1
Egremont Rd ME15 75 F2
Eider Cl CT6 22 D2
Eighteen Acre La TN29 200 D8
Elder Cl ME17 99 D2
Elder Ct ME8 33 B6
Elders The CT3 68 F1
Eldon Pl 4 CT10 30 B4
Eldon St ME4 10 A4
Eleanor Dr ME10 36 E8
Elfrida Cl CT9 29 C8
Elgar Bretts Ct 10 CT1 87 F7
Elgar Pl CT11 52 D7
Elham CE Prim Sch CT4 144 F4
Elham Cl Gillingham ME8 11 B3
Margate CT9 8 C1
Elham Rd CT1 87 E6
Elham Valley Railway Mus★
CT18 177 A8
Elham Valley Vineyards★
CT4 128 D4
Elham Way CT10 30 A2
Eling Ct ME15 97 A8
Eliot Coll CT2 66 E4
Elizabeth Carter Ave
CT14 116 F4
Elizabeth Ct
Broadstairs CT10 30 B6
Canterbury CT1 88 B6
Chatham ME5 32 A7
Gillingham ME8 11 C1
Herne Bay CT6 22 F5
Elizabeth Dr CT18 164 B2
Elizabeth Gdns CT21 176 B1
Elizabeth Ho
Maidstone ME14 75 A6
Rochester ME1 9 C4
Elizabeth Kemp Ct CT12 29 C1
Elizabeth Rd CT11 52 F6
Elizabeth St CT17 166 D6
Elizabeth Way CT6 23 B3
Elizabethan Ct TN27 120 C7
Ellen Ave CT11 29 E2
Ellen Ct CT3 89 F8
Ellen's Hill CT14 116 E3
Ellen's Pl ME9 35 C6
Ellenden Ct CT2 66 C4
Ellens Rd CT14 116 F2
Ellenswood Cl ME15 76 A1
Ellesmere Mews TN28 202 C8
Ellingham Leas ME15 97 C7
Ellingham Way TN23 156 A5
Ellington Ave CT9 28 B8
Ellington Inf Sch CT11 52 C7
Ellington Pl CT11 52 C7
Ellington Rd CT11 52 D7
Ellington Sch for Girls
CT11 52 C7
Elliot Cl CT1 67 C3
Elliot Ct CT6 23 C4
Elliots Pl ME13 62 D7
Elliott Park Sch ME12 4 A7
Ellis Dr TN28 202 C8
Ellis Ho 7 ME14 75 B4
Ellis Rd CT5 21 A3
Ellis Way CT6 23 C2
Ellison Cl CT5 21 C1
Ellison Ct ME13 62 E6
Ellison Way ME8 12 A2
Ellisons Wlk CT1 88 C8
Elm Ave ME4 9 E1
Elm Cl TN27 118 F3
Elm Cotts TN25 122 E3
Elm Court Ind Est ME7 32 E3
Elm Ct CT8 27 E8
Elm Fields TN29 201 A6
Elm Gdns CT21 176 E2
Elm Gr Maidstone ME15 75 B3
Manston CT12 28 D1
Sittingbourne ME10 37 B4
Westgate-on-S CT8 27 E8
Elm Ho 11 CT21 176 B2
Elm La ME12 4 E5
Elm Park Gdns CT17 165 F7
Elm Pl TN23 155 F7
Elm Rd Aylesham CT3 112 E5
7 Folkestone CT19 178 E6
Gillingham ME7 10 E6
St Mary's Bay TN29 194 F3
Elm Tree Ave ME9 14 D4
Elm Tree Dr ME1 9 A2
Elm Wood Cl CT5 21 C2
Elm Wood W CT5 21 C2
Elmfield Gillingham ME8 11 A3
Tenterden TN30 179 B8
Elmfield Ct
Coxheath ME17 96 C3
Tenterden TN30 179 B8
Elmhurst Cl TN25 138 F4
Elmhurst Cvn Pk ME12 5 F6
Elmhurst Gdns ME4 9 E3
Elmleigh Rd CT3 90 A8
Elmley Ind Est ME11 3 A2
Elmley Marshes Nature
Reserve★ ME12 16 F4
Elmley Rd ME12 4 D3
Elmley Way CT9 28 F6
Elms Ave CT11 52 D6
Elms Hill CT15 165 D6
Elms The Hersden CT3 46 E1
Teynham ME9 39 A2
Elms Vale Rd CT15,CT17 165 E7
Elmsmead TN31 197 B4
Elmstead Pl 12 CT20 178 E5
Elmstone Cl ME16 74 B2
Elmstone Gdns CT9 8 E2
Elmstone Hole Rd
ME17 100 D1
Elmstone La ME16 74 B2
Elmstone Rd
Gillingham ME8 33 D7
Ramsgate CT11 52 D7
Elmton La CT15 114 C1
Elmtree TN26 181 C1
Elmway ME12 5 F6
Elmwood Ave CT10 30 A8
Elmwood Cl CT10 30 A7
Elventon Cl CT19 177 E7
Elverland La ME13,ME9 61 B2
Elvington Cl ME16 74 D5
Elvington La CT18 162 E2
Elwick La 13 TN23 139 B2
Elwick Rd TN23 139 B2
Ely Cl ME8 11 E2
Embassy Cl ME7 10 F1
Emelina Way CT5 43 B6
Emerald Cl ME1 31 D7
Emerald Cres ME10 36 D6
Emerald View ME12 6 E4
Emily Rd ME5 32 B6
Emmerson Gdns CT5 21 D3
Emperor Way TN23 155 F4
Empire Terr CT9 28 E8
Empress Gdns ME12 6 D4
Emsworth Gr ME14 75 D6
Enbrook Rd CT20 177 E4
Enbrook Valley CT20 177 E5
Encombe CT20 177 D3
Endeavour Foyer The 8
ME4 10 B2
Enfield Rd CT14 117 D7
Engineers Ct 1 TN23 139 B2
English Martyrs' RC Prim
Sch ME2 9 B8
Ennerdale ME13 62 E6
Ennerdale Gdns CT3 112 F6
Ennerdale Ho ME15 97 E7
Enterprise Bsns Est ME2 9 E7
Enterprise Cl ME2 9 D8
Enterprise Ctr TN24 156 E7
Enterprise Ctr The ME5 54 C8
Enterprise Rd
Maidstone ME15 75 A1
Margate CT9 29 A6
Enticott Cl CT5 21 A1
Epaul La ME1 9 C6
Eppe Cl 2 ME2 9 B8
Epping Cl CT6 23 B2
Epple Bay Ave CT7 27 B8
Epple Bay Rd CT7 27 A8
Epple Rd CT7 27 B8
Epps Rd ME10 36 E3
Epsom Cl ME15 97 F6
Eric Rd CT17 149 B2
Erith Cl ME14 75 A8
Erith St CT17 149 B1
Ernest Dr ME16 74 B5
Ernest Rd ME4 10 A3
Ernwell Rd CT19 178 D6
Ersham Rd CT1 88 A7
Eskdale Ave CT11 52 A7
Esmonde Dr CT12 27 F2
Esmonde Ho 15 ME7 10 A6
Esplanade Dover CT17 166 D6
Rochester ME1 9 B5
Westgate-on-S CT8 7 C1
Essella Pk TN24 139 E1
Essella Rd TN24 139 E1
Essetford Rd TN23 156 A7
Essex Ave CT6 22 B4
Essex Gdns CT7 26 F6
Essex Rd Canterbury CT1 88 D7
Maidstone ME15 97 E6
Westgate-on-S CT8 27 F8
Essex St CT5 43 D8
Estelle Cl ME1 31 D7
Esther Ct ME10 36 E8
Estuary Rd ME12 1 C1
Estuary Way CT5 21 E3
Etchden Rd TN26 154 A8
Ethel Rd CT10 29 F5
Ethel-Maud Ct ME7 10 D7
Ethelbert Cres CT9 8 A3
Ethelbert Gdns CT9 7 J3
Ethelbert Rd
Birchington CT7 26 D8
Canterbury CT1 88 B6
Deal CT14 95 C1
Dover CT17 166 C8
Faversham ME13 62 C6
Folkestone CT19 178 D7
Margate CT9 7 J3
Ramsgate CT11 52 D6
Rochester ME1 9 C4
Ethelbert Road Inf Sch
ME13 62 C6
Ethelbert Sq CT8 7 C1
Ethelbert Terr Margate CT9 8 A3
Westgate-on-S CT8 7 C1
Ethelburga Dr CT18 161 B7
Ethelred Ct ME13 62 C6
Ethelred Rd CT8 7 C1
Eton Cl ME5 31 F4
Ettrick Terr CT21 176 A2
Eurogate Bsns Pk TN24 139 B5
Eurolink Bsns Pk ME10 37 B5
Eurolink Way ME10 36 F4
Eva Rd ME7 10 D3
Evans Rd TN24 157 A7
Evelings Alley 18 CT5 20 D2
Evelyn Cl ME2 9 C8
Evelyn Ct CT21 177 A2
Evelyn Ho
9 Folkestone CT20 178 D5
5 Rochester ME2 9 C8
Evelyn Rd ME16 74 E3
Evenhill Rd CT3 89 E8
Everard Way ME13 62 B8
Everglades The ME7 32 F6
Evergreen Cl
Gillingham ME7 33 A5
Iwade ME9 14 D4
Everist Ct CT18 161 C6
Eversleigh Rise CT5 43 F7
Eversley Cl ME16 74 C6
Eversley Coll CT20 177 F4
Eversley Rd CT21 177 B3
Eversley Way CT20 177 F5
Evington Pottery★
TN25 142 D7
Evison Cl CT16 149 B2
Evorg Ho 6 ME4 10 B2
Ewart Rd ME4 9 E1
Exchange St CT14 117 D7
Exchange The CT5 20 E3
Exeter Cl CT19 177 D6
Exeter Wlk ME1 31 C7
Exmoor Rise TN24 139 B4
Exmouth Rd ME7 10 C7
Exton Cl ME5 32 C2
Exton Gdns ME14 75 F5
Eye The ME4 9 F5
Eyhorne St ME17 77 D2
Eynsford Cl CT9 8 F2
Eynsford Rd ME16 74 D7
Eythorn Court Barn
CT15 131 B7
Eythorne Cl TN24 139 D5
Eythorne Elvington Com Prim
Sch CT15 131 C8
Eythorne Rd CT15 130 E6
Eythorne Sta CT15 131 C8

F

Faggs Wood Forest Wlks★
TN26 170 D2
Fagus Cl ME5 32 B1
Fair St CT10 29 E4
Fair View Com Inf Sch
ME8 33 C5
Fair View Com Jun Sch
ME8 33 C5
Fairacre CT10 29 E4
Fairacres Cl CT6 23 C4
Fairbourne Heath Cotts
ME17 100 B1
Fairbourne La ME17 100 C4
Fairfax Bsns Ctr ME15 97 F4
Fairfax Cl
Folkestone CT20 177 D5
Gillingham ME8 33 D5
Fairfax Dr CT6 23 F5
Fairfax Ho ME15 97 F5
Fairfield Deal CT14 116 F6
Elham CT4 144 F5
Fairfield Cl TN28 202 B7
Fairfield Pk CT10 29 E4
Fairfield Rd
Broadstairs CT10 29 E4
Minster (Thanet) CT12 50 B7
New Romney TN28 202 B7
Ramsgate CT11 29 E2
Fairfield Terr TN26 183 A7
Fairhurst Dr ME15 96 B4
Fairings The TN30 179 B8
Fairlawn CT5 21 D1
Fairlawn Rd CT12 29 B3
Fairlead Rd ME1 9 D1
Fairleas ME10 37 B2
Fairlight Ave CT12 52 B8
Fairlight Cotts 8 ME13 62 C7
Fairlight Rd CT21 176 A3
Fairmeadow ME14 74 F4
Fairoaks CT6 23 B3
Fairservice Cl ME10 37 C5
Fairview CT21 175 A3
Fairview Ave ME8 33 B5
Fairview Cl CT9 8 A2
Fairview Cotts
Maidstone ME15 96 F5
Wormshill ME9 79 C7
Fairview Dr TN24 156 D6
Fairview Gdns
Deal CT14 117 A2
Sturry CT2 68 A6
Fairview Ind Pk TN26 183 D7
Fairview Rd
Elvington CT15 114 B1
Sittingbourne ME10 37 A3
Fairway CT13 95 A7
Fairway Ave CT19 178 A7
Fairway Cl Rochester ME1 9 C1
St Mary's Bay TN29 194 F3
Fairway Cres CT5 43 A7
Fairway The Deal CT14 117 C8
Herne Bay CT6 22 D2
Hythe CT21 176 C1
Littlestone-on-Sea TN28 202 D6
Rochester ME1 9 C1
Sittingbourne ME10 36 E1
St Mary's Bay TN29 195 A5
Fairways The ME13 62 A6
Fairwood Ind Est TN23 139 A1
Fairwood Ind Pk TN23 138 F2
Falcon Cl CT6 45 F7
Falcon Ct ME10 37 A2
Falcon Gdns ME12 4 D7
Falcon Ho 3 ME10 37 A4
Falcon Way TN23 155 E7
Falkland Pl ME5 31 E1
Fallowfield Chatham ME5 32 B8
Sittingbourne ME10 37 A2
Fallowfield Cl ME14 75 E4
Fan The CT16 166 H8
Fanconi Rd ME5 32 B3
Fancy Row ME14 76 C5
Fane Way ME8 33 D4
Fans La ME9 14 D4
Fant La ME16 74 B2
Faraday Ho ME1 9 D5
Faraday Rd ME14 75 C7
Fareham Wlk 10 ME15 97 F6
Farington Cl ME16 74 B4
Farleigh Ct ME16 74 A2
Farleigh Hill ME15 74 E1
Farleigh Hill Ret Pk
ME15 74 E1
Farleigh La ME16 74 A1
Farleigh Rd CT2 67 A3
Farleigh Trad Est ME15 74 E1
Farley Cl Chatham ME5 32 D2
Shadoxhurst TN26 155 A1
Farley Rd CT9 28 F7
Farleys Way TN31 196 B2
Farm Cl TN23 155 E7
Farm Cres ME10 37 A2
Farm Gdns TN31 196 C2
Farm House Cl CT5 43 F8
Farm La CT14 116 F6
Farm Rd Chatham ME5 31 E3
Hamstreet TN26 183 A7
Farmer Cl Hythe CT21 176 D3
Leeds ME17 99 A6
Farmhouse Cl CT4 128 F7
Farnborough Cl ME16 74 C2
Farncombe Way CT16 149 B7
Farne Cl ME15 97 A6
Farnham Cl ME8 12 B1
Farningham Cl ME14 75 C6
Farraday Cl ME1 31 D8
Farrar Rd CT7 27 A6
Farrers Wlk TN23 156 B4
Farrier Cl Ashford TN23 138 F5
Maidstone ME14 75 E5
Farrier St CT14 117 D7
Farriers Ct ME8 34 C8
Farrow Ct TN23 156 A6
Farthing Cnr ME9 33 E3
Farthingloe Cotts CT15 165 F5
Farthingloe Ct CT17 166 A6
Farthingloe Rd CT17 166 A6
Farthings Cotts ME14 53 F1
Farthings Ct CT2 66 C4
Fauchon's Cl ME14 75 F3
Fauchon's La ME14 75 F4
Faulkners La CT2 66 A1
Faussett Hill CT4 109 F8
Faustina Dr TN23 155 F4
Faversham Cottage Hospl
ME13 62 C7
Faversham Ind Est ME13 62 F7
Faversham Miniature Rly★
ME13 62 B4
Faversham Rd
Boughton Lees TN24,TN25 122 E5
Challock ME13,TN27 104 C3
Charing TN27 103 E1
Lenham ME17 101 E7
Lewson Street ME13,ME9 61 B5
Pested TN25,ME13 105 B4
Whitstable CT5 42 C6
Wichling ME17,ME9 80 B4
Faversham Reach ME13 62 D8
Faversham Sta ME13 62 D6
Faversham Stone Chap★
ME13 61 E7
Favourite Rd CT5 43 B6
Fawley Cl ME14 74 E7
Fay Cl ME1 9 B3
Featherbed La Iwade ME9 14 E2
Selling ME13 84 A7
Featherby Cotts ME7 10 F6
Featherby Inf Sch ME8 11 A3
Featherby Jun Sch ME8 11 A3
Featherby Rd
Gillingham ME8 11 A3
Gillingham,Grange ME7 11 A5
Felborough Cl CT4 107 C8
Felderland Cl
Maidstone ME17 97 E5
Sandwich CT14 93 F5
Felderland Dr ME17 97 E5
Felderland La CT14 93 E4
Felderland Rd ME17 97 E5
Feldspar Cl Chatham ME5 32 A1
Sittingbourne ME10 36 D6
Fellows Cl ME8 33 B6
Fennel Cl ME16 74 B3
Fennell Cl ME1 9 B3
Fenner Cl CT20 177 E4
Fenoulhet Way CT6 23 A5
Fenton Ct CT14 117 B6
Ferdi Lethert Ho TN24 139 E5
Ferguson Cl CT21 176 F2
Ferguson Rd TN29 207 F6
Ferguson Way CT21 176 A1
Fern Bank Cres CT19 178 D6
Fern Cl Hawkinge CT18 163 C6
Whitstable CT5 21 C1
Fern Ct Broadstairs CT10 30 B5
Dover CT16 149 D1
Fern Wlk ME10 37 C5
Fernbank Cl ME5 31 F2
Ferndale Cl ME12 3 D6
Ferndale Ct CT7 27 A6
Ferndale Rd ME7 10 E5
Ferndown CT7 26 D8
Ferndown Cl ME7 33 A5
Ferne La CT15 147 D3
Ferne Way CT20 177 E6
Fernfield CT18 163 C6
Fernfield La CT18 163 C7
Fernhill Rd ME16 74 A2
Fernlea Ave CT6 22 E4
Fernleigh Cl ME13 64 B3
Fernley Ct 11 CT20 178 D5
Ferrier Cl ME8 33 E4
Ferry Rd Iwade ME9 14 E4
Queenborough ME11,ME12 3 D1
Ferry View ME11 2 F3
Fiddling La TN25 159 E6
Field Ave CT1 67 D3
Field Cl ME5 31 E6
Field End TN24 140 A1
Field End Pl ME13 64 A3
Field Mill Rd TN27 119 B5
Field View
Kingsnorth TN23 156 B4
Whitstable CT5 43 B7
Field Way CT2 67 F5
Fielder Cl ME10 37 C5
Fielding St ME13 62 C7
Fieldings The ME10 36 E2
Fieldview Cl ME12 3 C6
Fieldworks Rd ME7 10 A7
Fiesta Wlk CT1 88 C7
Fife Rd CT6 22 B3
Fifth Ave CT9 8 B3
Fig Tree Rd CT10 29 F7
Fig Tree Wlk CT15 131 C7
Fiji Terr ME14 75 A7
Filer Rd ME12 3 E7
Filmer Rd CT4 88 F1
Finch Ct ME14 74 E7

Finch Gr CT21 187 D8
Finch Mews CT14 117 C4
Finches The
Sittingbourne ME10 36 F3
St Nicholas at Wade CT7 25 E2
Findlay Cl ME8 33 D6
Findlay Ct 9 CT21 176 B2
Finglesham Ct ME15 97 C8
Finglesham Farm Barns
CT14 116 A8
Finlay Cl ME13 62 B7
Finn Farm Ct TN23 156 D1
Finn Farm Rd TN23 156 C2
Finsbury Ct CT11 52 E8
Finsbury Rd CT11 52 E8
Fintonagh Dr ME14 75 B6
Finwell Rd ME8 12 A2
Fir Ct TN24 139 F1
Fir Tree Cl CT11 52 C6
Fir Tree Gr Bredhurst ME7 33 B1
Chatham ME5 32 D1
Fir Tree Hill CT13 93 B6
Firbank Gdns CT9 28 D7
Firbanks CT5 43 F8
Firethorn Cl ME7 10 E6
Firmin Ave ME17 97 D5
Firs Cl CT19 177 D7
Firs La CT19 177 D7
Firs Rd CT4 112 F1
Firs The Deal CT14 117 C8
Hersden CT3 46 E1
First Ave Broadstairs CT10 8 F2
Chatham ME4 10 C2
Eastchurch ME12 5 E5
Gillingham ME7 10 E3
Margate CT9 8 B3
Rushenden ME11 2 F3
Sheerness ME12 1 D1
First La ME17 76 E2
Firtree Cl CT2 66 B3
Fish Market CT19 178 E5
Fisher Cl CT21 176 D1
Fisher Rd Canterbury CT2 66 D1
Chatham ME5 32 B7
Fisher St Maidstone ME14 75 A6
Sandwich CT13 73 A1
Fisher Street Rd ME13 83 E2
Fisherman's Wharf
CT13 73 A1
Fishermans Ctyd CT14 117 D3
Fishers TN28 202 E5
Fishmonger's La 8
CT16 166 E7
Fitzgerald Ave CT6 22 C4
Fitzmary Ave CT9 7 E1
Fitzroy Ave
Broadstairs CT10 8 G2
Margate CT9 8 B1
Ramsgate CT12 29 B2
Fitzroy Rd CT5 20 F2
Fitzthorold Ho ME7 10 E7
Fitzwalter Ct 1 CT16 149 B3
Fitzwilliam Rd ME14 75 F5
Five Acre Wood Sch
ME15 97 B7
Five Bells La 5 ME1 9 D4
Five Vents La TN29 201 B8
Five Ways Ct ME4 10 A4
Fiveways 6 CT17 166 C8
Fiveways L Ctr ME4 10 A4
Fiveways Rise CT14 116 F5
Flamingo Cl ME5 32 A7
Flamingo Dr CT6 22 E3
Flanders Cl ME10 14 F1
Flanders Field TN25 157 E4
Flax Court La CT15 131 C7
Flaxman Ct 13 ME7 10 A6
Flaxman Dr ME16 74 C6
Flaxpond Rd TN23 155 F7
Fleet Ave ME12 1 C1
Fleet Rd Rochester ME1 9 D1
St Margaret's at Cliffe
CT15 134 A1
Fleet Villas TN24 139 D7
Fleets La CT2 66 D7
Fleetwood Ave CT6 22 D4
Fleetwood Cl ME12 4 B6
Fleming Rd CT13,CT3 92 D6
Fleming Way CT19 178 E8
Fletcher Battery Camp Site
ME12 6 A6
Fletcher Rd CT5 21 B1
Fletchers Way CT14 117 A5
Flete Rd CT9 28 D5
Fleur de Lis Heritage Ctr*
ME13 62 D7
Flimwell TN23 155 D6
Flint Cl ME10 36 E8
Flint Cotts CT7 26 F6
Flint Gn ME5 32 C3
Flint Gr CT10 29 E5
Flint Ho CT9 7 J3
Flint La ME17 79 C1
Flodden Rd CT14 116 F3
Flood Hatch ME15 74 D2
Flood La ME13 62 C8
Flood St TN25 157 D2
Flora Rd CT11 52 E8
Florence Ave CT5 43 B7
Florence Cotts CT11 52 D6
Florence Ct CT9 8 B3
Florence Rd
Maidstone ME16 74 E3
3 Ramsgate CT11 52 D6
Florence St 3 ME2 9 B8
Florida Cl CT16 149 B3
Florin Dr ME1 9 B4
Flower Rise ME14 74 F7
Flume End ME15 74 D2
Flying Horse La 6 CT16 166 E7
Foads Hill CT12 51 D6
Foads La CT12 51 D5
Focal Point Rd CT16 148 F4
Fodbury Ct CT8 7 C1
Foley Cl TN24 157 A7
Foley St ME14 75 A5
Folkestone Ent Ctr
CT19 177 F8
Folkestone Harbour Sta
CT20 178 E4
Folkestone Mus* CT20 178 D5
Folkestone Race Course
CT21 175 A6
Folkestone Rd
Brookland TN31 198 B3
Church Hougham CT15 165 D4
Dover CT17,CT15 166 B7
Folkestone Sch for Girls The
CT20 177 F4
Folkestone West Sta
CT18 177 F5
Folkestone, Christ Church CE
Prim Sch CT20 178 C5
Folkestone, St Mary's CE
Prim Sch CT19 178 F6
Folkestone, St Peter's CE
Prim Sch CT19 178 E5
Folks Wood Way CT21 175 A4
Folkstone Ho 4 ME15 97 F6
Folkestone, St Martin's CE
Prim Sch CT18 177 B5
Folly Rd CT20 178 E6
Fonblanque Rd ME12 1 D2
Fontwell Cl ME15 97 F6
Foord Almshouses ME1 9 B3
Foord Rd ME17 101 D5
Foord Rd N CT19,CT20 178 D5
Foord Rd S 14 CT20 178 D5
Foord St ME1 9 D4
Forbes Rd ME13 62 C6
Ford Cl Bridge CT4 88 F1
Herne Bay CT6 22 A4
Ford Hill CT3,CT6 46 E8
Ford Way TN23 138 F1
Ford Wlk CT5 43 A3
Fordcombe Cl ME15 97 F7
Fordingbridge Cl ME16 74 B5
Fordoun Rd CT10 29 F5
Fordwich Cl ME16 74 B7
Fordwich Gn ME8 11 C3
Fordwich Gr CT10 29 E7
Fordwich Pl CT13 93 F8
Fordwich Rd CT2 67 F4
Fordwich TH* CT2 68 A4
Foreland Ave
Folkestone CT19 178 F6
Margate CT9 8 D1
Foreland Ct
Birchington CT7 26 D8
Ramsgate CT11 52 D5
St Margaret's at Cliffe
CT15 151 A5
Foreland Hts CT10 30 B7
Foreland Park Ho CT10 30 B7
Foreland Rd CT15 151 A4
Foreland Sch The CT10 30 A6
Foreland The CT1 88 B5
Forelands Sq CT14 117 B3
Foreness Cl CT10 8 G3
Forest Ave TN25 138 E4
Forest Cotts TN25 105 C2
Forest Dr ME5 31 F2
Forest Hill ME15 74 F1
Forestall Mdw TN23 156 B4
Forestdale Rd ME5 54 A8
Foresters Cl ME5 31 F2
Foresters Way CT20 178 D5
Forestry Cotts CT4 125 B7
Forge Cl Eythorne CT15 131 C7
Sellindge TN25 159 D1
Sturry CT2 67 F5
Forge Cotts
Boyden Gate CT3 47 C8
Broadstairs CT10 30 B5
Faversham ME13 63 D8
Forge Field CT15 164 E5
Forge Hill
Aldington TN25 173 A5
Bethersden TN26 153 E5
Forge Ho Canterbury CT1 87 E6
Ickham CT3 69 C1
Forge La Ashford TN23 139 B2
Boxley ME14 54 C2
Boyden Gate CT3 47 C8
Bredhurst ME7 33 A1
East Farleigh ME15 96 C7
Egerton Forstal TN27 118 C1
Gillingham ME7 10 E7
Leeds ME17 98 F7
Maidstone ME14 76 C4
Ramsgate CT11 52 C7
Sutton CT15 133 A6
Upchurch ME9 12 F3
Whitfield CT16 149 A8
Whitstable CT5 43 D8
Forge Mdw
Harrietsham ME17 100 D6
Stone in Oxney TN30 190 A4
Forge Meads TN30 188 E3
Forge Path CT16 149 A8
Forge Rd ME10 36 E6
Forgefield TN26 153 D5
Forgefields CT6 46 B8
Forrens The 15 CT1 67 A1
Forrester Cl CT1 67 C2
Forson Cl TN30 179 B8
Forstal Cotts Forstal ME20 53 B2
Lenham Heath ME17 102 A1
Forstal La ME17 96 D4
Forstal Rd
Egerton Forstal TN27 118 C1
Forstal ME20 53 C2
Woolage Village CT4 112 E1
Forstal The
Lenham Heath ME17 102 A1
Preston CT3 70 B6
Wye TN25 123 E2
Forsters ME17 98 E4
Forsyth Ct 7 ME7 10 C7
Fort Amherst Heritage Pk &
Caverns* ME4 9 F5
Fort Burgoyne (Casemated
Barracks) CT15 149 E2
Fort Burgoyne Rd CT16 149 E1
Fort Cl TN29 206 E6
Fort Cotts CT10 30 B4
Fort Cres CT9 7 J3
Fort Hill CT9 7 I3
Fort Lower Prom CT9 7 J3
Fort Luton (Mus)* ME4 10 A1
Fort Paragon CT9 7 J3
Fort Pitt Gram Sch ME4 9 E4
Fort Pitt Hill ME1,ME4 9 E4
Fort Pitt St ME4 9 E3
Fort Prom CT9 7 J3
Fort Rd Broadstairs CT10 30 B4
Hythe CT21 176 A2
Margate CT9 7 I3
Fort St ME1 9 D4
Fortuna Ct CT11 52 D7
Forty Acres Hill ME12 4 C4
Forty Acres Rd CT2 66 E2
Forum The 2 ME10 36 F4
Forum Way TN23 155 E5
Forward Way ME1 31 C6
Fostall Gn TN23 155 F7
Fostall Rd ME13 40 C1
Foster Cl CT19 177 E7
Foster Clark Est ME15 75 B2
Foster Clarke Dr ME17 97 D5
Foster Rd TN24 157 A6
Foster St ME15 75 A3
Foster Way CT14 117 B5
Foster's Ave CT10 29 E7
Foster's Ct CT13 94 A7
Fostington Way ME5 31 F1
Fougeres Way TN24 139 A4
Foulds Cl ME8 33 B5
Foundry Wharf ME1 9 E4
Fountain Inn Ct CT9 7 I3
Fountain La
Maidstone ME16 74 A2
Sheerness ME12 1 B2
Fountain St
2 Sittingbourne ME10 36 E4
3 Whitstable CT5 20 D2
Fountains Cl TN24 140 A1
Four Horseshoes Pk
ME13 41 D1
Four Oaks ME13 61 E8
Four Turnings CT3 70 B3
Four Wents
Langley Heath ME17 98 E3
Maidstone ME17 97 F2
Fouracre Cotts ME9 34 E6
Fourth Ave Eastchurch ME12 5 F5
Gillingham ME7 10 E4
Fowey Cl ME5 32 C5
Fowler Cl ME8 33 C3
Fox Cl CT18 161 B7
Fox Hill ME10,ME9 37 D3
Fox Holt Rd CT15 146 B2
Fox St ME7 10 C6
Fox Way CT4 128 F8
Fox's Cross CT5 43 B4
Fox's Cross Hill CT5 43 A3
Fox's Cross Rd CT5 43 C3
Foxborough Cl CT13 93 B6
Foxborough Hill CT13 93 B5
Foxborough La CT12 50 C6
Foxburrow Cl ME8 33 D5
Foxden Dr ME15 75 F1
Foxdene Ct CT5 42 F6
Foxdene Rd CT5 42 F6
Foxdown Cl CT2 66 E2
Foxglove Cres ME5 31 E4
Foxglove Gn TN24 139 F2
Foxglove Rd TN24 139 E1
Foxglove Rise ME14 74 E7
Foxgrove ME10 36 E7
Foxgrove Rd CT5 21 A1
Foxhunter Pk The CT12 49 D6
Foxley Rd ME11 3 A5
Frampton Rd CT21 176 A2
France Rd CT16 149 A5
Frances Gdns CT11 52 F8
Francis Cl CT12 51 D5
Francis Dr ME5 32 A2
Francis La ME15 97 F5
Francis Rd Ashford TN23 156 B8
Broadstairs CT10 30 B7
Frank Edinger Cl TN24 139 D4
Frank Walters Bsns Pk The
CT10 29 D3
Frankapps Cl ME9 35 B6
Franklin Dr ME14 75 D4
Franklin Rd ME7 10 D5
Franklins Cotts ME15 96 C5
Franklyn Ho CT2 67 F5
Franklyn Rd CT2 87 C8
Franks Ct ME8 11 B2
Freathy La TN25 139 C8
Freda Cl CT10 29 F1
Frederick Rd Deal CT14 117 A3
Gillingham ME7 10 C4
Frederick St ME10 36 E4
Freedown The CT15 151 A7
Freeman Ct 3 ME10 36 E4
Freeman Gdns ME4 9 F2
Freeman Way ME15 97 E7
Freeman's Cl CT5 43 A6
Freeman's Rd CT12 50 B6
Freemen's Way CT14 117 B3
Freesia Cl ME7 10 F6
Fremantle Rd CT20 177 E5
Fremlins Rd ME14 76 C4
French's Row ME9 38 D2
Frencham Cl CT2 67 A4
Frensham Cl ME10 37 B4
Frensham Wlk ME5 31 F1
Freshfield La CT21 176 B4
Freshland Rd ME16 74 B4
Freshlands CT6 23 E5
Freshwater Cl CT6 22 B3
Freshwater Rd ME5 32 B7
Friars Ave ME5 31 F2
Friars Cl CT5 21 A1
Friars Sch TN23 155 B8
Friars The CT1 66 F1
Friars Way CT16 149 A3
Friary Pl 3 ME2 9 B7
Friary Prec ME2 9 B7
Friary Way CT2 66 D2
Frid Cnr TN26 153 E7
Friendly Cl CT9 8 D1
Friends Ave CT9 29 D8
Friesian Way TN24 139 C8
Frindsbury Rd ME2 9 B8
Frinstead Wlk ME16 74 B7
Frinsted Cl ME8 11 C3
Frinsted Rd ME9 58 E2
Friston Way ME1 31 D8
Frith Bsns Pk TN25 172 B6
Frith Rd
Aldington Frith TN25 172 C6
Dover CT16 149 C1
Frithwood Cl ME15 75 F1
Frittenden Cl TN23 155 E6
Frobisher Cl ME10 36 E7
Frobisher Ct 2 CT11 52 F8
Frobisher Gdns ME1 9 C2
Frog Farm Cotts ME9 13 A4
Frog La CT4 111 C6
Frogmore Wlk ME17 101 C5
Frognal Cl ME9 38 B2
Frognal Gdns ME9 38 C2
Frognal La ME9 38 B2
Front Brents ME13 62 D8
Front Rd TN26 169 A1
Front St CT14 133 F5
Front The CT15 151 A4
Frost Cres ME5 32 A7
Frostland La TN26,TN29 184 C1
Froyle Cl ME16 74 C6
Fruiterer's Cl ME9 59 B7
Fulbert Dr ME14 75 F5
Fulbert Rd CT16 149 B5
Fulham Ave CT9 28 C7
Fullers Cl ME14 76 A4
Fullers Yd CT9 7 J2
Fulmar Ct TN29 194 F3
Fulmar Mews CT18 163 A3
Fulmar Way CT6 23 F4
Fulsam Pl CT9 7 H1
Fulston Manor Sch ME10 36 F2
Fulston Pl ME10 37 A3
Furfield Cl ME17 97 E5
Furley Park Prim Sch
TN23 156 C2
Furrell's Rd ME1 9 D5
Furze Hill Cres ME12 3 E6
Fusilier Ave CT20 177 B5
Fyndon Ho CT1 88 C7

G

Gabriel's Hill ME15 75 A4
Gadby Rd ME10 36 C5
Gads Hill ME7 10 F6
Gadsby La TN26 153 A3
Gagetown Terr 1 ME14 74 F7
Gainsboro Rd 4 CT7 26 F8
Gainsborough Ave CT9 29 C8
Gainsborough Cl
Folkestone CT19 178 A7
Gillingham ME8 33 D6
Sittingbourne ME10 36 B5
Gainsborough Dr
Herne Bay CT6 23 E5
Maidstone ME16 74 B4
Gainsborough Ho ME1 9 D5
Galena Cl Chatham ME5 32 A1
Sittingbourne ME10 36 C6
Gallants La ME15 96 A2
Galleon Cl ME1 31 C8
Galliard St CT13 94 A8
Gallow's Cnr CT21 176 A2
Galloway Dr TN25 139 C8
Galloways Rd TN29 205 C5
Gallwey Ave CT7 26 E7
Galway Rd ME12 1 D1
Gammon's Farm La
TN29 185 B3
Gammons Yd 6 CT2 66 F1
Gandy's La ME17 97 C2
Gange Mews 3 ME13 62 D7
Gann Rd CT5 20 F2
Gaol La 13 CT16 166 D7
Gap House Sch CT10 30 B2
Gap The Blean CT2 66 A7
Canterbury CT1 88 B5
Garden Cl Maidstone ME15 97 E7
Rough Common CT2 66 A2
Garden Cotts CT3 91 A7
Garden Hall The TN25 124 A1
Garden of England Pk
(Mobile Home Pk)
ME17 100 B7
Garden Pl TN24 139 E6
Garden Rd CT19 178 D6
Garden St ME7 10 A6
Gardeners Pl CT4 86 F1
Gardens The
Coxheath ME17 96 C3
Ivychurch TN29 192 F4
Gardiner St ME7 10 C6
Gardiner's Hill TN31 197 B6
Gardner Cl CT18 162 F3
Garfield Pl 4 ME13 62 D7
Garfield Rd
Gillingham ME7 10 D6
Margate CT9 7 H2
Garlinge Green Rd CT4 108 E6
Garlinge Inf Sch CT9 28 C8
Garlinge Jun Sch CT9 28 B8
Garrard Ave CT9 28 B8
Garrington Cl ME14 75 C6
Garrison Rd ME12 1 B3
Garton Way TN23 155 C7
Gas House Rd ME1 9 C6
Gas La ME13 63 F3
Gas Rd Sittingbourne ME10 36 F5
Sittingbourne,Murston
ME10 37 B6
Gas St CT1 87 F7
Gascoyne Cl ME15 76 B2
Gasworks La TN23 139 B2
Gatcombe Cl
Chatham ME5 32 A5
Maidstone ME16 74 B5
Gate La CT4 144 A4
Gate Quays CT9 7 I2
Gateacre Rd CT5 43 A6
Gatefield La 9 ME13 62 D7
Gatekeeper Chase ME8 33 F8
Gateway Ct 21 CT11 52 F7
Gateway The CT16 166 E7
Gatland La ME16 74 B2
Gault Cl ME15 76 A2
Gaunt's Cl CT14 117 A4
Gayhurst Cl ME8 33 D6
Gayhurst Dr ME10 36 C5
Gaze Hill Ave ME10 37 A3
Gazedown TN29 194 F3
Gean Cl ME5 54 A8
Geddes Cl CT18 162 F3
Genesta Ave CT5 43 B7
Genesta Cl ME10 36 E7
Geneva Ave ME8 11 A2
Gentian Cl
4 Chatham ME5 31 E4
Maidstone ME14 75 E5
Geoffrey Ct CT7 27 A7
George Alley CT14 117 D6
George Cooper Ho 11
CT20 178 C4
George Gurr Cres CT19 178 D8
George Hill Rd CT10,CT9 8 E1
George La
Boughton Street ME13 63 F3
Folkestone CT20 178 D4
Leeds ME17 99 B7
New Romney TN28 202 B7
Rochester ME1 9 C6
George Marsham Ho
ME15 96 F3
George Parris Ct ME12 4 C6
George Pk CT9 7 F1
George Roche Rd CT1 88 A6
George Spurgen Com Prim
Sch CT19 178 E7
George St Ashford TN23 139 B1
Deal CT14 117 D7
Dover CT17 149 C1
Maidstone ME15 75 A3
Ramsgate CT11 52 E7
Sittingbourne ME10 37 B4
George Stone Ho 25
CT20 178 E5
George Summers Cl ME2 9 E8
George V Ave CT9 28 C8
George Warren Ct 1 CT9 7 J1
George Williams Way
TN24 139 E5
George Wood Cl TN29 205 C6
George's Ave CT5 43 A7
Georgian Cl ME11 3 A3
Georgian Dr ME17 96 D3
Georgian Way ME8 33 C4
Gerald Ave ME4 9 F2
Gerald Palmby Ct CT14 117 C7
Geraldine Rd CT19 177 F6
Gerlac Ho TN24 139 C5
Gerrard Ave ME1 31 E8
Gerrards Dr ME10 36 F2
Gibbons Rd ME10 36 B5
Gibraltar Ave ME7 10 B7
Gibraltar Hill ME4 9 F4
Gibraltar La
Hawkinge CT18 163 A2
Maidstone ME14 74 F8
Gibraltar Sq CT15 149 E3
Gibson St ME10 36 E4
Gidd's Pond Cotts ME14 75 E6
Giddyhorn La ME16 74 C5
Gifford Cl ME8 11 C3

Gigger's Green Rd TN25 .185 C7
Gilbert Cl ME7 .33 A5
Gilbert Pl 9 CT20 .177 E3
Gilbert Rd
4 Ashford TN24 .139 B2
Ramsgate CT11 .52 D8
Gilbert Terr 2 ME14 .74 F7
Gilbert Way CT1 .87 E6
Gilchrist Ave CT6 .22 C2
Giles Gdns CT9 .28 F8
Giles La CT2 .66 D4
Giles-Young Ct 7 ME10 .36 E5
Gilford Rd CT14 .117 D5
Gilham Gr CT14 .117 B4
Gill La
Aldington Frith TN25 .172 A8
Ruckinge TN26 .171 C2
Gillett Rd TN29 .205 D7
Gillingham Coll The ME7 .10 F4
Gillingham Gate ME7 .10 C8
Gillingham Gate Rd ME7 .10 C8
Gillingham Gn ME7 .10 E6
Gillingham Rd ME7 .10 D5
Gillingham Sta ME7 .10 D5
Gillman Cl CT18 .162 F4
Gillon Mews 9 CT1 .67 B2
Gills Terr ME8 .12 C3
Ginsbury Cl ME2 .9 E6
Giraud Dr ME13 .62 B8
Glack Rd CT14 .116 F4
Glade The Chatham ME5 .32 A2
Deal CT14 .116 F6
Gladstone Ct CT10 .29 F4
Gladstone Dr ME10 .37 C4
Gladstone Rd
Ashford TN24 .156 E7
Broadstairs CT10 .29 F4
Chatham ME4 .9 E2
Deal CT14 .117 C4
Folkestone CT19 .178 E6
Maidstone ME14 .75 A6
Margate CT9 .7 I1
Whitstable CT5 .20 D2
Gladwyn Cl ME8 .33 D4
Glamis Cl ME5 .32 A5
Glanville Rd
Gillingham ME7 .10 D5
Rochester ME2 .9 A8
Glasgow Ho 8 ME15 .97 E7
Gleaming Wood Dr ME5 .54 D8
Gleaners Cl ME14 .75 E4
Gleanings Mews ME1 .9 C5
Glebe Cl Smarden TN27 .135 B2
St Margaret's at Cliffe CT15 .150 F6
Glebe Cotts ME13 .81 E7
Glebe Ct CT12 .50 B5
Glebe Gdns
Lenham ME17 .101 E5
6 Margate CT9 .28 B8
Glebe La Maidstone ME16 .74 A1
Sittingbourne ME10 .37 B2
Glebe Rd Gillingham ME7 .10 E3
Margate CT9 .28 B8
Glebe The TN27 .120 D7
Glebe Way Ashford TN24 .139 D6
Whitstable CT5 .43 D8
Glebeland TN27 .118 F4
Glebelands Alkham CT15 .147 D1
Ash CT3 .71 C2
Mersham TN25 .157 E4
Glemsford Cotts CT2 .65 E1
Glen Ave CT6 .23 C5
Glen Gr CT17 .166 B7
Glen Iris Ave CT2 .66 C2
Glen Iris Cl CT2 .66 C2
Glen Rd CT14 .134 C6
Glen The
Minster (Sheppey) ME12 .4 B7
Shepherdswell CT15 .130 D5
Upstreet CT3 .47 D3
Glen Wlk CT5 .43 A3
Glenavon Ho CT10 .30 B7
Glenbervie Dr CT6 .23 E5
Glenbrook Cl CT6 .23 D5
Glenbrook Gr ME10 .36 E7
Glencoe Jun Sch ME4 .10 A2
Glencoe Rd Chatham ME4 .10 A2
Margate CT9 .8 A1
Glendale CT20 .178 E4
Glendale Rd ME12 .4 B7
Gleneagles Ct ME5 .31 F2
Gleneagles Dr ME15 .75 A1
Glenfield Rd CT16 .149 B3
Glenside CT5 .44 A8
Glenside Ave CT1 .67 B2
Glenwood TN30 .167 B3
Glenwood Cl
Chatham ME5 .10 C1
Gillingham ME7 .33 A7
Maidstone ME16 .74 C5
Tenterden TN30 .167 B3
Glenwood Dr ME12 .4 C6
Glistening Glade ME8 .33 E6
Globe La ME4 .9 F5
Gloster Cl CT18 .163 B3
Gloster Ropewalk CT17 .166 C5
Gloster Way CT17 .166 C5
Gloucester Ave
Broadstairs CT10 .29 F3
Margate CT9 .8 D2
Gloucester Cl ME8 .34 A8
Gloucester Mews TN28 .202 C8
Gloucester Pl 17 CT20 .178 D5
Gloucester Rd
Maidstone ME15 .97 D8
Whitstable CT5 .20 F2
Glover Cl ME10 .14 F1
Glover Rd TN24 .139 E1
Glovers Cres ME10 .36 F3
Glovers Mill ME4 .9 D3
Glynne Cl ME8 .33 D6
Goad Ave ME5 .32 B3
Goat Lees La TN25 .139 D8
Gobery Hill CT3 .70 B1
Godden Rd CT2 .67 A4
Godden Way ME8 .11 A4
Goddings Dr ME1 .9 A3
Goddington La ME17 .100 B6
Goddington Rd ME2 .9 B8
Godfrey Gdns CT4 .86 F1
Godfrey Ho CT5 .43 E8
Godfrey Wlk TN23 .156 B8
Godfrey's Grave ME13 .64 B7
Godfreys Cotts ME13 .105 C8
Godinton* TN23 .138 C4
Godinton La TN23,TN26 .138 D5
Godinton Prim Sch TN23 .138 D3
Godinton Rd TN23 .139 A2
Godinton Way TN23 .139 A2
Godinton Way Ind Est TN23 .139 B2
Godwin Bglws CT9 .8 B3
Godwin Cl ME10 .14 F1
Godwin Cotts CT9 .8 A3
Godwin Rd Canterbury CT1 .87 C6
Dover CT16 .166 F8
Margate CT9 .8 A3
Godwyn Gdns CT20 .178 A4
Godwyn Rd Deal CT14 .117 C8
Folkestone CT20 .178 A4
Godwyne Cl CT16 .166 D8
Godwyne Ct CT16 .149 D1
Godwyne Rd CT16 .149 D1
Gogway CT4 .126 B4
Gold Hill TN25 .121 D4
Goldcrest Wlk CT5 .43 B6
Golden Acre La CT8 .27 D7
Golden Cl CT8 .27 D7
Golden Hill CT5 .43 F6
Golden Sq
New Romney TN28 .202 A6
Tenterden TN30 .179 B8
Golden St CT14 .117 D7
Golden Wood Cl ME5 .54 D8
Goldfinch Cl
Faversham ME13 .40 C1
Herne Bay CT6 .23 C2
Golding Cl ME1 .9 E1
Goldings The ME8 .33 C8
Goldsmith Ct TN30 .167 B1
Goldsmith Rd ME8 .33 E5
Goldstone Dro CT3 .71 E7
Goldstone Wlk ME5 .32 A1
Goldthorne Cl ME14 .75 C5
Goldups La CT4 .84 C1
Goldups Lane Cotts CT4 .84 C1
Goldwell Cl TN25 .173 A6
Goldwell Hos TN25 .173 A6
Goldwell La
Aldington TN25 .173 B7
Great Chart TN23,TN26 .154 F8
Golf Ct CT14 .95 C1
Golf Rd CT14 .117 C8
Golf Road Pl CT14 .117 C8
Gooch Cl ME16 .74 D8
Good Hope CT14 .116 F4
Good Intent Cotts TN27 .119 A5
Goodall Cl ME8 .33 E5
Goodban Sq CT3 .71 D1
Goodcheap La TN25 .140 D2
Goodfellow Way 3 CT16 .166 D8
Goodnestone CE Prim Sch CT3 .91 C2
Goodnestone Gdns* CT3 .91 C1
Goodnestone Hill CT3 .91 D2
Goodnestone Rd
Sittingbourne ME10 .37 B4
Wingham CT3 .91 B5
Goodwin Ave CT5 .21 E2
Goodwin Ct CT9 .8 D3
Goodwin Dr ME14 .75 B8
Goodwin Pk CT9 .29 A5
Goodwin Rd
Ramsgate CT11 .52 B5
St Margaret's at Cliffe CT15 .151 A4
Goodwood Cl ME15 .97 F6
Goose Cl ME5 .32 A7
Goose Farm CT2 .67 D7
Goosefields ME13 .41 E1
Gordon Ave ME11 .3 A4
Gordon Cl Ashford TN24 .139 D2
Sittingbourne ME10 .37 C4
Gordon Cotts ME9 .58 B6
Gordon Ct ME17 .96 E3
Gordon Gr CT8 .7 C1
Gordon Inf Sch ME2 .9 A8
Gordon Jun Sch ME2 .9 A8
Gordon Rd Canterbury CT1 .87 F7
Chatham ME4 .10 A7
Chatham,Luton ME4 .10 B2
Dover CT16 .149 A5
Faversham ME13 .62 E8
Folkestone CT20 .177 D6
Gillingham ME7 .10 E5
Herne Bay CT6 .22 F4
Margate CT9 .8 A3
Margate,Westwood CT9 .29 A5
Ramsgate CT11 .52 D8
Rochester ME2 .9 A8
Whitstable CT5 .43 D8
Gordon Sq Birchington CT7 .26 F7
Gordon Sq *continued*
Faversham ME13 .62 E7
Gordon Terr Lydd TN29 .205 C5
Rochester ME1 .9 C4
Gore Cl CT13 .93 B3
Gore Cotts ME9 .12 E1
Gore Court Rd
Maidstone ME15 .97 F5
Sittingbourne ME10 .36 E2
Gore Ct TN24 .139 C3
Gore End Cl CT7 .26 F7
Gore Farm CT13 .93 B3
Gore Farm Trails* ME9 .12 D1
Gore La CT13 .93 B2
Gore Mews 3 CT1 .67 B2
Gore Rd Eastry CT13 .93 B3
Silver Street ME9 .57 F5
Gore Street Farm Cotts CT12 .49 A7
Gore Terr CT13 .93 B3
Gorely Ho 14 CT17 .166 D7
Goretop La CT14 .94 C6
Gorham Dr ME15 .76 A1
Gorrell Rd CT5 .20 E1
Gorse Ave ME5 .31 F5
Gorse La CT6 .23 C2
Gorse Mead TN23 .155 F8
Gorse Rd ME10 .37 C5
Gorst St ME7 .10 C5
Goschen Rd CT17 .166 B8
Gosfield Rd CT6 .23 A4
Goshawk Ho 1 ME10 .37 A4
Gosmere Farm Barns
Doddington ME13 .80 E7
Sheldwich ME13 .83 E7
Goss Hall La CT3 .72 A2
Gosselin St CT5 .43 E8
Goteley Mere TN24 .139 C7
Gothic Cl CT14 .117 B1
Gothic Cotts TN26 .121 A1
Goudhurst Cl
Canterbury CT2 .67 A4
Maidstone ME16 .74 E4
Goudhurst Rd ME8 .11 B3
Gough Rd CT20 .177 E3
Gould Rd ME5 .32 B3
Gower Ho ME14 .75 A6
Grace Ave ME16 .74 D6
Grace Ct 16 CT20 .178 D5
Grace Hill CT20 .178 D5
Grace Mdw CT16 .149 A7
Grace Rd ME12 .1 B1
Grace Sch CT20 .178 D5
Grace Wlk CT14 .117 A5
Grafton Ave ME1 .31 E8
Grafton Rd
Broadstairs CT10 .29 F8
Sittingbourne ME10 .36 F4
Grafton Rise CT6 .22 C4
Graham Cl ME4 .9 F6
Grain Rd ME8 .33 C3
Grainey Field ME9 .34 E4
Gram's Rd CT14 .134 C8
Grampian Way ME15 .76 A1
Grampion Cl TN24 .139 C4
Granada Ho 8 ME15 .75 A4
Granada St 9 ME15 .75 A4
Granary Cl Gillingham ME8 .11 F1
Maidstone ME14 .75 E5
Granary Court Rd TN25 .159 A4
Granary Pl CT5 .43 D8
Grand Ct
6 Folkestone CT20 .178 B3
7 Gillingham ME7 .10 C6
Littlestone-on-Sea TN28 .202 E5
Grand Dr CT6 .22 C4
Grand Mans CT10 .30 B3
Grand Par TN28 .202 E5
Grand Pavilion CT5 .20 F3
Grand The 4 CT20 .178 B3
Grange Cres TN30 .167 A3
Grange Ct
1 Folkestone CT20 .178 C4
9 Ramsgate CT11 .52 C6
Grange Hill ME5 .10 B3
Grange Ho ME16 .74 A2
Grange La ME14 .54 A1
Grange Rd
Broadstairs CT10 .29 F6
Deal CT14 .117 B5
Folkestone CT19 .177 E6
Gillingham ME7 .11 A6
Herne Bay CT6 .23 C4
Hythe CT21 .176 B4
Ramsgate CT11 .52 C6
Rochester ME2 .9 B7
Tenterden TN30 .167 A3
Grange Rdbt ME7 .11 A6
Grange The
Shepherdswell CT15 .130 D5
Whitstable CT5 .43 A6
Grange Way
Broadstairs CT10 .29 F2
Rochester ME1 .9 C3
Grant Cl Broadstairs CT10 .29 E6
Gillingham ME7 .11 B1
Grant Dr ME15 .97 D6
Grant's Cotts ME17 .101 B5
Grantham Ave CT14 .117 A5
Grantley Cl TN23 .156 A8
Granville Ave
Broadstairs CT10 .30 B3
Ramsgate CT12 .29 B1
Granville Cl ME13 .62 C7
Granville Ct Deal CT14 .117 C2
Maidstone ME14 .75 A6
Granville Dr CT6 .22 B2
Granville Farm Mews 24 CT11 .52 F7
Granville Ho 18 CT11 .52 F7
Granville Marina 20 CT11 .52 F7
Granville Par CT20 .177 E3
Granville Pl
Folkestone CT20 .177 F3
Sheerness ME12 .1 D2
Granville Rd
Broadstairs CT10 .30 B3
Deal CT14 .117 C2
Gillingham ME7 .10 E5
Kingsdown CT14 .134 D3
Maidstone ME14 .75 A6
Sheerness ME12 .1 D2
St Margaret's at Cliffe CT15 .151 B6
Granville Rd E CT20 .177 F3
Granville St Deal CT14 .117 D5
Dover CT16 .149 C1
Granville The CT15 .151 B6
Grapple Rd ME14 .75 A7
Grasmere Ave CT11 .52 A7
Grasmere Gdns CT19 .178 B7
Grasmere Pk CT5 .44 B8
Grasmere Rd
Ashford TN24 .139 C6
Whitstable CT5 .44 B8
Grasmere Way CT3 .112 F6
Grasslands Ashford TN23 .155 D7
Langley Heath ME17 .98 E4
Grassmere TN29 .194 E3
Grassy Glade ME7 .33 B6
Gravel Castle Rd CT4 .129 A8
Gravel Hill ME13 .103 C8
Gravel La CT15 .165 A4
Gravel Wlk
3 Ashford TN23 .139 B3
12 Canterbury CT1 .87 F8
Rochester ME1 .9 D5
Gravelly Bottom Rd ME17 .99 B2
Gravelly Field TN23 .155 C8
Graveney Prim Sch ME13 .41 E1
Graveney Rd
Faversham ME13 .62 F7
Maidstone ME15 .97 F7
Gray Cl CT18 .163 C5
Graylen Cl CT14 .117 C7
Graylings Ct ME10 .36 C2
Graylings The ME1 .9 B3
Grays Way CT1 .87 B6
Grayshott Cl ME10 .36 F3
Graystone Rd CT5 .21 A2
Great Basin Rd ME12 .1 A2
Great Burton Ho TN24 .139 E5
Great Chart Prim Sch TN23 .155 D8
Great Conduit St CT21 .176 C2
Great Ivy Mill Cotts ME15 .96 F7
Great Lines ME7 .10 B5
Great Oaks Small Sch CT13 .93 B2
Great South Ave ME4 .10 A1
Great Stour Pl 3 CT2 .66 F1
Greatstone Prim Sch TN28 .202 D2
Grebe Apartments 15 ME15 .97 E5
Grebe Cl CT18 .163 A4
Grebe Cres CT21 .187 C8
Grecian St ME14 .75 A6
Green Acres CT15 .131 D7
Green Acres Cl CT6 .23 B3
Green Bank Cl ME7 .33 A5
Green Cl Hawkinge CT18 .163 B4
Rochester ME1 .9 D2
Green Cloth Mews 2 CT1 .67 B2
Green Ct Bridge CT4 .89 A1
Folkestone CT19 .178 E7
Green Dell CT2 .66 F4
Green Gates CT16 .149 A8
Green Hedges TN30 .179 B8
Green Hill ME15 .76 B1
Green Hill La ME17 .100 D1
Green Hills CT4 .128 D8
Green La Alkham CT15 .147 D3
Ashford TN23 .155 E5
Bethersden TN26 .153 A2
Broadstairs CT10 .29 E5
Capel-le-F CT18 .164 B3
Challock TN25 .105 A2
Deal CT14 .117 B1
Dover CT16 .149 B3
Eythorne CT15 .131 D7
Folkestone CT19 .178 E7
Goodnestone CT3 .92 B3
Hythe CT21 .176 A2
Langley Heath ME17 .98 E3
Maidstone ME17 .97 C3
Margate CT9 .29 E8
Old Wives Lees CT4 .85 C2
Platt's Heath ME17 .100 F2
Rhodes Minnis CT4,CT18 .143 E2
Rodmersham ME9 .59 B7
Smarden TN27 .135 A1
St Margaret's at Cliffe CT15 .133 F1
Temple Ewell CT16 .148 E6
Whitfield CT16 .148 F7
Whitstable CT5 .43 D8
Yelsted ME9 .34 F1
Green Lane Ave CT21 .176 A2
Green Lane Cotts ME17 .98 E3
Green Leas CT5 .21 D1
Green Lees ME13 .61 E2
Green Mdws TN29 .186 D2
Green Porch Cl ME10 .36 F7
Green Rd Birchington CT7 .26 F8
Stalisfield Green ME13 .103 C6
Green Sands ME5 .54 C8
Green St ME7 .10 C5
Green The Blean CT2 .66 A6
Burmarsh TN29 .186 C4
Chartham CT4 .86 D3
East Farleigh ME15 .96 B7
Harbledown CT2 .65 E1
Hythe CT21 .176 B4
Littlebourne CT3 .89 F7
Lower Halstow ME9 .13 B3
Lydd TN29 .205 B5
Manston CT12 .28 D1
Sheerness ME12 .1 I1
Warehorne TN26 .182 D6
Woodchurch TN26 .169 A2
Woolage Village CT4 .112 E1
Wye TN25 .123 E2
Green Way Lydd TN29 .205 C5
Maidstone ME16 .74 B3
Green's Cotts ME15 .96 A4
Greenacre CT4 .111 D3
Greenacre Cl ME5 .32 A5
Greenacre Dr CT14 .117 C1
Greenacre Sch ME5 .31 F5
Greenacres CT14 .95 B4
Greenbank Ashford TN24 .139 D6
Chatham ME5 .32 B8
Greenbanks CT18 .161 C6
Greenborough Cl ME15 .97 E6
Greencroft TN23 .155 E6
Greenfield Cl ME20 .53 A6
Greenfield Cotts
Boxley ME14 .54 C3
9 Canterbury CT1 .87 F7
Greenfield Rd
Folkestone CT19 .178 E7
Gillingham ME7 .10 D6
Ramsgate CT12 .29 C2
Greenfields
Maidstone ME15 .97 E8
Sellindge TN25 .159 E2
Greenfinches ME7 .32 F6
Greenhill Bridge Rd CT6 .22 D3
Greenhill Cl CT12 .50 B7
Greenhill Gdns
Herne Bay CT6 .22 D3
Minster (Thanet) CT12 .50 B7
Greenhill La TN27 .135 F7
Greenhill Rd CT6 .22 C2
Greenhithe 3 ME15 .75 A3
Greenhouse La CT2 .66 E2
Greenleas 1 CT20 .178 B3
Greenlees Cl ME10 .36 B5
Greenly Way TN28 .202 C6
Greensand Rd ME15 .76 A2
Greenside
High Halden TN26 .167 E7
Maidstone ME15 .75 B3
Greenside Ho CT9 .7 F1
Greensole La CT12 .28 E1
Greenvale Gdns ME8 .11 B2
Greenvale Inf Sch ME4 .10 A2
Greenview Wlk ME8 .11 A4
Greenway Chatham ME5 .31 D6
Faversham ME13 .62 B8
Greenway Court Farm Cotts ME17 .78 A1
Greenway Court Rd ME17 .78 A1
Greenway La ME17 .100 A7
Greenways
Lower Halstow ME9 .13 B3
Maidstone ME14 .75 F5
Sittingbourne ME10 .37 B3
Greenwich Cl
Chatham ME5 .32 B4
Maidstone ME16 .74 D4
Gregory Cl Gillingham ME8 .33 E4
Sittingbourne ME10 .37 A8
Gregory Ct TN25 .123 E2
Grenadier Cl
Gillingham ME8 .12 B2
Maidstone ME15 .75 F2
Grenham Bay Ave CT7 .26 E8
Grenham Rd CT7 .26 F8
Grenville Gdns CT7 .26 E8
Grenville Way CT10 .29 E4
Gresham Ave CT9 .7 E1
Gresham Cl 3 ME8 .11 F1
Gresham Rd ME17 .96 D3
Greville Ho CT17 .166 C7
Greville Homes CT13 .93 B2
Grey Friars Cotts 8 CT1 .87 F8
Grey Wethers ME14 .53 E4
Grey Willow Gdns TN23 .155 D8
Greyfriars Cl ME16 .74 D5
Greyfriars Ct CT10 .8 F1
Greystones Rd
Cliffs End CT12 .51 D5
Maidstone ME15 .76 A2
Grice Cl CT18 .162 F3
Grieveson Ho ME4 .10 A4
Griffin Cotts TN26 .181 C2
Griffin St CT14 .117 D7
Griffin's Cnr TN25 .140 E7
Grimshill Ct CT2 .66 C4
Grimshill Rd CT5 .43 E8
Grimston Ave CT20 .178 B4
Grimston Gdns CT20 .178 B4
Grimthorpe Ave CT5 .43 C7
Grinsell Hill CT12 .50 E6

Grisbrook Farm Cl
TN29 205 D6
Grisbrook Rd TN29 205 D6
Grizedale Cl ME1 31 D8
Groom Way ME17 101 E6
Groombridge Sq 13 ME15 97 F6
Grosvenor Ave ME4 9 E3
Grosvenor Cotts CT7 27 B3
Grosvenor Gdns CT9 7 I1
Grosvenor Hill CT9 7 I2
Grosvenor Ho 5 ME15 97 F5
Grosvenor Pl CT9 7 I2
Grosvenor Rd
Ashford TN24 139 D7
Broadstairs CT10 30 A4
Gillingham ME7 11 A1
Ramsgate CT11 52 C7
Whitstable CT5 43 D7
Grotto Gdns 6 CT9 7 J2
Grotto Hill CT9 7 J2
Grotto Rd 5 CT9 7 J2
Grove Ave ME12 6 G2
Grove Cl ME13 62 A6
Grove Cotts TN30 179 B6
Grove Court Farm ME13 64 A3
Grove Ct 4 ME2 9 B7
Grove Dairy Farm ME9 36 A6
Grove Ferry Hill CT3 47 E3
Grove Ferry Rd CT3 48 A2
Grove Gdns 6 CT9 7 G1
Grove Green La ME14 75 E5
Grove Green Rd ME14 75 F5
Grove Ho TN27 136 C3
Grove La Brookland TN29 191 D3
Iden TN31 197 C4
Grove Park Ave ME10 36 B5
Grove Park Prim Sch
ME10 36 B6
Grove Pl ME13 62 A6
Grove Rd Chatham ME4 10 B2
Deal CT14 117 D3
Folkestone CT20 178 E6
Gillingham ME7 11 A6
Maidstone ME15 97 C7
Preston CT3 70 B8
Ramsgate CT11 52 D6
Rochester ME2 9 B8
Selling ME13 84 B4
Staple CT3 91 F6
Wickhambreaux CT3 69 D6
Grove Road Cotts
Wickhambreaux CT3 69 C2
Wickhambreaux,Frognall
CT3 69 C3
Grove Terr CT1 87 E7
Grove The Ashford TN24 139 E6
Barham CT4 128 F8
Deal CT14 117 C6
Dover CT16 149 C1
Herne Bay CT6 22 C2
Maidstone ME14 76 A3
Westgate-on-S CT8 27 F8
Grove Way CT3 70 C7
Grovehurst Ave ME10 14 F1
Grovehurst Rd ME10,ME9 14 E2
Grovelands ME17 101 E5
Groveway ME12 6 F2
Grovewood Ct ME14 75 E4
Grovewood Dr ME14 75 D6
Grummock Ave CT11 52 B7
Grundy's Hill 13 CT11 52 E6
Guardian Ct ME8 11 C1
Guernsey Way TN24 139 C7
Guestling Mill Ct 1 CT13 72 F1
Guildcount La 5 CT13 72 F1
Guildford Ave CT8 27 E8
Guildford Lawn 1 CT11 52 E6
Guildford Rd CT1 87 F6
Guildhall Ct 10 CT20 178 D5
Guildhall Mus* ME11 2 F5
Guildhall Mus The* ME1 9 C6
Guildhall St
4 Canterbury CT1 87 F8
18 Folkestone CT20 178 D5
Guildhall St N CT19,
CT20 178 D5
Guilford Ave CT16 149 A8
Guilford Ct CT14 117 D2
Guilford Ho CT13 95 A7
Guilford Rd CT13 94 E8
Guilton CT3 71 B1
Guldeford La TN29,TN31 198 F3
Guldeford Lane Cnr
TN31 198 D2
Gulland Ho 4 ME14 75 B4
Gullands ME17 98 E4
Gun La ME2 9 B7
Gun Tower Mews ME1 9 B4
Gundulph Rd ME1 9 E4
Gundulph Sq ME1 9 C6
Gunnis Cl ME8 33 D4
Gurling Rd CT15 133 F1
Guston CE Prim Sch
CT15 149 E3
Guston Rd
East Langdon CT15 150 A8
Maidstone ME14 75 C6
Guthrie Gdns CT17 148 E3
Guy Cl CT10 30 A7
Gwyn Rd CT12 29 C2
Gypsy Cnr CT5 44 D3

H

Hackfield TN23 138 F1
Hackington Cl CT2 66 E4
Hackington Pl CT2 66 F2
Hackington Rd CT2 66 E7
Hackington Terr CT2 66 F2
Hacklinge Hill CT14 94 B2
Hackney Rd ME16 74 C2
Haddon Dene Sch CT10 29 F4
Hadleigh Ct ME7 33 A3
Hadleigh Gdns CT6 23 B5
Hadley Gdns ME17 77 E2
Hadlow Coll CT1 88 B8
Hadlow Dr CT9 8 E2
Hadlow Rd ME14 75 C5
Hadrian Gdns TN23 155 F5
Haffenden Mdw TN27 120 C8
Haffenden Rd TN30 167 B1
Haig Ave Chatham ME1 9 D1
Chatham,Luton ME4 10 A2
Gillingham ME7 10 E4
Haine Ind Est CT12 28 F1
Haine Rd CT12,CT10 28 F2
Halden Cl ME15 97 F6
Hales Cl TN30 179 B8
Hales Ct TN30 179 B8
Hales Dr CT2 66 F3
Hales Rd ME10 36 D1
Haleys Pl ME1 53 A8
Halfmile Ride CT9 28 E6
Halford Cl CT6 23 B2
Halfpenny Cl ME16 74 A2
Halfway Houses Prim Sch
ME12 3 D6
Halfway Rd ME12 3 D8
Halifax Cl ME5 32 B6
Hall Ave TN24 156 F6
Hall By The Sea Rd CT9 7 H2
Hall Cl ME10 36 E6
Hall Cres CT14 116 F5
Hall Rd ME5 32 C3
Hallcroft Ct CT11 52 C7
Hallett Wlk 10 CT1 67 B2
Halliday Ct CT21 176 A2
Halliday Dr CT14 117 D3
Hallsfield Rd ME5 31 D2
Hallwood Cl ME8 33 D5
Hallwood Ho ME5 32 C2
Halstatt Rd CT14 117 A3
Halstead Cl CT2 67 B4
Halstead Gdns CT9 8 F3
Halstead Wlk ME16 74 C7
Halstow Cl ME15 97 B6
Halstow Way TN23 155 F8
Halt The Elham CT4 144 F4
Whitstable CT5 44 A7
Ham Farm Cotts CT14 93 F2
Ham La Gillingham ME7 32 E3
Lenham ME17 101 C5
Ham Mill La TN26,TN29 183 A2
Ham Rd ME13 40 C1
Ham Shades La CT5 21 A1
Ham Street Sta TN26 183 A8
Hambledon Ct ME16 74 B3
Hambrook Cl CT4 107 B8
Hambrook La CT4 107 C8
Hambrook Wlk ME10 36 F8
Hamele The CT2 67 F5
Hamelin Rd ME7 32 F8
Hamill Terr CT1 67 B2
Hamilton Cl
Littlestone-on-Sea TN28 202 E5
Ramsgate CT12 29 B1
Hamilton Cres ME10 36 C3
Hamilton Ct Chatham ME5 10 C1
Rochester ME1 9 B4
Hamilton Ho
Coxheath ME17 96 C3
Maidstone ME15 97 F5
Hamilton Rd
Ashford TN24 156 D6
Deal CT14 117 C4
Dover CT17 166 B8
Gillingham ME7 10 D7
Lydd TN29 205 C6
Whitstable CT5 20 D1
Hammond Cl CT15 113 E5
Hammond's Cnr TN29 201 E6
Hammond's Rd CT20 177 E5
Hamond Hill 6 ME4 9 E4
Hampden La TN23 156 A7
Hampden Mews TN23 156 A7
Hampden Rd TN23 156 A6
Hampshire Cl ME5 32 C7
Hampshire Dr ME15 97 C8
Hampshire Rd CT1 88 D7
Hampshires The ME17 100 C6
Hampson Way ME14 76 A4
Hampton Cl Chatham ME5 32 A5
Herne Bay CT6 22 A3
Hampton Gdns CT6 22 A3
Hampton La TN25 141 C3
Hampton Pier Ave CT6 22 B4
Hampton Prim Sch CT6 22 C4
Hampton Rd ME14 75 C6
Hampton Vale CT21 177 B4
Hamstreet Prim Sch
TN26 182 F8
Hamstreet Rd
Bromley Green TN26 170 E5
Hamstreet TN26 183 C7
Hamwick Gn ME5 32 C1
Hancocks Field CT14 117 A5
Hangman's La CT14 133 F5
Hanover Cl Ashford TN23 138 F2
Deal CT14 117 D2
Hanover Cl *continued*
Margate CT9 8 E2
Sittingbourne ME10 36 E2
Hanover Ct
Broadstairs CT10 29 F4
Faversham ME13 62 B8
Hythe CT21 176 C1
Maidstone ME14 75 B5
Hanover Dr ME8 33 C4
Hanover Ho 6 CT20 178 C4
Hanover Pl CT2 66 F2
Hanover Rd ME17 96 C3
Hanover Sq CT6 22 F5
Hanover St CT6 22 F5
Hanscomb Ho CT2 66 E2
Hanslett's La ME13 61 D3
Hanson Dr ME15 96 F3
Hanway ME8 11 A2
Happy Valley Holiday Camp
ME12 6 E2
Harbledown Gdns CT9 8 E3
Harbledown Ho ME16 74 B2
Harbledown Manor ME8 11 B3
Harbledown Pk CT2 66 C1
Harbour Approach Rd
CT20 178 E4
Harbour Par CT11 52 E6
Harbour Point CT19 178 F5
Harbour Sch CT15 165 E7
Harbour St
Broadstairs CT10 30 B4
Folkestone CT20 178 E5
Ramsgate CT11 52 E6
Whitstable CT5 20 D2
Harbour Twrs 16 CT11 52 E6
Harbour View Rd CT17 166 B8
Harbour Way CT20 178 E5
Harbourland Cl ME14 75 B8
Harbourne La TN26,
TN30 167 E5
Harcourt Dr
Canterbury CT2 66 D2
Herne Bay CT6 22 B5
Harcourt Gdns ME8 33 E4
Harcourt Prim Sch
CT19 177 E7
Harcourt Rd CT19 177 F7
Harden Rd TN29 205 D7
Harden's View TN26 182 D6
Hardinge Cl ME8 33 D4
Hardinge Rd TN24 139 C3
Hardres Court Rd CT4 110 A3
Hardres Rd CT11 52 E8
Hardres St CT11 52 E7
Hards Town ME4 10 A4
Hardwick Ho ME15 97 E8
Hardwick Rd CT20 178 A4
Hardwicke Ho TN27 120 B7
Hardwicke Rd CT17 166 B6
Hardy Cl Ashford TN24 157 A7
Canterbury CT2 66 C1
Chatham ME5 32 B6
Hardy Lodge ME1 9 B4
Hardy Rd
Greatstone-on-Sea TN28 202 D3
St Margaret's at Cliffe
CT15 150 E8
Hardy St ME14 75 A6
Hare St 2 ME4 10 B3
Harebell Cl
3 Chatham ME5 31 F4
Maidstone ME14 75 E5
Minster (Sheppey) ME12 4 A4
Harebrook CT11 29 F1
Haredale Cl ME1 31 D7
Harkness Ct 6 ME10 37 B4
Harkness Dr CT2 66 E2
Harling Cl ME17 97 D5
Harman Ave CT21 174 F3
Harman Ct ME5 32 B3
Harmers Way TN27 118 F3
Harmsworth Gdns CT10 30 A5
Harnet St 6 CT13 72 F1
Harold Ave Gillingham ME7 10 E4
Westgate-on-S CT8 27 E8
Harold Ct ME13 62 C6
Harold Rd Birchington CT7 26 E8
Deal CT14 117 D8
Margate CT9 8 B3
Sittingbourne ME10 37 B4
Harold St Dover CT16 166 D8
Queenborough ME11 3 A4
Harold's Rd CT16 166 E8
Harp Farm Rd ME14 54 C6
Harper Rd TN23 155 F8
Harple La ME14 54 F1
Harps Ave ME12 4 C6
Harpswood ME17 77 F1
Harpswood La CT21 176 A4
Harptree Dr ME5 31 F5
Harrier Dr ME10 37 A2
Harriestsham Sta ME17 100 D6
Harriet Dr ME1 9 B3
Harriets Cnr CT5 43 B5
Harrietsham Ho 18 ME16 74 A3
Harrietsham Prim Sch
ME17 100 E6
Harringe La CT21,TN25 174 A6
Harriot Cl CT19 178 B7
Harris Gdns ME10 37 C5
Harris Rd ME12 1 D2
Harris's Alley CT3 91 A7
Harrison Ct 4 ME8 11 F1
Harrison Dr ME17 100 E6
Harrison Rd 4 CT11 52 D6
Harrison Terr ME13 40 A2
Harrow Ct Chatham ME5 32 C4
Stockbury ME9 56 D8
Harrow Dene CT10 29 E6
Harrow Rd ME7 32 F6
Harrow Way
Ashford TN23 155 E5
Maidstone ME14 75 E5
Harry Pay Cl TN24 139 D4
Harry Wells Rd CT6 22 B3
Harrys Rd ME9 38 D3
Hart Cl CT18 163 A4
Hart Hill TN27 103 A2
Hart St ME16 74 F3
Hart Street Bsns Ctr
ME16 74 F3
Hartington St ME4 10 A3
Hartley Cl ME15 97 F6
Hartley Mews ME8 11 B3
Hartlip CE Prim Sch ME9 34 D5
Hartlip Cl ME12 3 B7
Hartlip Hill ME9 34 F7
Hartnup St ME16 74 C2
Hartpiece Cl ME8 11 F2
Hartridge Farm ME15 96 A7
Harts Cotts TN26 183 A8
Harts Holiday Camp ME12 6 G1
Harts La 6 CT5 20 D2
Hartsdown Rd CT9 28 D8
Hartsdown Tech Coll
CT9 28 D8
Harty Ave ME8 33 B3
Harty Ferry Cotts ME13 40 C5
Harty Ferry Rd ME12 18 E4
Harty Ferry View CT5 43 C6
Harty Terr ME12 5 A5
Harvest La CT4 126 E5
Harvest Way
Ashford TN23 155 D7
Hawkinge CT18 163 B4
Harvesters Cl ME8 33 E7
Harvesters Way ME14 75 D4
Harvey Ave CT14 117 C3
Harvey Ct CT19 178 A6
Harvey Dr
Sittingbourne ME10 37 A2
Whitstable CT5 21 B1
Harvey Gram Sch The
CT19 178 A6
Harvey Pl
21 Folkestone CT20 178 D5
9 Folkestone CT20 178 E5
Harvey Rd Ashford TN24 139 F1
Gillingham ME8 33 E8
Harvey St CT20 178 E5
Harville Rd TN25 123 C2
Harwich St CT5 43 D8
Harwick Dr TN28 202 C8
Harwood Ho TN25 123 E1
Harwood Rd ME8 12 B1
Hasborough Rd CT19 178 F6
Haskard Cl CT18 162 F4
Haslemere Est ME15 97 F5
Haslewood Cl TN27 135 B2
Hassall Reach CT1 87 B6
Hassell St TN25 124 F2
Haste Hill Cl ME17 97 B3
Haste Hill Rd ME17 97 B3
Hasted Rd ME9 35 B7
Hasteds ME17 77 D2
Hastings Ave CT9 8 A1
Hastings Pl CT13 93 F8
Hastings Rd ME15 75 B3
Hatch La CT4 86 C5
Hatch Rd ME17 101 C5
Hatch St 3 ME13 62 C7
Hatfield Rd Margate CT9 7 G2
Ramsgate CT11 52 D7
Rochester ME2 9 A8
Hathaway Ct
Gillingham ME8 33 D8
Rochester ME1 9 B5
Hatherall Rd ME14 75 B6
Hatherley Ct CT9 8 A3
Hatton Rd ME5 32 C3
Havant Wlk 8 ME15 97 F6
Havelock Pl CT3 71 E1
Havelock Rd CT14 117 C3
Havelock St CT1 67 A1
Haven Cl ME1 9 C2
Haven Dr Hawkinge CT18 163 A4
Herne Bay CT6 23 F6
Haven The
Ashford TN23 155 F5
Brenzett TN29 192 A3
Hythe CT21 187 C8
Haventhorpe TN24 139 C3
Havisham Cl ME1 9 D2
Hawbeck Rd ME8 33 C3
Hawe Cl CT2 67 A4
Hawe Farm Way CT6 23 B2
Hawe La CT2 68 A7
Hawes Ave CT11 52 B7
Hawk Cl CT5 43 C7
Hawk's La CT1 87 F8
Hawkesbury St CT17 166 D5
Hawkhurst Cl CT7 27 B8
Hawkhurst Rd ME8 11 B3
Hawkhurst Way CT10 30 A2
Hawkinge Prim Sch
CT18 163 B4
Hawkins Cl Chatham ME7 10 A6
Sittingbourne ME10 36 E7
Hawkins Rd CT19 177 D6
Hawks Hill La ME9 58 C4
Hawks Rd CT6 22 B2
Hawks Way TN23 155 E7
Hawksdown CT14 134 B8
Hawksdown Rd CT14 134 C8
Hawkshill Rd CT14 134 D8
Hawkwood ME16 74 B5
Hawkwood Cl ME1 9 D5
Hawley Ct ME16 74 E4
Hawley Sq CT9 7 J2
Hawley St CT9 7 I2
Hawser Rd ME1 9 C1
Hawthorn TN26 190 D8
Hawthorn Ave
Canterbury CT2 67 A2
West Minst ME12 3 A8
Hawthorn Cl
Aylesham CT3 112 E4
Crabble CT17 148 E2
Hythe CT21 187 E8
Ramsgate CT11 29 E1
St Mary's Bay TN29 194 F3
Hawthorn Cnr
Herne Bay CT6 24 A3
Old Romney TN29 200 E3
Hawthorn Farm Cvn &
Camping Site CT15 133 C1
Hawthorn Ho
5 Chatham ME5 31 F5
10 Sittingbourne ME10 36 E4
Hawthorn Rd
Kingsnorth TN23 156 B4
Sittingbourne ME10 36 E4
Hawthorne Ave ME8 11 C2
Hawthorne Cl CT15 131 D7
Hawthorne Ho 4 ME16 74 A3
Hawthorns ME5 31 F1
Hawthorns The
Broadstairs CT10 29 C4
Chatham ME5 31 F6
Hay Hill CT13,CT14 93 D2
Hay Ho CT21 176 B2
Hay La CT14 93 F2
Haydon Cl ME16 74 B4
Hayes Alley 17 CT5 20 D2
Hayes La ME9 56 F6
Hayfields ME5 32 D2
Haygate Ho ME1 9 C4
Hayle Mill Cotts ME15 96 F8
Hayle Mill Rd ME15 96 F8
Hayle Rd ME15 75 A3
Haymakers La TN23 155 D8
Haymen St ME4 9 E3
Haynes Ho 3 ME14 75 B4
Hayrick Cl ME14 75 E5
Haysel ME10 37 A2
Hayton Rd TN25 160 A2
Haywain Cl Ashford TN23 155 E5
Maidstone ME14 75 F4
Hayward Ave ME2 9 B8
Hayward Cl
Ashford TN24 157 A8
Deal CT14 117 A4
Hayward's Cl TN28 202 B6
Hayward's Hill ME13 82 C4
Hayward's Ho ME1 9 C6
Hazebrouck Rd ME13 62 A7
Hazel Ave ME16 74 C5
Hazel Cl CT15 131 C7
Hazel Ct Birchington CT7 26 D8
Hersden CT3 68 D8
Hazel Gr Chatham ME5 32 B8
Sheerness ME12 1 H1
Hazel Hts TN25 138 E5
Hazel Street Rd ME9 57 A4
Hazel Wlk CT10 29 C4
Hazeldene Chalet Pk
ME12 5 F5
Hazeldown Cl CT17 148 E2
Hazels The ME8 33 B5
Hazelwood Dr ME16 74 B4
Hazelwood Mdw CT13 93 F7
Hazlemere Dr
Gillingham ME7 11 A5
Herne Bay CT6 23 D5
Hazlemere Rd CT5 43 A7
Hazling Dane CT15 130 F5
Hazlitt Dr ME16 74 D5
Head Hill ME13 63 D7
Head Hill Rd ME13 63 D8
Head Race The ME15 74 D2
Headcorn Dr CT2 67 B4
Headcorn Gdns CT9 8 E2
Headcorn Rd
Gillingham ME8 11 B4
Platt's Heath ME17 100 F1
Headingley Rd ME16 74 B6
Heard Way ME10 37 B5
Hearne Cl ME10 37 B5
Heart In Hand Cnr CT3 23 F2
Heart In Hand Rd CT6 23 F2
Heart's Delight La CT3 70 B3
Hearts Delight ME9 36 B1
Hearts Delight Rd ME9 36 B1
Heath Cl CT2 67 F7
Heath Ct CT15 150 F6
Heath Farm Sch TN27 119 C7
Heath Gr ME16 74 A2
Heath Ho CT3 46 E5
Heath Rd Coxheath ME17 96 C3
Langley Heath ME17 98 E4
Maidstone ME16 74 A2
Maidstone,Cock Street
ME17 97 C2
Heath The
Appledore Heath TN26 181 C1
Whitstable CT5 21 B1
Heath Villas TN26 181 C2
Heather Cl Chatham ME5 31 F4
Margate CT9 28 C8
Sittingbourne ME10 37 A3
Heather Dr
Maidstone ME15 75 B2
Tenterden TN30 167 B3
Heatherwood Cl ME17 99 E2

Heathfield ME17 . . . . .98 E4
Heathfield Ave
  Dover CT14 . . . . .149 B2
  Maidstone ME14 . . . . .75 C7
Heathfield Bglws ME17 . .102 B1
Heathfield Cl
  Chatham ME5 . . . . .32 B7
  Maidstone ME14 . . . . .75 B7
Heathfield Rd
  Ashford TN24 . . . . .139 C3
  Maidstone ME14 . . . . .75 C7
Heathfield Way CT14 . . . .128 F8
Heathorn St ME14 . . . . .75 B5
Heathside TN26 . . . . .181 C1
Heathside Ave ME17 . . . . . .96 C4
Heathwood Dr CT11 . . . . . . .29 E1
Heaton Rd CT1 . . . . .87 F6
Hedgend Ind Est CT7 . . . . . .25 F3
Hedgerow The ME14 . . . . . .75 E5
Hedgerows TN23 . . . . .155 D7
Hedges The ME14 . . . . .75 A7
Hedley St ME14 . . . . .75 B5
Heel La CT2 . . . . .67 C8
Heel Rd ME13 . . . . .104 D3
Heights Terr CT17 . . . . . . .166 C6
Heights The CT5 . . . . .43 C6
Helding Cl CT6 . . . . .23 B2
Helen Thompson Cl ME9 . .14 E4
Helena Ave CT9 . . . . .28 E4
Helena Corniche CT20 . . . .177 C3
Helena Rd CT18 . . . . .164 C2
Helena Villas CT21 . . . . . . .177 B3
Hellyar Ct ME1 . . . . .9 C4
Helmdon Cl CT12 . . . . .29 C2
Helvellyn Ave CT11 . . . . . . .52 B7
Hempstead Inf Sch ME7 . . .33 A5
Hempstead Jun Sch ME7 . .33 A5
Hempstead La ME9 . . . . .37 E3
Hempstead Rd ME7,ME8 . . .33 A5
Hempstead Valley Dr
  ME7 . . . . .33 A4
Hempstead Valley Sh Ctr
  ME7 . . . . .33 A3
Hempsted St [11] TN23 . . . .139 B2
Hempton Hill TN25 . . . . . .160 C5
Henbane Cl ME14 . . . . .75 E5
Hengist Ave CT9 . . . . .8 B1
Hengist Rd
  Birchington CT7 . . . . .26 C7
  Deal CT14 . . . . .117 D7
  Westgate-on-S CT8 . . . . . . .27 D8
  Westgate-on-S CT8 . . . . . . .27 E8
Henley Bsns Pk ME2 . . . . . . .9 D7
Henley Cl Chatham ME5 . . .32 A6
  Gillingham ME8 . . . . .33 D8
Henley Fields
  Maidstone ME14 . . . . .75 E6
  Tenterden TN30 . . . . .167 B2
Henley Mdws TN30 . . . . . .167 A2
Henley View TN30 . . . . . . .167 B2
Henniker Ct CT16 . . . . .149 A5
Henry Ct CT1 . . . . .87 F7
Henry St Chatham ME4 . . . .10 B3
  Gillingham ME8 . . . . .12 A1
Henwood TN24 . . . . .139 D3
Henwood Bsns Ctr
  TN24 . . . . .139 D2
Herbert Dane Ct [10]
  ME13 . . . . .62 D7
Herbert Rd Ashford TN24 .156 D6
  Chatham ME4 . . . . .10 A3
  Gillingham ME8 . . . . .33 E8
  Ramsgate CT11 . . . . .52 C6
Herbert St CT17 . . . . .149 B1
Herdson Rd CT20 . . . . .178 A5
Hereford Cl
  Ashford TN24 . . . . .139 C7
  Gillingham ME8 . . . . .11 D2
Hereford Gdns CT6 . . . . . . .26 F6
Hereford Rd ME15 . . . . .97 D3
Hereson Rd CT11 . . . . .52 F8
Hereson Sch The CT10 . . . . .30 A3
Hereward Ave CT7 . . . . .26 E8
Heritage Cl CT5 . . . . .43 A6
Heritage Ct [19] CT1 . . . . . .87 F8
Heritage Dr ME7 . . . . .10 F1
Heritage Gdns CT16 . . . . .166 E8
  Folkestone CT20 . . . . .177 D6
Heritage Rd Chatham ME5 . .32 A6
Herman Terr ME4 . . . . .10 A4
Hermitage Cl CT21 . . . . . .176 B2
Hermitage La
  Detling ME14 . . . . .55 B4
  Maidstone ME16 . . . . .74 A4
Herne Ave CT6 . . . . .23 A4
Herne Bay High Sch CT6 . .22 D3
Herne Bay Inf Sch CT6 . . . .22 F4
Herne Bay Jun Sch CT6 . . .22 F4
Herne Bay Mus★ CT6 . . . . .22 F5
Herne Bay Rd Sturry CT3 . . .45 E2
  Whitstable CT5 . . . . .21 C3
Herne Bay Sta CT6 . . . . . . .22 F4
Herne Bay West Ind Est
  CT6 . . . . .22 C3
Herne CE Inf Sch CT6 . . . .46 A8
Herne CE Jun Sch CT6 . . . .46 A8
Herne Ct CT19 . . . . .177 C6
Herne Dr CT6 . . . . .22 C2
Herne Rd ME8 . . . . .11 C2
Herne St CT6 . . . . .46 A8
Herne Windmill★ CT6 . . . .23 B2
Herneville Gdns CT6 . . . . . .23 B4
Hernhill CE Prim Sch
  ME13 . . . . .64 B7
Hero Ho ME12 . . . . .1 C1
Hero Wlk ME1 . . . . .31 C7
Heron Apartments [3]
  ME15 . . . . .97 F5

Heron Cl ME9 . . . . .13 B3
Heron Dr ME12 . . . . .4 B5
Heron Forestall Ave
  CT18 . . . . .163 B4
Heron Ho TN23 . . . . .138 F1
Heron Lodge [6] CT16 . . . .149 B2
Heron Way ME5 . . . . .32 B7
Heron Wlk TN23 . . . . .155 E8
Heron's Brook TN25 . . . . . .140 E6
Heron's Way CT21 . . . . . . .187 D8
  Maidstone ME15 . . . . .97 F4
Heronden View TN13 . . . . . .93 A2
Herons Cl CT14 . . . . .107 C8
Herschell Rd CT7 . . . . .26 F8
Herschell Rd E CT14 . . . . .117 C3
Herschell Rd W CT14 . . . . .117 C3
Herschell Sq CT14 . . . . . . .117 C3
Hersden Com Prim Sch
  CT3 . . . . .46 E1
Hertford Ct CT1 . . . . .88 C8
Hertford Ho
  Herne Bay CT6 . . . . .23 A5
  [17] Ramsgate CT11 . . . . . .52 E6
Hertford Pl CT11 . . . . .52 E6
Hertford Rd CT9 . . . . .29 C8
Hertford St CT11 . . . . .52 E6
Herts Cres ME15 . . . . .96 F3
Hever Cl ME15 . . . . .97 F6
Hever Gdns ME16 . . . . .74 E3
Hever Pl Canterbury CT2 . . .67 A3
  Sittingbourne ME10 . . . . . . .36 D3
Hewitt Cl Gillingham ME7 . .10 F6
  Maidstone ME16 . . . . .74 D7
Hewitt Rd [1] CT16 . . . . . . .166 D8
Hewitts Pl TN24 . . . . .139 F1
Hextable Cl
  Ashford TN23 . . . . .155 F6
  Maidstone ME16 . . . . .74 D7
Heyford Cl CT18 . . . . .163 B4
Hibernia St [6] CT11 . . . . . .52 E6
Hickory Dell ME7 . . . . .33 A5
Hicks Forstal Rd CT3 . . . . .46 B5
Higgins' La ME1 . . . . .9 F5
High Bank ME1 . . . . .9 D2
High Banks ME5 . . . . .96 F5
High Dewar Rd ME8 . . . . . . .34 A4
High Elms ME8 . . . . .11 C4
High Halden CE Prim Sch
  TN26 . . . . .167 E7
High Knocke TN29 . . . . . . .195 B6
High Mdw CT17 . . . . .149 C1
High Minnis CT14 . . . . . . .143 F8
High Oak Hill ME9 . . . . .35 D8
High Ridge TN23 . . . . .155 C7
High Snoad Wood TN25 . .105 A1
High St Ashford TN23 . . . .139 C2
  Bridge CT4 . . . . .89 A1
  Broadstairs CT10 . . . . .29 E5
  Broadstairs,St Peter's
    CT10 . . . . .30 A4
  Brookland TN29 . . . . .199 E8
  Canterbury CT1 . . . . .87 F8
  [8] Canterbury,Northgate
    CT1 . . . . .67 A1
  Chatham ME4 . . . . .10 A4
  Chatham,Brompton ME7 . . .10 A6
  Deal CT14 . . . . .117 D6
  Dover CT16 . . . . .166 C8
  Dymchurch TN29 . . . . . . .195 C6
  Eastchurch ME12 . . . . .5 D3
  Eastry CT13 . . . . .93 B2
  Elham CT4 . . . . .144 F5
  Fordwich CT2 . . . . .68 A4
  Forstal ME20 . . . . .53 A3
  Gillingham ME7 . . . . .10 C5
  Gillingham,Rainham ME8 . .33 F8
  Herne Bay CT6 . . . . .22 F5
  Hythe CT21 . . . . .176 C2
  Lenham ME17 . . . . .101 D5
  Littlebourne CT3 . . . . .89 F7
  Lydd TN29 . . . . .205 C6
  Lyminge CT18 . . . . .161 C6
  Maidstone ME14 . . . . .74 F4
  Manston CT12 . . . . .51 D8
  Margate CT9 . . . . .7 I2
  Margate,Garlinge CT9 . . . . .28 B7
  Minster (Sheppey) ME12 . . .4 D6
  Minster (Thanet) CT12 . . . .50 C6
  New Romney TN28 . . . . . .202 B6
  Newington ME9 . . . . .35 C6
  Queenborough ME11 . . . . . .2 F5
  Ramsgate CT11 . . . . .52 E7
  Rochester ME1 . . . . .9 C6
  Rochester,Strood ME2 . . . . .9 B7
  Sandwich CT13 . . . . .73 A1
  Sheerness ME12 . . . . .1 C1
  Sheerness,Blue Town ME12 . .1 B3
  Sittingbourne ME10 . . . . . .36 F4
  Sittingbourne,Milton Regis
    ME10 . . . . .36 E6
  St Margaret's at Cliffe
    CT15 . . . . .150 F6
  Sturry CT2 . . . . .67 F5
  Temple Ewell CT16 . . . . . .148 D5
  Tenterden TN30 . . . . .179 A7
  Whitstable CT5 . . . . .20 D2
  Wingham CT3 . . . . .91 A8
  Wye TN25 . . . . .123 E2
High St The TN27 . . . . .120 C7
High Street St Lawrence
  CT11 .52 B7
High Trees CT14 . . . . .157 A8
High View Ave CT6 . . . . .22 B5
Higham Cl ME15 . . . . .74 E2
Higham La CT4 . . . . .111 B8

Higham Park & Gdns★
  CT4 .111 C8
Higham View ME14 . . . . . . .53 E4
Highbury Gdns CT12 . . . . . .29 B3
Highbury La TN30 . . . . .179 A7
Highbury Wlk CT12 . . . . . . .29 B2
Highcroft Gn ME15 . . . . . . .97 F4
Highfield Cl
  Gillingham ME8 . . . . .33 D7
  Hythe CT21 . . . . .176 A4
  Ramsgate CT12 . . . . .29 B3
  Rough Common CT2 . . . . . .66 B3
Highfield Ct
  Herne Bay CT6 . . . . .22 E4
  [5] Margate CT9 . . . . .8 B2
  Ramsgate CT12 . . . . .29 B2
Highfield Gdns CT9 . . . . .7 H1
Highfield Ind Est CT19 . . .178 F6
Highfield La TN24,TN25 . .157 C6
Highfield Rd
  Ashford TN23 . . . . .157 A8
  Gillingham ME8 . . . . .33 D7
  Halfway Houses ME12 . . . . .3 E6
  Ramsgate CT12 . . . . .29 B3
Highfields Ave CT6 . . . . . . .23 D4
Highfields View CT6 . . . . . .23 C4
Highgate Rd CT5 . . . . .21 B1
Highgrove Rd ME5 . . . . .32 A5
Highland Cl CT20 . . . . .177 F4
Highland Rd
  Chartham CT4 . . . . .86 D1
  Maidstone ME15 . . . . .97 E6
Highlands Cres TN29 . . . . . .195 A7
Highlands Glade CT12 . . . . .28 E1
Highpoint TN23 . . . . .139 D3
Highridge Gillingham ME7 . .10 F1
  Hythe CT21 . . . . .177 A3
Highridge Cl ME14 . . . . .75 F5
Highsted Gram Sch ME10 . .36 F2
  Borden ME9,ME10 . . . . .36 F1
Highstreet Rd
  Waterham ME13 . . . . .42 D2
  Yorkletts CT5,ME13 . . . . . . .42 E2
Highview Cl
  Boughton Street ME13 . . . .64 B3
  Loose ME15 . . . . .97 A8
Highview Dr ME5 . . . . .31 D5
Highview Pk Cvn Pk
  CT18 . . . . .178 G8
Highview Rd ME12 . . . . .4 C7
Highview Sch CT19 . . . . . .178 D6
Highworth Gram Sch for
  Girls TN24 . . . . .139 A3
Hilary Cl CT6 . . . . .23 C4
Hilda Rd Chatham ME4 . . . .10 A3
  Halfway Houses ME12 . . . . .3 D6
Hildenborough Cres
  ME16 . . . . .74 C7
Hildersham Cl CT10 . . . . . . .29 C5
Hill Ave CT15 . . . . .130 E5
Hill Brow Maidstone ME14 . .76 A5
  Sittingbourne ME10 . . . . . . .36 D2
Hill Chase ME5 . . . . .31 E3
Hill Cres Aylesham CT3 . . . .112 E5
  Lenham ME17 . . . . .101 D5
Hill Ct TN27 . . . . .103 E1
Hill Dr CT13 . . . . .93 B3
Hill Green Rd ME9 . . . . .56 D8
Hill House Dr CT12 . . . . . . .50 C7
Hill La CT18 . . . . .162 B1
Hill Rd Burham ME5 . . . . . . .31 A3
  Folkestone CT19 . . . . .178 E8
  Folkestone,Foord CT19 . . .178 E7
  Rochester ME1 . . . . .9 A2
Hill Rise CT5 . . . . .138 E5
Hill The Charing TN27 . . . .120 D8
  Littlebourne CT3 . . . . .89 F8
Hill Top Cotts ME17 . . . . . . .96 E2
Hill Top Rd CT6 . . . . .23 B5
Hill View Ashford TN24 . . .139 C3
  Margate CT9 . . . . .28 D7
Hill View Ct CT4 . . . . .111 E2
Hill View Terr CT18 . . . . . .161 D3
Hill View Way ME5 . . . . .31 E5
Hill's Terr ME4 . . . . .9 F3
Hillary Rd ME14 . . . . .75 A7
Hillborough Bsns Pk CT6 . .23 F4
Hillborough Dr CT6 . . . . . . .23 F5
Hillborough Gr ME5 . . . . . . .32 A3
Hillborough Rd CT6 . . . . . . .23 B5
Hillbrow Ave
  Herne Bay CT6 . . . . .23 B2
  Sturry CT2 . . . . .67 F7
Hillbrow La TN23 . . . . .138 F1
Hillbrow Rd
  Ashford TN23 . . . . .139 A1
  Ramsgate CT11 . . . . .52 D8
Hillcrest TN23 . . . . .155 B8
Hillcrest Cl TN24 . . . . .139 E6
Hillcrest Gdns
  Deal CT14 . . . . .117 A2
  Ramsgate CT11 . . . . .52 B6
Hillcrest Rd Chatham ME4 . . .9 F2
  Hythe CT21 . . . . .176 B3
  Kingsdown CT14 . . . . .134 D4
  Littlebourne CT3 . . . . .89 E8
Hillcroft Rd CT6 . . . . .23 B3
Hillden Shaw ME15 . . . . . . .97 A8
Hiller Cl CT10 . . . . .30 A6
Hillfield Villas TN26 . . . . . .167 F8
Hillman Ave CT6 . . . . .22 A4
Hillside
  [1] Folkestone CT20 . . . . . .177 E3
  Rochester ME1 . . . . .9 A2
Hillside Ave
  Canterbury CT2 . . . . .66 C2
  Rochester ME2 . . . . .9 B8
  Rushenden ME11 . . . . .2 F3

Hillside Cotts CT3 . . . . .70 A1
Hillside Ct Hythe CT21 . . . .176 C2
  [2] Rochester ME2 . . . . .9 A7
Hillside Ind Est CT20 . . . . .177 E4
Hillside Rd Chatham ME4 . .10 A4
  Dover CT17 . . . . .149 A2
  Minster (Sheppey) ME12 . . .4 B7
  Stalisfield Green ME13 . . .103 E6
  Whitstable CT5 . . . . .21 A1
Hillside St CT21 . . . . .176 C2
Hillstone Ct [5] CT16 . . . . .166 E8
Hilltop CT5 . . . . .43 D7
Hilltop Ho CT2 . . . . .66 C3
Hilltop Rd ME12 . . . . .4 A5
Hillview Rd
  Canterbury CT2 . . . . .66 C2
  Whitstable CT5 . . . . .43 D8
Hillyfield Rd TN23 . . . . . . .156 A8
Hillyfields Rise TN23 . . . . .139 A1
Hilton Bsns Ctr TN23 . . . .156 B6
Hilton Cl ME13 . . . . .62 D6
Hilton Dr ME10 . . . . .36 B6
Hilton Rd TN23 . . . . .138 F2
Hinchliffe Way CT9 . . . . . . .29 C8
Hind Cl TN29 . . . . .195 C8
Hinde Cl ME10 . . . . .36 F7
Hinde Ho ME10 . . . . .36 F6
Hines Terr ME5 . . . . .14 C1
Hinton Cres ME7 . . . . .33 A6
Hinxhill Rd TN24,TN25 . . .140 D1
Hirst Cl CT16 . . . . .149 B4
Historic Dockyard The★
  ME4 .10 A8
Hither Field TN27 . . . . . . .120 C7
Hoad Rd CT15,CT18 . . . . . .146 A2
Hoades Wood Rd CT2 . . . . .68 A7
Hoads Wood Gdns
  TN25 . . . . .138 E6
Hoath Cl ME8 . . . . .33 B7
Hoath Farm The CT3 . . . . . .88 F7
Hoath La ME8 . . . . .33 B7
Hoath Prim Sch CT3 . . . . . .46 E5
Hoath Rd CT3 . . . . .46 C3
Hoath Way ME7,ME8 . . . . . .33 B5
Hobart Cres CT16 . . . . .149 C3
Hobart Gdns ME10 . . . . . . .36 C4
Hobart Rd CT12 . . . . .29 A1
Hockeredge Gdns CT8 . . . .27 F8
Hockers Cl ME14 . . . . .76 A8
Hockers La ME14 . . . . .76 A8
Hodge's Gap CT9 . . . . .8 C3
Hodgson Rd CT5 . . . . .42 F7
Hog Gn CT4 . . . . .144 F4
Hog Hill ME14 . . . . .76 B5
Hogarth Cl CT6 . . . . .23 C5
Hogarth Ho ME11 . . . . .2 F5
Hogbarn La ME17 . . . . .79 A3
Hogben Cl CT18 . . . . .161 B7
Hogben's Hill ME13 . . . . . . .84 D4
Hogbrook Hill La CT15 . . . .164 D8
Hogg La CT4 . . . . .109 E2
Hogpound Cnr TN30 . . . . .189 B6
Holbeam Rd ME13 . . . . .82 A1
Holborn La ME4 . . . . .9 F5
Holbourn Cl CT6 . . . . .46 B8
Holbrook Dr CT12 . . . . .29 B1
Holcombe Rd Chatham ME4 . .9 F2
  Rochester ME1 . . . . .9 C3
Holdenhurst TN23 . . . . . . .155 E6
Holder Cl ME5 . . . . .32 C6
Holding St ME8 . . . . .11 F1
Holland Cl Broadstairs CT10 . .8 G2
  Sheerness ME12 . . . . .1 C1
Holland Ho ME1 . . . . .9 D5
Holland Rd Chatham ME5 . . .32 A5
  Maidstone ME14 . . . . .75 B5
Hollands Ave CT19 . . . . . . .178 F7
Hollicondane Rd CT11 . . . . .52 E8
Hollingbourne Hill ME17 . .77 F4
Hollingbourne Prim Sch
  ME17 . . . . .77 E2
Hollingbourne Rd ME8 . . .11 C2
Hollingbourne Sta ME17 . .77 C3
Hollington Pl TN24 . . . . . .139 B3
Hollingworth Ct ME14 . . . .75 C3
Hollingworth Rd ME15 . . . .97 F5
Hollow La Canterbury CT1 . .87 E5
  Hartlip ME9 . . . . .34 E5
Hollow Rd CT3 . . . . .47 B6
Hollow St CT3 . . . . .47 C5
Hollow Wood Rd CT17 . . . .165 E8
Hollowmede CT1 . . . . .87 E6
Holly Cl Broadstairs CT10 . . .29 C4
  Chatham ME5 . . . . .32 C8
  Eastry CT13 . . . . .93 C4
  Folkestone CT19 . . . . .178 E7
  Gillingham ME7 . . . . .10 E6
  Hythe CT21 . . . . .176 D3
Holly Farm Rd ME15 . . . . . .98 C6
Holly Gdns
  Maidstone ME14 . . . . .75 B7
  Margate CT9 . . . . .8 C7
Holly Hill Rd ME13 . . . . . . .64 D5
Holly La CT9 . . . . .8 C2
Holly Mdws TN23 . . . . .138 D3
  St Mary's Bay TN29 . . . . . .194 F4
Holly Tree Cl ME17 . . . . . . .99 E2
Hollybank Hill ME10 . . . . . .36 D4
Hollybush Cnr CT4 . . . . .90 A3
Hollybush La CT3 . . . . .69 A4
Holm Hill La ME17 . . . . . . .100 B6
Holman Rd CT15 . . . . .88 A7
Holme Oak Cl CT1 . . . . .87 F6
Holmes Ct [5] CT1 . . . . .88 B8
Holmes Way CT12 . . . . .29 A3
Holmesdale Cl ME15 . . . . . .96 F3

Hea – Hop 225

Holmesdale Terr [14]
  CT20 . . . . .178 D4
Holmestone Rd CT17 . . . . .148 E1
Holmlea Cl TN24 . . . . .139 E1
Holmoaks Gillingham ME8 . .11 E2
  Maidstone ME14 . . . . .75 C5
Holmscroft Rd CT6 . . . . . . .23 D5
Holmside ME7 . . . . .10 E3
Holmside Ave ME12 . . . . .5 E7
Holmwood Rd TN23 . . . . . .155 E7
Holness Rd CT3 . . . . .71 D2
Holt St CT15 . . . . .113 C4
Holters Mews [13] CT1 . . . .88 A8
Holters Mill CT2 . . . . .66 F2
Holton Cl CT7 . . . . .27 A6
Holtwood Cl ME8 . . . . .33 D6
Holtye Cres ME15 . . . . .75 B2
Holy Family RC Prim Sch
  ME15 . . . . .97 F4
Holy Trinity & St John's CE
  Prim Sch CT9 . . . . .7 J2
Holy Trinity CE Prim Sch
  CT10 . . . . .30 A1
Holyrood Dr ME12 . . . . .4 A5
Holywell Ave CT19 . . . . . . .178 D8
Holywell Ho CT19 . . . . .178 D8
Holywell La ME7 . . . . .12 F2
Holywell Prim Sch ME9 . . .12 F3
Home Farm Cotts CT14 . .115 E6
Homebirch Ho [6] CT7 . . . . .26 F8
Homefern Ho 7 I3
Homefield Ct CT14 . . . . . . .117 B6
Homefield Dr ME8 . . . . .12 B2
Homefield Row CT14 . . . . .117 B6
Homefleet Ho [13] CT11 . . . .52 F7
Homelands Cl TN25 . . . . . .159 D1
Homeleigh Rd CT12 . . . . . . .29 B3
Homepeak Ho [12] CT21 . .176 B2
Homepine Ho [8] CT20 . . .178 C4
Homersham CT1 . . . . .87 D6
Homeside Farm CT14 . . . .126 F6
Homespire Ho [19] CT1 . . . .67 A1
Homestall Ct CT2 . . . . .66 C4
Homestall La ME13 . . . . . . .63 B5
Homestall Rd ME9 . . . . .60 D3
Homestead TN23 . . . . .155 D8
Homestead Cl [7] CT9 . . . . . .7 J1
Homestead Ct CT14 . . . . . .117 A4
Homestead La CT15 . . . . . .132 C7
Homestead View ME9 . . . . .36 B2
Homestead Village CT5 . . . .52 C5
Homevale Rd [3] CT20 . . . .177 E3
Homeview [3] ME10 . . . . . . .37 B4
Homeview Terr [2] ME10 . .37 B4
Homewood Ave ME10 . . . . .36 D3
Homewood Inf Sch ME10 . .36 D4
  Tenterden TN30 . . . . .167 B2
Homewood Rd Sturry CT2 . .68 A6
Homewood Sch & Sixth Form
  Ctr TN30 . . . . .167 B3
Honduras Terr [8] ME14 . . .75 A7
Hone St ME2 . . . . .9 B8
Honey Bee Glade ME8 . . . . .33 E6
Honey Cl ME7 . . . . .33 A5
Honey Hill CT2,CT5 . . . . . . .65 F8
Honey La ME15 . . . . .98 B6
Honeyball Wlk ME9 . . . . . . .38 C2
Honeycrock Hill ME9 . . . . . .56 F8
Honeyfield TN23 . . . . .138 E1
Honeypot Cl ME2 . . . . .9 B8
Honeysuckle Cl
  [3] Chatham ME5 . . . . .31 E4
  Gillingham ME7 . . . . .32 E4
  Margate CT9 . . . . .28 C8
Honeysuckle Ct ME10 . . . . .37 B5
Honeysuckle Rd CT11 . . . . .52 F8
Honeysuckle Way CT6 . . . .23 D2
Honeywood Cl
  Canterbury CT1 . . . . .67 B2
  Dover CT16 . . . . .149 A6
  Lympne CT21 . . . . .175 A4
Honeywood Ho CT16 . . . . .149 A6
Honeywood Parkway
  CT16 . . . . .149 B5
Honeywood Rd CT16 . . . . .149 A6
Honfleur Rd CT13 . . . . .93 F8
Honiton House Sch CT9 . . . .8 A3
Honner Cl CT18 . . . . .162 F3
Honywood Rd ME17 . . . . . .101 C4
Hoo Farm CT12 . . . . .49 F6
Hook Cl Chatham ME5 . . . . .31 E4
  Folkestone CT20 . . . . .177 F5
Hook La Brookland TN29 . .199 C6
  Charing TN27 . . . . .120 A7
  Harrietsham ME17 . . . . . . .100 C6
Hook Wall TN29 . . . . .199 C5
Hookstead TN26 . . . . .167 C2
Hooper's Pl ME1 . . . . .9 C4
Hooper's Rd ME1 . . . . .9 C4
Hoopers La CT6 . . . . .23 D3
Hop Garden Way CT1 . . . . .87 E6
Hop Gdn TN26 . . . . .181 C1
Hope La
  New Romney TN28 . . . . . .202 A8
  St Mary in the Marsh TN29 . .193 F2
Hope Rd CT14 . . . . .117 D5
Hope St Chatham ME4 . . . . .10 A3
  Maidstone ME14 . . . . .74 F6
  Sheerness ME12 . . . . .1 C2
Hope Villas CT1 . . . . .87 D6
Hope's La CT12 . . . . .49 E1
Hopes Gr TN26 . . . . .167 D7
Hopeville Ave CT10 . . . . . . .29 E6
Hopewell Bsns Ctr ME5 . . .32 C8
Hopewell Dr ME5 . . . . .32 C8

Hopewell Sch TN23 155 E7
Hoppers Way TN23 155 D8
Hopsons Pl ME12 4 C5
Horatio Pl ME1 9 B4
Horn Hill ME9 58 E2
Horn St CT19,CT20,CT21 177 B4
Hornash La TN26 170 D8
Hornbeam Ave ME5 32 B2
Hornbeam Cl TN23 138 F3
Hornbrook La TN26 181 C7
Hornes Place Chapel* TN26 181 D2
Hornet Cl CT10 29 D3
Horsa Rd Birchington CT7 26 D7
Deal CT14 117 D8
Horse Wash La ME1 9 C6
Horsebridge Rd CT5 20 D2
Horselees Rd ME13 64 A2
Horseshoe Cl
Gillingham ME7 32 F5
Maidstone ME14 75 E5
Horseshoes La ME17 98 E4
Horsford Wlk ME13 62 A8
Horsham Hill ME9 12 E4
Horsham La ME8,ME9 12 D3
Horshams The CT6 23 D5
Horsley Cl CT18 163 B4
Horsley Rd ME1 9 B4
Horsted Ave ME4 9 E1
Horsted Inf Sch ME4 31 D5
Horsted Jun Sch ME5 31 D5
Horsted Ret Pk ME5 31 D5
Horsted Way ME1 31 D7
Horton Cotts CT4 86 E4
Horton Downs ME15 75 F1
Horton Gdns CT4 86 E4
Horwood Cl ME1 31 B8
Hoser Gdns CT7 27 A7
Hospital Hill CT20,CT21 177 C3
Hospital La
Canterbury CT1 87 F8
3 Chatham ME1 9 E4
Hospital Meadow Cotts CT3 91 D2
Hospital of Thomas the Martyr Eastbridge The* CT1 87 F8
Hospital Rd ME17 99 E8
Hotel Rd Gillingham ME8 11 A2
St Margaret's at Cliffe CT15 151 B6
Hothfield Common Nature Reserve* TN26 137 F8
Hothfield Rd ME8 11 F1
Hothfield Village Prim Sch TN26 137 F7
Hougham Court La CT15 165 A3
Houghton Ave ME7 33 B3
Houghton Green La TN31 197 C2
Houghton Ho CT19 178 C5
Houghton La TN31 197 C3
House Mdw TN23 155 C7
Housefield TN24 139 F2
Housefield Rd ME13 104 C6
Hovenden Cl CT2 67 A4
Howard Ave Rochester ME1 9 D3
Sittingbourne ME10 36 D6
Howard Cl ME12 4 C7
Howard Dr ME16 74 B5
Howard Rd CT10 30 A3
Howard Sch The ME8 33 D8
Howbury Wlk ME8 33 D4
Howfield La CT4 86 E5
Howland Mews CT1 87 E6
Howletts Oast CT4 89 C5
Howletts Wild Animal Pk* CT4 89 D6
Hoxton Cl TN23 155 D8
Hoystings Cl The CT1 88 A7
Hubbard's La ME15 97 A3
Hubbards Cotts ME8 12 C2
Hubbards Hill ME17 102 B6
Hubble Dr ME15 97 E7
Hubert Way CT10 29 E6
Huckleberry Cl ME5 32 B3
Hudson Cl
7 Dover CT16 149 B3
Gillingham ME8 11 C1
Sturry CT2 67 F6
Hudson Rd CT1 67 B2
Hugh Pl 5 ME13 62 D7
Hugh Price Cl ME10 37 C5
Hugin Ave CT10 29 E7
Hulkes La ME1 9 E4
Hull Pl CT14 116 F6
Hull Rd TN29 206 E6
Humber Ave CT6 21 F4
Hume Ct CT21 176 D1
Humphrey Terr CT18 162 F4
Hundreds Cl CT8 27 D7
Hunger Hatch La TN27 119 F4
Hunstanton Cl ME8 33 E3
Hunt Cl CT18 163 A4
Hunter Ave TN24 156 E8
Hunter Cl TN24 156 E8
Hunter Rd TN24 139 E1
Hunters Bank CT4 144 F4
Hunters Chase
Herne Bay CT6 23 C2
Whitstable CT5 43 E7
Hunters Ct 5 ME7 10 C7
Hunters Forstal Rd CT6 23 C2
Hunters Way
Gillingham ME7 10 E1
Sheldwich ME13 83 C5
Hunters Way W ME5 10 E1
Hunters Wlk CT14 117 B6
Huntersfield Cl ME5 32 C1
Hunting Gate CT7 26 F8
Huntingdon Wlk 2 ME15 97 E7
Huntington Rd ME17 96 B3
Hunton Gdns CT2 67 A4
Hunton Hill ME15 96 A2
Huntsfield Ind Est CT20 177 D4
Huntsman La ME14 75 B4
Huntsman's Cnr ME4 31 E8
Huntsmans Cl ME1 9 E1
Huntswood TN23 138 E1
Hurst Cl ME5 31 E6
Hurst Gr CT12 29 C1
Hurst Hill ME5 31 E2
Hurst La Capel-le-F CT18 164 B4
Charing Heath TN27 119 E6
Sittingbourne ME10 14 F1
Hurst Pl ME8 33 F8
Hurst Rd TN24 139 C7
Hurstford La TN26,TN27 120 C2
Hurstings The ME15 74 D2
Hurstwood ME5 31 E4
Hurstwood Rd
Bredhurst ME7 33 B1
Warren Street ME13 102 E8
Hussar Ho ME1 9 C3
Hustlings Dr ME12 5 B5
Hutchings Cl ME10 37 C5
Hutsford Cl ME8 33 D5
Huxley Ct 3 ME1 9 D4
Hybrid Cl ME1 9 D1
Hyde Ct CT17 166 C7
Hyde Pl CT3 112 F5
Hyde Rd ME16 74 D6
Hyde The CT4 86 B2
Hylands Cotts TN26 169 A2
Hythe Cl CT20 177 F5
Hythe Com Sch CT21 176 B1
Hythe Pl CT13 94 A8
Hythe Rd Ashford TN24 139 E1
Dymchurch TN29 186 E1
Lympne CT21 175 D4
Sittingbourne ME10 36 D5
Smeeth TN25,TN24 158 C3
Hythe Sta* CT21 176 A2
Hythe, St Leonard's CE Jun Sch CT21 176 B2
Hyton Dr CT14 117 B6

I

Ian's Wlk CT21 177 A3
Ibis Cl CT5 43 B6
Ice Bowl The* ME8 11 A1
Ickham Court Farm CT3 69 C1
Iden La TN27 119 B4
Iden Rd TN31 197 B3
Idenwood Cl ME8 33 D6
Iffin La CT4 87 E2
Ifield Cl ME15 97 F7
Ilex Rd CT19 177 F6
Illustrious Cl ME5 32 A6
Imbert Cl TN28 202 C6
Imperial Ave ME12 4 D7
Imperial Dr ME12 6 E4
Imperial Rd ME7 10 C3
Imperial Way TN23 155 C8
Impton La ME5 32 A1
Ince Rd CT2 67 F7
Ingle Cl CT7 27 B7
Ingle Rd ME4 9 F2
Ingleden Cl ME10 36 F8
Ingleden Park Rd TN30 167 C1
Ingles La 8 CT20 178 D5
Ingles Mews 4 CT20 178 C4
Ingles Rd CT20 178 C4
Ingoldsby Rd
Birchington CT7 26 E7
Canterbury CT1 87 D6
Folkestone CT19 178 E7
Ingram Cl CT18 162 F3
Ingram Rd ME7 10 E6
Inner Lines ME7 10 A6
Institute Rd Chatham ME4 10 A4
Faversham ME13 62 D7
Inverary Ct CT11 29 E1
Inverness Ho 7 ME15 97 E7
Inverness Terr CT10 30 A3
Invicta Ct ME10 36 F7
Invicta Gram Sch ME14 75 C4
Invicta Ho Canterbury CT1 87 F7
Margate CT9 8 C1
Invicta Rd
Folkestone CT19 178 D7
Lydd TN29 207 I6
Margate CT9 29 B8
Sheerness ME12 1 D2
Whitstable CT5 43 F8
Invicta Villas ME14 76 C4
Inward Car Lanes CT16 166 G8
Inward Freight Lanes CT16 166 G8
Iona Cl ME5 32 D1
Iona Rd ME15 97 A7
Irchester St 11 CT11 52 F7
Ireland Ct TN24 139 D2
Irene Astor Ct 7 CT20 178 D5
Iris Cl ME5 54 A8
Iron Bar La 4 CT1 88 A8
Ironside Cl ME5 32 A8
Irvine Dr CT9 29 C8
Isis Cl CT21 175 A3
Island Rd
Upstreet CT3,CT7 47 D2
Westbere CT2,CT3 68 C7
Island Wall CT5 20 C1
Isle of Sheppey Holiday Village ME12 6 F2
Ito Way ME8 11 A3
Ivanhoe Rd Herne Bay CT6 23 A4
Westgate-on-S CT8 7 C1
Ivens Way ME17 100 D6
Iversgate Cl ME8 11 F2
Ives Holiday Camp ME12 6 G1
Ivory Cl ME13 40 A1
Ivy Cl Etchinghill CT18 161 D3
Kingswood ME17 99 D2
Ivy Cottage Hill CT12 50 E7
Ivy Cotts TN23 155 C8
Ivy Ct CT2 66 E6
Ivy House Rd CT5 20 F1
Ivy La Canterbury CT1 88 A8
Ramsgate CT11 52 D6
Ivy Mews ME17 99 E2
Ivy Pl Canterbury CT1 87 E7
Deal CT14 117 D7
Rochester ME1 9 A2
Ivy St ME8 33 F8
Ivy Way CT19 178 E7
Ivychurch Gdns CT9 8 E2
Ivychurch Rd TN29 192 B3
Ivyside CT8 7 C1
Iwade Com Prim Sch ME9 14 D4

J

Jaarlen Rd TN29 205 B6
Jacinth Dr ME10 36 C6
Jacklin Cl ME5 31 F2
Jackson Ave ME1 31 E8
Jackson Cl ME8 11 C1
Jackson Rd CT1 87 E7
Jacksons La 8 TN30 179 A7
Jacksons Stables CT8 7 D1
Jacob Cl CT9 28 E7
Jacob Yd 8 ME13 62 D7
Jacobs Ho ME12 1 D2
Jacobs Oak TN24 156 D6
Jade Cl ME10 36 C7
Jaffa Ct CT5 43 D8
Jamaica Terr ME14 75 A7
James Allchin Gdns TN24 139 F4
James Cl Ash CT3 71 D2
Lyminge CT18 161 C7
James Ct
Folkestone CT20 178 A4
2 Margate CT9 8 B2
James Hall Gdns CT14 117 C3
James Haney Dr TN24 139 F5
James Morris Ct 3 CT20 177 F3
James St Ashford TN23 139 A2
5 Chatham ME4 9 F4
Folkestone CT19 178 D6
Gillingham ME7 10 C6
Maidstone ME14 75 A5
8 Ramsgate CT11 52 D6
Rochester ME1 9 C4
Sheerness ME12 1 E2
James Whatman Way ME14 74 F5
Japonica Cl ME5 32 C2
Jarman's Field TN25 123 F2
Jarrett Ho 10 CT20 178 C4
Jarrett's Ct 1 ME10 37 B4
Jarvis Dr TN24 157 A7
Jarvis Pl TN30 167 B3
Jarvist Pl CT14 134 D6
Jasmine Cl Chartham CT4 86 E1
2 Chatham ME5 31 F4
Jasper Ave ME1 9 D2
Jayne Wlk CT5 43 B6
Jefferson Cl TN23 138 F1
Jefferson Dr ME8 11 C1
Jefferson Rd ME12 1 E2
Jefferstone Gdns TN29 194 E4
Jefferstone La TN29 194 E4
Jeffery St ME7 10 C6
Jeffrey St ME14 75 A5
Jellicoe Cl TN24 157 A7
Jemmett Rd TN23 156 A8
Jenkins Dr ME15 97 E5
Jenkins' Dale ME4 9 F3
Jenner Rd ME1 9 C4
Jenner's Way TN29 194 F3
Jennifer Gdns CT9 29 C8
Jersey Cl TN24 139 C8
Jersey La CT4 109 C6
Jersey Rd ME2 9 A8
Jesmond St 3 CT19 178 D6
Jesse's Hill CT4 111 B1
Jessica Mews
2 Canterbury CT1 67 B1
Sittingbourne ME10 36 E7
Jesson Cl TN29 195 A4
Jesson Court Cvn Pk TN29 194 F4
Jesuit Cl CT2 67 A4
Jesus Hospl CT1 67 A1
Jetty Rd Sheerness ME12 1 B3
Warden ME12 6 E4
Jewry La CT1 87 F8
Jeyes Rd ME7 10 C4
Jezreels Rd ME7 10 D3
Jillian Way TN23 155 E7
Jiniwin Rd ME1 31 D7
Jo-Ann's Ct 5 CT10 30 A4
Johannesburg Ho 2 ME15 97 F5
Johannesburg Rd CT16 149 C4
John Anderson Ct 11 ME13 62 D7
John Badger Cl TN24 139 E5
John Bowley Ho CT19 177 F6
John Dutton Way TN24 139 E4
John Graham Ct CT1 88 A6
John Hall Cl ME13 40 B2
John Nash Cl ME9 60 B8
John Newington Cl TN24 139 F5
John St Broadstairs CT10 30 B4
Maidstone ME14 75 A6
Rochester ME1 9 C4
John Tapping Cl CT14 117 B1
John Wilson Bsns Pk CT5 21 B1
John's Gn CT13 93 E6
Johnson Ave ME7 10 C7
Johnson Cl TN24 157 A7
Johnson Ct ME13 40 B1
Johnson Ho ME10 36 D4
Johnson Rd ME10 36 D4
Johnson Way ME12 4 A7
Johnson's Cnr TN26 183 A4
Joiners Ct ME4 10 B2
Jointon Rd CT20 178 B4
Jordan Cl ME15 97 E5
Joseph Conrad Ho CT2 66 D1
Joseph Wilson Ind Est CT5 44 A7
Joss Gap Rd CT10 8 H1
Joy La CT5 43 B8
Joy Lane Inf Sch CT5 43 C7
Joy Lane Jun Sch CT5 43 C7
Joy Wood ME17 97 D5
Joyes Cl Folkestone CT19 178 E7
Whitfield CT16 149 B7
Joyes Rd
Folkestone CT19 178 E7
Whitfield CT16 149 B7
Jubilee Cl CT21 187 D8
Jubilee Cotts Staple CT3 92 B6
Throwley ME13 82 D1
Worth CT14 94 B4
Jubilee Cres ME11 2 F5
Jubilee Ct
19 Broadstairs CT10 30 B4
17 Ramsgate CT11 52 F7
Whitstable CT5 21 A3
Jubilee Dr CT14 117 D3
Jubilee Field TN30 188 E4
Jubilee Fields ME8 12 D2
Jubilee Ho CT20 178 B4
Jubilee Rd
Littlebourne CT3 89 F8
Sandwich CT13 93 F8
Worth CT14 94 B4
Jubilee St ME10 36 E5
Jubilee Terr ME7 10 C6
Jubilee Way CT15,CT16 150 A2
Judd Rd ME13 62 A7
Judkins Cl ME5 32 C6
Julian Ct CT19 178 B5
Julian Rd CT19 178 B6
Julie Cl CT10 30 A7
Julien Pl TN24 157 A8
Junction Rd
Gillingham ME7 10 D4
Herne Bay CT6 22 C2
Junior King's Sch CT2 67 E5
Juniper Cl Ashford TN23 138 E2
Canterbury CT1 88 A6
Chatham ME5 32 A4
Maidstone ME16 74 B6
Whitstable CT5 20 F1
Jupiter La TN23 155 E5
Jury's Gap Coastguard Cotts TN31 203 E1
Jury's Gap Rd TN29 205 A5

K

Kain Ct CT12 29 B1
Kake St CT4 125 E7
Katherine Ct ME5 32 B2
Kearsney Abbey* CT16 148 D4
Kearsney Ave CT16 148 E4
Kearsney Ct CT16 148 D4
Kearsney Sta CT16 148 D4
Keat Farm Cl CT6 23 F5
Keating Cl ME1 9 A3
Keddow's Cl CT21 187 D8
Kedleston Rd CT16 149 C5
Keefe Cl ME5 31 D1
Keel Ct ME2 9 D8
Keeley Mews ME7 10 E3
Keeper's Hill CT4 89 D2
Keith Ave CT12 52 A8
Kellaway Rd ME5 32 A2
Kelly Dr ME7 10 C7
Kelly Ho ME1 31 C7
Kelvedon Rd CT14 117 C2
Kemp Alley 2 CT5 20 D1
Kemp Cl ME5 31 E4
Kemp Rd CT5 21 C2
Kempes Pl TN25 123 E2
Kempton Cl ME5 32 C2
Kemsdale Rd ME13 63 F6
Kemsing Gdns CT2 67 B4
Kemsley Down Sta ME10 15 C1
Kemsley Mill Railway Mus* ME10 15 C1
Kemsley Sta ME10 14 E1
Kemsley Street Rd ME7 33 C1
Kenardington Rd TN26 181 E3
Kenbrook TN24 139 C7
Kendal Cl CT11 52 B6
Kendal Mdw CT5 21 E1
Kendal Rise CT10 30 A5
Kendal Way ME8 33 D8
Kendall Pl 1 ME15 97 D8
Kendon Bsns Pk ME2 9 D8
Kenfield Rd CT4 109 A6
Kengate Ind Est CT21 175 F1
Kenilworth Cl CT15 151 A6
Kenilworth Ct ME10 36 C5
Kenilworth Dr ME8 33 D6
Kenilworth Gdns ME8 33 D7
Kenilworth Ho ME16 74 B2
Kennedy Cl ME13 62 D8
Kennedy Dr CT14 117 B2
Kennedy Ho 8 CT11 52 F7
Kennel Barn Rd ME9 57 C5
Kennel Hill CT15 131 E6
Kennelling Rd ME13, TN27 103 D5
Kennels The CT15 131 E6
Kennett Dr CT14 117 A2
Kennett La TN25 175 B8
Kennett Lane Cotts TN25 175 B8
Kennington CE Jun Sch TN24 139 E7
Kennington Cl
Gillingham ME8 11 B4
Maidstone ME15 97 F7
Kennington Pl TN24 139 D7
Kennington Rd TN24 140 A1
Kensington Ho ME16 74 A2
Kensington Rd CT1 67 C4
Kent & Canterbury Hospl CT1 88 A5
Kent & East Sussex Rly Mus* TN30 179 A8
Kent Ave Ashford TN24 139 B3
Canterbury CT1 88 D8
Maidstone ME15 75 C1
Minster (Sheppey) ME12 4 B6
Sittingbourne ME10 36 D3
Kent Battle of Britain Mus* CT18 162 F4
Kent Cl ME1 31 C8
Kent Coll CT2 66 C3
Kent Coll Inf & Jun Sch CT2 66 A1
Kent County Optholmic & Aural Hospl ME14 75 A4
Kent County Show Gd ME14 55 C3
Kent Gdns CT7 26 F7
Kent Ho
4 Broadstairs CT10 30 A4
Folkestone CT20 178 B4
Kent Inst of Art & Design
Maidstone ME16 74 C3
Rochester ME1 9 E4
Canterbury CT1 88 B7
Kent International Airport CT12 28 B1
Kent Music Sch CT1 66 F1
Kent Pl CT11 52 F6
Kent Rd Folkestone CT19 177 E7
Margate CT9 29 B8
Sheerness ME12 1 C1
Kent Science Pk ME9 58 D6
Kent St CT5 43 D8
Kent Terr Gillingham ME8 12 C2
Ramsgate CT11 52 F6
Kent View Dr ME12 5 D1
Kentish Ct 8 ME16 74 E4
Kentmere Ave CT11 51 F7
Kenton Gdns CT12 50 B6
Kentstone Ct ME4 10 A4
Kenward Rd ME16 74 C5
Kenwood Ave ME5 32 A4
Kenya Terr 7 ME14 75 A7
Kenyon Wlk ME8 33 B3
Kerry Hill Way ME14 74 E6
Kerton Rd TN29 209 D7
Keston Ct ME8 11 A2
Kestrel Cl
Kingsnorth TN23 156 C3
Sittingbourne ME10 37 A2
Kestrel Ct
4 Sittingbourne ME10 37 A4
Whitstable CT5 21 A3
Kestrel Ho ME7 10 B6
Kestrel Rd ME5 32 C2
Keswick Ave ME10 37 C3
Keswick Ct ME7 11 A5
Keswick Dr ME16 74 B5
Kettle Dr CT18 163 B5
Kettle Hill ME13 81 F4
Kettle Hill Rd
Eastling ME13 81 F5
Throwley ME13 82 A4
Kevin Dr CT11 52 B6
Kewlands ME14 75 C6
Key St ME10 36 A5
Keycol Hill ME9 35 F5
Keyes Ave ME4 9 F2
Keyes Pl CT19 178 E7
Keynes Coll CT2 66 D4
Keys The CT18 163 C5
Keyworth Mews 7 CT1 67 B2
Khartoum Rd ME7 10 A6
Khartoum Sq CT16 149 A6
Khyber Rd ME4,ME7 10 B7
Kilbride Ct CT11 29 F1
Kilburn Ho 6 ME14 75 A5
Kiln Cl Challock TN25 105 B1
Sittingbourne ME10 37 A3

Kiln Cnr CT21 176 B4
Kiln Field TN30 179 C7
Kiln La TN26 153 F5
Kiln Rd TN25 172 F4
Kilnbridge Cl ME15 96 B7
Kilnbridge Wks ME15 96 B7
Kilndown Cl
Ashford TN23 155 E6
Maidstone ME16 74 C7
Kilndown Gdns
Canterbury CT2 67 A4
Margate CT9 8 E2
Kimberley Cl CT16 149 C3
Kimberley Cnr CT10 29 F8
Kimberley Ct CT8 7 C1
Kimberley Gr CT5 42 F6
Kimberley Rd
Gillingham ME7 10 D3
Ramsgate CT12 29 A1
Kimberley Way TN24 156 C7
Kimberly Terr CT18 161 C7
King Arthur Ct ME10 36 E3
King Arthur Rd CT12 51 D7
King Charles Ct CT14 117 D2
King Edward Ave
Broadstairs CT10 30 A4
Herne Bay CT6 23 B4
King Edward Ct CT6 23 B4
King Edward Rd
Birchington CT7 27 A5
Chatham ME4 9 F2
Deal CT14 117 D8
Gillingham ME7 10 F6
Maidstone ME15 74 F2
1 Ramsgate CT11 52 C6
Rochester ME1 9 C5
King Edward St CT5 20 D1
King Ethelbert Sch CT7 27 C7
King George Rd ME5 31 E4
King George V Meml Houses
ME8 11 C2
King George Villas CT14 94 B3
King Lear's Way CT17 166 B5
King St Brookland TN29 191 D2
Canterbury CT1 66 F1
Chatham ME4 10 A4
Deal CT14 117 D6
Deal, Walmer CT14 117 D3
Dover CT16 166 D7
Fordwich CT2 68 A4
Gillingham ME7 10 C6
Maidstone ME14 75 A4
Margate CT9 7 J3
Ramsgate CT11 52 E7
Rochester ME1 9 C4
Sandwich CT13 73 A1
Sheerness ME12 1 B2
Sittingbourne ME10 36 E5
King William Rd 6 ME7 10 C7
King's Ave Ashford TN23 139 A2
Birchington CT7 26 D7
Broadstairs CT10 30 B6
Ramsgate CT12 29 B1
Rochester ME1 9 C3
Sandwich CT13 95 A8
Whitstable CT5 20 E1
King's Bastion ME7 10 A5
King's Cl CT14 134 D6
King's Head Alley ME12 1 B3
King's Orch ME1 9 C5
King's Pk CT1 67 B1
King's Pl 5 CT11 52 E6
King's Prospect TN24 156 E6
King's Rd Birchington CT7 27 A6
Chatham ME5 10 D1
Faversham ME13 62 C7
Herne Bay CT6 22 F5
Ramsgate CT11 52 D8
King's Sch ME1 9 C5
King's Sch Canterbury The
CT1 67 A1
King's Sch The CT1 88 A8
Kingfisher Apartments 13
ME15 97 E5
Kingfisher Ave CT21 187 D8
Kingfisher Cl
Ashford TN24 157 A7
Iwade ME9 14 E4
Margate CT9 28 B8
Whitstable CT5 43 C7
Kingfisher Com Prim Sch
ME5 32 B7
Kingfisher Ct
Herne Bay CT6 22 D3
11 Maidstone ME15 75 B4
Kingfisher Dr ME5 32 C7
Kingfisher Gdns CT21 187 C8
Kingfisher Ho TN23 138 F1
Kingfisher Wlk CT10 29 F5
Kingly Way CT17 166 A7
Kings Acre ME15 76 A1
Kings Chase TN24 140 A2
Kings Cotts ME17 98 F6
Kings Ct CT14 117 D3
Kings Mdw TN24 139 E7
Kings Mews 7 CT1 67 A1
Kings Mill Cl ME10 36 E5
Kings Oak Mews ME5 31 F4
Kings Par 7 TN24 139 B2
Kings Rd Aylesham CT3 112 F6
Dover CT17 166 A7
Folkestone CT20 177 D6
Minster (Sheppey) ME12 4 D7
Kings Reach ME15 97 D8
Kings Ropewalk CT17 166 B5
Kings Row
1 Maidstone ME15 75 A1
Rochester ME1 9 B4
Kings Wlk ME14 75 B5
Kings Wood Forest Wlks★
TN25 105 F1
Kingsbridge Ct 11 CT20 178 E5
Kingsdale Ct ME5 10 C1
Kingsdown & Ringwould CE
Prim Sch CT14 134 C5
Kingsdown Cl
Gillingham ME7 33 B4
Maidstone ME16 74 E4
Kingsdown Cotts ME9 59 E4
Kingsdown Hill CT14 134 D4
Kingsdown Park Holiday
Village CT14 134 D5
Kingsdown Pk CT5 20 F2
Kingsdown Rd
Kingsdown CT14 134 D7
Lynsted ME9 59 D4
St Margaret's at Cliffe
CT15 151 A7
Kingsfield Rd CT6 23 B2
Kingsford Cl TN25 157 E4
Kingsford Ct CT17 149 B1
Kingsford St TN25 157 D5
Kingsgate Ave CT10 8 F1
Kingsgate Bay Rd CT10 8 H2
Kingsgate Castle CT10 8 H2
Kingsgate Cl ME16 74 C4
Kingsgate Coll CT10 30 A8
Kingsgate La TN30 188 C5
Kingsland Gdns CT14 134 B8
Kingsland Hollow TN29 195 A4
Kingsland La
Egerton Forstal TN27 118 E1
Westwell TN25 121 F1
Kingsley Rd
Maidstone ME15 75 A3
Whitstable CT5 43 E8
Kingsmarsh La TN29 201 C5
Kingsmead
Folkestone CT19 178 B8
Westgate-on-S CT8 7 C1
Kingsmead Prim Sch
CT1 67 A1
Kingsmead Rd CT1,CT2 67 A2
Kingsnorth CE Prim Sch
TN23 156 B3
Kingsnorth Ct 2 CT20 178 B5
Kingsnorth Gdns CT20 178 C5
Kingsnorth Rd
Ashford TN23 156 A6
Faversham ME13 62 C6
Gillingham ME8 11 C4
Kingston Ave CT9 28 C7
Kingston Cl Crabble CT17 148 F3
Herne Bay CT6 23 F5
Ramsgate CT12 29 B2
Kingston Cres ME5 32 C4
Kingston Dr ME15 97 A8
Kingstone Ct 3 CT20 178 B5
Kingsway Chatham ME5 10 D1
Dymchurch TN29 186 E2
Gillingham ME7 10 E1
Kingswear Gdns ME2 9 C7
Kingswood Ave ME4 9 F2
Kingswood Cl TN24 139 D5
Kingswood Ho 12 ME16 74 A3
Kingswood Prim Sch
ME17 99 E2
Kingswood Rd
Gillingham ME7 10 D6
Kit's Coty ME20 53 D8
Kingswood Villas CT17 149 A2
Kinross Cl ME5 32 B7
Kipling Rd TN23 139 B2
Kipping Cl CT18 163 A4
Kirby's Hts 8 CT2 66 F1
Kirby's La CT2 66 F1
Kirk Gdns CT14 117 B2
Kirk View TN23 155 C8
Kirkdale ME15 96 F5
Kirkdale Cl ME5 32 D1
Kirkdale Cotts ME15 96 F5
Kirkdale Rd ME15 96 F6
Kirkstone Ave CT11 51 F7
Kirkwood Ave TN26 169 A1
Kirton Cl CT18 162 F4
Kit Hill ME13 84 D8
Kit Hill Ave ME5 31 E3
Kit's Coty Ho★ ME20 53 C6
Kitchener Ave ME4 10 A1
Kitchener Cl CT4 128 F8
Kitchener Rd
Dover CT17 166 A7
Rochester ME2 9 A8
Kitchener Sq CT19 178 E6
Kite Farm CT5 21 D3
Kitewell La TN29 205 D8
Kither Rd TN23 156 A7
Kitsbridge La
Hamstreet TN26 183 C4
Ruckinge TN25,TN26 184 B6
Kittiwake Cl CT6 23 F5
Klondyke Ind Est ME11 2 F4
Knatchbull Way TN25 158 E5
Knavesacre Ct ME8 33 D5
Knell La CT3 71 C3
Knight Ave
Canterbury CT2 87 D8
Gillingham ME7 10 D7
Knight Rd ME2 9 A6
Knight's Ave CT10 30 B6
Knight's Rd CT16 166 E8
Knightrider Ct ME15 75 A3
Knightrider St
Maidstone ME15 75 A3
Sandwich CT13 73 A1
Knights Alley 20 CT5 20 D2
Knights Ct Dover CT17 149 B1
Sittingbourne ME10 36 E3
Knights Pk ME2 9 A6
Knights Templars CT17 166 C6
Knights Way CT16 149 A3
Knightsfield Rd ME10 36 D7
Knock Hill TN30 190 A2
Knock Rd TN23 156 A7
Knockholt Rd CT9 8 F3
Knockhurst Ct TN30 167 C1
Knockwood Rd TN30 167 C1
Knold Pk CT9 28 E8
Knole Rd ME5 32 C3
Knole The ME13 62 B7
Knoll Ct CT20 178 C4
Knoll Hill TN25 173 C3
Knoll La TN23 155 E7
Knoll Pl CT14 117 C2
Knoll The CT15 151 A6
Knoll Way ME12 6 D4
Knott Cres TN24 157 A7
Knott Ct ME14 74 F6
Knott's La 20 CT1 67 A1
Knotts La CT15 150 F6
Knotts Sq TN23 139 C2
Knowle Rd ME14 75 B6
Knowler Way CT6 23 C5
Knowlton Gdns ME16 74 B2
Knowlton Wlk 1 CT1 67 B2
Kohima Pl CT15 149 F2
Kyetop Wlk ME8 33 D6

L

La Belle Alliance Sq 9
CT11 52 E7
La Galamina TN28 206 E8
La Providence ME1 9 C5
La Rocco TN28 206 E8
La Tausco TN28 206 D8
La-Tene CT14 117 B2
Laburnum Ave CT13 93 F8
Laburnum Cl CT16 148 E4
Laburnum Gr ME12 1 I1
Laburnum Ho ME12 1 C2
Laburnum La CT2 68 B7
Laburnum Pl ME10 36 E4
Labworth Cl ME12 3 E6
Lacey Cl ME17 98 E4
Lachlan Way 2 CT20 177 F3
Lackenden Cotts CT3 89 D6
Lacock Gdns Loose ME15 97 A8
Maidstone ME15 75 A1
Lacton Oast TN24 157 B8
Lacton Way TN24 157 A8
Lacy Cl ME16 74 D7
Ladbrooke Ho 7 ME14 75 A5
Ladds Cnr ME7 11 B5
Lade Fort Cotts TN29 206 E6
Lade Fort Cres TN29 206 E6
Ladies Wlk CT21 176 C1
Lady Garne Rd CT15 164 F5
Lady Joanna Thornhill
Endowed Prim Sch
TN25 123 E2
Lady Wootton's Gn 6
CT1 88 A8
Ladyfields Chatham ME5 32 D2
Herne Bay CT6 23 D2
Ladyfields Cl ME9 35 F5
Ladysmith Gr CT5 42 F6
Ladysmith Rd CT5 43 C5
Ladywell 7 CT16 166 D8
Ladywell Ho 2 CT16 166 D8
Ladywood Rd CT2 67 F7
Lagos Ave CT12 29 A1
Lakelands
Harrietsham ME17 100 E6
Loose ME15 97 A7
Lakemead TN23 155 E8
Laker Ho ME14 75 A6
Laker Rd ME1 31 C6
Lakeside TN23 155 E8
Lakeside Gdns TN26 120 F1
Lakeside Pk ME2 9 E7
Lakesview International Bsns
Pk CT3 47 A1
Lakewood Dr ME8 33 C6
Laking Ave CT10 30 B7
Laleham Gdns CT9 8 B2
Laleham Rd CT9 8 B1
Laleham Sch CT9 8 B1
Laleham Wlk CT9 8 B1
Lamb's Wlk CT5 43 C6
Lambard Ho 8 ME14 75 A5
Lambden Rd TN27 136 C6
Lamberhurst Farm ME13 42 F1
Lamberhurst Gn ME8 11 B3
Lamberhurst Rd ME16 74 B7
Lamberhurst Way CT9 8 F3
Lambert Ho CT14 117 B3
Lambes Ct ME8 33 D5
Lambeth Cl ME5 32 B4
Lambeth Rd CT1 67 C4
Lambourn Way ME5 32 C2
Lambourne Pl ME8 12 A2
Lambourne Rd ME15 75 F2
Lambourne Wlk CT1 88 C8
Lambsfrith Gr ME7 33 B3
Lambton Rd CT17 149 A1
Laming Rd CT7 27 B6
Lammas Dr ME10 36 E6
Lammas Gate ME13 62 D8
Lamplighters Cl ME7 32 F5
Lancashire Rd ME15 97 E7
Lancaster Ave CT18 164 C2
Lancaster Cl
Hamstreet TN26 183 A8
Ramsgate CT12 29 B1
Lancaster Ct ME8 33 C7
Lancaster Gdns
Birchington CT7 26 F6
Herne Bay CT6 23 D5
Lancaster Ho Deal CT14 117 A5
3 Dover CT17 166 D7
Lancaster Rd
Canterbury CT1 87 F6
Dover CT17 166 D7
Lancaster The CT10 30 B3
Lance Cl ME10 36 F8
Lancelot Cl CT14 117 A3
Lancer Ho ME1 9 C3
Lancet La ME15 97 A6
Lanchester Cl CT6 22 A3
Landbury Wlk TN23 138 F4
Landon Rd CT6 23 C4
Landor Ct ME7 33 A3
Landrail Rd ME9 13 B3
Landway The ME14 76 A4
Lane End CT6 22 D5
Lane The CT15 149 F6
Lane's Wlk CT5 20 E2
Lanes The CT12 50 D6
Lanfranc Gdns CT2 66 C1
Lanfranc Ho 5 CT1 67 A1
Lanfranc Rd CT14 117 C8
Lang Ct CT5 21 C3
Langdale TN23 155 E8
Langdale Ave CT11 52 A7
Langdale Cl ME8 11 D1
Langdale Rise ME16 74 C5
Langdon Ave CT3 71 F1
Langdon Cl CT15 150 F5
Langdon Cross CT15 150 C7
Langdon Prim Sch
CT15 133 A1
Langdon Rd
Folkestone CT19 177 D7
Rochester ME1 9 C4
Langham Cl CT9 7 F1
Langham Gr ME16 74 C4
Langholm Rd TN23 156 A7
Langhorne Gdns 9
CT20 178 C4
Langley Gdns CT9 8 E3
Langley Ho 11 ME16 74 A3
Langley Rd ME10 36 F7
Langney Dr TN23 155 E6
Langport Rd TN28 202 C6
Langton Cl ME14 75 C5
Langton Cotts CT3 70 B5
Langton La CT4 88 A4
Lankester Parker Rd
ME1 31 C6
Lansdown Rd
Canterbury CT1 88 A7
Sittingbourne ME10 37 C4
Lansdowne Ave ME15 97 C6
Lansdowne Ct 9 ME4 9 F4
Lansdowne Prim Sch
ME10 37 C3
Lansdowne Rd ME4 9 E2
Lanthorne Rd CT10 30 A6
Lapwing Cl
Hawkinge CT18 163 A3
Minster (Sheppey) ME12 4 B5
Lapwing Dr
Ashford TN23 156 D3
Lower Halstow ME9 13 B3
Larch Cl CT10 29 D4
Larch Rd CT15 114 B1
Larch Terr ME12 3 A8
Larch Wlk TN24 139 C6
Larch Wood Cl ME5 32 D1
Larchcroft ME5 32 A4
Larches The
Faversham ME13 62 A8
Whitstable CT5 43 C8
Larkey View CT4 86 E1
Larkfield Ave
Gillingham ME7 10 E4
Sittingbourne ME10 36 E6
Larking Dr ME16 74 D7
Larkscliff Ct CT7 26 D8
Larksfield Rd ME13 40 C1
Larkspur Rd ME5 31 E4
Lascelles Rd CT17 166 A6
Laser Quay ME2 9 D6
Latchgate CT20 177 C3
Lathe Barn★ TN29 186 D5
Latimer Cl CT6 22 B2
Latimer Pl 4 ME7 10 C7
Launder Way ME15 74 E2
Laundry Rd CT12 50 D7
Laura Pl ME1 9 A2
Laura Villas CT6 22 E5
Laureate Cl CT9 8 B2
Laurel Ave TN29 194 F4
Laurel Cl CT20 177 E6
Laurel Gr ME17 99 D2
Laurel Ho ME12 1 C2
Laurel Rd ME7 10 C7
Laurel Way CT4 86 E1
Laurel Wlk ME8 33 E6
Laurels The ME16 74 C2
Laurensfield CT12 50 C7
Laureston Pl CT16 166 E8
Laurice Ct 6 CT11 52 C6
Laurie Gray Ave ME5 31 D1
Lauriston Cl CT11 52 A5
Lauriston Mount CT10 30 A5
Lausanne Rd CT9 7 J2
Lausanne Terr 11 CT9 7 J2
Lavenda Cl ME7 33 A4
Lavender Cl
1 Chatham ME5 31 E4
Margate CT9 28 C8
Whitstable CT5 21 C2
Lavender Ct ME10 37 A3
Lavender Ho 3 ME15 97 D8
Lavender La CT12 51 C5
Lavender Mews CT1 87 F8
Laverstoke Rd ME16 74 C8
Lawley Cl CT12 29 C1
Lawn Cl ME4 10 B2
Lawn Rd Broadstairs CT10 30 A4
Deal CT14 117 C1
Lawn Villas CT11 52 E6
Lawns The 15 CT11 52 F7
Lawrence Cl
Folkestone CT19 177 F6
Loose ME15 97 A7
Lawrence Ct CT19 178 E6
Lawrence Gdns CT6 23 C4
Lawrence St ME7 10 C5
Laws La TN25 172 D7
Lawson Cl CT4 86 D2
Laxey The ME15 74 E1
Laxton Cl ME15 75 F3
Laxton Dr ME17 98 A1
Laxton Way
Canterbury CT1 88 C7
Faversham ME13 62 E5
Sittingbourne ME10 36 D6
Whitstable CT5 21 C1
Lay La CT3 71 D2
Layfield Cotts ME9 14 D1
Layfield Rd ME7 10 F7
Laylam Cl CT10 29 D5
Lazarus Hart Havens of Rest
The 4 CT11 52 F8
Le Roux Cl CT18 162 F4
Lea Cl CT21 176 B4
Lea Ct ME4 9 E1
Leach Ho ME13 64 A3
Leacon Cotts TN27 120 E4
Leacon Cotts The TN27 120 E4
Leacon Rd TN23 138 F2
Leafield TN25 159 D1
Leafy Glade ME8 33 B6
Leahurst Ct CT16 148 E4
Leake Ho 2 ME1 9 C1
Leamington Dr ME16 74 B4
Leander Rd ME1 31 C7
Learoyd Rd TN28 202 C6
Leas Gn CT10 29 D4
Leas Rd CT14 117 B4
Leas The Faversham ME13 62 B8
Folkestone CT20 178 C4
Kingsdown CT14 134 D3
Minster (Sheppey) ME12 4 C8
Sheerness ME12 1 I1
Whitstable CT5 21 D1
Leaside Cotts CT21 176 B3
Leatt Cl CT10 29 F4
Leaveland Cl TN23 155 F6
Leaveland Cotts ME13 83 B2
Leda Cotts TN25 120 F3
Lee Ho CT14 117 C1
Leech Ct ME1 9 D5
Leeds & Broomfield CE Prim
Sch ME17 99 A7
Leeds Castle★ ME17 99 D7
Leeds Rd ME17 98 E3
Leeds Sq ME8 11 B3
Leelands Ho CT14 117 B1
Lees Cl The TN25 158 D5
Lees Court Rd ME13 83 C5
Lees Rd Ashford TN24 140 A1
Brabourne Lees TN25 158 E6
Lees Terr CT4 85 C2
Lees The CT6 23 C5
Leeswood TN24 140 B1
Leet Cl Gillingham ME7 10 E6
Minster (Sheppey) ME12 5 B5
Leeward Rd ME1 9 C1
Leggett's La 10 CT5 20 D2
Leicester Ave CT9 8 C2
Leicester Ct CT9 8 D3
Leicester Gdns ME12 6 E3
Leicester Rd ME15 97 D7
Leigh Ave ME15 97 B6
Leigh Ct ME12 3 F5
Leigh Green Ind Est
TN30 179 E6
Leigh Rd CT12 28 F1
Leighton Ct 3 CT16 149 C1
Leighton Rd CT16 149 C1
Leighville Dr CT6 22 D4
Leitch Row ME7 10 A7
Leivers Rd CT14 117 A3
Len Valley Wlk ME15 75 F1
Lenacre Ave CT16 148 F7
Lenacre La CT16 148 F8
Lenacre St TN25,TN26 122 B2
Lendrim Cl 11 ME7 10 A6
Lenfield Ave ME14 75 B4
Length The CT7 25 F2
Lenham Cl CT10 30 A2
Lenham Ct 10 ME15 75 B4
Lenham Forstal Rd
ME17 119 B8
Lenham Gdns CT9 28 B8
Lenham Heath Rd ME17 101 C2
Lenham Ho ME17 101 E5
Lenham Prim Sch ME17 101 C5
Lenham Rd ME17 100 C1
Lenham Sta ME17 101 C4
Lenham Way ME8 11 A3

Lennard Ct 4 CT20 .....178 E5
Lennard Rd CT20 .....178 E5
Lenside Dr ME15 .....76 A2
Leona Ct 8 CT9 .....8 B2
Leonard Cl ME16 .....74 B6
Leonard Rd
　7 Chatham ME4 .....10 B3
　Greatstone-on-S TN28 .....206 E7
Leonard's Ave CT11 .....29 E1
Leonie Ct CT6 .....22 D4
Leopold Rd
　2 Chatham ME4 .....10 A3
　Ramsgate CT11 .....52 E8
Leopold St CT11 .....52 E6
Lerryn Gdns CT10 .....29 F8
Les Spickett Cl ME13 .....62 E6
Lesley Ave CT1 .....88 A6
Lesley Chalk Ho TN23 .....139 C2
Lesley Pl ME16 .....74 E5
Leslie Ave CT9 .....28 B8
Leslie Cres TN30 .....167 B2
Leslie Rd Birchington CT7 .....27 A8
　Gillingham ME7 .....10 D7
Leslie Smith Dr ME13 .....62 C7
Lested La ME17 .....98 B1
Lester Rd ME4 .....10 A3
Letchworth Ave ME4 .....9 F1
Leviathan Way ME4 .....10 A8
Lewd La TN27 .....135 A3
Lewis Ave ME8 .....11 B2
Lewis Cl ME13 .....62 A7
Lewis Court Dr ME17 .....97 C3
Lewis Cres CT9 .....8 B3
Lewis Ct TN23 .....155 F7
Lewisham Rd CT17 .....148 E3
Lewson Street Rd ME9 .....60 E8
Leybourn Rd CT10 .....30 B2
Leybourne Cl ME5 .....32 A2
Leybourne Dr CT9 .....28 B8
Leyburne Dr CT16 .....166 D8
Leycroft Cl CT2 .....66 E3
Leys The CT12 .....28 D1
Leysdown Rd
　Eastchurch ME12 .....5 E3
　Leysdown-on-S ME12 .....6 C1
Leysdown View CT5 .....43 C6
Leyton Ave ME7 .....10 E1
Library Rd CT2 .....66 D4
Libya Terr 6 ME14 .....75 A7
Lichfield Cl CT1 .....88 B6
Lichfield Cl ME8 .....11 D2
Lichfield Ho 12 ME15 .....97 E7
Lidsing Rd ME14 .....54 E6
Liege Cl ME10 .....14 F1
Lighthouse Rd CT15 .....151 A5
Lilac Ct TN23 .....138 E3
Lilk Hill ME14 .....76 C3
Lillian Rd CT11 .....52 F8
Lilyvale Cotts TN25 .....158 F4
Lilyvale Rd TN25 .....158 F4
Lime Cl Ashford TN23 .....138 F3
　Chartham CT4 .....86 E1
Lime Ct ME8 .....33 C3
Lime Gr
　Halfway Houses ME12 .....3 D5
　Sittingbourne ME10 .....37 A4
Lime Kiln Rd CT1 .....87 F6
Lime Kiln Wharf ME11 .....3 A5
Lime Villas CT4 .....144 F5
Limekiln Rdbt CT17 .....166 D6
Limekiln St CT17 .....166 D5
Limepits Cross ME9 .....35 F3
Limes Cl TN30 .....179 C8
Limes Pl 15 ME13 .....62 D7
Limes Rd Dover CT16 .....149 C1
　Folkestone CT19 .....177 F6
Limes The Ashford TN23 .....156 A5
　Lenham ME17 .....101 D5
　Old Romney TN29 .....201 A7
Limetree Cl ME5 .....32 B8
Limetree Terr ME17 .....101 E6
Linces The CT16 .....149 B4
Lincoln Rd ME7 .....10 D7
Lincoln Ave CT1 .....88 B7
Lincoln Cl CT5 .....21 D3
Lincoln Gdns CT7 .....26 F7
Lincoln Rd ME15 .....97 D8
Lindale Flats CT14 .....117 C2
Linden Ave
　Broadstairs CT10 .....30 B5
　Herne Bay CT6 .....22 E4
　Whitstable CT5 .....20 F1
Linden Chase CT2 .....66 E1
Linden Cl
　Sittingbourne ME10 .....36 D3
　Westgate-on-S CT8 .....27 E7
Linden Cres CT19 .....178 D6
Linden Dr ME12 .....3 A7
Linden Gr CT2 .....66 E1
Linden Grove Prim Sch
　TN23 .....155 F6
Linden Ho 5 ME5 .....31 F4
Linden Rd Ashford TN24 .....139 D1
　Chartham CT4 .....86 E1
　Coxheath ME17 .....96 C4
　Gillingham ME7 .....10 E5
　Westgate-on-S CT8 .....27 F8
Lindens CT1 .....176 D2
Lindenthorpe Rd CT10 .....30 A6
Lindfield Cotts ME13 .....62 A6
Lindisfarne Gdns ME16 .....74 E1
Lindridge Cl CT6 .....46 A8
Lineacre Cl ME8 .....33 D6
Linen Ct CT1 .....87 F8
Lines Terr ME4 .....10 A4

Linington Rd CT7 .....27 A6
Link Hill La TN27 .....118 D3
Link La CT1 .....88 A8
Link Rd Broadstairs CT10 .....29 F7
　Tyler Hill CT2 .....66 E6
Link The TN23 .....155 E7
Links Cl CT6 .....23 A3
Links Cres TN29 .....195 A4
Links Ct CT14 .....95 C1
Links Rd CT14 .....117 C8
Links The ME5 .....32 B8
Links Way TN28 .....202 D6
Linksfield Ct CT8 .....27 D7
Linksfield Rd CT8 .....27 D7
Linksway CT19 .....178 B8
Linksway Ct CT19 .....178 B8
Linkway ME9 .....14 A8
Linley Rd CT10 .....29 E7
Linnet Ave CT5 .....43 B6
Linton Gore ME17 .....96 D3
Linton Rd ME15 .....96 F4
Lion Ct CT14 .....117 C5
Lion Field ME15 .....62 B7
Lion Yd Faversham ME13 .....62 A6
　3 Sittingbourne ME10 .....36 F4
Lion's Rd TN28 .....202 A6
Lionard Ho 3 CT2 .....66 E1
Liphook Way ME16 .....74 C8
Lisa Ct CT5 .....21 A2
Lismore Cl ME15 .....97 D3
Lismore Rd Herne Bay CT6 .....23 D5
　Whitstable CT5 .....44 B8
Liss Rd CT13 .....93 A1
List The CT3 .....69 C2
Lister Cl 1 Deal CT14 .....117 C5
　Dover CT17 .....149 B1
Lister Ho CT9 .....29 A8
Lister Rd CT9 .....29 A8
Lister Way CT20 .....177 F3
Listmas Rd ME4 .....10 B3
Listways Cotts CT3 .....113 B6
Little Acres TN25 .....171 E7
Little Ave CT14 .....116 F3
Little Brook Rd TN23 .....139 A3
Little Buckland Ave
　ME16 .....74 D6
Little Charles St CT6 .....22 F5
Little Chequers TN25 .....123 E2
Little Copse Cl CT4 .....86 E1
Little Ct ME16 .....74 D2
Little Glovers ME15 .....36 F3
Little Groves Cvn & Chalet Pk
　ME12 .....6 F2
Little Groves Holiday Camp
　ME12 .....6 F2
Little Hempen TN23 .....155 D8
Little Hill TN30 .....167 B2
Little John Ave ME5 .....31 F2
Little Kit's Coty Ho ★
　ME20 .....53 C5
Little Knoll TN23 .....155 F8
Little Mdw CT2 .....65 E1
Little Orch ME17 .....96 D3
Little Paddocks CT5 .....44 D7
Little Robhurst TN26 .....167 D8
Little Stone Stile Cotts
　ME13 .....84 F4
Little Switzerland CT19 .....178 A8
Little Walton TN13 .....93 C3
Little York Mdws ME17 .....11 C4
Littlebourne Ave ME8 .....11 B4
Littlebourne CE Prim Sch
　CT3 .....89 F8
Littlebourne Rd
　Canterbury CT1,CT3 .....88 E8
　Maidstone ME14 .....75 C6
Littlebrook Cl TN23 .....139 A3
Littlefield Rd ME8 .....12 B2
Littlemead CT17 .....178 A7
Littlestone Ct TN28 .....202 E5
Littlestone Ho TN28 .....202 E5
Littlestone Rd TN28 .....202 D6
Liverpool Lawn 18 CT11 .....52 E6
Liverpool Rd CT14 .....117 D2
Livingstone Bldgs ME7 .....10 D5
Livingstone Circ ME7 .....10 D5
Livingstone Rd TN29 .....187 D4
Livingstone Rd
　Broadstairs CT10 .....29 E6
　Gillingham ME7 .....10 E5
Livingstone Wlk 6 ME15 .....97 F5
Lloyd Ct CT14 .....117 D7
Lloyd Rd CT10 .....30 A5
Lloyds Gn TN30 .....188 D4
Loading Bay App CT13 .....73 A8
Loaland Bsns Ctr ME2 .....9 D8
Lobelia Cl ME7 .....10 E6
Locarno Ave ME8 .....11 A2
Lock La ME14 .....53 D1
Lock St ME7 .....10 C5
Lockham Farm Ave
　ME17 .....97 D5
Lockholt Cl TN23 .....138 E3
Lockington Gr ME1 .....9 C5
Locksley Cl ME12 .....31 E2
Lockswood ME16 .....74 D7
Loddington La ME17 .....97 A1
Loder Cl ME17 .....101 B5
Lodge Field Rd CT5 .....21 D1
Lodge Rd ME4 .....75 D5
Lodge Wood Dr TN25 .....138 E5
Lomas Rd ME10,ME9 .....37 D4
Lombard St CT9 .....7 I3
Lombardy Cl ME7 .....33 A6
Lombardy Dr ME14 .....75 C5
London Pl 24 CT20 .....178 E5
London Rd Canterbury CT2 .....66 D1
　Deal CT14 .....117 B5

London Rd continued
　Dover CT16,CT17 .....149 B1
　Dunkirk ME13 .....64 E2
　Faversham ME13 .....62 B6
　Gillingham ME8 .....11 C1
　Hartlip ME8,ME9 .....34 D7
　Hythe CT21 .....175 F3
　Maidstone ME16 .....74 C6
　Newington ME9 .....35 A6
　Ramsgate CT11 .....52 B6
　Rochester ME1 .....9 A7
　Sittingbourne ME10 .....36 C4
　Temple Ewell CT15,CT16 .....148 B6
　Teynham ME9 .....38 C1
London Road (River)
　CT16,CT17 .....148 F4
London Road Temple Ewell
　CT16 .....148 D5
London Road Trad Est
　ME10 .....36 D4
London St CT20 .....178 E5
Londonderry Ho 15 ME15 .....97 E7
Lone Barn Rd ME17 .....102 B8
Lonefield TN26 .....155 B1
Long Acre Cl CT2 .....66 E2
Long Barrow The TN24 .....156 E6
Long Beech TN23 .....138 E1
Long Catlis Rd ME8 .....33 D4
Long Dr CT13 .....93 C2
Long Hill CT4 .....85 C1
Long La CT15 .....130 D7
Long Length TN23 .....155 D4
Long Mdw CT12 .....49 D6
Long Meadow Way CT2 .....67 A4
Long Reach Cl CT5 .....43 C6
Long Rock CT21 .....21 D3
Long Row TN25 .....157 D2
Long Wlk TN23 .....138 E4
Long's Acre TN25 .....123 E1
Longacre CT5 .....21 D1
Longacre Rd TN23 .....155 D7
Longage Hill CT18,CT4 .....144 A1
Longbridge TN24 .....140 B1
Longbridge Terr CT21 .....175 F1
Longdown Ho ME5 .....31 F6
Longfellow Rd ME7 .....10 C3
Longfield TN30 .....179 A6
Longfield Cl CT5 .....21 D2
Longfield Cl CT5 .....21 D2
Longfield Pl ME15 .....97 C8
Longfield Rd CT17 .....166 B7
Longfields Dr ME14 .....76 A5
Longford Cl ME8 .....34 A8
Longford Ct ME8 .....34 A8
Longford Terr 9 CT20 .....178 D4
Longford Way 10 CT20 .....178 D4
Longham Copse ME15 .....75 F1
Longhill Ave ME5 .....10 B3
Longhurst Dr ME5 .....31 F2
Longley Rd Gillingham ME8 .....11 F1
　Rochester ME1 .....9 C4
Longmarket 2 CT1 .....88 A8
Longmead Cl CT6 .....22 C3
Longmete Rd CT3 .....70 C5
Longmore Dr ME12 .....5 C1
Longparish Cl ME15 .....97 F6
Longport CT1 .....88 B8
Longridge ME10 .....37 B2
Longsfield TN25 .....173 A6
Longshaw Rd ME15 .....97 F5
Longtail Rise CT6 .....22 E2
Longtye Dr CT5 .....44 C7
Longwood ME5 .....32 B1
Lonsdale Ave CT9 .....8 C3
Lonsdale Ct CT16 .....149 D1
Lonsdale Dr
　Gillingham ME8 .....33 E7
　Herne Bay CT6 .....22 B5
　Sittingbourne ME10 .....36 C5
Lookers La CT21 .....176 B3
Loop Court Mews 9
　CT13 .....72 F1
Loop St CT13 .....72 F1
Loose Down Rd ME13 .....104 F7
Loose Inf & Jun Schs
　ME15 .....97 A6
Loose Rd ME15 .....97 A7
Lord Cornwallis Ct
　CT19 .....178 C8
Lord Romney's Hill ME14 .....75 F3
Lord Warden Ave CT14 .....117 D2
Lord Warden Ho CT17 .....166 D5
Lord Warden Sq CT17 .....166 D5
Lords Cl ME9 .....37 E2
Lords Cotts ME13 .....83 C4
Lords Wood Cl ME5 .....32 B2
Lords Wood La ME5 .....32 B3
Lordswood Ind Est ME5 .....54 C8
Lordswood Inf & Jun Sch
　ME5 .....32 B3
Lorenden Park Nature
　Reserve ★ ME13 .....61 F3
Lorenden Prep Sch ME13 .....61 E3
Lorien Flats TN24 .....139 D7
Lorimar Ct ME10 .....36 C7
Lorina Rd CT12 .....52 C8
Lorne Cotts CT14 .....117 C7
Lorne Rd
　Dover CT16,CT17 .....149 B2
　Ramsgate CT11 .....52 C6
Lorraine Ct 1 CT19 .....178 E6
Loudon Ct TN23 .....138 E3
Loudon Path TN23 .....138 E3
Loudon Way TN23 .....138 E3
Loughborough Ct 2
　CT11 .....52 E7
Louisville Ave ME7 .....10 D4
Lourdes Manor Cl TN25 .....159 D1

Love La Adisham CT3 .....90 F2
　12 Canterbury CT1 .....88 A8
　Faversham ME13 .....62 F6
　Margate CT9 .....7 I3
　Minster (Sheppey) ME12 .....4 D7
　Rochester ME1 .....9 C5
Love Street Cl CT6 .....22 C2
Lovelace Cl ME8 .....33 D4
Lovelace Ct TN26 .....153 C5
Lovell Rd
　Minster (Sheppey) ME12 .....4 A5
　Rough Common CT2 .....66 B3
Loves Holiday Camp ME12 .....6 F3
Lower Bannister Cotts
　ME9 .....36 B2
Lower Blackhouse Hill
　CT21 .....176 D3
Lower Bloors La ME8 .....11 E3
Lower Boxley Rd 10
　ME14 .....75 A5
Lower Bridge St CT1 .....88 A8
Lower Chantry La CT1 .....88 A8
Lower Denmark Rd
　TN23 .....156 C8
Lower Ensden Rd CT4 .....85 D4
Lower Fant Rd ME16 .....74 D2
Lower Gore La CT13 .....93 B3
Lower Halstow Prim Sch
　ME9 .....13 B2
Lower Hartlip Rd ME9 .....34 E5
Lower Herne Rd CT6 .....45 E8
Lower Lees Rd CT4 .....85 D2
Lower Mill La CT14 .....117 C5
Lower Northdown Ave
　CT9 .....8 B2
Lower Norton La ME9 .....39 A1
Lower Queens Rd TN24 .....139 C3
Lower Rainham Rd
　Gillingham ME7 .....11 D5
　Gillingham,Lower Rainham
　ME8 .....12 A3
Lower Rd
　East Farleigh ME15 .....96 B7
　Eastchurch ME12 .....5 B3
　Faversham ME13 .....61 C8
　Maidstone ME15 .....75 B3
　Minster (Sheppey) ME12 .....3 E4
　River CT17 .....148 E3
　Staple CT3 .....92 B6
　Stone in Oxney TN30 .....189 D5
　Temple Ewell CT16 .....148 D5
　Teynham ME9 .....38 B3
　Teynham,Lower Newlands
　ME9,ME13 .....38 E2
　Woodchurch TN26 .....169 B1
Lower Rd E CT16 .....166 H8
Lower Rd W CT16 .....166 G8
Lower Rowling Cotts
　CT3 .....92 B2
Lower Sandgate Rd
　CT20 .....178 C3
Lower Sands TN29 .....186 E2
Lower Santon La CT3 .....70 D7
Lower St Eastry CT13 .....93 B1
　Leeds ME17 .....99 A7
　Tilmanstone CT14 .....115 A2
Lower Stone St ME15 .....75 A3
Lower Tovil ME15 .....74 E2
Lower Twydall La ME7,
　ME8 .....11 C4
Lower Vicarage Rd
　TN24 .....139 D7
Lower Wall Rd
　Burmarsh CT21 .....186 D8
　Dymchurch CT21 .....187 A7
Lower Warren Rd ME20 .....53 E6
Lower Woodlands Rd
　ME7 .....11 A6
Lowfield Rd ME12 .....3 E6
Lowslip Hill CT15 .....165 A5
Lowther Rd CT17 .....166 B8
Loxwood Cl CT16 .....149 B1
Lubbock Cl ME15 .....97 E5
Lubbock Wlk ME8 .....33 D5
Lucerne Cl CT5 .....42 F6
Lucerne Dr CT5 .....42 F6
Lucerne La CT15 .....133 C2
Lucerne St ME14 .....75 A5
Lucilla Ave TN23 .....155 F4
Luckhurst Gdns CT9 .....8 E3
Luckhurst Rd
　Ashford TN24 .....157 A7
　Crabble CT17 .....148 E3
Luckley Ho TN25 .....123 E3
Lucknow Ct CT15 .....149 F3
Lucy Ave CT19 .....178 B7
Lucy's Hill CT21 .....176 B2
Luddenham Cl
　Ashford TN23 .....155 F6
　Maidstone ME14 .....75 C6
Luddenham Sch ME13 .....39 E1
Ludgate Rd ME9 .....59 F5
Lukes Cl CT17 .....149 B1
Lukin Ho CT21 .....175 F1
Lullingstone Cl ME7 .....33 B3
Lullingstone Cl 15 CT1 .....87 F8
Lullingstone Rd ME16 .....74 C7
Lumsden Terr 8 ME4 .....9 E4
Lushington Rd ME14 .....74 E7
Luton Ave CT10 .....29 F3
Luton Ct CT10 .....29 F3
Luton High St ME5 .....10 C2
Luton Inf Sch ME5 .....10 C2
Luton Jun Sch ME4 .....10 C2
Luton Rd
　Chatham ME4,ME5 .....10 B2
　Faversham ME13 .....62 F6
Lyall Way ME8 .....33 E4

Lychfield Dr ME2 .....9 A8
Lydbrook Cl ME10 .....36 D4
Lydd Airport TN29 .....206 A2
Lydd Prim Sch TN29 .....205 C6
Lydd Rd Chatham ME5 .....32 B5
　New Romney TN28,TN29 .....201 F4
Lydd Town Crossing
　TN29 .....205 D8
Lydd Town Mus ★ TN29 .....205 C6
Lydden Hill CT15 .....130 C1
Lydden International Motor
　Racing Circuit CT4 .....129 F3
Lydden Prim Sch CT15 .....147 F8
Lydia Rd CT14 .....117 A2
Lydos Cl TN29 .....206 C5
Lyeat Ct CT2 .....66 C4
Lyell Cl CT21 .....176 A1
Lyell Ct 5 CT7 .....26 F8
Lyell Rd CT7 .....26 F8
Lyle Cl ME2 .....9 A8
Lyle Ct ME5 .....74 C5
Lyminge CE Prim Sch
　CT18 .....161 C7
Lyminge Cl ME8 .....11 C2
Lyminge Way CT9 .....8 C1
Lymington Ct ME15 .....97 F4
Lymington Rd CT8 .....27 E7
Lympne Castle ★ CT21 .....174 F2
Lympne CE Prim Sch
　CT21 .....175 A3
Lympne Hill CT21 .....175 A4
Lympne Ind Pk CT21 .....174 E3
Lyn Ct CT20 .....178 A5
Lynacre CT2 .....66 C1
Lyndhurst Ave
　Gillingham ME8 .....33 C3
　Margate CT9 .....8 B2
Lyndhurst Cl CT2 .....66 C3
Lyndhurst Gr ME10 .....36 E2
Lyndhurst Rd
　Broadstairs CT10 .....30 A4
　Crabble CT17 .....148 E2
　Dymchurch TN29 .....195 C6
　Maidstone ME15 .....97 C8
　Ramsgate CT11 .....52 F8
Lyndon Way CT18 .....161 C7
Lyngate Ct CT9 .....8 D2
Lynmouth Dr ME12 .....4 C7
Lynstead Ho ME16 .....74 A1
Lynsted & Norton Prim Sch
　ME9 .....60 A7
Lynsted Cl TN23 .....155 F4
Lynsted La ME9 .....60 B7
Lynsted Rd Gillingham ME8 .....11 B3
　Halfway Houses ME12 .....3 B3
Lynton Court Mans CT9 .....8 B3
Lynton Dr ME5 .....32 B3
Lynton Pl CT4 .....89 A1
Lynton Rd CT21 .....176 C1
Lynwood CT19 .....178 C7
Lysander Cl
　Broadstairs CT10 .....29 C3
　Littlebourne CT3 .....89 E4
Lysander Wlk CT18 .....163 A4
Lytham Ave CT6 .....22 D1

M

Mabledon Ave TN24 .....139 D1
Mabledon Cl TN28 .....202 B6
Macdonald Par CT5 .....43 A6
Macdonald Rd
　Dover CT17 .....149 A1
　Gillingham ME7 .....10 D6
Mace Ind Est TN24 .....139 C3
Mace La TN24 .....139 C2
Mace Terr TN26 .....155 A1
Mackenders Cl ME20 .....53 A6
Mackenders Gn ME20 .....53 A6
Mackenders La ME20 .....53 A6
Mackenzie Dr CT20 .....177 E5
Mackeson Ct 8 CT21 .....176 B2
Macklands Ho ME8 .....12 A2
Macklands Way ME8 .....12 A2
Madden Ave ME5 .....31 E5
Madeira Ct CT20 .....178 B3
Madeira Rd
　Littlestone-on-Sea TN28 .....202 E6
　Margate CT9 .....8 A2
Madeira Wlk CT11 .....52 E6
Madginford Cl ME15 .....76 A2
Madginford Park Inf Sch
　ME15 .....76 A2
Madginford Park Jun Sch
　ME15 .....76 A2
Madginford Rd ME15 .....75 F2
Madras Ho 2 ME15 .....97 E5
Mafeking Rd ME5 .....31 F3
Magazine Rd TN24 .....139 B3
Magdala Rd
　Broadstairs CT10 .....29 E6
　Dover CT17 .....149 B1
Magdalen Cl ME7 .....33 C4
Magdalen Ct
　Broadstairs CT10 .....30 A6
　Canterbury CT1 .....88 B7
Magness Rd CT14 .....117 A2
Magnolia Ave
　Gillingham ME8 .....33 B5
　Margate CT9 .....8 D2
Magnolia Dr CT4 .....86 E1
Magnolia Ho 3 ME16 .....74 A3
Magnolia Rise CT6 .....23 D2
Magpie Ct ME12 .....4 A6
Magpie Hall Rd
　Chatham ME4 .....10 A2
　Stubb's Cross TN26 .....155 E2

Magpie La
Rhodes Minnis CT4 144 B3
Yelsted ME9,ME14 33 F1
Magpie Lodge 4 CT16 149 B2
Magwitch Cl ME1 9 B4
Maida Rd ME4 10 B2
Maiden La CT1 87 D6
Maidstone Barracks Sta ME16 74 E5
Maidstone East Sta ME14 74 F5
Maidstone Gram Sch ME15 75 B2
Maidstone Gram Sch for Girls ME16 74 E5
Maidstone Hospl The ME16 74 A4
Maidstone Ind Ctr ME14 74 F5
Maidstone L Ctr ME15 75 C2
Maidstone Mus & Bentlif Art Gallery★ ME14 74 F5
Maidstone Rd
Bredhurst ME7,ME8 33 B2
Charing TN25,TN26,TN27 120 D6
Chatham ME4 9 F2
Chatham,Walderslade ME5 31 D4
Danaway ME9 35 D4
Five Wents ME17 98 E2
Gillingham ME8 33 C6
Lenham ME17 101 D5
Potters Corner TN25,TN26 138 D7
Rochester ME1 9 C3
Maidstone St Michaels CE Jun Sch ME16 74 E3
Maidstone West Sta ME16 74 F3
Mailyns The ME8 33 D7
Main Gate Rd ME4 9 F7
Main Rd
Queenborough ME11,ME12 3 B5
Sellindge TN25 159 C1
Sheerness ME12 1 B3
Main St Iden TN31 197 B4
Peasmarsh TN31 196 B2
Maine Cl CT16 149 B3
Maison Des Fleurs ME16 74 C2
Maison Dieu★ ME13 62 A6
Maison Dieu Pl 4 CT16 166 D8
Maison Dieu Rd CT16 166 D8
Maitland Ct ME13 40 B1
Majestic Par CT20 178 C4
Major Cl CT5 43 B6
Makenade Ave ME13 62 E6
Malcolm Sargent Rd TN23 156 B5
Malden Dr ME14 75 A8
Malham Dr CT9 8 A1
Mall The ME13 62 C6
Mallard Apartments 14 ME15 97 E5
Mallard Cl CT6 22 E2
Mallard Cres ME9 14 D4
Mallard Ct ME12 4 A6
Mallards TN24 156 D7
Mallards Way ME15 76 A1
Malling Terr ME16 74 C4
Mallings Dr ME14 76 C4
Mallings La ME14 76 C4
Mallory Cl CT12 29 C2
Mallow Way 1 ME5 31 F4
Mallows The ME14 74 E7
Malmains Rd CT17 166 A6
Malmedy Ct CT14 117 A1
Malt House La TN30 179 A7
Malt Mews ME1 9 C5
Malta Ave ME5 32 A7
Malta Ho 17 CT1 67 B2
Malta Terr 5 ME14 75 A7
Malthouse Cl ME17 101 D5
Malthouse Cotts
Boughton Lees TN25 122 F4
New Romney TN28 202 A6
Malthouse Hill
10 Hythe CT21 176 B2
Maidstone ME15 96 F4
Malthouse La
Hamstreet TN26 170 D1
Peasmarsh TN31 196 D2
Malthouse Rd CT2 66 F2
Malthouse The ME16 96 A8
Malthouses The
Birchington CT7 26 F7
Brabourne TN25 159 B8
Maltings Bsns Pk The TN31 196 C2
Maltings Hall The CT11 52 D7
Maltings The
7 Canterbury,St Dunstan's CT2 66 E1
10 Canterbury,St Martin's CT1 88 A8
Deal CT14 134 B8
Faversham ME13 62 D8
Gillingham ME8 34 A8
Littlebourne CT3 89 F7
Loose ME17 97 B4
Maidstone, Grove Green ME14 75 E5
Peasmarsh TN31 196 C2
Malus Cl ME5 32 B1
Malvern Mdw CT16 148 E5
Malvern Pk CT6 23 D4
Malvern Rd
Ashford TN24 139 B4
Dover CT17 166 C7
Gillingham ME7 10 E3
Temple Ewell CT16 148 E5
Mamignot Cl ME14 76 A5
Manchester Cl ME5 32 C6
Manciple Cl CT2 87 C8
Mandarin La CT6 22 E2
Mandeville Ct 1 ME14 75 A5
Mandeville Rd CT2 66 E2
Mangers La CT16 149 A2
Mangers Pl CT16 149 A3
Mangravet Ave ME15 97 C7
Manktelow Ct CT10 29 F2
Manley Cl CT16 149 A7
Manley Ho CT16 149 A7
Mannering Cl CT17 148 F3
Mannock Ho 6 CT1 67 B1
Manns Hill CT4 127 A6
Manor Ave CT14 117 B4
Manor Cl Canterbury CT1 87 C5
Deal CT14 117 A4
Herne Bay CT6 23 F6
Maidstone ME14 76 B3
Rushenden ME11 3 A3
Manor Cotts
Hernhill ME13 64 B6
Langley ME17 98 C5
Manor Ct Canterbury CT1 87 F7
Gillingham ME7 11 C4
Maidstone ME14 76 B3
Manor Dr CT7 26 F6
Manor Farm Cl CT21 175 A4
Manor Gdns Chatham ME5 31 F4
Whitfield CT16 149 A8
Manor Gr ME10 36 D3
Manor Ho 14 ME7 10 A6
Manor Ho The
Canterbury CT2 66 F2
5 Folkestone CT20 178 B3
Sarre CT7 48 D6
Manor House Dr
Ashford TN23 156 D3
Maidstone ME16 74 D3
Manor La ME1 9 A2
Manor Lea Rd CT7 25 F1
Manor Leaze TN25 158 F5
Manor Mews CT14 133 F5
Manor Pound La TN25 158 F7
Manor Rd
3 Broadstairs CT10 30 A4
Chatham ME4 9 F4
Deal CT14 117 A4
Dover CT17 166 A6
Folkestone CT20 178 C4
Herne Bay CT6 23 F6
Lydd TN29 205 C6
Milstead ME9 58 F2
Rushenden ME11 3 A3
St Nicholas at Wade CT7 25 F1
Whitstable CT5 21 A2
Manor Rise Dover CT17 166 A6
Maidstone ME14 76 B3
Manor St ME7 10 A6
Manor Way Ashford TN23 138 F4
Leysdown-on-S ME12 6 H2
Warden ME12 6 D6
Manorfield Ashford TN23 155 E8
Elham CT4 144 F4
Manse Field TN25 158 E5
Mansel Dr ME1 9 A2
Mansell La CT15 146 B4
Mansfield Dr ME9 14 D3
Mansfield Wlk ME16 74 E2
Mansion Gdns CT16 149 A4
Mansion Row ME7 10 A6
Mansion St CT9 7 I3
Mansions The CT10 29 E4
Manston Court Cotts CT12 28 C2
Manston Court Rd CT12, CT9 28 D3
Manston Pk CT12 27 D2
Manston Rd
Acol CT12,CT7 27 D4
Margate CT12,CT9 28 C4
Ramsgate CT11,CT12 52 A8
Mansum Ct CT7 25 F2
Mantles Hill CT14 116 D1
Manwood Almshouse CT2 66 F3
Manwood Ave CT2 66 F3
Manwood Cl ME10 36 F2
Manwood Rd CT13 94 A8
Maple Ave Gillingham ME7 10 E6
Maidstone ME16 74 C6
Maple Cl Ashford TN23 138 E3
Broadstairs CT10 8 E1
Rough Common CT2 66 B3
Maple Ct CT3 68 E8
Maple Dr Hawkinge CT18 163 C5
St Mary's Bay TN29 194 F4
Maple Gdns CT3 68 E8
Maple St ME12 1 D1
Maplefields Gdns CT18 163 C5
Maples The
Broadstairs CT10 29 D4
Minster (Sheppey) ME12 4 B6
Maplesden Noakes Sch The ME16 74 E6
Maplins Cl 5 ME8 11 F1
Mara Ct ME4 9 F1
Marathon Paddock ME7 10 D4
Marc Brunel Way ME4 10 A7
Marconi Way ME1 31 D7
Marcroft CT10 30 B7
Mardale Cl ME8 12 A1
Marden Ave CT12 52 B8
Mardol Rd TN24 139 C5
Maresfield Cl CT16 149 B2
Margaret Ct CT6 22 F4
Margaret St 10 CT20 178 E5
Margate Caves★ CT9 7 J3
Margate Cl ME7 10 E6
Margate Hill CT7 27 C4
Margate Rd
Herne Bay CT6 23 C3
Herne Bay,Broomfield CT6 23 D2
Ramsgate CT10,CT12,CT11 29 B3
Margate Sta CT9 7 H2
Marian Ave ME12 4 A7
Marigold Way ME16 74 A3
Marilyn Cres CT7 27 B7
Marina Ct Deal CT14 117 D8
Hythe CT21 176 C1
Marina Dr ME12 4 A7
Marina Espl CT11 52 F7
Marina Rd CT11 52 F7
Marina The CT14 117 D8
Marine Ave TN29 186 F3
Marine Cres
7 Folkestone CT20 178 D4
Whitstable CT5 21 B3
Marine Ct 15 Dover CT16 166 E7
Whitstable CT5 20 F3
Marine Dr Broadstairs CT10 8 G3
Margate CT9 7 I2
Marine Gap CT5 20 C1
Marine Gdns CT9 7 I2
Marine Ho CT5 20 F3
Marine Hts CT8 7 D1
Marine Par Dover CT16 166 E7
Folkestone CT20 178 E4
Hythe CT21 176 C1
Littlestone-on-Sea TN28 202 E5
Sheerness ME12 1 F2
Whitstable CT5 21 A3
Marine Parade Mews CT20 178 E4
Marine Point CT20 178 A3
Marine Rd CT14 117 D4
Marine Terr
Folkestone CT20 178 E4
Margate CT9 7 H2
Whitstable CT5 20 C1
Marine Walk St CT21 176 C2
Mariners Ct CT5 43 D8
Mariners Lea CT10 29 D4
Mariners Lee CT5 20 E3
Mariners The ME1 9 B4
Mariners View ME7 10 F7
Marion Cl ME5 32 A2
Marion Cres ME15 97 B8
Maritime Ave CT6 23 C4
Maritime Cl ME2 9 D8
Maritime Est ME2 9 D8
Maritime Pl CT14 117 D7
Maritime Way ME4 10 A8
Marjan Cl CT17 149 A1
Mark Ave CT11 52 B5
Mark St ME4 10 A2
Market Bldgs 4 ME14 74 F4
Market Colonnade 3 ME14 74 F4
Market Hill CT21 176 C2
Market La 12 TN23 139 B2
Market Pl Aylesham CT3 112 F5
Charing TN27 120 C7
1 Faversham ME13 62 D7
20 Folkestone CT20 178 D5
Margate CT9 7 I3
Market Sq 12 CT16,CT17 166 D7
Market St
Deal CT14 117 D6
Faversham ME13 62 D7
Herne Bay CT6 22 F5
Margate CT9 7 I3
Sandwich CT13 73 A1
Market View CT3 112 F5
Market Way CT2 67 A2
Markland Rd CT17 165 F7
Marlborough Cl
Broadstairs CT10 29 E3
Littlestone-on-Sea TN28 202 D6
Marlborough Ct
Folkestone CT20 178 B4
Hythe CT21 176 D1
Marlborough Ho
4 Gillingham ME8 33 F8
Margate CT9 8 C3
Marlborough Rd
Deal CT14 117 A2
Dover CT17 165 F7
Gillingham ME7 10 B5
Margate CT9 7 I1
6 Ramsgate CT11 52 D6
Whitstable CT5 43 D5
Marlborough Road Ind Est CT14 117 A3
Marlborough Way TN24 139 F7
Marler Rd CT19 177 E6
Marley Ct CT2 66 C4
Marley La Chislet CT3 47 A5
Finglesham CT14 116 A8
Kingston CT4 111 B1
Marley Rd ME17 100 F6
Marley Way ME1 9 C2
Marlow Cl CT5 21 B1
Marlow Copse ME5 31 F1
Marlow Ho CT7 27 B7
Marlow Mdws CT2 67 F5
Marlowe Arc 11 CT1 87 F8
Marlowe Ave CT1 87 F8
Marlowe Ct 13 CT1 87 F8
Marlowe Rd
Ashford TN23 139 B2
Dover CT16 149 B3
Margate CT9 29 C8
Marlpit Cotts ME17 97 E2
Marmion Way TN23 155 C8
Marquis Dr ME7 33 B3
Marr Cl ME12 3 F7
Marrians View 1 ME5 10 C2
Marrose Ave CT12 29 B3
Marrowbone Hill ME12 5 B5
Marsh Cres TN28 202 B6
Marsh Farm Rd CT12 50 B4
Marsh La Deal CT14 117 A7
Teynham Street ME9 39 A4
Marsh Rd TN26 183 F6
Marsh Rise ME10 15 A1
Marsh St ME2 9 B7
Marsh View CT21 187 C8
Marshall Cres
Broadstairs CT10 29 E4
Rushenden ME11 2 F3
Marshall Rd ME8 33 C8
Marshall St CT19 178 E7
Marshalls Land TN30 167 A3
Marsham Cres ME17 98 B1
Marsham St ME14 75 A4
Marshborough Rd CT13 93 B7
Marshlands TN29 195 B7
Marshlands Cl TN29 195 B7
Marshwood Cl CT1 67 C3
Marstan Cl ME9 12 E2
Marston Cl ME5 31 E3
Marston Dr ME14 75 C5
Marston Wlk ME5 31 E3
Martello Cotts CT21 187 E8
Martello Dr CT21 175 F1
Martello Ind Ctr CT19 178 F6
Martello Rd
Folkestone CT20 178 E6
Folkestone, Sandgate CT20 177 E3
Martello Terr 1 CT20 177 F3
Martello Tower Mus TN29 195 C7
Martello Tower Visitor Ctr★ CT19 178 A6
Martello Twr★ TN29 195 C7
Marten Rd CT20 178 B5
Martha Cl CT19 178 B7
Martin Ct ME7 33 A3
Martin Dale Cres CT15 133 C2
Martin Ho TN25 123 E2
Martin Mill Sta CT15 133 C2
Martin Rd ME2 9 B8
Martin's Cl CT12 29 C2
Martin's Way CT21 187 D8
Martindale Cl CT1 88 A7
Martindown Rd CT5 43 C7
Martins Cl TN30 179 C8
Martins The TN26 168 A8
Martyrs' Field Rd CT1 87 F7
Mary Ct ME4 10 A2
Mary Green Wlk 5 CT1 67 B2
Mary Hougham Almshouses CT14 117 D7
Mary Rd CT14 117 A3
Maryland Ct
Gillingham ME8 33 E5
Hythe CT21 176 D3
Maryland Gr CT1 88 C6
Mason's Rise CT10 30 A5
Masons Rd CT17 149 B1
Matfield Cres ME14 75 C5
Matilda Cl ME8 33 B8
Matthew's Pl 9 CT16 149 C1
Matthews Cl CT14 117 C6
Matthews Rd CT6 22 C2
Mattinson Pl ME9 78 F7
Matts Hill Rd ME9 33 E2
Maugham Ct CT5 43 D8
Maundene Sch ME5 32 B5
Maunders Cl ME5 32 C8
Maunsell Pl TN24 156 D7
Maurice Ct CT9 8 B3
Maxine Gdns CT10 29 F5
Maxted Ct CT6 23 C4
Maxton Cl Dover CT17 166 A6
Maidstone ME14 75 F5
Maxton Ct CT17 166 A6
Maxton Rd CT17 166 A6
Maxwell Dr ME16 74 B6
Maxwell Pl CT14 117 C4
Maxwell Rd ME7 10 A6
May Lodge CT14 117 D5
May Rd Gillingham ME7 10 C4
Rochester ME1 9 C3
May St CT6 23 F4
May Terr 2 ME7 10 A7
Maybrook Ind Est CT1 67 D4
Maydowns Rd CT5 21 D2
Mayers Rd CT14 117 A1
Mayfair 2 ME2 9 C8
Mayfair Ave ME15 97 A8
Mayfield Ave CT16 149 C2
Mayfield Cl Chatham ME5 32 A1
Gillingham ME8 11 E2
Mayfield Ct 3 CT16 149 B2
Mayfield Gdns CT16 149 C2
Mayfield Rd
Herne Bay CT6 23 A3
Lyminge CT18 161 C6
Whitfield CT16 149 A7
Mayflower Ho ME1 9 B4
Mayfly Dr CT18 163 A4
Mayford Rd ME5 32 D2
Mayforth Gdns CT11 52 B6
Mayhew Cl TN23 156 A8
Maylam Gdns ME10 36 B4
Maymills Cotts CT13 93 B2
Maynard & Cotton's Spital 9 CT1 87 F8
Maynard Ave CT9 28 B8
Maynard Pl ME5 10 D2
Maynard Rd CT1 87 E7
Mayor's Pl 11 TN30 179 A7
Maypits TN23 155 F8
Maypole La CT3 46 E6
Maypole Rd CT3 46 E6
Mays Rd 3 CT11 52 C6
Maystreet Cross CT6 23 F3
Mayton La CT2 45 C1
Maytree Cotts CT14 133 D8
Mayville Rd CT10 29 E6
Mayweed Ave ME5 31 E4
Mc Kenzie Rd ME5 32 A3
McAlpine Cres ME15 96 F3
McCarthy Ave CT2 67 F7
McClean Wlk ME12 17 C8
McCudden Row 8 ME7 10 A6
McKinlay Ct CT7 26 D8
Mead Gn ME5 32 C3
Mead Rd Ashford TN24 156 E7
Folkestone CT19 178 D6
Mead Way CT2 66 E1
Mead Wlk TN23 155 E8
Meade The CT18 162 F4
Meadow Bank ME13 61 F2
Meadow Brook Ct CT20 177 E4
Meadow Cl Bridge CT4 89 A1
Chatham ME5 31 F5
Chilham CT4 107 E8
Hawkinge CT18 163 B4
Herne Bay CT6 23 C4
Iwade ME9 14 D4
Meadow Cotts
East Studdal CT15 132 D8
Goodnestone CT3 92 A2
Meadow Ct Margate CT9 29 B8
Westenhanger CT21 175 B6
Meadow Dr CT5 44 D8
Meadow Gr TN25 174 D8
Meadow Hill Cotts CT15 147 D1
Meadow Ho ME9 36 B2
Meadow Rd
Ashford TN23 139 A4
Canterbury CT2 66 C2
Margate CT9 7 F1
Sturry CT2 67 F6
Meadow Rise ME9 14 D4
Meadow View
Hothfield TN26 138 A6
Monkton CT12 49 D6
Meadow View Ind Est TN26 183 C7
Meadow View Rd
Maidstone ME17 97 B3
Shepherdswell CT15 130 E5
Meadow Way
Eythorne CT15 131 C8
Hythe CT21 187 D8
Meadow Wlk
Maidstone ME15 75 B3
Whitstable CT5 43 C6
Meadowbank Rd ME4 10 A4
Meadowbrook CT20 177 E4
Meadowbrook Cl TN24 139 D6
Meadowbrook Rd TN24 139 D6
Meadowdown ME14 75 E4
Meadowdown Cl ME7 33 A4
Meadows The
Herne Bay CT6 23 D2
3 Maidstone ME15 74 E2
New Romney TN28 202 C6
Sittingbourne ME10 36 F2
Wittersham TN30 188 D4
Meadowsweet Ho TN23 138 F1
Meads Ave The ME10 36 D7
Meads Way TN29 194 E3
Meadside Wlk ME5 31 F6
Meadway CT17 148 E3
Medina Ave CT5 43 B7
Medlar Cl ME9 58 A6
Medlar Gr ME7 33 A4
Medlars The ME14 75 D6
Medway City Est ME2 9 D7
Medway Cl ME10 36 D4
Medway Com Coll ME4 10 A1
Medway Ent Ctr ME2 9 D8
Medway Gdns ME4 9 F7
Medway Heritage Ctr★ ME4 9 F5
Medway Ho 7 ME14 74 F4
Medway Hts 5 ME4 9 E4
Medway Maritime Hospl ME7 10 B4
Medway Rd
Gillingham ME7 10 C7
Sheerness ME12 1 C1
Medway St Chatham ME4 9 F5
Maidstone ME14 74 F4
Medway Trad Est ME16 74 F3
Medway Villas ME15 96 B7
Meehan Rd TN28 202 E4
Meehan Rd S TN28 202 E3
Meeres Court La ME10 37 C5
Meeson's Cl ME13 81 E6
Meeting Ct CT9 7 I3
Meeting House La 2 ME4 9 F4
Meeting St CT11 52 E7
Megan Cl TN29 205 D7
Megby Cl ME8 33 D6
Meggett La CT15 164 C7
Megone Cl CT18 163 A4
Meirs Court Rd ME8 33 E6
Melbourne Ave
Dover CT16 149 C4
Ramsgate CT12 29 B1
Melbourne Com Prim Sch CT16 149 C4

Melbourne Rd ME4 10 A3
Melbury Mews TN28 202 C8
Melford Dr ME16 74 C4
Mellanby Cl CT7 27 A6
Mellor Row ME10 14 F1
Melody Cl Gillingham ME8 33 C4
Warden ME12 6 E4
Melon La TN26,TN29 193 B6
Melrose Cl ME15 97 A7
Melsetter Cl CT7 27 B7
Melville Ct ME4 9 F6
Melville Lea CT13 93 C7
Melville Rd ME15 75 A3
Memorial (General) Hospl ME10 36 F3
Mendfield St 5 ME13 62 C7
Mendip Rise TN24 139 B4
Menin Rd ME10 14 F1
Mentmore Ho CT12 29 C3
Mentmore Rd CT12 29 C3
Menzies Ave CT14 117 B1
Menzies Ct ME12 4 A5
Menzies Rd CT16 149 A5
Mercer Dr ME17 100 F6
Mercer Way ME17 98 B1
Mercery La 5 CT1 87 F8
Merchant Store The 7 CT2 66 F1
Merchants Way CT2 87 C8
Mercury Cl ME1 9 A3
Mere Gate CT9 7 I1
Meredale Sch ME8 12 A1
Meredith Cl ME17 98 F7
Meresborough Cotts ME8 33 F5
Meresborough La ME8, ME9 34 B5
Meresborough Rd ME8 34 A7
Mereworth Cl ME8 11 A3
Meriden Wlk CT18 161 D3
Meridian Ct
Ashford TN23 155 E7
Maidstone ME16 74 E4
Meridian Pk ME2 9 E6
Merino Way TN23 155 E5
Merivale Gr ME5 32 B4
Merleburgh Dr ME10 36 F8
Merlin Cl ME10 37 A3
Merlin Ho Chatham ME4 10 B8
2 Sittingbourne ME10 37 A4
Mermaid Cl ME5 32 A6
Merritt Rd TN28 202 E2
Merrivale Hts CT10 30 A2
Merrywood Gr CT6 23 D2
Mersham Prim Sch TN25 157 E3
Merton Cl ME5 32 C5
Merton La CT4 87 F4
Merton Rd ME15 75 F2
Meryl Gdns CT14 117 C1
Metcalfe Mews 1 CT1 67 B2
Meteor Ave CT5 43 B7
Meteor Cl ME10 36 E8
Metropole Ct 2 CT20 178 B3
Metropole Rd E CT20 178 B3
Metropole Rd W CT20 178 B3
Metropole The 3 CT20 178 B3
Meverall Ave CT12 51 E5
Mews The
1 Maidstone ME16 74 E5
Sittingbourne ME10 36 F2
Meyrick Rd ME12 1 D2
Micawber Cl ME5 32 A1
Michael Ave CT11 52 G8
Michelle Gdns CT9 28 A8
Micketts Gdns ME10 36 B4
Mickleburgh Ave CT6 23 B4
Mickleburgh Hill CT6 23 B4
Mid Kent Coll (City Way Ctr) ME1 9 D4
Mid Kent Coll of H & F Ed ME16 74 C3
Mid Kent Coll of Higher & F Ed ME5 31 E6
Mid Kent Sh Ctr The ME16 74 C7
Middelburg Ho CT19 177 D6
Middelburg Sq CT20 178 D4
Middle Cl TN23 138 C1
Middle Deal Rd CT14 117 B5
Middle Mead CT19 178 B7
Middle Row
Ashford TN23 139 C2
2 Faversham ME13 62 D7
6 Maidstone ME14 74 F4
Middle St Ashford TN23 139 B2
4 Chatham ME7 10 A6
Deal CT14 117 D6
Middle Wall CT5 20 D2
Middle Way ME10 37 B3
Middlefields ME8 34 A8
Middlesex Rd ME15 97 D7
Middleton Cl ME8 33 E4
Middleton Cotts TN25 122 E3
Middleton Ct 9 ME10 36 E4
Middletune Ave ME10 36 E7
Midhurst Ct ME15 75 A3
Midley Cl ME16 74 C7
Midsummer Hill TN24 139 D6
Miers Court Prim Sch ME8 33 F7
Mierscourt Cl ME8 34 A8
Mierscourt Rd ME8 33 E6
Mikyle Ct CT1 88 A6
Milbourne Gr ME10 36 E7
Milburn Rd ME7 10 C7
Mildred Cotts CT19 177 F7
Mile Rd CT12 48 F6
Miles Ct CT3 91 A8
Miles Pl ME1 9 D3
Miles Way CT7 26 F7
Milestone Cl CT19 178 A7
Milestone Rd CT14 117 B5
Milford Cl ME16 74 D5
Military Rd
Canterbury CT1 67 A1
Chatham ME4 9 F5
2 Dover CT17 166 D7
Folkestone CT20 177 E4
Houghton Green TN31 197 E3
Hythe CT21 176 B2
Ramsgate CT11 52 E6
Stone in Oxney TN26,TN30 190 B4
Mill Bank TN29 205 B6
Mill Bank Cotts CT13 93 A2
Mill Bay CT20 178 E5
Mill Cl Crabble CT17 148 F2
Lenham ME17 101 C4
Sandwich CT13 72 E2
Wickhambreaux CT3 69 C2
Mill Cotts
Queenborough ME11 3 A5
Ramsgate CT11 52 D6
Worth CT14 94 A4
Mill Court Cl CT6 23 B2
Mill Ct Ashford TN24 139 D2
Sittingbourne ME10 37 A3
Mill Field Ash CT3 71 E1
Broadstairs CT10 29 F5
Mill Fields Rd CT21 175 F2
Mill Gn CT13 93 A2
Mill Hamlet CT3 69 C2
Mill Hill CT14 117 A3
Mill Ho CT17 148 F3
Mill La Ashford TN24 140 A1
Birchington CT7 26 F6
Bonnington TN25 172 E5
Bridge CT4 88 F1
Canterbury CT1 66 F1
Canterbury,Harbledown CT2 87 C8
Chatham,Bluebell Hill ME5 31 D1
Chatham,Luton ME5 10 C1
Chilham CT4 107 D7
Coxheath ME17 96 D4
10 Dover CT16 166 E7
Eastry CT13 93 B2
Hartlip ME9 34 E6
Hawkinge CT18 163 B5
Herne Bay CT6 23 B2
Lydd TN29 205 D7
Lynsted ME9 60 C5
Maidstone ME14 74 F6
Margate CT9 7 I2
Newchurch TN29 184 F3
Nonington CT15 113 F4
Northbourne CT14 115 F4
Preston CT3 70 D6
Shepherdswell CT15 130 F5
Smarden TN27 135 A2
Stelling Minnis CT4 126 F2
Tenterden TN30 167 B1
Whitfield CT16 149 A8
Worth CT14 94 A4
Mill Lane Cotts CT14 116 A4
Mill Mews CT14 117 B4
Mill Pl ME13 62 D8
Mill Race CT17 148 F3
Mill Rd Bethersden TN26 153 E5
Bramling CT3 90 E6
Deal CT14 117 C4
Dymchurch TN29 195 B7
Gillingham ME7 10 C6
Hoath CT3 46 F5
Hythe CT21 176 D2
Lydd TN29 205 D7
Rochester ME2 9 B8
Staple CT3 92 B5
Sturry CT2 67 F5
Mill Row CT7 26 F6
Mill St Maidstone ME15 74 F4
Maidstone,Loose ME15 96 F5
Sittingbourne ME10 36 E5
Temple Ewell CT16 148 D5
Mill Terr Bridge CT4 88 F1
Chartham CT4 86 D3
Mill View Ashford TN24 156 F8
Woodchurch TN26 169 A3
Mill View Rd CT6 23 A1
Mill Wall Pl CT13 94 A8
Mill Way ME10 36 F6
Mill Wlk ME16 74 A3
Millais Rd CT16 149 C1
Millbank La TN29 200 E7
Millbank Rd TN23 155 F5
Millbrook CT21 176 D2
Millbrook Cl ME15 74 F1
Millbrook Mdw TN23 138 E1
Milldale Cl CT14 117 B4
Millen Rd ME10 36 E5
Millen's Row ME13 83 B3
Millenium Terr CT1 87 C6
Millennium Way
Broadstairs CT10 29 C4
Sheerness ME12 1 C2
Miller Ave CT2 87 D8
Miller Cl Ashford TN24 139 D2
Deal CT14 117 C8
Sittingbourne ME10 37 A8
Miller Cotts TN24 139 D2
Miller Ct ME12 4 A5
Millers Ct Ramsgate CT12 29 B1
Whitstable CT5 43 D7
Millers La CT12 49 C7
Millers Wharf 1 ME15 74 E2
Millers Yd CT1 87 E7
Millfield Ashford TN23 155 D8
Folkestone CT20 178 D5
Hawkinge CT18 163 C5
High Halden TN26 167 D7
Sittingbourne ME10 37 A3
St Margaret's at Cliffe CT15 150 F7
Millfield Cl CT18 163 B5
Millfield Manor CT5 20 E1
Millfield Rd
Faversham ME13 62 E7
Ramsgate CT12 29 B3
Millfields Chatham ME5 32 D2
Shepherdswell CT15 130 E4
Millmead Ave CT9 8 D1
Millmead Gdns CT9 8 D1
Millmead Rd CT9 8 C1
Millpond Cl ME2 9 B8
Mills Cl ME12 3 F6
Mills Terr ME4 10 A3
Millstock Terr 2 ME15 74 E2
Millstream Cl
Faversham ME13 62 C7
Whitstable CT5 20 E1
Millstream Cotts CT5 43 E8
Millstream Gn TN24 156 F7
Millstrood Rd CT5 43 E8
Millwood Ct 4 ME4 9 F4
Millyard Way CT15 114 D1
Milne Rd TN24 156 F8
Milner Cl CT15 114 B1
Milner Cres CT3 112 E5
Milner La CT2 67 F5
Milner Rd Elvington CT15 114 B1
Gillingham ME7 10 D7
Whitstable CT5 43 A6
Milners ME17 98 F6
Milstead & Frinstead CE Prim Sch ME9 58 E1
Milstead Cl
Maidstone ME14 75 C5
West Minst ME12 3 B7
Milsted Rd ME8 11 C3
Milton Ave CT9 7 J1
Milton Cl Canterbury CT1 88 C6
Dover CT16 149 B4
Milton Court Prim Sch ME10 36 E6
Milton Rd Ashford TN23 139 B2
Canterbury CT1 88 A6
Dover CT16 149 B4
Gillingham ME7 10 C3
Sittingbourne ME10 36 E4
Milton Regis Halt ME10 37 A6
Milton Sq 4 CT9 7 J1
Milton St ME16 74 C2
Mincers Cl ME5 32 C2
Miners Way CT3 113 A5
Minerva Ave CT16 149 C2
Minerva Ho 4 CT11 52 D7
Minerva Rd ME2 9 A8
Minnis Field CT4 126 E2
Minnis Gn CT4 126 E2
Minnis La CT15,CT17 148 C2
Minnis Rd CT7 26 E7
Minnis Terr CT17 149 A2
Minnis Way CT14 94 B5
Minster Abbey★ ME12 4 D6
Minster Abbey★ CT12 50 C5
Minster Agriculture & Rural Life Mus★ CT12 50 C5
Minster CE Prim Sch CT12 50 B5
Minster Cl CT10 30 A2
Minster Coll ME12 3 F6
Minster Dr Herne Bay CT6 22 D4
Minster (Sheppey) ME12 4 B8
Minster Gatehouse Mus★ ME12 4 D6
Minster Lodge 4 CT11 52 C6
Minster Rd Acol CT12,CT7 27 C2
Faversham ME13 62 E7
Gillingham ME8 11 C3
Minster (Sheppey) ME12 4 B6
Ramsgate CT11 52 B5
Westgate-on-S CT8 27 F7
Minster Sta CT12 50 C5
Minster-in-Sheppey Prim Sch ME12 4 C7
Mint The CT2 66 C1
Mintching Wood La ME9 58 F2
Minter Ave CT18 162 F7
Minter Cl CT18 162 F7
Minterne Ave ME10 36 D2
Minterne Com Jun Sch ME10 36 D2
Minters Ind Est CT14 117 B6
Miranda Ct ME12 1 C1
Misling La CT4 143 C7
Missenden Ct 6 CT20 178 D5
Mitcham Rd TN29 195 C8
Mitchell Ave Chatham ME4 9 F2
Hawkinge CT18 163 B5
Mitchell Cl ME17 101 C5
Mitchell St CT19 177 D6
Mitre Rd ME1 9 B4
Mittell Ct TN29 205 B6
Moat Farm Cl CT19 178 C7
Moat Farm Rd CT19 178 C7
Moat Ho Canterbury CT1 87 F7
Charing TN27 120 C7
Moat La Ash CT3 71 E1
Fordwich CT2 68 A3
Rough Common CT2 66 B4
Moat Pk TN27 120 C6
Moat Sole CT13 72 F1
Moat The TN27 120 C7
Moat Way ME11 3 A5
Moatfield Mdw TN23 156 B4
Mock La TN23 155 B6
Mockett Ct 4 ME10 36 E4
Mockett Dr CT10 29 F7
Molehill Cnr CT5 44 D8
Molehill Copse Prim Sch ME15 97 D7
Molehill Rd Herne Bay CT6 22 A1
Whitstable CT5,CT6 44 E8
Molineux Rd CT12 50 B6
Molland Cl CT3 71 C2
Molland La
Ash,Guilton CT3 71 C2
Ash,Paramour Street CT3 71 D6
Molland Lea CT3 71 C2
Molloy Rd TN26 155 B1
Monarch Cl ME5 32 A6
Monastery Ave CT16 149 E1
Monastery St CT1 88 A8
Monckton's Ave ME14 74 F7
Monckton's Dr ME14 74 E7
Monckton's La ME14 74 F7
Moncrif Cl ME14 76 B4
Mongeham Church Cl CT14 116 D3
Mongeham Prim Sch CT14 116 F4
Mongeham Rd CT14 116 E3
Mongeham View CT14 116 E4
Monica Cl ME13 84 E6
Monins Rd Dover CT17 166 B7
Iwade ME9 14 D3
Monkdown ME15 76 A1
Monkery La TN25,TN27 104 D2
Monks Cl Canterbury CT2 67 A2
Faversham ME13 62 B8
Monks Hill Cotts TN26 182 E6
Monks Way CT16 149 A3
Monks Wlk TN27 120 C7
Monkshill Rd ME13 42 B2
Monkton CE Prim Sch CT12 49 D7
Monkton Court La CT15 131 D7
Monkton Gdns CT9 8 E3
Monkton Manor CT12 49 C7
Monkton Pl CT11 52 D7
Monkton Rd CT12 50 A6
Monkton Rdbt CT12 49 D8
Monkton St CT12 49 D7
Monkwood Cl ME1 31 B8
Monmouth Cl ME8 11 D2
Mons Ct ME10 14 F1
Montacue Ct CT20 178 B4
Montague Ct ME12 1 C1
Montague Rd CT11 52 E8
Montague St CT6 22 D5
Montefiore Ave
Broadstairs CT10 30 A1
Ramsgate CT11 29 F1
Montefiore Cotts CT11 52 F8
Montfort Cl
Ashford TN23 155 F7
Canterbury CT2 67 A4
Montfort Rd Chatham ME5 31 F2
Rochester ME2 9 A8
Montgomery Ave ME5 32 A7
Montgomery Rd ME7 10 C3
Montgomery Sch CT2 68 C8
Montgomery Way CT19 178 E8
Montpelier Ave CT5 43 D6
Montpelier Bsns Pk TN23 138 F1
Montpelier Gate ME16 74 B5
Montreal Cl 8 CT16 149 B3
Montrose Ave ME5 10 E2
Monument Way TN24 156 F5
Moon Hill CT15 130 E4
Moonfleet Cl ME10 15 A1
Moonstone Dr ME5 32 B2
Moonstone Sq ME10 36 D6
Moor La Ivychurch TN29 192 D4
Woodchurch TN26 180 E6
Moor Park Cl ME8 34 A8
Moor St ME8 34 B8
Moore Cl TN29 192 A3
Moore St ME2 9 A8
Moorfield CT2 66 F4
Mooring Rd ME1 9 D1
Moorings The ME9 38 E6
Moorland Rd CT15 130 E4
Moorstock La TN25 159 C2
Moorwell Dr CT15 130 D5
Moray Ave CT7 26 F8
Mordaunt Ave CT8 27 E8
Morden St ME1 9 C4
Morehall Ave CT19 177 F6
Morehall Prim Sch CT19 177 F6
Morella Wlk ME17 101 C5
Morello Cl ME9 38 C2
Moreton Ct CT14 117 C2
Moreton Terr TN26 155 A1
Morgan Kirby's Gdn ME13 83 D5
Morgan Rd ME2 9 A8
Morris Ave CT6 21 F4
Morris Cl ME17 97 D5
Morris Court Cl ME9 37 D2
Morrison Rd CT20 178 E6
Morry La ME17 99 D1
Mortimer Cl TN23 156 B7
Mortimer Rd CT16 166 F8
Mortimer St CT6 22 F5
Morton Cl ME15 97 D6
Moss End Mews CT11 29 E2
Mossbank ME5 32 A3
Mossy Glade ME8 33 E6
Mostyn Rd ME14 75 C4
Mote Ave ME15 75 B3
Mote Hall Villas ME14 76 C4
Mote Pk ME15 75 D2
Mote Rd ME15 75 A3
Motney Hill Rd ME8 12 A4
Mouat Ct ME5 32 A3
Mount Castle La ME17 101 F1
Mount Charles Wlk CT4 88 F1
Mount Dr ME14 76 B4
Mount Ephraim★ ME13 64 A4
Mount Field
Faversham ME13 62 B6
Queenborough ME11 3 A5
Mount Green Ave CT12 51 D5
Mount La Hartlip ME9 34 D4
Maidstone ME14 76 B4
Mount Lodge ME1 9 B2
Mount Pleasant
Aldington TN25 173 A6
Blean CT2 66 A6
Chatham ME5 10 B3
Faversham ME13 40 B2
Forstal ME20 53 A3
Kingsdown CT14 134 D5
Minster (Thanet) CT12 50 C8
Tenterden TN30 179 C8
Mount Pleasant Cl CT18 161 C7
Mount Pleasant Dr ME14 76 A5
Mount Pleasant Rd 4 CT20 178 D5
Mount Pleasant Terr ME17 100 E2
Mount Rd Canterbury CT1 88 C6
Chatham ME4 9 F3
Dover CT17 166 A6
Rochester ME1 9 B2
Mount St CT21 176 C2
Mount View ME13 62 A5
Mount View Ct 3 ME4 9 F3
Mount View Rd CT6 23 A2
Mountain St CT4 107 B6
Mountbatten Ave ME5 32 A7
Mountbatten Ho CT14 117 D3
Mountbatten Way TN25 158 E6
Mountfield Rd TN28 202 C6
Mountfield Way CT8 27 D6
Mounts Cl CT14 117 A5
Mounts View TN23 138 F4
Mountsfield Cl ME16 74 D5
Mountview ME9 36 B2
Moyes Cl CT12 51 D5
Moyle Cl ME8 33 D4
Mozart Ct ME4 9 E3
Muddy Bush Cnr CT3 90 F2
Muddy La ME10 37 B2
Muir Rd
Maidstone ME15 75 A2
Ramsgate CT11 52 F8
Mulberry Cl
Gillingham ME7 33 A4
Ramsgate CT11 52 F8
Mulberry Ct
Canterbury CT1 87 F8
Hythe CT21 176 D3
Littlestone-on-Sea TN28 202 E5
Maidstone ME14 75 B5
Mulberry Field CT13 72 F1
Mulberry Hill CT4 85 D1
Mulberry Rd TN23 138 D3
Mummery Ct ME13 61 E2
Munday Bois Cotts TN27 135 F8
Munday Bois Rd TN27 118 E1
Mundella Prim Sch CT19 178 D6
Mungeam Ho ME1 9 C4
Munn's La ME9 34 E6
Munsgore La ME9 35 E3
Murrain Dr ME15 76 A1
Murray Rd ME2 9 C8
Murston Inf Sch ME10 37 B4
Murston Jun Sch ME10 37 B5
Murston Rd ME10 37 B4
Murthwaite Ct ME12 4 A5
Murton Pl ME13 41 E1
Muscovy Rd TN25 139 C7
Muscovy Way CT6 22 E3
Museum of Canterbury★ CT1 87 F8
Museum of Kent Rural Life★ ME14 53 D1
Musgrave Cl CT12 27 F2
Musgrave Rd ME10 36 F6
Musgrove TN23 156 A8
Musket La
Eyhorne Street ME17 77 C2
Leeds ME17 77 A2
Mustards Rd ME12 6 D2
Mutrix Gdns CT9 7 E1
Mutrix Rd CT9 28 B8
Mutton La ME13 62 A6
Mymms Cl CT5 44 C8
Mynn Cres ME14 76 A4
Myrtle Cres ME5 31 F5
Myrtle Gn TN23 138 D4
Myrtle Rd 5 CT19 178 E6
Mystole Ho CT4 108 B8
Mystole La CT4 108 C8

N

Nacholt Cl CT5 21 A2
Nackington Ct CT1 88 B6

Nackington Pk CT4 88 A4
Nackington Rd CT1,CT4 88 A3
Nag's Head La ME1 9 D4
Nagpur Ho 4 ME15 97 E5
Nailbourne Cl CT4 111 D3
Nailbourne Ct CT18 161 C7
Naildown Cl CT21 177 A3
Naildown Rd CT21 177 A3
Nairne Cl TN26 170 A8
Naldera CT10 30 C7
Namur Pl CT15 149 F3
Napchester Rd CT16 149 A8
Napier Cl ME10 36 C4
Napier Com Sch ME7 10 D4
Napier Ct ME14 74 F7
Napier Gdns CT21 176 C1
Napier Rd
  Broadstairs CT10 29 E6
  Dover CT16 149 B2
  Gillingham ME7 10 D4
Napleton Ct 7 CT11 52 C6
Napleton Rd
  Faversham ME13 62 C7
  Ramsgate CT11 52 C6
Napoleon Wlk ME17 101 C5
Napwood Cl ME8 33 D6
Nares Rd ME8 33 D4
Nargate Cl CT3 90 A8
Nargate St CT3 90 A8
Narrabeen Rd CT19 177 E6
Narrowbush La TN29 200 B7
Naseby Ave CT20 177 D5
Nash Cl ME5 32 C2
Nash Court Farming World★
  ME13 63 D4
Nash Court Gdns CT9 28 F8
Nash Court Rd CT9 28 F8
Nash Gdns CT10 30 B4
Nash Hill CT18 161 D6
Nash La CT9 28 F7
Nash Rd Margate CT9,CT10 28 F7
  Wingham CT3 70 D2
Nashenden Farm La ME1 31 A8
Nashenden La ME1 9 A2
Nasmyth Rd CT7 27 A8
Nat's La TN25 141 A5
Natal Rd Chatham ME4 10 A3
  Dover CT16 149 C4
Nativity Cl ME10 36 E4
Nautilus Cl ME12 4 A6
Nautilus Dr ME12 4 A6
Naval Terr ME12 1 B3
Naylands CT9 7 H1
Naylor's Cotts ME7 33 B1
Neal's Place Rd CT2 66 C3
Neale St ME4 9 F2
Neame Rd CT7 27 A7
Neames Forstal ME13 84 E7
Neason Ct CT19 178 F6
Neason Way CT19 178 F6
Neath Rd TN29 204 A2
Neatscourt Cotts ME12 3 C4
Nelson Ave ME12 4 D5
Nelson Cl Ashford TN24 157 B8
  West Minst ME12 3 A8
Nelson Cres CT11 52 E6
Nelson Ct Birchington CT7 26 E8
  Chatham ME5 10 C1
Nelson Gdns ME13 62 C6
Nelson Ho 8 ME15 97 F5
Nelson Mews TN28 202 E5
Nelson Park Rd CT15 150 E8
Nelson Pl CT10 30 B5
Nelson Rd Gillingham ME7 10 D4
  Whitstable CT5 20 D1
Nelson St Deal CT14 117 D7
  Faversham ME13 62 C6
Nelson Terr ME5 10 C1
Nelson Wlk ME10 36 B5
Neptune Bsns Pk ME2 9 E7
Neptune Cl ME2 9 E7
Neptune Terr ME12 1 E2
Neptune Way ME2 9 E6
Nesbit Rd TN29 194 F4
Ness Rd TN29 205 C6
Ness The CT1 88 B5
Nether Ave TN28 202 D6
Nethercourt Cir CT12 52 A6
Nethercourt Farm Rd
  CT11 52 B7
Nethercourt Gdns CT11 52 B6
Nethercourt Hill CT11 52 B6
Nethergong Hill CT3 47 D3
Netherhale Farm Rd CT7 26 B3
Nethersole Cl CT2 67 A4
Nethersole Rd CT4 112 F1
Netley Cl ME14 75 D6
Nettlefield TN24 139 E5
Nettlepole La TN27 119 D1
Nevill Gdns CT14 117 B1
Neville Cl ME14 75 B8
Neville Ho CT14 117 D6
Neville Rd ME4 9 E2
New Barns Rd ME14 75 A8
New Beach Holiday Centre
  TN29 187 A4
New Beverley Ho CT2 66 F2
New Bridge 12 CT16 166 E7
New Bridge Way TN29 194 E3
New Cotts Guston CT15 149 E6
  Harbledown CT2 65 E1
  Teynham ME9 38 A4
New Covenant Pl 4 ME1 9 D4
New Cross St CT9 7 I2
New Cut Chatham ME4 9 F4
  East Farleigh ME15 96 D7
New Cut Rd
  Chilham CT4,ME13 85 A3
New Cut Rd *continued*
  Harbledown ME13 65 A1
  Maidstone ME14 75 D5
New Delhi Ho 5 ME15 97 E5
New Dover Rd
  Canterbury CT1,CT4 88 C6
  Capel-le-F CT18 164 C2
New Forest La CT4 85 B3
New Gardens Rd ME9 38 C2
New Haine Rd CT12 29 A3
New Hall Cl TN29 195 C8
New House Cl CT1 87 E4
New House La CT4 87 C2
New Inn Cotts ME15 96 C7
New Kempes Ho TN25 123 E2
New La TN29 205 C6
New Lincoln Ho CT19 178 D8
New Rd Chatham ME4 9 F4
  Egerton TN27 119 A2
  Elham CT4 144 F4
  Eythorne CT15 131 C7
  Harbledown CT2 65 D3
  Herne CT2,CT6 45 C4
  Hythe CT21 176 B1
  Hythe, Saltwood CT21 176 B4
  Langley ME17 98 C5
  Minster (Sheppey) ME12 4 C6
  Rochester ME1 9 D4
  Rough Common CT2 66 B3
  Sheerness ME12 1 B1
New Rectory La TN23 156 B4
New Rents 5 TN23 139 B2
New Road Ave ME4 9 E4
New Road Cotts CT6 45 E5
New Road Hill TN25 172 F4
New Road Ind Est ME12 1 B1
New Road Sch ME4 10 A3
New Romney Pl CT13 93 F8
New Romney Sta TN28 202 C6
New Ruttington La CT1 67 A1
New St Ash CT3 71 E1
  Ashford TN24 139 B2
  Canterbury CT1 87 E7
  Canterbury,St Dunstan's
  CT2 66 E1
  Chatham ME4 9 E3
  Deal CT14 117 D7
  12 Dover CT16,CT17 166 D8
  Folkestone CT20 178 D5
  Herne Bay CT6 22 F5
  Lydd TN29 205 C6
  Margate CT9 7 I2
  Sandwich CT13 94 A8
  Sheerness ME12 1 C1
  2 Whitstable CT5 20 D2
New Strs ME4 9 F6
New Town Gn TN24 156 D8
New Town St
  Canterbury CT1 67 B2
  Chartham CT4 86 C5
New Villas ME15 96 C7
Newark Ct 1 ME2 9 B7
Newark Yd ME2 9 B7
Newbridge Ave ME10 36 E7
Newbury Ave ME16 74 C6
Newbury Cl
  Birchington CT7 27 B6
  Dover CT17 165 F7
  Folkestone CT20 177 D5
Newcastle Hill 8 CT11 52 E7
Newchurch La TN26 193 A7
Newchurch Rd ME15 75 A1
Newcomen Rd ME12 1 D2
Newenden Cl
  Ashford TN23 155 F6
  Maidstone ME14 75 D6
Newgate Gap CT9 8 A3
Newgate Lower Prom CT9 8 A3
Newgate Prom CT9 8 A3
Newhouse Cnr CT3 48 D1
Newhouse Farm Cotts
  ME13 83 E7
Newhouse La ME13 83 D7
Newing Cl CT3 89 E8
Newington CE Prim Sch
  ME9 35 B7
Newington Ct CT12 29 B1
Newington Ent Ctr ME9 35 C8
Newington Ind Est ME9 34 F6
Newington Inf Sch CT12 52 B8
Newington Jun Foundation
  Sch CT12 52 A8
Newington Rd
  Peene CT18 177 A8
  Ramsgate CT12,CT11 29 B1
Newington Sta ME9 35 B6
Newington Wlk ME14 75 C6
Newland Green La
  TN27 135 D8
Newland Rd ME12 2 F7
Newlands Ashford TN23 155 D6
  St Mary's Bay TN29 194 F3
  Whitfield CT16 149 B6
Newlands Ave ME10 36 B5
Newlands Dr CT14 134 B8
Newlands Farm Cotts
  ME13 104 C4
Newlands Ho CT11 29 E2
Newlands La CT12 29 D2
Newlands Prim Sch CT11 29 E1
Newlands Rd
  Charing TN27 119 F5
  Ramsgate CT12 29 D1
Newlyn Ct 1 ME14 75 A4
Newlyn's Mdw CT15 147 D1
Newman Ct CT21 176 B1
Newman Dr ME10 37 A8
Newman Rd CT3 112 E5
Newmans Cl CT10 30 A6
Newnham Cl ME8 11 C2
Newnham La ME9,ME13 81 D7
Newnham St ME4 10 B3
Newport Ct CT1 88 B6
Newton Cl Chatham ME5 32 C2
  1 Maidstone ME16 74 E3
Newton Rd
  Faversham ME13 62 D7
  Whitstable CT5 21 B2
Newtown Rd TN23,TN24 156 D7
Nicholas Cl ME16 74 A3
Nicholas Dr CT12 51 D5
Nicholas Rd TN24 139 B6
Nicholls Ave CT10 29 F2
Nicklaus Dr ME5 31 F3
Nickle Cotts CT4 86 A4
Nickleby Cl ME1 9 C2
Nickley Wood Rd TN26 170 C6
Nightingale Ave
  Hythe CT21 187 D8
  Whitstable CT5 43 B6
Nightingale Cl
  Ashford TN24 157 B7
  Chartham CT4 86 C6
  Gillingham ME8 33 E6
Nightingale La CT15 113 C2
Nightingale Pl CT9 8 A2
Nightingale Rd
  Dover CT16 149 C2
  Faversham ME13 62 C7
  Herne CT6 45 F7
Nile Rd ME7 10 C4
Nine Acres TN24 139 C5
Nine Ash La ME13 63 D3
Ninn La TN23 138 B2
Nixon Ave CT12 29 C1
No Name St 3 CT13 73 A1
Noah's Ark Rd CT17 166 A8
Noah's Ark Terr CT17 166 B8
Noakes Mdw TN23 156 A8
Nobel Cl ME9 38 C2
Nobel Ct ME13 62 C7
Noble Ct CT9 28 A8
Noble Gdns CT9 28 A8
Nonington CE Prim Sch
  CT15 113 C5
Nonington Ct CT15 113 E5
Nonsuch Cl CT1 88 C8
Nore Cl Gillingham ME7 10 E1
  Sheerness ME12 1 D1
Noreen Ave ME12 4 A6
Norfolk Cl Chatham ME5 32 C3
  Gillingham ME8 11 D2
Norfolk Dr TN23 139 A2
Norfolk Rd Canterbury CT1 87 E6
  Maidstone ME15 97 C8
  Margate CT9 8 B3
  Margate,Lydden CT9 28 D5
Norfolk Sq CT12 29 B2
Norfolk St CT5 43 D8
Norman Castle★ CT1 87 F7
Norman Cl Gillingham ME8 33 B5
  Maidstone ME14 75 B6
Norman Rd
  Ashford TN23,TN24 156 B7
  Broadstairs CT10 29 F6
  Canterbury CT1 88 A7
  Faversham ME13 62 C7
  Ramsgate CT11 52 B6
  St Margaret's at Cliffe
  CT15 151 B6
  Warden ME12 6 A6
  Westgate-on-S CT8 7 D1
  Whitstable CT5 43 E8
Norman St 8 CT17 166 D8
Norman Tailyour Ho
  CT14 117 D5
Norreys Rd ME8 33 E7
Norrie Rd CT7 27 A6
Norrington Mead 3
  CT19 178 A7
Norrington Rd ME15 97 B6
North Ave CT11 52 D6
North Barrack Rd CT14 117 D4
North Borough Jun Sch
  ME14 75 A6
North Camber Way
  CT16 150 B1
North Cl CT20 177 D4
North Close Bsns Ctr
  CT20 177 D4
North Court Cl CT3 91 A8
North Court La CT14 115 A4
North Court Rd CT3 91 A8
North Cres ME17 96 D4
North Ct Deal CT14 117 C7
  2 Maidstone ME15 75 A1
  Ramsgate CT12 29 B2
North Dane Way ME5 32 C4
North Down View ME17 100 F6
North Downs Cl CT4 85 C2
North Eastling Rd ME13 81 F8
North Exit Rd CT16 166 H8
North Foreland Ave CT10 30 B7
North Foreland Hill CT10 30 B8
North Foreland Rd CT10 30 B7
North Holmes Rd CT1 88 B8
North La Canterbury CT2 66 F1
  Faversham ME13 62 C8
  7 Folkestone CT20 177 E3
  Selling ME13 84 F8
North Lea CT14 117 C7
North Lockside Rd ME4 10 D8
North Lyminge La CT18 161 C7
North Military Rd CT17 166 C7
North Pends TN24 139 E5
North Pondside Rd ME4 10 A8
North Quay Conyer ME9 38 E6
  Faversham ME13 40 D1
North Rd Chatham ME4 10 B8
  Chatham,Brompton ME4,
  ME7 10 A7
  Cliffs End CT13 51 A1
  Deal CT14 134 D6
  Dover CT17 166 C8
  Folkestone CT20 177 D4
  Hythe CT21 176 B2
  Queenborough ME11 2 F5
  Sandwich CT13 95 A7
North Rd W CT21 176 A3
North Return Rd CT16 166 G8
North Sch The TN24 139 D1
North Side Three Rd
  ME4 10 C8
North St Ashford TN23 139 C2
  Deal CT14 117 D7
  Dover CT17 166 B7
  Folkestone CT19 178 E5
  Herne Bay CT6 23 A5
  New Romney TN28 202 A6
  Rochester ME2 9 B7
  Sheldwich ME13 83 C8
  Sittingbourne ME10 36 F7
  Warmlake ME17 98 E1
North View Hersden CT3 46 F1
  Maidstone ME15 75 B1
North View Cotts ME15 96 C7
North Way
  Finglesham CT14 116 A7
  Maidstone ME14 75 B7
Northbourne Ave CT17 166 B8
Northbourne CE Prim Sch
  CT14 115 F5
Northbourne Court Gdns★
  CT14 116 B5
Northbourne Park Sch
  CT14 115 C6
Northbourne Park Sch
  (Annexe) CT14 115 D6
Northbourne Rd
  East Studdal CT15 115 E1
  Gillingham ME8 11 B4
  Great Mongeham CT14 116 C4
Northbourne Way CT9 8 E2
Northbrooke TN24 139 C3
Northbrooke La TN24 139 C3
Northcliffe Gdns CT10 30 A7
Northcote Rd Deal CT14 117 D5
  Kingsdown CT14 134 D4
  Rochester ME2 9 A7
Northdown Ashford TN24 139 C4
  Doddington ME9 80 F7
  Stockbury ME9 56 D8
Northdown Ave CT9 8 B2
Northdown Bsns Pk
  ME17 101 F6
Northdown Cl
  Lenham ME17 101 F6
  Maidstone ME14 75 B7
Northdown Hill CT10,CT9 29 D7
Northdown Park Rd CT9 8 C1
Northdown Prim Sch CT9 8 C1
Northdown Rd
  Broadstairs CT10 29 E6
  Margate CT9 8 B2
Northdown Way CT9 8 C1
Northdowns Cl CT15 132 B6
Northern By-Pass TN27 120 C8
Northfleet Cl ME14 75 C5
Northgate Canterbury CT1 67 A1
  Rochester ME1 9 C6
Northleigh Cl ME15 97 A6
Northpoint Bsns Est ME2 9 D8
Northumberland Ave
  Ashford TN24 139 D5
  Gillingham ME8 11 E1
  Margate CT9 8 C2
Northumberland Ct
  Maidstone ME15 97 D7
  Margate CT9 8 C3
Northumberland Rd
  ME15 97 D8
Northwall Ct CT14 117 C7
Northwall Mews CT14 117 C7
Northwall Rd CT14 117 B8
Northwood Dr ME10 36 F1
Northwood Rd
  Broadstairs, Ramsgate
  CT10,CT12 29 C3
  Whitstable CT5 20 F2
Norton Ave CT6 46 A8
Norton Dr CT12 50 B6
Norton Gr ME5 31 E3
Norton Knatchbull Sch The
  TN24 139 E2
Norton La TN26 153 D5
Norton Rd
  Five Wents ME17 98 D1
  Lewson Street ME13,ME9 60 E5
Norview Rd CT5 43 B7
Norway Dro CT15 151 A8
Norway Terr 4 ME14 75 A7
Norwood Gdns TN23 139 B2
Norwood La TN29 193 E8
Norwood Rise ME12 4 C7
Norwood St TN23 139 B2
Norwood Wlk E ME10 36 C5
Norwood Wlk W ME10 36 B5
Notley St CT1 67 A1
Notley Terr 3 CT1 67 A1
Nottingham Ave ME15 97 D7
Nottingham Rd CT7 26 F5
Nouds La ME9 60 D6
Nouds Rd ME9 60 D7
Nunnery Fields CT1 88 A7
Nunnery Fields Hospl
  CT1 87 F6
Nunnery Rd CT1 87 F7
Nursery Ave
  Maidstone ME16 74 B6
  Maidstone,Bearsted ME14 76 B3
Nursery Cl Densole CT18 163 A7
  Ramsgate CT11 52 C7
  Sheerness ME12 1 E1
  Whitstable CT5 21 A1
Nursery Fields Acol CT7 27 B3
  Hythe CT21 176 A2
Nursery Gdns CT10 8 E1
Nursery La Densole CT18 163 A7
  Sheldwich ME13 83 D5
  Whitfield CT16 148 F7
Nursery Rd ME8 33 D8
Nursery Wlk CT2 66 E2
Nurserylands CT6 22 F3
Nutberry Cl ME9 38 D2
Nutfield Cl ME5 32 B8
Nutfields ME10 37 B3
Nutley Cl TN24 139 C3
Nutts Ave ME12 6 G2
Nutts Cvn Site ME12 6 H1
Nutwood Cl ME14 75 E4

O

Oak Ave Eythorne CT15 131 D5
  Gillingham ME7 10 E6
  Minster (Sheppey) ME12 4 F6
Oak Bglws TN29 205 C6
Oak Caer TN25 172 F4
Oak Cotts
  Barrowhill TN25 174 D7
  East Studdal CT15 132 E8
  Selling ME13 84 D4
Oak Dr
  Boughton Street ME13 64 A3
  Hawkinge CT18 163 B5
  St Mary's Bay TN29 194 F3
Oak Gr CT15 114 B2
Oak Hall Pass CT21 176 C2
Oak Hill CT13 93 B6
Oak Ho 6 ME5 31 F4
Oak La Lydd TN29 205 B6
  Minster (Sheppey) ME12 4 F7
  Upchurch ME9 12 D2
Oak Lodge Rd TN28 202 B7
Oak Rd ME10 37 C5
Oak Ridge TN26 183 F8
Oak St CT14 117 D6
Oak Tree Ave ME15 97 C7
Oak Tree Gr CT9 28 A8
Oak Tree Prim Sch
  TN23 155 F8
Oak Tree Rd TN23 155 F8
Oak Trees Com Sch
  ME15 97 C7
Oak Wlk CT21 176 C2
Oakapple Ho 10 ME16 74 A3
Oakapple La ME16 74 A3
Oakdale Rd CT6 23 A4
Oakdene Rd CT12 29 C1
Oakenpole TN23 138 E1
Oakfield Ct CT12 52 B8
Oakfield Rd TN24 139 D5
Oakfields ME10 36 C3
Oakham Dr TN29 205 D7
Oakhurst Cl ME5 31 F3
Oakland Cl ME5 31 F3
Oakland Ct Cliffs End CT12 51 C5
  Herne Bay CT6 22 E5
Oaklands Ashford TN23 138 F1
  Mersham TN25 157 E4
  Sturry CT2 68 B7
Oaklands Ave CT10 29 E5
Oaklands Inf & Jun Sch
  ME5 31 F4
Oaklands Way CT2 68 B7
Oakleigh Cl ME5 31 E2
Oakleigh Ho TN23 155 E8
Oakleigh La CT4 89 B5
Oakleys The CT15 130 D5
Oakridge CT10 8 G1
Oaks Ave CT6 22 D2
Oaks Bsns Village The
  ME5 32 C1
Oaks Com Inf Sch The
  ME10 36 D2
Oaks Dene ME5 31 F1
Oaks Pk CT2 66 B3
Oaks Rd Folkestone CT20 177 D6
  Tenterden TN30 179 B8
Oaks The Broadstairs CT10 29 F7
  Hawkinge CT18 163 B3
  Hersden CT3 46 F1
  St Nicholas at Wade CT7 25 F2
  Whitstable CT5 43 B6
Oaks View CT21 187 C8
Oakside Rd CT3 112 E5
Oaktree Ho ME10 37 B3
Oakum Ct ME4 10 B2
Oakvale Cl CT17 166 B7
Oakwood CT9 29 C8
Oakwood Ct ME16 74 D3
Oakwood Dr CT5 21 A1
Oakwood Ind Est CT10 29 E6
Oakwood Park Gram Sch
  ME16 74 C3
Oakwood Rd
  Maidstone ME16 74 D3
  Sturry CT2 68 A7

Oakwood Terr ME10 37 C4
Oakwood Villas CT11 29 E1
Oare Marshes Nature Reserve* ME13 40 B6
Oare Marshes Nr & Watch Tower Info Ctr* ME13 40 C6
Oare Rd ME13 40 C1
Oast Cotts Dargate ME13 64 D8
Sheldwich ME13 83 C8
Wormshill ME9 79 C5
Oast Ct Margate CT9 28 F8
Sittingbourne ME10 36 E2
Oast Ho CT4 85 C2
Oast Ho The
Canterbury CT3 88 F8
3 Gillingham ME8 33 F8
Oast La ME13 104 E6
Oast Mdw TN24 139 F1
Oast Paddock The CT3 92 A6
Oast The Canterbury CT1 88 B6
Staple CT3 92 A6
Oasthouse Field TN29 192 F4
Oasts The ME14 76 C4
Oastview ME8 34 A8
Oaten Hill CT1 88 A7
Oaten Hill Pl CT1 88 A7
Oaze The CT5 43 C6
Occupation Rd TN25 123 F2
Ocean Cl CT7 27 B8
Ocean View
Broadstairs CT10 30 A1
Herne Bay CT6 23 F6
Ocelot Ct 6 ME4 10 B3
Octavia Ct ME5 32 B3
Octavian Dr CT21 175 A3
Octavian Way TN23 155 E5
Odiham Dr ME16 74 C7
Odo Rd CT17 166 C8
Officers Terr ME4 9 F7
Officers' Rd ME4 10 B8
Offley Cl CT9 8 C1
Ogilvy Ct CT10 29 E7
Okehampton Cl TN24 139 F7
Olantigh Ct CT7 27 A7
Olantigh Rd TN25 123 F3
Olave Rd CT9 8 B1
Old Ash Cl TN24 139 C5
Old Ashford Rd
Charing TN27 120 C7
Lenham ME17 101 E5
Old Badgins Rd ME13 83 B6
Old Bailey The ME17 100 E6
Old Bakery Cl TN29 194 F4
Old Bakery Mews ME13 63 F4
Old Bakery The ME12 3 F5
Old Barn Cl ME7 32 F6
Old Billet La ME12 5 C6
Old Boundary Rd CT8 7 D1
Old Bridge Rd CT5 20 E1
Old Carriageway The ME7 32 F4
Old Castle Wlk ME8 33 D4
Old Charlton Rd CT16 149 D2
Old Chatham Rd
Kit's Coty ME20 53 D6
Sandling ME14 53 F1
Old Church Rd CT4 86 E1
Old Coachworks The 10 CT13 72 F1
Old Coal Yd The 7 CT5 20 D1
Old Coastgaurd Cotts TN29 209 D3
Old Corn Stores The ME14 76 C4
Old Court Hill CT15,CT3 113 C6
Old Crossing Rd 1 CT9 28 B8
Old Dairy Cl 4 CT11 52 F7
Old Dairy Yd CT12 52 C7
Old Dover Rd
Barham CT4 112 B1
Canterbury CT1 88 B6
Capel-le-F CT18 164 C1
Old Dr ME15 96 F6
Old Dungeness Lighthouse* TN29 209 D2
Old Farm Cl CT5 43 C6
Old Farm Rd CT7 26 D7
Old Ferry Rd ME9 14 E7
Old Flour Mill The CT17 149 B2
Old Fold CT5 44 C8
Old Folkestone Rd CT17 166 A4
Old Forge La ME9 56 F3
Old Garden Ct CT4 86 E1
Old Gate Rd ME13 62 B8
Old Green Rd
Broadstairs CT10 29 F7
Margate CT9 8 C1
Old Hall Dr CT12 51 C5
Old Halls The 8 CT5 20 D2
Old Ham La ME17 101 A4
Old High St The CT20 178 E5
Old Hockley Rd ME13 82 C2
Old Hook Rd ME12 4 F2
Old Hop Gdn The TN31 196 C2
Old House La ME9 34 E4
Old Kingsdown Cl CT10 29 E3
Old Lain ME17 100 F6
Old Lenham Rd ME9 80 C4
Old London Rd CT21 175 F2
Old Loose Cl ME15 96 F5
Old Loose Hill ME15 96 F4
Old Maidstone Rd ME9 35 F5
Old Mead CT19 178 A7
Old Mill La ME20 53 C3
Old Mill Mews CT19 177 F7
Old Mill Rd ME17 76 F1
Old Oast Bsns Ctr The ME20 53 A1
Old Orch TN23 155 D8
Old Orch The ME8 34 A8
Old Palace Rd CT4 89 C3
Old Park Ave
Canterbury CT1 67 C2
Dover CT16 149 A3
Old Park Cl CT16 149 A4
Old Park Ct CT1 67 C2
Old Park Hill CT16 149 B4
Old Park Rd CT16 149 B2
Old Pattens La ME4 9 D2
Old Police Sta The 4 CT5 20 D2
Old Pond Rd TN23 155 F8
Old Print Ho 4 CT16 166 E7
Old Priory Sch The CT11 52 D6
Old Railway Works (Ind Est) TN24 156 D8
Old Rd Chatham ME4 9 F4
Elham CT4 144 F4
Sarre CT7 48 C6
Old Rectory Cl
Hawkinge CT18 163 B4
Mersham TN25 157 E5
Old Rectory The TN25 122 E2
Old Roman Rd CT15 133 C1
Old Ruttington La CT1 67 A1
Old Saltwood La CT21 176 B4
Old Saw Mill The TN26 153 E6
Old School Cl
Lenham ME17 101 D4
Sturry CT2 67 F6
Old School Ct
Egerton TN27 118 F3
Folkestone CT20 178 B4
Old School Gdns CT9 8 A1
Old School Mews CT4 86 C2
Old School Pl ME14 75 A5
Old School The TN24 156 D8
Old School Yd 2 CT10 29 E5
Old Stables The CT11 52 C5
Old Surrenden Manor TN26 154 C5
Old Surrenden Manor Rd TN26 154 C5
Old Timber Yard Ind Est CT11 52 A7
Old Tovil Rd ME15 75 A2
Old Town Gaol Mus* CT17 166 D8
Old Town Hall Mus* CT9 7 I3
Old Trafford Cl ME16 74 B6
Old Tree La ME17 97 D3
Old Tree Rd CT3 47 B7
Old Valley Rd CT4 128 F7
Old Vicarage Gdn CT2 67 F6
Old Vicarage Gdns TN25 123 E2
Old Vicarage The CT13 93 C7
Old Way TN26 190 D7
Oldborough Manor Com Sch ME15 97 B6
Oldchurch Ct 3 ME16 74 E3
Oldfield Cl Gillingham ME8 33 D8
Maidstone ME15 75 E1
Oldhawe Hill CT3,CT6 46 D7
Oldhouse La TN29 191 E1
Oldstairs Rd CT14 134 D4
Olive Gr 2 CT11 52 F7
Oliver Cl ME4 10 B2
Oliver Twist Cl ME1 9 B4
Olivers Row ME14 76 C4
Olivine Cl Chatham ME5 54 A8
Sittingbourne ME10 36 C7
Olliffe Cl ME5 31 F2
Omer Ave CT9 8 C2
Onslow Rd ME1 9 D3
Ontario Way CT16 149 B3
Opal Gn ME5 32 B2
Opie Wlk CT18 162 F3
Orache Dr ME14 75 E5
Orange St CT1 87 F8
Orange Terr ME1 9 D5
Orbit Cl ME5 54 A8
Orbital Pk TN24 156 F6
Orchard Ave CT14 117 B5
Orchard Bank ME17 98 B1
Orchard Bsns Ctr ME16 74 C8
Orchard Cl Canterbury CT2 66 F4
Coxheath ME17 96 C3
Langley Heath ME17 98 E4
Littlebourne CT3 89 F7
Mersham TN25 157 E3
Minster (Thanet) CT12 50 B7
Ramsgate CT12 29 B3
Whitfield CT16 148 F8
Whitstable CT5 20 F3
Wingham CT3 91 A7
Orchard Cotts ME16 96 A8
Orchard Ct
Chillenden CT3 113 F8
Herne Bay CT6 22 F1
Orchard Cvn Pk TN29 186 D3
Orchard Dr Crabble CT17 148 E3
Hythe CT21 176 B1
Littlestone-on-Sea TN28 202 E6
Maidstone ME14 75 E4
Newington ME9 35 A5
Wye TN25 123 F1
Orchard End CT11 52 A5
Orchard Field TN26 153 D4
Orchard Fields CT21 160 E2
Orchard Flats CT1 88 D7
Orchard Gdns CT9 28 A8
Orchard Gr ME12 4 C6
Orchard Ho 9 ME13 62 C7
Orchard Hts TN23 138 F5
Orchard Ind Est ME15 97 F3
Orchard La Ashford TN24 139 F6
Challock TN25 105 B2
Monkton CT7,CT12 49 A8
St Nicholas at Wade CT7 25 F1
Orchard Mews CT14 117 D5
Orchard Pk CT6 23 D4
Orchard Pl
Faversham ME13 62 D7
2 Maidstone ME16 74 E3
Sittingbourne ME10 37 A3
Orchard Rd Eastry CT13 93 B3
Herne Bay CT6 22 F3
Margate CT9 28 A8
St Mary's Bay TN29 195 A5
Tenterden TN30 167 A3
Orchard Residences The CT1 88 A5
Orchard Row CT6 23 A1
Orchard Sch The CT1 87 F6
Orchard St Canterbury CT2 66 E1
Gillingham ME8 33 E8
Maidstone ME15 75 A3
Orchard The
Maidstone ME14 76 B4
Monkton CT12 49 D6
Orchard Valley CT21 176 A2
Orchard View Ash CT3 71 F1
Detling ME14 76 A8
Tenterden TN30 179 C8
Teynham ME9 38 C3
Orchard Villas
1 Chatham ME4 9 F3
Kearsney CT17 148 E4
Orchard Way
Eastchurch ME12 5 D1
Peasmarsh TN31 196 C1
Orchards The CT4 144 F4
Orchid Cl ME12 4 A4
Orchids The
Etchinghill CT18 161 D4
Mersham TN25 157 E4
Ordnance St ME4 9 E3
Ordnance Terr 9 ME4 9 E4
Orgarswick Ave TN29 195 C7
Orgarswick Way TN29 195 C7
Orient Pl CT2 66 F1
Orion Rd ME1 31 C7
Orion Way TN24 156 E8
Orlestone Villas TN26 183 A8
Ormonde Ct CT21 176 C1
Ormonde Rd
11 Folkestone CT20 178 E6
Hythe CT21 176 C1
Ormsby Gn ME8 33 E3
Orpins Cl TN25 158 D6
Orr Cl CT18 162 F4
Osborne Gdns CT6 23 D4
Osborne Rd
Ashford TN24 156 F8
Gillingham ME7 10 C5
Kingsdown CT14 134 C6
Osborne Terr CT9 7 J1
Osbourn Ave CT8 27 E8
Osbourne Rd CT10 29 F4
Oscar Rd CT10 30 B4
Osier Field TN24 139 E7
Osier Rd ME9 38 E3
Osprey Ave ME5 10 E2
Osprey Cl CT5 43 C7
Osprey Ct 2 Dover CT16 149 B2
Hawkinge CT18 162 F3
Sittingbourne ME10 37 A3
Ospringe CE Prim Sch ME13 62 A6
Ospringe Pl ME13 62 B6
Ospringe Rd ME13 62 B7
Ospringe St ME13 62 A6
Ostend Ct ME10 14 F1
Ostlers La CT7 48 D6
Oswald Pl CT17 149 B2
Oswald Rd CT17 149 B2
Otham Cl CT2 67 A4
Otham La ME15 76 C2
Otham St Maidstone ME15 76 C2
Otham ME15 98 B7
Ottawa Cres CT16 149 C3
Ottawa Way CT16 149 B3
Otterbourne Pl ME15 75 E1
Otterden Cl TN23 155 F6
Otterden Rd ME13 81 D3
Otterham Quay La ME8 12 B2
Otteridge Rd ME14 76 A3
Otterpool La CT21,TN25 174 D4
Otway St Chatham ME4 10 A3
Gillingham ME7 10 D6
Otway Terr 1 ME4 10 A3
Out Elmstead La CT4 111 F2
Outfall Ave TN29 209 C2
Oval The TN29 186 D1
Overland La CT3 71 A3
Overton Ho ME12 1 D2
Owen Sq CT14 117 B2
Owen's Cl CT21 177 B3
Owens Court Cotts ME13 83 F8
Owens Way ME7 11 A6
Owl's Hatch Rd CT6 22 C1
Owletts Cl ME15 97 D8
Ox La TN30 167 B2
Oxen Lease TN23 155 E8
Oxenden Cnr CT3 23 F1
Oxenden Cres CT3 91 A8
Oxenden Park Dr CT6 22 E4
Oxenden Rd CT20 177 E4
Oxenden St CT6 22 E5
Oxenden Way CT4 128 F8
Oxenturn Rd TN25 140 E8
Oxford Cl 5 CT5 20 D1
Oxford Ct CT1 87 F7
Oxford Mans 6 CT5 20 D1
Oxford Rd Canterbury CT1 87 F7
Gillingham ME7 10 D3
Maidstone ME15 97 D8
Oxford St 6 Margate CT9 7 J1
Whitstable CT5 20 D1
Oxford Terr CT20 178 D4
Oxney Cl CT7 26 F7
Oxney Cotts TN30 190 A4
Oyster Cl Herne Bay CT6 22 B3
Sittingbourne ME10 36 E6
Oyster Mews 4 CT5 20 D1

P

Packer Pl ME5 32 A8
Packer's La 5 CT11 52 E7
Pad's Hill ME15 75 A4
Padbrook La CT3 70 D6
Paddock Cl Deal CT14 116 F5
Folkestone CT20 177 F5
Lydd TN29 205 B6
Paddock Rd
Ashford TN23 155 E7
2 Birchington CT7 27 A7
Paddock The
Canterbury CT1 88 B8
Chatham ME4 9 F4
Dover CT16 166 D8
Old Wives Lees CT4 85 C2
Woodchurch TN26 169 A1
Paddock View CT5 43 E7
Paddocks The
Ashford TN23 138 C1
Broadstairs CT10 29 F7
Densole CT18 163 A8
Gillingham ME7 33 A5
Herne Bay CT6 23 F5
Margate CT9 8 C1
Padsole La ME15 75 A4
Padstow Manor 1 ME7 10 C6
Padwell La TN23 155 C8
Paffard Cl CT2 67 F6
Paffard Ct CT2 67 F6
Page Pl CT19 178 D8
Page Rd CT18 162 F3
Paget Row ME7 10 C5
Paget St ME7 10 C5
Pagitt St ME4 9 E3
Paine Ave TN29 205 C6
Painesfield Cl TN29 186 C4
Painter's Forstal Rd ME13 61 E3
Painters Farm Camping & Cvn Site ME13 61 E3
Palace Ave ME15 75 A4
Palace Cl CT5 21 B2
Palace Cotts ME9 80 F8
Palace Ct Gillingham ME5 10 D2
Hythe CT21 176 C2
Palace Ind Est ME15 97 F4
Palace St 17 CT1 67 A1
Palace Wood Inf Sch ME16 74 C6
Palace Wood Jun Sch ME16 74 C6
Palm Bay Ave CT9 8 D3
Palm Bay Gdns CT9 8 C3
Palm Bay Prim Sch CT9 8 D3
Palm Ct CT8 7 C1
Palm Tree Cl CT15 131 D7
Palm Tree Way CT18 161 B7
Palmar Rd ME16 74 D6
Palmars Cross Hill CT2 66 A1
Palmarsh Ave CT21 187 D7
Palmarsh Cres CT21 187 D7
Palmarsh Prim Sch CT21 187 D8
Palmbeach Ave CT21 187 D8
Palmer Cl CT6 46 B8
Palmer Cres CT9 29 C8
Palmer Rd CT3 91 A8
Palmerston Ave
Broadstairs CT10 30 B3
Deal CT14 117 C2
Palmerston Ct CT14 117 D2
Palmerston Rd
Chatham ME4 9 F1
Dover CT16 148 F4
Palmerston St 4 CT19 178 D6
Palmerston Wlk ME10 37 C4
Palting Way CT20 178 B4
Pamela Ct ME7 10 D5
Pannell Dr CT18 162 F4
Panteny La ME9 37 E2
Pantheon Gdns TN23 155 F5
Panton Cl ME5 32 C4
Paper La TN24 156 F6
Papion Gr ME5 31 E2
Papworth Cl 1 CT19 178 A7
Parade CT1 87 F8
Parade Rd CT20 177 F3
Parade The
Ashford TN24 156 F5
Birchington CT7 26 D8
Eastry CT13 93 B2
Folkestone CT20 178 E5
Greatstone-on-S TN28, TN29 206 E7
Margate CT9 7 I3
Sittingbourne ME10 36 F2
Paradise CT11 52 D7
Paradise Cotts ME9 34 E5
Paradise Row CT13 72 F1
Paragon CT11 52 E5
Paragon St CT11 52 D5
Paraker Way CT21 177 B4
Pardoner Cl CT2 87 C7
Pardoners Way CT16 149 A3
Parfitt Way CT16 149 B2
Parham Cl CT1 67 B2
Parham Ct CT1 67 B2
Parham Rd
Canterbury CT1 67 B2
Chatham ME4 9 F2
Paris Cnr TN26 153 F6
Parish Rd Chartham CT4 86 C3
Minster (Sheppey) ME12 4 A5
Park Ave Birchington CT7 27 A6
Broadstairs CT10 29 E2
Deal CT14 117 C5
Dover CT16 149 D1
Gillingham ME7 10 D3
Leysdown-on-S ME12 6 G1
Maidstone ME17 96 E2
Maidstone, Penenden Heath ME14 75 B6
Queenborough ME11 3 B4
Sittingbourne ME10 36 E1
Whitstable CT5 20 F3
Park Avenue Holiday Village ME12 6 G1
Park Barn Rd ME17 99 C5
Park Chase CT10 29 E2
Park Cl Hawkinge CT18 163 A4
Margate CT9 8 D1
Park Cotts Preston CT3 70 B6
Ramsgate CT11 29 E2
Park Cres ME4 31 F8
Park Crescent Rd CT9 8 A1
Park Ct ME13 62 E7
Park Dr Hothfield TN26 138 A6
Sittingbourne ME10 36 D1
Park Farm Cl
Folkestone CT19 178 C8
Shadoxhurst TN26 155 A1
Tyler Hill CT2 66 E6
Park Farm Prim Sch CT19 178 C6
Park Farm Rd CT19 178 C7
Park Gate CT10 29 F2
Park Ho Dover CT16 149 D1
Maidstone ME14 75 B6
Park La Bethersden TN26 154 C8
Birchington CT7 27 A6
Bishopsbourne CT4 111 C5
Elham CT4 144 F5
Maidstone, Cock Stone ME17 97 D2
Maidstone, Ringlestone ME14 74 F7
Margate CT9 8 A2
Park Lea CT14 117 C5
Park Mall 2 TN24 139 B2
Park Manor ME7 10 B5
Park Mews 6 CT16 166 D8
Park Par TN29 195 C7
Park Pl
Ashford, Beaver TN23 156 B7
Ashford, Willesborough TN24 156 F8
Dover CT16 166 D8
Herne CT6 46 A8
Margate CT9 7 I1
Park Rd Ashford TN24 139 D6
Broadstairs CT10 30 B6
Dover CT16 149 B2
Faversham ME13 62 D7
Folkestone CT19 177 E6
Herne Bay CT6 22 F4
Hythe CT21 176 B1
Littlestone-on-Sea TN28 202 E5
Margate CT9 8 A2
Preston CT3 70 D7
Queenborough ME11 2 F5
Ramsgate CT11 52 C7
Sheerness ME12 1 E1
Sittingbourne ME10 36 E3
Temple Ewell CT16 148 D5
Westgate-on-S CT7 27 D6
Park Rd N TN24 139 B3
Park Side CT14 117 C5
Park St Ashford TN24 139 C2
Deal CT14 117 D6
Dover CT16 166 D8
Lydd TN29 205 C6
Park Terr Throwley ME13 82 D1
Woodnesborough CT13 93 D7
Park Vale TN24 139 D6
Park View
Folkestone CT19 178 E7
Margate CT9 8 A2
Peasmarsh TN31 196 B2
Sturry CT2 67 F6
Park View Cl CT3 91 D2
Park View Ct ME15 75 E1
Park View Rise CT15 113 D4
Park View Terr 2 TN30 179 A7
Park Villas ME14 75 E4
Park Way Coxheath ME17 96 D3
Maidstone ME15 75 B1
Park Way Prim Sch ME15 75 B1
Park Wood Cl TN23 156 B5
Park Wood Forest Wlks* TN26 181 C4
Park Wood Gn ME8 33 D5
Park Wood Par ME15 97 F5
Park Wood Rd CT2 66 C4
Park Wood Trad Est
Maidstone ME15 97 F4
Otham ME15 98 A4

Parker Cl Gillingham ME8 ... 33 E5
Hamstreet TN26 ... 183 A7
Parker Pl CT18 ... 163 C5
Parkfield Rd
Folkestone CT19 ... 178 C6
Gillingham ME8 ... 11 F1
Parkland Ct CT10 ... 29 F6
Parkside Com Prim Sch CT1 ... 67 D2
Parkside Ct Herne Bay CT6 ... 22 F5
Ramsgate CT11 ... 52 D7
Parkside Pl CT1 ... 67 D3
Parkway The CT7 ... 27 B7
Parkwood TN31 ... 197 B4
Parkwood Cl CT10 ... 29 F2
Parkwood Inf Sch ME8 ... 33 E5
Parkwood Jun Sch ME8 ... 33 E5
Parr Ave ME7 ... 10 D6
Parrs Head Mews ME1 ... 9 C6
Parsonage Chase ME12 ... 3 F5
Parsonage Cotts ME9 ... 58 A5
Parsonage Farm ME13 ... 82 F4
Parsonage Farm (Rural Heritage Ctr)★ CT4 ... 145 A6
Parsonage Fields CT12 ... 49 C7
Parsonage La
Rochester ME2 ... 9 C8
Sittingbourne ME9 ... 36 A8
Parsonage Oast CT12 ... 49 C7
Parsonage Rd CT6 ... 23 A3
Parsonage Stocks Rd ME13 ... 82 F5
Parsonage Villas CT15 ... 165 C5
Partridge Cl CT6 ... 23 C3
Partridge La ME13 ... 62 D7
Pasley Rd ME4,ME7 ... 10 A7
Pasley Rd E ME7 ... 10 B7
Pasley Rd N ME4 ... 10 B7
Pasley Rd W ME7 ... 10 A7
Pastime Cl ME10 ... 36 E8
Pasture The
Ashford TN24 ... 139 D6
Hawkinge CT18 ... 163 B4
Patchways TN29 ... 184 E3
Path Field Cotts CT15 ... 164 E5
Patricia Way CT10 ... 29 D3
Patrixbourne Ave ME8 ... 11 C2
Patrixbourne Rd CT4 ... 89 B2
Pattens Gdns ME1 ... 9 E2
Pattens La ME1,ME4 ... 9 E1
Pattens Pl ME1 ... 9 D2
Patterson Cl CT14 ... 117 A4
Pattison Farm Cl TN25 ... 172 F4
Paul's Pl 8 CT16 ... 149 C1
Pavement The TN30 ... 167 B3
Pavilion Cl CT14 ... 117 C8
Pavilion Ct CT20 ... 178 E4
Pavilion Dr ME10 ... 14 F1
Pavilion Mdw CT17 ... 148 E4
Pavilion Rd CT19 ... 178 D6
Pavings The ME17 ... 77 C2
Paxton Ave CT18 ... 162 F3
Pay St CT18 ... 162 F7
Payden St ME17 ... 102 D8
Payers Pk CT20 ... 178 D5
Payne's La ME15 ... 97 B7
Pays La TN25 ... 104 D1
Payton Cl CT9 ... 29 A7
Payton Mews 4 CT1 ... 67 B1
Peacock Mews 7 ME16 ... 74 E4
Peacock Pl ME13 ... 84 A6
Peacock Rise ME5 ... 32 A4
Peafield Wood Rd CT4 ... 127 E4
Peak Dr CT13 ... 93 B3
Pean Court Rd CT5 ... 43 D3
Pean Hill CT5 ... 43 D2
Pear Tree Alley 2 ME10 ... 36 E5
Pear Tree Cl CT10 ... 29 C4
Pear Tree La
Dymchurch TN29 ... 186 D1
Gillingham ME7 ... 32 E7
Loose ME15 ... 97 B6
Pear Tree Row ME17 ... 98 B5
Pear Tree Wlk ME9 ... 35 A5
Pearmain Wlk CT1 ... 88 C7
Pearman Cl ME8 ... 12 A1
Pearson's Way CT10 ... 29 E7
Peartree Cotts ME8 ... 34 B8
Peartree Rd CT6 ... 23 C3
Peasmarsh CE Prim Sch TN31 ... 196 B1
Peckham Cl ME2 ... 9 C8
Pedding Hill CT3 ... 71 A1
Pedding La CT3 ... 92 A8
Peel Dr ME10 ... 37 C4
Peel St ME14 ... 75 A6
Peelers Ct CT2 ... 66 F1
Peene Cotts CT18 ... 162 B1
Pegwell Ave CT11 ... 52 A5
Pegwell Bay Ctry Pk★ CT12 ... 51 C2
Pegwell Bay Nature Reserve★ CT12 ... 51 C3
Pegwell Cl CT11 ... 52 A5
Pegwell Ct CT11 ... 52 B5
Pegwell Rd CT11 ... 52 B5
Pelham Gdns CT20 ... 178 A4
Pelwood Rd TN31 ... 203 A2
Pemberton Ct CT21 ... 177 B3
Pemberton Rd TN24 ... 139 D2
Pemberton Sq 4 ME2 ... 9 C8
Pembroke ME4 ... 10 B8
Pembroke Ave CT9 ... 7 F1
Pembroke Ct
Chatham ME4 ... 10 A4
Folkestone CT19 ... 178 E6
1 Ramsgate CT11 ... 52 E7
Pembroke Gdns ME8 ... 33 E4
Pembroke Ho TN28 ... 202 E5
Pembroke Lodge Mus & Art Gall CT7 ... 26 F7
Pembroke Mews TN28 ... 202 C8
Pembroke Rd ME17 ... 96 C3
Pembroke Rise ME4 ... 10 A7
Pembury Ct 6 ME10 ... 36 E4
Pembury Gdns ME16 ... 74 D3
Pembury Pl TN25 ... 138 F4
Pembury St ME10 ... 36 E4
Pembury Way ME8 ... 11 E2
Penbury CT14 ... 117 C1
Pencester Ct 3 CT16 ... 166 E8
Pencester Rd CT16 ... 166 D8
Penderel Mews TN30 ... 179 B8
Penenden Ct ME14 ... 75 B7
Penenden Heath Rd ME14 ... 75 C7
Penenden St ME14 ... 75 A6
Penfield La ME9 ... 59 A4
Penfold Cl Chatham ME5 ... 32 B7
Maidstone ME15 ... 97 E5
Penfold Gdns CT15 ... 130 E5
Penfold Hill ME17 ... 99 B8
Penfold Rd CT19 ... 178 F6
Penfold Way ME15 ... 96 F6
Pengelly Pl CT2 ... 66 F2
Penhurst Cl ME14 ... 75 F5
Penlee Point TN24 ... 139 D5
Penn Cl ME10 ... 37 B2
Penn Hill TN23 ... 155 E6
Pennant Rd ME1 ... 31 C7
Pennine Way
Ashford TN24 ... 139 B4
Maidstone ME15 ... 76 A1
Pennington Cl CT2 ... 68 C7
Penny Cress Gdns ME16 ... 74 C3
Penny Cress Rd ME12 ... 4 A4
Penny Pot La CT4 ... 108 B4
Penny Spring Farm (Cvn Pk) ME14 ... 55 B2
Pennypot Ind Est CT21 ... 175 F1
Penrith Ct ME7 ... 11 A5
Penrose Ct CT21 ... 176 C1
Penryn Manor 4 ME7 ... 10 C6
Pensand Ho CT21 ... 176 D1
Penshurst Cl
Canterbury CT2 ... 67 A3
Gillingham ME8 ... 11 E2
Penshurst Gdns CT9 ... 8 F2
Penshurst Rd CT11 ... 52 F7
Penshurst Rise ME13 ... 62 B8
Penstocks The ME15 ... 74 D2
Pent Vale Cl CT19 ... 178 A6
Pent Valley Sch CT19 ... 177 F7
Pentagon Sh Ctr ME4 ... 9 F4
Pepy's Way ME2 ... 9 A8
Pepys Ave ME12 ... 1 C2
Percival Terr CT17 ... 166 B7
Percy Ave CT10 ... 8 F2
Percy Rd Broadstairs CT10 ... 29 F5
Margate CT9 ... 8 A3
Ramsgate CT11 ... 52 D8
Peregrine Cl CT21 ... 187 D8
Peregrine Dr ME10 ... 37 A2
Peri Ct CT1 ... 87 E6
Peridot Ct ME15 ... 97 E5
Perie Row 9 ME7 ... 10 A6
Perimeter Rd CT16 ... 166 G8
Periwinkle Cl ME10 ... 36 E5
Periwinkle Ct 3 ME10 ... 36 E5
Perkins Ave CT9 ... 28 F8
Perries Mead CT19 ... 178 B7
Perrot Way CT18 ... 163 B5
Perry Court Rudolf Steiner Sch CT4 ... 108 E7
Perry La CT3 ... 70 C3
Perry St Chatham ME4 ... 9 E3
Maidstone ME14 ... 74 F6
Perry Wood Local Nature Reserve★ ME13 ... 84 D4
Perryfield St ME14 ... 74 F6
Perth Gdns ME10 ... 36 C4
Perth Way CT16 ... 149 C3
Pested Bars Rd ME17 ... 97 D5
Pested La TN25 ... 105 C4
Petchell Mews 11 CT1 ... 67 B2
Peter Candler Way TN24 ... 139 E4
Peter St Deal CT14 ... 117 D7
Dover CT16 ... 166 C8
Folkestone CT20 ... 178 E5
Petfield Cl ME12 ... 4 C6
Petham Gn ME8 ... 11 C2
Petham Prim Sch CT4 ... 109 C3
Petlands ME17 ... 97 D5
Petrel Cl CT6 ... 23 F4
Petrel Way CT18 ... 163 A3
Pett Bottom Rd CT4 ... 110 C5
Pett Hill CT4 ... 88 F1
Pett La Charing TN27 ... 120 D7
Silver Street ME9 ... 57 B7
Pett's Cres CT12 ... 50 B5
Pettfield Hill Rd ME13 ... 82 B1
Pettman Cl CT6 ... 22 F3
Pettman Ct 5 CT10 ... 29 E5
Pettmans Mews CT5 ... 20 C2
Petts La CT3 ... 91 A8
Peverel Dr ME14 ... 76 A5
Peverel Gn ME8 ... 33 D4
Peverell Rd CT16 ... 149 B4
Pewter Ct CT1 ... 87 F7
Pharos Dr CT16 ... 149 E1
Pheasant La ME15 ... 97 B8
Pheasant Rd ME4 ... 10 C2
Pheasants' Hall Rd CT4 ... 110 F2
Philip Corby Cl CT9 ... 8 B2
Philipine Craft Ctr★ TN29 ... 199 A6
Philippa Ho CT19 ... 178 F6
Phillip Rd CT19 ... 177 E6
Phillippa Ct ME10 ... 36 E8
Phillips Ct ME8 ... 11 B2
Phillips Rd CT7 ... 27 A6
Phoenix Com Prim Sch TN24 ... 139 D5
Phoenix Ct 11 ME7 ... 10 C6
Phoenix Ind Est ME2 ... 9 D7
Phoenix Pk ME15 ... 97 F4
Phoenix Rd ME5 ... 32 B2
Piccadilly Apartments 4 ME5 ... 10 B3
Pickelden La CT4 ... 107 F8
Pickering St ME15 ... 97 B6
Pickhill Oast TN30 ... 179 B4
Pickneybush La TN29 ... 194 A7
Pickwick Cres ME1 ... 9 C3
Picton Rd CT11 ... 52 C7
Pie Factory Rd CT15 ... 113 E2
Pier Approach Rd ME7 ... 10 D7
Pier Ave Herne Bay CT6 ... 22 E4
Whitstable CT5 ... 21 A2
Pier Rd ME7 ... 10 E7
Pier Rd Ind Est ME7 ... 10 D7
Pier The CT16 ... 148 F8
Pierpoint Rd CT5 ... 43 D7
Pierremont Ave CT10 ... 30 A4
Pigeon La CT6 ... 23 A2
Pigtail Cnr ME12 ... 4 E6
Pike Cl CT19 ... 178 A7
Pike Rd CT14,CT15 ... 114 E4
Pikefields ME8 ... 11 C2
Pilar Ct CT8 ... 7 D1
Pilckem Cl CT1 ... 67 D1
Pilgrim Spring CT19 ... 178 D8
Pilgrims Ct TN27 ... 120 C7
Pilgrims La Chilham CT4 ... 85 E1
Whitstable CT5 ... 43 B4
Pilgrims Lakes ME17 ... 100 E6
Pilgrims Rd CT1 ... 88 C7
Pilgrims View ME14 ... 53 E3
Pilgrims Way
Boughton Aluph TN25 ... 123 A4
Boxley ME14 ... 54 E3
Broad Street ME14,ME17 ... 77 C6
Canterbury CT1 ... 88 C7
Charing TN27 ... 120 E8
Detling ME14 ... 55 B1
Dover CT16 ... 149 A3
Eccles ME20 ... 53 B6
Hollingbourne ME17 ... 77 F3
Lenham ME17 ... 101 B7
Thurnham ME14 ... 76 E8
Westwell TN25 ... 121 D5
Pilgrims Way Prim Sch CT1 ... 88 C7
Pilgrims' Way TN25 ... 159 E8
Pilot Rd ME1 ... 31 C8
Pilot's Farm Rd CT4 ... 110 A4
Pilots Ave CT14 ... 117 A4
Pimp's Court Cotts ME15 ... 96 E6
Pimp's Court Farm Ctr ME15 ... 96 E6
Pimpernel Cl ME14 ... 76 B4
Pimpernel Way ME5 ... 31 E4
Pin Hill CT1 ... 87 F7
Pincus Ho ME10 ... 36 D5
Pine Cotts ME14 ... 74 E8
Pine Gr Gillingham ME7 ... 33 A5
Maidstone ME14 ... 75 B6
Pine Ho 3 Chatham ME5 ... 31 F5
5 Maidstone ME14 ... 75 B4
Pine Lodge ME16 ... 74 C3
Pine Lodge Ct CT14 ... 117 B5
Pine Lodge Touring Pk ME17 ... 76 F2
Pine Pl ME15 ... 74 E1
Pine Tree Ave CT2 ... 66 E2
Pine Tree Cl CT7 ... 27 B7
Pine Way CT19 ... 177 D7
Pine Wlk CT6 ... 23 E5
Pineham Rd CT15 ... 149 D6
Pines Gardens The★ CT15 ... 151 B5
Pines The
Broadstairs CT10 ... 29 D4
Canterbury CT1 ... 88 A6
Pineside Rd CT3 ... 89 E8
Pinetree Cl CT5 ... 20 F3
Pinewood Cl CT12 ... 29 C1
Pinewood Dr ME5 ... 54 D8
Pinks Cnr CT12 ... 50 D6
Pinners Hill CT15,CT3 ... 113 C6
Pinners La CT15 ... 113 C5
Pintail Dr ME9 ... 14 E3
Pintail Way CT6 ... 23 C2
Pioneer Bsns Pk CT11 ... 52 C8
Pioneer Rd CT16 ... 149 A3
Pippin Ave CT4 ... 111 B8
Pippin Cl Coxheath ME17 ... 96 B2
Sittingbourne ME10 ... 36 D6
Pippin Croft ME7 ... 33 A6
Pirbright Cl ME5 ... 32 D2
Pitstock Rd ME9 ... 59 B5
Pitt Rd
Chartway Street ME17 ... 99 A2
Maidstone ME16 ... 74 B1
Pittlesden TN30 ... 179 A7
Pittlesden Pl 1 TN30 ... 179 A7
Pittock Ho CT14 ... 117 B3
Pivington La TN27 ... 119 C2
Pivington Mill Ind Est TN27 ... 119 C2
Pixwell La CT14 ... 116 D3
Place La Hartlip ME9 ... 34 D4
Place La *continued*
Woodchurch TN26 ... 169 B3
Place The CT4 ... 112 F1
Plain Cotts CT20 ... 178 A4
Plain Rd
Brabourne Lees TN25 ... 158 F5
Folkestone CT20 ... 178 B4
Plains Ave ME15 ... 75 C1
Plains of Waterloo CT11 ... 52 F7
Plaistow Sq ME14 ... 75 C6
Plantation Cl TN26 ... 138 A7
Plantation La ME14 ... 76 A3
Plantation Rd
Faversham ME13 ... 62 C7
Gillingham ME7 ... 11 A6
Whitstable CT5 ... 21 D2
Platt's Heath Prim Sch ME17 ... 100 F2
Platters The ME8 ... 33 C7
Playdell Ct 12 CT20 ... 178 D4
Playden La TN31 ... 197 C3
Playing Fields CT13 ... 93 E7
Playstool Cl ME9 ... 35 B6
Playstool Rd ME9 ... 35 A6
Plaza Ct 7 ME10 ... 37 A4
Pleasance Rd N TN29 ... 206 E5
Pleasance Road Central TN29 ... 209 D7
Pleasant Row 10 ME7 ... 10 A6
Pleasant Valley La ME15 ... 96 B4
Pleasent Pl ME12 ... 3 E6
Plenty Brook Dr CT6 ... 22 F3
Plewis Ho ME7 ... 10 E7
Pleydell Cres CT2 ... 67 F7
Pleydell Gdns CT20 ... 178 D4
Plimsoll Ave CT19 ... 178 E8
Plomley Cl ME8 ... 33 D4
Plough Cotts ME17 ... 98 D2
Plough Ct CT6 ... 23 D2
Plough Hill CT15 ... 165 C4
Plough La CT5 ... 21 D3
Plough Rd ME12 ... 5 C5
Plough Wents Rd ME17 ... 98 B2
Ploughmans Way
Ashford TN23 ... 155 D5
Chatham ME5 ... 32 A1
Gillingham ME8 ... 33 E6
Plover Cl Chatham ME5 ... 32 D1
Herne Bay CT6 ... 23 F5
Plover Rd Hawkinge CT18 ... 162 F3
Minster (Sheppey) ME12 ... 4 A5
Pluckley CE Prim Sch TN27 ... 136 D7
Pluckley Cl ME8 ... 11 C3
Pluckley Gdns CT9 ... 8 E2
Pluckley Rd
Bethersden TN26 ... 153 D7
Charing TN27 ... 120 B5
Hothfield TN26,TN27 ... 137 B4
Smarden TN27 ... 135 D2
Pluckley Sta TN27 ... 136 C3
Plum Tree Gdns TN26 ... 169 B1
Plum Tree La ME9 ... 56 B8
Plumford Rd ME13 ... 62 A2
Plumpton Wlk
5 Canterbury CT1 ... 67 B1
9 Maidstone ME15 ... 97 F6
Plumpudding La ME13 ... 42 E1
Plumstone Rd CT7 ... 26 F1
Plumtree Gr ME7 ... 33 A4
Plumtrees ME16 ... 74 A2
Plurenden Manor Farm Cotts TN26 ... 168 D7
Plurenden Rd TN26 ... 168 E7
Poachers Cl ME5 ... 32 C5
Pochard Cres CT6 ... 22 E3
Podkin Wood ME5 ... 53 F8
Poets Cnr CT9 ... 7 J1
Poets Wlk CT14 ... 117 C1
Poison Cross CT13 ... 93 B4
Poldark Ct 22 CT11 ... 52 F7
Poles The ME9 ... 12 E4
Polhill Dr ME5 ... 31 F2
Pollard Cl TN23 ... 155 F8
Pollard Ct ME7 ... 10 C5
Pollard Pl CT5 ... 43 C6
Polo Way CT5 ... 21 D1
Pomfret Ho CT4 ... 86 D1
Pomfret Rd CT4 ... 86 D1
Pommeus La CT14 ... 133 D7
Poncia Rd TN23 ... 156 A7
Pond Cotts Herne Bay CT6 ... 23 D2
Sittingbourne ME10 ... 58 D8
Pond Dr ME10 ... 37 A2
Pond Farm Rd
Hucking ME17 ... 56 D1
Oad Street ME9 ... 35 F1
Pond Hill CT3 ... 90 D1
Pond Hill Rd CT20 ... 177 C5
Pond La
St Margaret's at Cliffe CT15 ... 150 D7
Womenswold CT4,CT3 ... 112 D3
Pondmore Way TN25 ... 138 F4
Ponycart La CT4 ... 126 E3
Poorhole La CT10 ... 29 B5
Poot La ME9 ... 12 E5
Pope House La TN30 ... 167 B4
Pope St Godmersham CT4 ... 107 E4
Maidstone ME16 ... 74 C2
Popes La CT2 ... 67 F7
Popes Wood ME14 ... 75 F6
Poplar Cl TN23 ... 138 F3
Poplar Dr Elvington CT15 ... 114 B2
Herne Bay CT6 ... 22 D2
Poplar Field TN30 ... 188 D4
Poplar Gr ME16 ... 74 C5
Poplar La TN29 ... 205 D7
Poplar Rd
Broadstairs CT10 ... 29 E6
Ramsgate CT11 ... 52 D7
Wittersham TN30 ... 188 D4
Poplar View ME13 ... 63 E3
Poplars TN26 ... 182 A7
Poplars The
Ashford TN23 ... 156 A7
Bethersden TN26 ... 153 E5
Hersden CT3 ... 46 F1
Poppy Cl Gillingham ME7 ... 10 E5
Maidstone ME16 ... 74 D3
Poppyfield TN31 ... 197 C1
Popsal La CT3 ... 91 B6
Porchester Cl ME15 ... 97 A6
Port Cl Chatham ME5 ... 32 B3
Maidstone ME14 ... 76 A5
Port Lympne Wild Animal Pk★ CT21 ... 174 D2
Port Rise ME4 ... 9 F3
Portal House Sch CT15 ... 151 A6
Portebello Ct CT14 ... 117 D7
Porter Cl ME12 ... 4 A6
Porter's La ME13 ... 62 B2
Porters Wlk ME17 ... 98 E4
Portery The CT14 ... 117 D6
Portland Ave ME10 ... 37 C4
Portland Cl
Ashford TN24 ... 139 C7
Hythe CT21 ... 176 B2
Portland Ct
3 Hythe CT21 ... 176 B2
Ramsgate CT11 ... 52 E7
Portland Rd
Gillingham ME7 ... 10 E6
Hythe CT21 ... 176 B2
Portland St 1 ME4 ... 10 B2
Portland Terr
Ripple CT14 ... 133 D8
Sheerness ME12 ... 1 D2
Portlight Pl CT5 ... 43 A6
Portree Mews ME7 ... 10 E3
Portsdown Cl ME16 ... 74 B2
Portway CT5 ... 43 C8
Post Barn Rd ME4 ... 9 F2
Post Office Row CT4 ... 84 D1
Postley Commercial Ctr ME15 ... 75 A2
Postley Rd ME15 ... 75 A1
Postling TN23 ... 138 E1
Postling Rd CT19 ... 177 E7
Postling Wents CT21 ... 175 F8
Postmill Dr ME15 ... 74 F1
Pot Kiln La TN26 ... 152 E4
Potten Street Rd CT7 ... 25 E3
Potter St CT13 ... 73 A1
Potteries The ME9 ... 12 E3
Potters Cl TN24 ... 138 E6
Potters Cnr TN24 ... 138 E6
Pottery Cotts TN25 ... 140 E5
Potyn Ho ME1 ... 9 C4
Pouces Cotts CT12 ... 27 F1
Poulders Gdns CT13 ... 93 E8
Poulders Rd CT13 ... 93 E8
Poulsen Ct 8 ME10 ... 37 B4
Poulton Cl CT17 ... 165 F8
Poulton Close Bsns Pk CT17 ... 148 E1
Poulton La CT3 ... 92 C8
Pound Ct TN23 ... 156 A3
Pound Farm Cotts CT18 ... 177 A7
Pound Ho TN23 ... 156 B8
Pound La Ashford TN23 ... 155 F4
Brabourne Lees TN25 ... 158 F5
Canterbury CT1 ... 66 F1
Elham CT4 ... 144 F4
Molash CT4 ... 105 F4
Poundhurst Rd TN26 ... 171 C3
Powell Cl ME20 ... 53 A3
Powell Cotton Dr CT7 ... 27 B6
Powell Sch The CT16 ... 149 B4
Powell-cotton Mus★ CT7 ... 27 B5
Power Station Rd ME12 ... 3 E7
Pratling St ME20 ... 53 C4
Precincts The CT1 ... 88 A8
Premier Bsns Ctr ME4 ... 10 C1
Prentis Cl ME10 ... 36 C5
Prentis Quay ME10 ... 36 F5
Prescott Cl CT15 ... 149 E6
Prescott Ho TN28 ... 202 A7
Prestedge Ave CT11 ... 29 E2
Preston Ave
Faversham ME13 ... 62 E6
Gillingham ME7 ... 10 E1
Preston Ct ME13 ... 62 D6
Preston Gr ME13 ... 62 D6
Preston Hall Gdns ME12 ... 6 E4
Preston Hill CT3 ... 70 B1
Preston La
Faversham ME13 ... 62 D6
Preston CT3 ... 70 B5
Preston Malt Ho ME13 ... 62 D6
Preston Par CT5 ... 42 F7
Preston Pk ME13 ... 62 D6
Preston Prim Sch CT3 ... 70 C6
Preston Rd Manston CT12 ... 28 E2
Stourmouth CT3 ... 48 D1
Wingham CT3 ... 70 B3
Preston St ME13 ... 62 D7
Preston Way ME8 ... 11 B2
Pretoria Ho 8 ME15 ... 97 E5
Pretoria Rd
Canterbury CT1 ... 88 B8
Chatham ME4 ... 9 F2

Pretoria Rd *continued*
Gillingham ME7 10 D3
Price's Ave Margate CT9 8 B2
Ramsgate CT11 52 C6
Prices Ct 5 ME10 37 B4
Priest & Sow Cnr CT5 21 B3
Priest Ave CT2 87 C7
Priest Fields CT6 23 F5
Priest Wlk CT5 21 C3
Priestdale Ct ME4 9 E3
Priestfield Rd ME7 10 E5
Priestfield Stad (Gillingham FC) ME7 10 E5
Priestfields ME1 9 B3
Primrose Ave ME8 33 B5
Primrose Cl ME4 31 E7
Primrose Dr TN23 156 B4
Primrose Gr ME9 58 A6
Primrose Hill CT4 86 B7
Primrose Ho 10 ME15 97 E7
Primrose La ME9 58 A6
Primrose Pl CT17 149 B1
Primrose Rd CT17 149 A1
Primrose Way
Cliffs End CT12 51 C5
Whitstable CT5 21 C1
Prince Andrew Rd CT10 29 E7
Prince Arthur Rd ME7 10 B6
Prince Charles Ave
Chatham ME5 32 B4
Minster (Sheppey) ME12 4 C6
Sittingbourne ME10 37 C3
Prince Charles Rd CT10 29 E7
Prince of Wales Rdbt CT17 166 D6
Prince Of Wales Residential Pk CT21 187 E8
Prince Of Wales Terr CT14 117 D5
Prince William Ct CT14 117 D7
Prince's Ave CT12 29 B1
Prince's Gdns CT9 8 C2
Prince's Rd CT11 52 D8
Prince's St Margate CT9 7 J2
9 Ramsgate CT11 52 E6
Rochester ME1 9 C4
Prince's Wlk CT9 8 D3
Princes Ave Chatham ME5 32 B5
Minster (Sheppey) ME12 4 D7
Princes Cl CT7 26 D7
Princes Cres 10 CT9 7 J2
Princes Dr CT13 95 A8
Princes Gate 18 CT20 178 E5
Princes Par CT21 176 E2
Princes St Deal CT14 117 D7
11 Dover CT16 166 D7
Maidstone ME14 75 A5
Princes Terr CT21 175 F1
Princes Way
Canterbury CT2 66 E1
Detling ME14 55 A1
Princess Anne Rd CT10 29 E7
Princess Cl CT5 21 C3
Princess Margaret Ave
Margate CT9 8 E2
Ramsgate CT12 29 A1
Princess Mary Ave ME4 10 B7
Princess Rd CT5 21 C3
Princess St CT19 178 E6
Prinys Dr ME8 33 C4
Prior Rd TN28 206 E8
Prior's Lees 8 CT20 178 D4
Prioress Rd CT2 87 D8
Prioress Wlk CT16 149 A3
Priory Cl Broadstairs CT10 29 F3
East Farleigh ME15 96 B8
New Romney TN28 201 F6
Priory Ct Gillingham ME8 11 A2
Leysdown-on-S ME12 6 G1
Rochester ME1 9 D5
Priory Fields Sch CT17 166 B8
Priory Gate 4 ME14 75 A5
Priory Gate Rd CT17 166 C8
Priory Gdns
Canterbury CT1 88 A6
Folkestone CT20 178 D4
Priory Gr CT17 166 C8
Priory Hill CT17 166 C8
Priory Hill Camp ME12 6 H1
Priory Ho CT17 166 C7
Priory Inf Sch CT11 52 D7
Priory La Herne Bay CT6 23 A3
Sellindge TN25 159 D4
Priory of St Jacob CT1 87 E6
Priory Pl ME13 40 C1
Priory Rd
Aldington Frith TN25 172 C4
Dover CT16,CT17 166 D8
Faversham ME13 62 C8
Gillingham ME8 11 A2
Maidstone ME15 75 A3
Ramsgate CT11 52 D6
Rochester ME2 9 A6
Priory Row ME13 62 C8
Priory St 10 CT16 166 D8
Priory Station Approach Rd CT17 166 C7
Priory The TN29 205 C6
Priory Way TN30 179 C7
Pritchard Ct ME7 10 C3
Pritchard Dr CT18 163 A4
Probyn Mews CT18 162 F3
Proctor Wlk CT18 162 F4
Progress Est The ME15 98 A4
Promenade
Birchington CT7 26 F8
Deal CT14 117 D3
Promenade The ME12 6 G2
Prospect Ave ME2 9 B8
Prospect Cl CT8 27 E7
Prospect Cotts
Boughton Lees TN25 122 E3
Harbledown CT2 65 E1
Shepherdswell CT15 130 D4
Prospect Ct 20 CT11 52 E6
Prospect Gdns CT12 50 B7
Prospect Hill CT6 23 A5
Prospect Mews CT21 176 C2
Prospect Pl
7 Broadstairs CT10 30 B4
Canterbury CT1 88 A7
Dover CT17 149 B1
Eastling ME13 81 E6
Hamstreet TN26 182 F7
Maidstone ME16 74 E3
St Nicholas at Wade CT7 25 E1
Prospect Rd
Birchington CT7 26 F7
Broadstairs CT10 30 B4
Folkestone CT20 177 D3
Hythe CT21 176 C2
Minster (Thanet) CT12 50 B6
Prospect Row
Chatham ME4 10 A3
Chatham,Brompton ME7 10 A6
Prospect Terr Elham CT4 144 F4
21 Ramsgate CT11 52 E6
Prospect Way TN25 158 E5
Provender La ME13,ME9 61 A6
Provender Way ME14 75 E5
Providence St TN23 156 C8
Puckle La CT1 88 A6
Pudding La Ash CT3 71 D1
Maidstone ME14 74 F4
Pudding Rd ME8 33 F8
Puffin Ct CT18 163 A3
Puffin Rd CT6 23 F4
Pullman Cl CT12 52 C8
Pump La
Gillingham ME7,ME8 11 D3
1 Margate CT9 7 J2
Purbeck Rd ME4 9 E2
Purchas Ct CT2 66 C4
Purchase La TN26 154 E8
Purr Wood CT4 107 B2
Purser Way ME7 10 C7
Puttney Dr ME10 37 A8
Pye Alley La CT5 43 C3
Pym Ho TN27 120 D7
Pynson's Ind Est CT10 29 D4
Pyott Mews 3 CT1 67 B1
Pyrus Cl ME5 54 A8
Pyson's Rd CT10,CT12 29 D3
Pyson's Road Ind Est CT10 29 D3

Q

Quain Ct CT20 178 C4
Quantock Dr TN24 139 B4
Quantock Gdns CT12 29 B3
Quarries The ME17 97 C4
Quarrington La TN25 158 B8
Quarry Cotts TN30 189 C3
Quarry Rd Hythe CT21 176 B3
Maidstone ME15 75 A2
Quarry Sq ME14 75 A5
Quarry View TN23 155 D7
Quarry Wlk CT21 177 A3
Quarry Wood TN25 173 A6
Quay Cotts ME9 38 E6
Quay Ct CT5 20 E2
Quay La Faversham ME13 62 D8
Sandwich CT13 73 A1
Quay The ME9 38 E6
Quayside ME4 10 B8
Queen Anne Rd ME14 75 B4
Queen Bertha Rd CT11 52 C6
Queen Bertha's Ave CT7 27 C8
Queen Elizabeth Ave CT9 8 D1
Queen Elizabeth Rd CT16 166 F8
Queen Elizabeth Sq ME15 97 D6
Queen Elizabeth the Queen Mother Hospl CT9 28 F8
Queen Elizabeth's Gram Sch ME13 62 D8
Queen Mother Ct CT14 117 D2
Queen Mother Ct The ME1 9 B4
Queen St Ashford TN23 139 B2
Chatham ME4 10 A4
Deal CT14 117 D6
Dover CT16,CT17 166 D7
Folkestone CT20 178 E5
Herne Bay CT6 22 F5
Margate CT9 7 I2
Ramsgate CT11 52 E6
Rochester ME1 9 C4
Queen Victoria Meml Hospl CT6 23 B4
Queen's Ave
Birchington CT7 26 D7
Broadstairs CT10 30 B6
Maidstone ME16 74 D5
Margate CT9 7 I1
Ramsgate CT12 29 B1
Queen's Ct CT6 23 A4
Queen's Gate Rd CT11 52 C8
Queen's Gdns CT16,CT17 166 D8
Queen's Lea CT15 164 E5
Queen's Prom CT9 8 B3
Queen's Rd Ash CT3 71 D2
Ashford TN24 140 A1
Broadstairs CT10 30 B4
Chatham ME5 10 D1
Faversham ME13 62 B7
Gillingham ME7 10 C4
Littlestone-on-Sea TN28 202 D6
Lydd TN29 205 C6
Maidstone ME16 74 C4
Ramsgate CT11 52 F7
Westgate-on-S CT8 27 F8
Queen's Rise CT14 133 F5
Queen's Way ME12 3 A8
Queenborough Dr ME12 4 B7
Queenborough Fst Sch ME11 3 B5
Queenborough Rd
Halfway Houses ME12 3 C6
Queenborough ME12 3 C4
Queenborough Sta ME11 3 A5
Queendown Ave ME8 33 D5
Queendown Rd CT7 28 A3
Queens Ave
Canterbury CT2 66 E1
Dover CT17 166 A7
Folkestone CT20 177 B6
Herne Bay CT6 23 D5
Queens Ct Ashford TN24 139 C3
Gillingham ME8 34 A8
Hythe CT21 176 B1
Margate CT9 8 A3
Queens Gdns
Broadstairs CT10 30 B3
Herne Bay CT6 22 F5
Queens Ho ME16 74 B3
Queens Lodge CT9 8 B3
Queens Mews CT14 117 D6
Queens Par
12 Faversham ME13 62 D7
Margate CT9 8 A3
Queens Rd Aylesham CT3 112 F5
Minster (Sheppey) ME12 4 D7
Whitstable CT5 21 A2
Queens The CT14 117 D5
Queens Way ME14 55 A1
Queensbridge Dr CT6 22 C4
Queensdown Rd CT14 134 D4
Queensway
Dymchurch TN29 186 E2
Lydd TN29 205 C6
Queenswood Rd ME20 53 D7
Quern Rd CT14 117 A2
Quern The ME15 74 E1
Querns Pl CT1 88 B8
Querns Rd CT1 88 C8
Quested Rd CT19 177 E6
Quested Way ME17 100 C6
Quetta Rd CT12 28 F1
Quex Ct CT7 27 B6
Quex House & Gdns★ CT7 27 B5
Quex Rd CT8 27 F8
Quex View Rd CT7 27 A5
Quickstep Cl ME10 36 F8
Quickthorn Cres ME5 31 E5
Quince Orch TN26 183 A7
Quinion Cl ME5 54 A8
Quinnell St ME8 11 E1
Quinton Rd ME10 36 C7

R

Rabbit Hole CT4 129 A7
Racecourse Cvn Site CT21 175 B7
Radcliffe Ct CT21 176 B2
Radfall Cnr CT5 44 C6
Radfall Gate CT5 44 C6
Radfall Hill CT5 44 D5
Radfall Rd CT5 44 D4
Radfall Ride CT5 44 C5
Radleigh Gdns ME1 9 E1
Radley Cl CT10 30 A6
Radnor Bridge Rd CT19, CT20 178 E5
Radnor Chambers 13 CT20 178 D4
Radnor Cl Herne Bay CT6 23 B1
Maidstone ME14 74 E7
Radnor Cliff CT20 178 A3
Radnor Cliff Cres CT20 178 A3
Radnor Park Ave CT19 178 C6
Radnor Park Cres CT19 178 C5
Radnor Park Gdns CT19 178 C6
Radnor Park Ho CT19 178 C6
Radnor Park Rd CT19 178 C6
Radnor Pk W CT19 178 B6
Radnor St 20 CT19 178 E5
Raggatt Pl ME15 75 B2
Raglan Pl 10 CT10 30 B4
Ragstone Hollow TN25 173 A6
Ragstone Rd ME15 76 A2
Railway Ave CT5 20 E1
Railway Cotts ME9 38 D3
Railway Hill CT4 128 E8
Railway Rd ME12 1 C2
Railway St Chatham ME4 9 F4
Gillingham ME7 10 D6
Railway St Ind Pk ME7 10 D6
Railway Terr Margate CT9 7 H1
Queenborough ME11 3 A5
Rainham Cl ME15 75 A1
Rainham Mark Gram Sch ME8 11 D2
Rainham Rd ME5 10 C3
Rainham Sch for Girls ME8 33 C8
Rainham Sh Ctr 2 ME8 11 F1
Rainham Sta ME8 11 F1
Raleigh Cl Ashford TN24 157 A8
Chatham ME5 32 A6
Raleigh Ct 1 CT11 52 F8
Raleigh Way ME12 3 E6
Ram La TN25,TN27 137 C8
Ramillies Cl ME5 32 A6
Ramp A CT16 166 H8
Ramp B CT16 166 H8
Ramp C CT16 166 G8
Ramp D CT16 166 G8
Rampart Rd CT21 176 B2
Ramparts The CT13 94 A8
Rampion Cl ME14 75 E5
Ramsey Cl CT2 66 E1
Ramsey Ho
8 Canterbury CT1 87 F7
Deal CT14 117 C3
Ramsgate Maritime Mus★ CT12 52 E6
Ramsgate Model Village★ CT11 52 D5
Ramsgate Motor Mus★ CT11 52 D5
Ramsgate Rd
Broadstairs CT10 30 B4
Broadstairs,Dumpton CT10, CT11 29 F2
Margate CT10,CT9 29 A6
Sandwich CT13 73 A7
Ramsgate Sch The CT12 29 A2
Ramsgate Sta CT12 52 C8
Ramstone Cl TN25 158 E5
Rancorn Rd CT9 7 G1
Randall Rd ME4 9 E1
Randall St ME14 74 F6
Randalls Row ME15 96 F5
Randle Way ME9 37 E2
Randolph Cl CT1 88 A7
Randolph Ct CT8 7 C1
Randolph Gdns TN24 139 E5
Randolph Ho
15 Folkestone CT20 178 E5
Gillingham ME7 10 C5
Randolph La TN31 197 B3
Randolph Rd Dover CT17 149 B1
Gillingham ME7 10 C5
Randolph Sq CT9 7 J3
Ranelagh Gdns 1 CT10 29 E5
Ranelagh Gr CT10 29 E5
Ranelagh Rd Deal CT14 117 D5
Sheerness ME12 1 D2
Range Rd Eastchurch ME12 5 D1
Hythe CT21 176 B1
Range Road Ind Est CT21 176 B1
Ransley Gn TN26 183 F8
Ransome Way CT7 26 F6
Raspberry Hill La ME9 14 D6
Ratling Rd CT3 112 F7
Rattington St CT4 86 E2
Ravelin Ho ME12 1 D2
Ravenlea Rd CT20 178 A5
Ravens Dane Cl ME15 76 A1
Ravensbourne Ave CT6 23 B3
Ravenscourt Rd
Deal CT14 117 C5
Rough Common CT2 66 B3
Ravenswood Ave ME2 9 B8
Rawdon Rd
Maidstone ME15 75 A3
Ramsgate CT11 52 C6
Rawling St ME9 58 F3
Rayham Rd CT5 44 A8
Rayleigh Cl ME16 74 D7
Rayleigh Ho 2 ME15 97 D8
Raymer Rd ME14 75 B8
Raymond Ave CT1 88 A6
Raymond Fuller Way TN24 139 E4
Raymoor Ave TN29 195 A4
Rayner Hill Cotts ME17 102 C5
Rayners Hill ME17 102 C5
Raywood Office Complex TN27 120 B4
Reach Cl CT15 150 F5
Reach Mdw CT15 151 A6
Reach Rd Lympne CT21 174 D2
St Margaret's at Cliffe CT15 150 F5
Reachfields CT21 176 A1
Readers La TN31 196 F5
Reading Cl CT14 117 B1
Reading Ho 4 ME15 97 F5
Reading Rd CT17 165 F7
Reading St
Broadstairs CT10 29 F8
Tenterden TN30 180 C2
Reading Street Rd CT10, CT9 29 E8
Readscroft Rd ME8 33 D5
Rebecca Ct 6 CT9 8 B2
Recca La CT15,CT18 146 A4
Recreation Cl ME14 75 B6
Recreation Ground Rd TN30 179 B7
Recreation Way ME10 15 A1
Rectory Bglws TN26 169 F8
Rectory Cl TN26 169 A2
Rectory Gdns CT5 21 D2
Rectory Grange ME1 9 C2
Rectory La Barham CT4 112 A2
Harrietsham ME17 100 E5
Hythe CT21 176 B5
Lyminge CT18 161 C6
Rectory La *continued*
Maidstone ME16 74 A1
Rectory Rd
Broadstairs CT10 30 B5
Deal CT14 116 F4
Sittingbourne ME10 37 B3
St Mary in the Marsh TN29 194 B4
Rectory Way TN24 139 C5
Rectory Wlk TN26 183 A7
Reculver Ave CT7 26 E8
Reculver CE Prim Sch CT6 24 A4
Reculver Cl CT6 23 F5
Reculver Ctry Pk★ CT6 24 B6
Reculver Dr CT6 23 E5
Reculver La CT6 24 B6
Reculver Rd CT6 23 D5
Reculver Wlk ME15 97 F7
Reculvers Rd CT8 27 F7
Red Brick Cotts ME13 85 A6
Red Ho The TN28 202 E6
Red Lion Ct 6 CT21 176 B2
Red Lion La 11 CT5 20 D2
Red Lion Sq 7 CT21 176 B2
Red Rd CT2 64 D5
Red Robin Cotts ME9 35 B6
Red Tree Orch TN23 155 E7
Redan Pl ME12 1 E2
Redberry Rd TN23 156 B5
Redbridge Cl ME5 32 C4
Redbrook St TN26 168 D5
Redbrooks Way CT21 175 F2
Redcliffe La ME14 75 B7
Redcot La CT2 68 B7
Redfern Ave ME7 10 E5
Redhill Rd CT8 27 E8
Redhouse Farm CT14 95 B1
Redhouse La CT4 109 D6
Redhouse Wall CT14 95 B1
Redington TN24 139 C3
Redland Shaw ME4 9 E1
Redlands Ct CT17 148 E4
Redmill Cl CT20 177 E5
Redoubt Way TN29 187 B4
Redruth Manor 3 ME7 10 C6
Redsells Cl ME15 76 A1
Redsull Ave CT14 117 A3
Redvers Cotts CT16 148 E5
Redvers Rd ME4 10 A2
Redwing Rd ME5 32 B7
Redwood Cl
Canterbury CT2 66 E2
Chartham CT4 86 E1
Chatham ME5 32 B2
Redyear Cotts TN24 140 A1
Redyear Ct TN24 140 A1
Reece Adams Ho CT18 164 B1
Reed Ave CT1 67 D3
Reed Cres TN23 156 C3
Reedland Cres ME13 62 C8
Reedmace Cl TN23 155 D8
Reeds Cl CT6 23 C4
Reeves Alley 1 CT5 20 D1
Reeves Pas 7 ME13 62 C7
Reeves Way CT5 21 C2
Reeves Yd CT5 20 D2
Reform Rd ME4 10 B2
Regency Cl
Gillingham ME8 33 C3
Sheerness ME12 1 B3
Whitstable CT5 43 F7
Regency Ct ME10 36 D4
Regency Pl CT1 67 B2
Regency Villas CT4 129 C5
Regent Dr ME15 97 A8
Regent Rd ME7 10 C4
Regent St CT5 20 D2
Regents Ct 14 TN23 139 B2
Regents Pl TN23 139 B2
Regents Wlk CT6 23 D5
Reginald Rd ME16 74 E3
Regis Bsns Pk ME12 1 B1
Regis Cres ME10 36 F7
Regis Manor Com Prim Sch ME10 36 E7
Regvlbivm Roman Fort & Reculver Twrs★ CT6 24 D7
Reinden Gr ME15 75 F1
Remston Mews 12 CT1 67 B2
Remus Cl TN23 155 F4
Renault Cl CT6 22 A4
Rendezvous St CT20 178 D5
Rendezvous The CT9 7 I3
Renown Rd ME5 32 C2
Rentain Rd CT4 86 D2
Repton Cl CT10 29 F6
Repton Manor Rd TN23 139 A3
Repton Way ME5 31 F4
Reservoir Ave TN29 209 D2
Reservoir Rd CT5 20 E2
Resolution Cl ME5 32 A6
Rest Harrow ME13 83 C5
Restharrow Rd ME14 75 E4
Retreat The
Birchington CT7 27 B8
Doddington ME9 80 D7
Ramsgate CT12 52 B8
Rettendon Dr ME10 36 F8
Revenge Rd ME5 54 C8
Reynolds Cl CT6 23 B4
Reynolds La CT3 24 D3
Rhee Wall TN26 190 D7
Rheims Ct CT2 66 D1
Rheims Way CT1,CT2 87 E8
Rhodaus Cl CT1 87 F7
Rhodaus Ho CT1 87 F7
Rhodaus Town CT1 87 F7
Rhode St ME4 10 A4

Rhodes Gdns CT10 .. 30 A6
Rhodes Ho 5 ME5 .. 10 C2
Rhodewood Cl ME15 .. 76 A1
Richard Ct 7 CT9 .. 8 B2
Richard St Chatham ME4 .. 9 F4
Rochester ME1 .. 9 C3
Richardson Way CT12 .. 51 D5
Richborough Castle & Mus★ CT13 .. 72 E5
Richborough Rd CT8 .. 27 F7
Richborough Way TN23 .. 155 E5
Richbourgh Rd CT13 .. 72 E3
Richdore Rd CT4 .. 125 C6
Richmond Ave CT9 .. 8 B1
Richmond Cl ME5 .. 32 B4
Richmond Ct CT16 .. 149 D1
Richmond Dr
Herne Bay CT6 .. 23 E5
New Romney TN28 .. 202 C8
Sittingbourne ME10 .. 36 E7
Richmond First Sch ME12 .. 1 E2
Richmond Gdns CT2 .. 66 C2
Richmond Ho 26 CT20 .. 178 E5
Richmond Inf Sch ME7 .. 10 C6
Richmond Meech Dr TN24 .. 139 E4
Richmond Rd
Gillingham ME7 .. 10 C7
Ramsgate CT11 .. 52 D6
Whitstable CT5 .. 21 B1
Richmond St
Folkestone CT19 .. 177 D6
Herne Bay CT6 .. 22 F5
Sheerness ME12 .. 1 E2
Richmond Way ME15 .. 97 A8
Riddles Rd ME10,ME9 .. 36 C3
Ridge Meadow Prim Sch ME5 .. 31 F6
Ridge The TN24 .. 139 E6
Ridgeway Lympne CT21 .. 175 A3
Whitstable CT5 .. 21 C1
Ridgeway Cliff CT6 .. 22 C5
Ridgeway Rd CT6 .. 46 A7
Ridgeway Terr TN25 .. 158 C5
Ridgeway The
Boughton Street ME13 .. 64 A3
Broadstairs CT10 .. 29 F3
Chatham ME4 .. 31 E7
Crabble CT17 .. 148 E2
Gillingham ME7 .. 10 C7
Margate CT9 .. 8 B1
Smeeth TN25 .. 158 B5
Ridgeway Wlk CT6 .. 46 A7
Ridgway ME16 .. 74 B2
Ridham Ave ME10 .. 15 A1
Ridham Dock ME9 .. 15 B6
Riding Hill TN24 .. 139 C6
Ridings The
7 Canterbury CT1 .. 67 B1
Margate CT9 .. 8 F3
Whitstable CT5 .. 21 D1
Ridlands CT1 .. 88 A5
Ridley Cl CT6 .. 46 A8
Ridley Rd ME1 .. 9 B4
Rigden Rd TN23 .. 156 B7
Rigden's Ct 6 ME10 .. 36 E5
Rigshill Rd ME13 .. 103 B6
Riley Ave CT6 .. 21 F4
Rimpton Ct CT10 .. 29 F7
Ring Wall CT14 .. 94 E2
Ringlestone Cres ME14 .. 74 F8
Ringlestone Rd ME17 .. 78 D4
Ringold Ave CT12 .. 52 A8
Ringsloe Ct CT7 .. 26 D8
Ringwood Cl
Canterbury CT2 .. 66 E3
Gillingham ME8 .. 33 D8
Ringwood Rd ME15 .. 97 C8
Ringwould Rd
Kingsdown CT14 .. 134 B5
Ringwould CT14,CT15 .. 133 D4
Ripley Rd TN24 .. 157 A8
Ripon Cl ME8 .. 11 D3
Ripper's Cross TN26 .. 137 D4
Ripple Cross CT14 .. 133 F6
Ripple Rd CT14 .. 133 F7
Ripple Sch The CT14 .. 133 D8
Ripplevale Sch CT14 .. 133 E8
Risborough La CT19, CT20 .. 177 D5
Risborough Way CT20 .. 177 E6
Risdon Cl CT2 .. 67 F6
Rise The Ashford TN23 .. 155 E7
Borden ME9 .. 36 B2
Chatham ME4 .. 10 A7
Gillingham ME7 .. 33 A3
Halfway Houses ME12 .. 3 C5
Kingsdown CT14 .. 134 D5
Rochester ME1 .. 9 D3
St Margaret's at Cliffe CT15 .. 151 B6
Rising Rd TN23 .. 139 A1
River Bank Cl 8 ME15 .. 75 B4
River Cl ME15 .. 96 A7
River Ct Chartham CT4 .. 86 D3
Crabble CT17 .. 148 F2
River Dale CT17 .. 148 F3
River Dr CT17 .. 148 F2
River Mdw CT17 .. 148 F3
River Prim Sch CT17 .. 148 E3
River Rd CT13 .. 73 B4
River St 6 Chatham ME7 .. 10 A6
River CT17 .. 148 E3
River View Gillingham ME8 .. 11 D3
Maidstone ME15 .. 74 F2
Rushenden ME11 .. 2 F3
Sturry CT2 .. 67 F7
River View Cl 6 ME4 .. 9 F3
Riverbank Way TN24 .. 156 D6
Riverbourne Ct 6 ME10 .. 36 F4
Riverdale Rd CT1 .. 67 B2
Riverhead Cl
Maidstone ME16 .. 74 D6
Margate CT9 .. 8 B1
Sittingbourne ME10 .. 36 C3
Rivermead Sch ME7 .. 10 E6
Rivers Rd ME9 .. 38 D2
Rivers Wlk ME17 .. 101 C5
Riversdale Rd
Ashford TN23 .. 156 C8
Ramsgate CT12 .. 29 B1
Riverside Chartham CT4 .. 86 C3
Crabble CT17 .. 148 F3
Temple Ewell CT16 .. 148 C5
Riverside Bsns Pk TN24 .. 139 D2
Riverside Cl Bridge CT4 .. 89 A1
Kingsnorth TN23 .. 156 A4
Riverside Ct 11 CT2 .. 66 F1
Riverside Ctry Pk & Visitor Ctr★ ME7 .. 11 D5
Riverside Ind Est CT21 .. 175 B1
Riverside Mews CT4 .. 89 A1
Riverside Pk ME16 .. 96 A8
Riverside Prim Sch ME8 .. 12 A1
Riverside Rd CT13 .. 51 A1
Riverside Ret Pk CT1 .. 87 D6
Riverside Sch TN23 .. 138 F1
Riverview TN23 .. 138 E1
Riviera Ct 6 CT20 .. 177 E3
Riviera Rd CT20 .. 178 A3
Riviera The CT20 .. 177 F3
Roach St ME2 .. 9 A7
Road of Remembrance CT20 .. 178 D4
Robert Brundett Cl TN24 .. 139 E5
Robert Napier Sch The ME7 .. 10 E3
Robert St CT14 .. 117 D7
Roberts Cl ME10 .. 36 D7
Roberts Rd
Gillingham ME8 .. 33 E8
Greatstone-on-Sea TN28 .. 202 E1
Whitstable CT5 .. 42 F6
Robeshaw ME9 .. 58 E2
Robin Ct 6 Rochester ME1 .. 9 D4
Whitstable CT5 .. 21 A3
Robin Ho 5 ME16 .. 74 E4
Robin Hood La
Chatham ME5 .. 31 D1
Lydd TN29 .. 205 C5
Robin Hood Lane (Lower) ME5 .. 31 F2
Robin Hood Lane (Upper) ME5 .. 31 E1
Robin La TN29 .. 205 C6
Robin's Cl CT21 .. 187 C8
Robina Ct CT9 .. 8 D3
Robins Ave ME17 .. 101 C5
Robins Cl ME17 .. 101 C4
Robins Ct ME14 .. 75 B7
Robson's Yd CT17 .. 166 C8
Robus Cl CT18 .. 161 C7
Robus Terr CT18 .. 161 C7
Robyn Cotts TN26 .. 167 E8
Rochester Airport ME1, ME5 .. 31 C6
Rochester Airport Ind Est ME1 .. 31 C5
Rochester Ave
Canterbury CT1 .. 88 B7
Rochester ME1 .. 9 C4
Rochester Castle★ ME1 .. 9 C6
Rochester Cath★ ME1 .. 9 C6
Rochester Ct
Canterbury CT1 .. 88 B6
Rochester ME2 .. 9 E8
Rochester Gate ME1 .. 9 D5
Rochester Gram Sch for Girls The ME1 .. 9 C2
Rochester Ho 1 ME15 .. 97 D7
Rochester Ind Coll ME1 .. 9 D4
Rochester Rd
Burham ME1 .. 53 A8
Chatham ME1,ME5 .. 31 C4
Pratling Street ME20 .. 53 B4
Rochester St ME4 .. 9 E3
Rochester Sta ME1 .. 9 D5
Rock Ave ME7 .. 10 C3
Rock Hill Rd TN27 .. 118 E2
Rock Rd Maidstone ME14 .. 75 A6
Sittingbourne ME10 .. 36 E4
Rockingham Pl CT6 .. 23 B2
Rockstone Way CT12 .. 29 A1
Rocky Bourne Rd TN25 .. 172 D5
Rocky Hill ME16 .. 74 E4
Rocky Hill Terr 2 ME16 .. 74 E4
Rodmer Cl ME12 .. 4 C8
Rodmersham Gn ME9 .. 59 B7
Rodmersham Sch ME9 .. 59 B7
Rodney St CT11 .. 52 D6
Roebuck Ho ME1 .. 9 E5
Roebuck Rd
Faversham ME13 .. 62 A7
Rochester ME1 .. 9 C5
Roentgen Ho ME10 .. 36 D5
Roethorne Gdns TN30 .. 179 B8
Roffen Rd ME1 .. 9 C2
Rogersmead TN30 .. 179 A7
Rokesley Rd CT16 .. 149 B5
Rolfe La TN28 .. 202 B7
Roll's Ave ME12 .. 5 C1
Rolvenden Ave ME8 .. 11 C3
Rolvenden Dr ME10 .. 36 B5
Roly Eckhoff Ho CT16 .. 149 B3
Roman Amphitheatre★ CT13 .. 72 E4
Roman Cl Chatham ME5 .. 31 D1
Deal CT14 .. 117 B6
Roman Hts ME14 .. 75 C6
Roman Rd
East Studdal CT15 .. 132 C5
Faversham ME13 .. 62 C7
Ramsgate CT12 .. 29 C2
Whitfield CT15 .. 149 D8
Roman Sq ME10 .. 36 F3
Roman Way
Elvington CT15 .. 114 B2
Folkestone CT19 .. 177 C6
Kingsnorth TN23 .. 156 C4
St Margaret's at Cliffe CT15 .. 150 F5
Romany Ct ME5 .. 10 D1
Romany Rd ME8 .. 11 C2
Romden Rd TN27 .. 152 B8
Rome House Cnr TN28 .. 202 A6
Rome Rd TN28 .. 202 A6
Rome Terr ME4 .. 9 F4
Romilly Gdns CT12 .. 29 C2
Romney Ave CT20 .. 177 F5
Romney Cl
4 Birchington CT7 .. 27 A7
Maidstone ME14 .. 76 A3
Romney Ct ME10 .. 36 E5
Romney Marsh Ho TN29 .. 195 C7
Romney Marsh Rd TN23, TN24 .. 156 B6
Romney Pl ME15 .. 75 A4
Romney Rd
Ashford TN24 .. 139 E1
Chatham ME5 .. 32 B5
Hamstreet TN26 .. 183 A7
New Romney TN29 .. 201 E3
Romney Sands Holiday Village TN28 .. 206 D8
Romney Sands Sta TN28 .. 206 E8
Romney Warren Ctry Pk★ TN28 .. 194 D1
Romney Way CT21 .. 175 F1
Romney, Hythe & Dymchurch Rly★ CT21 .. 176 A2
Romsey Cl TN24 .. 140 A2
Romulus Gdns TN23 .. 155 F4
Ronalds Ct 6 ME10 .. 37 A4
Rook La ME9 .. 35 F6
Rookery Cl Ashford TN24 .. 139 D7
Bredgar ME9 .. 58 A6
Rookston Cnr CT3 .. 48 D1
Roonagh Ct ME10 .. 36 E2
Roosevelt Ave ME5 .. 32 A8
Roosevelt Rd CT16 .. 149 B3
Rope Walk Mews CT13 .. 93 F8
Rope Wlk ME4 .. 9 F5
Ropemakers Ct ME4 .. 10 A1
Roper Cl Canterbury CT2 .. 66 E1
Gillingham ME8 .. 33 C3
Roper Rd Canterbury CT2 .. 66 E1
Teynham ME9 .. 38 D3
Rosamund Ct CT19 .. 178 C6
Rose Acre Rd CT3 .. 89 F7
Rose Cotts Hythe CT21 .. 176 B4
Lenham Heath ME17 .. 119 B8
Ramsgate CT12 .. 28 F2
Rose Ct ME17 .. 96 D1
Rose Farm La TN27 .. 136 A5
Rose Gdns Birchington CT7 .. 26 F6
Eythorne CT15 .. 131 D7
Herne Bay CT6 .. 23 C4
Minster (Thanet) CT12 .. 50 B6
Rose Hill
11 Ramsgate CT11 .. 52 E6
Wittersham TN30 .. 189 B5
Rose La
Bishopsbourne CT4 .. 111 C6
Canterbury CT1 .. 87 F8
Lenham Heath ME17 .. 119 B8
Rose St Rochester ME1 .. 9 D3
Sheerness ME12 .. 1 C2
Rose Street Prim Sch ME12 .. 1 C2
Rose Terr ME13 .. 62 D5
Rose Wlk CT18 .. 163 A4
Rose Yd ME14 .. 75 A4
Roseacre Cl CT2 .. 66 E1
Roseacre Ct CT9 .. 8 E2
Roseacre Gdns ME14 .. 76 A3
Roseacre Jun Sch ME14 .. 76 A4
Roseacre La ME14 .. 76 A4
Rosebery Ave
Herne Bay CT6 .. 23 E5
Ramsgate CT11 .. 29 F1
Rosebery Cl ME10 .. 37 D4
Rosebery Rd Chatham ME4 .. 9 E2
Gillingham ME7 .. 10 D7
Rosedale Rd CT9 .. 8 A1
Roseholme ME16 .. 74 D2
Roselands CT14 .. 117 C1
Roselands Gdns CT2 .. 66 D2
Roselawn Gdns 3 CT9 .. 28 B8
Roselea Ave CT6 .. 22 F3
Roseleigh Ave ME16 .. 74 C5
Roseleigh Rd ME10 .. 36 D2
Rosemary Ave
Broadstairs CT10 .. 30 A3
Halfway Houses ME12 .. 3 D6
Rosemary Cl 4 ME5 .. 31 F4
Rosemary Cnr TN29 .. 199 D8
Rosemary Ct 1 ME1 .. 9 D4
Rosemary Gdns
Broadstairs CT10 .. 29 F2
Whitstable CT5 .. 44 A8
Rosemary La 16 CT1 .. 87 F8
Rosemary Rd ME15 .. 76 A3
Rosemount Cl ME15 .. 96 F4
Rosetower Ct CT10 .. 29 F8
Rosewood Dr TN25 .. 138 F4
Rosewood Way CT7 .. 27 B7
Rosiers Ct 1 CT2 .. 66 E1
Ross Gdns CT2 .. 66 B3
Ross St ME1 .. 9 D4
Ross Way CT20 .. 177 E5
Rossendale Ct 10 CT20 .. 178 E6
Rossendale Gdns 8 CT20 .. 178 E6
Rossendale Rd CT20 .. 178 E6
Rossetti Ct CT7 .. 26 F7
Rossetti Rd CT7 .. 26 F8
Rossland Rd CT12 .. 52 A8
Rosslyn Gn ME16 .. 74 B5
Rothbrook Dr TN24 .. 139 C7
Rother Vale ME5 .. 32 C3
Rothley Cl TN30 .. 179 B8
Rothsay Ct CT11 .. 29 F1
Rough Common Rd CT2 .. 66 B3
Round Wood Cl ME5 .. 32 A1
Roundel Cl ME9 .. 38 D2
Roundel The ME10 .. 36 F2
Roundwell ME14 .. 76 D3
Rover Rd ME5 .. 32 B2
Row The Ash CT3 .. 71 E5
Chillenden CT3 .. 113 F8
Elham CT4 .. 144 F5
Ruckinge TN26 .. 183 F8
Rowan Cl Ashford TN23 .. 138 E2
Staple CT3 .. 92 A6
Sturry CT2 .. 67 F6
Rowan Ct Ashford TN24 .. 156 E8
Broadstairs CT10 .. 30 A5
Rowan Ho
4 Chatham ME5 .. 31 F5
7 Maidstone ME16 .. 74 A3
Rowan Lea ME5 .. 10 B1
Rowan Tree Pk CT5 .. 43 B6
Rowan Wlk ME4 .. 9 E3
Rowans The ME12 .. 4 B7
Rowbrocke Cl ME8 .. 33 D3
Rowe Cl CT9 .. 28 F7
Rowena Rd CT8 .. 7 C1
Rowetts Way ME12 .. 5 D3
Rowland Ave ME7 .. 10 E2
Rowland Cl
Gillingham ME7 .. 10 E1
Maidstone ME16 .. 74 E3
Rowland Cotts CT21 .. 174 F3
Rowland Cres CT6 .. 23 E5
Rowland Dr CT6 .. 22 C2
Roxburgh Rd CT8 .. 7 D1
Royal Ave CT5 .. 43 C5
Royal Cl CT10 .. 29 F4
Royal Cres Margate CT9 .. 7 H2
Ramsgate CT11 .. 52 D5
Royal Ct CT5 .. 21 A3
Royal Eagle Cl ME2 .. 9 E7
Royal Engineers Mus★ ME7 .. 10 B6
Royal Engineers' Rd ME14 .. 74 F7
Royal Espl Margate CT9 .. 7 F1
Ramsgate CT11 .. 52 C5
Royal Fountain Mews ME12 .. 1 B2
Royal Harbour App CT11 .. 52 C5
Royal Mews 16 CT11 .. 52 F7
Royal Military Ave CT20 .. 177 D5
Royal Military Rd
Aldington TN25 .. 173 D1
Hythe CT21 .. 175 D1
Royal Mus & art Gallery with Buffs Regimental Mus★ CT1 .. 87 F8
Royal Par CT11 .. 52 E6
Royal Rd Ramsgate CT11 .. 52 D6
Sheerness ME12 .. 1 D2
Royal School for Deaf Children CT9 .. 7 J2
Royal Sovereign Ave ME4 .. 10 B7
Royal St George's Golf Links★ CT13 .. 73 E2
Royal Star Arc 5 ME14 .. 74 F4
Royal Victoria Hospl CT19 .. 178 C6
Royal Victoria Pl 5 CT16 .. 166 D8
Royds Rd TN24 .. 156 D6
Royston Gdns CT15 .. 150 F6
Royston Rd ME15 .. 76 A3
Roystons Cl ME8 .. 11 F2
Royton Ave ME17 .. 101 D5
RSPB Dungeness Nature Reserve★ TN29 .. 208 F5
Rubery Dro CT3 .. 72 C7
Ruckinge Cnr TN26 .. 183 F8
Ruckinge Rd TN26 .. 183 A7
Ruckinge Way ME8 .. 11 C3
Rudge Cl ME5 .. 32 D2
Ruffets Wood TN23 .. 156 C3
Rugby Cl Broadstairs CT10 .. 29 F5
Chatham ME5 .. 31 F4
Rugby Gdns TN23 .. 156 C8
Rugby Rd CT17 .. 166 A6
Ruins Barn Rd ME10,ME9 .. 58 D6
Rule Ct ME12 .. 3 B8
Rumfields Rd CT10 .. 29 D4
Rumstead La ME17,ME9 .. 56 D4
Rumstead Rd ME9 .. 56 E4
Rumwood Ct ME17 .. 98 B5
Runcie Ho 6 CT1 .. 87 F7
Runcie Pl CT2 .. 66 D1
Runham La ME17 .. 100 E3
Running Horse Rdbt The ME14 .. 53 E1
Runnymede Gdns ME15 .. 97 A8
Runnymede Mews ME13 .. 62 C7
Rush Cl Chatham ME5 .. 32 A3
Dymchurch TN29 .. 195 B6
Rusham Rd CT3 .. 70 C1
Rushenden Ct ME11 .. 2 F3
Rushenden Rd ME11 .. 3 A4
Rushmead Cl CT2 .. 66 D2
Rushmead Dr ME15 .. 97 A7
Ruskins View CT6 .. 23 A1
Russell Cl ME10 .. 36 C3
Russell Ct ME4 .. 10 B3
Russell Dr CT5 .. 21 D3
Russell Pl ME13 .. 40 B3
Russell Rd
1 Folkestone CT19 .. 178 D6
Kit's Coty ME20 .. 53 D7
Russell St Dover CT16 .. 166 E7
Sheerness ME12 .. 1 C2
Russells Ave ME8 .. 34 A8
Russet Ave ME13 .. 62 E5
Russet Ct ME17 .. 96 C3
Russets The
Maidstone ME16 .. 74 B5
Whitstable CT5 .. 21 D1
Russett Rd CT1 .. 88 C8
Ruth Ho 2 ME16 .. 74 E5
Ruth St ME4 .. 10 A2
Rutherford Coll CT2 .. 66 E4
Rutherford Rd TN24 .. 139 B5
Rutland Ave CT9 .. 8 C2
Rutland Cl CT1 .. 88 D7
Rutland Gdns
Birchington CT7 .. 26 F7
Margate CT9 .. 8 C2
Rutland Ho 3 CT9 .. 8 B2
Rutland Pl ME8 .. 33 C3
Rutland Rd CT16 .. 149 B3
Rutland Way ME15 .. 97 E8
Ryan Dr ME15 .. 76 A2
Rycault Cl 4 ME16 .. 74 E3
Rycaut Cl ME8 .. 33 D3
Rydal Ave CT11 .. 52 B7
Rydal Ho ME15 .. 97 E7
Ryde Cl ME5 .. 32 B8
Ryde St CT2 .. 66 E1
Ryder's Ave CT8 .. 27 D8
Rye Ct TN23 .. 155 D7
Rye Rd Brookland TN29 .. 199 D8
Peasmarsh TN31 .. 196 E2
Wittersham TN30 .. 189 A2
Rye Wlk CT6 .. 23 C2
Ryegrass Cl ME5 .. 32 C6
Ryland Ct 5 CT20 .. 178 E5
Ryland Pl 6 CT20 .. 178 E5
Rylands Rd TN24 .. 139 D5
Rype Cl TN29 .. 205 C5
Ryswick Mews TN28 .. 202 C8

S

Sabre Ct ME7 .. 11 A1
Sackett's Gap CT9 .. 8 C3
Sacketts Hill CT10 .. 29 C6
Sackville Cl TN26 .. 138 A7
Sackville Cres TN23 .. 139 A2
Saddlebrook Pk ME12 .. 6 E2
Saddler's Wall La TN29 .. 191 B1
Saddlers Cl ME14 .. 75 E5
Saddlers Hill CT3 .. 91 D2
Saddlers Mews CT5 .. 21 D1
Saddlers Way TN23 .. 156 B5
Saddleton Gr CT5 .. 43 D8
Saddleton Rd CT5 .. 43 D8
Sadlers Cl ME5 .. 31 D2
Saffron Cl ME16 .. 74 B3
Saffron Way
1 Chatham ME5 .. 31 F5
Sittingbourne ME10 .. 36 F7
Saffron's Pl 14 CT20 .. 178 E5
Sage Rd ME1 .. 9 B3
Sailfield Ct ME4 .. 9 F7
Sailmakers Ct 5 ME4 .. 10 B2
St Agnes Gdns ME12 .. 1 D1
St Alban's Rd CT3 .. 46 E1
St Albans Cl ME7 .. 10 E7
St Alphege CE Prim Sch CT5 .. 20 D1
St Alphege Cl CT5 .. 43 B7
St Alphege La 17 CT1 .. 66 F1
St Alphege Rd 4 CT16 .. 149 C1
St Ambrose Gn TN25 .. 123 E2
St Andrew Terr CT17 .. 149 A2
St Andrew's Cl
Maidstone ME16 .. 74 A2
Whitstable CT5 .. 43 E7
St Andrew's Gdns CT15 .. 130 E5
St Andrew's Lees CT13 .. 94 A8
St Andrew's Rd
Deal CT14 .. 117 C6
Littlestone-on-Sea TN28 .. 202 E6
Maidstone ME16 .. 74 A3
Ramsgate CT11 .. 52 F8
St Andrews CT19 .. 178 E5
St Andrews Cl
Canterbury CT1 .. 87 E7
Folkestone CT19 .. 178 B7
Herne Bay CT6 .. 23 A4
Margate CT9 .. 28 F7
St Andrews Gdns CT17 .. 149 B2
St Andrews Pk ME16 .. 74 A3

St Andrews Rd ME7 10 D7
St Andrews Sch ME1 9 C4
St Andrews Way CT14 115 A3
St Angela's Sch CT8 27 D7
St Ann's Rd
Dymchurch TN29 195 B7
Faversham ME13 62 B7
St Anne's Ct
1 Dover CT16 149 B2
Herne Bay CT6 22 E5
St Anne's Dr CT6 22 D4
St Anne's Gdns CT9 28 F8
St Anne's Rd
Ashford TN23 155 F7
Whitstable CT5 20 F2
St Annes Ct ME16 74 E4
St Anselm's RC Sch CT1 88 C5
St Anthony's Sch CT9 8 C1
St Anthony's Way CT9 8 C1
St Augustine of Canterbury RC Prim Sch ME8 33 D3
St Augustine's Abbey CT11 52 D5
St Augustine's Abbey (rems of)★ CT1 88 A8
St Augustine's Ave CT9 28 F8
St Augustine's Cres CT5 21 D3
St Augustine's Ct 3 CT1 88 B8
St Augustine's Pk CT11 52 C6
St Augustine's RC Prim Sch CT21 176 E2
St Augustine's Rd
Canterbury CT1 88 B7
Deal CT14 116 F4
Ramsgate CT11 52 D5
St Augustines Bsns Pk CT5 21 E3
St Augustines Ct CT6 22 F2
St Barnabas Cl
Ashford TN23 155 F7
Gillingham ME7 10 D3
Maidstone ME16 74 C8
St Bart's Cl 5 CT17 166 C8
St Bart's Rd CT13 93 F8
St Bartholemews Cl 4 CT17 166 C8
St Bartholomew's Hospl ME1 9 E4
St Bartholomew's Hospl CT13 94 A7
St Bartholomew's La 4 ME1 9 E4
St Bartholomew's Terr 2 ME1 9 E4
St Benedict's Lawn CT11 52 D5
St Benedicts RC Prim Sch ME5 32 C2
St Benet's Rd CT8 27 E7
St Benets Ct TN30 179 B8
St Benets Way TN30 179 B8
St Catherine's Dr ME13 62 D6
St Catherine's Gr CT12 28 D1
St Catherine's Hospl ME1 9 D4
St Catherines TN29 201 A7
St Catherines Ct
Ramsgate CT11 29 F1
Rochester ME1 9 D5
St Cecilia Ho CT14 117 B1
St Christopher Cl CT9 29 D8
St Christopher's Sch CT1 88 B6
St Christophers Gn CT10 29 F5
St Clare Rd CT14 117 C1
St Clement's Ct CT6 23 A3
St Clement's Ho ME1 9 D5
St Clement's Rd CT8 7 C1
St Clements 8 CT13 73 A1
St Clements Cl ME12 6 D2
St Clements Ct
Broadstairs CT10 29 E6
Folkestone CT20 178 F5
Ramsgate CT11 52 D7
St Clements Rd ME12 6 E3
St Cosmus Cl TN25 105 B1
St Crispin's Com Prim Inf Sch CT8 27 E7
St Crispin's Rd CT8 27 E7
St Cuby CT10 30 C7
St David's Cl
Birchington CT7 27 B8
Whitstable CT5 43 E8
St David's Rd Deal CT14 117 C6
Ramsgate CT11 29 F1
St Davids Ave CT17 166 A5
St Davids Gate ME16 74 A2
St Denys Rd CT18 163 B5
St Dunstan's Cl CT2 66 E1
St Dunstan's Rd CT9 8 A2
St Dunstan's St CT2 66 E1
St Dunstan's Terr CT2 66 E1
St Dunstans Ct 4 CT2 66 E1
St Eanswythe Way 19 CT20 178 D5
St Eanswythe's CE Prim Sch CT20 178 D4
St Edmund's RC Sch CT16 149 D2
St Edmund's Rd CT14 116 E4
St Edmund's Sch CT2 66 C3
St Edmunds Rd CT1 87 F8
St Edmunds Way ME8 12 B1
St Edward's RC Prim Sch ME12 1 C2
St Elisabeth Ho CT1 67 A1
St Ethelbert's RC Prim Sch CT11 52 F8
St Faith's at Ash Sch CT3 71 C1
St Faith's La ME14 76 B4
St Faith's St ME14 74 F4
St Francis Cl Deal CT14 116 F4
Maidstone ME14 75 B7
Margate CT9 29 D8
St Francis RC Prim Sch ME15 74 C4
St Francis Rd CT19 177 F6
St Gabriel's Ct 12 CT20 178 E6
St George's Ave
Herne Bay CT6 22 D4
Sheerness ME12 1 C1
St George's Bsns Ctr TN23 138 F2
St George's CE Foundation Sch CT10 29 C5
St George's CE Mid Sch ME12 4 E6
St George's Cl CT5 43 E7
St George's Ct ME12 3 B8
St George's Lees CT13 94 A8
St George's Pas CT14 117 D6
St George's Pl
Canterbury CT1 88 A8
Hythe CT21 187 D8
St George's Rd
Broadstairs CT10 30 A4
Deal CT14 117 D6
Folkestone CT19 177 F6
Gillingham ME7 10 C6
Ramsgate CT11 52 F8
Sandwich CT13 94 A8
St George's Sq
3 Ashford TN24 139 B2
Maidstone ME16 74 E3
St George's St CT1 88 A8
St George's Terr CT6 22 E5
St Georges Ave ME12 5 D2
St Georges Bsns Pk ME10 37 B4
St Georges Cres CT17 166 B5
St Georges Ct CT17 149 A2
St Georges La CT1 88 A8
St Georges Pl
Sandwich CT13 94 B8
St Margaret's at Cliffe CT15 150 F6
St Georges St CT1 88 A8
St Giles Cl CT17 166 B5
St Giles Rd CT17 166 B5
St Giles Wlk CT17 166 B5
St Gregory's 9 CT1 67 A1
St Gregory's Cl CT14 116 F4
St Gregory's Ct CT1 67 B1
St Gregory's RC Prim Sch CT9 28 E8
St Gregory's Rd CT1 67 B1
St Helen's Rd ME12 1 E1
St Helier's Cl ME16 74 B2
St Hilda Rd CT19 177 E6
St Hilda's Rd CT21 176 B1
St Jacob's Pl CT1 87 D6
St James Cl ME12 6 E4
St James La 7 CT16 166 E7
St James Rd CT14 134 D5
St James St CT16 166 E7
St James' Ave
Broadstairs CT10 29 E5
Ramsgate CT12 29 B1
St James' Gdns CT5 43 D8
St James' Park Rd CT9 28 A8
St James's Terr CT7 27 B8
St Jean's Rd CT8 27 E7
St John Bsns Ctr The 10 CT9 7 J1
St John Fisher RC Comp (Lower) Sch ME4 9 F2
St John Fisher RC Comp Sch ME4 9 E3
St John's Ave
Ramsgate CT12 29 A1
Sittingbourne ME10 37 B3
St John's CE Inf Sch ME4 9 E3
St John's CE Prim Sch ME14 75 E4
St John's Church Rd CT19 178 C6
St John's Cl CT18 163 A7
St John's Commandery (rems of)★ CT15 146 E4
St John's Cotts
Bethersden TN26 153 D5
12 Sandwich CT13 72 F1
St John's Ct TN24 157 A6
St John's Hospl 6 CT1 67 A1
St John's La
Ashford TN23,TN24 139 C2
Canterbury CT1 87 F8
St John's Pl CT1 67 A1
St John's Rd Dover CT17 166 C7
Faversham ME13 62 D7
Gillingham ME7 10 C3
Margate CT9 7 J2
New Romney TN28 202 A6
Whitstable CT5 21 D3
St John's St
Folkestone CT20 178 D5
7 Margate CT9 7 J2
St John's Way CT18 163 A7
St Johns Cres CT2 66 D6
St Johns Rd
Elvington CT15 114 B2
Hythe CT21 176 A3
St Johns Way ME1 9 A2
St Joseph's RC Prim Sch
Aylesham CT3 113 A5
Broadstairs CT10 29 F5
St Julien Ave CT1 67 D1
St Katherine Rd ME12 3 E7
St Laurence Ave ME16 74 C8
St Laurence Cl ME9 37 D2
St Laurence Ct CT11 52 C7
St Laurence In Thanet CE Jun Sch CT11 52 B8
St Lawrence Ave CT11 52 B5
St Lawrence Cl CT1 88 B6
St Lawrence Coll CT11 52 D8
St Lawrence Coll Jun Sch CT11 52 E8
St Lawrence Ct TN28 202 A6
St Lawrence Forstal CT1 88 B6
St Lawrence Gd (Kent Cty Cricket Club) CT1 88 B6
St Lawrence Ind Est CT11 52 B7
St Lawrence Rd CT1 88 B6
St Leonard's Rd CT14 117 B4
St Leonards Ave ME4 9 F2
St Leonards Ct CT21 176 B1
St Leonards Mews CT21 176 B1
St Leonards Rd
Hythe CT21 176 B1
Maidstone ME16 74 C8
St Louis Gr CT6 22 C4
St Luke's Ave
Maidstone ME14 75 B5
Ramsgate CT11 52 E8
St Luke's Cl CT8 27 E8
St Luke's Rd
Maidstone ME14 75 B5
Ramsgate CT11 52 E8
St Luke's Wlk CT18 162 F4
St Lukes Cl CT5 43 E7
St Lukes Ct Ashford TN23 155 F7
Maidstone ME14 75 A6
St Magnus Cl CT7 27 A8
St Magnus Ct CT7 27 A8
St Malo Ct 2 CT20 178 C4
St Margaret's at Troy Town CE Prim Sch ME1 9 C4
St Margaret's Banks ME1 9 D5
St Margaret's CE Jun Sch ME8 33 E8
St Margaret's Cl CT5 43 A6
St Margaret's Ct 6 ME8 33 F8
St Margaret's Inf Sch ME8 33 E8
St Margaret's Mews ME1 9 C5
St Margaret's Rd
St Margaret's at Cliffe CT15 151 A5
Westgate-on-S CT8 27 E7
St Margaret's St
Canterbury CT1 87 F8
Rochester ME1 9 C5
St Margaret's-at-Cliffe Prim Sch CT15 151 A6
St Margarets Cl ME16 74 B2
St Margarets Ct 1 CT20 178 B5
St Margarets Dr
Deal CT14 134 B8
Gillingham ME8 33 C5
St Margarets Rd
St Margaret's at Cliffe CT15 134 A1
Westgate-on-S CT7 27 F3
St Mark's Cl CT20 177 D5
St Marks Cl CT5 43 E8
St Marks Ho ME7 10 C5
St Martin's Cl
Detling ME14 55 A1
Dover CT17 166 B5
St Martin's Hill CT1 88 C8
St Martin's Hospl CT1 88 D8
St Martin's Pl CT1 88 B8
St Martin's Rd
Canterbury CT1 67 B1
Deal CT14 116 F4
Dover CT15 149 E4
St Martin's Sch CT17 166 A7
St Martin's Terr CT1 88 B8
St Martin's View CT6 46 A8
St Martins Ave CT1 88 B8
St Martins Cl
Canterbury CT1 88 B8
Newington ME9 35 C7
St Martins Ct 4 CT1 88 B8
St Martins Cvn Site CT3 88 E8
St Martins Ho CT17 166 D5
St Martins Rd
Folkestone CT20 177 D6
New Romney TN28 202 B6
St Mary Ct 13 ME13 62 D7
St Mary of Charity CE Prim Sch ME13 62 D7
St Mary's Ave Margate CT9 8 D1
Margate CT9 29 D8
St Mary's Bay Sta TN29 194 F4
St Mary's CE Prim Sch
Ashford TN23 139 A3
Chilham CT4 107 B8
Dover CT16 166 E8
St Mary's Church★ CT6 24 C7
St Mary's Cl Eastry CT13 93 C2
Hamstreet TN26 183 A8
Nonington CT15 113 C5
Woodnesborough CT13 93 B6
St Mary's Ct 17 CT1 87 F8
St Mary's Ct CT6 22 E4
St Mary's Gdns
Chatham ME4 10 B7
St Mary's Gdns *continued*
St Mary's Bay TN29 195 A5
Upstreet CT3 47 E3
St Mary's Gr
Tilmanstone CT14 115 A4
Whitstable CT5 42 F7
St Mary's Mdw CT3 91 A8
St Mary's Pl ME9 35 C7
St Mary's Prim Sch ME2 9 B7
St Mary's RC Prim Sch
Deal CT14 116 F3
Gillingham ME7 10 D6
Whitstable CT5 20 F2
St Mary's Rd
5 Broadstairs CT10 30 B4
Deal CT14 117 C1
Elham CT4 144 F4
Faversham ME13 62 D7
Gillingham ME7 10 C6
Minster (Thanet) CT12 50 B6
Patrixbourne CT4 89 B3
Rochester ME2 9 B7
St Mary in the Marsh TN28,TN29 194 C5
West Hythe CT21 175 B1
St Mary's Row ME12 4 A6
St Mary's St CT1 87 F8
St Mary's Terr 2 CT20 178 E5
St Mary's View ME9 35 C7
St Mary's Westbrook CT20 178 A5
St Marys Cl CT18 161 D3
St Marys Dr CT18 161 D3
St Marys Gn TN24 139 E7
St Marys Mews TN24 156 F8
St Matthew's CE Inf Sch ME1 9 A2
St Matthew's Cl ME9 35 C7
St Matthews Dr ME1 9 A2
St Mawes CT8 7 C1
St Michael & All Angels Church CT14 117 C4
St Michael's Alley 14 CT11 52 E6
St Michael's CE Inf Sch ME16 74 E3
St Michael's CE Prim Sch TN31 197 C2
St Michael's CE Prim Sch TN30 167 A3
St Michael's Cl
Chatham ME4 9 F3
5 Sittingbourne ME10 36 F4
St Michael's Ct
8 Folkestone CT20 178 E5
6 Rochester ME2 9 B8
St Michael's Pl CT2 66 E2
St Michael's RC Prim Sch ME4 9 F3
St Michael's Rd
Canterbury CT2 66 E2
Maidstone ME16 74 D3
Sittingbourne ME10 36 F4
St Michael's St CT20 178 E5
St Michael's Terr TN30 167 A3
St Michael's Wlk CT18 162 F4
St Michaels Ave CT9 29 D8
St Michaels Cl
Canterbury CT2 66 A1
Pratling Street ME20 53 C3
St Mildred's Ave
Birchington CT7 26 E8
Broadstairs CT10 30 A4
Ramsgate CT11 52 B5
St Mildred's Cl 4 TN30 179 A7
St Mildred's Gdns CT8 7 D1
St Mildred's Prim Inf Sch CT10 30 A4
St Mildred's Rd
Margate CT9 8 A2
Minster (Thanet) CT12 50 B5
Ramsgate CT11 52 C6
Westgate-on-S CT8 7 C1
St Mildreds Ct
Canterbury CT1 87 E8
Deal CT14 117 C1
Westgate-on-S CT8 7 D1
St Mildreds Pl CT1 87 E7
St Monicas Deal CT14 134 D6
Dover CT17 166 C7
St Monicas Rd CT14 134 D6
St Nicholas at Wade CE Prim Sch CT7 25 E2
St Nicholas CE Inf Sch ME2 9 A7
St Nicholas CE Prim Sch TN28 202 B7
St Nicholas Cl Deal CT14 116 F4
Sturry CT2 67 F7
St Nicholas Cnr CT7 25 F1
St Nicholas Ho CT3 71 D2
St Nicholas Hospl CT2 66 C1
St Nicholas Rd
Canterbury CT1 87 D6
Faversham ME13 62 A7
Hythe CT21 176 A2
Littlestone-on-Sea TN28 202 E6
St Nicholas Rdbt CT7 26 B2
St Nicholas Sch CT1 87 F6
St Nicholas Terr 1 CT21 176 B2
St Patrick's Cl Deal CT14 117 C6
Whitstable CT5 43 E7
St Patrick's Rd
Deal CT14 117 C6
Ramsgate CT11 52 F8
St Patrick's Row ME9 59 B7
St Patricks Rd CT17 166 A4
St Paul's Ave ME13 62 A7
St Paul's Ct CT20 177 E4
St Paul's Rd CT9 8 A3
St Paul's St ME10 36 E5
St Paul's Way CT20 177 F4
St Pauls Cres ME13 64 A3
St Pauls Inf Sch ME14 75 A7
St Pauls Rd ME13 64 A3
St Pauls Terr CT1 88 A8
St Peter St ME1 9 D4
St Peter's Bridge ME14 74 F4
St Peter's CE Prim Sch ME20 53 A3
St Peter's Cl ME12 3 D6
St Peter's Ct
Broadstairs CT10 29 F5
Faversham ME13 62 A7
St Peter's Footpath
Margate CT9 7 J1
Margate,Drapers Mill CT9 29 A8
St Peter's Gr CT1 87 F8
St Peter's Inf Sch ME1 9 C3
St Peter's La CT1 66 F1
St Peter's Meth Prim Sch CT1 87 F8
St Peter's Park Rd CT10 29 F5
St Peter's Path ME1 9 D5
St Peter's Pl CT1,CT2 87 F8
St Peter's RC Prim Sch ME10 36 D2
St Peter's Rd
Boughton Street ME13 64 A3
Broadstairs CT10 29 F5
Margate CT10,CT9 29 A7
Whitstable CT5 20 D2
St Peter's Row TN26 153 D5
St Peter's St
Canterbury CT1,CT2 87 F8
Sandwich CT13 73 A1
St Peter's Way TN26 170 A8
St Peter-in-Thanet CE Jun Sch CT10 29 F7
St Peters Cotts 5 CT5 20 D2
St Peters Pl ME9 60 A6
St Peters St ME16 74 F4
St Philip Howard RC Prim Sch CT6 22 E5
St Philip's Ave ME15 75 B2
St Pierre Ct CT14 117 D5
St Radigund's Com Prim Sch CT17 149 A1
St Radigund's Ct CT17 149 A1
St Radigund's Pl CT1 67 A1
St Radigund's Rd CT17 149 A1
St Radigunds St CT1 66 F1
St Richard's RC Prim Sch CT16 149 D1
St Richard's Rd CT14 116 F3
St Richard's Wlk CT17 166 A4
St Ronan's Cl ME15 97 C7
St Saviour's Cl ME13 62 E7
St Saviour's Hospl CT21 176 F2
St Saviours CE Jun Sch CT8 27 E8
St Saviours Cl CT19 178 D7
St Saviours Ct CT8 27 E8
St Saviours Rd ME15 97 D6
St Simon of England RC Prim Sch TN23 156 A8
St Simon Stock Sch ME16 74 C4
St Stephen's Cl
Canterbury CT2 66 F2
Newington ME9 35 C7
St Stephen's Ct CT2 66 F2
St Stephen's Fields CT2 66 F1
St Stephen's Gn CT2 66 F3
St Stephen's Hill CT2 66 E4
St Stephen's Inf Sch CT2 66 F3
St Stephen's Jun Sch CT2 66 F3
St Stephen's Lodge CT2 66 F2
St Stephen's Manor CT10 30 B7
St Stephen's Mews TN23 156 A6
St Stephen's Rd CT2 66 F2
St Stephen's Sq ME15 74 E2
St Stephen's Way CT20 177 F4
St Stephen's Wlk TN23 155 F7
St Stephens Fields 5 CT2 66 F1
St Stephens Ho 1 CT2 66 F1
St Stephens Mews ME1 31 E8
St Stephens Pathway 4 CT2 66 F1
St Swithin's Rd CT5 21 B3
St Teresa's RC Prim Sch TN24 139 B4
St Theresa's Cl TN24 139 B3
St Thomas Hill CT2 66 D3
St Thomas More RC Prim Sch ME5 32 A5
St Thomas of Canterbury RC Prim Sch ME8 11 B2
St Thomas' Cross TN26 170 E3
St Thomas' RC Prim Sch CT1 67 A1
St Thomas's Hospl CT13 72 F1
St Vincent Rd CT15 150 F7
St Vincent's Cl
Littlebourne CT3 68 F1
Whitstable CT5 43 E7
St Welcome's Way ME17 100 E6
St William of Perth RC Prim Sch ME1 9 B2
St William's Way ME1 9 D2

St Winifred Rd CT19 177 F6
Salbris Cl TN29 195 D8
Salem St ME15 75 A3
Salisbury Ave
Broadstairs CT10 29 F2
Gillingham ME8 33 D8
Ramsgate CT11 52 F8
Salisbury Cl ME10 37 C4
Salisbury Ho
Canterbury CT2 66 D2
4 Maidstone ME15 97 D7
Salisbury Rd
Canterbury CT2 66 E2
Chatham ME4 10 A3
Deal CT14 117 B2
Dover CT16 149 D1
Folkestone CT19 177 E7
Herne Bay CT6 23 C5
Kit's Coty ME20 53 D7
Maidstone ME14 75 A6
St Margaret's at Cliffe CT15 151 B6
Whitstable CT5 43 D8
Sally Port ME7 10 A6
Sally Port Gdns ME7 10 B6
Salmestone Grange★ CT9 28 E8
Salmestone Prim Sch CT9 28 E8
Salmestone Rd CT9 28 F8
Salmestone Rise CT9 28 E8
Salmon Cres ME12 3 F6
Salt Marsh La 21 CT5 20 D2
Salt's Ave ME15 96 F3
Salt's Dr CT10 29 E5
Salter's La TN29 199 C8
Salters La ME13 62 D4
Salthouse Cl TN29 199 D8
Saltings The
Littlestone-on-Sea TN28 202 E5
16 Whitstable CT5 20 D2
Salts Cl CT5 20 D1
Salts La ME15 97 A4
Saltwood CE Prim Sch CT21 176 B4
Saltwood Gdns CT9 8 E2
Saltwood Rd ME15 74 F1
Samara Cl ME5 32 A1
Samian Cres CT19 177 C6
Samphire Cl ME14 75 E4
Samphire Ct CT16 166 E8
Samphire Hoe Ctry Pk★ CT15 165 E2
Samuel Ct CT9 8 A3
Samuel Mews TN29 205 D7
San Remo CT8 7 C1
Sancroft Ave CT2 66 C1
Sanctuary Cl
Broadstairs CT10 29 F2
Kearsney CT17 148 D4
Sanctuary Rd ME8 11 A3
Sanctuary The CT13 95 A7
Sand Ct ME12 6 G2
Sand End CT5 43 C6
Sandalwood Dr CT7 25 F1
Sandbach Ho CT9 8 B3
Sandbanks Rd ME13 41 C2
Sandbourne Dr ME14 53 F1
Sandcroft TN28 202 F7
Sanderling Rd CT6 23 F5
Sanderling Way ME9 14 D5
Sanders Ct ME12 4 A5
Sandford Rd ME10 36 B5
Sandgate Ct ME8 33 F4
Sandgate Espl CT20, CT21 177 D2
Sandgate High St CT20 177 E3
Sandgate Hill CT20 178 A4
Sandgate Prim Sch CT20 177 F4
Sandgate Rd CT20 178 C4
Sandgates CT4 143 E7
Sandhills Cvn Pk CT14 95 B1
Sandhurst Cl
Canterbury CT2 67 A4
Gillingham ME8 11 C3
Sandhurst Rd CT9 8 F2
Sandilands TN24 139 E2
Sandle's Rd CT7 26 F7
Sandling Cl TN23 155 F6
Sandling Ct ME14 75 B7
Sandling La ME14 75 A8
Sandling Prim Sch ME14 75 B8
Sandling Rd Hythe CT21 175 F6
Maidstone ME14 74 F6
Maidstone,Ringlestone ME14 74 F7
Sandling Sta CT21 175 F6
Sandown Cl CT14 95 D1
Sandown Cotts
Margate CT9 8 A3
Teynham ME9 38 E1
Sandown Ct CT14 117 C7
Sandown Dr
Gillingham ME8 33 D7
Herne Bay CT6 22 D4
Sandown Lees CT13 94 D8
Sandown Pl CT14 117 C7
Sandown Rd Deal CT14 117 D8
Sandwich CT13 94 B8
Sandown Sch CT14 117 C7
Sandpiper Ct
3 Birchington CT7 26 F8
Margate CT9 7 I3
Sandpiper Rd
Chatham ME5 32 D2
Hawkinge CT18 163 A3
Whitstable CT5 43 B7
Sandpit Hill CT3 47 C4
Sandra Ct 5 ME2 9 B8
Sandringham Ho ME1 9 B4
Sandringham Rd ME8 33 E3
Sandstone Ct CT20 178 A3
Sandstone Dr ME10 36 E8
Sandstone Rise ME5 54 C8
Sandway Rd ME17 100 F4
Sandwich Bay Bird Obsy★ CT13 94 E7
Sandwich Cl CT20 177 F5
Sandwich Ind Est CT13 73 B1
Sandwich Inf Sch CT13 72 F1
Sandwich Jun Sch CT13 93 F7
Sandwich Rd Ash CT3 71 F1
Cliffs End CT12 51 D4
Eastry CT13 93 C3
Eythorne CT15 131 C8
Nonington CT15,CT3 113 F6
Sandwich CT13,CT14 93 D5
Whitfield CT15,CT16 149 A7
Woodnesborough CT13 93 D7
Sandwich Sta CT13 94 A8
Sandwich Tech Sch CT13 93 F6
Sandwich Town Mus★ CT13 72 F1
Sandwood Rd
Ramsgate CT10 29 F1
Sandwich CT13 93 F8
Sandy Cnr TN26 154 F5
Sandy Dell ME7 33 A3
Sandy La Ashford TN24 140 B1
Daniel's Water TN26 154 E6
Hythe CT20,CT21 177 B3
Maidstone,Harbourland ME14 75 C8
Maidstone,Penenden Heath ME14 75 C7
Maidstone,Ware Street ME14 76 B5
Tenterden TN30 179 B7
Sandy Mount ME14 76 B5
Sandy Pl TN25 158 D5
Sandyhurst La TN25 139 B8
Sanger Cl CT9 7 I1
Sangro Pl CT1 67 D1
Sanspareil Ave ME12 4 A6
Santon La CT3 70 E8
Sappers Wlk ME7 10 C5
Sapphire Cl ME10 36 C7
Saracen Cl ME7 11 A1
Saracen Fields ME5 54 C8
Sarafand Ho ME1 9 B4
Sarah Gdns CT9 29 D8
Sark Cl TN29 195 C8
Sarre Ct CT7 48 D6
Sarre Mill★ CT7 48 D7
Sarre Pl CT13 93 F8
Sarsen Hts ME5 31 F1
Sassoon Cl CT18 163 A4
Satis Ave ME10 36 E7
Satmar La CT15,CT18 164 E4
Satmore La CT18 164 C4
Saunders La CT3 71 F1
Saunders St
7 Chatham ME4 9 F3
Gillingham ME7 10 C6
Saunders Way TN31 203 A2
Savage Rd ME5 32 B3
Savernake Dr CT6 23 B2
Savoy The 8 CT11 52 C6
Saw Lodge Field TN23 156 C4
Sawpit Rd ME9 59 B2
Sawyers Ct ME4 10 B2
Saxon Ave ME12 4 B6
Saxon Cl CT21 176 E2
Saxon Rd Bridge CT4 89 A1
Faversham ME13 62 C7
Ramsgate CT11 52 B6
Westgate-on-S CT8 7 D1
Saxon Shore
Sittingbourne ME10 15 A1
Whitstable CT5 43 C8
Saxon St 9 CT17 166 D8
Saxon Way Prim Sch ME7 10 E6
Saxon Wlk ME9 14 D4
Saxons Cl CT14 117 C8
Saxons Dr ME14 75 B7
Saxton Rd TN29 206 E5
Saxton St ME7 10 C5
Sayer Rd TN27 120 C8
Sayers La 6 TN30 179 A7
Scanlons Bridge Rd CT21 176 A2
Scarborough Dr ME12 4 C8
Scarlett Cl ME5 32 C5
Sceales Dr CT12 51 D6
Sceptre Way CT5 43 B7
School Ave ME7 10 E4
School Cl The CT8 7 C1
School Hill CT4 107 B8
School Ho ME10 36 E3
School La
Bekesbourne CT4 89 C4
Blean CT2 66 A6
Borden ME9 35 F4
Boughton Street ME13 63 F3
Fordwich CT2 68 A4
Goodnestone CT3 91 D2
Herne Bay CT6 23 B1
Hoath CT3 46 E6
Ickham CT3 90 C8
Iwade ME9 14 C4
Lower Halstow ME9 13 B2
Lower Hardres CT4 110 B6
Maidstone ME15 75 E1
Newington ME9 35 B7
School La *continued*
Peasmarsh TN31 196 B2
Platt's Heath ME17 100 F2
Ramsgate CT11 52 E7
Sittingbourne ME9 37 D2
Stalisfield Green ME13 103 D6
Staple CT3 92 A6
Stourmouth CT3 48 E2
Wingham CT3 91 A7
School Path CT3 89 F7
School Rd
Appledore Heath TN26 181 C1
Ash CT3 71 C2
Bethersden TN26 153 D4
Charing TN27 120 C8
Densole CT18 162 E7
Faversham ME13 62 C6
Hothfield TN26 138 A7
Hythe CT21 176 B4
Sandwich CT13 72 F1
Sittingbourne ME10 37 B3
Tilmanstone CT14 114 F4
School View ME9 58 C8
Schrieber Mews ME7 10 D5
Scimitar Cl ME7 11 A1
Scocles Cotts ME12 4 C5
Scocles Rd ME12 4 C5
Scoggers Hill ME13 85 A7
Scoones Cl ME9 37 E2
Scot's La TN25 159 F8
Scotby Ave ME5 32 B4
Scotchmen Cl ME12 3 E7
Scott Ave Canterbury CT1 87 E6
Gillingham ME8 12 A1
Scott St ME14 74 F6
Scott's Terr ME4 9 F3
Scotteswood Ave ME4 9 F2
Scotton St TN25 123 F2
Scragged Oak Cvn Pk ME14 55 B2
Scragged Oak Rd
Detling ME14 55 C5
Hucking ME17 56 C1
Scraps Hill ME9 37 F4
Scrapsgate Rd ME12 4 A7
Scrubbs La ME16 74 D4
Sea App ME12 6 E4
Sea Rd Deal CT14 134 D6
Hythe CT21 177 A2
Westgate-on-S CT8 7 C1
Sea St Herne Bay CT6 22 C3
St Margaret's at Cliffe CT15 151 A6
Whitstable CT5 20 D2
Sea View Ave CT7 26 E8
Sea View Cl CT18 164 B1
Sea View Cotts ME9 13 B3
Sea View Gdns ME12 6 E3
Sea View Hts CT7 26 D8
Sea View Rd
Birchington CT7 26 E8
Broadstairs CT10 30 A6
Cliffs End CT12 51 D6
Herne Bay CT6 23 C5
St Margaret's at Cliffe CT15 150 F4
Sea View Sq CT6 22 F5
Sea View Terr
Folkestone CT20 177 D3
Margate CT9 7 G2
Minster (Sheppey) ME12 5 A5
Sea Wall
Dymchurch TN29 195 D8
Whitstable CT5 20 D2
Seabourne Cl TN29 195 B6
Seabourne Way TN29 195 B7
Seabrook CE Prim Sch CT21 177 B2
Seabrook Ct CT21 177 B3
Seabrook Gdns CT21 177 B2
Seabrook Gr CT21 177 A2
Seabrook Rd CT21 176 E2
Seabrook Vale CT21 177 B4
Seacroft Rd CT10 30 A1
Seadown Cl CT21 177 A4
Seafield Rd
Broadstairs CT10 30 A4
Ramsgate CT11 52 C6
Whitstable CT5 21 B3
Seaford Ct ME1 9 B5
Seagar Rd ME13 40 B1
Seager Rd ME12 1 F2
Seagrave Cres CT19 178 F6
Sealand Ct ME1 9 B5
Seamark Cl CT12 49 D7
Seamark Rd CT12,CT7 26 E2
Seapoint Rd CT10 30 B3
Seasalter Beach CT5 43 A7
Seasalter Cl ME12 6 E4
Seasalter Cross CT5 43 A6
Seasalter La CT5 43 A5
Seasalter Rd ME13 41 E3
Seascape 10 CT20 177 E3
Seaside Ave ME12 4 C8
Seathorpe Ave ME12 4 C8
Seaths Cnr CT3 91 A7
Seaton Ave CT21 176 B3
Seaton Cotts TN25 122 E3
Seaton Rd Gillingham ME7 10 E3
Wickhambreaux CT3 69 D2
Seaview Ave ME12 6 H1
Seaview Cotts 6 CT10 30 B4
Seaview Ct CT10 30 B3
Seaview Cvn & Chalet Pk CT5 21 E4
Seaview Ho CT19 178 D8
Seaview Holiday Camp ME12 6 E3
Seaview Hts TN29 195 C7
Seaview Rd
Gillingham ME7 10 C4
Greatstone-on-Sea TN28 202 E1
Seaville Dr CT6 23 E5
Seaway Cotts CT5 20 C1
Seaway Cres TN29 194 F4
Seaway Gdns TN29 194 F4
Seaway Rd TN29 195 A4
Second Ave
Broadstairs CT10 8 G2
Chatham ME4 10 C1
Eastchurch ME12 5 F5
Gillingham ME7 10 E3
Margate CT9 8 B3
Rushenden ME11 2 F3
Sheerness ME12 1 C1
Secretan Rd ME1 9 B1
Sedge Cres ME5 31 E4
Sedgemoor Ho ME1 9 E5
Sedley Cl ME8 33 C3
Seeshill Cl CT5 43 E8
Segrave Rd CT19 178 F5
Selbey Cl CT6 23 C4
Selborne Ho CT17 166 C7
Selborne Rd CT9 29 B8
Selbourne Rd ME7 10 D7
Selbourne Terr CT17 166 C7
Selbourne Wlk ME15 97 F6
Selby Field Cvn Pk CT21 186 D8
Selby Rd ME15 97 F4
Selkirk Rd CT16 149 B3
Sellindge Prim Sch TN25 159 C1
Selling CE Prim Sch ME13 84 B6
Selling Ct ME13 84 C5
Selling Rd Chilham CT4 85 B3
Faversham ME13 62 F3
Selling ME13 84 E6
Selling St ME13 84 B6
Selling Sta ME13 84 E7
Sellinge Grn ME8 11 C3
Selsea Ave CT6 22 D4
Selstead Cl ME8 11 C2
Selsted CE Prim Sch CT15 146 C6
Selway Ct CT14 117 B3
Selwood Cl ME12 3 E6
Selwyn Ct CT10 29 F5
Selwyn Dr CT10 29 F5
Semaphore Rd CT7 26 F8
Semple Cl CT12 50 C7
Semple Gdns ME4 9 E3
Senacre La ME15 97 E6
Senacre Sq ME15 97 F7
Senacre Tech Coll ME15 97 D6
Senacre Wood Prim Sch ME15 97 F7
Sene Pk CT21 176 D3
Senlac Cl CT11 52 B6
Serene Ct 12 CT10 30 B4
Serene Pl 9 CT10 30 B4
Sessions House Sq ME14 74 F5
Setford Rd ME5 32 C6
Setterfield Ho CT21 176 D2
Setterfield Rd CT9 7 J1
Settington Ave ME5 10 C1
Sevastopol Pl CT1 67 D1
Seven Stones Dr CT10 30 A1
Sevenacre Rd ME13 62 C8
Sevenscore CT12 51 A5
Sevenscore Farm Cotts CT12 51 A5
Severn Rd ME5 32 C5
Sevington La TN24 157 A7
Sevington Pk ME15 96 F6
Sewell Cl CT7 27 A6
Sexburga Dr ME12 4 B8
Sextant Pk ME2 9 E6
Seymour Ave
Westgate-on-S CT9 7 D1
Whitstable CT5 20 E1
Seymour Cl CT6 23 B1
Seymour Pl CT1 87 E7
Seymour Rd
1 Chatham ME5 10 B3
Gillingham ME8 12 C1
St Margaret's at Cliffe CT15 150 F8
Seymour Villas 10 CT20 177 F3
Shackleton Cl ME5 32 B6
Shadoxhurst Rd TN26 169 C7
Shaftesbury Ave CT19 177 E7
Shaftesbury Ct CT14 117 D2
Shaftesbury Dr ME16 74 C4
Shaftesbury Rd
Canterbury CT2 66 F3
Hersden CT3 46 E1
Whitstable CT5 20 D1
Shaftsbury St CT11 52 F7
Shah Pl CT11 52 D7
Shakespeare Ct CT17 166 B7
Shakespeare Pas CT9 7 H2
Shakespeare Rd
Birchington CT7 27 A8
Dover CT17 166 B6
Gillingham ME7 10 C3
Margate CT9 7 J1
Sittingbourne ME10 37 A4
Shakespeare Terr 12 CT20 178 C4
Shalder Ho ME7 10 D7
Shalfleet Cl 1 ME5 32 A7
Shalloak Rd CT2 67 D6
Shallows Rd CT10 29 D6
Shalmsford Ct CT4 86 C2
Shalmsford Rd CT4 85 E2
Shalmsford St CT4 86 B2
Shamel Bsns Ctr ME2 9 C7
Shamley Rd ME5 32 D2
Shamrock Ave CT5 43 B7
Shanklin Cl ME5 32 C8
Shapland Cl CT6 23 C3
Share & Coulter Rd CT5 21 D1
Sharfleet Cres ME9 14 D4
Sharon Cres ME5 31 F4
Sharps Gn ME8 11 D5
Sharsted Hill ME9 81 C8
Sharsted Way
Gillingham ME7 33 A3
Maidstone ME14 76 B5
Shaw Cl ME14 75 C7
Shaw Cross TN24 139 D5
Shawdon Ave CT13 95 A7
Shaws Way ME1 9 C3
Shawstead Rd ME7,ME7 32 D5
Sheal's Cres ME15 75 A2
Sheals Ct ME15 75 A2
Shear Way TN29 186 C5
Shearers Cl ME14 75 E4
Shearwater ME16 74 B5
Shearwater Ave CT5 43 C7
Shearwater Ct ME12 3 B8
Shearwater Ho TN29 195 A3
Shearway Rd CT19 177 F7
Sheen Ct CT9 7 I2
Sheepfold La TN23 156 C4
Sheerness Harbour Est ME12 1 B3
Sheerness Heritage Ctr (Mus)★ ME12 1 D2
Sheerness-on-Sea Sta ME12 1 C2
Sheerstone ME9 14 D4
Sheerwater Rd CT3 70 F5
Sheerways ME13 62 A6
Sheet Glass Rd ME11 3 A3
Sheffield Gdns CT14 117 C4
Shelden Dr ME8 33 F8
Sheldon Bsns Ctr ME2 9 D8
Sheldon Cl CT3 113 A6
Sheldwich Cl TN23 156 A6
Sheldwich Prim Sch ME13 83 C6
Shell Grotto★ CT9 7 J2
Shell Ness Nature Reserve★ ME12 19 E4
Shellbeach ME12 19 D6
Shelley Ave CT1 67 C2
Shelley Rd ME16 74 C2
Shelley Rise ME1 9 A3
Shellness Rd ME12 19 D7
Shellons St CT20 178 D5
Shelvin La CT4 129 C3
Shenley Gr ME14 53 F2
Shepherd Cl TN23 155 E5
Shepherd Dr TN24 157 A8
Shepherd's Close Rd CT4 89 E1
Shepherd's Cross CT15 132 B1
Shepherds Gate ME7 32 F5
Shepherds Gate Dr ME14 75 E6
Shepherds Way
Langley Heath ME17 98 E4
Whitstable CT5 44 C8
Shepherds Well Sta CT15 130 D5
Shepherds Wlk
Hythe CT21 175 E1
Whitstable CT5 44 C8
Shepherdsgate CT2 66 F1
Shepherdsgate Dr CT6 46 A8
Shepherdswell Rd CT15 131 A7
Shepperton Cl ME5 32 C4
Sheppey Beach Villas ME12 6 H2
Sheppey Cl 3 CT7 27 A7
Sheppey Coll ME12 1 C3
Sheppey Com Hospl ME12 4 C7
Sheppey Community Hospl ME12 4 A5
Sheppey Cotts ME12 1 E2
Sheppey Rd ME15 97 A7
Sheppey St ME12 1 B2
Sheppey Terr ME12 4 F5
Sheppey View CT5 43 C6
Sheppey Way Iwade ME9 14 F6
Queenborough ME12,ME9 3 D2
Sittingbourne ME9 36 B7
Shepway TN24 139 E5
Shepway Cl CT19 178 D6
Shepway Cross CT21 175 B3
Shepway Ct ME15 97 C8
Shepway Inf Sch ME15 97 E8
Shepway Jun Sch ME15 97 E8
Sheraton Ct ME5 31 F1
Sherbourne Dr ME16 74 B2
Sheridale Bsns Ctr ME2 9 A6
Sheridan Cl Chatham ME5 32 C7
Maidstone ME14 74 E8
Sheridan Ct ME1 9 A2
Sheridan Rd CT16 149 B3
Sheriff Dr ME5 32 A2
Sheringham Cl ME16 74 D7
Sheringham Ho 5 ME15 97 D8
Sherman Cl ME7 11 B1
Shernold Sch ME16 74 D5
Shernolds ME15 97 B7
Sheron Cl CT14 117 A5
Sherriffs Court La CT12 49 E6
Sherwood Ave ME5 32 A2

Sherwood Cl
Ashford TN24 139 D7
Faversham ME13 40 B1
Herne Bay CT6 23 C2
Whitstable CT5 43 C6
Sherwood Ct CT8 7 C1
Sherwood Dr CT5 43 C6
Sherwood Gdns CT11 29 E1
Sherwood Ho ME5 32 A3
Sherwood Rd CT7 26 F5
Shillingheld Cl ME14 75 F5
Ship Cl TN29 195 C8
Ship La ME1 9 E4
Ship St CT19 178 D6
Shipland Hos TN27 136 D8
Shipley Ct ME14 75 A4
Shipley Mill CL TN23 156 C4
Shipman Ave CT2 87 C8
Shipmans Way CT16 149 A3
Shipway Ho CT21 176 D1
Shipwrights Ave ME4 10 B2
Shipwrights Lee CT5 20 C2
Shipyard Area ME13 40 D1
Shire La ME13 103 C6
Shireway Cl CT19 178 A7
Shirkoak Pk TN26 169 A5
Shirley Ave Chatham ME5 31 D5
Ramsgate CT11 29 E1
Shirley Ct ME15 97 E5
Shirley Way ME15 76 A3
Shoebury Terr ME12 5 A5
Sholden Bank CT14 116 E4
Sholden CE Prim Sch CT14 116 F5
Sholden New Rd CT14 116 F6
Shooter's Hill 5 CT17 149 C1
Shooters Hill CT15 131 C8
Shore Cl Birchington CT7 26 D8
Herne Bay CT6 22 B3
Shorefields ME8 12 B2
Shoregate La ME9 12 F6
Shoreham La TN30 167 A3
Shoreham Wlk ME15 97 F7
Shorland Ct ME1 9 B5
Shorncliffe Cres CT20 177 E5
Shorncliffe Ind Est CT20 177 D4
Shorncliffe Rd CT20 177 F5
Short La Alkham CT15 147 D1
Snargate TN29 191 D6
Short St 3 Chatham ME4 10 B3
Chillenden CT3 114 A8
5 Sandwich CT13 73 A1
Sheerness ME12 1 C2
Short's Prospect ME12 17 C8
Shortlands Gn ME15 97 F5
Shortlands Rd ME10 37 B4
Shorts Way ME1 9 A3
Shotfield Cl CT3 70 C6
Shottendane Rd CT9,CT8 28 C7
Shottenden La CT4 106 A7
Shottenden Rd
Gillingham ME7 10 D7
Shottenden CT4,ME13 105 D8
Shrimpton Cl CT4 85 B3
Shropshire Terr 1 ME15 97 E7
Shrub Hill Rd CT5 44 D7
Shrubbery The CT14 117 C1
Shrubcote TN30 179 C7
Shrubsole Ave ME12 1 D1
Shrubsole Dr ME14 53 F3
Shuart La CT7 25 F4
Shurland Ave
Leysdown-on-S ME12 6 H1
Minster (Sheppey) ME12 4 B6
Sittingbourne ME10 36 F1
Shurland Pk ME12 5 E5
Shuttle Rd CT10 30 B5
Shuttlesfield La CT4 144 D1
Sibert's Cl CT15 130 F5
Sibertswold CE Prim Sch CT15 130 E4
Sidings The
Dymchurch TN29 195 B7
Lyminge CT18 161 C7
Whitstable CT5 20 E2
Sidney Rd Gillingham ME7 10 C7
Rochester ME1 9 A2
Sidney St
Folkestone CT19 178 E7
Maidstone ME16 74 C2
Signal Ct 6 ME8 11 F1
Silchester Ct ME14 75 C7
Silecroft Ct TN23 138 E1
Silvanus Ho 5 CT11 52 D7
Silver Ave CT7 27 B6
Silver Bank ME5 32 A6
Silver Birch Ct TN26 155 A1
Silver Birch Gr TN23 156 B4
Silver Birches
Chatham ME5 32 A3
Sheerness ME12 1 H1
Silver Birches Mobile Homes Pk TN26 171 A4
Silver Hill Chatham ME4 9 F3
Rochester ME1 9 A2
Tenterden TN30 167 B1
Silver Hill Gdns
Ashford TN24 140 A1
4 Chatham ME4 9 F3
Silver Hill Rd TN24 140 A1
Silver St Deal CT14 117 D7
Silver Street ME9 57 F5
Silver Tree ME5 32 B1
Silverdale ME16 74 A2
Silverdale Ave ME12 4 A6
Silverdale Dr
Gillingham ME8 33 F7
Herne Bay CT6 23 D2
Silverdale Gr ME10 36 D3
Silverdale Rd CT11 52 A5
Silverlands Rd CT18 161 C7
Silvers The CT10 29 C4
Silverspot Cl ME8 33 F7
Silverweed Rd ME5 31 F4
Simmonds La ME15 98 B6
Simmonds Rd CT1 87 E7
Simon Ave CT9 8 D2
Simon Langton Girls Gram Sch CT1 88 C5
Simon Langton Gram Sch for Boys CT4 88 A4
Simon's Ave TN23 155 F7
Simone Weil Ave TN24 139 B4
Simpson Rd ME10 36 C5
Sinclair Cl ME8 33 E5
Sindal Shaw Ho ME5 31 E4
Singapore Dr ME7 10 B5
Singer Ave CT6 22 B4
Singledge Ave CT16 148 F6
Singledge La CT15 131 C2
Singleton Cl CT12 50 B6
Singleton Ctr The TN23 155 D8
Singleton Hill TN23 155 D8
Singleton Rd TN23 138 C1
Sion Hill CT11 52 E6
Sion Pass 12 CT11 52 E6
Sir Evelyn Rd ME1 9 B1
Sir John Hawkins Hospl ME4 9 E4
Sir John Hawkins Way ME4 9 F4
Sir John Moore Ave CT21 176 B2
Sir John Moore Ct 5 CT20 177 E3
Sir Joseph Williamson's Mathematical Sch ME1 9 C1
Sir Roger Manwood's Sch CT13 94 B8
Sir Thomas Longley Rd ME2 9 E6
Siskin Cl Ashford TN25 139 B7
Hawkinge CT18 162 F4
Sissinghurst Dr ME16 74 B4
Sittingbourne & Kemsley Light Rly★ ME10 37 A7
Sittingbourne Com Coll ME10 37 C2
Sittingbourne Ind Pk ME10 36 F5
Sittingbourne Rd
Maidstone,Detling ME14 75 E8
Maidstone,Penenden Heath ME14 75 B6
Sittingbourne Retail Pk ME10 36 F5
Sittingbourne Sta ME10 36 F4
Six Bells Pk TN26 169 A3
Six Fields Path TN30 179 A7
Sixth Ave ME12 6 A5
Skeete Rd CT18 160 E7
Skene Cl ME8 12 A1
Skinner Rd TN29 205 C6
Skinner St Chatham ME4 9 F3
Gillingham ME7 10 C5
Skinner Street Prim Sch ME7 10 C6
Skinner's Alley 3 CT5 20 D1
Skinner's Way ME17 98 E4
Skinners Cl ME20 53 A6
Skye Cl ME15 97 A7
Skylark Way TN23 156 D3
Slade Cl ME5 32 B2
Slade Rd ME17 102 D8
Slades Cl CT5 44 C8
Slatin Rd ME2 9 B8
Sleigh Rd CT2 67 F6
Slicketts Hill ME4 10 A4
Slip La CT15 147 C2
Slipway Rd ME12 1 A3
Sloe La CT10,CT9 29 B6
Slough Rd ME9 59 A3
Small Hythe Cl ME15 76 B2
Small Hythe Rd TN30 179 B4
Smallhythe Pl★ TN30 179 C1
Smallhythe Place (Mus)★ TN30 188 C8
Smarden Prim Sch TN27 135 A1
Smarden Rd TN27 136 B6
Smarden Wlk ME8 12 B1
Smarts Cotts ME14 76 C4
Smeed Cl 4 ME10 37 B4
Smeed-Dean Ctr The ME10 37 A4
Smeeth Com Prim Sch TN25 158 D5
Smith Rd ME5 32 B3
Smith St ME2 9 A6
Smiths Orch ME9 57 F5
Smithy Dr TN23 156 C4
Smuggler's Way CT7 27 A8
Smugglers Leap Cvn Pk CT12 50 C8
Snakes Hill CT3 91 A5
Snargate La TN29 191 C5
Snargate St CT17 166 D7
Snelgrove Ho 14 CT16 166 D8
Snell Gdns CT6 22 B2
Snipe Cl TN25 139 C7
Snodhurst Ave ME5 31 E5
Snodhurst Ho 2 ME5 32 A7
Snow Ho ME7 10 E7
Snowbell Rd TN23 156 B4
Snowdon Ave ME14 75 B5
Snowdon Cl ME5 32 B7
Snowdon Par ME14 75 C5
Snowdown Caravan Site CT15 113 A4
Snowdown Ct CT3 112 F5
Snowdown Sta CT15 113 B3
Snowdrop Cl CT19 178 C8
Sobraon Way CT1 67 D1
Solar Ct CT12 52 C7
Sole Street Cotts CT4 125 B7
Solent Gdns ME5 32 B8
Soleshill Rd CT4 84 E1
Solomon Ho CT14 117 B3
Solomon Rd ME8 12 A1
Solomons La ME13 62 D7
Solomons Rd ME4 9 F4
Somerfield Barn Ct TN25 174 C8
Somerfield Cl ME16 74 D5
Somerfield Hospl The ME16 74 E5
Somerfield La ME16 74 D4
Somerfield Rd ME16 74 D4
Somerset Cl Chatham ME5 32 C8
Sittingbourne ME10 36 C4
Whitstable CT5 43 B7
Somerset Ct
2 Broadstairs CT10 30 A4
Deal CT14 117 B3
Ramsgate CT12 29 B2
Somerset Rd
Ashford TN24 139 B3
Canterbury CT1 88 D8
Deal CT14 117 C3
Folkestone CT19 177 E6
Maidstone ME15 97 C8
Somme Ct CT1 67 D1
Sommerville Cl ME13 62 E7
Somner Cl CT2 66 D1
Somner Wlk ME15 97 F4
Sondes Cl CT6 23 A2
Sondes Rd CT14 117 D5
Sonora Way ME10 36 C7
Sorrell Rd ME5 31 F4
Sotherton TN24 156 E7
Souberg Cl CT14 117 C8
South Ave
Aylesham CT15 113 A3
Gillingham ME8 11 B2
Sittingbourne ME10 37 A3
South Avenue Jun & Inf Schs ME10 37 A3
South Barham Rd CT4 128 E6
South Borough Prim Sch ME15 75 A2
South Brooks Rd TN29 207 H6
South Bush La ME8 34 B6
South Camber Way CT16 150 B1
South Canterbury Rd CT1 88 A6
South Cl CT1 88 A8
South Cliff Par CT10 30 B1
South Court Dr CT3 91 A7
South Cres ME17 96 C4
South Ct Deal CT14 117 D6
Ramsgate CT12 29 B2
South Deal Prim Sch CT14 117 B4
South Eastern Rd
Ramsgate CT11 52 D7
Rochester ME2 9 C7
South Exit Rd CT16 166 G8
South Goodwin Ct CT14 117 D8
South Green La ME9 56 F6
South Kent Coll
Dover CT16 166 D8
Folkestone CT20 178 B5
South Kent Coll Jemmett Campus TN23 156 A8
South Kent Coll of Tech TN23 139 C1
South Kent Coll South Ashford Campus TN23 155 F6
South Lea TN23 156 A3
South Lodge CT5 20 E3
South Lodge Cl CT5 20 E3
South Military Rd CT17 166 C5
South Motto TN23 156 B5
South of England Rare Breeds Ctr★ TN26 169 D1
South Park Bsns Village ME15 75 A1
South Park Rd ME15 75 C1
South Pondside Rd ME4 10 A8
South Quay ME13 40 D1
South Rd Chatham ME4 10 B7
Chatham,Brompton ME4, ME7 10 A7
Dover CT17 166 B8
Faversham ME13 62 C7
Herne Bay CT6 23 A5
Hythe CT21 176 D1
Kingsdown CT14 134 D5
Sandwich CT13 73 A8
South Side Three Rd ME4 10 C8
South St Canterbury CT1 67 C2
Deal CT14 117 D6
Folkestone CT20 178 E4
Lydd TN29 205 C6
Queenborough ME11 2 F5
Selling ME13 84 F8
Whitstable CT5 44 A7
South Stour Ave TN23 156 C8
South Street Rd ME9 56 C7
South Swale Nature Reserve★ ME13 41 A6
South Turbine Hall Rd TN29 209 C2
South View CT3 46 F1
South View Gdns ME12 1 D1
South View Rd CT5 43 D6
South Wall CT14 117 B7
Southall Cl CT12 50 C7
Southbourne TN23 155 E5
Southbourne Gr ME5 32 A4
Southbourne Rd CT19 178 E5
Southdown Rd ME12 3 E6
Southenay La TN25 159 C4
Southern Way CT19 178 E6
Southernwood Rise CT20 177 F4
Southfields ME1 9 C3
Southgate Rd TN30 179 C7
Southill Rd ME4 9 F3
Southland's Com Comp Sch TN28 202 B7
Southlees La ME9 56 F3
Southmead Cl CT19 178 A6
Southover Ct 2 CT20 177 E3
Southsea Ave ME12 4 C8
Southsea Dr CT6 22 D4
Southstone Ct CT21 176 C1
Southstreet Crossing CT5 44 A7
Southwall Ind Est CT14 117 B7
Southwall Rd CT14 117 B6
Southwold Pl CT8 27 E7
Southwood Gdns CT11 52 B6
Southwood Hts CT11 52 C6
Southwood Rd
Ramsgate CT11 52 C6
Whitstable CT5 21 B2
Sovereign Bvd ME7,ME8 10 F2
Sovereigns The ME16 74 D4
Sowell St CT10 29 F5
Spade La ME9 34 C6
Spanton Cres CT21 176 A3
Sparrow Castle 3 CT9 7 J1
Speakman Ct 5 CT11 52 C6
Spearhead Rd ME14 74 F7
Spearpoint Cnr TN24 139 F5
Spectrum Bsns Ctr ME2 9 E8
Spectrum Bsns Est ME15 97 F4
Speedwell Ave ME5 31 F4
Speedwell Cl
Gillingham ME7 10 E5
Maidstone ME14 75 E5
Speedwell Rd CT5 43 B6
Speke Rd CT10 29 E6
Spekes Rd ME7 33 B6
Spelders Hill TN25 141 A5
Speldhurst Cl TN23 155 E5
Speldhurst Ct ME16 74 D4
Speldhurst Gdns CT9 8 F3
Spembley Ct ME4 9 E4
Spence Cl CT18 163 A4
Spencer Cl ME5 32 A5
Spencer Flats ME5 32 B8
Spencer Ho 3 CT20 177 F5
Spencer Rd CT7 27 A8
Spencer Sq CT11 52 D6
Spencer St 9 CT11 52 D6
Spencer Way ME15 97 E7
Spenlow Dr ME5 54 A8
Spenser Rd CT6 22 E4
Spicer Homes ME10 36 F2
Spicer's Pl CT3 69 C2
Spicers Ct CT21 176 C1
Spicers Field CT6 23 D2
Spiers The ME7 11 C5
Spillett Cl ME13 62 B6
Spillway The ME15 74 D2
Spindle Glade ME14 75 C5
Spindlewood Cl ME5 32 B3
Spindlewood End TN23 138 D4
Spinnaker Ct 4 ME1 9 C1
Spinnens Acre Com Jun Sch ME5 32 C1
Spinney La CT3 112 E4
Spinney The
Ashford TN23 138 E3
Chatham ME5 32 B1
Crabble CT17 148 E2
Maidstone ME15 75 B3
Margate CT9 8 E1
Spire Ave CT5 44 A8
Spires The Canterbury CT2 66 F2
Maidstone ME16 74 D4
Spitalfield La TN28 201 F6
Spitalfield Terr TN28 201 F6
Spitfire & Hurricane Memls Mus★ CT12 28 A2
Spitfire Cl ME5 32 B6
Spitfire Way CT18 163 B3
Split Ho CT17 149 A1
Split La CT4 127 A5
Sportsfield ME14 75 B5
Spot La ME15 76 A2
Spratling La CT12 28 F1
Spratling St CT12 28 E1
Sprig The ME14 76 A4
Spring Farm TN29 192 D5
Spring Grove Sch TN25 123 C2
Spring Ho CT21 176 C2
Spring Hollow TN29 195 A4
Spring La Canterbury CT1 88 C7
Fordwich CT2 68 A4
Hythe CT21 177 A4
Spring Terr 15 CT20 178 D5
Spring Vale ME16 74 E4
Spring Wlk CT5 43 C7
Springett Way ME17 96 D3
Springfarm Rd TN29 192 C5
Springfield Ave
Maidstone ME14 74 F7
Tenterden TN30 167 C2
Springfield Cl CT11 29 E2
Springfield Pass CT21 176 B2
Springfield Rd
Dover CT16 149 B2
Gillingham ME7 10 E6
Margate CT9 8 E3
Sittingbourne ME10 36 D5
Springfield Terr 7 ME4 9 F4
Springfield Way CT21 177 B3
Springhead Rd ME13 40 D1
Springside Terr CT18 161 C6
Springvale Gillingham ME8 33 C6
Iwade ME9 14 D4
Springwood Cl
Ashford TN23 138 E3
1 Maidstone ME16 74 A3
Springwood Ct TN28 202 B6
Springwood Dr TN23 138 E3
Springwood Rd ME16 74 A3
Sprotlands Ave TN24 139 F1
Sprotshill Cl ME10 36 E6
Spurgeons Cotts ME17 96 E2
Spurway ME14 76 A4
Square Hill ME15 75 B4
Square Hill Rd ME15 75 B4
Square The
Birchington CT7 27 A7
Chilham CT4 107 B8
Elham CT4 144 F4
Lenham ME17 101 D5
Selling ME13 84 A6
Sittingbourne ME10 14 F1
Squeeze Gut Alley 14 CT5 20 D2
Squire Ave CT2 87 C8
Squires Ct ME12 5 E3
Squires Way CT16 149 A3
Squirrel La TN25 138 F5
Stable Cl ME5 32 C5
Stable Ct Chilham CT4 107 B7
Faversham ME13 62 D6
Stablemead CT19 178 A7
Stace Cl TN30 179 C8
Staceys St ME14 74 F5
Stade St CT21 176 C1
Stade The CT19 178 E5
Stadium Way ME10 37 C6
Stadler Cl ME16 74 D7
Staffa Rd ME15 97 A7
Stafford Cl TN23 138 F2
Stafford St ME7 10 C5
Staffordshire St 11 CT11 52 E7
Stag Rd ME5 32 B5
Stagshaw Cl ME15 75 A2
Staines Hill CT2 68 B7
Staines Pl CT10 30 B5
Stalham Ct ME7 33 B4
Stalin Ave ME5 32 B8
Stalisfield Rd
Charing TN27 103 E3
Stalisfield Green ME13, TN27 103 C5
Throwley ME13 82 C6
Stamford Villas ME12 5 C2
Stampers The ME15 74 D2
Stanbury Cres CT19 178 F7
Stancomb Ave CT11 52 C5
Standard Ave CT6 22 A4
Standen Cl ME8 33 E4
Standen La CT18 163 E5
Staner Ct CT12 52 A8
Staner Hill CT12 51 F8
Stanford Dr ME16 74 C3
Stangate Dr ME9 14 D4
Stanhope Ave ME10 37 A3
Stanhope Cl ME14 74 E7
Stanhope Rd
Ashford TN23 155 E6
Deal CT14 117 D6
Dover CT16 149 C2
Rochester ME2 9 A7
Stanhope Sq TN23 155 F6
Stanley Ave
Minster (Sheppey) ME12 4 D7
Queenborough ME11 3 A4
Stanley Cl TN29 187 B4
Stanley Gdns CT6 22 F3
Stanley Pl
Broadstairs CT10 30 A4
Ramsgate CT11 52 E7
Stanley Rd
Broadstairs CT10 30 A6
Chatham ME5 32 C6
Deal CT14 117 D5
Folkestone CT19 177 E6
Gillingham ME7 10 C6
Herne Bay CT6 22 F4
Margate CT9 8 A3
Ramsgate CT11 52 D8
Whitstable CT5 43 D7
Stanmore Ct CT1 88 B7
Stansfeld Ave CT18 163 A4
Stansted Cl ME16 74 D7
Staple Cl ME10 36 E5
Staple Rd CT3 91 C6
Staple St ME13 63 F5
Staple Vineyard★ CT3 91 F5
Staplehurst Ave CT10 30 A2
Staplehurst Gdns CT9 8 E2
Staplehurst Lodge Ind Est ME10 36 D5
Staplehurst Rd
Gillingham ME8 11 B3

Staplehurst Rd *continued*
Sittingbourne ME10 36 D5
Staplers Ct ME14 75 B8
Staplestreet Rd ME13 64 A4
Star Hill ME1 9 D5
Star La Folkestone CT19 177 D7
Gillingham ME7 33 A7
Margate CT9 29 A5
Star Mill Ct ME5 10 D2
Star Mill La ME5 10 D2
Star Rd TN24 139 D2
Starle Cl CT1 67 B1
Starnes Ct 5 ME14 75 A5
Starvation Cnr 1 CT5 20 D2
Starveacre La ME9 36 B1
Station App Adisham CT3 112 E8
Birchington CT7 26 F7
Maidstone ME16 74 F3
Martin Mill CT15 133 C2
Minster (Thanet) CT12 50 C5
New Romney TN28 202 C6
Station Approach Rd
CT11 52 D8
Station Cotts ME13 84 E7
Station Dr CT14 117 A1
Station Hill Cotts ME15 96 A7
Station Mews Elham CT4 144 F4
3 Tenterden TN30 179 A7
Station Rd Adisham CT3 90 E1
Ashford TN23 139 C2
Bekesbourne CT4 89 C4
Birchington CT7 27 A7
Bridge CT4 88 F2
Charing TN27 120 C7
Chartham CT4 86 D3
Deal CT14 117 B1
Dymchurch TN29 195 B7
East Farleigh ME15 96 A7
Faversham ME13 62 D6
Folkestone CT19 177 F5
Gillingham ME8 12 A2
Harrietsham ME17 100 D6
Herne Bay CT6 22 E4
Hythe CT21 176 D3
Lydd TN29 205 D7
Lyminge CT18 161 C6
Maidstone ME14 74 F5
Margate CT9 7 H2
Martin Mill CT15 133 D1
Minster (Thanet) CT12 50 C5
New Romney TN28 202 C6
Newington ME9 35 B6
Pluckley TN27 136 C5
Rochester ME2 9 C7
Shepherdswell CT15 130 D5
Smeeth TN25 158 B3
St Margaret's at Cliffe CT15 150 E8
Tenterden TN30 179 A7
Teynham ME9 38 D2
Westgate-on-S CT8 7 D1
Whitstable CT5 20 E2
Station Rd E CT1 87 F7
Station Rd W CT2 66 F1
Station Row ME9 38 D3
Station St ME10 36 F4
Station Terr TN28 202 C6
Stede Hill ME17 78 F3
Steed Cl CT6 46 B8
Steeds Cl TN23 156 A1
Steeds La TN23,TN26 156 B1
Steele St ME2 9 A8
Steerforth Cl ME1 9 C2
Stella Maris RC Prim Sch
CT19 178 C6
Stelling Minnis CE Prim Sch
CT4 126 F6
Stembrook CT16 166 D8
Stembrook Ct 4 CT16 166 D7
Stempe Cl CT18 163 B3
Step Style ME10 37 B2
Stephen Cl CT10 30 A4
Stephen Ct 2 CT20 178 D5
Stephen's Cl CT9 28 B7
Stephens Cl
Faversham ME13 62 B8
Ramsgate CT11 52 C8
Stephenson Rd CT2 66 F3
Steps Hill Rd ME9 56 D6
Sterling Ave ME16 74 C5
Sterling Cl CT10 29 E7
Sterling Ct 12 CT1 66 F1
Sterling Rd
Queenborough ME11 3 A5
Sittingbourne ME10 36 D1
Sterry Gdns ME15 97 E7
Steven Cl ME4 10 A3
Stevens Cl TN27 118 F3
Stevens Cotts TN30 179 A7
Stevens Ho CT17 166 C8
Stevenson Cl ME15 74 F3
Stickfast La ME9 14 A1
Stiles Cl Folkestone CT19 178 A7
Minster (Sheppey) ME12 4 A6
Stirling Cl Gillingham ME8 33 E4
Rochester ME1 9 A3
Stirling Way CT12 29 A2
Stirlng Rd TN24 156 D7
Stisted Way TN27 118 F3
Stock La TN25 158 A4
Stockbury Dr ME16 74 D7
Stockbury Gdns CT9 8 E2
Stockdale Gdns CT14 117 C4
Stocker's Hill ME13 63 E4
Stockers Brow ME9 59 A7
Stockers Hill ME9 59 A7
Stockett La ME15 96 D6
Stockham Ct CT19 177 E7
Stocks Rd TN30 188 F3
Stocks The ME13 83 C6
Stockton Cl ME14 75 B8
Stockwood Chase CT2 66 A2
Stoddart Rd CT19 177 E6
Stodmarsh National Nature Reserve★ CT3 69 D8
Stodmarsh Rd CT3 68 C3
Stombers La CT18 163 C6
Stonar Cl Ramsgate CT11 29 E1
Sandwich CT13 73 A1
Stonar Gdns CT13 73 A2
Stone Barn Ave CT7 27 A6
Stone Bay Sch CT10 30 B6
Stone Cnr TN30 189 A6
Stone Cross Lees CT13 93 F7
Stone Gdns CT10 30 B5
Stone Gn TN30 189 F4
Stone Hill TN25 159 A2
Stone Hill Rd TN27 118 F2
Stone Ho CT10 30 B7
Stone House Mews CT10 30 B7
Stone Rd CT10 30 B5
Stone St Faversham ME13 62 C7
Lympne CT21 175 A4
Stanford TN25 160 C3
Stelling Minnis CT4 126 D4
Westenhanger TN25,CT21 175 B6
Stone Stile La CT4 84 D1
Stoneacre★ ME15 98 B7
Stoneacre Cl ME8 33 D5
Stoneacre Ct 7 ME15 75 A1
Stoneacre La ME15 98 B7
Stonebridge TN25 141 A5
Stonebridge Cotts TN23 156 B8
Stonebridge Green Rd
TN27 119 A4
Stonebridge Way ME13 62 B7
Stonecross Lea ME5 10 C1
Stonedane Ct ME13 62 C8
Stonegate TN25 123 E2
Stonehall Rd CT15 147 F8
Stoneheap Rd CT14, CT15 115 E1
Stonestile Farm Rd
TN27 103 A3
Stoneway Pk CT4 126 D7
Stoney Bank ME7 10 F1
Stoney Rd ME13 64 B3
Stony La ME1 31 C5
Stonyway La CT15 165 C5
Stopford Rd ME7 10 D4
Storehouse Wharf ME12 1 A3
Stour Cl Ashford TN23 138 E1
Chartham CT4 86 D2
Stour Cres CT1 67 D3
Stour Ct 7 Canterbury CT1 87 F8
8 Sandwich CT13 72 F1
Stour Rd CT4 86 D2
Stour St CT1 87 F8
Stour Valley Cl CT3 47 D3
Stour Valley Ind Est CT4 86 E4
Stourfields TN24 139 D4
Stourmouth Rd CT3 70 C8
Stourside Studios 13 CT1 66 F1
Stourville 9 CT1 87 F8
Stowell Cl TN23 155 C8
Stowting CE Prim Sch
TN25 160 B8
Stowting Hill TN25 143 A1
Straight La TN29 191 F1
Strakers Hill CT15 132 D8
Strand Approach Rd ME7 10 E7
Strand Rdbt The ME7 10 E7
Strand St CT13 72 F1
Strand The CT14 117 D4
Stranger's Cl CT1 87 C6
Stranger's La CT1 87 C6
Strangford Pl CT6 23 B2
Strangford Rd CT5 20 F2
Strasbourg St CT9 29 A6
Stratford Ave ME8 33 D8
Stratford Dr ME15 97 D6
Stratford La 2 ME8 33 F8
Straw Mill Hill ME15 74 E1
Stream Wlk CT5 20 D2
Street End CT3 71 E1
Street End Rd ME5 10 B1
Street The Acol CT7 27 B3
Adisham CT3 112 C8
Appledore TN26 190 D8
Ash CT3 71 D1
Ashford,Great Chart TN23 138 C1
Ashford,Kennington TN24 139 E6
Ashford,Willesborough Lees TN24 157 B8
Barham CT4 111 F1
Bethersden TN26 153 D5
Bishopsbourne CT4 111 C6
Borden ME9 36 B2
Bossingham CT4 127 A7
Boughton Street ME13 64 A3
Boxley ME14 54 C3
Brabourne TN25 159 C8
Bredgar ME9 58 A5
Bredhurst ME7 33 B1
Brook TN25 141 B6
Chilham CT4 107 B8
Deal CT14 116 F6
Denton CT4 129 B3
Detling ME14 55 A1
Doddington ME9 80 E7
East Langdon CT15 133 A1
Eastling ME13 81 E6
Egerton TN27 118 F3
Eythorne CT15 131 D7
Faversham ME13 40 B2
Finglesham CT14 116 B8
Street The *continued*
Godmersham CT4 107 B2
Goodnestone CT3 91 D2
Guston CT15 149 E6
Hamstreet TN26 183 A7
Hartlip ME9 34 D5
Hastingleigh TN25 142 B6
Hawkinge CT18 163 B5
Hothfield TN26 138 A6
Ickham CT3 69 C1
Iwade ME9 14 E4
Kingston CT4 111 D3
Lower Halstow ME9 13 B3
Lympne CT21 174 F2
Lynsted ME9 60 A6
Maidstone ME14 76 C4
Martin Mill CT15 133 B3
Mersham TN25 157 E4
Molash CT4 105 F4
Newnham ME9 81 C8
Nonington CT15 113 D1
Northbourne CT14 116 A5
Patrixbourne CT4 89 B3
Peene CT18 177 A7
Petham CT4 109 B3
Pluckley TN27 136 D7
Postling CT21 160 F2
Preston CT3 70 C6
Selling ME13 84 B6
Shadoxhurst TN26 170 A8
Sittingbourne ME9 37 E3
Smarden TN27 135 A1
St Nicholas at Wade CT7 25 F2
Staple CT3 91 F6
Stockbury ME9 56 E8
Stone in Oxney TN30 190 A5
Stourmouth CT3 48 E1
Upchurch ME9 12 F4
West Hougham CT15 164 F5
Wickhambreaux CT3 69 C2
Wittersham TN30 188 D3
Womenswold CT4 112 D2
Woodnesborough CT13 93 C7
Wormshill ME9 79 A7
Worth CT14 94 B5
Streete Court Rd CT8 27 F8
Streete Ct CT8 27 F8
Streetfield CT6 46 B8
Streetfield Rd ME8 11 F1
Stretton Ct CT14 117 D5
Stringer Dr CT7 27 A6
Strode Cres ME12 1 D2
Strode Park Rd CT6 23 A2
Strond St CT17 166 D6
Strood Ret Pk ME2 9 B7
Strood Sta ME2 9 C7
Strouts Rd TN23 155 D7
Strover St ME7 10 C7
Stuart Cl ME14 75 C6
Stuart Ct Canterbury CT1 88 A6
Dover CT17 166 C8
Stuart Ho CT14 117 A5
Stuart Rd
Folkestone CT19 178 E6
Gillingham ME7 10 D3
Studds Cotts CT6 22 A3
Studfall Cl CT21 187 D8
Studio Cl TN24 139 E6
Stumble La TN23 156 B1
Stuppington Court Farm
CT1 87 E4
Stuppington La CT1 87 F5
Sturdee Ave ME7 10 E4
Sturdy Cl CT21 176 D2
Sturges Rd TN24 139 B3
Sturla Rd ME4 10 A3
Sturmer Cl CT1 88 C7
Sturry CE Prim Sch CT2 68 A7
Sturry Court Mews CT2 67 F5
Sturry Hill CT2 67 F6
Sturry Rd CT1,CT2 67 C3
Sturry Sta CT2 67 F5
Sturry Way ME8 11 C2
Style Cl ME8 33 E4
Styles La ME14 54 C3
Subdown Cotts TN25 159 C8
Sudbury Pl CT8 27 E7
Suffolk Ave
Gillingham ME8 11 F1
Westgate-on-S CT8 27 D7
Suffolk Ct 7 ME8 11 F1
Suffolk Dr TN23 139 A2
Suffolk Gdns CT17 165 F7
Suffolk Rd Canterbury CT1 88 D8
Maidstone ME15 97 D8
Suffolk St CT5 43 D8
Sugarloaf Wlk CT19 178 D8
Sultan Mews ME5 32 C2
Sultan Rd ME5 32 C2
Summer Cl Hythe CT21 175 F2
Tenterden TN30 167 C1
Summer Ct
Canterbury CT2 66 C1
Whitstable CT5 21 C2
Summer Hill CT2 66 C1
Summer Hill Pk TN24 157 C7
Summer La CT2 66 E6
Summer Leeze TN24 156 E8
Summer Leeze Gdns
TN24 156 E8
Summer Rd CT7 25 E1
Summerfield Ave CT5 20 F1
Summerfield Rd CT9 8 E2
Summerhill TN23 155 E6
Summerville Ave ME12 4 A5
Sumpter Way ME13 61 F7
Sun La Hythe CT21 176 C2
St Nicholas at Wade CT7 25 F2
Sun Rise TN25 138 F5
Sun St CT1 87 F8
Sun Terr ME5 32 B4
Sun Valley Way CT15 131 C8
Sunbeam Ave CT6 21 F4
Sunderland Cl ME1 9 A3
Sunderland Dr ME8 34 A8
Sunderland Ho 3 ME7 10 C7
Sundew Gr CT11 52 E8
Sundridge Cl CT2 67 A4
Sundridge Dr ME5 32 A4
Sunningdale Ave 4
CT19 178 A7
Sunningdale Cl ME8 33 D6
Sunningdale Ct ME15 75 B4
Sunningdale Dr ME8 33 D6
Sunningdale Wlk CT6 22 D1
Sunny Bank
Eythorne CT15 131 B8
Hythe CT21 175 F2
Sittingbourne ME10 37 B5
Sunny Cnr CT17 166 B5
Sunnyfields Cl ME8 33 E8
Sunnyfields Dr ME12 3 C6
Sunnyhill Rd CT6 22 C4
Sunnymead CT2 66 D7
Sunnymead Ave ME7 10 E5
Sunnymead Camp ME12 5 E5
Sunnymead Cvn Pk ME12 5 F5
Sunnyside Doddington ME9 80 E7
Littlestone-on-Sea TN28 202 D6
Lydd TN29 205 B6
Sunnyside Ave ME12 4 A6
Sunnyside Chalet Pk ME12 5 E5
Sunnyside Cl CT14 116 D1
Sunnyside Cotts CT14 117 C6
Sunnyside Cvn Pk ME12 5 E5
Sunnyside Gdns CT13 93 E8
Sunnyside Rd CT20 177 D3
Sunray Ave CT5 43 B7
Sunset Cl Eastchurch ME12 5 F6
Whitstable CT5 43 C6
Sunshine Ct 1 ME8 33 F8
Sunstone Dr ME10 36 C7
Superabbey Est ME20 53 B2
Surf Cres ME12 5 F6
Surrenden Rd CT19 177 F6
Surrey Cl CT12 29 B1
Surrey Gdns CT7 26 F7
Surrey Rd Canterbury CT1 88 D7
Maidstone ME15 97 D8
Margate CT9 8 B3
Surtees Cl TN24 156 E6
Susan's Hill TN26 168 E3
Sussex Ave Ashford TN24 139 B3
Canterbury CT1 88 D7
Margate CT9 7 J1
Sussex Cl CT6 22 B4
Sussex Dr ME5 32 A4
Sussex Gdns
Birchington CT7 26 F7
Herne Bay CT6 22 B4
Westgate-on-S CT8 7 D1
Sussex Mans CT8 7 D1
Sussex Rd
5 Folkestone CT19 178 D6
Maidstone ME15 97 D8
New Romney TN28 202 A6
Sussex St CT11 52 E7
Sussex Wlk CT1 88 D7
Sutherland Cl CT21 176 A2
Sutherland Dr CT7 27 B6
Sutherland Gdns ME8 33 E6
Sutherland Ho CT21 176 C1
Sutherland Rd CT14 117 C6
Sutton Baron Rd ME9 58 A8
Sutton Cl
Folkestone CT19 178 A7
Gillingham ME8 34 A8
Sutton Cotts ME13 84 C3
Sutton La CT14 133 F5
Sutton Rd Hersden CT3 46 E1
Langley ME17 98 C5
Maidstone ME15 97 D6
Ripple CT14 133 C8
Sutton Row CT14 117 B5
Sutton St ME14 76 D4
Suttons The TN31 203 A1
Swadelands Cl ME17 101 C5
Swadelands Sch ME17 101 C5
Swain Rd Gillingham ME8 33 B6
Tenterden TN30 167 D3
Swakeley Wlk CT5 21 D3
Swale Ave Rushenden ME11 2 F3
Sheerness ME12 1 C1
Swale Cl CT6 23 A3
Swale Ho ME11 2 F5
Swale Sta ME9 15 A7
Swale View ME13 64 B6
Swalecliffe Ave CT6 22 B4
Swalecliffe Com Prim Sch
CT5 21 B2
Swalecliffe Court Dr CT5 21 D3
Swalecliffe Rd CT5 21 B2
Swallow Ave CT5 43 B6
Swallow Cl CT9 28 C8
Swallow Ct CT6 45 F7
Swallow Ho Dover CT17 166 A6
4 Maidstone ME16 74 E4
Swallow Rise ME5 32 A5
Swallowfield TN24 156 E7
Swallows The CT13 94 A8
Swamp Rd TN29 201 B4
Swan Apartments 12
ME15 97 E5
Swan Cl ME10 37 B4
Swan Cotts TN30 188 D3
Swan Gn TN25 159 D1
Swan La TN25 159 E2
Swan St TN30 188 C3
Swanfield Rd CT5 43 D8
Swann Way CT18 163 A4
Swanstree Ave ME10 37 B2
Swanton La
Littlebourne CT3 68 D2
Lydden CT15 147 C6
Swanton Mill★ TN25 157 B2
Swarling Hill Rd CT4 109 C7
Swaynes Way CT13 93 B2
Sweechbridge Rd CT6 23 F3
Sweechgate CT2 67 E7
Sweet Bay Cres TN23 138 D3
Sweet Briar Ct ME16 74 D5
Sweetbriar La CT15 114 B2
Sweetlove Pl CT3 91 A8
Sweyn Rd CT9 8 A3
Swift Cres ME5 32 C6
Swift Ho 6 ME16 74 E4
Swinburne Ave CT10 30 A3
Swinford Gdns CT9 29 C8
Swinford Manor Sch
TN23 138 B4
Swingate Cl ME5 32 B2
Swingate Inf Sch ME5 32 C1
Swiss Way CT19 178 F7
Switch House Ave TN29 209 C2
Sycamore Ave CT3 112 E5
Sycamore Cl
Broadstairs CT10 29 C4
Chartham CT4 86 F1
Dymchurch TN29 195 C8
Herne Bay CT6 23 C5
Hythe CT21 175 E1
Lydd TN29 205 D7
Margate CT9 28 E7
Sycamore Cres ME16 74 C5
Sycamore Dr CT14 117 B4
Sycamore Gdns TN29 195 C8
Sycamore Grange CT11 29 F1
Sycamore La TN23 138 E4
Sycamores The CT3 68 E8
Sydcot Dr CT14 117 D8
Sydenham Rd CT14 117 D7
Sydenham St CT5 20 D2
Sydney Ave ME10 36 C4
Sydney Cooper Cl CT2 66 B2
Sydney Rd Chatham ME4 10 A3
Deal CT14 117 A1
Ramsgate CT11 52 F8
Whitstable CT5 43 E8
Sydney St TN23 156 C8
Sylewood Cl ME1 31 B8
Sylvan Glade ME5 54 A8
Sylvan Rd ME8 33 C8
Symmonds Dr ME10 37 A6
Symons Ave ME4 10 A2
Syndale Pl 5 CT11 52 F7
Syndale Valley Vineyard★
ME9 81 C7

T

Tabret Cl TN24 139 D6
Tadburn Gn ME5 32 B4
Taddington Wood La
ME5 31 E2
Taddy Gdns CT9 29 C8
Tadley Ct Gillingham ME7 10 F6
Rochester ME1 31 C8
Tadworth Rd TN24 139 D5
Tail Race The ME15 74 E2
Taillour Cl ME10 36 F7
Talavera Rd CT1 88 D8
Talbot Ave CT6 22 B3
Talbot Rd Maidstone ME16 74 C6
Margate CT9 8 B2
Tall Trees Cl ME17 99 D2
Tally Ho Rd TN26 155 C2
Tamarind Cl ME7 33 A4
Tamarisk ME12 19 E5
Tame La CT21,TN29 185 F6
Tamley La TN25 142 B6
Tams Gdns ME12 4 D6
Tangier Cl CT15 149 E3
Tanglewood Cl ME8 33 C6
Tangmere Cl ME7 10 F5
Tanhouse La TN31 196 A2
Tanker Hill ME8 33 D6
Tankerton Cir CT5 20 F3
Tankerton Ct CT5 21 B3
Tankerton Hts CT5 20 E3
Tankerton Mews CT5 20 E3
Tankerton Rd CT5 20 F3
Tanner's Hill CT21 176 C3
Tanner's Hill Gdns CT21 176 C3
Tanners St ME13 62 C7
Tannery Ct 5 ME10 36 E5
Tannery La Ashford TN23 139 C2
11 Sandwich CT13 72 F1
Tapleys Hill CT4 110 B5
Taplin Ct 5 CT7 27 A7
Target Bsns Ctr ME15 97 F4
Target Firs CT16 148 D5
Tariff Reform Cotts
ME13 62 D5
Tarragon Rd ME16 74 B3
Tartane La TN29 195 C8
Taryes Ho 2 CT11 52 C6
Tasker Cl ME15 76 B3
Tassell's Wlk CT5 21 D3
Taswell Cl CT16 166 E8
Taswell Rd ME8 12 A1

Taswell St CT16 166 E8
Tatchell Dr TN27 120 C7
Tatler Cl ME5 32 D2
Tatsfield Cl ME8 11 A2
Tattershall Rd ME15 75 A1
Taunton Cl ME15 97 F6
Taverners Rd ME8 33 E7
Tavistock Cl Chatham ME5 31 F1
  Gillingham ME8 33 E7
  Sittingbourne ME10 36 D4
Tavistock Rd CT11 29 E1
Tay Cl ME5 32 B5
Taylers Yd TN25 123 E2
Taylor Cl ME17 100 D6
Taylor Rd
  Folkestone CT19 177 E6
  Lydd-on-S TN29 206 E6
  Minster (Thanet) CT12 50 B6
Taylor's La ME2 9 B7
Taylors Cl TN29 194 F3
Taylors Hill CT4 107 B8
Taylors La TN29 194 F3
Taymouth Ho 1 CT16 166 E8
Taywood Cl TN24 139 F1
Teal Cl CT18 162 F3
Teal Dr CT6 22 E2
Teal Way ME9 14 E3
Teasaucer Hill ME15 96 F8
Teasel Cl ME14 75 F4
Teasel Rd ME5 31 F4
Teddars Leas Rd CT18 161 E4
Tedder Ave ME5 32 A7
Teddington Cl CT1 67 B2
Teelin Cl TN29 195 A4
Telegraph Hill Ind Pk CT12 50 D7
Telegraph Rd CT14 117 B3
Telescope Alley ME12 1 E2
Telford Ct
  Folkestone CT19 178 E6
  Herne Bay CT6 22 C2
Telford Ho 1 ME14 75 A6
Telford St CT6 22 E5
Telham Ave CT12 52 B8
Temeraire Hts CT20 177 C3
Temeraire Manor 2 ME7 10 A6
Templar Ct
  9 Canterbury CT2 66 F1
  11 Dover CT17 149 C1
Templar Rd CT16 148 D5
Templar St CT17 166 C8
Temple Cl Ashford TN23 155 F5
  Temple Ewell CT16 148 D6
Temple Ct CT2 66 D1
Temple Ewell CE Prim Sch CT16 148 D5
Temple Gdns
  Rochester ME2 9 A6
  Sittingbourne ME10 37 B3
Temple Manor★ ME2 9 A6
Temple Mews 10 CT1 87 F8
Temple Rd CT2 66 D1
Temple Side CT16 148 D6
Temple Way CT14 94 A4
Templeman Liby CT2 66 E4
Ten Acre Way ME8 12 B1
Ten Perch Rd CT1 87 D6
Tennyson Ave CT1 67 D3
Tennyson Gdns CT3 112 F6
Tennyson Ho CT1 67 D3
Tennyson Pl
  Canterbury CT1 67 D3
  Folkestone CT19 178 E7
Tennyson Rd
  Ashford TN23 156 A6
  Gillingham ME7 10 C3
Tenterden & District Mus★ TN30 179 A7
Tenterden CE Jun Sch TN30 179 B7
Tenterden Dr CT2 67 A4
Tenterden Inf Sch TN30 179 B7
Tenterden Rd
  Appledore Heath TN26 181 B1
  Chatham ME5 32 B5
Tenterden Station Est TN30 179 A8
Tenterden Town Sta★ TN30 179 A8
Tenterden Vineyard★ TN30 179 C1
Tenterden Way CT9 8 C1
Terance Butler Ave ME2 9 E8
Terence Cl ME4 10 A2
Terlingham La CT18 163 A2
Terminus Dr CT6 23 D5
Terminus Rd ME16 74 A2
Terminus Wlk 3 CT20 178 E5
Terrace Apartments The CT21 176 C1
Terrace Cotts CT4 127 A6
Terrace Rd
  Elvington CT15 114 B1
  Maidstone ME16 74 E3
  Sittingbourne ME10 37 B3
Terrace The
  Canterbury CT2 66 F3
  Faversham ME13 62 A7
  Pluckley TN26 120 A1
  Rochester ME1 9 C5
  Shepherdswell CT15 130 D5
Terry's La CT5 20 D2
Teynham Cl CT9 8 F2
Teynham Dr CT5 20 F2
Teynham Gn ME8 11 A4
Teynham Parochial CE Prim Sch ME9 38 C2
Teynham Rd CT5 20 F2
Teynham St ME9 38 F4
Teynham Sta ME9 38 D3
Thames Ave
  Gillingham ME8 33 E8
  Sheerness ME12 1 C1
Thames Ct ME12 6 G2
Thames View Inf Sch ME8 11 D2
Thames View Jun Sch ME8 11 D2
Thanet Cl CT10 30 B5
Thanet Coll
  Broadstairs CT10 30 A3
  Margate CT9 7 I2
Thanet Ent Ctr CT10 29 D7
Thanet Gdns CT19 178 F6
Thanet Ho 7 ME15 97 F5
Thanet Place Gdns CT10 30 B6
Thanet Rd
  Broadstairs CT10 30 B4
  Margate CT9 7 J2
  Ramsgate CT11 52 F7
  Westgate-on-S CT8 27 D8
Thanet Reach Bsns Pk CT10 29 C4
Thanet Terr TN26 138 A6
Thanet View
  Eythorne CT15 131 B8
  St Nicholas at Wade CT7 25 F2
Thanet Way
  Boughton Street ME13 63 D6
  Herne Bay CT6 23 C3
  Whitstable CT5 21 C2
  Yorkletts CT5,ME13 42 E2
Thanington Ct Farm CT1 87 C6
Thanington Rd CT1 87 C6
Thatchers The ME16 74 B5
Theatre Sq 7 TN30 179 A7
Theatre St CT21 176 C2
Theodore Pl ME7 10 C5
Theresa Rd CT21 176 B1
Third Ave Chatham ME5 10 C1
  Eastchurch ME12 5 F6
  Gillingham ME7 10 F4
  Margate CT9 8 B3
Thirlemere Cl ME16 74 D8
Thirlmere TN24 139 D6
Thirlmere Ave CT11 51 A7
Thirlmere Cl ME7 11 A5
Thirlmere Gdns CT3 112 F6
Thirsk Ho 6 ME15 97 F6
Thistle Dr CT5 43 B6
Thistle Hill Way
  Minster (Sheppey) ME12 4 A4
  Minster (Sheppey) ME12 4 C5
Thistle Wlk ME10 37 B5
Thistlebank ME5 32 A3
Thistledown ME14 75 F4
Thistledown Cl ME7 33 A4
Thomas Aveling Sch The ME1 31 C8
Thomas Ct 9 ME10 37 B4
Thomas Rd
  Faversham ME13 62 D7
  Sittingbourne ME10 37 B4
Thomas Seth Bsns Pk ME11 3 A3
Thomas St ME1 9 C3
Thompson Cl Deal CT14 134 B8
  Folkestone CT19 178 B7
  Gillingham ME8 34 A8
Thomson Rd TN25 139 B5
Thorn Cl ME5 31 D1
Thorn Est The TN27 136 B6
Thorn Gdns CT11 29 E1
Thorn Hill Rd ME12 6 D4
Thorn La CT4 126 C2
Thorn Wlk ME10 37 C5
Thornbridge Rd CT14 117 B2
Thorndale Cl ME5 31 D4
Thornden Cl CT6 22 B2
Thornden Ct CT2 66 C4
Thornden Wood Rd
  Herne Bay CT6 22 B1
  Whitstable CT6 44 E4
Thorndike Cl ME4 31 F8
Thorndike Ho ME4 31 F8
Thorndike Rd TN29 186 C4
Thorne Hill CT12 51 A6
Thorne Rd CT12 50 B6
Thorney Croft Cl ME17 99 D2
Thorneycroft Rd ME13 103 D5
Thornham Rd ME8 11 C3
Thornhill Pl ME14 75 A6
Thornhurst CT6 23 D4
Thornlea TN23 138 E2
Thornton Cl TN24 140 A1
Thornton La CT13,CT14 114 E7
Thornton's La 9 CT16 166 E7
Thorold Rd ME5 10 D3
Thorpe Wlk ME8 33 D3
Thrale Way ME8 33 E4
Thread La ME13 64 B4
Three Acres Site CT19 178 B8
Three King's Yd CT13 73 A1
Threshers Dr ME14 75 E5
Throwley Dr CT6 22 C4
Throwley Rd ME13 82 D5
Thrupp Paddock CT10 8 G1
Thrush Cl ME5 32 B7
Thruxted La CT4 86 B1
Thundersland Rd CT6 23 B4
Thurlow Ave CT6 23 C5
Thurnham CE Inf Sch ME14 76 A4
Thurnham La ME14 76 C7
Thurston Pk CT5 20 E1
Thurstone Ct ME14 74 F6
Thyme Wlk ME16 74 B3
Tiber Cl CT19 177 C6
Tichborne Cl ME16 74 C6
Tickham La ME9 60 C5
Tickner's La TN29 192 B1
Tideway The ME1 31 C8
Tilbury Rd ME8 12 A2
Tilden Cl TN26 167 D7
Tilden Ct TN26 167 E7
Tilden Gill Rd TN30 179 C7
Tile Fields ME17 77 D2
Tile Ho The CT21 176 C2
Tile Kiln Hill CT2 66 B5
Tile Kiln La CT19 177 F7
Tile Kiln Rd TN24 139 C7
Tile Lodge Cotts TN27 119 E8
Tile Lodge Rd TN27 119 E8
Tillard Cl CT4 109 B3
Tillery La TN29 200 A8
Timber Tops ME5 54 D8
Timberbank ME5 32 A6
Timeball Tower Mus★ CT14 117 D5
Timperley Cl CT14 117 B6
Tina Gdns CT10 30 A6
Tinbridge Pk ME13 63 A5
Tinker's Alley ME4 9 F7
Tintagel Manor 6 ME7 10 C6
Tintern Rd ME16 74 D7
Titchfield Cl 5 ME15 97 F6
Titchfield Rd ME15 97 F6
Tithe Barn La TN23 155 D8
Tithe Yd ME17 101 D5
Tivoli Brooks CT9 7 I1
Tivoli Park Ave CT9 7 H1
Tivoli Rd CT9 28 E8
Tobruk Way ME5 31 F6
Toby Rd TN29 206 E6
Todd Cres ME10 37 A8
Toddington Cres ME5 31 D1
Toke Cl TN23 138 C1
Tolgate La ME2 9 B7
Tolgate Way ME14 53 E4
Toll Gate CT14 117 A4
Toll La TN27 120 E7
Tollemache Cl CT12 27 F2
Tollgate Cl CT5 43 C8
Tolputt Ct CT19 178 E6
Tolsford Cl
  Etchinghill CT18 161 D3
  Folkestone CT19 177 D6
Tomar Owl Sanctuary★ TN25 156 F2
Tomay Cotts CT6 24 A3
Tomlin Dr CT9 29 C8
Tonbridge Ct ME16 74 D3
Tonbridge Rd ME16 74 C3
Tonford La Canterbury CT1 87 B6
  Harbledown CT2 87 A7
Tonge Rd ME10 37 C4
Tontine St CT20 178 E5
Tookey Rd TN28 202 B6
Top Rd TN30 189 E3
Topaz Dr ME10 36 C6
Tormore Mews CT14 117 A4
Tormore Pk CT14 117 A4
Toronto Cl 6 CT16 149 B3
Toronto Rd ME7 10 E4
Torrington Cotts CT12 50 D7
Torrington Rd TN23 156 C8
Tothill St CT12 50 C7
Tourmaline Dr ME10 36 C6
Tournay Cl TN23 155 F8
Tourney Cl CT21 174 F3
Tourney Rd TN29 205 C5
Tourtel Rd CT1 67 A1
Tovil Gn ME15 74 E2
Tovil Green Bsns Pk ME15 74 E1
Tovil Hill ME15 74 E2
Tovil Rd ME15 74 F2
Tovil, St Stephen's CE Inf Sch ME15 74 E2
Tower Bglws CT7 27 A8
Tower Ct 4 CT20 177 E3
Tower Est TN29 186 E2
Tower Gdns Hythe CT21 176 C1
  Maidstone ME14 76 B4
Tower Hamlets Rd CT17 166 C8
Tower Hamlets St 1 CT17 166 C8
Tower Hill Dover CT17 166 C8
  Whitstable CT5 20 E3
Tower La ME14 76 B4
Tower Par CT5 20 E3
Tower Rd CT5 20 E2
Tower St CT17 166 C8
Tower View CT4 86 F1
Tower Way 1 CT1 87 F8
Towers Point ME1 9 B4
Towers Sch The TN24 139 D8
Towers The TN27 103 E1
Towers View TN24 139 C7
Town Hill CT4 88 F2
Town La CT4 86 C6
Town Rd CT4 109 C5
Town Wlk CT20 178 D4
Townley St CT11 52 D6
Townsend Farm Rd CT15 150 F6
Townsend Terr CT17 166 B5
Townwall St CT16 166 E7
Toy Mus★ CT5 20 E3
Tracies The ME9 35 C6
Tradewinds CT5 43 B6
Trafalgar Par ME12 4 B6
Trafalgar Rd CT7 27 F3
Trafalgar St ME7 10 C5
Tram Rd The CT20 178 E5
Tramways ME5 10 C2
Transformer Ave TN29 209 C2
Transom Ho 3 ME1 9 C1
Trapfield Cl ME14 76 C4
Trapfield La ME14 76 C4
Trapham Rd ME16 74 D5
Travers Gdns ME9 57 F5
Travers Rd CT14 117 A5
Travertine Rd ME5 32 B1
Treasury View CT3 90 C8
Trefoil The ME9,ME13 60 E6
Trefor Jones Ct CT16 149 B2
Trelawn Cres ME5 32 B2
Trenley Dr CT3 67 F1
Trent Rd ME5 32 B5
Trenton Cl ME16 74 B7
Trevale Rd ME1 9 B1
Trevino Dr ME5 31 F2
Trevor Dr ME16 74 C5
Tribune Ct ME12 3 B8
Tribune Dr ME10 36 F6
Trident Cl ME2 9 E7
Trigg's Row ME9 38 D2
Triggs Cotts ME9 38 D2
Trilby Way CT5 43 B6
Trimworth Rd CT19 177 F6
Trinity Cres CT20 178 B4
Trinity Ct Deal CT14 117 A4
  Forstal ME20 53 A3
  Margate CT9 7 J3
Trinity Gdns CT20 178 C4
Trinity Hill CT9 7 J3
Trinity Homes CT14 117 C1
Trinity Pl Deal CT14 117 A4
  Ramsgate CT11 52 F7
Trinity Rd Ashford TN24 139 B7
  Folkestone CT20 178 B4
  Gillingham ME7 10 C6
  Sheerness ME12 1 D2
  Sittingbourne ME10 36 F7
Trinity Sch ME1 9 D4
Trinity Sq
  Broadstairs CT10 29 F7
  Margate CT9 7 J3
Trinity Trad Est ME10 36 F6
Tritton Cl TN24 139 F7
Tritton Fields TN24 139 F7
Tritton Gdns TN29 186 D1
Tritton La TN28 202 B6
Troodos Hill ME14 74 F8
Trotts Hall Gdns ME10 36 F3
Trotwood Cl ME5 54 A8
Trotwood Pl 14 CT10 30 B4
Troubridge Cl TN24 157 B7
Troughton Mews CT9 7 H1
Trove Ct 7 CT11 52 F7
Troy Mews ME1 9 C4
Troy Town La TN25 141 B5
Troys Mead ME17 77 D2
Trueman Cl CT2 66 A7
Trumpet Ho TN23 156 B8
Truro Cl ME8 11 D3
Truro Rd CT11 52 F7
Tudor Ave
  Dymchurch TN29 186 D1
  Maidstone ME14 75 B6
Tudor Byway TN24 139 D6
Tudor Cl CT7 27 B8
Tudor Ct Canterbury CT2 66 C4
  Whitstable CT5 21 A3
Tudor End TN24 139 D5
Tudor Farm Cl TN23 156 A3
Tudor Gr ME8 33 F8
Tudor Ho Deal CT14 117 A5
Tudor Ho★ CT9 7 J3
Tudor Mews CT14 117 B4
Tudor Rd Ashford TN24 139 D5
  Canterbury CT1 87 E7
  Folkestone CT19 177 D6
Tufa Cl ME5 32 B1
Tufton Rd Ashford TN24 139 D2
  Gillingham ME8 11 F1
  Hothfield TN26 138 A7
Tufton St Ashford TN23 139 B2
  Maidstone ME14 75 A4
Tufton Wlk 9 TN23 139 B2
Tunbridge Way TN23 155 C8
Tunbury Ave ME5 31 F1
Tunbury Ave S ME5 31 F1
Tunbury Prim Sch ME5 31 F1
Tunis Ct CT1 67 D1
Tunis Row CT10 30 B5
Tunstall CE Prim Sch ME9 58 C8
Tunstall Rd
  Canterbury CT2 67 A4
  Sittingbourne ME10,ME9 58 D8
Tupman Cl ME1 9 B4
Turbine Hall Ave TN29 209 C2
Turgis Cl ME17 98 E4
Turketel Rd CT20 178 A4
Turmine Ct ME12 4 A5
Turnagain La 3 CT1 87 F8
Turnden Gdns CT9 8 E2
Turner Cl Ashford TN24 156 E7
  Sittingbourne ME10 37 A7
Turner Ct
  5 Folkestone CT20 177 F5
  Margate CT9 8 A2
Turner St CT11 52 E7
Turners Ave TN30 179 B8
Turners Cl ME12 1 D1
Turnpike Cl CT21 176 A2
Turnpike Hill CT21 176 A3
Turnstone Cl ME9 14 E4
Turnstone Ct TN29 194 F3
Turnstone Rd ME5 32 C1
Turrets The Deal CT14 117 C1
  9 Sittingbourne ME10 37 A4
Tuscan Dr ME5 32 C1
Tweed Terr CT21 176 A1
Twelve Acres TN24 156 F8
Twiss Ave CT21 176 D2
Twiss Gr CT21 176 D2
Twiss Rd CT21 176 D2
Twydall Ent Ctr ME8 11 C4
Twydall Gn ME8 11 B3
Twydall Inf Sch ME8 11 B2
Twydall Jun Sch ME8 11 B2
Twydall La ME8 11 B2
Twyford Cl ME8 12 A2
Twyford Ct ME14 75 D6
Twymans Mill ME13 62 C7
Twyne Cl CT2 68 A6
Twysden Ct TN25 123 E2
Tydeman Rd ME15 75 F2
Tydeman's Ave CT5 21 C1
Tyland Barn Wildlife Conservation Ctr★ ME14 53 E3
Tyland La ME14 53 F3
Tyler Cl CT2 66 F3
Tyler Dr ME8 33 E4
Tyler Hill Rd CT2 66 C6
Tyler Way CT5 21 E3
Tyndale Pk CT6 23 B5
Tyne Cl ME5 32 C5
Tyrwhitt-Drake Mus of Carriages★ ME15 75 A3
Tysoe Ct ME12 4 A5
Tyson Ave CT9 7 E1
Tyson Rd CT19 178 E7

U

Uden Rd TN29 187 B4
Uffington Ct CT3 91 A2
Ufton Cl ME15 75 E1
Ufton La ME10 36 E3
Ulcombe Gdns CT2 67 A3
Ulcombe Hill ME17 99 F1
Ulcombe Rd ME17 98 E3
Ulley Rd TN24 139 D7
Ullswater Gdns CT3 112 F6
Ullswater Ho 5 ME15 97 E7
Ulster Rd CT9 28 F8
Undercliff CT20 177 E3
Undercliffe Rd CT14 134 D5
Underdown Ave ME4 9 F1
Underdown La CT6 22 F2
Underdown Rd
  Dover CT17 166 B7
  Herne Bay CT6 22 F5
Underhill Cotts CT18 177 B8
Underhill Rd CT20 177 B5
Underwood CT18 163 C6
Underwood Cl
  Ashford TN24 139 D6
  Canterbury CT4 88 B5
  Maidstone ME15 74 F2
Underwood Ct CT1 88 B6
Unicorn Cotts CT4 89 B5
Unicumes La ME16 74 C2
Union Cres CT9 7 J2
Union Pk ME15 97 F4
Union Pl
  4 Canterbury CT1 67 A1
  Chatham ME4 10 A4
Union Rd Bridge CT4 88 F1
  Deal CT14 117 D6
  Minster (Sheppey) ME12 4 C7
  Ramsgate CT11 52 F8
Union Row CT9 7 J2
Union Sq 3 CT10 30 B4
Union St Canterbury CT1 67 A1
  Chatham ME4 10 A3
  Dover CT17 166 D6
  Faversham ME13 62 C7
  Maidstone ME14 75 A5
  12 Ramsgate CT11 52 E7
  Rochester ME1 9 C5
  Sheerness ME12 1 B2
Unity Pl 3 CT11 52 F7
Unity St Sheerness ME12 1 E2
  Sittingbourne ME10 36 E3
Univ of Greenwich ME4 10 B8
Univ of Kent at Canterbury CT2 66 D4
University Rd CT2 66 D3
Unwin Cl ME20 53 A3
Upbury Arts Coll ME7 10 B4
Upbury Way ME4 10 A4
Upchurch Wlk CT9 8 E2
Updown Way CT4 86 F1
Uphill CT18 163 B4
Uplands CT2 66 F4
Uplands Way ME12 3 C5
Uplees Cotts ME13 39 F5
Uplees Rd ME13 40 A3
Upnor Ho ME15 97 E8
Upper Approach Rd CT10 30 A3
Upper Brents ME13 62 D8
Upper Bridge St
  Canterbury CT1 88 A8
  Wye TN25 123 F2
Upper Britton Pl ME7 10 B5
Upper Chantry La CT1 88 A7

Upper Corniche CT20 ...177 C3
Upper Dane Ct CT9 ...8 B1
Upper Dane Rd CT9 ...8 B1
Upper Denmark Rd TN23 ...156 B8
Upper Dumpton Park Rd CT11 ...52 E8
Upper East Rd ME4 ...10 B8
Upper Fans La ME9 ...14 C4
Upper Fant Rd ME16 ...74 D2
Upper Field Rd ME10 ...37 B5
Upper Free Down CT6 ...23 B2
Upper Gore La CT13 ...93 A2
Upper Gr CT9 ...7 J2
Upper Hunton Hill ME15 ...96 A3
Upper Luton Rd ME5 ...10 C2
Upper Malthouse Hill CT21 ...176 B2
Upper Maltings Pl CT7 ...26 F7
Upper Queens Rd TN24 ...139 B3
Upper Rd
Dover CT15,CT16 ...150 C2
Dover,Eastern Docks CT16 ...166 G8
Maidstone ME15 ...75 B2
Upper St
Hollingbourne ME17 ...77 E3
Kingsdown CT14 ...134 D5
Leeds ME17 ...98 F5
Tilmanstone CT14 ...115 A3
Upper St Ann's Rd ME13 ...62 B6
Upper Stone St ME15 ...75 A3
Upper Strand St CT13 ...73 A1
Upper Tickham Cotts ME9 ...60 D6
Upper Vicarage Rd TN24 ...139 D7
Upstreet CT18 ...161 D3
Upton Cl CT19 ...178 A7
Upton Jun Sch CT10 ...29 F4
Upton Rd CT10 ...29 F5
Urquhart Cl ME5 ...32 A5
Ursuline Dr CT8 ...27 D7

V

Vale Cotts ME9 ...57 A8
Vale Ct 10 CT11 ...52 D6
Vale Dr ME5 ...31 E6
Vale Pl CT11 ...52 D6
Vale Rd Broadstairs CT10 ...29 F4
Maidstone ME15 ...96 E4
Ramsgate CT11 ...52 D6
Ripple CT14,CT15 ...133 B8
Whitstable CT5 ...43 D8
Vale Sq CT11 ...52 D6
Vale The CT10 ...30 A4
Vale View Com Sch CT17 ...166 B7
Vale View Rd
Aylesham CT3 ...112 E5
Dover CT17 ...166 B7
Valebrook Cl CT20 ...177 C5
Valence Ho ME15 ...97 C7
Valenciennes Ho ME4 ...10 A4
Valenciennes Rd ME10 ...36 E3
Valentine Cl ME7 ...11 A1
Valentine Rd ME15 ...97 E7
Valerian Cl ME5 ...31 E4
Valestone Cl CT21 ...177 B4
Valetta Way ME1 ...9 B4
Valiant Rd ME5 ...32 C2
Valkyrie Ave CT5 ...43 C7
Vallance The ME9 ...60 A6
Valley Cotts
Alkham CT15 ...147 C1
Stalisfield Green ME13 ...103 D8
Valley Dr ME15 ...96 F6
Valley Park Com Sch ME14 ...75 C4
Valley Rd Barham CT4 ...111 E2
Canterbury CT1 ...87 E6
Crabble CT17 ...148 E3
Folkestone CT20 ...177 E4
Gillingham ME7 ...10 E4
Margate CT9 ...28 E4
Valley Rise ME5 ...31 F1
Valley The ME17 ...96 D3
Valley View CT15 ...131 C8
Valley View Rd ME1 ...9 B1
Valley Wlk CT21 ...177 B3
Vancouver Dr ME8 ...11 C1
Vancouver Rd CT16 ...149 C3
Vange Cottage Mews ME1 ...9 B4
Vanguard Way ME2 ...9 E8
Vanity Holiday Village ME12 ...6 G2
Vanity La ME17 ...96 D1
Vanity Rd ME12 ...6 F2
Varne Ct 6 CT20 ...177 F3
Varne Lodge 5 CT20 ...177 F3
Varne Mews TN28 ...202 E4
Varne Pl CT19 ...178 F5
Varne Rd CT19 ...178 F5
Vaughan Dr ME10 ...36 F8
Vauxhall Ave
Canterbury CT1 ...67 C3
Herne Bay CT6 ...22 A3
Vauxhall Cres CT1 ...67 C3
Vauxhall Industrial Rd CT1 ...67 D4
Vauxhall Rd CT1,CT2 ...67 C4
Vectis Dr ME10 ...36 F8
Ventnor Cl ME5 ...32 C8
Ventnor La 12 CT9 ...7 J2
Venture Cl TN29 ...186 D1
Vere Rd CT10 ...30 A4
Vereth Rd 2 CT11 ...52 D6
Verity Farm Holiday Camp ME12 ...6 F1
Vernon Pl Canterbury CT1 ...88 A7
Deal CT14 ...117 D8
Verwood Cl CT2 ...66 E2
Vespasian Way TN23 ...155 F4
Vesper Ct TN27 ...135 A1
Vestey Ct CT8 ...7 C1
Viaduct Cl CT12 ...52 C8
Viaduct Terr TN26 ...182 F7
Viaduct The CT17 ...166 D5
Viburnum Cl TN23 ...138 E2
Vicarage Cotts ME9 ...13 C3
Vicarage Cres 8 CT9 ...7 J1
Vicarage Ct ME9 ...35 B7
Vicarage Gdn CT12 ...49 C7
Vicarage Gdns CT3 ...91 A7
Vicarage Hill CT4 ...109 B4
Vicarage La
Ashford TN23 ...139 C2
Blean CT2 ...66 A6
Charing Heath TN27 ...119 C7
Deal CT14 ...116 F5
East Farleigh ME15 ...96 B6
Elham CT4 ...144 F4
Faversham ME13 ...62 A4
Lower Halstow ME9 ...13 C3
Nonington CT15 ...113 C5
4 Sandwich CT13 ...72 F1
Selling ME13 ...84 C6
St Margaret's at Cliffe CT15 ...150 F6
Tilmanstone CT14 ...115 A3
Vicarage Pl CT9 ...7 J1
Vicarage Rd
Folkestone CT20 ...177 F3
Gillingham ME7 ...10 C5
Minster (Sheppey) ME12 ...4 D7
Rochester ME2 ...9 B8
Sittingbourne ME10 ...36 E6
Vicarage St
Broadstairs CT10 ...29 E5
Faversham ME13 ...62 D8
Vicary Way ME16 ...74 D5
Vickers Cl CT18 ...163 A4
Victor Ave CT9 ...8 D2
Victoria Ave
Broadstairs CT10 ...29 E8
Hythe CT21 ...176 B2
Margate CT9 ...8 B1
St Margaret's at Cliffe CT15 ...151 B6
Westgate-on-S CT8 ...27 F8
Victoria Cl ME5 ...31 D2
Victoria Cres
Ashford TN23 ...139 B1
Dover CT16 ...166 D8
Victoria Ct Hythe CT21 ...176 C1
6 Maidstone ME16 ...74 E3
Victoria Dr CT6 ...22 C5
Victoria Gr
12 Folkestone CT20 ...178 D5
Hythe CT21 ...177 B2
Victoria Ho 7 CT5 ...20 D2
Victoria Hospl CT14 ...117 B5
Victoria Mews
Deal CT14 ...117 C6
Westgate-on-S CT8 ...7 D1
Victoria Orch ME16 ...74 B3
Victoria Par
Broadstairs CT10 ...30 B4
Ramsgate CT11 ...52 F7
Victoria Park Mews 2 CT16 ...166 E8
Victoria Pk Dover CT16 ...166 E8
Herne Bay CT6 ...23 A5
Victoria Pl
Faversham ME13 ...62 C7
Hythe CT21 ...176 B4
Victoria Rd Ashford TN23 ...139 B1
Broadstairs CT10 ...29 E6
Canterbury CT1 ...87 E7
Capel-le-F CT18 ...164 B2
Chatham,Kit Hill ME5 ...31 E3
Chatham,Luton ME4 ...10 B2
Deal CT14 ...117 D5
Folkestone CT19 ...178 C5
Hythe CT21 ...176 C1
Kingsdown CT14 ...134 C4
Littlestone-on-Sea TN28 ...202 E5
Margate CT9 ...7 J2
Margate,Lydden CT9 ...28 D4
Ramsgate CT11 ...52 F7
Sittingbourne ME10 ...36 D4
Victoria Rd W TN28 ...202 E5
Victoria Road Prim Sch TN23 ...139 B1
Victoria Row
Canterbury CT1 ...67 A1
Ramsgate CT11 ...52 C5
Victoria St Dover CT17 ...149 B1
Gillingham ME7 ...10 D6
Maidstone ME16 ...74 E3
New Romney TN28 ...202 A6
Rochester ME1 ...9 D5
Rochester,Strood ME2 ...9 B7
Sheerness ME12 ...1 D1
Whitstable CT5 ...20 D2
Victoria Terr Hythe CT21 ...177 B2
Minster (Sheppey) ME12 ...5 A5
Rochester ME1 ...9 A2
Sittingbourne ME10 ...36 D4
Victoria Yd 22 CT1 ...67 A1
Victory Manor 1 ME7 ...10 A6
Victory Pk ME2 ...9 E7
Victory Rd CT15 ...133 F1
Victory St ME12 ...1 C2
Vidal Manor ME7 ...10 C5
Viewlands ME5 ...10 C3
Viewpoint ME14 ...75 C8
Vigo Terr ME9 ...38 C1
Viking Cl CT7 ...26 D8
Viking Ct Broadstairs CT10 ...30 B3
Canterbury CT2 ...66 F2
Margate CT9 ...8 A2
Viking Ship★ CT12 ...51 E5
Village View ME5 ...10 C2
Village Way TN26 ...183 A7
Villas The CT3 ...47 A1
Villiers Ct CT17 ...166 C7
Villiers Ho CT10 ...30 B7
Villiers Rd CT1 ...67 D1
Vincent Cl
Broadstairs CT10 ...29 C3
Folkestone CT20 ...177 E5
Vincent Ct ME12 ...1 D1
Vincent Gdns ME12 ...1 D1
Vincent Pl TN24 ...139 F4
Vincent Rd
Kit's Coty ME20 ...53 C7
Margate CT9 ...28 C4
Sittingbourne ME10 ...37 C3
Vine Cl CT11 ...29 E2
Vine End CT11 ...29 E2
Vine Lands TN29 ...205 B6
Vine Lo CT11 ...29 E2
Vineries The ME7 ...10 E5
Viners Cl ME10 ...36 F1
Vines La ME1 ...9 C5
Viney's Gdns TN30 ...167 C1
Vineyard Cres ME8 ...12 B1
Vinson Cl ME13 ...41 D1
Vinten Cl CT6 ...46 B8
Vinters Rd ME14 ...75 B4
Vintners Way ME14 ...75 E4
Violet Ave CT12 ...29 C2
Violet Cl ME5 ...54 A8
Virginia Rd
Gillingham ME7 ...10 C7
Whitstable CT5 ...44 A8
Vixen Cl ME5 ...32 C6
Vlissingen Dr CT14 ...117 C8
Volante Dr ME10 ...36 E7
Vulcan Cl Chatham ME5 ...32 B7
Whitstable CT5 ...43 C7

W

Wacher Cl CT2 ...66 F2
Waddenhall Barns CT4 ...126 B5
Waddington Dr CT18 ...163 A4
Waddle Cnr TN30 ...189 D3
Wades Cl TN29 ...194 B4
Wadham Pl ME10 ...37 B2
Waghorn St ME4 ...10 B2
Wagoners Cl ME14 ...75 E4
Wain Ct ME12 ...4 A5
Wainwright Ct CT10 ...30 B6
Wainwright Pl TN24 ...156 D8
Wake Rd ME1 ...31 C8
Wakefield Way CT21 ...176 B1
Wakefield Wlk CT21 ...176 D1
Wakehurst Cl ME17 ...96 B3
Wakeley Rd ME8 ...12 A1
Wakeleys Cotts ME8 ...34 B8
Walcheren Cl CT14 ...117 C8
Walcot Pl CT6 ...23 B3
Waldens The ME17 ...99 E2
Waldershare Ave CT13 ...95 A7
Waldershare Ho CT15 ...131 D5
Waldershare La CT15 ...132 E2
Waldershare Rd CT15 ...132 A5
Walderslade Ctr ME5 ...32 A3
Walderslade Girls Sch ME5 ...31 F5
Walderslade Prim Sch ME5 ...32 A3
Walderslade Rd ME5 ...31 F6
Walderslade Woods ME5 ...31 E2
Waldron Dr ME15 ...96 F6
Waldron Rd CT10 ...30 B2
Walk The ME17 ...99 E2
Walker La CT7 ...26 D8
Wall Rd TN24 ...139 B3
Wall The ME10 ...36 E5
Wallace Mews CT19 ...178 D7
Wallace Rd ME1 ...31 E8
Wallace Way CT10 ...29 E4
Wallbridge La ME8 ...12 D3
Waller Rd TN28 ...206 E7
Wallers Rd ME13 ...62 A7
Wallis Ave ME15 ...97 E5
Wallis Rd TN24 ...139 D2
Wallwood Rd CT11 ...52 F8
Walmer Castle★ CT14 ...117 D1
Walmer Castle Rd CT14 ...117 C1
Walmer Ct 3 ME14 ...75 A5
Walmer Gdns
Cliffs End CT12 ...51 D5
Deal CT14 ...117 A2
Sittingbourne ME10 ...36 D5
Walmer Rd CT5 ...43 E8
Walmer Sch CT14 ...117 B2
Walmer Sta CT14 ...117 A1
Walmer Way Deal CT14 ...117 A2
1 Folkestone CT20 ...177 F5
Walmsley Ho 4 CT19 ...178 E6
Walmsley Rd CT10 ...29 F5
Walner Gdns TN28 ...202 B7
Walner La TN28 ...202 B7
Walnut Cl Ashford TN24 ...139 D6
Broadstairs CT10 ...29 F2
Chatham ME5 ...32 B8
Walnut Ridge TN25 ...173 A6
Walnut Tree Ave ME15 ...97 A5
Walnut Tree Cl 6 CT7 ...27 A7
Walnut Tree Cotts ME13 ...84 E8
Walnut Tree Dr ME10 ...36 D4
Walnut Tree La
Loose ME15 ...97 A5
Westbere CT2 ...68 D7
Walpole Rd CT9 ...7 J3
Walsby Dr ME10 ...37 A8
Walsham Rd ME5 ...31 F1
Walshaw Ho 2 ME14 ...75 A6
Walsingham Cl ME8 ...33 D3
Walsingham Ho 3 ME14 ...75 A6
Waltham Cl
Ashford TN24 ...140 A2
Margate CT9 ...8 E2
Waltham Rd
Gillingham ME8 ...11 C3
Waltham CT4 ...108 F1
Walton Gdns CT19 ...178 D7
Walton Manor Cl CT19 ...178 D7
Walton Rd CT19 ...178 D6
Waltons The CT19 ...178 C8
Wanden La TN27 ...135 C8
Wanstall Ct CT7 ...27 A7
Wantsum Cl CT6 ...23 F5
Wantsum Mews 7 CT13 ...72 F1
Wantsum Way CT7 ...25 E3
Wantsume Lees CT13 ...72 E2
Warblers Cl 3 ME2 ...9 A7
Warden Bay Pk ME12 ...6 E3
Warden Bay Rd ME12 ...6 E3
Warden Cl ME16 ...74 C4
Warden Ct 10 CT17 ...149 C1
Warden House Mews CT14 ...117 A4
Warden House Prim Sch CT14 ...117 A5
Warden Point Way CT5 ...43 C6
Warden Rd Rochester ME1 ...9 C2
Warden ME12 ...6 B5
Warden Spring Cvn Pk ME12 ...6 D5
Warden Terr ME12 ...5 A6
Warden View Gdns ME12 ...6 D1
Warden Way ME12 ...6 B5
Wardour Cl CT10 ...30 B4
Wards Hill Rd ME12 ...4 C8
Wardwell La ME9 ...13 C1
Ware St ME14 ...76 A5
Warehorne Rd TN26 ...183 A7
Warlingham Cl ME8 ...12 A1
Warmlake ME17 ...98 F1
Warmlake Bsns Est ME17 ...98 E1
Warmlake Rd ME17 ...98 C1
Warner St ME4 ...9 F3
Warnford Gdns ME15 ...97 A8
Warre Ave CT11 ...52 C5
Warren Cl
Folkestone CT19 ...178 F6
Sittingbourne ME10 ...37 B2
Warren Dr CT10 ...29 E5
Warren Dr The CT8 ...27 D7
Warren Hos TN27 ...119 E8
Warren Hts TN25 ...158 E5
Warren La Ashford TN24 ...139 A4
Lydden CT15 ...147 D6
Yelsted ME9 ...34 C3
Warren Lo CT1 ...87 B6
Warren Rd
Folkestone CT19 ...178 F6
Kit's Coty ME5 ...53 D7
Littlestone-on-Sea TN28 ...202 D6
Warren Ret Pk TN24 ...139 B4
Warren St
Stalisfield Green TN27 ...103 A3
Warren Street ME17 ...102 D7
Warren The
Brabourne Lees TN25 ...158 E5
Selling ME13 ...84 E7
Whitstable CT5 ...43 C6
Warren View TN23 ...138 F4
Warren Way CT19 ...178 F6
Warren Wood Com Prim Sch & Language Unit ME1 ...31 C8
Warren Wood Rd ME1 ...31 C7
Warten Rd CT11 ...29 F1
Warwick Cres ME10 ...36 C5
Warwick Dr CT11 ...52 B5
Warwick Pl ME16 ...74 E3
Warwick Rd
Ashford TN24 ...139 E5
Canterbury CT1 ...88 C8
Deal CT14 ...117 D2
Margate CT9 ...8 B2
Whitstable CT5 ...20 D2
Washford Farm Rd TN23 ...155 E5
Washington Cl 4 CT16 ...149 B3
Washington Ho ME15 ...97 E5
Washington La TN29 ...200 C6
Wass Dro CT3 ...71 B7
Wat Tyler Way ME15 ...75 A4
Watchester Ave CT11 ...52 C5
Watchester La CT12 ...50 B5
Watchmans Terr 6 ME5 ...10 C2
Water Farm CT4 ...144 F4
Water La Canterbury CT1 ...87 F8
6 Faversham ME13 ...62 C7
Harrietsham ME17 ...100 B5
Kingswood ME17 ...99 F3
6 Maidstone ME15 ...75 A4
Maidstone,Bearsted ME14 ...76 E6
Painters Forstal ME13 ...61 F4
Sturry CT2 ...67 F5
Water Mdws CT2 ...67 F4
Water St CT14 ...117 D7
Waterbrook Ave TN24 ...157 A4
Watercress Ho TN23 ...138 F1
Watercress La
Ashford TN23 ...155 F8
Wingham CT3 ...90 F6
Waterditch La ME17, TN27 ...102 E5
Waterfall Rd TN26 ...138 B6
Waterham Rd ME13 ...42 C1
Waterlock Cotts CT3 ...91 A7
Waterloo Cres CT16, CT17 ...166 E7
Waterloo Hill ME12 ...4 D6
Waterloo Mans 14 CT16, CT17 ...166 E7
Waterloo Pl 10 CT11 ...52 F7
Waterloo Rd
Folkestone CT20 ...177 D5
Gillingham ME7 ...10 C4
Sittingbourne ME10 ...36 D5
Whitstable CT5 ...20 D2
Waterloo St ME15 ...75 A3
Waterloo Terr ME12 ...5 A5
Waterlow Rd ME14 ...75 A6
Waterman Ho TN23 ...156 B8
Watermead Cl TN23 ...155 F7
Watermeadow Cl ME7 ...32 F6
Watermill Cl
Maidstone ME16 ...74 B5
Rochester ME2 ...9 C8
Waters Edge ME15 ...74 F2
Waters Pl ME7 ...33 A6
Watersend CT16 ...148 D5
Waterside Ashford TN24 ...139 F1
Maidstone ME14 ...74 F5
Waterside Cl ME13 ...40 D1
Waterside Ct
5 Hythe CT21 ...176 B2
Rochester ME2 ...9 E6
Waterside Dr CT8 ...7 D1
Waterside Gate ME16 ...74 F5
Waterside La ME7 ...10 F7
Waterside Terr TN23 ...138 C1
Waterside View ME12 ...6 E4
Watersmeet Cl ME15 ...75 A1
Waterstone Pl ME13 ...62 A6
Waterworks Hill CT15 ...133 B3
Waterworks La CT15 ...133 B3
Watery La CT4 ...109 C5
Watkin Rd CT19 ...178 C6
Watling Ave ME5 ...10 D2
Watling Pl ME10 ...37 A3
Watling St Canterbury CT1 ...87 F8
Gillingham ME5 ...10 D2
Watson Ave ME5 ...31 D5
Watsons Cl TN25 ...139 C8
Watsons Hill ME10 ...36 E5
Wattle Cnr TN30 ...189 D3
Watts Cotts TN24 ...139 D7
Watts Yd 13 CT13 ...72 F1
Watts' Ave ME1 ...9 C4
Watts' St ME4 ...9 E3
Wauchope Rd CT5 ...42 F6
Wave Crest CT5 ...20 C1
Waverley Ave ME12 ...4 B7
Waverley Cl Chatham ME5 ...32 D2
Coxheath ME17 ...96 C3
Waverley Rd CT9 ...28 C8
Way Farm Cotts CT12 ...50 E7
Way Hill CT12 ...50 E7
Wayborough Hill CT12 ...50 D7
Wayfield Com Prim Sch ME5 ...32 A7
Wayfield Rd ME5 ...32 A7
Wayne Cl CT10 ...29 E5
Wayside TN30 ...167 B2
Wayside Ave TN30 ...167 B3
Wayside Flats TN30 ...167 B2
Weald Cl ME15 ...97 C6
Weald Ct Charing TN27 ...103 E1
Sittingbourne ME10 ...36 D2
Weald The TN24 ...139 C3
Wealden Ave TN30 ...167 B1
Wealden Ct 5 ME5 ...10 B3
Wealdhurst Pk CT10 ...29 D5
Wear Bay Cres CT19 ...178 F6
Wear Bay Rd CT19 ...178 F5
Weatherall Cl ME13 ...64 B2
Weatherly Cl ME1 ...9 C4
Weatherly Dr CT10 ...29 F2
Weavering Cotts ME14 ...75 E3
Weavering St ME14 ...75 F4
Weavers The ME16 ...74 B5
Weavers Way
Ashford TN23 ...155 E7
Dover CT16 ...149 A3
Webb Cl CT19 ...178 A7
Webster Rd ME8 ...11 F1
Webster Way CT18 ...163 B4
Weddington La CT3 ...71 E2
Wedgewood Cl ME16 ...74 B5
Wedgewood Dr ME5 ...32 A7
Weeds Wood Rd ME5 ...31 F4
Week St ME14 ...75 A4
Weekes Ct ME11 ...3 A5
Weigall Pl CT11 ...52 C7
Weighbridge Way CT16 ...166 H8
Welcombe Ct ME8 ...33 D8
Well Cl CT2 ...68 A6
Well La Fordwich CT2,CT3 ...68 A3
Painters Forstal ME13 ...61 B3
St Margaret's at Cliffe CT15 ...150 F6
Well Rd Lyminge CT18 ...161 C6
Maidstone ME14 ...75 A5
Queenborough ME11 ...3 A5
Rushenden ME11 ...2 F3

Well St ME15,ME17 ....96 E4
Well Winch Rd ME10 ....36 D5
Weller Ave ME1 ....9 D2
Wellesley Ave CT14 ....117 C3
Wellesley Cl
  Broadstairs CT10 ......29 E3
  Westgate-on-S CT8 .....27 E7
Wellesley Ho CT14 .....117 C1
Wellesley Rd
  Ashford TN23 ....139 C2
  Dover CT16 ....166 E7
  Margate CT9 ....8 B1
  Sheerness ME12 ....1 E2
  Westgate-on-S CT8 .....27 E7
Wellesley Terr CT13 ....94 A8
Wellesley Villas TN24 .139 C3
Wellfield Rd CT20 .....178 A5
Wellington Cl CT1 ......7 C1
Wellington Cres CT11 ..52 F6
Wellington Ct CT14 ....117 D3
Wellington Gdns
  2 Dover CT16 ....149 B3
  Margate CT9 ....7 J3
Wellington Ho
  6 Maidstone ME15 ....97 E5
  Margate CT9 ....8 C3
Wellington Par
  Deal CT14 ....134 D7
  Kingsdown CT14 ......134 E6
Wellington Pl
  Folkestone CT20 .....177 D3
  Maidstone ME14 ......74 F6
Wellington Rd
  Deal CT14 ....117 D5
  Folkestone CT20 .....177 D5
  Gillingham ME7 ......10 C4
  Margate CT9 ....28 D4
  Sittingbourne ME10 ..36 B6
  Temple Ewell CT16 ..148 D5
  Westgate-on-S CT8 ...27 E7
Wellington St CT5 .....43 D5
Wellington Terr CT20 .177 D3
Wellis Gdns CT9 ....7 G1
Wells Ave CT1 ....88 B7
Wells Cl
  New Romney TN28 ....202 C6
  Tenterden TN30 ......179 B8
Wells Ho ME10 ....37 B4
Wells Rd CT19 ....177 F6
Wells Way ME13 ....40 B1
Welsdene Rd CT9 ....28 B8
Welson Rd CT20 ....178 A5
Wemmick Cl ME1 ....31 D7
Wemyss Ct **13** CT1 .....67 B2
Wemyss Ho **14** CT1 .....67 B2
Wemyss Way CT1 ....67 C1
Wenderton La CT3 ......70 A2
Wenham's La TN29 ....192 E2
Wents Wood ME14 ......75 F5
Wentworth Ave CT9 .....7 E1
Wentworth Cl CT18 ...161 C6
Wentworth Dr
  Gillingham ME8 ......33 E7
  Ramsgate CT12 ....29 A1
  Sittingbourne ME10 ..36 C5
Wentworth Gdns CT6 ..22 D2
Wentworth Ho ME10 ...36 C5
Wesley Terr CT18 ....161 C7
West Beach CT5 ....20 C1
West Borough Prim Sch
  ME16 ....74 B3
West Cliff CT5 ....20 D1
West Cliff Arc **10** CT11 .52 E6
West Cliff Ave CT10 ...30 B3
West Cliff Ct CT10 ....30 B3
West Cliff Dr CT10 ....22 B4
West Cliff Gdns
  Folkestone CT20 .....178 A4
  Herne Bay CT6 ....22 B4
West Cliff Prom CT11 ..52 D5
West Cliff Rd
  Broadstairs CT10 .....30 B3
  Ramsgate CT11 ....52 B5
West Cliff Terr CT11 ..52 B6
West Cliff **3** ME15 .....75 A1
West Dr ME5 ....31 D5
West Dumpton La CT11 .29 E1
West End TN26 ....168 F3
West End Cotts ME9 ...80 D7
West Gn ME10 ....14 F1
West Hill Rd CT6 ......22 C5
West Hythe Rd CT21 ..187 A8
West La Sheerness ME12 .1 B2
  Sittingbourne ME10 ..37 A4
West Lane Trad Est
  ME10 ....37 A4
West Lawn Gdns CT20 ..177 D3
West Lea CT14 ....117 C7
West Minster Prim Sch
  ME12 ....3 B8
West Motney Way ME8 ..12 A3
West Norman Rd CT16 ..166 E8
West Par CT21 ....176 B1
West Park Ave CT7 .....8 D1
West Park Farm North Ret Pk
  CT19 ....178 B8
West Park Rd ME15 ....75 B2
West Pas ME12 ....1 B2
West Pl TN29 ....199 D8
West Ramp CT16 ......166 G8
West Rd Chatham ME4 ..10 A7
  Cliffs End CT13 ......51 A1
  Folkestone CT20 .....177 C4
West Ridge ME10 ......36 D3
West Side CT15 ....133 A1

West St Ashford TN23 ..139 B2
  Deal CT14 ....117 D6
  Dover CT17 ....166 C8
  Faversham ME13 ......62 C7
  Gillingham ME7 ....10 D6
  Harrietsham ME17 ...100 C6
  Hothfield TN26 ......137 F7
  Lenham ME17 ....79 E1
  New Romney TN28 ....202 A6
  Queenborough ME11 ...2 F5
  Sheerness ME12 ....1 B2
  Sittingbourne ME10 ..36 E4
West Street Cotts CT14 .94 A1
West Tank Farm Rd
  TN29 ....209 C2
West Terr CT20 ....178 D4
West View CT19 ......178 D8
West View Cl CT6 ......22 C2
West Wlk ME16 ....74 B3
West Wood Rd ME9 ....56 B8
Westbere La CT2 ......68 B7
Westbourne TN23 .....155 D6
Westbourne Gdns CT20 .178 B4
Westbourne St ME10 ...36 E4
Westbrook Ave CT9 .....7 F1
Westbrook Cotts CT9 ...7 G1
Westbrook Gdns CT9 ...7 G1
Westbrook La CT9 .....22 B3
Westbrook Prom CT9 ...7 G2
Westbrook Rd CT9 .....7 G2
Westbrooke Cl ME4 ....10 A2
Westbury Cres CT17 ..166 B6
Westbury Hts CT17 ...166 B6
Westbury Rd Dover CT17 .166 B6
  Westgate-on-S CT8 ...27 E8
Westcliff Dr ME12 ......4 D8
Westcliff Gdns CT9 .....7 F1
Westcliff Ho **4** CT20 ..178 D4
Westcliff Rd CT9 ....7 G1
Westcourt La CT15 ...130 C5
Westcourt Rd ME7 .....10 A6
Westdean CT17 ....148 E2
Westenhanger Sta
  TN25 ....175 B7
Westerham Cl
  Canterbury CT2 ......67 A4
  Gillingham ME8 ......11 B3
  Margate CT9 ....8 F1
Westerham Rd ME10 ...36 C3
Westerhill Rd ME17 ...96 C1
Westerhout Cl CT14 ..117 C8
Westerly Mews **5** CT2 ..66 E1
Western Ave
  Ashford TN23 ....139 A3
  Bridge CT4 ....89 A1
  Chatham ME4 ....10 A8
  Halfway Houses ME12 ..3 D6
  Herne Bay CT6 ......22 E4
Western Cl CT17 .....166 C6
Western Espl
  Broadstairs CT10 .....30 B2
  Herne Bay CT6 ......22 C5
Western Gdns CT9 ...156 E8
Western Heights Rdbt
  CT17 ....166 C5
Western Ho CT14 ....117 C7
Western Hts ★ CT17 ...166 C6
Western Link ME13 ...62 A8
Western Rd Deal CT14 .117 C7
  Maidstone ME16 .....74 C2
  Margate CT9 ....29 C8
Western Service Rd
  CT16 ....166 G8
Western Undercliff CT11 .52 C5
Westfield CT2 ....66 A6
Westfield Bsns Ctr ME2 ..9 C7
Westfield Cotts ME9 ..13 A2
Westfield Gdns ME9 ...35 C3
Westfield La CT18 ....161 C3
Westfield Rd
  Birchington CT7 ......27 A7
  Margate CT9 ....28 C8
Westfield Sole Rd ME5,
  ME14 ....54 D8
Westgate Ave CT7 .....28 A4
Westgate Bay Ave CT8 ..7 C1
Westgate Cl CT7 ......66 C1
Westgate College for Deaf
  People CT9 ....7 J2
Westgate Court Ave CT2 .66 D1
Westgate Ct **8** CT2 ....66 E1
Westgate Garden Flats
  CT2 ....87 E8
Westgate Gr CT2 ....66 F1
Westgate Hall Rd **14** CT1 .66 F1
Westgate Rd ME13 ....62 E7
Westgate Terr CT5 ....20 E2
Westgate-on-Sea Sta
  CT8 ....27 E8
Westland Way CT18 ..163 B3
Westlands Ave ME10 ..36 B4
Westlands Rd CT6 .....22 C3
Westlands Sch The ME10 .36 B4
Westlea CT21 ....178 A3
Westleigh Rd CT8 .....27 D8
Westmarsh Cl ME15 ...97 F7
Westmarsh Dr CT9 .....8 E2
Westmarsh Dro CT3 ...71 A8
Westmeads Com Inf Sch
  CT5 ....20 E2
Westmeads Rd CT5 ....20 E2
Westminster Rd CT1 ...67 C4
Westminster Sq ME15 .74 B4
Westminster Wlk CT12 .29 C1
Westmoors TN25 .....155 E6
Westmoreland Dr ME9 .13 C3
Westmorland Cl ME15 .97 E7

Westmorland Gn ME15 ..97 E7
Westmorland Rd ME15 .97 E7
Westmount Ave ME4 ....9 F3
Westmount Ho **4** CT9 ...8 B2
Weston Rd ME2 ....9 A8
Westonville Ave CT9 ...7 F1
Westover Gdns CT10 ..29 E7
Westover Rd CT10 ....29 E6
Westree Ct **7** ME16 ....74 E3
Westree Rd ME16 .....74 E3
Westside Apartments **10**
  CT2 ....66 F1
Westway ME17 ....96 C3
Westwell Ct TN25 ....121 E3
Westwell La
  Charing TN25,TN27 ..120 F5
  Potters Corner TN24,TN25 .138 E7
  Westwell TN25,TN26 .121 B4
Westwood Ct ME13 ...62 E3
Westwood Pl ME13 ....62 D5
Westwood Rd
  Broadstairs CT10 ....29 C4
  Loose ME15 ....97 A7
Westwood Ret Pk CT10 .29 A5
Westwood Wlk ME9 ...35 B7
Wetheral Dr ME5 ......32 B4
Wey Cl ME5 ....32 C5
Wey St TN26 ....183 D3
Weybridge Cl ME5 .....32 C4
Weyburn Dr CT12 .....29 A1
Weyhill Cl ME14 ......75 C6
Weymouth Cl CT19 ...177 D7
Weymouth Rd CT19 ..177 D6
Weymouth Terr CT19 .177 D7
Whalf Rd CT13 ....73 B4
Wharf Rd Gillingham ME7 .10 C7
  Maidstone ME15 .....74 E2
Wharfedale Rd CT9 ....8 A1
Wharton Gdns TN24 ..156 E8
Whatman Cl ME14 ....75 C6
Whatman Ho ME13 ....63 F4
Whatmer Cl CT2 ......68 A6
Wheatcroft Cl ME10 ..37 B4
Wheatcroft Gr ME8 ...33 F7
Wheatear Way ME5 ....32 B7
Wheatfields Chatham ME5 .32 D2
  Maidstone ME14 .....75 D4
Wheatley Rd
  Ramsgate CT12 ....29 C1
  Whitstable CT5 ....20 E2
Wheatsheaf Cl
  Boughton Street ME13 .64 A3
  Loose ME15 ....97 B8
Wheatsheaf Gdns ME12 ..1 C1
Wheatsheafe La CT15 .133 B2
Wheeler St ME14 ......75 A5
Wheelers The ME8 ....33 B6
Wheelwrights The
  ME17 ....100 D6
Wheelwrights Way CT13 .93 B2
Wheler Ct ME13 ....62 A7
Wheler Rd TN27 .....120 C8
Whewell Terr **1** CT20 .178 E5
Whiffen's Ave ME4 .....9 F5
Whiffen's Ave W ME4 ..9 F5
Whigham Cl TN23 ....155 D7
Whimbrel Cl ME10 ....36 F8
Whimbrel Wlk ME5 ...32 C1
Whinfell Ave CT11 ....51 F7
Whinless Rd CT17 ...166 A8
Whiston Ave TN26 ...153 C4
Whitbourne Ct CT5 ...43 D8
Whitby Rd CT20 .....177 D6
Whitchurch Cl ME16 ..74 E4
Whitcombe Cl ME5 ...32 C3
White Acre Dr CT4 ..134 B8
White Cliffs **11** CT20 .178 D4
White Cliffs Bsns Ctr
  CT16 ....149 A6
White Cliffs Bsns Pk
  CT16 ....149 B6
White Ct **8** CT20 ....177 E3
White Hart Mans CT9 ..7 I3
White Hill
  Boughton Aluph TN25 .123 B6
  Challock TN25 ......105 E1
  Chilham CT4 ....85 E1
White Hill Cl CT4 ....110 A8
White Hill Rd ME9,ME14 .33 D1
White Horse Hill CT18 .163 C3
White Horse La
  6 Canterbury CT1 ....87 F8
  Otham Hole ME15 ....98 A6
  Rhodes Minnis CT4 .144 A3
White House Farm Ct
  CT15 ....113 E5
White Marsh Ct CT5 ...20 E2
White Mill & Folk Mus ★
  CT13 ....72 E2
White Post ME17 ......78 B5
White Post Gdns CT3 ..71 E1
White Rd ME4 ....10 A2
White Rock Ct ME16 ..74 E3
White Rock Pl **5** ME16 .74 E3
White Willow CT24 ..156 D6
White Wood Rd CT13 ..93 B1
Whiteacre La CT4 ....125 E4
Whitebeam **1** TN23 .138 D4
Whitebeam Dr ME17 ..96 B3
Whitecliff Way CT19 .178 F6
Whitefriars Mdw **15** CT13 .72 F1
Whitefriars Way **14** CT13 .72 F1
Whitegate CT8 ....33 D5
Whitehall
  Brookland TN29 .....199 E8
  Sandwich CT13 ......95 A7
Whitehall Bridge Rd CT2 .87 E8

Whitehall Cl CT2 ......87 E8
Whitehall Dr ME17 ....99 D3
Whitehall Gdns CT2 ..66 E1
Whitehall Rd
  Broad Street ME14 ...77 A6
  Canterbury CT2 ......87 E8
  Canterbury,Harbledown
    CT2 ....87 D7
  Ramsgate CT12 ....29 C1
  Sittingbourne ME10 ..36 E2
Whitehall Way TN25 .159 D1
Whiteheads La ME14 ..76 B4
Whitehorse Hill ME5 ..10 B3
Whitehouse Cres ME11 .53 A8
Whitehouse Dro CT13,
  CT3 ....72 D7
Whitelocks Cl CT4 ...111 D3
Whitenbrook CT21 ...177 A3
Whitenbrook Dell CT21 .177 A3
Whiteness Gn CT10 ....8 F1
Whiteness Rd CT10 ....8 G2
Whitepost **12** CT5 .....20 D2
Whites Hill CT13 .....115 B2
Whitewall Rd ME2 .....9 D7
Whitewall Way ME2 ...9 D7
Whiteway Rd ME11,ME12 .2 F6
Whitfeld Rd TN23 ...156 B8
Whitfield Ave
  Broadstairs CT10 .....29 E7
  Dover CT16 ....149 E7
Whitfield Cotts TN23 .156 B8
Whitfield Ct CT16 ...149 A6
Whitfield Hill
  Dover CT16 ....148 F4
  Temple Ewell CT16 .148 A4
Whitfield Lodge CT16 .149 A4
Whitfield Rdbt CT16 .149 A6
Whitfield Sch & Aspen Specl
  Unit CT16 ....149 A7
Whitgift Ct CT2 ......66 D1
Whiting Cres ME14 ...62 A8
Whiting Ho TN29 ....205 C5
Whitmore St ME16 ...74 D2
Whitstable & Seasalter CE
  Jun Sch CT5 ....20 D1
Whitstable & Tankerton
  Hospl CT5 ....21 A2
Whitstable & Tankerton Sta
  CT5 ....20 E1
Whitstable Jun Sch CT5 .20 D1
Whitstable Mus & Art
  Gallery ★ CT5 ....20 D1
Whitstable Rd
  Canterbury CT2 ......66 D2
  Faversham ME13 ......62 E7
  Faversham, Goodnestone
    ME13 ....63 B6
  Herne Bay CT5,CT6 ..22 B3
  Rough Common CT2 ..66 B4
Whittaker St ME4 .....10 A4
Whittington Terr CT15 .130 D4
Whybornes Chase ME12 ..4 C7
Whyman Ave ME4 .....10 A1
Whytecliffs CT10 .....30 A2
Wichling Cl CT2 ......67 A3
Wick La CT4 ....129 E7
Wicken Ho ME16 ......74 E4
Wicken La TN25,TN27 .120 E6
Wickenden Cres TN24 .157 A8
Wickets The TN24 ...156 F7
Wickham Ave CT11 ...52 G8
Wickham Cl ME9 ......35 B6
Wickham Court La CT3 .69 B3
Wickham La CT3 ......69 B1
Wickham Mill CT3 ....69 C2
Wickham Pl ME17 ...101 D5
Wickham Rd CT3 .....69 B2
Wickham Terr ME11 ...2 F5
Wickhambreaux CE Prim Sch
  CT3 ....69 C2
Widgeon Wlk CT18 ..163 B3
Widred Rd CT17 .....166 C8
Wierton La ME17 .....97 E1
Wife Of Bath Hill CT2 ..87 C8
Wigmore Cotts CT15 .131 C8
Wigmore La CT15 ....131 C8
Wigmore Rd ME8 .....33 B4
Wigmore Wood CT15 .131 C8
Wigwam Paddocks CT7 ..2 A8
Wihtred Rd ME9 ......37 D2
Wilberforce Rd
  Coxheath ME17 ......96 D3
  Folkestone CT20 ....177 E3
Wilbrough Rd CT7 ....27 A7
Wilcox Cl CT3 ....112 D5
Wild Air CT7 ....26 F7
Wild wood Wealden Forest
  Pk ★ CT2,CT6 ....45 D4
Wilderness Hill CT9 ...8 A2
Wildfell Cl ME5 ....54 C8
Wildish Rd ME13 .....62 A8
Wildman Cl ME8 ......33 D3
Wildwood Cl ME17 ....99 E2
Wildwood Glade ME7 ..33 B4
Wildwood Rd CT2 .....67 F6
Wiles Ave TN28 .....202 B6
Wiles Ho TN28 ......202 B6
Wilfred Rd CT11 ......52 C8
Wilgate Green Rd ME13 .82 F6
Wilkes Rd ME10 ......29 E4
Wilkie Rd CT7 ....27 A8
Wilkinson Dr CT14 ...117 D3
Wilks Cl ME8 ....12 B2
Will Adams Ct **9** ME7 ..10 C6
Will Adams Rdbt ME7 .10 C6
Will Adams Way ME8 ..10 F1

Willement Rd ME13 ...62 B7
Willesborough Ct TN24 .140 A2
Willesborough Ind Pk
  TN24 ....140 A1
Willesborough Inf & Jun
  Schs TN24 ....157 A8
Willesborough Rd TN24 .139 F4
Willesborough Windmill ★
  TN24 ....140 A1
Willetts Hill CT12 ....49 D7
William Ave
  Folkestone CT19 ....178 B2
  Margate CT9 ....29 C8
William Gibbs Ct **14**
  ME13 ....62 D7
William Harvey Hospl
  TN24 ....140 C1
William Judge Cl TN30 .179 D7
William Muge Ho **15**
  CT16 ....166 D8
William Pitt Ave CT14 .117 B6
William Pitt Cl CT21 .176 D2
William Rd TN23 .....156 B8
William Rigby Dr ME12 ..3 D7
William St
  Faversham ME13 ......62 D7
  Gillingham ME8 ......12 A1
  Herne Bay CT6 ......22 F5
  Sittingbourne ME10 ..36 E4
  Whitstable CT5 ......20 D2
Williamson Rd TN29 .206 E5
Willingdon TN23 .....155 E5
Willingdon Pl CT14 ..117 C1
Willingdon Rd CT16 .149 A5
Willington Gn ME15 ...97 E2
Willington St ME15 ...75 F2
Willis Ct ME12 ....3 F5
Willis Ho ME1 ....9 C4
Willop Cl TN29 ......186 F3
Willop Way TN29 ....186 F3
Willoughby Ct **14** CT1 .87 E8
Willow Ave
  Broadstairs CT10 .....29 C4
  Faversham ME13 ......62 A4
Willow Bank Ind Est ME9 .14 E6
Willow Cl Canterbury CT2 .67 A2
  Hythe CT21 ....175 E1
  Margate CT9 ....8 C2
Willow Ct
  Broadstairs CT10 .....30 A5
  Folkestone CT20 ....177 E4
  Loose ME15 ....97 A6
Willow Dr
  Hamstreet TN26 .....183 A7
  St Mary's Bay TN29 .194 F3
Willow Farm Way CT6 .23 C2
Willow Ho Ashford TN23 .138 F1
  2 Chatham ME5 ......31 F5
  8 Maidstone ME16 ...74 A3
  Sheerness ME12 ....1 C2
  Sittingbourne ME10 ..37 B3
Willow Lodge CT19 ..178 D7
Willow Rd
  Great Mongeham CT14 .116 C3
  Whitstable CT5 ......43 C5
Willow Rise ME15 ....75 F1
Willow Tree Cl
  Ashford TN24 ....139 F1
  Herne Bay CT6 ......23 B4
Willow Way
  Maidstone ME15 .....75 A3
  Margate CT9 ....28 C8
  Whitstable CT5 ......44 C8
Willow Waye CT15 ...131 D7
Willowbank Cl TN29 .195 A4
Willowbank Ct **12** ME15 .75 B4
Willowby Gdns ME8 ...33 E4
Willows Ct CT2 ......66 C4
Willows The
  Ashford TN24 ....139 E6
  Gillingham ME8 ......11 E2
  Newington ME9 ......35 B6
  Sheerness ME12 ....1 I1
  Sittingbourne ME10 ..14 F1
Wills La TN29 ....184 C4
Willson's Rd CT11 ....52 D6
Wilmecote Ct ME8 ....33 B4
Wilmington Way ME8 ..11 B2
Wilmott Pl CT13 ......93 B2
Wilson Ave Deal CT14 .116 F4
  Rochester ME1 ....31 E7
Wilson Cl Ashford TN24 .140 A1
  Maidstone ME15 .....97 E7
Wilsons La ME15 ......96 A5
Wiltie Ct CT19 ......178 C5
Wiltie Gdns CT19 ....178 C5
Wilton Cl CT14 ......117 C5
Wilton Rd
  Folkestone CT19 ....178 B6
  Ramsgate CT12 ....28 F1
Wilton Terr ME10 .....36 B5
Wiltshire Cl ME5 ......32 C8
Wiltshire Way **4** ME15 .97 E8
Wimborne Pl CT12 ....52 B8
Wimbourne Dr ME8 ...33 D6
Win Pine Ho CT21 ...176 A1
Winant Way CT16 ...149 B3
Wincheap CT1 ....87 E7
Wincheap Foundation Prim
  Sch CT1 ....87 E6
Wincheap Gn **4** CT1 ...87 F7
Wincheap Ind Est CT1 .87 D7
Winchelsea Ct CT17 .166 C7
Winchelsea Rd
  Chatham ME5 ....32 B5
  Dover CT17 ....166 B7
Winchelsea St CT17 .166 B7
Winchelsea Terr CT17 .166 B7

Winchester Ave ME5 . . . . . . .31 F4
Winchester Gdns CT1 . . . . . .88 A6
Winchester Ho **3** ME15 . . .97 D7
Winchester Mews CT14 . . .117 B3
Winchester Pl **9** ME14 . . .75 A5
Winchester Way ME8 . . . . . .34 A8
Wind Hill TN27 . . . . .119 E7
Wind Hill La TN27 . . . . . . .119 E7
Windermere ME13 . . . . .62 E6
Windermere Ave CT11 . . . .52 A7
Windermere Ct TN24 . . . .139 C4
Windermere Dr ME8 . . . . . .33 D7
Windermere Gdns CT3 . . . .112 F6
Windermere Gr ME10 . . . . .36 D3
Windermere Ho **4** ME15 . .97 E7
Winding Hill ME13 . . . . .83 F6
Windmill Ave CT12 . . . . . . .29 B3
Windmill Cl
  Ashford TN24 . . . . .140 A1
  Bridge CT4 . . . . .89 A1
  Canterbury CT1 . . . . .88 C8
  Herne Bay CT6 . . . . .23 A2
Windmill Ct
  Maidstone ME17 . . . . .97 B3
  Whitstable CT5 . . . . .43 C7
Windmill Hill ME17 . . . . . .100 B1
Windmill Hts ME14 . . . . . . .76 B4
Windmill La ME13 . . . . .40 B1
Windmill Manor ME7 . . . . .10 C4
Windmill Par CT11 . . . . .52 C6
Windmill Quay Rd ME12 . . . .4 E2
Windmill Rd
  Canterbury CT1 . . . . .88 C8
  Gillingham ME7 . . . . .10 C4
  Herne Bay CT6 . . . . .23 A2
  Sittingbourne ME10 . . . . . .36 D6
  Whitstable CT5 . . . . .43 D7
Windmill Rise ME12 . . . . .4 E6
Windmill Row ME17 . . . . . . .98 D2
Windmill St CT21 . . . . . . .176 B1
Windmill View CT9 . . . . .29 A8
Windmill Wlk CT17 . . . . . . .29 B1
Windsor Ave
  Chatham ME4 . . . . .9 F2
  Margate CT9 . . . . .8 B1
Windsor Cl
  Broadstairs CT10 . . . . .29 E5
  Maidstone ME14 . . . . .75 B6
Windsor Ct Deal CT14 . . .117 C2
  Gillingham ME7 . . . . .10 D5
  Margate CT9 . . . . .8 B1
Windsor Dr ME10 . . . . .36 D2
Windsor Gdns
  Herne Bay CT6 . . . . .22 B3
  Warden ME12 . . . . .1 D2
Windsor Ho Deal CT14 . . .117 A5
  6 Dover CT17 . . . . .166 D7
  Whitstable CT5 . . . . .20 D1
Windsor Mews
  9 Margate CT9 . . . . .7 J2
  New Romney TN28 . . . . . .202 C8
Windsor Rd
  Canterbury CT1 . . . . .87 C6
  Cliffs End CT12 . . . . .51 D7
  Gillingham ME7 . . . . .10 D5
Windward Rd ME1 . . . . .9 C1
Windyridge ME7 . . . . .10 E1
Winehouse La CT18 . . . . . .164 D3
Wineycock ME9 . . . . .81 C8
Winford Mews ME1 . . . . .9 A2
Wing Ho ME12 . . . . .6 H1
Wing Rd ME12 . . . . .6 H1
Wingate Ct **7** ME8 . . . . . .36 E4
Wingate Rd CT19 . . . . .178 D7
Wingham Cl
  Gillingham ME8 . . . . .11 C3
  Maidstone ME15 . . . . .97 F7
Wingham Ind Est CT3 . . . .91 B6
Wingham Prim Sch CT3 . .91 A7
Wingham Rd CT3 . . . . .90 D8
Wingham Well La CT3 . . . .90 F5
Wingham Wildlife Pk★
  CT3 . . . . .70 C1
Wingrove Dr
  Maidstone ME14 . . . . .75 E5
  Rochester ME2 . . . . .9 C7
Wingrove Hill CT17 . . . . . .148 E2
Wings Cl CT10 . . . . .30 B5

Winifred Ave CT12 . . . . .29 C2
Winifred Rd ME15 . . . . .75 F3
Winkle Cl CT6 . . . . .22 B3
Winnipeg Cl CT16 . . . . . . .149 C3
Winstanley Cres CT11 . . . .52 D8
Winstanley Rd ME12 . . . . . . .1 D2
Winston Cl CT1 . . . . .88 C7
Winston Ct CT7 . . . . .27 A8
Winston Gdns CT6 . . . . . . .23 D4
Winston Ho **4** CT20 . . . .177 F5
Winter Dr CT18 . . . . .163 B5
Winterage La CT18 . . . . . .162 C7
Winterstoke Cres CT11 . . .52 G8
Winterstoke Way CT11 . . .52 F8
Winton Way TN29 . . . . . . .195 A5
Wirrals The ME5 . . . . .32 A4
Wises La ME10,ME9 . . . . . .36 A4
Wish The TN26 . . . . .181 F6
Wissenden La TN26 . . . . .153 B6
Wisteria Ho **11** ME15 . . . .97 E7
Withersdane Cotts
  TN25 . . . . .124 A2
Witley Wlk CT16 . . . . .149 B7
Wittersham CE Prim Sch
  TN30 . . . . .188 D2
Wittersham Cl ME5 . . . . . . .32 B5
Wittersham La TN31 . . . . .197 B5
Wittersham Rd
  Iden TN31 . . . . .197 B7
  Stone in Oxney TN30 . . . .189 C3
  Wittersham TN30 . . . . . . .188 C5
Wivenhoe TN23 . . . . .155 E5
Wivenhoe Ct ME8 . . . . .12 A2
Wold Cvn Pk The ME12 . . . .5 F6
Wolf Ho ME4 . . . . .10 B8
Wolfe Ct CT14 . . . . .117 D3
Wolfe Rd ME16 . . . . .74 B2
Wollaston Cl ME8 . . . . .33 D3
Wollaston Rd CT14 . . . . . .117 D4
Wolseley Ave CT6 . . . . .22 A4
Wolseley Pl **4** TN24 . . . .139 B3
Wolseley Terr CT11 . . . . . .205 C5
**Women's Land Army Mus
  The★** CT15 . . . . .165 E5
Wood Ave CT19 . . . . .178 E7
Wood Cottage La CT19 . .177 D7
Wood Hill CT2 . . . . .66 E6
Wood La TN23 . . . . .156 D3
Wood Rd CT21 . . . . .176 B1
Wood St Chatham ME7 . . .10 A6
  Dover CT17 . . . . .166 D8
  Lynsted ME9 . . . . .59 F8
  Sheerness ME12 . . . . .1 D2
Wood View CT3 . . . . .46 E5
Wood Yd CT14 . . . . .117 D6
Wood's Pl CT17 . . . . .149 B2
Woodberry Dr ME10 . . . . . .37 C3
Woodberry Flats CT11 . . . .30 A3
Woodbridge Dr ME15 . . . . .74 F1
Woodbrook TN27 . . . . .120 D7
Woodbury La TN30 . . . . . .179 A7
Woodbury Rd ME5 . . . . . . .31 F1
Woodchurch CE Prim Sch
  TN26 . . . . .169 A2
Woodchurch Cl ME5 . . . . . .32 B5
Woodchurch Cotts CT7 . . .27 F4
Woodchurch Cres ME8 . . . .11 C2
Woodchurch Ho ME8 . . . . .11 C2
Woodchurch Rd
  Appledore Heath TN26 . . .181 C4
  Margate CT7,CT9 . . . . .28 A5
  Shadoxhurst TN26 . . . . . .155 A1
  Tenterden TN30 . . . . .179 D8
  Westgate-on-S CT7 . . . . . .27 F3
Woodchurch Windmill (dis)★
  TN26 . . . . .169 A3
Woodcock Gdns CT18 . . .163 A4
Woodcote CT5 . . . . .21 D1
Woodcourt CT ME10 . . . . . .36 E2
Woodcut ME14 . . . . .75 A8
Woodfield Ave CT19 . . . . .177 E7
Woodfield Cl CT19 . . . . . .177 E7
Woodford Ave CT11,CT12 . .29 D1
Woodford Ct CT7 . . . . .27 A7
Woodford Rd ME16 . . . . . . .74 B2
Woodgate CT4 . . . . .110 E3
Woodgate Cl ME13 . . . . . . .62 C8

Woodgate Ct ME13 . . . . . . .84 E7
Woodgate La ME9 . . . . .35 C2
Woodgates Cl TN26 . . . . . .167 D7
Woodhall Terr ME11 . . . . . . .3 A5
Woodhurst ME5 . . . . .31 D4
Woodland Ave
  Aylesham CT3 . . . . .112 E5
  Birchington CT7 . . . . .27 B6
Woodland Cl CT17 . . . . . . .148 E2
Woodland Cotts CT18 . . . .161 B7
Woodland Dr ME12 . . . . .4 B7
Woodland Rd
  Herne Bay CT6 . . . . .22 B2
  Lyminge CT18 . . . . .160 E8
Woodland View TN30 . . . .188 E4
Woodland Way
  Broadstairs CT10 . . . . .8 G1
  Canterbury CT2 . . . . .66 D4
  Dymchurch TN29 . . . . . . .187 A5
  Maidstone ME14 . . . . .75 B7
  Woodnesborough CT13 . . .93 C6
Woodlands Blean CT2 . . . . .65 F7
  Chatham ME5 . . . . .32 A2
  Coxheath ME17 . . . . .96 B3
  Hernhill ME13 . . . . .64 C7
Woodlands Cl
  Maidstone ME14 . . . . .75 B7
  Peasmarsh TN31 . . . . .196 C2
Woodlands Ct ME5 . . . . . . .31 F3
Woodlands Dr CT21 . . . . .177 A4
Woodlands Prim Sch
  ME7 . . . . .10 F4
Woodlands Rd
  Adisham CT3 . . . . .112 C8
  Ashford TN24 . . . . .139 F2
  Gillingham ME7 . . . . .10 F4
  Sittingbourne ME10 . . . . . .37 B3
Woodlands Terr ME7 . . . . . .10 F3
Woodlawn St CT5 . . . . .20 D2
Woodlea TN24 . . . . .139 C3
Woodman Ave CT5 . . . . . . .21 E3
Woodnesborough La
  CT13 . . . . .93 B3
Woodnesborough Rd
  CT13 . . . . .93 E7
Woodpecker Dr ME9 . . . . . .14 E4
Woodpecker Glade ME8 . .33 D6
Woodrow Chase CT6 . . . . .23 A1
Woodruff Cl ME8 . . . . .12 D4
Woods Hill CT4 . . . . .125 C5
Woods Ley CT3 . . . . .71 D2
Woodshole Cotts ME9 . . . .14 D1
Woodside Ashford TN23 . . .155 E6
  Boughton Street ME13 . . . .64 B2
  Gillingham ME8 . . . . .33 C6
Woodside Ave CT4 . . . . . . .86 D2
Woodside Cl CT16 . . . . . . .148 E4
Woodside Cotts ME13 . . . .64 B2
Woodside Gdns ME10 . . . . .36 D2
Woodside Rd
  Maidstone ME15 . . . . .97 C7
  Sturry CT2 . . . . .67 F7
Woodstock Rd
  Deal CT14 . . . . .117 C4
  Rochester ME2 . . . . .9 A7
  Sittingbourne ME10 . . . . . .36 E1
Woodstock Way TN24 . . . .139 E7
Woodvale Ave CT5 . . . . . . .44 C8
Woodville Cl CT1 . . . . .87 D6
Woodville Rd
  Maidstone ME15 . . . . .75 A2
  Ramsgate CT12 . . . . .29 C1
Woolaston Cl ME15 . . . . . . .74 F1
Woolbrook Cl ME8 . . . . .12 B2
Woolcomber St CT16 . . . .166 E7
Wooldeys Rd ME8 . . . . .11 F2
Woolett Rd ME10 . . . . .36 C5
Woollets Cl CT6 . . . . .22 C3
Woolley Rd ME15 . . . . .97 F7
Woolmer Dr TN24 . . . . . . .157 A7
Woolpack Hill TN25 . . . . . .158 D5
Woolreeds Rd TN23 . . . . . .156 A7
Woolwich Cl ME5 . . . . .32 A7
Wootton Cl CT4 . . . . .109 A4
Wootton Dr CT4 . . . . .109 A4
Wootton Gn ME8 . . . . .11 D3

Wootton La CT15,CT4 . . . .146 C7
Wopsle Cl ME1 . . . . .31 D7
Worcester Cl
  Faversham ME13 . . . . .62 E6
  Minster (Sheppey) ME12 . . .4 C6
Worcester Dr ME10 . . . . . . .36 D6
Worcester Gr CT10 . . . . . . .29 F6
Worcester La CT3 . . . . .88 E7
Worcester Rd ME15 . . . . . . .97 D7
Wordsworth Cl ME5 . . . . . .32 C7
Wordsworth Gdns CT3 . . .112 F6
Wordsworth Rd ME14 . . . . .75 B7
Workhouse La ME15 . . . . . .96 C4
Workhouse Rd
  Chartway Street ME17 . . . .99 A1
  Throwley ME13 . . . . .82 F1
World's End ME9 . . . . .60 E7
Wormdale Hill ME9 . . . . . . .35 B3
Wormdale Rd ME9 . . . . .35 B4
Worsfold Ct **5** ME15 . . . .75 A1
Worth La CT20 . . . . .177 E3
Worth Prim Sch CT14 . . . .94 B5
Worthgate Pl **2** CT1 . . . .87 F7
Worthington St **11** CT16,
  CT17 . . . . .166 D8
Wotton Cl ME15 . . . . .97 E5
Wotton Rd TN23 . . . . .156 B6
Wotton Trad Est TN23 . . .156 B6
Wraightsfield Ave TN29 .195 D8
Wraik Hill CT5 . . . . .43 C5
Wrangleden Cl ME15 . . . . .97 E5
Wrangleden Rd ME15 . . . . .97 E5
Wreight Ct ME13 . . . . .40 B1
Wren Way ME5 . . . . .32 B6
Wren's Cross ME15 . . . . . . .75 A3
Wrens Ct ME9 . . . . .58 A8
Wrens Rd ME9 . . . . .58 A7
Wrentham Ave CT6 . . . . . . .22 B2
Wright Cl ME8 . . . . .11 C2
Wright's Way ME12 . . . . . . .17 C8
Wrights Cl TN30 . . . . .179 A8
Wrotham Ave **20** CT10 . . .30 B4
Wrotham Rd CT10 . . . . .30 B4
Wyatt Ho **1** ME2 . . . . .9 A7
Wyatt Pl ME2 . . . . .9 A7
Wyatt St ME14 . . . . .75 A4
Wych Elm Way CT21 . . . . .187 E8
Wycherley Cres CT16 . . . .149 B4
Wye Coll (Imperial Coll
  London) TN25 . . . . .123 F2
Wye Gdns CT16 . . . . .8 F2
Wye National Nature
  Reserve★ TN25 . . . . . . .141 D7
Wye Rd TN25 . . . . .122 F3
Wye Sta TN25 . . . . .123 D2
Wyke Manor Rd ME14 . . . .75 A4
Wykeham Cl ME11 . . . . .2 F3
Wykeham Cotts ME17 . . . .96 F2
Wykeham Gr ME17 . . . . . . .99 A7
Wykeham Rd ME10 . . . . . . .37 B4
Wykeham St ME2 . . . . .9 B8
Wyles Rd ME4 . . . . .9 E2
Wyles St ME7 . . . . .10 C7
Wyllie Cl ME10 . . . . .36 E7
Wynd The TN27 . . . . .103 D1
Wyndham Ave CT10 . . . . . . .8 B2
Wyndham Rd Chatham ME4 . .9 E2
  Dover CT17 . . . . .166 B8
Wyndy La CT5 . . . . .138 F4
Wynn Ellis Ho CT5 . . . . . . .20 E3
Wynn Rd CT5 . . . . .21 A2
Wytchlings The ME17 . . . . .99 D2
Wytherling Cl ME14 . . . . . .75 F5
Wyvern Cl ME10 . . . . .36 E7
Wyvern Sch The TN23 . . .138 E1
Wyvern Way TN24 . . . . . . .139 E3
Wyvill Cl ME8 . . . . .33 E5

Y

Yard The Barham CT4 . . . . .111 F1
  Chatham ME5 . . . . .32 B3
Yardhurst Gdns CT9 . . . . . . .8 F3
Yardley Ho CT10 . . . . .30 B7
Yarrow Cl CT10 . . . . .30 A3

Yarrow Ct ME14 . . . . .75 F5
Yarrow Rd ME5 . . . . .31 F4
Yates Cl TN31 . . . . .203 A2
Yaugher La ME9 . . . . .34 C3
Yeates Dr ME10 . . . . .37 A8
Yellow Sands ME12 . . . . . . .19 E5
Yelsted La Chatham ME14 . .54 D7
  Yelsted ME9 . . . . .34 A1
Yelsted Rd ME9 . . . . .56 A7
Yeoman Ct ME14 . . . . .76 B3
Yeoman Dr ME7 . . . . .10 F1
Yeoman Gdns TN24 . . . . . .157 B8
Yeoman Ho ME1 . . . . .9 D4
Yeoman La ME14 . . . . .76 B4
Yeoman Pk ME15 . . . . .76 A2
Yeoman Way ME15 . . . . . . .76 A2
Yeomans Sq TN23 . . . . . . .155 D8
Yevele Cl ME11 . . . . .3 A5
Yew Cl TN23 . . . . .138 E2
Yew Tree Cl
  Broadstairs CT10 . . . . .29 D4
  Chatham ME5 . . . . .32 D1
  Deal CT14 . . . . .117 A4
  Stanford TN25 . . . . .160 B1
Yew Tree Cotts ME14 . . . . .53 F1
Yew Tree Farm CT3 . . . . . .114 A8
Yew Tree Gdns
  Birchington CT7 . . . . .27 A7
  Fordwich CT2 . . . . .68 A4
Yew Tree Mews CT14 . . . .117 A3
Yew Tree Pk ME17 . . . . . . .102 F1
Yew Tree Pk Cvn & Camping
  Site CT4 . . . . .109 D2
Yew Tree Pl ME7 . . . . .33 B1
Yew Tree Rd TN29 . . . . . . .194 F3
Yewhedges ME13 . . . . .81 E4
Yewtree Cross CT18 . . . . .161 C8
Yewtree Ho **2** ME1 . . . . . . .9 D4
Yoakes La TN29 . . . . .192 F1
Yoakley Sq CT9 . . . . .28 F8
Yoke Cl ME9 . . . . .9 B8
Yokosuka Way ME7,ME8 . . .11 A7
York & Albany Cl CT14 . . .117 B1
York Ave
  18 Broadstairs CT10 . . . .30 B4
  Chatham ME5 . . . . .31 F3
  Gillingham ME7 . . . . .10 C4
York Cl CT5 . . . . .22 D4
York Hill ME5 . . . . .10 C2
York Ho **10** CT17 . . . . . . .166 D7
York Mews CT19 . . . . .177 E7
York Rd Ashford TN24 . . .139 D5
  Canterbury CT1 . . . . .87 E7
  Deal CT14 . . . . .117 D4
  Herne Bay CT6 . . . . .22 D5
  Maidstone ME15 . . . . .75 C2
  Rochester ME1 . . . . .9 C3
York St Broadstairs CT10 . . .30 B4
  Dover CT16,CT17 . . . . . . .166 D7
  Ramsgate CT11 . . . . .52 E6
York Street Rdbt CT16,
  CT17 . . . . .166 D7
York Terr CT7 . . . . .27 B7
Young Cl CT14 . . . . .117 B6
Young's Pl CT15 . . . . .164 F5
Ypres Ct CT1 . . . . .67 D1
Ypres Dr ME10 . . . . .14 F1

Z

Zarena Ct **8** CT20 . . . . . .177 F3
Zealand Rd CT1 . . . . .87 F6
Zetland Ave ME7 . . . . .10 E2
Zillah Gdns ME8 . . . . .33 C6
Zion Pl CT9 . . . . .7 J3

Addresses

Name and Address	Telephone	Page	Grid reference

Name and Address	Telephone	Page	Grid reference

Grid square letters (map, left side)

NG NH NJ NK

NM NN NO NP

NR NS NT NU

NX NY NZ

SC SD SE TA

SH SJ SK TF TG

SM SN SO SP TL TM

SR SS ST SU TQ TR

SW SX SY SZ TV

Any feature in this atlas can be given a unique reference to help you find the same feature on other Ordnance Survey maps of the area, or to help someone else locate you if they do not have a Street Atlas.

The grid squares in this atlas match the Ordnance Survey National Grid and are at 500 metre intervals. The small figures at the bottom and sides of every other grid line are the National Grid kilometre values (**00** to **99** km) and are repeated across the country every 100 km (see left).

To give a unique National Grid reference you need to locate where in the country you are. The country is divided into 100 km squares with each square given a unique two-letter reference. Use the administrative map to determine in which 100 km square a particular page of this atlas falls.

The bold letters and numbers between each grid line (**A** to **F**, **1** to **8**) are for use within a specific Street Atlas only, and when used with the page number, are a convenient way of referencing these grid squares.

Example   The railway bridge over DARLEY GREEN RD in grid square B1

Step 1: Identify the two-letter reference, in this example the page is in **SP**

Step 2: Identify the 1 km square in which the railway bridge falls. Use the figures in the southwest corner of this square: Eastings **17**, Northings **74**. This gives a unique reference: **SP 17 74**, accurate to 1 km.

Step 3: To give a more precise reference accurate to 100 m you need to estimate how many tenths along and how many tenths up this 1 km square the feature is (to help with this the 1 km square is divided into four 500 m squares). This makes the bridge about **8** tenths along and about **1** tenth up from the southwest corner.

This gives a unique reference: **SP 178 741**, accurate to 100 m.

Eastings (read from left to right along the bottom) come before Northings (read from bottom to top). If you have trouble remembering say to yourself "Along the hall, THEN up the stairs"!

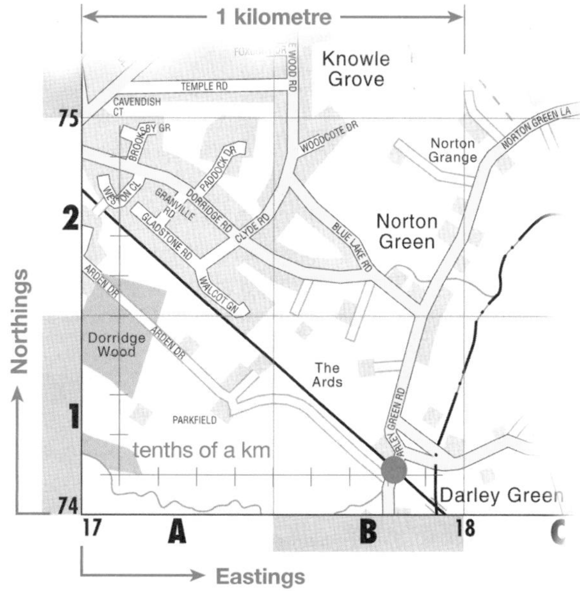

PHILIP'S MAPS

the Gold Standard for serious driving

◆ Philip's street atlases cover every county in England and Wales, plus much of Scotland.

◆ All our atlases use the same style of mapping, with the same colours and symbols, so you can move with confidence from one atlas to the next

◆ Widely used by the emergency services, transport companies and local authorities.

◆ Created from the most up-to-date and detailed information available from Ordnance Survey

◆ Based on the National Grid

BEST BUY • BEST BUY
Auto EXPRESS
BEST BUY • BEST BUY

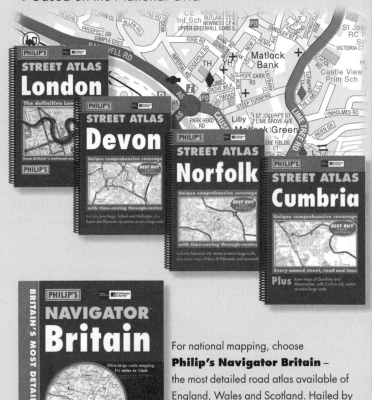

STREET ATLAS **London**
The definitive Lon...
from Britain's national ma...

STREET ATLAS **Devon**
Unique comprehensive coverage
Includes Lyme Regis, Sidbach and Wellington, plus Exeter and Plymouth city centres at extra-large scale
with time-saving through-routes

STREET ATLAS **Norfolk**
Unique comprehensive coverage
Includes Norwich city centre at extra-large scale, plus town maps of Bury St Edmunds and Lowestoft
with time-saving through-routes

STREET ATLAS **Cumbria**
Unique comprehensive coverage
Every named street, road and lane
Plus town maps of Dumfries and Morecambe, with Carlisle city centre at extra-large scale

BRITAIN'S MOST DETAILED ROAD ATLAS
PHILIP'S
NAVIGATOR **Britain**
Ultra-large scale mapping 1⅓ miles to 1 inch
50 fully indexed town plans
'Extremely clear maps with the most detail by far' Auto Express
Recommended by the Institute of Advanced Motorists

For national mapping, choose **Philip's Navigator Britain** – the most detailed road atlas available of England, Wales and Scotland. Hailed by Auto Express as 'the ultimate road atlas', this is the only one-volume atlas to show every road and lane in Britain.

Street atlases currently available

England
Bedfordshire
Berkshire
Birmingham and West Midlands
Bristol and Bath
Buckinghamshire
Cambridgeshire
Cheshire
Cornwall
Cumbria
Derbyshire
Devon
Dorset
County Durham and Teesside
Essex
North Essex
South Essex
Gloucestershire
North Hampshire
South Hampshire
Herefordshire Monmouthshire
Hertfordshire
Isle of Wight
Kent
East Kent
West Kent
Lancashire
Leicestershire and Rutland
Lincolnshire
London
Greater Manchester
Merseyside
Norfolk
Northamptonshire
Northumberland
Nottinghamshire
Oxfordshire
Shropshire
Somerset

All England and Wales coverage

Staffordshire
Suffolk
Surrey
East Sussex
West Sussex
Tyne and Wear
Warwickshire
Birmingham and West Midlands
Wiltshire and Swindon
Worcestershire
East Yorkshire Northern Lincolnshire
North Yorkshire
South Yorkshire
West Yorkshire

Wales
Anglesey, Conwy and Gwynedd
Cardiff, Swansea and The Valleys
Carmarthenshire, Pembrokeshire and Swansea
Ceredigion and South Gwynedd
Denbighshire, Flintshire, Wrexham
Herefordshire Monmouthshire
Powys

Scotland
Aberdeenshire
Ayrshire
Edinburgh and East Central Scotland
Fife and Tayside
Glasgow and West Central Scotland
Inverness and Moray

How to order

Philip's maps and atlases are available from bookshops, motorway services and petrol stations. You can order direct from the publisher by phoning **01903 828503** or online at **www.philips-maps.co.uk**
For bulk orders only, phone 020 7644 6940